Fodor's 2013

IRELAND

D1124945

Fodor's Travel Publications · New York, Toronto, London, Sydney, Auckland

www.fodors.com

FODOR'S IRELAND 2013

Writers: Paul Clements, Alannah Hopkin, Anto Howard

Editors: Jess Moss, Mark Sullivan, Salwa Jabado
Editorial Contributors: Robert I. C. Fisher, Jacinta O'Halloran, Daniel Mangin

Production Editors: Carolyn Roth, Elyse Rozelle
Maps & Illustrations: David Lindroth, Mark Stroud, *cartographers;* Rebecca Baer, *map editor;* William Wu, *information graphics*
Design: Fabrizio La Rocca, *creative director;* Tina Malaney, Chie Ushio, Jessica Ramirez, *designers;* Melanie Marin, *associate director of photography;* Jennifer Romains, *photo research*
Cover Photos: Front cover: (Dunguaire Castle, Kinvara, Galway) SIME/eStock Photo. Back cover (from left to right): Geray Sweeney/Tourism Ireland; © Mustang79 | Dreamstime.com; Holger Leue/Tourism Ireland. Spine: nhtg/Shutterstock.
Production Manager: Angela L. McLean

COPYRIGHT

ISBN 978-0-87637-124-4

ISSN 0071-6464

SPECIAL SALES

This book is available at special discounts for bulk purchases for sales promotions or premiums. Special editions, including personalized covers, excerpts of existing books, and corporate imprints, can be created in large quantities for special needs. For more information, write to Special Markets/Premium Sales, 1745 Broadway, MD 3-1, New York, NY 10019, or e-mail specialmarkets@randomhouse.com.

AN IMPORTANT TIP & AN INVITATION

Although all prices, opening times, and other details in this book are based on information supplied to us at press time, changes occur all the time in the travel world, and Fodor's cannot accept responsibility for facts that become outdated or for inadvertent errors or omissions. So **always confirm information when it matters**, especially if you're making a detour to visit a specific place. Your experiences—positive and negative— matter to us. If we have missed or misstated something, **please write to us.** Share your opinion instantly through our online feedback center at fodors.com/contact-us.

PRINTED IN COLOMBIA

10 9 8 7 6 5 4 3 2 1

CONTENTS

Fodor's Features

MAPS

ABOUT THIS GUIDE

Fodor's Ratings

Everything in this guide is worth doing—we don't cover what isn't—but exceptional sights, hotels, and restaurants are recognized with additional accolades. Fodor'sChoice★ indicates our top recommendations; ★ highlights places we deem highly recommended; and **Best Bets** call attention to notable hotels and restaurants in various categories. Care to nominate a new place? Visit Fodors.com/contact-us.

Trip Costs

We list prices wherever possible to help you budget well. Hotel and restaurant price categories from **$** to **$$$$** are noted alongside each recommendation. For hotels, we include the lowest cost of a standard double room in high season. For restaurants, we cite the average price of a main course at dinner or, if dinner isn't served, at lunch. For attractions, we always list adult admission fees; discounts are usually available for children, students, and senior citizens.

Hotels

Our local writers vet every hotel to recommend the best overnights in each price category, from budget to expensive. Unless otherwise specified, you can expect private bath, phone, and TV in your room. For expanded hotel reviews, facilities, and deals visit Fodors.com.

TripAdvisor ◎◎

Our expert hotel picks are reinforced by high ratings on TripAdvisor. Look for representative quotes in this guide, and the latest TripAdvisor ratings and feedback at Fodors.com.

Ratings		Hotels & Restaurants	
★	Fodor's Choice	🏨	Hotel
★	Highly recommended	⤵	Number of rooms
☾	Family-friendly	❘❍❘	Meal plans
Listings		✕	Restaurant
✉	Address	⌅	Reservations
✉	Branch address	👘	Dress code
☎	Telephone	▭	No credit cards
🖷	Fax	💲	Price
⊕	Website		
✍	E-mail	**Other**	
🎫	Admission fee	⇨	See also
☉	Open/closed times	☞	Take note
Ⓜ	Subway	🏌	Golf facilities
⊹	Directions or Map coordinates		

Restaurants

Unless we state otherwise, restaurants are open for lunch and dinner daily. We mention dress code only when there's a specific requirement and reservations only when they're essential or not accepted. To make restaurant reservations, visit Fodors.com.

Credit Cards

The hotels and restaurants in this guide typically accept credit cards. If not, we'll say so.

Experience
Ireland

WHAT'S NEW

From Boom to . . . ?

If your only contact with Ireland has been through the international media, you might be moved to pity and fear at the plight of this fragile, little island. In the last few years, the Irish have suffered the classic Greek tragedy (incidentally so have the Greeks). Years of double-digit growth had led to the pride and vanity of the Celtic Tiger, so the fall was far and deep when the international financial crisis swept across the old sod in a tsunami of bad debt.

A massive economic bailout by the European Union and the IMF mean that Ireland has effectively lost its financial sovereignty, something truly precious to every citizen, as it was won with blood and sacrifice less than a century ago in rebellion against the British. The blight of emigration has returned, with many of our overeducated young people forced to say good-bye to a homeland that cannot sustain their hopes and ambitions.

The ongoing negative fallout is familiar the world over, except deeper and scarier: property prices have nearly halved, unemployment has tripled, government budget cuts have slashed public services, and "The Great Recession" has replaced "the boom" as the most boring thing to bring up in the midst of a good pub conservation. While some commentators dare to suggest there are the first hints of hints of a recovery, and Ireland has been the only bailed-out country in Europe to hit it's fiscal targets, it will be years before the country is truly back on its own feet.

Even though it all ended in tears, the decade-long period of rapid growth and expansion changed the face of timeless Ireland forever. The paw print of the "Tiger" is everywhere: brash modern buildings; state-of-the-art highways; well-educated, confident young people; a slew of new immigrants from all corners of the globe; and the highest mobile phone usage in Europe—the Ireland of idyllic postcard simplicity (if it ever existed) is truly gone forever, and with it, all those images of red-haired colleens leading turf-laden donkeys to thatched cottages.

But beneath the headlines and the grimness of the financial news, real Ireland—the things that were never for sale—goes on, and perhaps even shows signs of prospering. The landscape is still ancient, empty, and breathtakingly beautiful. History, drama, and passion shine from every ruined castle wall and old Irish poem.

The Culture Industry

People tend to reassess what really matters in a crisis. In Ireland, one result of the boom has been a refocusing of attention on culture as a window into the damaged soul of the nation, and as a possible creative drive to help us right the listing ship. In late 2011, the country took the bold step to elect a poet and intellectual, Michael D. Higgins, as president, beating a celebrity businessman into a distant second place. While his power is limited, the symbolic value of the move was clear; we value things other than money. Funding for the arts may have been cut, but affordable spaces have become available for galleries and plays and people are turning again to artists to look deeper at the true state of the nation. Small theatre companies are springing up in unexpected places and film is actually one of the few growth industries. Rich in technical and acting talent, and suddenly affordable once again, Ireland has recently become a prized location for the world's top film and TV producers: don't be surprised to run into one of your favorite marauding characters from Game of Thrones (filmed largely in Northern Ireland) on your travels.

Titanic Belfast

Sometimes it's hard to believe that a ship that sank on its maiden voyage, causing an international scandal and untold tragedy, has become one of the world's great iconic stories. Belfast isn't complaining. In early 2012, on the centenary of the launch and sinking of the *Titanic*, the city that built the mighty leviathan began a huge waterfront development to return life to the once proud dockyard district. At the heart of the project is the majestic new Titanic Belfast, a museum dedicated to the construction and story of the doomed ocean liner. Slick, ambitious, and high-tech (sounds a bit like a press release for the original ship), the museum sets out to take ownership of the story for Belfast and continue the revival and regeneration of that long-blighted city. With a wealth of hotels, restaurants, bars, and cultural spaces planned for the whole docklands, there's a feeling that the city that refused to sink might just be able to relaunch itself as the coming place to visit on the island of Ireland.

Co-op is the New Zeitgeist

While Cork, the "other capital city" is blessed with the elegant and lively Victorian-style English Market, Dublin has for years lacked anything that could truly be called a city market. Enter the Dublin Food Co-op in Newmarket Square, a colorful, "muck on your potatoes" covered market set up in an old warehouse space left empty by the great economic bubble-popping.

A true organic food market every Saturday, and, alternatively, a vintage furniture, children's, and bric-a-brac market on Sundays, the Co-op has captured the zeitgeist of New Dublin better than any other space. Loose, humble, democratic, fun, and, most of all, real, it replaces glitz and PR with hard work, community, generosity, and creativity.

Local bakers, cheese makers, veggie growers, and craftspeople have come together to make something out of nothing. The little ad-hoc café at the back serves some of the best-value food around—their fresh blueberry pancakes taste all the better for the lack of hype and hyperbole in the air.

If you want to see the Irish at their best, coping with the tragedy that has befallen their nation, you could do worse than spend a Saturday morning in Newmarket Square.

WHAT'S WHERE

Numbers refer to chapters.

2 Dublin. A transformed city since the days of O'Casey and Joyce, Ireland's capital may have replaced its legendary tenements with modern high-rises but its essential spirit remains intact. One of Europe's most popular city-break destinations, it has art, culture, Georgian architecture, and, of course, hundreds of pubs where conversation and vocal dexterity continue to flourish within an increasingly multicultural mix. Get spirited (pun intended) at the Guinness Brewery, "Rock 'n' Stroll" your way through hip Temple Bar, and be illuminated by the *Book of Kells* at Trinity College's great library.

3 Dublin Environs. The counties outside the Pale are a treasure trove of history, monastic settlements, ancient tombs, battlefields, and peaceful valleys only an hour from the hubbub of the capital's center. From the lush greenery of Kildare and Wicklow, to the mythology and traditions of Meath and Louth, the historic timeline encompasses many of the pivotal pre-Christian and early Church locales of Ireland's past. Listen for ancient echoes at the Hill of Tara, hike into prehistory at Newgrange, and opt for opulence at Castletown House.

4 The Midlands. Overlooked by many visitors due to the region's relative absence of wow-factor attractions, this verdant oasis of bog and lake harks back to the simpler, and slower, life of Ireland 40 years ago. Friendly, almost shy natives, old-style pubs, unspoiled vistas and walks, plus a wealth of historic ruins make for a relaxing adventure into the way we were. Tree-hug one of the great yews at Tullynally Gardens, lift your spirits at Clonmacnoise, and take a river cruise down the Shannon.

5 The Southeast. Ireland's sunniest corner (with almost double the national average), the coastal counties have long been the favored hideaway of Dublin folk on vacation. Quiet seaside villages, country houses, and some of the nation's best land all offer delightful reasons to tarry. Inland, counties like Kilkenny and Tipperary offer a lion's share of history and important monuments in the main towns, Wexford and Waterford. Follow in the footsteps of St. Patrick at the Rock of Cashel, dig the ducal lifestyle at Lismore, and romp in the brisk waters of the pristine beaches around the fishing village of Ardmore.

6 County Cork. After exploring the delights of Cork City—museums, lively pubs, quirky cafés, and lots of good music, trad and otherwise—use it as a base to explore Ireland's largest county, as nearly everyone heads to get the gift of gab by kissing the famous Blarney Stone. Get your fill of five-star scenery by traveling east to Shanagarry—teach yourself good taste at Ballymaloe House, pioneer of the new Irish cuisine. Due south is the "Irish St-Tropez," fashionable Kinsale, while westward lies Bantry, one of Ireland's finest stately homes, which sits atop a breathtaking bluff over Bantry Bay. From here a cliff-top road with stunning views leads to ruggedly beautiful Glengarriff.

WHAT'S WHERE

7 The Southwest. The counties of Kerry and Limerick have sights that top every tourist's must-see list. The most brazenly scenic coastal drive in the land, the Ring of Kerry, will use up your entire flash card in a jiffy! While there, take a wet and wonderful ride out to the sea-wrapped Skellig islands, whose twin peaks rise out of the sea. The Gap of Dunloe lets you walk through the heart of Killarney's purple mountains and cross the glittering blue lake of Killarney. And don't forget to have your Nikon handy for Ireland's prettiest village, Adare. Everywhere, the glories of Ireland's coastline combine to paint a canvas that still casts a potent spell upon the stranger.

8 County Clare, Galway, and the Aran Islands. Set with postcard-perfect villages like Doolin, the lunar landscape of the Burren, and the towering Cliffs of Moher (they'll give you a new understanding of the word "awesome"), County Clare is pure tourist gold. For a complete change of pace, head to nearby Galway City: one of Ireland's liveliest, it has a compact historic center bursting with artistic energy and a lively pub culture. This is also the place to organize your trip to the Oileáin Árainn (Aran Islands), three outposts of Gaelic civilization, which still have a strong whiff of the "old ways"—and not just the whiff of turf smoke.

9 Connemara and County Mayo. With the most westerly seaboard in Europe, this region remains a place apart—the most Irish part of Ireland. Connemara is an almost uninhabited landscape of misty bogland, studded with deep blue lakes under huge Atlantic skies, and distant purple hills: painters and photographers have strived for generations to capture the ever-changing light. Nearby is the delightful village of Cong, setting for *The Quiet Man*, where fetching ivy-covered thatched cottages contrast with the baronial splendor of Ashford Castle. For bright lights, head to Clifden and Westport, both lively small towns of great charm.

10 The Northwest. Sligo, Leitrim, and Donegal are homelands of rugged, self-sufficient people and roads where wandering sheep and cows are still the norm. Weatherwise, the area gets more than its fair share of the elements—a condition more than compensated for in its warm welcomes. Take a poetry break beside Yeats's grave near Ben Bulben, discover hidden Glencolumbkille, and immerse yourself in Irish in Sligo town.

11 Northern Ireland. This region has positively bloomed since the peace dividend of recent times, which finally nailed the coffin lid upon "the Troubles." From the beauty of Antrim's coastline to the vibrant cultural renaissance of Derry and Belfast, Northern Ireland has finally emerged from the yoke of its sectarian past into a present full of promise and possibility. Cross the Giant's Causeway, slide into a cozy snug in a pub on Belfast's Golden Mile, and trail after Eire's "wee folk" in the shimmery Glens of Antrim.

9

MAYO

Achill Island

Clare Island

Clew Bay

Inishturk

Inishbofin

Lough Corrib

Oileáin Árainn
(Aran Islands)

Galway

Kilrush

Mouth of the Shannon

Listowel

Tralee

Corca Dhuibhne
[Dingle Peninsula]

Blasket Islands

Dingle Bay

Killarney

Iveragh Peninsula

KERRY

Skellig Rocks

7

Beara Peninsula

Kenmare Bay

Bantry Bay

Mizen Head

Malin Head

Rathlin Island

SCOTLAND
(United Kingdom)

Toraigh
(Tory Island)

North Channel

Portrush

Coleraine

Lough Foyle

Ariann Mhor
(Aranmore Island)

Letterkenny

Derry City

ANTRIM

DONEGAL

DERRY

Ballymena

Larne

Strabane

**NORTHERN
IRELAND**

Island Magee

*Gweebarra
Bay*

Donegal
Town

(United Kingdom)

Omagh

Cookstown

Lough
Neagh

BELFAST

Newtownards

Belfast Lough

11

*Donegal
Bay*

Ballyshannon

*Lower
Lough Erne*

TYRONE

Dungannon

DOWN

*Killala
Bay*

*Sligo
Bay*

LEITRIM

FERMANACH

Armagh City

Ballina

Sligo Town

*Upper
Lough Erne*

Monaghan
City

ARMAGH

Newcastle

10

Newry

*ough
Conn*

SLIGO

River Shannon

MONAGHAN

Dundalk

Castlebar

ROSCOMMON

Cavan

CAVAN

Dundalk Bay

*Lough
Mask*

Knock

Longford

LOUTH

Drogheda

LONGFORD

MEATH

GALWAY

WESTMEATH

Mullingar

DUBLIN

Ballinasloe

Athlone

DUBLIN

Bay

Galway City

OFFALY

Naas

Dún Laoghaire

8

Birr

KILDARE

Bray

Irish Sea

REPUBLIC OF IRELAND

Portlaoise

WICKLOW

Wicklow

Ennis

LAOIS

Athy

Roscrea

CLARE

Nenagh

Arklow

Shannon

TIPPERARY

Kilkenny
City

CARLOW

Gorey

Limerick

Thurles

LIMERICK

City

Cashel

KILKENNY

WEXFORD

Newcastle
West

Tipperary
Town

Clonmel

Carrick-on-Suir

Wexford Town

Mallow

Farahy

WATERFORD

Waterford

CORK

Midleton

Youghal

St. George's Channel

Cork City

Cobh

Kinsale

Skibbereen

| 0 | | 50 mi |

| 0 | | 50 km |

IRELAND PLANNER

Safety

Ireland is still essentially a safe country, but you do need to observe some basic precautions.

Don't leave valuables in a rental car: this is advice countless visitors neglect with sad consequences. Most car theft is opportunistic—if there's nothing visible like a pocketbook, a bag, a camera, even maps or guides within the car, most likely your petty criminal will amble past toward more available pickings.

Likewise, when parking in urban areas, use a car park—this also guards against auto clampers (a recent scourge of Irish towns, where fines to release your car cost up to €130).

Carry only the minimal amount of cash with perhaps one credit card when strolling around the streets and shops—while handbag snatching is infrequent, there's no point in making yourself a possible target.

Getting Here

Dublin Airport is the main arrival point for the whole country, with regular flights from most of the world's major destinations. With the new road system, it is relatively easy to get from the airport to even the most isolated area in a few hours. Shannon Airport in County Clare also has direct flights from the United States and is a good starting point if you plan to explore in the West and Southwest. Belfast is the main airport in Northern Ireland and has direct flights from the East Coast of the United States. Smaller airports at Cork and Knock have regular flights to the United Kingdom and mainland Europe. Ferries from Britain and France arrive at ports in Dublin, Rosslare, Larne, and Cork.

Getting Around

The Irish bus and rail network made great strides in recent decades, but recent cutbacks may see a reduction in service and routes. All urban centers and towns are now interconnected by bus and rail, and you shouldn't have difficulty crisscrossing the country in any direction.

But if you can, opt for a car—its greater flexibility, combined with the possibility of meandering down byways and country lanes, opens up a great many more vistas than any train will do. Rental rates are on par with most EU countries, and offices are located at all airports, ferry terminals, and town centers. During the summer months, it's wise to book in advance.

FROM DUBLIN TO	BY CAR	BY TRAIN
Cork	3 hr 5 min	3 hr
Belfast	2 hr 15 min	2 hr
Galway	2 hr 20 min	2 hr 10 min
Kilkenny	1 hr 30 min	1 hr 45 min
Killarney	3 hr 50 min	3 hr 20 min
Limerick	2 hr 20 min	2 hr
Sligo	2 hr 50 min	3 hr 5 min

Restaurant Basics

For too many years the restaurant scene in Ireland was a bit of a joke among locals and visitors alike: exactly how many ways can you serve potatoes? One welcome legacy of the false boom was an explosion of modern, metropolitan eateries. An influx of immigrants played its part, particularly the Chinese colonization of Parnell Street in Dublin and the sprouting up of real Italian enotecas like Delle Langhe. But Irish chefs also rose to the challenge, using Ireland's nonpareil produce to reimagine Irish cuisine, with places like One Pico in Dublin and the Cliff House in Ardmore Waterford leading the way. The downturn has seen a cull of some of the more ostentatious restaurants, but fresh and cool new places have been popping up—literally—all over town; a crop of exciting, unscripted, temporary, "Pop-Up" eateries have been opening in the premises of closed down Celtic Tiger vanities. Crackbird in Dublin is a prime example of this spirit of make-do and daring.

Overall, there's a return to good food, good quality, and good service. The locavore movement has taken root in Ireland and the demand for organic and locally sourced produce, as well as, in general, health-conscious options is reflected on Irish menus around the country. Visitors are often surprised to find how celiac-friendly Irish restaurants are; look for the "C" for celiac on nearly every menu in town—there's even a separate line for gluten-free communion in Mass!

Hotel Basics

Determining your budget is the key here—are you content with B&Bs and small hotels, or do you want to splurge on castles and grand country houses? It's best when planning your trip to Ireland to set aside a few hours of Web browsing to familiarize yourself with costs and standards. Certainly prices have fallen drastically in the last few years, and value is there to be had with careful planning, plus a bit of haggling if you are game. As well as our own site— ⊕ *Fodors.com*—which should be your first stop, try ⊕ *www.goireland.com* and ⊕ *www.visitdublin.ie*. The Irish Tourist Board's website— ⊕ *www.discoverireland.com*—is a mine of information and a good overview of the whole country. For a week's stay in Ireland, consider small city-center hotels in Dublin, Cork, and Galway. For at least one night, consider staying in a castle or country house— it'll be costly, but very memorable. Check out ⊕ *www. irelandsbluebook.com* for a select listing.

Stretching Your Dollar

At this writing, the dollar is struggling against the euro—($1.32 to €1)—but the situation is pretty fluid. While nobody wants to penny-pinch on vacation, a few changes can yield savings without upsetting your holiday.

For starters, take a bus from the airport—it'll be one-quarter the cost of a cab and will get you into town twice as fast on dedicated bus corridors now operating in all cities.

Stay at B&Bs. They're well located and they'll have comfy bedrooms, good food, and an all-knowing landlady to answer all your questions. Listen carefully to her advice on bargain shopping, as she's got an inside line you'll not find on any website. In restaurants, opt for the house wine—the Irish have become serious wine-drinkers in recent years and the house stuff is no longer just "plonk" for unsophisticated palates.

At lunchtime, why not try a picnic? After all, you're here to see scenery, and given that the changeable weather does allow for some dazzling sunshine most days, why not pack a few sandwiches and some drinks or coffee? Ireland is full of wonderful road pull-ins where you can park, walk a few minutes, and dine in glorious isolation to the sound of gurgling streams, lowing cows, or wind echoing across an open plain.

IRELAND TODAY

Politics

There's nothing like the worst economic crisis in living memory to shake up the political waters. Fianna Fáil, a center-right party that was in power for most of the last two decades, was crushed in the 2010 elections due to its part in inflating Ireland's property bubble and spectacularly mishandling the economy. They have been replaced by a coalition made up of center-right Fine Gael and the center-left Labour Party. With a huge majority this coalition has begun to see its popularity plummet as it implements the tough austerity measures agreed to in the bailout deal with the IMF and the European Union. That deal means, in effect, that the Irish government has lost sovereignty over the country's finances, a humbling situation for any country, especially one relatively recently freed from the shackles of imperialism. There is much talk of a "new politics," with transparency and honesty now the favorite buzzwords, but it remains to be seen whether the men in power (and in Ireland they are still mostly men) have learned anything. At any bar, talk of politics will lead directly to the ailing economy or the Irish health service and its poor state—everybody will tell you a story of taking their kid to the local emergency room and waiting five hours for someone to look at a broken finger. One recent government minister described the health portfolio as "Angola," a concise definition that spoke volumes. Ireland's a great country with wonderful people, goes the common view—just don't get sick (unless you have good travel insurance).

Economics

What is there to say? If Ireland's economy were a patient, then it would be on life support, crippled by an illness brought on by years of excess and self-delusion. Strangely, Ireland's exports are climbing at record rates, with food processing and IT two growth areas, but the domestic market has completely collapsed. Nobody is buying, selling, or building houses, and ghost estates around the country testify to the surplus of properties built (usually in the wrong place) during the madness of the last years of the Tiger. The locals are saving like frightened squirrels, meaning that there's precious little money to ignite consumer sales. So travelers are valued more than ever, adding greatly to your haggling power.

Media

As the church confessional is no longer the purge-zone of choice for the majority of Irish people, radio and TV talk shows have stepped in to fill the void. Every topic under the sun is squeezed and caressed over the airwaves on a daily basis—lesbian nuns, love on the Web, cheap retirement in Bulgaria, mother-and-daughter double-date rules, not to mention one beer-tasting show where brands from around the world are digested in an ever-downward spiral of drunken hilarity. Not quite Howard Stern, you understand, but eons beyond Vatican II. Newspapers include the major three dailies: the *Irish Times,* the *Irish Independent,* and the *Irish Examiner.* A host of U.K. tabloids have also entered the market in recent years, with the *Mail,* the *Sun,* and the *Mirror* being the leading lights. So-called freesheets—morning commuter giveaway papers containing a condensed version of the day's news plus heaps of advertising—are similarly flexing their literary muscles.

People

For all of their dangerous propensity to rack up the biggest credit card debt in Europe on BMWs, boob jobs, and second homes on Capri, most Irish were, at heart, as confused by life in Celtic Tiger Ireland as the tourists might have been. It all came to us too fast and too flashy, how could we say no? The Irish, when they have a job, still work some of the longest hours, on average, in Europe, but despite their breezy, world-weary air, they remain largely as enthusiastic and comic about life as they ever were. One caller to a radio show summed up his ideal life: "a two-car garage, sex with my wife twice a week, a 12 handicap, and kids who won't call me a loser to my face." The average Joe is in there somewhere.

Religion

Priests and bishops (and even the Pope) continue to hit the headlines through sex scandals and revelations of criminal pedophilia cover-ups that have rocked Ireland for more than a decade. The church has fallen a long way in the estimation of most of the population, and suddenly the media is not afraid to ask some searing questions about the church's past and future. Older people are struggling to come to terms with this national loss of trust in their hallowed institution, while increasing numbers of younger folks are turning their backs on regular Mass-going.

Irish-born men entering the priesthood is down to a handful each year and African priests are often shipped in to fill the breach. A majority of the population will still go to church for births, marriages, and funerals but there is a noted decrease in involvement of priests in the social fabric of Irish life. The Catholic Church in Ireland, it seems, will have to quickly redefine and rebrand itself if it is not to go the way of the Church of England in the United Kingdom and become a minority sideshow.

Sports

In these dark times the enduring love affair between the Irish and their sports has taken on an added importance. Major victories for golfers like Darren Clarke and Rory McIlroy lift the nation's spirits for a day or two. Football and hurling are still enshrined as the national pastimes—but only just ahead of rugby, soccer, and horse racing.

For a small nation, Ireland has consistently punched above its weight in the global arena, as exemplified by the recent qualification for Euro 2012 by the much-maligned soccer team. Every second pub has a satellite dish pulling down anything from badminton in Bhutan to sumo wrestling in Tokyo. It's no surprise that images of winning football teams reside in pride of place on many pub walls.

Culture

Neither the World Wide Web, cellular texting, nor Internet gaming will dent the nation's fondness for the written word. Although there have been few to match the talent of Shaw, Wilde, and Joyce, the huge-selling works of Joe O'Connor, Roddy Doyle, Colum McCann, and Colm Tóbín underline the country as one of the biggest book-buying populations in Europe.

In the movies, time and tide have taken us a long way from John Wayne in *The Quiet Man* to the modern romance of *Once* and writer-directors like Neil Jordan, Jim Sheridan, and Noel Pearson and their warts-and-all visions of modern Ireland.

IRELAND
TOP ATTRACTIONS

The Rock of Cashel

(A) The center of tribal and religious power for more than a thousand years, it became the seat of the Munster Kings in the 5th century. Handed over to the early Christian Church in 1101, the medieval abbey perched on a limestone mount in Tipperary contains rare Romanesque sculpture and carvings celebrating St. Patrick's visit there in 450.

The Giant's Causeway

(B) Irish mythology claims that the warrior Fionn Mac Cumhaill (Finn McCool) laid the Antrim causeway himself to enable easy crossing to his lover on Staffa Island off the Scottish coast, where similar basalt columns are found. Formed by volcanic eruptions more than 60 million years ago, the area is a magical mix of looming cliffs and thundering surf—and an awesome reminder of nature's power.

Newgrange

(C) Stonehenge and the pyramids at Giza are spring chickens compared to Newgrange, one of the most fascinating sites near Dublin. Built around 5,200 years ago, Newgrange is a passage tomb—a huge mound of earth with a stone passageway leading to a burial chamber constructed entirely of dry stone (mortar wasn't invented yet). Steeped in Celtic myth and lore, these graves were built for the Kings of Tara. Untouched for centuries, the main chamber was excavated in the 1960s and revealed itself as the world's oldest solar observatory, where the sun's rays light up the interior on December 21 each year.

Book of Kells

(D) If you visit only one attraction in Dublin, let it be this extraordinary creation housed in Trinity College. Often called "the most beautiful book in the world," the manuscript dates to the 8th or 9th century and remains a marvel of intricacy and creativity. Fashioned by monks probably based on the Hebridean island of Iona, and worked with reed pens and iron-gall ink on a folded section of vellum, the manuscript demonstrates a sense of sublime balance and beauty in elaborate interlaces, abstractions, and "carpet-pages."

The Blarney Stone

(E) One of the country's most enduring myths, wherein kissing a stone high upon the battlements of a ruined Cork castle bestows a magical eloquence on the visitor, may also be one of its most ludicrous. Grasped by the ankles and hanging perilously upside down to pucker upon ancient rock, you'll certainly have a tall tale to tell the folks back home. Despite the difficulty, there's generally a long line waiting to scale the skeletal remains of Blarney Castle, a strangely derelict edifice in the otherwise neatly groomed estate; try to visit in the very early morning.

Ring of Kerry

(F) Ireland's most popular scenic route, the Ring of Kerry is one of Europe's grandest drives, combining mountainous splendor with a spectacularly varied coastline. It's best to escape the tour buses that choke its main road by taking to the hills on foot, by horseback, or by bike.

Aran Islands

(G) Famed for their haunting beauty, these three islands set in Galway Bay have lured artists, writers, and multitudes of curious visitors for decades. On Inishmore, Inishmaan, and Inisheer you'll find a mode of life that reflects man's struggle against nature. Topped with the stone forts and crisscrossed by ancient "garden" walls, they epitomize solitude—one reason Irish bards like playwright J. M. Synge visited them many times.

FESTIVALS AND EVENTS

Make Like a Bird

Happening on the May Bank Holiday Weekend, the **Kinvara Cuckoo Fleadh** (⊕ *www.kinvara.com*) is perfectly timed to welcome in the warmer evenings of early summer. A well-established and richly deserved reputation has ensured that the fleadh has become a showcase for the best in traditional music, attracting musicians from all over the country and beyond. An added bonus is having it in one of the country's prettiest towns in beautiful County Galway

Sonatas in Ancient Grandeur

Among the architectural grandeur that is Bantry House in Cork, the annual music festival (⊕ *www.westcorkmusic.ie*) allows for languid sunsets, picnics on the lawns, and sublime sounds from some of Europe's top classical musicians. The notes may be highbrow, but the vibe is indelibly Irish-mellow. The festival runs from the last week in June until the first week in July.

The Write Stuff

Fancy getting up close and personal with Lawrence Block, Roddy Doyle, Colm Tóbín, Neil Jordan, Anne Enright, and a host of other literary greats? **Listowel Writer's Week** (⊕ *www.writersweek.ie*) is a chaotic and seriously democratic gathering devoted to all things literary—including numerous workshops by the greats where info on writing your own masterpiece is there for the asking. This being Kerry, expect discussions to last well toward dawn. It takes place all over the town of Listowel on the first weekend in June.

Lark in the Park

Every June, Cork city struts its artistic stuff with the **Midsummer Festival** (⊕ *www.corkmidsummer.com*), a mix of music, film, and theater. Be sure to get tickets for whatever the Corcadorca Theatre Company is doing—in the past they've taken Shakespeare to the local courthouse, the city morgue, and the expansive green spaces of Fitzgerald's Park: a very different experience from a company constantly pushing the envelope. It runs from the 21st of June to the end of the month.

Blooming Forth

Even though it is now reckoned that more Americans and Japanese attend the events surrounding **Bloomsday** (⊕ *www.jamesjoyce.ie*) than Irish people, it hasn't taken away a jot from an event that continues to grow regardless. Most Irish, if they're being honest, will probably admit to "never having actually finished *Ulysses*," but are still happy to discourse at length over devilled kidneys and other Joycean delights on the hidden meanings within this legendary work. Bloomsday is June 16th.

Extend Your Stay

With almost 100 acts in more than 25 venues across Dublin, the fledgling **10 Days in Dublin** (⊕ *www.10daysindublin.ie*) festival, inaugurated in 2011, showcases the best of emerging Irish music, film, spoken word, theater, comedy, and visual art for 10 days in early July. Highlights in 2012 included Trinity Orchestra performing "Dark Side of the Moon," Patrick Kelleher and his Cold Dead Hands, Donal Dineen, and Matthew Halpin Trio. Events are €10 or less.

Have a Flutter on the Nags

Galway Race Week (⊕ *www.galwayraces. com*) is one of the country's biggest events with most of Dublin, Cork, and Limerick decamping to the City of the Tribes for an end of July week of celebration centered half around equine excellence and half around pub sessions. Every politician worth his salt hits the races to press the flesh, followed by legions of supporters and onlookers out for the "craic"—of which there is an endless supply.

Good for the Sole

On the last Sunday in July, join the thousands of pilgrims/adventurers who climb Mayo's **Croagh Patrick** (⊕ *www.croaghpatrick.com*)—and in your bare feet for the full purging of your misdeeds. A ghostly hill, tricky loose stones underfoot, and a Mass overlooking Clew Bay: it all adds up to an experience that is difficult but hugely rewarding.

Acting the Goat

Puck Fair in Kerry (⊕ *www.puckfair.ie*) is the oldest festival in Ireland, dating back to pagan times, where a goat is made king for three days of drinking, dancing, and general abandon. In the town of Killorglin, County Kerry, pubs stay open all night, traveler folk sell horses and cows on Main Street, and up to 100,000 people crowd this tiny town of 58 pubs for a mad three-day weekend. Held on the second weekend in August, it's all in all, truly one of Ireland's most unusual festivals.

Gather Those Boats

Cruínniu na mBád (⊕ *www.kinvara.com/cruinniu*), or the Gathering of the Boats, is basically a big booze-up and regatta to celebrate the unique and beautiful boat that is the Galway Hooker—a sleek, dark little sailing vessel with rusty red sails originally used to transport turf and other necessities along the harsh Atlantic coast of Ireland. The event takes place around the third weekend in August around southern County Galway, with traditional boat races the excuse for a "hooley," or party of trad music and late nights.

Clash of the Ash

Usually happening on the first Sunday in September, the **All-Ireland Hurling Final** (⊕ *www.gaa.ie*), at Dublin's Croke Park, is a uniquely Irish sporting spectacle. Thirty highly amped players clutching ash hurleys whack a heavy leather ball, or sliothar, at warp speeds around the pitch as they slug it out for the sport's highest prize. Raw emotions, brilliant color, and Harry Potter–ish skills that you won't see back home make it memorable.

Food, Glorious Food

Long noted for its cuisine innovations, the **Kinsale Gourmet Festival** (⊕ *www. kinsalerestaurants.com*) is all about the happy pursuit of great food and wine plus the excitable bravado of this infectious coastal town. Buy a weekend ticket, have breakfast on a boat, lunch at a pierside pub, and dinner at any of the dozens of great eateries in this amazingly friendly town. It takes place on the second weekend in October.

What a Wonderful World

For jazz lovers, the **Cork Jazz Festival** (⊕ *www.guinnessjazzfestival.com*) on the Halloween bank holiday weekend in October is a perfect antidote to the approaching dark evenings of winter. George Melly, one of the music legends who visits regularly, puts it thus: "I forget where I've parked, where I'm meant to be playing, and, sometimes, even who I am—but it all works out in the end." A fair description of a festival with heart and soul.

QUINTESSENTIAL IRELAND

The Pub: Pillar of Irish Social Life

It's been said that the pub is the poor man's university. If this is true, Ireland has more than 10,000 opportunities for higher education. Even if you only order an Evian, a visit to a pub (if not two or three) is a must.

The Irish public house is a national institution—down to the spectacle, at some pubs, of patrons standing at closing time for the playing of Ireland's national anthem. Samuel Beckett would often repair to a pub, believing a glass of Guinness stout was the best way to ward off depression.

Pubs remain pillars of Irish social life—places to chat, listen, learn, gossip, and, of course, enjoy a throaty sing-along.

Impromptu concerts often break out, and if you're really enjoying the craic—quintessentially Irish friendly chat and lively conversation—it's good form to buy a pint for the performers.

Wherever you go, remember that when you order a Guinness, the barman first pours it three-quarters of the way, then lets it settle, then tops it off and brings it over to the bar.

The customer should then wait again until the top-up has settled, at which point the brew turns a deep black.

The mark of a perfect pint? As you drink the liquid down, the brew will leave thin rings on the glass to mark each mouthful.

"Fleadhs" and Festivals

From bouncing-baby competitions to traditional-music festivals, the tradition of the fleadh (festival, pronounced "flah") is alive and well in Ireland year-round.

Before you leave home, check on regional Irish tourist websites or, upon arrival, discuss the local happenings with local tourist boards or your hotel concierge.

Music festivals rule the roost—Kinvara's Cuckoo Fleadh, Galway's Festival of Irish

If you want to get a sense of Irish culture and indulge in some of its pleasures, start by familiarizing yourself with the rituals of daily life. These are a few highlights—things you can take part in with relative ease.

Popular Music, the giant Fleadh Cheoil na hÉireann, and the World Irish Dancing Championships (held every April in Ennis) are some major events.

But there are also village festivals dedicated to hill walking, fishing, poetry, art, and food; the Mullaghmore Lobster Festival in August always proves mighty tasty.

Keep A'Clappin' and A'Tappin'

Ceol agus craic, loosely translated as "music and merriment," are not simply recreations in Ireland. They are part of the very fabric of the national identity.

Ask most Irish men or women in exile what they miss most about home and, more than likely, those words "the craic" will be uttered.

And the beat and rhythm that accompany Irish fun are the "4/4" of the reel and the jig. Wherever you go you'll find that every town buzzes with its own blend of styles and sounds.

In its most exciting form, "trad" music is an impromptu affair, with a single guitar or fiddle player belting out a few tunes until other musicians—flute, whistle, uilleann pipes, concertina, and bodhrán drum—seem to arrive out of the pub's dark corners and are quickly drawn into the unstoppable force of the session.

A check of local event guides will turn up a wealth of live entertainment—if you're lucky you'll find a world-class artist in performance whose talents are unsung outside a small circle of friends and fans.

On some nights, Dublin itself—with more than 120 different clubs and music pubs to choose from—almost becomes one giant traditional-music jam session. Where to head first? Just take a walk down Grafton Street and keep your ears open.

WHEN TO GO

You don't come to Ireland for the weather. As the saying goes, "If you could put a roof on the country it'd be perfect." That said, in summer the weather can be pleasant: the ever-present rain clouds responsible for the evergreen countryside often take a vacation; the sun comes out (and everything in the country comes to a halt to appreciate it!); and the days are long, with daylight lasting until after 10 in late June and July. As British and Irish school vacations overlap from late June to mid-September, vacationers descend on popular coastal resorts in the South, West, and East. There are crowds in popular holiday spots, and prices for accommodations are at their peak. Festival season is also at its peak; in the summer months the country is host to festival events big and small, offering a wide variety of music festivals like Electric Picnic, Castlepalooza, and Spirit of Folk Festival, as well as events celebrating everything from food and comedy, to surfing, goats, and Irish beauty. Local sports also heat up in the summer months as counties battle it out to reach the All-Ireland hurling and football finals in September. In short, if you can afford the flights and peak rates, summer is the time to visit.

If the purse strings are a little unforgiving, it's best to visit Ireland outside peak travel months. Fall and spring are good times to travel (late September can be dry and warm, although the weather can be unpredictable). Seasonal hotels and restaurants close from early or mid-November until mid-March or Easter. During this off-season, prices are lower than in summer, but your selection is limited, and some minor attractions close. St. Patrick's Week gives a focal point to a spring visit, but some Americans may find the saint's-day celebrations a little less enthusiastic than the ones back home.

Festivals

If you plan to visit the biggest festivals in Ireland, book well in advance. In March, Ireland's major St. Patrick's event is the **Dublin Festival and Parade** (⊕ *www.stpatricksday.ie*), which includes fireworks and bands from the U.S. In April, see the spectacular **World Irish Dancing Championships**. In May, the **Fleadh Nua**, the annual festival of traditional Irish music, song, and dance, takes place at a town (on a yearly rotation) in County Clare. August a "trad" music highlight: the **Fleadh Cheoil na hEireann** (⊕ *www.fleadhcheoil.ie*), held the last weekend of August or the first weekend in September, an extravaganza across the country. In October, the **Dublin Theatre Festival** (⊕ *www.dublintheatrefestival.com*) puts on 10 international productions, 10 Irish plays, and a fringe of 60-plus plays. In October, the **Wexford Opera Festival** (⊕ *www.wexfordopera.com*) is high glamour.

IF YOU LIKE

Beautiful Irish Villages

Nearly everyone has a mind's-eye view of the perfect Irish village. Cozy huddles filled with charming calendar cottages, mossy churchyards, and oozing with thatched-roof-pewter-and-china-dog atmosphere, these spots have a sense of once-upon-a-timefied tranquility that not even tour buses can ruin. Should you be after medicine for overtired nerves—a gentle peace in beautiful surroundings with a people so warm you'll be on first-name terms in five minutes—these will be your Arcadias. Many are so nestled away they remain the despair of motorists, but then no penciled itinerary is half as fun as stumbling upon these four-leaf clovers. Here are four of the most famous—but why not summon up courage, venture out on the lesser roads, and throw away the map?

Kinvara, Co. Galway. This village is picture-perfect, thanks to its gorgeous bayside locale, great walks, and numerous pubs. North of the town is spectacularly sited Dunguaire Castle, noted for its medieval-banquet evenings.

Cong, Co. Mayo. John Ford's *The Quiet Man* introduced this charmer to the world and the singular beauty of its whitewashed single-story cottages with tied-on thatched roofs.

Adare, Co. Limerick. Right out of a storybook, this celebrated village of low-slung Tudor cottages is adorned with ivied churches and a moated castle from the days when knighthood was in flower.

Lismore, Co. Tipperary. Set within some of Ireland's lushest pasturelands and lorded over by the Duke of Devonshire's castle, dreamy Lismore is popular with both romantic folk and anglers (the sparkling Blackwater here teems with salmon).

Celtic Sites

From rush hour on busy O'Connell Street in Dublin it's a long way to Tipperary's Cashel of the Kings, a group of ancient church relics—the largest in all Ireland—perched high above the plain on its famous rock. The journey is worth it, since it takes you back in time to the legendary days when Celtic Christianity conquered the isle of Eire. Beginning in the 5th century AD, hallowed shrines and monasteries sprung up across the land, often dotted with treasures sacred—the famous High Crosses, inscribed with biblical symbols and stories—and profane, such as the lofty Round Towers, lookouts for Viking raids. Just north of Dublin, around the Boyne Valley, you'll find two great sites: Tara, where "The Harp That Once Through Tara's Halls" played, and also Newgrange, once seat of the High Kings of Ireland.

Clonmacnoise, Co. Offaly. The isolated monastery at the confluence of two rivers was famous throughout Europe as a center of learning. It's also a royal burial ground.

Glendalough, Co. Wicklow. A monastery founded by a hermit in the 6th century, attacked by Vikings in the 10th century, and plundered by the English in the 12th century—your typical Irish ruins.

Rock of Cashel, Co. Tipperary. A cluster of ruins—cathedral, chapel, round tower—crowning a circular, mist-shrouded rock that rises from a plain.

Tara, Co. Meath. Fabled home of one of Ireland's titular High Kings, the ageless Hill of Tara has fired up people's imaginations from early Christians to Scarlett O'Hara.

Stately Houses

Ireland's stately homes are either proud reminders of a shared history with Britain or symbols of an oppressive colonial past. If you're interested in luxurious pomp and reliving the decadence of yesteryear, there's no denying the magnificence of these country estates and lavish mansions, erected by the Anglo-Irish Protestant Ascendancy in the 17th, 18th, and 19th centuries. The wealthy settlers constructed ornate houses in various architectural styles, with Palladian designs popular in the first half of the 18th century, before the Neoclassical and neo-Gothic influences took over. In the last century, several majestic piles—notably Ashford Castle in Cong and Dromoland Castle in Newmarket-on-Fergus—became hotels, so anyone can now enjoy a queen-for-a-stay fantasy.

Castle Ward, Co. Down. An architectural curiosity, in that it was built inside and out in two distinct styles, Classical and Gothic—perhaps because Viscount Bangor and his wife never could agree on anything.

Bantry House, Bantry, Co. Cork. Set in Italianate gardens and perched over one of Ireland's most spectacular bays, this manor has a Continental air, thanks to its extensive art collection, tapestries, and fine French furniture.

Castletown House, Co. Kildare. Renaissance architect Andrea Palladio would surely have approved of this exceedingly large and grand Palladian country house.

Florence Court, Co. Down. With magnificent Georgian-period stuccoed salons, this shimmering white mansion is strikingly set against the Cuilcagh Mountains where, legend has it, you can hear the "song of the little people."

Retail Therapy

Once you get past all the traditional Irish leprechauns with "made in China" stickers on their bottoms, you'll find that Ireland has some of Europe's finest-quality goods. Objects like a Donegal tweed hat or a hand-knit Aran sweater, a Belfast linen tablecloth, or a piece of Waterford or Cavan crystal can be pricey but will last a lifetime. In Dublin look for antiques, vintage books, or au courant European and Irish fashions, many showcased at cool shops like Costume and Platform. Galway has its share of galleries and offbeat boutiques and is a great spot for book shopping. Keep an eye open for signs indicating crafts workshops, where independent craftspeople sell directly from their studios. The best of the North's traditional products, many made according to time-honored methods, include exquisite linen, laces, and superior handmade woolen garments. Traditional music CDs and the unadorned blackthorn walking stick are two good choices at the other end of the price scale.

Kilkenny Design Craft Centre, Co. Kilkenny. Ireland's favorite emporium for Irish-designed crafts includes the best of Irish knitwear, crystal, jewelry, and pottery.

O'Sullivan Antiques, Dublin. Mia Farrow and Liam Neeson are just two fans of this purveyor of 19th-century delights.

Ardmore Pottery and Craft Gallery, Ardmore, Co. Waterford. Home to potter Mary Lincoln, this is one of the most beloved, creative, and cleverly stocked craft shops in the country.

Avoca, Co. Wicklow. The birthplace of the legendary Avoca mill, you can shop for vibrant throws, rugs, and scarves and meet the weavers at work.

Natural Wonders

It's not always easy to conjure up leprechauns and druids in today's Ireland, but head to any of its famously brooding landscapes and those legendary times will seem like yesterday. With its romantic coastlines, wild bogs, and rugged seascapes, the Emerald Isle is especially rich in rugged, wildly gorgeous spectacle. Around its natural splendors, the countryside is dotted with villages where sheep outnumber residents by 100 to 1. Unfortunately, sheep don't also outnumber tourists.

The Aran Islands, Galway Bay. The islands battle dramatically with sea and storm and now welcome droves of visitors who fall under the spell of their brooding beauty.

The Skelligs, Ring of Kerry. Be warned: these spectacular pinnacles of rock soaring out of the sea will haunt you for days.

The Burren, Co. Clare. A 300-square-km (116-square-mile) expanse that is one of Ireland's strangest landscapes, the Burren stretches off as far as the eye can see in a gray, rocky, lunar landscape that becomes a wild rock garden in spring.

Cliffs of Moher, Co. Clare. One of Ireland's most breathtaking natural sights, these majestic cliffs stretch for 8 km (5 miles). At some points, the only thing separating you from the sea, 700 feet below, is a patch of slippery heather.

Giant's Causeway, Co. Antrim, Northern Ireland. There are equal measures of legend and science surrounding this rock formation—a cluster of 37,000-odd volcanic basalt pillars.

Literary Haunts

Irish literature developed its distinctive traits largely because of Ireland's physical and political isolation. Yet the nation has produced a disproportionately large number of internationally famous authors for a country of her size, including four Nobel Prize winners—George Bernard Shaw, W. B. Yeats, Samuel Beckett, and Seamus Heaney. The list of literary notables is a whole lot longer and includes James Joyce, Oscar Wilde, Sean O'Casey, Sean O'Faolain, Brian Friel, and Edna O'Brien. Indeed, the country's literary heritage is evident everywhere you go. In Dublin you'll find Joyce's Liffey; Dean Swift's cathedral; and the Abbey Theatre, a potent symbol of Ireland's great playwrights. Yeats opens up the county of Sligo; the Aran Islands were the inspiration of J. M. Synge; and Cork inspired the works of Frank O'Connor. Wherever you are in Ireland, its literary heritage is never far away.

Trinity College, Dublin. Founded by Queen Elizabeth I, this university provided the greats—Beckett, Wilde, Stoker—with 30 acres of stomping grounds.

Limerick City, Co. Limerick. Frank McCourt's *Angela's Ashes* had thousands heading here to tour Angela's city and partake of the tearfulness of it all.

Sligo Town, Co. Sligo. Take in the town where William Butler Yeats grew up, then visit his grave in Drumcliff to view his beloved mountain, Ben Bulben.

Aran Islands, Co. Galway. See what inspired the dark genius of Synge's *Playboy of the Western World* and the black comedy of Martin McDonagh's *Cripple of Inishmaan.*

GREAT ITINERARIES

THE EAST AND THE SOUTH

5 to 10 days

Dublin's literary charm and Georgian riches, and rugged County Wicklow and the historic Meath plains are all just a few hours' drive from each other. Here you'll find the Boyne Valley, the cradle of native Irish civilization—no one will want to miss sacred Tara, Kells, Newgrange, and Glendalough, all time-burnished sites that guard the roots of Irishness. More idyllic pleasures can be found at Powerscourt, the grandest gardens in the land. In the south you'll find fishing towns and bustling markets, coastal panoramas, and—just outside crazy Killarney (oh, and it is crazy, an emerald-green Orlando)—stunning mountain-and-lake scenery.

Dublin

1 to 3 days. Dublin's pleasures are uncontainable. James Joyce's Dublin holds treasures for all sorts. Literary types: explore Trinity College, Beckett's stomping grounds, and its legendary *Book of Kells*. Visit key Joyce sites and the Dublin Writers Museum, and indulge in the Dublin Literary Pub Crawl. Joyce fanatics: arrive a week before Bloomsday (June 16) for Bloomstime celebrations. Literary or not, stroll around the city center and take in the elegant Georgian architecture around St. Stephen's Green, austere Dublin Castle, and the national treasures in the museums around Merrion Square and pedestrianized Grafton Street. Check out Temple Bar, Dublin's party zone, and join locals in this city-of-1,000-pubs for a foamy pint in the late afternoon. Pubs are the center of Dublin activity, and the locals never lose their natural curiosity about "strangers." You will frequently be asked, "Are you enjoying your holiday?"

"Yes" is not good enough: What they're really after is your life story, and if you haven't got a good one you might want to make one up. Pay your respects by taking a tour of the ever-popular Guinness Brewery and Storehouse. Night options: catch a show at W. B. Yeats's old haunt, the Abbey Theatre; see some Victorian music hall shows at the Olympia Theatre; or listen to traditional or alternative music at a pub or other venue. Last call arrives early at pubs, even here, so if you're still revved, go to Lesson Street and hit the nightclubs. For a dose of unmitigated Irish enthusiasm, join the roaring crowds at Croke Park and see some traditional Gaelic football and hurling.

Boyne Valley and County Wicklow

2 days. Walt Disney couldn't have planned it better. The small counties immediately to the north, south, and west of Dublin—historically known as the Pale—seem expressly designed for the sightseer. The entire region is like an open-air museum, layered with legendary Celtic sites, spectacular gardens, and elegant Palladian country estates. First head to the Boyne Valley, a short trip north of the capital. Spend the morning walking among the Iron Age ruins of the rolling Hill of Tara. After a picnic lunch on top of the hill, drive through ancient Kells—one of the centers of early Christianity in Ireland—and then to Newgrange, famous for its ancient passage graves. One thousand years older than Stonehenge, the great white-quartz structure merits two or three hours. Spend the rest of your day driving through the low hills and valleys of County Meath and to Georgian-era Slane, a manorial town planned by the Conynghams. Dominating the town are elegant Slane Castle and 500-foot Slane Hill. Backtrack to Kells or continue to

Drogheda and spend the night. The following day, head south of Dublin through the County Wicklow mountains. You might want to stop in one of the small, quiet towns along the Wicklow Way hiking trail and go for a short hike. Drive on to stately Powerscourt House, whose gardens epitomize the glory and grandeur of the Anglo-Irish aristocracy. From the profane to the sacred, head next to the "monastic city" of Glendalough and the medieval monastery of the hermit St. Kevin. Repair to Ireland's highest village, Roundwood, for lunch at the town's 17th-century inn.

West Cork and Kerry

4 days. Head about 250 km (155 miles) southwest to Cork City, filled with tall Georgian houses and old quays and perfect for a half day of walking. The place has few don't-miss attractions, but that's not the point: unlike many other towns, Cork is very much alive. As Europe's 2005 City of Culture, it has a progressive university, art galleries, offbeat cafés, a formidable pub scene, and some of the country's best traditional music. Drive south to Kinsale, once heralded as the gourmet capital of Ireland, an old fishing town turned resort, with many good restaurants. A slow three- or four-hour drive

along the coast and up through the small towns of West Cork takes you through the kind of landscape that inspired Ireland's nickname, the Emerald Isle. Spend the night in the market town of Skibbereen. Next morning, cross into County Kerry and head straight for Killarney, at the center of a scattering of azure lakes and heather-clad mountains. Although it has been almost transformed into a Celtic theme park by a flood of tourists, it's a good base for exploring your pick of two great Atlantic-pounded peninsulas: the strikingly scenic Ring of Kerry and the beloved Dingle Peninsula. Both offer stunning ocean views, hilly landscapes (like the Macgillycuddy's Reeks mountains), and welcoming towns with good B&Bs. To do justice to the fabulous views of the Ring, you need a minimum of two days, especially if traveling by bus. The five-hour drive back to Dublin takes you through Limerick City and the lakes of the Midlands.

THE WEST AND THE NORTH

6 to 7 days

"To hell or to Connaught" was the choice given the native population by Cromwell, and indeed the harsh, barren landscape of parts of the West and North might appear cursed to the eye of an uprooted farmer. But there's an appeal in the very wildness of counties Clare, Galway, Mayo, Sligo, and Donegal, with their stunning, steep coastlines hammered and shaped for eons by the Atlantic. Here, in isolated communities, you'll hear locals speaking Irish as they go about their business. The arrival of peace has opened the lush pastures of long-suffering Northern Ireland to travelers.

Galway and Clare

2 days. A three-hour drive west from Dublin leads straight to the 710-foot-high Cliffs of Moher, perhaps the single most impressive sight in Ireland. Using the waterside village of Ballyvaughan as your base, spend a day exploring the lunar landscape of the harsh, limestone Burren. In spring it becomes a mighty rock garden of exotic colors. The next morning, head north out of Ballyvaughan toward Galway City. On the way you'll pass 2-million-year-old Ailwee Cave and the picture-perfect village of Kinvara. Galway City, spectacularly overlooking Galway Bay, is rapidly growing, vibrant, and packed with culture and history. If time allows, drive west to Ros an Mhil (Rossaveal) and take a boat to the fabled Aran Islands. Spend the night in Galway City.

North and West to Donegal

2 days. Northwest of Galway City is tiny Clifden, with some of the country's best Atlantic views. From here, head

east through one of the most beautiful stretches of road in Connemara—through Kylemore Valley, home of Kylemore Abbey, a huge Gothic Revival castle. After seeing the castle and its grounds, head north through tiny Leenane (the setting of the hit Broadway play, *The Beauty Queen of Leenane*) and on to the most attractive town in County Mayo, Westport. It's the perfect spot to spend the night: the 18th-century planned town is on an inlet of Clew Bay, and some of the West Coast's finest beaches are nearby. Your drive north leads through the heart of Yeats Country in Sligo. Just north of cozy Sligo Town is the stark outline of a great hill, Ben Bulben, in whose shadow poet Yeats wanted to be buried. South of town, follow the signposted Yeats Trail around woody, gorgeously scenic Lough Gill. Continuing north, you pass Yeats's simple grave in unassuming Drumcliff, a 3000 BC tomb in Creevykeel, and small Donegal Town. Head north through Letterkenny on the tight, meandering roads, into the windswept mountains and along the jagged coastline of northern Donegal. A trip on a fishing boat to one of the many islands off the coast is a must, as is a slow drive along the coast from the Gweedore Headland, covered with heather and gorse, to the former plantation village of Dunfanaghy (Dun Fionnachaid), heart of Donegal's Irish-speaking Gaeltacht region and a friendly place to spend the night.

Northern Ireland

2 days. Begin exploring the province in historic, divided Derry City (called Londonderry by Unionists), Northern Ireland's second city. A few hours are sufficient to take in the views from the old city walls and the fascinating murals of the Catholic Bogside district. Continue on to two of the region's main attractions, the 13th-century Norman fortress of Dunluce Castle and the Giant's Causeway, shaped from volcanic rock some 60 million years ago. Heading south, sticking to coastal roads for the best scenery, you'll soon pass through the Glens of Antrim, whose green hills roll down into the sea. Tucked in the glens are a number of small, unpretentious towns with great hotels. Early in the morning, head straight to Northern Ireland's capital, Belfast. The old port city, gray and often wet, is a fascinating place, recovering from years of strife. A morning of driving through its streets will have to suffice before you head west through the rustic, pretty countryside to Lough Neagh, the largest lake in the British Isles. It's time to head back to Dublin, but if you're ahead of schedule, take the longer route that passes through the glorious Mountains of Mourne and around icy-blue Carlingford Lough.

BY CAR: SOME TIPS

Road signs are generally in both Irish and English, although in Gaeltacht (Irish speaking) areas new laws now mandate signs in Irish *only* (most such regions are located in the counties along the western coast of the country, Donegal and Connemara in particular). Thus, if traveling in these areas, invest in a good, detailed map with both Irish and English names.

Another new law has mandated that all speed limit signs now need to be posted in kilometers—not miles—per hour (a bit of a nuisance, as most cars have speedometers in miles). Signage is currently being changed throughout Ireland.

Remember to slow down on smaller, countryside lanes and roads: traffic jams can sometimes be caused by flocks of sheep and herds of cattle, not cars.

Brand-new divided highways are the fastest way to get from one point to another, but use caution: highways sometimes end as abruptly as they begin.

GREAT OUTDOORS

TOP BOATING TRIPS

Imagine the scene: gentle waves lap at the edges as your boat heads for open water drawing a perfect silver line across the tranquil mirror-flat surface. Every sound is crystal clear: a dog barks, a kingfisher whirrs past flying low across the water, and fellow-sailors shout a hearty welcome. This magical moment can easily be yours in Ireland, thanks to the wealth of possibilities for either guided tours or private hires.

Coast or Inland?

Ireland's indented western seaboard from Donegal to Cork has many first-class sailing opportunities. The main towns have sailing clubs in scenic areas. The best option is to choose an area such as West Cork and spend a week sailing from port to port. If you want to enjoy the very heart of Ireland, the River Shannon offers an unequalled choice of boating trips from the north Midlands down to Limerick. Cruisers can be hired at Carrick-on-Shannon, Banagher, and Portumna. Crossing the Irish border, the Shannon–Erne Waterway has opened up a little-known area of untamed beauty. And the renaissance of Ireland's canals is a recent regeneration success.

The Five Best Boating Trips?

River Barrow: Hire a traditional steel canal boat at Rathangan in Co. Kildare for a 120-km (70-mile) trip along the idyllic Barrow—Ireland's oldest navigation—passing through a Chaucerian landscape and dropping anchor at Graiguenamanagh (known as Graig); en route sign up for a canalways pub crawl.

West Cork Sailing: The harbors of the ports of call along this coast, such as Kinsale, Glandore, Baltimore, and Bantry, offer delightful overnight stays.

River Shannon Cruising: One of the best places to hire from is the delightful boating town of Carrick-on-Shannon—putter your leisurely way down to Lough Ree or as far as the Lower Shannon.

Fermanagh Lakes: With 700 km (430 miles) of rivers, lakes, and canals, Fermanagh is tops. Upper and Lower Lough Erne are dotted with islands topped with castles or Round Towers ideal for exploring.

Royal Canal: With its reconstructed locks and bridges, the 145 km (90 miles) canal is perfect for those on narrow boats, and in 2010 it became fully navigable from Dublin to Richmond Harbor in County Longford. Towpaths run from the Liffey all the way to the Shannon.

Guided Tours or Private Hire?

A first-time boater? Get some courses under your belt by contacting the International Sailing Schools Association. Of course, if you want to sit back and have it all done for you, book half-day or full-day guided pleasure cruises. *For more info, see "Cruising on the Shannon" in the Midlands.*

Information, Please?

The best websites about boating in Ireland include ⊕ *www.sailing.ie*; ⊕ *www.sailingschools.org*; ⊕ *www.discoverireland.ie/lakelands*; ⊕ *www.waterwaysireland.org*; ⊕ *www.iwai.ie*; Emerald Star Cruisers: ⊕ *www.emeraldstar.ie*; Riversdale Barge Holidays: ⊕ *www.riversdalebargeholidays.com*; Canalways Ireland: ⊕ *www.canalways.ie*; Royal Canal Cruisers: ⊕ *www.royalcanalcruisers.com*.

BEST WALKS AND HIKES

Catch the right day and an Irish hilltop can seem like a slice of heaven. The country is laced with 33 well-marked walking trails. If you're not feeling adventurous, strolls through a forest park or a lakeside dander are wonderful options. If you're going for bragging rights, consider walking the newly added extension to the world-renowned International Appalachian Trail, stretching along the spectacular coastal cliffs of Slieve League in County Donegal.

The Top Hiking Regions?
The Reeks of Kerry: Munster, in the Southwest of the country, has Ireland's biggest mountains with the MacGillicuddy's Reeks in Kerry (1,039 meters, 3,414 feet) leading the way in the hierarchy of height. They attract serious hill walkers and serious gongoozlers (those who like to gaze up at the peaks).

West Is Best: Many of Ireland's West Coast walking routes are framed by spectacular Atlantic scenery: Connemara, Sligo, and Donegal are renowned for the allure of their hills with thrilling views.

Ulster Way: Relaunched in 2009, the 1,000 km (625 miles) circular Ulster Way crosses the most stunning upland areas of Northern Ireland including the impressive Mountains of Mourne.

The Five Top Walks?
Burren, Co. Clare: An unforgettable trip into an otherworldly place, this lunar-like landscape is threaded with looped walks, rare flowers, and ancient ruins, many with a backdrop of unbeatable views across Galway Bay. The entire Burren Way is a 15-km (21-mile), five-hour pleasure-filled walk.

Silent Valley, Co. Down: Catch a bus from Newcastle and, after a two-hour (undemanding) walk around this idyllic place, you will realize why it was so named.

Glendalough, Co. Wicklow: The gentle, three-hour circular Spink Walk takes you across a wooden bridge, along a boardwalk, through conifer woodland and alongside the Upper Lake with sweeping views over the valley.

Slievenamon, Co. Tipperary: An unmistakable landmark famed in song, there is an easy track to the top where a burial cairn reputedly contains the entrance to the Celtic underworld.

The Barrow Way, Co. Carlow: Follow the Barrow river on a 70-mile meander through the forgotten midlands, where countless historical sights pepper the pastoral landscape. It's a feast for wildlife lovers as well.

Weather or Not?
Irish weather is fickle, mist comes down quickly, and it's easy to get lost. Check the forecast and leave word with someone at your hotel about where you are going. Layers of waterproof gear and fleeces are a good bet so you can strip off when the sun comes out (don't worry, it will appear if you wait long enough!). Even though signposting is generally good in hill areas, bring a map: free walking guides are available from regional tourism offices, but invest in Ordnance Survey Discovery maps available at newsagents for €8. Wear comfy boots and bring fruit or chocolate and a warm or hydrating drink.

Information, Please?
The two best websites are ⊕ *www. discoverireland.ie/walking* and ⊕ *www. walkni.com.*

IRISH FAMILY NAMES

Antrim
Lynch
McDonnell
McNeill
O'Hara
O'Neill
Quinn

Armagh
Hanlon
McCann

Carlow
Kinsella
Nolan
O'Neill

Cavan
Boylan
Lynch
McCabe
McGovern
McGowan
McNally
O'Reilly
Sheridan

Clare
Aherne
Boland
Clancy
Daly
Lynch
McGrath
McInerney
McMahon
McNamara
Molon(e)y
O'Brien
O'Dea
O'Grady
O'Halloran
O'Loughlin

Cork
Barry
Callaghan
Cullinane
Donovan
Driscoll
Flynn
Hennessey
Hogan
Lynch
McCarthy
McSweeney
Murphy
Nugent
O'Casey

O'Cullane
(Collins)
O'Keefe
O'Leary
O'Mahony
O'Riordan
Roche
Scanlon
Sheridan

Derry
Cahan
Hegarty
Kelly
McLaughlin

Donegal
Boyle
Clery
Doherty
Friel
Gallagher
Gormley
McGrath
McLoughlin
McSweeney
Mooney
O'Donnell

Down
Lynch
McGuinness
O'Neil
White

Dublin
Hennessey
O'Casey
Plunkett

Fermanagh
Cassidy
Connolly
Corrigan
Flanagan
Maguire
McManus

Galway
Blake
Burke
Clery
Fah(e)y
French
Jennings
Joyce
Kelly
Kenny
Kirwan
Lynch

Madden
Moran
O'Flaherty
O'Halloran

Kerry
Connor
Fitzgerald
Galvin
McCarthy
Moriarty
O'Connell
O'Donoghue
O'Shea
O'Sullivan

Kildare
Cullen
Fitzgerald
O'Byrne
White

Kilkenny
Butler
Fitzpatrick
O'Carroll
Tobin

Laois
Dempsey
Doran
Dunn(e)
Kelly
Moore

Leitrim
Clancy
O'Rourke

Limerick
Fitzgerald
Fitzgibbon
McKeough
O'Brien
O'Cullane
(Collins)
O'Grady
Woulfe

Longford
O'Farrell
Quinn

Louth
O'Carroll
Plunkett

Mayo
Burke
Costello
Dugan

Gormley
Horan
Jennings
Jordan
Kelly
Madden
O'Malley

Meath
Coffey
Connolly
Cusack
Dillon
Hayes
Hennessey
Plunkett
Quinlan

Monaghan
Boylan
Connolly
Hanratty
McKenna
McMahon
McNally

Offaly
Coghlan
Dempsey
Fallon
Malone
Meagher
(Maher)
Molloy
O'Carroll
Sheridan

Roscommon
Fallon
Flanagan
Flynn
Hanley
McDermot
McKeogh
McManus
Molloy
Murphy

Sligo
Boland
Higgins
McDonagh
O'Dowd
O'Hara
Rafferty

Tipperary
Butler
Fogarty
Kennedy

Lynch
Meagher
(Maher)
O'Carroll
O'Dwyer
O'Meara
Purcell
Ryan

Tyrone
Cahan
Donnelly
Gormley
Hagan
Murphy
O'Neill
Quinn

Waterford
Keane
McGrath
O'Brien
Phelan
Power

Westmeath
Coffey
Dalton
Daly
Dillon
Sheridan

Wexford
Doran
Doyle
Hartley
Kavanagh
Keating
Kinsella
McKeogh
Redmond
Walsh

Wicklow
Cullen
Kelly
McKeogh
O'Byrne
O'Toole

ANCESTOR-HUNTING

Over 46 million Americans claim Irish ancestry, and the desire to trace those long-lost roots back in the "auld sod" can run deep. Here are some pointers for how you can make your trip to Ireland a journey into your past.

Before You Go

The more you can learn about your ancestors, the more fruitful your search is going to be once you're on Irish soil. Crucial facts include:

- The name of your ancestor
- Names of that ancestor's parents/ spouse
- His or her date of birth, marriage, or death
- County and parish of origin in Ireland
- Religious denomination

The first place to seek information is directly from members of your family. A grandparent or a great aunt with a story to tell can be the source of important clues. And relatives may have documents stored away that can help with your sleuthing—old letters, wills, diaries, birth certificates, photos.

If family resources aren't leading you anywhere, try turning to the Mormon Church. They've made it their mission to collect mountains of genealogical information, much of which it makes available free of charge at ⊕ *familyresearch*.org; plug in the name a relative, and you may find records that include parents' names and places of origin.

On the Ground in Ireland

National Library of Ireland. Ancestor hunters have long traveled throughout Ireland to comb parish church records, but most of these records are now available on microfilm in Dublin at the National Library of Ireland. The library is a great place to begin your hunting; you can consult a research adviser there free of charge. ⊠ *Kildare St., Dublin, Co. Dublin* ☎ *01/603–0200* ⊕ *www.nli.ie.*

General Register Office. Civil records— dating back to 1865—are available at the General Register Office. Records for Anglican marriages date from 1845. ⊠ *8–11 Lombard St. E, Dublin* ☎ *01/635– 4000* ⊕ *www.groireland.ie.*

National Archives. The Curracloe Beach has census records and, like the National Library, provides free genealogy consultations. ⊠ *Bishop St., Dublin* ☎ *01/407– 2300* ⊕ *www.nationalarchives.ie.*

Centre for Migration Studies. For Northern Ireland, you can find information at the Centre for Migration Studies at the Ulster American Folk Park and ⊠ *Mellon Rd., Castletown, 2 Mellon Rd., Omagh* ☎ *028/8225–6315* ⊕ *www.qub.ac.uk/cms/.*

Public Records Office. the Public Records Office ⊠ *Balmoral Ave., 2 Titanic Blvd., Belfast, Northern Ireland* ☎ *28/9053– 4800* ⊕ *www.proni.gov.uk.*

None of these places has actual records available online, but their websites provide information about genealogical research.

If you'd rather not spend your vacation in a record hall, you can hire a professional to do your spadework. The **Association of Professional Genealogists** in Ireland (⊕ *www.irishgenealogy.ie*) will present you with a "package of discovery" upon your arrival.

The *Irish Times* newspaper also has ancestor-hunting resources (⊕ *www.ireland. com/ancestor*). And the National Library provides references for professionals.

BEST IRISH GREENS

The wonderfully alive, challenging natural terrain is one of the things that makes Irish golf so remarkable. Of the estimated 150 top-quality links courses in the world, 39 of them are in Ireland. Most of these leading courses were designed by celebrated golf architects, such as Tom Morris, James Braid, Harry Colt, and Alister MacKenzie, who capitalized on spectacular landscapes. Others—such as Jack Nicklaus, with his new course at Killeen Castle in County Meath—will continue in their steps.

The Weather Factor

You see all kinds of weather in Ireland—driving winds, rain, sleet, and sunshine—and you may see it all in one round. There are no rain checks here. You play unless there's lightning, so pack your sweaters, waterproof shoes, and rain gear, especially if you're planning your trip between fall and spring.

The Sunday Bag Factor

If you don't have a golf bag that's light enough for you to carry for 18 holes, invest in one before your trip. Electric carts are generally available only at the leading venues, so you usually have the option of using a caddy or caddy car (pull cart)—or of carrying your own bag. Many courses have caddies but don't guarantee their availability because they're not employed by the course, so you may have to tote your bag yourself. Be prepared with a carryall or a Sunday bag.

The Northern Ireland Factor

Some of the best and most beautiful courses are in Northern Ireland, where the leading venues—like Royal County Down and Royal Portrush—are less remote than in the republic. Remember that this part of the island is under British rule, so all currency is in U.K. pounds, although many clubs and businesses will accept the euro. There are no restrictions when traveling from one part of the country to the other.

The Private Club Factor

Unlike those in America, most private golf clubs in Ireland are happy to let visitors play their courses and use their facilities. It's important to remember, however, that such clubs place members first; guests come second. In some, you'll need a letter of introduction from your club in America to secure your playing privilege. There are often preferred days for visitors; call in advance to be sure that a club can make time for you.

The Downturn Factor

The recent rapid economic downturn in Ireland has seen a few courses close and a slew of them—mostly in the republic—continue to drop their highly inflated prices to a much more reasonable rate for 2011 and 2012. Ireland is now packed with newer premium courses all competing to undercut each other pricewise—the "perfect storm" for the price-conscious visitors who still want to test themselves against the best golf courses the country has to offer.

The Perfect Links

Ballybunion Golf Club, Co. Kerry. On the Old Course, one of the country's classics, each and every hole is a pleasure. Set on the shore of the Atlantic at the southern entrance to the Shannon River, Ballybunion is famed for tough but pleasant golf, epitomized by the huge dunes—great for a stroll but hellish to play out of.

The K Club, Co. Kildare. You'd have to be a nongolfer and a hermit not to have heard of this course, one of the country's most prestigious and demanding. Arnold Palmer designed the main course, famed for its water obstacles and inland links feel. The on-site facilities are the best in Ireland.

Portmarnock Golf Club, Co. Dublin. One of the nation's "Big Four" golf clubs (along with Ballybunion, Royal County Down, and Royal Portrush), Portmarnock is a links course near Dublin. Located on a sandy peninsula, it has hosted regular Irish Opens with its 100-plus bunkers ready to trap amateur and pro alike.

Royal County Down, Northern Ireland. A lunar landscape makes this course as beautiful as it is difficult. It has recently ousted St. Andrews as *Golf Digest*'s best course outside the United States. The sea of craterlike bunkers and long rough reward the straight and punish the proud.

Old Head, Co. Cork. Set on a spectacular peninsula jutting out into the wild Atlantic below, the Old Head is the romantic favorite of Irish golf lovers. Often compared to the Pacific sections of Pebble Beach, expect your pulse to race at the stunning views and wildlife.

Royal Portrush, Northern Ireland. This grand old course has made it into *Golf Digest*'s top 10 non-U.S. courses. It's a sea of sand hills and curving fairways, with the White Rocks par-5 5th set on the edge of a cliff. Word has it (okay, Royal Portrush recommends) that a long carry over the mounds to the right of the white stone will be rewarded with a much shorter approach to the green.

Donegal Golf Club, Co. Donegal. This wild and wonderful course sits between the shores of beautiful Donegal Bay and the shadow of the majestic Blue Stack Mountains. From the 5th to the 9th you enter the "Valley of Tears," a fearsome challenge of four perilous holes made all the more challenging by feisty winds.

Doonbeg, Co. Clare. Doonbeg is a new, creative addition to the great tradition of Irish links. Gamblers beware at the treacherous 15th; anything long could run off the green and never be seen again. Making it to the 18th is rewarded with mighty views of the ocean.

Dublin

WORD OF MOUTH

"A band of enthusiastic volunteers from the Dublin area is available to meet any visitors to help them plan their stay in the city. The idea is to match the interests of the visitor with that of the local, and they will meet in the city center and adjourn for a complimentary cup of tea or a drink at one of three nearby hostelries—the Merrion Hotel, Bewley's Café, or the Porterhouse Bar."

—See Dee

WELCOME TO DUBLIN

TOP REASONS TO GO

★ **Georgian Elegance:** Dublin's signature architectural style makes its most triumphant showing in Merrion, Fitzwilliam, Mountjoy, and Parnell squares.

★ **The Guinness Brewery and Storehouse:** A high-tech museum tells the story of Guinness, Dublin's black blood. At the top, the Gravity Bar has the city's best views.

★ **Toe-Tapping "Trad":** If your head is still throbbing from last night's sing-along at the pub, head to other music-mad venues like the Olympia Theatre for the best in Irish folk music.

★ **Magnificent Museums:** From the Renoirs at the Hugh Lane to the Tara Brooch at the National Museum and the first editions of Joyce at the Dublin Writers Museum, Dublin is one big treasure chest.

★ **Trinity College:** An oasis of books, granite, and grass sits at the heart of the city. Highlights are the exquisitely illustrated *Book of Kells* and the ornate Long Room.

1 The Southside. Between Christ Church Cathedral and Trinity College lies a concentration of famous sights. Merrion Square is the heart of the Georgian district; to its west, four major museums sit side by side. Southwest from here is quaint St. Stephen's Green, which connects to Trinity via stylish, pedestrian-only Grafton Street.

2 Temple Bar. The cobblestone streets and small lanes bounded by Wellington Quay and Dame Street have been transformed into Dublin's trendiest neighborhood. The nightlife doesn't stop at "last call," and on weekends the streets are packed with young people from all over Europe.

GETTING ORIENTED

Despite the seismic changes of the infamous boom-and-bust Celtic Tiger economy, Dublin happily remains an intimate capital that mixes elegant Georgian buildings, wrought-iron bridges, a battalion of booksellers, and more than 1,000 pubs. The heart of the city is the River Liffey, which runs east to west, splitting Dublin neatly in two. The more affluent Southside has a greater concentration of sights, and it can seem a world apart from the more working-class Northside. North or south, Dublin is compact and easily navigated, making it a great walking city.

It's the green lungs of the city, home to Dublin Zoo, and perfect for a stroll or cycle. A handful of other cultural attractions near the park also merit a visit.

3 The Northside. Less affluent but more eloquent than the Southside, this neighborhood was once home to James Joyce; today it's the site of the Dublin Writers Museum and the James Joyce Centre. Other highlights are the grand Custom House, historic O'Connell Street, and Dublin's two great theaters, the Abbey and the Gate.

4 Dublin West. This former industrial district stretches from Christ Church west to that other Dublin shrine, the Guinness Brewery. Imposing Dublin Castle houses the Chester Beatty Library—arguably the most impressive museum in Ireland.

5 Phoenix Park and Environs. Phoenix Park, Europe's largest public city park, hugs the north bank of the Liffey

Updated by
Anto Howard

Ask any Dubliner what's happening and you may hear echoes of one of W. B. Yeats's most-quoted lines: "All changed, changed utterly." No matter that the decade-long "Celtic Tiger" boom era has been quickly followed by the Great Recession—for visitors Dublin remains one of Western Europe's most popular and delightful urban destinations. Whether or not you're out to enjoy the old or new Dublin, you'll find it a colossally entertaining city, all the more astonishing considering its intimate size.

It is ironic and telling that James Joyce chose Dublin as the setting for his famous *Ulysses, Dubliners,* and *A Portrait of the Artist as a Young Man* because it was a "center of paralysis" where nothing much ever changed. Which only proves that even the greats get it wrong sometimes. Indeed, if Joyce were to return to his once genteel hometown today—disappointed with the city's provincial outlook, he left it in 1902 at the age of 20—and take a quasi-Homeric odyssey through the city (as he so famously does in *Ulysses*), would he even recognize Dublin as his "Dear Dirty Dumpling, foostherfather of fingalls and dotthergills"?

For instance, what would he make of Temple Bar—the city's erstwhile down-at-the-heels neighborhood, now crammed with restaurants and trendy hotels and suffused with a nonstop, international-party atmosphere? Or the simple sophistication of the open-air restaurants of the tiny Italian Quarter (named Ouartie Bloom after his own creation), complete with sultry tango lessons? Or of the hot/cool Irishness, where every aspect of Celtic culture results in sold-out theaters, from *Once,* the cult Indie movie and Broadway hit, to *Riverdance,* the old Irish mass-jig recast as a Las Vegas extravaganza? Plus, the resurrected Joyce might be stirred by the songs of U2, fired up by the sultry acting of Michael Fassbender, and moved by the poems of Nobel laureate Seamus Heaney. As for Ireland's capital, even after the Celtic Tiger party has faded, elegant shops and hotels, galleries, coffeehouses, and a stunning variety

2

of new, creative little restaurants can be found on almost every street in Dublin, transforming the provincial city that suffocated Joyce into a place almost as cosmopolitan as the Paris to which he fled.

The recent economic downturn has provoked a few Dublin citizens to protest that the boomtown transformation of their heretofore-tranquil city has permanently affected its spirit and character. These skeptics (skepticism long being a favorite pastime in the capital city) await the outcome of "Dublin: The Sequel," and their greatest fear is the possibility that the tattered old lady on the Liffey has become a little less unique, a little more like everywhere else.

Oh ye of little faith: the rare ole gem that is Dublin is far from buried. The fundamentals—the Georgian elegance of Merrion Square, the Norman drama of Christ Church Cathedral, the foamy pint at an atmospheric pub—are still on hand to gratify. Most of all, there are the locals themselves: the nod and grin when you catch their eye on the street, the eagerness to hear half your life story before they tell you all of theirs, and their paradoxically dark but warm sense of humor.

DUBLIN PLANNER

WHEN TO GO

When is it best—and worst—to pay a call on the Irish capital? The summer offers a real lift, as the natives spill out of the pubs into the slew of sidewalk cafés and open-air restaurants. The week around St. Patrick's Day (March 17) is, naturally, a nonstop festival of parades, cultural happenings, and "hooleys" (long nights of partying) throughout the city. Christmas in Dublin seems to last a month, and the city's old-style illuminations match the genteel, warm mood of the locals. The downside quickly follows, however, for January and February are damp hangover months. A warm sweater is a must all year round, as even summer nights can occasionally get chilly. Dublin gets its share of rain (though a lot less than other parts of Ireland), so an umbrella is a good investment—and best to make it a strong one, as the winds show no mercy to cheaper models.

PLANNING YOUR TIME

IF YOU HAVE ONE DAY

Touring the largest city in Ireland in the space of a day sounds like an impossible goal, but if you're determined you can do it in the span of a single sunrise-to-sunset day. Think Dublin 101. Begin with Trinity College—the oldest seat of Irish learning and home to the Old Library, the staggering Long Room, and Ireland's greatest art treasure—the *Book of Kells*, one of the world's most famous illuminated manuscripts.

Leave the campus and take a stroll along Grafton Street, Dublin's busiest shopping street and the pedestrian spine of the Southside. Take in a few shops and entertaining buskers on the street and at the end of Grafton you will find yourself at the northwest corner of **St. Stephen's Green,** Dublin's favorite relaxation spot. Head over to the northeast corner of the park to find ground zero for the city's cultural institutions. Here, surrounding the four points of Leinster House (built by the

CLOSE UP

Dublin Past and Present

Until AD 500, Dublin was little more than a crossroads—albeit a critical one—for four of the main thoroughfares that traversed the country. It had two names: Baile Atha Cliath, meaning City of the Hurdles, bestowed by Celtic traders in the 2nd century AD; and Dubhlinn, or "dark pool," after a body of water believed to have been where Dublin Castle now stands.

In 837, Norsemen carried out the first invasion of Dublin, to be followed by new waves of warriors staking their claim to the city—from the 12th-century Anglo-Normans to Oliver Cromwell in 1651.

Not until the 18th century did Dublin reach a golden age, when the patronage of wealthy nobles turned the city into one of Europe's most prepossessing capitals. But the era of "the glorious eighteenth" was short-lived; in 1800, the Act of Union brought Ireland and Britain together into the United Kingdom, and power moved to London.

The 19th century proved to be a time of political turmoil, although Daniel O'Connell, the first Catholic lord mayor of Dublin, won early success with the introduction of Catholic Emancipation in 1829. During the late 1840s, Dublin escaped the worst effects of the famine that ravaged much of southern and western Ireland.

The city entered another period of upheaval in the first decades of the 20th century, marked by the Easter Uprising of 1916. A war for independence from Britain began in 1919, followed by establishment of the Irish Free State in December 1921 and subsequent civil war. In its aftermath Dublin entered an era of political and cultural conservatism, which continued until the late 1970s. A major turning point occurred in 1972, when Ireland joined the European Economic Community.

In the 1980s, while the economy remained in recession, Irish musicians stormed the American and British barricades of rock-and-roll music, with U2 climbing to the topmost heights.

The 1990s and first years of the 21st century have truly been Ireland's boom time, set in motion to a great extent by the country's participation in the European Union. When Ireland approved the new EU treaty in 1992, it was one of the poorest member nations, qualifying it for grants of all kinds.

Ireland quickly transformed itself into the economic envy of the world, propelled by massive investment from multinational corporations, particularly in the telecommunications, software, and service industries. In 2000 the government announced that Ireland was the world's largest exporter of software. But the later years of the Tiger were fueled by a monumental property bubble, and Dublin, like most of the world, suddenly woke up with one doozy of an economic hangover.

Today, roughly a third of the Irish Republic's 4.1 million people live in Dublin and its suburbs. It's a city of young people—astonishingly so (students from all over Ireland attend Trinity College and the city's dozen other universities). Many of them have their eyes feverishly focused on the future.

Meeting the Dubs

The most appealing thing about Dublin isn't the sights, or even the great pubs and restaurants. It's the people—the citizens, the Dubs. They're fun, funny, and irreverent, and most of them love nothing better than talking to strangers. So, to get the most out of your visit, make a point of rubbing elbows with the locals. The pub is a natural spot to do this (see "A Trip to the Pub"), but almost any place will do. Ask for directions on a street corner (even if you don't need them), and you might be on your way to a brilliant conversation.

And mind the slag. "Slagging" is the Dubliner's favorite type of humor. It consists of mildly—or not so mildly—insulting a friend or a soon-to-be-friend in sharp but jovial fashion. It's best employed to deflate vanity or hubris, but clearly marks out the victim as well-liked and worthy. Packed buses and late-night chip shops are classic slagging venues.

earl of Kildare, Ireland's first patron of Palladianism), are the National Museum, replete with artifacts and exhibits dating from prehistoric times; the National Gallery of Ireland (don't miss the Irish collection and the Caravaggio *Taking of Christ*); the National Library; and the Natural History Museum. Depending on your interests, pick one to explore, and then make a quick detour westward to Merrion Square—among Dublin's most famous Georgian landmarks.

For a lovely lunch, head back to St. Stephen's Green and the Victorian-era Shelbourne—the lobby salons glow with Waterford chandeliers and blazing fireplaces. From St. Stephen's Green walk west for 10 minutes to pay your respects to St. Paddy—St. Patrick's Cathedral. If, instead, the Dublin of artists and poets is more your speed, hop a double-decker bus and head north of the Liffey to the Dublin Writers Museum. End the day with a performance at the nearby Gate Theatre, another Georgian eye-knocker, or spend the evening exploring the cobbled streets and the many cafés and shops of Dublin's bohemian quarter, the compact Temple Bar area, back on the south bank of the Liffey. Because you couldn't fit in a stop at the Guinness Brewery and Storehouse, top the evening off with a pint at the Stag's Head pub just across Dame Street.

IF YOU HAVE THREE DAYS

Dedicate your second day to the areas north and west of the city center. In the morning, cross the Liffey via O'Connell Bridge and walk up O'Connell Street, the city's widest thoroughfare, stopping to visit the General Post Office—the besieged headquarters of the 1916 rebels—on your way to the Dublin Writers Museum (if you didn't have a chance to visit on your first day) and the Dublin City Gallery, the Hugh Lane. Be sure to join the thousands of Dubliners strolling down Henry, Moore, and Mary streets, the Northside's pedestrian shopping area. In the afternoon, head back to the Liffey for a quayside walk by Dublin's most imposing structure, the Custom House; then head west to the Guinness Brewery and Storehouse. Hop a bus or catch a cab back into the city for a blowout dinner at the glamorous Tea Room in Temple Bar's Clarence hotel. Spend the evening on a literary pub crawl to see where the likes of Beckett and Behan held court, perhaps joining a special guided tour. On the third day tour the northern outskirts of Dublin from Glasnevin Cemetery and the National Botanic Gardens across to the sublime Marino Casino in Marino and the quaint fishing village of Howth. Back in the city, have tea at Bewley's and catch a musical performance at the Olympia Theatre or a play at the Abbey Theatre.

GETTING HERE AND AROUND

AIR TRAVEL

Dublin Airport, 10 km (6 miles) north of the city center, serves international and domestic flights.

Airport Dublin Airport ☎ *01/814–1111* ⊕ *www.dublinairport.com.*

AIRPORT TRANSFERS: BUSES AND TAXIS
Dublin Bus operates the Airlink shuttle service between Dublin Airport and the city center, with departures outside the arrivals gateway. Journey time from the airport to the city center is normally 30 minutes, but it may be longer in heavy traffic. The single fare is €6 and round-trip is €10; pay the driver inside the bus or purchase a one-day bus pass for the same price. If you have time, you can save money by taking a regular bus for €2. Aircoach's comfortable coaches run from the airport to the city center 24 hours a day for €7 one-way and €12 round-trip. The service stops at major hotels. A taxi is a quicker alternative than the bus to get from the airport to Dublin center. A line of taxis waits by the arrivals gateway; the fare for the 30-minute journey to any of the main city-center hotels is about €20 to €23 plus tip (tips don't have to be large). Ask about the fare before leaving the airport.

BOAT AND FERRY TRAVEL

Irish Ferries runs a regular high-speed car and passenger service into Dublin port from Holyhead in Wales. The crossing takes 1 hour and 50 minutes on the faster *Dublin Swift* and 3 hours and 15 minutes on the huge *Ulysses*. Stena Line has services to both Dublin and nearby Dun Laoghaire port from Holyhead (3½ hours). They also run a high-speed service, known as HSS, which takes about 1 hour and 40 minutes. Prices and departure times vary according to season, so call to confirm. In summer, reservations are strongly recommended; book online or through a travel agent. Dozens of taxis wait to take you into town from both ports, or you can take DART or a bus to the city center.

Ferry Contacts Irish Ferries ⊠ *Alexandra Rd., Ferryport, Northside, Dublin, Co. Dublin* ☎ *0818/300–400, 01/607–5700* ⊕ *www.irishferries.com.* **Stena Line** ⊠ *Ferryport, Dun Laoghaire, South County Dublin, Dublin, Co. Dublin* ☎ *01/204–7777* ⊕ *www.stenaline.ie.*

BUS TRAVEL

Busaras, just behind the Custom House on the Northside, is Dublin's main station for buses to and from the city. Dublin Bus runs the city's regular buses. Bus Éireann is the main intercity bus company, with service throughout the country. Aircoach has direct bus connections to Cork and Belfast, and is usually a bit cheaper than Bus Éireann.

2

In town, there's an extensive network of buses, most of which are green double-deckers.

Some bus services run on cross-city routes, including the smaller "Imp" buses, but most buses start in the city center.

Buses to the north of the city begin in the Lower Abbey Street–Parnell Street area, while those to the west begin in Middle Abbey Street and in the Aston Quay area. Routes to the southern suburbs begin at Eden Quay and in the College Street area. Several buses link the DART stations, and another regular bus route connects the two main provincial railway stations, Connolly and Heuston. If the destination board indicates "an lár," that means that the bus is going to the city center.

Museumlink is a shuttle service that links up the National Museum of Natural History, National Museum of Archaeology and History, and the National Museum of Decorative Arts and History. You can catch it outside any of the three museums.

BUS FARES AND SCHEDULES
In the city, fares begin at €1.40 and are paid to the driver, who will accept inexact fares, but you'll have to go to the central office in Dublin to pick up your change as marked on your ticket. Change transactions and the city's heavy traffic can slow service considerably. Most bus lines run until 11:30 at night, but some Nitelink buses run Friday to Saturday until 4:30 am on some major routes; the fare is €5.

Bus Information Aircoach ☎ 01/844–7118 ⊕ www.aircoach.ie. **Busaras** ✉ Store St., Northside, Dublin, Co. Dublin ☎ 01/830–2222. **Bus Éireann** ☎ 01/873–4222 ⊕ www.buseireann.ie. **Dublin Bus** ✉ 59 Upper O'Connell St., Northside, Dublin, Co. Dublin ☎ 01/873–4222 ⊕ www.dublinbus.ie.

CAR TRAVEL
Renting a car in Dublin is very expensive, with high rates and a 12.5% local tax. Gasoline is also expensive by U.S. standards, at around €2 a liter. Peak-period car-rental rates begin at around €260 a week for the smallest stick models, like a Ford Fiesta. Dublin has many car-rental companies, and it pays to shop around and to avoid "cowboy" outfits without proper licenses. A dozen car-rental companies have desks at Dublin Airport; all the main national and international firms also have branches in the city center.

Traffic in Ireland has increased exponentially in the last few years, and nowhere has the impact been felt more than in Dublin, where the city's complicated one-way streets are congested not only during the morning and evening rush hours but often during much of the day. If possible, avoid driving a car except to get in and out of the city (and be sure to ask your hotel or guesthouse for clear directions to get you out of town).

TAXI TRAVEL
There are taxi stands beside the central bus station, and at train stations, O'Connell Bridge, St. Stephen's Green, College Green, and near major hotels; the Dublin telephone directory has a complete list. The initial charge is €4.10, with an additional charge of about €1.03 per kilometer thereafter. The fare is displayed on a meter (make sure it's on). You may, instead, want to phone a taxi company and ask for a cab to meet you

at your hotel, but this may cost up to €2 extra. Each extra passenger costs €1, but there is no charge for luggage.

Hackney cabs, which also operate in the city, have neither roof signs nor meters and will sometimes respond to hotels' requests for a cab.

Although the taxi fleet in Dublin is large, the cabs are nonstandard, and some cars are neither spacious nor in pristine condition. NRC Taxis has a reliable track record. Globas Taxis is one of the city's biggest but also the busiest. SCR Taxis has some of the friendliest drivers.

Taxi Companies NRC Taxis ☎ *01/677–2222* ⊕ *www.radiocabs.ie.* **Global Taxis** ☎ *01/473–1333* ⊕ *www.globaltaxis.ie.* **SCR Taxis** ☎ *01/473–1166.*

TRAIN AND TRAM TRAVEL

As a delightfully compact city, Dublin does not have—or need—a subway system. But its LUAS trams and DART electric railway are a great way to get around the city center and beyond. The DART (Dublin Area Rapid Transit) connects Dublin with the fishing village of Howth to the north and the seaside resort of Bray to the south on a fast, efficient, superscenic train line that hugs the coastline, providing one spectacular view after another. But this line also runs through the center city with three convenient stations and then continues to such seaside destinations as Dun Laoghaire, Dalkey, and Bray.

As for the LUAS tram service, it runs two lines right into the heart of the city, facilitating easy access to sights like the Guinness Storehouse (James Street Stop), O'Connell Street (the Northside Abbey Street stop), and St. Stephen's Green.

Tickets can be bought at stations, but it's also possible to buy weekly rail tickets, as well as weekly or monthly rail-and-bus tickets, from the Irish Rail Travel Centre.

Train Information Connolly Station ⊠ *Amiens St., Northside, Dublin, Co. Dublin.* **DART** ☎ *01/836–6222* ⊕ *www.irishrail.ie/dart.* **Heuston Station** ⊠ *End of Victoria Quay, Dublin West, Dublin, Co. Dublin.* **Irish Rail–Iarnod Éireann** ☎ *01/836–6222* ⊕ *www.irishrail.ie.* **LUAS** ☎ *800/300–604* ⊕ *www.luas.ie.* **Pearse Station** ⊠ *Westland Row, Southside, Dublin, Co. Dublin.*

TRAIN AND TRAM FARES AND SCHEDULES

DART service starts at 6:30 am and runs until 11:30 pm; at peak periods—8 to 9:30 am and 5 to 7 pm—trains arrive every five minutes. At other times of the day, the intervals between trains are 15 to 25 minutes. Individual fares begin at €1.80 and range up to €4.70 one-way. You'll pay a heavy penalty for traveling the DART without a ticket. LUAS trams run from 5:30 am until 12:30 am Monday to Saturday and 7 am until 11:30 pm on Sunday. They come every 7 to 10 minutes at peak times and every 15 to 20 minutes after that. Fares range from €1.60 to €2.60 according to the number of zones traveled.

TRAINS TO AND FROM DUBLIN

Irish Rail (Iarnród Éireann) runs intercity trains connecting Dublin with the rest of Ireland. Connolly Station provides train service to and from the East Coast, Belfast, the North (with stops in Malahide, Skerries, and Drogheda), the Northwest, and some destinations to the South, such as Wicklow. Heuston Station is the place for trains to and from the South and West including Galway, Limerick, and Cork. Trains also run from here to Kildare Town, Newbridge, and other west of Dublin stops.

For more information on getting here and around, see Travel Smart Ireland.

RESTAURANTS

With the Irish food revolution long over and won, Dublin now has a city full of fabulous, hip, and suavely sophisticated restaurants. Award-winning Euro-toques and their sous-chefs continue to come up with new and glorious ways to abuse your waistline. Instead of just spuds, glorious spuds, you'll find delicious new entries to New Irish cuisine like roast scallop with spiced pork belly and cauliflower au gratin topped with a daring caper-and-raisin sauce or sautéed rabbit loin with Clonakilty black pudding. Okay, there's a good chance spuds will still appear on your menu—and most likely, offered in several gloriously different ways.

As for lunches or munchies on the run, there are scores of independent cafés serving excellent coffee, and often good sandwiches. Other eateries, borrowing trends from all around the world, serve inexpensive pizzas, focaccia, pitas, tacos, and wraps (which are fast gaining in popularity over the sandwich). And, yes, alas, Starbucks long ago planted its ubiquitous flag in Dublin.

Dubliners dine later than the rest of Ireland. They stay up later, too, and reservations are usually not booked before 6:30 or 7 pm and up to around 10 pm. Lunch is generally served from 12:30 to 2:30. Pubs often serve food through the day—until 8:30 or 9 pm. Most pubs are family-friendly and welcome children until 7 pm. The Irish are an informal bunch, so smart-casual dress is typical. *Prices in the reviews are the average cost of a main course at dinner or, if dinner is not served, at lunch.*

HOTELS

A reduction in demand for rooms means that Dublin's boom-time high rates have fallen somewhat but are still in line with the best hotels of any major European or North American city. Service charges range from 15% in expensive hotels to zero in moderate and inexpensive ones. Be sure to inquire when you make reservations.

As a general rule of thumb, lodgings on the north side of the River Liffey tend to be more affordable than those on the south. Bed-and-breakfasts charge as little as €46 a night per person, but they tend to be in suburban areas—generally a 15-minute bus ride from the center of the city. This is not in itself a great drawback, and savings can be significant. Many hotels have a weekend, or "B&B," rate that's often 30% to 40% cheaper than the ordinary rate; some hotels also have a midweek special that provides discounts of up to 35%. *Prices in the reviews are the lowest cost of a standard double room in high season. For expanded reviews, facilities, and current deals, visit Fodors.com.*

TOUR OPTIONS

Of course, Dublin is a walker's city, and it's a city full of storytellers. Put two and two together, and it's little surprise that Dublin is a particularly good place for guided walking tours.

BUS TOURS

Dublin Bus has three- and four-hour tours of the north and south coast-lines, taking in sights like the James Joyce Tower and the Casino at Marino. The one-hour city tour takes in the city-center sights like Trinity College, the Royal Hospital Kilmainham, and Phoenix Park. The one-hour city tour, with hourly departures, allows you to hop on and off at any of the main sights. Tickets are available from the driver or Dublin Bus. There's also a continuous guided open-top bus tour (€18), run by Dublin Bus, which allows you to hop on and off the bus as often as you wish and visit some 23 sights along its route.

The company also conducts a north-city coastal tour, going to Howth, and a south-city tour, traveling as far as Enniskerry. Gray Line Tours runs city-center tours that cover the same sights as the Dublin Bus itineraries. Bus Éireann organizes day tours out of Busaras, the main bus station, to country destinations such as Glendalough.

Information Bus Éireann ☎ *01/836–6111* ⊕ *www.buseireann.ie.* **Dublin Bus** ☎ *01/873–4222* ⊕ *www.dublinbus.ie.* **Gray Line Tours** ☎ *01/670–8822* ⊕ *www.grayline.com.*

PUB AND MUSICAL TOURS

Dublin Tourism has a booklet on its self-guided Rock 'n' Stroll trail, which covers 16 sights with associations to such performers as Bob Geldof, Christy Moore, Sinéad O'Connor, and U2. Most of the sights are in the city center and Temple Bar. The Traditional Musical Pub Crawl begins at Oliver St. John Gogarty and moves on to other famous Temple Bar pubs. Led by two professional musicians who perform songs and tell the story of Irish music, the tour is given April–October, daily at 7:30 pm, and from Thursday to Saturday, at 7:30 pm, the rest of the year; the cost is €12. The Viking Splash Tour is a big hit with kids. The amphibious ex–U.S. military vehicle tours the city center before launching onto the water by the IFSC (International Financial Service Center, near the Custom House). Kids get a helmet to wear and love terrifying native pedestrians with the "Viking roar." An adult ticket is €20. Colm Quilligan arranges highly enjoyable evening tours of the literary pubs of Dublin, where "brain cells are replaced as quickly as they are drowned."

Information Colm Quilligan ☎ *01/454–0228* ⊕ *www.dublinpubcrawl.com.* **Traditional Musical Pub Crawl** ✉ *20 Lower Stephens St., Southside, Dublin, Co. Dublin* ☎ *01/478–0191* ⊕ *www.discoverdublin.ie.* **Viking Splash Tours** ☎ *01/707–6000* ⊕ *www.vikingsplash.ie* 💶 *€20.*

WALKING TOURS

Dublin Tourism has an iWalk tour with a podcast audio guide narrated by well-known historian and artist Pat Liddy. Historical Walking Tours of Dublin, run by Trinity College history graduate students, are excellent two-hour introductions to the city. The Fáilte Ireland–approved tours take place from May to September, starting at the front gate of Trinity College, daily at 11 am and 3 pm, with an extra tour on weekends at noon. These tours are also available October and April daily at 11 am and November to March, Friday–Sunday at 11 am. The cost is €12. Dublin Footsteps conducts a Georgian/Literary Walking Tour that leaves from the Grafton Street branch of Bewley's Oriental Café June–September, Monday, Wednesday, Friday, and Saturday at 11; each tour lasts approximately two hours and costs €10.

Trinity Tours organizes walks of the Trinity College campus on weekends from March 17 (St. Patrick's Day) through mid-May and daily from mid-May to September. The half-hour tour costs €10 and includes the *Book of Kells* exhibit; tours start at the college's main gate every 40 minutes from 10:15 am. There are generally nine tours a day. The 1916 Rebellion Tour is an exciting walk that outlines the key areas and events of the violent Dublin rebellion that began Ireland's march to independence. The guides are passionately political and the two-hour tour never flags. They meet at the International Bar on Wicklow Street and operate February through October, Monday to Saturday at 11:30 am and Sunday at 1 pm. The cost is €12.

Information **Dublin Footsteps** ☎ *01/496–0641* ⊕ *www.visitdublin.com.* **Historical Walking Tours of Dublin** ☎ *87/6889412* ⊕ *www.historicalinsights.* **ie. Trinity Tours** ☎ *01/608–2320* ⊕ *www.tcd.ie/Library/bookofkells/tour-attractions.* **1916 Rebellion Walking Tour** ☎ *086/858–3847* ⊕ *www.1916rising.com* 🖃 *€12.*

VISITOR INFORMATION

The main Fáilte Ireland tourism center (known as Dublin Discover Ireland Centre) is in the former (and still spectacular) St. Andrew's Church on Suffolk Street and is open July–August, Monday–Saturday 9–7, Sunday 10:30–3, and October–June, Monday–Saturday 9–5:30, Sunday 10:30–3. There is a smaller Northside branch on O'Connell Street that is open Monday–Saturday 9–5. The Dublin Airport branch is open daily 8 am–10 pm; the branch at the Ferryport, Dun Laoghaire, is open Monday–Friday 9:30–1:15 and 2:30–5.

Dublin Discover Ireland Centre ✉ *Suffolk St. off Grafton St., Southside, Dublin, Co. Dublin* ☎ *1850/230330* ⊕ *www.visitdublin.com.*

Tourist Office O'Connell Street ✉ *Upper O'Connell St., Northside, Dublin, Co. Dublin* ☎ *01/605–7700, 1850/230330* ⊕ *www.visitdublin.com.*

DUBLIN PASS   Like many tourist capitals around the world, Dublin now features a special pass to help travelers save on admission prices. In conjunction with Fáilte Ireland (Suffolk Street Office and at many other Irish tourist offices throughout Ireland), the Dublin Pass is issued for one, two, three, or six days, and allows free (or, rather, reduced, since the cards do cost something) admission to 30 sights, including the Guinness Brewery, the Dublin Zoo, the Dublin Writers Museum, and Christ Church Cathedral. Prices are €35 for one day; €55 for two days; €65 for three days; and €95 for six days; children's prices are much lower (only €19 for one day). You can buy your card online and have it waiting for you at one of Dublin's tourist information offices when you arrive. Another plus: you can jump to the head of any line at participating museums and sights.

EXPLORING DUBLIN

"In Dublin's fair city, where the girls are so pretty"—so went the centuries-old ditty. Today, there are parts of the city that may not be fair or pretty, but although you may not be conscious of it while you're in the center city, Dublin *does* boast a beautiful setting: it loops around the edge of Dublin Bay and is on a plain at the edge of the gorgeous, green Dublin and Wicklow mountains, which rise softly just to the south. From the glass-wall top of the Guinness Storehouse in the heart of town, the sight of the city, the bay, and the mountains will take your breath away. From the city's noted vantage points, such as the South Wall, which stretches far out into Dublin Bay, you can nearly get a full measure of the city. From north to south, Dublin stretches 16 km (10 miles); in total, it covers 28,000 acres—but Dublin's heart is far more compact than these numbers indicate. Like Paris, London, and Florence, a river runs right through it. The River Liffey divides the capital into the Northside and the Southside, as everyone calls the two principal center-city areas, and virtually all the major sights are well within less than an hour's walk of one another.

SOUTHSIDE

The River Liffey provides a useful aid of orientation, flowing as it does through the direct middle of Dublin. If you ask a native Dubliner for directions—from under an umbrella, as it will probably be raining in the approved Irish manner—he or she will most likely reply in terms of "up" or "down," up meaning away from the river, and down toward it. Until recently, Dublin's center of gravity was O'Connell Bridge, a diplomatic landmark in that it avoided locating the center either north or south of the river—strong local loyalties still prevailed among "Northsiders" and "Southsiders," and neither group would ever accept that the city's center lay elsewhere than on their own side. The 20th century, however, saw diplomacy fall by the wayside—Dublin's heart now beats loudest southward across the Liffey, due in part to a large-scale refurbishment and pedestrianization of Grafton Street, which made this already upscale shopping address the main street on which to shop, stop, and be seen. At the foot of Grafton Street is the city's most famous and recognizable landmark, Trinity College; at the top of it is Dublin's most popular strolling retreat, St. Stephen's Green, a 27-acre landscaped park with flowers, lakes, bridges, and Dubliners enjoying their time-outs.

TOP ATTRACTIONS

Bank of Ireland. Across the street from the west facade of Trinity College stands one of Dublin's most striking buildings, formerly the original home of Irish Parliament. A pedimented portico fronted by six massive Corinthian columns dominates the grand facade, which follows the curve of Westmoreland Street as it meets College Green, once a Viking meeting place and burial ground. Inside, stucco rosettes adorn the coffered ceiling in the pastel-hue, colonnaded, clerestoried main banking hall, at one time the Court of Requests, where citizens' petitions

Reflected in the waters of the Liffey, the Custom House is just one of the many famed Dublin landmarks spectacularly illuminated at night.

were heard. Just down the hall is the original House of Lords, with an oak-panel nave, a 1,233-drop Waterford glass chandelier, and tapestries depicting the Battle of the Boyne and the Siege of Derry; ask a guard to show you in. Visitors are welcome during normal banking hours; the Dublin historian and author Éamonn Mac Thomáis conducts brief guided tours every Tuesday at 10:30, 11:30, and 1:45. ⊠ *2 College Green, Southside, Dublin, Co. Dublin* ☎ *01/661–5933* ⊕ *www. visitdublin.com* ✉ *Free* ⊙ *Mon.–Wed. and Fri. 10–4, Thurs. 10–5.*

Grafton Street. It's no more than 200 yards long and about 20 feet wide, but brick-lined Grafton Street, open only to pedestrians, can claim to be the most humming street in the city, if not in all of Ireland. It's one of Dublin's vital spines: the most direct route between the front door of Trinity College and St. Stephen's Green, and the city's premier shopping street, with Dublin's most distinguished department store, Brown Thomas, as well as tried and trusted Marks & Spencer. Grafton Street and the smaller alleyways that radiate off it offer dozens of independent stores, a dozen or so colorful flower sellers, and some of the Southside's most popular watering holes. In summer, buskers from all over the world line both sides of the street, pouring out the sounds of drum, whistle, pipe, and string.

QUICK BITES

Bewley's Oriental Café. The granddaddy of the capital's cafés, and an essential part of the character of Grafton Street, Bewley's Oriental Café, came within a heartbeat of extinction a few years back, after having served coffee and sticky buns to Dubliners since its founding by the Quakers in 1840. Fortunately, the old dame was saved and turned into a combination

Dublin Southside

café, pizza, and pasta joint. Best of all, a revamp brought back some of the old grandeur associated with Bewley's, including the exotic picture wallpaper and trademark stained-glass windows, designed by the distinguished early-20th-century artist Harry Clarke. The place is worth a visit if only to sit in the supercomfortable velvet seats over a cup of quality coffee, and people-watch just like Dubliners have for well over 150 years. There's even a cute little theater upstairs with lunchtime shows. The ticket price (€8–€12) includes homemade soup and brown bread. ⊠ *78 Grafton St., Southside, Dublin, Co. Dublin* ☎ *01/672–7700* ⊕ *bewleys.com/ bewleys-grafton-street-cafe.*

Fodor'sChoice
★

Iveagh Gardens. Dublin's best-kept secret has to be this 1865 Ninian Niven–designed "English landscape" walled garden that shockingly few natives seem to even know about. The architect showed off his dramatic flair in the rustic grotto and cascade, the sunken panels of lawn with their fountains, the blooming rosarium, and wonderful little wooded areas. This public park has no playground, but kids really love the "secret garden" feel to the place and the fact that the waterfall has rocks from every one of Ireland's 32 counties. Restoration of the gardens began in 1995 and has left the city with a Victorian treasure complete with a perfect box hedge and a working sundial. Access is from Hatch Street. ⊠ *Clonmel St., Southside, Dublin, Co. Dublin* ☎ *01/475–7816* ⊕ *www.heritageireland.ie/en/dublin/theiveaghgardens* ⊡ *Free* ☉ *Mon.– Sat. 8–sunset Sun. 10–sunset.*

Fodor'sChoice
★

Merrion Square. Created between 1762 and 1764, this tranquil square a few blocks east of St. Stephen's Green is lined on three sides by some of Dublin's best-preserved Georgian town houses, many of which have brightly painted front doors crowned by intricate fanlights. Leinster House, the National Museum of Natural History, and the National Gallery line the west side of the square. It's on the other sides, however, that the Georgian terrace streetscape comes into its own—the finest houses are on the north border. Even when the flower gardens here are not in bloom, the vibrant, mostly evergreen grounds, dotted with sculpture and threaded with meandering paths, are worth strolling through. Several distinguished Dubliners have lived on the square, including Oscar Wilde's parents, Sir William and "Speranza" Wilde (No. 1); Irish national leader Daniel O'Connell (No. 58); and authors W. B. Yeats (Nos. 52 and 82) and Sheridan LeFanu (No. 70). Until 50 years ago the square was a fashionable residential area, but today most of the houses serve as offices. At the south end of Merrion Square, on Upper Mount Street, stands the Church of Ireland St. Stephen's Church. Known locally as the "pepper canister" church because of its cupola, the structure was inspired in part by Wren's churches in London. An open-air art gallery featuring the works of local artists is held on the square on Sundays. ⊠ *Southeast Dublin, Dublin, Co. Dublin* ⊕ *www. merrionsquareart.com* ☉ *Daily sunrise–sunset.*

Fodor'sChoice
★

National Gallery of Ireland. Caravaggio's *The Taking of Christ* (1602), Van Gogh's *Rooftops of Paris* (1886), Vermeer's *Lady Writing a Letter with Her Maid* (circa 1670) . . . you get the picture, or rather, you'll *find* the picture here. Established in 1864, and designed by Francis Fowke (who also designed London's Victoria & Albert Museum), the National Gallery of Ireland is one of Europe's finest smaller art museums, with "smaller" being a relative term: the collection holds more than 2,500 paintings and some 10,000 other works. But unlike Europe's largest art museums, the National Gallery can be thoroughly covered in a morning or afternoon without inducing exhaustion.

A highlight of the museum is the major collection of paintings by Irish artists from the 17th through 20th centuries, including works by Roderic O'Conor (1860–1940), Sir William Orpen (1878–1931), and William Leech (1881–1968). The Yeats Museum section contains works by members of the Yeats family, including Jack B. Yeats (1871–1957), the brother of writer W. B. Yeats, and by far the best-known Irish painter of the 20th century.

> ## WHAT A CHARACTER!
>
> If you want to size up a real Irish character, check out one of the National Gallery's most eye-knocking paintings, Sir Joshua Reynolds's *First Earl of Bellomont* (1773). Depicted in pink silks and ostrich plumes, Charles Coote was a notorious womanizer (leading to his nickname, the "Hibernian Seducer") and was shot in the groin for his troubles by rival Lord Townshend. Famously, Coote gave his inaugural speech as quartermaster general of Ireland in *French*, continually referred to his County Cavan neighbors as "Hottentots," and wound up marrying the daughter of the superrich Duke of Leinster.

The collection also claims exceptional paintings from the 17th-century French, Dutch, Italian, and Spanish schools, and works by French impressionists Monet, Sisley, and Renoir. The amply stocked gift shop is a good place to pick up books on Irish artists. Free, guided tours are available on Saturday at 2 and on Sunday at 1 and 2. ✉ *Merrion Sq. W, Southeast Dublin, Dublin, Co. Dublin* ☎ *01/661–5133* ⊕ *www. nationalgallery.ie* ✉ *Free; special exhibits €10* ☉ *Mon.–Wed., Fri., and Sat. 9:30–5:30, Thurs. 9:30–8:30, Sun. noon–5:30.*

QUICK BITES

Café Joly. The National Library's light-filled tearoom, Café Joly is usually one of the city's more serene lunchtime spots. There's a light, French country influence to the fare, with top specials including crumbly quiches and a hearty chicken bake. Their organic sandwiches and coffees are also top quality. It's open Monday–Wednesday 9:30–7, Thursday–Friday 9:30–4:45, and Saturday 9:30–4:30. ✉ *Kildare St., Southside, Dublin, Co. Dublin* ☎ *160/30200* ⊕ *www.nli.ie/en/cafe-and-shop.aspx.*

National Library. Along with works by W. B. Yeats (1923), George Bernard Shaw (1925), Samuel Beckett (1969), and Seamus Heaney (1995), the National Library contains first editions of every major Irish writer, including books by Jonathan Swift, Oliver Goldsmith, and James Joyce (who used the library as the scene of the great literary debate in *Ulysses*). In addition, almost every book ever published in Ireland is kept here, along with an unequaled selection of old maps and an extensive collection of Irish newspapers and magazines—more than 5 million items in all.

Topped by half-moon fanlights, the brightly hued doorways of Merrion Square are icons of Dublin's 18th-century Georgian style.

The library is housed in a rather stiff neoclassical building with colonnaded porticoes and an excess of ornamentation—it's not one of Dublin's architectural showpieces. But inside, the main Reading Room, opened in 1890 to house the collections of the Royal Dublin Society, has a dramatic dome ceiling, beneath which countless authors have researched and written. The personal papers of greats such as W. B. Yeats are also on display. The library also has a free genealogical consultancy service that can advise you on how to trace your Irish ancestors. ⊠ *Kildare St., Southeast Dublin, Dublin, Co. Dublin* ☎ *01/603–0200* ⊕ *www.nli.ie* 🖅 *Free* ⊙ *Mon.–Wed. 9:30–9, Thurs. and Fri. 9:30–5, Sat. 9:30–4:30.*

★ **National Museum of Archaeology.** Just south of Leinster House is Ireland's National Museum of Archaeology, one of four branches of the National Museum of Ireland, and home to a fabled collection of Irish artifacts dating from 7000 BC to the present. Organized around a grand rotunda, the museum is elaborately decorated, with mosaic floors, marble columns, balustrades, and fancy ironwork. It has the largest collection of Celtic antiquities in the world, including gold jewelry, carved stones, bronze tools, and weapons.

The Treasury collection, including some of the museum's most renowned pieces, is open on a permanent basis. Among the priceless relics on display are the 8th-century Ardagh Chalice, a two-handled silver cup with gold filigree ornamentation; the bronze-coated iron St. Patrick's Bell, the oldest surviving example (5th–8th century) of Irish metalwork; the 8th-century Tara Brooch, an intricately decorated piece made of white bronze, amber, and glass; and the 12th-century bejeweled oak Cross of Cong, covered with silver and bronze panels.

The "*Or*: Ireland's Gold" exhibition gathers together the most impressive pieces of surprisingly delicate and intricate prehistoric gold work—including sun disks and the late Bronze Age gold collar known as the Gleninsheen Gorget—that range in dates from 2200 to 500 BC. Upstairs, Viking Ireland is a permanent exhibit on the Norsemen, featuring a full-size Viking skeleton, swords, and leatherworks recovered in Dublin and surrounding areas, and a replica of a small Viking boat. The newest attraction is an exhibition entitled "Kinship and Sacrifice," centering on a number of Iron Age "bog bodies" found along with other objects in Ireland's peat bogs.

The 18th-century Collins Barracks, near Phoenix Park (*see Phoenix Park*), houses the National Museum of Decorative Arts and History, a collection of glass, silver, furniture, and other decorative arts. ⊠ *Kildare St. Annex, 7–9 Merrion Row, Southeast Dublin, Dublin, Co. Dublin* ☎ *01/677-7444* ⊕ *www.museum.ie* ☐ *Free* ⊙ *Tues.–Sat. 10–5, Sun. 2–5.*

Newman House. One of the finest examples of Georgian Dublin, Newman House is actually two imposing town houses joined together. The earlier of the two, No. 85 St. Stephen's Green (1738), has two landmarks of Irish Georgian style: the Apollo Room, decorated with stuccowork depicting the sun god and his muses; and the magnificent Saloon, crowned with an exuberant ceiling aswirl with cupids and gods, created by the Brothers Lafranchini–the finest *stuccadores* (plasterers) of 18th-century Dublin. Next door at No. 86 (1765), the staircase, set against pastel walls, is one of the city's most beautiful rococo examples—with floral swags and musical instruments picked out in cake-frosting white. To explore the rich history and architecture of the houses you must join a guided tour. At the back of Newman House hides Dublin's "secret garden" (*see Iveagh Gardens*). ⊠ *85–86 St. Stephen's Green, Southside, Dublin, Co. Dublin* ☎ *01/475-7255* ⊕ *www.ucd. ie/campusdevelopment/developmentprojects* ☐ *House and garden €5* ⊙ *Tours June–Aug., Tues.–Fri. at 2, 3, and 4.*

Old Library and the Book of Kells. Home to Ireland's largest collection of books and manuscripts, the Old Library's principal treasure is the Book of Kells, generally considered to be the most striking manuscript ever produced in the Anglo-Saxon world and one of the great masterpieces of early Christian art. The book, which dates to the 9th century, was re-bound in four volumes in 1953, two of which are usually displayed at a time, so you typically see no more than four original pages. However, such is the incredible workmanship of this illuminated version of the Gospels that one folio alone is worth the entirety of many other painted manuscripts. The most famous page shows the "XPI" monogram (symbol of Christ), but if this page is not on display, you can still see a replica of it, and many of the other lavishly illustrated pages, in library's "Turning Darkness into Light" exhibition—dedicated to the history, artistry, and conservation of the book—through which you must pass to see the originals.

Because of the fame and beauty of the Book of Kells, it's all too easy to overlook the other treasures in the library. Highlights include the Long Room—the narrow main room of the library and home to approximately 200,000 of the 3 million volumes in Trinity's collection as well as one of the remaining copies of the 1916 Proclamation of the Irish Republic; a grand series of marble busts, of which the most famous is Roubiliac's depiction of Jonathan Swift; carved Royal Arms of Queen Elizabeth I–the only surviving relic of the original college buildings; a beautiful early Irish harp; the Book of Armagh, a 9th-century copy of the New Testament that also contains St. Patrick's Confession; and the legendary Book of Durrow, a 7th-century Gospel book from County Offaly. You may have to wait in line to enter the library if you don't get here early in the day. ✉ *Front Sq., Southside, Dublin, Co. Dublin* 🕾 *01/896–2320* ⊕ *www. tcd.ie/Library/bookofkells/old-library* 🎫 *€9, includes Book of Kells* ⊗ *May–Sept., Mon.–Sat. 9:30–5, Sun. 9:30–4:30; Oct.–Apr., Mon.– Sat. 9:30–5, Sun. noon–4:30.*

Powerscourt Townhouse Centre. One of the finest 18th century mansions in Dublin, the Powerscourt Townhouse Centre has a little something for everyone—magnificent architecture, quality shopping, and an Irish dancing museum and show. Designed by Robert Mack in 1771, it's a massive edifice that towers over the little street it sits on (note the top story, framed by large volutes, which was intended as an observatory). Inside, there are rococo salons designed by James McCullagh, splendid examples of plasterwork in the Adamesque style, and a shopping atrium filled with high-quality Irish crafts shops, installed in and around the covered courtyard. The mall exit leads to St. Teresa's Carmelite Church and Johnson's Court. Beside the church, a pedestrian lane leads onto Grafton Street.

The recently opened Story of Irish Dance (⊕ *www.jig.ie*) is a combination museum and performance space dedicated to traditional Irish dance. The small museum houses old dancing costumes and a multimedia exhibition of the history of dance in Dublin. *Jig* is a 90-minute virtuoso dance performance held at 1 and 6 pm from Wednesday to Sunday. *Hop Up* is a combination performance and dance lesson where you can join in. It lasts one hour and takes place Tuesday to Sunday at 3 pm. You can even get one-on-one dance classes. Check the website for details. ✉ *59 S. William St., Southside, Dublin, Co. Dublin* 🕾 *67/94144* ⊕ *www.powerscourtcentre.com* 🎫 *Jig €17.50, Hop Up €15* ⊗ *Mon.–Wed. and Fri. 10–6, Thurs. 10–8, Sat. 9–6, Sun. noon–6; limited shops open Sun.*

Fodor'sChoice
★ **St. Stephen's Green.** Dubliners call it simply Stephen's Green, and green it is (year-round)—a verdant, 27-acre Southside square that was used for the public punishment of criminals until 1664. After a long period of decline, it became a private park in 1814—the first time in its history that it was closed to the public. Its fortunes changed again in 1880, when Sir Arthur Guinness paid for it to be laid out anew. Flower gardens, formal lawns, a Victorian bandstand, and an ornamental lake

with lots of waterfowl are all within the park's borders, connected by paths guaranteeing that strolling here or just passing through will offer up unexpected delights (such as palm trees). Among the park's many statues are a memorial to W. B. Yeats and another to Joyce by Henry Moore. In the 18th century the walk on the north side of the green was referred to as the Beaux Walk because most of Dublin's gentlemen's clubs were in town houses here. Today it's dominated by the legendary Shelbourne hotel. On the south side is the alluring Georgian Newman House. ⊠ *Southside, Dublin, Co. Dublin* ⌨ *Free* ⊙ *Daily sunrise–sunset.*

Shelbourne Hotel. The iconic, redbrick, white-wood-trim Shelbourne hotel commands "the best address in Dublin" from the north side of St. Stephen's Green, where it has stood since 1865. You don't have to stay to take advantage of the gorgeous location; stop in for afternoon tea in the very opulent Lord Mayor's Lounge, a true Dublin treat, and bask in the history, grandeur, and other tasty dining options available at Dublin's most iconic hotel. In 1921 the Irish Free State's constitution was drafted here, in a first-floor suite. Elizabeth Bowen wrote her novel *The Hotel* about this very place. ⊠ *27 St. Stephen's Green, Southside, Dublin, Co. Dublin* ☎ *166/34500* ⊕ *www.marriott.co.uk/hotels/travel/ dubbr-the-shelbourne-dublin-a-renaissance-hotel.*

Fodor'sChoice   **Trinity College Dublin.** Founded in 1592 by Queen Elizabeth I to "civi-
★   lize" (Her Majesty's word) Dublin, Trinity is Ireland's oldest and most famous college. The memorably atmospheric campus is a must; here you can track the shadows of some of the noted alumni, such as Jonathan Swift (1667–1745), Oscar Wilde (1854–1900), Bram Stoker (1847–1912), and Samuel Beckett (1906–89). Trinity College, Dublin (familiarly known as TCD), was founded on the site of the confiscated Priory of All Hallows. For centuries Trinity was the preserve of the Protestant Church; a free education was offered to Catholics—provided that they accepted the Protestant faith. As a legacy of this condition, until 1966 Catholics who wished to study at Trinity had to obtain a dispensation from their bishop or face excommunication.

Trinity's grounds cover 40 acres. Most of its buildings were constructed in the 18th and early 19th centuries. The extensive **West Front,** with a classical pedimented portico in the Corinthian style, faces College Green and is directly across from the Bank of Ireland; it was built between 1755 and 1759, and is possibly the work of Theodore Jacobsen, architect of London's Foundling Hospital. The design is repeated on the interior, so the view is the same from outside the gates and from the quadrangle inside. On the lawn in front of the inner facade stand statues of two alumni, orator Edmund Burke (1729–97) and dramatist Oliver Goldsmith (1730–74). On the right side of the cobblestone quadrangle of **Parliament Square** (commonly known as Front Square) is Sir William Chambers's theater, or Examination Hall, dating from the mid-1780s, which contains the college's most splendid Adamesque interior, designed by Michael Stapleton. The hall houses an impressive organ retrieved from an 18th-century Spanish ship and a gilded oak chandelier from the old House of Commons; concerts are sometimes held here. The chapel, left of the quadrangle, has stucco ceilings and fine woodwork. The looming campanile, or bell tower, is the symbolic heart of the college; erected in 1853, it dominates the center of the square. ☎ *01/896–1000* ⊕ *www.tcd.ie.*

Douglas Hyde Gallery. Trinity College's starkly modern Arts and Social Sciences Building, with an entrance on Nassau Street, houses the **Douglas Hyde Gallery of Modern Art**, which concentrates on contemporary art exhibitions and

has its own bookstore. Also in the building, down some steps from the gallery, is a snack bar serving coffee, tea, and sandwiches, where students willing to chat about life in the old college frequently gather. ⊠ *Nassau St., Southside, Dublin, Co. Dublin* ☎ *18/96111* ⊕ *www.douglashydegallery.com* ☒ *Free* ☉ *Mon.–Wed. and Fri. 11–6, Thurs. 11–7, Sat. 11–4:45.*

Berkeley Library. The Berkeley Library, the main student library at Trinity, was built in 1967 and is named after the philosopher and alumnus George Berkeley (pronounced "Barkley," like the basketball player). The small open space in front of the library contains a spherical brass sculpture designed by Arnaldo Pomodoro. A very modern, sleek extension dominates the Nassau Street side of the campus. The library is not open to the public. ⊠ *Nassau St., Southside, Dublin, Co. Dublin* ☎ *01/896–1661* ⊕ *www.tcd.ie* ☉ *Grounds daily 8 am–10 pm.*

Science Gallery. This kid-friendly museum occupies a funky building at the rear of Trinity College. Its constantly changing exhibitions aim to allow art and science to meet—or collide, as the case may be, with an emphasis on fun and joining in off-the-wall experiments. ⊠ *Pearse St., Southside, Dublin, Co. Dublin* ☎ *01/896–4091* ⊕ *ww.sciencegallery.com* ☒ *Free* ☉ *Hrs vary with each exhibition.*

WORTH NOTING

Dublin Discover Ireland Centre. Medieval St. Andrew's Church, deconsecrated and fallen into ruin, has been resurrected as the Dublin home of Fáilte Ireland (the tourism board), and provides the most complete information on Dublin's sights, restaurants, and hotels; you can even rent a car and book theater tickets here. The office has reservations facilities for all Dublin hotels, as well as guided tours, a plethora of brochures, a gift shop, and even a pleasant café. ⊠ *St. Andrew's Church, Suffolk St., Southside, Dublin, Co. Dublin* ☎ *53/1605–7700 in Ireland* ⊕ *www.visitdublin.com* ☉ *July–Sept., Mon.–Sat. 8:30–6, Sun. 11–5:30; Oct.–June, daily 9–6.*

George's Street Arcade. This Victorian covered market fills the block between Drury Street and South Great George's Street. Two-dozen or so stalls sell books, prints, clothing (new and secondhand), exotic foodstuffs, and trinkets. ⊠ *S. Great George's St., Southside, Dublin, Co. Dublin* ⊕ *www.georgesstreetarcade.ie* ☉ *Mon.–Wed. and Fri.–Sat. 9–6:30, Thurs. 9–8, Sun. 9–6.*

Continued on page 70

LITERARY DUBLIN
A PLAYWRIGHT ON EVERY CORNER

As any visit to the Dublin Writers Museum will prove, this city packs more literary punch per square foot than practically any other spot on the planet. While the Irish capital may be relatively small in geographic terms, it looms huge as a country of the imagination. Dubliners wrote some of the greatest works of Western literature, including these immortal titles: *Ulysses*, *Gulliver's Travels*, *Dracula*, *The Importance of Being Earnest*, and *Waiting for Godot*. Today Dublin is a veritable literary theme park: within a few minutes' walk you can visit the birthplace of George Bernard Shaw, see where Sean O'Casey wrote *Juno and the Paycock*, and pop into the pub where Brendan Behan loved to get marinated.

Dubliners

by JAMES JOYCE

THE ALBATROSS

Ulysses, First American Edition

Dublin Writers Museum, Gallery of Writers

A WAY WITH WORDS

As tellers of the tallest tales, speakers of Gaelic (reputedly the world's most perfect medium for prayers, curses, and seduction), and the finest practitioners of the art of blarney, it's little surprise that the Hibernian race produced no fewer than four Nobel prize winners: Shaw, W. B. Yeats, Samuel Beckett, and Seamus Heaney. But what is surprising is that this tiny, long-colonized island on the outskirts of Europe somehow managed to maneuver itself to the very heart of literature in the language of the invader itself, English. And at that heart's core lies Dublin.

A ramble through literary Dublin is a crash course in Irish soul.

FOR BETTER OR VERSE

By the 18th century, the Gaelic tradition was trumped by the boom of literature written in English, often by second- or third-generation descendants of English settlers, such as William Congreve, Richard Brinsley Sheridan, and Oliver Goldsmith. With the Easter Uprising of 1916, so many Irish writers found themselves censored that "being banned" became a matter of prestige (it also did wonders for book sales abroad, with a smuggled copy of *Ulysses* becoming the ultimate status symbol). Sadly, many writers became exiles; most famously, Joyce was joined in Paris by Beckett in 1932.

DUBLIN B(U)Y THE BOOK

Book lovers know that a guidebook to this city is an anthology of Irish literature in itself. Dublin's Northside is studded with landmarks immortalized in James Joyce's novels. A stone's throw from the Liffey is the Abbey Theater, a potent symbol of Ireland's great playwrights. To the south lies Trinity College, alma mater of Jonathan Swift, Bram Stoker, Oscar Wilde, and Samuel Beckett. And scattered around the city are thousands of pubs where storytelling evolved as the incurable Irish "disease." They are the perfect places to take a time-out while touring Dublin's leading literary shrines and sites.

THE TRAIL OF TALES

Allowing you to turn the pages of the city, as it were, with your feet, a literary ramble through Dublin is a magical mystery tour through more than 400 years of Irish history.

The view from Parliament Square, Trinity College

DUBLIN WRITERS MUSEUM. The best place to start any literary tour of the city, this gloriously restored 18th-century mansion was once the home of the Jameson Whiskey family (booze and writers are never too far apart in Dublin). Its Edwardian rooms are filled with inky treasures like the 1804 edition of Swift's *Gulliver's Travels* and the 1899 first edition of Stoker's *Dracula*. ⊠ 18 Parnell Sq. N ☎ 01/872-2077 ⊕ www.writersmuseum.com.

GATE THEATER. Landmarked by its noble Palladian portico, this magnificent Georgian theater (built 1784) today sees the premieres of some of Ireland's most talked-about plays. Orson Welles and James Mason got their starts here. ⊠ Cavendish Row ☎ 01/874-4045 ⊕ www.gate-theater.ie.

JAMES JOYCE CENTRE. Now an extensive library dedicated to arguably the greatest novelist of the 20th century, this sumptuously decorated 18th-century town house was featured in *Ulysses* as a dancing academy. Letters from Beckett, Joyce's guitar and cane, and a Joyce edition illustrated by Matisse are collection highlights. ⊠ 35 N. Great George's St. ☎ 01/878-8547 ⊕ www.jamesjoyce.ie.

SEAN O'CASEY HOUSE. A one-time construction laborer, O'Casey became Ireland's greatest modern playwright and this is the house where he wrote all his famous Abbey plays, including *Juno and the Paycock* and *The Plough and the Stars*. ⊠ 422 N. Circular Rd.

ABBEY THEATRE. Hard to believe this 1950s modernist eyesore is the fabled home of Ireland's national theater company, established on a wave of nationalist passion by Yeats and his patron, Lady Gregory, in 1904. Here premiered J. M. Synge's scandalous *Playboy of the Western World* and the working-class plays of Sean O'Casey. The foyer and bar display mementos of the theater's fabled "Abbeyists." ⊠ Lower Abbey St. ☎ 01/878-7222 ⊕ www.abbeytheater.ie.

TRINITY COLLEGE DUBLIN. This 400-year-old college has an incredible record for turning out literary giants like Swift, Goldsmith, Wilde, Synge, Stoker, and Beckett. Majestically presiding over its famous library is the 9th-century Book of Kells, mother of all Irish tomes. ⊠ Front Sq. ☎ 01/896-2320 ⊕ www.tcd.ie/library.

NATIONAL LIBRARY. Joyce used the 1890 Main Reading Room, with its dramatic domed ceiling, as the scene of the great literary debate in *Ulysses*. At No. 30 Kildare Street a plaque marks a former residence of *Dracula*'s creator, Bram Stoker. ⊠ Kildare St. ☎ 01/603-0200 ⊕ www.nli.ie.

MERRION SQUARE. An elegant mansion, which can be toured, No. 1 Merrion Square is the former Oscar Wilde family residence. A statue of Oscar reclines in

Neary's Pub

the park opposite. Around the square, note the plaques that indicate former residents, including W. B. Yeats and Sheridan le Fanu, Dublin's most famous ghost-story teller.

ST. STEPHEN'S GREEN. This pretty, flower-filled little park is home to a wonderful statue of Joyce.

GEORGE BERNARD SHAW BIRTHPLACE. Shaw lived in this modest Victorian terrace house until he was 10 and the painstaking restoration of the rooms highlights a cramped, claustrophobic atmosphere Eliza Doolittle would have felt at home in. ✉ 33 Synge St. ☎ 01/475–0854 ⊕ www.-visitdublin.com.

NEARY'S PUB. The Victorian-style interiors here were once haunted by Dublin's literary set, most notably the raconteur Brendan Behan. ✉ 1 Chatham St. ☎ 01/677–7371.

See main Exploring for full texts on these landmarks.

Shaw Birthplace

A DUBLIN PANTHEON

JONATHAN SWIFT

"Where fierce indignation can no longer tear his heart": Swift, one of the great satirists in the English language, willed these words be carved on his tomb at Dublin's St. Patrick's Cathedral. Swift was born on November 30, 1667, in the Liberties area of Dublin. Life would deal him many misfortunes, but he gave as good as he got, venting his great anger with a pen sharper than any sword. His rage at the British government's mistreatment of the Irish was turned into the brilliant satire *A Modest Proposal* where he politely recommends a solution to the dual problems of hunger and overpopulation: breed babies for meat. Best remembered for the brilliant moral fable *Gulliver's Travels*, he died on October 19, 1745, and is buried in Dublin's St. Patrick's Cathedral, where he was dean.

OSCAR WILDE

The greatest wit of his age and arguably any other, Wilde was born on October 16, 1834, at 21 Westland Row in Dublin, the son of an eminent eye doctor. He was educated at Trinity College, where he was a promising boxer and was quoted as saying his greatest challenge was learning to live up to the blue china he had installed in his rooms. Wilde moved to London in 1879, where he married, had children, and became celebrated for the plays *The Importance of Being Earnest* and *Salome* and his titillating novel *The Picture of Dorian Gray*. But his life was always more famous than his work and a scandalous affair with the aristocratic Alfred Douglas finally led to his ruin and imprisonment.

W. B. YEATS

Poet, dramatist, and prose writer, Yeats—winner of the Nobel Prize for Literature in 1923—stands as one of the greatest English-language poets of the 20th century. And yet in Ireland itself he is best remembered for his key role in the struggle for Irish freedom and the revival of Irish culture, including his part in forming the Abbey Theatre (National Theatre). Born in the seaside suburb of Sandymount in Dublin in 1865, his fascination with Celtic folklore and the stories of Cuchulainn can be seen throughout his early poems and plays. But many of his greatest poems are haunted by the dashing figure of Maud Gonne, actress, revolutionary, and unrequited love. He died in 1939 in Paris but his body was buried in Drucliffe, at the foot of Ben Bulben mountain in his beloved County Sligo.

GEORGE BERNARD SHAW

G. Bernard Shaw—he hated George, and never used it either personally or professionally—was born in Dublin in 1856. His father was a boozing corn merchant and his mother a professional singer. When Shaw was a boy his mother ran away with her voice coach, and it may be no coincidence that his plays are dotted with problem child/parent relationships. In 1886 he went to London where plays such as *Pygmalion* and *Saint Joan* helped propel him to international stardom. Pacifist, socialist, and feminist, Shaw was a true original; a radical in the real sense of the word, his work always challenged the norms of his day. He lived to the ripe old age of 94 and died in 1950 after falling off a ladder while trimming trees outside his house.

SEAN O'CASEY

The first working-class Irish literary great, dramatist O'Casey was born at 85 Upper Dorset Street in the inner-city Dublin slums in 1880. Problems with his eyes as a child kept him indoors where he gleaned a love of reading. An early advocate of Yeats's Celtic Revival, he later found his true faith in the socialism of union leader Jim Larkin. His trilogy of great tragicomedies—*Shadow of a Gunman, Juno and the Paycock,* and *The Plough and the Stars*—all deal with ordinary families caught up in the maelstrom of Irish politics and were performed at Yeats's Abbey in the 1920s. Their playful language and riotous action have made them classics ever since. He spent his later life in England and died in Devon in 1964.

BRENDAN BEHAN

Writer, fighter, drinker, and wit, Brendan Francis Behan was born in Dublin's Holles Street Hospital in 1923 into an educated, political working-class family. Urged on by his fiercely patriotic grandmother, he joined Fiánna Eireann, the youth wing of the IRA and in 1939 was jailed for three years for possessing explosives. In prison he began to write but it wasn't until the 1950s that he hit it big with *The Quare Fellow*, a play based on his prison experiences, and later works *The Hostage* and *Borstal Boy*. But it was in the bars of Dublin that the "demon drinker" Behan delivered many of his greatest lines—alas, lost now forever. A self-proclaimed "drinker with a writing problem," he died in 1964 at the age of only 41.

REJOICE!: The Darlin' Dublin of James Joyce

If Joyce fans make one pilgrimage in their lives, let it be to Dublin on June 16th for Bloomsday. June 16th, of course, is the day Leopold Bloom toured Dublin in *Ulysses*, and commemorative events take place all week long leading up to the big day (and night).

Grown men and women stroll the streets attired in black suits and carrying fresh bars of lemon soap in their pockets, imitating the unassuming hero of what is arguably the 20th century's greatest novel. Denounced as obscene, blasphemous, and unreadable when it was first published in 1922 (and then banned in the U.S. until 1933), this 1,000-page riff on Homer's *Odyssey* portrays three characters—Leopold Bloom, a Jewish ad salesman, his wife, Molly, and friend Stephen Dedelus—as they wander through Dublin during the span of one day, June 16th, 1904. Dedicated Joyceans flock to the weeklong event, now called "Bloomstime," for Bloomsday breakfasts (where they can enjoy, like Bloom himself,

"grilled mutton kidneys . . . which gave to his palate a fine tang of faintly scented urine"), readings, performances, and general merriment.

But don't despair if you miss Bloomsday, because you can experience the Dublin that inspired the author's novels year-round. James Joyce (1882-1941) set all his major works—*Dubliners, A Portrait of the Artist as a Young Man, Ulysses,* and *Finnegans Wake*—in the city where he was born and spent the first 22 years of his life. Joyce knew and remembered Dublin in such detail that he bragged (and that's the word) that, if the city were destroyed, it could be rebuilt in its entirety from his written works.

Left, Joyce Statue, Earl Street;
Top left, a portrait of James Joyce, 1915
Top right, Bloomsday celebrations

IN THE FOOTSTEPS OF A POET: A James Joyce Walk

Begin in the heart of the Northside, on Prince's Street, next to the GPO (General Post Office), where the office of the old and popular *Freeman's Journal* newspaper (published 1763–1924) was once located and where Bloom once worked.

Head north up O'Connell Street down Parnell Square before turning right onto Dorset Street and then left onto Eccles Street. Leopold and Molly Bloom's fictional home stood at 7 Eccles Street, north of Parnell Square.

Head back to Dorset Street and go east. Take a right onto Gardiner Street and then a left onto Great Denmark Street and Belvedere College. Between 1893 and 1898, Joyce studied at Belvedere College (☎ 01/874–3974) under the Jesuits; it's housed in a splendid 18th-century mansion. The **James Joyce Centre** (☎ 01/878–8547 ⊕ www.jamesjoyce.ie), a few steps from Belvedere College on North Great George's Street, is the hub of Bloomsday celebrations.

Go back to Gardiner Street and then south until you come to Railway Street on your left. The site of **Bella Cohen's Brothel** (⊠ 82 Railway St.) is in an area

that in Joyce's day contained many houses of ill repute. A long walk back down O'Connell Street to the bridge and then a right will take you to Ormond Quay. On the western edge of the Northside, the **Ormond Quay Hotel** (⊠ Upper Ormond Quay ☎ 01/872–

1811) was an afternoon rendezvous spot for Bloom.

Across the Liffey, walk up Grafton Street to **Davy Byrne's Pub** (⊠ 21 Duke St., ☎ 01/671–1298). Here, Bloom comes to settle down for a glass of Burgundy and a Gorgonzola cheese sandwich, and meets his friend Nosey Flynn. Today, the pub has gone very upscale from its pre-World War II days, but even Joyce would have cracked a smile at the sight of the shamrock-painted ceiling and the murals of Joycean Dublin by Liam Proud.

After a stop at Davy Byrne's, proceed via Molesworth Street to the **National Library**— where Bloom has a near meeting with Blazes Boylan, his wife's lover. Walk up Molesworth Street until you hit Trinity. Take a right and walk to Lincoln Place. No establishment mentioned by Joyce has changed less since his time than **Sweny's Pharmacy** (⊠ Lincoln Pl.), which still has its black-and-white exterior and an interior crammed with potions and vials.

As seen here on Parliament Square, memorial statues stand as tribute to Trinity College's famed alumni, including Oliver Goldsmith and Samuel Beckett.

Long Hall Pub. With its mahogany bar, mirrors, and plasterwork ceilings, the Long Hall Pub is one of Dublin's most ornate traditional taverns. It's a good place to take a break for a cup of tea or a cheeky daytime pint of Guinness. ⊠ *51 S. Great George's St., Southside, Dublin, Co. Dublin* ☎ *01/475–1590.*

Government Buildings. The swan song of British architecture in the capital, this enormous complex, a landmark of Edwardian baroque, was the last neoclassical edifice to be erected by the British government. It was designed by Sir Aston Webb, who did many of the similarly grand buildings in London's Piccadilly Circus, to serve as the College of Science in the early 1900s. Following a major restoration, these buildings became the offices of the Department of the *taoiseach* (the prime minister, pronounced *tea*-shuck) and the *tánaiste* (the deputy prime minister, pronounced tawn-*ish*-ta). Fine examples of contemporary Irish furniture and carpets populate the offices. A stained-glass window, known as "My Four Green Fields," was made by Evie Hone for the 1939 New York World's Fair. It depicts the four ancient provinces of Ireland: Munster, Ulster, Leinster, and Connacht. The government offices are accessible only via 35-minute guided tours on Saturday. They are dramatically illuminated every night. ⊠ *Upper Merrion St., Southeast Dublin, Dublin, Co. Dublin* ☎ *01/662–4888* ⊕ *www.taoiseach.gov.ie* ✉ *Free; pick up tickets from National Gallery on day of tour* ☉ *Tours Sat. 10:30–3:30.*

Huguenot Cemetery. One of the last such burial grounds in Dublin, this cemetery was used in the late 17th century by French Protestants who had fled persecution in their native land. The cemetery gates are rarely open, but you can view the grounds from the street—it's on the northeast corner across from the square. ⊠ *27 St. Stephen's Green N, Southside, Dublin, Co. Dublin.*

Mansion House. The mayor of Dublin resides at the Mansion House, which dates from 1710. It was built for Joshua Dawson, who later sold the property to the government on the condition that "one loaf of double-refined sugar of six pounds weight" be delivered to him every Christmas. In 1919 the Declaration of Irish Independence was adopted here. The house is not open to the public. ⊠ *Dawson St., Southeast Dublin, Dublin, Co. Dublin* ☎ *01/222–6200* ⊕ *www.dublincity.ie/yourcouncil/lordmayordublin.*

✿ **National Museum of Natural History.** One of four branches of the National Museum of Ireland, this museum is little changed from Victorian times and remains a fascinating repository of mounted mammals, birds, and other flora and fauna. The Irish Room houses the most famous exhibits: skeletons of the extinct, prehistoric, giant "Irish elk." The International Animals Collection includes a 65-foot whale skeleton suspended from the roof. Another highlight is the very beautiful Blaschka Collection, finely detailed glass models of marine creatures, the zoological accuracy of which has never been achieved again in glass. Built in 1856 to hold the Royal Dublin Society's rapidly expanding collection, it was designed by Frederick Clarendon to sit in harmony with the National Gallery on the other side of Leinster Lawn. When it was completed, it formed an annex to Leinster House and was connected to it by a curved, closed Corinthian colonnade. In 1909 a new entrance was constructed at the east end of the building on Merrion Street. ⊠ *Merrion St., Southeast Dublin, Dublin, Co. Dublin* ☎ *01/677–7444* ⊕ *www.museum.ie* ⊠ *Free* ☽ *Tues.–Sat. 10–5, Sun. 2–5.*

No. 29. Everything in this carefully refurbished 1794 home, known simply as Number Twenty-Nine, is in keeping with the elegant lifestyle of the Dublin middle class between 1790 and 1820, the height of the Georgian period, when the house was owned by a wine merchant's widow. From the basement to the attic—in the kitchen, nursery, servants' quarters, and the formal living areas—the National Museum has re-created the period's style with authentic furniture, paintings, carpets, curtains, paint, wallpapers, and even bell pulls. ⊠ *29 Fitzwilliam St. Lower, Southeast Dublin, Dublin, Co. Dublin* ☎ *01/702–6165* ⊕ *www.esb.ie/numbertwentynine* ⊠ *€6* ☽ *Tues.–Sat. 10–5, Sun. noon–5.*

Royal Hibernian Academy. The Royal Hibernian Academy, an old Dublin institution, is housed in a well-lighted building, one of the largest exhibition spaces in the city. The gallery holds adventurous exhibitions of the best in contemporary art, both from Ireland and abroad. ⊠ *15 Ely Pl., off St. Stephen's Green, Southside, Dublin, Co. Dublin* ☎ *01/661–2558* ⊕ *www.royalhibernianacademy.ie* ⊠ *Free* ☽ *Mon.–Tues., 11–5, Wed.–Sat. 11–7, Sun. 2–5.*

Royal Irish Academy. The country's leading learned society houses important documents in its 18th-century library, including a large collection of ancient Irish manuscripts, such as the 11th- to 12th-century *Book of*

Dating from 1123, the bejeweled oak Cross of Cong is among the greatest treasures on view at the National Museum of Archaeology and History.

the Dun Cow, and the library of the 18th-century poet Thomas Moore. ⊠ *19 Dawson St., Southeast Dublin, Dublin, Co. Dublin* ☏ *53/1676–2346* ⊕ *www.ria.ie* ▣ *Free* ⊙ *Mon.–Thurs. 10–5:30, Fri. 10–5.*

St. Ann's Church. A plain, neo-Romanesque granite exterior, built in 1868, belies the rich Georgian interior of this church, which Isaac Wills designed in 1720. Highlights of the interior include polished-wood balconies, ornate plasterwork, and shelving in the chancel dating from 1723—and still in use for organizing the distribution of bread to the parish's poor. ⊠ *Dawson St., Southeast Dublin, Dublin, Co. Dublin* ☏ *01/676–7727* ⊕ *www.stannschurch.ie* ▣ *Free* ⊙ *Weekdays 10–4, Sun. for services only.*

Sandymount Strand. South of the city center, a few blocks west of the Sydney Parade DART station, the Sandymount Strand stretches for 5 km (3 miles) from Ringsend to Booterstown. It was cherished by James Joyce and his beloved, Nora Barnacle from Galway, and it figures as one of the settings in *Ulysses;* it's also a popular spot with strolling Dubliners today. (The beach is "at the lacefringe of the tide," as Joyce put it.) When the tide recedes, the beach extends for 1½ km (1 mile) from the foreshore, but the tide sweeps in again very quickly. A sliver of a park lies between Strand Road and the beach, the water of which is not suitable for swimming. At the end of the strand there's a wonderful walk out along the south harbor wall to the Poolbeg Lighthouse, which has eye-popping views of Dublin Bay.

Shaw Birthplace. "Author of many plays" is the simple accolade to George Bernard Shaw (1856–1950) on the plaque outside his birthplace. The Nobel laureate was born here to a once prosperous family fallen on

CLOSE UP

Dublin's Gorgeous Georgians

"Extraordinary Dublin!" sigh art lovers and connoisseurs of the 18th century. It was during the "Gorgeous Eighteenth" that this duckling of a city was transformed into a preening swan, largely by the Georgian style of art and architecture that flowered between 1714 and 1820 during the reigns of the four English Georges.

Today Dublin remains in good part a sublimely Georgian city, thanks to enduring grace notes: the commodious and uniformly laid-out streets, the genteel town squares, the redbrick mansions accented with demilune (half-moon) fan windows. The great 18th-century showpieces are **Merrion, Fitzwilliam, Mountjoy,** and **Parnell squares. Merrion Square East,** the longest Georgian street in town, reveals scenes of decorum, elegance, polish, and charm, all woven into a "tapestry of rosy brick and white enamel," to quote the 18th-century connoisseur Horace Walpole.

Setting off the facades are fanlighted doors (often lacquered in black, green, yellow, or red) and the celebrated "patent reveal" window trims—thin plaster linings painted white to catch the light. These half-moon fanlights—as iconic of the city as clock towers are of Zurich—are often in the neoclassical style known as the Adamesque (which was inspired by the designs of the great English architect Robert Adam).

Many facades appear severely plain, but don't be fooled: just behind their stately front doors are entry rooms and stairways aswirl with tinted rococo plasterwork, often the work of *stuccadores* (plasterers) from Italy (including the talented Lafranchini brothers). Magnificent **Newman**

House (⊠ *85–86 St. Stephen's Green, Southside* ☎ *01/716–7422* ⊕ *www. visitdublin.com* ✉ *House and garden €5*), one of the finest of Georgian houses, is open to the public.

The Palladian style—as the Georgian style was then called—began to reign supreme in domestic architecture in 1745, when the Croesus-rich Earl of Kildare returned from an Italian grand tour and built a gigantic Palladian palace called **Leinster House** in the seedy section of town.

"Where I go, fashion will follow," he declared, and indeed it did. By then, the Anglo-Irish elite had given the city London airs by building the **Parliament House** (now the Bank of Ireland), the **Royal Exchange** (now City Hall), the **Custom House,** and the **Four Courts** in the new style.

But this phase of high fashion came to an end with the Act of Union: according to historian Maurice Craig, "On the last stroke of midnight, December 31, 1800, the gaily caparisoned horses turned into mice, the coaches into pumpkins, the silks and brocades into rags, and Ireland was once again the Cinderella among the nations."

It was nearly 150 years before the spotlight shone once again on 18th-century Dublin. In recent decades, the conservation efforts of the **Irish Georgian Society** (⊠ *74 Merrion Sq., Southside* ☎ *01/676–7053* ⊕ *www.igs. ie*) have done much to restore Dublin to its Georgian splendor. Thanks to its founders, the Hon. Desmond Guinness and his late wife, Mariga, many historic houses, including that of George Bernard Shaw on Synge Street, have been saved and preserved.

2

hard times. Shaw lived in this modest, Victorian terrace house until he was 10 and remembered it as having a "loveless" feel. The painstaking restoration of the little rooms highlights the cramped, claustrophobic atmosphere. All the details of a family home—wallpaper, paint, fittings, curtains, furniture, utensils, pictures, rugs—remain, and it appears as if the family has just gone out for the afternoon. You can almost hear one of Mrs. Shaw's musical recitals in the tiny front parlor. The children's bedrooms are filled with photographs and original documents and letters that throw light on Shaw's career. ⊠ *33 Synge St., Southeast Dublin, Dublin, Co. Dublin* ☎ *01/475–0854* ⊕ *www.visitdublin.com* ✆ *€6* ☺ *June–Aug., Tues.–Fri., 10–1 and 2–5, Sat. 2–5.*

> **WORD OF MOUTH**
>
> "We passed row after row of identical Georgian houses, all with different brightly painted doors and rounded window arches. The story is that men were too drunk after a night at the pub to know which door was the right one unless it was painted a bright, strong color (red, blue, etc.). I don't know if the story is true, but it certainly makes sense!"
>
> —Green Dragon

TEMPLE BAR

Locals complain about the late-night noise, and visitors sometimes say the place has the feel of a Dublin theme park, but a visit to modern Dublin wouldn't be complete without spending some time in the city's most famously vibrant area. More than any other neighborhood in the city, Temple Bar represents the dramatic changes (good and bad) and ascending fortunes of Dublin that came about in the last decade of the 20th century. The area, which takes its name from one of the streets of its central spine, was targeted for redevelopment in 1991–92 after a long period of neglect, having survived widely rumored plans to turn it into a massive bus depot and/or a giant parking lot. Temple Bar took off as Dublin's version of New York's SoHo, Paris's Bastille, or London's Notting Hill—a thriving mix of high and alternative culture distinct from what you'll find in any other part of the city. Dotting the area's narrow cobblestone streets and pedestrian alleyways are apartment buildings (inside they tend to be small and uninspired), vintage-clothing stores, postage-stamp-size boutiques selling overpriced gewgaws, art galleries, roaring traditional music bars aimed at tourists, a hotel resuscitated by U2, hip restaurants, pubs, clubs, European-style cafés, and a smattering of cultural venues.

Temple Bar's regeneration was no doubt abetted by that one surefire real-estate asset that appealed to the Viking founders of the area: location. The area is bordered by Dame Street to the south, the Liffey to the north, Fishamble Street to the west, and Westmoreland Street to the east. In fact, Temple Bar is situated so perfectly between everywhere else in Dublin that it's difficult to believe this neighborhood was once largely forsaken. It's now sometimes called the "playing ground of young Dublin," and for good reason: on weekend evenings and daily in summer it teems with young people—not only from Dublin but from all over Europe—drawn by its pubs, clubs, and lively *craic* (good conversation and fun).

TOP ATTRACTIONS

Gallery of Photography. Dublin's premier photography gallery has a permanent collection of early-20th-century Irish photography and also puts on monthly exhibitions of work by contemporary Irish and international photographers. The gallery is an invaluable social record of Ireland. The bookstore is the best place in town to browse for photography books and to pick up arty postcards. ⊠ *Meeting House Sq. S, Temple Bar, Dublin, Co. Dublin* ☎ *01/671–4654* ⊕ *www.galleryofphotography. ie* ⊠ *Free* ☉ *Tues.–Sat. 11–6, Sun. 1–6.*

Ha'penny Bridge. Every Dubliner has a story about meeting someone on this cast-iron Victorian bridge, a heavily trafficked footbridge that crosses the Liffey at a prime spot—Temple Bar is on the south side, and the bridge provides the fastest route to the thriving Mary and Henry streets shopping areas to the north. Until early in the 20th century, a halfpenny toll was charged to cross it. Congestion on the Ha'penny has been relieved with the opening of the Millennium Footbridge a few hundred yards up the river. A refurbishment, including new railings, a return to the original white color, and tasteful lighting at night, has given the bridge a new lease on life.

Irish Film Institute (IFI). The opening of the IFI in a former Quaker meetinghouse helped to launch the revitalization of Temple Bar. It has two comfortable art-house cinemas showing revivals and new independent films, the Irish Film Archive, a bookstore for cineastes, and a popular bar and restaurant-café, all of which make this one of the neighborhood's most vital cultural institutions and *the* place to be seen. On Saturday nights in summer, the center screens films outdoors on Meeting House Square. ⊠ *6 Eustace St., Temple Bar, Dublin, Co. Dublin* ☎ *01/679–5744* ⊕ *www.ifi.ie* ⊠ *Event ticket prices vary* ☉ *Weekdays 9:30 am–midnight, weekends 11 am–midnight.*

QUICK BITES

Irish Film Institute Café. This buzzing café is a pleasant place for a lunchtime break. Sandwiches are large and healthful, with plenty of vegetarian choices, and the people-watching is unmatched. ⊠ *6 Eustace St., Temple Bar, Dublin, Co. Dublin* ☎ *01/679–5744.*

Meeting House Square. The square, which is behind the Ark and accessed via Curved Street, takes its name from a nearby Quaker meetinghouse. Today it's something of a gathering place for Dublin's youth and artists. Numerous summer events—classic movies (Saturday night), theater, games, and family programs—take place here. (Thankfully, seats are installed.) The square is also a favorite site for the continuously changing street sculpture that pops up all over Temple Bar (artists commissioned by the city sometimes create oddball pieces, such as half of a Volkswagen protruding from a wall). Year-round, the square is a great spot to sit, people-watch, and take in the sounds of the performing buskers who swarm to the place. There's also an organic food market here every Saturday morning.

Continued on page 82

A TRIP TO THE PUB

For any visitor to Ireland who wants to see the natives in their bare element—to witness them at full pace, no-holds-barred—a trip to a busy pub is a must. Luckily for you, a pub is above all a welcoming place, where a visitor is seen as a source of new, exotic stories and, more importantly, as an unsullied audience for the locals and their tall tales.

The term "pub" is shorthand for "public house," which is an apt name for one of Ireland's great institutions. Stepping into a pub (and there seems to be one on every corner) is the easiest way to transport yourself into the thick of Irish life. A pub, of course, is a drinking establishment, and for better or worse the Irish have a deep, abiding relationship with drink—particularly their beloved black stout.

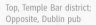

The point, however, isn't what you drink, but where: in the warmth of the public house, in company. It's the place to tell stories, most of them true, and to hear music. It's where locals go to mark the key stages of their lives: to wet a new baby's head; to celebrate a graduation; to announce an engagement; and finally to wake a corpse.

Top, Temple Bar district;
Opposite, Dublin pub

HOW TO CHOOSE A PUB

Not all pubs are created equal. Throughout this book we recommend some of the finest, but here are a few ways to distinguish the real gold from the sparkling pyrite:

■ Qualified, experienced bar staff—not grubby students dreaming of the round-the-world trip they are working to save up for. A uniform of white shirt and black trousers is often a good sign.

■ At least one man over sixty (preferably with a cap of some description) drinking at the bar (not at a table). He should know the good bars by now, right?

■ No TV. Or, if there is a TV it should be hidden away in a corner, only to be used for horse racing and other major sporting events.

■ No recorded music. A pub is a place to talk and listen. Occasional live music is okay, especially a traditional session.

■ Bathrooms are clean but not *too* clean. They are purely functional, not polished chambers for hanging out and chatting with friends about your new Blackberry.

THE QUEST FOR THE CRAIC

Pub-going at its best has a touch of magic to it: conversation flows, spirits rise, and inhibitions evaporate. There's a word in Gaelic for this happy condition: the craic, which roughly translates as "lively talk and good times." The craic is the sort of thing that's difficult to find only when you're looking too hard for it. Large crowds, loud music, and one pint too many can also make the craic elusive. When your companions all seem clever and handsome, and you can't imagine better company in the world, that's when you know you've found it.

Top left, pub signs in O'Connell Street, Ennis, County Clare; Right, the Long Hall Pub, Dublin

PUB ETIQUETTE

■ First, if you want to meet people and get into the craic, belly up to the bar counter and pass up a seat at a table.

■ Always place your drink order at the bar and don't heckle the barkeepers to get their attention. They're professionals—they'll see you soon enough.

■ If you do take a table, bring your dirty glasses back to the bar before you leave, or when you order another round.

■ In present-day Ireland, male and female pubgoers usually get equal treatment. At the most traditional places, though, it's still customary in mixed company for the man to order drinks at the bar while the woman takes a table seat.

■ Don't tip the barkeepers, except at Christmas, when you can offer to buy them a drink.

■ Never sip from your Guinness until it has fully settled. You'll know this from the deep black color and perfectly defined white head.

■ Don't smoke in the bar; it's against the law. But feel free to gather outside in the rain and chat with the other unfortunates. It's a great spot to start a romance.

■ You have to be at least 18 years old to *drink* in a pub, but kids are welcome during the day, and nondrinking minors as young as 14 are often tolerated at night.

MAKING THE ROUNDS

You may get caught up in the "rounds" system, in which each pub mate takes turns to "shout" an order. Your new friends may forget to tell you when it's your round, but any failure to "put your hand in your pocket" may lead to a reputation that will follow you to the grave. To miss your "shout" is to become known for "short arms and long pockets" and to be shunned by decent people.

LAST CALL

Technically, pubs have to stop serving at 11:30 Mon.–Thurs., 12:30 Fri.–Sat., and 11 Sun. At the end of the night, ignore the first five calls of "Time please, ladies and gentlemen!" from the barman. You'll know he's getting serious by the roar of his voice.

THE "BLACK STUFF"

Rich, creamy head.

Nearly black in color, with a very slight coffee-like aftertaste.

As you drink, the head will leave "rings of pleasure" down the side of the glass.

THE POUR

The storage and pouring of a pint of stout is almost as important as the brewing. The best quality is usually found in older bars that sell a lot of pints—meaning the beer you get hasn't been sitting in the keg too long and the pipes are well coated.

Pouring a pint consists of two stages: The glass is filled three-quarters full, then allowed to sit. After the head settles, the glass is filled to the top (stage two).

Why the painstaking ritual? Because the barkeeper knows you don't want your first sip to be a mouthful of foam. And because the flavor's that much sweeter for the waiting.

Stout, a dark beer made using roasted malts or barley, originated in Ireland, and it's the country's national drink, consumed in pubs with unflagging allegiance.

GUINNESS. For most Irish, the name Guinness is synonymous with stout. With massive breweries in Africa and the Americas, it really is a world brand, but the "true" pint still flows from the original brewery at St. James Gate in Dublin. While some old-timers still drink the more malty bottled version, draught Guinness is now the standard. A deep, creamy texture and slightly bitter first taste is followed by a milder, more "toasty" aftertaste.

MURPHY'S. The Murphy Brewery was founded by James Murphy in 1856 in Cork City. Murphy's is very much a Cork drink, and often suffers from "second city" complex in relation to its giant rival Guinness. Corkonians say Murphy's has a less bitter, more nutty flavor than the "Dublin stout."

BEAMISH. Another Cork drink, a little sweeter and less dry than either Guinness or Murphy's, and so a little easier on the novice palate. Beamish and Crawford Brewery began making beer in 1792.

WELCOME TO IRELAND'S LIVING ROOM . . .

Pub food is a lunchtime thing; the prices are reasonable, and the quality can be quite good. Ask for a menu at the bar. If you're near a coast, look for sea-food specialties, from oysters and mussels to smoked salmon. With beef-and-Guinness stew, you can drink your stout and eat it too.

Although the majority of your companions will be drinking stout, you do have other options.

A lager is always available—Heineken and Carlsberg are the most popular brands.

If you're thirsting for something stronger, take a nip of Irish whiskey, which tends to be less smoky and intensely flavored than its Scotch cousin. Jameson and Bushmills, both smooth blends, are the standard varieties, and you can usually find a single-malt as well.

On the other hand, if the booze isn't your thing, you can always choose tea, soda, or a bottle of water. (Ballygowan is the Irish Evian.) It's fine to order nonalcoholic drinks—many people who drive do so.

"TRAD" MUSIC IN ITS NATURAL DOMAIN

The pub is an ideal place to hear traditional Irish music. Performances can have a spontaneous air to them, but they don't start up just anywhere. Pubs that accommodate live sessions have signs saying so; and they're more common outside Dublin than in the city. To learn more about Irish music, see "Gael Force" in chapter 8.

Top, musicians performing at Gus O'Connor's pub in Doolin, County Clare; Right, oysters and a (half) pint, Galway

★ **Olympia Theatre.** One of the most atmospheric places in Europe to see musical acts, the Olympia is Dublin's second-oldest theater, and one of its busiest. This classic Victorian music hall, built in 1879, has a gorgeous red wrought-iron facade. The Olympia's long-standing Friday and Saturday series, "Midnight at the Olympia," has brought numerous musical performers to Dublin, and the theater has also seen many notable actors strut across its stage, including Alec Guinness, Peggy Ashcroft, Noël Coward, and even the old-time Hollywood team of Laurel and Hardy. Big-name performers like Van Morrison often choose the intimacy of the Olympia over larger venues. It's really a hot place to see some fine performances, so if you have a chance, by all means, go. Conveniently, there are two pubs here—through doors directly off the back of the theater's orchestra section. ⊠ *72 Dame St., Temple Bar, Dublin, Co. Dublin* ☎ *167/93323* ⊕ *www.mcd.ie/olympia* ⊠ *Event ticket prices vary.*

★ **Wall of Fame.** If you're strolling through Temple Bar and suddenly come upon a group of slack-jawed young people staring wide-eyed at a large wall, then you've probably stumbled upon the Wall of Fame. The whole front wall of the Button Factory music venue has become a giant tribute to the giants of Irish rock music. Twelve huge photos adorn the wall, including a very young and innocent U2, a very beautiful Sinead O'Connor, and a very drunk Shane McGowan. ⊠ *Curved St, Temple Bar, Dublin, Co. Dublin* ☎ *01/607–9202.*

QUICK BITES

The Bakery. This no-frills little bakery café at the heart of Temple Bar is bursting with fresh, authentic Irish cream cakes, fruit flans, and apple turnovers. Their coffee is a favorite with in-the-know caffeine junkies. ⊠ *Pudding Row, 2 E. Essex St. West, Temple Bar, Dublin, Co. Dublin* ☎ *01/672–9882.*

WORTH NOTING

☉ **The Ark.** A self-described cultural center for children, the Ark engages and inspires young imaginations through a variety of creative endeavors and activities like music, poetry readings, film, dance, painting, interactive exhibitions, and more. Its theater opens onto Meeting House Square for outdoor performances in summer. A gallery and workshop space host ongoing activities. ⊠ *11a Eustace St., Temple Bar, Dublin, Co. Dublin* ☎ *01/670-7788* ⊕ *www.ark.ie* ⊠ *Free* ☉ *Weekdays 10–4:30, weekends only if there's a show.*

National Library Photographic Archive. This important photographic resource holds regular exhibitions in its stylish modern building in Temple Bar. The collection comprises approximately 600,000 photographs, most of which are Irish, making up a priceless visual history of the nation. Although most of the photographs are historical, dating as far back as the mid-19th century, there's also a large number of contemporary pictures. Subject matter ranges from topographical views to studio portraits, from political events to early tourist photographs. You can also buy a print of your favorite photo. ⊠ *Meeting House Sq., Temple Bar, Dublin, Co. Dublin* ☎ *53/1603–0200* ⊕ *www.nli.ie/en/national-photographic-archive.aspx* ⊠ *Free* ☉ *Weekdays 10–5, Sat. 12–5.*

NORTHSIDE

"What do you call a Northsider in a suit? The accused." So went the old joke. But faded stereotypes about the Northside being Dublin's poorer and more deprived half were partly washed away beneath the wave of Celtic Tiger development. Locals and visitors alike are discovering the no-nonsense, laid-back charm of the Northside's revamped Georgian wonders, understated cultural gems, high-quality restaurants, and buzzing ethnic diversity.

If you stand on O'Connell Bridge or the pedestrian-only Ha'penny span, you'll get excellent views up and down the River Liffey, known in Gaelic as the *abha na life*, transcribed phonetically as Anna Livia by James Joyce in *Finnegans Wake*. Here, framed with embankments like those along Paris's Seine, the river nears the end of its 128-km (80-mile) journey from the Wicklow Mountains to the Irish Sea. And near the bridges, you begin a pilgrimage into James Joyce country—north of the Liffey, in the center of town—and the captivating sights of Dublin's Northside, a mix of densely thronged shopping streets and genteelly refurbished homes.

For much of the 18th century, the upper echelons of Dublin society lived in the Georgian houses in the Northside—around Mountjoy Square—and shopped along Capel Street, which was lined with stores selling fine furniture and silver. But development of the Southside—the Georgian Leinster House in 1745, Merrion Square in 1764, and Fitzwilliam Square in 1825—changed the Northside's fortunes. The city's fashionable social center crossed the Liffey, and although some of the Northside's illustrious inhabit-

> **TOO GREAT A TOLL**
>
> William Butler Yeats was one of many Dubliners who found the halfpenny toll of Ha'penny Bridge too steep. He detoured to O'Connell Bridge instead.

ants stuck it out, the area gradually became run-down. The Northside's fortunes have now changed back, however. Once-derelict swaths of houses, especially on and near the Liffey, have been rehabilitated, and large shopping centers have opened on Mary and Jervis streets. The high-rise Docklands area, east of the Custom House, is pocked with modern high-rise apartments. More importantly, the new Daniel Libeskind–designed, 2,000-seat, Grand Canal Theatre has shifted the cultural tectonic plates of Dublin toward this area. In addition, the beginnings of a little Chinatown are forming on Parnell Street, while a swing bridge has been added between City Quay and the Northside. O'Connell Street itself has been partially pedestrianized, and most impressive of all is the Spire, the street's 395-foot-high stainless-steel monument.

TOP ATTRACTIONS

Custom House. Seen at its best when reflected in the waters of the Liffey during the short interval when the high tide is on the turn, the Custom House is the city's most spectacular Georgian building. Extending 375 feet on the north side of the river, this is the work of James Gandon, an English architect who arrived in Ireland in 1781, when the building's construction commenced (it continued for 10 years). Crafted from gleaming Portland stone, the central portico is linked by arcades to pavilions at either end. A statue of Commerce tops the copper dome, whose puny circumference, unfortunately, is out of proportion to the rest of the building. Statues on the main facade are based on allegorical themes. Note the exquisitely carved lions and unicorns supporting the arms of Ireland at the far ends of the facade. After Republicans set fire to the building in 1921, it was completely restored and reconstructed to house government offices. A visitor center traces the building's history and significance, and the life of Gandon. ⊠ *Custom House Quay, Northside, Dublin, Co. Dublin* 🕾 *01/888–2538* ⊕ *www.visitdublin. com* 🖃 *Free* ⊗ *Mid-Mar.–Oct., weekdays 10–12:30, weekends 2–5; Nov.–mid-Mar., Wed.–Fri. 10–12:30, Sun. 2–5.*

★ **Dublin City Gallery, The Hugh Lane.** The Francis Bacon studio, reconstructed here exactly as the artist left it on his death (including his diary, books, walls, floors, ceiling, and even dust!), makes this already impressive gallery a must-see for art lovers and fans of the renowned British artist. Built as a town house for the Earl of Charlemont in 1762, this residence was so grand that the Parnell Square street on which it sits was nicknamed "Palace Row" in its honor. Sir William Chambers, who also built the Marino Casino for Charlemont, designed the structure in the best Palladian manner. Its delicate and rigidly correct facade, extended by two demilune (half-moon) arcades, was fashioned from

Dublin Northside

Abbey Presbyterian
Church **5**

Custom House **15**

Dublin City Gallery,
The Hugh Lane **7**

Dublin Writers
Museum **6**

GAA Museum **12**

Garden of
Remembrance **8**

Gate Theatre **4**

General Post Office **3**

James Joyce
Centre **10**

Mountjoy Square **11**

O'Connell Street **1**

Pro-Cathedral **14**

Rotunda Hospital **9**

St. Francis Xavier
Church **13**

The Spire **2**

the "new" white Ardmulcan stone (now seasoned to gray). Charlemont was one of the cultural locomotives of 18th-century Dublin—his walls were hung with Titians and Hogarths, and he frequently dined with Oliver Goldsmith and Sir Joshua Reynolds—so he would undoubtedly be delighted that his home is now a gallery, named after Sir Hugh Lane, a nephew of Lady Gregory (W. B. Yeats's aristocratic patron). Lane collected both impressionist paintings and 19th-century Irish and Anglo-Irish works. A complicated agreement with the National Gallery in London (reached after heated diplomatic dispute) stipulates that a portion of the 39 French paintings amassed by Lane shuttle between London and here. Time it right and you'll be able to see Pissarro's *Printemps,* Manet's *Eva Gonzales,* Morisot's *Jour d'Été,* and, the jewel of the collection, Renoir's *Les Parapluies.*

Irish artists represented include Roderic O'Conor, well known for his views of the West of Ireland; William Leech, including his *Girl with a Tinsel Scarf* and *The Cigarette*; and the most famous of the group, Jack B. Yeats (W. B.'s brother). The museum has a dozen of his paintings, including *Ball Alley* and *There Is No Night.* The mystically serene Sean Scully Gallery displays seven giant canvasses by Ireland's renowned abstract modernist. ⊠ *Parnell Sq. N, Northside, Dublin, Co. Dublin* ☎ *01/222–5550* ⊕ *www.hughlane.ie* ⊠ *Free* ☉ *Tues.–Thurs. 10–6, Fri. and Sat. 10–5, Sun. 11–5.*

★ **Dublin Writers Museum.** "If you would know Ireland—body and soul— you must read its poems and stories," wrote W. B. Yeats in 1891. Further investigation into the Irish way with words can be found at this unique museum, in a magnificently restored 18th-century town house on the north side of Parnell Square. The mansion, once the home of John Jameson, of the Irish whiskey family, centers on the Gallery of Writers, an enormous drawing room gorgeously decorated with paintings, Adamesque plasterwork, and a deep Edwardian lincrusta frieze. Rare manuscripts, diaries, posters, letters, limited and first editions, photographs, and other mementos commemorate the lives and works of the nation's greatest writers—and there are many of them, so leave plenty of time—including Joyce, Shaw, J. M. Synge, Lady Gregory, W. B. Yeats, Beckett, and others. On display are an 1804 edition of Swift's *Gulliver's Travels,* an 1899 first edition of Bram Stoker's *Dracula,* and an 1899 edition of Wilde's *Ballad of Reading Gaol.* There's a "Teller of Tales" exhibit showcasing Behan, O'Flaherty, and O'Faoláin. Readings are periodically held, and there's a room dedicated to children's literature. The bookshop and café make this an ideal place to spend a rainy afternoon. ⊠ *18 Parnell Sq. N, Northside, Dublin, Co. Dublin* ☎ *01/872–2077* ⊕ *www.writersmuseum.com* ⊠ *€7.50* ☉ *Mon.–Sat. 10–5, Sun. 11–5.*

Gate Theatre. The show begins here as soon as you walk into the auditorium, a gorgeously Georgian masterwork designed by Richard Johnston in 1784 as an assembly room for the Rotunda Hospital complex. The Gate has been one of Dublin's most important theaters since its founding in 1929 by Mícheál MacLiammóir and Hilton Edwards, who also founded Galway City's An Taibhdhearc as the national Irish-language theater. The Gate stages many established productions by Irish as well as foreign playwrights—and plenty of foreign actors have performed here, including Orson Welles (his first paid performance) and James Mason (early in his career). ⊠ *Cavendish Row, Northside, Dublin, Co. Dublin* ☎ *01/874–4045* ⊕ *www. gate-theatre.ie* 🎫 *Event ticket prices vary* ☉ *Shows Mon.–Sat.*

> ### THE SCARS OF HISTORY
>
> Look for the bullet marks on the pillars of the General Post Office—they're remnants of the 1916 Easter Uprising.

General Post Office (GPO). One of the great civic buildings of Dublin's Georgian era, the GPO's fame is based on the role it played in the Easter Uprising. The building, with its impressive neoclassical facade, was designed by Francis Johnston and built by the British between 1814 and 1818 as a center of communications. This gave it great strategic importance—and was one of the reasons it was chosen by the insurgent forces in 1916 as a headquarters. Here, on Easter Monday, 1916, the Republican forces, about 2,000 in number and under the guidance of Pádraig Pearse and James Connolly, stormed the building and issued the Proclamation of the Irish Republic. After a week of shelling, the GPO lay in ruins; 13 rebels were ultimately executed, including Connolly, who was dying of gangrene from a wound in a leg shattered in the fighting and had to be propped up in a chair in front of the firing squad. Most of the original building was destroyed, though the facade survived, albeit with the scars of bullets on its pillars. Rebuilt and reopened in 1929, it became a working post office with an attractive two-story main concourse. The 1916 Proclamation and the names of its signatories are inscribed on the green marble plinth. The little museum deals with the history of the building, and the role of the Post Office in Ireland. ⊠ *O'Connell St., Northside, Dublin, Co. Dublin* ✉ *heritage@anpost.ie* ⊕ *www.anpost.ie/AnPost/History+and+Heritage/ Museum/Museum.htm* 🎫 *€2* ☉ *Weekdays 10–5, Sat. 10–4.*

NEED A BREAK?

The Sackville Lounge. For a classic Dublin pub with a cozy, warm atmosphere, stop in to this place, famously popular with theater folk and old flat-cap Dublin men, for a smooth pint of the black stuff. ⊠ *Sackville Pl., Northside, Dublin, Co. Dublin* ☎ *01/874–5222.*

James Joyce Centre. Few may have read him, but everyone in Ireland has at least heard of James Joyce (1882–1941)—especially since owning a copy of his censored and suppressed *Ulysses* was one of the top status symbols of the early 20th century. Joyce is of course now acknowledged as one of the greatest modern authors, and his *Dubliners, Finnegan's Wake,* and *A Portrait of the Artist as a Young Man* can even be read as quirky "travel guides" to Dublin. Open to the public, this restored 18th-century Georgian town house, once the dancing academy of Professor Denis J. Maginni (which many will recognize from a reading of *Ulysses*), is a center for Joycean studies and events related to the author. It has an extensive library and archives, exhibition rooms, a bookstore, and a café. The collection includes letters from Beckett, Joyce's guitar and cane, and a celebrated edition of *Ulysses* illustrated by Matisse. The interactive "James Joyce and Ulysses" exhibition allows you to delve into the mysteries and controversies of the novel. The center is the main organizer of "Bloomstime," which marks the week leading up to the Bloomsday celebrations. (Bloomsday, June 16, is the single day *Ulysses* chronicles, as Leopold Bloom winds his way around Dublin in 1904.) ⊠ *35 N. Great George's St., Northside, Dublin, Co. Dublin* ☎ *01/878–8547* ⊕ *www.jamesjoyce.ie* ✆ *€5, guided tour €10* ☾ *Tues.– Sat. 10–5, Sun. noon–5.*

O'Connell Street. Dublin's most famous thoroughfare, which is 150 feet wide, was previously known as Sackville Street, but its name was changed in 1924, two years after the founding of the Irish Free State. After the devastation of the 1916 Easter Uprising, the Northside street had to be almost entirely reconstructed, a task that took until the end of the 1920s. At one time the main attraction of the street was Nelson's Pillar, a Doric column towering over the city center and a marvelous vantage point, but it was blown up in 1966, on the 50th anniversary of the Easter Uprising. A major cleanup and repaving have returned the street to some of its old glory. The large monument at the south end of the street is dedicated to Daniel O'Connell (1775–1847), "The Liberator," and was erected in 1854 as a tribute to the orator's achievement in securing Catholic Emancipation in 1829. Look closely and you'll notice that O'Connell is wearing a glove on one hand, as he did for much of his adult life, a self-imposed penance for shooting a man in a duel. But even the great man himself is dwarfed by the newest addition to O'Connell Street: the 395-foot-high Spire was built in Nelson's Pillar's place in 2003, and today this gigantic, stainless-steel monument dominates the street.

St. Mary's Pro-Cathedral. Dublin's principal Catholic cathedral (also known as St. Mary's) is a great place to hear the best Irish male voices: a Palestrina choir, in which the great Irish tenor John McCormack began his career, sings in Latin here every Sunday morning at 11. The cathedral, built between 1816 and 1825, has a classical church design— on a suitably epic scale. The church's facade, with a six-Doric-pillared portico, is based on the Temple of Theseus in Athens; the interior is modeled after the Grecian-Doric style of St. Philippe du Roule in Paris. But the building was never granted full cathedral status, nor has the identity of its architect ever been discovered; the only clue to its creation is in the church ledger, which lists a "Mr. P." as the builder. ⊠ *83 Marlborough St., Northside, Dublin, Co. Dublin* ☎ *01/874–5441* ⊕ *www. procathedral.ie* ✆ *Free* ☾ *Weekdays 7:30–6:45, Sat. 7:30–7:15, Sun. 9–1:45 and 5:30–7:45.*

The Spire. Christened the "Stiletto in the Ghetto" by local smart alecks, this needlelike monument is the most exciting thing to happen to Dublin's skyline in decades. The Spire, also known as the Monument of Light, was originally planned as part of the city's millennium celebrations. But Ian Ritchie's spectacular 395-foot-high monument wasn't erected until the beginning of 2003. Seven times taller than the nearby General Post Office, the stainless-steel structure rises from the spot where Nelson's Pillar once stood. Approximately 10 feet in diameter at its base, the softly lighted monument narrows to only 1 foot at its apex—the upper part of the Spire sways gently when the wind blows. The monument's creators envisioned it serving as a beacon for the whole of the city, and it will certainly be the first thing you see as you drive into Dublin from the airport. ⊠ *O'Connell St., Northside, Dublin, Co. Dublin.*

DID YOU KNOW?

The Champs-Élysées of Dublin, O'Connell Street is home to the city's St. Patrick's Day parade and is lined with important landmarks, including the General Post Office, scene of the Easter Rising of 1916.

WORTH NOTING

Abbey Presbyterian Church. Built on the profits of sin—well, by a generous wine merchant actually—and topped with a soaring Gothic spire, this church anchors the northeast corner of Parnell Square, an area that was the city's most fashionable address during the gilded days of the 18th-century Ascendancy. Popularly known as Findlater's Church, after the merchant Alex Findlater, the church was completed in 1864 with an interior that has a stark Presbyterian mood despite stained-glass windows and ornate pews. For a bird's-eye view of the area, climb the small staircase that leads to the balcony. ⊠ *Parnell Sq., Northside, Dublin, Co. Dublin* ☎ *01/837–8600* ⌨ *Free* ⊙ *Hrs vary.*

🦆 **GAA Museum.** The Irish are sports crazy and reserve their fiercest pride for their native games. In the bowels of Croke Park, the main stadium and headquarters of the GAA (Gaelic Athletic Association), this museum gives you a great introduction to native Irish sport. The four Gaelic games (football, hurling, camogie, and handball) are explained in detail, and if you're brave enough you can have a go yourself. High-tech displays take you through the history and highlights of the games. *National Awakening* is a really smart, interesting short film reflecting the key impact of the GAA on the emergence of the Irish nation and the forging of a new Irish identity. The exhilarating *A Day in September* captures the thrill and passion of All Ireland finals day—the annual denouement of the intercounty hurling and Gaelic football seasons—which is every bit as important to the locals as the Super Bowl is to sports fans in the United States. Tours of the stadium, the fourth largest in Europe, are available. ⊠ *St. Joseph's Avenue, Croke Park Stadium, North County Dublin, Dublin, Co. Dublin* ☎ *01/819–2300* ⊕ *museum.gaa.ie* ⌨ *Museum €6, museum and stadium tour €11* ⊙ *July and Aug., Mon.–Fri. 9:30–6, Sun. 10:30–5; Sept.–June, Mon.–Sat. 9:30–5, Sun. 11:30–5.*

Garden of Remembrance. Opened 50 years after the Easter Uprising of 1916, the garden in Parnell Square commemorates those who died fighting for Ireland's freedom. At the garden's entrance is a large plaza; steps lead down to the fountain area, graced with a sculpture by contemporary Irish artist Oisín Kelly, based on the mythological Children of Lír, who were turned into swans. The garden serves as an oasis of tranquility in the middle of the busy city. ⊠ *Parnell Sq., Northside, Dublin, Co. Dublin* ☎ *01/821–3021* ⊕ *www.heritageireland.ie* ⌨ *Free* ⊙ *Apr.–Sept., daily 8:30–6; Oct.–Mar., daily 9:30–4.*

Mountjoy Square. Irishman Brian Boru, who led his soldiers to victory against the Vikings in the Battle of Clontarf in 1014, was said to have pitched camp before the confrontation on the site of Mountjoy Square. Playwright Sean O'Casey lived here, at No. 35, and used the square as a setting for *The Shadow of a Gunman*. Built over the course of the two decades leading up to 1818, this Northside square was once surrounded by elegant terraced houses. Today only the northern side remains intact. The houses on the once derelict southern side have been converted into apartments.

St. Francis Xavier Church. One of the city's finest churches in the classical style, the Jesuit St. Francis Xavier's was begun in 1829, the year of Catholic Emancipation, and was completed three years later. The building is designed in the shape of a Latin cross, with a distinctive Ionic portico and an unusual coffered ceiling. The striking, faux-marble high altarpiece, decorated with lapis lazuli, came from Italy. The church appears in James Joyce's story "Grace." ⊠ *Upper Gardiner St., Northside, Dublin, Co. Dublin* ☎ *01/836–3411* ⊕ *www.gardinerstparish.ie* ☜ *Free* ☉ *Daily 7 am–8:30 pm.*

DUBLIN WEST

A cornucopia of things quintessentially Dublin, this area is studded with treasures and pleasures ranging from the opulent 18th-century salons of Dublin Castle to time-burnished St. Patrick's Cathedral, and from the Liberties neighborhood—redoubt of the city's best antiques stores—to the Irish Museum of Modern Art (housed at the strikingly renovated Royal Hospital Kilmainham). You can time-travel from the 10th-century crypt at Christ Church Cathedral—the city's oldest surviving structure—to the modern plant of the Guinness Brewery and its storehouse museum. You can also cross the Liffey for a visit to Smithfield, Dublin's old (but recently revitalized) market area where flowers, fruit, vegetables, and even horses have been sold for generations. Traditional music bars sit side by side here with modern hotels and the Old Jameson Distillery museum.

Keep in mind that Dublin is compact. The following sights aren't far from those in the other city-center neighborhoods. In fact, City Hall is just across the street from Temple Bar, and Christ Church Cathedral is a short walk farther west. The westernmost sights covered here—notably the Royal Hospital and Kilmainham Gaol—are, however, at some distance, so if you're not an enthusiastic walker, you may want to drive or catch a cab, bus, or LUAS tram to them.

TOP ATTRACTIONS

Fodor's Choice ★ **Chester Beatty Library.** A connoisseur's delight, this "library" is considered one of the overlooked treasures of Ireland. After Sir Alfred Chester Beatty (1875–1968), a Canadian mining millionaire and a collector with a flawless eye, assembled one of the most significant collections of Islamic, Early Christian, and Far Eastern art in the Western world, he donated it to Ireland. Housed in the gorgeous clock-tower building of Dublin Castle, exhibits include clay tablets from Babylon dating from 2700 BC, Japanese wood-block prints, Chinese jade books, early papyrus bibles, and Turkish and Persian paintings. The second floor, dedicated to the major religions, houses 250 manuscripts of the Koran from across the Muslim world, as well as one of the earliest Gospels. The first-floor "Arts of the Book" exhibition looks at the different origins and finest examples of books throughout the world. Guided tours of the library are available on Tuesday and Saturday at 2:30 pm. On sunny days the garden is one of the most tranquil places in central Dublin. ⊠ *Castle St., Dublin West, Dublin, Co. Dublin* ☎ *01/407–0750* ⊕ *www.cbl.ie* ☜ *Free* ☉ *May–Sept., weekdays 10–5, Sat. 11–5, Sun. 1–5; Oct.–Apr., Tues.–Fri. 10–5, Sat. 11–5, Sun. 1–5.*

The Silk Road Café. A great-value, Middle Eastern delight hidden away in the Chester Beatty Library, the Silk Road Café has a buffet-style menu always full of exotic surprises. The light-filled room (open Tues.–Fri. 10–4:30, Sat. 11–4:30, and Sun. 1–4:30) and serene atmosphere make you want to linger longer than you should. ⊠ *Chester Beatty Library, Castle St., Dublin West, Dublin, Co. Dublin* ☎ *01/407–0770* ⊕ *www.silkroadcafe.ie.*

★ **Christ Church Cathedral.** From its exterior, you'd never guess that the first Christianized Danish king built a wooden church at this site in 1038; because of the extensive 19th-century renovation of its stonework and trim, the cathedral looks more Victorian than Anglo-Norman. Construction on the present Christ Church—the flagship of the Church of Ireland and one of two Protestant cathedrals in Dublin (the other is St. Patrick's just to the south)—was begun in 1172 by Strongbow, a Norman baron and conqueror of Dublin for the English Crown, and continued for 50 years. By 1875 the cathedral had deteriorated badly; a major renovation gave it much of the look it has today, including the addition of one of Dublin's most charming structures: a Bridge of Sighs–like affair that connects the cathedral to the old Synod Hall, which now holds the Viking multimedia exhibition, Dublinia. Strongbow himself is buried in the cathedral, beneath an impressive effigy. The vast, sturdy **crypt,** with its 12th- and 13th-century vaults, is Dublin's oldest surviving structure and the building's most notable feature. The Treasures of Christ Church exhibition includes manuscripts, various historic artifacts, and the tabernacle used when James II worshiped here. But the real marvel are the mortified bodies of a cat and rat—they were trapped in an organ pipe in the 1860s—who seem caught in a cartoon chase for all eternity. At 6 pm on Wednesday and Thursday, you can enjoy the glories of a choral evensong and the bell ringers usually practice on Fridays at 7 pm. ⊠ *Christ Church Pl. and Winetavern St., Dublin West, Dublin, Co. Dublin* ☎ *01/677–8099* ⊕ *www.cccdub.ie* ☜ *€6* ⊙ *June–Aug., weekdays 9:45–6:15, Sat. 9:45–6:15, Sun. 12:30–2:30 and 4:30–6:15; Sept.–May, Mon.–Sat. 9:45–4:15, Sun. 12:30–2:30.*

City Hall. Facing the Liffey from Cork Hill at the top of Parliament Street, this grand Georgian municipal building (1769–79), once the Royal Exchange, marks the southwest corner of Temple Bar. Today it's the seat of the Dublin Corporation, the elected body that governs the city. Thomas Cooley designed the building with 12 columns that encircle the domed central rotunda, which has a fine mosaic floor and 12 frescoes depicting Dublin legends and ancient Irish historical scenes. The 20-foot-high sculpture to the right is of Daniel O'Connell, "The Liberator." He looks like he's about to begin the famous speech he gave here in 1800. The building houses a multimedia exhibition—with artifacts, kiosks, graphics, and audiovisual presentations—tracing the evolution of Ireland's 1,000-year-old capital. ⊠ *Dame St., Dublin West, Dublin, Co. Dublin* ☎ *01/222–2204* ⊕ *www.dublincity.ie/RecreationandCulture* ☜ *€4* ⊙ *Mon.–Sat. 10–5:15.*

Dublin Castle. As seat and symbol of the British rule of Ireland for more than seven centuries, Dublin Castle figured largely in Ireland's turbulent history early in the 20th century. It's now mainly used for Irish and EU

Dublin West and Phoenix Park

TO
ASHTOWN CASTLE
& DUBLIN ZOO

Phoenix Park

Memorial Park

Phoenix Park

Infirmary Rd.

Chesterfield Ave.

Conyngham Rd.

River Liffey

St. John's Rd. West

South Circular Rd.

Inchicore Rd.

Kilmainham La.

Old Kilmainham

Mil. Brown

Bow Bridge

Military Rd.

Parkgate St.

Montpelier Hill

Arbour Hill

Benburb St.

Wolfe Tone Quay

Victoria Quay

Ellis Quay

Ellis Quay

Usher's Island

Arran Quay

Usher's Quay

Bridgefoot St.

Oliver Bond St.

W. Thomas St.

Thomas St.

Bridge St.

Merchants Quay

Inns Quay

Chancery St.

Mary's La.

Green St.

Capel St.

Abbey St.

Strand St.

Ormond Quay

Liffey St.

Bolton St.

Parnell St.

Mary St.

Jervis St.

Church St.

King St.

Bow St.

Brunswick St.

Blackhall Pl.

Queen St.

Manor St.

Smithfield

King St. North

Church St. North

Steevens' Lane

Seán Heuston Br.

Bow La. W.

James's St.

Watling St.

Crane St.

Marrowbone Lane

Dame St.

Castle St.

Ship St.

Great Georges St.

Fishamble St.

Christ Church Pl.

Winetavern St.

High St.

Nicholas St.

Patrick St.

Kevin St.

Bride St.

Golden Ln.

John's La.

Francis St.

Dillon St.

Cornmarket

Meath St.

The Coombe

Swift's Alley

Dean St.

St. Patrick's Park

St. Augustine St.

Dublin Castle

The Liberties

1 · 3 · 2 · 4 · 5 · 6 · 7 · 8 · 9 · 10 · 11 · 12 · 13 · 14 · 15 · 16 · 17 · 18

0   1/4 mi
0   1/2 km

governmental purposes. The sprawling Great Courtyard is the reputed site of the Black Pool (Dubh Linn, pronounced *dove*-lin) from which Dublin got its name. In the Lower Castle Yard, the Record Tower, the earliest of several towers on the site, is the largest remaining relic of the original Norman buildings, built by King John between 1208 and 1220. The clock-tower building houses the fabulous Chester Beatty Library. The State Apartments (on the southern side of the Upper Castle Yard)—formerly the residence of the English viceroys and now used by the president of Ireland to host visiting heads of state and EU ministers—are lavishly furnished with rich Donegal carpets and illuminated by Waterford glass chandeliers. The largest and most impressive of these chambers, St. Patrick's Hall, with its gilt pillars and painted ceiling, is used for the inauguration of Irish presidents. The Round Drawing Room, in Bermingham Tower, dates from 1411 and was rebuilt in 1777; numerous Irish leaders were imprisoned in the tower from the 16th century to the early 20th century. The blue oval Wedgwood Room contains Chippendale chairs and a marble fireplace. The Church of the Holy Trinity features carved oak panels, stained glass depicting the viceroy's coat of arms, and an elaborate array of fan vaults. More than 100 carved heads adorn the walls outside; among them, St. Peter, Jonathan Swift, St. Patrick, and Brian Boru.

Enter the castle through the Cork Hill Gate, just west of City Hall. One-hour guided tours are available every half hour, but the rooms are closed when in official use, so call ahead. The Castle Vaults hold an elegant little patisserie and bistro. ⊠ *Castle St., Dublin West, Dublin, Co. Dublin* ☏ *01/645–8813* ⊕ *www.dublincastle.ie* ▱ *State Apartments €4.50 including tour* ⊙ *Mon.–Sat. 10–4:45, Sun. 2–4:45.*

Four Courts. The stately Corinthian portico and the circular central hall warrant a visit to the seat of the High Court of Civil Law in Ireland. The distinctive copper-cover dome topping a colonnaded rotunda makes this one of Dublin's most instantly recognizable buildings. The view from the rotunda is terrific. Built between 1786 and 1802, the Four Courts is James Gandon's second Dublin masterpiece—close on the heels of his Custom House, located downstream on the same side of the River Liffey. In 1922, during the Irish Civil War, the Four Courts was almost totally destroyed by shelling—the adjoining Public Records Office was gutted, and many priceless legal documents, including innumerable family records, were destroyed. Restoration took 10 years. Tours of the building are not given, but you're welcome to sit in while the courts are in session. ⊠ *Inns Quay, Dublin West, Dublin, Co. Dublin* ☏ *01/872–5555* ⊕ *www.courts.ie* ⊙ *Daily 10–1 and 2:15–4.*

Fodor'sChoice ★ **Guinness Storehouse.** Ireland's all-dominating brewery—founded by Arthur Guinness in 1759 and at one time the largest stout-producing brewery in the world—spans a 60-acre spread west of Christ Church Cathedral. Not surprisingly, it's the most popular tourist destination in town—after all, the Irish national drink is Guinness stout, a dark brew made with roasted malt. The brewery itself is closed to the public, but the Guinness Storehouse is a spectacular attraction, designed to woo— some might say brainwash—you with the wonders of the "dark stuff." In a 1904 cast-iron-and-brick warehouse, the museum display covers six floors built around a huge, central glass atrium that is shaped like a giant pint glass. Beneath the glass floor of the lobby you can see Arthur Guinness's original lease on the site, for a whopping 9,000 years. The exhibition elucidates the brewing process and its history, with antique presses and vats, a look at bottle and can design through the ages, a history of the Guinness family, a fascinating archive of Guinness advertisements, and a chance to pull your own perfect pint. The star attraction is undoubtedly the top-floor **Gravity Bar,** with 360-degree floor-to-ceiling glass walls that offer a nonpareil view out over the city at sunset while you sip your free pint. One of the bar's first clients was one William Jefferson Clinton. You'll find the Guinness logo on everything from piggy banks to underpants in the Guinness Store on the ground floor. ⊠ *St. James' Gate, Dublin West, Dublin, Co. Dublin* ☎ *01/408–4800* ⊕ *www.guinness-storehouse.com* ⊠ *€14.40* ⊙ *July and Aug., daily 9:30–7; Sept.–June, daily 9:30–5.*

★ **Kilmainham Gaol.** Leaders of many failed Irish rebellions spent their last days in this grim, forbidding structure, and it holds a special place in the myth and memory of the country. The 1916 commanders Pádraig Pearse and James Connolly were held here before being executed in the prison yard. Other famous inmates included the revolutionary Robert Emmet and Charles Stewart Parnell, a leading politician. You can visit the prison only as part of a very moving and exciting guided tour, which leaves every hour on the hour. The cells are a chilling sight, and the guided tour and a 30-minute audiovisual presentation relate a graphic account of Ireland's political history over the past 200 years—from an Irish Nationalist viewpoint. A new exhibition explores the history of the prison and its restoration. A small tearoom is on the premises. ⊠ *Inchicore Rd., Dublin West, Dublin, Co. Dublin* ☎ *01/453–5984* ⊕ *www.heritageireland.ie* ⊠ *€6* ⊙ *Apr.–Sept., daily 9:30–5; Oct.–Mar., Mon.–Sat. 9:30–4, Sun. 10–5.*

★ **Royal Hospital Kilmainham.** This replica of Les Invalides in Paris is regarded as the most important 17th-century building in Ireland. Commissioned as a hospice for disabled and veteran soldiers by James Butler—the Duke of Ormonde and viceroy to King Charles II—it was completed in 1684, making it the first building erected in Dublin's golden age. It survived into the 1920s as a hospital, but after the founding of the Irish Free State in 1922, the building fell into disrepair. The entire edifice has since been restored. The architectural highlight is the hospital's baroque chapel, distinguished by its extraordinary plasterwork ceiling and fine wood carvings. ⊕ *www.rhk.ie.*

Irish Museum of Modern Art. The Royal Hospital also houses the Irish Museum of Modern Art, which concentrates on the work of contemporary Irish artists such as Richard Deacon, Richard Gorman, Dorothy Cross, Sean Scully, Matt Mullican, Louis Le Brocquy, and James Coleman. The museum also displays works by some non-Irish 20th-century greats, including Picasso and Miró, plus recent hotshots like Damien Hirst, and regularly hosts touring shows from major European museums. The Grass Roots Café serves light fare such as soups and sandwiches. The hospital is a short ride by taxi or bus from the city center. ⊠ *Kilmainham La., Dublin West, Dublin, Co. Dublin* ☎ *01/612–9900*

⊕ *www.imma.ie* ▱ *Free* ☉ *Royal Hospital: Mon, Tues., and Thurs.–Sat. 10–5:30, Wed. 10:30–5:30, Sun. noon–5:30. Museum: Tues. and Thurs.–Sat. 10–5:30, Wed. 10:30–5:30, Sun. noon–5:30; tours Wed. and Fri. at 2:30, Sat. at 11:30.*

Fodor'sChoice **St. Patrick's Cathedral.** The largest cathedral in Dublin and also the
★ national cathedral of the Church of Ireland, St. Patrick's was built in honor of Ireland's patron saint, who—according to legend—baptized many converts at a well on this site in the 5th century. The original building, dedicated in 1192 and early English Gothic in style, was an unsuccessful attempt to assert supremacy over the capital's other Protestant cathedral, Christ Church Cathedral. At 305 feet, this is the longest church in the country, a fact Oliver Cromwell's troops found useful as they made the church's nave into their stable in the 17th century.

■TIP➔ While in the shadow of St. Patrick's Cathedral, head from Patrick Close to Patrick Street; look down the street toward the Liffey for a fine view of Christ Church.

Make sure you see the gloriously heraldic Choir of St. Patrick's, hung with colorful medieval banners, and find the tomb of the most famous of St. Patrick's many illustrious deans, Jonathan Swift, immortal author of *Gulliver's Travels,* who held office from 1713 to 1745. Swift's tomb is in the south aisle, not far from that of his beloved "Stella," Mrs. Esther Johnson. Swift's epitaph is inscribed over the robing-room door. W. B. Yeats—who translated it thus: "Swift has sailed into his rest; Savage indignation there cannot lacerate his breast"—declared it the greatest epitaph of all time. Other memorials include the 17th-century Boyle Monument, with its numerous painted figures of family members, and the monument to Turlough O'Carolan, the last of the Irish bards and one of the country's finest harp players. "Living Stones" is the cathedral's permanent exhibition celebrating St. Patrick's place in the life of the city. If you're a music lover, you're in for a treat; matins (9:40 am) and evensong (5:45 pm) are still sung on many days. ⊠ *Patrick St., Dublin West, Dublin, Co. Dublin* ☎ *01/453–9472* ⊕ *www.stpatrickscathedral.ie* ▱ *€5.50* ☉ *Mar.–Oct., weekdays 9–5, Sat. 9–5:30, Sun. 9–11, 12:30–3, and 4:30–5:30; Nov.–Feb., weekdays 9–5, Sat. 9–5:30, Sun. 9–11 and 12:30–2:30.*

WORTH NOTING

☺ **Dublinia.** Ever wanted a chance to put your head in the stocks? Dublin's Medieval Trust has set up an entertaining and informative reconstruction of everyday life in medieval Dublin. The main exhibits use high-tech audiovisual and computer displays; you can also see a scale model of what Dublin was like around 1500, a medieval maze, a life-size reconstruction based on the 13th-century dockside at Wood Quay, and a fine view from the tower. Dublinia is in the old Synod Hall (formerly a meeting place for bishops of the Church of Ireland), joined via a covered stonework Victorian bridge to Christ Church Cathedral. An exhibition on "The Viking World" consists of a similar reconstruction of life in even earlier Viking Dublin, including a Viking burial. An exhibition called "Historical Hunters" puts you in the role of archaeologist with interactive digs and a lab to test your newfound knowledge.

Inside gloriously heraldic St. Patrick's Cathedral is the hallowed tomb of Jonathan Swift, author of *Gulliver's Travels* and former cathedral dean.

There's a guided tour at 2:30 pm every day. ⊠ *St. Michael's Hill, Dublin West, Dublin, Co. Dublin* ☎ *01/679–4611* ⊕ *www.dublinia.ie* ⊠ *Exhibit €7.50* ⊗ *June–July, daily 9:30–5; Mar.–May and Aug.–Sept., daily 10–5; Oct.–Feb., daily 10–4:30.*

Marsh's Library. When Ireland's first public library was founded and endowed in 1701 by Narcissus Marsh, the Archbishop of Dublin, it was made open to "All Graduates and Gentlemen." The two-story brick Georgian building has remained virtually the same since then. It houses a priceless collection of 250 manuscripts and 25,000 15th- to 18th-century books. Many of these rare volumes were locked inside cages, as were the readers who wished to peruse them. The cages were to discourage the often-impecunious students, who may have been tempted to make the books their own. The library has been restored with great attention to its original architectural details, especially in the book stacks. It's a short walk west from St. Stephen's Green and is accessed through a charming little cottage garden. ⊠ *St. Patrick's Close off Patrick St., Dublin West, Dublin, Co. Dublin* ☎ *01/454–3511* ⊕ *www.marshlibrary. ie* ⊠ *€2.50* ⊗ *Mon. and Wed.–Fri. 9:30–1 and 2–5, Sat. 10–1.*

The National College of Art & Design. The delicate welding of glass and iron onto the redbrick Victorian facade of this onetime factory makes this school worth a visit. A walk around the cobblestone central courtyard often gives the added bonus of viewing students working away in glass, clay, metal, and stone. The glass-fronted new gallery combines work by local, national, and international avant-garde artists. ⊠ *100 Thomas St., Dublin West, Dublin, Co. Dublin* ☎ *53/1636–4200* ⊕ *www.ncad. ie* ⊠ *Free* ⊗ *Weekdays 9–7.*

Old Jameson Distillery. Founded in 1791, this distillery produced one of Ireland's most famous whiskeys for nearly 200 years, until 1966, when local distilleries merged to form Irish Distillers and moved to a purpose-built, ultramodern distillery in Middleton, County Cork. Part of the complex was converted into the group's head office, and the distillery itself became a museum. There's a short audiovisual history of the industry, which had its origins 1,500 years ago in Middle Eastern perfume making. You can also tour the old distillery, and learn about the distilling of whiskey from grain to bottle, or view a reconstruction of a former warehouse, where the colorful nicknames of former barrel makers are recorded. The 40-minute tour includes a complimentary tasting; four attendees are invited to taste different brands of Irish whiskey and compare them against bourbon and Scotch. If you have a large group and everyone wants to do this, phone in advance to arrange it. You can also get tutored—complete with certification—in whiskey tasting. ⊠ *Bow St., Dublin West, Dublin, Co. Dublin* 🕾 *01/807–2348* ⊕ *www.tours.jamesonwhiskey.com* 🎟 *€13* 🕙 *Mon.–Sat. 9–6, Sun. 10–6; tours every ½ hr up to 5:30.*

St. Michan's Church. However macabre, St. Michan's main claim to fame is down in the vaults, where the totally dry atmosphere has preserved several corpses in a remarkable state of mummification. They lie in open caskets. Most of the resident deceased are thought to have been Dublin tradespeople (one was, they say, a religious crusader). Except for its 120-foot-high bell tower, this Anglican church is architecturally undistinguished. The church was built in 1685 on the site of an 11th-century Danish church (Michan was a Danish saint). If preserved corpses are not enough of a draw, you can also find an 18th-century organ, which Handel supposedly played for the first performance of *Messiah*. Don't forget to check out the Stool of Repentance—the only one still in existence in the city. Parishioners judged to be "open and notoriously naughty livers" used it to do public penance. ⊠ *Lower Church St., Dublin West, Dublin, Co. Dublin* 🕾 *01/872–4154* ⊕ *www.visitdublin.com* 🎟 *€4* 🕙 *Mid-Mar.–Oct., weekdays 10–12:45 and 2–4:45, Sat. 10–12:45, Sun. service at 10 am; Nov.–mid-Mar., weekdays 12:30–3:30, Sat. 10–12:45, Sun. service at 10 am.*

St. Nicholas of Myra's Church. A grand neoclassical style characterizes this church, completed in 1834. The highly ornate chapel inside includes ceiling panels of the 12 apostles, and a pietà raised 20 feet above the marble altar, guarded on each side by angels sculpted by John Hogan while he was in Florence. The tiny nuptial chapel to the right has a small Harry Clarke stained-glass window. ⊠ *St. Nicholas St., Dublin West, Dublin, Co. Dublin* 🕾 *01/454–2172* 🎟 *Free* 🕙 *Hrs vary.*

PHOENIX PARK AND ENVIRONS

Far and away Dublin's largest park, Phoenix Park (the name is an anglicization of the Irish *Fionn Uisce,* meaning "clear water") is a vast, green, arrowhead-shaped oasis north of the Liffey, about a 20-minute walk from the city center. It's the city's main escape valve and sports center (cricket, soccer, Gaelic games, and polo), and the home of the noble creatures of the Dublin Zoo. A handful of other cultural sights near the park also merit a visit.

2

TOP ATTRACTIONS

Fodor's Choice ★ **National Museum of Decorative Arts and History.** Here, in one gigantic treasure chest, is the full panoply of the National Museum's collection of glass, silver, furniture, and other decorative arts. The setting is spectacular: the huge Collins Barracks, named for the assassinated Irish Republican leader Michael Collins (1890–1922). Built in the early 18th century, and designed by Captain Thomas Burgh, these erstwhile "Royal Barracks" were stylishly renovated to become a showcase for the museum, which opened in September 1997. The displays are far ranging, covering everything from one of the greatest collections of Irish silver in the world to Irish period furniture—you'll see that the country's take on Chippendale was far earthier than the English mode. "The Way We Wore: 250 Years of Irish Clothing and Jewelry" and a thousand years of Irish coins are other highlights. Headlining the collections are some extraordinary objects, including the Fonthill Vase, the William Smith O'Brien Gold Cup, and the Lord Chancellor's Mace. ⊠ *Benburb St., Dublin West, Dublin, Co. Dublin* ☎ *01/677–7444* ⊕ *www.museum. ie* 🎫 *Free* ⊗ *Tues.–Sat. 10–5, Sun. 2–5.*

☺ **Phoenix Park.** Europe's largest public park, which extends about 5 km (3 miles) along the Liffey's north bank, encompasses 1,752 acres holds a lot of verdant green lawns, woods, lakes, and playing fields. Sunday is the best time to visit: games of cricket, football (soccer), polo, baseball, hurling (a traditional Irish sport that resembles a combination of lacrosse, baseball, and field hockey), and Irish football are likely to be in progress. Old-fashioned gas lamps line both sides of Chesterfield Avenue, the main road that bisects the park for 4 km (2½ miles), which was named for Lord Chesterfield, a lord lieutenant of Ireland, who laid out the road in the 1740s. To the right as you enter the park is the People's Garden, a colorful flower garden designed in 1864. Rent bikes (including tandems) at the main gate to get the most from the park's hidden corners. ⊕ *www.phoenixpark.ie.*

Ashtown Castle. Also within Phoenix Park is a visitor center, in the 17th-century fortified Ashtown Castle; it has information about the park's history, flora, and fauna. Admission to the center is free and they run guided tours of the park throughout the year. Hours are April to December, daily 9:30–4:30; November to February, Wednesday–Sunday 9:30–4:30. ⊠ *Dublin West, Dublin, Co. Dublin* ☎ *01/677–0095* ⊕ *www.phoenixpark.ie.* 🎫 *Free.*

Dublin Zoo. Founded in 1830, Dublin Zoo may be the third-oldest public zoo in the world but a major renovation completed in 2007 gave new life and luster to the old place. Animals from tropical climes are kept in unbarred enclosures, and Arctic species swim in the lakes close to the reptile house. Some 700 lions have been bred here since the 1850s, one of whom became familiar to movie fans the world over when MGM used him for its trademark. (As they will tell you at the zoo, he is in fact yawning in that familiar shot: an American lion had to be hired to roar and the "voice" was dubbed.) The African Plains section houses the zoo's larger species; the Nakuru Safari is a 25-minute tour of this area. World of Primates is a gathering of the usual suspects from tiny colobus monkeys to big gorillas. In summer the Lakeside Café serves

Home to the city zoo and plenty of cricket fields, Phoenix Park—the largest urban park in Europe—is a favorite escape for stressed-out Dubliners.

ice cream and drinks. ⊠ *Dublin West, Dublin, Co. Dublin* ☎ 47/48900 ⊕ *www.dublinzoo.ie* 🖃 *€15.50* ⊙ *Mar.–Sept. 9:30–5, Jan. 9:30–3:30, Feb 9:30–4, Oct. 9:30–4:30, Nov.–Dec. 9:30–3:00.*

Farmleigh House. This 78-acre Edwardian estate, situated to the northwest of the park, includes a working farm, walled and sunken gardens, wonderful picnic-friendly grounds, a regular organic food market, and a house full of antique furnishings and historic art. Admission is free. ⊠ *Phoenix Park, Dublin West, Dublin, Co. Dublin* ☎ *01/677–1425* ⊕ *www.farmleigh.ie* ⊙ *Daily 10–4:30.*

NEED A BREAK?

Ryan's Pub. One of Dublin's last remaining genuine late-Victorian-era pubs, Ryan's has changed little since its last remodeling—in 1896. It's right near the entrance to Phoenix Park. The small restaurant upstairs does a mean steak. ⊠ *28 Parkgate St., Dublin West, Dublin, Co. Dublin* ☎ *01/677–6097.*

WORTH NOTING

Heritage Ireland. All 14 Irishmen executed by the British following the 1916 Easter Uprising are buried here, including Pádraig Pearse, who led the rebellion; his younger brother Willie, who played a minor role in the uprising; and James Connolly, a socialist and labor leader wounded in the battle. Too weak from his wounds to stand, Connolly was tied to a chair and then shot. The burial ground is a simple but formal area, with the names of the dead leaders carved in stone beside an inscription of the proclamation they issued during the uprising. ⊠ *Arbour Hill, Dublin West, Dublin, Co. Dublin* ☎ *01/821–3021* ⊕ *www.heritageireland.ie/en/Dublin/ArbourHillCemetary* 🖃 *Free* ⊙ *Weekdays 8–4, Sat. 11–4, Sun. 9:30–4.*

WHERE TO EAT

If you arrive thinking you're going to eat potatoes, potatoes, and more potatoes, be prepared to have your preconceptions overturned, and to be enthralled and very happily sated in the process. Ireland has undergone a food revolution, and some of Dublin's chefs are leading the charge—taking advantage of the fact that Ireland has some of the best "raw materials" in the world.

Given that it is a small island on which one is never farther than an hour-and-a-half drive from the coast, it is not only its seaside restaurants that can claim to serve fish on the same day it's caught. In addition, the freshest Limerick hams, tastiest Cork *crubins* (pigs' trotters), and most succulent Galway Bay oysters arrive in the city every day.

Ethnic restaurants now have a firm foothold in the city's foodie culture—thanks to the influx of immigrants during the Celtic Tiger prosperity—so you can indulge your passion for superb French or Italian food one day, then enjoy Korean barbecue the next. This interest in far-flung food has heralded a new wave of internationally trained professionals who have stamped their own *blás* (Irish for "gloss") on traditional ingredients. *Prices in the reviews are the average cost of a main course at dinner or, if dinner is not served, at lunch. Use the coordinate (✢ 1:B2) at the end of each listing to locate a site on the corresponding Where to Eat in Dublin map.*

SOUTHSIDE

$ ✕ **Busyfeet & Coco Café.** This bustling, quirky bohemian café emphasizes
CAFÉ good, wholesome food. Organic ingredients play a prominent role on a menu that's laden with delicious salads and sandwiches. Try the grilled goat-cheese salad served with walnut-and-raisin toast and sun-dried-tomato tapenade on a bed of arugula. The delicious Mediterranean quesadilla wrap—with roasted vegetables, napolitana sauce, and mature cheddar—is a must. It's also one of the city center's best-situated spots for a bit of people-watching, as Dublin's young and hip stroll by all day long. Live music every Saturday night. ⑤ *Average main: €8* ⊠ *41–42 S. William St., Southside, Dublin, Co. Dublin* ☎ *01/671–9514* ⬧ *Reservations not accepted* ✢ *1:C4.*

$ ✕ **Cake Café.** When the head of the Slow Food Dublin movement opens a
CAFÉ café, expectations are going to be high. Michelle Darmody's dreamy little
Fodor'sChoice Cake Café fulfills every one of them. As it is in a plant-filled courtyard at
★ the back of the restored Daintree building, try to snag an outside table if the weather is decent. Then chill out and chow down on simple savory and sweet delights, all made with a loving, homey touch. Local, organic, and seasonal are the words to live by here and the terrine of Cashel Blue cheese with hazelnut is a typically delicious lunch dish. Save room for the delicate tarts and moist chocolate-chocolate brownie. This is also the perfect summer spot for a cheeky daytime glass of prosecco with a few nibbles in the courtyard. And don't forget their fun cookery classes: they are the talk of the town. ⑤ *Average main: €11* ⊠ *The Daintree Building, Pleasants Pl., Southside, Dublin, Co. Dublin* ☎ *01/478–9394* ⊕ *www.thecakecafe.ie* ☽ *Closed Sun. No dinner Mon. and Sat.* ✢ *1:B5.*

BEST BETS FOR DUBLIN DINING

With hundreds of restaurants to choose from, how will you decide where to eat? Fodor's writers and editors have selected their favorite restaurants by price, cuisine, and experience in the lists here. You can also search by neighborhood for excellent eating experiences—just peruse the following pages. Or find specific details about a restaurant in the full reviews, which are listed alphabetically.

Fodor's Choice ★

Cake Café, $, p. 101
Chapter One, $$$$, p. 116
Dunne and Crescenzi, $, p. 103
Enoteca delle Langhe, $, p. 117
Fallon & Byrne, $$, p. 104
L'Gueuleton, $$, p. 105
Musashi Noodles and Sushi Bar, $, p. 118
One Pico, $$$, p. 108
Patrick Guilbaud, $$$$, p. 108
The Winding Stair, $$, p. 118

By Price

$

Cake Café, p. 101
Dunne and Crescenzi, p. 103
Enoteca delle Langhe, p. 117
French Paradox, p. 119

The Good World, p. 104
Kingfisher, p. 117
Musashi Noodles and Sushi Bar, p. 118
The Pepper Pot, p. 108
Soup Dragon, p. 118

$$

Eden, p. 113
L'Gueuleton, p. 105
The Green Hen, p. 104
The Winding Stair, p. 118

$$$

Dax, p. 103
One Pico, p. 108
Unicorn, p. 112

$$$$

Chapter One, p. 116
Les Frères Jacques, p. 114
Patrick Guilbaud, p. 108
Thornton's, p. 109

By Type

CHILD-FRIENDLY

Cake Café, $, p. 101
Dunne and Crescenzi, $, p. 103
Enoteca delle Langhe, $, p. 117
The Good World, $, p. 104
The Steps of Rome, $, p. 109

EXPENSE ACCOUNT

Chapter One, $$$$, p. 116
Patrick Guilbaud, $$$$, p. 108
Shanahan's on the Green, $$$$, p. 109
Town Bar and Grill, $$$, p. 109

GREAT VIEWS

Cake Café, $, p. 101
Eden, $$, p. 113
The Winding Stair, $$, p. 118

HOT SPOT

Cake Café, $, p. 101
Crackbird, $, p. 113
The Green Hen, $$, p. 104
Hop House, $, p. 117
Musashi Noodles and Sushi Bar $, p. 118

LOTS OF LOCALS

Busyfeet & Coco Café, $, p. 101
The Good World, $, p. 104
L'Gueuleton, $$, p. 105
L. Mulligan Grocer, $, p. 117
The Pepper Pot, $, p. 108

MOST ROMANTIC

Chapter One, $$$$, p. 116
L'Gueuleton, $$, p. 105
One Pico, $$$, p. 108

DELICIOUS DECOR

Cake Café, $, p. 101
Chapter One, $$$$, p. 116
Patrick Guilbaud, $$$$, p. 108
The Pepper Pot, $, p. 108
The Tea Room, $$, p. 115

$$
ASIAN

✕**Chai-Yo.** Watch and learn . . . and then eat. The Japanese teppanyaki area at this classy Pan Asian restaurant on bustling Baggot Street, where the chef cooks your food right on your tabletop, is a feast for the eye as well as the palate. Choose from a selection of scallops, sea bass, steak, teriyaki chicken, and prawns, and watch as a beautiful grilled dish is whipped up before your eyes. The white walls and dark lacquered furnishings give Chai-Yo a serene ambience, enhanced by the delicate glassware and fine, green-washed-porcelain plates. The menu picks the best from Chinese, Thai, and Japanese dishes, with the Asian tapas a good eat-and-go option. The miso soup with tofu, seaweed, and spring onions is a simple but tasty starter, and the green-shell mussels and pineapple curry is a chef specialty. $ *Average main: €19* ⊠ *100 Lower Baggot St., Southside, Dublin, Co. Dublin* ☎ *01/676–7652* ⊕ *www. chaiyo.ie* ⊘ *No lunch weekends* ✛ *1:E5.*

$$$
FRENCH

✕**Dax.** When is a wine bar not just a wine bar? When it's one of the city's most talked-about restaurants. Opened as a basement wine bar by Olivier Meisonnave, the former sommelier at stellar Thornton's, Dax has quickly become one of the dining spots of choice for Dubliners who care about food. You can choose to drink or dine (tapas-style) at the bar, in the lush armchairs of the open-plan lounge, or in the more formal, restrained-modern dining room. The roast partridge with celeriac mousse, dates, pancetta, hazelnut crunch, and white port and balsamic dressing is an adventurous starter, while the braised veal cheek with linguini, caramelized salsify, pearl onions, and vanilla foam is a standout main course. The cold-meat platter is a finger-lickin' little bar dish. With Olivier in charge, the wine list is the envy of many a more expensive eatery, and with two-dozen wines poured by the glass you can dare to try something really special. $ *Average main: €27* ⊠ *23 Pembroke St., Southside, Dublin, Co. Dublin* ☎ *01/676–1494* ⊕ *www.dax.ie* ☖ *Reservations essential* ⊘ *Closed Sun. and Mon. No lunch Sat.* ✛ *1:D5.*

$$
ECLECTIC

✕**Dillinger's.** Paper napkins, no tablecloths, and a lively buzz emphasize the no-fuss vibe at culinary heavyweights Temple Garner and John Farell's new American eatery in Ranelagh village. The no-fuss vibe extends to the menu, too; the chef is more interested in quality and comfort than originality and complexity. Steak is their standard-bearer, but their mussels in white wine with fries and roast cod fillet with yellow split-pea dal are also favorites. The New England clam chowder with smoked haddock and bacon is a nice twist on a classic. $ *Average main: €20* ⊠ *47 Ranelagh Village, Southside, Dublin, Co. Dublin* ☎ *149/78010* ⊕ *www.dillingers.ie* ☖ *Reservations essential* ⊘ *No lunch Mon.–Thurs.* ✛ *1:C6.*

$
ITALIAN
Fodor'sChoice
★

✕**Dunne and Crescenzi.** Nothing succeeds like success. So popular is this classy little Italian joint just off Nassau Street that they've expanded into the premises two doors down. Pity the poor little coffee shop in between trying to compete with the unpretentious brilliance of this brother-and-sister restaurant and deli. The menu is extensive but simple: panini (sandwiches), a horde of antipasti choices, a few choice pasta specials, and some evening meat dishes and desserts. The all-Italian kitchen staff work wonders with high-quality imported ingredients. The *tagliere della casa*—a selection of typical Italian salumi and farmhouse cheeses garnished with preserves and served on warm bread—makes a great light lunch. A couple of long tables make it perfect for a group, and the hundreds of bottles of wine on shelves cover every inch of the walls. They have opened a second café in nearby Sandymount. $ *Average main: €14* ⊠ *14 S. Fredrick St., Southside, Dublin, Co. Dublin* ☎ *01/677–3815* ⊕ *www.dunneandcrescenzi.com* ✦ *1:D4.*

$$ ╳ **Ely Winebar.** Almost equidistant from the twin dames of Dublin hotel
IRISH elegance, the Shelbourne and the Merrion, Ely started out as a mere wine bar—and oh, what a selection of wines they have—but it has quickly grown into a wonderful little eatery with organic meat and vegetables from the owner's family farm in County Clare. Dishes tend to be simple—for example, their pea, organic ham, and crab risotto—but incredibly fresh and succulent. The plate of mature Irish and Continental cheeses is the perfect finish—with a glass of wine, of course. $ *Average main: €22* ⊠ *22 Ely Pl., Southside, Dublin, Co. Dublin* ☎ *01/676–8986* ⊕ *www.elywinebar.ie* ⊘ *Closed Sun. No lunch Sat.* ✦ *1:D5.*

$$ ╳ **Fallon & Byrne.** A fresh, one-stop-shop for everything organic and
FRENCH delicious in Dublin, Fallon & Byrne combines a huge deli with a cozy
Fodor's Choice cellar wine bar and expansive second-floor French brasserie. Located on
★ the top floor of a beautiful old telephone exchange building, the high-ceiling, light-filled dining room has a bustling, city-center atmosphere. The menu covers everything from burgers to loin of rabbit, but the pan-fried silver bream with sweet potato, cauliflower purée, pink grapefruit, and beurre blanc and the goat cheese ravioli with sautéed red chard and tomberries, candied beetroot, and tomato broth are typical. Leave room for the lemon-ricotta cheesecake with ginger ice cream. You can pick up a bottle of wine in the wine cellar and enjoy it for a small corkage fee. $ *Average main: €23* ⊠ *11–17 Exchequer St., Southside, Dublin, Co. Dublin* ☎ *01/472–1010* ⊕ *www.fallonandbyrne.com* ⌫ *Reservations essential* ✦ *1:C3.*

$ ╳ **The Good World.** When Dublin's growing Chinese population wants
CHINESE a big, uptown night out they come here. The surroundings are modest,
★ with large round tables—ideal for groups—in a somewhat dark but comfortable room. But the food is authentic and inspired—ask for the black-cover Chinese menu, not the standard, dumbed-down one. The dim sum selection is nonpareil in Ireland, with the scallop dumplings a standout, and the chili-salt squid melts in the mouth. It's the perfect spot to order a load of dishes to be shared by an adventurous group. As is often the case with Chinese restaurants in Ireland, the desserts are not really worth trying. $ *Average main: €14* ⊠ *18 S. Great George's St., Southside, Dublin, Co. Dublin* ☎ *01/677–5373* ✦ *1:C3.*

$$ ╳ **The Green Hen.** It can be hard to re-create that classic bistro feel outside
FRENCH of France, but this intimate spot at the heart of busy Dublin has managed to get the mix of bustle and tranquility just right. A mix of warm brick walls dotted with black-and-white snaps of French film stars from the 1950s and wood paneling with tongue-in-cheek French movie posters keeps the vibe informal. A quick glance at the gilt-framed mirrored menu reveals that this kitchen is all about rich, evocative French fare—two winners are the tian of crab with beetroot remoulade and salmon caviar and the roast rump of lamb with boudin noir and rösti potato

spinach. The rhubarb crème brûlée is a clever Irish take on the Gallic standard. Lunch is a great value, and keep an eye out for adventurous *plat du jours* and lively wine list. ⑤ *Average main: €20* ⊠ *33 Exchequer St., Southside, Dublin, Co. Dublin* ☎ *01/670–7238* ⊕ *www.thegreenhen. com* ☉ *No lunch weekends. No dinner Mon.* ✛ *1:C3.*

$$ ⤬ **Il Primo.** Owners John Farrell and Anita Thoma like to run this little
ITALIAN two-story Italian restaurant like an intimate dinner party. A little quote board outside offers a daily pearl of wisdom, and old wooden tables and chairs give the two small dining rooms a casual feel. The friendly, if cramped, surroundings attract a devoted clientele and John's collection of contemporary art adds a dash of flair to the walls. The slow-cooked beef cheek with duck-fat-roasted potatoes and root vegetables is a standout evening dish. Risotto is a house specialty and the version with pancetta, leeks, and taleggio is a must. The wine list—heavy with Italian influences—is, to quote a local phrase, as long as your arm. ⑤ *Average main: €20* ⊠ *16 Montague St., off Harcourt St., Southside, Dublin, Co. Dublin* ☎ *01/478–3373* ⊕ *www.ilprimo.ie* ☉ *No dinner Sun.* ✛ *1:C4.*

$ ⤬ **Jaipur.** Call to mind all the stereotypes of bad, production-line Indian
INDIAN restaurants. Then consign them to the flames, for Jaipur is something different altogether. A spacious room with a sweeping staircase and contemporary furnishings reflects Jaipur's modern, cutting-edge approach to Indian cuisine. Mixed with traditional dishes, such as chicken tikka masala, are more unusual preparations, such as *pork vindaloo* (tandoor-cooked pork chop with home-ground red chilis, Goan spiced paste, a hint of coconut vinegar and palm sugar). The delightful *karwari* is a sweet-and-sour butterfish in a tamarind-flavor broth redolent of coastal-south-Indian spices. Try the Jaipur Jugalbandi, a selection of five appetizers. Dishes can be toned down or spiced up to suit your palate, and service is courteous and prompt. Another plus: the wine list is well thought out. They also have locations in the suburbs of Dalkey and Malahide. ⑤ *Average main: €15* ⊠ *41 S. Great George's St., Southside, Dublin, Co. Dublin* ☎ *01/677–0999* ⊕ *www.jaipur.ie* ⚑ *Reservations essential* ✛ *1:B4.*

$$ ⤬ **L'Gueuleton.** Dubliners don't do waiting, but you'll see hungry crowds
FRENCH doing just that outside this no-reservations-accepted, exceptional eat-
Fodor's Choice ery just off George's Street. L'Gueuleton's lost a little of its intimacy
★ when it expanded, but the crowds still come for authentic French food at a fair price. Start with the duck egg mayonnaise with celery salt and watercress. For a main course, the slow-roasted pork belly with choucroute and Lyonnaise potatoes somehow manages to be hearty and adventurous at the same time. Desserts have a devilishly childish touch to them—passion-fruit cake with white chocolate sauce is a typical example. Although you can't phone in a reservation, you can go there early in the evening and put your name and phone number down for a table, and then pop next door to Hogan's bar while you're waiting. ⑤ *Average main: €21* ⊠ *1 Fade St., Southside, Dublin, Co. Dublin* ☎ *01/675–3708* ⊕ *www.lgueuleton.com* ✛ *1:B4.*

$$ ⤬ **La Maison Restaurant.** Closing one of the city's favorite little bakery/
FRENCH cafés would have been a crime if it hadn't been replaced by such an intimate, classy little eatery. La Maison des Gourmets became simply

DUBLIN'S SEAFOOD BOUNTY

Clarenbridge oysters, Carlingford Lough mussels, Ballina wild smoked salmon, Donegal crab—the menus of the top restaurants in Dublin are now full of some of the most flavorsome seafood on the planet. Surprisingly, Ireland has only recently fallen in love with its own array of briny treasures, and thereby hangs a fish tale.

(above) The Irish treasure of the deep—smoked salmon; (right, top) When it comes to fish and chips, some say the greasier the better; (right, bottom) Seaweed is a chic new condiment.

A somewhat apocryphal story about Ireland joining the EEC (European Economic Community) in 1973 has the government given a stark choice: you can farm or you can fish, but you can't do both. They chose to protect farming, and the result was the massive overfishing by giant Spanish factory ships off Irish waters. This fact may, in part, explain why Ireland—a relative pollution-free, sea-surrounded nation—is not one of the first places gourmands think of for great seafood. Historically, there was also a certain snobbery about eating fish, as it was seen as peasant food only suitable for fasting Fridays. Well, things have certainly changed in the last two decades as a new breed of homegrown chefs has pushed the importance of locally sourced seafood on their menus.

TOP FISHY JOINTS

Some standout joints in Dublin go that extra mile. The oyster stall at the Temple Bar Farmer's Market every Saturday is something of a Dublin institution, where affordable Atlantic oysters and white wine are downed alfresco. Les Fréres Jacques delivers true Gallic panache to its lobsters. The no-frills Kingfisher is noted for its whole rainbow trout.

2

SMOKED SALMON

From all corners of Ireland small producers are now making some of Europe's finest smoked salmon. Obviously, and perhaps unfortunately, the wild Atlantic salmon still has a richer, more piquant taste than its farmed cousin. The word "wild" in the description will tell you the fish isn't farmed. The traditional smoking method uses only Irish oak, which gives it a very distinctive, subtle flavor, and deep orange color. The best way to enjoy smoked salmon is over some toasted Dublin brown bread with a simple squeeze of lemon and some coarse black pepper to add that little extra tang.

IRISH CHOWDER

It's the pint of heavy cream and density of mussels tossed into the mix that makes Irish seafood chowder such a great snack on the run. It's also a dish that even the most humble of eateries doesn't usually mess up, although the general rule still applies: the nearer to the coast the eatery is located, the better its chowder. Regular fish stock is often used but clam juice—an Irish specialty—also adds to the unique flavor.

FISH-AND-CHIPS

Every Dubliner will argue about the best place to get their favorite fast-food dish of fish-and-chips, but few will quarrel with the fact that cod, ray, and haddock are the top three battered delights to go

for. Interestingly, the descendants of 1950s Italian immigrants—with names like Macari and Borza—are the recognized masters of the battering art, and you'll find one of their eponymously named shops in almost every neighborhood. Tip: a single portion is usually enough to feed two!

SEAWEED

Yes, the Irish are slowly discovering the delights of farming native seaweed for use in the kitchen and elsewhere. Irish seaweed is usually gathered along the western seaboard, dried, and then sold in small packets, a bit like herbs. Look closely at restaurant menus and you'll find dulse, carrageen moss, and various kelps and wracks all turning up to add spice to risottos, salads, soups, breads, and even ice cream. The local spa industry has cottoned on, developing "algotherapies," including wraps, aging creams, and even full-on seaweed baths. Enjoy chowders at Ireland's great seafood festivals: the Galway Oyster Festival, the event in Baltimore in West Cork, and the Killybegs festival.

La Maison and, although the delicious pastries were lost forever, this bustling, unpretentious bistro now boasts one of the most inviting and good-value menus in the city. The look is very much casual bistro, a satisfying backdrop for starters like the hot smoked salmon rillette with dill crème fraîche and sourdough toasts and such mouthwatering mains as the roast cod with artichoke barigoule, girolle mushrooms, and green asparagus. The chocolate fondant is a dessert to die for. $ *Average main: €20* ⊠ *15 Castle Market, Southside, Dublin, Co. Dublin* ☎ *01/672–7258* ⊕ *www.lamaisonrestaurant.ie* ✛ *1:C4.*

$ × **Mao.** Everything is Asian fusion at this bustling café—which has
ASIAN quickly blossomed into a mini-franchise across the city—from the little Andy Warhol pastiche of Chairman Mao on the washroom door to the eclectic mix of dishes on the menu, which combine Thai, Vietnamese, and other Southeast Asian elements. Top choices include the chicken lemongrass salad, chili squid, crispy whole sea bass with scallops, and the *nasi goreng* (Indonesian fried rice with chicken and shrimp). $ *Average main: €10* ⊠ *2 Chatham Row, Southside, Dublin, Co. Dublin* ☎ *01/670–4899* ⊕ *www.cafemao.com* ✍ *Reservations not accepted* ✛ *1:B5.*

$$$ × **One Pico.** Chef-owner Eamonn O'Reilly cuts quite a dash, but it's his
MODERN IRISH sophisticated, daring, contemporary cuisine that tends to seduce visitors
Fodor's Choice to his little restaurant tucked away in a quiet lane only a few minutes from
★ Stephen's Green. Try the incredible organic golden beetroot with Ryefield goat cheese to start. Dishes such as roast rump of veal with fricassee of girolles, pearl onion, and truffle, and *pomme sarladaise* (a southern France version of mashed potatoes) demonstrate a savvy use of native ingredients. Follow this with the mango cheesecake with mango and lime foam. As is usual with Dublin's luxe eateries, the fixed-price lunch and preheater menus offer great value. $ *Average main: €29* ⊠ *5–6 Molesworth Pl., off Schoolhouse La., Southside, Dublin, Co. Dublin* ☎ *01/676–0300* ⊕ *www.onepico.com* ✍ *Reservations essential* ✛ *1:D4.*

$ × **The Pepper Pot.** The hodgepodge collection of old tablecloths, cutlery,
CAFÉ and cups creates a warm, family atmosphere in this sweet little café on the balcony level of the Powerscourt Town House Centre. Weary shoppers resuscitate with the simple menu, fresh-baked goods, TLC, and people-watching. The soups and sandwiches are top-notch but the salads have a cult following, with the panfried goat cheese with Gubeen chorizo and vine tomatoes enough to serve as a filling main. Tarts are seasonal and cakes are old school; the Victoria sponge and lemon and poppy seed are two standouts. $ *Average main: €7* ⊠ *Powerscourt Town Centre, First Floor Balcony, S. William St., Southside, Dublin, Co. Dublin* ☎ *01/707–1610* ⊕ *www.thepepperpot.ie* ✍ *Reservations not accepted* ⊘ *No dinner. Closed Sun.* ✛ *1:C4.*

$$$$ × **Restaurant Patrick Guilbaud.** Also known as "Dublin's finest restau-
FRENCH rant," this do-be-impressed place on the ground floor of the Merrion
Fodor's Choice Hotel boasts a menu described as French, but chef Guillaume Lebrun's
★ genius lies in his occasional daring use of traditional Irish ingredients— so often taken for granted—to create the unexpected. The best dishes are flawless: Clogher Head lobster ravioli, veal sweetbreads and licorice, or the slow-cooked pork with pomme purée, lemon star anise, and licorice. Follow that, if you can, with the *assiette au chocolat* (a tray of five

hot and cold chocolate desserts). The ambience is just as delicious—if you're into lofty, minimalist dining rooms and Irish modern art (the Roderick O'Connors and Louis LeBrocquys are all from the owner's private collection). Nearly as impressive is the 70-page wine list, the view of the Merrion's manicured gardens, and the two-course lunch special for €38. Soaring white vaults and white walls won't make you feel warm and cozy, but you can always go somewhere else for that. ⑤ *Average main: €55* ⊠ *21 Upper Merrion St., Southside, Dublin, Co. Dublin* ☎ *01/676–4192* ⊕ *www.restaurantpatrickguilbaud.ie* ⌂ *Reservations essential* ☉ *Closed Sun. and Mon.* ✢ *1:D5.*

\$\$\$\$
AMERICAN ✕**Shanahan's on the Green.** Glowing with gilded chandeliers and graced with a few marble fireplaces, this American-style steak house in a restored Georgian town house offers a sleekly elegant setting in which to chow down on some of the tenderest Irish Angus beef this side of the Atlantic (they cook it in a special high-temperature oven, searing the outside to keep the inside good and juicy). If steak doesn't float your boat, they also do a mean panfried wild sea bass with wild garlic, Morteau sausage, and morel mushrooms. Oreo-cookie-crust cheesecake is the perfect way to finish off the feast, but many will consider the decor—think sash windows, gilt mirrors, and plush carpets—rich enough. ⑤ *Average main: €42* ⊠ *119 St. Stephen's Green, Southside, Dublin, Co. Dublin* ☎ *01/407–0939* ⊕ *www.shanahans.ie* ⌂ *Reservations essential* ☉ *No lunch Sat.–Thurs.* ✢ *1:C4.*

\$
ITALIAN ✕**The Steps of Rome.** Discerning natives flock to this place for a cheap lunch, or a good takeout. Just a few steps from Grafton Street, this Italian eatery is also popular for a late-night bite. Slices of delicious, thin-crust pizza, with all the traditional toppings, are the main attraction. The *funghi* (mushroom) pizza is particularly good. The few tables are usually full, but it's worth waiting around for the classic Italian pasta dishes like the cannelloni. Some diners just opt for the fresh salads with focaccia. Follow it all with cheesecake or tiramisu, and good strong espresso. ⑤ *Average main: €12* ⊠ *1 Chatham Ct., Southside, Dublin, Co. Dublin* ☎ *01/670–5630.*

\$\$\$\$
FRENCH
★ ✕**Thornton's Restaurant.** Forget the stretched metaphors: if you're passionate about food, this place is a must. Kevin Thornton's cooking style is light, and his dishes are small masterpieces of structural engineering, piled almost dangerously high in towers of food. Dinner is a set, three-course menu and a highlight is the magret of duck with chestnut purée, braised red cabbage, potato soufflé, and morel sauce. Desserts range from apple tarte tatin to prune and Armagnac soufflé, and the cheese course is supplied by famed Sheridans of Dublin. The dining room is simple and elegant—there's little to distract you from the exquisite food. ■ TIP➔ **The Canapé Bar is the perfect spot for a pre- or post-theater snack with a glass of champagne.** ⑤ *Average main: €40* ⊠ *Fitzwilliam Hotel, 128 St. Stephen's Green, Southside, Dublin, Co. Dublin* ☎ *01/478–7008* ⊕ *www.thorntonsrestaurant.com* ⌂ *Reservations essential* ☉ *Closed Sun. and Mon. No lunch Tues. and Wed.* ✢ *1:C4.*

\$\$\$
ITALIAN ✕**Town Bar and Grill.** Once an old wine merchant's cellar, this Kildare Street spot is now a modern-Italian trattoria with an elegant, New York–vibe dining room, a definite buzz, live music some nights, and

Map 1: Where to Eat in Dublin

A **B** **C** **D**

1

Chapter One

Parnell Square

Hop House

N. Great George's St.

Hill St.

Summerhill

Sean McDermott St.

Railway St.

Lower Domnick St.

Bolton St.

Green St.

Parnell St.

Lower O'Connell St.

Parnell St.

Marlborough St.

Gardiner St.

Foley St.

Kingfisher

2

Beresford St.

Bow St.

Church St.

Mary's La.

Parnell St.

Capel St.

Jervis St.

Mary St.

Henry St.

Prince's St. N.

Earl St. N.

Talbot St.

101 Talbot

CUSTOM HOUSE

Juno
L. Mulligan Grocer
Nancy Hands

Musashi Noodles and Sushi Bar

Enoteca Delle Langhe

Upper Abbey St.

Middle Abbey St.

Lower Abbey St.

Sackville Pl.

Custom House Quay

Custom Br.

Butt Br.

Talbot Br.

Arran St. E.

Mary's Abbey

Liffey St.

Lotts

Bachelor's Walk

River Liffey

Eden Quay

George's Quay

TARA ST. STATION

Soup Dragon

Strand St. Great

Aston Quay

Burgh Quay

Poolbeg St.

3

Whitworth Br.

The Winding Stair

Inns Quay

Merchant's Quay

Ormond Quay

Grattan Br.

Wellington Quay

Temple Bar

Cope St.

See "Where to Eat in Temple Bar" map

Wood Quay

Essex Quay

Fownes St.

Anglesea St.

Fleet St.

Westmoreland St.

College St.

Pearse St.

Townsend St.

Cook St.

Winetavern St.

Fishamble St.

Crackbird

Lord Edward St.

Dame St.

College Green

College St.

Suffolk St.

TRINITY COLLEGE

High St.

Back Ln.

Thomas Davis St.

Burdock's

Castle St.

The Good World

Stag's Head

The Green Hen

Nassau St.

Lord Edward

DUBLIN CASTLE

Yamamori

Fallon And Byrne

La Maison

Il Primo

Davy Byrne's

Dunne and Crescenzi

Wicklow St.

Leinster St.

Lincoln Place

Clare St.

Lovin Catering

Francis St.

Ship St. Great

Golden La.

L'Gueuleton

Jaipur

Great George's St.

Drury St.

William St.

One Pico

Duke St.

Anne St.

Dawson St.

Molesworth St.

Frederick La. S.

4

The Coombe

Patrick St.

St. Patrick's Close

St. Patrick's Park

Aungier St.

The Pepper Pot

Busyfeet & Coco Café

The Steps of Rome

Wagamama

Thornton's

St. Stephen's Green N.

Kildare St.

LEINSTER HOUSE

Upper Merrion St.

Merrion Sq. West

Town Bar and Grill

Unicorn

Merrion Row

Patrick Guilbaud

New Row

New Bride St.

Mercer St.

York St.

Shanahan's on the Green

St. Stephen's Green W.

Cliffe St.

St. Stephen's Green

St. Stephen's Green E.

Ely Winebar

5

Blackpitts

Clanbrassil St.

Arnott St.

Heytesbury St.

Camden St.

Lower Kevin St.

Camden Row

Mao

Cake Café

Pleasants St.

Harcourt St.

Iveagh Garden

St. Stephen's Green S.

Earlsfort Ter.

Lower Leeson St.

Pembroke St.

Dax

Upper Fitzwilliam St.

Bibi's Café

Lombard St. W.

Ovoca Rd.

Curzon St.

Grantham St.

Charlotte St.

Upper Hatch St.

Lower Hatch St.

Harrington St.

Harcourt Rd.

Adelaide Rd.

6

Longwood Av.

Bloomfield Av.

Victoria St.

Lennox St.

S. Richmond St.

Charlemont St.

Charlemont Mall

Dillinger's

Charlemont Pl.

Grand Parade

Dartmouth Sq. North

Dartmouth Sq. South

Upper Leeson St.

Sussex St.

Windsor Terrace

Portobello Rd.

Grand Canal

Canal Rd.

A **B** **C** **D**

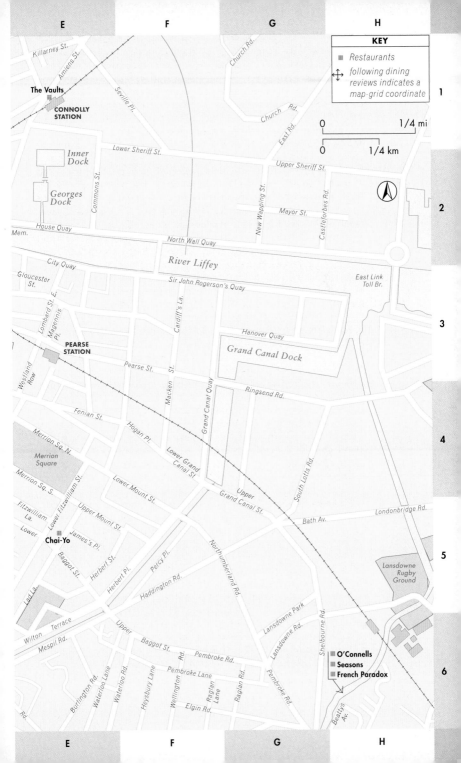

KEY

■ Restaurants
✛ following dining reviews indicates a map-grid coordinate

E   **F**   **G**   **H**

Killarney St.

Amiens St.

The Vaults

CONNOLLY STATION

Seville Pl.

Church Rd.

Church Rd.

East Rd.

0   1/4 mi

0   1/4 km

1

Inner Dock

Lower Sheriff St.

Commons St.

Upper Sheriff St.

New Wapping St.

Mayor St.

Castleforbes Rd.

2

Georges Dock

House Quay

Mem.

North Wall Quay

River Liffey

City Quay

Gloucester St.

Sir John Rogerson's Quay

East Link Toll Br.

3

Lombard St. E.

Magennis Pl.

PEARSE STATION

Cardiff's La.

Hanover Quay

Grand Canal Dock

Westland Row

Pearse St.

Macken St.

Grand Canal Quay

Ringsend Rd.

Fenian St.

Hogan Pl.

Lower Grand Canal St.

Upper Grand Canal St.

South Lotts Rd.

4

Merrion Sq. N.

Merrion Square

Merrion Sq. S.

Lower Fitzwilliam St.

Upper Fitzwilliam St.

Lower Mount St.

Bath Av.

Londonbridge Rd.

Fitzwilliam La.

Lower

James's Pl.

Chai-Yo

Baggot St.

Upper Mount St.

Herbert St.

Herbert Pl.

Percy Pl.

Haddington Rd.

Northumberland Rd.

Lansdowne Park

Lansdowne Rd.

Shelbourne Rd.

Lansdowne Rugby Ground

5

Lad La.

Wilton Terrace

Mespil Rd.

Upper Baggot St.

Burlington Rd.

Waterloo Rd.

Waterloo Lane

Pembroke Rd.

Pembroke Lane

Pembroke Lane

Wellington Rd.

Heytsbury Lane

Raglan Lane

Raglan Rd.

Pembroke Rd.

O'Connells
Seasons
French Paradox

Beatty's Av.

6

Rd.

Elgin Rd.

E   **F**   **G**   **H**

an Irish celebrity clientele. Chef Philip likes to take traditional Italian classics and give them just a little twist. The beef carpaccio with seared foie gras, dressed rocket, horseradish crème fraîche, and pomegranate vinaigrette is one of the most exciting starters. For mains try the char-grilled veal loin with almond potatoes, wilted spinach, and salsa verde. Pecan pie with ginger, cardamom ice cream, and confit orange is a nice guilty way to finish. [$] *Average main: €26* ⊠ *21 Kildare St., Southside, Dublin, Co. Dublin* ☎ *166/24800* ⊕ *www.townbarandgrill. com* ⌂ *Reservations essential* ✛ *1:D4.*

$$$
MEDITERRANEAN
★

✕ **Unicorn.** In the art of finding the perfect place to get slightly sozzled over some quality eats, the Unicorn is a Southside masterwork. Posher locals love to head here when they want to let their hair down in some wine-fuelled, late-evening craic. The atmosphere is loose and relaxed, especially on the little terrace overlooking Merrion Court, and the menu is scrumptious Italian. Hot antipasti include chicken livers Marsala and calamari fritti, and tempting main courses include roast rack of lamb with celeriac, green beans wrapped in parma ham and champ, or the linguini with Dublin Bay prawns, courgettes, garlic, chili, and white wine. To dine here, you must turn your mobile phone to silent—how cool is that? [$] *Average main: €27* ⊠ *12B Merrion Ct., Southside, Dublin, Co. Dublin* ☎ *91/5998–4874* ⊕ *www.unicornrestaurant.com* ⌂ *Reservations essential* ☉ *Closed Sun. No lunch Sat.* ✛ *1:D4.*

$
JAPANESE

✕ **Wagamama.** Modeled on a Japanese canteen, Wagamama, with its long wooden tables and benches and high ceilings with exposed metal piping, ensures a unique communal dining experience. It attracts a young, loud crowd and is constantly busy. Formal courses aren't acknowledged—food is served as soon as it's ready, and appetizers and main courses arrive together. Steamed and salted edamame are a delicious starter, followed with filling bowls of *ginger chicken udon* (teppan-fried udon noodles with chicken, egg, bean sprouts, spring onion, and chili) or chili beef ramen, and washed down with fresh fruit or vegetable juice. There's also a fine selection of beers and sakes for the less abstemious. [$] *Average main: €14* ⊠ *S. King St., Southside, Dublin, Co. Dublin* ☎ *01/478–2152* ⊕ *www.wagamama.ie* ✛ *1:C4.*

$$
JAPANESE

✕ **Yamamori Noodles.** The culinary backlash to years of spuds, spuds, and more spuds hit Dublin a few years ago and Yamamori jumped to the top of the list for noodle addicts. The novelty has worn off slightly but the open plan and family-style tables have kept it popular with the hip crowd. The meals-in-a-bowl are a splendid slurping experience, and although you'll be supplied with a small Chinese-style soupspoon, the best approach is with chopsticks. The *yasai yaki soba,* Chinese-style noodles with Asian vegetables and egg, garnished with *menma* (dried bamboo) and spring onions, is a favorite example. You can also get sushi and sashimi, delicious chicken teriyaki, or house specials like baked lobster. ■ TIP➔ **The bento box combo meal is the best value here.** [$] *Average main: €20* ⊠ *72 S. Great Georges St., Southside, Dublin, Co. Dublin* ☎ *01/475–5001* ⊕ *www.yamamorinoodles.ie* ✛ *1:B3.*

TEMPLE BAR

$
DINER

$\times$ **Crackbird.** Originally a "pop-up" restaurant, this busy fried-chicken joint has quickly become the hot spot for young Dubliners looking for something affordable but different. Always bustling, the place thrives off the energy of its young staff and the over the top decor of the fancy Chinese restaurant that formerly occupied the space. The menu is basically chicken done in a few mouthwatering ways; the buttermilk and soy garlic being two standouts. The real treat is the wonderfully prepared sides like the burnt-lemon-and-feta dip or the best potato salad in town. For lunch try the tortilla with hummus and chicken brochette. It's perfect for groups, with large tables and the option to get a bucket of chicken to share. They're so cool they don't have a phone number, but you can tweet your bookings (@CrackBIRDdublin) . . . that is, if you're cool, too. $ *Average main: €11* ⊠ *60 Dame Street, Temple Bar, Dublin, Co. Dublin* ✛ *1:B3.*

$$
MODERN IRISH

$\times$ **Eden.** A favorite haunt of arty and media types, Eden has an open kitchen, a high wall of glass through which you can observe one of Temple Bar's main squares, and patio-style doors that lead to an outdoor eating area—a major plus in a city with relatively few alfresco dining spots. On weekend nights in summer you can enjoy an outdoor movie in Meeting House Square while you eat. Seasonal menus are in vogue here, but standout dishes include potted mushroom and soft cheese with pickled pearl onions, butternut squash and warm toast, and Castletownebere scallops with crispy potato cake, creamed leeks, and prawn bisque. Desserts include a tempting Belgian hot chocolate pudding. $ *Average main: €20* ⊠ *Meeting House Sq., Temple Bar, Dublin, Co. Dublin* ☎ *01/670–5372* ⊕ *www.edenrestaurant.ie* ✍ *Reservations essential* ✛ *2:B2.*

$
AMERICAN

$\times$ **Elephant & Castle.** The Elephant was long established in Temple Bar before the Tiger (Celtic, that is) came and went and changed the neighborhood forever. Large windows are great for people-watching in the city's trendiest area, but "nothing fancy" would be a good motto for the traditional American food. Charcoal-grilled burgers, salads, omelets, sandwiches, and pasta make up the much-thumbed menu. Sunday brunch is usually busy. The portions are some of the most generous in Dublin. When the service is good, the turnover tends to be quick, although you may be inclined to linger. New Yorkers, take note: yes, this is a cousin of the restaurant of the same name in Greenwich Village. $ *Average main: €17* ⊠ *18 Temple Bar, Temple Bar, Dublin,*

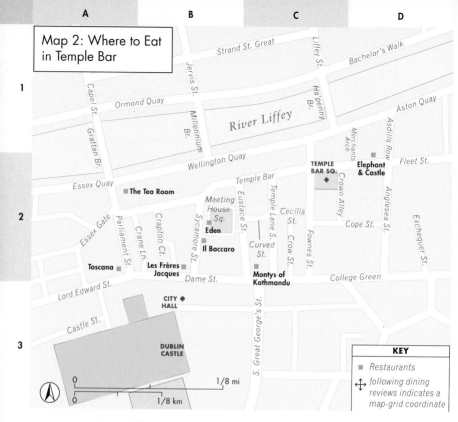

Map 2: Where to Eat in Temple Bar

A   B   C   D

Strand St. Great

Capel St.

Jervis St.

Liffey St.

Bachelor's Walk

Ormond Quay

Grattan Br.

Millennium Br.

River Liffey

Ha'penny Br.

Aston Quay

Wellington Quay

Essex Quay

The Tea Room

Temple Bar

Meeting House Sq.

Eden

Il Baccaro

Eustace St.

Temple Lane S.

Merchants Arch

TEMPLE BAR SQ.

Elephant & Castle

Asdill's Row

Fleet St.

Crown Alley

Cecilia St.

Cope St.

Anglesea St.

Exchequer St.

Essex Gate

Parliament St.

Crane Ln.

Crampton Ct.

Sycamore St.

Curved St.

Crow St.

Fownes St.

Toscana

Les Frères Jacques

Dame St.

Montys of Kathmandu

College Green

Lord Edward St.

CITY HALL

Castle St.

S. Great George's St.

DUBLIN CASTLE

1/8 mi

1/8 km

KEY

■ *Restaurants*

✥ *following dining reviews indicates a map-grid coordinate*

Co. Dublin ☎01/679–3121 ⊕ *www.elephantandcastle.ie* ⌕ *Reservations not accepted* ✥ *2:D2.*

$$ ✕ **Il Baccaro.** One of the more romantic locations in the city has to be the tiny candlelit dining room of this authentic Italian osteria in a vaulted basement off Meeting House Square. The menu is small and focused, with classic pastas and traditional starters like the air-cured Valtellina beef marinated with lemon and served with strips of Parmesan cheese. Roast pork finished on the grill with a mixed mushroom sauce and panfried chicken breast topped with roasted red peppers, baby potatoes, and pancetta are two trusty mains. Selling house wine by the half or full carafe is a good value touch. $ *Average main: €19* ⊠ *Meeting House Sq., Temple Bar, Dublin, Co. Dublin* ☎01/671–4597 ⊕ *www. ilbaccarodublin.com* ⊙ *No lunch* ✥ *2:B2.*

ITALIAN

$$$$ ✕ **Les Frères Jacques.** Many restaurants call themselves French, but this elegant eatery next to the Olympia Theatre positively reeks of Gallic panache. Old prints of Paris and Deauville hang on the green-paper walls, and the French waiters, dressed in white Irish linen and black bow ties, exude a European charm without being excessively formal. Expect traditional French cooking that nods to the seasons. Seafood is a major attraction, and fresh lobster is typically roasted and flambéed with Irish whiskey. Others prefer the fillet of beef with mushroom farce, roast baby potatoes, and cognac juices. Also recommended are the seasonal

FRENCH

game specialties. A piano player performs Friday and Saturday evenings and on the occasional weeknight. $ *Average main: €33* ⊠ *74 Dame St., Temple Bar, Dublin, Co. Dublin* ☎ *01/679–4555* ⊕ *www. lesfreresjacques.com* ⌘ *Reservations essential* ☾ *Closed Sun. No lunch Sat.* ✛ *2:B2.*

> **A TASTY TIP**
>
> Patrick Guilbaud, Chapter One, One Pico, and other high-end places prove the simple adage: great chefs make great restaurants. Many have fixed-price lunch menus that are excellent bargains for the cash-conscious epicurean.

$$

ASIAN

✕ **Montys of Kathmandu.** Montys proudly (and yet, somehow unshockingly) declares itself the "only Nepalese restaurant in Dublin." The bland decor is nothing to write home about, but the food at this little eatery in the middle of hypermodern Temple Bar is as authentic as it is unique. *Poleko* squid (lightly spiced and barbecued in a tandoori oven and served in a sizzler) and lamb *Choila* (with fresh chilis, ginger, garlic, herbs, and a dash of red wine) are the more adventurous starters. For a main course try *Momos,* dumplings served with momo chutney, a favorite street dish in Kathmandu. They even have a celiac-friendly menu. The wine cellar is surprisingly varied. $ *Average main: €19* ⊠ *28 Eustace St., Temple Bar, Dublin, Co. Dublin* ☎ *01/670–4911* ⊕ *www. montys.ie* ☾ *No lunch* ✛ *2:C2.*

$$

MODERN IRISH

✕ **The Tea Room.** In the Clarence Hotel, you can sit around all day and hope that Bono and the boys of U2—they own the joint, after all— might turn up for a quick snack. Other stars of stage and screen often stay at the hotel and stop in at the Tea Room. Minimalistically hued in golden oak, eggshell white, and light yellows, the high-ceiling room is a perfect stage for off-duty celebs. The contrast between this high-vaulted cocoon and busy Essex Street—whose madding crowds can be glimpsed through the double-height windows—could not be more dramatic. The menu has been slimmed down in recent times with a focus on a smaller number of dramatic dishes, including the butterfly breaded rainbow trout with silk mash potatoes, anchovy butter, and lime fish sauce and the wild mushroom risotto. $ *Average main: €19* ⊠ *Clarence Hotel, 6–8 Wellington Quay, Temple Bar, Dublin, Co. Dublin* ☎ *01/407–0813* ⊕ *www.theclarence.ie* ⌘ *Reservations essential* ✛ *2:A2.*

$$

ITALIAN

✕ **Toscana.** A genuine trattoria in the heart of crazy Temple Bar, Toscana buzzes with chatter all evening long and offers a popular pretheater menu. A Mediterranean slant to the simple dining room includes plenty of Italian landscapes, cream tones, and wood. A typical starter is the panfried crab claws in garlic. The *penne entrecote* is strips of Irish beef panfried with onions, garlic, and olive oil and tossed in a plum tomato and cream sauce. The meat and pizza dishes are also always reliable and the Bailey's cheesecake with chocolate sauce is a dessert that will send you home with a smile on your face. $ *Average main: €18* ⊠ *3 Cork Hill, Dame St., Temple Bar, Dublin, Co. Dublin* ☎ *01/670–9785* ⊕ *www.toscana.ie* ✛ *2:A2.*

Cuisine Irelandaise mixes new French cuisine with old Irish ingredients and results—such as this squab in Irish whiskey sauce at Les Frères Jacques—are *très delicieux.*

NORTHSIDE

$$
MEDITERRANEAN

✗ **101 Talbot.** The 101 on 101 Talbot is that it has that certain buzz that comes only from restaurants popular with the artistic and literary set. Close to the Abbey and Gate theaters, so there's no danger of missing a curtain call, this slightly frantic upstairs restaurant showcases an ever-changing exhibition of local artists' work. The creative contemporary food—with eclectic Mediterranean and Eastern influences—uses fresh local ingredients. Try the char-grilled breast of Irish chicken stuffed with black pudding and goat cheese and served with spring onion mash. The char-grilled prawn kebab with baby spinach salad also impresses. Healthful options and several vegetarian choices make this a highly versatile restaurant. $ *Average main: €19* ⊠ *101 Talbot St., Northside, Dublin, Co. Dublin* ☎ *01/874–5011* ⊕ *www.101talbot.ie* ⌖ *Reservations essential* ⊗ *Closed Sun. and Mon.* ✦ *1:D2.*

$$$$
MODERN IRISH
Fodor'sChoice
★

✗ **Chapter One.** This wonderful, culture-vulture favorite gets its name from its location, downstairs in the vaulted, stone-wall basement of the Dublin Writers Museum; the natural stone-and-wood setting makes it cozily cavelike. The contemporary French eatery is currently the culinary king of the Northside, thanks to chef-proprietor Ross Lewis's way with such dishes as feta cheese mousse with organic beetroot essence, pear purée, spiced apple, and pumpkin oil. Yeats himself would have loved the John Dory overflowing with leeks stewed in white truffle butter, light vermouth sauce, and sautéed chanterelles, while Synge probably would have fancied the Dublin version of Proust's madeleine: rich bread-and-butter pudding, a favorite of working-class Irish mothers for generations, here turned into an outrageously filling work of art. $ *Average main: €33* ⊠ *18–19 Parnell Sq., Northside, Dublin, Co. Dublin* ☎ *01/873–2266* ⊕ *www.chapteronerestaurant.com* ⌫ *Reservations essential* ⊘ *Closed Sun. and Mon. No lunch Sat.* ✛ *1:B1.*

$ ✕ **Enoteca delle Langhe.** Officially called Quartier Bloom in tribute to Joyce's most famous character, a charming little (very little) Italian quarter has sprung up just off Ormond Quay, bringing a chorus of approval from Dubliners long starved of quality, down-to-earth Italian food. It consists of a communal plaza area, a fabulous mural that's a modern take on Leonardo da Vinci's *The Last Supper*, and a couple of places to eat, including Enoteca delle Langhe. Italian-owned and -operated, Langhe serves up the full enoteca experience: quality, affordable Italian wines (more than 75% are sourced from the Langhe district); a limited but enticing selection of appetizers—try the perfect bruschetta with scrumptious toppings like sundried-tomato pesto and sautéed zucchini—warm, friendly, family-style service; and a constant buzz in the air. In summer, tango dancers perform outside. $ *Average main: €11* ⊠ *Blooms Lane, Northside, Dublin, Co. Dublin* ☎ *01/888–0834* ✛ *1:B2.*

ITALIAN
Fodor'sChoice
★

$ ✕ **Hop House.** A unique Korean-Japanese standout in the slew of cheap and cheerful Chinese eateries that have opened on Parnell Street (some local wags are already calling it Chinatown), Hop House is a restaurant and pub in one. Part of the old Shakespeare pub has been transformed into the friendliest, best-value new restaurant in the city. The dining room is bright and busy, with little table buzzers for service and the sounds of music spilling over from the bar next door. Traditional Korean specialties like kimchi are augmented with a large selection of sushi rolls, including the mouthwatering Black Tiger Roll with avocado, crab, eel, and teriyaki sauce. Hot dishes include spicy pork and squid. $ *Average main: €13* ⊠ *160 Parnell St., Northside, Dublin, Co. Dublin* ☎ *01/872–8318* ⊕ *www.hophouse.ie* ✛ *1:C1.*

KOREAN FUSION

$ ✕ **Kingfisher Restaurant.** Don't let the down-at-the-heel canteen decor put you off—this place has been around for a long time and is a master of the art of fish-and-chips. Their mammoth-value menu is full of seafood surprises like such Dublin favorites as cod and ray (or more unusual choices like halibut) and you can even order a whole sea bass and rainbow trout. Kingfisher's huge Irish breakfasts have won awards with all the meats sourced fresh from the owners' own farm. The Northside locals love this place and give it a lively community atmosphere. $ *Average main: €16* ⊠ *166–168 Parnell St., Northside, Dublin, Co. Dublin* ☎ *01/872–8732* ⊕ *www.kingfisherdublin.com* ✛ *1:C1.*

IRISH

$ ✕ **L. Mulligan Grocer.** This gem of an old Dublin boozer—which was once also the local grocer—has recently been turned into a gastropub and world beer emporium, without losing too much of its real Dublin feel. Microbrewery beers are hard to come by in Ireland, so the wide selection of small-label ales, lagers, and stouts is reason enough to make the trip to the evocatively named village of Stoneybatter on the Northside. The menu doesn't fuss around with too many choices, but the potted crab with sourdough soldiers is a great starter and the pork bell with colcannon, roasted fennel, and carrot and celeriac crisps is the pick of the hearty mains. Mulligan's is the perfect spot for a quick

IRISH

pint of ale and a plate of black pudding (with pear relish and red chard) if you don't feel like a full sit-down meal. $ *Average main: €17* ⊠ *18 Stoneybatter, Northside, Dublin, Co. Dublin* ☎ *01/670–9889* ⊕ *www. lmulligangrocer.com* ⊙ *No lunch Mon.–Fri.* ✛ *1:A2.*

$

SUSHI

Fodor's Choice

★

✕ **Musashi Noodles and Sushi Bar.** This hot new sushi bar on unfashionable Capel Street is the talk of the money-conscious-town because it's finally made the Japanese staple affordable in Dublin. The interior is simple and unfussy; a long, narrow room with dark wood floors and rows of pinewood tables and seats dotted with red cushions. Japanese owned and run, the flair is saved for the fresh and flavorful dishes—all the sushi standards you'd expect but better than anything else in the city. They also do a mean tempura and gyoza for those who don't fancy raw fish. Another treat is the BYOB policy on wine, with a very fair €4 corkage charge. $ *Average main: €14* ⊠ *15 Capel St., Northside, Dublin, Co. Dublin* ☎ *01/532–8068* ⊕ *www.musashidublin.com* ✛ *1:B2.*

$

IRISH

✕ **Soup Dragon.** This tiny café and take-out soup shop serves an astonishing array of fresh soups daily, with standout value on their daily deals. Soups come in three sizes, and you can get vegetarian soup or soups with meat- or fish-based broth. Best bets include red pepper, tomato, and goat cheese soup; fragrant Thai chicken soup; beef chili; and hearty mussel, potato, and leek soup. The friendly staff make fine coffee and delicious smoothies. The cost of soup includes bread and a piece of fruit for dessert—an excellent value—and they also do a decent grab-and-go breakfast. A second Soup Dragon recently opened around the corner on Ormond Quay. $ *Average main: €6* ⊠ *168 Capel St., Northside, Dublin, Co. Dublin* ☎ *01/872–3277* ⊕ *www.soupdragon.com* ▬ *No credit cards* ⊙ *Closed Sun. No dinner* ✛ *1:B2.*

$

ITALIAN

✕ **The Vaults.** Come eat under the train station. Not exactly the best sales pitch you've ever heard, but this wonderful, long-neglected space beneath Connolly Station was imaginatively revamped to create one of the city's trendiest dining spots by day (and club venues by night). Cavernous arches, smooth Portland stone floors, and dramatic lighting create the background for a mostly young business set. Each of the 10 interlinked vaults is decorated in its own style, ranging from hypermodern to turn-of-the-20th-century elegant. Cocktails are a specialty, although it's worth a visit for the food alone. The chef makes everything from scratch, including the pizza dough. A wide-ranging menu covers light snack options alongside more substantial dishes like the house pizza, a blend of tomato, mozzarella, prawns, red onion, and herbs. Be sure to leave room for the excellent bread-and-butter pudding. Note that dinner is served only until 8. $ *Average main: €14* ⊠ *Harbourmaster Pl., Northside, Dublin, Co. Dublin* ☎ *01/605–4700* ⊕ *www. thevaults.ie* ⊙ *Closed weekends* ✛ *1:E1.*

$$

IRISH

Fodor's Choice

★

✕ **The Winding Stair.** Once Dublin's favorite secondhand bookshop-café, the Winding Stair now houses an atmospheric, buzzing little restaurant, replete with old wooden floors, simple decor, a downstairs bookshop, and grand views of the Ha'penny Bridge and the river Liffey. Upstairs, former habitués will enjoy seeing the old bookcases around the walls (some of which are now stacked with wine). Hearty portions of upmarket traditional Irish food best describes the terrific menu, which is greatly helped by locally sourced ingredients, and reads like a list of small, artisan Irish producers. The wild venison cushion with colcannon bake, buttered kale and wild mushrooms is a standout, as is the Irish cheese potato cake with oyster mushrooms, wilted spinach, truffle oil, and chive crème fraiche. An inventive wine list and a wonderful Irish farmhouse cheese selection are two more treats on offer. Your sweet tooth insists that you try the bread-and-butter pudding for dessert. $ *Average main: €23* ⊠ *40 Ormond Quay, Northside, Dublin, Co. Dublin* ☎ *01/872–7320* ⊕ *www.winding-stair.com* ✢ *1:A3.*

BALLSBRIDGE

$ ✕ **The French Paradox.** Relaxed, simple, but chic would best describe this
FRENCH little restaurant above a wine shop in the heart of Ballsbridge; it also
★ describes the people of the south of France who inspired the place. Wine buffs, Francophiles, and gourmets flock here for the hearty traditional fare and Mediterranean ambience. Share the *assiette le fond de barrique,* a selection of charcuterie, pâté, and cheese, or perhaps indulge in a selection of cured Irish fish or a choice from the foie gras menu. Select a nice bottle from the ground-floor wine shop (mostly French labels) and sip it in situ for a mere €8 corkage fee along with a few "French tapas." Seating is limited. $ *Average main: €11* ⊠ *53 Shelbourne Rd., Ballsbridge, Dublin, Co. Dublin* ☎ *01/660–4068* ⊕ *www.thefrenchparadox. com* ⌆ *Reservations essential* ☉ *Closed Sun.* ✢ *1:H6.*

$$$ ✕ **O'Connells in Donnybrook.** When it comes to cooking, pedigree counts.
MODERN IRISH Owner Tom O'Connell is a brother to Ireland's favorite celebrity chef, Darina Allen, famed for her "slow food" Ballymaloe Cookery School in Cork. Tom, now based in the heart of Donnybrook village, follows the family blueprint by showcasing fresh Irish produce and focusing on locally produced meats and game that can be traced to their source (in many cases, an individual farm). Altogether you have the makings of a feast that is deliciously, quintessentially Irish. Spiced beef is prepared according to an old Cork recipe, salmon fillet is "hot smoked" by the restaurant itself, while McCarthy's Black Pudding is handmade in Kanturk, County Cork. You can also try the roast Castletownbere cod with braised leek and lemon-butter sauce or the braised shoulder of lamb with buttered cabbage and braised leeks. Desserts continue the homegrown theme including a warm chocolate brownie with Gathabawn vanilla ice cream. The cheese board is a who's who of Irish farmhouse cheeses, including the Ferguson family's tangy Gubbeen. $ *Average main: €29* ⊠ *135 Morehampton Rd., Donnybrook, Ballsbridge, Dublin, Co. Dublin* ☎ *01/269–6116* ⊕ *www.oconnellsdonnybrook.com* ✢ *1:H6.*

$$$$ ✕ **Seasons.** Although the restaurant at the Dublin branch of the vaunted
MODERN IRISH Four Seasons hotel took a little time to find its feet in and out of the kitchen, it has finally staked its claim in Dublin's dining scene—Sunday brunch here has become a ritual for many well-to-do Dublin Southsiders. Dramatic dishes, served in the large and slightly overwhelming silver-service dining room, creatively incorporate local (and often organic) ingredients. A starter of Cromane Bay Irish mussels with lime leaf coriander and char-grilled baguette might be followed by slow-roasted loin of veal with blanquette sauce, garlic potato purée, and

autumn vegetables. Manager Simon Keegan was the sommelier so the wine list is one of the best in the country. ⑤ *Average main: €35* ⊠ *Four Seasons Hotel, Simmonscourt Rd., Ballsbridge, Dublin, Co. Dublin* ☎ *01/665–4642* ⊕ *www.fourseasons.com/dublin* ⚠ *Reservations essential* ✛ *1:H6.*

DUBLIN WEST

$ × **Bibi's Cafe.** Sisters Maisha and Petria Lenehan had the clever idea of
CAFÉ combining elegant shopping and dining in this little gem in the middle
★ of a quiet, off-the-beaten-track, residential street. Their small menu specializes in creative breakfasts and lunch (and brunch on the weekend) with a local twist. The pan-toasted sandwich with ham, Gubeen cheese, and homemade chutney is typical, as is their wonderful brioche French toast with Irish bacon and maple syrup. ■ **TIP**➡ **You might want to hit the sisters' cute clothes boutique, Dolls, next door before you hit up their devilishly tempting cake selection.** ⑤ *Average main: €9* ⊠ *14b Emorville Ave., Dublin West, Dublin, Co. Dublin* ☎ *01/454–7421* ⊕ *www.bibis. ie* ⊘ *Closed Mon. No Dinner* ✛ *1:A6.*

$ × **Leo Burdock.** Old man Burdock has moved on and the place hasn't
IRISH been the same since, but the hordes still join the inevitable queue at Dublin's famous hundred-year-old, takeout fish-and-chips shop, right next door to the Lord Edward pub. You can't eat here, but why would you anyway, when you can sit in the gardens of St. Patrick's Cathedral a few minutes way. Fresh cod is a classic, and the battered sausage a particular Dublin favorite, but the real stars here are the long, thick, freshly cut chips, which have a slightly smoky aftertaste. ■ **TIP**➡ **Look like a local and ask to season your chips with "crispy bits."** ⑤ *Average main: €9* ⊠ *2 Werburgh St., Christchurch, Dublin West, Dublin, Co. Dublin* ☎ *01/454–0306* ⊕ *www.leoburdock.com* ═ *No credit cards* ✛ *1:A3.*

$$ × **Lord Edward Restaurant.** Culinary trends and fashions may come and
SEAFOOD go but Dublin's oldest seafood restaurant remains resolutely traditional. On the cozy top floor above a lovely old bar of the same name, the Lord Edward looks out on the front entrance of Christ Church Cathedral. They do a mean Irish stew but the stars here are definitely the seafood dishes, usually smothered in a totally unhip but delicious, calorie-packed cream sauce. The salmon and the cod are two favorites, and the lobster Mornay is also special. ⑤ *Average main: €24* ⊠ *23 Christ Church Pl., Dublin West, Dublin, Co. Dublin* ☎ *01/454–2420* ⊕ *www. lordedward.ie* ⊘ *Closed Sun. No lunch Sat.* ✛ *1:B3.*

$ × **Lovin Catering.** This unasuming little shop on Francis Street conjures
CAFÉ up some of the best pastries in town. There's no seating in this powerhouse patisserie, but long counters allow space for perching your coffee and tucking into the finest sweet and savory treats. Pop in for a morning coffee and an apple and almond tartlet; try the quiche or salmon roulade with homemade salsa for lunch; or simply take afternoon tea with a scrumptious scone. Expect queues at lunchtime, and be sure to buy in bulk for the tastiest take-out picnic in town. ⑤ *Average main: €9* ⊠ *49 Francis St., Liberties, Dublin, Co. Dublin* ☎ *01/454–4912* ⊕ *www.lovincatering.com* ⊘ *Closed Sun. No dinner* ✛ *1:A4.*

PHOENIX PARK AND ENVIRONS

$ ✕ **Juno's Café.** Located at the gates of the Phoenix Park and perfect for a
CAFÉ post- or pre-amble dinner, this little gem of a café has few culinary frills but delivers plenty of hearty bang for your precious euros. Finnish head chef Juha Salo, formerly of the Mermaid Café and 101 Talbot, knows what the Irish like to eat and he manages to add a little magic dust to some old reliables. His fish-and-chips—with a wafer-light batter and chunky, crisp chips—has to be one of the best in the city. Home produce and seasonal choices predominate, and the chicken schnitzel with cherry tomatoes, capers, parsley, grilled lemon, and home-cut chips is a delicious belly filler. Dishes like the Bellingham Blue Cheese Polenta with roast sweet corn salsa and rocket lettuce satisfy more adventurous tastes. ⑤ *Average main: €16* ✉ *26 Parkgate St., Dublin West, Dublin, Co. Dublin* ☎ *01/670–9820* ⊕ *www.junoscafe.com* ☾ *No dinner Sun.– Wed.* ✛ *1:A2.*

$$ ✕ **Nancy Hands Bar & Restaurant.** There's a fine line between recreating
ECLECTIC tradition and looking like a theme bar but Nancy Hands just about pulls it off. A galleylike room juxtaposes old wood, raw brick, and antiques with contemporary art to create a convivial, cozy dining area. The bar food is good, but the upstairs restaurant operates on a more serious level. Hearty specialties include scallops of turkey panfried with wild mushrooms and served with a creamy penne pasta and the leg of rabbit with steamed dumplings. Numerous wines are served by the glass, and the selection of spirits is one of the most impressive in the country. ⑤ *Average main: €18* ✉ *30–32 Parkgate St., Dublin West, Dublin, Co. Dublin* ☎ *01/677–0149* ⊕ *www.nancyhands.ie* ✍ *Reservations essential* ✛ *1:A2.*

WHERE TO STAY

The economic slowdown abruptly halted the "absolute avalanche of new hotels" as the *Irish Times* characterized Dublin's accommodation boom. But visitors still have an impressive choice of elegant lodgings all over the city, including the classy and intimate La Stampa on Dawson Street, the totally revamped landmarks of the Shelbourne and the Westbury, and some tempting choices found in Ballsbridge, an inner "suburb" that's a 20-minute walk from the city center. For something uniquely Dublin, you can always stay at one of the elegant guesthouses that occupy former Georgian town houses found on both sides of the Liffey.

The economic downturn means prices have fallen, especially at the high and medium end, and Dublin now has a good selection of quality affordable accommodations, including many moderately priced hotels with basic but agreeable rooms. Most guesthouses, long the mainstay of the economy end of the market, have thankfully upgraded their facilities and now provide rooms with private bathrooms or showers, as well as cable color televisions, direct-dial telephones, and Internet connections. The bigger hotels are all equipped with Wi-Fi. If you've rented a car and you're not staying at a hotel with parking, it's worth considering a location out of the city center, such as Dalkey or Killiney, where the surroundings are more pleasant and you won't have to worry about parking on city streets.

Prices in the reviews are the lowest cost of a standard double room in high season. For expanded reviews, facilities, and current deals, visit Fodors.com. Use the coordinate (✛ B2) at the end of each listing to locate a site on the corresponding Where to Stay in Dublin map.

SOUTHSIDE

$$
HOTEL
Brooks Hotel. It has nearly 100 rooms, but this hotel—minutes from Grafton Street—likes to describe itself as a boutique property, and it does manage to convey the personal touch of a much smaller establishment. **Pros:** next to Grafton Street; live piano music in bar; rooms refurbished every six years. **Cons:** office-block exterior; business clientele makes for slightly flat atmosphere; standard rooms on small side. **TripAdvisor:** "friendly," "super location and super clean," "comfortable accommodations." ⑤ *Rooms from: €150 ✉ Drury St., Southside, Dublin, Co. Dublin* ☎ *01/670–4000* ⊕ *www.brookshotel.ie* ⟿ *98 rooms* ✛ *C4.*

$$
HOTEL
Fodor's Choice
★
Central Hotel Dublin. Every city center needs its little oasis, and the Central's book-and-armchair-filled Library Bar—warmed by a Victorian fireplace—nicely fits the bill. **Pros:** delightful Library Bar; original 1887 facade; old-fashioned feel. **Cons:** rooms a bit snug; street noise in some rooms; you have to prepay up front! **TripAdvisor:** "great stay," "perfect," "fantastic location." ⑤ *Rooms from: €140 ✉ 1–5 Exchequer St., Southside, Dublin, Co. Dublin* ☎ *01/679–7302* ⊕ *www.centralhotel.ie* ⟿ *67 rooms, 3 suites* ◉ *Breakfast* ✛ *C3.*

$$$
HOTEL
Conrad Dublin International. The best thing about the ugly-on-the-outside, seven-story, redbrick and smoked-glass Conrad is the spectacular views out over the city, so ask for—no, insist on—a room on one of the top three floors. **Pros:** Gary the concierge; great views on higher floors; marble bathrooms; just off St. Stephen's Green. **Cons:** drab, 1970s-style corridors; slightly cramped standard rooms; poor views on lower floors. **TripAdvisor:** "luxurious as always," "great location," "five-star bedroom." ⑤ *Rooms from: €199 ✉ Earlsfort Terr., Southside, Dublin, Co. Dublin* ☎ *01/602–8900* ⊕ *www.conradhotels.com* ⟿ *182 rooms, 10 suites* ✛ *D5.*

$
HOTEL
Grafton Guest House. A stone's throw from the famous shopping street that gave it its name, this Victorian Gothic–style building has been tastefully transformed into one of central Dublin's best bargains. **Pros:** best value in city center; warm, unfussy service; simple but cool design. **Cons:** some rooms are cramped; can suffer from street noise; no elevator. **TripAdvisor:** "suited our needs," "great location," "fab." ⑤ *Rooms from: €94 ✉ 26–27 S. Great George's St., Southside, Dublin, Co. Dublin* ☎ *01/648–0010* ⊕ *www.graftonguesthouse.com* ⟿ *16 rooms* ◉ *Breakfast* ✛ *C3.*

$
HOTEL
Fodor's Choice
★
Kellys Hotel Dublin. With buzzing Hogan's bar and the classy L'Gueuleton restaurant right downstairs, this cool little hotel is already at the epicenter of trendy Dublin living. **Pros:** killer city-center location; cool vibe; one of the city's best restaurants downstairs; great spot to

BEST BETS FOR DUBLIN LODGING

Fodor's offers a selective listing of high-quality lodging experiences at every price range, from the city's best budget options to its most sophisticated luxury hotel. Here, we've compiled our top recommendations by price and experience. The very best properties—those that provide a particularly remarkable experience—are designated with a Fodor's Choice symbol.

Fodor'sChoice ★

Castle Hotel, $, p. 127

Central Hotel, $$, p. 122

Four Seasons Hotel Dublin, $$$$, p. 130

Kelly's Hotel, $, p. 122

La Stampa, $$, p. 125

Merrion, $$$$, p. 125

Number 31, $$$, p. 125

Pembroke Townhouse, $, p. 132

Schoolhouse Hotel, $$$, p. 132

Shelbourne, $$$, p. 126

Westbury Hotel Dublin, $$$$, p. 126

By Price

$

Ariel Guest House, p. 130

Bewley's Hotel at Newlands Cross, p. 132

Charleville Lodge, p. 127

Grafton Guest House, p. 122

Jurys Inn, Christchurch, p. 133

Kelly's Hotel, p. 122

Pembroke Townhouse, p. 132

$$

Brooks Hotel, p. 122

Central Hotel, p. 122

La Stampa, p. 125

Paramount Hotel, p. 127

$$$

Number 31, p. 125

Schoolhouse Hotel, p. 132

Shelbourne, p. 126

$$$$

Four Seasons Hotel Dublin, p. 130

Merrion, p. 125

Westbury Hotel Dublin, p. 126

By Type

GORGEOUS GEORGIANS

Merrion, $$$$, p. 125

Number 31, $$$, p. 125

Pembroke Townhouse, $, p. 132

BEST DESIGN

The Clarence, $$$, p. 126

La Stampa, $$, p. 125

Number 31, $$$, p. 125

Shelbourne, $$$, p. 126

Westin Dublin, $$$$, p. 126

MOST CHARMING

Charleville Lodge, $, p. 127

Number 31, $$$, p. 125

Pembroke Townhouse, $, p. 132

Schoolhouse Hotel, $$$, p. 132

BEST VIEWS

Conrad Dublin International, $$$, p. 122

Herbert Park Hotel, $$, p. 132

Shelbourne, $$$, p. 126

MOST ROMANTIC

Dylan Hotel, $$$, p. 130

La Stampa, $$, p. 125

The Morrison, $$, p. 129

Number 31, $$$, p. 125

BEST BARS

Central Hotel, $$, p. 122

Kelly's Hotel, $, p. 122

Paramount, $$, p. 127

Shelbourne, $$$, p. 126

Westbury Hotel Dublin, $$$$, p. 126

BEST GRANDE DAME

Burlington Hotel, $$, p. 130

Shelbourne, $$$, p. 126

Westbury Hotel Dublin, $$$$, p. 126

2

Castle Hotel

Kellys Hotel Dublin

Charleville Lodge

bump into interesting Dubliners. **Cons:** some rooms are cramped; can suffer from street noise; no elevator. **TripAdvisor:** "good location," "gem in the heart of the city," "chic." $ *Rooms from: €90* ⊠ *36 S. Great Georges St., Southside, Dublin, Co. Dublin* ☎ *01/648–0010* ⊕ *www.kellysdublin.com* ⊃ *15 rooms, 2 suites* |◎| *Breakfast* ✢ *C3.*

$ | **B&B/INN** | **★** | ⊞ **Kilronan House Hotel.** Just a five-minute walk from St. Stephen's Green, this mid-19th-century terraced guesthouse, with its elegant white facade and cozy sitting-room fire, will welcome you home at the end of a long day's sightseeing. **Pros:** great price for location; beautiful, calming facade; cozy sitting room. **Cons:** public areas a bit worn; uncreative room furnishings; no Internet in rooms; no elevator. **TripAdvisor:** "super staff," "yummy breakfast," "a great experience." $ *Rooms from: €99* ⊠ *70 Adelaide Rd., Southside, Dublin, Co. Dublin* ☎ *01/475–5266* ⊕ *www.kilronanhouse.com* ⊃ *12 rooms* |◎| *Breakfast* ✢ *D5.*

$$ | **HOTEL** | **Fodor's Choice** | **★** | ⊞ **La Stampa Hotel & Spa Dublin.** Overlooking the mansion house, home to the luxe and popular Balzac restaurant, and 50 yards from Trinity College, this intimate town-house hotel is one of the classiest boutique hotels on the Dublin scene. **Pros:** great luxury for the price; choice of three quality restaurants; spa oasis in the city. **Cons:** small hotel fills up quickly; no parking; one could overdose on the Asian theme. **TripAdvisor:** "staff was nice," "quirky," "good location and service." $ *Rooms from: €120* ⊠ *35 Dawson St., Southside, Dublin, Co. Dublin* ☎ *01/677–4444* ⊕ *www.lastampa.ie* ⊃ *23 rooms, 5 suites* ✢ *D4.*

$$$$ | **HOTEL** | **Fodor's Choice** | **★** | ⊞ **Merrion Hotel.** Stately and spiffy, and splendidly situated directly across from Government Buildings between Stephen's Green and Merrion Square, this luxurious hotel actually comprises four exactingly restored Georgian town houses. **Pros:** Patrick Guilbaud restaurant; infinity pool; city-center location; attentive staff; ranked No. 1 Dublin on TripAdvisor. **Cons:** you'll pay extra for a room in the original house; some rooms are overdecorated. **TripAdvisor:** "pitch perfect," "quiet Georgian refuge," "luxury like no other." $ *Rooms from: €230* ⊠ *Upper Merrion St., Southside, Dublin, Co. Dublin* ☎ *01/603–0600* ⊕ *www.merrionhotel.com* ⊃ *123 rooms, 19 suites* ✢ *E4.*

$$$ | **B&B/INN** | **Fodor's Choice** | **★** | ⊞ **Number 31.** Whether your lodging style is sublime Georgian elegance or serene cool modern, this one-in-a-million guesthouse, a short walk from St. Stephen's Green, serves up both . . . as well as the best made-to-order breakfast in town. **Pros:** the king and queen of guesthouse hosts; serene decor and art; best breakfast in the city. **Cons:** a few rooms can be a little noisy; no elevator; a little pricey. **TripAdvisor:** "best breakfast in Dublin," "very good service," "unbelievably wonderful." $ *Rooms from: €190* ⊠ *31 Leeson Close, Southside, Dublin, Co. Dublin* ☎ *01/676–5011* ⊕ *www.number31.ie* ⊃ *21 rooms* ✢ *E5.*

$$ | **HOTEL** | ⊞ **Premier Suites Dublin.** Get a top-floor suite at this modernized Georgian town house just off St. Stephen's Green and lord it over the whole Southside. **Pros:** top-floor suites have spectacular city views; ground-floor suites have private entrances. **Cons:** decor is modern, motel-functional. **TripAdvisor:** "great property," "spacious room with modern amenities," "fantastic location." $ *Rooms from: €149* ⊠ *14–17 Lower Leeson St., Southside, Dublin, Co. Dublin* ☎ *01/638–1111* ⊕ *www. premiersuitesdublin.com* ⊃ *30 suites* ✢ *D5.*

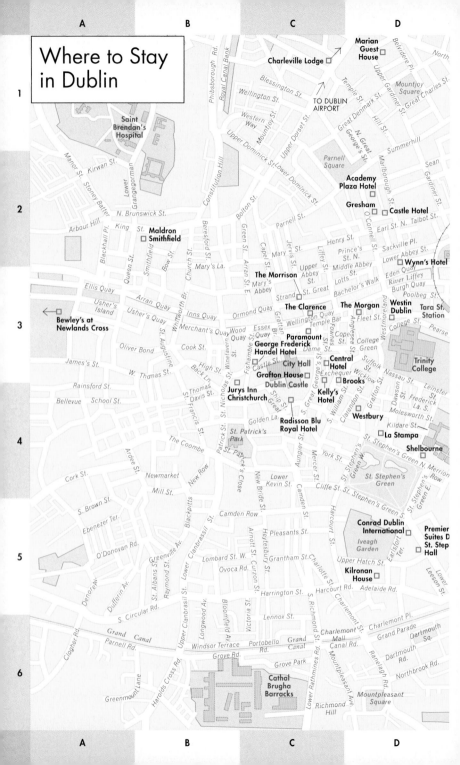

Where to Stay in Dublin

A   **B**   **C**   **D**

Phibsborough Rd.

Royal Canal Bank

Marian Guest House

Belvidere Pl.

Charleville Lodge

North

1

Blessington St.

Wellington St.

Temple St.

Upper Gardiner St.

Mountjoy Square

Great Charles St.

TO DUBLIN AIRPORT

Western Way

Mountjoy St.

Great Denmark St.

Hill St.

Saint Brendan's Hospital

Upper Dominick St.

Lower Dominick St.

Upper Dorset St.

Great George's St.

N. Great Denmark St.

Summerhill

Manor St.

Kirwan St.

Lower Grangegorman

Marlborough St.

Sean

Gardiner St.

Parnell Square

Academy Plaza Hotel

2

Arbour Hill

King St.

N. Brunswick St.

Bolton St.

Parnell St.

Gresham

O'Connell St.

Earl St. N. Talbot St.

Castle Hotel

Blackhall Pl.

Smithfield

Bow St.

Beresford St.

Green St.

Maldron Smithfield

Henry St.

Prince's St. N.

Sackville Pl.

Lower Abbey St.

Wynn's Hotel

Ellis Quay

Arran Quay

Usher's Island

Usher's Quay

Whitworth Br.

Inns Quay

Church St.

Mary's La.

Capel St.

Jervis St.

Mary St.

Liffey St.

Middle Abbey St.

Lotts

Eden Quay

River Liffey

Burgh Quay

Poolbeg St.

The Morrison

Upper Abbey St. Great

St. Mary's Abbey

Strand St. Great

Bachelor's Walk

Westin Dublin

Tara St. Station

Bewley's at Newlands Cross

Merchant's Quay

Ormond Quay

Wood Quay

Essex Quay

Wellington Quay

Temple Bar

Fleet St.

College St.

Pearse

3

James's St.

Oliver Bond

Cook St.

High St.

Fishamble St.

Grattan Br.

The Clarence

Copeco St.

Fownes St.

Anglesea St.

The Morgan

Westmoreland

College Green

Trinity College

Rainsford St.

W. Thomas St.

Back Ln.

St. Nicholas St.

Winetavern St.

Paramount

George Frederick Handel Hotel

Dame St.

Exchequer St.

Suffolk St.

Nassau St.

Dawson St.

Leinster St.

Bellevue

School St.

St. Francis St.

St. Thomas Davis St.

City Hall

Grafton House

Dublin Castle

Central Hotel

Brooks

Wicklow St.

S. William St.

Clarendon St.

Grafton St.

S. Frederick La. S.

Molesworth St.

4

The Coombe

Patrick St.

St. Patrick's Park

St. Pat's Close

Jurys Inn Christchurch

Ship St.

S. Great George's St.

Kelly's Hotel

Westbury

Kildare St.

La Stampa

Golden La.

Radisson Blu Royal Hotel

Aungier St.

Mercer St.

York St.

St. Stephen's Green W.

St. Stephen's Green

St. Stephen's Green N.

Merrion Row

Shelbourne

Cork St.

Newmarket

New Row

Blackpitts

Camden Row

Lower Kevin St.

Cliffe St.

Camden St.

St. Stephen's Green S.

St. Stephen's Green E.

Mill St.

S. Brown St.

Ebenezer Ter.

Greenville Av.

Lower Clanbrassil St.

Arnott St.

Heytesbury St.

Pleasants St.

Grantham St.

Charlotte St.

Upper Hatch St.

Conrad Dublin International

Iveagh Garden

Earlsfort Ter.

Premier Suites D St. Step Hall

5

O'Donovan Rd.

St. Albans Rd.

Raymond St.

Lombard St. W.

Ovoca Rd.

Curzon St.

Victoria St.

Harrington St.

Harcourt Rd.

Adelaide Rd.

Kilronan House

Lower Leeson St.

Denore Rd.

Dufferin Av.

S. Circular Rd.

Longwood Av.

Bloomfield Av.

Lennox St.

Richmond St.

Charlemont St.

Charlemont Pl.

Grand Parade

Dartmouth Rd.

Dartmouth Sq.

Clogher Rd.

Grand Canal

Parnell Rd.

Harolds Cross Rd.

Windsor Terrace

Portobello Rd.

Grand Canal Rd.

Charlemont Mall

Mountpleasant Ave.

Ranelagh Rd.

Northbrook Rd.

6

Greenmount Lane

Greenmount St.

Grove Rd.

Grove Park

Cathal Brugha Barracks

Lower Rathmines Rd.

Richmond Hill

Mountpleasant Square

A   **B**   **C**   **D**

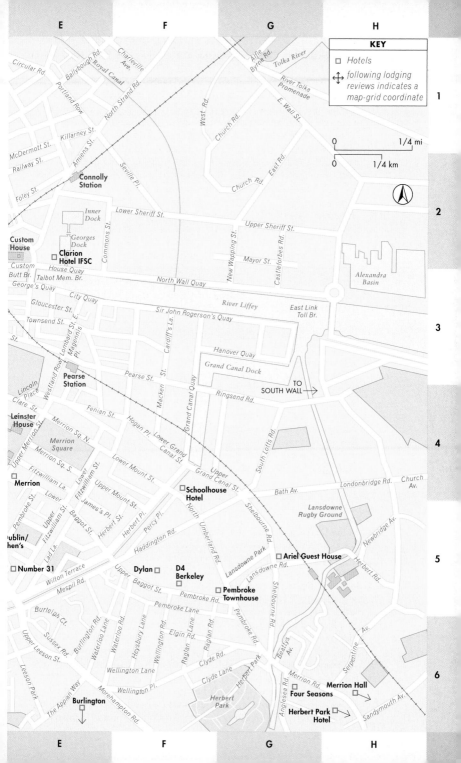

$$$
HOTEL
Fodor's Choice
★
The Shelbourne Dublin, Renaissance. Paris has the Ritz, New York has the Pierre, and Dublin has the Shelbourne—today, newly resplendent in its broad, ornamented, pink-and-white, mid-Victorian facade after a no-expense-spared renovation by the big Marriott chain. **Pros:** afternoon tea in Lord Mayor's Lounge; Irish art worth gazing at; new spa and wellness center; all-around luxury. **Cons:** some noise in front rooms; pricey; feels a little stuffy at times. **TripAdvisor:** "good food and good style," "elegant," "lots of history and tradition." $ *Rooms from: €209* ⊠ *27 St. Stephen's Green, Southside, Dublin, Co. Dublin* ☎ *01/663–4500, 800/543–4300 in U.S.* ⊕ *www.marriott.co.uk/hotels/travel/dubbr-the-shelbourne-dublin-a-renaissance-hotel* ⤴ *246 rooms, 19 suites* ✢ *D4.*

$$$$
HOTEL
Fodor's Choice
★
Westbury Hotel Dublin. This luxurious, chandelier-filled, modern hotel, just off Grafton Street is a favorite with elegantly dressed Dubliners who often stop for afternoon tea in the Gallery, the spacious mezzanine-level main lobby, furnished with a grand piano and a grand view out onto the bustling streets. **Pros:** great service; prime people-watching from the Gallery; great shopping location just off Grafton Street; the art deco glamour of the Marble bar. **Cons:** tries a little too hard to be posh. **TripAdvisor:** "I wish there were six stars to give," "best hotel in the world," "great location." $ *Rooms from: €228* ⊠ *Grafton St., Southside, Dublin, Co. Dublin* ☎ *01/679–1122* ⊕ *www.doylecollection. com* ⤴ *187 rooms, 18 suites* ✢ *D4.*

$$$$
HOTEL
The Westin Dublin. Reconstructed from three 19th-century landmark buildings across the road from Trinity College, the Westin is all about location, but the marble pillars, tall mahogany doorways, blazing fireplaces, Palladian marble busts, and period details are not too shabby either. **Pros:** beside Temple Bar but not in Temple Bar; overlooks Trinity College; in-room spa treatments. **Cons:** on a busy traffic corner; windowless bar; mediocre restaurants; fee for Wi-Fi. **TripAdvisor:** "great and quiet place," "wonderful staff," "terrific location." $ *Rooms from: €220* ⊠ *College Green, Southside, Dublin, Co. Dublin* ☎ *01/645–1000* ⊕ *www.thewestindublin.com* ⤴ *141 rooms, 22 suites* ✢ *D3.*

TEMPLE BAR

$$$
HOTEL
The Clarence. Temple Bar's most prestigious hotel, and occasional home to your potential new best friends/elevator buddies, co-owners Bono and the Edge of U2, this renovated 1852 grand old hotel is the place to be to sample Temple Bar's nightlife, even if your pals are too busy rocking to hang. **Pros:** stylish Octagon Bar; the owners might be on-premises; Tea Room restaurant. **Cons:** rooms a bit small; some rooms suffer from street noise; paying a premium for "cool." **TripAdvisor:** "terrific downtown location," "a real pleasure," "nice hotel." $ *Rooms from: €189* ⊠ *6–8 Wellington Quay, Temple Bar, Dublin, Co. Dublin* ☎ *01/407–0800* ⊕ *www.theclarence.ie* ⤴ *44 rooms, 5 suites* ✢ *C3.*

$
HOTEL
George Frederic Handel Hotel. Right in the heart of Temple Bar, this basic but well-run hotel somehow manages to feel like something of an oasis from the hustle of this lively neighborhood. **Pros:** great location for nightlife in Temple Bar; great value; staff extra attentive. **Cons:** rooms are small; noisy neighborhood; a little short on amenities. **TripAdvisor:**

"terrific location," "spacious room," "excellent staff." Ⓢ *Rooms from: €99* ✉ *16–18 Fishamble St., Temple Bar, Dublin, Co. Dublin* ☎ *01/670–9404* ⊕ *www.georgefrederichandelhotel.com* ⤳ *40 rooms* ✛ *C3.*

$$ Ⓣ **The Morgan.** A sparkling gem among a lot of very drab hotels in
HOTEL Temple Bar, the Morgan boasts about its chic design and decor, and the
★ excitingly designed bedrooms and luxurious, colorful bathrooms are indeed pleasing to the eyes of many fashionistas and photographers who love this place. **Pros:** individually designed bathrooms; great cocktail bar; extended-stay apartments are good value. **Cons:** a little overdesigned in places; no parking; no restaurant. **TripAdvisor:** "great location," "amazing," "party time." Ⓢ *Rooms from: €126* ✉ *10 Fleet St., Temple Bar, Dublin, Co. Dublin* ☎ *01/643–7000* ⊕ *www.themorgan. com* ⤳ *107 rooms, 14 suites* ✛ *D3.*

$$ Ⓣ **Paramount Hotel.** Classic 1930s American movies seem to have been
HOTEL the inspiration for the look of this medium-size hotel in the heart of Temple Bar—dark woods and subtle colors decorate the bedrooms, continuing the look that seems very 1930s (if not Bogie and Bacall). **Pros:** stylish, integrated design; right in the heart of Temple Bar's action; good value during the week. **Cons:** street noise can be a problem; no a/c; fills up on weekends. **TripAdvisor:** "very pleasant stay," "in the heart of it," "it's worth the location." Ⓢ *Rooms from: €139* ✉ *Parliament St. and Essex Gate, Temple Bar, Dublin, Co. Dublin* ☎ *01/417–9900* ⊕ *www.paramounthotel.ie* ⤳ *64 rooms* ✛ *C3.*

NORTHSIDE

$ Ⓣ **Academy Plaza Hotel.** This modern, architecturally uninspired Best
HOTEL Western Plus hotel is centrally located just off O'Connell Street and
★ offers lots of comfort at an affordable, slightly-unfashionable-neighborhood price. **Pros:** soundproof windows; recently renovated; choice of restaurants. **Cons:** unfashionable location; rooms are not huge; bland exterior. **TripAdvisor:** "very pleasant stay," "friendly staff," "lovely welcome." Ⓢ *Rooms from: €109* ✉ *10–14 Findlater Pl., Northside, Dublin, Co. Dublin* ☎ *01/878–0666* ⊕ *www.academyplazahotel.ie* ⤳ *274 rooms, 12 suites* ✛ *D2.*

$ Ⓣ **Castle Hotel.** Staying in a good-value Georgian house on the Northside
HOTEL can be a hit-and-miss affair quality-wise, but the Castle underwent a
Fodor's Choice major renovation, which makes the most of the lovely Georgian set-
★ ting by maintaining the period staircases, original plasterwork, antique mirrors, and open fires in the winter. **Pros:** owner-managed; great Georgian original features; newly renovated public areas; live trad music on weekends. **Cons:** small rooms; some street noise; fee for parking. **TripAdvisor:** "quite a pleasant stay," "nice Georgian stay," "good service." Ⓢ *Rooms from: €99* ✉ *2–4 Great Denmark St., Northside, Dublin, Co. Dublin* ☎ *01/874–6949* ⊕ *www.castle-hotel.ie* ⤳ *133 rooms* ✛ *D2.*

$ Ⓣ **Charleville Lodge.** If Dublin's city center is a Georgian wonder, a
B&B/INN short commute/15-minute walk to the historic Phibsborough area of Dublin's Northside will transport you to the Victorian 19th century and to this lodge comprising a row of completely restored terraced houses. **Pros:** good value; near Phoenix Park. **Cons:** outside the city center; two-night minimum on some rooms in summer weekends; no

Few other hotels enjoy such beloved and landmark status as the Shelbourne.

One of the new breed of boutique hotels, La Stampa delivers European high style.

elevator; few antiques. **TripAdvisor:** "an amazing stay," "nice little place," "comfortable." ⑤ *Rooms from: €75* ⊠ *268–272 N. Circular Rd., Northside, Phibsborough, Dublin, Co. Dublin* ☎ *01/838–6633* ⊕ *www.charlevillelodge.ie* ⤴ *30 rooms* ⦿⦿ *Breakfast* ✛ *C1.*

$ 🏨 **Clarion Hotel Dublin City (IFSC).** Built with business guests in mind, this
HOTEL high-rise hotel in the middle of the International Financial Services Centre has been a surprise hit with all travelers interested in the business of good value and clean, quiet rooms with good amenities. **Pros:** weekend bargains available; room to swing a couple of cats in big rooms; area rural-quiet at night. **Cons:** room design pretty functional; business clientele; no buzz at night. **TripAdvisor:** "great location," "great staff," "will definitely be back again." ⑤ *Rooms from: €115* ⊠ *IFSC, Northside, Dublin, Co. Dublin* ☎ *01/433–8800* ⊕ *www.clarionhotelifsc.com* ⤴ *165 rooms, 14 suites* ✛ *E2.*

$$ 🏨 **Gresham Hotel Dublin.** Opened in 1817, it's been a while since this
HOTEL O'Connell Street landmark was an upmarket place to stay north of the river—but an overhaul in 2006 and a drop in price have made the Gresham a solid city-center option again. **Pros:** great value for city center; great views down O'Connell Street. **Cons:** bar and public areas can get busy; room design unexciting; they can bump prices on busy weekends. **TripAdvisor:** "beautiful," "good staff," "great location." ⑤ *Rooms from: €125* ⊠ *23 Upper O'Connell St., Northside, Dublin, Co. Dublin* ☎ *01/874–6881* ⊕ *www.gresham-hotels-dublin.com* ⤴ *279 rooms, 9 suites* ✛ *D2.*

$ 🏨 **Marian Guest House.** A veritable Everest of fine Irish meats, the Mar-
B&B/INN ian's mighty Irish breakfast, with black pudding and smoked bacon, is reason enough to stay at this family-run redbrick guesthouse just off beautiful Mountjoy Square. **Pros:** excellent breakfast; family-owned and -run; small. **Cons:** located in a slightly run-down part of the city; gets some street noise; fairly basic rooms. **TripAdvisor:** "great little bed and breakfast," "highly recommended," "good base to explore." ⑤ *Rooms from: €70* ⊠ *21 Upper Gardiner St., Northside, Dublin, Co. Dublin* ☎ *01/874–4129* ⊕ *www.marianguesthouse.ie* ⤴ *6 rooms* ⦿⦿ *Breakfast* ✛ *D1.*

$$ 🏨 **The Morrison Hotel.** An 18th-century Georgian mansion + design over-
HOTEL haul (that includes toiletries and staff uniforms) by Ireland's top fashion guru, John Rocha = trendy boutique hotel and place to be seen by Dublin's nighthawks. **Pros:** people-watching in cocktail bar; intensely designed rooms; located near O'Connell Bridge. **Cons:** tries a little too hard to be cool; located on busy road. **TripAdvisor:** "nice rooms and lovely gym," "great location," "comfy bed." ⑤ *Rooms from: €130* ⊠ *Ormond Quay, Northside, Dublin, Co. Dublin* ☎ *01/887–2400* ⊕ *www.morrisonhotel.ie* ⤴ *120 rooms, 18 suites* ✛ *C3.*

$$ 🏨 **Wynn's Hotel.** A few doors down from the Abbey Theatre, Wynn's
HOTEL began its life as a Dublin boarding house in 1845 and its beautiful stained-glass awning has become something of a landmark—as a romantic meeting spot for locals—on the Northside. **Pros:** great location for theater fans; feels like a genuine full-service hotel; a touch of history about the place. **Cons:** decor can fell a bit hodge-podge; rooms aren't huge; can be some noise from ballroom downstairs.

TripAdvisor: "hotel with real character," "absolutely perfect," "very friendly." ⑤ *Rooms from: €129* ✉ *35–39 Lower Abbey St., Northside, Dublin, Co. Dublin* ☎ *01/874–5131* ⊕ *www.wynnshotel.ie* ⤳ *65 rooms* ⦿ *No meals* ✛ *D2.*

BALLSBRIDGE

$ 🏠 **Ariel Guest House.** The homemade preserves and oven-warm scones are reason enough to stay at this redbrick 1850 Victorian guesthouse, in one of Dublin's poshest tree-lined suburbs and a 15-minute walk from St. Stephen's Green. **Pros:** four-poster beds in larger rooms; fantastic collection of Victoriana throughout the house; good price for smaller rooms. **Cons:** no longer run by owner; no elevator; a good walk to the city center. **TripAdvisor:** "gorgeous house and amazing staff," "stunning breakfasts," "elegant." ⑤ *Rooms from: €110* ✉ *52 Lansdowne Rd., Ballsbridge, Dublin, Co. Dublin* ☎ *01/668–5512* ⊕ *www.ariel-house.net* ⤳ *37 rooms* ⦿ *Breakfast* ✛ *G5.*

$$ 🏨 **Burlington Hotel.** If you want to meet the Ballsbridge locals, then spend
HOTEL a night at the Burlington. **Pros:** a Dublin institution; large, light-filled rooms; part of a small, Irish-owned group. **Cons:** looks a little bit like a parking garage; staff not as experienced as they used to be; very big. **TripAdvisor:** "great staff," "friendly, efficient service," "super hotel." ⑤ *Rooms from: €150* ✉ *Upper Leeson St., Ballsbridge, Dublin, Co. Dublin* ☎ *01/618–5600* ⊕ *www.burlingtonhotel.ie* ⤳ *500 rooms, 6 suites* ✛ *E6.*

$$ 🏨 **D4 Berkley.** This former high-end favorite has been reborn as a more
HOTEL modest, contemporary hotel experience with much lower prices to match. **Pros:** great price for the upmarket location; facilities of nearby sister hotels available to guests; huge suites are good value for families. **Cons:** attracts a lot of conferences; service not as strong as it used to be. **TripAdvisor:** "extremely friendly," "very nicely appointed," "good choice of food." ⑤ *Rooms from: €130* ✉ *Pembroke Rd., Ballsbridge, Dublin, Co. Dublin* ☎ *143/73444* ⊕ *www.d4berkeley.ie* ⤳ *156 rooms, 26 suites* ✛ *F5.*

$$$ 🏨 **Dylan Hotel.** A symphony of "Victorian Contemporary Fusion" with
HOTEL Arts and Crafts stained glass, bordello brocades, spray-painted silver furnishings, and lordly antiques, this unique hotel in an old Victorian building is a racy addition to the sometimes-staid Dublin scene. **Pros:** great spot for a romantic weekend; individually designed rooms; property is big enough to ensure privacy, small enough to still feel intimate. **Cons:** hit-or-miss restaurant; hasn't fully adjusted prices in downturn. **TripAdvisor:** "so very chic," "very cool and nonchalant," "Dublin in style." ⑤ *Rooms from: €209* ✉ *Eastmoreland Pl., Ballsbridge, Dublin, Co. Dublin* ☎ *01/660–3000* ⊕ *www.dylan.ie* ⤳ *38 rooms, 6 suites* ✛ *F5.*

$$$$ 🏨 **Four Seasons Hotel Dublin.** Set within the showgrounds of the Royal
HOTEL Dublin Society, this Victorian-Georgian hybrid—topped by gigantic
Fodor'sChoice eaves and a lovely cupola—looks like the real McCoy but was in fact
★ an extravaganza built during the boomtime excesses of the brash Celtic Tiger era. **Pros:** one of the country's top spas; prices have dropped considerably; Lobby Lounge great for afternoon tea. **Cons:** a bit of an architectural mishmash; room design not the most inventive. **TripAdvisor:**

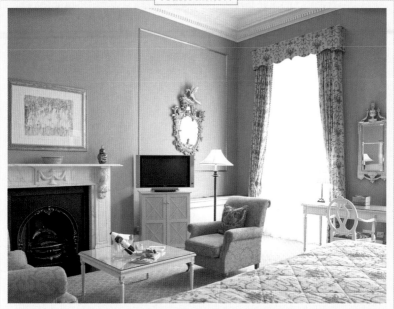

The Merrion began life as the residence of the first Duke of Wellington.

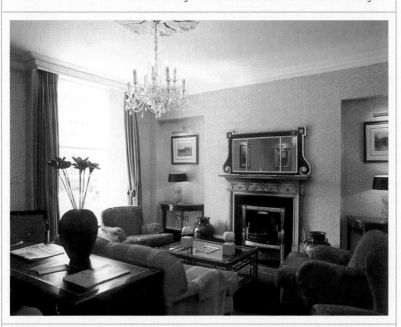

The Pembroke Townhouse gives Georgian style a delightful 21st-century spin.

"favorite hotel in Dublin," "a regular and a favorite," "great service." ⑤ *Rooms from: €230* ✉ *Simmonscourt Rd., Ballsbridge, Dublin, Co. Dublin* ☎ *01/665–4000* ⊕ *www.fourseasons.com/dublin* ⤳ *157 rooms, 40 suites* ✣ *G6.*

$$
HOTEL

🛏 **Herbert Park Hotel.** You're only a short distance from the city but you'll feel much farther away in this independently owned hotel, nestled next to leafy Herbert Park and the doddering Dodder River. **Pros:** independently owned hotel; terrace dining in summer; Sunday jazz buffet is a treat. **Cons:** looks like an office block; rooms not too exciting; a bit outside the city center. **TripAdvisor:** "lovely," "a comfortable stay," "nice modern hotel." ⑤ *Rooms from: €129* ✉ *Merrion Rd., Ballsbridge, Dublin, Co. Dublin* ☎ *35/3667–2200* ⊕ *www.herbertparkhotel.ie* ⤳ *150 rooms, 3 suites* ✣ *H6.*

$$
B&B/INN

🛏 **Merrion Hall.** Ivy covers this secluded redbrick Edwardian town house, and a *Room with a View* atmosphere is created with a wonderfully stuffy afternoon tea (and also fine wines) served in the bay-windowed drawing room overlooking the Ballsbridge street. **Pros:** lovely Edwardian building; luxurious suites; beautiful neighborhood. **Cons:** suites are relatively expensive; limited facilities; no elevator. **TripAdvisor:** "old-school flavor with modern convenience," "one of the best," "amazing experience." ⑤ *Rooms from: €120* ✉ *54 Merrion Rd., Ballsbridge, Dublin, Co. Dublin* ☎ *01/668–1426* ⊕ *www.merrionhall.com* ⤳ *34 rooms* ✣ *H6.*

$
B&B/INN
Fodor'sChoice
★

🛏 **Pembroke Townhouse.** "Townhouse" does not do justice to the splendor of the place, but it does hint at the cozy, relaxed atmosphere of the Pembroke, a superb example of classic 18th-century grandeur. **Pros:** a Georgian wonderland; big, airy rooms; privately owned. **Cons:** 15-minute trip to the city center; often books out early; no a/c. **TripAdvisor:** "excellent accommodation," "genuine hospitality," "lovely breakfast." ⑤ *Rooms from: €99* ✉ *90 Pembroke Rd., Ballsbridge, Dublin, Co. Dublin* ☎ *01/660–0277* ⊕ *www.pembroketownhouse.ie* ⤳ *41 rooms, 7 suites* ✣ *F5.*

$$$
HOTEL
Fodor'sChoice
★

🛏 **Schoolhouse Hotel.** Excuse the pun, but this converted Victorian parochial school just off the Grand Canal really is A-plus—set in a gorgeous example of Irish 19th-century architecture complete with turrets and soaring nave (now the setting for the restaurant), this may be the most uniquely recycled hotel in Ireland. **Pros:** unique building; top-class Irish restaurant; in-room spa treatments. **Cons:** a trip to the city center; fills up quickly; no minibars; no elevator. **TripAdvisor:** "first class," "beautiful hotel with wonderful food," "helpful staff." ⑤ *Rooms from: €175* ✉ *2–8 Northumberland Rd., Ballsbridge, Dublin, Co. Dublin* ☎ *01/667–5014* ⊕ *www.schoolhousehotel.com* ⤳ *31 rooms* ✣ *F4.*

DUBLIN WEST

$
HOTEL

🛏 **Bewley's Hotel Newlands Cross.** This four-story franchise hotel on the southwest outskirts of the city is, in two words, cheap and cheerful. **Pros:** great value for families; good location for further travels; Bewley's delicious coffee in the morning. **Cons:** mainly business clientele; not convenient to the city center; overlooks the expressway. **TripAdvisor:** "amazing metro-meets-modern accommodation," "comfortable stay," "well worth a visit." $ *Rooms from: €69* ⊠ *Newlands Cross at Naas Rd., Dublin West, Dublin, Co. Dublin* ☎ *01/464–0140* ⊕ *bewleyshotels. com/newlands_cross* ⟲ *299 rooms* ✛ *A3.*

$ ⚆ **Jurys Inn Christchurch.** Expect few frills at this functional budget hotel,
HOTEL   on a hill facing Christ Church Cathedral and within walking distance
of most city-center attractions. **Pros:** good value for families; views
of Christ Church; near Temple Bar. **Cons:** ugly building; basic, func-
tional rooms; tends to be popular with bachelor(ette) parties. **Trip-
Advisor:** "comfortable," "fantastic stay," "great location." $ *Rooms
from: €109* ⊠ *Christ Church Pl., Dublin West, Dublin, Co. Dublin*
☎ *01/454–0000* ⊕ *dublinhotels.jurysinns.com/jurysinn_christchurch*
⟲ *182 rooms* ✛ *B4.*

$ ⚆ **Maldron Hotel Smithfield.** On Smithfield Plaza, this snazzy, good-value
HOTEL   hotel is at the heart of Dublin's refurbished old-market district area.
Pros: located on an open plaza; great views from rooms in front on
higher floors; under-floor heating in bathrooms. **Cons:** no proper res-
taurant. **TripAdvisor:** "a little out of the way," "excellent service,"
"terrific stay." $ *Rooms from: €99* ⊠ *Smithfield Village, Dublin West,
Dublin, Co. Dublin* ☎ *01/485–0900* ⊕ *www.maldronhotels.com* ⟲ *85
rooms, 7 suites* ✛ *B2.*

$$ ⚆ **Radisson Blu Royal Hotel, Dublin.** The sleek glass-and-concrete Radis-
HOTEL   son, just off South Great George's Street, offers to-the-point business
accommodations with a dash of cool contemporary style, proof positive that it is possible to be elegant and functional at the same time.
Pros: right in the heart of "real Dublin"; stylish, understated decor;
landscaped rooftop terrace. **Cons:** looks out over a block of flats; restaurant is hit or miss; mostly business clientele. **TripAdvisor:** "prime location," "comfortable," "excellent quality and location." $ *Rooms from:
€140* ⊠ *Golden La., Dublin West, Dublin, Co. Dublin* ☎ *01/898–2900*
⊕ *www.radissonblu.ie/royalhotel-dublin* ⟲ *138 rooms, 12 suites* ✛ *C4.*

NIGHTLIFE AND THE ARTS

Long before Stephen Dedalus's excursions into "Nighttown" in James
Joyce's *Ulysses,* Dublin was proud of its lively after-hours scene, particularly its thriving pubs. But the now tamed Celtic Tiger economy, once
the envy of all Europe, turned Dublin into one of the most happening
destinations on the whole continent. Things have calmed down in the
last few years, but the city's 900-plus pubs are still its main source of
entertainment; many public houses in the city center have live music—
from rock to jazz to traditional Irish.

Theater is an essential element of life in the city that was home to
O'Casey, Synge, W.B. Yeats, and Beckett. Today Dublin has seven major
theaters that reproduce the Irish "classics," and also present newer fare
from the likes of Martin McDonagh and Conor McPherson. Opera,
long overlooked, now has a home in the restored old Gaiety Theatre.

Check the *Irish Times* and the *Evening Herald* newspapers for event
listings, as well the *Big Issue* and the *Event Guide*—weekly guides to
film, theater, and musical events around the city. In peak season, consult
the free Fáilte Ireland (Irish Tourist Board) leaflet "Events of the Week."

NIGHTLIFE

Live music has replaced DJs in a lot of Dublin nightspots, but in Dublin's dance clubs the dominant sound is still hip-hop and house music, and the crowd that flocks to them every night of the week is of the trendy, under-30 generation. Leeson Street—just off St. Stephen's Green, south of the Liffey, and known as "the strip"—is a slightly frayed and uncool nightclub area aimed at the over-30 crowd that revs up at pub closing time and stays active until 4 am. The dress code at Leeson Street's dance clubs is informal, but jeans and sneakers are not welcome. Most of these clubs are licensed only to sell wine, and the prices can be exorbitant (up to €30 for a mediocre bottle); the upside is that most don't charge to get in.

Despite rampant remodeling during the boom years, the traditional pub has steadfastly clung to its role as the primary center of Dublin's social life. The city has nearly 1,000 pubs ("licensed tabernacles," writer Flann O'Brien calls them). And although the vision of elderly men enjoying a chin wag over a creamy pint of stout has become something of a rarity, there are still plenty of places where you can enjoy a quiet (or not so quiet) drink and a chat. Last drinks are called at 11:30 pm Monday to Thursday, 12:30 am Friday and Saturday, and 11 pm on Sunday. Some city-center pubs have extended opening hours and don't serve last drinks until 1:45 am.

As a general rule, the area between Grafton and Great George's streets is a gold mine for classy pubs. Another good bet is the Temple Bar district (though some of the newer ones are all plastic and mirrors). And if it's real spit-on-the-floor hideaways you're after, head across the Liffey to the areas around Parnell Square or Smithfield. Beware of the tourist-trap, faux-traditional pubs where you can hardly hear the music for the roar of the seven flat-screen TVs.

Most pubs serve food at lunchtime, many throughout the day and into the early evening. This is an inexpensive way to eat out, and the quality of the food is often quite good.

■TIP→ If you will need late-night transportation, try to arrange it with your hotel before you go out.

Use the coordinate (✛ B2) at the end of each pub listing to locate a site on the corresponding Dublin Pubs map.

SOUTHSIDE
IRISH CABARET, MUSIC, AND DANCING

★ **Bewley's Café Theatre.** With its intimate nights in this small, Victorian venue, Bewley's Café Theatre has become the atmospheric cabaret hot spot in Dublin. Set in the Oriental Room on the second floor above the glorious, stained-glass jewel that is the Grafton Street restaurant, the unique lunchtime performances here—a one-act play by O'Casey or Wilde with a bowl of soup and soda bread—are also noteworthy. ⊠ *Grafton St., 78/79 Grafton St., 2nd floor, Southside, Dublin, Co. Dublin* ☎ *086/878–4001* ⊕ *www.bewleyscafetheatre.com.*

The Sugar Club. A landmark venue with tables, the Sugar Club has regular performance (some touted as "burlesque") nights. ⊠ *8 Lwr. Leeson St., Southside, Dublin, Co. Dublin* ☎ *01/678–7188* ⊕ *www.thesugarclub.com.*

2

JAZZ

Ha'penny Bridge Inn. In its tiny but buzzing upstairs room, the Ha'penny Bridge regularly hosts blues and jazz nights. ✉ *42 Wellington Quay, Southside, Dublin, Co. Dublin* ☎ *01/677–0616.*

JJ Smyth's. An old-time jazz venue, JJ Smyth's hosts the Pendulum Club—a popular hangout for all "jazz heads"—on Sundays. Live music all week. ✉ *12 Aungier St., Southside, Dublin, Co. Dublin* ☎ *01/475–2565* ⊕ *www.jjsmyths.com.*

The Mint Bar. A basement venue set in a former bank vault, the Mint Bar presents the Velvet Lounge band and other jazz groups on Wednesday to Saturday nights. ✉ *Westin Hotel, College Green, Southside, Dublin, Co. Dublin* ☎ *01/645–1000* ⊕ *www.thewestindublin.com/the-mint-bar.*

NIGHTCLUBS

ALT. Once a bastion of experimental theatre, Andrew's Lane Theatre has been reborn as ALT, a cozy club with regular live indie gigs. ✉ *Andrews Lane, Southside, Dublin, Co. Dublin* ☎ *01/478–0766* ⊕ *www. andrewslane.com.*

Fodor's Choice ★ **Lillie's Bordello.** Once the hot spot for celebs, Lillie's Bordello is now more for regular Joes: a popular hangout for a young late-night crowd. Hot or not, the decor remains a knockout: Victorian brocaded velvets and gilded frames plus pink and purple neon lasers. Take a rest from the dance floor in the gorgeous Library room. ✉ *Grafton St., Southside, Dublin, Co. Dublin* ☎ *01/679–9204* ⊕ *www.lilliesbordello.ie.*

Rí Ra. Part of the hugely popular Globe bar, Rí Ra has lost some of its shine in recent years. The name means "uproar" in Irish, and on most nights the place does go a little wild. Upstairs is more low-key. ✉ *Dame Ct., Southside, Dublin, Co. Dublin* ☎ *01/677–4835* ⊕ *www.rira.ie.*

PUBS

Cassidy's. Once a quality neighborhood pub with a tasty pint of stout, Cassidy's has morphed into an often overcrowded but very popular spot with young revelers. ✉ *42 Lower Camden St., Southside, Dublin, Co. Dublin* ☎ *01/475–6540* ✛ *D5.*

Cellar Bar. An 18th-century wine vault with bare brick walls and vaulted ceilings, this spot at the superstylish Merrion Hotel tends to draw a well-heeled crowd. ✉ *24 Upper Merrion St., Southside, Dublin, Co. Dublin* ☎ *01/603–0600* ⊕ *www.merrionhotel.com* ✛ *E4.*

Davy Byrne's. A noted pilgrimage stop for Joyceans, Davy Byrne's is where Leopold Bloom stops in for a glass of Burgundy and a Gorgonzola-cheese sandwich in *Ulysses* (and ruminates before helping a blind man cross the road). Unfortunately, the decor—quite an eyeful, with its gaudily painted ceiling, stained-glass cupola, and blush pastels—is greatly changed from Joyce's day ("He entered Davy Byrnes. Moral pub."), but it still serves some fine pub grub. ✉ *21 Duke St., Southside, Dublin, Co. Dublin* ☎ *167/75217* ⊕ *www.davybyrnes.com* ✛ *D4.*

Doheny & Nesbitt. A traditional spot with snugs, dark wooden furnishings, and smoke-darkened ceilings, Doheny & Nesbitt has hardly changed over the decades. ✉ *4–5 Lower Baggot St., Southside, Dublin, Co. Dublin* ☎ *01/676–2945* ⊕ *dohenyandnesbitts.com* ✛ *E4.*

Doyle's In Town. A small, cozy pub, Doyle's is a favorite with journalists from the *Irish Times* office, just across the street. ⊠ *9 College St., Southside, Dublin, Co. Dublin* ☎ *01/671–0616* ⊕ *www.doylesintown.com* ⊹ *E3.*

George. Dublin's two-floor main gay pub, George draws an almost entirely male crowd; its nightclub stays open until 2:30 am nightly except Tuesday. The "alternative bingo night," with star drag act Miss Shirley Temple Bar, is a riot of risqué fun. SaturGays are always packed. ⊠ *89 S. Great George's St., Southside, Dublin, Co. Dublin* ☎ *01/478–2983* ⊕ *www.thegeorge.ie* ⊹ *D3.*

The Globe. Once the hippest café-bar in town, Globe still draws trendy, hipster Dubliners who sip espresso drinks by day and pack the place at night. There's live Rockabilly on Sunday. ⊠ *11 S. Great George's St., Southside, Dublin, Co. Dublin* ☎ *01/671–1220* ⊕ *www.globe.ie* ⊹ *D3.*

Fodor'sChoice
★ **Grogans.** Also known as the Castle Lounge, Grogans is a small place packed with creative folk. Owner Tommy Grogan is known as a patron of local artists, and his walls are covered with their work. ⊠ *15 S. William St., Southside, Dublin, Co. Dublin* ☎ *01/677–9320* ⊹ *D3.*

Hogan's. A huge space on two levels, Hogan's gets jammed most nights, but the old place maintains its style through it all. ⊠ *35 S. Great George's St., Southside, Dublin, Co. Dublin* ☎ *01/677–5904* ⊹ *D4.*

★ **Horseshoe Bar.** A recent massive face-lift, along with the rest of the Shelbourne hotel, made the Horseshoe Bar the hottest ticket in town. There's comparatively little space for drinkers around the famous semicircular bar—but this does wonders for making friends quickly. ⊠ *Shelbourne, 27 St. Stephen's Green, Southside, Dublin, Co. Dublin* ☎ *01/676–6471* ⊕ *www.marriott.co.uk* ⊹ *E4.*

Kehoe's. Popular with Trinity students and cynical journalists, Kehoe's has a tiny back room that is nice and cozy, while the upstairs is basically the owner's old living room, open to the public. ⊠ *9 S. Anne St., Southside, Dublin, Co. Dublin* ☎ *01/677–8312* ⊹ *D4.*

Lesson Lounge. This has the look of a classic old Dublin "boozer," with one notable exception: it has a television. The Lesson is known as a place to watch televised sports of all kinds, and it's always pleasant and inclusive. ⊠ *148 Upper Lesson St., Southside, Dublin, Co. Dublin* ☎ *01/660–3816* ⊹ *E6.*

★ **Library Bar.** The place to go when you're ready to get away from all the madness, the Library has book-lined shelves, big armchairs and

> ### WORD OF MOUTH
>
> "Here's a cool marketing fact we never knew before: Do you know the *Guinness World Records*? Of course you do. Well, it was originally created as an advertising tool. One of the execs back in the 1950s wanted to settle a barroom bet he made with someone, and didn't have a way of finding an answer—so he came up with the idea to publish a book containing every record imaginable. That way, they could sell them for use in bars around the world, so that the Guinness name would always be there to settle bets. Who knew?"
>
> —Erin74

sofas, and a blazing fireplace—all in all, this first-floor hideaway is one of the most serene nighttime spots in Dublin. ⊠ *Central Hotel, 1–5 Exchequer St., Southside, Dublin, Co. Dublin* ☎ *01/679–7302* ⊕ *www. centralhoteldublin.com* ✛ *D3.*

Long Hall Pub. One of Dublin's most ornate traditional taverns, the Long Hall has Victorian lamps, a mahogany bar, mirrors, chandeliers, and plasterwork ceilings, all more than 100 years old. The pub serves sandwiches and an excellent pint of Guinness. ⊠ *51 S. Great George's St., Southside, Dublin, Co. Dublin* ☎ *01/475–1590* ✛ *D4.*

McDaid's. A landmark that once attracted boisterous Brendan Behan and other leading writers in the 1950s, McDaid's wild literary reputation still lingers, although the bar has been discreetly modernized and is altogether quieter. ⊠ *3 Harry St., Southside, Dublin, Co. Dublin* ☎ *01/679–4395* ✛ *D4.*

Mulligan's. Synonymous in Dublin with a truly perfect pint of Guinness, Mulligan's started life as a *shebeen* (unlicensed drinking venue) and then, pub lore tells us, was listed as "legal" since 1782. Until a few years ago no women were admitted. Today journalists, locals, and students of both sexes flock here for a good pint. ⊠ *8 Poolbeg St., Southside, Dublin, Co. Dublin* ☎ *01/677–5582* ⊕ *www.mulligans.ie* ✛ *E3.*

Neary's. With an exotic, Victorian-style interior, Neary's was once the haunt of music-hall artists and a certain literary set, including Brendan Behan. Join the actors from the adjacent Gaiety Theatre for a good pub lunch. ⊠ *1 Chatham St., Southside, Dublin, Co. Dublin* ☎ *01/677–7371* ✛ *D4.*

O'Donoghue's. A cheerful, tourist-friendly hangout, O'Donoghue's has impromptu musical performances that often spill out onto the street. ⊠ *15 Merrion Row, Southside, Dublin, Co. Dublin* ☎ *01/676–2807* ⊕ *www.odonoghues.ie* ✛ *E4.*

The Old Stand. One of the oldest pubs in the city, the Old Stand is named after the now demolished Old Stand at Lansdowne Road stadium, home to Irish rugby and football. The pub is renowned for great pints and fine steaks. ⊠ *37 Exchequer St., Southside, Dublin, Co. Dublin* ☎ *01/677–7220* ✛ *D3.*

Peter's Pub. The epitome of the cozy little boozer, Peter's Pub hugs a busy corner where people-watching becomes an art at the outside tables in summer. ⊠ *Johnson Place, Southside, Dublin, Co. Dublin* ☎ *01/677–8588* ✛ *D4.*

Fodor'sChoice ★ **The Secret Bar.** Considering itself too hip to even have a name when it opened, the Secret has finally decided to play on its hidden-away vibe. Above the wonderful L'Gueuleton restaurant this open-plan, buzzing bar even has a cute little covered patio. ⊠ *1 Fade St., Southside, Dublin, Co. Dublin* ☎ *01/675–3708* ✛ *D4.*

Fodor'sChoice ★ **Stag's Head.** A Victorian beaut, the Stag's Head dates from 1770 and was rebuilt in 1895. Theater people from the nearby Olympia, journalists, and Trinity students gather around the unusual Connemara red-marble bar, study their reflections in the many mirrors, and drink in all the oak carvings. ⊠ *1 Dame Ct., Southside, Dublin, Co. Dublin* ☎ *01/679–3701* ✛ *D3.*

Toner's. Though billed as a Victorian bar, Toner's actually goes back 200 years, with an original flagstone floor to prove its antiquity, as well as wooden drawers running up to the ceiling—a relic of the days when bars doubled as grocery shops. Oliver St. John Gogarty, who was the model for Buck Mulligan in James Joyce's *Ulysses*, accompanied W. B. Yeats here, in what was purportedly the latter's only visit to a pub. ⊠ *139 Lower Baggot St., Southside, Dublin, Co. Dublin* ☎ *01/676–3090* ⊕ *www.tonerspub.ie* ✢ *E5.*

TEMPLE BAR
NIGHTCLUBS

Button Factory. A happening music venue, the Button mixes top DJs and up-and-coming live acts. ⊠ *Curved St., Temple Bar, Dublin, Co. Dublin* ☎ *01/670–9202* ⊕ *www.buttonfactory.ie.*

Club M. Club M is an old-school-disco-type venue, popular with the suburban crowd in town for the night. Their theme nights—like "school disco"—tend to pack the place. ⊠ *Cope St., Temple Bar, Dublin, Co. Dublin* ☎ *01/671–5274* ⊕ *www.clubm.ie.*

The Turk's Head. The Turk's Head pub-cum-nightclub is known for its extravagant mosaics, Moroccan woodwork, bits of Arabian Nights decor, and its world culture (i.e., Latin, reggae, funk, and flamenco) late nights. ⊠ *Paramount Hotel, 27–30 Parliament St., Temple Bar, Dublin, Co. Dublin* ☎ *01/679–9701* ⊕ *www.paramounthotel.ie/turks-head.html* ✢ *C3.*

The Workman's Club. This no-frills, hip spot specializes in Indie club nights and attracts an artistic and hipster crowd. It has three floors of music and live gigs. Check the website for upcoming nights. ⊠ *10 Wellington Quay, Temple Bar, Dublin, Co. Dublin* ☎ *01/670–6692* ⊕ *www.theworkmansclub.com.*

PUBS

The Front Lounge. A modern pub, the Front Lounge caters to a mixed crowd of young professionals, both gay and straight. ⊠ *33–34 Parliament St., Temple Bar, Dublin, Co. Dublin* ☎ *01/670–4112* ⊕ *www.thefrontlounge.ie* ✢ *D3.*

Oliver St John Gogarty. A lively bar that attracts all ages and nationalities, the Oliver St. John Gogarty overflows with patrons in summer. On most nights there's traditional Irish music upstairs. ⊠ *57 Fleet St., Temple Bar, Dublin, Co. Dublin* ☎ *01/671–1822* ⊕ *www.gogartys.ie* ✢ *D3.*

Palace Bar. Scarcely changed since the 1940s, the Palace Bar is tiled and rather barren looking, but is popular with journalists and writers (the *Irish Times* is nearby). The walls are lined with cartoons drawn by newspaper illustrators. ⊠ *21 Fleet St., Temple Bar, Dublin, Co. Dublin* ☎ *01/677–9290* ✢ *D3.*

The Porterhouse. One of the few bars in Ireland to brew its own beer, the Plain Porter has won the best stout award at the "Brewing Oscars," beating out the mighty Guinness. The tasteful interior is all dark woods and soft lighting. ⊠ *16–18 Parliament St., Temple Bar, Dublin, Co. Dublin* ☎ *01/679–8847* ⊕ *www.porterhousebrewco.com* ✢ *C3.*

THE NORTHSIDE
NIGHTCLUBS

The Academy. A music mecca with four floors of entertainment of every kind, the Academy is anchored by big-name local and international DJs and gigs. It attracts a young, dance-crazy crowd who like to party until the wee hours. ⊠ *57 Middle Abbey St., Northside, Dublin, Co. Dublin* ☎ *01/877–9999* ⊕ *www.theacademydublin.com.*

The Church. The sacrilege of bopping the night away in a former church might add a little spice at this mainstream weekend club. Non-dancing churchgoers can check out the pub and restaurant upstairs. ⊠ *Jervis St., Northside, Dublin, Co. Dublin* ☎ *01/828–0102* ⊕ *www.thechurch. ie/club.aspx.*

PUBS

The Flowing Tide. Directly across from the Abbey Theatre, the Flowing Tide draws a lively pre- and post-theater crowd. No TVs, quality pub talk, and a great pint of Guinness make it a worthwhile visit (although the decor won't win any prizes). ⊠ *Lower Abbey St., Northside, Dublin, Co. Dublin* ☎ *01/874–0842* ✛ *E2.*

Morrison Bar. A modern, stylish bar in one of Dublin's most designer-friendly hotels, this loungy spot overlooks the river it's named after and attracts a crowd that likes to dress up and talk about dressing up. ⊠ *Morrison Hotel, Upper Ormond Quay, Northside, Dublin, Co. Dublin* ☎ *01/878–2999* ⊕ *www.morrisonhotel.ie* ✛ *D3.*

Pantibar. A new, amusingly named gay bar fronted by the infamous Dublin drag queen Panti, this happening place has loud music at night but is pretty chilled-out during the day. ⊠ *7-8 Capel St., Northside, Dublin, Co. Dublin* ☎ *01/874–0710* ⊕ *www.pantibar.com* ✛ *C2.*

BALLSBRIDGE
PUBS

The 51 Bar. Famous for its collection of whiskies from around the world, the 51 has a beer garden that is always buzzing with activity in fine weather. ⊠ *51 Haddington Rd., Ballsbridge, Dublin, Co. Dublin* ☎ *01/660–0150* ⊕ *www.the51bar.com* ✛ *G5.*

The Horse Show House. A Ballsbridge institution, the Horse Show House is a favorite of the boisterous but welcoming rugby and show-jumping set. Great spot to watch sports of any kind. ⊠ *32 Merrion Rd., Ballsbridge, Dublin, Co. Dublin* ☎ *01/668–9424* ✛ *H6.*

DUBLIN WEST
PUBS

★ **Brazen Head.** Reputedly Dublin's oldest pub (the site has been licensed since 1198), the Brazen Head doesn't have much of a time-burnished decor—except for one big exception: an enchanting stone courtyard that is intimate, charming, and delightful. The front is a faux one-story castle, complete with flambeaux, while the interior looks modern day (except for the very low ceilings). People love to jam the place not for its history but for its traditional-music performances and lively sing-along sessions on Sunday evenings. On the south side of the Liffey quays, it's a little difficult to find—turn down Lower Bridge Street and make a

Some say Dubliners now give the Temple Bar district the brush-off; others still find it the pulsing aorta of the city's nightlife.

right onto the old lane. ⊠ *20 Lower Bridge St., Dublin West, Dublin, Co. Dublin* 🕾 *01/677–9549* ⊕ *www.brazenhead.com* ⊹ *B3*.

Cobblestone. A glorious house of ale in the best Dublin tradition, Cobblestone is popular with Smithfield Market workers. Its chatty imbibers and live traditional music are attracting a more varied, younger crowd from all over town. ⊠ *N. King St., Dublin West, Dublin, Co. Dublin* 🕾 *01/872–1799* ⊹ *B2*.

★ **Fallons.** Somehow you always get a seat in this tiny sliver of a pub—a warm, old-school boozer at its best—tucked away on a corner near St. Patrick's Cathedral. ⊠ *129 The Coombe, Dublin West, Dublin, Co. Dublin* 🕾 *01/454–2801* ⊹ *B4*.

★ **Ryan's Pub.** One of Dublin's last genuine, late-Victorian-era pubs, Ryan's has changed little since its last (1896) remodeling. ⊠ *28 Parkgate St., Dublin West, Dublin, Co. Dublin* 🕾 *01/677–6097* ⊹ *A2*.

THE ARTS

CLASSICAL MUSIC AND OPERA
SOUTHSIDE
Grand Canal Theatre. Housed in a spanking new, brash Daniel Liebskind–designed building in the growing docklands area of the city, the Grand Canal Theatre has a 2,000-plus capacity, making it Ireland's biggest theater space. Its calendar includes the best of international ballet, classical music, pop gigs, and even Broadway musicals. ⊠ *Grand Canal Sq., Southside, Dublin, Co. Dublin* 🕾 *01/677–7999* ⊕ *www.grandcanaltheatre.ie.*

★ **The National Concert Hall.** Just off St. Stephen's Green, the National Concert Hall is Dublin's main theater for classical music of all kinds, from symphonies to chamber groups. The slightly austere neoclassical building was transformed in 1981 into one of Europe's finest medium-size concert halls. It houses the cream of Irish classical musicians, the National Symphony Orchestra of Ireland. A host of guest international conductors and performers—Maxim Vengerov, Radu Lupu, and Pinchas Zukerman are just a few of the soloists who have appeared—keep the standard very high, and performances continue throughout the year. The concert year picks up speed in mid-September and sails through to June; July and August also get many dazzling troupes. The smaller, more intimate John Field and Carolan rooms are perfect for chamber music. ⊠ *Earlsfort Terr., Southside, Dublin, Co. Dublin* ☎ *01/417–0000* ⊕ *www.nch.ie.*

St. Stephen's Church. Under its glorious "pepper canister" cupola, St. Stephen's Church stages a tempting program of choral and orchestral events. ⊠ *Upper Mount St., Southside, Dublin, Co. Dublin* ☎ *01/288–0663* ⊕ *peppercanister.ie.*

St. Patrick's Cathedral. Along with some regular concert performances, you can catch some beautiful church singing at evensong at St. Pat's most weekdays around 5:30 pm. ⊠ *Saint Patrick's Close, Dublin West, Dublin, Co. Dublin* ☎ *01/453–9472* ⊕ *www.stpatrickscathedral.ie* 🎟 *€5.50.*

Royal Hospital Kilmainham. Frequent classical concerts are hosted by the Royal Hospital Kilmainham in its magnificent 17th-century interior. ⊠ *Military Rd., Dublin West, Dublin, Co. Dublin* ☎ *01/612–9900* ⊕ *www.rhk.ie.*

Opera Theatre Company. Ireland's only touring opera company, the Opera Theatre company performs at venues in Dublin and throughout the country. ⊠ *Temple Bar Music Centre, Curved St., Temple Bar, Dublin, Co. Dublin* ☎ *01/679–4962* ⊕ *www.opera.ie.*

THE NORTHSIDE

Cineworld Cinemas. A 17-screen theater just off O'Connell Street, Cineworld is the city center's only multiplex movie house; it shows the latest commercial features. ⊠ *Parnell Center, Parnell St., Northside, Dublin, Co. Dublin* ☎ *81/8304204* ⊕ *www.cineworld.ie.*

Savoy Cinema. Just across from the General Post Office, the Savoy is a four-screen theater with the largest screen in the country. ⊠ *O'Connell St., Northside, Dublin, Co. Dublin* ☎ *01/874–6000* ⊕ *www.omniplex.ie.*

DUBLIN WEST

Lighthouse Cinema. Rescued from the jaws of bankruptcy, the Lighthouse is a serene art-house cinema complex with a regular selection of international and local movies. ⊠ *Market Sq., Smithfield, Dublin West, Dublin, Co. Dublin* ☎ *01/872–8006* ⊕ *www.lighthousecinema.ie.*

Don't forget that U2 hails from Dublin. You'll find a calendar packed with rock, techno, and break-beat in the city's many clubs and concert halls.

ROCK AND CONTEMPORARY MUSIC

SOUTHSIDE

★ **ALT.** Andrew's Lane Theatre, an intimate old theater, has been transformed into a hopping music venue. ✉ *9–11 Andrew's Lane, Southside, Dublin, Co. Dublin* ☎ *01/679–5720.*

International Bar. A long-established, tiny, get-close-to-the-band venue upstairs, International Bar also hosts theater in the afternoon. ✉ *Wicklow St., Southside, Dublin, Co. Dublin* ☎ *01/677–9250.*

The Village. Set in a striking, glass-front building, the Village isn't too fussy about the kind of bands it hosts, so long as their amps are turned up full and the lead singer knows how to scream. ✉ *26 Wexford St., Southside, Dublin, Co. Dublin* ☎ *01/475–8555* ⊕ *www.thevillagevenue.com.*

Whelan's. Just off the southeastern corner of St. Stephen's Green, Whelan's is one of the city's best—and most popular—music venues. Well-known performers play everything from rock to folk to traditional music. ✉ *25 Wexford St., Southside, Dublin, Co. Dublin* ☎ *01/478–0766* ⊕ *www.whelanslive.com.*

TEMPLE BAR

★ **Button Factory.** A new music venue and club rolled into one, the Button Factory buzzes with activity every night of the week. Live acts range from rock bands to world music to singer-songwriters. ✉ *Curved St., Temple Bar, Dublin, Co. Dublin* ☎ *01/670–9202* ⊕ *www.buttonfactory.ie.*

Olympia Theatre. Everything from rock to country is presented at the Olympia, which is noted for its "Midnight from the Olympia" shows every Friday and Saturday from midnight to 2 am. ⊠ *72 Dame St., Temple Bar, Dublin, Co. Dublin* ☎ *01/679–3323* ⊕ *www.mcd.ie/olympia.*

NORTHSIDE

The O2. Home to the grandest, big-gig concerts by rock stars and dance luminaires, the O2 Arena is a high-tech, 14,500-capacity venue. ⊠ *Northwall Quay, Northside, Dublin, Co. Dublin* ☎ *01/836–3633* ⊕ *www.theo2.ie.*

DUBLIN WEST

Vicar Street. Across from Christ Church Cathedral, Vicar Street is a venue for intimate concerts. It often plays host to folk music, jazz, and comedy, as well as rock performances. ⊠ *58–59 Thomas St., Dublin West, Dublin, Co. Dublin* ☎ *01/775–5800* ⊕ *www.vicarstreet.com.*

THEATER

SOUTHSIDE

Fodor'sChoice ★ **Gaiety Theatre.** When this shimmering red-and-gold 19th-century theater is not showing musical comedy, drama, and revues, the sumptuous Gaiety on weekends is taken over by Opera Ireland for one of their big shows. ⊠ *S. King St., Southside, Dublin, Co. Dublin* ☎ *01/677–1717* ⊕ *www.gaietytheatre.ie.*

Samuel Beckett Centre. Home to Trinity College's drama department, as well as visiting European groups, the Samuel Beckett Centre also hosts dance performances by visiting troupes; the theater was built in 1992 and stands near the center of Trinity's campus. ⊠ *Trinity College, Southside, Dublin, Co. Dublin* ☎ *01/608–2266* ⊕ *www.tcd.ie/Drama/samuel-beckett-theatre.*

TEMPLE BAR

The New Theatre. A troupe with a political agenda, the New Theatre often favors productions by Irish working-class writers like Sean O'Casey and Brendan Behan in its newly renovated space. ⊠ *43 E. Essex St., Temple Bar, Dublin, Co. Dublin* ☎ *01/670–3361* ⊕ *www.thenewtheatre.com.*

Olympia Theatre. Dublin's oldest and premier multipurpose theatrical venue, the Olympia hosts drama and live comedy in addition to its high-profile musical performances. ⊠ *72 Dame St., Temple Bar, Dublin, Co. Dublin* ☎ *01/677–7744* ⊕ *www.olympia.ie.*

Project Arts Centre. A theater and performance space in an ugly modern building at the center of Temple Bar, the Project Arts Center is home to fringe and mainstream theater, contemporary music, and experimental art events. ⊠ *39 E. Essex St., Temple Bar, Dublin, Co. Dublin* ☎ *01/881–9613* ⊕ *www.projectartscentre.ie.*

Smock Alley Theatre. Smock Alley is a wonderfully atmospheric theater space tucked down a little lane. Now housed in a lovely 19th-century Irish Neo-Gothic structure, it stands on the site of a famous 17th-century Dublin theater. ⊠ *Lower Exchange St., Temple Bar, Dublin, Co. Dublin* ☎ *01/677–0014* ⊕ *www.smockalley.com.*

NORTHSIDE

Fodor's Choice ★ **Abbey Theatre.** One of the most fabled theaters in the world, the Abbey is the home of Ireland's national theater company. In 1904 W. B. Yeats and his patron, Lady Gregory, opened the theater, which became a major center for the Irish literary renaissance—the place that first staged works by J. M. Synge and Sean O'Casey, among many others. Plays by recent Irish drama heavyweights like Brian Friel, Tom Murphy, Hugh Leonard, and John B. Keane have all premiered here, and memorable productions of international greats like Mamet, Ibsen, and Shakespeare have also been performed. You should not, however, arrive expecting 19th-century grandeur: the original structure burned down in 1951. Unfortunately, an ugly concrete boxlike auditorium was built in its place—but what it may lack in esthetics it makes up for in space and acoustics. Some say the repertoire is overly reverential and mainstream, but such chestnuts as Dion Boucicault's *The Shaughran* wind up being applauded by many. Happily, the Abbey's sister theater at the same address, the Peacock, offers more experimental drama. But the Abbey will always be relevant since much of the theatergoing public still looks to it as a barometer of Irish culture. ⊠ *Lower Abbey St., Northside, Dublin, Co. Dublin* ☎ *01/878–7222* ⊕ *www.abbeytheatre.ie.*

★ **Gate Theatre.** An intimate 371-seat theater in a jewel-like Georgian assembly hall, the Gate produces the classics and contemporary plays by leading Irish writers, including Beckett, Wilde (the production of *Salome* was a worldwide hit), Shaw, and the younger generation of dramatists, such as Conor McPherson. ⊠ *Cavendish Row, Parnell Square, Northside, Dublin, Co. Dublin* ☎ *01/874–4045* ⊕ *www.gate-theatre.ie.*

SHOPPING

The only known specimens of leprechauns or *shillelaghs* in Ireland are those in souvenir-shop windows, and shamrocks mainly bloom around the borders of Irish linen handkerchiefs and tablecloths. But in Dublin's shops you can find much more than kitschy designs. There's a tremendous variety of stores here, many of which are quite sophisticated—as a walk through Dublin's central shopping area, from O'Connell to Grafton Street, will prove. Department stores stock internationally known fashion-designer goods and housewares, and small (and often pricey) boutiques sell Irish crafts and other merchandise. Don't expect too many bargains here. And be prepared, if you're shopping in central Dublin, to push through crowds—especially in the afternoons and on weekends. Most large shops and department stores are open Monday to Saturday 9 to 6, with late hours on Thursday and Friday until 9. Although nearly all department stores are closed on Sunday, some smaller specialty shops stay open. *Those with later closing hours are noted below.* You're particularly likely to find sales in January, February, July, and August.

SOUTHSIDE

SHOPPING CENTERS

Powerscourt Centre. Once the regal former town home of Lord Powerscourt (built in 1771), this was largely gutted two decades ago to make room for an interior roofed-over courtyard and a space shared by a mix of restaurants, cafés, antiques stores, and boutiques of original Irish fashions by young designers. A pianist often plays on the dais at ground-floor level. ✉ *59 S. William St., Southside, Dublin, Co. Dublin* ☎ *01/679–4144* ⊕ *www.powerscourtcentre.com.*

Royal Hibernian Way. On the former site of the two-century-old Royal Hibernian Hotel, a coaching inn that was demolished in 1983, this complex is home to pricey, stylish shops—about 20 or 30, many selling fashionable clothes and accessories—including Clarke Irish and Celtic Jewellers. ✉ *Off Dawson St., between S. Anne and Duke Sts., Southside, Dublin, Co. Dublin* ☎ *01/679–5919.*

Fodor'sChoice
★ **St. Stephen's Green Centre.** Dublin's city center's largest and most ambitious shopping complex, St. Stephen's Green Centre resembles a giant greenhouse, with Victorian-style ironwork. On three floors overlooked by a giant clock, the 100 mostly small shops sell crafts, fashions, and household goods. ✉ *Northwest corner of St. Stephen's Green, Southside, Dublin, Co. Dublin* ☎ *01/478–0888* ⊕ *www.stephensgreen.com.*

Westbury Mall. An upmarket shopping mall, the Westbury is where you can buy a stylish range of designer jewelry, antique rugs, and decorative goods. ✉ *Westbury Hotel, off Grafton St., Southside, Dublin, Co. Dublin.*

DEPARTMENT STORES

Fodor'sChoice
★ **Brown Thomas.** Dublin's most exclusive department store, Brown Thomas stocks the leading designer names (including leading Irish designers) in clothing and cosmetics, plus lots of stylish accessories. There's also a good selection of crystal. ✉ *Grafton St., Southside, Dublin, Co. Dublin* ☎ *01/605–6666* ⊕ *www.brownthomas.com.*

Dunnes Stores. Ireland's largest chain of department stores, all Dunnes branches stock fashion (including the exciting Savida range), household, and grocery items, and have a reputation for value and variety. ✉ *St. Stephen's Green Centre, Southside, Dublin, Co. Dublin* ☎ *01/478–0188* ⊕ *www.dunnesstores.ie* ✉ *Henry St., Northside, Dublin, Co. Dublin* ✉ *Ilac Center, Mary St., Northside, Dublin, Co. Dublin* ☎ *01/873–0211.*

Dublin Shopping Streets

CLOSE UP

SOUTHSIDE

Dawson Street. Just east of Grafton Street between Nassau Street to the north and St. Stephen's Green to the south, Dawson Street is the city's primary bookstore avenue. Waterstone's and Hodges Figgis face each other from opposite sides of the street.

Francis Street. Part of the Liberties, the oldest part of the city and the hub of Dublin's antiques trade, Francis Street and surrounding areas, such as the Coombe, have plenty of shops where you can browse. If you're looking for something in particular, dealers will gladly recommend the appropriate store to you. It's also home to a couple of hot new galleries.

Grafton Street. Dublin's bustling pedestrian-only main shopping street, Grafton Street has two department stores: down-to-earth Marks & Spencer and *trés* chic Brown Thomas. The rest of the street is taken up by shops, many of them branches of international chains, such as the Body Shop and Bally, and many British chains. This is also the spot to buy fresh flowers, available at reasonable prices from outdoor stands. On the smaller streets off Grafton Street—especially Duke Street, South Anne Street, and Chatham Street—are worthwhile crafts, clothing, and designer housewares shops.

Nassau Street. Dublin's main tourist-oriented thoroughfare, Nassau has some of the best-known stores selling Irish goods, but you won't find many locals shopping here. Still, if you're looking for classic Irish gifts to take home, you should be sure at least to browse along here.

TEMPLE BAR

Temple Bar Cultural Trust. Once dubbed Dublin's hippest neighborhood, Temple Bar is still dotted with small, precious boutiques—mainly intimate, quirky shops that traffic in a small selection of trendy goods, from vintage clothes to some of the most avant-garde Irish garb anywhere in the city. ⊕ *www.templebar.ie.*

NORTHSIDE

Henry Street. Running westward from O'Connell Street, Henry Street is where cash-conscious Dubliners shop. Arnotts department store is the anchor here; smaller, specialty stores sell CDs, footwear, and clothing. Henry Street's continuation, Mary Street, has a branch of Marks & Spencer and the Jervis Shopping Centre.

O'Connell Street. The city's main thoroughfare, O'Connell Street is more downscale than Southside city streets (such as Grafton Street), but it is still worth a walk. One of Dublin's largest department stores, Clery's, is here, across from the GPO. On the same side of the street as the post office is Eason's, a large book, magazine, and stationery store.

Marks & Spencer. More affordable than high-end Grafton Street competitor Brown Thomas, Marks & Spencer stocks everything from fashion (including lingerie) to tasty, unusual groceries. ⊠ *Grafton St., Southside, Dublin, Co. Dublin* ☎ *01/679–7855* ⊕ *www.marksandspencer.com* ⊠ *Henry St., Northside, Dublin, Co. Dublin* ☎ *01/872–8833.*

Shop-'til-you-droppers love Grafton Street, a store-lined address custom-made for serious retail therapy.

OUTDOOR MARKETS

George's Street Arcade. Opened in 1881 as South City Markets, this classic Victorian market right in the heart of town is home to a small but eclectic collection of clothes, books, food and jewelry stalls. It's covered, but feels outdoors, and open every day. ⊠ *S. Great George's St., Southside, Dublin, Co. Dublin* ⊕ *www.georgesstreetarcade.ie.*

BOOKS

Books Upstairs. An excellent selection of special-interest books is available here, including Irish literature, gay and feminist literature, psychology, and self-help books. ⊠ *36 College Green, Southside, Dublin, Co. Dublin* ☎ *01/679–6687.*

Fodor's Choice ★ **Cathach Books.** Head here for a fine array of first editions of Irish literature and many other books of Irish interest, plus old maps of Dublin and Ireland. ⊠ *10 Duke St., Southside, Dublin, Co. Dublin* ☎ *01/671–8676* ⊕ *www.rarebooks.ie.*

Fodor's Choice ★ **Hodges Figgis.** Dublin's leading independent bookstore, Hodges Figgis stocks 1½ million books on three floors. Once considered Ireland's oldest, its "independent" claim is a bit bogus, as a giant chain bought it some years ago. That noted, it has a stock, staff, look, and even an aroma of an independent bookstore, and might even still please James Joyce (who alludes to it in his *Ulysses*). ⊠ *56–58 Dawson St., Southeast Dublin, Dublin, Co. Dublin* ☎ *01/677–4754.*

Hughes & Hughes. This noted bookseller has strong travel and Irish-interest sections (there's also a store at Dublin Airport). ⊠ *St. Stephen's Green Centre, Southside, Dublin, Co. Dublin* ☎ *01/478–3060* ⊕ *www. hughesandhughes.ie.*

Dublin à la Mode

The success of shops like Costume and Dolls has given young Irish designers the confidence to produce more original and impressive work. One of Costume's most popular designers, **Helen James**, graduated from National College of Art and Design in textile design in 1992. She went straight to New York, where she worked for Donna Karan, among others. She returned to Ireland in 2002 and developed her line of unique, hand-printed textile accessories. Many people say there is a delicate Japanese feel to her work.

Footwear has long been an area overlooked by Irish designers, but Irishwoman **Eileen Shields** has been living and working in New York since 1988; for almost 10 years she designed footwear for Donna Karan. Her own premiere collection is all about clean, bold lines. Materials include antique kid, fine suede, python, and soft patent leather. Textures are often strongly contrasting, while colors are sensual and sophisticated. You can get the shoes online at ⊕ www.eileenshields.com.

The Tucker family has been a key player in Irish fashion since the 1960s, and new-generation **Leigh Tucker** has quickly established herself as one of Dublin's classiest young designers. Fine tailoring is her trademark—the finish on her eveningwear is nonpareil—and beaded French lace and draped jersey are her favorite materials. Her line can be found in boutiques across Ireland and at Costume in Dublin, and she's now making wedding dresses as well.

Reads. Somehow Reads manages to sell best sellers cheaper than any of its rivals. Also, it has a decent Irish section. ⊠ *24–25 Nassau St., Southside, Dublin, Co. Dublin* ☎ *01/679–6011.*

Fodor'sChoice ★ **Stokes Books.** A gem of an antique bookstore, Stokes has a great used-book section and specializes in Irish history and literature. While on the small side, Stokes is a treasure trove that will turn on most book-lovers. ⊠ *George's Street Arcade, Southside, Dublin, Co. Dublin* ☎ *01/671–3584* ⊕ *www.georgesstreetarcade.ie/stokes-books/index.php.*

CHINA, CRYSTAL, CERAMICS, AND JEWELRY

Appleby Jewellers. This is the best known of the several classy, old-style jewelry shops that line tiny Johnson's Court, a delightful little lane off busy Grafton Street. ⊠ *Johnson's Ct., Grafton St., Southside, Dublin, Co. Dublin* ☎ *01/679–9572* ⊕ *www.appleby.ie.*

Fodor'sChoice ★ **Barry Doyle Design.** A true original with his Celtic modern jewelry, Barry Doyle is a master who allows you to watch him at work in his adjoining studio as he fashions beautiful wedding rings and his lovely Lilac Collection baubles. ⊠ *George's Street Arcade, Upstairs, Southside, Dublin, Co. Dublin* ☎ *01/671–2838* ⊕ *www.barrydoyledesign.com.*

★ **House of Ireland.** For Irish goods and crafts, this is a great one-stop shopping resource with an extensive selection of crystal, jewelry, tweeds, sweaters, and other upscale goods. ⊠ *37–38 Nassau St., Southside, Dublin, Co. Dublin* ☎ *01/671–1111* ⊕ *www.houseofireland.com.*

Kilkenny Shop. Specializing in contemporary Irish-made ceramics, pottery, and silver jewelry, Kilkenny Shop regularly holds exhibits of exciting new work by Irish craftspeople and has a wide array of gifts fashioned by Orla Kiely and other top Irish designers. ⊠ *6–15 Nassau St., Southside, Dublin, Co. Dublin* ☎ *01/677–7066* ⊕ *www. kilkennyshop.com.*

Trinity Crafts. Your one-stop shop for everything cheesy Irish, head to Trinity Crafts for such trashy treasures as "The leprechauns made me do it" mugs and Guinness-logo underwear. ⊠ *27 Nassau St., Southside, Dublin, Co. Dublin* ☎ *01/672–5663.*

★ **Weir & Sons.** Dublin's most prestigious jeweler, Weir & Sons sells not only jewelry and watches, but also china, glass, lamps, silver, and leather. Founded in 1869, its flatiron building has long been a landmark on Grafton Street. ⊠ *96 Grafton St., Southside, Dublin, Co. Dublin* ☎ *01/677–9678* ⊕ *www.weirandsons.ie.*

CLOTHING STORES

A-Wear. Something of a fashion institution for local women, A-Wear stocks leading Irish designers, including John Rocha and his steady stream of exciting new looks. ⊠ *Grafton St., Southside, Dublin, Co. Dublin* ☎ *01/872–4644* ⊕ *www.awear.com.*

BT2. This is swanky Brown Thomas's impressive attempt to woo a younger crowd. Most of the major labels are present, including DKNY and Paul Smith. ⊠ *Grafton St., Southside, Dublin, Co. Dublin* ☎ *01/605–6666* ⊕ *www.bt2.ie.*

Fodor's Choice **Costume.** A classy boutique where Dubliners with fashion sense and
★ money like to shop for colorful, stylish clothes. Costume showcases local designers include Leigh, Helen James, and Helen Steele; Temperley and Preen are among the international designers featured. ⊠ *10 Castel Market, Southside, Dublin, Co. Dublin* ☎ *01/679–4188* ⊕ *www. costumedublin.ie.*

★ **Indigo and Cloth.** This has quickly become the place where Irish men with a bit of taste come for quality, slightly edgy clothing. Designers like Oliver Spencer and Velour dominate, and they also have a small, but classy, women's section. Check out their website's amazing "Minizine." ⊠ *Basement 27, South William St., Southside, Dublin, Co. Dublin* ☎ *01/670–6403* ⊕ *www.indigoandcloth.com.*

★ **Smock.** This tiny designer shop with great, left-field taste stocks international labels that include Pearson, Veronique, and A. F. Vandevoft. They also carry a beautiful line in fine jewelry. ⊠ *31 Drury St., Southside, Dublin, Co. Dublin* ☎ *01/613–9000* ⊕ *www.smock.ie.*

MUSIC

Celtic Note. Aimed at the tourist market, Celtic Note has lots of compilations and greatest-hits formats. ⊠ *14/15 Nassau St., Southside, Dublin, Co. Dublin* ☎ *01/670–4157* ⊕ *www.celticnote.com.*

★ **Gael Linn.** A specialist in traditional Irish music and Irish-language recordings, Gael Linn is where the aficionados go. ⊠ *35 Dame Street, Southside, Dublin, Co. Dublin* ☎ *01/675–1200* ⊕ *www.gael-linn.ie.*

HMV. HMV somehow withstands the digital music revolution responsible for the downfall of other mega music stores worldwide, and continues to supply Dublin with the latest in music, movies, and videogames, as well as gig tickets. ⊠ *65 Grafton St., Southside, Dublin, Co. Dublin* ☎ *01/679–5334* ⊕ *www.hmv.com* ⊠ *18 Henry St., Northside, Dublin, Co. Dublin* ☎ *01/872–2095.*

McCullogh Piggott. This is the best place in town to buy instruments, sheet music, scores, and books about music. ⊠ *11 South William Street, Southside, Dublin, Co. Dublin* ☎ *01/670–6702* ⊕ *www. mcculloughpigott.com.*

> ### ANTIQUES
>
> Dublin is one of Europe's best cities in which to buy antiques, largely due to a long and proud tradition of restoration and high-quality craftsmanship. The Liberties, Dublin's oldest district, is, fittingly, the hub of the antiques trade, and is chockablock with shops and traders. Bachelor's Walk, along the quays, also has some decent shops. It's quite a seller's market, but bargains are still possible.

SWEATERS AND TWEEDS

★ **Avoca Handweavers.** This is a beautiful store with an eclectic collection of knitwear, jewelry, ceramics, and housewares from contemporary Irish designers. ⊠ *11–13 Suffolk St., Southside, Dublin, Co. Dublin* ☎ *01/274–6900* ⊕ *www.avoca.ie.*

Cleo. Hand-knit sweaters and accessories made only from natural fibers are a specialty at Cleo. ⊠ *18 Kildare St., Southeast Dublin, Dublin, Co. Dublin* ☎ *01/676–1421* ⊕ *www.cleo-ltd.com.*

Fodor's Choice
★ **Kevin and Howlin.** A quintessential Irish store, Kevin and Howlin stocks spiffy fashions, with lots of stylish handwoven-tweed men's jackets, suits, and hats, along with an array of treasures woven from tweedy fabrics. All in all, this is a fabulous, one-stop shop for traditional clothes with flair. Wait until you see the whole wall devoted to headgear—eat your heart out, Ralph Lauren! ⊠ *31 Nassau St., Southside, Dublin, Co. Dublin* ☎ *01/677–0257* ⊕ *www.kevinandhowlin.com.*

Monaghan's. If you're into cashmere, you should get yourself into Monaghan's. ⊠ *Royal Hibernian Way, 15–17 Grafton St., Southside, Dublin, Co. Dublin* ☎ *01/677–0823* ⊕ *www.monaghanscashmere.ie.*

TEMPLE BAR

MUSIC

Claddagh Records. Head here for a good selection of traditional and folk music. ⊠ *2 Cecilia St., Temple Bar, Dublin, Co. Dublin* ☎ *01/677–0262* ⊕ *www.claddaghrecords.com.*

OUTDOOR MARKETS

★ **Cows Lane Market.** Held every Saturday from February to September at the west edge of Temple Bar, Cows Lane is home to some of the most innovative young fashion and accessory designers in the country. ⊠ *Temple Bar, Dublin, Co. Dublin* ⊕ *templebar.ie/Market/Designer_Mart.*

Meeting House Square Market. Held Saturday morning in the heart of Temple Bar, this is a good place to buy homemade foodstuffs: cheeses, breads, chocolate, and organic veggies.

NORTHSIDE

SHOPPING CENTERS

The chq Building. While this has not turned out to be the glittering, beating heart of shopping in the Docklands area as it promised at its launch, it does have a few tempting stores, including Irish tailors Louis Copeland and Fran & Jane, the mother and daughter boutique. ⊠ *IFSC, Docklands, Northside, Dublin, Co. Dublin* ⊕ *www.chq.ie.*

Ilac Centre. Dublin's first large, modern shopping center, Ilac Centre boasts two department stores, hundreds of specialty shops, and several restaurants. The stores are not as exclusive as those at some of the other centers, but there's plenty of free parking. ⊠ *Henry St., Northside, Dublin, Co. Dublin* ☎ *01/878–2775* ⊕ *www.ilac.ie.*

Jervis Shopping Centre. A slightly high-end center, Jervis houses some of the major British chain stores. It has a compact design and plenty of parking. ⊠ *Jervis and Mary Sts., 125 Abbey St. Upper, Northside, Dublin, Co. Dublin* ☎ *01/878–1323* ⊕ *jervis.ie.*

DEPARTMENT STORES

Arnotts. Fully filling three floors, Arnotts stocks a wide selection of clothing, household accessories, and sporting goods. It is known for matching quality with value. There is a Gap section downstairs. ⊠ *Henry St., Northside, Dublin, Co. Dublin* ☎ *01/805–0400* ⊕ *www.arnotts.ie.*

Clery's. Once the city's most fashionable department store, Clery's is still worth a visit. You'll find all kinds of merchandise—from clothing to home appliances—on its four floors. Note that goods sold here reflect a distinctly modest, traditional sense of style. ⊠ *18-27 Lower O'Connell St., Northside, Dublin, Co. Dublin* ☎ *01/878–6000* ⊕ *www.clerys.com.*

Debenhams. The U.K. chain store, Debenhams has opened in the city center and includes a Zara section along with its own clothing and homeware lines. ⊠ *Henry St., Northside, Dublin, Co. Dublin* ☎ *01/814–7200* ⊕ *www.debenhams.ie.*

Eason & Son. Known primarily for its large selection of books, magazines, and stationery, Eason also sells an array of tapes, CDs, videos, and other audiovisual goodies at its main O'Connell Street branch; all in all, it has about 50 bookstores throughout Ireland. ⊠ *O'Connell St., Northside, Dublin, Co. Dublin* ☎ *01/873–3811* ⊕ *www.eason.ie.*

CHINA, CRYSTAL, CERAMICS, AND JEWELRY

McDowells. Popular with Dubliners, this jewelry shop has been in business for more than 100 years. ⊠ *3 Upper O'Connell St., Northside, Dublin, Co. Dublin* ☎ *01/874–4961* ⊕ *www.mcdowellsjewellers.com.*

DUBLIN WEST

ANTIQUES

Christy Bird. Dublin's oldest furniture shop, Christy Bird was recycling household items before anyone else dreamed of it. You have to hunt for anything that is true quality and most of the goods here are now repro and mass-market. ⊠ *32 S. Richmond St., Dublin West, Dublin, Co. Dublin* ☎ *01/475–4049* ⊕ *www.christybird.com.*

Martin Fennelly Antiques. A stalworth of Dublin's traditional antiques quarter around Francis Street, Fennelly's specializes in early furniture and decorative items like candlesticks, tea caddies, and fitted jewelry caskets. ⊠ *60 Francis St., Dublin West, Dublin, Co. Dublin* ☎ *01/473–1126* ⊕ *www.fennelly.net.*

Fodor's Choice
★
O'Sullivan Antiques. Specializing in 18th- and 19th-century furniture, with a high-profile clientele (including Mia Farrow and Liam Neeson), the O'Sullivan "look" has been so successful that it now runs a full-time sister shop in New York. ⊠ *43–44 Francis St., Dublin West, Dublin, Co. Dublin* ☎ *01/454–1143, 01/453–9659* ⊕ *www.osullivanantiques.com.*

CLOTHING STORES

★ **Dolls.** An independent boutique, Dolls likes to boast of its unusual designer pieces. Featured international designers include Karen Walker and Future Classics. The adjoining lovely little café is ideal for a shopping time-out. Say hello to Bobo the dog for us! ⊠ *Emorville Avenue, Dublin West, Dublin, Co. Dublin* ☎ *01/672–9004.*

OUTDOOR MARKETS

★ **Dublin Food Co-op.** A breath of eco-fresh air on the Dublin food-shopping scene, this member-run co-op has a quality food market in a wonderful old space in Newmarket at the heart of the Liberties district every Thursday and Saturday. They even encourage the use of a few words of Irish among the locals as they shop for organic veggies, flowers, cheeses, and wines. They have also just started a flea market on the last Sunday of the month and a furniture market on the third Sunday. ⊠ *12 Newmarket St., Dublin West, Dublin, Co. Dublin* ⊕ *www.dublinfood.coop.*

Liberty Market. Just minutes from Christchurch Cathedral, this working class favorite is a great place to get a feel for Dubliners at play. The stalls vary from knickknacks to children's clothing and candy. Open Thursday to Saturday. ⊠ *Meath St., Dublin West, Dublin, Co. Dublin* ⊕ *www.libertymarket.ie.*

SPORTS AND THE OUTDOORS

FOOTBALL

Soccer—called football in Europe—is very popular in Ireland, largely due to the euphoria resulting from the national team's underdog successes since the late 1980s.

Football Association of Ireland. League of Ireland matches take place throughout the city on Friday evening or Sunday afternoon from March to November. For details, contact the Football Association of Ireland. ✉ *80 Merrion Sq. S, Southeast Dublin, Dublin, Co. Dublin* ☎ *01/676–6864* ⊕ *www.fai.ie.*

GAELIC GAMES

Gaelic Athletic Association (*GAA*). The traditional games of Ireland, Gaelic football and hurling, attract a huge following, with roaring crowds cheering on their county teams. Games are held at Croke Park, the stunning, high-tech national stadium for Gaelic games, just north of the city center. For details of matches, contact the Gaelic Athletic Association. ✉ *Croke Park, North County Dublin, Dublin, Co. Dublin* ☎ *01/836–3222* ⊕ *www.gaa.ie.*

GOLF

Fodor's Choice ★ **Portmarnock Golf Club.** The hoo-ha and court battles over Portmarnock's refusal to admit women members often overshadows the club's position as the most famous of Ireland's "Big Four" (Ballybunion, Royal County Down, and Royal Portrush are the others). This links course, on a sandy peninsula north of Dublin, has hosted numerous major championships and Tom Watson often used it as a preparation for the Open. Known for its flat fairways and greens and its 100-plus bunkers, it provides a fair test for any golfer who can keep it out of the heavy rough. Greens fees include lunch. ✉ *Portmarnock, Co. Dublin* ☎ *01/846–2968* ⊕ *www.portmarnockgolfclub.ie* ✉ *Greens fees: €175* ⅃ *27 holes. Yardage: 7,382, 3,449. Par 72, 37. Practice area, driving range, caddies (reserve in advance), caddy carts, club rental, catering* ☉ *Visitors: daily.*

HORSE RACING

Horse racing—from flat to hurdle to steeplechase—is one of the great sporting loves of the Irish. The sport is closely followed and betting is popular, but the social side of attending races is equally important to Dubliners.

The Curragh Rececourse. Southwest of Dublin off M7, the Curragh hosts the five Classics, the most important flat races of the season, from May to September. There are numerous bars here and two restaurants. ✉ *Off Exit 12 of M7 between Newbridge and Kildare Town* ☎ *045/441–205* ⊕ *www.curragh.ie.*

Fairyhouse Racecourse. Every Easter Monday, Fairyhouse hosts the Grand National, the most popular steeplechase of the season. ✉ *Ratoath* ☎ *01/825–6167* ⊕ *www.fairyhouseracecourse.ie.*

Leopardstown Racecourse. The main course in Dublin is Leopardstown, an ultramodern course that in February hosts the Hennessey Gold Cup, one of Ireland's most prestigious steeplechases. Summertime is devoted to flat racing, and the rest of the year to racing over fences. You can also nip in for a quick meal at the restaurant. ✉ *Leopardstown Rd., South County Dublin, Dublin, Co. Dublin* ☎ *01/289–3600* ⊕ *www. leopardstown.com.*

RUGBY

For many years Rugby was a "garrison sport" in Ireland, the preserve of "West Brits" and private-school boys. The success of the Irish team internationally, and Leinster and Munster in European club competitions, has changed that somewhat, and you might see an oval ball being tossed around by kids in any area of the country.

Aviva Stadium. The home of Irish Rugby, Aviva's state-of-the-art arena opened in 2010 (on the site of the old Lansdowne Stadium) and can accommodate 50,000 fans. ✉ *62 Lansdowne Rd., Ballsbridge, Dublin, Co. Dublin* ☎ *01/238–2300* ⊕ *www.avivastadium.ie.*

SIDE TRIPS: NORTH COUNTY DUBLIN

Dublin's northern suburbs remain largely residential, but there are a few places worth the trip, such as the architectural gem Marino Casino. As with most suburban areas, walking may not be the best way to get around. It's good, but not essential, to have a car. Buses and trains serve most of these areas.

MARINO CASINO

Take Malahide Road from Dublin's north city center for 4 km (2½ miles). Or take Bus 20A or Bus 24 to Casino from Cathal Brugha Street in north city center.

Marino Casino. One of Dublin's most exquisite, yet also most underrated, architectural landmarks, the Marino Casino (the name means "little house by the sea," and the building overlooks Dublin Harbour) is a small-scale, Palladian-style Greek temple, built between 1762 and 1771 from a plan by Sir William Chambers. Often compared to the Petit Trianon at Versailles, it was commissioned by the great Irish grandee Lord Charlemont as a summerhouse. Inside, highlights are the china-closet boudoir, the huge golden sunset in the ceiling of the main drawing room, and the signs of the zodiac in the ceiling of the bijou library. When you realize that the structure has, in fact, 16 rooms—there are bedrooms upstairs—Sir William's sleight-of-hand is readily apparent: from its exterior, the structure seems to contain only one room. It makes a good stop on the way to Malahide, Howth, or North Bull Island. ✉ *Malahide Rd., Marino, North County Dublin,*

Marino, Co. Dublin ☎*01/833–1618* ⊕*www.heritageireland.ie* ✉*€3*
⊙ *May–Oct., daily 10–5.*

MALAHIDE

*By car, drive from north city center on R107 for 14½ km (9 miles).
Or catch hourly train from Connolly Station. Or board Bus 42 to
Malahide, which leaves every 15 minutes from Beresford Place behind
Custom House.*

ℭ **Malahide Castle.** This township is chiefly known for its glorious Malahide Castle, a picture-book castle occupied by the Talbot family from
1185 until 1976, when it was sold to the local County Council. The
great expanse of parkland around the castle has more than 5,000 different species of trees and shrubs, all clearly labeled. The castle itself
combines styles and crosses centuries; the earliest section, the three-
story tower house, dates from the 12th century. Hung with many family portraits, the medieval great hall is the only one in Ireland that is
preserved in its original form. Authentic 18th-century pieces furnish
the other rooms. Within the castle, the **Fry Model Railway Museum**
houses rare, handmade models of the Irish railway and one of the
world's largest miniature railway displays, which covers an area of
2,500 square feet. Tara's Palace, a dollhouse that was made to raise
funds for children's charities, is also here; it has 25 rooms, all fully
furnished in miniature. A new addition, scheduled to open in September 2012, includes an Avoca restaurant and shop. ✉ *10 km (6 miles)
north of Howth on Coast Rd., North County Dublin, Malahide, Co.
Dublin* ☎*01/846–2184* ⊕*www.malahidecastle.com* ✉*Castle €7.50,
castle and railway museum €11.50* ⊙ *Apr.–Sept., Mon.–Sat. 10–5, Sun.
11–6; Oct.–Mar., Mon.–Sat. 10–5, Sun. 11–5.*

Fodor's Choice **Newbridge House and Farm.** One of the greatest stately homes of Ire-
★ land, Newbridge House, in Donabate, was built between 1740 and
ℭ 1760 for Charles Cobbe, Archbishop of Dublin. A showpiece in the
Georgian and Regency styles, the house is less a museum than a home
because the Cobbe family still resides here, part of a novel scheme
the municipal government allowed when they took over the house
in 1985. The sober exterior and even more sober entrance hall—all
Portland stone and Welsh slate—don't prepare you for the splendor of
Newbridge's Red Drawing Room, perhaps Ireland's most sumptuous
18th-century salon. Cobbe's son, Thomas, and his wife, Lady Betty
Beresford, sister of the marquess of Waterford, had amassed a great
collection of paintings and needed a hall in which to show them off,
so they built a back wing of the house to incorporate an enormous
room built for entertaining and impressing others. That it does, thanks
to its crimson walls, fluted Corinthian columns, dozens of old masters, and glamorous rococo-style plaster ceiling designed by the Dublin
stuccadore Richard Williams. Elsewhere in the house are fascinating
family heirlooms: the kitchens still have their original utensils; crafts
workshops and some examples of old-style transportation, such as
coaches, are in the courtyard; and there is even a Museum of Curiosi-
ties, complete with the mummified ear of an Egyptian bull and relics
of Lady Betty's medical practice (her chilblain plaster became famous).

Some fine paintings are left, but the greatest were sold centuries ago in order to build proper houses for the estate servants. Beyond the house's walled garden are 366 acres of parkland and a restored 18th-century animal farm. The coffee shop is renowned for the quality and selection of its homemade goods. You can travel from Malahide to Donabate by train, which takes about 10 minutes. From the Donabate train station, it's a 15-minute walk to the Newbridge House grounds. ⊠ *Donabate, 8 km (5 miles) north of Malahide, signposted from N1, North County Dublin, Malahide, Co. Dublin* ☎ *01/843–6534* ⊕ *www. newbridgehouseandfarm.com* ✉ *€7* ⊗ *Apr.–Sept., Tues.–Sat. 10–1 and 2–5, Sun. noon–6; Oct.–Mar., weekends noon–5.*

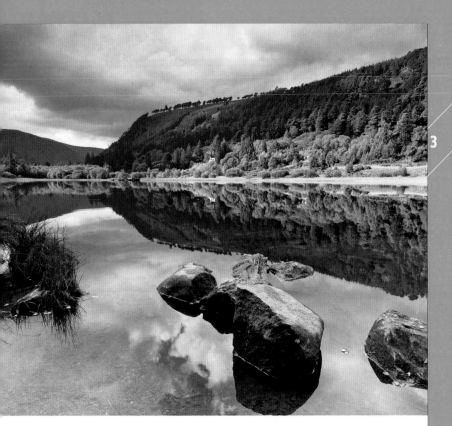

Dublin Environs

INCLUDING COUNTIES CAVAN, DUBLIN, KILDARE, LOUTH, MEATH, AND WICKLOW

WORD OF MOUTH

"I would definitely do Newgrange—so rich in history, and it absolutely will stir your imagination! But also do Knowth—you can climb right on top of it!"

—suspire

WELCOME TO DUBLIN ENVIRONS

TOP REASONS TO GO

★ **Newgrange:** Just standing amid these 5,000-year-old tombs (which predate the pyramids), you'll wonder: how did they build them?

★ **A Day at the Races:** The Irish may like a drink, but they really love to gamble, as you'll discover in Kildare, center of the Irish bloodstock world. Punchestown in spring and the Curragh in summer are both unique, passionate racecourse experiences.

★ **Spectacular Georgian Country Houses:** Modesty never struck the rich Anglo-Irishman, whose propensity to flaunt his riches led to such over-the-top stately homes as Castletown, Russborough, and Powerscourt.

★ **Wicklow Is for Walkers:** There's no better way to meet the locals and see the land than trekking out on the 132-km-long (82-mile-long) Wicklow Way, Ireland's most popular trail.

★ **Early Morning at Glendalough:** Before the tour buses arrive, channel the spirit of the 6th-century, isolation-seeking St. Kevin.

1 The Boyne Valley. Set 48 km (30 miles) north of Dublin, this entire area is redolent with prehistoric and pagan sites. You don't have to be an Indiana Jones to be awed by the Hill of Tara or Newgrange, a Neolithic burial ground and solar observatory still evocative of the mysteries of pre-Celtic civilization.

2 County Wicklow. Set with dense woods and idyllic lakes, "the garden of Ireland" is a favorite day out for Dubliners, thanks to sylvan estates like Powerscourt and Glendalough, a 6th-century monastic site so serene you may be tempted to renounce the profane world.

3 County Kildare. After visiting stately Castletown—a monument to Ireland's Georgian age of elegance—check out Derby Day at the Curragh racecourse. The grinning bookmakers are just waiting to take your money.

New Inn

CAVAN

N3

N52

Cloghan

WESTMEATH

Kinnegad   N4

Tyrrellspass

OFFALY

Cherryville

N7

Mountrath

Athy

LAOIS

Abbeyleix

Durrow

0   10 mi
0   10 km

NORTHERN IRELAND

ARMAGH
DOWN

Annayalla
Castleblayney
MONAGHAN
Omeath
N53
Dundalk
Inniskeen
N2
Dundalk Bay
M1
Ardee
N52
N2
LOUTH
Irish Sea
Kells
BOYNE VALLEY
Slane
Drogheda
N3
Newgrange
M1
Navan
N51
Hill of Tara
N2
MEATH
DUBLIN
Lambay Island
M3
Swords
M1
Drumleck Point
DUBLIN
Dublin Bay
KILDARE
Castletown
N81
Russborough House
M7
M11
Naas
Bray
Powerscourt
Kildare
The Curragh
Kilcullen
WICKLOW
Kilmacanoge
N78
N11
WICKLOW MOUNTAINS
Ballinalea
Glendalough
Wicklow
Wicklow Head
M9
CARLOW
N11
Arklow
WEXFORD

GETTING ORIENTED

3

The Dublin environs include three main regions: County Wicklow's coast and mountains, the Boyne Valley, and County Kildare. The Boyne Valley includes much of counties Meath and Louth to the north and east of Dublin. Kildare and Wicklow are to the southeast and south of the capital. Tour this small region, or opt for day trips from Dublin, especially to the Wicklow Mountains, which rise up suddenly at the fringes of the city.

IRELAND'S HISTORIC HEART

Stone Age, Celtic, early Christian, and Norman: the country is scattered with sites that act as signposts in the long and twisting story called "Ireland." But by circumstance of geography and mystical significance many of the great stone ghosts to ancient Ireland are concentrated in the counties immediately surrounding Dublin.

(top) Newgrange is a spectacular passage tomb; (right, top) The Stone of Destiny rests on the Hill of Tara; (right, bottom) Graves and High Crosses hallow the grounds of Glendalough.

Here, often so closely thrown together as to make an almost Disneyesque mockery of the vastness of time and history, stand the man-made wonders that are impressive but slightly melancholic reminders of more heroic and more savage ages. In fact, a tour down the valley of the River Boyne is a trip into the past, back beyond history, to the Neolithic tombs of Newgrange, the Druidic holy place of the Hill of Tara, the monasteries of early Christianity, and the Norman castles of the chain-mailed invader who brought a bloody end to so much of Celtic Ireland. Not far from Dublin, chart the rise and fall of Irish culture at their glorious monuments.

THE HIGH CROSS

The Celtic High Cross is an endearing symbol of Ireland, and Monasterboice—a former monastic settlement—has more of them than anywhere in Ireland. Dating to AD 923, the 20-foot-high Muireadach Cross is the best preserved, as its panels depicting the slaying of Abel, David and Goliath, and the Last Judgment prove. The nearby 110-foot round tower gives you a view of the once-glorious monastic site.

NEWGRANGE

Built in the fourth millennium BC, a thousand years before Stonehenge, Newgrange is not only one of the world's pristine surviving passage tombs but also a great granite reminder of the ingenuity, spirituality, and perseverance of modern Ireland's Neolithic ancestors. How did they move 250,000 tons of stone? How did they align it to perfectly capture the first rays of the dawn sun on the winter solstice? The thrill of visiting and entering the somber tomb at Newgrange lies not only in what you discover but in the awesome mysteries that can only be answered by the imagination.

GLENDALOUGH

A single early morning hour spent in the isolated and serene Glendalough Valley—green jewel set amidst the Wicklow Mountains—should be enough to convince you St. Kevin the monk made the perfect choice when he was searching for 6th-century solitude and peace. The simplicity, separation, and sparseness that were at the heart of early Christianity in Ireland are sublimely apparent in the hermit's cave called St. Kevin's Bed and the ruins of the tiny Church of the Oratory.

HILL OF TARA

Visitors are sometimes disappointed when they finally see the mythical Hill of Tara, spiritual and regal heart of Celtic

and Druidic Ireland. It is now just a hill after all—300 feet high with awesome views out over the flat central plains of Ireland and all the way to Galway in the West. But with a little reading at the interpretive center and a lot of imagination, you can picture the Iron Age fort that once stood here and the huge *feis* or national assembly where Celtic Ireland passed its laws and settled its tribal disputes. It is a place that is both beyond history and made of it.

MELLIFONT ABBEY

As well as war, the Normans brought great stone-church building to Ireland; one of their greatest religious monuments is Mellifont Abbey. Founded in 1142 by St. Malachy, the main parts of the abbey were built a little later in the Norman style, including the two-story chapter house and the octagonal Lavabo, where the monks used to wash. Although much of the abbey is in ruins, it still manages to illustrate the medieval church's rise to wealth and power in Ireland. Incidentally, the term "Celtic" is derived from the tribes that arrived on Irish shores around 700 BC, first called Galli by the Romans and then named Gaels in Ireland.

Updated by
Anto Howard

Walt Disney himself couldn't have planned it better. The small counties immediately north, south, and west of Dublin—historically known as the Pale—seem expressly designed to entertain and enchant the sightseer. The entire region is rich with legendary Celtic sites, gorgeous gardens, and the most elegant Palladian country estates in Ireland.

Due to its location on the Irish Sea, facing Europe, the region was the first to attract the earliest "tourists"—conquerors and rulers—and the first over which they exercised the greatest influence. Traces of each new wave remain: the Celts chose Tara as the center of their kingdom; the Danes sailed the rivers Boyne and Liffey to establish many of today's towns; and the region's great Protestant-built houses of the 18th century remind us that the Pale (originally the Pale referred to the area of eastern Ireland ruled directly by the Normans) was the starting point and administrative center for the long, violent English colonization of the whole island.

The Dublin environs include three basic geographical regions. North of Dublin lies the Boyne Valley, with its abundant ruins of Celtic Ireland extending from counties Meath to Louth. In pagan times this area was the home of Ireland's high kings, and the center of religious life. All roads led to Tara, the fabled Hill of Kings, the royal seat, and the place where the national assembly was held. Today, time seems to stand still—and you should, too, for it's almost sacrilegious to introduce a note of urgency here.

South of the capital is the mountainous county of Wicklow, where the gently rounded Wicklow Mountains contain the evocative monastic settlement at Glendalough, many later abbeys and churches, and the great 18th-century estates of the Anglo-Irish aristocracy, such as Castletown, Powerscourt, and Russborough.

Southwest of Dublin are the flat pastoral plains of County Kildare, which stretch between the western Midlands and the foothills of the Dublin and Wicklow Mountains—both names actually refer to the same mountain range, but each marks its county's claim to the land. Kildare is the flattest part of Ireland, a natural playing field for breeding, training, and racing some of the world's premier Thoroughbreds.

DUBLIN ENVIRONS PLANNER

WHEN TO GO

While certainly not the wettest part of Ireland (the West gets that dubious distinction), the counties around Dublin do get their fair share of rain. June, July, August, and September tend to be the driest months, and the good news is that the rain in the region in summer is usually light and short-lived. Wicklow, with all its hills and valleys, seems to have an obscure microclimate of its own, so don't rely too much on the weatherman to get it right.

PLANNING YOUR TIME

IF YOU HAVE THREE DAYS

Most people who explore Dublin Environs base themselves in the city and use day trips to sample the very different landscapes around the capital. Driving distances from downtown Dublin to the Environs are less than two hours (in decent traffic). Just don't plan on visiting both the north and south of Dublin in the same day—each region is worth its own day or half-day trip from the city.

Visits to Newgrange and Glendalough are musts, and the latter of these could be combined with a country house visit to Powerscourt. For the more active visitor a one-day walk along the Wicklow Way might pair best with an overnight stay in the cozy Hunter's Hotel.

GETTING HERE AND AROUND

BUS TRAVEL

Bus Éireann services link Dublin with the main and smaller towns in the area. All buses for the region depart from Dublin's Busaras, the central bus station, at Store Street. Dublin Bus serves some towns and estates in the region as well.

Bus Information Dublin Bus ☎ *01/873–4222* ⊕ *www.dublinbus.ie.*

CAR TRAVEL

The easiest and best way to tour Dublin's environs is by car, because many sights are not served by public transportation, and what service there is, especially to outlying areas, is infrequent. To visit destinations in the Boyne Valley, follow N3, along the east side of Phoenix Park, out of the city and make Trim and Tara your first stops. Alternatively, leave Dublin via N1/M1 toward Belfast. To reach destinations in County Kildare, follow the quays along the south side of the River Liffey (they are one-way westbound) to St. John's Road West (N7/M7); in a matter of minutes, you're heading for open countryside. Avoid traveling this route during the evening peak rush hours, especially on Friday, when Dubliners are themselves making their weekend getaways. To reach destinations in County Wicklow, N11/M11 is the fastest and most clearly marked route. The two more scenic routes to Glendalough are R115 to R759 to R755, or R177 to R755.

TRAIN TRAVEL

Irish Rail (Iarnród Éireann) trains run the length of the east coast, stopping at towns between Dundalk to the north in County Louth to Arklow along the coast in County Wicklow. From Heuston Station, the

Arrow, a commuter train service, runs westward to Celbridge, Naas, Newbridge, and Kildare Town.

For more information on getting here and around, see Travel Smart Ireland.

RESTAURANTS

Dining out in the area is essentially a casual affair, but the innovations and experimentation of Dublin's top restaurateurs are influencing the cooking—and the prices—at the finer establishments outside the capital. Even so, you'll find some truly stylish places here, including La Serre, in the running for the most dazzlingly decorated restaurant in the country (with a top-rated chef holding down the kitchen, to boot). As in the Southwest, chefs hereabouts have a deep respect for fresh, locally grown and raised produce. You'll find everything from Continental-style meals to hearty ploughman's lunches.

Prices in the reviews are the average cost of a main course at dinner or, if dinner is not served, at lunch.

HOTELS

A lot of people opt to stay in Dublin and take day trips to the environs. If that's the case, a hotel on the south side of the city or in South County Dublin might be a good idea if you're planning to spend time in Wicklow or East Kildare. For Meath and Louth, a hotel on the north side or to the west of the city might work better. If you don't want to "commute" from the city, the noted country-house hotels around Kildare and Wicklow are great options. They are surprisingly good value for the unique, luxurious experience they offer. Bed-and-breakfasts are another good option, and though the ones in this region tend to be a little more expensive than in other parts of Ireland, they also are a little classier and more stylish.

Prices in the reviews are the lowest cost of a standard double room in high season. For expanded reviews, facilities, and current deals, visit Fodors.com.

TOUR OPTIONS

Bus Éireann runs guided bus tours from Dublin to many of the historic and scenic locations throughout the Dublin environs daily in summer. Visits include trips to Glendalough in County Wicklow; Boyne Valley and Newgrange in County Louth; and the Hill of Tara, Trim, and Navan in County Meath. Irish Sightseeing Tours, a privately owned touring company, also runs many guided bus tours throughout the Dublin environs between May and September. Their Grand Wicklow Tour lasts seven hours, as does their day trip to Newgrange and Mellifont Abbey. Prices start at €32. Wild Wicklow Tours uses minibuses that can handle smaller groups and take you off the beaten track. Their full-day trips to Glendalough also take in Avoca Handweavers and a Dublin coastal drive. Prices start at €28. Railtours Ireland has a half-day rail tour into the Wicklow Mountains. The train stops at Arklow, and then a bus takes you through Avoca and on to Glendalough. The cost is €39.

Tour Information **Bus Éireann** ☎ *01/836–6111* ⊕ *www.buseireann.ie.*
Irish Sightseeing Tours ☎ *01/458–0054* ⊕ *www.loveireland.com.*
Railtours Ireland ☎ *01/856–0045* ⊕ *www.railtoursireland.com.*
Wild Wicklow Tours ☎ *01/280–1899* ⊕ *www.wildwicklow.ie.*

VISITOR INFORMATION

For information on travel in the Dublin environs, contact one of the
following tourist information offices (TIOs) year-round: Dublin Tour-
ism/Bord Fáilte, Dundalk, or Wicklow Town. In summer, temporary
TIOs are open throughout the environs, in towns such as Drogheda
and Dundalk in County Louth and Kildare Town in County Kildare.
East Coast Midlands Tourism is the department of Bord Fáilte directly
responsible for the Dublin environs area.

Tourism Information **County Kildare Tourism** ☎ *045/898–888*
⊕ *www.visitkildare.ie.* **County Louth Tourism** ☎ *042/933–5457*
⊕ *www.louthholidays.com.* **County Meath Tourism** ☎ *046/9097060*
⊕ *www.meath.ie/tourism.* **County Wicklow Tourism** ☎ *40/1847–1000*
⊕ *www.visitwicklow.ie.* **East Coast Midlands Tourism** ☎ *1850/230330*
⊕ *www.discoverireland.ie/places-to-go/Dublins-doorstep.*

THE BOYNE VALLEY

For every wistful schoolboy in Ireland the River Boyne is a name that
resonates with history and adventure. It was on the banks of that river in
1014 that the Celtic chieftain Brian Boru defeated the Danish in a deci-
sive battle that returned the east of Ireland to native rule. It was also by
this river that Protestant William of Orange defeated the Catholic armies
of exiled James II of England, in 1690. In fact, this whole area, only 48
km (30 miles) north of cosmopolitan Dublin, is soaked in stories and legends that predate the pyramids. You can't throw a stick anywhere in the
valley without hitting some trace of Irish history. The great prehistoric,
pagan, and Celtic monuments of the wide arc of fertile land known as
the Boyne Valley invariably evoke a sense of wonder. You don't have to
be an archaeologist to be awed by Newgrange and Knowth—set beside
the River Boyne—or the Hill of Tara, Mellifont Abbey, or the High Cross
of Monasterboice. One way to approach exploring this area is to start
at the town of Trim, the locale closest to Dublin, and work your way
north. Keep in mind that Omeath and the scenic Cooley Peninsula at the
end of this section are on the border of Northern Ireland.

TRIM

51 km (32 miles) northwest of Dublin.

The heritage town of Trim, on the River Boyne, contains some of the
finest medieval ruins in Ireland. In 1359, on the instructions of King
Edward III, the town was walled and its fortifications were strengthened.
In the 15th century, several parliaments were held here. Oliver Cromwell
massacred most of its inhabitants when he captured the town in 1649. In
the old town hall, the visitor center has an audiovisual display depicting
the arrival of the Normans and the story of medieval Trim.

Boyne Valley

NORTHERN IRELAND

CAVAN

LOUTH

MEATH

DUBLIN

Irish Sea

Castleblayney
Cootehill
Omeath
Carlingford Lough
Carlingford
Kilkeel
Greenore
Inniskeen
Dundalk
Carrickmacross
Rathnetty
Louth
Dundalk Bay
Bailieborough
Kingscourt
Virginia
Ardee
Dunleer
Lough Ramor
Monasterboice
Clogherhead
Collon
Mellifont Abbey
Baltray
King William's Glen
Kells
Slane
Drogheda
Crossakiel
Newgrange
Navan
Duleek
Rathcairn
Balbriggan
Delvin
Athboy
Skerries
Hill of Tara
Kilmessan
Garristown
Rush
Trim
Newtown
Laracor
Summerhill
Swords
Malahide
Kinnegad
Kilcock
Enfield

0   6 miles
0   9 km

GETTING HERE AND AROUND

By car, Trim is just over 48 km (30 miles) northwest of Dublin on the M3 and then the R154. Once in town, parking isn't a problem. There is no train but regular Bus Éireann buses serve the town from Busáras in the Dublin city center. The car or bus trip takes about an hour.

ESSENTIALS

Visitor Information Trim Visitor Center ⊠ *Old Town Hall, Castle St., Trim, Co. Meath* ☎ *046/943-7227* ⊕ *www.meath.ie/tourism.*

EXPLORING

TOP ATTRACTIONS

Cnoc an Linsigh. An attractive area south of Summerhill with forest walks and picnic sites, Cnoc an Linsigh is ideal for a half day of meandering. Many of the lanes that crisscross this part of County Meath provide delightful driving between high hedgerows, and afford occasional views of the lush, pastoral countryside.

Laracor. At Laracor, 3 km (2 miles) south of Trim on R158, a wall to the left of the rectory marks the now-destroyed building where Jonathan Swift (1667–1745), the satirical writer, poet, and author of *Gulliver's Travels,* was rector from 1699 until 1713, when he was made dean of St. Patrick's Cathedral in Dublin. Nearby are the walls of the cottage where Esther Johnson, the "Stella" who inspired much of Swift's writings, once lived. ⊠ *Co. Meath.*

Newtown. Located 1¼ km (¾ mile) east of Trim on the banks of the River Boyne, Newtown contains the ruins of what was once the largest cathedral in Ireland, built beginning in 1210 by Simon de Rochfort, the first Anglo-Norman bishop of Meath. ⊠ *Co. Meath.*

Royal Mint. Facing the river is the Royal Mint, a ruin that illustrates Trim's political importance in the Middle Ages. It produced coins with colorful names like "Irelands" and "Patricks" right up into the 15th century. ⊠ *Trim, Co. Meath.*

St. Patrick's Cathedral. The Church of Ireland St. Patrick's Cathedral dates from early in the 19th century, but the square tower is from an earlier structure built in 1449. Bishops were enthroned here as early as 1536. The stained glass in the west window was the first commission of Edward Burne Jones. ⊠ *Loman St., Trim, Co. Meath.*

Summerhill. One of the most pleasant villages of south County Meath, Summerhill, 8 km (5 miles) southeast of Laracor along R158, has a large square and a village green with a 15th-century cross. ⊠ *Summerhill, Co. Meath.*

Trim Castle. The largest Anglo-Norman fortress in Ireland, Trim Castle dominates present-day Trim from its 2½-acre site, which slopes down to the river's placid waters. Built by Hugh de Lacy in 1173, the castle was soon destroyed, and then rebuilt from 1190 to 1220. The ruins include an enormous keep with 70-foot-high turrets flanked by rectangular towers. The outer castle wall is almost 500 yards long, and five D-shaped towers survive. So impressive is the castle that it was used as a medieval backdrop in Mel Gibson's movie *Braveheart*. The admission price includes a house tour. ⊠ *Trim, Co. Meath* ☎ *046/943–8619* ⊕ *www.heritageireland.ie* 🖃 *Keep and grounds €4, grounds only €3* ☉ *Mid Mar.–Sept., daily 10–6; Oct. daily 9:30–5:30; Nov.–Jan. weekends 9–5; Feb.–mid Mar., weekends 9:30–5:30.*

Yellow Steeple. Overlooking Trim from a ridge situated opposite the castle, the Yellow Steeple was built in 1368 and is a remnant of the Augustinian abbey of St. Mary's, founded in the 13th century. This constituted the site of a great medieval pilgrimage to a statue of the Blessed Virgin. Much of the tower was deliberately destroyed in 1649 to prevent its falling into Cromwell's hands, and today only the striking, 125-foot-high east wall remains. ⊠ *Trim, Co. Meath.*

WORTH NOTING

Meath Heritage Centre. If your ancestors are from County Meath, take advantage of the family-history tracing service at this genealogy center. ⊠ *Castle St., Trim, Co. Meath* ☎ *046/943–6633* ⊕ *www.meathroots.com* 🖃 *Free* ☉ *Mon.–Thurs. 9–1 and 1:30–5, Fri. 9–2.*

WHERE TO STAY

For expanded hotel reviews, visit Fodors.com.

$

B&B/INN

🖽 **Tigh Catháin.** About 1 km (½ mile) outside of town on the Longwood road, the "House of O'Catháin" is a Tudor-style country cottage with four artfully decorated guest rooms and lovely gardens out back and in front, which are perfect for lounging around in the sun. **Pros:** family-owned and -run; big, hearty breakfast; glorious gardens. **Cons:** small and often booked up; half a mile to nearest town; few facilities. **TripAdvisor:** "gracious host," "beautiful stay," "comfortable room." ⑤ *Rooms from: €76* ✉ *High St., Trim, Co. Meath* ☎ *046/943–1996* ⊕ *www.tighcathain-bnb.com* ⮎ *4 rooms* ⦿| *Breakfast.*

HILL OF TARA

8 km (5 miles) northeast of Trim, 40 km (25 miles) northwest of Dublin.

GETTING HERE AND AROUND

The Hill of Tara is an hour's drive from Dublin just off the N3/M3 motorway. From Belfast it's a 1½-hour drive; take the M1 and connect with the N51 at Drogheda. There is ample parking near the site. You can also take Bus Éireann route to Navan that passes within 1 km (2 miles) of the site and walk; ask the driver to drop you at the Tara Cross and follow the signs. Or a taxi from Navan to Tara costs about €15.

TOURS

Mary Gibbons Tours operates bus tours from Dublin Monday through Saturday. They charge €35, which includes a round-trip ticket and admission to the Hill of Tara and Newgrange. Tours depart from outside the Dublin Tourism office on Suffolk Street, as well as from some of the major hotels.

Transportation Contacts Mary Gibbons Tours ☎ *086/335–1355* ⊕ *www.newgrangetours.com.*

EXPLORING

★ **Hill of Tara.** In the legends and the popular imagination of the Irish this ancient site has taken on mythic proportions. As with much of the idealization of the Celtic past, it was the 19th-century revival led by W. B. Yeats and Lady Gregory that was responsible for the near-religious veneration of this site, set at the junction of the five ancient roads of Ireland, and known in popular folklore as the seat of the High Kings of Ireland. The 19th-century ballad by Thomas Moore, "The Harp That Once Through Tara's Halls," was also a major factor in the long over-romanticized view of Tara. Today, its ancestral banqueting hall and great buildings (one was the former palace of the Ard Rí, or High King) have all vanished but for a few columns. Still, the site is awe-inspiring.

From the top of the Hill of Tara—it rises more than 300 feet above sea level—you can see across the flat central plain of Ireland, with the mountains of east Galway visible from nearly 160 km (100 miles) away. In the mid-19th century, the nationalist leader Daniel O'Connell staged a mass rally here that supposedly drew more than a million people—which would be nearly a third of Ireland's current population. On-site, first pay a call on the Interpretative Center housed in an old Church of Ireland church on the hillside. Here, you can learn the story of Tara and its legends. Without this background it will be difficult to identify many of the earthworks at Tara. Or just call upon your imagination to evoke the millennia-old spirit of the place and picture it in its prime, with the tribes congregating for some great pagan ceremony.

Systematic excavation by 20th-century archaeologists has led to the conclusion that the largest remains are those of an Iron Age fort that had multiple ring forts, some of which were ruined in the 19th century by religious zealots from England searching for the Ark of the Covenant here. The "Mound of the Hostages," a Neolithic passage grave, most likely gave the place its sacred air. During the hill's reign as a royal seat, which lasted to the 11th century, a great *feis* (national assembly) was held here every third year, during which laws were passed and tribal disputes settled.

FIRES OF FAITH

The Hill of Tara's decline was predicted one Easter Eve in the 5th century when, in accordance with the Druid religion, the lighting of fires was forbidden. Suddenly, on a hillside some miles away, flames were spotted. "If that fire is not quenched now," said a Druid leader, "it will burn forever and will consume Tara." The fire had been lighted by St. Patrick at Slane to celebrate the Christian rites of the Paschal.

Tara's influence waned with the arrival of Christianity; the last king to live here was Malachy II, who died in 1022. But as with so many other prominent sites of the Irish pre-Christian era, Christianity remade Tara in its own image.

Today a modern statue of St. Patrick stands here, as does a pillar stone that may have been the coronation stone (it was reputed to call out in approval when a king was crowned). In the graveyard of the adjacent Anglican church is a pillar with the worn image of a pagan god, and a Bronze Age stone standing on end. ✉ *Co. Meath* ☎ *046/902–5903* ⊕ *www.heritageireland.ie* 🎟 *€3* ⏱ *May 28–Sept. 16, daily 10–6.*

WHERE TO EAT AND STAY
For expanded hotel reviews, visit Fodors.com.

$$
MODERN IRISH
★

✕ **Eden.** One of Dublin's endearingly favorite chic restaurants has set up a second home in the vaulted cellar of Bellinter House. Eden sticks to its seasonal ethos with menus based on locally sourced produce. Boxty (potato cake) salad is an interesting twist on a traditional starter, and the slow cooked lamb shank with mashed potato, green beans, and caramelized baby onion is an exciting main. 💲 *Average main: €21* ✉ *Bellinter House, 4 km (2 miles) northwest of Hill of Tara and 7 km (5 miles) south of Navan, Navan, Co. Meath* ☎ *46/9030900* ⊕ *www.bellinterhouse.com* 🍴 *Reservations essential.*

$$
B&B/INN
Fodor's Choice
★

🏨 **Bellinter House.** Surrounded by 12 acres on the banks of the Boyne, new owners of this splendid 1750 country house have refurbished the property, restoring the old glories of the place while adding a few modern twists. **Pros:** stunningly authentic four original rooms; serene infinity pool; great value. **Cons:** newer rooms not quite up to old house standard; staff can be a little inexperienced. **TripAdvisor:** "beautiful and relaxing," "18th-century charm," "lovely house and location." 💲 *Rooms from: €130* ✉ *7 km (4½ miles) south of Navan and 4 km (2½ miles) northwest of Hill of Tara, Navan, Co. Meath* ☎ *046/903–0900* ⊕ *www.bellinterhouse.com* 🛏 *34 rooms* 🍴 *Breakfast.*

SPORTS AND THE OUTDOORS

GOLF

Killeen Castle. The great Jack Nicklaus had a hands-on involvement in the design and construction of this championship-level course and golf school set in the serene woodlands of Norman Killeen Castle in Meath. Covering twice the acreage of an average championship course—you might need a buggy to get around—Nicklaus really had room to let his imagination run free and the natural water features and stonework are a special treat. Check out the wonderful Paul Ferriter sculpture of the great man himself near the first tee box. ⊠ *Co. Meath* ☎ *01/689–3000* ⊕ *www.killeencastle.com* ✉ *Greens fees: Apr.–Oct., Mon.–Thurs. and Sun. €100, Fri. and Sat. €125; Nov.–Mar., daily €75* ⅄ *18 holes. Yardage: 7,700. Par 72. Practice area, driving range, caddies, caddy carts, buggies, club rental, shoe rental, catering, golf school* ⊗ *Visitors: weekdays.*

KELLS

67 km (41 miles) northwest of Dublin.

In the 9th century, a group of monks from Iona in Scotland took refuge at Kells (Ceanannus Mór) after being expelled by the Danes. St. Columba had founded a monastery here 300 years earlier, and although some historians think it was indigenous monks who wrote and illustrated the *Book of Kells*—the Latin version of the four Gospels, and one of Ireland's greatest medieval treasures—most scholars now believe that the Scottish monks brought it with them. Reputed to have been fished out of a watery bog at Kells, the legendary manuscript was removed for safekeeping during the Cromwellian wars to Trinity College, Dublin, where it remains. A large exhibit is now devoted to it in the college's Old Library, where a few of the original pages at a time are on view.

GETTING HERE AND AROUND

Kells is a 50-minute drive northwest of Dublin on the M3 motorway. There is ample parking in and around the town. Bus Éireann has regular busses from Dublin; the trip takes 1 hour and 25 minutes.

EXPLORING

Kells Heritage Centre. Temporarily located in the Kells Town Hall tourist office, this center was scheduled at this writing to move into the old Courthouse building sometime in 2013. The prize exhibit is a brilliant copy of the *Book of Kells*—it's a more pleasant, less rushed, and less expensive way to see this medieval masterpiece compared with the madness of Trinity College in high season. ⊠ *Headfort Place, Kells, Co. Meath* ☎ *046/9248856* ✉ *Free* ⊗ *Weekdays 9:30–1 and 2–5.*

Round Tower. The nearly 100-foot-high Round Tower, adjacent to St. Colmcille's House, dates to before 1076 and is in almost perfect condition. The tower was likely used as a defensive hideout by local monks during an invasion; they would climb up the rope ladder with their valuables and pull it up after them. Its top story has five windows, not the usual four, each facing an ancient entrance into the medieval town. ⊠ *Kells, Co. Meath.*

St. Colmcille's House. Similar in appearance to St. Kevin's Church at Glendalough and Cormac's Chapel at Cashel, St. Colmcille's House is a small, two-story, 7th-century church measuring about 24 feet square and nearly 40 feet high, with a steeply pitched stone roof. ⊠ *Kells, Co. Meath.*

St. Columba's. Four elaborately carved High Crosses stand in the church graveyard; you'll find the stump of a fifth in the marketplace—during the 1798 uprising against British rule it was used as a gallows. ⊠ *Kells, Co. Meath.*

> **WINTER SOLSTICE AT NEWGRANGE**
>
> A visit to Newgrange's passage grave during the winter solstice is considered to be a memorable experience. You'll have to get on the nine-year waiting list to reserve one of the 24 places available on each of the five mornings (December 19–23). And then pray that no clouds obscure the sun and ruin the light show the Bronze Age builders intended.

NEWGRANGE

21 km (13 miles) east of Kells, 28 km (17 miles) northwest of Dublin.

Fodor's Choice ★

Expect to see no less than one of the most spectacular prehistoric tombs in Europe when you come to Newgrange. Built in the 4th millennium BC—which makes it roughly 1,000 years older than Stonehenge—Newgrange was constructed with some 250,000 tons of stone, much of which came from the Wicklow Mountains, 80 km (50 miles) to the south. The Brú na Bóinne Visitor Centre, near the village of Donore, is the starting point for all visits to and tours of Newgrange and Knowth. Arrive early if possible, because you can't book ahead of time and Newgrange often sells out in high season.

GETTING HERE AND AROUND

From Dublin it's about a 50-minute drive to Newgrange: take the M1 motorway north to the Donore exit before Drogheda; Brú na Bóinne is clearly signposted before the exit. Drive about 6 km (4 miles) to the village of Donore, turn right and travel about half a mile to the visitor center. There is ample parking at the center. The Bus Éireann route from Dublin to Drogheda stops at Newgrange, and Mary Gibbons Tours combines a visit to this site with the Hill of Tara on its bus tour. Over the Top Tours also runs a daily shuttle bus from Dublin to Newgrange.

ESSENTIALS

Transportation Contacts **Mary Gibbons Tours** ☎ *086/335–1355* ⊕ *www.newgrangetours.com.* **Over the Top Tours** ☎ *01/860–0404, 1800/424252* ⊕ *www.overthetoptours.com.*

Visitor Information **Brú na Bóinne Visitor Centre** ⊠ *Off N2, near Donore village, Kells, Co. Meath* ⊕ *www.heritageireland.ie* ☉ *Nov.–Jan., daily 9–5; Feb.–Apr. and Oct., daily 9:30–5:30; May, daily 9–6:30; June–mid-Sept., daily 9–7; mid- to late Sept., daily 9–6:30. Last tour leaves from visitor center 1 hour and 45 minutes before closing.*

Built between 3100 and 2900 BC, Newgrange is strikingly adorned with boulders carved with Neolithic triple spirals and diamonds.

EXPLORING

Knowth. The prehistoric sites of Dowth and Knowth have been under excavation since 1962, and although Dowth is still closed to the public, Knowth is now open. The great tumulus at Knowth is comparable in size and shape to Newgrange, standing at 40 feet and having a diameter of approximately 214 feet. Some 150 giant stones, many of them beautifully decorated, surrounded the mound. More than 1,600 boulders, each weighing from one to several tons, were used in the construction. The earliest tombs and carved stones date from the Stone Age (3000 BC), although the site was in use until the early 14th century. In the early Christian era (4th–8th century AD), it was the seat of the High Kings of Ireland. Much of the site is still under excavation, and you can often watch archaeologists at work here. Tours of the site depart from the Brú na Bóinne Visitor Centre. *Knowth and interpretive center €5 ☉ Nov.–Jan., daily 9–5; Feb.–Apr. and Oct., daily 9:30–5:30; May, daily 9–6:30; June–mid-Sept., daily 9–7; mid- to late Sept., daily 9–6:30. Last tour leaves from visitor center 1 hour and 45 minutes before closing.*

Fodor's Choice ★ **Newgrange.** How the people who built the Newgrange tumulus transported the stones to the spot remains a mystery. The mound above the tomb measures more than 330 feet across and reaches a height of 36 feet at the front. White quartz stone was used for the retaining wall, and egg-shaped gray stones were studded at intervals. The passage grave may have been the world's earliest solar observatory. It was so carefully constructed that, for five days on and around the winter solstice, the rays of the rising sun still hit a roof box above the lintel at the entrance to the grave. The rays then shine for about 20 minutes down the main interior passageway to illuminate the burial chamber. The site was restored in 1962 after years of neglect and quarrying. The geometric designs on some stones at the center of the burial chamber continue to baffle experts. Tours of the site depart from the Brú na Bóinne Visitor Centre. ⊕ *www. heritageireland.ie* ✉ *Newgrange and interpretive center €6* ⊗ *Nov.–Jan., daily 9–5; Feb.–Apr. and Oct., daily 9:30–5:30; May, daily 9–6:30; June–mid-Sept., daily 9–7; mid- to late Sept., daily 9–6:30. Last tour leaves from visitor center 1 hour and 45 minutes before closing.*

> ## WORD OF MOUTH
>
> "The massive entrance stone to Newgrange is covered with swirling designs. Back then, it must have taken weeks to carve this complex design, during an era when time spent not farming meant not eating."
>
> —GreenDragon

SLANE

2½ km (1½ miles) north of Newgrange, 46 km (29 miles) northwest of Dublin.

Slane Castle is the draw at this small Georgian village, built in the 18th century around a crossroads on the north side of the River Boyne.

GETTING HERE AND AROUND

Slane is a 40-minute drive (47 km [29 miles]) northwest of Dublin on the N2 major road. There is plenty of parking around the town and at the castle. Bus Éireann runs a regular service from Busáras in Dublin; it takes about an hour and 10 minutes.

ESSENTIALS

Slane Tourism ☎ *041/988–4077* ⊕ *slanetourism.com.*

EXPLORING

Hermitage. The 16th-century building known as the Hermitage was constructed on the site where St. Erc, a local man converted to Christianity by St. Patrick himself, led a hermit's existence. All that remains of his original monastery is the faint trace of the circular ditch, but the ruins of the later church include a nave and a chancel with a tower in between. ✉ *Co. Meath.*

♻ **Newgrange Farm.** A two-hour tour of farmer Willie Redhouse's fully functioning arable and livestock farm includes feeding the ducks, bottle-feeding the lambs, a tour of the aviaries with their exotic birds, and a straw maze for the kids. A blacksmith gives demonstrations of his ancient art, and there is a nice tractor-trailer ride around the farm. Every Sunday at 3 pm the Sheep Derby takes place, with teddy bears tied astride the animals in the place of jockeys. Visiting children are made "owners" of individual sheep for the duration of the race. ✉ *N51, 3 km (2 miles) east of Slane, Co. Meath* ☎ *041/982–4119* ⊕ *www. newgrangefarm.com* ✉ *€9* ⊗ *Mar. 17–Sept. 9, daily 10–6.*

★ **Slane Castle.** The stately 18th-century Slane Castle is beautifully situated overlooking a natural amphitheater. In 1981 the castle's owner,

Anglo-Irish Lord Henry Mount Charles, staged the first of what have been some of Ireland's largest outdoor rock concerts; REM's show holds the record for attendance, with 70,000, while other stars that have appeared here have included Madonna, Bob Dylan, and the Rolling Stones. As for the Gothic-style castle itself, after a decade of renovation following a devastating fire, it reopened to the public in 2001. The tour includes the main hall, with its delicate plasterwork and beautiful stained glass, the dazzling red, neo-Gothic ballroom completed in 1821 for the visit of King George IV, and other rooms. The stunning parklands were laid out by Capability Brown, the famous 18th-century landscape gardener. ☎ 41/9820643 ⊕ *www.slanecastle.ie* ☒ €7 ⊘ *June 3–Sept. 1, Sun.–Thurs. noon–5.*

Slane Hill. North of Slane town is the 500-foot-high Slane Hill, where St. Patrick proclaimed the arrival of Christianity in 433 by lighting the Paschal Fire. From the top, you have sweeping views of the Boyne Valley. On a clear day, the panorama stretches from Trim to Drogheda, a vista extending 40 km (25 miles).

WHERE TO STAY

For expanded hotel reviews, visit Fodors.com.

$$$$
B&B/INN
Fodor'sChoice
★

☒ **Tankardstown House.** Voted the best private-house hotel in Ireland in a national newspaper, Tankardstown is a sumptuous Georgian-era manor house with a classic walled garden and 80 acres of breathtaking parkland, located 3 km (2 miles) from Slane. **Pros:** authentic Georgian exterior and interiors; idyllic natural setting; cottages a great option for families. **Cons:** not cheap in the current climate; limited facilities for the price. **TripAdvisor:** "restaurant with style," "fantastic house," "beautiful setting." ⑤ *Rooms from: €315* ☒ *2.5 km (1 mile) from the gates of Slane Castle, Slane, Co. Meath* ☎ *041/982–4621* ⊕ *www.tankardstown. ie* ⏎ *6 rooms, 5 suites, 7 cottages* ⋈ *Breakfast.*

DROGHEDA

15½ km (9 miles) east of Slane, 45 km (28 miles) north of Dublin.

Drogheda (pronounced draw-*hee*-da) is one of the most enjoyable and historic towns on the east coast of Ireland—and a setting for one of the most tragic events in Irish history, the siege and massacre wrought by Oliver Cromwell's English army. It was colonized in 911 by the Danish Vikings; two centuries later, the town was taken over by Hugh de Lacy, the Anglo-Norman lord of Trim, who was responsible for fortifying the towns along the River Boyne. At first, two separate towns existed, one on the northern bank, the other on the southern bank. In 1412, already heavily walled and fortified, Drogheda was unified, making it the largest English town in Ireland. Today, large 18th-century warehouses line the northern bank of the Boyne. The center of town, around West Street, is the historic heart of Drogheda.

GETTING HERE AND AROUND

Thanks to the M1 motorway, Drogheda is a short 45-minute trip north of Dublin. Paid parking is available throughout the town. Bus Éireann operates Expressway and regular services connecting Drogheda to

Dublin (40 minutes), Belfast (1 hour 30 minutes), Dundalk (30 minutes), and Navan (40 minutes), while Irish Rail connects the town to Hueston Station in Dublin (51 minutes [express]), Belfast (1 hour 40 minutes), and Dundalk (20 minutes) on the same line. The bus station is just south of the river on the corner of John Street and Donore Road and the train station is south of the river and east of the town center on the Dublin Road.

ESSENTIALS

Visitor Information Drogheda Tourist Office ⊠ *The Tholsel, West St., Drogheda, Co. Louth* ☎ *041/987–2843* ⊕ *www.drogheda.ie.*

EXPLORING

TOP ATTRACTIONS

Drogheda Museum Millmount. Perhaps the main attraction in Drogheda lies across the river from the town center. The museum and Martello Tower, off the Dublin road (N1) south of Drogheda, shares space in a renovated British Army barracks with crafts workshops, including a pottery- and picture-gallery and studio. It was on the hill at Millmount that the townsfolk made their last stand against the bloodthirsty Roundheads of Cromwell. Perhaps in defiance of Cromwell's attempt to obliterate the town from the map, the museum contains relics of eight centuries of Drogheda's commercial and industrial past, including painted banners of the old trade guilds, a circular willow-and-leather coracle (the traditional fishing boat on the River Boyne), and many instruments and utensils from domestic and factory use. Most moving are the mementos of the infamous 1649 massacre of 3,000 people by Cromwell. There are also geological and archaeological displays. The exhibit inside the Martello Tower adjacent to the museum focuses on the military history of Drogheda. ⊠ *Millmount, Drogheda, Co. Louth* ☎ *041/983–3097* ⊕ *www.droghedamuseum.ie* ⊠ *Museum €3.50, tower €3* ⊙ *Mon.–Sat. 9:30–5:30, Sun. 2–5.*

St. Laurence's Gate. One of the two surviving entrances from Drogheda's original 11 gates in its town walls, the 13th-century St. Laurence's Gate has two four-story drum towers and is one of the most perfect examples in Ireland of a medieval town gate. ⊠ *Drogheda, Co. Louth.*

WORTH NOTING

Butler's Gate. One of the original 11 town entrances, Butler's Gate predates St. Laurence's Gate by 50 years or more, making it one of the earliest surviving Norman urban structures in Ireland. It's near the Millmount Museum. ⊠ *Millmount, Drogheda, Co. Louth.*

St. Peter's. A severe, 18th-century church within an enclosed courtyard, the Anglican St. Peter's is rarely open except for Sunday services. It's worth a peek for its setting and the fine views over the town from the churchyard. ⊠ *Fair St., Drogheda, Co. Louth* ⊕ *stpetersdrogheda.ie.*

St. Peter's Church. The Gothic-Revival Roman Catholic St. Peter's Church houses the preserved head of St. Oliver Plunkett. Primate of all Ireland, he was martyred in 1681 at Tyburn in London; his head was pulled from the execution flames. ⊠ *West St., Drogheda, Co. Louth.*

Tholsel. This bank building has an 18th-century square granite edifice with a cupola. ⊠ *West St. and Shop St., Drogheda, Co. Louth.*

Victorian Railway Viaduct. The center of town, around West Street, is the historic heart of Drogheda. Among the town's leading landmarks is the long railway viaduct, which towers over the river. Built around 1850 as part of the railway line from Dublin to Belfast, it's still used and is a splendid example of Victorian engineering. Its height above the river makes the viaduct Drogheda's most prominent landmark.

WHERE TO STAY

For expanded hotel reviews, visit Fodors.com.

$$
B&B/INN
🏠 **Boyne Valley Hotel and Country Club.** A 1-km (½-mile) drive leads to this 19th-century mansion that was once owned by a Drogheda brewing family and now offers contemporary-style guest lodgings. **Pros:** great activity facilities; lovely grounds. **Cons:** uninspired decor; newer building a touch functional; restaurant only open weekends. **TripAdvisor:** "lovely place to visit," "the food is very good," "wonderful staff." ⑤ *Rooms from: €138* ⊠ *Dublin Rd., Drogheda, Co. Louth* 🕾 *041/983–7737* ⊕ *www.boyne-valley-hotel.ie* ⇗ *71 rooms* ⦙◎⦙ *Breakfast.*

$
HOTEL
🏠 **The D Hotel.** A dramatic location on the south bank of the Boyne easily makes up for the slightly functional exterior of this trendy new hotel in the center of medieval Drogheda—happily, the guest rooms are very Swedish modern in feel, making for a very restful stay. **Pros:** dramatic riverside location; extra comfy big beds; great terrace for drinks and people-watching. **Cons:** only some rooms have great views; uninspired exterior design; restaurant open weekends only off season. **TripAdvisor:** "great place to stay," "lovely," "well recommended." ⑤ *Rooms from: €99* ⊠ *Scotch Hall, Drogheda, Co. Louth* 🕾 *041/987–7700* ⊕ *www.thedhotel.com* ⇗ *104 rooms* ⦙◎⦙ *Breakfast.*

SPORTS AND THE OUTDOORS

GOLF

County Louth Golf Club. This course is better known by the name of its hometown, Baltray, and covers 190 acres by the Irish Sea at the mouth of the River Boyne. This wonderful links course manages to keep a relatively low profile, which means less crowds in summer. Long hitters will love the atypical layout, a par-72 that features five par-5s, but beware the well-protected, undulating greens. ⊠ *Drogheda, Co. Louth* 🕾 *041/988–1530* ⊕ *www.countylouthgolfclub.com* ⛳ *Greens fees: Nov.–Mar., weekdays €65, weekends €85; Apr. weekdays €80, weekends €100; May–Jul., weekdays €100, weekends €135; Aug.–Sept weekdays €95, weekends €130; Oct. weekdays €75.* 🏌 *18 holes. Yardage: 6,936. Par 72. Practice area, caddies (reserve in advance), caddy carts, club rental, catering* ⊗ *Visitors: Mon. and Wed.–Sun. No weekends Oct.–Dec.*

MELLIFONT ABBEY

10 km (8 miles) northwest of Drogheda.

GETTING HERE AND AROUND

The abbey is a 13-km (8-mile) drive northwest of Drogheda off the R168 (Drogheda to Collon Road). From Dublin just take the M1 to Drogheda and the smaller road from there. There is ample parking at the site. There is no public transport to the abbey, but you can get a taxi from Drogheda.

EXPLORING

★ **Mellifont Abbey.** On the eastern bank of the River Mattock, which creates a natural border between counties Meath and Louth, lie the remains of Mellifont Abbey, the first Cistercian monastery in Ireland. Founded in 1142 by St. Malachy, archbishop of Armagh, it was inspired by the formal structure surrounding a courtyard of St. Bernard of Clairvaux's monastery, which St. Malachy had visited.

Among the substantial ruins are the two-story chapter house, built in 12th-century English-Norman style and once a daily meeting place for the monks; it now houses a collection of medieval glazed tiles. Four walls of the 13th-century octagonal lavabo, or washing place, still stand, as do some arches from the Romanesque cloister. At its peak Mellifont presided over almost 40 other Cistercian monasteries throughout Ireland, but all were suppressed by Henry VIII in 1539 after his break with the Catholic Church. Adjacent to the parking lot is a small **architectural museum** depicting the history of the abbey and the craftsmanship that went into its construction. ✉ *Near Collon, Co. Louth* ☏ *041/982–6459* ⊕ *www.heritageireland.ie* ☑ *€3* ◷ *Late April–Sept., daily 10–5:15.*

WHERE TO EAT

$$$
IRISH
★

✕ **Forge Gallery Restaurant.** For generations the local forge was the burning heart of any rural Irish community, and this well-established restaurant is still something of a beacon to locals and visitors for miles around. Warm rose and plum tones and antique furnishings decorate this two-story eatery in a converted forge, and an old fireplace fills the place with a comforting warmth and light. The cuisine mixes French Provençal with a strong hint of traditional Irish cooking. Two popular specialties are roast duckling served on a bed of greens, with spring onion, soy, and ginger sauce, and tagine of mussels, scallops, and crab claws served in a creamy saffron sauce. Make sure you try one of the seasonal homemade soups. Paintings by local artists hang in the reception area and are for sale. Reservations are essential on weekends. 💲 *Average main: €31* ✉ *N2, north of Slane, Collon, Co. Louth* ☏ *041/982–6272* ⊕ *www.forgegalleryrestaurant.ie* ◷ *Closed Mon. and Tue. No dinner Sunday. No lunch Wed.–Sat.*

ARDEE

14½ km (9 miles) northwest of Mellifont Abbey.

The road from Mellifont Abbey to Ardee passes through Monaster-boice, home to some of Ireland's finest medieval High Crosses. Near the village's Round Tower, you'll find the famed Muireadach Cross and, nearby, the West Cross, the tallest in all the country. Once you take in these noted medieval sculptures, continue on to the market town of Ardee, found at the northern edge of the Pale. Here stand two 13th-century castles: Ardee Castle and Hatch's Castle. The town of Ardee (Baile Átha Fhirdia or Ferdia's Ford), interestingly, was named after the ford where the mythical folk hero Cuchulainn fought his foster brother Ferdia. There's a statue depicting this battle at the start of the riverside walk.

GETTING HERE AND AROUND

Take the M1 motorway north from Dublin and exit at junction 14, then take the roundabout onto the N33 (signposted Ardee). There is a regular bus Éireann service from Dublin. Parking is readily available around the town.

EXPLORING

Ardee Castle. The one with square corners, Ardee Castle was founded by Roger de Peppard in 1207, but much of the present building dates to the 15th century and later. The castle faces north—its objective to protect the Anglo-Irish Pale from the untamed Celtic tribes of Ulster. It was converted into a courthouse in the 19th century. ⊠ *Ardee, Co. Louth.*

Hatch's Castle. The one with rounded corners, Hatch's Castle is a private residence and not open to the public. Built in the 13th century, it was given by Cromwell as a gift to the loyal Hatch family. If you look closely you can see it still flaunts two 18th-century cannons at its entrance.

St. Mary's Church of Ireland. Set on Main Street, St. Mary's Church of Ireland incorporates part of a 13th-century Carmelite church burned by Edward the Bruce in 1316, including the holy-water font. The current building was constructed in the 19th century. ⊠ *Main St., Ardee, Co. Louth* ☎ *183/23019.*

WHERE TO EAT

$

SEAFOOD

★

✕ **The Glyde Inn.** Sitting right on the edge of Dundalk Bay and overlooking the Cooley and Mourne mountains, this stolid little guesthouse ("inn" is pushing it) and pub now also features a quality surf-and-turf restaurant. You'd never know the Glyde was established way back in 1700, as it is now such a casual, no-fuss place. Happily, the hospitality matches the delicious locally sourced food and great vistas. The menu ranges from fish-and-chips—comfort food at its best—to lobster (the poor critters are housed in a tank tiny enough to make some people lose their appetite). Their four-course special is a great deal and they also do a mean Irish breakfast. You can really enjoy that if you book one of the inn's few B&B rooms. ⑤ *Average main: €14* ⊠ *Annagassan, Co. Louth* ☎ *042/937–2350* ⊕ *www.theglydeinn.ie.*

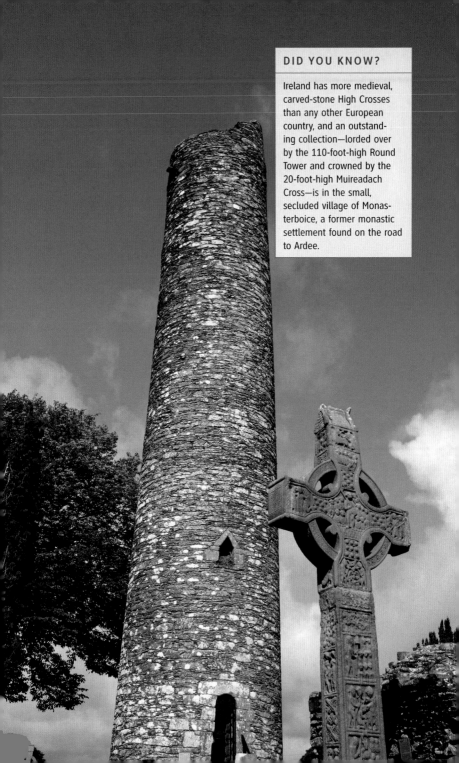

DUNDALK

14½ km (9 miles) east of Inniskeen, 20 km (12.5 miles) northeast of Ardee, 80 km (50 miles) north of Dublin.

Perfectly positioned as a hub to explore the region north and south of the border, Dundalk—only 9½ km (6 miles) from Northern Ireland—is the main town of County Louth (Ireland's smallest county). Its earliest settlement dates from the early Christian period, around the 7th century. In May the town hosts an avant-garde "fringe" drama and visual arts festival (with a nice schedule of children's events).

THE LEGENDARY CUCHULAINN

The area around Dundalk is closely connected with Cuchulainn (pronounced *coo*-chu-lain)—"a greater hero than Hercules or Achilles," as Frank McCourt, in *Angela's Ashes,* quotes his father. Cuchulainn, the warrior of the Irish epic *Táin Bó Cuailnge* (Cattle Raid of Cooley), heroically defended this area of ancient Ulster against invaders.

GETTING HERE AND AROUND

From Dublin take the M1 north and exit at junction 16 onto the roundabout. Take the first exit onto the N52 to Dundalk. Bus Éireann runs regular buses from Dublin to the town's bus station on Long Walk near the main shopping center; the trip takes 1 hour and 30 minutes. Routes from Belfast and Drogheda also connect to Dundalk. Serviced by Irish Rail, Clarke Train Station is on Carrickmacross Road. There are daily trains to Dublin (1 hour 20 minutes); Belfast (1 hour 20 minutes); and Drogheda (20 minutes).

ESSENTIALS

Visitor Information Dundalk Tourist Office ⊠ *Jocelyn St., Dundalk, Co. Louth* ☎ *042/933–5484* ⊕ *www.dundalk.ie.*

EXPLORING

Bell Tower. Dundalk is an uninspiring, frontier town but has some fine, notable historic buildings. On Mill Street, the bell tower of a Franciscan monastery with Gothic windows dates from the 13th century. ⊠ *Dundalk, Co. Louth.*

County Museum Dundalk. Set in a beautifully restored 18th-century warehouse, this museum is dedicated to preserving the history of the dying local industries, such as beer brewing, cigarette manufacturing, shoe and boot making, and railway engineering. Other exhibits deal with the history of Louth from 7500 BC to the present. ⊠ *Joycelyn St., Dundalk, Co. Louth* ☎ *042/932–7056* ⊕ *www.dundalkmuseum. ie* ⊗ *Tues.–Sat. 10–5.*

Dundalk District Court Office. The Market House, the Town Hall, and the Courthouse are examples of the town's 19th-century heritage; the Courthouse is the most impressive of the three, built in the 1820s in a severe Greek Revival style, with Doric columns supporting the portico. It stands north of St. Patrick's Cathedral. ⊠ *Dundalk, Co. Louth* ☎ *42/9392350.*

St. Patrick's Cathedral. Built between 1835 and 1847, this grand cathedral was designed when the Gothic Revival was at its height. With its buttresses and mosaics lining the chancel and the side chapel walls, it was modeled on the 15th-century King's College Chapel at Cambridge, England. The fine exterior was built in Newry granite, and the high altar and pulpit are of carved Caen stone. ⊠ *Town center, Dundalk, Co. Louth* ☏ *42/9334648* ⊕ *www.stpatricksparishdundalk. org* ☏ *€5.50* ☉ *Daily 8–6.*

WHERE TO EAT AND STAY

For expanded hotel reviews, visit Fodors.com.

$ ✕ **Restaurant Number Thirty Two.** A cozy, local spot with a wonderfully
EUROPEAN warm welcome, Thirty Two is situated in a quiet part of town near the county museum. The light-filled dining room has simple decor and ideal people-watching windows, while the menu offers quality, uncomplicated fare. To start, try the pan-seared squid with citrus sour yogurt and chili-and-red-pepper jam. Follow up with the duck confit, served with glazed shallots, Puy lentil cassoulet, and port and ginger jellies. Their early evening menu is an incredibly good value. ⑤ *Average main: €15* ⊠ *32 Chapel St., Dundalk, Co. Louth* ☏ *042/933–1113* ☉ *Closed Sun. No lunch.*

$$ 🏨 **Ballymascanlon House Hotel.** Just north of Dundalk, this Victorian man-
HOTEL sion with a slightly severe but elegant modern addition sits on 130 acres on the scenic Cooley Peninsula. **Pros:** guest rooms big enough to get lost in; cheap golf for residents; good weekend, all-inclusive deals. **Cons:** a little pricey for the area; in-room facilities sparse; popular for weddings. **TripAdvisor:** "wonderful experience," "beautiful gardens," "lovely short break." ⑤ *Rooms from: €160* ⊠ *Dundalk, Co. Louth* ☏ *042/935–8200* ⊕ *www.ballymascanlon.com* ⤳ *90 rooms* ⏝⏝ *Breakfast.*

$ 🏨 **Innisfree House.** An early-20th-century redbrick gem in the heart of
B&B/INN Dundalk, Innisfree House is a shockingly good value considering the
★ genteel, stylish atmosphere created by the beautiful Edwardian furniture and antiques throughout. **Pros:** genuine afternoon tea served; option of evening dining; authentic Edwardian furnishings. **Cons:** not in the most picturesque area; maybe a little overdecorated; short on facilities. **TripAdvisor:** "sumptuous luxury," "great place to stay," "a true treat." ⑤ *Rooms from: €65* ⊠ *Carrick Rd., Dundalk, Co. Louth* ☏ *042/933–4912* ⊕ *www.innisfreehouse.ie* ⤳ *9 rooms* ⏝⏝ *Breakfast.*

COUNTY WICKLOW

Make your way to the fourth or fifth story of almost any building in Dublin that faces south and you can see off in the distance—amazingly, not *that* far off in the distance—the green, smooth hills of the Dublin and Wicklow mountains. On a clear day the mountains are even visible from some streets in and around the city center. If your idea of solace is green hills, and your visit to Ireland is otherwise limited to Dublin, County Wicklow—or Cill Mhantain (pronounced kill *wan*-tan), as it's known in Irish—should be on your itinerary.

Counties Kildare
and Wicklow

Not that the secret isn't out; rugged and mountainous with dark, wooded forests, central Wicklow, known as the "garden of Ireland," is a popular picnic area among Dubliners. It has some of Ireland's grandest 18th-century mansions, including Russborough and Powerscourt, and cradles one of the country's earliest Christian retreats: Glendalough. Nestled in a valley of dense woods and placid lakes, Glendalough and environs can seem (at least during the off-season) practically untouched since their heyday 1,000 years ago. The granite mountains that have protected Glendalough all these years run into the sea along the east coast, which has several popular sandy beaches.

BLESSINGTON

23 km (14 miles) southwest of Dublin.

On the western shore of the Poulaphouca Reservoir, known locally as Blessington Lakes, the small market town of Blessington, with its wide main street lined on both sides by tall trees and Georgian buildings, is one of the most charming villages in the area. It was founded in the late 17th century, and was a stop on the Dublin–Waterford mail coach service in the mid-19th century. Until 1932, a steam train ran from here to Dublin. Just outside the village are two of the marvels of Ireland:

18th-century **Russborough House** *(see "Treasure Hunt: the Anglo-Irish Georgian House")* and the adjacent Paulaphauca Reservoir.

GETTING HERE AND AROUND

You can reach Blessington by car from Dublin via the N81; the drive takes half an hour. Dublin bus runs a daily service to Blessington.

EXPLORING

Poulaphouca Reservoir. Known locally as the Blessington Lakes, Poulaphouca (pronounced pool-a-*fook*-a) is a large, meandering, artificial lake minutes from Russborough House that provides Dublin's water supply. You can drive around the entire perimeter of the reservoir on minor roads; on its southern end lies Hollywood Glen, a particularly beautiful natural spot. ⊕ *www.coillteoutdoors.ie/*.

OFF THE
BEATEN
PATH

Piper's Stones. Beyond the southern tip of the Poulaphouca Reservoir, 13 km (8 miles) south of Blessington on N81, look for a small sign for the Piper's Stones, a Bronze Age stone circle that was probably used in a ritual connected with worship of the sun. It's just a short walk from the road.

WHERE TO STAY

For expanded hotel reviews, visit Fodors.com.

$$$
HOTEL
Fodor's Choice
★

Rathsallagh House. A lovely hotel set in 530 acres of parkland, Rathsallagh House first came into being when low-slung, ivy-covered Queen Anne stables were converted into a farmhouse in 1798. **Pros:** large, luxurious rooms; superb dining room. **Cons:** books up easily; some variance in room quality; expensive food. **TripAdvisor:** "cozy," "absolutely charming," "lovely country house." ⑤ *Rooms from: €190* ⊠ *Dunlavin, Co. Wicklow* ☎ *045/403–112* ⊕ *www.rathsallagh.com* ⤚ *29 rooms* ⦿⦿ *Multiple meal plans.*

SPORTS AND THE OUTDOORS

HIKING

Church Mountain. You can take in splendid views of the Blessington Lakes from the top of Church Mountain, which you reach via a vigorous walk through Woodenboley Wood, at the southern tip of Hollywood Glen. Follow the main forest track for about 20 minutes and then take the narrow path that heads up the side of the forest to the mountaintop for about another half hour.

BRAY

22 km (14 miles) south of Dublin on N11, 8 km (5 miles) east of Enniskerry on R755.

One of Ireland's oldest seaside resorts, Bray is a trim, growing village known for its summer cottages and sand-and-shingle beach, which stretches for 2 km (1 mile). When the trains first arrived from Dublin in 1854, Bray became the number-one spot for urban vacationers and subsequently took on the appearance of an English oceanfront town. Some Dubliners still flock to the faded glory of Bray's boardwalk to push baby carriages and soak up the sun. Uncrowded trails for hiking and mountain biking crisscross the mountains bordering Bray to the south.

GETTING HERE AND AROUND

From Dublin take the N81 south to the M50 southbound. Exit onto the M11, and at junction 5 take the second exit at the roundabout to the R761 (signposted Bray). The drive takes about half an hour. The DART train runs regularly to Bray from Dublin, as do a number of city buses. There is plenty of parking around the town.

EXPLORING

Killruddery. The 17th-century formal gardens at Killruddery House are precisely arranged, with fine beech hedges, Victorian statuary, and a parterre of lavender and roses. The Brabazon family, the earls of Meath, have lived here since 1618. In 1820 they hired William Morris to remodel the house as an Elizabethan Revival mansion. The estate also has a Crystal Palace conservatory modeled on those at the botanic gardens in Dublin. Killruddery Arts organizes year-round arts events including the kid-friendly Enchanted Garden in late June and an old-fashioned Easter egg hunt. The tea house in the old dairy is a perfect spot for a light snack. ⊠ *Bray–Greystones Rd., 3 km (2 miles) south of Bray, Killruddery, Co. Wicklow* ☎ *01/286–3405* ⊕ *www. killruddery.com* ☞ *House and gardens €11, gardens only €6* ⊗ *Gardens: Apr. and Oct., weekends 9:30–5; May–Sept., daily 9:30–5; house July–Sept., daily 1–5.*

National Sealife. National Sealife is an aquarium and museum dedicated to the creatures of the sea, with an emphasis on those that occupy the waters around Ireland. Besides massive sea tanks that contain all manner of swimming things, there's a major conservation project with captive breeding of sea horses. **FinZone** is an undersea adventure trail perfect for kids, including puzzles to solve, and Nemo's Kingdom is a coral reef tank with all the fish portrayed in the Disney movie. Touch-screen computers and video games give the whole thing a high-tech feel. There are also regular feeding demonstrations during the day. In winter, call to confirm opening times before visiting. ⊠ *Strand Rd., Bray, Co. Wicklow* ☎ *01/286–6939* ⊕ *www.visitsealife.com/bray* ☞ *€8* ⊗ *Mar.–Oct., daily 10–5; Nov.–Feb. weekdays 11–4, weekends 10–5.*

One Martello Terrace. One Martello Terrace, at the harbor, is Bray's most famous address. James Joyce (1882–1941) lived here between 1887 and 1891 and used the house as the setting for the Christmas dinner in *A Portrait of the Artist as a Young Man.* Today the house is owned by an Irish *Teachta Dála* (member of Parliament, informally known as a "TD"). Although the residence has been renovated, the dining room portrayed in Joyce's novel maintains the spirit of his time. ⊠ *1 Martello Terrace, Bray, Co. Wicklow* ☎ *01/286–8407 TD constituency office, call Thurs. 10–1.*

WHERE TO EAT

$ ✕ **Campo de Fiori.** The most unassuming of exteriors hides one of Ireland's most authentic, award-winning Italian eateries. Owners Laura and Marco Roccasalvo (he's also the chef) and their Italian staff give this little place a warm, informal vibe. The old posters, "picturesque" fishing nets, and wine bottles on show might hint of tourist trap but the truth is a chilled-out spot that is introducing locals to the delights of hearty,

ITALIAN

★

no-frills Italian cuisine. Along with their kitchen, this place also offers an adorable blog and "Il Club dei Buongustai" (The Gourmets' Club), whose members sponsor theme nights and tasting-menu evenings (Sardinia was held in July). Year-round, their pizza and pasta specials are always worth checking out as well as such fine mains as the cod steak on a cream of chickpea, with capers and olives. The wine list is large and the staff loves to help you match your *vino* to your food. $ *Average main: €16* ⊠ *1 Albert Ave., Bray, Co. Wicklow* ☎ *01/276–4257* ⊕ *www.campodefiori.ie.*

$

SEAFOOD

Fodor's Choice

★

✕ **The Hungry Monk.** The cloisters- and refectory-style decor is definitely tongue-in-cheek at this upbeat, fun bistro in sleepy Greystones, an old-fashioned seaside resort a couple of miles south of Bray. Owner Pat Keown is a great host and his laughter and love of good food and fine wine are catching. Dinner is served by candlelight and the menu specializes in uncluttered seafood dishes in summer and wild game on those cold winter nights. The Seafood Symphony is a particular favorite, as is the Wicklow lamb-and-feta cheeseburger. Sunday lunches are famous for their length (they often last into the early evening) and for the lively atmosphere. $ *Average main: €17* ⊠ *1 Church Rd., Greystones, Co. Wicklow* ☎ *01/287–5759* ⊕ *www.thehungrymonk.ie* ⊗ *Closed Mon.– Wed. No lunch Thurs.–Sat. No dinner Sun.*

SPORTS AND THE OUTDOORS

HIKING

Bray Head. A well-marked path leads from the beach to the 10-foot-tall cross that crowns the spiny peak of Bray Head, a rocky outcrop that rises 791 feet from the sea. The semi-difficult, one-hour climb affords stunning views of Wicklow Town and Dublin Bay.

Wicklow Way. Whether you're a novice or veteran hiker, Wicklow's gentle, rolling hills are a terrific place to begin an Irish walking vacation. Devoted hikers come from all over the world to traverse the 137-km (85-mile) Wicklow Way, the first long-distance trail to open in Ireland, and one of the best. Wicklow is Ireland's little Alps, with bracing fresh air guaranteed among the blue skies and mountain heather and gorse. Much of the route lies above 1,600 feet and follows rough sheep tracks, forest firebreaks, and old bog roads (rain gear, windproof clothing, and sturdy footwear are essential). The trail starts in the outskirts of Dublin suburbs, in Marlay Park, just south of Dublin city center, then ascends into the Wicklow mountain foothills, before passing glens, farms, and historic sights like Rathgall, home to the Kings of Leinster, and the Mill of Purgatory—a venerated "wardrobe" in Aghowle Church—before finishing up in Clonegal. If your feet are less than bionic, you can just do any number of the short walks along the Way, or you might opt for biking, another excellent way to see the area.

Consider participating in one of the walking festivals held at Easter, in May, and in autumn. The autumn Footfalls Wicklow Walking Festival is a two-day event based in the Glenmalure area. It costs €18 a day, or €130 for a two-night B&B package. ☎ *0404/45152* ⊕ *www. wicklowway.com.*

POWERSCOURT HOUSE, GARDENS, AND WATERFALL

25 km (16 miles) south of Dublin on R117, 22 km (14 miles) north of Glendalough on R755.

One of the grandest estates and gardens in Ireland, Powerscourt is one of the main reasons that people head to Enniskerry, but just one among many. Within the shadow of famous Sugar Loaf Mountain, Enniskerry remains one of the prettiest villages in Ireland. It's built around a sloping central triangular square with a backdrop of the wooded Wicklow Mountains. That noted, Enniskerry is the gateway to get to Powerscourt.

GETTING HERE AND AROUND

Powerscourt is about a half-hour drive from Dublin. Head south from Dublin on the N81 to the M50 southbound. Take the exit for the M11, which becomes the N11, then take the R117 for Enniskerry and continue on to Powerscourt House and Gardens. You can also take the bus from Dublin to Enniskerry and walk the mile to Powerscourt. Alternatively, you can take the Irish Rail's DART train line from Dublin city center to Bray and then take Dublin bus No. 185c (€1.35) from outside the DART station in Bray all the way to Powerscourt. Be careful, as not all No. 185 buses go to Powerscourt, only the 185c buses. Check the bus timetable or ask the driver before you get on to make sure you have the right bus.

EXPLORING

Fodor'sChoice ★ **Powerscourt House & Gardens.** They really had the life, those old aristocrats. At more than 14,000 acres, including stunning formal gardens and a 400-foot waterfall, Powerscourt must have been some place to call home. The grounds were originally granted to Sir Richard Wingfield, the first viscount of Powerscourt, by King James I of England in 1609. Richard Castle (1690–1751), the architect of Russborough House, was hired to design the great house. His was an age not known for modesty, and he chose the grand Palladian style. The house took nine years to complete and was ready to move into in 1740. It was truly one of the great houses of Ireland and, indeed, all of Britain.

Unfortunately, you won't be able to see much of it. A terrible fire almost completely destroyed the house in 1974, cruelly on the eve of a huge party to celebrate the completion of a lengthy restoration by the Slazenger family of golfing manufacturing fame. A second period of renovation is currently underway and the original ballroom on the first floor—once "the grandest room in any Irish house," according to historian Desmond Guinness—is the only room that gives a sense of the place's former glory. It was based on Palladio's version of the "Egyptian Hall" designed by Vitruvius, architect to Augustus, emperor of Rome.

Powerscourt Gardens, considered among the finest in Europe, were laid out from 1745 to 1767 following the completion of the house—and were radically redesigned in the Victorian style, from 1843 to 1875, by Daniel Robertson. The Villa Butera in Sicily inspired him to set these gardens with sweeping terraces, antique sculptures, and a circular pond and fountain flanked by winged horses. There's a celebrated view of the Italianate patterned ramps, lawns, and pond across the beautiful, heavily wooded Dargle Valley, which stairsteps to the horizon and the noble profile of Sugar Loaf Mountain. The grounds include many specimen trees (plants grown for exhibition), an avenue of monkey puzzle

> **GENIUS IN A BOTTLE**
>
> Powerscourt's grand Victorian gardens were designed by an eccentric boozer, Daniel Robertson, who liked to be tooled around the gardens-in-progress in a wheelbarrow while taking nips from a bottle of sherry.

trees, a parterre of brightly colored summer flowers, and a Japanese garden. The kitchen gardens, with their modest rows of flowers, are a striking antidote to the classical formality of the main sections. A cute café, crafts and interior design shops, a garden center, and a children's play area are also in the house and on the grounds. ⊠ *Enniskerry, Co. Wicklow* ☎ *01/204–6000* ⊕ *www.powerscourt.ie* ⊒ *€8.50* ⊗ *Mon.– Sat. 9:30–5:30, Sun. 10–5:30.*

Powerscourt Waterfall. One of the most inspiring sights to the writers and artists of the Romantic generation, the 400-foot Powerscourt Waterfall, 5 km (3 miles) south of the gardens, is the highest in the British Isles. ⊠ *Enniskerry, Co. Wicklow* ☎ *01/204–6000* ⊒ *€5.50* ⊗ *Mar., Apr., Sept., and Oct., daily 10:30–5:30; May–Aug., daily 9:30–7; Nov.–Feb., daily 10:30–4. Closed two weeks before Christmas.*

WHERE TO EAT AND STAY

For expanded hotel reviews, visit Fodors.com.

$$$$
FRENCH
★
✕**Gordon Ramsay at Powerscourt.** Star of the bleep-ridden *Hell's Kitchen* TV show, Scottish superchef, and bad boy of English cuisine Gordon Ramsay has now set up shop in Ireland at the spectacular Ritz-Carlton hotel. The eponymous chef doesn't actually cook here but his inventive stamp can be seen all over the menu. Low ceilings give the very formal dining room a slightly overbearing feel, but large windows open onto a big terrace that is ideal for summer dining. The food is constantly exciting and innovative, and the six-course tasting menu is a great value. Starters include the stunning ravioli of lobster and Clare Island salmon with a lemongrass sauce. Top mains include the panfried hake with samphire, brown shrimp, and shellfish sauce. ⑤ *Average main: €33* ⊠ *Ritz-Carlton Powerscourt, Enniskerry, Co. Wicklow* ☎ *01/274–9377* ⊕ *www.ritzcarlton.com* ⊴ *Reservations essential.*

$
IRISH
✕**Poppies Country Cooking.** This cozy café—with a pine-panel ceiling, farmhouse furniture, and paintings of poppies on the walls—is a great place for breakfast, lunch, or late-afternoon tea. Expect potato cakes, shepherd's pie, lasagna, vegetarian quiche, house salads, and soup. But the most popular dishes are Poppies chicken (a casserole-like concoction) and homity pie (potpie with potatoes, onion, garlic, and cream cheese). For dessert try the apple pie or the rhubarb crumble, which is so good that the Irish rugby team stops by for it after practice. ⑤ *Average main: €7* ⊠ *The Square, Enniskerry, Co. Wicklow* ☎ *01/282–8869* ⊕ *www.poppies.ie* ⊗ *No dinner.*

3

$$$$ ⊞ **The Ritz-Carlton Powerscourt.** Set on the regal Powerscourt estate, the
RESORT   gargantuan Palladian-style exterior of this Xanadu may seem out of
★   place, but luxury always makes itself at home, and no one can carp
about the views of the fabled Sugar Loaf peak outside the soaring windows. **Pros:** sumptuous pool and spa; top restaurant; beautiful setting
in Powerscourt grounds. **Cons:** some people have called the exterior
over-the-top; garden rooms don't have a great view; can feel very busy at
times. **TripAdvisor:** "nice restaurant," "lovely staff," "charming location." ⑤ *Rooms from: €260* ⊠ *Powerscourt Estate, Enniskerry, Co.*
Wicklow ☎ *35/3274–8888* ⊕ *www.ritzcarlton.com/Powerscourt* ➵ *107*
rooms, 93 suites ⑩ *Breakfast.*

SPORTS AND THE OUTDOORS
GOLF

Fodor's Choice   **Druids Glen Resort.** The beautiful Druids Glen Golf Course has hosted the
★   Irish Open on four occasions since it opened in 1995 and is known in
golfing circles as the "Augusta of Europe." The wonderful landscaping
and the extensive use of water in the layout explain the comparisons to
the home of the Masters. It's essentially an American-style target course
incorporating some delightful changes in elevation, and its forbidding,
par-3 17th has an island green, like the corresponding hole at TPC
Sawgrass. A second course, Druids Heath, is a marvelous attempt to
combine the best of links, heath land, and parkland golf. ⊠ *Newtown-*
mountkennedy, Co. Wicklow ☎ *01/287–3600* ⊕ *www.druidsglenresort.*
com ▦ *Greens fees: Glen: Oct.–Apr., Mon.–Thurs., €60, Fri.–Sun., €50;*
May–Sept., Mon.–Thurs., €80, Fri.–Sun., €95. Heath: Oct.–Apr., Mon.–
Thurs., €35, Fri.–Sun., €45; May–Sept. Mon.–Thurs., €45, Fri.–Sun.,
€55. ⅄ *36 holes. Yardage: 7,046 (Glen), 7,434 (Heath). Both courses:*
Par 71. Practice area, caddies, caddy carts, buggies, club rental, shoe
rental, catering ☾ *Visitors: daily.*

Fodor's Choice   **Powerscourt Golf Club.** These two recently built courses are nestled in the
★   foothills of the Wicklow Mountains on the ancient Powerscourt lands,
home to a legendary 18th-century stately home and garden. Panoramic
views to the sea and Sugarloaf Mountain—and all those 200-year-old
trees—give the impression that the course has been here for years. The
older East course is a largely parkland course, but some holes have
certain links characteristics. The course's tiered greens will test even
the best golfers. The more recently built West course is even more
challenging and is designed with top-class tournament golf in mind.
⊠ *Enniskerry, Co. Wicklow* ☎ *53/1204–6000* ⊕ *www.powerscourt.ie*
▦ *Greens fees: Apr.–Sept. €120, Oct.–Mar. €79* ⅄ *36 holes. Yardage:*
7,022 (East), 6,938 (West). Both courses: Par 72. Practice area, driv-
ing range, caddies, caddy carts, club rental, catering ☾ *Visitors: daily.*

ROUNDWOOD

18 km (11 miles) south of Enniskerry on R755.

★   At 800 feet above sea level, Roundwood is the highest village in Ireland.
It's also surrounded by spectacular mountain scenery. The Sunday afternoon market in the village hall, where cakes, jams, and other homemade
goods are sold, livens up what is otherwise a sleepy place. From the

broad main street, by the Roundwood Inn, a minor road leads west for 8 km (5 miles) to two lakes, Lough Dan and Lough Tay, lying deep between forested mountains like Norwegian fjords.

GETTING HERE AND AROUND

Drive south from Dublin on the N81 to the M50 southbound, then take the exit for the M11, which becomes the N11. At junction 12, exit onto the R772 into Newtown Mount Kennedy. Turn right onto the R765 for Roundwood. St. Kevin's bus runs a regular service here from Dublin.

WHERE TO EAT

$
IRISH
★

✕ **Roundwood Inn.** Travel back to the 17th century at this inn evocatively furnished in a traditional style, with wooden floors, dark furniture, and diamond-shaped windows. The place is best known for its wonderful, hearty, reasonably priced bar food (served in a nook of the bar), available at lunch and dinner—try the glorious cream of seafood soup. The restaurant area opens only for Friday and Saturday dinner and Sunday lunch. Menu offerings present a combination of Continental and Irish cuisines, reflecting the traditions of the German proprietor, Jurgen Schwalm, and his Irish wife, Aine. Highlights include an excellent seafood platter of salmon, oysters, lobster, and shrimp along with a very gamey pheasant casserole. ⑤ *Average main: €15* ⊠ *Main St., Roundwood, Co. Wicklow* ☎ *01/281–8107* ⚫ *Reservations essential.*

GLENDALOUGH

9 km (6 miles) southeast of Roundwood via R755 and R756.

GETTING HERE AND AROUND

If you're driving, consider taking the scenic route along R115, but be prepared for awesome, austere mountain passes. Don't take this route if you're in a hurry—it takes about an hour and 45 minutes, while the faster route on the N11 takes one hour—and don't expect a lot of signage—just concentrate on the nifty views.

St. Kevin's Bus has daily service between Dublin and Glendalough, with a stop in Bray. The trip takes 1½ hours. There is no direct train to Glendalough, but you can take the Irish Rail train from Dublin as far as Rathdrum (1 hour 20 minutes) and then take a taxi (approximately €10) the 11 km (7 miles) from there to Glendalough.

ESSENTIALS

Transportation Contacts St. Kevin's Bus ☎ *01/281–8119* ⊕ *www.glendaloughbus.com.*

EXPLORING

Fodor's Choice
★

Glendalough. Nestled in a lush, quiet valley deep in the rugged Wicklow Mountains, among two lakes, trees, and acres of windswept heather, Gleann dá Loch ("glen of two lakes") is one of Ireland's premier monastic sites. The hermit monks of early Christian Ireland were drawn to the Edenlike quality of some of the valleys in this area, and this evocative settlement remains to this day a sight to calm a troubled soul. Stand here in the early morning (before the crowds and the hordes of school-trippers arrive), and you can appreciate what drew the solitude-seeking St. Kevin to this spot. St. Kevin—or Coemghein, "fair begotten" in

Irish (d. 618)—was a descendant of the royal house of Leinster who renounced the world and came here to live as a hermit before opening the monastery in 550. Glendalough then flourished as a monastic center until 1398, when English soldiers plundered the site, leaving the ruins that you see today.

Glendalough's visitor center is a good place to orient yourself and pick up a useful pamphlet. Many of the ruins are clumped together beyond the visitor center, but some of the oldest surround the Upper Lake, where signed paths direct you through spectacular scenery devoid of crowds. Most ruins are open all day and are freely accessible.

Probably the oldest building on the site, presumed to date from St. Kevin's time, is the **Teampaill na Skellig** (Church of the Oratory), on the south shore of the Upper Lake. A little to the east is **St. Kevin's Bed,** a tiny cave in the rock face, about 30 feet above the level of the lake, where St. Kevin lived his hermit's existence. It's not easily accessible; you approach the cave by boat, but climbing the cliff to the cave can be dangerous. At the southeast corner of the Upper Lake is the 11th-century **Reefert Church,** with the ruins of a nave and a chancel. The saint also lived in the adjoining, ruined beehive hut with five crosses, which marked the original boundary of the monastery. You get a superb view of the valley from here.

The ruins by the edge of the Lower Lake are the most important of those at Glendalough. The **gateway,** beside the Glendalough Hotel, is the only surviving entrance to an ancient monastic site anywhere in Ireland. An extensive **graveyard** lies within, with hundreds of elaborately decorated crosses, as well as a perfectly preserved six-story **round tower.** Built in the 11th or 12th century, it stands 100 feet high, with an entrance 25 feet above ground level.

The largest building at Glendalough is the substantially intact 7th- to 9th-century **cathedral,** where you can find the nave (small for a large church, only 30 feet wide by 50 feet long), chancel, and ornamental oolite limestone window, which may have been imported from England. South of the cathedral is the 11-foot-high Celtic **St. Kevin's Cross.** Made of granite, it's the best-preserved such cross on the site. **St. Kevin's Church** is an early barrel-vaulted oratory with a high-pitched stone roof. ⊠ *Glendalough, Co. Wicklow* ☎ *0404/45325* ⊕ *www. heritageireland.ie* ✉ *Ruins free, visitor center €3* ☉ *Ruins daily 24 hrs. Visitor center mid-Mar.–mid-Oct., daily 9:30–6; mid-Oct.–mid-Mar., daily 9:30–5; last admission 45 mins before closing.*

WHERE TO STAY

For expanded hotel reviews, visit Fodors.com.

$ 🏠 **Derrymore House.** On 6 acres of woodland above the Lower Lake in
B&B/INN   Glendalough Valley, Derrymore is one of the most serene B&Bs in Wicklow. **Pros:** family-owned and -run; music played in the house by family; Victorian beds. **Cons:** room decor is basic; gets fully booked easily; family lives in house. **TripAdvisor:** "beautiful spot and comfortable room," "lovely location," "best people." ⑤ *Rooms from: €90* ⊠ *Roundwood, Co. Wicklow* ☎ *0404/45493* ⊕ *www.glendaloughaccommodation.com* ↪ *3 rooms* ⊟ *No credit cards* ❙◯❙ *Breakfast.*

Even though destroyed by Viking raids and then disbanded as a monastery by the Reformation, medieval Glendalough remains magical and magnificent.

MOUNT USHER GARDENS

18 km (11 miles) east of Glendalough via R755 and R763.

GETTING HERE AND AROUND

From Dublin, Mount Usher Gardens is under an hour's drive. Take the N81 to the M50 southbound and exit onto the M11. At junction 15 exit onto the R772 to Ashford and turn left to the signposted Mount Usher Gardens. Bus Éireann runs a regular bus to Ashford from Dublin.

EXPLORING

★ **Mount Usher Gardens.** Covering more than 20 acres on the banks of the River Vartry, the gardens here were first laid out in 1868 by textile magnate Edward Walpole. Succeeding generations of the Walpole family further planted and maintained the grounds, which today have more than 5,000 species. The "Robinsonian" (that is, informal) gardener has made the most of the riverside locale by planting eucalypti, azaleas, camellias, and rhododendrons. The river is visible from nearly every place in the gardens; miniature suspension bridges bounce and sway underfoot as you cross the river. Near the entrance, you'll find a cluster of crafts shops (including a pottery workshop) as well as a bookstore and self-service tearoom. The twin villages of Ashford and Rathnew are to the south and east, and Newtownmountkennedy is to the north. ✉ *Ashford, Co. Wicklow* ☎ *404/40205* ⊕ *www.mountushergardens.ie* 🎫 *€7.50* ⊗ *Mar.–Oct., daily 10:30–5:20.*

WHERE TO STAY

For expanded hotel reviews, visit Fodors.com.

$$ **HOTEL** ★ **Hunter's Hotel.** On 2 acres of flower gardens (the Knot Garden is an award winner) beside the Vartry River, the beautiful white Hunter's Hotel is the oldest coaching inn in Ireland. **Pros:** pleasing period atmosphere; enchanting gardens; fine restaurant. **Cons:** books up easily; bedrooms aren't huge. **TripAdvisor:** "absolutely charming," "real character," "peaceful." $ *Rooms from: €160* ✉ *Newrath Bridge, Rathnew, Co. Wicklow* ☎ *404/40106* ⊕ *www.hunters.ie* ⌁ *16 rooms* ⦿*Breakfast.*

$$$ **HOTEL** **Tinakilly Country House Hotel.** This beautifully restored Victorian-Italianate mansion, built in the 1870s by seafaring Captain Robert Halpin, is now decorated with mementos of his nautical exploits, including paintings and ship models. **Pros:** authentic Victorian old house; great strolling garden. **Cons:** newer rooms not as unique as older ones; large number of guest rooms make for less intimacy; a little pricey in high season. **TripAdvisor:** "what a beautiful house," "a lovely Irish stay," "superb cuisine." $ *Rooms from: €210* ✉ *Rathnew, Co. Wicklow* ☎ *404/69274* ⊕ *www.tinakilly.ie* ⌁ *51 rooms, 5 suites* ⦿*Breakfast.*

WICKLOW TOWN

26 km (16 miles) east of Glendalough, 51 km (32 miles) south of Dublin.

At the entrance to the attractive, tree-lined Main Street of Wicklow Town sprawl the extensive ruins of a 13th-century Franciscan friary. Wicklow, from the Danish *wyking alo,* means "Viking meadow," testifying to the very ancient roots of this region.

GETTING HERE AND AROUND

A 50-minute drive south on the N81 and then the N11/M11 takes you from Dublin straight into Wicklow Town. Parking is available throughout the town. There are also daily train and bus routes here from Dublin.

ESSENTIALS

Visitor Information Wicklow County Tourism ✉ *Unit C23, Wicklow Enterpirse Park, The Murrough, Wicklow Town, Co. Wicklow* ☎ *0404/69117* ⊕ *www.visitwicklow.ie.*

EXPLORING

Black Castle. Immediately south of the harbor, perched on a promontory that has good views of the Wicklow coastline, is the ruin of the Black Castle. This structure was built in 1169 by Maurice Fitzgerald, an Anglo-Norman lord who arrived with the English invasion of Ireland. The ruins (freely accessible) extend over a large area; with some difficulty, you can climb down to the water's edge. ✉ *Wicklow Head, Co. Wicklow.*

Friary. The friary was closed down during the 16th-century dissolution of the monasteries, but its ruins are a reminder of Wicklow's stormy past, which began with the unwelcome reception given to St. Patrick on his arrival in AD 432. Inquire at the nearby priest's house to see the ruins. The streets of Wicklow ran with blood during the 1798 rebellion when Billy Byrne, member of a wealthy local Catholic family, led rebels from south and central Wicklow against the forces of the Crown.

Byrne was eventually captured and executed at Gallow's Hill just outside town. There is a memorial to him in the middle of Market Square. ⊠ *Main St., Wicklow Town, Co. Wicklow* ☎ *0404/67196 priest's house.*

Protestant Church. Between one bank of the River Vartry and the road to Dublin stands the Protestant Church, which incorporates various unusual details: a Romanesque door, 12th-century stonework, fine pews, and an atmospheric graveyard. The church is topped off by a copper, onion-shaped cupola, added as an afterthought in 1771. ⊠ *Dublin Rd., Wicklow Town, Co. Wicklow* ☎ *Free* ☾ *Daily 10–6.*

Wicklow Harbor. The harbor is Wicklow Town's most appealing area. Take Harbour Road down to the pier; a bridge across the River Vartry leads to a second, smaller pier, at the northern end of the harbor. From this end, follow the shingle beach, which stretches for 5 km (3 miles); behind the beach is the broad lough, a lagoon noted for its wildfowl.

Wicklow's Historic Gaol. The old jail, just above Market Square, has been converted into a museum and heritage center, where it's possible to trace your genealogical roots in the area. Computer displays and life-size models tell the gruesome history of the jail, from the 1798 rebellion to the late 19th century. ⊠ *Market Sq., Wicklow Town, Co. Wicklow* ☎ *404/61599* ⊕ *www.wicklowshistoricgaol.com* ☎ *€7.30* ☾ *Feb.–Dec., Mon.–Sat. 10:30–4:30, Sun. 11–4:30; Jan. daily noon–3.*

WHERE TO EAT AND STAY

For expanded hotel reviews, visit Fodors.com.

$$$
FRENCH
★
✕ **The Strawberry Tree.** Claiming to be Ireland's only "certified organic restaurant," this spot has been getting top reviews for its serious approach to all-natural but always stylish cuisine. Idyllically located at the heart of the vast BrookLodge Spa hotel, the mod/trad complex is tucked away in a rural Wicklow valley. The glossy decor—midnight-blue walls, mirrored ceiling, and gleaming mahogany furniture—consequently comes as a dramatic contrast but cues you into the classy service and creative menu. Wild woodpigeon terrine, carrot and orange sorbet, and steamed wild pollock with green beans and beurre blanc comprise part of the feast, one that can be enjoyed at the Big Table, which seats up to 40. After dessert, check out the spectacular wine cellar. ⑤ *Average main: €30* ⊠ *Brooklodge, Macreddin Village, Wicklow Town, Co. Wicklow* ☎ *0402/36444* ⊕ *www.brooklodge.com* ☾ *Nov.–Mar. closed Mon.–Wed.; April, May and Oct. closed Mon–Tue; June–Mid July and Sept, closed Mon.*

$$$$
RENTAL
🏠 **Wicklow Head Lighthouse.** This 95-foot-high stone tower—first built in 1781—once supported an eight-sided lantern, and has been renovated by the Irish Landmark Trust as a delightfully quirky lodging. **Pros:** unique lodging experience; stunning views; inexpensive if you have a group of people. **Cons:** a lot of stairs; books out easily; minimum stay is two nights. **TripAdvisor:** "a very unique experience," "once in a lifetime," "an amazing place." ⑤ *Rooms from: €260* ⊠ *Wicklow Head, Co. Wicklow* ☎ *01/670–4733* ⊕ *www.irishlandmark.com* ⇲ *2 rooms* ⦿ *No meals.*

COUNTY KILDARE

Horse racing is a passion in Ireland—just about every little town has at least one betting shop—and County Kildare is the country's horse capital. Nestled between the basins of the River Liffey to the north and the River Barrow to the east, its gently sloping hills and grass-filled plains are perfect for breeding and racing Thoroughbreds. For some visitors, the fabled National Stud Farm just outside Kildare Town provides a fascinating glimpse into the world of horse breeding. And don't forget the Japanese Gardens, adjacent to the National Stud, which are among Europe's finest. You may want to head to this area from Glendalough— the spectacular drive across the Wicklow Gap, from Glendalough to Hollywood, makes for a glorious entrance into Kildare.

MAYNOOTH

21 km (13 miles) southwest of Dublin.

A few minutes south of the tiny Georgian town of Maynooth is the hamlet of Celbridge, official address to Ireland's largest country house, **Castletown** *(see "Treasure Hunt: The Anglo-Irish Georgian House").*

GETTING HERE AND AROUND

From Dublin take the N4/M4 in the direction of Galway/Sligo, then exit at junction 7 and take the R406 to Maynooth. The drive takes around half an hour. Dublin Bus serves Maynooth from Merrion Square in the city center, and there is a regular train service from Connolly station in Dublin.

EXPLORING

St. Patrick's College. After touring Castletown, head slightly to the west to find Maynooth's St. Patrick's College. What was once a center for the training of Catholic priests is now one of Ireland's most important lay universities. The visitor center chronicles the college's history and that of the Catholic Church in Ireland. Stroll through the university gardens—the Path of Saints or the Path of Sinners. At the entrance to St. Patrick's College are the ruins of Maynooth Castle, the ancient seat of the Fitzgerald family. The Fitzgeralds' fortunes changed for the worse when they led the rebellion of 1536 (it failed). The castle keep, which dates from the 13th century, and the great hall are still in decent condition. ⊠ *Maynooth, Co. Kildare* ☎ *01/628–5222, 01/628–6744 castle tours* ⊕ *www.nuim.ie* ⊠ *Free* ⊙ *Castle tours: May 24–Sept. 26, daily 10–6 (call for exact times).*

SPORTS AND THE OUTDOORS

GOLF

Carton House Golf Club. This just-outside-of-Dublin estate has quickly become one of the brightest stars in the Irish golfing universe. It's in a majestic 1,100-acre park that was the ancestral home of the earls of Kildare, presided over by an enormous and very grand 18th-century stately house. The parkland Mark O'Meara course makes use of the estate's rolling hills, specimen trees, and the River Rye. The highlight comprises the 14th, 15th, and 16th stretch: a pair of classy par-3s wrapped around a heroic par-5. The second 18 holes, created by Colin

Montgomerie, make up an inland links-style course, which is flatter and virtually treeless. There's a good mix of long par-4s backed up with tricky short ones. Recessed pot bunkers lie in wait to pick up off-line shots. ⊠ *Maynooth, Co. Kildare* ☎ *01/651–7720* ⊕ *www. cartonhousegolf.com* ⊠ *Greens fees: May–Oct., Mon.–Thurs. €75, Fri.–Sun. €85; Nov.–Apr., Mon.–Thurs. €60, Fri.–Sun. €70 ⅃ 36 holes. Yardage: 7,006 (O'Meara), 7,301 (Montgomerie). Both courses: Par 72. Practice area, caddies, caddy carts, buggies, club rental, shoe rental, catering* ⊗ *Visitors: daily.*

STRAFFAN

5 km (3 miles) southwest of Castletown House, 25½ km (16 miles) southwest of Dublin.

Its attractive location on the banks of the River Liffey, its unique butterfly farm, and the Kildare Hotel and Country Club—where Arnold Palmer designed the K Club, one of Ireland's most renowned 18-hole golf courses—are what make Straffan so appealing.

GETTING HERE AND AROUND
To get here by car from Dublin, take the N4/M4 (toward Galway/Sligo) and exit at junction 7 to the R406 (toward Naas). At the roundabout take the second exit onto Baberstown Road (signposted Straffan). Bus Éireann runs a regular service here from Dublin.

EXPLORING
The Steam Museum. This museum covers the history of Irish steam engines, handsome machines used both in industry and agriculture—for churning butter or threshing corn, for example. There's also a fun collection of model locomotives. Engineers are present on "live steam days" every Sunday and bank holiday. The adjoining Lodge Park Walled Garden is included in the price and is perfect for a leisurely summer stroll. ⊠ *Lodge Park, Straffan, Co. Kildare* ☎ *01/627–3155* ⊕ *www. steam-museum.com* ⊠ *€7.50* ⊗ *June–Aug., Wed.–Sun. 2–6; May and Sept., by appointment only.*

Straffan Butterfly Farm. The only one of its kind in Ireland, this farm has a tropical house with exotic plants, butterflies, and moths. Mounted and framed butterflies are for sale. ⊠ *Straffan, Co. Kildare* ☎ *01/627–1109* ⊕ *www.straffanbutterflyfarm.com* ⊠ *€8* ⊗ *June–Aug., daily noon–5:30.*

WHERE TO STAY
For expanded hotel reviews, visit Fodors.com.

$$$$
HOTEL
Fodor's Choice
★

☒ **Barberstown Castle.** With a 13th-century castle keep at one end, an Elizabethan section in the middle, a large Georgian country house at the other end, and a whole new modern wing, Barberstown represents 750 years of Irish history. **Pros:** 20 acres of serene gardens; privately run; real fires in public spaces. **Cons:** prices still a little Celtic Tiger–like; newer wings not as special as old house. **TripAdvisor:** "a beautiful hotel," "nice lunch," "lovely." Ⓢ *Rooms from: €230* ⊠ *Straffan, Co. Kildare* ☎ *01/628–8157* ⊕ *www.barberstowncastle.ie* ⟳ *57 rooms* ⦿ *Multiple meal plans.*

$$$$
RESORT
⌖ **Kildare Hotel and Country Club.** Manicured gardens and the renowned Arnold Palmer–designed K Club golf course surround this mansard-roof country mansion. **Pros:** all-around luxury; quality spa; spacious, comfortable rooms. **Cons:** very expensive year-round. **TripAdvisor:** "nice staff," "beautiful property," "fantastic room." ⑤ *Rooms from: €330* ✉ *Straffan, Co. Kildare* ☎ *01/601–7200* ⊕ *www.kclub.ie* ⤳ *60 rooms, 9 suites, 23 apartments* ⑩ *Multiple meal plans.*

SPORTS AND THE OUTDOORS

GOLF

Fodor'sChoice
★
The K Club. "Home to the 2006 Ryder Cup" says all a golfer needs to know about the pedigree of the K Club. It remains Ireland's premier luxury golf resort, with two full championship parkland courses. The Palmer course is named after its designer, the legendary Arnold Palmer, and offers a round of golf in lush, wooded surroundings bordered by the River Liffey. The generous fairways and immaculate greens are offset by formidable length, which makes it one of the most demanding courses in the Dublin vicinity. The Smurfit course is essentially an "inland links" course. The signature 7th hole wows visitors with its water cascades and man-made rock-quarry feature. The on-site facilities are terrific and include a 95-room resort with three restaurants, a health club, tennis and squash courts, a pool, and massage and other spa treatments. ✉ *Kildare Country Club, Straffan, Co. Kildare* ☎ *01/601–7321* ⊕ *www. kclub.com* ⛳ *Greens fees: Palmer €100–€295; Smurfit €70–€195* ⛳ *36 holes. Yardage: 7,350 (Palmer), 7,277 (Smurfit). Both courses: Par 72. Practice area, driving range, caddies, caddy carts, club rental, shoe rental, catering* ⊗ *Visitors: daily.*

NAAS

13 km (8 miles) south of Straffan, 30 km (19 miles) southwest of Dublin.

The seat of County Kildare and a thriving market town in the heartland of Irish Thoroughbred country, Naas (pronounced nace), is full of pubs with high stools where short men (trainee jockeys) discuss the merits of their various stables.

GETTING HERE AND AROUND
To get here from Dublin, take the N81 to the N7 (Naas Road) in the direction of Limerick. Exit at junction 9 to the R445 (signposted Naas). The drive takes about 35 minutes. Bus Éireann runs a regular service from Dublin. Parking is available throughout the town.

SPORTS AND THE OUTDOORS

HORSE RACING
Punchestown Racecourse. Naas has its own small racecourse, but Punchestown Racecourse has a wonderful setting amid rolling plains, with the Wicklow Mountains a spectacular backdrop. Horse races are held regularly here, but the most popular event is the Punchestown National Hunt Festival in April, a real pilgrimage for fans of steeplechase racing. ✉ *R411, 3 km (2 miles) south of Naas, Naas, Co. Kildare* ☎ *045/897–704* ⊕ *www.punchestown.com.*

Continued on page 208

TREASURE HUNT

THE ANGLO-IRISH GEORGIAN HOUSE

For an up-close look at the lifestyles of the rich and famous, 18th-century style, nothing beats a visit to the great treasure houses of Castletown and Russborough. Set just a half-hour south of Dublin and located only 20 miles apart, they offer a unique peek through the keyhole into the extravagant world of Ireland's "Princes of Elegance and Prodigality."

Castletown House and its impressive grounds.

When the Palladian architectural craze swept across England, the Anglo-Irish—determined not to be outdone—set about building palaces in their own domain that would be the equal of anything in the mother country. Both Castletown House and Russborough House set new benchmarks in symmetry, elegance, and harmony for the Georgian style, which reigned supreme from 1714 to 1830 and was named after the four Georges who successively sat on the English throne.

This style was greatly influenced by the villa designs of the 16th-century Italian architect Andrea Palladio.

Although Castletown remains the largest private house in Ireland, and Russborough has the longest façade of any domicile in the country, Georgian groupies know that the real treasures lie inside: ceilings lavishly worked in Italianate stuccowork, priceless Old Master paintings, and an intimate look at the glory and grandeur of the Anglo-Irish lords.

CASTLETOWN: A GEORGIAN VERSAILLES

Reputedly the inspiration for a certain building at 1600 Pennsylvania Avenue, Castletown remains the finest example of an Irish Palladian–style house.

In 1722, William Conolly (1662–1729) decided to build himself a house befitting his new status as the speaker of the Irish House of Commons and Ireland's wealthiest man. On an estate 20 km (12 mi) southwest of Dublin, he began work on Castletown, designed in the latest Neoclassical fashion by the Florentine architect Alessandro Galilei. As it turns out, a young Irish designer and Palladian aficionado by the name of Sir Edward Lovett Pearce (1699–1733) was traveling in Italy, met Galilei, and soon signed on to oversee the completion of the house. Inspired by the use of outlying wings to frame a main building—the "winged device" used in Palladio's Venetian villas—Lovett Pearce added Castletown's striking colonnades and side pavillons in 1724. It is said that between them a staggering total of 365 windows were built into the overall design of the house—legend has it that a team of four servants were kept busy year-round keeping them all clean.

Conolly died before the interior of the house was completed, and work resumed in 1758 when his great nephew Thomas, and more importantly, his 15-year-old wife, Lady Louisa Lennox, took up residence there. Luckily, Louisa's passion for interior decoration led to the creation of some of Ireland's most stunning salons, including the Print Room and the Long Gallery. Little of the original furnishings remain today, but there is plenty of evidence of the ingenuity of Louisa and her artisans, chief among whom were the Lafranchini brothers, master craftsmen who created the famous wall plasterwork, considered masterpieces of their kind. Rescued in 1967 by Desmond Guinness of the brewing family, Castletown was deeded to the Irish state and remains the headquarters for the Irish Georgian Society.

Above left: Castletown House facade
Above right: The family crest of William Conolly.

CASTLETOWN HOUSE

✉ Celbridge
☎ 01/628–8252
🌐 www.castletownhouse.ie
💶 € 4.50
🕐 Open Apr.—Oct., Tues.–Sat. 10–5, Sun. 10–6.

THE ENTRANCE HALL

Studded with 17th-century hunting scenes painted by Paul de Vos, this soaring white-on-white entryway showcases one of Ireland's greatest staircases. Also extraordinary are the walls festooned with plasterwork sculpted by the Brothers Lafranchini, famous for their stuccoed swags, flora, and portraits.

THE LONG GALLERY

Upstairs at the rear of the house, this massive room—almost 80 feet by 23 feet—is the most notable of the public rooms. Hued in a vibrant cobalt blue and topped by a coved ceiling covered with Italianate stuccowork and graced by three Venetian Murano glass chandeliers, it is a striking exercise in the antique Pompeian style.

THE PRINT ROOM

Smaller but even more memorable is the Print Room, the only example in Ireland of this elegant fad. Fashionable young women loved to glue black-and-white prints—here, looking like oversize postage stamps in a giant album—onto salon walls. This was the 18th-century forerunner of today's teens covering their walls with posters of rock-star icons.

Above left: The Grand Staircase. Upper right: 18th–century Italian engravings decorate the Print Room. Bottom right: A marble statue within the Long Gallery. Far right: Mahogony bureau made for Lady Louisa, circa 1760.

WHAT A WAY TO GO

"I do not get any idea of the beauty of my house if I live in it…only if I can gaze upon the house from far off," proclaimed Lady Louisa in 1821 of her beloved Castletown. In her late seventies, she had a tent built on the front lawn so she could study the house at her leisure. After one evening on the lawn she promptly caught a chill and died.

5 OTHER GREAT GEORGIAN HOUSES

Newbridge, County Dublin

Emo Court, County Laois

Westport House, County Mayo

Florence Court, County Fermanagh

Castle Coole, County Fermanagh

RUSSBOROUGH: A TEMPLE TO ART

An Irish Xanadu, Russborough House pulls out all the stops to achieve Palladian perfection.

Another conspicuously grand house rising seemingly in the middle of nowhere—actually the western part of County Wicklow—Russborough was an extravagance paid for by the wages of beer. In 1741, a year after inheriting a vast fortune from his brewer father, Joseph Leeson commissioned architect Richard Castle to build him a home of palatial stature, and was rewarded with this slightly over-the-top house, whose monumental 700-foot-long façade one-upped every other great house in Ireland. Following Castle's death, the project was taken over and completed by his associate, Francis Bindon. Today, the house serves as a showcase for the celebrated collection of Old Master paintings of Sir Alfred Beit, a descendant of the De Beers diamond family, who had bought and majestically restored the property in 1952.

PRINCELY MAGNIFICENCE

The first sight of Russborough draws gasps from visitors: a mile-long, beech-lined avenue leads to a distant embankment on which sits the longest house frontage in Ireland. Constructed of silver-gray Wicklow granite, the façade encompasses a seven-bay central block, from either end of which radiate semicircular loggias connecting the flanking wings—the finest example in Ireland of Palladio's "winged device."

The interiors are full of grand period rooms that were elegantly refurbished in the 1950s by their new, moneyed owner under the eye of the legendary 20th-century decorator, Lady Colefax. The Hall is centered around a massive black Kilkenny marble chimneypiece and has a ceiling modeled after one in the Irish Parliament. Four 18th-century Joseph Vernet marine landscapes—once missing

Top left: A look at the 700-foot façade of Russborough House. Bottom left: The grand Saloon. Above right: The Hall. Opposite, top: Drawing Room. Opposite: Vermeer's *Lady Writing a Letter*.

RUSSBOROUGH
HOUSE

✉ Off N81, Blessington
☎ 045/865-239
🌐 www.russborough.ie
🎫 € 10
🕐 Open Apr.-Oct., Tues.-
Sat 10-5, Sun. 10-6.

3

IN FOCUS TREASURE HUNT: THE ANGLO-IRISH GEORGIAN HOUSE

but found by Sir Alfred—once again grace the glorious stucco moldings created to frame them in the Drawing Room. The grandest room, the Saloon, is famed for its 18th-century stucco ceiling by the Lafranchini brothers; fine Old Masters hang on walls covered in 19th-century Genoese velvet. The views out the windows take in the foothills of the Wicklow Mountains and the famous Poulaphouca reservoir in front of the house.

VERMEER, DIAMONDS, AND GANGSTERS

If it can be said that beer paid for the house, then diamonds paid for the paintings. Russborough House is today as famed for its art collection—and the numerous attempts, some successful, to steal it—as for its architecture. Credit for this must go to Sir Alfred Beit (1903–1994), nephew of the cofounder of De Beers Diamonds. One evening in 1974 while Alfred was enjoying a quiet dinner with his wife, the door burst open and in marched Rose Dugdale, an English millionaire's daughter turned IRA stalwart. Her gang "liberated" 19 of the Beit masterpieces, including Vermeer's fabled *Lady Writing a Letter*, hopefully to bargain for the release of two IRA members jailed in London. Once the paintings were recovered a week later, Sir Alfred decided to donate 17 works to the National Gallery of Ireland. Alas, a week before the handing-over ceremony in 1986, Sir Alfred and his wife were again settling down to dine when in marched Martin Cahill, a.k.a. "The General," Dublin's most notorious underworld boss (and subject of three major movies). He made off with the Vermeer and 16 other paintings. They were returned and now sit safely (we hope) in the National Gallery.

STUCCADORES

Sounds better than plaster-workers, no? Baroque exuberance reigns in the house's lavishly ornamented plasterwork ceilings executed by celebrated stuccadores the Brothers Lafranchini, who originally hailed from Switzerland and worked in other great houses in Ireland, including Castletown. Their decorative flair adorns the Music Room and Library, but even these pale compared to the plasterwork done by an unknown artisan in the Staircase Hall—an extravaganza of whipped-cream moldings, cornucopias, and Rococo scrolls: "the ravings of a maniac," according to one 19th-century critic, who guessed that only an Irishman would have had the blarney to pull it off.

THE CURRAGH

8 km (5 miles) southwest of Naas, 25½ km (16 miles) west of Poula-phouca Reservoir.

The broad plain of the Curragh, bisected by the main N7 road, is the biggest area of common land in Ireland, encompassing about 31 square km (12 square miles) and devoted mainly to grazing.

SPORTS AND THE OUTDOORS

HORSE RACING

★ **Curragh Racecourse.** Curragh is Ireland's major racing center, and the course is its main showplace. It's a flat-racing mecca for enthusiasts from all over the world, and the Irish Derby and other international horse races are run here. ⊠ *N7, Naas, Co. Kildare* ☎ *045/441–205* ⊕ *www.curragh.ie* ⊡ *€15.*

KILDARE TOWN

5 km (3 miles) west of the Curragh, 51 km (32 miles) southwest of Dublin.

Horse breeding is the cornerstone of County Kildare's thriving economy, and Kildare Town is the place to come if you're crazy about horses. But, in addition to all things equine, Kildare boasts other stellar attractions, including the famous Japanese Gardens.

GETTING HERE AND AROUND

Kildare Town is about 45 minutes from Dublin; take the N81 south to the N7/M7, exit at junction 13, and take the third exit at the round-about to the R415 (signposted Kildare). Parking is available throughout the town. Kildare Town is a major rail junction serviced by Irish Rail and has trains to Dublin (45 minutes), Galway (2 hours), Limerick (1 hour 45 minutes), and Cork (2 hours 25 minutes). The town's train station is just outside town but a free bus service meets the trains and drops you into the center of town. Bus Éireann runs a regular bus service between Dublin and Kildare Town (1 hour).

ESSENTIALS

Visitor Information Kildare Tourist Office ⊠ *Market House, Kildare Town, Co. Kildare* ☎ *455/30672* ⊕ *kildare.ie/tourism.*

EXPLORING

Irish National Stud. If you're a horse aficionado, or even just curious, check out this stud farm, a main center of Ireland's racing industry. The Stud was founded in 1900 by brewing heir Colonel William Hall-Walker, and transferred to the Irish state in 1945. It's here that breeding stallions are groomed, exercised, tested, and bred. Spring and early summer, when mares have foals, are the best times to visit. The **National Stud Horse Museum,** also on the grounds, recounts the history of horses in Ireland. Its most outstanding exhibit is the skeleton of Arkle, the Irish race-horse that won major victories in Ireland and England during the late 1960s. The museum also contains medieval evidence of horses, such as bones from 13th-century Dublin, and some early examples of equestrian equipment. ⊠ *1½ km (1 mile) south of Kildare Town, Kildare Town, Co. Kildare* ☎ *045/521–617* ⊕ *www.irish-national-stud.ie* ⊡ *€12.50,* *includes entry to Japanese Gardens ⊙ Mid-Feb.–Dec. daily 9:30–5.*

★ **Japanese Gardens.** Adjacent to Kildare's National Stud Farm, the Japanese Gardens were created between 1906 and 1910 by the Stud's founder, Colonel Hall-Walker, and laid out by a Japanese gardener, Tassa Eida, and his son Minoru. The gardens are recognized as among the finest Asian gardens in the world, although they're more of an East–West hybrid than authentically Japanese. The Scots pine trees, for instance, are an

appropriate stand-in for traditional Japanese pines, which signify long life and happiness. The gardens symbolically chart the human progression from birth to death, although the focus is on the male journey.

A series of landmarks runs along a meandering path: the Tunnel of Ignorance (No. 3) represents a child's lack of understanding; the Engagement and Marriage bridges (Nos. 8 and 9) span a small stream; and from the Hill of Ambition (No. 13), you can look back over your joys and sorrows. It ends with the Gateway to Eternity (No. 20), beyond which lies a Zen Buddhist meditation sand garden. This is a worthwhile destination any time of the year, though it's particularly glorious in spring and fall. ⊠ *About 2½ km (1½ miles) south of Kildare Town, clearly signposted off Market Sq., Kildare Town, Co. Kildare* ☎ *045/521–617* ⊕ *www.irish-national-stud.ie* ☜ *€11, includes entry to National Stud Farm* ⊙ *Mid-Feb.–Dec., daily 9:30–5.*

Round tower, graveyard of St. Brigid's Cathedral. This 108-foot-high round tower dating from the 12th century is the second highest in Ireland (the highest is in Kilmacduagh in County Galway). Extraordinary views across much of the Midlands await you if you're energetic enough to climb the stairs to the top. ☎ *045/521–229* ☜ *€4* ⊙ *May–Sept., Mon.–Sat. 10–1 and 2–5, Sun. 2–5.*

St. Brigid's Cathedral. The Church of Ireland St. Brigid's Cathedral is where the eponymous saint founded a religious settlement in the 5th century. The present cathedral, with its stocky tower, is a restored 13th-century structure. It was partially rebuilt around 1686, but restoration work wasn't completed for another 200 years. The stained-glass west window of the cathedral depicts three of Ireland's greatest saints: Brigid, Patrick, and Columba. In pre-Christian times Druids gathered around a sacred oak that stood on the grounds and from which Kildare (*Cill Dara*), or the "church of the oak," gets its name. Also on the grounds is a restored fire pit reclaimed from the time of Brigid, when a fire was kept burning—by a chaste woman—in a female-only fire temple. Interestingly, Brigid started the place for women, but it was she who asked monks to move here as well. ⊠ *Off Market Sq., Kildare Town, Co. Kildare* ☜ *€2* ⊙ *May–Sept., Mon.–Sat. 10–1 and 2–5, Sun. 2–5.*

Silken Thomas. Right off Kildare's main market square, the Silken Thomas pub re-creates an old-world atmosphere with open fireplaces, dark wood, and leaded lights; it's a good place to stop for lunch before exploring the sights here. They also have a restaurant and rooms to stay. ⊠ *The Square, Kildare, Co. Kildare* ☎ *045/522–232* ⊕ *www. silkenthomas.com.*

WHERE TO EAT AND STAY

For expanded hotel reviews, visit Fodors.com.

$$$

MEDITERRANEAN

Fodor's Choice

★

✕ **La Serre.** Choosing between a table in the sheltered courtyard or the splendid Turner-designed conservatory is the hardest thing about dining at this restaurant—nearly everything on chef Paul Carroll's menu is a winner. He masterfully mixes Mediterranean moods in such dishes as the chicken liver terrine with apricot and roasted almond chutney on toasted brioche, or his signature pork loin with duck fat rösti, caramelized onion purée, and girolles. But the tastiest thing here may be the conservatory: one of the most gorgeous dining rooms in all Europe, its hard-rock walls and Victorian glasshouse windows create a swooningly delicious ambience. There are barbecues in the courtyard every Sunday in summer. La Serre is part of the Village at Lyons complex that is built up around an historic canal stop and manor estate. $ *Average main: €28* ⊠ *Celbridge, Kildare Town, Co. Kildare* ☎ *01/630–3500* ⊕ *www. villageatlyons.com* ✪ *Closed Mon. and Tues. No dinner Sun.*

$$

HOTEL

▥ **Keadeen Hotel.** The luxurious spa and health center are the big attractions at this family-owned hotel on 10 acres of flower-filled gardens. **Pros:** good spa and pool; light-filled rooms. **Cons:** uninspired architecture; popular for weddings; can feel very busy at times. **TripAdvisor:** "first class," "very nice stay," "best hotel in Ireland." $ *Rooms from: €130* ⊠ *Newbridge, Co. Kildare* ☎ *045/431–666* ⊕ *www.keadeenhotel. ie* ⤺ *75 rooms* ⦿ *Multiple meal plans.*

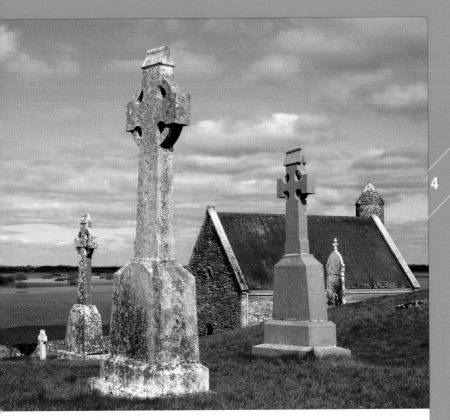

The Midlands

INCLUDING COUNTIES CAVAN, LAOIS, LEITRIM, LONGFORD, MONAGHAN, OFFALY, ROSCOMMON, AND WESTMEATH

WORD OF MOUTH

"If you like an old-fashioned Irish pub that still has some sawdust on the floor, Sean's Bar on the Connaught (western) side of [Athlone] is worth a look and there is usually music of some sort on over a holiday weekend. Apart from Clonmacnoise and Birr Castle, Athlone itself has a castle that houses a town museum."

—SeeDee

WELCOME TO THE MIDLANDS

TOP REASONS TO GO

★ **Stately Clonmacnoise:** Atmospheric and still spirit-warm, this great early Christian monastery survived Viking, Norman, and English invaders over the centuries.

★ **Green Mansions:** While known for its rich farmlands, the Midlands is also home to stately homes and gardens, including fairy-tale Tullynally Castle and Birr Castle.

★ **Hiking the Slieve Bloom Mountains:** Dip in and out of the 20-mile Slieve Bloom Trail, ideal hiking country for those with a yen to rise above their surroundings.

★ **Athlone:** The restored 13th-century castle along with the quirky shops and Europe's oldest pub are worth taking time to visit.

★ **The Treasure House of Emo:** A quintessential landmark of 18th-century Palladian elegance, Emo—the former home of the Earl of Portarlington—has a spectacular rotunda inspired by Rome's Pantheon.

1 The Eastern Midlands. Just an hour from Dublin, this region is essentially rich farmland but is studded with even richer sights: grand homes such as Emo Court, Belvedere House, and Tullynally Castle; once-upon-a-time villages such as Abbeyleix; and the historic treats of Fore Abbey and Kilbeggan Distillery. Leaving the ancient kingdom of Leinster, you come to two counties of Ulster: Cavan and Monaghan. Beyond Cavan Town you enter the heart of the Northern Lakelands, dotted with hundreds of beautiful lakes.

2 The Western Midlands. One of the corners of "hidden Ireland," this region is unblighted by crowds. While some of the country's most distinctive boglands are here, cultural treasures also beckon: stately Birr Castle and Strokestown House, and the great early Christian monastery of Clonmacnoise, burial place of the Kings of Tara.

GETTING ORIENTED

4

Perfect for the relaxed visitor who values the subtle over the spectacular, the flat, fertile plain at the center of Ireland is full of relatively undiscovered historic towns, abbey ruins, and grand houses. Though just two hours from the chaotic rush of Dublin, Cork, or Galway, the region is carpeted with countryside perfect for bicycling: no wonder stressed-out Dubliners love to head here to chill out.

CRUISING ON THE SHANNON

Whether you opt for a one-hour or one-week journey—and choose between a guided boat tour or private boat hire—cruising on the River Shannon is a never-to-be-forgotten experience, giving a new perspective on 'ole Ireland.

(top) A great vacation along the Shannon River; (right, top) Many travelers opt to boat 'n' bike downriver to the boating hub of Athlone; (right, bottom) Ireland's "inland sea," Lough Derg

Think of blissful relaxing times on the river, mooring for lunch at a quayside inn, or sampling traditional culture with gregarious lockkeepers. Along the Shannon's 334-km (207-mile) length you can head to major boating hubs like Athlone, or to historic stretches where it meanders past ancient settlements (such as Clonmacnoise), or to lakes aplenty. The biggest is Ireland's "inland sea," Lough Derg, bordered by easygoing villages like Terryglass and Mountshannon that offer appealingly quiet streets, stone-built cottage restaurants, and rustic harborside bars with picnic tables (many with evening music or Irish dancing sessions). Remember, the motto of Shannon cruising is "There's no hurry"—the boats travel at only 11 kph (7 mph), so a river journey is a slow affair with time to drink in the history, wildlife, and inland gems of an older Ireland many thought had disappeared.

WHEN TO GO

Good times to cruise are in May through early June. Rentals are cheaper, the waterways are less crowded, the weather is generally favorable, and daylight stretches well into late evening. Whenever you go, get the scoop on permits, moorings, and river by-laws from Waterways Ireland (⊕ *www. waterwaysireland.org*).

A WONDERFUL DAY ON THE WATER

On the map, the scale of the Shannon may look daunting—it *is* the longest river in Ireland or Britain—but that's one reason why many people opt for an idyllic daylong exploration. If you only have time for a short guided journey, then one of the best is upriver from Athlone to Lough Ree on a three-hour trip on board the *Viking* boat, costing €10–€20. Or opt to go downriver to magnificent Clonmacnoise. You can also board pleasure cruisers at Killaloe and Dromineer. If you're feeling romantic, try an evening cruise with the Moon River company, which operates a luxurious 100-seater from Carrick-on-Shannon. A detailed commentary is provided on these cruises.

Guided Cruises **Moon River** ✉ *Carrick-on-Shannon, Co. Leitrim* ☎ *071/962–1777* ⊕ *www.moonriver.ie.*

Silver Line Cruisers ✉ *Banagher, Co. Offaly* ☎ *057/915–1112* ⊕ *www.silverlinecruisers.com.*

The Spirit of Killaloe ✉ *Killaloe, Co. Clare* ☎ *086/814–0559* ⊕ *www.spiritofkillaloe.com.*

Viking Ship Cruises ✉ *7 St. Mary's Pl., Athlone, Co. Westmeath* ☎ *090/647–3383* ⊕ *www.vikingtoursireland.ie.*

GOING WITH THE SHANNON FLOW

As the Shannon has its own slow-paced signature—a place where you are alive to the layers of history along the

riverside and sequestered villages, which are a joy to explore—why not consider your own boat hire? The beauty of a personal cruise is that you can concoct your own itinerary, moving at your own speed and stopping off where the notion, and the motion, takes you.

There are four main boating towns for hiring cruisers: Carrick-on-Shannon, Portumna, Banagher, and Williamstown. From luxury cabin cruisers to barges or smaller boats, a glittering array of vessels is available for rent. Prices range from €650 for a two- to four-berth cruiser for one week in the quieter off-season, and from €1,750 in the more expensive summer months. With most companies, you can also rent for three-night/four-day short breaks. Rates start from €450 for the fall and early spring periods, rising to €1,600 in summer. In addition to guided tours, Silver Line Cruisers offers boat rentals.

Boat Hires **Carrick Craft** ✉ *Carrick-on-Shannon, Co. Leitrim* ☎ *071/962–1777* ⊕ *www.carrickcraft.com.*

Emerald Star ✉ *Portumna, Co. Galway* ☎ *071/962–3711* ⊕ *www.emeraldstar.ie.*

Shannon Castle Line ✉ *Williamstown Harbor, Whitegate, Co. Clare* ☎ *061/927–042* ⊕ *www.shannoncruisers.com.*

Updated by
Paul Clements

Irish schoolchildren were once taught to think of their country as a saucer, with mountains edging the rim and a dip in the middle. The dip is the Midlands—or the Lakelands, as it's sometimes called—and this often-overlooked region comprises nine counties: Cavan, Laois (pronounced leash), Westmeath, Longford, Offaly, Roscommon, Monaghan, Leitrim, and Tipperary.

Ask people from other parts of Ireland what the purpose of the Midlands is and they will jest that the region exists simply to hold the rest of the country together. The perception is a bit true: with flat plains and no major city in the region (Dublin lies to the east, Galway and Limerick to the west, and Cork to the south), the Midlands remains a quiet and geographically unspectacular place. Night owls should probably keep going—the wildest thing in these parts is the wind.

But that is precisely why many travelers consider the Midlands a gem in the making. For when it comes to studying how Ireland gets on with its daily life, there are few better places. Here, the pace of life is slower, every neighbor's face is familiar, and you can get to know the locals simply by walking along a village's main street. Spend enough time in the region and you might even get to recognize the difference between a Cavan twang and a Tipperary brogue.

The tourist sun also shines brightly on the region because of its notable cultural highlights. Among them are Clonmacnoise, Ireland's most important monastic ruins; historic towns with age-old industries, such as lace making and crystal making; the gorgeous gardens of Birr Castle; and some of Ireland's finest Anglo-Irish houses, including Strokestown Park House, Emo Court, and some of Ireland's most historically delightful hotels.

As for scenic pleasures, this region has its fair share of Ireland's 800 bodies of water, and much of the landscape is blanket bog. The River Shannon, one of the longest rivers in Europe and the longest in Britain or Ireland, bisects the Midlands from north to south, piercing a series of *loughs* (lakes): Lough Allen, Lough Ree, and Lough Derg. The Royal Canal and the Grand Canal cross the Midlands from east to west, ending in the Shannon north and south of Lough Ree.

THE MIDLANDS PLANNER

WHEN TO GO

C'mon, this is Ireland, after all—a rain mac or windbreaker should never be far from your side when you visit the Midlands. Though, in fairness, it must be said that the legendary "soft" weather has become noticeably more clement; since 2000, Ireland has been recording more hours of sunshine. The best time to visit the Midlands is the spring and summer when there's at least a better chance of some sunshine, although bring a rain mac just in case.

FESTIVALS AND EVENTS

APRIL   **Festival of Fires.** At the end of April, this event at Westmeath's Hill of Uisneach (the historic residence of the High Kings of Ireland and a gathering place for tribes and clans) features theater and music and is Europe's oldest festival. ⊕ *www.festivalofthefires.com.*

JULY   **Percy French Summer School.** In mid-July, one of Ireland's best-loved songwriters, Percy French, is celebrated in Roscommon town and at Castlecoote House with a summer school, complete with concerts and lectures. French was born at Cloonyquinn House near Elphin; his best-known songs include "Are Ye Right There Michael?" and "Phil the Fluther's Ball." ⊕ *www.percyfrench.ie.*

AUGUST   **Castle Palooza Festival.** Music dominates at this festival, held at Charleville Castle in Tullamore over the August summer-bank holiday weekend. ⊕ *www.castlepalooza.com.*

Flat Lake Festival. County Monaghan holds the Flat Lake Festival in Clones in mid-August. The event focuses on arts, books, films, and music, with numerous literary readings in tents and straw-filled barns—there's even sheep karaoke. ⊕ *www.theflatlakefestival.com.*

Terryglass Arts Festival. This event in North Tipperary presents music, dance, and street theater for five days in the third week of August. ⊕ *www.terryglassartsfestival.ie.*

Tullamore Show. Ireland's biggest agricultural gathering attracts 60,000 annually in early August to the Butterfield estate near Blueball on the road to Birr. An international visitor center caters to the huge crowds of overseas visitors who flock to see the largest assembly of cattle anywhere in Ireland competing in 1,000 classes for 42 national titles. ⊕ *www.tullamoreshow.com.*

OCTOBER   **Pumpkin Festival.** You'll see some of Europe's largest pumpkins at this annual festival in Co. Cavan's Virginia, held on the October holiday weekend. ⊕ *www.virginia.ie.*

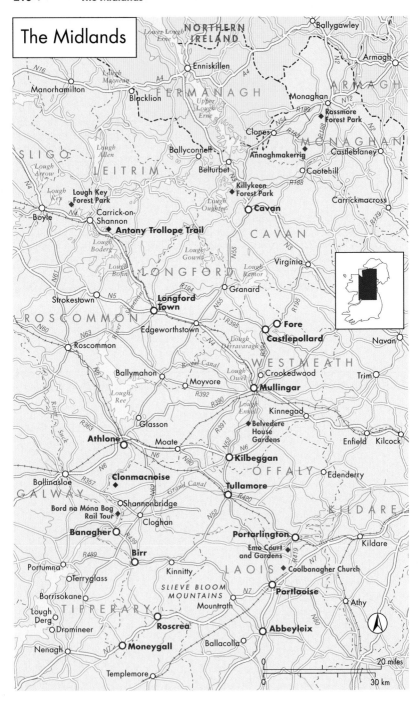

The Midlands

NORTHERN IRELAND

Ballygawley

Lower Lough Erne

Enniskillen

Armagh

N16

Manorhamilton

Lough Macnean

Blacklion

FERMANAGH

Monaghan

N12

ARMAGH

Upper Lough Erne

R189

Rossmore Forest Park

SLIGO

Lough Allen

Ballyconnell

Clones

R184

MONAGHAN

Castleblaney

Lough Arrow

N4

LEITRIM

Belturbet

Annaghmakerrig

Cootehill

Lough Key

Lough Key Forest Park

Killykeen Forest Park

R188

Carrickmacross

Boyle

N4

Carrick-on-Shannon

Lough Oughter

Cavan

R179

Antony Trollope Trail

CAVAN

Lough Boderg

Lough Gowna

N55

N3

Virginia

Lough Bofin

LONGFORD

Lough Ramor

R195

Strokestown

N5

R194

Granard

N61

Longford Town

N55

R395

Fore

Castlepollard

Navan

ROSCOMMON

N60

N63

Edgeworthstown

N4

Lough Derravaragh

WESTMEATH

Roscommon

N61

Ballymahon

Royal Canal

Lough Owel

Crookedwood

Trim

N6

Moyvore

R392

R390

Mullingar

Lough Ree

R363

Glasson

R391

N52

Lough Ennel

Kinnegad

Enfield

Kilcock

Athlone

Moate

N6

N6

N80

N52

Belvedere House Gardens

River Suck

Ballinasloe

R357

Clonmacnoise

N62

Grand Canal

Kilbeggan

Tullamore

R420

OFFALY

Edenderry

GALWAY

Bord na Móna Bog Rail Tour

Shannonbridge

R439

Cloghan

N52

KILDARE

Banagher

R489

Birr

Portarlington

Kildare

Portumna

Terryglass

Kinnitty

Emo Court and Gardens

R419

N7

Coolbanagher Church

Borrisokane

SLIEVE BLOOM MOUNTAINS

LAOIS

Lough Derg

TIPPERARY

Mountrath

N7

Portlaoise

Athy

Dromineer

Roscrea

N80

Nenagh

N7

Moneygall

Ballacolla

Abbeyleix

Templemore

0   20 miles

0   30 km

PLANNING YOUR TIME

The Midlands is a slice of old Ireland. Spend a few days traveling around the unspoiled countryside with its traditional hay meadows and you will comes across ancient humped bridges, handsome square tower-houses, and curious-looking castles.

IF YOU HAVE THREE DAYS

If you come from the Greater Dublin area (the Midlands is easily accessible from the city in less than two hours) or surrounding counties such as Wicklow and Kildare, then a grand kickoff to a tour is at Portarlington to visit the nearby Emo Court and Gardens, a large country house designed by James Gandon, the architect responsible for much of Georgian Dublin. Head on to Tullamore, stopping at the elegantly restored 19th-century bonded warehouse of Tullamore Dew Irish Whiskey Distillery (based in the heritage center). Consider an overnight in Tullamore, which has a good selection of hotels and B&Bs.

On Day 2 drive across to Birr for a morning's exploration of its Georgian architecture and a wander around the castle grounds. The formal gardens contain the tallest box hedges in the world; in spring you will see a dazzling display of flowering magnolias, cherries, crab apples and naturalized narcissi. Half an hour's drive takes you to Clonmacnoise, Ireland's most important monastic settlement, where it's worthwhile joining a guided tour that will give you a sense of the place and its past in less than an hour. The next day head for Athlone on the River Shannon and walk around the quirky Left Bank, full of crafts and antiques shops as well as secondhand book shops, cafés, and Sean's Bar (which lays claim, sometimes disputed, to be Ireland's oldest). Make time for a two-hour cruise along the Shannon to get a different perspective on the Midlands.

GETTING HERE AND AROUND

AIR TRAVEL

Dublin Airport is the principal international airport that serves the Midlands; car-rental facilities are available here. Sligo Airport has daily flights from Dublin on Aer Lingus.

Airport Information Sligo Airport ☎ 071/916–8280 ⊕ www.sligoairport.com.

BIKE TRAVEL

One of the best ways to immerse yourself in the Midlands is to meander through the region on a bike. Although the area may not offer the spectacular scenery of the more hilly coastal regions, its level, Netherlands-like terrain means a less strenuous ride.

The twisting roads are generally in good (well, good enough) condition. There are picnic spots galore in the many state-owned forests just off the main roads. The more rural regions of Laois allow you to spend days exploring beautiful glens, waterfalls, nature trails, and wooded regions around the Slieve Bloom Mountains. Try to avoid the major trunk roads that bisect the region. After all, this is an area that deserves thorough and leisurely exploration! Contact the regional and township tourist offices for all the details.

CLOSE UP

Walk the Slieve Bloom Mountains

Crystal clear freshwater streams, gushing waterfalls, lush forests, and no fewer than 27 glens are all part of the Slieve Bloom Mountain experience. The mountains stretch across the southern end of Offaly and are shared with neighboring county Laois. At one time, the summit—Arderin—was considered to be the highest point in Ireland. Whether you come for serious hiking, a gentle stroll, or just to drink in the spectacular views, you won't be disappointed. Looped walks, some led by guides, range from 4 km (3 miles) to 15 km (12 miles). Popular trailheads start from the villages of Kinnitty, Cadamstown, and Clonaslee, or you can make your base in the beautiful heritage town of Birr. Information and guided walking leaflets are available from the tourist information offices in Birr and Tullamore.

BUS TRAVEL

With a much more extensive network than trains, buses are a better bet for exploring much of the Midlands. Most small towns and villages are serviced by at least one bus per day, while trains are generally limited to towns on main lines linking cities. Bus Éireann runs express buses from Dublin to many Midlands towns, and regular-speed buses connect others. The train stations for Athlone, Cavan, and Longford also act as their bus depots.

CAR TRAVEL

The roads of the Midlands offer an easier intro to Irish driving than the hairpin bends of West Cork and Connemara. Because the area has a decent network of main arteries and off-the-beaten-track byroads, a car may be your best option for covering the widest itinerary.

Don't be surprised to round a bend only to confront a herd of sheep idly grazing with little hurry about them—do what the locals do, slow to a stop and wait for an opening in the woolly mass to occur. The same goes for cows. Refrain from honking your horn on these occasions—it will only confirm your status as an impatient tourist, and, besides, the cows won't take a bit of notice.

TRAIN TRAVEL

All trains are run by Irish Rail. The main Midlands towns that have train connections lie on cross-country routes linking the cities, either east–west or north–south. Intercity trains make only a few stops at smaller towns, while slower trains stop at small towns and some villages. You can connect from one Midlands town to another by train, but check in advance on the regularity of services. There are no exclusively local train services—they all continue on to cities.

Train Information **Sligo Railway Station** ☎ *071/916-9888.*

For more information on getting here and around, see Travel Smart Ireland.

RESTAURANTS

The Midlands town of Birr may be known as the "bellybutton of Ireland" because of its central location, not because this region is regarded as one of the cuisine centers of Ireland. No matter that Ireland's best restaurant (according to some)—Neven Maguire's MacNean's, near Cavan town—is in the Midlands, nor the fact that the region is also home to Wineport Lodge, Ireland's first "wine hotel," you'll find that most restaurants here are simple eateries, ranging in price from inexpensive to moderate, and are often attached to family hotels.

Nevertheless, there are those restaurants that will entice you right in off the street, especially those offering beef—Mullingar, in the center of the Midlands, is the beef capital of Ireland—and fish specialties, as the many lakes and rivers of the region provide an abundance of fresh salmon and trout (in fact, since no place is more than an hour and a half from the sea, expect to find lots of fresh ocean fish).

Prices in the reviews are the average cost of a main course at dinner or, if dinner is not served, at lunch.

HOTELS

The Irish bed-and-breakfast offers great value in the Midlands—farmhouses and homes geared to paying guests provide direct contact with local families and the lore of their area. Time was when these kinds of accommodations veered toward the spartan—not anymore. Good beds, decent heating, en-suite bathrooms, and the legendary Irish breakfast are now the norm; broadband, flat-screen TVs, and computer games courtesy of the landlady's kids are often part of the bargain.

Although B&Bs may not offer the same kind of privacy as hotels, they still work delightfully well as the ultimate way to meet genuine Irish folk—a bird's-eye view into working families and the organized chaos of a country household. As commercial progress has blossomed in the Midlands, so, too, have the options in hotels, country houses, and cottage rentals increased. Pretty much every town now has more than one decent hotel—most with health centers and spa facilities.

From June to early September, tourism gets into serious stride, bolstered by the many Irish families using their holiday homes and getaway cottages in the region. Finding accommodation is never a major problem—except for those weekends when a town is holding an annual music festival.

Prices in the reviews are the lowest cost of a standard double room in high season. For expanded reviews, facilities, and current deals, visit Fodors.com.

TOURS

To plan a trip within any particular county or area, you're best off starting with the local tourist office. They will have a thorough list of the must-see attractions in their areas. Several of the region's larger travel agencies also organize tours.

Four Midlands Tourist Information Offices (TIOs) are open all year: Cavan, Monaghan, Mullingar, and Portlaoise. The Mullingar TIO has information on Counties Westmeath, Offaly, Monaghan, Cavan, and Laois. Another five Midlands TIOs are open seasonally: Athlone (April–October), Birr (May–September), Longford (June–September), and Tullamore (mid-June–mid-September). *Find tourist office addresses, phone numbers, and websites listed under the main town sections throughout this chapter.*

THE EASTERN MIDLANDS

The eastern fringe of the Midlands is about an hour's drive from Dublin, and a visit to the area could easily be grafted onto a trip to the Dublin environs. In spite of its proximity to the capital, or perhaps because of it, this area is a bit removed from the regular tourist trail and is a source of constant surprises. Unspoiled Georgian villages, ruined castles, and "towns that time forgot" dot the landscape. There are also plenty of opportunities for hill walking, horseback riding, and other outdoor pursuits. Lovers of stately homes are in for a treat, as Emo Court and Gardens, Charleville Forest Castle, Belvedere House Gardens, and Tullynally Castle await them. If rare plants, mixed annuals, or specimen trees get you excited then head off on the County Laois Garden Trail, a delightful journey to 10 formal and not-so-formal gardens where you may find a perfumed pergola to stimulate your senses.

The Eastern Midlands fan out from the central point of Mullingar. With richer farmland than is found in the northern area of the Midlands, the eastern region tends toward agriculture. But the Dublin commuter culture means that you're as likely to be delayed on a back road by a badly parked BMW as by a slow-moving tractor on its way home from the dairy.

ABBEYLEIX

99 km (61 miles) southwest of Dublin.

Fodor's Choice ★ One of the most elegant small towns in Ireland, Abbeyleix has retained its Georgian ambience and its broad main street, which is lined with well-appointed stone-cut buildings and original shop fronts in the traditionally ornate Irish style. The entire tree-lined village was built in the 18th century, on the orders of the Viscount de Vesci, to house servants and tradesmen working on his nearby estate. Many town houses and vernacular buildings date from the 1850s, but more recent buildings, including the Market House, erected in 1906, and the Hibernian Bank, from 1900, contribute greatly to the town's refined character.

GETTING HERE AND AROUND

Drivers between Cork and Dublin can now bypass Abbeyleix via the N8, which has partially alleviated the town's traffic problems. However, on busy summer holiday weekends, congestion still occurs so add a little extra time in case of delays. Allow 75 minutes driving time to Dublin or 90 minutes to Dublin airport. The nearest large town is Portlaoise, a 10-minute drive, while Kilkenny is 30 minutes south on the N77. Free on-street car parking and several car parks are available in town. Daily buses connect Abbeyleix to Dublin or Cork; the former is just under two hours away, the latter a 2¾-hour trip.

> ### WRECKED RUGS
>
> The carpets for the ill-fated *Titanic* were woven at a now-defunct carpet factory in Abbeyleix.

EXPLORING

Heritage House. Also known as the former North Boys School, the Heritage House has fascinating informative displays on the history of Abbeyleix and the de Vescis, an Anglo-Norman family who, in 1699, came to live at an estate nearby. They were instrumental in building and developing the new town of Abbeyleix in 1770. The school was originally constructed for the education of Catholics (at the other end of the town you'll find the South School, built for Protestants). Also accessible through the Heritage House is the original Sexton's House (no extra charge), which boasts a stylish interior from the turn of the 19th century. The center also has a crafts shop. ✉ *Top of town, Abbeyleix, Co. Laois* ☎ *057/873–1653* ⊕ *www.heritagehousemuseum.com* ☜ *€3* ⊙ *Apr.–Aug., weekdays 9–5, weekends 1–5; Sept.–Mar., weekdays 9–5.*

Heywood Gardens. Ballinakill, a pretty Georgian village about 5 km (3 miles) south of Abbeyleix, contains the Heywood Gardens, designed by the English architect Sir Edwin Lutyens in the early 20th century within an existing 18th-century park. The Lutyenses' house burned down, but the gardens, with landscaping most likely attributable to the famed Gertrude Jekyll, are worth a detour. Guided one-hour tours are available through this gardener's paradise, where a formal lawn flanked by traditional herbaceous borders leads to a sunken Italian garden. Highlights include a rose called Natalie Naples and Johnston's Blue geraniums. ✉ *Ballinakill, Abbeyleix, Co. Laois* ☎ *057/873–3563* ⊕ *www.heritageireland.ie* ☜ *Free* ⊙ *Daily 9–dusk, tour at 3 pm.*

★ **Morrissey's Pub and Grocery Store.** Don't miss Morrissey's. A working public house since 1775, this is one of Ireland's best-loved drinking emporiums and has a dark, wood-panel interior furnished with antique bar fittings. Customers can warm themselves by an ancient potbelly stove. Until 2005 this establishment still functioned as a shop, and while it retains its stocks of groceries, they are no longer for sale. An evocative time capsule, it serves as a reminder of times when you could purchase a pound of butter, the newspaper, and cattle feed while enjoying the obligatory pint of Guinness. They serve soup and sandwiches in the afternoon, which you can enjoy alfresco at picnic tables at the front of the bar. ✉ *Main St., Abbeyleix, Co. Laois* ☎ *057/873–1281.*

WHERE TO STAY

For expanded hotel reviews, visit Fodors.com.

$
B&B/INN
The Foxrock Inn. The main attraction of this modest 200-year-old guesthouse, set in the tiny village of Clough right in the heart of the County Laois countryside, is the genuinely warm welcome extended by its owners, Sean and Marian Hyland, one that is delightfully seconded

by a friendly red settler by the name of Shannon and a terrier called Marley. **Pros:** well off the tourist track but plenty of activities in surrounding area; friendly owners who are knowledgeable about the area. **Cons:** no frills; rooms don't come with any extras. $ *Rooms from: €80* ⊠ *Clough, Ballacolla, Co. Laois* 🖶 *057/873–8637* ⊕ *www.foxrockinn.com* 🛏️ *5 rooms* 🍽️ *Breakfast.*

PORTLAOISE

14 km (9 miles) north of Abbeyleix.

Near the heart of County Laois, the rich farmland south and west of Portlaoise is one of Ireland's undiscovered gems. Golf, fishing, hiking, and horseback riding are traditional sports here, and the development of the Grand Canal for recreational purposes is adding to the area's attractions. Explore the pretty villages and romantic, ivy-covered ruins by car, follow one of the many hiking trails, or drive the new Garden Trail.

Portlaoise's name is derived from the Irish for "Fort of Laois" and refers to the town's strife-filled history. In terms of its architecture, it's rather eclectic—it feels as if bits of other towns were picked up and dropped randomly onto the site. Once best known for having Ireland's highest-security prison, which housed the IRA's most notorious members during the 1970s and '80s and still looms over the town, Portlaoise is undergoing a renaissance. The main street, which once formed part of the main Dublin–Cork road, is now largely given over to pedestrians; pubs and restaurants are flourishing; and the thriving Dunamaise Arts Centre adds an extra dash of culture.

GETTING HERE AND AROUND

Portlaoise is an hour by train, bus, or car from Dublin. Kilkenny is 45 minutes south on the N8 and then N77. Roads from Portlaoise also lead south and west to Cork, Galway, and Limerick. There is no free parking anywhere in town; paid parking is available on James Fintan Lawlor Ave., next to County Hall, and at shopping centers.

Portlaoise has several daily Irish Rail trains to the capital and is on the main line linking it with Cork, Limerick, and Tralee. The small station is five minutes from the town center. Bus routes leading to Ireland's three main cities—Dublin, Cork, and Limerick—converge at Portlaoise. In addition to Bus Éireann, an independent operator, J. J. Kavanagh & Sons, serves the town, and Dublin Coach offers a route to Dublin Airport. ■ TIP→ Staying in Portlaoise gives you a good base from which to explore the surrounding countryside and helps you to avoid the heavy traffic that can clog the main N7 Dublin road.

ESSENTIALS

Transportation Contacts **Dublin Coach** 🕿 *018/627–566* ⊕ *www.dublincoach.ie.* **JJ Kavanagh** 🕿 *056/883–1106* ⊕ *www.jjk.ie.*

Visitor Information **Portlaoise Tourist Office** ⊠ *James Fintan Lawlor Ave., Portlaoise, Co. Laois* 🕿 *057/862–1178* ⊕ *www.discoverireland.ie/eastcoast.*

EXPLORING

Laois Garden Trail. A new driving route promotes the area's horticultural heritage, connecting 10 of the county's celebrated formal gardens and expertly maintained privately owned ones. There's no set order for visiting the gardens; start the trail wherever you wish, and spend as long as you'd like in each garden. To do unhurried justice to all 10 gardens, it'll take you at least two days, better still, three if time permits. Stops include the state-run gardens at Emo Court and Heywood House, as well as Gash Gardens in Castletown, which offers a delightful river walk along the banks of the Nore; the demesne gardens of Castle Durrow, with its glorious scented roses; and the organically managed potager-style kitchen garden of Dunmore Country School, just outside Durrow. There is a charge for some while admission to others is free. ✉ *Portlaoise, Co. Laois* ⊕ *www.laoistourism.ie.*

Laois Heritage Trail. Stop by the Portlaoise Tourist Office to pick up a map of the Laois Heritage Trail, a signposted, daylong drive on quiet back roads that takes in 13 heritage sites, ranging from Abbeyleix to Emo Court. The circular trail starts in Borris-in-Ossory on N7. ⊕ *www. laois.ie/LeisureandCulture/Heritage/LaoisHeritageTrail/.*

Rock of Dunamase. A dramatic 150-foot-high limestone outcrop, the famous Rock of Dunamase dominates the landscape east of Portlaoise. For this reason, it was used as a military stronghold. As far back as AD 140 its occupants kept watch against marauders, and it was fought over in turn by the Vikings, Normans, Irish, and English. Today it's crowned by the ruins of a 12th-century castle, once home to Diarmuid MacMurrough, king of Leinster, who precipitated the Norman invasion when he invited the famed and feared Norman leader Strongbow to Ireland to marry his daughter. Some of the castle's thick walls still stand. The main reason for visiting the Rock today is to take the short walk to its summit to enjoy the view of the Slieve Bloom Mountains to the north and the Wicklow Mountains to the south. ✉ *N80 (Stradbally Rd.), 5 km (3 miles) east of Portlaoise, Portlaoise, Co. Laois.*

WHERE TO EAT AND STAY

For expanded hotel reviews, visit Fodors.com.

$ ✕ **Kingfisher.** In the town center, this is a particularly lively and stylish
INDIAN spot. The high-ceiling room was once a banking hall, but now its softly
★ lighted walls glow with warm terra-cotta tones, the perfect complement to the slightly spicy Punjabi cuisine. *Pappadams* (crunchy lentil-flour breads) and condiments appear on the table before you order, and the friendly staff in traditional dress can guide you expertly through the long menu. Dishes vary from mild and creamy meat kormas to fresh cod with a mild blend of spices and lemon juice to chicken "cooked with angry green chilis." Last orders for dinner are taken as late as 10:45 pm, so this is definitely the place to go when your tummy rumbles late on a summer's eve. $ *Average main: €17* ✉ *Old AIB Bank, Main St., Portlaoise, Co. Laois* ☎ *057/866–2500* ⊕ *www.kingfisherrestaurant. com* ☼ *No lunch Sat.–Tues.*

$$$
EUROPEAN
Fodor's Choice
★

✕ **The Lemon Tree.** This spot combines an informal atmosphere with modern-but-cozy surroundings. Starters might include duck confit with hoisin sauce; many enjoy the prime Irish Angus sirloin for the main course or loin of Slaney valley lamb roasted in bacon. The popular fresh fish dishes that tantalize the taste buds include scallops, and fillet of sea bass grilled with black olive tapenade. Lunch is available only to groups, by advance reservation. The restaurant is on the first floor of the premises; downstairs, Delaney's pub serves bar food during the day. ⑤ *Average main: €25* ✉ *67 Main St. Portlaoise, Co. Laois* ☎ *057/866–2200* ⊕ *www.lemontreerestaurant.net* ☾ *No dinner Mon. No lunch.*

$$
RESORT
Fodor's Choice
★

⊡ **Heritage Golf & Spa Resort.** Step into this hotel's spacious, light-filled atrium with its touches of marble, cherrywood, and mahogany and you quickly realize you have entered another world. **Pros:** a haven of peace, calm, and elegance; the smoked haddock at breakfast is a winner. **Cons:** the grass-cutters start early so prepare for a lawnmower wake-up around 6:30; isolated from any nearby towns. **TripAdvisor:** "excellent staff," "lovely hotel," "a hidden-away delight." ⑤ *Rooms from: €120* ✉ *Killenard, Co. Laois* ☎ *057/864–5500* ⊕ *www.theheritage.com* ➳ *98 rooms, 13 suites* ⏐◎⏐ *Breakfast.*

$
B&B/INN
★

⊡ **Ivyleigh House.** Owners Dinah and Jerry Campion say they like to give their guests "the best of everything," and that maxim is certainly evident the minute you step inside this elegant Georgian town house next to the Portlaoise train station—open fires, antiques, and sumptuously cozy sofas await you in the beige-on-brown, wood-accented sitting room. **Pros:** breakfasts are lavish, filling, and imaginative; luxury linens. **Cons:** no baths, so it's a power shower only; the town lacks much in the way of evening activities. **TripAdvisor:** "perfect place for some rest and relaxation," "lovely hospitality," "fresh bread and great food." ⑤ *Rooms from: €110* ✉ *Bank Place, Church Street, Portlaoise, Co. Laois* ☎ *057/862–2081* ⊕ *www.ivyleigh.com* ➳ *6 rooms* ⏐◎⏐ *Breakfast.*

NIGHTLIFE AND THE ARTS

★ **Anchor Inn.** Also known as Turley's Bar, this canal-side spot, 10 km (6 miles) east of Portlaoise on N80, is popular for its lively Monday-night traditional-music sessions, which start around 10. Sessions take place more frequently in spring and summer. Fishing, boating, and canal-bank walks are all accessible from this location. ✉ *Grand Canal near Stradbally, Vicarstown, Co. Laois.*

Dunamaise Arts Centre. This lively arts center has a 240-seat theater, an art gallery, and a friendly coffeehouse (open daily 8:30–5:30). You may catch a professional production on tour or a local amateur show. The exhibition space displays the work, usually of a surprisingly high standard, of contemporary Irish artists. It's built into the back of the 18th-century stone courthouse on Church Street in a space that used to be the town jail. ✉ *Main St., Portlaoise, Co. Laois* ☎ *057/866–3355* ⊕ *www.dunamaise.ie.*

4

SPORTS AND THE OUTDOORS
GOLF
Heath Golf Club. From early spring the dazzling blaze of yellow furze—also known as gorse—decorates the open heath land at this 18-hole course. The area has a colorful history, too, as the popular Irish politician Daniel O'Connell held meetings here in the mid-1830s. They've been playing golf on the Heath since the 1890s and the club dates from 1930. The course incorporates three natural lakes and is referred to as an "inland links." Good value deals for visitors include special rates combining golf with a meal; or you can settle for a drink in the friendly "19 Hole" bar. ⊠ *5 km (3 miles) northeast of Portlaoise on main Dublin Rd., Portlaoise, Co. Laois* ☏ *057/864–6533* ⊕ *www.theheathgc. ie* ⊠ *Greens fees: Weekdays €18, weekends €20* ⚘ *18 holes. Yardage 6120. Par 72. Two practice areas, putting green, indoor driving range, buggies, pull carts, catering* ⊙ *Visitors: daily.*

The Heritage Golf and Spa Resort. Millions of dollars were spent on developing this Celtic Tiger arrival to the Irish golf scene—and it shows. This 18-hole championship course is a challenge for the pros but somehow manages to be forgiving to the amateur at the same time. Heritage has second-to-none facilities including a 38,000-square-foot clubhouse. A life-size bronze of Seve Ballesteros (by the renowned sports sculptor Paul Ferriter) greets you at the entrance to the course he designed here, which is noted for its mix of challenging doglegs and water traps (including five on-course lakes). Add four demanding par-5s to the mix and the result is a truly world-class parkland course. The development of luxury on-site accommodation has also increased the club's attractiveness to the visiting golfer. ⊠ *Killenard, Co. Laois* ☏ *57/8645500* ⊕ *www.theheritage.com* ⊠ *Greens fees: May–Oct., weekdays €30–€50, weekends €40–€50; Nov.–Apr., weekdays €30, weekends €40.* ⚘ *18 holes. Yardage: 7,319. Par 72. Practice area, driving range, caddies, caddy carts, buggies, club rental, shoe rental, catering* ⊙ *Visitors: daily.*

PORTARLINGTON

13 km (8 miles) northeast of Portlaoise.

Built on the River Barrow in the late 17th century, Portarlington was originally an English settlement. Later, a Huguenot colony developed here, and French surnames are still common in the area. Some good examples of Georgian architecture can be seen in the town.

GETTING HERE AND AROUND
On the road between Mullingar and Portlaoise, Portarlington is a small crossroads town relatively free of traffic—it's well clear of the N7 so it misses out on the motorway trade. Tullamore is a 30-minute drive away, Portlaoise is 20 minutes, and Dublin is a 45-minute drive. There are several free parking lots in town. The Dublin–Cork train stops at Portarlington and there are regular Bus Éireann connections to the bigger towns and to Dublin.

EXPLORING

★ **Emo Court and Gardens.** A quintessential landmark of Irish Palladian elegance lies just 7 km (4½ miles) south of Portarlington. Emo Court is one of the finest large-scale country houses near Dublin that is open to the public. Even if you elect to skip over much of the Midlands, try to tack on a visit to Emo, especially if you're in Kildare or Wicklow counties. To come upon the house from the main drive, an avenue lined with magisterial Wellingtonia trees, is to experience one of Ireland's great treasure-house views. Begun in 1790 by James Gandon, architect of the Custom House and the Four Courts in Dublin, Emo (the name derives from the Italian version of the original Irish name Imoe) is thought to be Gandon's only domestic work matching the grand scale of his Dublin civic buildings. Construction continued on and off for 70 years, as family money troubles followed the untimely death of Emo's original patron and owner, the first earl of Portarlington.

In 1996 Emo's English-born owner donated the house to the Irish nation. The ground-floor rooms have been beautifully restored and decorated and are prime examples of life on the grand scale. Among the highlights are the entrance hall, with trompe l'oeil paintings in the apses on each side, and the library, which has a carved Italian-marble mantel with putti frolicking among grapevines. But the showstopper, and one of the finest rooms in Ireland, is the dome rotunda—the work of one of Gandon's successors, the Irish architect William Caldbeck—inspired by the Roman Pantheon. Marble pilasters with gilded Corinthian capitals support the rotunda's blue-and-white coffered dome. Emo's 55 acres of grounds include a 20-acre lake, lawns planted with yew trees, a small garden (the Clocker) with Japanese maples, and a larger one (the Grapery) with rare trees and shrubs. There's also a tearoom on the premises. ⊠ *Emo, Co. Laois* ☎ *057/862–6573* ⊕ *www.heritageireland.ie* ✉ *Gardens free, house €3* ☉ *Gardens daily 9– dusk, house mid-June–mid-Sept., daily 10–6; last tour at 5.*

WHERE TO STAY

For expanded hotel reviews, visit Fodors.com.

$ ⊞ **Eskermore House.** In summer, a delightful display of rambling roses
B&B/INN   adorns the doorway of this charming farmhouse, which, located 9 km (6 miles) west of Edenderry on R402, is a good base for hiking in the Slieve Bloom Mountains. **Pros:** great-value accommodations in peaceful surroundings; the open fire is a pure delight. **Cons:** few frills on offer; rooms are basic. ⑤ *Rooms from: €70* ⊠ *Mount Lucas, Edenderry, Co. Offaly* ☎ *86/824–9574* ⊕ *www.eskermore.com* ⟿ *3 rooms* ◎I *Breakfast.*

$$ ⊞ **Roundwood House.** As you arrive, you'll note the dreamlike beauty
B&B/INN   of this chateau-esque mansion set on the slopes of the Slieve Bloom
Fodor's Choice   mountains—a dark tree-lined avenue suddenly opens up to reveal a
★   dramatically gorgeous Palladian villa as a flock of white geese, some ducks and hens as well as a Labrador called Rococo often form the welcoming party. **Pros:** friendly hosts; mature woodland is ideal for walks. **Cons:** dinner sometimes served at a communal table; not easy to drag yourself away at stay's end. **TripAdvisor:** "high-class cooking," "very special and unique," "kick back and relax." ⑤ *Rooms from: €140* ⊠ *Mountrath, Co. Laois* ☎ *057/873–2120* ⊕ *www.roundwoodhouse. com* ⟿ *10 rooms, plus 2 self-catering cottages* ◎I *Breakfast.*

In the spring, the gardens at Emo Court rival the splendor of its neoclassical-style salons—here, a section of parkland abloom with bluebells.

TULLAMORE

27 km (17 miles) northwest of Portarlington.

The county seat of Offaly, Tullamore is a bustling market town that thrived during Ireland's Celtic Tiger boom in the mid-1990s and, like many parts of Ireland, has suffered in the economic downturn. The town's historical success was based on its location on the Grand Canal, one of Ireland's most important trading links during the 18th and 19th centuries.

GETTING HERE AND AROUND

A medium-size Midlands town, Tullamore is a transportation hub. Six roads converge here, meaning that market days at the end of the week are especially busy and free street parking is first-come, first-served. Dublin is just over an hour's drive, while the neighboring towns of Athlone, Mullingar, and Portlaoise are approximately 30 minutes away. Travelers are reasonably well served by Bus Éireann buses here; routes connect to Dublin (two hours east) as well as towns north, south, and west of Tullamore. By train, Tullamore is 70 minutes from Dublin, 90 minutes from Galway, and two hours from Sligo. Train and bus services coalesce at Cormac Street in town.

ESSENTIALS

Visitor Information Tullamore Tourist Office ⊠ *Bury Quay, Tullamore, Co. Offaly* ☎ *057/935–2617* ⊕ *ww.tullamore.org* ☉ *Mid-June–mid-Sept. only.*

EXPLORING

Charleville Forest Castle. One relic of Tullamore's former splendor is found on the southwestern edge of town, where, if you take the road heading to Birr from the center of Tullamore, you'll find a storybook vision in splendid Tin Soldier Fortress style: Charleville Forest Castle. Perhaps the finest Neo-Gothic, British-style 19th-century castle in Ireland, its flag tower and turrets rise above its domain of 30 acres of woodland walks and gardens. The Georgian–Gothic Revival house was built as a symbol of English might triumphing over French force (the French revolutionary forces, to be exact, who had become a little too cozy with the Irish locals). In fact, the floor plan is even modeled on the Union Jack. Commissioned by Baron Tullamore and dating from 1812, the castle is a rural example of the work of architect Francis Johnston, who was responsible for many of Dublin's stately Georgian buildings. The interiors are somewhat the worse for wear—most are gigantic chambers with a few sticks of furniture—but the William Morris–designed dining room still has its original stenciled wallpaper.

Descended through the Bury family, who eventually lost their fortune and left no heirs, the castle became an orphan in the 1960s but has been slowly restored. The surrounding forest is said to be haunted by the spirits of the ancient Druids. Guided tours leave every 40 minutes in the summer between 1 pm and 5 pm. ⌂ *1½ km (1 mile) outside Tullamore on N52 to Birr, Tullamore, Co. Offaly* ☎ *057/932–3040* ⊕ *www.charlevillecastle.ie* ⌂ *€20 for one adult or couple. Additional members of same party €6* ☾ *Daily 1–5.*

★ **Lough Boora Parklands.** This open expanse of rehabilitated land is a
☾ place to potter and ponder. The old commercial, now exhausted, bog has been restored for a variety of leisure activities, from hiking and cycling to coarse angling and bird-watching (more than 150 species make their home here). Best of all, Lough Boora is now home to one of Ireland's most unique sculpture parks. Along the **Sculpture Walk**, where golden plovers, lapwings, and starlings may accompany you, 20 large-scale sculptures made from local materials (including glacial stone, water, and willow) have been created by artists influenced by the legacy of the bogs. The result is some of the most creative environmental outdoor artwork anywhere in Ireland. To cite one instance, the installation artist Mike Bulfin has turned a rusty old bog train into a cartoonish curve whose image will remain imprinted in your mind long after your visit to this magical place. ⌂ *Boora, 2 miles north of Kilcormac, Tullamore, Co. Offaly* ☎ *057/934–5978* ⊕ *www. loughbooraparklands.com* ⌂ *Free.*

Tullamore Dew Heritage Center. The Tullamore Dew Heritage Center underwent a makeover in 2012, adding new whiskey tours and tasting sessions. Tullamore Dew Irish Whiskey can trace its roots to 1829, when the Tullamore Distillery was founded. It was greatly expanded under the aegis of Daniel E. Williams, whose family became joint shareholders, and his own initials, D-E-W, were added to the whiskey's name, inspiring the slogan "Give every man his Dew" (which appeared on the bottles for many years). Today it's the world's second-largest and fastest-growing Irish whiskey. Check the website for tour and tasting schedules. ✉ *Bury Quay, Tullamore, Co. Offaly* ☎ *057/932–5015* ⊕ *www.tullamoredew.com* 🎫 *€6 self-guided, €8 guided tour* ⊙ *May–Sept., Mon.–Sat. 9–6, Sun. noon–5; Oct.–Apr., Mon.–Sat. 10–5, Sun. noon–5.*

WHERE TO STAY

For expanded hotel reviews, visit Fodors.com.

$ 🏨 **Annaharvey Farm.** Just 6 km (4
B&B/INN miles) outside of Tullamore town on the Portarlington road, this
family farmhouse dedicated to all things equestrian was once an old-world grain barn but has been converted into an elegant accommodation, replete with pitch-pine floors, massive roof beams, and open fireplaces. **Pros:** well away from the main road, secluded location; the clear Offaly night skies are filled with thousands of stars. **Cons:** bathrooms are small; noisy neighing horses may disturb your slumber. **TripAdvisor:** "wonderful family," "a haven of peace and tranquility," "perfect getaway." ⑤ *Rooms from: €75* ✉ *Tullamore, Co. Offaly* ☎ *057/934–3544* ⊕ *www.annaharveyfarm.ie* 🛏 *7 rooms* ⊙ *Closed Dec. and Jan.* 🍴 *Breakfast.*

SPORTS AND THE OUTDOORS

GOLF

Esker Hills Golf Club. Studded with natural lakes and woodlands, as well as excellent sand-based greens and valleys, Esker Hills is an 18-hole championship course. Masterfully designed by Christy O'Connor Jr., it is regarded as one of Ireland's leading inland links-type courses and is playable all year round. The club takes its name from eskers, or mounds of sand or gravel left by streams of melted ice, which provide the dramatic undulations, never mind the challenges, of the course. ✉ *N80, 5 km (3 miles) north of Tullamore, Tullamore, Co. Offaly* ☎ *057/935–5999* ⊕ *www.eskerhillsgolf.com* 🎫 *Greens fees: Weekdays €35, weekends €45* ⛳ *18 holes. Yardage: 6626. Par: 71. Practice putting area, caddies, buggies, catering* ⊙ *Visitors: daily except Sunday morning until 11 am.*

KILBEGGAN

11 km (7 miles) north of Tullamore.

GETTING HERE AND AROUND

The small town of Kilbeggan is on the main M6 Dublin–Athlone route; the nearest large town is Tullamore, 15 minutes south on the N52. There is free parking in town. Regular buses serving the busy Dublin–Galway route stop at Kilbeggan. Athlone is a 15-minute journey by bus, and Dublin is an 80-minute ride.

> ### BRIGHT ELIXIR
>
> Kilbeggans know "Irish" is a straight pot-still whiskey, and it has a characteristic flavor that distinguishes it from Scotch, bourbon, or rye. Irish is not drunk until it has matured for at least seven years in wooden casks. It's best quaffed without a mixer, so try it straight or with water.

4

EXPLORING

Kilbeggan Distillery Experience. It's the whiskey (the Irish spell their traditional tipple with an "e") that brings most people to the unassuming little town of Kilbeggan, home of the Kilbeggan Distillery Experience, the oldest pot-still distillery in the world and the last of its type in Ireland. This whiskey-lover's mecca was established in 1757 but was closed down as a functioning distillery in 1954. It has found new life as a museum of industrial archaeology illustrating the process of Irish pot-whiskey distillation and the social history of the workers. A tour plus tasting takes one hour, while a self-guided tour is 40 minutes. After you've watched the mashing and fermenting processes you can enjoy homemade food available in the Pantry restaurant. ☎ 057/933–2134 ⊕ www.kilbeggandistillery.com ⊠ €7.50 ☉ Apr.–Oct., daily 9–6; Nov.–Mar., daily 10–4.

MULLINGAR

24 km (15 miles) northeast of Kilbeggan.

The Irish are great ones for wrapping an insult up in a lyrical turn of phrase. Rather than describe a woman as overweight they'll say with a wink she's "beef to the ankle, like a Mullingar heifer." Of course, the phrase also illustrates Mullingar's role as Ireland's beef capital, a town surrounded by rich countryside where cattle trading has historically been one of the chief occupations. It's also County Westmeath's major town—a busy commercial and cattle-trading center on the Royal Canal, midway between two large, attractive lakes, Lough Owel and Lough Ennel. Although best used as a base to tour the surrounding countryside, Mullingar has some sights worthy of your time.

GETTING HERE AND AROUND

Mullingar is a busy town on the N4 Longford–Dublin route. Although it is bypassed by the highway, traffic in town can still come to a standstill at certain times of the day. The Dublin–Sligo train stops at Mullingar, and buses run to Athlone (1 hour) and Dublin (90 minutes).

ESSENTIALS

Visitor Information Mullingar Discover Ireland Centre ⊠ *Market Sq., Mullingar, Co. Westmeath* ☎ *35/3934–8650* ⊕ *www.discoverireland.ie/eastcoast.*

EXPLORING

★ **Belvedere House & Gardens.** A stately mid-18th-century hunting lodge
♨ with extensive gardens, Belvedere House occupies a beautiful spot on the northeast shore of Lough Ennel. Access to the mansion is through the servants' entrance—so you can see what life behind the scenes was like back then. The interiors are a quirky mix of Georgian stateliness and Victorian charm. The noted bow and Palladian windows have great parkland views sloping down to the lake and its islands.

Built in 1740 by architect Richard Cassels for Robert Rochfort, first earl of Belvedere, it became a byword for debauchery and dissipation, thanks to the high jinks of Rochfort's wife, the "very handsome" Mary Molesworth. After falling passionately in love with Rochfort's younger brother (and bearing him a child), she was locked up in another family

4

house for decades. Robert regaled guests with the "scandal" while offering sumptuous dinners at this house under its great plasterwork ceilings. He spent much of his family fortune dotting the gardens of the estate with "follies," including the Jealous Wall, a gigantic mock-castle ruin that served to cover up a view of the adjoining estate, owned by another brother, also hated.

You can walk around the 160 acres of the estate and woodland trails. Also on the grounds are a restaurant, a coffee shop, an animal sanctuary, and two children's play areas. ⊠ *N52, 4 km (2½ miles) south of Mullingar, Mullingar, Co. Westmeath* ☎ *044/934–9060* ⊕ *www.belvederehouse.ie* ✉ *House and parkland €8.75* ☉ *Mar.–Apr. and Sept.–Oct., daily 10–7; May–Aug., daily 10–8; Nov.–Feb., daily 10:30–3:30.*

Cathedral of Christ the King. The town's largest structure is the Renaissance-style Catholic Cathedral of Christ the King, completed in 1939. Note the facade's finely carved stonework, and the mosaics of St. Patrick and St. Anne by the Russian artist Boris Anrep in the spacious interior. There's a museum in the cathedral, and tours are available in the spring and summer (call for times). ⊠ *Mary St., Mullingar, Co. Westmeath* ☎ *044/934–8338* ⊕ *www.mullingarparish.ie* ☉ *Daily 8–8.*

WHERE TO STAY

For expanded hotel reviews, visit Fodors.com.

$$

HOTEL

★

⊡ **Temple Country Retreat and Spa.** If you're hoping to recharge your batteries, this is just the place: a modern retreat surrounded by 100 acres of parkland with all you could want in terms of relaxation therapy. **Pros:** serene and peaceful, the perfect escape; top-class food in comfortable surroundings. **Cons:** no TVs. **TripAdvisor:** "chilled-out break," "just OK," "excellent." ⑤ *Rooms from: €120* ⊠ *Horseleap, Moate, Co. Westmeath* ☎ *057/933–5118* ⊕ *www.templespa.ie* ⤵ *18 rooms, 2 suites* ☉ *Closed Christmas wk* ¶⊙| *All meals.*

SPORTS AND THE OUTDOORS

GOLF

Delvin Castle Golf Club. This historic 18-hole course in the stately parkland setting of Clonyn Castle demesne has beautiful views across north Westmeath. Mature trees and woodland surround you, and the ruins of the original Delvin Castle are visible at the 10th hole. A pleasant, rewarding course, it is playable all year round—the only difficulty may be occasional severe frost in the winter. ⊠ *Delvin, Co. Westmeath* ☎ *044/966–4315* ✉ *Greens fees: Mon., Wed., and Fri., €20; Tues. and Thurs., €10; weekends €25* ⚑ *18 holes. Yardage: 6103. Par 70. Practice area, putting green, caddies, buggies, catering* ☉ *Visitors: daily.*

CASTLEPOLLARD

21 km (13 miles) north of Mullingar.

A pretty village of multihued 18th- and 19th-century houses laid out around a large, triangular green, Castlepollard is also home to Tullynally Castle and Gardens, the largest castle in Ireland that still functions as a family home.

GETTING HERE AND AROUND

The small rural town of Castlepollard sits at a crossroads between Cavan and Mullingar, which is the nearest large town, 20 minutes south on the narrow R394. Free parking is available in the Square or on side streets. There is a daily bus service to Dublin (the trip takes 2 hours), and a route once a week to Mullingar.

EXPLORING

Fodor's Choice   ★   **Tullynally Castle and Gardens.** It's hard to figure out which is more famous: Tullynally's storybook castle or the magical parklands that surround this fabled family seat. And this is not just any family: the Pakenhams are the famous Irish tribe that has given us Elizabeth Longford (whose biography of Queen Victoria is in most libraries) and Antonia Fraser, wife of the late playwright Harold Pinter and best-selling biographer of Mary, Queen of Scots, among others. In fact, Tullynally—the name, literally translated, means "Hill of the Swans"—has been the home of 10 generations of this family, which also married into the earldom of Longford. Lady Fraser's brother Thomas, a historian, is the current earl but does not use the title.

As a result of an 18th-century "Gothicization," the former Georgian house was transformed into a faux castle by architect Francis Johnston; the resulting 600 feet of battlements were not just for bluff, as the earls were foes of Catholic emancipation. Inside, the family has struggled to make the vast salons warm and cozy—a bit of a losing battle. The house really comes into its own as a stage set for the surrounding park—the gray-stone structure is so long and has so many towers it looks like a miniature town from a distance. The total circumference of the building's masonry adds up to nearly ½ km (¼ mile) and includes a motley agglomeration of towers, turrets, and crenellations that date from the first early fortified building (circa 1655) up through the mid-19th century, when additions in the Gothic Revival style went up one after another.

Today, more attention is given to the beautiful parkland, in part because Thomas Pakenham is a tree-hugger extraordinaire. He is the author of several books, his most famous being *Meetings with Remarkable Trees* (1996), an exceptional art book that includes many of his magnificent photographs. The estate's rolling parkland was laid out in 1760, much along the lines you see today, with fine rhododendrons, numerous trees, and two ornamental lakes. A garden walk through the grounds in front of the castle leads to a spacious flower garden, a pond, a grotto, and walled gardens. The kitchen garden here is one of the largest in Ireland, with a row of old Irish yew trees. Don't miss the forest path, which takes you around the perimeter of the parkland and affords excellent views of the romantic castle. After your energetic tour, enjoy a visit to the coffee shop in the courtyard. ⊠ *1½ km (1 mile) west of Castlepollard on the R395 road to Granard, Castlepollard, Co. Westmeath* ☎ *044/966–1159* ⊕ *www.tullynallycastle.com* ⊠ *€6* ☉ *May–mid-Aug., Thurs.–Sun., daily 1–6.*

FORE

5 km (3 miles) east of Castlepollard.

You've heard of the seven wonders of the ancient world, but here in the heart of the Irish Midlands is a tiny village with seven wonders all to itself! According to Irish myth, this is the place where water runs uphill, where there's a tree that will not burn and water that will not boil, among other fantastical occurrences. The village is known not only for its legend, but also for its medieval church and the remains (supposedly the largest in Ireland) of a Benedictine abbey.

GETTING HERE AND AROUND

Fore is on a quiet country road between Castlepollard and Oldcastle on the R195. The nearest main town is Mullingar, a 30-minute drive. There's free parking in the village. Fore cannot be reached by train or bus.

EXPLORING

Fore Abbey. The spectacular remains of Fore Abbey dominate the simple village—its structure is massive and its imposing square towers and loophole windows make it resemble a castle rather than an abbey.

CAVAN

36 km (22 miles) north of Fore, 114 km (71 miles) northwest of Dublin.

Like all the larger towns of the region, Cavan is growing and prosperous. It is perhaps best known for its crystal factory. But as one of the main transportation hubs of the Midlands, Cavan has also attracted an impressive array of restaurant and hotels, so this is a fine base for exploring this region, which lies near the border to Northern Ireland. There are two central streets: with its pubs and shops, Main Street is like many other streets in similar Irish towns; Farnham Street has Georgian houses, churches, a courthouse, and a bus station.

GETTING HERE AND AROUND

Cavan is a thriving market town on the main N3 from Navan to Enniskillen in Northern Ireland. There is metered pay-parking in the town center. The town and surrounding south Ulster area, including neighboring Monaghan, relies on an extensive bus network for public transport. Cavan is equidistant from Belfast and Galway with a 3-hour travel time to both cities by bus. Bus Éireann serves Cavan on Galway–Belfast, Athlone–Belfast, and Dublin–Donegal Expressway routes, and there is weekday service to small towns throughout Cavan and Monaghan.

ESSENTIALS

Transportation Information Cavan Bus Office ☎ *049/433–1709.*

Visitor Information Cavan Tourist Office ✉ *Farnham St., Cavan, Co. Cavan* ☎ *049/433–1942* ⊕ *www.cavantourism.com.*

EXPLORING

Bear Essentials Ireland. A fun stop for children of all ages, you can view the largest collection of teddy bears in Ireland here. Each bear is hand-crafted in the workshop from the finest mohair. The Bear Essentials

Tullynally Castle—the largest in Ireland (just a small portion is shown here)—is surrounded by spectacular parkland, forest paths, and kitchen gardens.

Showroom and gift shop is next door. There's also a "Teddy Bear Hospital" on-site, where you can bring your damaged teddy for repair or redesign. ⊠ *Tirnawannagh, 23 km (18 miles) northwest of Cavan town, Bawnboy, Co. Cavan* ☏ *049/952–3461* ⊕ *www.bearessentials.ie* ✉ *Free* ⊘ *Mon.–Sat. 9–6, Sun. 11–6.*

WHERE TO EAT AND STAY
For expanded hotel reviews, visit Fodors.com.

$$$$
IRISH
Fodor's Choice
★

✕ **MacNean's House & Restaurant.** Quality doesn't come cheap but every bite in Neven Maguire's restaurant is a sublime taste sensation. No surprise—this is one of the best restaurants in Ireland. The five-course dinner menu, priced at €67, is an unhurried affair—it even comes with pre-starters and pre-desserts. Winning appetizers include an artistically presented study of shellfish, and the confit of Thornhill duck leg served with balsamic jelly. Top mains include a rare breed of caramelized pork belly and pan-seared turbot. The Menu Prestige, at €127 (including wine), delivers a staggering nine courses: your taste buds may never again experience such an explosion of epicurean delights. The five-course Sunday lunch at €37.50 is a great value. As many diners have learned, the 65-km (40-mile) detour to Blacklion makes a lot more sense if you are heading from Dublin northwest to Sligo or Donegal and also take in an overnight—there are 19 rooms available. But be warned: this restaurant is perpetually busy, and there's a waiting list of up to 12 months for weekends. ⑤ *Average main: €67* ⊠ *Blacklion, Main St., Cavan, Co. Cavan* ☏ *071/985–3022* ⊕ *www.nevenmaguire. com* ⟋ *Reservations essential* 🏛 *Jacket required* ⊘ *Mon.–Sat. no lunch; closed Jan. and Feb.–Dec. Mon. and Tues.* ⦿| *Breakfast.*

$$$$
IRIS H
Fodor's Choice
★

✕ The Olde Post Inn. The magic formula of a genuine Irish welcome and immaculate food with a culinary flourish is what draws people to the restaurant in the Olde Post Inn. In a restored stone former post office set in an elegantly landscaped garden, the restaurant has won a clutch of awards and, as a result, is often booked solid. Chef-owner Gearóid Lynch gives a dramatic modern twist to some Irish classics, including Irish venison with rösti potatoes, monkfish with bacon-and-cabbage terrine, and the positively mouthwatering suckling pig with *poitín* liquor sauce. A Lynch specialty is chicken stuffed with potato, apple, bacon, and herbs served with a whiskey sauce. Ingredients highlight local and regional foods. To get here, take the N53 to Cloverhill from Cavan Town. If you feel like staying overnight, six guest bedrooms, all in the original part of the postmaster's residence, have been modernized with contemporary bathrooms and plasma-TVs. $ *Average main: €55* ✉ *Cloverhill, Cavan, Co. Cavan* ☎ *047/55555* ⊕ *www.theoldepostinn. com* ☾ *Closed Mon. No lunch Tues.–Sat.*

$$
HOTEL
★

Cabra Castle. With its collection of mock-Gothic towers, turrets, and crenellations, along with rumors of paranormal activity, Cabra Castle has been deemed one of the world's scariest hotels; the Irish Ghosthunters Association has confirmed that it was indeed a place visited by spirits. **Pros:** stunning views of the surrounding countryside; a romantic retreat with attentive personal service. **Cons:** emphasis appears to be on weddings; the ghostly goings-on cannot be guaranteed but the signs are positive. **TripAdvisor:** "relaxing getaway," "fit for a king," "beautiful scenery and very accommodating." $ *Rooms from: €150* ✉ *Carrickmacross Rd., 65 km (40 miles) south of Cavan, on R179, Kingscourt, Co. Cavan* ☎ *042/966–7030* ⊕ *www.cabracastle.com* ⤶ *80 rooms, 5 suites, 21 self-catering lodges* ⦿ *Breakfast.*

SPORTS AND THE OUTDOORS

GOLF

County Cavan Golf Club. Visitors are welcome at this beautifully manicured 18-hole course set amid parkland in Drumelis, the heart of the Cavan lakelands. The Cavan Club has a long pedigree stretching back to 1894; it moved to its present location in 1920. The fairways are lined with mature trees and present a challenge, especially on holes 14–18. The 180m 10th is difficult from a tee-box in front of the clubhouse to a new green under an old chestnut tree. The club pro, Bill Noble, holds regular lessons. Golfers can warm up and sharpen their pitching, chipping, bunker, and putting techniques in a top-notch practice area. ✉ *Arnmore House, Drumelis, Cavan, Co. Cavan* ☎ *049/433–1283* ⊕ *www.cavangolf.com* ⛳ *Greens fees: Daily €20* ⛳ *18 holes. Yardage: 6164. Par 70. Practice area, floodlit driving range, buggies, catering* ☾ *Visitors: daily.*

LONGFORD TOWN

37 km (23 miles) southwest of Cavan, 124 km (77 miles) northwest of Dublin.

Longford, the seat of County Longford and a typical small market-town community, is rich in literary associations, though after Oliver Goldsmith, the names in the county's pantheon of writers may draw a blank from all but the most dedicated Irish literature enthusiasts. Long-ford Town provides a good base for exploring the largely untouristed countryside surrounding it. A day trip to the pretty heritage village of Ardagh (10 km [7 miles] southeast of Longford Town), with its quaint houses and village green, is a popular option.

GETTING HERE AND AROUND

Longford is on the N4 linking Mullingar and Carrick-on-Shannon. It's easily accessible by car, and town parking is generally not a problem. Shop around, as some parking is free while other streets are metered. Unlike many Midlands towns, Longford is doubly blessed with both train and bus links. Convenient for making connections, buses stop outside Longford train station. Bus Éireann routes fan out in all directions. Dublin airport and city are 2¼–2½ hours away, and Belfast is a four-hour ride. There's also a cross-border bus from Longford to Derry operated in conjunction with Ulsterbus; journey time is four hours. The town is on the main Irish Rail Dublin–Sligo railway line: Dublin is 1¾ hours away and Sligo is 1¼ hours.

ESSENTIALS

Transportation Information **Longford Railway Station** ☎ *043/3345208.*

Visitor Information **Longford Town Tourist Office** ⊠ *Market Sq., Longford, Co. Longford* ☎ *043/334–2577.*

EXPLORING

Bogwood Sculptures. A lovely spot near Longford Town is Newtown-cashel, on the banks of Lough Ree, where you can visit Bogwood Sculptures, a fascinating workshop run by sculptors Michael and Kevin Casey. The center displays sculptures and keepsakes made from bog-wood, which is hewn from the 5,000-year-old trees submerged and ultimately preserved by the area's ancient peat lands. To get there from Longford drive 14 km (9 miles) on the N63 to Lanesborough, then take the R392 for 2 km (1 mile) and follow signs for Turreen–Newtown-cashel. ⊠ *Barley Harbour, Newtowncashel, Co. Longford* ☎ *043/332–5297* ⊕ *www.bogwood.net* 🎫 *Free* ⊙ *Mon.–Sat. 10–6.*

The Genealogy Centre. This genealogy research center is worth visiting to search for your roots. Call in advance. ⊠ *17 Dublin St., Longford, Co. Longford* ☎ *043/334–1235* ⊕ *www.longfordgenealogy.com.*

Strokestown Park House & Famine Museum. The highlight of a trip to Strokestown in County Roscommon is the Irish National Famine Museum in the stable yard of Strokestown Park House. The museum tells the story of the devastating Irish potato blight in the 1840s, which is now regarded as one of the greatest social disasters in 19th-century Europe. Two million people—about a quarter of the population of Ireland—either died or emigrated and their harrowing story is well worth exploring. Museum exhibits include original famine documents found during the restoration of the house; it's a remarkable contrast to the opulent surroundings of the Georgian Palladian mansion and its six acres of garden. The Strokestown Park House landlord, Major Denis Mahon, was assassinated in November 1847 at the height of the famine. Strokestown is a 30-minute drive west of Longford town on the N5. ✉ *Strokestown, Co. Roscommon* ☎ *071/963–3013* ⊕ *www. strokestownpark.ie* 🖳 *Museum and gardens €13.08. House, museum, or gardens, €8.72* ☉ *Daily 10:30–5:30.*

WHERE TO EAT AND STAY
For expanded hotel reviews, visit Fodors.com.

$$ ✕**The Purple Onion.** A perfect resting place for tired and hungry travelers on the road to the west of Longford Town, this pub and restaurant

IRISH

Fodor's Choice
★

is on the main street of a tiny Shannon-side village. This place was originally a standard public house with low ceilings, nooks, crannies, and snugs, but under the patronage of Pauline Roe and Paul Dempsey it has been transformed into a gourmet's delight—a special gastropub, now abustle with locals, cruise-boat tourists, and food lovers from all over. Specialties include Thornhill duck or a Cavan roast on braised red cabbage with Chardonnay vinegar and honey glaze. Potatoes and vegetables are abundant and even served (atypically, for an Irish pub) al dente. It's worth leaving space for the Toblerone cheesecake, which has become the sweet talk of Longford. An upstairs gallery has work by some of the finest and best-known Irish artists, including Jack B. Yeats and Paul Henry, among 100 others. To get here from Longford Town drive 10 km (6 miles) west on the N5. ⑤ *Average main: €22* ✉ *Tarmonbarry, Co. Longford* ☎ *043/335–9919* ⊕ *www.purpleonion. ie* ☉ *Closed Mon. No lunch Tues.–Sat.*

$ 🛏 **Keenan's Boutique Hotel.** The B&B on the west side of its first-rate restaurant and its hotel accommodations overlooking the Shannon make

HOTEL
★

Keenan's a virtual village within a village at this East Midlands junction. **Pros:** friendly and helpful family-run operation. **Cons:** Tarmonberry is best as a one-night stand on your way east or west. **TripAdvisor:** "a complete relaxing break," "beautiful hotel," "wonderful staff." ⑤ *Rooms from: €90* ✉ *Tarmonbarry, Longford, Co. Roscommon* ☎ *043/332–6052* ⊕ *www.keenanshotel.ie* ⟿ *12 rooms* ☉ *Breakfast.*

$ 🛏 **Viewmount House.** An exquisite Georgian home once owned by the Earl of Longford, Viewmount has been restored to its former charm by

B&B/INN
★

James and Beryl Kearney. **Pros:** wonderfully restored house; comfort and hospitality are the order of your stay. **Cons:** 20-minute walk into town; limited amount to do in Longford. **TripAdvisor:** "peace and tranquility," "an unexpected oasis of calm," "beautiful retreat." ⑤ *Rooms from: €70* ✉ *Dublin Rd., Longford, Co. Longford* ☎ *43/3341919* ⊕ *www.viewmounthouse.com* ⟿ *12 rooms, 7 suites* ☉ *Breakfast.*

THE WESTERN MIDLANDS

This section of the Midlands covers the area's western fringe, making its way from the heart of the region, the town of Longford, and skirting the hilly landscape of County Leitrim, dappled with lakes and beloved of anglers for its fish-filled waters. The area is the country's most sparsely populated, though it has a light sprinkling of villages and, until his death in 2006, was the home of one of Ireland's leading writers, John McGahern; at the end of July, the John McGahern International Seminar and Summer School—a series of lectures, workshops, and tours—is held in Carrick-on-Shannon in his honor. Moving south through Roscommon, western Offaly, and the northern part of Tipperary, the scenery is generally low on spectacle but high on unspoiled, lush, and undulating countryside. The towns are small and undistinguished, except Birr and Strokestown, both designed to complement the "big houses" that share their names. This is one of the parts of the country where you're most likely to encounter the "hidden Ireland," a place unblighted by the plastic leprechaun syndrome of the more touristy areas to the south and west. The historic highlight of this region is the ancient site of Clonmacnoise, an important monastery of early Christian Ireland.

ANTONY TROLLOPE TRAIL

Trail starts in the village of Drumsna, 16 km (10 miles) north of Longford town.

GETTING HERE AND AROUND

The Trollope Trail is centered in Drumsna, a village 10 minutes from Carrick-on-Shannon and 30 minutes from Longford town. Dublin is a two-hour drive along the N4. Sligo lies 30 minutes north on the N4. Head west across the Plains of Mayo and two hours driving will take you to Galway.

EXPLORING

Anthony Trollope Trail. This trail, created to honor the celebrated English Victorian novelist Anthony Trollope (1815–82), takes in 27 locations throughout Leitrim and incorporates many fascinating topographical spots, including an area along the River Shannon known as Flaggy Bottoms. Trollope, a senior civil servant, was sent to Drumsna in 1843 to investigate the financial affairs of the postmaster. While living there he wrote his first novel *The Macdermots of Ballycloran*, drawing inspiration from the nearby ruin of Headford House. A leaflet and information on the trail is available from the tourist office in Carrick-on-Shannon (☎ 071/962–0170).

ATHLONE

34 km (21 miles) southeast of Longford Town, 127 km (79 miles) west of Dublin, 121 km (75 miles) east of Limerick.

Fodor'sChoice ★ The mighty Shannon flows majestically through the heart of Athlone, yet for years it seemed as if the town was happy to turn its back on one of Europe's great waterways. That trend has been well and truly reversed and with it has come a real buzz of regeneration. The area around Athlone Castle has been transformed into a veritable "Left Bank." On both sides of the Shannon, new restaurants and stylishly modern architecture have sprung up along streets lined with 200-year-old buildings that have been given some imaginative repurposing alongside one of Ireland's most architecturally dazzling churches. Once upon a time, tourists were few and far between in what was cuttingly termed the "dead center" of Ireland, but the renaissance has made Athlone an increasingly attractive destination.

GETTING HERE AND AROUND

Athlone is one of the Midlands' largest towns and on busy days its long main street can take 30 minutes to drive end to end. Although the main Dublin N6 motorway has considerably eased congestion this is still a place where delays are inevitable. Parking is available on the street, in paid lots, and at shopping centers. The drive to Dublin takes 2 hours, while Galway is 90 minutes west.

A GREAT IRISH TENOR

Count John McCormack (1884–1945) was perhaps the finest lyric tenor Ireland has produced. Born in Athlone, he recorded 600 records from 1914 to 1918 and made the Hollywood film *Song of My Heart*. A memorial bust stands on Grace Road by the Shannon.

With its central location, Athlone is an important Bus Éireann hub with connecting Expressway services to more than 20 principal towns and cities as well as dozens of smaller destinations across Ireland. Some routes are operated in conjunction with Ulsterbus. Trains branch out in three main directions from Athlone: southwest to Galway, west to Westport, and east to Dublin. The east–west intercity Irish Rail Galway–Dublin service takes 1¾ hours to reach Dublin.

ESSENTIALS

Transportation Information **Athlone Railway Station** ☎ 090/647–3300.

Visitor Information **Athlone Tourist Office** ✉ *Athlone Castle, Athlone, Co. Westmeath* ☎ *090/649–4630* ⊕ *www.discoverathlone.ie* ☾ *Apr.–Oct. only.*

EXPLORING

Athlone Castle. Beside the River Shannon, at the southern end of Lough Ree, stands Athlone Castle, a Norman stronghold built in the 13th century. After their defeat at the Battle of the Boyne in 1691, the Irish retreated to Athlone and made the river their first line of defense. The castle, which celebrated its 800th anniversary in 2010, is a fine example of a Norman stronghold with a strategic role in Irish history. It houses a small museum of artifacts relating to Athlone's eventful past, and the castle gatehouse serves as the town's tourist office. ✉ *Town Bridge, Athlone, Co. Westmeath* ☎ *090/649–2100* ⊕ *www.athlone.ie/athlone-castle* 🎫 *€6* ☾ *May–Sept., daily 10–5; Oct.–Apr., by appointment.*

St. Peter and St. Paul Catholic Church. St. Peter and St. Paul Catholic Church sparkles with its restored granite walls—it's a striking ecclesiastical and architectural baroque landmark that many come to see. Built in a completely different style from that generally adopted in Ireland, the church opened on June 29, 1937 (the feast day of the patron saints of St. Peter and St. Paul). In recent years, repair work on the impressive interior has included redecoration of the vaulted ceiling, walls, floors, and pews. Dominating the skyline for many miles around, the twin campanili symbolize the saints, while the squat copper dome adds to the overall grace of this much-loved building. Look out, too, for the six fine stained-glass windows from the famed Harry Clarke Studios in Dublin. The tribute window to St. Patrick is a riot of glorious color. ✉ *Market Sq., Athlone, Co. Westmeath* ☎ *090/649–2171* ⊕ *www.drum. ie/parish* ☾ *Daily 9–6.*

An entry in Fodor's "Show Us Your Ireland" contest, this photo submitted by Bartholomew shows a young lass at the Birr Arts Festival.

WHERE TO EAT

$

THAI

✕ **Kin Khao Thai Restaurant.** You can't miss (and you'd be foolish to pass by) the distinctive yellow-and-red insignia of what is widely regarded as the leading Thai restaurant in the Midlands, if not in all of Ireland. Adam Lyons runs a slick first-floor operation in a 650-year-old building on the west bank. The extensive menu features dishes rarely available outside Thailand, including the Crying Tiger (grilled fillet of beef on a sizzling hot platter with a hot chili sauce) and Jungle Curry (an extremely hot curry made with mixed vegetables and chicken, beef, or prawns). Ceiling fans and balloon bamboo lights help create the perfect gastronomic scene—it's not hard to imagine yourself in Chiang Mai. Just keep the water jug handy, as the smooth richness of coconut milk doesn't offset this fiery food. ⑤ *Average main: €17* ✉ *Abbey La., Athlone, Co. Westmeath* ☎ *090/649–8805* ⊕ *www.kinkhaothai.ie* ☾ *Lunch Mon, Tue, Sat.*

$$

ASIAN

Fodor's Choice

★

✕ **The Left Bank Bistro.** One of Athlone's culinary gems, this bistro is noted for its early-bird menu which now runs through the evening, filled with such delights as roast salmon fillet, beef Stroganoff, or South Indian vegetable curry with rice and yogurt. Later on, the beige-on-brown dining room fills up with people happy to choose Asian fusion dishes from the main dinner menu, which favors steaks, fish, and duck. For lunch the most popular dish is tandoori chicken breast on focaccia bread with sautéed potatoes. Irresistible desserts include Mississippi mud pie, pavlova roulade, and lemon-and-lime cheesecake. If you don't feel too hungry there is also a tapas menu to pick and choose from. Ask Annie McNamara, one of the joint owners, about the Left Bank dressing, a specially bottled vinaigrette that people come from all across Ireland to buy. $ *Average main: €23* ⊠ *Fry Pl., Athlone, Co. Westmeath* ☎ *090/649–4446* ⊕ *www.leftbankbistro. com* ☾ *Closed Sun. and Mon.*

WHERE TO STAY

For expanded hotel reviews, visit Fodors.com.

$

B&B/INN

Bastion Bed & Breakfast. An inviting glow hits you as you step into the long narrow corridor of this unconventional B&B, all nooks and little staircases, and with a high funky-and-fun quotient. **Pros:** healthy buffet breakfasts offer up cereal, fresh breads, fruit and cheese; minimalist chic and no clutter; historic character of neighborhood. **Cons:** bathrooms are small; no phones, TVs, or elevators. **TripAdvisor:** "fabulous and friendly," "very eclectic," "quirky little B&B." $ *Rooms from: €70* ⊠ *2 Bastion St., Athlone, Co. Westmeath* ☎ *090/649–4954* ⊕ *www. thebastion.net* ⟿ *7 rooms* ⊠ *Breakfast.*

$$$

HOTEL

Fodor'sChoice

★

Glasson Country House Hotel and Golf Club. With views extending out to Hare Island and beyond to Lough Ree, this 1780 stone manor house has seen its popularity rise with golfers every year since 1993, when the welcoming hosts Tom and Breda Reid turned a 70-acre field into a challenging course. **Pros:** family-run; an enthralling place to de-stress with woodland walks and boat trips all nearby. **Cons:** strong winds can whip in off the lake on breezy days—bring a sweater; bunker discussions dominate the conversation at breakfast, so be prepared. **TripAdvisor:** "top class," "memory lane," "amazing surroundings." $ *Rooms from: €170* ⊠ *Glasson, Co. Westmeath* ☎ *090/648–5120* ⊕ *www. glassongolfhotel.ie* ⟿ *65 rooms, 9 suites* ⊠ *Breakfast.*

$

HOTEL

Radisson Blu Hotel, Athlone. In a prime location on the banks of the Shannon, this 127-room property has a distinctive water theme, not surprisingly so, as more than half the units have superb views of the meandering river with a lovely look at the Sts. Peter and Paul across the way. **Pros:** stunning views; top-notch location for exploring the town, castle, and Left Bank; free parking. **Cons:** precooked breakfasts are mediocre; good pool but no spa. **TripAdvisor:** "a perfect place," "comfortable stay," "top class." $ *Rooms from: €100* ⊠ *Northgate St., Athlone, Co. Westmeath* ☎ *090/644–2600* ⊕ *www.radissonblu.ie/ hotel-athlone* ⟿ *128 rooms, 10 suites* ⊠ *Breakfast.*

$$$

HOTEL

★

Wineport Lodge. Catch the right sunset, and this is one of the most enchanting hideaways in Ireland . . . or perhaps we mean Sweden: this place is so stylishly modern and light-filled, thanks to all the orange cedarwood and plate-glass windows, that the locale could easily be Scandinavian. **Pros:** magical lake and forest setting; the under-floor bathroom heating is luxurious. **Cons:** the serenity is occasionally broken by jet-skiers on the lough; restaurant service can be slow. **TripAdvisor:** "very relaxing," "excellent staff," "a magical place." $ *Rooms from: €188* ⊠ *0123 Athlone, Glasson, Co. Westmeath* ☎ *090/643–9010* ⊕ *www.wineport.ie* ⟿ *29 rooms, 14 suites* ⊠ *Breakfast.*

4

Goldsmith Country

All that glitters may not be Goldsmith, but that hasn't prevented the Irish tourist board from promoting the Northern Lakelands to the burgeoning literary tourism market as "Goldsmith Country."

Yes, this is the region that gave birth to the writer Oliver Goldsmith (1730–74), celebrated for his farcical drama *She Stoops to Conquer* and his classic novel *The Vicar of Wakefield.* Goldsmith left his homeland as a teenager and returned rarely. However, he is thought to have drawn on memories of his native Longford for his most renowned poem, "The Deserted Village." At Goldsmith's childhood home in Lissoy in County Longford, only the bare walls of the family house remain standing. At Pallas, near Ballymahon in County Longford, his birthplace, there's a statue in his memory but little else. The plot of *She Stoops to Conquer* involves a misunderstanding in which a traveler mistakes a private house for an inn. This actually happened to Goldsmith at Ardagh House, now a college, in the center of the village of Ardagh (just off N55) in County Longford. In the same play the character Tony Lumpkin sings a song about a pub called the Three Jolly Pigeons; today the pub of the same name, on the Ballymahon road (N55) north of Athlone, is the headquarters of the Oliver Goldsmith Summer School.

Every year on the first weekend in June, leading academics from around the world speak on Goldsmith at this pub and other venues, and there are readings by the best of Ireland's contemporary poets and evening traditional music sessions in the tiny, atmospheric, country pub. Call the Athlone Tourist Office (☎ 090/649–4630) for more information.

NIGHTLIFE

Sean's Bar. In Athlone's buzzing Left Bank sector, Sean's Bar styles itself as the world's oldest pub (a claim some cynics dispute although a framed certificate from the *Guinness Book of Records* says otherwise), dating to AD 900. Sawdust on the floor of this dimly lighted, low-ceiling, long narrow bar helps give it a rustic look and soaks up spillages. Framed pictures and prints line the walls alongside maps of the Shannon navigation system, and the beer garden stretches almost down to the water. There's traditional music most nights. ✉ *13 Main St., Athlone, Co. Westmeath* ☎ *090/649–2358* ⊕ *www.seansbar.ie.*

SHOPPING

The Left Bank district is a jumble of lanes and small streets lined with pubs, antiques shops, bookstores, and one of the few surviving Irish bookbinders.

Ballinahown Irish Designer Craft Village. Make time for a stop at this craft village, home to two separate and distinctive stores, Core Crafted Design and Celtic Roots Studio. Both sell distinctive local crafts, ranging from bog-oak sculpture to honey as well as an outstanding choice of ceramics, jewelry, glasswork, and textiles. It's the last village in Westmeath as you travel to Clonmacnoise. Core is based in the

Old Schoolhouse, and Celtic Roots Studio is next door. ✉ *N62, south from Athlone to Limerick, Athlone, Co. Westmeath* ☎ *090/643–0222* ⊕ *www.irishdesignercraftvillage.com.*

Bastion Gallery. An Aladdin's cave of a place in which to browse, the funky Bastion Gallery sells quirky gifts, books, and toys. It's no surprise to learn that Michael Jackson, on a recording trip to the Irish Midlands, spent two hours in the shop one evening in 2006. ✉ *6 Bastion St., Athlone, Co. Westmeath* ☎ *090/649–4948* ⊕ *www. bastiongallery.com.*

★ **John's Bookshop.** Owned and run since 1997 by the affable John Donohue, this book shop is exactly the way a secondhand bookstore should be: cluttered, disorganized, and heaving with rare and signed Irish-related, and general books. ✉ *9 Main St., Athlone, Co. Westmeath* ☎ *090/649–4151* ⊕ *www.johnsbookshop.com.*

SPORTS AND THE OUTDOORS

BICYCLING

Buckleys Cycles. A combination of unfrequented back roads and lakeside scenery makes this attractive biking country, so head to this place to rent a bike. ✉ *Kenna Centre, Dublin Rd., Athlone, Co. Westmeath* ☎ *090/647–8989* ⊕ *www.buckleycycles.ie.*

BOATING

A boat trip reveals the importance of Athlone's strategic location on the River Shannon as well as the beauty of the region. *For the complete scoop on getting out on the water, see our special section on "Cruising on the Shannon."*

Viking Tours. For a unique way to cruise the Shannon, take a ride on the *Viking.* A replica of a Viking longboat, it travels up-river to nearby Lough Ree. Originally built in 1923, it's the longest-serving timber passenger boat in Ireland or the United Kingdom. The cost is €10; sailings take place March through October. Check the website for schedules. ✉ *Athlone Castle, Athlone, Co. Westmeath* ☎ *86/2621136* ⊕ *www. vikingtoursireland.ie.*

GOLF

Athlone Golf Club. An 18-hole parkland course, founded in 1892, Athlone is one of Ireland's oldest clubs. Redesigned in 2005, the course stretches along the shores of the majestic Lough Ree at Hodson Bay. Tree-lined fairways, sandy greens, and undulating terrain all make for an idyllically sited location that visitors hold in high regard. The club has hosted many national and provincial competitions, and the resident head pro is the Irish golfer Kevin Grealy, who offers lessons to players of all abilities. Athlone represents excellent value alongside stunning views of the River Shannon. ✉ *Hodson Bay, Athlone, Co. Westmeath* ☎ *090/649–2073* ⊕ *www.athlonegolfclub.ie* ✍ *Greens fees: weekdays €30; weekends €35* ⅄ *18 holes. Yardage: 6001. Par 72. Practice area, caddies, caddy carts, buggies, catering* ☉ *Visitors: daily (some restrictions on Sunday).*

One of Ireland's greatest monastic settlements, Clonmacnoise was nearly leveled in places—including the Norman Castle seen above—but has other ruins that still inspire awe.

CLONMACNOISE

20 km (12 miles) south of Athlone, 93 km (58 miles) east of Galway.

Many ancient sites dot the River Shannon, but Clonmacnoise is early Christian Ireland's foremost monastic settlement and, like Chartres, a royal site. The monastery was founded by St. Ciaran between 543 and 549 at a location that was not as remote as it now appears to be: near the intersection of what were then two of Ireland's most vital routes— the Shannon River, running north–south, and the Eiscir Riada, running east–west. Like Glendalough, Celtic Ireland's other great monastic site, Clonmacnoise benefited from its isolation; surrounded by bog, it's accessible only via one road or via the Shannon.

GETTING HERE AND AROUND

It takes dedication to get here. As the easiest way to Clonmacnoise is by car, it can be crowded at high season, although many visitors also arrive on tours buses. Get here early—the main parking lot fills up quickly. The site is 20 minutes south of Athlone; take the N62 then turn off onto the narrow R444 in the direction of Shannonbridge. Birr is 35 minutes by car south along the R357 and then the N52. Parking here is free.

Clonmacnoise is well-nigh impossible to reach by public transport. If you don't have a car, it's best to book a trip with companies such as CIE Tours, Paddywagon, Shamrocker, or Midland Tours. Or opt to board a boat in Athlone for a 90-minute journey to the jetty beside Clonmacnoise visitor center. Trips are run on the *Viking*, and advance booking is necessary. The round-trip journey is €15.

EXPLORING

★ **Clonmacnoise.** Thanks to its location, this legendary monastery survived almost everything thrown at it, including raids by feuding Irish tribes, Vikings, and Normans. But when the English garrison arrived from Athlone in 1552, they ruthlessly reduced the site to ruin. Still, with a little imagination, you can picture life here in medieval times, when the nobles of Europe sent their sons to be educated by the local monks. The monastery was founded on an esker (natural gravel ridge) overlooking the Shannon and a marshy area known as the Callows, which today is protected habitat for the corncrake, a wading bird.

Numerous buildings and ruins remain. The small **cathedral** dates to as far as the 10th century but has additions from the 15th century. It was the burial place of kings of Connaught and of Tara, and of Rory O'Conor, the last high king of Ireland, who was buried here in 1198. The two round towers include **O'Rourke's Tower,** which was struck by lightning and subsequently rebuilt in the 12th century. There are eight **smaller churches,** the littlest of which is thought to be the burial place of St. Ciaran. The High Crosses have been moved into the visitor center to protect them from the elements (copies stand in their original places); the best preserved of these is the Cross of the Scriptures, also known as Flann's Cross. Some of the treasures and manuscripts originating from Clonmacnoise are now housed in Dublin, most at the National Museum.

Clonmacnoise has always been a prestigious burial place. Among the ancient stones are many other graves dating from the 17th to the mid-20th century. The whole place is time-burnished, though in midsummer it can be difficult to avoid the throngs of tourists. Repairs are sometimes being carried out to buildings. There are tours every hour during the summer season. ⊠ *Near Shannonbridge, Co. Offaly* ☎ *090/967–4195* ⊕ *www.heritageireland.ie* 🎫 *€6* ⊗ *Nov.–mid-Mar., daily 10–5:15; mid-Mar.–mid-May and mid-Sept.–Oct., daily 10–6; mid-May–mid-Sept., daily 9–7. Last admission 45 mins before closing.*

BANAGHER

31 km (19 miles) south of Clonmacnoise.

"Well, that beats Banagher!" This small Shannon-side town is best known in Ireland because of this common phrase, which dates from the 19th century when the town was the very worst example of a "rotten borough"—a corrupt electoral area controlled by the local landed gentry. In short, if something "beats Banagher" it's either pretty bad or rather extraordinary. Nowadays, Banagher is a lively marina town that is a popular base for water-sports enthusiasts. Charlotte Brontë (1816–55) famously spent her honeymoon here.

GETTING HERE AND AROUND

Midway between Athlone and Roscrea, Banagher is a small crossroads town. Athlone and Birr are both a 40-minute drive, and although the town is busy in summer, parking is generally not a problem. Kearns Transport operates daily services with links from Banagher to Birr (15 minutes), Tullamore (35 minutes), and Dublin (3 hours).

CLOSE UP

The Boglands

Like the Eskimos with their 100 different words for snow, the natives of the Midlands retain a historic attachment to their vast boglands and will extol their virtues at length if prompted by a stranger.

In rural parts, turf, or peat, still accounts for much of the winter fuel supply and locals can always be counted upon to discuss in great detail the quality and consistency of this uniquely native resource.

"Grand year for the turf" will generally indicate a sunny August—key drying time when the "sods" are cut and allowed to dry along the banks. Conversely, "wicked bad turf" denotes a typically soft Irish summer with poor drying.

Along country lanes, the sight of reeks of cut turf is still commonplace. If you're tired of using the weather as a conversational icebreaker, try turf as an alternative and virtually guaranteed discourse igniter.

No matter that from a distance an Irish peat bog looks like a flat, treeless piece of waterlogged land. A close-up view shows a much more exciting landscape.

Bogs support an extraordinary amount of wildlife, including larks and snipe, pale-blue dragonflies, and Greenland white-fronted geese. Amid the pools and lakes of the peat bog, amazing jewel-like wildflowers thrive, from purple bell heather to yellow bog asphodel, all alongside grasses, lichens, and mosses.

As you pass through the small town of Shannonbridge, 10 km (6 miles) south of Clonmacnoise, on either side of the road are vast stretches of chocolate-brown boglands and isolated industrial plants for processing the area's natural resource.

Bord na Móna, the same government agency that makes commercial use of other boglands, has jurisdiction over the area.

ESSENTIALS

Transportation Contacts **Kearns Transport** ☎ *057/912–0124* ⊕ *www.kearnstransport.com.*

EXPLORING

The River Queen. If you happen to be in Banagher in summer, consider taking a cruise along the Shannon aboard *The River Queen,* an enclosed launch run by Silver Line Cruisers Ltd. that seats 54 passengers and has a full bar on board. ✉ *The Marina, Banagher, Co. Offaly* ☎ *091/51112* ⊕ *www.silverlinecruisers.com* 🎫 *€12* ⊙ *Cruises June–mid-Sept., Sun. at 2.*

NIGHTLIFE

★ **J. J. Hough's.** Travelers love Hough's, where on spring and summer nights there's usually a sing-along around the German piano. Note the walls decorated with business cards, testifying to the pub's popularity the world over. Side rooms lead to a beer garden with wooden chairs and tables. ✉ *Main St., Banagher, Co. Offaly.*

DID YOU KNOW?

Still home to the earl of Rosse, Birr Castle is closed to the public but its "demesne"—nearly 100 acres of gardens—is open to showcase the family tradition of undertaking daring expeditions and bringing horticultural treasures back home. Find a secluded place for a picnic and dream an afternoon away.

SPORTS AND THE OUTDOORS

Shannon Adventure Canoeing and Camping Holidays. Paddling a canoe is a nice alternative to a river cruise. This outfitter rents Canadian-class canoes, which allow you to explore the Shannon and other waterways on your own terms. ☒ *The Marina, Banagher, Co. Offaly* ☎ *057/915–1411* ⊕ *www.discoverireland.ie* ⊙ *May–Oct., daily.*

BIRR

12 km (7 miles) southeast of Banagher, 130 km (81 miles) west of Dublin.

Beautifully reminiscent of an English country town with its tree-lined malls and well-preserved houses, the heritage town of Birr has roots that date to the 6th century. Still, the mid-18th-century Georgian building boom sets the tone. Birr Castle is the pièce de résistance and an ideal place to while away a morning or afternoon in an idyllic setting. For those who enjoy a riparian ramble, the Camcor River Walk opened in 2012, complementing the Active Age Park. Birr is also noted for its variety of festivals throughout the year, including the longest-running hot-air balloon championships in the world held at the end of September. Visit ⊕ *www.destinationbirr.ie* for information on upcoming events.

GETTING HERE AND AROUND

Six main roads meet at Birr. Limerick is 90 minutes south on the N52 and then the N7, while Athlone is 30 minutes north on the N52. There may be traffic delays along the town's narrow central streets. Several paid lots and on-street metered spaces provide parking. Buses leave from Emmet Square for Dublin (3½ hours away) and west for Limerick (75 minutes).

ESSENTIALS

Visitor Information Birr Tourist Office ☒ *Brendan St., Birr, Co. Offaly* ☎ *057/912–0110* ⊕ *www.discoverireland.ie/offaly* ⊙ *May–Sept. only.*

EXPLORING

Fodor'sChoice   **Birr Castle Demesne.** All roads in Birr lead to the gates of Birr Castle
★   Demesne, a gorgeous Gothic Revival castle (built around an earlier 17th-century castle that was damaged by fire in 1823) that is still the home of the earls of Rosse. It's not open to the public, but you can visit the surrounding 150 acres of gardens. The present earl and countess of Rosse continue the family tradition of making botanical expeditions all over the world for specimens of rare trees, plants, and shrubs. The formal gardens contain the tallest box hedges in the world (at 32 feet) and vine-sheltered hornbeam allées. In spring, check out the wonderful display of flowering magnolias, cherries, crab apples, and naturalized narcissi; in autumn, the maples, chestnuts, and weeping beeches blaze red and gold.

The grounds are laid out around a lake and along the banks of two adjacent rivers, above one of which stands the castle. The grounds also contain **Ireland's Historic Science Centre,** an exhibition on astronomy, photography, botany, and engineering housed in the stable block. The giant (72-inch-long) reflecting telescope, built in 1845, remained the largest in the world for 75 years. Allow at least two hours to see everything. There's a crafts shop, picnic and play area, and the Courtyard Café serves soup, salads, sandwiches, and daily lunch specials. ⊠ *Rosse Row, Birr, Co. Offaly* ☎ *057/912–0336* ⊕ *www. birrcastle.com* ⌑ *Castle grounds €9* ⊙ *Nov.–Mar., daily 10–4; Apr.– Oct., daily 9–6.*

WHERE TO EAT AND STAY

For expanded hotel reviews, visit Fodors.com.

MACREGOL THE SCRIBE

A facsimile of an early Christian illuminated manuscript—the MacRegol Gospel—is on display in the restored Birr Library. MacRegol was a scribe, bishop, and abbot in Birr. The original manuscript, which is now in Oxford's Bodleian Library, was produced around AD 800 and consists of 169 vellum folios or leaves.

$$ ✕ **The Thatch Bar.** It's worth venturing 2 km (1 mile) south of Birr, just off IRISH the N62 Roscrea road, into this thatched country pub and restaurant, which offers a warm welcome and imaginative food. Inexpensive meals are available at the bar at lunchtime and early evening (4 to 7:30); later at night, the restaurant offers a choice of a five-course dinner menu or an à la carte menu. Pigeon and rabbit terrines and sirloin steaks with mushrooms in garlic sauce vie for diners' attention with more exotic dishes such as kangaroo and locally farmed ostrich. ⑤ *Average main: €19* ⊠ *Crinkil, Co. Offaly* ☎ *057/912–0682* ⊕ *www.thethatchcrinkill. com* ⊙ *Open daily.*

$ ⛱ **Dooly's Hotel.** This unpretentious country hotel began life as a coach HOTEL house some 275 years ago and has retained its old-style charm. **Pros:** huge rooms with space for moving around in; a handy Midlands stopover, if you're on your way to the west coast. **Cons:** the weekend disco in the nightclub goes on until the early hours, so bring your earplugs; stairs can be difficult for the disabled or elderly. **TripAdvisor:** "lovely atmosphere," "friendly staff," "restaurant is very good." ⑤ *Rooms from: €79* ⊠ *Emmet Sq., Birr, Co. Offaly* ☎ *11/3535791* ⊕ *www.doolyshotel. ie* ⤶ *18 rooms* ⅼ◎ⅼ *Breakfast.*

$ ⛱ **The Maltings.** Sheltered beneath the eaves of Birr Castle on a riverbank, this converted cut-stone storehouse—built to store malt for B&B/INN Guinness in 1810—is a good option for families and offers special rates
Fodor's Choice for children. **Pros:** idyllic location; attractive rooms; great breakfasts.
★ **Cons:** beginning to show signs of wear and tear; no dinner available,
♻ but there are several restaurants in the area. **TripAdvisor:** "comfortable and quiet," "peaceful," "beautiful house." ⑤ *Rooms from: €70* ⊠ *Castle St., Birr, Co. Offaly* ☎☎ *057/912–1345* ⊕ *themaltingsbirr.com* ⤶ *10 rooms* ⅼ◎ⅼ *Breakfast.*

ROSCREA

19 km (12 miles) south of Birr.

Fodor's Choice Every corner you turn in this charming town will offer reminders of
★ its rich and sometimes turbulent past. Ancient castles, towers, and churches dot the skyline, proof of a heritage that dates to the 7th century. The road through town cuts right through the remains of a

monastery founded by St. Cronan. It also passes the west facade of a 12th-century Romanesque church that now forms an entrance gate to a modern Catholic church. Above the structure's rounded doorway is a hoodmold enclosing the figure of a bishop, probably St. Cronan.

GETTING HERE AND AROUND

Roscrea is on the main N7 road between Dublin and Cork, making it ideal as a stopover en route to the south. Limerick is one hour south on this route and roads from the town lead to all points of the Midlands compass. Cars park free on the main streets, and there is ample parking on side streets and in designated areas. The Bus Éireann Expressway from Dublin to Limerick stops in Roscrea, a 2½-hour journey. The Roscrea–Limerick leg of the route is 70 minutes. From Roscrea you can also catch a bus south to Cashel (2¼ hours) and Cork (3 hours) as well as north to Athlone (70 minutes) or as far northwest as Sligo, a journey of nearly 5 hours. The Irish Rail Dublin–Limerick train stops in Roscrea as well; the town is 90 minutes from each city.

EXPLORING

Roscrea Castle. In the very center of town is Roscrea Castle, a Norman fortress dating from 1314, given by King Richard II to the duke of Ormonde. Inside are vaulted rooms graced with tapestries and 16th-century furniture. A ticket to the castle also gains entry to the adjacent **Damer House**, a superb example of an early-18th-century town house on the grand scale. It was built in 1725 within the curtain walls of the castle, at a time when homes were often constructed beside or attached to the strongholds they replaced. The house has a plain, symmetrical facade and a magnificent carved-pine staircase inside; on display are exhibits about local history. To get here, start with your back to St. Cronan's monastery, turn left, and then turn right on to Castle Street. ⊠ *Castle St., Roscrea, Co. Tipperary* ☎ *0505/21850* ⊕ *www. heritageireland.ie* ⬚ *€4* ⊙ *May–Sept., daily 9:30–6; Oct.–Apr., weekends 10–5.*

The Southeast

INCLUDING COUNTIES CARLOW, KILKENNY, TIPPERARY, WATERFORD, AND WEXFORD

WORD OF MOUTH

"Re Kylemore Quay: It is a lovely little village of thatched houses and lots of flowers. Took a lot of pictures there. If the Silver Fox is still there, have supper there. I am not a foodie, but I remember that meal as wonderful! It is also a jumping-off point for a visit to the Saltee Islands for birding opportunities."

—irishface

WELCOME TO THE SOUTHEAST

TOP REASONS TO GO

★ **Sacred Ardmore:** St. Declan founded Ireland's first Christian settlement near this beautifully situated fishing village on the Waterford coast.

★ **Kilkenny, Ireland's Medieval Capital:** With its famous 14th-century "witch," Petronilla, *Camelot*-worthy Black Abbey, and fairy-tale Kilkenny Castle, the city still conjures up the days of knights and damsels.

★ **Pretty-as-a-postcard Lismore:** Presided over by the neo-baronial castle of the Dukes of Devonshire, this storybook village has attracted visitors ranging from Sir Walter Raleigh to Fred Astaire.

★ **Cashel of the Kings:** Ireland's "Rock of Ages," this spectacular 200-foot-tall rock bluff was the ancient seat of the Kings of Munster.

★ **Wexford and Waterford:** Big-city lights shine brightest here, thanks to such attractions as the famed Wexford Opera Festival and the reborn Waterford Crystal factory and visitor center.

1 Kilkenny City. Creativity is evident in every aspect of this town, from its medieval stonework to its array of modern and traditional craft and design found in galleries and studios as well as the many festivals and events held here year-round.

2 Southeast Inlands. Redolent of the Middle Ages, this once-upon-a-time-ified region is home to some thrilling medieval sights, including Leighlinbridge's Black Castle, the tiny village of Old Leighlin, and Jerpoint Abbey, the most famous Cistercian ruins in Ireland.

4 Southeast Coast. Combining the best of Ireland's climate with some wonderful sand-and-sea settings, this coastal headland is noted for quaint villages like Kilmore Quay and Ballyhack, the bustling and historic city of Waterford, and beachfront locations that attract Dubliners by the droves.

GETTING ORIENTED

Set around Tipperary—Ireland's largest inland county—the Southeast is a vast region that stretches from the town of Carlow near the border of County Wicklow in the north to Ardmore near the border of County Cork in the south. Although main towns can be packed with camera-wielding tourists, you can easily escape the tour buses thanks to endless expanses of tranquil countryside.

3 Wexford Town. The warm welcome, the ancient Viking streets, and the tiny, atmospheric Theatre Royal add to the cultural pleasures as this proud town puts on its Sunday best for the Wexford Opera Festival, a weeklong binge of arias and charm held every October.

5 County Tipperary and Around. The greatest group of monastic ruins in Ireland—the Rock of Cashel—lords it over miles of the idyllic region known as the Golden Vale along with some relentlessly romantic sights, like the 19th-century village of Lismore and Cahir's charming Swiss Cottage.

Updated by
Anto Howard

The Irish like to label their regions, and "Ireland's Sunny Southeast" is the tag they've applied to counties Wexford, Carlow, Kilkenny, Tipperary, and Waterford. The moniker is by no means merely fanciful: the weather station on the coast at Rosslare reports that this region receives more hours of sunshine than any other part of the country. Little wonder the outdoors-loving Irish have made the Southeast's coast a popular warm-weather vacation destination.

Receiving almost double the rays found anywhere else, the shore resorts buzz with activity from May to October. Thousands of families take their annual summer holidays here, where picnics and barbecues—often a rain-washed fantasy elsewhere in Ireland—are a golden reality.

The entire Southeast is rich with natural beauty—not the rugged and wild wonders found to the north and west, but a coast that alternates between long, sandy beaches and rocky bays backed by low cliffs, and an inland landscape of fertile river valleys and lush, undulating pastureland. The landscape of the region is diverse, the appeal universal: you'll find seaside fishing villages with thatched cottages, and Tipperary's verdant, picturesque Golden Vale. The region doesn't lack for culture, either. History-rich Ardmore, Carlow Town, the cities of Kilkenny and Waterford, and Wexford Town have retained traces of their successive waves of invaders—Celt, Viking, and Norman.

The most important of these destinations is Kilkenny City, a major ecclesiastic and political center until the 17th century and now a lively market town. Its streets still hold remnants from medieval times—most notably St. Canice's Cathedral—and a magnificent 12th-century castle that received a sumptuous Victorian makeover. Wexford's narrow streets are built on one side of a wide estuary, giving it a delightful maritime air. Waterford, although less immediately attractive than Wexford, is also built at the confluence of two of the region's rivers, the Suir and the Barrow. It offers a rich selection of Viking and Norman remains, some attractive Georgian buildings, and the visitor center and shop at the famed Waterford Glass Factory (which, a few years ago, stopped manufacturing here).

Deeper into the countryside, rustic charms beckon. The road between Rosslare and Ballyhack passes through quiet, atypical, flat countryside dotted with thatched cottages. In the far southwest of County Waterford, near the Cork border, Ardmore presents early Christian ruins on an exposed headland, while, in the wooded splendor of the Blackwater Valley, the tiny cathedral town of Lismore has a hauntingly beautiful fairy-tale castle.

THE SOUTHEAST PLANNER

WHEN TO GO

As well as having some of the richest land in the country, the Southeast is the envy of all Ireland for that most elusive element—sunshine. The region is also one of the driest in Ireland, which is saying something in a country where seldom do more than three days pass without some rain. Compared with an average of 80 inches on parts of the west coast, the Southeast gets as little as 40 inches of rainfall per year, varying from the finest light drizzle (a soft day, thank goodness!) to full-blown downpours.

FESTIVALS AND EVENTS

With practically every hamlet and village across the country glorying in its own festival/excuse for later pub opening, the Southeast delivers some of Ireland's most popular gatherings. Check with the tourist boards for listings and dates of all events, big and small.

JUNE **Eigse Arts Festival.** Carlow's Eigse Arts Festival is a 10-day celebration of visual arts in June. ⊕ *www.eigsecarlow.ie.*

AUGUST In August the Spraoi festival (⊕ *www.spraoi.com*) is a display of talented exuberance in Waterford City, using the city's extensive pedestrian areas.

Kilkenny Arts Festival. Kilkenny Arts Festival attracts many global premieres to its weeklong calendar in August. ⊕ *www. kilkennyarts.ie.*

OCTOBER In late October–early November, the two-week-long annual Wexford Opera Festival (⊕ *www.wexfordopera.com*) is the biggest social and artistic event in the entire Southeast. From mid-September until the final curtain comes down, Wexford becomes home to a colorful cast of international singers, designers, and musicians, as the town prepares for the annual staging of three grand opera productions at the brand new Wexford Opera House. The bad news: nearly every single bed within a large radius of Wexford is booked during the festival weeks, and usually for months before the actual event kicks off.

Wexford Fringe Festival. Running alongside the opera festival from late October to early November, the chaotic and theatrical Wexford Fringe is an eclectic mix of theatre, literature, music, dance, and street events. ⊠ *Wexford Town, Co. Wexford* ⊕ *www.wexfordfringe.ie.*

PLANNING YOUR TIME

IF YOU HAVE THREE DAYS

Distances are not great, but if you are here for a short stay—three days or fewer—you might want to base yourself in one of the cities or larger towns in the region; either Waterford, Kilkenny, or Wexford. All three are historic locations with plenty of places of cultural and historical interest accessible on foot. They are also growing shopping destinations. Day trips from Waterford and Wexford could include idyllic coastal villages like Ardmore, Dunmore East, and Kilmore Quay. From Kilkenny and Waterford the mountains and glens of Tipperary are only a short drive away. Spend a night at a coastal hotel like the Cliff House in Ardmore or the country manor of Ballyduff House in Thomastown. If you have more time in the region—say three to five days—you might want to drive the whole of the scenic coast from Wexford, down around spectacular Hook Head to Waterford and on to the winding road to Ardmore and Dungarvan. You want to take your time, avoid the motorway, and stop off at any village or watering hole that takes your fancy. The House restaurant in Ardmore and the Tannery in Dungarvan are two great places for food based on local produce. You still have plenty of time for a detour north into Tipperary along some beautiful mountain back roads and on to the historic town of Cashel to see the legendary Rock. From there it's a short, scenic hop back to medieval Kilkenny City.

GETTING HERE AND AROUND

AIR TRAVEL

Aer Arann flies between Waterford City and London's Luton and Southend Airports. There are also flights to Manchester, Birmingham, and Lorient in France in summer. Waterford Regional Airport is on the Waterford–Ballymacaw road in Killowen. Waterford City is less than 10 km (6 miles) from the airport. A hackney cab from the airport into Waterford City costs approximately €18.

Carrier **Aer Arann** ☎ *01/844-7700* ⊕ *www.aerarann.com.*

Airport Information **Waterford Airport** ☎ *051/875-589* ⊕ *www.waterfordairport.ie.*

BOAT AND FERRY TRAVEL

If you are coming to Ireland from England or the Continent, chances are you'll end up on a ferry bound for Rosslare Harbour, 19 km (12 miles) south of Wexford, one of Ireland's busiest ferry ports. There are two main companies that service Rosslare. Irish Ferries connects Rosslare to Pembroke, Wales (4 hours), and France's Cherbourg and Roscoff. Stena Line sails directly between Rosslare Ferryport and Fishguard, Wales (3 hours). They both have small information kiosks in the ultramodern terminal, which also has a tourist office, lockers, and a sprawling waiting room.

You can purchase ferry tickets at the terminal, but try to reserve a space in advance through the companies' Cork or Dublin office to avoid the frequent sellouts, particularly in summer and any time the Irish soccer team is playing in a major tournament abroad.

Reservations are also a must if you're traveling by car or motorcycle because onboard parking space is at a premium. Last time we checked, the journey from France to Ireland was free for EurailPass holders. Departure times vary from season to season; check the website for schedules.

Boat and Ferry Information **Irish Ferries** ☎ *053/913-3158* ⊕ *www.irishferries.com.* **Passage East Car Ferry Company** ☎ *051/382-480* ⊕ *www.passageferry.ie.* **Stena Line** ☎ *01/204-7777* ⊕ *www.stenaline.ie.*

BUS TRAVEL

Bus Éireann runs frequent buses between Waterford and Dublin, Limerick, Cork, and Rosslare. J. J. Kavanagh & Sons runs daily buses from Dublin to Carlow, Waterford, and Kilkenny.

Bus Information **Bus Éireann** ☎ *01/836-6111 in Dublin, 051/879-000 in Waterford* ⊕ *www.buseireann.ie.* **J. J. Kavanagh & Sons** ☎ *0818/333-222* ⊕ *www.jjkavanagh.ie.*

CAR TRAVEL

With new highways to Waterford and Kilkenny, a car is the best option for covering ground quickly and easily. Waterford City, the regional capital, is easily accessible from all parts of Ireland.

From Dublin, take N7 southwest, change to N9 in Naas and then to the M9, and continue along this as it bypasses Carlow Town and Thomastown until it terminates in Waterford. N25 travels east–west through Waterford City, connecting it with Cork in the west and Wexford Town in the east. From Limerick and Tipperary Town, N24 stretches southeast until it, too, ends in Waterford City. For the most part, the main roads in the Southeast are of good quality and are free of congestion. Side roads are generally narrow and twisting, and you should keep an eye out for farm machinery and animals on country roads.

TAXI TRAVEL

Taxis at Waterford Regional Airport connect to the major cities in the region; to Waterford City costs about €18; to Kilkenny, about €80; and to Wexford roughly €85. It costs €4.10 to hire a taxi on the street (€4.45 by night) in the larger towns: add €2 to book one by phone, and €1.03 per kilometer or part of a kilometer for the first 15 km. Full details of fares and conditions are on the Taxi Regulator website ⊕ *www.nationaltransport.ie.*

Taxi Companies **DJ Taxis Waterford** ☎ *087/410-4108* ⊕ *www.taxiswaterford. com.* **Celtic Cabs (Wexford)** ☎ *053/914-2434* ⊕ *www.celticcabs.com.* **Kilkenny Taxi** ☎ *056/772-2224* ⊕ *www.kilkennytaxi.com.*

TRAIN TRAVEL

Waterford City is linked by daily Irish Rail service to Dublin, with trains making stops at Thomastown, Kilkenny, Bagenalstown, and Carlow Town. The daily train between Waterford City and Limerick makes stops at Carrick-on-Suir, Clonmel, Cahir, and Tipperary Town. The train between Rosslare and Waterford City runs twice daily.

Train Information **Irish Rail** ☎ *01/836-6222 in Dublin, 051/873-401 in Waterford* ⊕ *www.irishrail.ie.* **MacDonagh Station** ⊠ *St. John's St..* **O'Hanrahan Station** ⊠ *Redmond Pl..* **Plunkett Station** ⊠ *Dock Rd., Co. Waterford.*

For more information on getting here and around, see Travel Smart Ireland.

RESTAURANTS

Food is usually prepared in a simple, country-house style, but be ready for some pleasant surprises, as there are a number of ambitious Irish chefs at work in the Southeast's restaurants and hotels. The best of the region's cuisine rests on modern interpretations of classic dishes. One leading light in the area, chef Kevin Dundon at Dunbrody House, expounds a philosophy of understated but delicious food both in his cooking school and in his cookbook, *Full On Irish*. Informed by his culinary experience, dishes such as tea-smoked chicken and tarragon-glazed lamb exemplify Dundon's modern, international take on his Irish roots. Another of the Southeast's prominent chefs, Paul Flynn of the Tannery is renowned among Irish foodies for his wonderful inventiveness using local ingredients with a French twist; his seafood dishes are often works of art. He's also the inspiration behind Dungarvan's Waterford Festival of Food every April. Martjin Kajuiter at the Cliff House in Ardmore has gained the region's only Michelin star for his daring use of local ingredients in a stunning cliff-side location. Other than its fabled strawberries, the Southeast is probably best known for its rich seafood, especially Wexford mussels, crabs, and locally caught salmon. Kilmore Quay, noted for lobster and deep-sea fishing, hosts an annual Seafood Festival the second week of July. Many restaurants serve local lamb, beef, and game in season. *Prices in the reviews are the average cost of a main course at dinner or, if dinner is not served, at lunch.*

HOTELS

Festivals, the good weather, and commerce make the Southeast popular, so plan way ahead for a stay in any of the main towns (and in many country manors, which usually have fewer than six bedrooms and fill up fast). As always, the local tourist offices can offer assistance if you arrive without reservations. *Prices in the reviews are the lowest cost of a standard double room in high season. For expanded reviews, facilities, and current deals, visit Fodors.com.*

TOURS

A Rural Experience runs day excursions and extended tours all over the Southeast, and their County Kilkenny tour is especially popular. The knowledgeable and delightful Jack Burtchaell of Burtchaell Tours

---

TUNE IN TO THE SOUTHEAST

As you'll no doubt spend a good portion of your time behind the wheel during your travels, tune in to Irish radio for another angle on the country. If you want to feel the true pulse of the nation, check out any of RTE Radio 1's morning and afternoon shows. In a country still reeling from the government mismanagement and social damage of the recent economic crash, the radio has become Ireland's modern confessional and a serious insight into what makes the Irish tick. Waterford Local Radio (95.1/97.5 FM) and South East Radio (95.6/96.4 FM) are the popular options around Waterford and Wexford respectively.

in Waterford City leads a Waterford walk at noon and 2 pm daily from March through September. Tours depart from the Granville Hotel. Walking tours of Kilkenny are arranged by Tynan Tours from the Kilkenny TIO. These tours take place daily April through October, and Tuesday through Saturday, November to March. Walking tours of historic Wexford Town can be prebooked for groups by contacting Wexford Walking Tours. Book tours through town tourist offices.

Walking Tours Burtchaell Tours of Waterford City ☎ *051/873–711* ⊕ *www.jackswalkingtours.com.* **A Rural Experience** ☎ *056/772–7590* ⊕ *www.aruralexperience.com.* **Tynan Tours of Kilkenny City** ☎ *087/265–1745* ⊕ *www.kilkennytourism.ie/tynans_walking_tours.*

VISITOR INFORMATION

Eight tourist information offices (TIOs) in the Southeast are open all year. They are Carlow Town, Dungarvan, Enniscorthy, Gorey, Kilkenny, Lismore, Waterford City, and Wexford Town. Another five TIOs are open seasonally: Cahir (May–September); Cashel (April–September); Rosslare (April–September); Tipperary Town (May–October); and Tramore (June–August). If traveling extensively by public transportation, be sure to load up on information (schedules, the best taxi-for-hire companies, etc.) upon arriving at the train and bus stations in Kilkenny City, Wexford Town, and Waterford City.

KILKENNY CITY

101 km (63 miles) southwest of Dublin.

Dubbed "Ireland's Medieval Capital" by its tourist board, and also called "the Oasis of Ireland" for its many pubs and watering holes, Kilkenny is one of the country's most alluring destinations. It demands to be explored by foot or bicycle, thanks to its easily circumnavigated town center, a 900-year-old Norman citadel that is now a lovely place of Georgian streets and Tudor stone houses. The city (population 25,000) is impressively preserved and attractively situated on the River Nore, which forms the moat of the magnificently restored Kilkenny Castle. In the 6th century, St. Canice (aka "the builder of churches") established a large monastic school here. The town's name reflects Canice's central role: Kil Cainneach means "Church of Canice." Kilkenny did not take on its medieval look for another 400 years, when the Anglo-Normans fortified the city with a castle, gates, and a brawny wall. Kilkenny City's central location means that it's not too far from anywhere else in Ireland.

GETTING HERE AND AROUND

From Dublin take the N7/M7 to the M9 and exit at Junction 8 for the N10 to Kilkenny. These are major motorways so the 62-mile trip takes only an hour and a half. Cork is a 2-hour drive, while Waterford City is only a 40-minute hop. There is plenty of paid parking around the town.

The bus station is a bit down from the train station on St. John's Street, and Bus Éireann runs eight buses a day to Dublin for a 2-hour 10-minute trip that costs €10.80 one-way and €12.15 round-trip. Three buses a day go to Cork for a three-hour trip that costs €16.70 one-way and €21.60 round-trip. J. J. Kava-nagh & Sons runs five buses a day from the station directly to Dublin airport for a three-hour journey that costs €18 one-way and €28 round-trip.

MacDonagh Station, the city train station, is a short walk from the city center at the top of St. John's Street. The station is on the Dublin—Waterford City line, which also serves Athy, Carlow, Bagenals-town, and Thomastown. Irish Rail runs six trains a day in each direction and the trip to Dublin takes about 1 hour 45 minutes and costs €18 each way. There is no direct train to Cork, but five trains a day go via Newbridge for a four-hour journey that costs €20.

ESSENTIALS

Visitor Information **Kilkenny Tourist Office** ⊠ *Shee Alms House, Rose Inn St., Kilkenny City, Co. Kilkenny* ☏ *056/775–1500* ⊕ *www.discoverireland.ie/kilkenny.*

EXPLORING

Kilkenny's city center is small, and despite the large number of historic sights and picturesque streets—in particular, Butter Slip and High Street—you can easily cover it in less than three hours. One of the most pleasant cities south of Dublin (and one of its most sports-minded—from July to September practically the only topic of conversation is the fate of the city's team at the All-Ireland Hurling Championship), Kilkenny City has become in recent years something of a haven for artists and craft workers seeking an escape from Dublin. At such venues as the Kilkenny Design Centre, you can find an array of quality Irish crafts. The city has more than 60 pubs, many of them on Parliament and High streets, which also support a lively music scene. Many of the town's pubs and shops have old-fashioned, highly individualized, brightly painted facades, created as part of the town's 1980s revival of this Victorian tradition. So after taking in Kilkenny Castle and the Riverfront Canal Walk—an overgrown pathway that meanders along the castle grounds—mosey down High and Kieran streets. These parallel avenues, considered the historic center of Kilkenny, are connected by a series of horse cart–wide lanes and are fronted with some of the city's best-preserved pubs and Victorian flats. Be sure to look up over the existing modern storefronts to catch a glimpse of how the city looked in years past, as many of the buildings still have second-floor facades reflecting historic decorative styles.

Kilkenny holds a special place in the history of Anglo-Irish relations. The infamous 1366 Statutes of Kilkenny, intended to strengthen English authority in Ireland by keeping the heirs of the Anglo-Norman invaders from assimilating into the Irish way of life, was an attempt at apartheid. Intermarriage became a crime punishable by death and the native Irish were forced to live outside the town walls in shantytowns.

While studded with plenty of historic sights, Kilkenny also welcomes the traveler with traditional and "characterful" pubs.

By the early 17th century, Irish Catholics began to chafe under such repression; they tried to bring about reforms with the Confederation of Kilkenny, which governed Ireland from 1642 to 1648, with Kilkenny as the capital. Pope Innocent X sent money and arms. Cromwell responded in 1650 by overrunning the town and sacking the cathedral, which he then used as a stable for his horses. This marked the end of Kilkenny's "Golden Age"; however, the succeeding centuries were not uneventful. In 1798 the city was placed under martial law due to a revolt by the United Irishmen; in 1904 King Edward VII paid a visit; and in 1923, at the height of Ireland's civil war, forces opposed to a government peace deal with the British briefly occupied Kilkenny Castle.

TOP ATTRACTIONS

★ **Black Abbey.** With a stained-glass, carved-stone interior that seems right out of the musical *Camelot*, the 13th-century Black Abbey is one of the most evocative and beautiful Irish medieval structures. Note the famous 1340 five-gabled Rosary Window, an entire wall agleam with ruby and sapphire glass, depicting the life of Christ. Home to a Dominican order of monks since 1225, the abbey was restored as a church by the order, whose black capes gave the abbey its name. Interestingly, it's also one of the few medieval churches still owned by the Roman Catholic Church, as most of the oldest churches in Ireland were built by the Normans and reverted to the Church of Ireland (Anglican) when the English turned to Protestantism. Nearby is the Black Freren Gate (14th century), the last remaining gateway to the medieval city of yore. ⊠ *South of St. Canice's Cathedral, Kilkenny City, Co. Kilkenny* ☎ *056/772–1279* 🖅 *Free* 🕙 *Daily 9–1 and 2–6.*

Kilkenny City

Kyteler's Inn. The oldest inn in town, Kyteler's is notorious as the place where Dame Alice Le Kyteler, a member of a wealthy banking family and an alleged witch and "brothel keeper," was accused in 1324 of poisoning her four husbands. So, at least, said the enemies of this apparently very merry widow. The restaurant retains its medieval aura, thanks to its 14th-century stonework and exposed beams down in the cellar, built up around Kieran's Well, which predates the house itself. Food and drink in this popular pub are as simple and plentiful as they would have been in Dame Alice's day—but minus her extra ingredients. ✉ *Kieran St., Kilkenny City, Co. Kilkenny* ☎ *056/772–1064* ⊕ *www. kytelersinn.ie.*

Fodor'sChoice **Kilkenny Castle.** Built in 1172 and set amid 50 acres of rolling lawns
★ beside the River Nore, Ireland's most recognizable castle is a bewitching marriage of Gothic and Victorian styles conjuring images of knights and damsels, dukes and duchesses. For more than 500 years, beginning in 1391, Kilkenny Castle served as the seat of one of the more powerful clans in Irish history, the Butler family, members of which were later designated earls and dukes of Ormonde. Around 1820, William Robert, son of the first marquess of Ormonde, overhauled the castle to make it a wonderland in the Victorian Feudal Revival style. In 1859, John Pollen was called in to redo the 150-foot-long, aptly

named Long Gallery–a refined, airy hall with dazzling green walls hung with a vast collection of family portraits and frayed tapestries, and a marvelously decorated ceiling, replete with oak beams carved with Celtic lacework and brilliantly painted animal heads. The main staircase was also redone in the mid-1800s to become a showpiece of Ruskinian Gothic. The castle's Butler Gallery, formerly the servants quarters, houses a superb collection of Irish modern art, including examples by Nathaniel Hone, Jack B. Yeats, Sir John Lavery, Louis Le Brocquy, and James Turrell. Be sure to stroll the grounds, and the Celtic-cross-shaped rose garden, after a spot of tea in the old Victorian kitchen. ⊠ *The Parade, Kilkenny City, Co. Kilkenny* ☎ *056/772–1450* ⊕ *www.kilkennycastle.ie* ⊠ *Castle tour €6, grounds and Butler Gallery free* ⊙ *Apr., May, and Sept., daily 9:30–5:30; June–Aug., daily 9:30–5:30; Oct.–Feb., daily 9:30–4:30, Mar., daily 9:30–5.*

★ **St. Canice's Cathedral.** In spite of Cromwell's defacements this is still one of the finest cathedrals in Ireland and the country's second-largest medieval church, after St. Patrick's Cathedral in Dublin. Behind the massive walls of this 13th-century structure (restored in 1866) is an exuberant Gothic interior, given a somber grandeur by the extensive use of a locally quarried black marble. Many of the memorials and tombstone effigies represent distinguished descendants of the Normans, some depicted in full suits of armor. Look for a female effigy in the south aisle wearing the old Irish, or Kinsale, cloak; a 12th-century black-marble font at the southwest end of the nave; and St. Ciaran's Chair in the north transept, also made of black marble, with 13th-century sculptures on the arms. In recent years, St. Canice's has achieved notoriety as the resting place of President Obama's great-great-great uncle, the Bishop of Ossory. The biggest attraction on the grounds is the 102-foot-high round tower, which was built in 847 by King O'Carroll of Ossory; if you have the energy, climb the tower's 167 steps for the tremendous 360-degree view from the top, as well as for the thrill of mounting 102 steps on makeshift wooden stairs. Next door is St. Canice's Library, containing some 3,000 16th- and 17th-century volumes. ⊠ *Dean St., Kilkenny City, Co. Kilkenny* ☎ *056/776–4971* ⊕ *www. stcanicescathedral.com* ⊠ *Cathedral €4, tower €3, both €6* ⊙ *Cathedral June–Aug., Mon.–Sat. 9–6, Sun. 2–6; Apr., May, and Sept., Mon.–Sat. 10–1 and 2–5, Sun. 2–5; Oct.–Mar., Mon.–Sat. 10–1 and 2–4, Sun. 2–4. Tower access depends on weather.*

WORTH NOTING

Rothe House. There's a feeling of time travel as you step off the busy main street and into one of the finest examples in Ireland of a Tudor-era merchant's house. Built by John Rothe between 1594 and 1610, this medieval complex with stone-wall courtyards (one of which houses a medieval well) is owned by the Kilkenny Archaeological Society and houses a collection of Bronze Age artifacts, ogham stones (carved with early Celtic symbols and messages), and period costumes. The reconstructed Burgage Garden recreates, down to the plant types themselves, a typical 17th-century Irish merchant's garden. There's also a genealogical research facility that can help you trace your ancestry. ⊠ *Parliament St., Kilkenny City, Co. Kilkenny* ☎ *056/772–2893* ⊕ *www.rothehouse.*

com 🖃 *€5, garden only €2* ☉ *Apr.–Oct., Mon.–Sat. 10:30–5, Sun. 3–5; Nov.–Mar., Mon.–Sat. 10:30–4:30.*

Tholsel. With its distinctive clock tower and grand entrance portico, this limestone-marble building on Parliament Street stands on the site of the execution of poor Petronilla, the "witch" burned at the stake in the 14th century in lieu of her mistress, Dame Alice Le Kyteler. Built in 1761, burned down in 1985, and then completely rebuilt, Tholsel now houses the city's municipal archives. Adjacent to the Tholsel is **Alice's Castle,** a town jail rather grandly fitted out in 18th-century architectural ornamentation.

Tourist Information Office (*TIO*). Housed in the Shee Alms House, off the east side of High Street, this building was erected in 1582 by Sir Richard Shee as a hospital for the poor and functioned as such until 1895. 🖃 *Rose Inn St., Kilkenny City, Co. Kilkenny* 🕾 *056/775–1500* ⊕ *www.discoverireland.ie/Places-To-Go/Kilkenny* ☉ *Apr.–Oct., Mon.–Sat. 9–6; Nov.–Mar., Mon.–Sat. 9:15–5.*

WHERE TO EAT

$$ × **Café Sol.** There's always a lively buzz about this small eatery, with its
MODERN IRISH tropics-tinted decor and chirpy staff. Chef Liam O'Hanlon gives European flair to the best of local produce, famous Kilkenny beef, and fish bought daily off the quays at Dunmore East. The emphasis is on contemporary Irish cuisine with a Mediterranean twist. The panfried hake with wilted spinach, crab, potato boxty, and saffron and vanilla velouté is one of the more delicious offerings. During the day, light meals and sandwiches are on offer; at night, dining is more formal. $ *Average main: €19* 🖃 *William St., Kilkenny City, Co. Kilkenny* 🕾 *056/776–4987* ⊕ *www.restaurantskilkenny.com.*

$ × **Langton's.** When it comes to restaurants and pubs, this is Kilkenny
IRISH Central. A landmark since the 1940s, Langton's is a labyrinth of inter-
Fodor's Choice connected bars and eateries. Most of the seating areas, all with open
★ fires, have different personalities—from the leather-upholstered gentlemen's club in the Horseshoe Bar to an attempt at art deco in the spacious dining room. Up front is one of Ireland's most famous "eating pubs," often crammed with punters to the rafters of its low ceiling. For more tranquil environs, head out back, where you can chow down in a neo-Gothic garden framed by a stretch of the old city walls. The main restaurant offers well-prepared traditional dishes, including (of course) Irish stew and a mean seafood chowder. They also have 30 art deco–style hotel rooms upstairs. $ *Average main: €15* 🖃 *69 John St., Kilkenny City, Co. Kilkenny* 🕾 *056/776–5133* ⊕ *www.langtons.ie.*

Extending 150 feet, Kilkenny Castle's Long Gallery is lined with family portraits and has a hammer-beam ceiling supported on carved stone corbels with gilded animal and bird heads on the cross beams.

$$ **✕ Ristorante Rinuccini.** A warm glow emanates from this excellent Italian
ITALIAN restaurant as you descend the steps into its dining room in the basement of a Georgian town house. Owner-chef Antonio Cavaliere is intensely involved in preparing such luscious pasta dishes as *rigatoni all' arrabbiata* (tubes of homemade egg pasta in a fresh tomato sauce with chili and garlic). Other specialties, such as rack of Irish lamb slow cooked with herbs and red wine, go particularly well with Antonio's garlic roasted potatoes—highly recommended as a side dish. A splendid all-Italian wine list complements the menu, and there's a host of delicious homemade desserts. This is one of the best Italian options in town. The restaurant accommodates overnight guests in the town house above. ⑤ *Average main: €23* ⊠ *1 The Parade, across from Kilkenny Castle, Kilkenny City, Co. Kilkenny* ☎ *056/776–1575* ⊕ *www.rinuccini.com* ⚫ *Reservations essential.*

WHERE TO STAY

For expanded hotel reviews, visit Fodors.com.

$$ **⌂ Butler House.** Who needs Kilkenny Castle when you can stay at the
HOTEL Dowager Duchess of Ormonde's 18th-century former town house, a charming piece of Georgian grandeur with an ivy-covered three-bay facade and an elegant walled garden (with a private entrance to Kilkenny Castle and courtyard). **Pros:** live in a castle for a few days; serene walled garden; breakfast in the old stables of Kilkenny Castle. **Cons:** books up quickly; no restaurant or bar; some rooms a lot smaller than others. **TripAdvisor:** "charming," "superlative hospitality," "grand accommodation." ⑤ *Rooms from: €140* ⊠ *16 Patrick St.,*

Kilkenny City, Co. Kilkenny ☎*056/776–5707* ⊕ *www.butler.ie* ↪*12 rooms, 1 suite* |◯| *Breakfast.*

$ ⊞ **Zuni Townhouse and Restaurant.** This popular, family-owned, city-
HOTEL center hotel boasts the chichi gloss of a big-city boutique lodging but without the icy-cool reception you get in some fashionable joints. **Pros:** right in the heart of the city; family-owned and -run; only 13 rooms. **Cons:** books up quickly; business clientele can stifle atmosphere; can get noisy outside on weekends. **TripAdvisor:** "excellent service," "great food," "brilliant atmosphere." ⑤ *Rooms from: €120* ⊠ *26 Patricks St., Kilkenny City, Co. Kilkenny* ☎ *056/772–3999* ⊕ *www.zuni.ie* ↪*13 rooms* |◯| *Breakfast.*

NIGHTLIFE AND THE ARTS

John Cleere's. If you're craving a pint, you have a choice of pubs along Parliament and High streets. John Cleere's is the best pub in town for a mix of live traditional music, poetry readings, and theatrical plays. ⊠ *22 Parliament St., Kilkenny City, Co. Kilkenny* ☎ *056/776–2573.*

Kilkenny Arts Festival. Every August, Kilkenny becomes the focus for Ire-land's culture vultures when the Kilkenny Arts Festival takes over the city for about two weeks. The emphasis in the past was on classical music, but the program has grown increasingly populist. Street theater, elaborate parades, and even a rock concert (staged in the aptly named Woodstock Desmesne) have lent the festival a more contemporary air. There's much speculation that Kilkenny's festivities might soon eclipse Ireland's premier arts festival in Galway. ☎ *056/776–3663* ⊕ *www.kilkennyarts.ie.*

Pumphouse. Offering a calendar of traditional music sessions during the week, the Pumphouse also offers live rock and pop on weekends. ⊠ *26–28 Parliament St., Kilkenny City, Co. Kilkenny* ☎ *056/776–3924* ⊕ *pumphousekilkenny.ie.*

Fodor'sChoice **Tynan's Bridge House.** Set on one of Kilkenny's famous "slips," Tynan's
★ Bridge House was first used as an exercise run for dray horses. Inside, you can guess that the pub is more than 200 years old from all the gas lamps, silver tankards, and historic teapots on display. Behind the horseshoe-shaped bar, you'll find antiquities from its days as a grocery and pharmacy, but it's best known these days for its Guinness and good conversation. ⊠ *2 Horseleap Slip, Kilkenny City, Co. Kilkenny* ☎ *056/772–1291.*

Widow McGraths. A good spot for live music, the Widow McGraths is famous for celebrating an American July 4th with a barbecue in its beer garden. ⊠ *29 Parliament St., Kilkenny City, Co. Kilkenny* ☎ *056/775–2520.*

Watergate Theatre. Hosting opera, plays, concerts, and comedy on its schedule, the Watergate hosts affordable local, national, and inter-national productions. ⊠ *Parliament St., Kilkenny City, Co. Kilkenny* ☎ *056/776–1674* ⊕ *www.watergatetheatre.com.*

SPORTS AND THE OUTDOORS

HURLING

Kilkenny GAA Grounds. The 1366 Statutes of Kilkenny expressly forbade the ancient Irish game of hurling. No matter: today, Kilkenny is considered one of the great hurling counties. Like its neighbor and archenemy, Wexford, Kilkenny has a long history of success in hurling, and as the annual All-Ireland Hurling Championships draws to its final stages during June and July, interest in the county's team runs to a fever pitch. Catch the home team at matches held at Kilkenny GAA Grounds. ⊠ *Nowlan Park, Kilkenny City, Co. Kilkenny* ☎ *056/776–5122* ⊕ *www. kilkennygaa.ie.*

SHOPPING

Kilkenny is a byword for attractive, original crafts that combine traditional arts with modern design elements.

Jerpoint Glass Studio. You can see glass being blown at this noted family-run studio, where the glass is heavy, modern, uncut, and hand finished using traditional tools and methods. The studio's factory shop is a good place to pick up a bargain. ⊠ *16 km (10 miles) south of Kilkenny in the valley of the River Nore, Stoneyford, Co. Kilkenny* ☎ *056/772–4350* ⊕ *www.jerpointglass.com.*

Kilkenny Design Centre. The town's leading outlet, and one of Ireland's favorite sources for Irish handcrafts, the Kilkenny Design Centre, in the old stable yard opposite the castle, sells ceramics, jewelry, sweaters, and handwoven textiles. They also have a restaurant specializing in hearty Irish fare. ⊠ *Kilkenny Castle, Kilkenny City, Co. Kilkenny* ☎ *056/772–2118* ⊕ *www.kilkennydesign.com.*

Murphy Jewellers. This county favorite specializes in heraldic jewelry. ⊠ *85 High St., Kilkenny City, Co. Kilkenny* ☎ *056/772–1127* ⊕ *www. murphyjewellers.com.*

Fodor's Choice ★ **Nicholas Mosse Pottery.** One of the best-known names in Irish ceramics, Mosse first set up his potter's wheel in an old flour mill in this quiet village (16 km [10 miles] south of Kilkenny) in 1975. Since then, the business has boomed and the rustic floral-pattern pottery created here is instantly recognizable for its "spongeware" designs. A visit here allows you to see the pottery being made, and the adjoining factory shop often has good bargains. ⊠ *Bennettsbridge, Co. Kilkenny* ☎ *056/772–7505* ⊕ *www.nicholasmosse.com.*

Rudolf Heltzel - Gold and Silversmith. Known for its striking, modern designs, Rudolf Heltzel mostly showcases gold and silver jewelry. ⊠ *10 Patrick St., Kilkenny City, Co. Kilkenny* ☎ *056/772–1497* ⊕ *www. heltzel.ie.*

Sweater Shop. You'll find a great selection of Irish knitwear and accessories for men, women, and children at this popular shop. ⊠ *81 High St., Kilkenny City, Co. Kilkenny* ☎ *056/776–3405* ⊕ *www.sweatershop.ie.*

Kilkenny Hurling: A Fast and Furious Sport

Get chatting with the locals in almost any pub across the Southeast, mention the sport of hurling, and an enthusiastic and often passionate conversation is bound to ensue. The region is the heartland of this ancient sport, whose followers have an almost religious obsession with the game.

Hurling is a kind of aerial field hockey with players wielding curved sticks. Its history comes from Ireland's Celtic ancestors, but it bears about the same relation to field hockey as ice hockey does to roller-skating. It's no accident that prowess on the hurling field is regarded as a supreme qualification for election to public office. A man who succeeds at hurling is eminently capable of dealing with anything that fate and the spite of other politicians can throw at him. Hurling is also an extremely skillful sport. A player must have excellent hand-eye coordination combined with an ability to run at high speeds while balancing a small golf-ball-size ball on his *camán* (hurling stick). Fans will proudly tell you it's also the world's fastest team sport.

Ireland's other chief sporting pastimes, including soccer and hurling's cousin, Gaelic football, take a backseat in this part of the country. Stars like Kilkenny's Henry Shefflin, rather than professional soccer players, are sporting icons for local kids. Counties Tipperary, Wexford, and Waterford are among the top teams in the region, but Kilkenny (nicknamed "The Cats") is currently the undisputed top team in the country. It has won eight of the last twelve All-Ireland Hurling Championships and is considered one of the best teams in history.

There's an intense rivalry between the counties, especially between old foes Tipperary and Kilkenny. When it gets down to club level, passions run even higher. Almost every parish in the region has a hurling club, and a quick inquiry with locals will usually be enough to find out when the next game is on. Even for the uninitiated, hurling is a great spectator sport. Sporty types wishing to give it a go, be warned; it's fast, furious, and entails more than a hint of danger, as players flail the air to capture the bullet-fast *sliotar* (hurling ball).

SOUTHEAST INLANDS

North of Kilkenny City is a region notably rich in historical sights. Travel through the farmlands of the Barrow Valley to the small county seat of Carlow Town, with scenic detours to Leighlinbridge's picturesque castle and Old Leighlin's time-stained cathedral.

LEIGHLINBRIDGE

14 km (9 miles) northeast of Kilkenny City.

★ **GETTING HERE AND AROUND**

From Kilkenny take the N77 to the N10 to the M9; exit at junction 7, then take the second exit onto the N9, and exit onto the R448 to Leighlinbridge. The trip takes about half an hour. Bus Éireann runs a regular service to the town from Dublin and Kilkenny. There is no train service.

EXPLORING

Black Castle. Poetically mirrored in the waters of the River Barrow, and framed by the bulk of a grandly medieval bridge, Black Castle was built in 1181 and has seen countless battles and sieges as one of the earliest Norman fortresses in Ireland. Its hulking, 400-year-old main tower still stands, and while it is not accessible it all but dares you to set up your easel and canvas on the adjoining ageless towpath. The bridge's five stone arches have spanned the river since 1320, making it one of the oldest functioning bridges in Europe and a magnificent repoussoir for the castle. ⊠ *Leighlinbridge, Co. Carlow.*

WHERE TO STAY

For expanded hotel reviews, visit Fodors.com.

$ 🖼 **Lord Bagenal Hotel.** Old and new, character and luxury, blend spec-
HOTEL tacularly at this noted hotel comprising a famous 19th-century pub surrounded by structures that mainly date to the early 1800s, as well as a modern wing constructed in the last decade, all set on the banks of the River Barrow. **Pros:** winning mix of ancient and modern, charming walled garden. **Cons:** uncommunicative staff. **TripAdvisor:** "a haven for relaxation," "great staff," "fantastic and stunning." ⑤ *Rooms from: €99* ⊠ *Main St., Leighlinbridge, Co. Carlow* ☎ *059/977–4000* ⊕ *www.lordbagenal.com* ↴ *39 rooms.*

OLD LEIGHLIN

5¾ km (3 miles) west of Leighlinbridge.

GETTING HERE AND AROUND

From Kilkenny take the N77 to the first exit onto the N78 to Old Leighlin. The trip takes about half an hour. There is no direct bus or train service, but the bus goes to nearby Leighlinbridge. There is parking around the town.

EXPLORING

St. Laserian's Cathedral. Home to one of Ireland's undiscovered gems of late-medieval architecture, the tiny village of Old Leighlin first found fame as the site of a monastery, founded in the 7th century by St. Laserian, that once accommodated 1,500 monks. The old monastery was rebuilt in the 12th century as St. Laserian's Cathedral. Sitting among green fields, with a castellated tower and Irish-Gothic windows, it evokes a stirring sense of Wordsworthian forlornness. Enlarged in the 16th century, its interior is noted for its 11th-century font, a 200-year-old grand wind organ, and a fine wood vaulted ceiling. Guided tours are available. General admission is free but a donation of €1 is suggested. ⊠ *Old Leighlin, Co. Carlow* ☎ *059/972–1570* ⊕ *cashel.anglican.org/information/diocese/cathedrals/leighlin.html* ☜ *Free* ☉ *Mid-June–Aug., weekdays 10–4.*

NIGHTLIFE

Carey's Pub. Carey's, which for centuries has served up glasses of ale to Old Leighlin residents, has been in the same family since 1542. A pub that survives this long deserves your patronage. ⊠ *Main St., Old Leighlin, Co. Carlow* ☎ *059/972–1214.*

THOMASTOWN

14½ km (9 miles) south of Kilkenny.

Thomastown, originally the seat of the kings of Ossory (an ancient Irish kingdom), is a pretty, stone-built village on the River Nore. It takes its name from Thomas FitzAnthony of Leinster, who encircled the town with a wall in the 13th century. Fragments of this medieval wall remain, as do the partly ruined 13th-century church of St. Mary, and Mullins Castle, adjacent to the town bridge.

GETTING HERE AND AROUND

From Kilkenny take the N77 to Thomastown exit. The 10-mile trip should take 20 minutes. Bus Éireann runs regular services from Dublin and Kilkenny. There is also regular train service from Dublin, Kilkenny, and Waterford.

EXPLORING

Fodor'sChoice ★ **Jerpoint Abbey.** Landmarked by its rearing and massive 15th-century tower, Jerpoint Abbey, near Thomastown, is one of the most notable Cistercian ruins in Ireland, dating from about 1160. The church, tombs, and the restored cloisters are must-sees for lovers of the Irish Romanesque. The vast cloister is decorated with affecting carvings of human figures and fantastical mythical creatures, including knights and knaves (one with a stomachache) and the assorted dragon or two. Dissolved in 1540, Jerpoint was taken over, as was so much around these parts, by the earls of Ormonde. The one part of the abbey that remains alive, so to speak, is its hallowed cemetery—the natives are still buried here. Guided tours of the impressive complex are available from mid-June to mid-September (last admission is 45 minutes before closing). ⊠ *2 km (1 mile) south of Thomastown on N9, Thomastown, Co. Kilkenny* ☎ *056/772–4623* ⊕ *www.heritageireland.ie/en/South-East/JerpointAbbey* ☜ *€3* ☉ *Mar.–Sept., daily 10–5:30; Oct., daily 9–5; Nov, daily 9:30–4.*

WHERE TO STAY

For expanded hotel reviews, visit Fodors.com.

$ | B&B/INN | ★   ▦ **Ballyduff House.** As the clematis-clad mansion comes into view at the top of a gently curving driveway you can understand why this

Southeast Inlands

wonderfully picturesque house was used as a location in the '90s movie adaptation of Maeve Binchy's *Circle of Friends*. **Pros:** family-owned and -run; stunningly authentic mansion; guests can use kitchen to prepare a picnic. **Cons:** only four rooms, so often full; few modern facilities. **TripAdvisor:** "a can't miss destination," "consummate host in a wonderful setting," "wonderful grand Irish country home." ⑤ *Rooms from: €100* ✉ *Thomastown, Co. Kilkenny* ☎ *056/775–8488* ⊕ *www. ballyduffhouse.com* ⟿ *4 rooms* ▬ *No credit cards* ⊘ *Closed Dec.–Feb.* ⎮⊙⎮ *Breakfast.*

$$ ▦ **Mount Juliet.** For many, the Jack Nicklaus–designed golf course—
HOTEL   which has hosted the Irish Open on three occasions—is the reason
★   to head here, but with luxurious accommodations, a lush 1,500-acre estate, a spa, equestrian center, salmon and trout fishing, and excellent dining options, there is *so* much more to this elegant three-story Georgian mansion than golf. **Pros:** great golf on your doorstep; pampering spa; period elegance with modern amenities; aside beautiful River Nore; relatively gentle room rates for such luxury. **Cons:** rooms outside main house a little inferior; some authentic charm sacrificed for modern comfort. **TripAdvisor:** "wonderful staff," "beautiful golf resort," "the Irish at their very best." ⑤ *Rooms from: €159* ✉ *Thomastown, Co. Kilkenny* ☎ *056/777–3000* ⊕ *www.mountjuliet.ie* ⟿ *29 rooms, 2 suites, 11 lodges.*

SPORTS AND THE OUTDOORS
GOLF

Fodor's Choice ★ **Mount Juliet Golf Course.** Attached to a magisterial country-house hotel, this Jack Nicklaus–designed championship parkland course, 19 km (11 miles) from Kilkenny Town, includes practice greens, a driving range, and, for those who feel a little rusty, a David Leadbetter golf academy. The heavily forested course has eight holes that play over water, including the wonderful 3rd hole—a par-3 over a stream from an elevated tee. The back 9 presents a series of difficult bunker shots. A sporting day out comes to a welcome end in the Hunter's Yard or Rose Garden lodge, which cater to both the thirsty and the hungry. Greens fees are above average, and although visitors are always welcome, a weekday round is best, since it's often crowded with members on weekends. ⊠ *Mount Juliet Estate, Thomastown, Co. Kilkenny* ☎ *056/777–3010* ⊕ *www. mountjuliet.ie* ✉ *Greens fees: May.–Sept., weekdays €75–€80, weekends €90; Nov.–Mar., weekdays €65, weekends €75; Apr. and Oct, weekdays €70–€75, weekends €85* ⅃ *18 holes. Yardage: 7,264. Par 72. Practice area, driving range, caddy carts, club rental, catering* ⊙ *Visitors: daily.*

ENNISCORTHY

32 km (20 miles) east of Graiguenamanagh.

Enniscorthy, on the sloping banks of the River Slaney and on the main road between Dublin and Wexford to the south of the popular resort of Gorey, is a thriving market town that is rich in history.

GETTING HERE AND AROUND

From Wexford town take the N1 to the N30 and enter Enniscorthy; the 20-mile trip takes about half an hour. From Dublin take the N11/M11 all the way to Enniscorthy; the trip takes about one hour and thirty minutes. There are regular bus and train services from Wexford and Dublin.

EXPLORING

★ **Enniscorthy Castle.** The town is dominated by Enniscorthy Castle, built in the first quarter of the 13th century by the Prendergast family. The imposing Norman castle was the site of fierce battles against Oliver Cromwell in the 17th century and during the Uprising of 1798. The castle has recently reopened after renovation, with an exhibition exploring the development of the building and the town. Exhibits also explore the 1916 Rising in Enniscorthy and the work of furniture designer and architect Eileen Gray, who was born in 1878 just outside town. Gray went on to become one of the founding designers of the modernist movement in the 1920s and now enjoys worldwide fame and staggering prices (one chair she designed brought $22 million at auction). The guided tour is a real treat, with a trip to the dungeon followed by a walk on the roof with impressive views out over the town and beyond. ☎ *053/923–4699* ⊕ *www.enniscorthycastle.ie* ✉ *€4* ⊙ *Weekdays 9:30– 4:30; weekends 12–4:30.*

National 1798 Centre. This small museum tells the tale of the United Irishmen and the ill-fated 1798 rebellion. ⊠ *Arnold's Cross, Enniscorthy, Co. Wexford* ☎ *053/923–7596* ⊕ *www.1798centre.ie* ✉ *€6* ⊙ *June–Aug., weekdays 9:30–4, weekends 12–4:30; Sept.–May, weekdays 9:30–4.*

★ **St. Aidan's Cathedral.** Standing on a commanding site overlooking the Slaney, the Gothic Revival structure of St. Aidan's was built in the mid-19th century under the direction of Augustus Welby Pugin, famed architect of the Houses of Parliament in London. ⊠ *Cathedral St., Enniscorthy, Co. Wexford* ☎ *053/923–5777* ⊕ *www.staidanscathedral. ie* ⊠ *Free* ☾ *Daily 10–6.*

WHERE TO STAY

For expanded hotel reviews, visit Fodors.com.

$$$

B&B/INN

Fodor's Choice

★

⊡ **Kilmokea Country Manor and Gardens.** A former Georgian rectory dating to 1794, Kilmokea presides over 7 acres of formal walled gardens blooming by the River Barrow and recently earned an Irish Heritage Garden certificate—a justifiable reward for owners Mark and Emma Hewlett, who have also managed to gild this lily with all manner of hostelry delights. **Pros:** family-owned and -run; incredible gardens; four-poster beds. **Cons:** no Internet in rooms; some rooms are expensive for this region; books up quickly. **TripAdvisor:** "lovely country house in tranquil setting," "great facilities," "peaceful and relaxing with warm welcome." ⑤ *Rooms from: €200* ⊠ *Great Island, Campile, Co. Wexford* ☎ *051/388–109* ⊕ *www.kilmokea.com* ⤴ *6 rooms* ⦿| *Breakfast.*

$

B&B/INN

⊡ **Salville House.** Gordon and Jane Parker have created a hilltop haven where food and relaxation are the order of the day, thanks to Gordon's way with inspired contemporary cuisine, the spacious guest rooms, with plenty of books on the shelves, and the great view of the River Slaney out the windows of this Victorian house. **Pros:** family-owned and -run; wonderful home-style food; great views. **Cons:** only five rooms; no air-conditioning; can be a little tricky to find. ⑤ *Rooms from: €100* ⊠ *Wexford Rd., Enniscorthy, Co. Wexford* ☎ *053/923–5252* ⊕ *www. salvillehouse.com* ⤴ *5 rooms* ⊟ *No credit cards* ⦿| *Breakfast.*

SHOPPING

Kiltrea Bridge Pottery. Garden pots, plant pots, and country kitchen crocks are just a few of the goodies stocked at this pottery studio and shop. ⊠ *Kiltrea, Caime, Co. Wexford* ☎ *053/923–5107* ⊕ *www. kiltreapottery.com.*

WEXFORD TOWN

19 km (12 miles) south of Enniscorthy, 62 km (39 miles) northeast of Waterford City, 115 km (72 miles) southwest of Dublin.

Wexford's history goes back to prehistoric times, though you'll find scant traces of them now. Much more obvious are the Viking and Norman associations, evident in alleys as well as in the town walls, some of which are still standing. Today, this coastal town is most famed for the Wexford Opera Festival, usually held in October, which has been seducing the world with wonderful productions of rare opera for more than 50 years. The warm and vivacious welcome, the narrow and ancient Viking streets, and the tiny, atmospheric Theatre Royal add to the pleasure of this event and of any visit to Wexford Town. Wexford is reached by car using the N11/M11 and the N25. The drive to Dublin on improved roads takes about two hours.

Wexford Town

GETTING HERE AND AROUND

From Dublin take the N11/M11 all the way to Wexford town; the trip takes about two hours and 10 minutes.

Intercity buses leave from O'Hanrahan train station on Redmond Place. Bus Éireann has nine buses a day going to Dublin (3 hours; €14.85 one-way, €17.55 round-trip), nine a day going to Rosslare (30 minutes; €4.50 one-way, €7.50 round-trip), and six a day Monday–Saturday, three on Sunday, going to Waterford City (3 hours; €7.50 one-way, €17.60 round-trip).

O'Hanrahan Station serves Irish Rail trains at the northern end of town on Redmond Place. Wexford is on the Dublin–Roslare line and three trains a day go to and from Dublin; the 2½-hour trip costs €22.50 one-way or same-day return and €28.50 open return. The short hop to Rosslare costs €4 and takes 25 minutes. There are no direct trains to Cork or Waterford.

ESSENTIALS

Visitor Information Wexford Tourist Office ⊠ *Crescent Quay, Wexford Town, Co. Wexford* ☎ *053/912–3111* ⊕ *www.discoverireland.ie.*

EXPLORING

From its appearance today, you would barely realize that Wexford is an ancient place, but in fact it was defined on maps by the Greek cartographer Ptolemy as long ago as the 2nd century AD. Its Irish name is Loch Garman, but the Vikings called it Waesfjord—the harbor of the mudflats—which became Wexford in English. Wexford became an English garrison town after it was taken by Oliver Cromwell in 1649.

The River Slaney empties into the sea at Wexford Town. The harbor has silted up since the days when Viking longboats docked here; nowadays only a few small trawlers fish from here. Wexford Town's compact center is on the south bank of the Slaney. Running parallel to the quays on the riverfront is the main street (the name changes several times), the major shopping street of the town, with a pleasant mix of old-fashioned bakeries, butcher shops, stylish boutiques, and a share of Wexford's many pubs. It can be explored on foot in an hour or two. Allow at least half a day in the area if you also intend to visit the Heritage Park at nearby Ferrycarrig, and a full day if you want to take in Johnstown Castle Gardens and its agricultural museum, or walk in the nature reserve at nearby Curracloe Beach. The town is at its best in late October and early November, when the presence of the Wexford Opera Festival and the Wexford Fringe creates a carnival atmosphere.

Rising above the town's rooftops are the graceful spires of two elegant examples of 19th-century Gothic architecture. These twin churches have identical exteriors, their foundation stones were laid on the same day, and their spires each reach a height of 230 feet. The **Church of the Assumption** is on Bride Street. The **Church of the Immaculate Conception** is on Rowe Street.

TOP ATTRACTIONS

★ ☾ **Irish National Heritage Park.** A 35-acre, open-air living-history museum beside the River Slaney, this is one of Ireland's most successful and enjoyable family attractions. In about 1½ hours, a guide takes you through 9,000 years of Irish history—from the first evidence of humans on this island, at around 7000 BC, to the Norman settlements of the mid-12th century. Full-scale replicas of typical dwelling places illustrate the changes in beliefs and lifestyles. Highlights of the tour include a prehistoric homestead, a *crannóg* (lake dwelling), an early Christian *rath* (fortified farmstead), a Christian monastery, a horizontal water mill, a Viking longhouse, and a Norman castle. There are also examples of pre-Christian burial sites and a stone circle. Most of the exhibits are "inhabited" by students in appropriate historic dress who will answer questions. The riverside site includes several nature trails. ⊠ *5 km (3 miles) north of Wexford Town on N11, Ferrycarrig, Co. Wexford* ☎ *053/912–0733* ⊕ *www.inhp.com* ⊠ *€8* ☾ *May–Aug., daily 9:30–5; Sept.–Apr., daily 9:30–4.*

Fodor'sChoice ★ **Johnstown Castle Gardens.** This massive, Victorian Gothic, gray-stone castle, set in a beautiful garden estate, looks like it was designed for a Disney fairy-tale set but it was in fact built for the Grogan-Morgan family between 1810 and 1855. Located 5 km (3 miles) southwest of Wexford following the N25 (direction Rosslare), the magnificent parklands—with splendid towering trees, lakes, and ornamental gardens—offer a grand frame to the castle. Unfortunately, you can't tour the building (it houses a national agricultural college) other than its entrance hall, but the well-maintained grounds are open to the public. The centerpiece is the 5-acre lake, one side of which has a terrace, lined with statues, from which to take in the panorama of the mirrored castle. Because there's such a variety of trees framing the view—Japanese cedars, Atlantic blue cedars, golden Lawson cypresses—there's color through much of the calendar. Nearby are the Devil's Gate walled garden—a woodland garden set around the ruins of the medieval castle of Rathlannon—and the **Irish Agricultural Museum.** The latter, housed in the quadrangular stable yards, shows what life was once like in rural Ireland. It also contains a 5,000-square-foot exhibition on the potato and the Great Famine (1845–49). ⊠ *Signposted just off N25, 6 km (4 miles) southwest of Wexford Town, Wexford Town, Co. Wexford* ☎ *053/914–2888* ⊕ *www.irishagrimuseum.ie* ⊠ *Gardens and Museum €8, Museum €6. Gardens are free Oct.–Mar.* ☾ *Gardens: daily 9–5:30. Museum: Apr.–Oct., weekdays 9–5, weekends 11–4:30; Nov.–Mar., weekdays 9–12:30 and 1:30–5.*

Westgate Tower. The largest of five fortified gateways in the Norman and Viking town walls, Westgate is the only one remaining. The early-13th-century tower has been sensitively restored. Keep an eye out as you wander this part of town for other preserved segments of the old town walls. ⊠ *Westgate., Wexford Town, Co. Wexford.*

Wexford Bull Ring. Once the scene of bull baiting, a cruel medieval sport that was popular among the Norman nobility, this arena was sad witness to other bloody crimes. Notoriously, in 1649, Cromwell's soldiers massacred 300 panic-stricken townspeople who had gathered here to

Viking longboats once docked where fishing trawlers now berth in Wexford's busy harbor.

pray as the army stormed their town. The memory of this heartless leader has remained a dark folk legacy for centuries and is only now beginning to fade. ⊠ *Quay St., back toward quays, Wexford Town, Co. Wexford.*

Wexford Wildfowl Reserve. A nature lover's paradise, Wexford Wildlife Reserve is just a short walk across the bridge from the main part of town. Today, it shelters one-third of the world's Greenland white-fronted geese. As many as 10,000 of them spend their winters on the mudflats, known locally as slobs, which also draw ducks, swans, and other waterfowl. Observation hides are provided for bird-watchers, and an audiovisual show and exhibitions are available at the visitor center. Lectures on the teeming birdlife of the reserve can be arranged on request. ⊠ *North Slob, Wexford Harbor, Wexford Town, Co. Wexford* ☎ *053/912–3406* ⊕ *www.wexfordwildfowlreserve.ie* ⊠ *Free* ☉ *Daily 9–5.*

WORTH NOTING

Commodore John Barry Statue. Standing in the center of Crescent Quay, this large bronze statue commemorates the man who came to be known as the father of the American Navy. Born in 1745 in nearby Ballysampson, Barry (1745–1803) settled in Philadelphia at age 15, became a brilliant naval fighter during the War of Independence (thus avenging his Irish ancestors), and trained many young naval officers who went on to achieve fame. ⊠ *Cresent Quay.*

Franciscan Friary. While Cromwell made a bonfire of the original 13th-century friary, this rebuilt 19th-century town landmark has a ceiling worth noting for its fine, locally crafted stuccowork and a relic and wax effigy of St. Adjutor—a young martyr slain by his own father. ⊠ *School St., Wexford Town, Co. Wexford* ☎ *053/912–2758* ☞ *Free* ⊙ *Daily 8:30–6:30.*

Selskar Abbey. This 12th-century abbey witnessed the first treaty between the Irish and the Normans signed in 1169. Today only ruins remain. ⊠ *Selskar St., south of Westgate Tower, Wexford Town, Co. Wexford.*

Tourist Information Office. A good starting point for a walking tour of Wexford Town, this also is a font of local information and leads to tours organized by local historians. ⊠ *Crescent Quay, Wexford Town, Co. Wexford* ☎ *053/912–3111.*

OFF THE BEATEN PATH

Curracloe Beach. Steven Spielberg filmed the terrifyingly gory D-Day landing scenes from his blockbuster *Saving Private Ryan* along this beautiful, soft, white-sand strand. In real life it's a popular swimming place in summer and a quiet home to many migratory birds in winter. It's 9 km (5½ miles) long, with a 1-km (½-mile) nature trail in the seashore sand dunes. The water is clean and there are 500 parking spaces at the White Gap entrance. Amenities are minimal, with lifeguards on duty only in summer on one stretch of the beach. **Amenities:** lifeguards, parking, showers. **Best For:** solitude in winter, swimming, walking, windsurfing. ⊠ *11 km (7 miles) northeast of Wexford Town on R742, Wexford Town, Co. Wexford* ⊕ *www.wexford.ie/wex/Departments/ Environment/Beaches/CurracloeBeach.*

WHERE TO EAT AND STAY
For expanded hotel reviews, visit Fodors.com.

$
ITALIAN
✕ **La Dolce Vita.** You might have to queue behind a few locals to get seated in this little Italian deli-eatery in a surprisingly serene spot just off the busy shopping area. Hearty food, high standards, and people's prices make it the perfect place to break up a day's sightseeing. Try the salmon fishcake with a balsamic vinaigrette; you also can't go wrong with their salads or genuinely fresh pasta dishes. ⑤ *Average main: €11* ⊠ *6 Trimmers La., Wexford Town, Co. Wexford* ☎ *053/917–0806* ⊙ *Closed Sun. No dinner.*

$$
IRISH
✕ **Reed Restaurant.** Local seafood is the big draw at this independent restaurant located at the family-popular Ferrycarrig hotel. Fresh-off-the-boat fish from Kilmore Quay is a favorite, but the Killurin lamb is just as local and tasty while more exotic dishes like ostrich fillet are also on offer. Check out the wine menu, one of the better ones in the Southeast. While the tables are formally appointed with crisp white linen, the light-filled dining room has a friendly, relaxed vibe. Try to grab a table that allows you to enjoy the romantic and serene riverfront view. ⑤ *Average main: €19* ⊠ *Ferrycarrig Hotel, Ferrycarrig Bridge, Wexford Town, Co. Wexford* ☎ *053/912–0999* ⊕ *www.ferrycarrighotel.ie/ reeds-restaurant.htm.*

$$$
HOTEL
☺ **Ferrycarrig.** A favorite with families, this spot, 4 km (2½ miles) outside town, offers a daycare facility and swimming pool for kids, a peaceful and tranquil riverside location for parents, and a well-equipped health center for both. **Pros:** family-friendly; good restaurant; riverside location. **Cons:** can get a bit hectic in summer; a little overpriced; some rooms better than others. **TripAdvisor:** "an unexpected pleasure," "a complete relaxing break," "excellent service." ⑤ *Rooms from: €179 ⊠ Ferrycarrig Bridge (3 km [2 miles] from Wexford Town on the N11), Wexford Town, Co. Wexford ☎ 053/912–0999 ⊕ www.ferrycarrighotel.ie ↴ 98 rooms, 4 suites ⓄⅠ Breakfast.*

$
B&B/INN
Fodor'sChoice
★
McMenamin's Townhouse. From opera divas to Hollywood stars, they've all stayed at this cozy Victorian town house, and not just because of Kay and Seamus McMenamin's homemade whiskey marmalade: this is a lodging of choice for stars of Wexford's opera fest each autumn who love the spacious bedrooms, highly polished Victorian furniture, while travelers consider this a last stopover before the Rosslare ferry takes them to France. **Pros:** family-owned and -run; great breakfast; beautiful antique beds in rooms. **Cons:** only four rooms so it books up quickly; no Internet in rooms; no TVs in rooms. **TripAdvisor:** "cozy historic Irish town house," "great rooms," "authentic Irish experience." ⑤ *Rooms from: €90 ⊠ 6 Glena Terr., Spawell Rd., Wexford Town, Co. Wexford ☎☎ 053/914–6442 ⊕ www.wexford-bedandbreakfast.com ↴ 4 rooms ⊙ Closed last 2 wks of Dec. ⓄⅠ Breakfast.*

NIGHTLIFE AND THE ARTS

Centenary Stores. As the saying goes, if you can find a street without at least one bar on it, you've left Wexford. Centenary Stores is a Victorian-style pub with an adjoining nightclub that makes it a popular place for the young crowd. Lunch is Monday through Saturday, and there's traditional music every Sunday morning. ⊠ *Charlotte St., Wexford Town, Co. Wexford ☎ 053/912–4424 ⊕ www.thestores.ie.*

★ **The Sky & the Ground.** One of the best pubs in town, the Sky and the Ground is a mecca for Irish music sessions, which pack in the crowds from Monday through Thursday. ⊠ *112 S. Main St., Wexford Town, Co. Wexford ☎ 053/912–1273 ⊕ www.theskyandtheground.com.*

Fodor'sChoice
★
Thomas Moore Tavern. Dating to the 13th century, the Thomas Moore Tavern is Wexford's oldest pub, named after the renowned Irish poet whose parents lived here. The pub has its original medieval walls and fine old beams along the ceiling, and a spot by the roaring fire is the perfect place for a quiet drink. Light lunches and snacks are served on weekdays between noon and 3. ⊠ *Cornmarket, Wexford Town, Co. Wexford ☎ 053/917–4688 ⊕ www.thomasmooretavern.com.*

Wexford Opera Festival. Wexford's grand and hoary landmark, the Theatre Royal has been entirely rebuilt to serve as the Wexford Opera Theatre for the world-famous Wexford Opera Festival, held here during the last two weeks of October and the beginning of November. The town's leading cultural event, the festival has been going strong since 1951 and features seldom-performed operas sung by top talent from all over the world. The strikingly modern, Keith Williams–designed building is custom built for opera and offers fabulous views out over

Mount Lenister to the northwest and Tuskar Rock lighthouse to the southeast. The surprisingly large main auditorium seats 749 with a smaller second space for 172. Along with an ever-expanding offering of more populist fare performed in small venues and pubs, the festival supplies a feast of concerts and recitals that start at 11 am and continue until midnight. Year-round, touring companies and local productions are also seen at these venues. ⊠ *27 High St., Wexford Town, Co. Wexford* ☎ *053/912–2144 box office* ⊕ *wexfordopera.com.*

SHOPPING

Barker's. Waterford crystal, Belleek china, local pottery, linens, and crafts are found here in tempting array. ⊠ *36 S. Main St., Wexford Town, Co. Wexford* ☎ *053/912–3159.*

Martin's Jewellers. This popular shop specializes in bespoke Celtic jewelry. ⊠ *Lower Rowe St., Wexford Town, Co. Wexford* ☎ *053/912–2635* ⊕ *www.martinsjewellers.ie.*

Westgate Design. A good selection of quality Irish crafts, clothing, pottery, candles, and jewelry is found at Westgate Design, along with a restaurant and deli. ⊠ *22 N. Main St., Wexford Town, Co. Wexford* ☎ *053/912–3787* ⊕ *www.westgatedesign.ie.*

SPORTS

GAELIC FOOTBALL
Wexford Park GAA. Wexford is mostly a hurling county, but you can watch both Gaelic football and hurling at the Wexford Park GAA. Check the website for upcoming games. ⊠ *Clonard Rd., Wexford Town, Co. Wexford* ☎ *053/914–4808* ⊕ *www.wexford.gaa.ie.*

THE SOUTHEAST COAST

This journey takes you along mainly minor roads through the prettiest parts of the coast in counties Wexford and Waterford, pausing midway to explore Waterford City—home of the dazzling cut glass—on foot. Along the way expect to see long golden beaches, quaint fishing villages like Kilmore Quay and Ballyhack, some of the country's best nature reserves, and Tramore, Ireland's most unredeemable family waterside resort. If you're coming from the Continent or England, chances are you'll end up on a ferry bound for Rosslare Harbour, one of Ireland's busiest ferry ports.

ROSSLARE

16 km (10 miles) southeast of Wexford Town.

Sometimes called Ireland's sunniest spot, the village of Rosslare is a seaside getaway with an attractive beach. Many vacationers head here to hike, golf, sun, and swim. But the truth is that most visitors are only here to take the ferry from the Rosslare-Europort terminal, the only reason (some point out) you should find yourself in this otherwise dull little town. As Rosslare is so well connected to the ferry port, the roads to major cities to and from here are very good: N81, N11, and N25. The car trip from Dublin takes around 2 hours 12 minutes. Cork is 179 km

(111 miles) northwest or 2 hours 45 minutes away via the N25. Rosslare is only 16 km (9 miles) southeast of Wexford Town on the R470.

GETTING HERE AND AROUND

From Dublin take the N11/M11 to the N25 and on to Rosslare. The trip takes about two hours and twenty minutes.

Stena Line Express sails May to September between Rosslare Harbour and Fishguard in Wales (adult €28, car and driver €117–€222; 2 hours; 2 sailings per day). Stena Line also runs its (slower) Superferry (adult €28, car and driver €72–€182; 3½ hours; 2 sailings per day) year-round on the same route. Irish Ferries sails to Pembroke in Wales (3¾ hours, twice daily). Single fares start at €30 for a foot passenger, €69 for a car and driver. Between April and December there are ferries to Cherbourg, France (19½ hours, up to three a week). ■TIP➜ Ferries to and from Rosslare frequently sell out, particularly in summer and any time the Irish soccer team is playing in a major tournament abroad. To be sure of getting a ticket on the boat of your choice, try to reserve your space in advance through the ferry companies' Cork or Dublin offices.

Bus Éireann has services from Rosslare-Europort to many cities and towns in Ireland, including Dublin (€16.65 one-way, €22.95 round-trip; 3 hours; 13 daily Monday–Saturday, 11 on Sunday) and Cork (€21.20 one-way, €30.20 round-trip; 4 hours; five daily Monday–Saturday, three on Sunday) that goes via Waterford City (€14.90 one-way, €20.70 round-trip; 1½ hours).

Irish Rail runs three trains daily on the Dublin–Rosslare Europort line via Wexford Town. The trip to Dublin takes three hours (€22.50 one-way, €28.50 round-trip) and to Wexford Town only 25 minutes (€5.90 one-way, €8.20 round-trip). Trains on the Rosslare Europort–Limerick route stop in Waterford City (€17 one-way, €28 round-trip; 1¼ hours) twice a day from Monday to Saturday.

EXPLORING

Rosslare Harbour. The terminus for car ferries from Fishguard and Pembroke in Wales (a four-hour trip) and from Cherbourg and Roscoff in France (a 22-hour trip), Rosslare Harbour, is located 8 km (5 miles) south of the village. The two ferry companies, **Irish Ferries** (⊕ *www.irishferries.com*) and **Stena Sealink** (⊕ *www.stenaline.ie*), serving Rosslare Harbour have small information kiosks in the ultramodern terminal, which also has lockers, a sprawling waiting room, and a café. You can purchase ferry tickets at the terminal. Reservations are also a must if you're traveling by car because onboard parking space is at a premium. Bus Éireann's Rosslare Harbour depot also adjoins the rail station. ⊕ *www.rosslareharbour.ie*.

Rosslare Harbour rail depot. The Rosslare Harbour rail depot, adjacent to the ferry terminal, is served by frequent trains to Dublin's Connolly Station and Cork (change at Limerick Junction). ☎ *053/915–7937* ⊕ *www.irishrail.ie*.

WHERE TO STAY

For expanded hotel reviews, visit Fodors.com.

$$$ ☷ **Kelly's Resort Hotel & Spa.** The Kelly family started this place in 1895
HOTEL and it has since become somewhat of a legend with Irish vacationers,
★ thanks to an overflowing sand-bucket of attractions: a stunning beach-
front location, second-to-none entertainment and leisure facilities, a
child-friendly approach, and a reputation for good food being just a
few. **Pros:** great value for families; lots of activities; quality spa on-
site. **Cons:** lots of kids make it hectic in summer; fairly basic facilities
in rooms; pricey in current climate. **TripAdvisor:** "a part of my life,"
"wonderful staff," "so relaxing." ⑤ *Rooms from: €175* ⊠ *Rosslare,
Co. Wexford* ☏ *053/913–2114* ⊕ *www.kellys.ie* ↘ *114 rooms, 4 suites*
⊙ *Closed Dec.–mid-Feb.* ⦿ *Multiple meal plans.*

NIGHTLIFE AND THE ARTS

The Porthole Bar. A trendy spot with designer decor featuring stonework
and fish tanks, the Porthole Bar is the main hangout at the Hotel Ross-
lare. It's particularly popular for live music on weekends. ⊠ *Rosslare
Harbour, Rosslare Harbour, Co. Wexford* ☏ *053/913–3110* ⊕ *www.
hotelrosslare.ie/the_portholes_bar.html.*

SPORTS

GOLF

Rosslare Golf Club. This popular course is a 30-hole championship links
built on a narrow peninsula with the Irish Sea on one side and the har-
bour on the other. On the 18-hole championship Old Course, the "Bar-
ber's Pole" is the index 1 and devilishly tricky par-4 11th. The 12-hole
Burrow Course was designed by Irish legend Christy O'Connor Junior.
⊠ *Rosslare Strand, Rosslare, Co. Wexford* ☏ *053/913–2203* ⊕ *www.
rosslaregolf.com* ⛳ *Greens fees: Old Course; weekdays €35 week-
ends €40. Burrow Course daily €20* ⅃ *30 holes. Yardage: 6,786 (Old
Course), 3956 (Burrow Course).*

St. Helens Bay Golf Resort. With panoramic views of the south Wex-
ford coastline and Tuskar Rock, 18-hole St. Helens Bay, a relatively
new course, is a classic Irish golf experience. There's a fun 9-hole golf
course right next door if you feel like extending your day. ⊠ *Kilrane,
Co. Wexford* ☏ *053/913–3234* ⊕ *www.sthelensbay.com* ⛳ *Greens fees:
Apr.–Oct., Mon.–Thurs. €35, Fri.–Sun. €40; Nov.–Mar., Mon.–Thurs.
€25, Fri.–Sun. €30* ⅃ *18 holes. Yardage 6,715.*

KILMORE QUAY

22 km (14 miles) south of Rosslare.

★ Noted for its fishing industry, this quiet, old-fashioned seaside village
of thatched and whitewashed cottages is also popular with recreational
anglers and bird-watchers. From the harbor there's a pleasant view to
the east over the flat coast that stretches for miles. Recent development
has turned the harbor into a popular leisure marina.

The Saltee Islands, Ireland's largest bird sanctuary, make a fine day trip
from Kilmore Quay. You can see kittiwakes, puffins, guillemots, cor-
morants, gulls, and petrels, especially in late spring and early summer

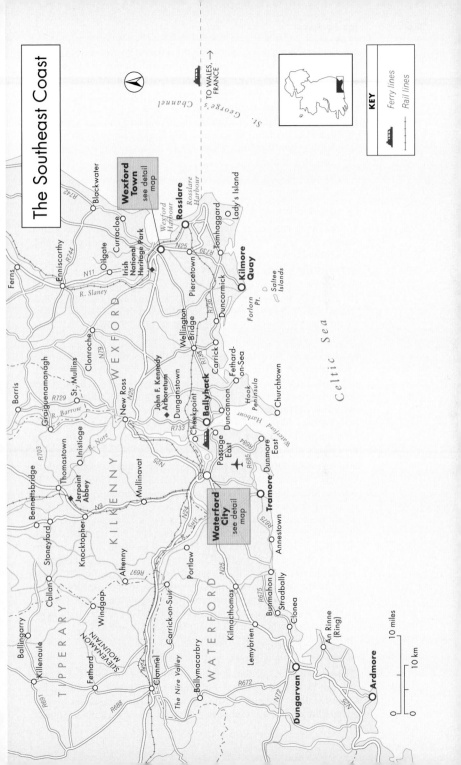

The Southeast Coast

KEY

▟ Ferry lines

Rail lines

TO WALES,
FRANCE →

St. George's Channel

Celtic Sea

TIPPERARY

Ballingarry
Killenaule
Fethard
SLIEVENAMON MOUNTAIN
Windgap
Ballinagarry
Ballingarry
Callan
Knocktopher
Stoneyford
Bennettsbridge
Thomastown
Jerpoint Abbey
Inistioge
Thomastown
R703
R729
Borris
Graiguenamanagh
St. Mullins
R.Barrow
Ferns
Enniscorthy
R744

KILKENNY

Ahenny
R697
Mullinavat
R.Nore
New Ross
N25
Clonroche
N79
R.Slaney

WEXFORD

Clonmel
Carrick-on-Suir
Ballymacarbry
The Nire Valley
R688
N24
Portlaw
R.Suir
N25
N24
John F. Kennedy Arboretum
Dunganstown
Cheekpoint
Ballyhack
Passage East
Wellington Bridge
Carrick
Fethard-on-Sea
Hook Peninsula
Duncannon
Churchtown

WATERFORD

N72
R672
Lemybrien
Kilmacthomas
R675
Bunmahon
Stradbally
Clonea
An Rinne (Ring)
Dungarvan
Ardmore
N25
Waterford Harbour
R684
R685
Dunmore East
Tramore
R675
Annestown
Waterford City see detail map

Ferns
Enniscorthy
Oilgate
Curracloe
Wexford Town see detail map
Blackwater
R742
N11
Irish National Heritage Park
Wexford Harbour
N25
Rosslare
Rosslare Harbour
Piercetown
Tomhaggard
Lady's Island
R739
Kilmore Quay
Duncormick
R736
Forlorn Pt.
Saltee Islands
R733

0 10 miles
0 10 km

when several million seabirds nest among the dunes and rocky scarp on the southernmost of the two islands. From mid-May to mid-September, look for boats at the village waterfront or on the marina to take you to the islands, weather permitting.

GETTING HERE AND AROUND

From Wexford take the N25 to the R739 and into Kilmore Quay. The trip should take about 35 minutes. Bus Éireann runs regular services from Dublin and Wexford. There is parking all over town, but it can get tricky in summer.

BALLYHACK

54 km (24 miles) west of Kilmore Quay.

Fodor's Choice
★

On the upper reaches of Waterford Harbor, this pretty village with a square castle keep, wooden buildings, thatch cottages, and a green, hilly background is admired by painters and photographers.

GETTING HERE AND AROUND

A small car ferry makes the five-minute crossing to Passage East and Waterford. From Wexford take the N25 west to the R373 and into Ballyhack. The 30-mile trip takes about an hour on these relatively narrow roads. There is regular bus service from Wexford Town.

EXPLORING

Ballyhack Castle. The gray-stone keep of Ballyhack Castle dates from the 16th century. It was once owned by the Knights Templars of St. John of Jerusalem, who held the ferry rights by royal charter. The first two floors have been renovated and house local-history exhibits. Guided tours are available by appointment, and the last admission is 45 minutes before closing. ☎ *051/389–468* ⊕ *www.heritageireland.ie/en/south-east/ballyahackcastle* ☒ *Free* ☉ *Late-June–late-Aug., weekdays 10–1 and 2–6, weekends 10–6.*

John F. Kennedy Arboretum. Twelve kilometers (8 miles) to the north of Ballyhack lies the John F. Kennedy Arboretum, with more than 600 acres of forest, nature trails, and gardens, plus an ornamental lake. The grounds contain some 4,500 species of trees and shrubs, and serve as a resource center for botanists and foresters. Go to the top of the park to get fine panoramic views. The arboretum is clearly signposted from New Ross on R733, which follows the banks of the Barrow southward for about 5 km (3 miles). The cottage where the president's great-grandfather was born is in Dunganstown; Kennedy relatives still live in the house. About 2 km (1 mile) down the road at Slieve Coillte you can see the entrance to the arboretum. ☒ *Dunganstown, Co. Wexford* ☎ *051/388–171* ⊕ *www.heritageireland.ie* ☒ *€3* ☉ *May–Aug., daily 10–8; Apr. and Sept., daily 10–6:30; Oct.–Mar., daily 10–5.*

WHERE TO EAT AND STAY

For expanded hotel reviews, visit Fodors.com.

$$$
CONTEMPORARY

✕ **Harvest Room.** Gourmands come in droves to the ruby-red dining room in Dunbrody House's restaurant, where master celebrity chef Kevin Dundon serves up Barbary duck in burnt-orange sauce, char-grilled fillet of slow-roasted pork belly with seared scallops and a lime confit, and a chocolate "selection of indulgences." If you're a DIY-Gourmand, you can learn how to cook Harvest Room's delights yourself; Kevin runs a cooking school on the premises, with classes scheduled for weekends. After a dinner that is likely to be memorable sip-to-sup, sit back with a goblet of Irish Mist in hand and catch a dramatic sunset fading over the Hook Peninsula. Sunday lunch here is the stuff of legend. $ *Average main: €30* ⊠ *Arthurstown, New Ross, Co. Wexford* 🕾 *051/389–600* ⊕ *www.dunbrodyhouse.com* 🕮 *Reservations essential* ⊘ *Closed Mon. and Tues. No lunch Mon.–Sat.*

> **SLOW BOAT TO WATERFORD**
>
> The Knights Templars of St. John of Jerusalem were required to keep a boat at Ballyhack to transport injured knights to the King's Leper Hospital at Waterford.

$$$$
HOTEL
Fodor's Choice
★

Dunbrody Country House. A rural jewel, this sprawling two-story 1830s Georgian manor house is graced with a bevy of allurements, thanks to current chatelains, Kevin and Catherine Dundon: the gardens are soul-restoring, the manse's public salons are a soigné symphony of mix-and-match tangerine-hue fabrics and stuffed armchairs, the views over the Barrow estuary are grand, and the guest rooms charm with a judiciously luxe combination of period antiques and fine reproductions. **Pros:** authentic Georgian feel; wonderful strolling gardens; great restaurant. **Cons:** expensive for this region; facilities limited for luxury hotel; giant Irish breakfast too good to resist. **TripAdvisor:** "an oasis of peace," "great welcome," "food to die for." $ *Rooms from: €225* ⊠ *Arthurstown, New Ross, Co. Wexford* 🕾 *051/389–600* ⊕ *www. dunbrodyhouse.com* 🛏 *15 rooms, 7 suites* ❑ *Breakfast.*

WATERFORD CITY

10 km (6 miles) west of Ballyhack by ferry and road, 62 km (39 miles) southwest of Wexford Town, 158 km (98 miles) southwest of Dublin.

The largest town in the Southeast and Ireland's oldest city, Waterford was founded by the Vikings in the 9th century and was taken over by Strongbow, the Norman invader, with much bloodshed in 1170. The city resisted Cromwell's 1649 attacks, but fell the following year. It did not prosper again until 1783, when George and William Penrose set out to create "plain and cut flint glass, useful and ornamental," and thereby set in motion a glass-manufacturing industry long without equal. The famed glassworks closed after the 2008 financial crisis, but Waterford Crystal has triumphantly risen again from the flames in a smaller, leaner version, opened in 2010 and now relocated to the Mall (*see our write-up under Shopping*).

GETTING HERE AND AROUND

From Dublin take the N7/M7 to the N9/M9 and all the way to Waterford City. This motorway is often quiet and the trip takes only two hours. It can be a long drive around the coast from Wexford to Waterford and the Passage East Car Ferry Company operates year-round from Passage East in Wexford to Ballyhack near Waterford City. The five-minute crossings are continuous from 7 am until 10 pm April through

September and until 8 pm the rest of the year (with first sailing on Sundays at 9:30 am). The cost is €8 one-way and €12 round-trip for a car and passengers and €2 one-way, €3 round-trip for a foot passenger.

Bus Éireann has a station on the waterfront at Merchant's Quay and runs regular buses to cities and towns all over the country, including Dublin (€12.15 one-way, €14.40 round-trip; 3 hours); Tramore (€2.50 one-way, €5 round-trip; 30 minutes); Wexford (€7.20 one-way, €17.60 round trip; 1½ hours); Dungarvan (€10.30 one-way, €13.70 round-trip; 50 minutes); and Cork (€17.10 one-way, €23.40 round-trip; 2¼ hours). Bus Éireann also runs a local city bus service in Waterford City, with five routes that cover the city center.

Plunkett Station is on the north side of the river in Waterford's city center. Irish Rail runs trains to Dublin (€10 one-way, €20 round-trip; 2¾ hours; four to six daily); Kilkenny (€10 one-way, €20 round-trip; 45 minutes; four to six daily); and Limerick (€17 one-way, €34 round-trip; 2¾ hours; three daily Monday–Saturday).

ESSENTIALS

Visitor Information **Waterford City Tourist Office** ✉ *41 The Quay, Waterford City, Co. Waterford* ☎ *051/875–823* ⊕ *www.discoverireland.ie.*

EXPLORING

Waterford has better-preserved city walls than anywhere else in Ireland but Derry. Initially, the slightly run-down commercial center doesn't look promising. You need to park your car and proceed on foot to discover the heritage that the city has made admirable efforts since the mid-1990s to preserve, in particular the grand 18th-century Georgian buildings that Waterford architect John Roberts (1714–96) built, including the town's Protestant and Catholic cathedrals.

If arriving by car, Cork is 125 km (77 miles) west on the N25 and N27 with the drive taking nearly two hours. It's only 52 km (32 miles) and 45 minutes to Kilkenny on the N9 and N10.

Waterford's compact town center can be visited in a couple of hours. Most visitors consider the Waterford Glass Visitor Centre and the impressive new duo of history museums as must-sees in any city tour.

■TIP➔ Off Colbeck Street along Spring Garden Alley, you can see one of the remaining portions of the old city wall; there are sections all around the town center.

TOP ATTRACTIONS

★ **Christ Church Cathedral.** Lovers of Georgian decorative arts will want to visit this late-18th-century Church of Ireland cathedral—the only neoclassical Georgian cathedral in Ireland—designed by local architect John Roberts. Inside, all is cup-of-tea elegance—yellow walls, white-stucco trim in designs of florets and laurels, grand Corinthian columns—and you can see why architectural historian Mark Girouard called this "the finest 18th-century ecclesiastical building in Ireland." It stands on the site of a great Norman Gothic cathedral. The then Bishop Cheneix wouldn't consider knocking that great edifice down but was convinced otherwise when a little rubble accidentally fell in his path a few times (with a little help from potential builders). Medievalists

Waterford City

River Suir

Adelphi Quay

Rose Lane

Johns R.

William St.

Bailey's New St.

The Quay

Custom House Parade

Henrietta St.

Greyfriar's St.

Olaf St.

Colbeck St.

High St.

Peter St.

City Wall

Gladam

Alley

Spring

Garden

Bishop's Palace

The Mall

Beau St.

Catherine St.

Parnell St.

Michael St.

Fire Station

Court House

PEOPLE'S PARK

Broad St.

Barronstrand St.

Patrick St.

Alexander St.

New St.

Browne's Lane

Castle St.

City Wall

Green

Mayors Walk

Ballybricken

Health Centre

Meagher's Quay

Great George's St.

Merchants Quay

O'Connell St.

Thomas St.

James St.

The Glen

Bridge St.

Summer Hill

Morgan St.

Lower Yellow Rd.

Barker St.

Granville Hotel

♦ Tourist Information Office

Arts Centre

Government Offices

0   1/8 mile

0   200 meters

Bishop's Palace **3**

Blackfriars Abbey **8**

Christ Church
Cathedral **5**

City Hall **2**

French Church **6**

Holy Trinity
Cathedral **9**

Reginald's Tower **1**

St. Olaf's Church **7**

Victorian
Clock Tower **10**

Waterford Crystal
at the Mall **4**

The circular Reginald's Tower, originally built by the Vikings, is one of the eye-catching sights along Waterford's Merchant's Quay, long the center of the city's social and economic scene.

will be sad, but those who prize Age of Enlightenment high style will rejoice. Try to catch one of the regular choral concerts held here to get the full atmospheric reward. ⊠ *Henrietta St., Waterford City, Co. Waterford* ☎ *051/858–958* ⊕ *www.christchurchwaterford.com* ▭ *€3* ⊙ *June–Sept., weekdays 9–1 and 2–6, Sat. 2–4; Oct. weekdays 10–5, Sat. 10–4 (rest of year by appointment only for tours).*

Fodor'sChoice ★ **House of Waterford Crystal.** Back from the dead after its recent bankruptcy, iconic Waterford Crystal is once again being produced in the city. The factory tour, which includes molding, blowing, sculpting, and cutting departments, is a must for any visitor who appreciates timeless craftsmanship and unique design. After watching a team of glassworkers create a twinkling masterpiece from a molten blob, you may have trouble resisting the retail store where you can select from the world's largest collection of Waterford crystal and have it engraved on the spot. ⊠ *The Mall, Waterford City, Co. Waterford* ☎ *051/317–000* ⊕ *www. waterfordvisitorcentre.com* ▭ *Factory Tour €11.50* ⊙ *Mar., Mon.–Sat. 9–3:15, Sun. 10–3:15; Apr.–Oct., Mon.–Sat. 9–4:15, Sun. 10–4:15; Nov.–Dec., weekdays 10–3:15.*

Fodor'sChoice ★ **Reginald's Tower.** Restored to its original medieval appearance as a striking showcase for the Viking and Norman sections of the Waterford Treasures exhibition, **Reginald's Tower**—a waterside circular tower on the east end of Waterford's quays—has marked the apex of a triangle containing the old walled city of Waterford for many centuries. Built by the Vikings for the city's defense in 1003, it has 80-foot-high, 10-foot-thick walls; an interior stairway leads to the top. The tower served in turn as the residence for a succession of Anglo-Norman kings (including

Henry II, John, and Richard II), a mint for silver coins, a prison, and an arsenal. It's said that Strongbow's marriage to Eva, the daughter of Dermot MacMurrough, took place here in the late 12th century, thus uniting the Norman invaders with the native Irish.

The impressive **Waterford Treasures exhibition** uses interactive audiovisual technology and exhibits to display Waterford's rich history and inheritance of rare and beautiful artifacts—from the Charter Roll of 1372, a list of all charters granted to Waterford up to that time, written in Latin on vellum, to the sword of King Edward IV. ⊠ *The Quay, Waterford City, Co. Waterford* ☎ *051/304–220* ⊕ *www.waterfordtreasures.com/reginalds-tower* ⊡ *€3* ☉ *June–mid-Sept., daily 10–6; Easter–May, daily 10–5; mid-Sept.–Easter, Wed.–Sun. 10–5.*

> ### ONE WAY OR ANOTHER
>
> Although there are several theories about the origin of the phrase, some experts credit Cromwell with coining the expression "by hook or by crook." Planning two siege routes to Waterford—one via Hook Head, the other via Crooke Village on the estuary of the River Suir—Cromwell declared that he would take the city "by Hooke or by Crooke."

Waterford City Hall. One of Waterford's finer Georgian buildings, the City Hall on the Mall, dates from 1783 and was designed by John Roberts, a native of the city. The arms of Waterford hang over the entrance, which leads into a spacious foyer that originally served as a town meeting place and merchants' exchange. The building contains two lovely theaters, an old Waterford dinner service, and an enormous 1802 Waterford glass chandelier, which hangs in the Council Chamber (a copy of the chandelier hangs in Independence Hall in Philadelphia). The Victorian horseshoe-shaped **Theatre Royal** is the venue for the annual Festival of Light Opera in September. Nearby are some good examples of domestic Georgian architecture—tall, well-proportioned houses with typically Irish semicircular fanlights above the doors. ⊠ *The Mall, Waterford City, Co. Waterford* ☎ *051/309–900* ⊡ *Free* ☉ *Weekdays 9–5.*

WORTH NOTING

Bishop's Palace. Among the most imposing of the city's remaining Georgian town houses, the Bishop's Palace is the new home to the Georgian part of the Waterford Treasures exhibition, mapping the history of what was Ireland's second city from 1700 to 1790. The most impressive part of the collection is the elegant silverware and, of course, fine glassmaking, including the oldest piece of Waterford Crystal on the planet—a decanter from the 1780s. ⊠ *Alongside City Hall on the Mall, Waterford City, Co. Waterford* ☎ *051/304–500* ⊕ *www.waterfordtreasures.com/bishops-palace* ⊡ *€5* ☉ *June–Aug., Mon.–Sat. 9–6, Sun. 11–6; Sept.–May, Mon.–Sat. 10–5, Sun. 11–5.*

Blackfriars Abbey. The ruined tower of Blackfriars belonged to a Dominican abbey founded in 1226 and returned to the Crown in 1541 after the dissolution of the monasteries. It was used as a courthouse until Cromwellian forces destroyed it in the 17th century. ⊠ *High St., Waterford City, Co. Waterford.*

5

City Quays. Located at the corner of Custom House Parade and Peter Street, the City Quays are a good place to begin a tour of Waterford City. The City Quays stretch for nearly 2 km (1 mile) along the River Suir and were described in the 18th century as the best in Europe. ⊠ *Custom House Parade and Peter St., Waterford City, Co. Waterford.*

French Church. Roofless ruins are all that remain of French Church, a 13th-century Franciscan abbey. The church, also known as Greyfriars, was given to a group of Huguenot refugees (hence the "French") in 1695. A splendid east window remains amid the ruins. The key is available at Reginald's Tower. ⊠ *Greyfriars St., Waterford City, Co. Waterford.*

Holy Trinity Cathedral. This Roman Catholic cathedral has a simple facade and a richly (some would say garishly) decorated interior with high, vaulted ceilings and ornate Corinthian pillars. It was designed in neoclassical style by John Roberts, who also designed Christ Church Cathedral and City Hall. Surprisingly, it was built in the late 18th century—when Catholicism was barely tolerated—on land granted by the Protestant city fathers. ⊠ *Barronstrand St., between High St. and clock tower on quays, Waterford City, Co. Waterford* ☎ *051/875–166* ⊕ *www.waterford-cathedral.com* ✉ *Free* ☉ *Daily 8:30–5:30.*

St. Olaf's Church. Built, as the name implies, by the Vikings in the mid-11th century, this church has one sole extant remnant: its original door, which has been incorporated into the wall of the existing building (a meeting hall). ⊠ *St. Olaf's St., Waterford City, Co. Waterford.*

WHERE TO EAT

$$ ✕ **Bodega Restaurant & Wine Bar.** A casual modern-Irish eatery, with food
MODERN IRISH   sourced locally, Bodega Restaurant is known as the fun place to eat in town. Bright colors and comfortable couches are festive, while the extensive wine menu gets everyone warmed up for lively dishes like Kilmore Quay fishcakes with Thai red curry oil followed by a delicious main course of slow-roasted pork belly, sautéed cabbage and bacon with broad bean cream. The place also hosts intimate gigs by some of Irelands top folk singers. ⑤ *Average main: €22* ⊠ *54 John's St., Waterford City, Co. Waterford* ☎ *051/844–177* ⊕ *www.bodegawaterford. com* ☉ *Closed Sun. No lunch Sat.*

$$$ ✕ **La Boheme.** Located in the historic Port of Waterford building, this
FRENCH   intimate eatery offers an authentic taste of France with all its warm
★   Gallic flair and old-world charm. Owners Christine and Eric Théze restored the arched-ceiling space, including the original flagstone floors and lime-washed walls, and they've made a showcase out of the beautiful pewter bar. The menu is a modern take on traditional French dishes, including a starter of Fenor Farm pork belly with cocoa bean salad and tomato jam; for a main course try the saddle of rabbit stuffed with carrots and prunes, and topped with a sweet potato purée and beetroot sauce. ⑤ *Average main: €27* ⊠ *2 George's St., Waterford City, Co. Waterford* ☎ *051/875–645* ⊕ *www.labohemerestaurant.ie* ☉ *No lunch. Closed Sun. and Mon.*

$$$$ ✕ **Munster Dining Room.** Nestled in the heart of the noted Waterford
FRENCH   Castle hotel, the Munster Dining Room's luxe decor—with oak pan-
★   eling darkened with age, and ancestral portraits spotlighted in gilt

CLOSE UP

Waterford Crystal

Silica sand + potash + litharge = Waterford crystal: it reads like cold science, but something magical happens when the craftsmen of Waterford produce arguably the top crystal in the world (although France's Baccarat might have something to say about that).

When the Waterford Glass Factory opened in 1783, it provided English royalty and nobility with a regular supply of ornate handcrafted stemware, chandeliers, and decorative knickknacks. Since then, Waterford crystal has graced the tables of heads of state the world over, and Waterford's earlier pieces have become priceless heirlooms.

The best Waterford glass was produced from the late 18th century to the early 19th century. This early work, examples of which can be found in museums and public buildings all over the country, is characterized by a unique, slightly opaque cast that is absent from the modern product.

Crystal glass is not cheap: each piece is individually fashioned by almost two-dozen pairs of hands before it passes final inspection and receives the discreet Waterford trademark.

The first thing on the itinerary of any visitor to Waterford was for many years a tour of the glass factory, a buzzing hive of master craftspeople. But the global downturn saw the landmark factory close. Happily, Waterford Crystal arose from the ashes in 2010 and now offers a smaller specialist facility at the Mall (⊕ www.waterfordvisitorcentre.com). The adjoining visitor center is already a must-see.

5

frames—hints at one of the most sophisticated menus around. The dress code is smart (jackets for the men) and the place does suggest a big night out. Dining options include a fixed-price, three-course menu featuring adventurous starters like wild rabbit tart with carrot puree and grain mustard jus; main course winners include the best of Irish steaks or the roast wild cod with pepperonata, aioli, tapenade, and Parmesan crisp. $ *Average main: €35* ⊠ *The Island, (2 km [1 mile] south of Waterford), Ballinakill, Co. Waterford* ☎ *051/878–203* ⊕ *www.waterfordcastle.com/dining* ☾ *No lunch.*

WHERE TO STAY
For expanded hotel reviews, visit Fodors.com.

$ **Dooley's Hotel.** Just a few minutes' walk from all the main attractions,
HOTEL this unpretentious hotel on the banks of the River Suir is popular both with families and business travelers, while the traditional-style bar is popular with locals. **Pros:** city-center location; large guest rooms; excellent service; popular bar is a good place to meet locals. **Cons:** attracts a business clientele; can get more luxury for same price elsewhere; can be a little noisy. **TripAdvisor:** "excellent customer service," "great location," "friendly and comfortable." $ *Rooms from: €80* ⊠ *30 The Quay, Waterford City, Co. Waterford* ☎ *051/873–531* ⊕ *www.dooleys-hotel. ie* ⊐ *113 rooms* ⋈ *Breakfast.*

$$ ⬚ **Foxmount Country House.** About 15 minutes northeast of Waterford
B&B/INN City, this stylish Georgian country house manages to be luxurious and
Fodor's Choice elegant and at the same time warm and personal. **Pros:** authenticity;
★ family-run; great value; rural but near the city. **Cons:** few facilities; no
restaurant. **TripAdvisor:** "wonderful and delightful," "a warm welcome
awaits you," "Georgian elegance in the country." $ *Rooms from:* €120
✉ *Passage East Rd., Waterford City, Co. Waterford* ☎ *051/874–308*
⊕ *www.foxmountcountryhouse.com* ⬚ *4 rooms* ▭ *No credit cards.*

$$$$ ⬚ **Waterford Castle Hotel & Golf Resort.** Not only does this fairy-tale cas-
HOTEL tle come with an 800-year history, its own 310-acre island, a private
Fodor's Choice ferry, and highly rated golf course, it also caters to lucky guests with
★ the best of Irish service and the grandest of Irish style. **Pros:** unique,
historic building; great golf course on-site; awe-inspiring Great Hall.
Cons: expensive for this region; books up early in summer; popular
with weddings. **TripAdvisor:** "best food and décor," "oasis of calm,"
"like a dream." $ *Rooms from:* €240 ✉ *The Island, 2 km (1 mile)
south of Waterford, Ballinakill, Co. Waterford* ☎ *051/878–203* ⊕ *www.
waterfordcastle.com* ⬚ *14 rooms, 5 suites.*

NIGHTLIFE AND THE ARTS

NIGHTLIFE

Geoffs. A dimly lighted pub, Geoffs is frequented by a mixed crowd
including students and locals. Big flagstones cover the floors, and seating
is on old wooden benches. An outdoor area is available for those keen to
avoid Ireland's smoking ban. A wide selection of food is served until 9,
every day. ✉ *9 John St., Waterford City, Co. Waterford* ☎ *051/874–787.*

Jack Meades. Known to the natives as Meade's Under the Bridge, Jack
Meades is snug under a time-stained stone bridge. In centuries past it
was a stop on the coach road from Waterford to Passage East. There's
a pub menu from May through September, and sing-along sessions
are held throughout the year on the weekends. In winter the fireplaces
roar, illuminating the wood beams and bric-a-brac. ✉ *Cheekpoint Rd.,
Halfway House, Ballycanavan, Co. Waterford* ☎ *051/873–187* ⊕ *www.
jackmeades.com.*

Old Ground. Housed in an 800-year-old building, this pub is highly
popular with the locals. Lunch is served daily, and traditional-music
sessions sometimes break out. ✉ *10 The Glen, Waterford City, Co.
Waterford* ☎ *051/852–283.*

★ **T & H Doolan's Bar.** The circa-1700 T & H Doolan's Bar, reputed to be
one of the oldest pubs in Ireland, hosts traditional Irish music most sum-
mer nights and Monday through Wednesday nights year-round. ✉ *32
George's St., Waterford City, Co. Waterford* ☎ *051/872–764.*

THE ARTS

Forum. A large multipurpose entertainment venue, the Forum often hosts
local productions or those of traveling theater companies. Two music
venues present big names as well as local acts performing all kinds of
music. ✉ *The Glen, Waterford City, Co. Waterford* ☎ *051/871–111*
⊕ *www.forumwaterford.com.*

★ **Garter Lane Arts Centre.** Culture buffs shouldn't miss the Garter Lane
Arts Centre, which has a nice schedule filled with concerts, exhibits,

A faux-baronial hotel first built as a homestead for the famous Fitzgerald family, Waterford Castle can indulge "queen-for-a-stay" fantasies.

and theater productions. Garter Lane is home to many productions of **Red Kettle** (⊕ *www.red-kettle.com*), Waterford's most successful theater company. ⊠ *22A O'Connell St., Waterford City, Co. Waterford* ☎ *051/855–038* ⊕ *www.garterlane.ie.*

★ **Spraoi Festival.** Billed as the "biggest street carnival in Ireland"—look for street theater, live music, and fireworks—the free outdoor Spraoi Festival, which appeals to children and adults, visitors and locals alike, takes place annually during the August bank holiday, the first weekend of the month. ☎ *051/841–808* ⊕ *www.spraoi.com.*

Theatre Royal Waterford. One of the oldest theaters in Ireland, Waterford's elegant Theatre Royal reopened after major renovations in 2009 with renewed vigor and devotion to large-scale theater and musical productions as well as live concerts. ⊠ *City Hall, The Mall, Waterford City, Co. Waterford* ☎ *051/874–402* ⊕ *www.theatreroyal.ie.*

SHOPPING

City Square Shopping Centre. With more than 40 shops ranging from small Irish fashion boutiques to large international department stores, City Square Shopping Centre also presents fashion shows and other forms of entertainment on the stage area in the center of the mall. ⊠ *City Sq., Waterford City, Co. Waterford* ☎ *051/853–528* ⊕ *www.city-square.ie.*

Kellys. This is a fine source for excellent Irish souvenirs, including traditional musical instruments, dolls, Irish linen, jewelry, Waterford crystal, and CDs. ⊠ *75–76 The Quay, Waterford City, Co. Waterford* ☎ *051/873–557.*

Penrose Crystal. Although the famed Waterford glassworks is now back in action, many shoppers also like to check out the goods at the town's other quality, handmade crystal manufactory. With a little notice, Penrose can have a personally engraved piece waiting for you when you arrive. ⊠ *32 John St., Waterford City, Co. Waterford* ☎ *051/876–537* ⊕ *www.penrosecrystal.com.*

SPORTS

GAELIC FOOTBALL

Waterford GAA Grounds. Watch exciting and spectacular Gaelic football and hurling at the Waterford GAA Grounds. ⊠ *Walsh Park, Waterford City, Co. Waterford* ☎ *051/591–5544* ⊕ *www.waterfordgaa.ie.*

GOLF

Faithlegg Golf Club. A perfectly manicured, 18-hole parkland course, Faithlegg is set in the mature landscape of a 200-acre estate on the banks of the River Suir. Problematic doglegs, blind shots, and nasty sand traps make it a lot trickier than it seems on first glance. ⊠ *Faithlegg House, Checkpoint, Co. Waterford* ☎ *051/382–241* ⊕ *www. faithlegg.com* 🏌 *Greens fees: Nov.–Feb. €20, Mar.–Apr. and Oct. weekdays €30, weekends €35, May–Sept. weekdays €35, weekends €40* 🏌 *Yardage 6,674.*

Waterford Castle Hotel & Golf Club. An elegant, 18-hole, parkland course, Waterford Castle claims to be Ireland's only true island course, being completely detached from the mainland on a privately owned 310-acre island. Designed by Irish golfing great Des Smyth, the tricky but playable course winds through mature woodland and features four internal water features in addition to the encroaching sea. Plenty of opportunities to hit one into the drink. ⊠ *The Island, Ballinakill, Co. Waterford* ☎ *051/871–633* ⊕ *www.waterfordcastle.com/golf* 🏌 *Greens fees: weekdays €30, weekends €40* 🏌 *Yardage 6,372.*

TRAMORE

🕐 *11 km (7 miles) south of Waterford City on R675, 4 km (2½ miles) west of Dunmore East.*

Tramore's 5-km-long (3-mile-long) **beach** is a popular escape for families from Waterford and other parts of the Southeast, as the many vacation homes and camper parks indicate. The beach is adjacent to the giant Tramore Amusement Park, which features all the usual rides, including a Ferris wheel, Crazy Mouse Spinning Roller Coaster, and old-fashioned dodgems. Kiddie heaven, in other words.

GETTING HERE AND AROUND

From Waterford take the R675 south to Tramore. The trip takes about fifteen minutes. Bus Éireann runs frequent daily buses from Tramore to Waterford City (€2.70 one-way, €5.40 round-trip; 30 minutes) where there are connecting buses to Dublin, Cork, and Kilkenny. This bus also goes to the train station in Waterford for rail connections. The Bus Éireann bus stop is outside the tourist office near Splashworld.

DUNGARVAN

42 km (26 miles) southwest of Tramore.

With their covering of soft grasses, the lowlands of Wexford and eastern Waterford gradually give way to heath and moorland; the wetter climate of the hillier western Waterford countryside creates and maintains the bog. The mountains responsible for the change in climate rise up behind Dungarvan, the largest coastal town in County Waterford. This bustling fishing and resort spot sits at the mouth of the River Colligan, which empties into Dungarvan Bay here. It's a popular base for climbers and hikers.

GETTING HERE AND AROUND

From Waterford, take the N25 west to Dungarvan. The trip takes 45 minutes.

Bus Éireann picks up and drops off on Davitt's Quay. They have regular daily services to and from Waterford (€10.30 one-way, €13.70 round-trip; 1 hour; 11 daily); Cork (€14.90 one-way, €20.70 round-trip; 1½ hours; 13 daily); and Dublin (14.40 one-way, 16.70 round-trip; 11 daily).

ESSENTIALS

Visitor Information Dungarvan & West Waterford Tourism ⊠ *The Courthouse, Dungarvan, Co. Waterford* ☎ *058/41741* ⊕ *www.dungarvantourism.com.*

EXPLORING

Ring (An Rinn). Unusual in the south and east of the country, Ring (An Rinn) is an unspoiled Gaeltacht area on Dungarvan Bay where you will find the Irish language still in daily use. Courses in Irish have been taught at Colaiste na Rinne, a language college, since 1909. This is a lovely spot for bikers, walkers, and bird-watchers, and a great place to experience Irish culture. ⊠ *7 km (4½ miles) southeast of Dungarvan, off R674, Dungarvan, Co. Waterford.*

WHERE TO EAT AND STAY

For expanded hotel reviews, visit Fodors.com.

$ ╳ **Nude Food.** Louise Clark's eclectic little café on O'Connell Street spe-
CAFÉ cializes in simple, delicious food with nothing to hide and everything
★ to love. For a pre-mountain-walk breakfast try the Ballinamult free-range baked egg and Marmite soldiers. When you come back down the mountain, try the traditional Irish stew with pearl barley, lamb, carrots, and homemade soda bread, or Nude's ploughman's platter, with honey-glazed ham, Carrigaline farmhouse cheese, and in-house pickles, preserves, and griddled sourdough bread. In fact, you might want to skip the mountain altogether so you can stay for the delightful almond tart with clotted cream. Nude has a lovely bakery and deli next door (so you can take a packed lunch to the mountain tomorrow). ⑤ *Average main: €11* ⊠ *86 O'Connell St., Dungarvan, Co. Waterford* ☎ *058/24594* ⊕ *www.nudefood.ie* ⊘ *No dinner Sun.–Wed.*

$$$ ╳ **The Tannery.** Clearly, the mountain air in Knockmealdown works won-
ECLECTIC ders for the creativity and vision of chef/culinary wizard Paul Flynn; it
Fodor's Choice also whets up quite an appetite in the flocks of Dubliners who besiege
★ what is commonly regarded as one of Ireland's leading restaurants every weekend. Flynn worked for almost a decade with London legend Nico

Ladenis and now wins raves from the likes of Sir Andrew Lloyd Webber. The menu is rustic but whimsical and always seasonal. Check out the gravlax of ocean trout with spring slaw and mustard dressing, or, if that doesn't tickle your taste buds, opt for the Barbary duck with chard, crispy parsnip, warm bacon, and hazelnut dressing. Fanatical foodies who want to stay as close to the culinary action as possible can now overnight in the adjoining guesthouse and attend the regular cooking school classes. Your waistline may never be the same again. ⑤ *Average main: €25* ⊠ *10 Quay St., Dungarvan, Co. Waterford* ☎ *58/45420* ⊕ *www.tannery.ie* ⊗ *Closed Mon. and 2 wks in Jan. No dinner Sun. Sept.–May. No lunch Mon.–Thurs. and Sat.*

$$ ▢ **The Gold Coast Golf Hotel.** Overlooking Dungarvan Bay, this hotel is HOTEL part of a family-run and family-friendly property that also includes ♻ self-catering holiday cottages (built around the hotel) and golf villas on the edge of a woodland course on a links setting. **Pros:** great location; owners love kids; great value even in high season. **Cons:** gets a bit hectic with all those kids around; guest rooms are a little mundane; no Internet in rooms. **TripAdvisor:** "lovely piece of paradise," "perfect location," "great pool and staff." ⑤ *Rooms from: €125* ⊠ *Dungarvan, Co. Waterford* ☎ *058/42249, 058/42416* ⊕ *www.goldcoastgolfresort.com* ⇆ *35 rooms, 2 suites, 16 cottages, 12 villas, 27 lodges* ⑩ *Breakfast.*

NIGHTLIFE AND THE ARTS

Colaiste na Rinne. A few miles outside Dungarvan, you can sit/join in on a *ceilí* (traditional Irish dance), held most nights in summer at Colaiste na Rinne, the school in this Irish-speaking community known for its strong tradition in Irish language, heritage, and culture. ⊠ *Ring, Co. Waterford* ☎ *058/46104* ⊕ *www.anrinn.com.*

ARDMORE

29 km (18 miles) southwest of Dungarvan.

Fodor's Choice Historic spiritual sites, white beaches, dramatic cliff walks, brawny fisher-
★ men—little Ardmore is a picture-postcard Irish town that packs a whole lot of wonder into a small peninsula at the base of a tall cliff. With a few notable exceptions—including John F. Kennedy and Gregory Peck—the cute but very real village is often overlooked by most overseas tourists.

GETTING HERE AND AROUND

From Waterford take the N25 west and exit left onto the R673 to Ardmore. The 46-mile trip takes about an hour with the last part of the drive traveled on a small country road. There are a few buses a day from Dungarvan and Youghal. Parking can be a problem around town in the high season.

EXPLORING

Cathedral of St. Declan and Round Tower. There's a story behind every ruin you pass in Ireland; behind many, there's a truly ancient story. Inside the ruined 12th-century Cathedral of St. Declan are some pillar stones decorated with ogham script (an ancient Irish alphabet) as well as the weathered but interesting biblical scenes carved on its west gable. St. Declan is reputed to have disembarked here in the 5th century—30 years before St. Patrick arrived in Ireland—and founded a monastery. The saint is said to be buried in St. Declan's Oratory, a small early Christian church that has been partially reconstructed.

On the grounds of the ruined cathedral, the 97-foot-high Round Tower, one of 70 round towers remaining in Ireland, is in exceptionally good condition. Round towers were built by the early Christian monks as watchtowers and belfries but came to be used as places of refuge for the monks and their valuables during Viking raids. This is the reason the doorway is 15 feet above ground level—once inside, the monks could pull the ladder into the tower with them.

WHERE TO EAT AND STAY

For expanded hotel reviews, visit Fodors.com.

$$$$
ECLECTIC
Fodor'sChoice
★

✕ **The House Restaurant.** Celebrated Dutch chef Martjin Kajuiter presides over the compact, award-winning little dining room of the Cliff House hotel. Go in summer, when you can eat out on the expansive terrace, which winds its way down the cliff side toward the sea. The food is all locally sourced and innovatively prepared—"trad" Irish is often the base but garnishes and sauces lend a festive, nouvelle air. Dinner is a fixed-price, three-course meal with the West Cork scallops with pork belly, purple kale and potato preparations, oyster leaves, and crystallized borage flower a stunning starter. And you can't go wrong with the Helvick Turbot Fillet with Dingle Bay crab ravioli, trumpet mushrooms, and leeks in a wine sauce as your main course. $ *Average main: €35* ✉ *Ardmore, Co. Waterford* ☎ *024/87800* ⊕ *www.thecliffhousehotel. com/dining* ⊗ *No lunch weekdays.*

$$$$
HOTEL
Fodor'sChoice
★

⊡ **Cliff House.** Tucked into the cliffs overlooking the fishing village of Ardmore, ageless nature confronts modernist design in this luxury hotel and spa—one of the most innovative additions to Irish accommodations in years. **Pros:** the sea is everywhere; great spa and pool; up the road from the wonderful Ardmore Pottery shop. **Cons:** pricey for the region; often has two-day minimums in summer; younger staff still learning their trade. **TripAdvisor:** "stunning views," "friendly people," "a truly memorable stay." $ *Rooms from: €300* ✉ *Ardmore, Co. Waterford* ☎ *024/87800* ⊕ *www.thecliffhousehotel.com* ⤴ *24 rooms, 15 suites.*

SHOPPING

Ardmore Pottery & Craft Shop. Home to potter Mary Lincoln, this is one of the most beloved, creative, and cleverly stocked craft shops in the country, with everything from Alan Ardiff gold jewelry to Veronica Molloy's famed homemade jams. You can even watch Mary at work at the wheel and purchase some of her own beautiful, delicate but simple designs. ✉ *The Cliff, Ardmore, Co. Waterford* ☎ *024/94152* ⊕ *www. ardmorepottery.com.*

SPORTS AND THE OUTDOORS

Ardmore Adventures. Ardmore and other nearby beaches have become meccas for water-sport lovers and this shop on Main Street is the hub for most of it. They organize snorkeling, kayaking, power boating, surfing, kids' camps, and anything else that involves fun and the sea. ✉ *Main St., Ardmore, Co. Waterford* ☎ *083/374–3889* ⊕ *www. ardmoreadventures.ie.*

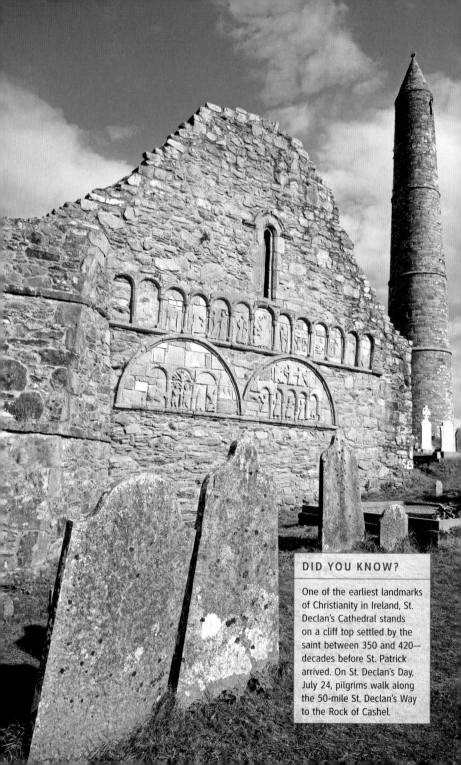

COUNTY TIPPERARY AND AROUND

"It's a long way to Tipperary . . . " So run the words of that famed song sung all over the world since World War I. Actually, Tipperary is *not* so far to go, considering that, as Ireland's biggest inland county, it's within easy striking distance of Waterford and Cork. Moving in from the coastline, you can travel through some of Ireland's lushest pasturelands and to some of its most romantic sights, such as Lismore Castle. The Blackwater Valley is renowned for its beauty, peacefulness, and excellent fishing. Some of the finest racehorses in the world are raised in the fields of Tipperary, which is also the county where you can find the Rock of Cashel—the greatest group of monastic ruins in all Ireland.

LISMORE

20 km (13 miles) northwest of Dungarvan.

Fodor'sChoice
★
Lismore is one of Ireland's grandest places to get lost in. Popular with both anglers and romantics, the enchanting little town of Lismore is built on the banks of the Blackwater, a river famous for its trout and salmon. From the 7th to the 12th century it was an important monastic center, founded by St. Carthac (or Carthage), and it had one of the most renowned universities of its time. The village has two cathedrals: a soaring Roman Catholic one from the late 19th century and the Church of Ireland's St. Carthage's, which dates from 1633 and incorporates fragments of an earlier church. Glamour arrived in the form of the dukes of Devonshire, who built their Irish seat here, Lismore Castle (their main house is Chatsworth in England); in the 1940s, Fred Astaire, whose sister, Adele, had married Lord Charles Cavendish, younger son of the ninth duke, would bend the elbow at the town's Madden's Pub. There were darker interludes in the town's history: Lismore was hard-hit by the Great Famine of 1845, and its Famine Graveyard bears poignant witness. Other architectural jewels include a quaint library funded by Andrew Carnegie and the Ballysaggartmore "folly"—a Gothic-style gateway to a 19th-century house that was so costly the house itself was never erected.

GETTING HERE AND AROUND

From Waterford take the N25 west to the N72 for Lismore. The trip takes about 55 minutes. There are regular buses from Dungarvan. In summer, parking spots are at a premium around the small town.

ESSENTIALS

Visitor Information **Lismore Tourist Office** ✉ *Lismore Heritage Centre, Lismore, Co. Waterford* ☎ *058/54975* ⊕ *www.discoverlismore.com.*

EXPLORING

Fodor'sChoice
★
Lismore Castle and Gardens. As you cross the bridge entering Lismore, take in the dramatic view of magnificent Lismore Castle, a vast, turreted, gray-stone building atop a rock that overhangs the River Blackwater. There has been a castle here since the 12th century, but the present structure, built by the sixth duke of Devonshire, dates from

In and Around County Tipperary

the mid-19th century. Today, the house remains the Irish estate of the Cavendish family and most of it is not open to the public (although you can call it your own for a very high rental fee). In 2007, however, an impressive new contemporary art gallery, designed by Cork architect Gareth O'Callaghan, opened in the west wing, perhaps a sign that the new duke, who inherited the family title in 2004, is intent on making his own mark. Happily, the upper and lower gardens, which consist of woodland walks, including an unusual yew walk said to be more than 800 years old (Edmund Spenser is said to have written parts of *The Faerie Queene* here), are open during certain months of the year. Comprising 7 acres set with 17th-century defensive walls, the gardens have an impressive display of magnolias, camellias, and shrubs, and are adorned with examples of contemporary sculpture. ☎ *058/54288* ⊕ *www.lismorecastle.com* ✉ *€8* ⊗ *Mid-Mar.–Sept., daily 11–4.*

★ **Lismore Heritage Center.** Almost the definitive example of an estate town, Lismore has in recent years taken the firm decision to project a pride of place linked with a deep sense of history. The Lismore Heritage Center in the former town courthouse lies at the core of the town, and its exhibits focus on the town's Celtic origins and its links to many famous people from Sir Walter Raleigh to Prince Charles to Fred Astaire. Lismore Experience, an impressive video presentation, charts the history of the town from its monastic 7th-century origins up to the present day. The center also has a large craft shop. ⊠ *The Old Courthouse, Lismore, Co. Waterford* 🕾 *058/54975* ⊕ *www.discoverlismore.com* 🖭 *€4.80 (Lismore Experience)* 🕙 *Apr.–Oct., weekdays 9:30–5:30, Sat. 10–5, Sun. noon–5; Nov.–Apr., weekdays 9:30–5:30.*

Mount Melleray Abbey. Mount Melleray Abbey was the first post-Reformation monastery, founded in 1832 by the Cistercian Order in what was then a barren mountainside wilderness. Over the years the order has transformed the site into more than 600 acres of fertile farmland. The monks maintain strict vows of silence, but you're welcome to join in services throughout the day and are permitted into most areas of the abbey. It's also possible to stay in the guest lodge by prior arrangement. If you're heading into the Knockmealdown Mountains from Lismore, you can easily stop on the way at the abbey for a visit. There's a small heritage center about the history of Irish monasticism with a few ogham stones and a short film. ⊠ *South of Vee Gap, signposted off R669, 13 km (8 miles) from Lismore, Cappoquin, Co. Waterford* 🕾 *058/54404* ⊕ *www.cappoquin.org/abbey.shtml* 🖭 *Free* 🕙 *Daily 8–8.*

Knockmealdown Mountains. Leaving Lismore, heading east on N72 for 6½ km (4 miles) toward Cappoquin, a well-known angling center, you can pick up R669 north into the Knockmealdown Mountains. Your route is signposted as the Vee Gap road, the Vee Gap being its summit, from where you'll have superb views of the Tipperary plain, the Galtee Mountains in the northwest, and a peak called Slievenamon in the northeast. If the day is clear, you should be able to see the Rock of Cashel, ancient seat of the Kings of Munster, some 32 km (20 miles) away. Just before you enter the Vee Gap, look for a 6-foot-high mound of stones on the left side of the road. It marks the grave of Colonel Grubb, a local landowner who liked the view so much that he arranged to be buried here standing up so that he could look out over the scene for all eternity.

WHERE TO EAT AND STAY

For expanded hotel reviews, visit Fodors.com.

$$
IRISH
✕ **O'Brien Chop House.** Producers from the surrounding town land fuel the menu at this recent addition to the Lismore dining scene, run by Justin and Jenn Green of nearby Ballyvolane House. You'll find carefully sourced meat from local farmers and butchers, honey from local beekeepers, and fruit and vegetables from the owners' own garden. Once an old Victorian pub, the restored interior is all wood and brass with an intimate and relaxed feel. The steak and chops are some of the best in the region; the chop-house beef and Black Rock Stout pie is classic, and you'll find a few seafood options, too. All in all, the ideal spot to while away a rainy evening. 💲 *Average main: €21* ⊠ *Main St., Lismore, Co. Waterford* 🕾 *058/53812* ⊕ *www.obrienchophouse.ie.*

$$
B&B/INN
★
🏠 **Richmond House.** It's been 300 years since the Earl of Cork and Burlington built this handsome country house and it still retains its imposing aura of courtly elegance, thanks to owners Claire and Paul Deevy who've added welcoming touches like log fires, traditional country-house decor, and a fabulous restaurant. **Pros:** excellent restaurant;

enchanting gardens. **Cons:** simple but boring guest rooms. **TripAdvisor:** "the place to go," "top class," "fantastic food and service." ⑤ *Rooms from: €125* ✉ *Cappoquin, Co. Waterford* ☎ *58/54278* ⊕ *www.richmondhouse.net* ⤳ *10 rooms* ⊘ *Closed late Dec.–mid-Jan.* ⑩ *Breakfast.*

CAHIR

37 km (23 miles) north of Lismore.

Cahir (pronounce it "Care") is a busy but easygoing market town with a pleasant Georgian square at its heart. It is built on the River Suir at the eastern end of the Galtee mountain range. The Suir is known for its good salmon and trout fishing, as is the Aherlow River, which joins it above town.

GETTING HERE AND AROUND

From Dublin, take the N7/M7 south to junction 19 and the N24. At junction 10, take the R670 to Cahir. The trip takes about two hours 10 minutes. There are regular bus services from Kilkenny and Waterford. There is also a train service from Dublin and Kilkenny.

ESSENTIALS

Visitor Information Cahir Tourist Office ✉ *Castle Car Park, Cahir, Co. Tipperary* ☎ *052/614–1453* ⊕ *www.discoverireland.ie.*

EXPLORING

Cahir Castle. The unavoidable focal point of the town, Cahir Castle is dramatically perched on a rocky island on the River Suir. Once the stronghold of the mighty Butler family and one of Ireland's largest and best-preserved castles, it retains its dramatic keep, tower, and much of its original defensive structure. An audiovisual show and guided tour are available upon request. ☎ *052/744–1011* ⊕ *www.heritageireland. ie* 🎟 *€3* ⊘ *Mid-Mar.–mid-June and Sept.–mid-Oct., daily 9:30–5:30; mid-June–Aug., daily 9–6:30; mid-Oct.–mid-Mar., daily 9:30–4:30; last entry 45 mins before closing.*

Fodor's Choice ★ **Swiss Cottage.** If there's little storybook allure to the brute mass of Cahir Castle, fairy-tale looks grace the first earl of Glengall's 1812 Swiss Cottage, a dreamy relic from the days when romanticism conquered 19th-century Ireland. A mile south of town on a particularly picturesque stretch of the River Suir, this "cottage *orné*" was probably designed by John Nash, one of the Regency period's most fashionable architects. Half thatch-roof cottage, half mansion, bordered by verandas constructed of branched trees, it was a veritable theater set that allowed the lordly couple to fantasize about being "simple folk" (down to the fact that secret doorways were constructed to allow servants to bring drinks and food without being noticed). Inside, some of the earliest Dufour wallpapers printed in Paris charm the eye. The cottage is signposted from the R670 along the Cahir-to-Ardfinnan road, or you can hike from Cahir Castle on a footpath along the enchanting river. In peak season, crowds can be fierce. ☎ *052/744–1144* ⊕ *www.heritageireland. ie* 🎟 *€3* ⊘ *Apr.–Oct., daily 10–6.*

The duke of Devonshire's Lismore Castle once sheltered Edmund Spenser when he was writing *The Faerie Queene*; today, his parklands are home to avant-garde artworks.

WHERE TO STAY

For expanded hotel reviews, visit Fodors.com.

$$ **HOTEL** **★** 🍽️ **Aherlow House Hotel & Lodges.** Built in 1928 to replace a house destroyed in Ireland's civil war, Aherlow is set on the slopes of Sliabh na Muc (Mountain of the Pigs), and comes with its own private forest and incredible views of the magnificent Galtee Mountains and the ancient Glen of Aherlow. **Pros:** rooms are big; families will love the lodges; stunning natural surroundings. **Cons:** popular with local weddings and parties; gets booked up summer weekends. **TripAdvisor:** "Irish hospitality at its best," "friendly staff," "great place to get away." ⑤ *Rooms from: €125* ✉ *Cahir, Glen of Aherlow, Co. Tipperary* ☎ *062/56153* ⊕ *www.aherlowhouse.ie* ⥥ *29 rooms, 15 lodges* ◐ *Closed Sun.–Thurs. during Jan.–Mar.*

$$$ **B&B/INN** **Fodor's Choice** **★** 🍽️ **The Old Convent.** A wonderfully tucked-away sanctuary—which began life as a prim and proper 19th-century convent set amidst spectacularly scenic vistas of the Knockmealdown Mountains—this retreat has now been tastefully restored by Christine and Dermot Gannon, with Dermot's well-established credentials as one of Ireland's most innovative chefs lovingly displayed in the restaurant here. **Pros:** passionate owner/manager couple; extra-comfortable mattresses; serenity of natural surroundings. **Cons:** a trek to the nearest town; not ideal for kids. **TripAdvisor:** "foodie's paradise with great accommodations," "gorgeous location," "a haven of delicious tranquility." ⑤ *Rooms from: €175* ✉ *Mount Anglesby, Clogheen, Co. Tipperary* ☎ *052/746–5565* ⊕ *www.theoldconvent.ie* ⥥ *7 rooms.*

TIPPERARY TOWN

22 km (14 miles) northwest of Cahir.

Tipperary Town, a dairy-farming center at the head of a fertile plain known as the Golden Vale, is a good starting point for climbing and walking in the hills around the Glen of Aherlow. The small country town, on the River Ara, is also worth visiting in its own right. In New Tipperary, a neighborhood built by local tenants during Ireland's Land War (1890–91), buildings such as Dalton's Heritage House have been restored; you can visit the Heritage House by calling the offices of Clann na Éireann. You can also visit the old Butter Market on Dillon Street; the Churchwell at the junction of Church, Emmet, and Dillon streets; and the grave of the grandfather of Robert Emmett—one of the most famous Irish patriots—in the graveyard at St. Mary's Church. A statue of Charles Kickham, whose 19th-century novel *The Homes of Tipperary* chronicled the devastation of this county through forced emigration, has a place of honor in the center of town. Adjacent to Bridewell Jail on St. Michael's Street is St. Michael's Church, with its stained-glass window depicting a soldier killed during World War I.

GETTING HERE AND AROUND

From Dublin, take the N7/M7 south to junction 19 and the M8. Take junction 9 to the N74 to Tipperary Town. There are bus services from Dublin, Cork, and Kilkenny, and regular train services from Dublin and Cork. There is ample parking around the town.

ESSENTIALS

Visitor Information Tipperary Tourist Office ⊠ *Mitchel St., Tipperary Town, Co. Tipperary* ☎ *062/80520* ⊕ *www.tipperary-excel.com.*

Tipperary Excel. The Tipperary Excel arts and culture center contains the local tourist office and the Tipperary Family History research center—a top spot for all those tracking down their Irish roots. ⊠ *Mitchel St., Tipperary Town, Co. Tipperary* ☎ *062/80520* ⊕ *www.tipperary-excel.com.*

CASHEL

17 km (11 miles) northeast of Tipperary Town.

Cashel is a market town on the busy Cork–Dublin road, with a lengthy history as a center of royal and religious power. From roughly AD 370 until AD 1101, it was the seat of the Kings of Munster, and it was probably at one time a center of Druidic worship. Here, according to legend, St. Patrick arrived in about AD 432 and baptized King Aengus, who became Ireland's first Christian ruler. One of the many legends associated with this event is that St. Patrick plucked a shamrock to explain the mystery of the Trinity, thus giving a new emblem to Christian Ireland.

GETTING HERE AND AROUND

By car, Cashel is on the busy N8/M8 motorway between Dublin and Cork. Dublin is 162 km (100 miles) or 2 hours northeast of Cashel on the N8/M8 and N7/M7. Cork City is 97 km (60 miles) or 1 hour 11 minutes south of Cashel on the N8/M8 and the N74.

Continued on page 313

TOWERING GLORY
The Rock of Cashel

Haunt of St. Patrick, Ireland's "rock of ages" is a place where history, culture, and legend collide.

Seat of the Kings of Munster and the hallowed spot where St. Patrick first plucked a shamrock to explain the mystery of the Trinity, the Rock of Cashel is Ireland's greatest group of ecclesiastical ruins. Standing like an ominous beacon in the middle of a sloped, treeless valley, the Rock has a titanic grandeur and majesty that create what one ancient scribe called "a fingerpost to Heaven."

Historians theorize the stupendous mass was born during the Ice Age. This being Ireland, however, fulsome myths abound: There are those who believe it was created when the Devil himself took a huge bite of the Slieve Bloom Mountains only to spit it out right in the middle of the Golden Vale. Today, the great limestone mass still rises 300 feet to command a panorama over all it surveys—fittingly, the name derives from the Irish *caiseal*, meaning stone fort, and this gives a good idea of the strategic importance of Cashel in days of yore.

For centuries, Cashel was known as the "city of the kings"—from the 5th century, the lords of Munster ruled over much of southern Ireland from here. In 1101, however, they handed Cashel over to the Christian fathers, and the rock soon became the center of the reform movement that reshaped the Irish Church. Along the way, the church fathers embarked on a centuries-long building campaign that resulted in the magnificent group of chapels, round towers,

SOUTHEASTERN VIEW OF THE ROCK

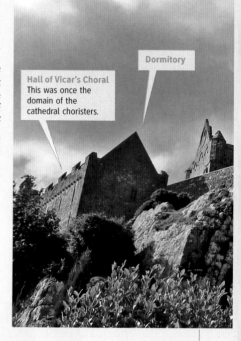

Hall of Vicar's Choral
This was once the domain of the cathedral choristers.

Dormitory

and walls you see at Cashel today. View them from afar on the N8 highway and the complex looks so complete you're surprised upon arriving to discover guides in modern dress and not knights in medieval uniform.

■TIP→ The best approach to the rock is along the Bishop's Walk, a 10-minute hike that begins outside the drawing room of the Cashel Palace hotel on Main Street in the town of Cashel, just to the south of the rock.

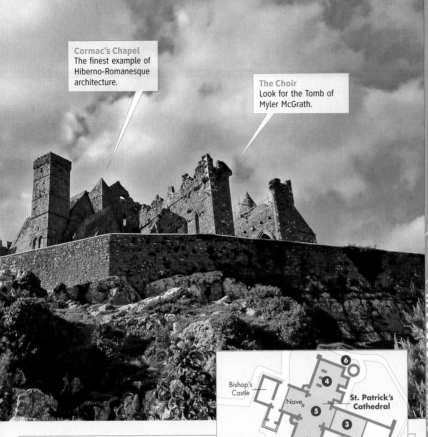

Cormac's Chapel
The finest example of Hiberno-Romanesque architecture.

The Choir
Look for the Tomb of Myler McGrath.

Bishop's Castle

Nave

St. Patrick's Cathedral

South Transept

Tickets

Dormitory

❶ HALL OF THE VICAR'S CHORAL
Built in the 15th century—though topped with a modern reconstruction of a beautifully corbeled medieval ceiling—this was once the domain of the cathedral choristers.

The Museum Located in the hall's undercroft, this collection includes the original St. Patrick's Cross and fast-forwards you to the present thanks to a striking audiovisual display on the Rock entitled the "Stronghold of the Faith."

❷ CORMAC'S CHAPEL
The real showpiece of Cashel is this chapel, built in 1127 by Cormac McCarthy, King of Desmond and Bishop of Cashel. A rare jewel in gleaming red sandstone, it is the finest example of Hiberno-Romanesque architecture. The entry archway carries a tympanum featuring a centaur in a helmet with a bow and arrow aimed at a lion, perhaps a symbol of good over evil. Such work was rare in Irish architecture and points to possible European influence. Preserved within the chapel is a splendid but broken sarcophagus, once believed to be Cormac's final resting place. At the opposite end of the chapel is the nave, where you can look for wonderful medieval paintings now showing through old plasterwork.

ST. PATRICK'S CATHEDRAL

With thick walls that attest to its origin as a fortress, this now-roofless cathedral is the largest building on the site. Built in 1169, it was dedicated on March 17th—St. Patrick's Day. On the theory that ancient churches were oriented to the sunrise on the feast day of their dedicated saint, the cathedral points east, a direction agreeing closely with March 17th. The original cathedral, constructed in a flamboyant variation on Irish Romanesque style, was destroyed by fire in 1495. In ❸ **The Choir**, look for the noted Tomb of Myler McGrath. Note the tombs in the ❹ **North Transept** whose carvings—of the apostles, other saints, and the Beasts of the Apocalypse— are remarkably detailed. The octagonal staircase turret that ascends the cathedral's central tower leads to a series of defensive passages built into the thick walls—from

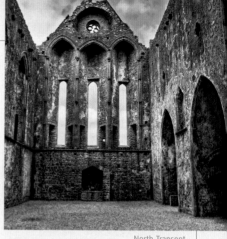

North Transept

the top of the tower, you'll have wonderful views. At the center of the cathedral is the area known as ❺ **The Crossing**, a magnificently detailed arch where the four sections of the building come together.

COMING OF AGE

AD 450—St. Patrick comes to Cashel, bringing the advent of Christianity when King Aengus accepts baptism from Ireland's patron saint.

990—Cashel is fortified by King Brian Boru, the legendary figure who broke the stranglehold of the Danes at the Battle of Clontarf in 1014.

1101—King Murtagh O'Brien, grandson of Brian Boru, proclaims the royal fortress "for God, St. Patrick, and St. Ailbe," making Cashel center of the Irish Church.

1317—The arrival of the Scots: Edward Bruce, brother of Robert I, is inaugurated king of Ireland, and attends Mass on the Rock where he later holds a parliament.

1749—Protestant archbishop Price earns undying infamy by pulling down the roof of the cathedral to rebuild his own church.

Detail of wooden ceiling in the Vicar's Choral, Rock of Cashel

NORTHERN VIEW OF THE ROCK

Bishop's Castle

Central Tower

❻ THE ROUND TOWER

As the oldest building on the Rock, the Round Tower rises 92 feet to command a panoramic view of the entire Vale of Tipperary. Dating back to 995, its construction followed the grim reality of the Viking invasions. A constant lookout was posted here to warn of any advancing armies, and food was always provisioned in the tower so as to outlast any prolonged siege. Note the door 10 feet from the ground, allowing ladders to be pulled up to thwart attackers, some of whom attempted to chip the rock at the base, to little effect.

❼ ST. PATRICK'S CROSS

Directly beyond the Rock's main entrance is this 7-foot-tall High Cross carved from one large block and resting upon what is said to have been the original coronation stone of the Munster kings. The cross was erected in the saint's honor to commemorate his famous visit to Cashel in 450. Upon both sides carved in high relief are two figures—the face of Christ crucified and a robed St. Patrick with his feet resting upon an ox head. Unique among High Crosses, this one has vertical supports on either side, perhaps allusions to the crosses of

the good and bad thieves. A sort of early Irish bible class, these large stone crosses (which were sculpted from the 9th to the 12th centuries) were perfect teaching tools for a population that was largely illiterate. This cross is a faithfully rendered replica—the original now rests in the site museum.

The Crossing

Nave

North Transept

THE ST. PATRICK CONNECTION

While many legends surround Saint Patrick, he was an actual historical figure—his writings, a Latin text dating from the 5th century AD, yield the few undisputed facts about him. Born into a wealthy family in Roman-occupied Britain, he was kidnapped as a young man by Irish marauders and enslaved for six years as a sheepherder on the slopes of Slemish in County Antrim. He escaped, and returned to Britain, but a vision called him back to Ireland to convert the people to Christianity. Arriving in 433, he defied the pagan priests of Tara by kindling the Easter fire on Slane but went on in a peaceful conversion of Ireland to Christianity—not a drop of blood was shed—until his death in AD 460.

St. Patrick's conversion of Ireland was characterized by clever diplomacy: his missionaries were careful to combine elements of then-current druidic ritual with new Christian practice. For example, the Irish Christian church popularized the Feast of all Saints, and arranged for it to be celebrated on November 1, the same day as the great Celtic harvest festival, Samhain. Today's Halloween evolved from this linking of Celtic and Christian holidays.

Clearly a skilled negotiator as well as missionary, St. Patrick wisely preserved the social structure of Ireland, converting the people tribe by tribe. He first attempted to establish the Roman system of dioceses and bishops, but—since Ireland had never been conquered by the Romans—this arrangement did not suit a society without large cities. Instead, the Celts preferred a religious institution introduced by the desert fathers: the monastery, an idea of a "family" of monks being easy to grasp in a tribal society. Over 70 monasteries were founded in the 5th and 6th centuries, and by AD 700 abbots had replaced bishops as the leaders of the Catholic church.

In 457 St. Patrick retired to Saul, where he died. The only relic that can be tied to him is the famous 5th-century iron bell in Dublin's National Museum. Even if it was not, as is traditionally believed, used by the saint, he carried one very like it, and used it to announce his approach.

ROCK OF CASHEL INFO
✉ *Rock of Cashel* ☎ *062/61437* ⊕ *www.heritageireland.ie* 🎟 *€6* ☺ *Mid-Mar.–early-June, daily 9:30–5:30; early-June–mid-Sept., daily 9–7; mid-Sept.–mid-Oct., daily 9–5:30; mid-Oct.–mid-Mar., daily 9–4:30.*

Above: Dublin, St. Patrick's Day parade

Bus Éireann runs buses between Cashel and Cork (€11.70 one-way and 19.80 round-trip; 1½ hours; eight daily) via Cahir (€3.90, 15 minutes) and Fermoy (€11.70, 1 hour 20 minutes). The bus stop for Cork is outside the Bake House on Main St. The Dublin stop (€11.70 one-way, €19.80 round-trip; 3 hours; six daily) is directly opposite. Tickets are available from the nearby Spar shop or you can buy them on the bus.

To head to the Rock of Cashel directly from Dublin, many travelers opt to use the Irish Rail route that heads to the small town of Thurles and then take a 20-minute bus or taxi ride to Cashel.

ESSENTIALS

Visitor Information Cashel Tourist Office ⊠ *Cashel Heritage Centre, Cashel, Co. Tipperary* ☎ *062/62511* ⊕ *www.discoverireland.ie.*

EXPLORING

Fodor's Choice
★

The awe-inspiring, often mist-shrouded **Rock of Cashel** is one of Ireland's most visited sites. *For complete information, see "Towering Glory: The Rock of Cashel."*

Cashel Heritage Centre. In the same building as the town TIO, the Cashel Heritage Centre explains the historic relationship between the town and the Rock and includes a scale model of Cashel as it looked during the 1600s. ⊠ *City Hall, Main St., Cashel, Co. Tipperary* ☎ *062/62511* ⊕ *www.cashel.ie* ⊡ *Free* ⊙ *Mar.–Oct., daily 9:30–5:50; Nov.–Feb., weekdays 9:30–5:30.*

G. P. A. Bolton Library. Located on the grounds of the St. John the Baptist Church of Ireland Cathedral, the G. P. A. Bolton Library has a particularly fine collection of rare books, manuscripts, and maps, some of which date to the beginning of the age of printing in Europe. ⊠ *John St., Cashel, Co. Tipperary* ☎ *062/61944* ⊡ *€2* ⊙ *Mon.–Thurs. 10–2:30.*

WHERE TO EAT AND STAY

For expanded hotel reviews, visit Fodors.com.

$$$$
MODERN IRISH
★

✕ **Chez Hans.** It's rather fitting that this restaurant is in a converted church, as it's become something of a foodies' shrine. Gourmands travel from Dublin and Cork to get their fix of chef Jason Matthia's cuisine, which is contemporary with a hint of nouvelle. He works wonders with fresh Irish ingredients, especially seafood. The cassoulet of seafood—half a dozen varieties of fish and shellfish with a delicate chive velouté—is legendary. Another specialty is panfried Dover sole with parsley butter and pickled cucumber. The atmosphere is wonderful, too, with dark wood and tapestries providing an elegant background for the white linen. They've opened a great café next door if you prefer something more informal. ⑤ *Average main: €33* ⊠ *Moore La., Cashel, Co. Tipperary* ☎ *062/61177* ⊕ *www.chezhans.net* ⌲ *Reservations essential* ⊙ *Closed Sun. and Mon. and late Jan.–early Feb. No lunch.*

$$
HOTEL
Fodor's Choice
★

🛏 **Cashel Palace Hotel.** This grand house truly is a palace in every sense: inside, red-pine paneling, barley-sugar staircases, Corinthian columns, and a surfeit of cosseting antiques all create an air of Georgian volupté, while outside the majestic manse is gorgeously offset by parkland with fountains and centuries-old trees. **Pros:** glorious period main house; great strolling gardens; good restaurant. **Cons:** expensive for this region;

popular for weddings; few in-room facilities. **TripAdvisor:** "lovely stay," "pleasant surprise," "lovely and special old estate." ⑤ *Rooms from: €160* ✉ *Main St., Cashel, Co. Tipperary* ☎ *062/62707* ⊕ *www. cashel-palace.ie* ↪ *21 rooms* ⏐◎⏐ *Breakfast.*

$$
HOTEL
★

⊡ **Dundrum House Hotel.** Nestled beside the River Multeen, 12 km (7½ miles) outside busy Cashel, this imposing, four-story 1730 Georgian house features elaborate plaster ceilings, attractive period furniture, open fires, an old convent chapel (stained-glass windows intact) which is now a cocktail bar, as well as a health spa and grand golf course. **Pros:** good value for Georgian comfort; wonderful parkland views; lively cocktail bar. **Cons:** main-house rooms superior to others; can get a bit noisy when full; attracts flush crowd. **TripAdvisor:** "nice grounds," "excellent escape," "fantastic." ⑤ *Rooms from: €140* ✉ *Dundrum, Co. Tipperary* ☎ *062/71116* ⊕ *www.dundrumhousehotel.com* ↪ *70 rooms, 16 holiday homes* ⏐◎⏐ *Breakfast.*

NIGHTLIFE AND THE ARTS

Bru Boru Cultural Centre. You can enjoy folksinging, storytelling, and dancing from mid-June through August Tuesday through Saturday, at the Bru Boru Centre at the foot of the Rock of Cashel. Entertainment usually begins at 7 pm and costs €20, €50 with dinner. The center also has the "Sounds of History" audiovisual exhibition open all day. ☎ *062/61122* ⊕ *www.bruboru.ie.*

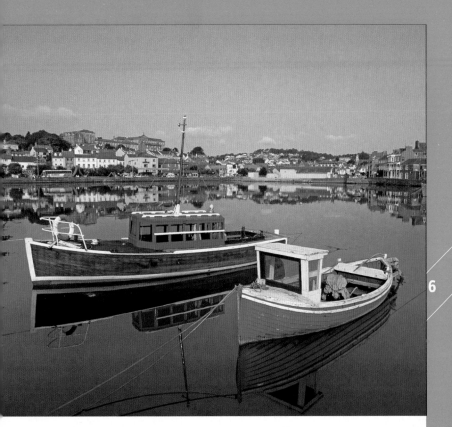

County Cork

WORD OF MOUTH

"The B&Bs in Ireland are much more basic and less elegant than many of the upscale ones in the U.S. As long as you are prepared for this, I think that this is the way to go. You will likely get a delicious breakfast and typically warm hosts who love to help."

—alevi7475

WELCOME TO COUNTY CORK

TOP REASONS TO GO

★ **Blarney Castle:** Visitors line up to kiss the Blarney Stone and acquire the gift of gab. This is an impressive 15th-century tower-house castle with unusual gardens, at their best in daffodil season—early to mid-March.

★ **Cobh:** If you have Irish roots, chances are your ancestors left from characterful Cobh. Its heritage center's Queenstown Story exhibits commemorate the 2.5 million emigrants who sailed from here.

★ **Kinsale:** This picturesque port, long a favored haven of sailors, is famed for its fine dining in tiny front-parlor eateries. It's also a chic place to see and be seen—the Irish St-Tropez.

★ **The Cork Coastline:** On the drive from Kinsale to Skibbereen you'll encounter charming little villages and unspoiled scenery.

★ **Bantry House:** One of Ireland's finest stately homes, packed with treasures from all over Europe, stands on a breathtaking bluff.

1 Cork City and Environs. Identifying Cork as Ireland's second-largest city is misleading—it has just one-tenth the population of Dublin, and its character is more along the lines of a college town, which it is, than a metropolis. That means lively pubs, quirky cafés, and lots of good music, trad and otherwise.

GETTING ORIENTED

After exploring the delights of Cork City, use it as a base to explore the county's famed wonders, including Blarney Castle. Embark on a gastronomic adventure by traveling east to Midleton and Shanagarry—famed respectively for their whiskey and culinary traditions. Shanagarry, in rich farming country, also has a local tradition of craft pottery. Due south is fashionable Kinsale, while westward lies Skibbereen and picture-perfect Bantry. From here a cliff-top road with stunning views leads to ruggedly beautiful Glengarriff.

6

2 East Cork. Products of the rich farming land east of Cork City used to include whiskey: see how it was made at the Jameson Experience in Midleton, just a short drive from Ballymaloe House, pioneer of the New Irish cuisine. The long, flat sandy beaches here—a summertime favorite with Irish holidaymakers—are great for windswept walks year-round.

3 West Cork. The resort town of Kinsale is the gateway to an attractive rocky coastline east and west of Skibbereen. The area is known for its atmospheric pubs and cottage restaurants.

4 Bantry Bay. At the top of the long sea inlet is the imposing Georgian mansion, Bantry House, just outside Bantry Town. The road between here and subtropical Glengarriff climbs high above the water, offering sweeping views of the bay; the hills of the Beara Peninsula are a scenic highlight.

Updated
by Alannah
Hopkin

The place names in this region have an undeniable Irish lilt: Blarney, where you can acquire the gift of the gab, famine-wracked Skibbereen, and beautiful Bantry Bay. But just as evocative is the scenery around every other turn in the road.

With its striking southwestern landscape, charming towns, mild climate, and deep-rooted history, the county of Cork is perennially popular with visitors. The county may be Ireland's largest, Cork may be Ireland's second-biggest city, and Kinsale the largest beep on the Irish foodie radar screen, but nearly everything else here is small-scale and friendly. The towns are tiny and the roads are narrow and twisting. Brightly painted villages and toy harbors encourage you to stop and linger. From Kinsale along the coast to Glengarriff, miles of pretty lanes meander through farmland. Indeed, this is Ireland's picture-postcard country.

But as you look over the fuchsia-laden hedges that ring thriving dairy farms or stop at a wayside restaurant to sample locally sourced beef, it's difficult to imagine that a century and a half ago this area was decimated by famine. Thousands perished in fields and workhouses, and thousands more took "coffin ships" from Cobh in Cork Harbour to the New World. The region was battered again during both the war for independence and the civil war that were fought with intensity in and around "Rebel Cork" between 1919 and 1921. Economic recovery didn't pick up until the late 1960s, and tourist development did not surge until the mid-1990s.

During the Irish economic boom, large sections of Cork's city center were rebuilt with an array of all-weather shopping malls. However, the landmark buildings survived and the streetscape got a much-needed face-lift in 2005, Cork's year as European Capital of Culture. The lilting up-and-down accent of Cork City's locals will immediately charm you, as will the generally festive air that prevails in its streets, making many visitors assume that some kind of festival is going on, even on those rare occasions when it is not. Cork has a reputation as Ireland's festival city, with jazz, film, and choral music festivals and the Midsummer Arts Festivals all attracting huge, good-natured crowds.

COUNTY CORK PLANNER

WHEN TO GO

The best times to visit County Cork are from mid-March to June and in September and October. July and August are the peak holiday periods. Roads are more crowded, prices are higher, and the best places are booked in advance. March can be chilly, with daily temperatures in the 40s and 50s. The average high in June is 18°C (65°F). May and June are the sunniest months, while May and September are the driest ones. From November to March, daylight hours are short, the weather is damp, and many places close.

FESTIVALS AND EVENTS

Cork is known as Ireland's festival city. The oldest event is the **Cork Film Festival** (⊕ *www.corkfilmfest.org*), in the second week in November, and the biggest the **Guinness Cork Jazz Festival** (⊕ *www.guinnessjazzfestival. com*), in late October. The **West Cork Chamber Music Festival** (⊕ www. westcorkmusic.ie) brings internationally renowned musicians to perform in the library of Bantry House for 10 days in late June. **Kinsale's Gourmet Festival** (⊕ *www.kinsalerestaurants.com*), a gourmand's delight, creates a party atmosphere all over town in early October.

PLANNING YOUR TIME

When you plan a trip to County Cork, you'll need to make a pick of the ports. The biggest one, Cobh, to the east of the Cork City, was the point of embarkation for most 19th-century Irish transatlantic passengers and it retains a strong whiff of nostalgia. Dominated by its tall-spired cathedral, the town, filled with 19th-century buildings, climbs vertiginously up- and downhill and faces southward out to sea. Kinsale is more of a village than a town, built by a hill at one end of an unspoiled fjordlike harbor. With its yacht marinas and tempting restaurants, Kinsale has a cosmopolitan air, but it also offers serious history at Charles Fort. Timoleague is a sleepy hamlet, nestled beside the romantic ruins of its abbey. Many visitors regard Castletownshend as the prettiest village, while others prefer the sheltered waters of subtropical Glengarriff.

IF YOU HAVE THREE DAYS

If you're here for a short stay—three days or fewer—you'd do well to base yourself in Cork City, which is easy to explore on foot. Allow a day to take in the sights of the city center, including the Crawford Art Gallery, the indoor English Market, and Patrick Street's boutiques. On the second day, visit Blarney Castle; from there it's a half-hour drive to Cork Harbour, where you can visit Fota Island and Cobh. On the third day head for Kinsale, worth a day itself, or you can head to the scenic coast of West Cork, which can be comfortably driven in a day. The narrow roads here meander through attractive waterside villages to the splendid prospect of Bantry Bay, overlooked by the stately Bantry House. A few miles farther west is another highlight, the sheltered inlet of Glengarriff. Return that night to Kinsale or Cork, both handy for the airport.

GETTING HERE AND AROUND

AIR TRAVEL

Cork Airport, 5 km (3 miles) south of Cork City on the Kinsale road, has direct flights daily to Dublin, London (Heathrow, Gatwick, and Stansted), Manchester, East Midlands, Paris, and Malaga, and direct flights to many other European cities. Shannon Airport, 26 km (16 miles) west of Limerick City, is the point of arrival for many transatlantic flights, including direct flights from Atlanta, Chicago, Philadelphia, Toronto (summer only), and New York City (from both JFK and Newark); it also has regular flights from the United Kingdom and many European cities.

Airports Cork Airport ☎ 021/431–3131 ⊕ www.corkairport.com. **Shannon Airport** ☎ 061/712–000 ⊕ www.shannonairport.com.

AIRPORT TRANSFERS Bus Éireann has a bus link between Cork Airport and the Cork Parnell Place Bus Station about every 30 minutes, and a route between the airport and Kinsale roughly every hour. Tickets for both destinations can be bought on the bus.

Shuttles Bus Éireann ☎ 90/648–4406 ⊕ www.buseireann.ie.

BUS TRAVEL

Bus Éireann and Aircoach operate express buses from Dublin, Galway, Shannon Airport, Limerick, Tralee, and Killarney to Cork City. Be warned: even so-called express buses from Dublin make at least two off-motorway stops en route, so the journey takes from four to five hours, depending on traffic. Citylink buses serve many Irish cities, including Cork City; book online for the best prices. Local buses tend to stop running in the early evening, which rules out many day trips—unless you want to spend most of the day on the bus. As a general rule, the smaller and more remote the town, the less frequent its bus service. Consult with hotel concierges, tourist board staffers, or the bus lines' websites for bus schedules.

Bus Information Aircoach ☎ 01/844–7118 ⊕ www.aircoach.ie. **Bus Éireann** ☎ 01/836–6111 in Dublin 021/450–8188 in Cork ⊕ www.buseireann.ie. **Citylink** ☎ 091/564–164 ⊕ www.citylink.ie. **Cork Bus Station Parnell Place** ✉ Parnell Pl. and Merchant's Quay, Cork City ☎ 021/450–8188, 021/422–2129 recorded message off-hrs [6 pm–9 am].

CAR TRAVEL

Scenery is the main attraction in County Cork, and unless you're a biker or hiker, the best option for taking it in is to rent a car, although regional buses do run on main roads. Once behind the wheel, plan to adopt the local pace—slow. Covering about 100 km (60 miles) a day is ideal, with many stops along the way. Speed is dictated to some degree by the roads: most are small, with one lane in each direction and plenty of bends and hills.

The main driving route from Dublin is the M7 motorway, connecting with the M8 in Portlaoise to continue 257 km (160 miles) on to Cork City. The journey from Dublin to Cork takes less than three hours. A car is the ideal way to explore this region's scenic routes and attractive but remote towns. Except for Cork City, where you're best off using a garage, parking is relatively easy to figure out.

ROAD CONDITIONS   County Cork has good, wide main roads (National Primary Routes) and better-than-average local roads (National Secondary Routes), both known as "N" routes. Regional ("R") routes can be narrow. They're also used by hikers and cyclists from Easter to October, as well as local traffic, which can take the form of school buses and huge trucks serving the local agricultural co-ops. The speed limit on these Regional routes is 80 km per hour (50 mph), but use your common sense and adjust your speed accordingly. If traffic builds up behind you, it is customary to signal to the left, and slow down (or pull off the road if there is space) to let the locals whiz past.

TAXI TRAVEL

Taxis at Shannon and Cork airports connect with those cities; Shannon to Limerick City costs about €40; from Cork to Cork City Railway Station, about €15. The Taxi Regulator website has full fare details.

Taxis and Information **Cork Taxi Co-op** ☎ *021/427–2222* ⊕ *www.corktaxi.ie.* **Taxi Regulator** ☎ *076/106-4000* ⊕ *taxiregulator.ie.*

TRAIN TRAVEL

Irish Rail–Iarnród Éireann runs direct hourly trains from Dublin Heuston Station to Cork's Kent Station; the trip takes just under three hours. Suburban trains serve Fota Island, Midleton, and Cobh. The journey time to Midleton or Cobh is about 25 minutes.

Train Information **Irish Rail–Iarnód Éireann** ☎ *01/836–6222 for inquiries and booking, 1850/366–222 in Ireland, 021/450–4777 in Cork* ⊕ *www.irishrail.ie.*

For more information on getting here and around, see Travel Smart Ireland.

RESTAURANTS

County Cork, home of the famous Slow Food Ireland movement, has become Ireland's top foodie destination. The mecca: Ballymaloe House, where Myrtle Allen pioneered New Irish cuisine and her daughter-in-law, the celebrated cookery author Darina Allen, learned her trade. Adventurous, well-traveled chefs throughout County Cork make the most of the first-rate local specialties: succulent beef and lamb, game in the winter, fresh seafood, and farmhouse cheeses. The best restaurants are not all in towns: even tiny villages might boast a gastro pub. *Prices in the reviews are the average cost of a main course at dinner or, if dinner is not served, at lunch.*

HOTELS

County Cork's great country-house accommodations include Ballymaloe House in east Cork, along with the guest wing at magnificent Bantry House. At the spectrum's other end is the uniquely Irish farmhouse bed-and-breakfast, such as the Glen Country House, where you are welcomed by the family dogs and treated as a long-lost friend. In between are excellent family-owned and -run traditional hotels, such as the Blarney Castle Hotel on Blarney's village green and the Seaview in Ballylickey on Bantry Bay. *Prices in the reviews are the lowest cost of a standard double room in high season. For expanded reviews, facilities, and current deals, visit Fodors.com.*

TOURS

Adams & Butler organizes self-driven or chauffeur-driven group tours with accommodations in private country houses and castles. It also conducts special-interest tours; topics include gardens, architecture, ghosts, and golf.

Irish Ways Walking Tours arranges group and self-guided walking tours on the Beara Way and the Sheep's Head Peninsula.

Adrian Wistreich of the Kinsale Pottery & Arts Centre puts together vacation packages that include hands-on pottery, jewelry making, stained-glass, and other workshops.

SouthWestWalks Ireland arranges themed walks along the coast of West Cork, around the Sheep's Head and Beara peninsulas in Bantry Bay.

Michael Martin's Titanic Trail is a 60-minute guided walking tour of Cobh that covers *Titanic* sites and history; it departs daily at 11 am from the Commodore Hotel (€9.50). Dermot Ryan, a native of Kinsale and a local history enthusiast, leads Kinsale Heritage Town Walks daily at 10:30 am and 4:30 pm (€5; children free). Don Herlihy's Historic Stroll in Old Kinsale departs from the town's tourist office daily at 11:15; you'll learn about Kinsale's links to "Man Friday" and the truth about Kinsale Hookers pirates.

Bus Éireann offers a range of daylong and half-day guided bus tours from June to September. Book these at the Cork Bus Station Parnell Place or at any tourist office. Full-day tours cost about €32, half-day €16. Bus Éireann also offers open-top bus tours of Cork City (€6) on some summer days.

Tour Contacts Bus Éireann Tours and Trips ☎ *021/450–8188 in Cork* ⊕ *www.buseireann.ie/inner.php?id=273.* **Adams & Butler** ✉ *58 Foster Ave., the Carriage House, Mount Merrion, Co. Dublin* ☎ *01/288–9355* ⊕ *www.adamsandbutler.com.* **Don & Barry's Kinsale Historic Stroll** ✉ *Kinsale* ☎ *021/477–2873* ⊕ *www.historicstrollkinsale.com.* **Irish Ways Walking Tours** ✉ *Belfield Bike Shop, University College, Dublin* ☎ *01/260–0749* ⊕ *www.irishways.com.* **Kinsale Heritage Town Walks** ✉ *Kinsale* ☎ *021/477–2729* ⊕ *www.kinsaleheritage.com.* **Kinsale Pottery & Arts Centre** ✉ *Olcote, Ballinacurra, Kinsale, Co. Cork* ☎ *021/477–7758* ⊕ *www.kinsaleceramics.com.* **SouthWestWalks Ireland** ✉ *6 Church St., Tralee* ☎ *066/712–8733* ⊕ *www.southwestwalksireland.com.* **The Titanic Trail** ✉ *Cobh* ☎ *021/481–5211* ⊕ *www.titanic.ie.*

VISITOR INFORMATION

Fáilte Ireland tourist information offices are open year-round in Bantry, Blarney, Clonakilty, Cobh (Cork Harbour), Cork Airport (Arrivals), Cork City, and Skibbereen. Those in Glengarriff, Kinsale, and Midleton are open from mid-March to mid-September or the end of October. Fáilte Ireland's Discover Cork Web page has details about locations and hours.

Discover Cork ⊕ *www.discoverireland.ie/Cork.*

CORK CITY AND ENVIRONS

The major metropolis of the South, Cork City makes a great base from which to explore the whole southern region. Though it's Ireland's second-largest city, it runs a distant second, with a population of 123,000, roughly one-tenth the size of Dublin. In the last decade, with high prices and overcrowding in Dublin, Cork became the new hot spot for urban thrills. Groups of Europeans frequently pop over for a weekend of partying, as the city is a spirited place, with a formidable pub culture, a lively traditional-music scene, a respected and progressive university, attractive art galleries, and offbeat cafés. Nearby Blarney, northwest of Cork City on R617, makes a perfect day trip. Blarney's attractions are Blarney Castle and the famous Blarney Stone.

CORK CITY

253 km (157 miles) southwest of Dublin.

Cork City received its first charter in 1185 from Prince John of Norman England, and it takes its name from the Irish word *corcaigh,* meaning "marshy place." The original 6th-century settlement was spread over 13 small islands in the River Lee. Major development occurred during the 17th and 18th centuries with the expansion of the butter trade, and many attractive Georgian-design buildings with wide bowfront windows were constructed during this time. As late as 1770 Cork's present-day main streets—Grand Parade, Patrick Street, and the South Mall—were submerged under the Lee. Around 1800, when the Lee was partially dammed, the river divided into two streams that now flow through the city, leaving the main business and commercial center on an island, not unlike Paris's Île de la Cité. As a result, the city has a number of bridges and quays, which, although initially confusing, add greatly to the port's unique character.

Cork can be very "Irish" (hurling, Gaelic football, televised plowing contests, music pubs, and peat smoke). But depending on what part of town you're in, Cork can also be distinctly un-Irish—the sort of place where hippies, gays, and farmers drink at the same pub.

PLANNING YOUR TIME

You can tour the city's center in a morning or an afternoon, depending on how much you plan to shop along the way. To really see everything, however, allow a full day, with a break for lunch at the Farmgate Café in the English Market. Note that the Crawford Art Gallery and the English Market are closed on Sunday.

GETTING HERE AND AROUND

The drive from Dublin to Cork City on the M7/M8 motorway takes just under three hours. The drive from Shannon Airport to Cork takes two-and-a-half hours, with motorway for some stretches. Use the tunnel (toll €1.80) to avoid traveling through the center of Limerick. Cork is about an hour-and-a-half drive from Killarney. Cork is well served by express buses. The main Cork Bus Station Parnell Place has luggage-storage facilities (manned from 9 to 6). Irish Rail–Iarnród Éireann direct trains from Dublin Heuston Station to Cork's Kent Station run hourly. The trip takes just under three hours.

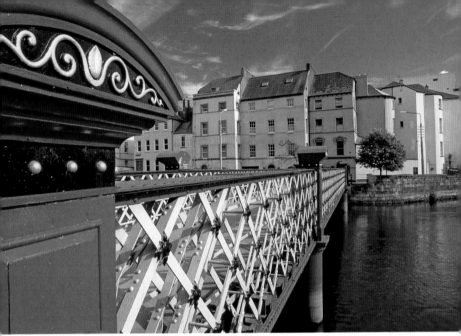

As the River Lee flows through Cork's center, delightful bridges and quays add to the city's unique character.

If you're driving within Cork City, it's advisable to use a multistory parking garage, as on-street parking can be hard to find and the process of paying for it can be difficult to master. Cork's city center is compact and walkable, but if you want to bus the mile to the university campus, pick up a No. 8 outside Debenham's department store on Patrick Street. A great introductory tour is the hop-on, hop-off Cork City Tour run by Cronin's Coaches, a double-decker bus that departs (March–October, €14) from the Tourist Information Office on Grand Parade between 9:30 am and 5 pm.

ESSENTIALS

Transportation Contacts **Cork Parnell Place Bus Station** ⊠ *Parnell Pl. and Merchant's Quay, Cork City, Co. Cork* ☎ *021/450–8188, 021/422–2129 recorded message off-hrs (6 pm–9 am).* **Cronin's Coaches** ☎ *021/430–9090* ⊕ *www.croninscoaches.com.* **Kent Station** ⊠ *Lower Glanmire Rd., Cork City, Co. Cork* ☎ *021/450–4544 for automated timetable.*

Visitor Information **Cork City Tourist Office** ⊠ *Grand Parade, Cork City, Co. Cork* ☎ *021/425–5100* ⊕ *www.discoverireland.ie/Corktio.*

EXPLORING

TOP ATTRACTIONS

Cork Vision Centre. In the renovated St. Peter's Church, an 18th-century building in what was the bustling heart of medieval Cork, this historical society provides an excellent introduction to the city's history and geography. The highlight is a detailed 1:500-scale model of the city, showing how it has changed over the ages. ⊠ *North Main St., Washington Village,*

Cork City, Co. Cork ☎ *021/427–9925* ⊕ *www.corkvisioncentre.com* ☑ *Free* ☉ *Tues.–Sat. 10–5.*

★ **Crawford Art Gallery.** The large red-brick building was built in 1724 as the customs house and is now home to Ireland's leading provincial art gallery. An imaginative expansion has added gallery space for visiting exhibitions and adventurous shows of modern Irish artists. The permanent collection includes landscape paintings depicting Cork in the 18th and 19th centuries. Take

WORD OF MOUTH

"On first trip with friends, we stayed in Cork. Let's just say we got lost, found the city confusing to drive. But, it was the best nightlife of our entire trip. Met some great locals and lost no more. Drank lots, stayed out till dawn, and learned how to insult each other the Cork way."

—uptowngirl2418

special note of works by Irish painters William Leech (1881–1968), Daniel Maclise (1806–70), James Barry (1741–1806), and Nathaniel Grogan (1740–1807). The café, run by the Allen family of Ballymaloe, is a good place for a light lunch or a homemade sweet. ☒ *Emmet Pl., City Center South, Cork City, Co. Cork* ☎ *021/490–7855* ⊕ *www.crawfordartgallery.ie* ☑ *Free* ☉ *Mon.–Sat. 10–5; Thurs. 10–8 pm.*

★ **English Market.** Food lovers (and, who, pray, isn't?): be sure to make a bee line for one of the misleadingly small entrances to this large and famous mecca for foodies. Fetchingly housed in an elaborate, brick-and-cast-iron Victorian building, it bears the official name of the Princes Street Market, but it's also known locally as the Covered Market along with its general nickname. Among the 140 stalls, keep an eye out for the Alternative Bread Co., which produces more than 40 varieties of handmade bread every day. Iago, Sean Calder-Potts's deli, has fresh pasta, lots of cheeses, and charcuterie. The Olive Stall sells olive oil, olive-oil soap, and olives from Greece, Spain, France, and Italy. Kay O'Connell's Fish Stall, in the legendary fresh-fish alley, purveys local smoked salmon. O'Reilly's Tripe and Drisheen is the last existing retailer of a Cork specialty, tripe (cow's stomach), and *drisheen* (blood sausage). Upstairs is the Farmgate, an excellent café. ☒ *Entrances on Grand Parade and Princes St., City Center South, Cork City, Co. Cork* ⊕ *www.corkenglishmarket.ie* ☉ *Mon.–Sat. 9:30–5:30.*

Patrick Street. Extending from Grand Parade in the south to Patrick's Bridge in the north, Panna (as it's known locally) is Cork's main shopping thoroughfare. It has been designed as a pedestrian-priority area with wide walks and special streetlights. A mainstream mix of department stores, boutiques, pharmacies, and bookshops lines the way. ■ **TIP→ If you look above some of the plate-glass storefronts, you can see examples of the bowfront Georgian windows that are emblematic of old Cork.** The street saw some of the city's worst fighting during the Irish War of Independence. ☒ *City Center South, Cork City, Co. Cork.*

Patrick's Bridge. From here you can look along the curve of Patrick Street and north across the River Lee to St. Patrick's Hill, with its tall Georgian houses. The hill is so steep that steps are cut into the pavement. Tall ships that served the butter trade used to load up beside the bridge at

Cork City

Merchant's Quay before heading downstream to the sea. The design of the large, redbrick shopping center on the site evokes the warehouses of old. ⊠ *Patrick St., City Center South, Cork City, Co. Cork.*

Paul Street. A narrow stretch between the River Lee and Patrick Street and parallel to both, Paul Street is the backbone of the trendy shopping district that now occupies Cork's old French Quarter. The area was first settled by Huguenots fleeing religious persecution in France. Musicians and other street performers often entertain passersby in the Rory Gallagher Piazza, named for the late rock guitarist, whose family was from Cork. The shops here offer the best in modern Irish design—from local fashions to hand-blown glass. ⊠ *City Center South, Cork City, Co. Cork.*

St. Anne's Church. The church's pepper-pot Shandon steeple, which has a four-sided clock and is topped with a golden, salmon-shaped weather vane, is visible from throughout the city and is the chief reason why St. Anne's is so frequently visited. The Bells of Shandon were immortalized in an atrocious but popular 19th-century ballad of that name. Your reward for climbing the 120-foot-tall tower is the chance to ring the bells, with the assistance of sheet tune cards, out over Cork. Beside the church, **Firkin Crane,** Cork's 18th-century butter market, houses two small performing spaces. Adjacent is the **Shandon Craft Market.** ⊠ *Church St., Shandon, Cork City, Co. Cork* ☎ *021/450–5906* 🎟 *€6* ⊙ *Easter–Oct., Mon.–Sat. 10–4; Nov.–Easter, Mon.–Sat. 11–3.*

St. Fin Barre's Cathedral. On the site that was the entrance to medieval Cork, this compact, three-spire Gothic cathedral, which was completed in 1879, belongs to the Church of Ireland and houses a 3,000-pipe organ. According to tradition, St. Fin Barre established a monastery on this site around AD 650 and is credited as being the founder of Cork. ⊠ *Bishop St., Washington Village, Cork City, Co. Cork* ☎ *021/496–3387* ⊕ *cathedral.cork.anglican.org* ⊙ *Weekdays 9:30–5, Sat. 10–5.*

Triskel Arts Centre. An excellent place to get the pulse of artsy goings-on in town, the Triskel occupies converted town houses and a former church. The lively, multidisciplinary community arts center has a popular coffee shop. ⊠ *Tobin St., Washington Village, Cork City, Co. Cork* ☎ *021/427–2022* ⊕ *www.triskelartscentre.ie* 🎟 *Free* ⊙ *Mon.–Sat. 9:30–5:30.*

★ **University College Cork.** The Doric, porticoed gates of UCC stand about 2 km (1 mile) from the city center. The college, which has a student body of roughly 10,000, is a constituent of the National University of Ireland. The main quadrangle is a fine example of 19th-century university architecture in the Tudor-Gothic style, reminiscent of many Oxford and Cambridge colleges. Several ancient ogham stones are on display in the North Quadrangle (near the visitor center), and the renovated Crawford Observatory's 1860 telescope can be visited. The Honan Collegiate Chapel, east of the quadrangle, was built in 1916 and modeled on the 12th-century, Hiberno-Romanesque style, best exemplified by the remains of Cormac's Chapel at Cashel. The UCC chapel's stained-glass windows, as well as its collection of art and crafts, altar furnishings, and textiles in the Celtic Revival style, are noteworthy. Three large, modern buildings have been successfully integrated with the old, including the Boole Library, named for mathematician George Boole (1815–64), who was a professor at the college. Both indoors and out the campus is enhanced by works of contemporary Irish art. The **Lewis Glucksman Gallery**, in a striking new building astride the college's entrance gates, displays works from the college's outstanding collection and hosts cutting-edge contemporary-art exhibitions. ⊠ *College Rd., Western Road, Cork City, Co. Cork* ☎ *021/490–1876*

> **GRANDDAD OF THE COMPUTER**
>
> George Boole (1815–64), a University College professor, is one of the heroes of the computer age. Despite growing up in a working-class family with limited access to education, he developed into a mathematical genius, inventing Boolean algebra—the foundation upon which computer science was built.

⊕ *www.ucc.ie* ⬛ *Free* ☉ *Visitor center weekdays 9–5; call for hrs Easter wk, July, Aug., and mid-Dec.–mid-Jan.; guided tours by arrangement.*

WORTH NOTING

Bishop Lucey Park. This tiny green park in the heart of the city opened in 1985 in celebration of the 800th anniversary of Cork's Norman charter. During its excavation, workers unearthed portions of the city's original fortified walls, now preserved just inside the arched entrance. Sculptures by contemporary Cork artists are found throughout the park. ⊠ *Grand Parade, Washington Village, Cork City, Co. Cork.*

☾ **Cork City Gaol.** This castlelike building contains an austere, 19th-century prison. Life-size wax figures occupy the cells, and sound effects illustrate the appalling conditions that prevailed into the 20th century. Also here, in the Governor's House, the **Radio Museum Experience** exhibits genuine artifacts from the 1923 radio station, 6CK, and tells the story of radio broadcasting in Cork. ⊠ *Sunday's Well Rd., Sunday's Well, Cork City, Co. Cork* ☎ *021/430–5022* ⊕ *www.corkcitygaol.com* ⬛ *€8* ☉ *Nov.–Feb., daily 10–4; Mar.–Oct., daily 9:30–5.*

Cork Opera House. This unattractive concrete hulk erected in 1965 replaced an ornate and much-loved opera house that was ruined in a fire. Later attempts to integrate the opera house with its neighbor, the Crawford Municipal Art Gallery, have softened the grim facade of what remains the only show in town for opera buffs. The piazza outside has sidewalk cafés and street performers. ⊠ *Emmet Pl., at Lavitt's Quay, City Center South, Cork City, Co. Cork* ☎ *021/427–0022* ⊕ *www.corkoperahouse.ie.*

Court House. A landmark in the very center of Cork, this magnificent classical building has an imposing Corinthian portico and is still used as the district's main courthouse. The exterior has been cleaned and fully restored and looks every bit as good as it did when it was built in 1835. ⊠ *Washington St., Washington Village, Cork City, Co. Cork* ☎ *021/427–2706* ☉ *Weekdays 9–5.*

☾ **Fitzgerald's Park.** This small, well-tended park is beside the River Lee's north channel in the west of the city. The park contains the **Cork Public Museum**, a Georgian mansion that houses a well-planned exhibit about Cork's history since ancient times, with a strong emphasis on the city's Republican history. ⊠ *Western Road, Cork City, Co. Cork* ☎ *021/427–0679* ⊕ *www.corkcity.ie/services/recreationamenityculture/museum* 🖼 *Free* 🕙 *Mon.–Sat. 11–1 and 2:15–5, Sun. 3–5; closed Sun. Oct.–Mar.*

General Post Office. Dominating a street otherwise occupied by boutiques, jewelry stores, and antiques shops, this neoclassical building with an elegant colonnaded facade was once Cork's opera house. ⊠ *Oliver Plunkett St., City Center South, Cork City, Co. Cork* ☎ *021/427–2000* 🕙 *Weekdays 9–5:30, Sat. 9–5.*

> **REBEL CORK**
>
> "Rebel Cork" suffered great damage during the Irish War of Independence (1919–21), when much of its center was burned down. Cork is now regaining some of its former glory as a result of sensitive commercial development and an ongoing program of inner-city renewal.

QUICK BITES

Long Valley. The friendly, old Long Valley pub, popular with artists, writers, students, and eccentrics, serves tea, coffee, pints, and sandwiches. The dark, mismatched interior is like a time warp taking you back to early-20th-century Cork. Some of the booths are built from wood salvaged from wrecked ocean liners—ask to be told the story. The generously filled sandwiches, made to order from home-cooked meat and thickly cut bread, also seem to belong to another age. ⊠ *Winthrop St., City Center South, Cork City, Co. Cork* ☎ *021/427–2144.*

Mardyke. This popular riverside walk links the city center with Fitzgerald's Park. Beside it is a field where cricket, very much a minority sport in Ireland, is played on summer weekends. ⊠ *Western Road, Cork City, Co. Cork.*

OFF THE BEATEN PATH

St. Mary's Pro-Cathedral. It's worth hiking up to St. Mary's, which dates from 1808, only if you're interested in tracing your Cork ancestors. Its presbytery has records of births and marriages dating from 1784. ⊠ *Cathedral Walk, Shandon, Cork City, Co. Cork* ☎ *021/430–4325* ⊕ *www.corkcathedral.ie* 🖼 *Free* 🕙 *Daily 9–6.*

WHERE TO EAT

$$

VEGETARIAN

★

✕**Café Paradiso.** The Mediterranean/Eastern fusion-style food here is so tasty that even dedicated meat eaters forget that it's vegetarian. Irish owner-chef Denis Cotter, who has published two acclaimed cookbooks, garners raves for his risottos with seasonal vegetables, his *gougère-choux* (cheese-flavor pastries) with savory fillings, and his homemade desserts. The simple café-style dining room is busy and colorful, with enthusiastic young waiters who love to recite the daily specials (which might include feta, pistachio, and couscous cake on citrus greens with sweet and hot pepper relish). The food is creatively arranged on massive platters or bowls, which add a sense of occasion. The restaurant is midway between the courthouse and the university. You can also stay the night here: there are two attractive rooms for two available for around €130 a night, or €200 including dinner. $ *Average main: €23* ⊠ *16*

Great resources like the English Market have made Cork a foodie mecca. Her Majesty Queen Elizabeth's walkabout here was a highlight of her first visit to Ireland, in 2011.

Lancaster Quay, Western Road, Cork City, Co. Cork ☎ *021/427–7939* ⊕ *www.cafeparadiso.ie* ⊗ *Closed Sun., Mon., and last 2 wks of Aug. No lunch Sun.–Thurs.*

$ ✕ **Farmgate Café.** One of the best—and busiest—informal lunch spots
IRISH in town is on a terraced gallery above the fountain at the Princes Street entrance to the atmospheric English Market. All ingredients used at the café are purchased in the market below. One side of the gallery opens onto the market and is self-service; the other side is glassed in and has table service (reservations advised). Tripe and *drisheen* (blood sausage) is one dish that is always on the menu; daily specials include less challenging but no less traditional dishes, such as corned beef with *colcannon* (potatoes and cabbage mashed with butter and seasonings) and loin of smoked bacon with *champ* (potatoes mashed with scallions or leeks). ⑤ *Average main: €14* ⊠ *English Market, City Center South, Cork City, Co. Cork* ☎ *021/427–8134* ⊕ *www.corkenglishmarket.ie* ⊗ *Closed Sun. No dinner.*

$$ ✕ **Fenn's Quay.** This tiny city-center restaurant, on the ground floor of
ECLECTIC a 250-year-old Georgian house, is always buzzing with a faithful local clientele—legal eagles from the nearby courthouse at lunch, theater- and moviegoers at dinner. The char-grilled fillet steak with chunky chips has achieved legendary status: some regulars can't bring themselves to order anything else. But there are other good options: fish from the nearby market is given robust, unfussy treatment, and vegetarian offerings include a twice-baked goat cheese soufflé with apple-and-walnut salad. The ginger-and-toffee sticky pudding is a dessert specialty. The decor is simple, with bright red café-style chairs and tan banquettes, but

striking modern paintings supply a dose of character. $ *Average main: €23* ✉ *Fenn's Quay, Sheares St., Washington Village, Cork City, Co. Cork* ☎ *021/427–9527* ⊕ *www.fennsquay.com* ☾ *Closed Sun.*

$$$

FRENCH

★

✕ **Flemings Silver Grange House.** On a hillside overlooking the river, this stately Georgian house is set in extensive grounds, which include a kitchen garden that supplies the restaurant. Classical French food is the forte of owner-chef Michael Fleming, and it's served, appropriately, in a dining room decorated in the French Empire style with plush Louis XV–style chairs, gilt-frame mirrors, and crystal chandeliers. Local ingredients are important: a starter of panfried foie gras is accompanied by black pudding from West Cork and glazed apple; it's a favorite with the regulars. Other standout items include the grilled monkfish from Fleming's hometown, Courtmacsherry, served with a basil oil dressing and red wine sauce, and the fillet of beef with wild mushrooms, red onion confit, and red wine sauce. Ask about the special-value dine-and-stay package at this "restaurant with rooms." $ *Average main: €31* ✉ *Silver Grange House, Lower Glanmire Rd., Tivoli, Cork City, Co. Cork* ☎ *021/482–1621* ⊕ *www.flemingsrestaurant.ie* ☾ *No lunch.*

$$$

EUROPEAN

Fodor's Choice

★

✕ **Greenes.** Tucked away on a cobbled patio accessible only on foot, this surprising haven is part of a Victorian warehouse conversion that also contains Hotel Isaacs. The stone and redbrick walls are the backdrop for a minimalist modern interior with tall-back green rattan chairs and small tables with linen place mats. The real surprise is out back where a gigantic rock-wall waterfall makes a stunning backdrop to a dining terrace. The ambitious French chef, Federic Desormeaux, has created a menu featuring classic French and Mediterranean cuisine. Highlights include the 10-ounce rib-eye steak with a brandy pepper sauce and dauphinoise potatoes and the king scallops and tiger prawns with fresh pappardelle pasta. Classic desserts with a twist include mango crème brûlée, and banoffee pie with crème anglaise. $ *Average main: €25* ✉ *Hotel Isaacs, 48 MacCurtain St., City Center North, Cork City, Co. Cork* ☎ *021/455–2279* ⊕ *www.greenesrestaurant.com* ☾ *No lunch Sat.–Mon.; closed Sun. except a few holidays.*

$

CONTEMPORARY

✕ **Isaacs.** Cross Patrick's Bridge to the River Lee's north side and turn right to reach this large, atmospheric brasserie in a converted 18th-century warehouse. Modern art, muted jazz, high ceilings, and well-spaced tables with colored wooden tops create a popular informal venue, where the food is taken seriously but the atmosphere is fun. The East-meets-Mediterranean menu features fresh local produce—which isn't so uncommon now, but was revolutionary when Isaac's came on the scene in 1992. Among the many tempting dishes are warm salads with Clonakilty black pudding, crispy duck confit with turnip and caramelized onion purée, and tempura of king prawns with eggplant, scallions, wasabi, pickled ginger, and soy dipping sauce. Service is friendly and efficient. Reservations are advisable Friday and Saturday evenings. $ *Average main: €18* ✉ *48 MacCurtain St., City Center North, Cork City, Co. Cork* ☎ *021/450–3805* ⊕ *www.isaacsrestaurant.ie* ☾ *No lunch Sun.*

$$$$

CONTEMPORARY

★

✕ **Ivory Tower.** Don't be put off by the seedy-looking street entrance to this second-floor restaurant: Seamus O'Connell, the American-born owner-chef here, is one of the stars of the Irish culinary scene. He describes his approach as "trans-ethnic fusion." He has cooked in Mexico and Japan, so his accomplished menu has such quirky, eclectic dishes as wild duck with vanilla, sherry, and jalapeños or pheasant tamale. His mastery of Japanese cooking is impressive, and he also works wonders with Irish staples: combining monkfish cheeks with pearl barley risotto, and in early spring serving a memorable nettle and wild garlic soup. Imaginative presentation, including a surprise taster to set the mood, compensates for the bare wooden floors and stark decor of the corner dining room, as does the house tradition that the maestro himself often serves the dishes he has created. The eight-course tasting menu is a great introduction to O'Connell's inimitable style. $ *Average main: €60* ⊠ *35 Princes St., Washington Village, Cork City, Co. Cork* ☎ *021/427–4665* ⊕ *www.ivorytower.ie* ⊟ *No credit cards* ⊗ *Closed Mon. and Tues., call to confirm Wed. and Sun. No lunch.*

$$$
EUROPEAN
Fodor'sChoice
★

✕ **Jacques.** Hidden away on a tiny side street is one of Cork's favorite restaurants. Its windowless interior, with its warm cream-colored walls and curved art deco–style bar, is carefully lighted to soothe and make you forget the world outside. Sisters Jacque and Eithne Barry have run the place for 25 years, and know their business. Food is always sourced locally from artisan food producers, so it's as fresh and wholesome as it comes. Jacques's cooking lets the flavor shine through, whether in a starter of smoked chicken, fennel, and orange salad, or a main course of roast breast of duck with potato stuffing, red cabbage, and apricot sauce. For dessert try the fruited bread-and-butter pudding, or indulge in a chocolate-and-hazelnut torte. There's a special-value three-course dinner menu at €35. $ *Average main: €25* ⊠ *Phoenix St., off Oliver Plunkett St. near GPO, City Center South, Cork City, Co. Cork* ☎ *021/427–7387* ⊕ *www.jacquesrestaurant.ie* ⊗ *No lunch. Closed Sun.*

$$$
FRENCH
★

✕ **Les Gourmandises.** With a Breton sommelier, Soizic, working the front of the house, and her U.K.- and Dublin-trained Irish husband, Pat Kiely, in the kitchen, you can expect a genuinely interesting eating experience. The restaurant is small, but it has high ceilings, and natural light pours in from an overhead skylight, brightening the quarry-tile floor and red-velvet chairs. Crisp white linen and fresh flowers are typical of Soizic's attention to detail. Pat's training with Marco Pierre White, John Burton Race, and Patrick Guilbaud shows in his mastery of a robust modern French repertoire. Roasted fillet of cod is served with pan-fried foie gras, braised lentils, and sherry-vinegar dressing, while roast pork belly comes with confit potato, black pudding, baked apple, and sage sauce. Good-value set menus are available before 9:30 pm on weekdays and from 6 to 7 pm on Saturdays. $ *Average main: €27* ⊠ *17 Cook St., City Center South, Cork City, Co. Cork* ☎ *021/425–1959* ⊕ *www. lesgourmandises.ie* ⊗ *Closed Mon., last wk in Aug., and 1st wk in Sept. No lunch Tues.–Sat. No dinner Sun.*

$
MODERN IRISH

✕ **Market Lane Restaurant & Bar.** All that remains of this corner building's former identity as a pub is the long mahogany bar. Today it is a popular bistro-style restaurant serving robust, freshly prepared food from an open kitchen. The small wooden-top tables with bentwood chairs or dark leather banquettes, the art deco hat-stands, and the predominantly black and white decor set a Parisian mood. Light floods in from large on-street windows on two sides during long summer evenings. The menu is on the no-frills paper tablemat: turn it over for the dinner menu. The menu is mainly contemporary Irish, with the emphasis on comfort food. Most ingredients are sourced from the city's nearby indoor food market, renowned for fresh fish, traditional butchery, and artisan produce. Meat lovers adore the braised ox-cheek stew, with smoked bacon and thyme mash, or the game pie of venison, pheasant, and wild boar. Other winners include the baked cod with buttered leeks and the homemade butcher's sausages with colcannon (potato mash with cabbage) and a creamy mustard sauce. Vegetarian? The many options include the feta salad with sesame crust, cucumber, olives, and char-grilled watermelon. $ *Average main: €16* ⊠ *5–6 Oliver Plunkett St., City Center South, Cork City, Co. Cork* ☎ *021/427–4710* ⊕ *www.marketlane.ie.*

$

IRISH

✕ **Strasbourg Goose Restaurant.** Tucked away in a pedestrian alley, this is the kind of personable restaurant you dream of finding on vacation and turning into a culinary home away from home. The decor is basic, and a little odd—a baronial wooden chimneypiece, dating from 1901, dominates the small, double-height room, which also has tables on an overhead balcony. (In summer, there are a few tables outside.) Photos of Hollywood stars, glass-block room dividers, and piquant lamps add to the pleasantly eccentric ambience, while the polished tabletops hold just a paper napkin and a knife and fork. People not only come here for the cheerful, bustling ambience but also for value. Choose a daily special like twice-cooked crispy lamb, or Barbary duck breast with gratin potatoes, or for a few euros more, go for the extensive 20-euro menu, served all evening. You can substitute a glass of wine for a dessert, which is good value, given Irish wine prices. $ *Average main: €15* ⊠ *17–18 French Church St., City Center South, Cork City, Co. Cork* ☎ *021/427–9534* ⊕ *www.strasbourggoosecork.com* ⊗ *Closed Mon. No lunch Tues.–Fri.*

WHERE TO STAY

For expanded hotel reviews, visit Fodors.com.

$

HOTEL

★

🏨 **Ambassador Hotel.** An imposing redbrick and cut-limestone Victorian-era nursing home now converted into a comfortable hotel may not be the fanciest hotel in Cork, nor the hippest, but it has the most character and the best view—which you pay for with a steep 10-minute walk up from the town center. **Pros:** strong local atmosphere; amazing views. **Cons:** steep hike up from city; some jarring notes in decor. **TripAdvisor:** "cleanliness and comfort," "beautiful Victorian redbrick house," "full of character." $ *Rooms from: €90* ⊠ *Military Hill, St. Luke's, City Center North, Cork City, Co. Cork* ☎ *021/453–9000* ⊕ *www.ambassadorhotelcork.ie* ⌂ *70 rooms* ◎ *Breakfast.*

$$

HOTEL

🏨 **Clarion Hotel Cork.** Occupying a corner block beside the River Lee, the Clarion is the first arrival of a huge docklands development—as you enter you'll spot black-clad receptionists standing behind simple wooden desks at the far end of the vast, marble-floor lobby, the first indication that this place aspires to boutique-hotel chic. **Pros:** funky; high-luxe rooms, great value. **Cons:** limited car parking; neighborhood quiet after dark; some rooms overlook internal atrium/staircase. **TripAdvisor:** "enjoyable stay," "friendly and comfortable," "best in

Ireland." ⑤ *Rooms from: €160* ✉ *Lapp's Quay, City Center South, Cork City, Co. Cork* ☎ *021/422–4900* ⊕ *www.clarionhotelcorkcity. com* ⤳ *191 rooms* ⦿ *Breakfast.*

$
B&B/INN

⌂ **Gabriel House.** On a bluff high above the railway station and the docks, this huge Victorian house is in Cork's boho northside quarter, a long (10-minute) hike uphill. **Pros:** young, enthusiastic staff; quiet location; oodles of character; rock-bottom prices. **Cons:** nearly hostel-like; some rooms very small; that long climb. **TripAdvisor:** "you get your exercise," "relaxed," "excellent location and wonderful bedrooms." ⑤ *Rooms from: €90* ✉ *Summerhill North, St. Luke's Cross, Montenotte District, Cork City, Co. Cork* ☎ *021/450–0333* ⊕ *www.gabriel-house. ie* ⤳ *28 rooms* ⦿ *Breakfast.*

$
B&B/INN
★

⌂ **Garnish House.** A pair of large Victorian town houses near the university are run by owner-manager Johanna Lucey, who will be offering you tea and homemade chocolate cake before you have even crossed the threshold of her home—the kind of old-fashioned hospitality that is fast disappearing in modern Ireland. **Pros:** a friendly welcome; a genuine Irish experience. **Cons:** seriously unhip; located on a busy main road; rooms book up well in advance. **TripAdvisor:** "exceptional service," "lovely place," "best welcome and breakfast." ⑤ *Rooms from: €98* ✉ *Western Rd., Washington Village, Cork City, Co. Cork* ☎ *021/427–5111* ⊕ *www.garnish.ie* ⤳ *14 rooms* ⦿ *Breakfast.*

$$$
B&B/INN
Fodor's Choice
★

⌂ **Hayfield Manor.** Ruddy with red brick and brightened by white-sash windows, Hayfield Manor's exterior hints at the comfy luxury within—beyond a splendid, carved-wood double staircase, lies a drawing room that's a symphony of gilded silk, with a white-marble fireplace, a 19th-century chandelier, and chic armchairs, a surprisingly soigné modern homage to the country-house style. **Pros:** stylish and chic; good value for luxury accommodations. **Cons:** a taxi or car ride to city center or a dull 15-minute walk; lack of scenic views. **TripAdvisor:** "very high quality and service," "genuine hospitality," "old-world elegance." ⑤ *Rooms from: €199* ✉ *College Rd. and Perrott Ave., Western Road, Cork City, Co. Cork* ☎ *021/484–5900* ⊕ *www.hayfieldmanor.ie* ⤳ *88 rooms* ⦿ *Breakfast.*

$$
HOTEL

⌂ **Imperial Hotel.** Though she cannot compete in size with the grande-dame hotels of bigger cities, the Imperial, which dates to 1813, plays this role with conviction in Cork society (that said, it's worth paying extra for one of the newer rooms, which are larger and quieter than the older ones). **Pros:** great central location; genuine Cork experience. **Cons:** some standard bedrooms are very small; quiet rooms have no view; popular venue for wedding receptions. **TripAdvisor:** "excellent location," "everything on your doorstep," "lovely friendly staff." ⑤ *Rooms from: €160* ✉ *South Mall, City Center South, Cork City, Co. Cork* ☎ *021/427–4040* ⊕ *www.flynnhotels.com/Imperial_Hotel_Cork* ⤳ *126 rooms, 1 suite* ⦿ *Breakfast.*

$$
HOTEL

⌂ **Hotel Isaacs Cork.** With a tone of boho shabby chic that appeals to the hotel's many regular guests, this stylish renovation transformed an old, city-center warehouse into a busy restaurant and hotel complex. **Pros:** location near bus and train stations; old-world character. **Cons:** heavy through-traffic outside; decor a bit worn at the edges; limited car parking. **TripAdvisor:** "good location," "clean and pleasant staff," "large rooms with atmosphere." ⑤ *Rooms from: €120* ⊠ *48 MacCurtain St., City Center North, Cork City, Co. Cork* ☎ *021/450–0011* ⊕ *www.isaacscork.com* ⇨ *50 rooms* ⊚⏐ *Breakfast.*

NIGHTLIFE AND THE ARTS

See the *Examiner* or the *Evening Echo* for details about movies, theater, and live music performances.

NIGHTLIFE

PUBS AND NIGHTCLUBS

Bierhaus. The huge world-beer selection, poker on Tuesday, and a DJ on Saturday lure a young hip crowd here. ⊠ *Pope's Quay, Shandon, Cork City, Co. Cork* ☎ *021/455–1648.*

Charlies Bar. Nightly music sessions are held here, with traditional Irish showcased on Sunday from 3 pm. ⊠ *2 Union Quay, South Docklands, Cork City, Co. Cork* ☎ *021/431–8342* ⊕ *www.charliesbarcork.com.*

Corner House. This popular bar, open daily, hosts Cajun, folk, or Irish music from Thursday to Sunday. ⊠ *7 Coburg St., City Center North, Cork City, Co. Cork* ☎ *021/450–0655.*

Counihan's. A classical string quartet plays every Sunday from midday noon, while evenings bring a blend of traditional Irish and Latin-rhythm music. ⊠ *11 Pembroke St., City Center South, Cork City, Co. Cork* ☎ *021/427–7850* ⊕ *www.counihans.com.*

Franciscan Well Brewery. This lively, award-winning microbrewery has a heated beer garden. ⊠ *North Mall, Shandon, Cork City, Co. Cork* ☎ *021/439–3434* ⊕ *www.franciscanwellbrewery.com.*

The Oliver Plunkett. You can hear live music here nightly—trad, blues, rock, swing, and soul. ⊠ *116 Oliver Plunkett St., City Centre South, Cork City, Co. Cork* ☎ *021/422–2779* ⊕ *www.theoliverplunkett.com.*

The Pavilion. A late-night bar, the Pavilion draws crowds with live entertainment and DJs Thursday to Sunday. ⊠ *13 Careys La., City Center South, Cork City, Co. Cork* ☎ *021/427–6230* ⊕ *www.pavilioncork.com.*

Sin É. Pronounced Shin-*ay*, Irish for "that's it," this is the place for live Irish music—fiddles, flute, banjo, and bodhrán. ⊠ *8 Coburg St., City Center North, Cork City, Co. Cork* ☎ *021/450–2266.*

THE ARTS

GALLERIES

The Lavit Gallery. The gallery showcases artworks and crafts by Cork Arts Society members and other Irish artists. ⊠ *5 Father Mathew St., off South Mall, City Center South, Cork City, Co. Cork* ☎ *021/427–7749* ⊕ *www.lavitgallery.com.*

Lewis Glucksman Gallery. The gallery exhibits art from the University College Cork's collection, stages temporary shows, and presents music, lectures, and other events. ⊠ *UCC Campus, Western Rd., corner of Donovan's Rd., Western Road, Cork City, Co. Cork* ☎ *021/490–1844* ⊕ *www.glucksman.org.*

Wandesford Quay Gallery. This ground-floor space exhibits works by students and staff of Cork's thriving Crawford College of Art and Design. ⊠ *Wandesford Quay, Washington Village, Cork City, Co. Cork* ☎ *021/455–5210* ⊕ *ccad-research.org/gallery.*

Thanks to streets lined with pubs and shops, a simple stroll around Cork can be a delightful way to while away the hours.

PERFORM-
ING ARTS
AND FILM
CIT Cork School of Music. Part of the Cork Institute of Technology, the school hosts concerts in its 450-seat Curtis Auditorium and smaller Stack Auditorium. ☒ *Union Quay, South Docklands, Cork City, Co. Cork* ☎ *021/427–0076* ⊕ *www.cit.ie.*

Cork Opera House. The city's major hall for touring productions also books dance, theater, and comedy and music events. ☒ *Lavitt's Quay, City Center South, Cork City, Co. Cork* ☎ *021/427–0022* ⊕ *www.corkoperahouse.ie.*

Everyman Palace Theatre. Modest-size theatrical productions are staged at the Everyman Palace, which has an ornate Victorian interior. ☒ *15 MacCurtain St., City Center North, Cork City, Co. Cork* ☎ *021/450–1673* ⊕ *www.everymanpalace.com.*

Triskel Arts Centre. The popular venue presents live music, classic and contemporary films, and offbeat art events and theater. ☒ *Tobin St., off S. Main St., Washington Village, Cork City, Co. Cork* ☎ *021/427–2022* ⊕ *www.triskelartscentre.ie.*

SHOPPING
DEPARTMENT STORES
Brown Thomas. Ireland's high-end department store carries items by Irish and international designers. The ground floor has an excellent cosmetics hall and a good selection of menswear and Irish crystal. Refuel at the coffee shop, which sells healthful open sandwiches and homemade soups. ☒ *18–21 Patrick St., City Center South, Cork City, Co. Cork* ☎ *021/480–5555* ⊕ *www.brownthomas.com.*

Debenham's. Cork's largest department store, a branch of the U.K. chain, occupies a beautiful landmark building with a central glass dome. ⊠ *12–17 Patrick St., City Center South, Cork City, Co. Cork* ☎ *1890/946–779* ⊕ *www.debenhams.ie.*

Dunnes Stores. Beginning in Cork as a family-owned drapery store, Dunnes became the place where all of Ireland buys its socks, underwear, and much more. ⊠ *Merchant's Quay, City Center South, Cork City, Co. Cork* ☎ *021/427–4200* ⊕ *www.dunnesstores.ie.*

Marks & Spencer. This British retail giant is as popular for its foods (great for picnics) and housewares as for its clothing basics. ⊠ *6–8 Patrick St., Merchant's Quay, City Center South, Cork City, Co. Cork* ☎ *021/427–5555* ⊕ *www.marksandspencer.com.*

Penneys. Head here for inexpensive rain gear, T-shirts, underwear, and any other garments you forgot to pack. ⊠ *Munster Arcade, 27 Patrick St., City Center South, Cork City, Co. Cork* ☎ *021/427–1935* ⊕ *primark.ie.*

MALLS

MahonPoint Shopping Centre. This massive out-of-town mall just south of the Lee Tunnel is known for its emphasis on fashion. ⊠ *Mahon Point, South Link Rd., Cork City, Co. Cork* ☎ *021/497–2800* ⊕ *www.mahonpointsc.ie.*

Merchant's Quay Shopping Centre. This large mall is conveniently located in the heart of downtown. ⊠ *Merchant's Quay, 1–5 Patrick St., City Center South, Cork City, Co. Cork* ☎ *021/427–5466* ⊕ *www.merchantsquaycork.com.*

Opera Lane. Topshop, Next, Gap, Viyella, Tommy Hilfiger, and other high-street fashion retailers do business in a gleaming covered arcade between Patrick Street and the Opera House. ⊠ *City Center South, Cork City, Co. Cork* ☎ *021/427–5008* ⊕ *www.operalane.com.*

ANTIQUES

Diana O'Mahony. This is a major spot for antique jewelry. ⊠ *8 Winthrop St., City Center South, Cork City, Co. Cork* ☎ *021/427–6599* ⊕ *www.dianaomahonyjewellery.com.*

Meadows & Byrne. You'll find the best of Irish contemporary design for the home, from cookware to Irish crystal, here. ⊠ *22 Academy St., City Center South, Cork City, Co. Cork* ☎ *021/427–2324* ⊕ *www.meadowsandbyrne.com.*

Stokes Fine Clocks and Watches. Packed with antique clocks and watches, Stokes often has a barograph or two (to measure atmospheric pressure). ⊠ *48B MacCurtain St., City Center North, Cork City, Co. Cork* ☎ *021/455–1195* ⊕ *www.stokesclocks.ie.*

BOOKS

Connolly's Bookshop. This shop is known for its good selection of Irish-interest titles and extensive stock of new and secondhand books. ⊠ *Paul St. Piazza, City Center South, Cork City, Co. Cork* ☎ *021/427–5366.*

Vibes & Scribes. Loyal, avid readers head here to peruse the extensive stock of new, secondhand, and discount books. The new bargain books are strong on art and Irish interest. ⊠ *21 Lavitt's Quay, City Center South, Cork City, Co. Cork* ☎ *021/427–9535* ⊕ *vibesandscribes.ie.*

6

Waterstones. Cork's biggest bookshop carries a wide selection of new fiction and nonfiction and stocks many locally published books. ⊠ 69 *Patrick St., City Center South, Cork City, Co. Cork* ☎ 021/427–6522 ⊕ *www.waterstones.com.*

CLOTHING

The Dressing Room. Fashion lovers adore the evening and business attire at this tiny but tony boutique opposite the entrance to the Cork Opera House. ⊠ 4 *Emmet Pl., City Center South, Cork City, Co. Cork* ☎ 021/427–0117.

Kuyichi. The international fashion chain with a sustainable-living ethos occupies a fine Queen Anne house. ⊠ 19 *Opera La., City Center South, Cork City, Co. Cork* ☎ 021/480–6671 ⊕ *www.kuyichi.com.*

Monica John. In addition to locally designed high-fashion ladies' wear, Monica John carries some imported lines. ⊠ *French Church St., City Center South, Cork City, Co. Cork* ☎ 021/427–1399.

Quills. A good selection of Irish-made apparel for women and men is always available at Quills. ⊠ 107 *Patrick St., City Center South, Cork City, Co. Cork* ☎ 021/427–1717.

Samui. Here's a stop for dramatic—often quirky, but always flattering—fashions from Ireland, France, Germany, and the United Kingdom. ⊠ 17 *Drawbridge St., City Center South, Cork City, Co. Cork* ☎ 021/427–8080 ⊕ *www.samuifashions.com.*

JEWELRY

Designworks Studio. A local favorite, Designworks is a top showcase for imaginative, modern jewelry. ⊠ *Cornmarket St., City Center South, Cork City, Co. Cork* ☎ 021/427–9420 ⊕ *designworksstudio.ie.*

The Swiss Gem. A trove of custom-made gold jewellery, this boutique also specializes in engagement rings. ⊠ 21 *Winthrop St., City Center South, Cork City, Co. Cork* ☎ 021/422–3892.

MUSIC

Pro Musica. Along with sheet music, Pro Musica stocks instruments for classical musicians. ⊠ 20 *Oliver Plunkett St., City Center South, Cork City, Co. Cork* ☎ 021/427–1659 ⊕ *www.promusica.ie.*

BLARNEY

10 km (6 miles) northwest of Cork City.

"On Galway sands they kiss your hands, they kiss your lips at Carney, but by the Lee they drink strong tea, and kiss the stone at Blarney." This famous rhyme celebrates one of Ireland's most noted icons—the Blarney Stone, which is the main reason most people journey to this small community built around a village green.

GETTING HERE AND AROUND

Blarney is about a 20-minute drive west of Cork City, midway between the N22 Killarney road and the N20 to Limerick. Local buses that depart from Cork Bus Station Parnell Place drop you at the Village Green, adjacent to the castle and the craft shops. There is a large car park (free). Taxis are available from Castle Cabs by phone reservation.

ESSENTIALS

Transportation Contacts Castle
Cabs ☎ 021/438–2222.

Visitor Information Blarney Tourist
Office ✉ *Blarney, Co. Cork* ☎ *021/438–
1624* ⊕ *www.cork-guide.ie/blarney*.

EXPLORING

★ **Blarney Castle.** In the center of Blarney is Blarney Castle, or what remains of it: the ruined central keep is all that's left of this mid-15th-century stronghold. The castle

contains the famed **Blarney Stone**; kissing the stone, it's said, endows the kisser with the fabled "gift of gab." It's 127 steep steps to the battlements. To kiss the stone, you must lie down on the battlements, hold on to a guardrail, and lean your head way back. It's good fun and not at all dangerous. Expect a line from mid-June to early September; while you wait, you can admire the views of the wooded River Lee valley and chuckle over how the word "blarney" came to mean what it does. As the story goes, Queen Elizabeth I wanted Cormac MacCarthy, Lord of Blarney, to will his castle to the Crown, but he refused her requests with eloquent excuses and soothing compliments. Exhausted by his comments, the queen reportedly exclaimed, "This is all Blarney. What he says he rarely means."

You can take pleasant walks around the castle grounds; Rock Close contains oddly shaped limestone rocks landscaped in the 18th century, and a grove of ancient yew trees that is said to have been a site of Druid worship. In early March there's a wonderful display of naturalized daffodils. ☎ *021/438–5252* ⊕ *www.blarneycastle.ie* 🎫 *€10* ⊗ *May and Sept., Mon.–Sat. 9–6:30, Sun. 9–5:30; June–Aug., Mon.–Sat. 9–7, Sun. 9–5:30; Oct.–Apr., Mon.–Sat. 9–sunset Sun. 9–5 or sunset.*

WHERE TO EAT AND STAY

For expanded hotel reviews, visit Fodors.com.

$$
EUROPEAN

✕**Blairs Inn.** Surrounded by woods a five minutes' drive from Blarney, Blairs Inn—noted for its exuberant window-box displays—is the perfect retreat from Blarney's tour-bus crowds. This is a real "local," complete with genial owner-hosts John and Anne, one son, Duncan, in the kitchen, and another son, Richard behind the bar. You can opt to dine at the bar ($) or in the quieter surroundings of the wood-paneled restaurant. In summer enjoy the beer garden; in winter, warm wood fires flicker in the hearth. Freshly prepared local produce is served in generous portions all day: best bets include Irish stew with lamb, carrots, and potatoes, as well as the house special, hot corned beef with parsley sauce, and a memorable gratin of prawns, crab, and salmon, served piping hot. There's live entertainment every Monday at 9 pm from May to October. ⑤ *Average main: €24* ✉ *Cloghroe, Co. Cork* ☎ *021/438–1470* ⊕ *blairsinn.ie.*

$
HOTEL

🛏**Blarney Castle Hotel.** Set on the village green only a minute's walk from the famed castle, this 1837 hotel occupies a traditional gabled building—guest rooms are on two stories above the bar, and five of them have views of the green. **Pros:** ideal touring base; good alternative to Cork City (5 miles); restaurant on premises; no smoking throughout. **Cons:** bar can get busy on Sunday night; some rooms overlook car park and yard. **TripAdvisor:** "what a lovely set of people," "superb location," "charming." ⑤ *Rooms from: €100* ⊠ *Blarney Village Green, Blarney, Co. Cork* ☎ *021/438–5116* ⊕ *www.blarneycastlehotel.com* ⊅ *13 rooms.*

$

B&B/INN

⌂ **The White House Bed and Breakfast Blarney.** A hacienda-style bungalow on an elevated site on the main road between the N20 and Blarney village (a five-minute walk from the latter), Blarney's White House has a distant view of the castle from its front door. **Pros:** good value for money; quiet and comfortable; home-cooked breakfast. **Cons:** won't win any style awards. ⑤ *Rooms from: €70* ⊠ *Shean Lower, Blarney, Co. Cork* ☎ *021/438–5338* ⊕ *www.thewhitehouseblarney.com* ⊅ *6 rooms.*

SHOPPING

Blarney Woollen Mills. With the largest stock and the highest turnover of Blarney's crafts shops, this noted emporium sells everything from Irish-made high fashion to Aran hand-knit items to leprechaun key rings. ☎ *021/451–6111* ⊕ *www.blarney.com.*

EAST CORK

Most visitors to Cork head west out of the city for the coastal areas between Cork and Glengarriff, but the county's eastern portions—Cork Harbour, Midleton, and Shanagarry, are also worth exploring.

CORK HARBOUR

16 km (10 miles) east of Cork City.

Cork City's nearby harbor district has seen plenty of history. Cork Harbour's draws include Fota Island—with an arboretum, a wildlife park, and the Fota House ancestral estate—and the fishing port of Cobh.

GETTING HERE AND AROUND

Cobh lies 16 km (10 miles) east of Cork City, and is signposted from the N25 (follow signs for Waterford). A suburban train from Cork's Kent Station stops at Fota Island and Cobh, and offers better harbor views than does the road.

TOURS

If the sight of Cork Harbour makes you want to take to the water, arrange an outing with Whale of a Time.

Transportation Contacts **Whale of a Time** ⊠ *East Ferry, Marlogue, Cobh, Co. Cork* ☎ *086/328–3250* ⊕ *www.whaleofatime.net.*

Visitor Information **Cobh Tourist Office** ⊠ *Sirius Arts Centre, Cobh, Co. Cork* ☎ *021/481–3301* ⊕ *www.visitcobh.com.*

EXPLORING

Fodor's Choice ★

Cobh Heritage Centre. Many of the people who left Ireland on immigrant ships for the New World departed from Cobh, which was formerly known as Queenstown. The center's Queenstown Story exhibit, in the old Cobh railway station, re-creates the experience of the 2.5 million emigrants who left from here between 1848 and 1950. It also tells the stories of great transatlantic liners, including the *Titanic,* whose last port of call was Cobh, and the *Lusitania,* which was sunk by a German submarine off this coast on May 7, 1915. Many of the *Lusitania*'s 1,198 victims are buried in Cobh, which has a memorial to them on the local quay. ⊠ *Old Railway Building, Lower Rd., Cobh, Co. Cork* ☎ *021/481–3591* ⊕ *www.cobhheritage.com* ⊠€*7.50* ⊘ *Nov.–Mar., Mon.–Sat. 9:30–5, Sun. 11–5; Apr.–Sept., daily 9:30–6.*

St. Colman's Cathedral. The best view of Cobh, well worth the uphill stroll, is from St. Colman's Cathedral, an exuberant neo-Gothic granite church designed by the eminent British architect E. W. Pugin in 1869, and completed in 1919. Inside, granite niches portray scenes of the Roman Catholic Church's history in Ireland, beginning with the arrival of St. Patrick. ☎ *021/481–3222* ⊕ *www.cobhcathedralparish.ie.*

Fota Island Wildlife Park. The 70-acre park is 12 km (7 miles) east of Cork via N25, R624, and the main Cobh road. It's an important breeding center for cheetahs and wallabies, and also is home to monkeys, zebras, giraffes, ostriches, flamingos, emus, and kangaroos. ☎ *021/481–2678* ⊕ *www.fotawildlife.ie* ⊠€*14* ⊘ *Mon.–Sat. 10–6, Sun. 11–6 (last entry 1 hr before closing).*

Fota House, Arboretum & Gardens. Next to the Fota Island Wildlife Park is Fota House, the Smith-Barry ancestral estate: its name is derived from the Irish *Fód te,* which means "warm soil," a tribute to the unique tidal estuary microclimate here and the reason why one of Ireland's most exotic botanical gardens was established here. The original lodge house was built in the mid-18th century for the Smith-Barry family, which owned vast tracts of land in South Cork, including the whole of Fota Island. The next generation of the powerful family employed the renowned architects Richard and William Vitruvius Morrison to convert the structure into an impressive Regency-style house that has now been painstakingly restored. The symmetrical facade is relatively unadorned and stands in contrast to the resplendent Adamesque plasterwork of the formal reception rooms (somewhat denuded of furniture). The servants' quarters are almost as big as the house proper. Fota's glories continue in the gardens, which include an arboretum, a Victorian fernery, an Italian garden, an orangerie, and a special display of magnolias. You can relax over cake and scones in the tearoom after visiting the gift shop. ☎ *021/481–5543* ⊕ *www.fotahouse.com* ⊠€*6* ⊘ *Apr.–Sept., Mon.–Sat. 9–5, Sun. 11–5; Oct.–Mar., Sat.–Sun.11–5.*

The Titanic Experience Cobh. Cobh was the last port of call for the ill-fated ocean liner *Titanic.* At 1:30 pm on April 11, 1912, tenders carried 123 passengers out to the ship from the offices of the White Star Line. These offices have now been converted into an interactive exhibition (cinema, holographs, touch-screen displays), allowing visitors to follow, literally, in the footsteps of the passengers as they embarked on the fateful voyage. ⊠ *The Promenade, Cobh, Co. Cork* ☎ *021/481–4412* ⊕ *www. titanicexperiencecobh.ie* ⊠€*7* ⊘ *Daily 9–6, last admission at 5.*

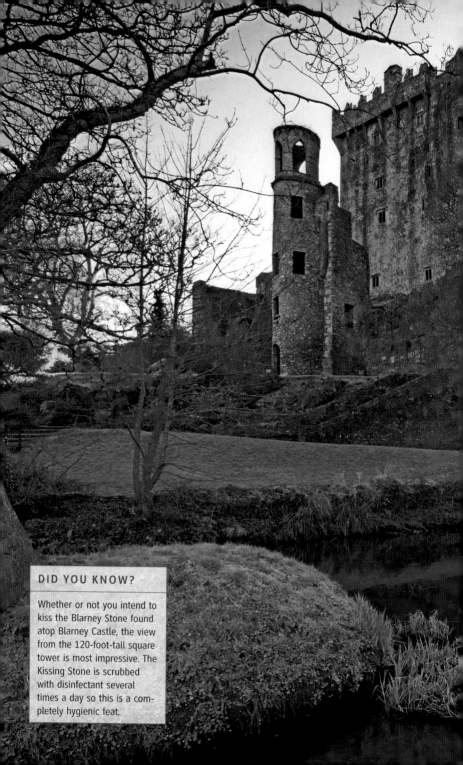

DID YOU KNOW?

Whether or not you intend to kiss the Blarney Stone found atop Blarney Castle, the view from the 120-foot-tall square tower is most impressive. The Kissing Stone is scrubbed with disinfectant several times a day so this is a completely hygienic feat.

East Cork

Mitchelstown
Castletownroche
Kanturk
N72
Mallow
Fermoy
River Blackwater
Lismore
N72
Dungarvan
N20
Rathcormac
C O R K
Cork City
see detail
map
Blarney
Midleton
N25
Youghal
R579
R617
Macroom
N22
Cork
Harbour
R629
Shanagarry
N22
N71
N28
Cobh
Cloyne
Ballycotton
Cork Airport
(ORK)
R600
Cork
Harbour
N71
Bandon
Kinsale
Kilbrittain
Charles Fort
Timoleague
R600
Celtic Sea
Clonakilty
Courtmacsherry
N71
Rosscarbery
0   20 miles
0   30 km

WHERE TO EAT

$

CONTEMPORARY

✕ **Gilbert's Restaurant & Townhouse.** Just below Cobh's cathedral, a short step from the waterfront, this handsome cut-stone house dates to 1824. Locals can be seen lingering over coffee and newspapers through the street-front windows. Parquet flooring links the café and bar area with the elegant bistro-style restaurant, where bentwood chairs and contemporary art combine to create a relaxed Continental atmosphere. The food is locally sourced and contemporary in style, with many light dishes on the menu. Start with the carpaccio of beetroot topped with goat's cheese fritters, or the smoked salmon, avocado and feta salad with honey mustard dressing, before sampling roasted loin of venison or linguine with prawns and mussels. The white chocolate mousse is a star among the desserts, but the lemon tart is equally popular. You can also spend the night here. The five bedrooms ($) are spacious, with woolen rugs on wooden floors, decorated in an uncluttered eclectic style. ⑤ *Average main: €18* ⊠ *11 Pearse Square, Cobh, Co. Cork* ☎ *021/481–1300* ⊕ *www.gilbertsincobh.com.*

MIDLETON

12 km (8 miles) east of Cork City.

Midleton is famous for its school, Midleton College, founded in 1696, and its distillery, founded in 1825 and modernized in 1975, which manufactures spirits—including Irish whiskey—for distribution worldwide. A pleasant market town set at the head of the Owenacurra River estuary, near the northeast corner of Cork Harbour, Midleton has many gray-stone buildings dating mainly from the early 19th century.

GETTING HERE AND AROUND

Midleton is 12 km (8 miles) east of Cork City on the main N25. It also has regular bus and rail connections with the city. The bus is best for visiting the Jameson distillery. Bus Éireann buses daily connect from Cork Bus Station Parnell Place to Midleton (30 minutes, €6.35 round-trip).

Midleton Station. Irish Rail trains from Cork's Kent Station serve Midleton Station (25 minutes, €6.50 round-trip) many times daily. ✉ *Midleton, Co. Cork* ☎ *021/450–6766 for timetable* ⊕ *www.irishrail.ie.*

EXPLORING

Jameson Experience. The experience here is a tour of the Old Midleton Distillery, on which you'll learn how Irish whiskey—*uisce beatha*, "the water of life"—was made in the old days. The old stone buildings are excellent examples of 19th-century industrial architecture, the impressively large old waterwheel still operates, and the pot still—a copper dome that can hold 32,000 imperial gallons of whiskey—is the world's largest. Early in the tour, requests are made for a volunteer "whiskey taster," so be alert if this option appeals. Tours end with a complimentary glass of Jameson's Irish whiskey (or a soft drink). A gift shop and café are also on the premises. ✉ *Old Midleton Distillery, Midleton, Co. Cork* ☎ *021/461–3594* ⊕ *www.tours.jamesonwhiskey. com* ▣ *€13.50* ۞ *Apr.–Oct., daily 9–5; Nov.–Mar., tours daily 11:30, 1:15, 2:30, and 4.*

SHANAGARRY

15 km (8 miles) southeast of Midleton, 17 km (11 miles) southeast of Cork Harbour.

There are three reasons to come to Shanagarry, a farming village known chiefly for its Quaker connections: Ballymaloe House, one of Ireland's first and still most famous country-house hotels; Ballymaloe Cookery School and Gardens, a top destination for chefs-in-training; and the gallery and shop of Stephen Pearce, a leading designer of earthenware pottery. All three enterprises are run by Quaker families, testimony to the religious roots of this community.

GETTING HERE AND AROUND

Shanagarry, on a rural back road, is about an hour's drive from Cork City or Cork Harbour on the N25 to the R632; from Midleton, take the R629. Or take the Ballycotton bus (there are five runs daily) from Cork Bus Station Parnell Place. The trip takes an hour and a quarter. The last return bus to Cork leaves Shanagarry at 4:45 pm.

EXPLORING

Shanagarry House. Shanagarry's most famous Quaker native son was none other than William Penn (1644–1718), the founder of the Pennsylvania colony, who grew up in Shanagarry House, still a private residence in the center of the village. The house's most famous tenant since William Penn was Marlon Brando, who stayed here in the summer of 1995 while filming *Divine Rapture* in nearby Ballycotton.

Shanagarry Design Centre. Run by the Kilkenny Shop, the spacious gallery and showroom (with scrumptious home baking in the café) is in the village center. On display are high-end Irish-made crafts including Newbridge silverware, Orla Kiely handbags, and potter Louis Mulcahy's huge bowls and lamps, as well as Irish-made clothing, woolen goods, Irish linen, and jewelry. Three artists have studios in the basement, where their work is also for sale. ⊠ *Next to Shanagarry Parish Church, Shanagarry, Co. Cork* ☎ *021/464–5838* 🖼 *Free* ☉ *Daily 10–6.*

Stephen Pearce Pottery. Potter Stephen Pearce has returned to the village where he grew up, and reopened the traditional craft pottery that launched his career in the late 1960s. The showroom sells his distinctive hand-thrown black and cream earthenware tableware, and the terra-cotta and white line, both beloved of collectors. Also for sale are a range of matching bowls and jugs. Book a pottery tour in advance, and ask about workshops. ⊠ *The Old Pottery, Shanagarry, Co. Cork* ☎ *021/464–6807* ⊕ *www.stephenpearce.com* ☉ *Mon.–Sat. 10–5, Sun. 11.30–5.*

WHERE TO STAY

For expanded hotel reviews, visit Fodors.com.

$$$$
B&B/INN
Fodor's Choice
★
☾

Ballymaloe House. Once past the entrance's demilune window of this Georgian manor, a symphony of whites and beiges that is the drawing room beckons to guests with its fine modern Irish paintings on the walls, a lovely touch for what is basically a farmhouse and family home, albeit a world-famous one: this is Ballymaloe, the fountainhead of New Irish cuisine. **Pros:** top restaurant; child-friendly family atmosphere; great wholesome food; quiet rural location near sandy beach. **Cons:** advance booking essential; village and beach not in walking distance. **TripAdvisor:** "can't wait to return," "just perfect," "a view of a gracious past." ⑤ *Rooms from: €250* ⊠ *Shanagarry, Co. Cork* ☎ *021/465–2531* ⊕ *www.ballymaloe.ie* ⏎ *29 rooms* ⏐⊙⏐ *Breakfast.*

WEST CORK

The historic old port—and now booming seaside town—of Kinsale is the perfect place to begin the 136-km (85-mile) trip, via Bantry Bay and through a variety of seascapes, to the lush vegetation of Glengarriff. If you tackle this scenic West Cork coastal route nonstop, the drive takes less than two hours, but the whole point of this journey is to linger in places that tickle your fancy. Must-sees include the famed 18th-century manse of Bantry House and the romantic island gardens of Ilnacullin.

Continued on page 354

A TASTE OF IRELAND

Queen scallops with aubergine caviar

Great ingredients and innovative chefs are shaping West Cork into one of the most foodie-friendly places on the planet.

The next time you wander into a time-burnished 19th-century Irish pub bent on downing a platter of steak, bland potatoes, and mushy peas, don't be surprised if you end up with a main course of skewered John Dory in Clonmel cider sauce and a dessert of Cooleeney Camembert ganache with lavender jelly. *Begorra*—you've encountered the much-vaunted Irish food revolution! Since the mid-1990s, the New Irish Cuisine has changed the beige, boiled, and boring food of yore into a bounty of gourmet delights. Today, haute-hungry gourmands packing chubby wallets (and the cookbooks of Margaret Johnson and Noel Cullen) are all abuzz discovering emerging culinary wizards; artisanal producers of farmhouse cheeses; organic beef and smoked fish; and some of the best farmers' markets and provisioners around. Leading the charge of Ireland's food revolution are superstar chefs, and few have done more to transform the Irish kitchen than Myrtle Allen and her daughter-in-law, Darina Allen. The trip to bountiful Ireland begins with them.

Gubbeen Farmhouse

BALLYMALOE: A TRIP TO BOUNTIFUL

One of the dining rooms; right, Ballymaloe Cookery School

When Myrtle Allen opened a restaurant at her Georgian farm-estate, Ballymaloe (east of Cork City and pronounced Bah-lee-mal-oo), in 1964, she hadn't set out to change the way Ireland eats.

Moving to the historic Quaker stronghold of Shangarry in 1948, she and her husband, Ivan, began the restoration of an old Georgian farm estate. Before too long, their 400-acre cropland became the breeding ground for a new gastronomy as the couple reaped harvests of sea kale, parsnips, carrageen moss, rutabagas, gooseberries, globe artichokes, and other heritage veggies. Long before organic became a buzzword, Myrtle made freshness her mantra: eggs from her own hens, produce from her own garden, freshly landed fish from nearby Ballycotton. So, when she opened The Yeats Room at Ballymaloe in 1964, food was embraced by a generation reared on frozen pizza. In no time, food critics were raving about Myrtle's everything-old-is-new-again-but-better take.

The Herb Garden at Ballymaloe

Myrtle Allen is now retired but chef Jason Fahey has a balanced touch that is is almost Quaker-like in its subtlety. Dinners here are the real thing: fresh-picked cori-ander from the greenhouse for the leg of lamb, the eggs in the Carageen Pudding—a custard mixed with Cork seaweed and bittersweet Irish-coffee sauce—the gift of hens with squatters' rights, and if the plaice weren't biting that day, it won't be on the menu. Under the hosts' celebrated collection of modern Irish paintings, diners can enjoy a kaleidoscope of specialties (selections change seasonally, weekly, and daily) be it a radish-leaf soup, a Ballymaloe cheddar cheese fondue, or a roast Ballycotton cod with Ulster champ. A final testimony to Myrtle's practice of supporting small-scale, local food purveyors is the adieu offering: the amazing cheese board, which conveys local artisanship at its best. Ballymaloe House has lovely overnight accommodations (☎ 021/465-2531 ⊕ www.ballymaloe.ie ⇨ *review under Shanagarry*), just one reason why many diners enjoy a leisurely repast at night.

NOW WE'RE COOKING

Darina Allen

If Myrtle Allen is the Alice Waters of Ireland, Darina Allen is its Martha Stewart. Thanks to her eight television series, her bestselling cookbooks, and the happy status of being the daughter-in-law of Myrtle, Darina's celebrity in Ireland is about on a par with U2's. She arrived in 1963 to apprentice at Ballymaloe and promptly fell in love with Myrtle's son, Tim, and her culinary dream. So, in 1983, she and Tim opened the Ballymaloe Cookery School, setting up shop two miles east on the other side of Shanagarry village at Kinoith House. The ultimate spot for a don't-just-visit, stay-and-become-an-Irish-chef experience, the school offers everything from two-hour starter lessons to the famed 12-week Certificate Course (run three times a year for 58 students), which many Irish chefs regard as a rite of passage. Half-day courses can be combined with an indulgent stay at Ballymaloe House—choose from "Sushi Made Simple," "The Magic of Phyllo," or "Discovering Tapas." A new departure is the "forgotten skills" series, day-long courses on chicken keeping, beekeeping, and organic gardening. Evidence that history repeats itself: Darina's daughter-in-law, Rachel Allen, is now making her second TV series and publishing her second cookbook.

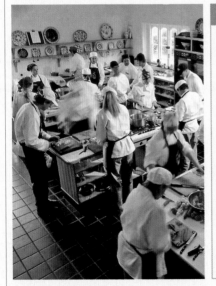

MENU BEST BETS

Goujons of Ballycotton Haddock with Tartare Sauce

John's Rosemary, Red Wine & Garden Leek Risotto

Gubbeen Ham Braised in Chablis & Cream Served with Peperonata & Chives

Roast East Cork Beef with Roast Garlic Mayonnaise, with Fondant Potato & Vegetable Pakoras

Ballymaloe Cheddar Cheese Fondue

Grilled Ballycotton Hake with Scallops & Lobster, Herb Relish & French Beans

THE BALLYMALOE COOKERY SCHOOL is in Kinoith, just outside Shanagarry (☎ 021/464–6785 ⊕ www.cookingisfun.ie). Classes range from afternoon demonstrations (€70) to half-day classes (€95) to 1, 2½, and 5 day courses to the full 12-week Certificate (€10,495). Students can stay in charming cottages on the grounds.

CORK CORNUCOPIA: THE FOOD ARTISANS

Compare a traditionally made butcher's sausage with the plastic-wrapped supermarket version, and you'll understand what all the fuss is about: flavor, texture, and general deliciousness.

You'll see why Ireland's new artisanal foodstuff makers, fed up with the formulaic, tasteless foods of big industry, have stepped in to pioneer the production of farmhouse cheeses, organic beef, and organic herb cultivation and fish smoking. They got a big boost with the 1998 founding of Slow Food Ireland (⊕ www.slowfoodireland.com), a loose collective of specialty producers and restaurateurs whose aim was to encourage careful food sourcing. West Cork has played an important role in the revival of Irish traditional foods, since incomers moving to the area seeking a change in lifestyle found that their small-business interests dovetailed with those of the traditional butchers, bakers, and farmers who had stayed put. These new artisans are now often listed on restaurant menus: Gubbeen Cheese, Ummera Smoked Salmon, Krawczyk's West Cork Salamis, Glenilen Dairy Products, and many others. Here are three of the best:

GUBBEEN FARMHOUSE PRODUCTS

Farmer Tom Ferguson tends a herd of prize cows, whose rich milk is made into creamy cheese by his wife Giana. The fresh-straw piggery allows its lucky pigs to have a view of Roaring Water Bay, one of the most scenic corners of Ireland. Tom and Giana's son, Fingal, runs the smokehouse (great smoked bacon, chorizo, and salamis), while daughter Clovisse grows organic vegetables and herbs. Products are sold at Neal's Yard in London and West Cork's farmer's markets. ✉ Gubbeen, Schull, near Skibbbereen, Co. Cork ☎ 028/28231 ⊕ www.gubbeen.com

BELVELLY SMOKEHOUSE Frank Hederman smokes his eels, mackerel, salmon, trout, and mussels over beech rather than oak, giving them an unusually mild flavor. His smoked salmon is sold in London's Fortnum & Mason. The smokehouse is open for tastings, and his products can be bought at Cork City's English Market and Midleton's farmers' market. ✉ Cobh ☎ 021/481–1089 ⊕ www.frankhederman.com

MACROOM OATMEAL Since the early 1800s, Donal Creedon's porridge oats have been hand-roasted on the traditional cast-iron plate at Walton's Mills before being shelled and ground, giving them a distinctive smoky, nutty flavor. Great for breadmaking, the meal is sold at many food shops. ✉ Kanturk, Co. Cork ☎ 026/41800 ⊕ macroomoatmealmills@eircom.net

BLESSED ARE THE CHEESEMAKERS

6

IN FOCUS A TASTE OF IRELAND

Thirty years ago Irish cheese came in bright-orange blocks and tasted like salted plastic. Today, a thriving cheesemaking culture—a mix of native ingenuity and French, Swiss, German, and Dutch expertise—produces a wide range of artisanal farmhouse cheeses from the milk of goats and sheep, as well as from purebred cows. **Here are the best:**

Ardsallagh Goat's Cheese. A popular salad ingredient, this cheese can be bought from its maker, Jane Murphy, at the Midleton Farmer's Market.

Cashel Blue. The most famous Irish blue, this mild, creamy delight is made in Fethard, Co. Tipperary—it is as much used in cooking as on the cheese board.

Crozier Blue. Made from sheep's milk, this has a cult following.

Gabriel and Desmond. Using only summer-season raw milk from local herds grazed near the sea, these hard cheeses created by Americans Bill Hogan and Sean Ferry have a long maturation period, resulting in a piquant, aromatic bouquet.

Knockalara Sheep's Milk Cheese. Made by Wolfgang and Agnes Schiebitz, this is popular with chefs thanks to its soft, crumbly texture.

Milleens. This pungent, washed-rind winner is made from the milk of cows raised by Norman and Veronica Steele on their Beara Peninsula family farm.

FINDING THE FEAST

Long known as the "belly of Ireland," the West Cork region is celebrated for its rich fishing and even richer farming. These days, gourmets are busy rooting out the best Irish chorizo, sampling a new Durrus cheese and nutmeg pizza, or wolfing down Galway Bay oysters (heaven when served with Guinness!). Like a world-class picnic, this cook's tour is the tastiest recipe for a day trip through the region.

The best places to track down top temptations from Cork's gastronomic cornucopia are the area's food markets, often set in small villages and averaging only about a dozen stalls. Low overheads mean bargains for the buyers, who enjoy an amazing array of artisanal foodstuffs, from organic vegetables to sauces and relishes, Breton pancakes, handmade bread, home-cured ham, preserves, smoked salmon, and a great range of cheeses. And the markets' festive atmosphere (often livened up with a jazz trio or street performers) is complemented by the camaraderie of the stall-holders—this is often their main contact with the buying public. Darina Allen, with typical energy, can be found most Saturday mornings selling produce from her Ballymaloe Cookery School at a stall in Midleton. Check out the ever-changing market scene on its website (⊕ www.bordbia.ie.com) for up-to-date information. Here is a tip sheet:

COUNTY CORK

BANTRY, Main Square, Friday 9 am to 1 pm. A traditional street market, with a strong presence of growers of organic plants and veggies.

CLONAKILTY, Friday, 10 am to 2 pm. The Friday market (mainly food) is in and around the covered alley beside O'Donovan's Hotel, Main St.

KINSALE, Market Square, Wednesday 10–1. Snack on a Breton crepe while stocking up on chutneys, smoked salmon, famhouse cheeses, fresh fish, and organic veg and fruit at this cute piazza market.

MIDLETON, Saturday 9:30 am–1 pm. One of the liveliest farmers' markets, it's held in a small car park, with buskers creating a festive vibe.

SCHULL, Sunday 11–3. At its best in summer and at Christmas, this foodie's market showcases superb products from local bakers, fish smokers and cheesemakers, and Gubbeen smoked pork products, all sold by their makers.

COUNTY KERRY

KENMARE, Wednesday 10 am–2 pm, closed Jan. and Feb. About 15 outdoor stalls offer local organic produce and a few exotic imports to an appreciative local clientele. Look out for Knockatee cheese from Tuosist down the road, Olivier's smoked trout from Killorglin, organic vegs, homemade pâtés, fresh fish, and French soaps and sweets.

DINGLE, Farmers' Market, Dykegate Street, Friday 10 am–2 pm. Held in the center of town, this is a lively affair, where local farmers offer homegrown vegetables, alongside freshly baked bread, farmhouse cheeses, homemade cupcakes and locally-made jams, as well as hot food to eat on the spot. Locally-made crafts are on sale too, and a community stall open to local charities also allows people to test-market new products.

MILLTOWN, Old Church Market, Saturday 10 am–2pm. Organic producers converge on this church, on the main road (N70) between Killorglin and Castlemaine—specialist bakers, organic growers, a wheatgrass stall, and an herbalist are highlights.

OTHER FOODIE FAVES

THE ENGLISH MARKET Today, this famous city-center covered market is a thriving hub of artisanal butchers, fishmongers, and greengrocers. Organic fruits and vegs, top-quality meat and fresh fish, imported coffees and teas, locally made charcuterie, farmhouse cheeses—even a champagne from a local wine merchant, Bubble Brothers. ⊠ *Grand Parade, Cork City* ⊕ *www.corkcity.ie*

THE LETTERCOLLUM SHOP Founders of the Lettercollum Kitchen Project, Con McLaughlin and Karen Austin are masters of the vegetarian and ethnic repertory (and also offer cooking classes). Their shop/bakery sells specialist breads, cooks'

ingredients, sandwiches, and savory herb tarts. Pick up a picnic. ⊠ *22 Connolly St., Clonakilty* ☎ *023/883-6938* ⊕ *www.lettercollum.ie*

URRU Once Ruth Healy took the Ballymaloe Certificate Cookery Course she left the corporate treadmill behind to open the ultimate cook's shop, which aims to bring urban chic to rural Ireland. Sip a latte while browsing among local artisanal foods, including homemade pâtés and patisserie, and a tempting range of cookbooks, cookwares, and chocolates. ⊠ *The Mill, MacSwiney Quay, Bandon, Co. Cork* ☎ *023/885-4731* ⊕ *www.urru.ie*

KINSALE

29 km (18 miles) southwest of Cork City.

Foodies flock to Kinsale, a picturesque port that pioneered the Irish small-town tradition of fine dining in unbelievably small restaurants. In the early 1980s, Kinsale had a village-size population of 2,000 and at least a dozen top-grade restaurants, mostly run by enthusiastic owner-chefs. Things have leveled out since then—the town has grown, while the number of restaurants has remained nearly the same, and most of the original chefs have moved on—but there is still a great buzz during the annual **Kinsale Gourmet Festival** (⊕ *www.kinsalerestaurants.com*) held in October. Year-round, head to Market Square (Tuesday 10–1) to find Kinsale Market, a cute piazza market where you can snack on a Breton crepe while stocking up on chutneys, smoked salmon, farmhouse cheeses, fresh fish, and organic goodies.

In Kinsale's town center, at the tip of the wide, fjordlike harbor that opens out from the River Bandon, upscale shops and eateries with brightly painted facades line small streets. Kinsale has two yacht marinas, and skippers with deep-sea angling boats offer day charters. The Kinsale Yacht Club hosts racing and cruising events during the sailing season, which runs from March to October for hardy souls and from June to August for everyone else.

GETTING HERE AND AROUND

Kinsale is 29 km (18 miles) southwest of Cork City on the R600, a half-hour drive, and is only a 15-minute drive from Cork Airport. Ground-level parking is easily available. Buses from Cork City stop at the airport and run about every hour. Kinsale's town center is compact, and there is no public transport, but taxis can be booked from Kinsale Cabs.

TOURS

For an overview of Kinsale's great natural harbor, take an hour-long cruise on the *Spirit of Kinsale*, offered by Kinsale Harbour Cruises. You'll hear informative commentary and view wildlife, including herons, seals, and otters.

ESSENTIALS

Transportation Contacts Kinsale Cabs ⊠ *Market Sq., Kinsale, Co. Cork* ☎ *021/477–2642* ⊕ *www.kinsalecabs.com.* **Kinsale Harbour Cruises** ⊠ *Pier Rd., Kinsale, Co. Cork* ☎ *086/250–5456* ⊕ *www.kinsaleharbourcruises. com* ⌑ *€12.50* ⊗ *Mid-Mar.–Sept., daily, weather permitting.*

Visitor Information Kinsale Tourist Office ⊠ *Pier Rd., Kinsale, Co. Cork* ☎ *021/477–2234* ⊕ *www.kinsale.ie.*

EXPLORING

★ **Charles Fort.** The British built Charles Fort on the east side of the Bandon River estuary in the late 17th century, after their defeat of the Spanish and Irish forces. One of Europe's best-preserved "star forts" encloses some 12 cliff-top acres and is similar to Fort Ticonderoga in New York State. If the sun is shining, take the footpath signposted Scilly Walk; it winds along the harbor's edge under tall trees and then through the

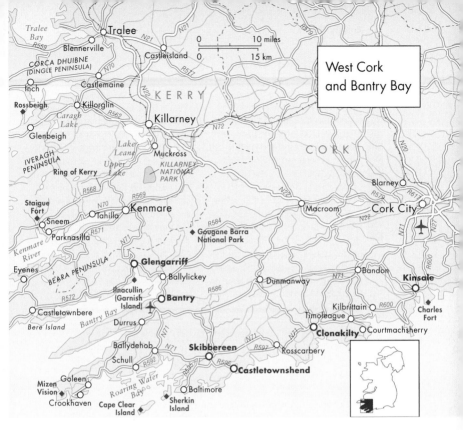

West Cork
and Bantry Bay

village of Summer Cove. ✉ *3 km (2 miles) east of town, Kinsale, Co. Cork* ☎ *021/477-2263* ⊕ *www.heritageireland.ie* 🎫 *€4* 🕓 *Mid-Mar.–Oct., daily 10–6; Nov.–mid-Mar., daily 10–5.*

Desmond Castle and the International Museum of Wine. This museum occupies a 15th-century fortified town house—originally a custom house—that has a dark history. It was used as a prison for French and American seamen in the 1700s, and was subsequently a jail and then a workhouse. Now it contains displays that tell the story of the wine trade and its importance to the Irish diaspora in France, America, Australia, and New Zealand. ✉ *Cork St., Kinsale, Co. Cork* ☎ *021/477-4855* ⊕ *www.winegeese.ie* 🎫 *€3* 🕓 *Mid-Apr.–mid-Oct., daily 10–6.*

Kinsale Museum. Memorabilia from the wreck of the *Lusitania* are among the artifacts in the Kinsale Museum, which is in a 17th-century, Dutch-style courthouse. The 1915 inquest into that ship's sinking took place in the wood-paneled courtroom. Downstairs is a fascinating collection of antique tradesman's tools. Because the staff consists of volunteers, it's best to call to confirm opening times. ✉ *Old Courthouse, Market Pl., Kinsale, Co. Cork* ☎ *021/477-7930* 🕓 *Apr.–Oct., daily 10–4.*

Spaniard Inn. The inn looks over the town and harbor from a hairpin bend on the road to Charles Fort. Inside, sawdust-covered floors and a

CLOSE UP

The Battle of Kinsale

Before Kinsale became the foodie capital of Ireland, it was chiefly famous for the Battle of Kinsale in 1601, when the Irish and the Spanish joined forces against the English—and lost. As generations of Irish schoolchildren could tell you, the Battle of Kinsale was a turning point in Irish history. It precipitated an event known as "the Flight of the Earls" (the subject of Brian Friels' play *Making History*), in which the Irish aristocracy left for Europe to seek help from the Catholic king of Spain. The Irish earls never returned, leaving their lands to be colonized by the English settlers, who also filled the power vacuum created by their absence. The Spanish influence that can be traced back to this battle can be seen in Kinsale's older houses, which have slate roofs and unusual slate fronts. Because of its geographical position—approximately 800 km (500 miles) of open sea due north of La Coruña—Kinsale continued to trade with Spain, and even today, Spanish trawlers fish in the waters off the coast of County Cork. Kinsale went on to become an important fishing port as well as a British army and naval base.

big open fireplace make this onetime fishermen's bar a cozy spot in winter. In summer you can take a pint to the restaurant's veranda and watch the world go by on land and sea. ⊠ *Scilly, Co. Cork* ☎ *021/477–2436* ⊕ *www.thespaniard.ie.*

WHERE TO EAT

$$ ✕ **Blue Haven.** A restaurant, bar, and small hotel occupy this attractive,
INTERNATIONAL yellow-stucco, blue-trim town house, with its landmark wall clock and welcoming flags. At this popular spot for casual dining you can sit near the open fire, outside on the patio, in a booth in the buzzing bistro section, or at a quieter table in the restaurant. The menu, a well-judged mix of old favorites, includes Caesar salad, sirloin steak, Thai red curry of vegetables with fragrant rice, and beer-battered fish-and-chips. The bar has live music nightly from May to September, and on Saturdays year-round. This is a good place to meet the locals, who can be hard to find in cosmopolitan Kinsale, and it's a fun place to stay, if you don't mind smallish rooms and the possibility of late-night noise. ⑤ *Average main: €18* ⊠ *Pearse St., Kinsale, Co. Cork* ☎ *021/477–2209* ⊕ *www. bluehavenkinsale.com.*

$$ ✕ **Crackpots.** A grocery was transformed into Carole Norman's "ceramic
ECLECTIC café," a simple but elegant eatery with warm yellow walls, an open fireplace, and cozy dining areas. The most popular tables are in the front "shop window" area. Behind the restaurant is Carole's pottery workshop; if you like your dinner plate, you can buy it. The eclectic menu has plenty of light dishes in the lower price range, with vegetarian options a strong point. Choices range from mussel and leek chowder to baked brill with a tapenade mash or Tuscan bean and curly-kale cassoulet. There's always steak, too. ⑤ *Average main: €18* ⊠ *3 Cork St., Kinsale, Co. Cork* ☎ *021/477–2847* ⊕ *www.crackpots.ie* ⊘ *Closed Mon.–Wed., Nov.–Mar. No lunch Mon.–Wed., Sept.–Easter.*

$ ✕ **Cucina.** Above the small bay windows of Cucina the bright blue sign
CONTEMPORARY   reads "Eat Drink Sleepover," indicating that something different is going on here. Ursula Roncken quit a high-flying international career in catering to live out her dream of opening a high-grade café offering light and healthy food in Kinsale. She had a gleaming polished-wood interior whipped up by a local craftsman and before long Cucina became the place to be seen mid-morning, reading the newspaper with a latte. Lunch entices with light bites like focaccia stuffed with Ardsallagh goat cheese, roasted tomato, crispy bacon, and baby spinach, plus daily backboard specials. In summer, and from Thursday to Saturday from November to March, Cucina serves a light dinner menu from 6 to 9 pm, with headliners like rib-eye steak over fried chips or a hot and cold fish platter featuring crispy squid, deep fried hake, salmon, crab, and prawns. The sleepover element consists of 4 simple rooms on the top floor, at 70 euros per room (breakfast not included). ⑤ *Average main: €10* ⊠ *9 Market St., Kinsale, Co. Cork* ☏ *021/477–0707* ⊕ *www.cucina.ie.*

$$ ✕ **Fishy Fishy Café.** Originally a café in a fish shop, Fishy Fishy has
SEAFOOD   moved up in the world and now occupies sumptuous indoor-outdoor
Fodor'sChoice   premises in the town park. The eatery's nautical style, with classy
★   wooden furniture and massive parasols, is modern and clean-lined.
☺   Crowds flock to stand in line for a table at peak times (1–2:30) because chef Martin Shanahan, who learned his craft in San Francisco, brings California pizzazz to his dishes. Look for wok-fried clams with spring onions, coriander, and ginger; "fishy fish" pie (white fish, salmon, and leeks in a hot cream sauce and mash au gratin); and seafood salad with a sweet chili dressing. It's all served by stylish young staffers who give the impression they are thrilled to be part of the show. Speaking of which, Martin's TV series, *Martin's Mad About Fish*, was a smash hit, especially with children, who can be seen leading their parents to the table here for a huge plate of battered fish and shoestring chips, Shanahan-style. The chef and his wife, Marie, do not take reservations for lunch, but they do for the limited dinner service (booking is advisable): until 9 pm from Tuesday to Saturday from March to October, and until 4:30 on Sunday and Monday. The rest of the year it's lunch only from Sunday to Wednesday, and dinner from Thursday to Saturday. ⑤ *Average main: €23* ⊠ *Crowley's Quay, Kinsale, Co. Cork* ☏ *021/470–0415* ⊕ *www.fishyfishy.ie.*

$$$ ✕ **Jim Edwards.** One of Ireland's original bar-restaurants, this is a famous
EUROPEAN   Kinsale institution known for its generous portions of local steak, lamb,
★   and duck, and fresh seafood, all prepared under the careful eye of the owner and his wife, Paula. Choose from the inexpensive daily specials in the busy bar ($), or have a more leisurely meal among the mahogany

> **WORD OF MOUTH**
>
> "When you visit Kinsale, if you do nothing else, make *sure* you take Don & Barry's Historic Kinsale Walking Tour. It was the best historical thing we did during our entire stay in Ireland. We had Barry Moloney as our guide and he was just fabulous! Lots of historical happenings in Kinsale to hear about, and loads of laughs."
> —Maggie1017

6

tables and dark-red decor of the somewhat baronial restaurant. With seafood this fresh, the preparation is kept simple: Kinsale oysters au naturel or crab claws tossed in garlic butter to start, followed by 10 ounces of prime fillet steak or medallions of monkfish (caught this morning) in a spring onion, ginger, and lime sauce. Fresh lobster from the tank is always available. The classic homemade desserts (profiteroles, crème brûlée) are substantial, and the Irish coffee is renowned. ⑤ *Average main: €26* ✉ *Market Quay, Kinsale, Co. Cork* ☎ *021/477–2541* ⊕ *www.jimedwardskinsale.com.*

$$$
FRENCH
✕ **Max's Wine Bar and Restaurant.** Polished antique tables, a large stone chimney, and bay windows facing the street lend the open-plan ground floor of this town house (more a restaurant than a wine bar) considerable charm. Lunches are light; it's a good place if you're keen on salads. At dinner, owner-chef Olivier Queva's classical French background is evident in his treatment of the daily catch, which includes fresh grilled lobster in the summer, and in his clever ways with such unusual cuts of meat as oxtail, trotters, and a wide range of offal. In winter, the catch of the day is replaced by game: quail, pheasant, wild duck, or venison. Olivier's Irish wife, Anne-Marie, ably tends the front of the house. The wine list is long and includes a good selection of French and New World wines. ⑤ *Average main: €27* ✉ *48 Main St., Kinsale, Co. Cork* ☎ *021/477–2443* ⊕ *www.maxs.ie* ⊙ *Closed Tues. and Dec.–mid-Mar.*

WHERE TO STAY

For expanded hotel reviews, visit Fodors.com.

$
B&B/INN
★
🖫 **Friar's Lodge.** A large Georgian town house has been tastefully converted into a cheerful guesthouse, with an array of facilities (but no bar or restaurant) that would do a hotel proud. **Pros:** private parking; quiet location; amazingly attentive service. **Cons:** no restaurant; no bar. **TripAdvisor:** "spacious rooms," "lovely service," "friendly place." ⑤ *Rooms from: €110* ✉ *Friar's St., Kinsale, Co. Cork* ☎ *021/477–7384* ⊕ *www.friars-lodge.com* ⇱ *18 rooms* ⊙ *Closed Christmas wk* ⎮○⎮ *Breakfast.*

$$
HOTEL
🖫 **Innishannon House.** A pretty country house built in 1720 in the châteaux style on the banks of the Bandon, Innishannon retains plenty of casual character. **Pros:** scenic riverside location; highly romantic; private car parking. **Cons:** a mile from nearest village; sometimes hosts wedding parties. **TripAdvisor:** "there's nowhere else as beautiful," "real traditional," "quaint." ⑤ *Rooms from: €130* ✉ *Innishannon, Co. Cork* ☎ *021/477–5121* ⊕ *www.innishannon-hotel.ie* ⇱ *12 rooms* ⎮○⎮ *Breakfast.*

$$
HOTEL
🖫 **Trident Hotel.** The modern three-story building may lack old-world charm, but the waterfront location more than compensates—built around three sides of a former dockyard on the edge of Kinsale's magnificent harbor, the Trident features large rooms with fabulous sea views. **Pros:** great sea views. **Cons:** bland decor; pool and spa at sister hotel a five-minute walk away. **TripAdvisor:** "will be back," "beautiful views and spacious bedrooms," "lovely staff." ⑤ *Rooms from: €150* ✉ *World's End, Kinsale, Co. Cork* ☎ *021/477–9300* ⊕ *www.tridenthotel.com* ⇱ *75 rooms* ⎮○⎮ *Breakfast.*

Thanks to locals painting their houses with bright colors the historic seaside village of Kinsale has become one of Ireland's most picturesque photo ops.

NIGHTLIFE

The Folk House. The friendly Folk House pub presents live music on weekends year-round, and midweek from May to October. ⊠ *Guardwell, Kinsale, Co. Cork* ☎ *021/477–2382* ⊕ *folkhousevenue.com.*

Shanakee. This club is renowned for live music—both rock and Irish traditional. ⊠ *Market St., Kinsale, Co. Cork* ☎ *021/477–4472.*

SPORTS AND THE OUTDOORS

GOLF

Fodor'sChoice
★

Old Head Golf Links. Golf doesn't get much more spectacular than this. On a celebrated 215-acre peninsula, which juts out into the wild Atlantic nearly 300 feet below, you can find an awe-inspiring spectacle that defies comparison. The only golfing stretches that could be likened to it are the 16th and 17th holes at Cypress Point and small, Pacific sections of Pebble Beach, from the 7th to the 10th, and the long 18th. Even if your golf is moderate, expect your pulse to race at the stunning views and wildlife. They've added 15 suites and a spa so you can now stay at the course for a few days. ⊠ *Kinsale, Co. Cork* ☎ *021/477–8444* ⊕ *www.oldhead.com* ⊠ *Greens fees: Apr. and Oct. €160; May–Sept. €200* ⌐ *18 holes. Yardage: 7,215. Par 72. Practice area, caddies (reserve in advance), caddy carts, club rental, catering* ⊗ *Visitors: daily. Closed Nov.–Mar.*

SHOPPING

ART

The Boathouse Gallery. Many of the works by locally based contemporary artists sold here are small enough to carry home. ⊠ *60 Main St., Kinsale, Co. Cork* ☎ *021/470–9981* ⊕ *www.theboathousegallery.ie.*

Giles Norman Photography Gallery. Black-and-white photographs of Irish scenes are featured at this local gallery. ⊠ *44 Main St., Kinsale, Co. Cork* ☎ *021/477–4373* ⊕ *www.gilesnorman.com.*

BOOKS

Kinsale Bookshop. Irish poetry and books on local history are the specialties of this fine bookshop. ⊠ *8 Main St., Kinsale, Co. Cork* ☎ *021/477–4244* ⊕ *www.kinsalebookshop.com.*

FOOD

Quay Food Company. Stock up on the Irish farmhouse cheeses and other local foods here for a great picnic. ⊠ *Market Square, Kinsale, Co. Cork* ☎ *021/470–4000.*

Tom's Artisan Bakery. The shop sells a wide range of breads baked daily, and irresistible cakes. Eat in or take away. ⊠ *18 Main St., Kinsale, Co. Cork* ☎ *021/470–6020.*

HOUSEWARES

Granny's Bottom Drawer. The shop carries a selection of fine linen and lace in classic and contemporary styles, and luxury designer knitwear. ⊠ *53 Main St., Kinsale, Co. Cork* ☎ *021/477–4839.*

Hilary Hale. This wood turner uses storm-felled locally grown timber to make lamps, bowls, and platters. ⊠ *Rincurran Hall, Summercove, Kinsale, Co. Cork* ☎ *021/477–2010* ⊕ *www.hilaryhale.com.*

Kinsale Crystal. This family-run studio sells handblown, hand-cut Irish crystal. ⊠ *Market St., Kinsale, Co. Cork* ☎ *21/477–4493* ⊕ *www. kinsalecrystal.ie.*

JEWELRY

Kinsale Silver. Silversmith Dominic Dolan crafts fine jewelry on the premises. ⊠ *Pearse St., Kinsale, Co. Cork* ☎ *021/477–4359* ⊕ *www. kinsalesilver.com.*

CLONAKILTY AND ENVIRONS

28 km (19 miles) west of Kinsale.

Clonakilty is a small market town to the west of Kinsale on a scenic, largely coastal road that passes through the village of Timoleague. Many of the storefronts in Clonakilty have charmingly traditional hand-painted signs and wooden facades. Clonakilty marks the western edge of the Seven Heads Peninsula, which stretches back eastward to Timoleague, whose ruined abbey dominates the view. Timoleague sits on the Argideen River estuary, renowned for its birdlife, especially great flocks of wintering migrants. From the abbey, you can see the road to Courtmacsherry, across the water. The sandy beach of this postcard-pretty village attracts many vacationers.

GETTING HERE AND AROUND

Clonakilty is 28 km (19 miles) west of Kinsale on the R600, Timoleague 19 km (12 miles). Follow the signposts from Timoleague to reach Courtmacsherry. Parking is easy in all three towns. There is no public transit between Kinsale and Clonakilty, but you can take the bus (about an hour) from Cork City.

EXPLORING

Timoleague Abbey. A mid-13th-century Franciscan abbey at the water's edge is Timoleague's most striking monument. The abbey was built before the estuary silted up, and its main business was the importing of wine from Spain. A tower and walls with Gothic-arch windows still stand, and you can trace the ground plan of the old friary—chapel, refectory, cloisters, and the extensive wine cellar. The English sacked the abbey in 1642, but like many other ruins of its kind it was used as a burial place until the late 20th century, hence the modern gravestones. ■TIP→ Walk around the back to find the entrance gate. The view of the sea framed by the structure's ruined Gothic windows is a don't-miss-it photo op. ⊠ *The Quay, Timoleague* ⊕ *www.timoleague.ie.*

OFF THE BEATEN PATH

Michael Collins Centre. It was in the village of Woodfield, 9 km (6 miles) west of Timoleague, that Michael Collins (1890–1922) had his last drink before he was shot in an ambush. The enthusiastic guide at this cottage-museum offers a lively introduction to the controversial hero of Irish independence, using slides, large photos, and film clips. Outside is a reconstruction of the ambush site, complete with Collins's armored Rolls-Royce and a Crossley tender. Directions to other Collins sites in the area are available, as are guided tours (pre-booking essential). ⊠ *Castleview, Woodfield, Co. Cork* ☎023/884–6107 ⊕ *www.michaelcollinscentre.com* ⊠ *€5* ⊙ *Mid-June–mid-Sept., weekdays 10:30–5, Sat. 11–2.*

WHERE TO EAT AND STAY

For expanded hotel reviews, visit Fodors.com.

$$
EUROPEAN
⊙

✕ The Pink Elephant. The legendary Pink Elephant looks out to sea and across the bay to wooded slopes. Huge windows frame the stunning view, and in good weather there is seating outside. The menu incorporates locally produced foods—organic leaves, farmhouse cheeses, smoked salmon, and the freshest fish and meats. Lunch includes a range of open sandwiches, a great beef burger, and healthy salads. Hearty mains dominate the dinner menu, on which you might find slow-roast shank of lamb with balsamic and red wine jus on scallion mash, roast monkfish with a tomato and mint salsa, even lentil moussaka. Desserts are substantial classics, including sticky toffee pie and raspberry and white chocolate cheesecake. This is also a popular bar, often made livelier by the banter between the friendly hosts, Jeremy and Niall, and their clientele. If not coming on a weekend, check the website or phone before traveling here, as opening times vary. ⑤ *Average main: €23* ⊠ *R600 between Kinsale and Timoleague, Harbour View, Kilbrittain, Co. Cork* ☎023/884–9608 ⊕ *www.pinkelephant.ie* ⊙ *Dinner Fri.–Sun., lunch Sat., Sun., and Wed. (daily in July and Aug.), otherwise phone to confirm.*

$$
B&B/INN
Fodor's Choice
★
⊙

Glen Country House. Midway between Kinsale and Clonakilty (9 miles from both) on the scenic R600, this elegant country hideaway—a lovely creeper-clad Victorian house—makes an excellent touring base, though many guests love to nestle down to enjoy the sheltered sea estuary and good walks. **Pros:** family atmosphere; gracious surroundings; great value. **Cons:** must drive, not walk, to nearest shops and eateries. **TripAdvisor:** "country class," "beautiful and peaceful home," "incredibly elegant property with wonderful hosts." $ *Rooms from: €120* ⊠ *Kilbrittain, Timoleague, Co. Cork* ☎ *023/884–9862* ⊕ *www.glencountryhouse.com* ⟿ *5 rooms* ⊙ *Closed Nov.–Mar.* ✝⃞ *Breakfast.*

$ ⊡ **Kilbrogan House.** This house at the highest point of Bandon, a mar-
B&B/INN ket town midway between Kinsale and Clonakilty, has been the community's architectural star since it was built in 1818—it's a good, peaceful base for touring that's off the beaten tourist trail. **Pros:** a haven of civilized style; out of the way; off-street parking. **Cons:** not much nightlife in town; limited restaurant scene in town. **TripAdvisor:** "amazing hospitality," "most comfortable bed," "superb accommodation." $ *Rooms from: €80* ⊠ *Kilbrogan Hill, Bandon, Co. Cork* ☎ *023/884–4935* ⊕ *www.kilbrogan.com* ⟿ *5 rooms* ⊙ *Closed Nov.–Feb.* ✝⃞ *Breakfast.*

SPORTS AND ACTIVITIES

BEACHES

Inchydoney Beach. The beach is on an island connected to the mainland by causeways, and accessible by car. It consists of two flat wide stretches of fine white sand divided by a rocky promontory. ■ TIP→ The east side is the most sheltered and has dunes that can be walked. The slope to the sea is so gentle, that at low tide it's a long walk to find deep water. Busy in July and August, its vast expanses offer exhilarating walks the rest of the year. **Amenities:** parking (free), lifeguards, toilets, water sports, hotel. **Best For:** walking, surfing, swimming. ⊠ *Inchydoney Island, 3 km (2 miles) south of town, Clonakilty, Co. Cork.*

SHOPPING

Clonakilty Market. Food producers sell fresh produce and artisan foods at this Friday market in a covered alley. ⊠ *Beside O'Donovan's Hotel, Main St., Clonakilty, Co. Cork* ⊙ *Fri. 9–2.*

Edward Twomey. This butcher's shop is famed for its Clonakilty Black Pudding, a breakfast product that's prominently featured on the shop's T-shirts—the ultimate West Cork souvenirs. ⊠ *16 Pearse St., Clonakilty, Co. Cork* ☎ *023/883–3365* ⊕ *www.clonakiltyblackpudding.ie.*

Etain Hickey Collections. Etain is one of Ireland's leading ceramic artists, and her shop stocks the best of contemporary crafts from local artists and fair-trade sources. ⊠ *40 Ashe St., Timoleague, Co. Cork* ☎ *023/882–1479* ⊕ *www.rossmorepottery.com.*

Lettercollum Kitchen Project. Owners Con McLaughlin and Karen Austin are masters of the vegetarian and ethnic repertory. Their bakery and deli sells specialty breads, cooks' ingredients, sandwiches, and savory herb tarts. You can assemble a superior picnic here. ⊠ *22 Connolly St., Clonakilty, Co. Cork* ☎ *023/883–6938* ⊕ *www.lettercollum.ie.*

SKIBBEREEN

33 km (20 miles) west of Clonakilty.
Skibbereen is the main market town in this neck of southwest Cork. The Saturday country market and the plethora of pubs, punctuated by bustling shops, supermarkets, and coffeehouses, keep the place jumping year-round.

> **GOING NATIVE**
>
> If you really want to see Skibbereen at its liveliest, come on a Wednesday when the cattle market is in full swing, and the sounds of men spitting and back-slapping fill the air.

GETTING HERE AND AROUND

Skibbereen is 85 km (53 miles) southwest of Cork City, a drive of an hour and 20 minutes on the N71, the main Bantry road. The town lies 33 km (20 miles) west of Clonakilty—about half an hour's drive. There is free parking on street and in several car parks. Buses depart from Cork Bus Station Parnell Place, but there's no local public transport. For local excursions, contact Long's Taxis. Skibbereen is a designated hub of the National Cycle Network, with three sign-posted routes of one-day and half-day trips. Book a bike in advance from Roycroft Cycles.

ESSENTIALS

Transportation Contacts Long's Taxis ✉ *Market Sq., Skibbereen, Co. Cork* ☎ *087/666–6666.* **Roycroft Cycles** ✉ *Ilen St., Skibbereen, Co. Cork* ☎ *028/21235* ⊕ *www.westcorkcycles.ie.*

Visitor Information Skibbereen Tourist Office ✉ *North St., Skibbereen, Co. Cork* ☎ *028/21766* ⊕ *www.discoverireland.ie/skibbereentio.*

EXPLORING

Mizen Vision Visitor Centre. Travel to this visitor center, set in a lighthouse at the tip of the Mizen Head (follow the R591 through Goleen to the end of the road), and you'll wind up reaching the Irish mainland's most southerly point. The lighthouse itself is on a rock at the tip of the headland; to reach it, you must cross a dramatic 99-step suspension footbridge. The lighthouse was completed in 1910; the Engine Room and Keepers' House have been restored by the local community. The exhilaration of massive Atlantic seas swirling 164 feet below the footbridge and the great coastal views guarantee a memorable outing. ✉ *Harbour Rd., Goleen, Co. Cork* ☎ *028/35115* ⊕ *www.mizenhead.ie* 🖾 *€4.50* ☉ *Mid-Mar.–May and Oct., daily 10:30–5; June–Sept., daily 10–6; Nov.–mid-Mar., weekends 11–4.*

Skibbereen Heritage Centre. A thoughtful renovation of a stone gasworks building has created an attractive, architecturally appropriate home for the Skibbereen Heritage Center. An elaborate audiovisual exhibit on the Great Famine presents dramatized firsthand accounts of what it was like to live in this community when it was hit hard by hunger. Other attractions include displays on area marine life, walking tours, access to local census information, and a varying schedule of special programs. ✉ *Upper Bridge St., Skibbereen, Co. Cork* ☎ *028/40900* ⊕ *www.skibbheritage. com* 🖾 *€6* ☉ *Mid-Mar.–mid-May and mid-Sept.–Oct., Tues.–Sat. 10–6; late May–mid-Sept., daily 10–6; mid-Nov.–mid-Mar., by appointment.*

WHERE TO EAT

$$$$ **✕ Island Cottage.** On Heir Island, this unlikely venture is a pilgrimage
EUROPEAN spot for food lovers, who praise the high standard of cooking and the
★ location. The five-course (no choices) set menu focuses on local produce, some of it picked in the wild on the island. Expect good, honest, unfussy food—the best of new Irish Traditional. The restaurant is
country-casual and tables seat 10, so be prepared to share. Cape Clear
turbot with sea spinach is typical; for dessert, you might have the terrine of vanilla ice cream with meringue in blackberry sauce. The proprietors, John Desmond and Ellmary Fenton, also operate "the world's
smallest cooking school" here. Advance booking is necessary for both
the restaurant and the cooking classes (lunch is for prebooked groups
only); call for details about the four-minute ferry ride to the island
from Cunnamore, which is about 15 km (9 miles) west of Skibbereen
(follow signs on the road to Ballydehob). ⑤ *Average main: €45* ✉ *Heir
Island, Skibbereen, Co. Cork* ☎ *028/38102* ⊕ *www.islandcottage.com*
⚞ *Reservations essential* ▭ *No credit cards* ⏰ *Closed mid-Sept.–mid-
June, Sun.–Tues. mid-June–mid-Sept.*

SHOPPING

West Cork Craft and Design Guild. About two-dozen elite craft makers
belong to this association; most of them welcome visitors to their studios by appointment. ☎ *028/21890* ⊕ *www.westcorkcraft.org.*

CASTLETOWNSHEND

8 km (5 miles) southeast of Skibbereen.

Castletownshend has an unusual number of large, stone houses, most
of them dating from the mid-18th century, when it was an important
port. The main street runs steeply downhill to the 17th-century castle
(built by the noted regional family of the Townshends) and the sea. The
sleepy town awakens in July and August, when its sheltered harbor
bustles. Sparkling views await from cliff-top St. Barrahane's Church,
which has a medieval oak altarpiece and three stained-glass windows
by early-20th-century Irish artist Harry Clarke.

GETTING HERE AND AROUND

Castletownshend lies southeast of Skibbereen on R596. The best way
to get here and around is by car. The 8-km (5-mile) drive takes about
10 minutes.

WHERE TO EAT

$$$ **✕ Mary Ann's.** Writer Edna O'Brien calls this low-beamed pub, one of
EUROPEAN Ireland's oldest, her favorite in the world. Mary Ann's mostly wealthy
★ visitors mingle happily with the few locals left in the village in the front
barroom, the quieter back room, or the large garden beyond. Owner-
manager Fergus O'Mahony is a brilliant host, always on the spot super-
vising the operations and contributing to the *craic* (lively conversation).
The bar-food menu ($) is served all day in the main bar area. Upstairs,
the 32-seat restaurant nearly always buzzes, so reservations are a good
idea. Try the trademark baked avocado stuffed with crabmeat, the mas-
sively generous platter of Castlehaven Bay shellfish and seafood, or the
succulent T-bone steak. This is a good place to sample a platter of the

local farmhouse cheeses, such as Durrus, Milleens, Gabriel, and Gubbeen. $ *Average main: €26* ⊠ *Main St., Castletownshend, Co. Cork* ☎ *028/36146* ⊕ *www.westcorkweek.com/maryanns* ☾ *Phone to confirm hours open Nov.–Mar. No bar food Mon., Nov.–Mar.*

BANTRY BAY

Between 6 and 8 miles wide, Bantry Bay is one of the largest natural harbors in the world. It was here that the French attempted to land a force of some 14,000 men in 1796, during the Napoleonic Wars. A combination of foul winds and naval incompetence proved their undoing. The chief market town for this part of Cork is Bantry, which lies at the head of Bantry Bay. This is a quiet rural area where small family farms, fishing, and shellfish farming are the main industries besides tourism.

BANTRY

25 km (16 miles) northwest of Skibbereen.

Fodor's Choice ★ The town of Bantry is situated at the head of Bantry Bay, between the Sheep's Head Peninsula to the southwest and the Beara Peninsula to the northwest. A somewhat unprepossessing town at first sight, Bantry is topped out with a large square that attracts artisans, craftspeople, and musicians to its Friday morning market in summer. If you approach Bantry heading west on the seaside road, before you reach town you'll spot the parking lot and visitor's entrance to the area's big attraction, Bantry House and Gardens.

GETTING HERE AND AROUND

Bantry is on the N71, midway between Skibbereen and Kenmare, an hour-and-a-half drive from Cork and an hour from Killarney. There is a large car park (free) in the main square. Buses from Cork Bus Station Parnell Place continue on to Glengarriff *(see Glengarriff)*. There is no other local public transport.

ESSENTIALS

Ireland can be expensive, but in this part of the country many of the best things are free. Ask at tourist information offices about the many coves and small beaches or the looped walks along sections of the Sheep's Head Walking Route. The Irish Trails website is a good resource for walks.

Visitor Information Bantry Tourist Office ⊠ *New Bantry St., Bantry, Co. Cork* ☎ *27/50229* ⊕ *www.bantry.ie.* **Irish Trails** ⊠ *Co. Cork* ⊕ *www.irishtrails.ie/trails. aspx?c=Cork.*

EXPLORING

Fodor's Choice ★ **Bantry House and Gardens.** One of Ireland's most famed manors, Bantry House and Gardens is noted for its picture-perfect perch: on a hillock above the south shore of Bantry Bay, the house is surrounded by a series of stepped gardens and parterres that make up "the stairway to the sky." Spreading out below the Georgian mansion lies the bay and, in the far distance, the spectacular range of the Caha Mountains—one of the great vistas of Ireland. Built in the early 1700s and altered and expanded later that century, the manor was the ancestral seat of the White family. The house is largely the vision of Richard White, the first earl of Bantry, who traveled extensively through Europe and brought a lot of it back with him: fabulous Aubusson tapestries said to have been commissioned by Louis XV adorn the Rose Drawing Room, while state portraits of King George III and Queen Charlotte glitter in floridly rococo gilt frames in the hypertheatrical, Wedgwood-blue and gold dining room. An antique or two is thought to have belonged to Marie-Antoinette.

Outside, the drama continues in the stepped garden terraces, set with marble statues, framed by stone balustrades, and showcasing such delights as an embroidered parterre of dwarf box. The tearoom serves light lunches, and features local artisan foods. In summer the house hosts concerts in the grand library room, notably the West Cork Chamber Music Festival (held during the first week of July). ☎ *027/50047* ⊕ *www.bantryhouse.ie* ✉ *House and gardens €11* ☉ *Apr.–Oct., daily 10–6; spring opening can vary.*

WHERE TO EAT AND STAY
For expanded hotel reviews, visit Fodors.com.

Bantry's hotels offer two distinct dining experiences The Seaview House is a good place for a quiet meal in elegant surroundings, while the Maritime has a busy bar and restaurant area, and a children's menu.

$$
SEAFOOD
✕ **O'Connors Seafood Restaurant.** Owner-chef Pat Kiely plies his trade in Bantry's main square, a stone's throw from the sea that provides the bulk of his menu. The sophisticated taupe and bronze shop front with model yachts in the windows indicates the presence of a restaurant with serious ambitions, while the unfussy cream and beige interior is calming and comfortable. Kiely has a way with fish: local oysters are baked with stout and walnuts, and monkfish is served with a wild smoked-venison risotto. Sea-fresh local mussels are served every which way: grilled and topped with garlic and herb breadcrumb, in a Thai coconut sauce, and à la marinara. A more conventional standout, the seafood pie, is topped with mashed-potato gratin. Meat and vegetarian dishes are also served. ⑤ *Average main: €24* ⊠ *Wolfe Tone Square, Bantry, Co. Cork* ☎ *027/55664* ⊕ *www.oconnorseafood.com* ☉ *Daily, lunch and dinner.*

$$$
B&B/INN
★
▥ **Bantry House.** When the day-trippers leave, you can play lord and lady of this celebrated manor for the night, thanks to 12 guest bedrooms— set in a self-contained wing off a long corridor with views of the south-facing garden and its famous stone terraces linked by the Hundred Steps, these are not the biggest nor the stateliest of stately-home guest bedrooms, but the ambience is truly memorable. **Pros:** a genuine heritage experience; unique location; friendly, helpful hosts; not as pricey as you'd think. **Cons:** a longish walk (or a short drive) into town; worth the premium only if you are into history and heritage. **TripAdvisor:** "unspoiled timeless elegance," "superb and memorable," "extremely helpful staff." ⑤ *Rooms from: €200* ⊠ *Bantry, Co. Cork* ☎ *027/50047* ⊕ *www.bantryhouse.ie* ⇱ *6 rooms* ☉ *Closed Nov.–mid-Mar.*

Divided by the Hundred Steps, the gardens of Bantry House are adorned with exotic plants due to the microclimate of its bay setting.

\$\$
HOTEL
Fodor's Choice
★
☾

The Maritime Hotel. A legacy of Ireland's boom years, this gleaming new waterfront hotel recalls times when building budgets were lavish, as the lobby—replete with black marble floor, flickering gas fire, modern chandeliers, and custom-made boat-shaped reception desk—reveals. **Pros:** great location, high comfort levels; top value for these medium-range rates. **Cons:** long, dimly lit internal corridors, some rooms accessible only via two elevators. **TripAdvisor:** "very nice," "great location," "modern rooms." ⑤ *Rooms from: €150* ⊠ *The Quay, Bantry, Co. Cork* ☎ *027/54700* ⊕ *www.themaritime.ie* ⇄ *110 rooms.*

\$\$\$
HOTEL

Seaview House Hotel. Among private, wooded grounds overlooking Bantry Bay, you'll find this large, three-story, 19th-century country house. **Pros:** unostentatious comfort; good food; low-key, friendly service. **Cons:** make your own entertainment; "village" is more a suburb of Bantry, with only one pub. **TripAdvisor:** "tranquility by the sea," "a little oasis of peace," "great staff and a friendly owner." ⑤ *Rooms from: €210* ⊠ *Ballylickey, Co. Cork* ☎ *027/50073* ⊕ *www.seaviewhousehotel. com* ⇄ *25 rooms* ☾ *Closed mid-Nov.–mid-Mar.* ⱐ⊙ⱐ *Breakfast.*

SHOPPING

Manning's Emporium. On the road between Bantry and Glengarriff, this shop is a showcase for locally made farmhouse cheeses, pâtés, and salamis—an excellent place to assemble a picnic or just to browse. ⊠ *Ballylickey, Co. Cork* ☎ *027/50456* ⊕ *www.manningsemporium.ie.*

GLENGARRIFF

14 km (8 miles) northwest of Bantry.

★ One of the jewels of Bantry Bay is Glengarriff, the "rugged glen" much loved by the writers William Thackeray and Sir Walter Scott. The drive from Bantry along the cliff top, with views of the islands of the bay and its shelter belt of mountains, is one of the scenic highlights of West Cork, while the descent into the sheltered wooded village reveals yet another landscape: thanks to the Gulf Stream, it's mild enough down here for subtropical plants to thrive. Trails along the shore are covered with rhododendrons and offer beautiful views of the nearby inlets, loughs, and lounging seals. You're very much on the beaten path, however, with crafts shops, tour buses, and boatmen soliciting your business by the roadside.

GETTING HERE AND AROUND

Glengarriff is a 10-minute drive 14 km (8 miles) from Bantry on the N71. There is a large public car park at Quill's Woolen Mills; on-street parking is easily found, too. Buses from Cork City stop here, and some continue to the Beara Peninsula. There is no public transport locally, but you can take a boat trip around the harbor, where huge seals bask in fine weather.

EXPLORING

Blue Pool Ferry. Buy a ticket at the kiosk beside the Quill's Woolen Mills car park, and follow the trail to an enchanting hidden harbor that's surrounded by rocks and overhanging trees. Boats leave from here for Garnish Island and Illnacullin Gardens. No need to land—you can take a round-trip tour and enjoy the wildlife of the bay, which includes a colony of comical basking seals. Cameras at the ready! ⊠ *Glengarriff, Co. Cork* ☏ *027/63333* ⊕ *www.bluepoolferry.com* ⊡ *€3.50* ☉ *Nov.–mid-Mar.*

Fodor'sChoice **Ilnacullin.** Many visitors head to Glengarriff because of that Irish Eden,
★ Ilnacullin. On Garnish Island, offshore from Glengarriff and beyond islets populated by comical-looking basking seals, you can find one of the country's horticultural wonders. In 1910 a Belfast businessman, John Annan Bryce, purchased this rocky isle, and, with the help of famed English architect Howard Peto and Scottish plantsman Murdo Mackenzie, transformed it into a botanical Disneyland. The main showpiece is a wisteria-covered "Casita"—a rather strange-looking half-shed, half-mansion that overlooks a sunken Italian garden. Ilnacullin has a little bit of everything, from a Grecian temple to a Martello tower to a "Happy Valley," all bedded with extraordinary shrubs, trees, and many unusual subtropical flowers.

You get to Ilnacullin by taking a Blue Pool ferry (10 minutes), which departs for the island from Glengarriff. George Bernard Shaw found Ilnacullin peaceful enough to allow him to begin his St. Joan here; maybe you'll find Garnish inspiring, too. ⊠ *Garnish Island, Co. Cork* ☏ *027/63040* ⊕ *www.heritageireland.ie/en/south-west* ⊡ *Gardens €4, ferry €12 round-trip* ☉ *July and Aug., Mon.–Sat. 9:30–6:30, Sun. 11–6:30; Apr.–June and Sept., Mon.–Sat. 10–6:30, Sun. noon–6:30; Oct., Mon.–Sat. 10–4:30, Sun. 1–5. Closed Nov.–Mar.*

Ring of Beara. Glengarriff is the gateway to the Ring of Beara, a 137-km (85-mile) scenic drive that circles the Beara Peninsula on R572. One of the main attractions is the Beara Way, a 196-km (120-mile) marked walking route that takes in prehistoric archaeological sites. Dursey Island is a bird-watcher's paradise that you reach by cable car. From Dursey Island, head for tiny Allihies, the former site of a huge copper mine, now the home of several leading Irish artists, some of whom invite studio visits (watch for signs). Continue along a breathtaking coastal road to Eyeries—a village overlooking Coulagh Bay—and then up the south side of the Kenmare River to Kenmare.

WHERE TO STAY

For expanded hotel reviews, visit Fodors.com.

$$

HOTEL

☑ **Glengarriff Eccles.** Fronted by a massive wrought-iron balcony, this stately landmark has looked out over the calm water of Glengarriff's harbor since before the Victorian novelist William Thackeray passed through. **Pros:** water's edge location; great sense of history; locals use the bar. **Cons:** 5-minute walk from village; a bit eerie when not busy. **TripAdvisor:** "quiet and friendly," "old-world," "best sea view ever." ⑤ *Rooms from: €140* ✉ *Glengarriff Harbour, Glengarriff, Co. Cork* ☎ *027/63003* ⊕ *www.eccleshotel.com* ↩ *66 rooms.*

6

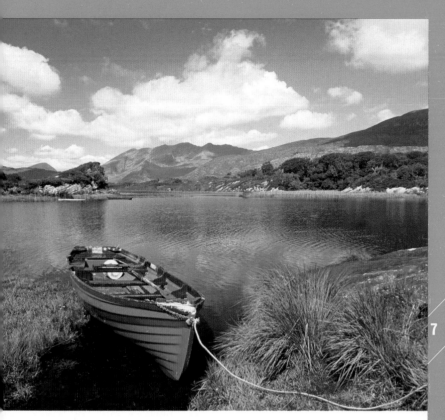

The Southwest

INCLUDING COUNTIES KERRY AND LIMERICK

WORD OF MOUTH

"Overall, the trip from Dublin to Dingle took eight hours total, and we drove 370 km. We were on the road for six of those eight hours, and stopped for two of them. The driving was so wonderful. We saw many beautiful scenes from the road, and stopped here and there to take in some particularly inspiring views."

—Haven17

WELCOME TO THE SOUTHWEST

TOP REASONS TO GO

★ **The Ring of Kerry:**
The most brazenly scenic coastal drive in Ireland might have been designed with the visitor in mind—get ready to use up your entire flash card in a jiffy!

★ **Skellig Michael:**
Take a wet and wonderful ride out to Ireland's most spectacular island, whose twin peaks, crowned with a medieval monastery, beckon to you along the Ring of Kerry.

★ **The Gap of Dunloe:**
A half-day tour lets you walk or ride horseback through the heart of Killarney's purple mountains and cross the glittering blue lake by rowboat.

★ **Adare:** Discover Ireland's prettiest village by taking a walk past its dinky thatched cottages to the banks of the River Maigue, where the remains of priories established by medieval monks still stand.

★ **"Castle Country":**
Limerick is studded with top attractions like King John's Castle on the banks of the Shannon.

1 Killarney and Environs.
Nineteenth-century visitors found the views of Killarney every bit as romantic and uplifting as the mountains of Switzerland; the unique combination of glacial landscape and abundant subtropical vegetation, studded by the bright blue waters of

GETTING ORIENTED

In the Southwest, five-star scenery is everywhere from the mountains and lakes of Killarney, out to Kerry's craggy western peninsulas. Brightly painted villages and small harbors encourage you to stop and linger—and when you do, you're rewarded with exceptional food, particularly in Kenmare and Dingle, towns that boast an extraordinary number of talented chefs in proportion to their size. Off the western coast, the Skelligs rank as the region's most awesome sight, though it takes an often-choppy boat ride to reach them. Adare, midway between Kerry and Limerick, is both picture-book pretty and rich in historical churches and monasteries. Limerick's historic center is the gateway to an area rich in mighty castles.

7

the lakes creates an unforgettable vista—and it smells good, too, with peat-fire smoke mingling with fresh mountain air.

2 The Ring of Kerry. One of Europe's great scenic drives, this route runs around the edge of this rocky peninsula, passing from the subtropical splendor of Sneem, on the sheltered Kenmare River, past Waterville, where the twin-peaked Skellig rocks hover on the horizon, to the starker views of Dingle Bay to the north.

3 Corca Dhuibhne: The Dingle Peninsula. Dingle Town is a-hopping, between the live traditional music in its numerous bars, and the sea-fresh seafood on offer in its eateries; head west to Slea Head for stunning coastal scenery, with vast sandy beaches, rocky islands, and Iron Age ruins.

4 North Kerry and Shannonside. Beyond the pretty and historic village of Adare with its dinky thatched cottages is the great River Shannon. Limerick City bears the scars of history from the 1691 Siege of Limerick—a confrontation with the English.

Updated
by Alannah
Hopkin

Ever since Killarney was first "discovered" by William Thackeray and Sir Walter Scott, visitors have been searching for superlatives to describe the deep blue lakes, dark green forests, and purple mountainsides of this romantic region. Perhaps it was no surprise that things couldn't remain low-key here forever. Today, the Ring of Kerry coastal drive can be packed with tour buses from April to October, and Killarney's town center, thronged with scurrying visitors, clearly has its eye on the tourist dollar.

But to be in a hurry in the Southwest is to be ill mannered. To truly enjoy the amazing array of scenic delights found here, remember that the locals of the Southwest—this region stretches from the Ring of Kerry in the south, the Dingle Peninsula in the west, through Killarney and north to Adare, Limerick, and the region's gateway, Shannon Airport—are unusually laid-back, even by Irish standards. They still remember what attracted tourists in the first place: uncrowded roads, unpolluted beaches and rivers, easy access to golf, and unspoiled scenery. So take your cue from them and venture onto the back roads. Meander along at your own pace, sampling wayside delights. Before you know it, you'll be far from Killarney Town's crowds and in the middle of the region's tranquil and incredibly stunning landscapes.

If Mother Nature doesn't cooperate, there is always the bounty of man-made attractions. Moving northward, scenery becomes less dramatic but much cozier, with Adare's thatched cottages giving the village the reputation as one of Ireland's prettiest. Head up to Limerick and a busy four-lane highway hurls you back into the 21st century. Metropolitan hub of southwest Ireland (and the Republic's third largest city), Limerick bears the scars of history, most notably from the Siege of Limerick, a face-off with the English that took place in 1691. Its other "scars" of history—described so memorably in Frank McCourt's best seller *Angela's Ashes*—lure travelers who discover that this is a compact, vibrant city.

THE SOUTHWEST PLANNER

WHEN TO GO

The best times to visit the Ring of Kerry, Killarney, and Dingle are mid-March to June, and September and October. In July and August it's the peak holiday period, meaning roads are more crowded, prices are higher, and the best places are booked in advance. March can be chilly, with daily temperatures in the 40s and 50s. The average high in June is 18°C (65°F), which is about as hot as it gets. May and June are the sunniest months, while May and September are the driest months. The farther west you go, the more likely you'll get rain. The weather is not such a crucial factor in Adare and the Limerick area, but from November to mid-March daylight hours are short, the weather is damp, and many smaller places on the Kerry coast and in Killarney are closed.

PLANNING YOUR TIME

If you're here for a short stay—three or fewer days—you'd do well to base yourself in Killarney and devote your time to exploring the surrounding area, then heading out to the Ring of Kerry or the Dingle Peninsula. With more time at your disposal, consider a half-day trip to Skellig Michael, an unforgettable remote, rock-hewn monastery, or Adare, one of Ireland's prettiest villages.

You also want to pick your peninsula, for two of Ireland's most scenic destinations sit side by side on the map: the Iveragh Peninsula (also known as the Ring of Kerry, for its scenic drive) and the Dingle Peninsula (also known by its Irish name, Corca Dhuibhne). If you like wild, rugged scenery, archaeological remains, and Irish music, Dingle is for you. In contrast, the Ring of Kerry is a longer drive with more varied scenery, ranging from lush subtropical vegetation to rocky coves and long sandy beaches near Glenbeigh. The scenery is punctuated by a series of small villages, all much quieter than Dingle.

IF YOU HAVE THREE DAYS

Spend day one driving the Ring of Kerry, pausing often to take in the varied coastal scenery. Spend the night in Kemare or Killarney, then head out the next morning to explore Killarney National Park either on a boat trip or in a horse-drawn jaunting car. Next head for Dingle and drive the Slea Head loop, before enjoying fresh seafood and live traditional music in Dingle Town, a good overnight stop. On your third morning, drive the Conor Pass to Tralee, heading away from the rugged coast to rich farmlands and a short walk around historic Adare. Finish the day with a walking tour and overnight stay in Limerick City.

GETTING HERE AND AROUND

AIR TRAVEL

The Southwest can be accessed from two international airports: Cork (ORK) on the southwest coast, and Shannon (SNN) in the west (26 km [16 miles] west of Limerick City). Cork Airport is about two hours' drive from both Killarney and Kenmare. Shannon Airport is 135 km (84 miles) from Killarney via Limerick, a journey that takes about 2½ hours. Kerry County Airport (KIR) at Farranfore, 16 km (10 miles) from Killarney, has daily flights from Dublin, London (Stansted and Luton), and Frankfurt (Hahn) operated by Ryanair.

Airport Information **Kerry County Airport** ☎ *066/976–4644* ⊕ *www.kerryairport.ie.*

AIRPORT
TRANSFERS

Bus Éireann runs a 40-minute bus route (€5) between Shannon Airport and Limerick City between 8 am and midnight. J. J. Kavannagh runs a popular bus shuttle to Shannon Airport, connecting with Limerick (45 minutes; €5 one-way).

Shuttles **J. J. Kavannagh Buses** ☎ *081/833–3222* ⊕ *www.jjkavanagh.ie.*

BUS TRAVEL

Bus Éireann operates express services from Dublin to Limerick City, and Tralee. Most towns in the region are served by the provincial Bus Éireann network. The main Bus Éireann bus stations in the region are at Limerick and Tralee, and there is also a bus station in Killarney. The bus stations are located outside the railway stations. Citylink (a private bus company) offers a reliable alternative to Bus Éireann, serving Dublin, Shannon, and Cork airports, and the city centers of Cork, Dublin, Limerick, and Galway.

Buses tend to stop running in the early evening, which is fine if you want to stay overnight and leave the next morning, but it rules out many day trips—unless you want to spend most of the day on the bus. As a general rule, the smaller the town, and the more remote, the less frequent its bus service: some of the smaller villages on the remote Corca Dhuibhne (Dingle Peninsula) have bus service only one day a week in winter. Bus Éireann runs a regular bus service around the Ring of Kerry between mid-June and mid-September, but there are only two buses a day, leaving Killarney at 8:45 am or 1:45 pm.

Bus Information **Citylink** ☎ *091/564164* ⊕ *www.citylink.ie.*

CAR TRAVEL

A car is the ideal way to explore this region, packed as it is with scenic routes, attractive but remote towns, and a host of out-of-the-way restaurants and hotels that deserve a detour. Road upgrades have not kept up with the increased usage, as a result prepare for peak-hour traffic jams.

The main driving route from Dublin is N7, which goes 192 km (120 miles) directly to Limerick City. If you land at Shannon Airport, access to the southwest is also via Limerick City; from there, pick up the N21 to Killarney. From Limerick it is about two hours to Killarney (111 km [69 miles]), and another half hour to Kenmare. An alternate, more scenic, route from Dublin leaves the N7 at Naas to join the N8 at Portlaoise, turning off the main Dublin–Cork road at Mitchelstown and following the N72 to Killarney. Both journeys from Dublin take about four hours; many people prefer to fly from Dublin to Kerry Airport (40 minutes) and pick up a rental car there.

TAXI TRAVEL

A taxi from Shannon Airport to Limerick City costs about €35. It costs €4.10 to hire a taxi on the street (€4.45 by night); add €2 to book one by phone, and €1.03 per kilometer.

Full details of fares and conditions are on the Taxi Regulator website. Taxis are also found at railway stations in Tralee, Killarney, and Limerick, and at Shannon and Kerry airports. Otherwise, they must be prebooked by phone: ask for the number of the local company at your hotel or B&B.

Taxi Companies All Route Taxis ✉ *Limerick* ☎ *061/300–777.* **Cork Taxi Co-Op** ✉ *6 Washington St. West, Cork* ☎ *021/427–2222* ⊕ *www.corktaxi.ie.* **Killarney Cabs** ✉ *Killarney* ☎ *064/663–7444.* **Taxi Regulator** ⊕ *www.taxiregulator.ie.* **Tralee Radio Taxis** ✉ *Tralee* ☎ *066/712–5451* ⊕ *www.traleeradiotaxis.com.*

TRAIN TRAVEL

The region is accessible by train from Dublin Heuston Station and from Cork's Kent Station. From Dublin the region is served by two direct rail links, to Limerick Junction (where you change trains for Limerick City), and on to Tralee (via Mallow and Killarney). The rail network is mainly useful for moving from one touring base to another.

For more information on getting here and around, see Travel Smart Ireland.

RESTAURANTS

The Southwest can almost be described as one big culinary hot spot. Kenmare, Dingle, and Killarney all have a high density of restaurants and gastro-pubs serving locally reared meat, artisan cheeses, and local seafood. Kerry mountain lamb has a unique flavor imparted by the wild herbs and grasses that those sheep you see on every hillside are busy munching on. Adare also has an array of tempting restaurants: choose between the low-ceilinged charm of the tiny rooms in the thatched cottage restaurant, the Wild Geese, and the genuine old-world hospitality at the blissfully comfortable Dunraven Arms, an old coaching inn still with some of its original antiques, that is now one of Ireland's leading hotels.

Prices in the reviews are the average cost of a main course at dinner or, if dinner is not served, at lunch.

HOTELS

For accommodations, the Southwest has some of the great country houses, including Adare Manor in County Limerick; Kenmare's unique duo of the magnificent Sheen Falls Lodge and the stately Park Hotel; the Cahernane House, which recalls Killarney's Victorian heyday; and finally the rambling landmark resort, the Parknasilla Resort in Sneem, a great place for a family break. At the other end of the spectrum is the uniquely Irish experience of a farmhouse bed-and-breakfast, such as Lakelands Farm Guesthouse in Waterville, with rowboats bobbing on Lough Currane at the bottom of the garden. In between is a range of excellent family-owned and -run traditional hotels, such as the Brook Lane Hotel in Kenmare, the Butler Arms in Waterville, and the secluded Carrig Country House at Glenbeigh near Killorglin.

Prices in the reviews are the lowest cost of a standard double room in high season.

TOUR OPTIONS

BUS TOURS

Bus Éireann offers a range of daylong and half-day guided tours from June to September. You can book them at the bus station in Killarney, or at any tourist office. A full-day tour costs about €30, half-day €15. The memorable Gap of Dunloe Tour (at €25) includes a coach or vintage bus and boat trip. Add €20 for a horse-drawn carriage ride through the Gap. There are three companies offering this tour, which can be booked through the Killarney Tourist Office. More conventional day trips can also be made to the Ring of Kerry, An Daingean (Dingle), and Ceann Sleibne (Slea Head), and to Caragh Lake and Rossbeigh. A full-day (10:30–5) tour costs from €20 to €30 per person, excluding lunch and refreshments. These can be booked through the Killarney TIO. Keating Coaches offers day trips and half-day tours of the Shannon region from Limerick City (book in advance). Themes include "castles and gardens"; "waterways, highways, and byways"; and "flying boats, monks, and dolphins."

Bus Tour Companies **Bus Éireann** ☎ *061/313–333 in Limerick, 066/716–4700 in Tralee* ⊕ *www.buseireann.ie.* **Keating Coaches** ☎ *69/68201* ⊕ *www.limericktours.com.*

SPECIAL-INTEREST TOURS

Adams and Butler organizes self-driven or chauffeur-driven group tours with accommodations in private country houses and castles. It also conducts special-interest tours, including gardens, architecture, ghosts, and golf, while Killorglin-based Go Ireland offers comprehensive packages for walking, cycling, fishing, golfing, and equestrian holidays on the Ring of Kerry and the Dingle Peninsula with experienced local guides.

Hidden Ireland Tours has two knowledgeable Irish-based guides, Con Moriarty of Killarney and Ann Curran of Dingle, who will tailor a package to suit your interests, catering for groups of 2 to 16 people, and upwards. Consider an eight-day walking tour with bases in Killarney and Dingle, or a luxurious car tour staying in some of the region's best country-house hotels. Slow Food, painting, literary tours, or antiques tours can also be arranged.

Tour Companies **Adams & Butler** ☎ *01/288–9355* ⊕ *www.adamsandbutler.com.* **Go Ireland** ☎ *066/976–2094* ⊕ *www.govisitireland.com.* **Hidden Ireland Tours** ☎ *087/258–1966* ⊕ *www.hiddenirelandtours.com.*

WALKING TOURS

SouthWestWalks Ireland has a variety of walks on the Ring of Kerry and around Killarney; some include accommodations and evening meals. Activity Ireland organizes customized walking and climbing tours on the Ring of Kerry. Outdoors Ireland offers hill walking and rock climbing in the Kerry hills. Irish Ways Walking Tours organizes walking tours for two or more in Dingle, Killarney, and Ring of Kerry. Richard Clancy, a noted historian, offers a two-hour guided walk (€9) in Killarney National Park daily at 11 am; departures are from O'Sullivan's

Bike Shop on Lower New Street in Killarney; book early for November–April. Limerick City Tours has city walks June to September; they can be booked at the Tourist Office. St. Mary's Action Centre has an *Angela's Ashes* Tour on request (book in advance).

Tour Information Outdoors Ireland ☎ 086/860–4563 ⊕ www.outdoorsireland.com. Irish Ways Walking Tours ☎ 353/1260–0749 ⊕ www.irishways.com. Limerick City Tours ☎ 087/235–1339. Richard Clancy ☎ 064/663–3471 ⊕ www.killarneyguidedwalks.com. St. Mary's Action Centre ☎ 061/318–106 ⊕ www.iol.ie/~smidp. SouthWestWalks Ireland ☎ 066/712–8733 ⊕ www.southwestwalksireland.com.

VISITOR INFORMATION

Fáilte Ireland provides a free information service; its tourist information offices (TIOs) also sell a selection of tourist literature. For a small fee it will book accommodations anywhere in Ireland. Seasonal TIOs in Waterville, Portmagee, Cahirciveen, and Listowelare open from May to October; the TIO in Kenmare is open April to October. All of the seasonal TIOs are generally open Monday–Saturday 9–6; in July and August they are also open Sunday 9–6. Year-round TIOs can be found in Adare, An Daingean/Dingle, Killarney, Limerick Shannon Airport, and Tralee. These offices are usually open Monday–Saturday 9–6 and also Sunday 9–6 in July and August.

KILLARNEY AND ENVIRONS

87 km (54 miles) west of Cork City, 19 km (12 miles) southeast of Killorglin, 24 km (15 miles) north of Glengarriff.

One of Southwest Ireland's most attractive locales, Killarney is also the most heavily visited town in the region (its proximity to the Ring of Kerry and to Shannon Airport helps to ensure this).

Killarney is famous for its lakes, not for the town, a point to bear in mind in order to avoid disappointment. Killarney town was one of the first places in Europe to owe its existence almost entirely to the tourism industry. Visitors started seeking out the region's dramatic lake scenery in the early 19th century, and the arrival of the railway ensured its growing popularity. Today Killarney is a small, low-key town lined with shops and eateries firmly targeted at the numerous visitors, but it's also a popular holiday destination for Irish visitors, and retains the traditional friendliness of less famous towns. There's a lively restaurant scene, and some good craft and clothing shops, but you may want to limit time spent there if discos, Irish cabarets, and singing pubs—the last of a local specialty with a strong Irish-American flavor—aren't your thing.

The nightlife is at its liveliest from May to September; the Irish and Europeans pack the town in July and August. Peak season for Americans follows in September and October. At other times, particularly from November to mid-March, when many of the hotels are closed, the town is quiet to the point of being eerie. Given the choice, go to Killarney in April, May, or early October.

Light rain is typical of the area, but because of the topography, it seldom lasts long. And the clouds' approach over the lakes and the subsequent showers can actually add to the scenery. The rain is often followed within minutes by brilliant sunshine and, yes, even a rainbow.

GETTING HERE AND AROUND

Killarney is about two hours from Cork on the N22, about three hours from Shannon Airport, on the N21/23/22, and two-and-a-half hours from Limerick. From Shannon Airport be sure to take the tunnel (toll €1.80) route when approaching Limerick, rather than driving through the center of the city. The main car park in Killarney is near the tourist information office in the town center, and there are others around the town, all operated on a "pay and display" basis during business hours. The town is well served by Expressway buses and has a rail link to Dublin (3 hours 20 minutes) and Cork (2 hours 20 minutes). The bus and rail stations are adjacent to each other, in the center of town, with taxi ranks. Most B&Bs and hotels offer a pick-up service. Elsewhere, taxis should be pre-booked by phone.

■TIP➔ There is no local bus service in Killarney Town; the traditional way to get around, especially if you plan to visit the car-free Muckross Park, is to hire one of the famous ponies and traps, known as a "jaunting car." The leading jaunting, bus, and boat tour operator is Killarney Jaunting Cars. An hour's "jaunt" for four people costs about €40. Jaunting cars can be prebooked or hired at the junction of Main Street and East Avenue. From mid-March to September you can view the National Park by taking a water-coach cruise on the Lily of Killarney boat from Ross Castle (1 hour, €10); book at the Killarney Tourist Office.

ESSENTIALS

Transportation Contacts **Killarney Bus and Train Station** ⊠ *East Ave. Rd., Killarney, Co. Kerry* ☎ *064/663–0011, 064/663–1067 for trains.*
Killarney Jaunting Cars ⊠ *Kinvara House, Muckross Rd., Killarney, Co. Kerry* ☎ *064/663–3358, 087/253–2770* ⊕ *www.killarneyjauntingcars.com.*

Visitor Information **Discover Ireland Centre** ⊠ *Aras Fáilte, Beech Rd., Killarney, Co. Kerry* ☎ *064/663–1633* ⊕ *www.killarney.ie.*

EXPLORING

With its glacial landscape enhanced by subtropical vegetation, the views found in and around Killarney are legendary. Yes, the lakes really are sapphire blue (at least when the sun is out), and seen from a distance, the MacGillicuddy's Reeks really are purple. Add a scattering of large gray rocks (large, as in big as a car), and acres of lush green flowering shrubs and trees, and you're starting to get the picture.

TOP ATTRACTIONS

★ **Gap of Dunloe.** Massive, glacial rocks form the side of the Gap of Dunloe, a narrow mountain pass that stretches for 6½ km (4 miles) between MacGillicuddy's Reeks and the Purple Mountains. The rocks create strange echoes: give a shout to test it out. Five small lakes are strung out beside the road. Cars are banned from the gap, but in summer the first 3 km (2 miles) are busy with horse and foot traffic, much of which turns back at the halfway point.

The entrance to the Gap is 10 km (7 miles) west of Killarney at Beaufort on the N72 Killorglin Road. If you drive or are on a tour bus, stop here and either hire a pony and trap or opt to walk. Many people amble through the parkland until Lord Brandon's Cottage, where they get a boat back to Killarney town—a strong reason why many choose to do the Gap on an organized tour so they will not end up back in Killarney with their car 7 miles away at the start of the Gap.

Kate Kearney's Cottage. At the entrance to the Gap of Dunloe, Kate Kearney's Cottage is a good place to rent a jaunting car or pony. Kate was a famous beauty who sold illegal *poteen* (moonshine) from her home, contributing greatly, one suspects, to travelers' enthusiasm for the scenery. Appropriately enough, Kearney's is now a pub and a good place to pause for an Irish coffee. ⊠ *Killarney, Co. Kerry* ☎ *064/664–4146* ⊕ *www.katekearneyscottage.com.*

Lord Brandon's Cottage. The gap's southern end is marked by Lord Brandon's Cottage, a tea shop serving soup and sandwiches. From here, a path leads to the edge of Upper Lake, where you can journey onward by rowboat. It's an old tradition for the boatman to carry a bugle and illustrate the echoes. The boat passes under Brickeen Bridge and into Middle Lake, where 30 islands are steeped in legends, many of which your boatman is likely to recount. Look out for caves on the left-hand side on this narrow stretch of water. ⊠ *7 km (4½ miles) west of Killarney, Killarney, Co. Kerry* ☉ *Easter–Sept., daily 10–dusk.*

Killarney National Park. Much of the area is part of Killarney National Park, which has more than 24,000 acres and is famous for such native habitats and species as oak holly woods, yew woods, and red deer; the park itself has no hours or admission. With a **National Park Visitor Centre** found at Muckross House, the park has signposted, self-guiding trails that thread these habitats.

At the park's heart is Muckross Park (or Demesne); the entrance to the Demesne area is 4 km (2½ miles) from Killarney on N71. Cars aren't allowed in Muckross Park; you either can walk, rent a bicycle, or take a traditional jaunting car—that is, a pony and a cart.

The air here smells of damp woods and heather moors. The red fruits of the Mediterranean strawberry tree (*Arbutus unedo*) are at their peak in October and November, which is also about the time when the bracken turns rust color, contrasting with the evergreens. In late April and early May, the purple flowers of the rhododendron *ponticum* put on a spectacular display. ⊕ *www.heritageireland.ie.*

★ **Ladies' View.** If the weather is fine, head southwest 19 km (12 miles) out of Killarney on N71 to Ladies' View, a famed panorama of the three lakes and the surrounding mountains. The name goes back to 1905, when Queen Victoria was a guest at Muckross House. Upon seeing the view, her ladies-in-waiting were said to have been dumbfounded by its beauty.

★ **Muckross House.** Hero of a 1,001 travel posters, the ivy-covered 19th-
☾ century Elizabethan-style manor known as Muckross House now houses the Kerry Folklife Centre. Downstairs, bookbinders, potters, and weavers demonstrate their crafts. Upstairs, elegantly furnished rooms portray the lifestyle of the landed gentry in the 1800s; in the basement

you can experience the conditions of servants employed in the house. Next door you'll find the Killarney National Park Visitor Centre.

The informal grounds are noted for their rhododendrons and azaleas, the water garden, and the outstanding limestone rock garden. In the park beside the house, the Muckross Traditional Farms comprise reconstructed farm buildings and outbuildings, a blacksmith's forge, a carpenter's workshop, and a selection of farm animals. It's a reminder of the way things were done on the farm before electricity and the mechanization of farming. Meet and chat with the farmers and their wives as they go about their work. The visitor center has a shop and a restaurant. ⊠ *Killarney National Park, Muckross Park, Muckross Rd. (N71), 6½ km (4 miles) south of Killarney, Killarney, Co. Kerry* ☎ *064/667–0144* ⊕ *www.muckross-house.ie* ☎ *House €7, farms €7.50, farms and house €12, visitor center free* ⊙ *House and visitor center: Nov.–mid-Mar., daily 9–5; mid-Mar.–June, Sept., and Oct., daily 9–6; July and Aug., daily 9–7. Farms: mid-Mar.–Apr., weekends 1–6; May and Sept, daily 1–6; June–Aug., daily 10–7; Oct., weekends 1–6.*

Ross Castle. A fully restored 14th-century stronghold, Ross Castle was the last place in the province of Munster to fall to Oliver Cromwell's forces in 1652. A later dwelling has 16th- and 17th-century furniture. ⊠ *Knockreer Estate, Muckross Rd. (N71), 2 km (1 mile) south of Killarney, Killarney, Co. Kerry* ☎ *064/663–5851* ⊕ *www.killarneynationalpark. ie/index.html* ☎ *€6* ⊙ *Mid-Mar.–Oct., daily 9:30–5:45.*

☺ **Torc Waterfall.** You reach this roaring cascade by a footpath that begins in the parking lot outside the gates of the Muckross Park. After your first view of the Torc, which will appear after about a 10-minute walk, it's worth the climb up a long flight of stone steps to the second, less-frequented clearing. ⊠ *Killarney National Park, Muckross Rd. (N71), 8 km (5 miles) south of Killarney, Killarney, Co. Kerry.*

WORTH NOTING

Aghadoe Heights. Here's an outstanding place to get a feel for what Killarney is all about: lake and mountain scenery. Stand beside Aghadoe's 12th-century ruined church and round tower, and watch the shadows creep gloriously across Lower Lake, with Innisfallen Island in the distance and the Gap of Dunloe to the west. ⊠ *R562, 5 km (3 miles) west of Killarney on Beaufort–Killorglin Rd., Killarney, Co. Kerry.*

Innisfallen Island. The romantic ruins on Innisfallen Island date from the 6th or 7th century. Between 950 and 1350 the *Annals of Innisfallen* were compiled here by monks. (The book survives in the Bodleian Library in Oxford.) To get to the island, which is on Lough Leane, you can rent a rowboat at Ross Castle (€5 per hour), or you can join a cruise (€10) in a covered, heated launch.

Muckross Friary. The 15th-century Franciscan Muckross Friary is amazingly complete, although roofless. The monks were driven out by Oliver Cromwell's army in 1652. An ancient yew tree rises above the cloisters and breaks out over the abbey walls. Three flights of stone steps allow access to the upper floors and living quarters, where you can visit the cloisters and what was once the dormitory, kitchen, and refectory. ⊠ *Killarney National Park, Muckross Park, Muckross Rd. (N71),*

4 km (2½ miles) south of Killarney, Killarney, Co. Kerry ☎ *64/6670144* ⊕ *www.heritageireland.ie* ✉ *Free* ⊙ *Mid-June–early Sept., daily 10–5.*

WHERE TO EAT

$$ \\ IRISH

✕ **Bricín.** In the unlikely event you didn't hit a craft shop in Killarney, you can browse the shelves of Bricín on your way to the restaurant on the second floor. This quirky little eatery set above the ground-floor craft emporium on Killarney's main street makes a change from pub grub, combining a warm welcome with a romantic atmosphere. Candles and an open fire shed light on Persian-style rugs and dark red walls hung with antique engravings of Killarney, while simple country-style wooden tables and stick-back chairs are set within "snug" areas created by stained-glass panels. The good value menu features boxty, an Irish potato pancake, with a choice of fillings including vegetarian. Other options include the baked salmon stuffed with crabmeat, the medallions of beef fillet, and the roast rack of lamb. ⑤ *Average main: €20* ⊠ *26 High St., Killarney, Co. Kerry* ☎ *064/663–4902* ⊙ *Closed Easter–Oct., Mon.; Nov.–Dec., Mon.–Weds.; and Jan.–mid-Mar. No lunch.*

$$$ \\ MODERN IRISH

✕ **Chapter Forty Restaurant.** People travel for miles to eat at this buzzing contemporary restaurant in Killarney's town center. While set in an old town house, the vibe inside is cool and contemporary, as announced by the bar salon, with its polished wood floors, plain walls, and gorgeous white and brown and cream leather chairs. Also beautifully presented are the nouvelle goodies that come parading out on huge square white platters or deep round bowls. The roast pork belly and salmon tartare, or the gravlax with asparagus salad and wasabi dressing, are among the best starters. Top mains are both trad and hip, and include the roast turbot with grilled prawns and seaweed tapenade or the roasted glazed rump of Kerry lamb with onion jam. All meat and dairy is Irish, and the seafood is predominantly local. Warning: few can resist the warm rhubarb crumble with caramel custard and candied ginger ice cream.
■TIP➔ Reduce costs by opting for a €25 or €35 prix-fixe menu. ⑤ *Average main: €25* ⊠ *40 New St., Killarney, Co. Kerry* ☎ *064/667–1833* ⊕ *www.chapter40.ie* ⊙ *Closed Sun. and Mon.*

$$$$ \\ SEAFOOD

✕ **Gaby's Seafood.** Expect the best seafood in Killarney from Belgian owner-chef Gert Maes. Inside the rustic exterior is a little bar beside an open fire; steps lead up to the main dining area, where ornate wooden stick-back chairs sit atop a plush gold and navy carpet. They match a huge wooden dresser that has adorned the room since the restaurant opened in 1978. In summer you can sip an aperitif in the small garden. Try the seafood platter (seven or eight kinds of fish in a cream-and-wine sauce) or lobster Gaby (shelled, simmered in a cream-and-cognac sauce, and served back in the shell). Turbot, salmon, and sole are also regular menu items. There is also a selection of fillet and sirloin steaks, au poivre or with garlic butter, and herb-scented rack of lamb. ⑤ *Average main: €32* ⊠ *27 High St., Killarney, Co. Kerry* ☎ *064/663–2519* ⊙ *Closed Sun.–Tues. Jan.–mid-Mar. No lunch.*

$$ ✕ **Treyvaud's.** Step behind the Victorian arched facade here and you'll
EUROPEAN discover a buzzing contemporary restaurant, masterminded by a pair
★ of brothers, chefs Paul and Mark Treyvaud. The decor is simple—pine
floorboards, wood-beam ceiling, lines of red-back chairs—so the food
takes center stage (only fitting considering all those diners who have
worked up a keen appetite out hiking). Winners include the shredded
duck confit with beetroot carpaccio, the homemade smoked haddock
fish cakes with garlic aioli, or the beef-and-Guinness pie with mashed
potatoes, renowned for its flavor. In winter Treyvaud's is famous for
its wide selection of game, including rabbit, wild boar, pheasant, and
quail. But even its seafood plate (Dover sole, tiger prawns, and crab
claws) will satisfy the hungriest hiker. $ *Average main: €23* ⊠ *62 High
St., Killarney, Co. Kerry* ☎ *064/663–3062* ⊕ *www.treyvaudsrestaurant.
com* ⊗ *Closed Mon. and Tues. Apr.–Oct.*

WHERE TO STAY

■ TIP➔ While the immediate region of Killarney has a vast array of accom-
modations, visitors should consider staying in hotels in Glenbeigh (about 20
minutes' drive away) if they really want to savor the region's peace and quiet.

For expanded hotel reviews, visit Fodors.com.

$$$$ ⊞ **Aghadoe Heights.** Once inside this large, modern hotel you'll soon for-
HOTEL get its blocklike external appearance, as the entrancing panorama of
Killarney's lakes spread out before you casts its spell. **Pros:** memorable
views; excellent spa; super-helpful staff. **Cons:** well out of town; a big
hotel by Irish standards. **TripAdvisor:** "sheer bliss," "true Kerry wel-
come," "the best of Ireland." $ *Rooms from: €275* ⊠ *off N22, 4 km (2½
miles) outside Killarney, on Tralee side, Killarney, Co. Kerry* ☎ *064/663–
1766* ⊕ *www.aghadoeheights.com* ⤴ *45 rooms, 26 suites* ⊙*Breakfast.*

$$$ ⊞ **Cahernane House Hotel.** Get a glimpse of the Killarney that attracted
HOTEL discerning 19th-century visitors at this imposing gray-stone house—
Fodor's Choice clearly, if you need a refuge from the touristy buzz of Killarney town,
★ this is the place. **Pros:** great old-world atmosphere; very luxe; fantastic
views. **Cons:** standard rooms are disappointingly plain; lots of weddings. **TripAdvisor:** "old beautiful house," "a quiet alternative to busy
Killarney," "friendly service." $ *Rooms from: €190* ⊠ *Muckross Rd.,
Killarney, Co. Kerry* ☎ *064/663–1895* ⊕ *www.cahernane.com* ⤴ *36
rooms, 2 suites* ⊗ *Closed Dec. 23–mid-Mar.* ⊙*Breakfast.*

$ ⊞ **Earls Court House.** In a quiet suburb within walking distance of
B&B/INN Killarney's center, this spacious guesthouse is furnished with interesting antiques collected by Emer Moynihan, who likes to greet her
guests by offering home-baked goods in front of the open fire. **Pros:**
quiet location; plenty of parking; warm welcome. **Cons:** long walk or
taxi ride to town; bland suburban location. **TripAdvisor:** "great location," "beautiful hotel," "a delightful place to return to." $ *Rooms
from: €100* ⊠ *Woodlawn Junct., Muckross Rd., Killarney, Co. Kerry*
☎ *064/663–4009* ⊕ *www.killarney-earlscourt.ie* ⤴ *30 rooms* ⊗ *Closed
mid-Nov.–mid-Mar.* ⊙*Breakfast.*

$ ⊞ **Friars Glen.** Set in its own 28 acres within Killarney National Park,
B&B/INN this stone house is a dream retreat for nature lovers. **Pros:** sylvan peace;
mountain air; friendly welcome. **Cons:** remote from town; limited choice

The beauty-measuring gauge flies off the scale at the Gap of Dunloe, considered by many to be the scenic star of the Lakes of Killarney region.

of restaurants nearby. **TripAdvisor:** "beautiful place and charming people," "comfortable and relaxing," "amazing hospitality." ⑤ *Rooms from: €100* ✉ *Mangerton Rd., Muckross, Co. Kerry* ☎ *064/663–7500* ⊕ *www.friarsglen.ie* ☞ *10 rooms* ⊘ *Closed Nov.–mid-Mar.*

$$ **HOTEL** ☷ **Loch Lein Country House Hotel.** A perfect rural retreat combining warm hospitality with a scenic location, this spacious country house is set 2 miles out of town near Killarney's famous golf courses. **Pros:** excellent value; friendly hosts; plenty of space. **Cons:** 2 miles from town; closed off-season. **TripAdvisor:** "perfect stay," "wonderful Irish inn," "Irish hospitality at its best." ⑤ *Rooms from: €130* ✉ *Fossa, Co. Kerry* ☎ *064/663–1260* ⊕ *www.lochlein.com* ☞ *25 rooms* ⊘ *Closed Nov.–mid-Apr.* ⑪ *Breakfast.*

NIGHTLIFE AND THE ARTS

Buckley's Bar. Located in the Arbutus Hotel, this popular spot has traditional Irish entertainment nightly from June to September. ✉ *Arbutus Hotel, College St., Killarney, Co. Kerry* ☎ *064/663–1037.*

The Danny Mann. Bars where a professional leads the songs and encourages audience participation and solos are popular in Killarney—and the Danny Mann may be the best. ✉ *New St., Killarney, Co. Kerry* ☎ *064/663–1640.*

Gleneagles. The place for big-name cabaret—from Sharon Shannon to the Wolfe Tones—Gleneagles also has a late-night disco. ✉ *Muckross Rd., Killarney, Co. Kerry* ☎ *064/663–1870.*

McSorleys Nite Club. A lively late-night venue, McSorleys attracts a younger crowd. ✉ *College St., Killarney, Co. Kerry* ☎ *064/663–9770.*

SPORTS AND THE OUTDOORS

BICYCLING

O'Sullivan's Cycles. A bicycle is the perfect way to enjoy Killarney's mild air, whether within the confines of Muckross Park or farther afield in the Kerry Highlands, and O'Sullivan's is a top place to rent cycles for either the day or the week. ⊠ *Bishop's La., off New St., Killarney, Co. Kerry* ☎ *064/663–1282* ⊕ *www.killarneyrentabike.com.*

FISHING

Salmon and brown trout populate Killarney's lakes and rivers.

John Lyne Fishing Tours. Call or email Mr. Lyne before you arrive in Killarney to organize a day or half day's salmon angling on the lakes. All gear, the license, and even the raincoats and trousers are included in the rate of 120 euros per half day. ⊠ *Gortagullane, Muckross, Killarney, Co. Kerry* ☎ *087/278–9335* ⊘ *johnmikelyne@gmail.com.*

GOLF

Fodor's Choice ★ **Killarney Golf and Fishing Club.** Freshwater fishing is the sport here, for this club is among a stunning mixture of mountains, lakes, and forests. There are three courses: Mahony's Point, along the shores of Lough Leane; the Lackabane, on the far side of the road from the main entrance; and the jewel in the crown, water-feature-packed Killeen. Despite the abundance of seaside links, many well-traveled golfers name Killarney their favorite place to play in Ireland. ⊠ *Mahony's Point, Killarney, Co. Kerry* ☎ *064/31034* ⊕ *www.killarney-golf.com* ⊠ *Greens fees: mid-Apr.–mid-Oct. €70 (Mahony's Point), €50 (Lackabane), €90 (Killeen); mid-Oct.–mid-Apr. €50 (Mahony's Point), €40 (Lackabane), €60 (Killeen)* ⌦ *54 holes. Yardage: 6,780 (Mahony's Point), 7,050 (Lackabane), 7,178 (Killeen). All courses: Par 72. Practice area, caddies, caddy carts, club rental, catering* ⊙ *Visitors: Mon.–Sat.*

HIKING

Cronin's Yard. Drive out to Beaufort—10 km (7 miles) west of Killarney on the N72 Killorglin road—and follow the signposts for Cronin's Yard, famed gateway to the MacGillicuddy's Reeks and the traditional starting point for the ascent of Carrauntoohil, Ireland's highest mountain (1038 m/3406 ft). This is the spot where outdoor types will definitely fall in love with Killarney. Park your car at the yard (2 euros all day). You can pre-book a guide for the ascent (about 6 hours round-trip). For a less strenuous outing, there is a self-guided 8-km (5-mile) loop of sandy paths and mountain tracks signposted from the Yard. On your return, enjoy a hot bowl of soup in their tearoom and, especially if the Irish weather has not been kind to you, enjoy a hot shower (available for a small fee). ⊠ *Mealis, Beaufort, Killarney, Co. Kerry* ☎ *064/662–4044* ⊕ *www.croninsyard.com* ⊙ *May–Sept., daily; Oct.–Easter, weekends or by prior arrangement.*

Kerry Way. This long-distance walking route passes through the Killarney National Park on its way to Glenbeigh. You can get a detailed leaflet about the route from the tourist information office. For the less adventurous, four safe and well-marked nature trails of varying lengths are in the national park. Try the 4-km (2½-mile) Arthur Young's Walk, which passes through old yew and oak woods frequented by sika deer. ⊕ *www.kerryway.net.*

Mangerton Walking Trail. You can reach the small, tarred road leading to this scenic trail that circles Mangerton Lake by turning left off N71 midway between Muckross Friary and Muckross House (follow the signs).

Mangerton Mountain. With a summit at 2,756 feet, Mangerton can be reached on foot in about two hours—less if you rent a pony. It's perfect if you want a fine, long hike with good views of woodland scenery.

SHOPPING

Bricín Craft Shop. For interesting handicrafts, including candles, ceramics, and woolens, head to the Bricín Craft Shop. ⊠ *26 High St., Killarney, Co. Kerry* ☎ *064/663–4902.*

Frank Lewis Gallery. Visit this noted gallery for a good selection of original paintings and sculptures. ⊠ *6 Bridewell Ln., beside General Post Office, Killarney, Co. Kerry* ☎ *064/663–1108* ⊕ *www.franklewisgallery.com.*

Kerry Woollen Mills. This mill was established in the 17th century and still uses the original buildings. Its range of traditional woolen products, from knitting yarns to hats and capes, make great gifts. The property is signposted off the main road between Killarney and Killorglin. ⊠ *Beaufort, Killarney, Co. Kerry* ☎ *064/664–4122* ⊕ *www.kerrywoollenmills.ie.*

The Kilkenny Shop. Peruse this shop's stock of contemporary Irish pottery, ironwork, woodwork, crystal, and jewelry. ⊠ *3 New St., Killarney, Co. Kerry* ☎ *064/663–5406* ⊕ *www.kilkennyshop.com.*

Killarney Bookshop. For a lovely array of local-interest books as well as fiction, biography, and travel titles check out the Killarney Bookshop. ⊠ *32 Main St., Killarney, Co. Kerry* ☎ *064/663–4108* ⊕ *www.killarneybookshop.ie.*

Killarney Outlet Centre. Bargain hunters should head for this discount shopping center (adjacent to the Great Southern Hotel and the train station), which has the Nike Factory Store and Blarney Woollen Mills as its anchor tenants. ⊠ *Fair Hill, Killarney, Co. Kerry* ☎ *064/663–6744* ⊕ *www.killarneyoutletcentre.com.*

MacBee's. This modern boutique stocks the best of Irish high fashion. ⊠ *26 New St., Killarney, Co. Kerry* ☎ *064/663–3622* ⊕ *macbees.ie.*

Mucros Craft Shop. Adjacent to Muckross House, the craft center has a wide range of gifts and clothing, as well as a resident weaver, a bookbindery, and Mucros Pottery. Margaret Whelan works on-site producing tableware in attractive blue and honey-colored glazes. ⊠ *Muckross House, Muckross Park, Killarney, Co. Kerry* ☎ *064/667–0153* ⊕ *www.muckross-house.ie.*

Quills Woolen Market. Stop here for the town's largest selection of Irish knitwear. Quills also carries tweeds, linens, and Celtic jewelry. ⊠ *Market Cross, Killarney, Co. Kerry* ☎ *064/663–2277.*

Retro Rose Bazaar. This shop has a gorgeous selection of vintage clothes, jewelry, and decorative items. ⊠ *37 New St., Killarney, Co. Kerry* ☎ *087/687–3364.*

THE RING OF KERRY

Running along the perimeter of the Iveragh Peninsula, the dramatic coastal road from Kenmare to Killorglin known as the Ring of Kerry is probably Ireland's single most popular tourist route. Stunning mountain and coastal views are around almost every turn. The only drawback: on a sunny day, it seems like half the nation's visitors are traveling along this two-lane road, packed into buses, riding bikes, or backpacking. The route is narrow and curvy, and the local sheep think nothing of using it for a nap; take it slowly.

Tour buses tend to start in Killarney and head for Killorglin to ply the Ring counterclockwise, so consider jumping ahead and starting in Killorglin ahead of the Killarney buses, or following the route clockwise, starting in Kenmare (although this means you risk meeting tour buses head-on on narrow roads). Either way, bear in mind that most of the buses leave Killarney between 9 and 10 am. The trip covers 176 km (110 miles) on N70 (and briefly R562 and N71) if you start and finish in Killarney; the journey will be 40 km (25 miles) shorter if you only venture between Kenmare and Killorglin. Because rain blocks views across the water to the Beara Peninsula in the east and the Dingle Peninsula in the west, hope for sunshine. It makes all the difference.

KENMARE

34 km (21 miles) south of Killarney, 336 km (209 miles) southwest of Dublin.

Situated slightly inland without a clear view of Kenmare Bay, Kenmare is a natural stopover for Ring of Kerry buses and travelers as it is the closest town to Killarney. Set at the head of the sheltered Kenmare River estuary, this small but bustling market town makes a lively touring base for those who wish to skip hectic Killarney altogether. The town was founded in 1670 by Sir William Petty (Oliver Cromwell's surveyor general, a multitasking entrepreneur), and most of its buildings date from the 19th century, when it was part of the enormous Lansdowne Estate—itself assembled by Petty.

It's currently a matter of some debate as to whether Kenmare has displaced Kinsale *(see "County Cork")* as the culinary capital of Ireland. Kenmare offers an amazing number of stylish little restaurants for a town its size, and also boasts a top-rated Kenmare Market, with dealers in organic goods and foodstuffs (Wednesdays, 10–5, March–December). The shopping is pretty good, too, with Irish high fashion, crafts, and original art vying for your attention.

GETTING HERE AND AROUND

Kenmare is at the junction of the N71 road that links Bantry and Glengarriff with Killarney, and the N70, which continues around the perimeter road known as the Ring of Kerry. Killarney and Glengarriff are both about 40 to 45 minutes away on scenic mountain roads. Kenmare is a natural stopover between Glengarriff (21 km [13 miles] south) and Killarney (34 km [21 miles] to the north). The mountain pass (N71) from Kenmare to Killarney via Ladies' View is a scenic highlight, offering a stunning first view of the lakes. There is ample parking in Kenmare town center.

The Ring of Kerry and Killarney

0 5 mi

0 5 km

Dingle Bay

Milltown

Killorglin

R563

R562

Ring of Kerry

Ring of Kerry

Glenbeigh

Rossbeigh

IVERAGH

PENINSULA

Macgillycuddy's Reeks

Kilgobnet

Kate Kearny's Cottage

Lord Brandon's Cottage

Cahciveen

Valentina Island

Ballinskelligs

Ballinskelligs Bay

Waterville

Ring of Kerry

N70

Staigue Fort

Sneem

Ring of Kerry

Parknasilla

Tahilla

R571

N70

Kenmare

R569

R568

Caragh Lake

KERRY

Kenmare River

BEARA PENINSULA

N71

Glengarriff

Kilgarvan

CORK

N22

N563

Ring of Kerry

Aghadoe

Beaufort

Innisfallen Island

Gap of Dunloe

Upper Lake

Ladies' View

Lough Leane

Lower Lake

Muckross Lake

Killarney

N72

Ross Castle

Muckross Friary

Muckross House

Torc Waterfall

Torc Mountain

Galways Bridge

Mangerton Mountain

KILLARNEY NATIONAL PARK

The Skelligs

A bus route connects Killarney to Kenmare; it continues on around the Ring of Kerry, stopping in all the villages between Kenmare and Killorglin before returning to Killarney. Otherwise, there is no public transport in this area.

TOURS

You can opt to base yourself in Kenmare and take a guided tour of the Ring by minibus (€25, May–September) with the local taxi company, Finnegan's Tours/Kenmare Coach and Cab. Their minibuses depart from the Square for the Ring on Monday, Wednesday, and Friday at 10 am. Other destinations include the Ring of Beara and Glengarriff. It is best to reserve by 10 pm the night before.

ESSENTIALS

Transportation Contacts **Finnegan's Tours/Kenmare Coach and Cab** ☎ 064/664–1491 ⊕ www.kenmarecoachandcab.com.

Visitor Information **Kenmare Tourist Office** ⊠ The Square, Kenmare, Co. Kerry ☎ 064/664–1233 ⊕ kenmare.com/tourism ⊙ Easter–Oct., Mon.–Sat. 9:30–5:30.

EXPLORING

Kenmare Heritage Centre. Come to this center in the tourist office to learn about the town's history. They can outline a walking route to Kenmare's places of interest. ⊠ The Square, Kenmare, Co. Kerry ☎ 064/664–1233 ⊕ www.kenmareireland.com ⊟ Free ⊙ Easter–Oct., Mon.–Sat. 9:30–5:30.

Stone Circle. Perhaps the town's most notable historic sight is this 3,000-year-old monument that dates from the early Bronze Age. Sometimes called the Druid Circle, it is within five minutes' walk of the village square (head down Market Street in front of the tourist office). It consists of 15 large stones arranged in a circle around a huge central boulder, which marks a rare Bronze Age burial site. ⊟ No credit cards.

WHERE TO EAT

$$
EUROPEAN
✕ **Lime Tree.** An open fire, stone walls, and a minstrel's gallery on a large balcony above the main room lend considerable character to this restaurant. Built in 1823 as a schoolhouse, it is located in its own leafy gardens at the top of town near the Park Hotel (where many of its staff trained). Tables are set with Irish linen napery, and in the long summer evenings light streams in from tall windows. Try one of the imaginative vegetarian options, such as hummus and blue cheese strudel, or go for roast loin of Kerry lamb with a red onion and sun-dried tomato tarte tatin. Leave room for the blackberry and pear fruit crumble. Advance booking is advisable. $ Average main: €23 ⊠ Shelburne St., Kenmare, Co. Kerry ☎ 064/664–1225 ⊕ www.limetreerestaurant.com ⊙ Closed Nov.–mid-Feb., and late Feb., Mar., and Oct. weekdays. No lunch.

$$
IRISH
✕ **Tom Crean Fish & Wine.** Owner Aileen d'Arcy recently renamed her restaurant, on the ground floor of a former bank, after her grandfather, the Arctic explorer Tom Crean. You can learn his story while browsing the menu, which is dominated by local produce. Top bets include the Sneem black pudding with apple and tomato chutney

GIFTS TO BRING HOME

You will soon notice that parts of County Kerry have more sheep than people: sheep means wool, and in this part of Ireland wool means sweaters, socks, and wooly hats. All three will come in very useful during your stay, and make great gifts, too.

Brían de Staic. Precious gifts would include modern jewelry in silver or gold by Brían de Staic. His ancient Irish designs can be found in Killarney, Dingle, and Tralee. ⊠ *Green St., Dingle* ☎ *066/915–1298* ⊕ *www. briandestaic.com.*

Louis Mulcahy Pottery. Ceramics are a strong point, too, with the Louis Mulcahy Pottery ceramics workshop and showrooms on Slea Head being the most western pottery in Europe. ⊠ *Clogher, Ballyferriter, Dingle* ☎ *066/915–6229* ⊕ *www.louismulcahy.com.*

Quills Woollen Market. This top gifts and/or souvenirs resource has outlets in Killarney, Kenmare, Sneem, and Dingle. Look out for "blackthorns": a traditional, craggy walking stick made from branches of the blackthorn tree, a handy accessory to have while you're here, and a great souvenir to take home. ⊠ *Market Cross, Killarney* ☎ *064/663–2277.*

baked in phyllo pastry and the local duck breast, panfried and served with roasted root vegetables and Puy lentils. Known for her warm welcome, Aileen learned her trade at Kenmare's famed Park Hotel, and shares the chef duties with her two sons. The main room is warmed by a large turf fire and has fully upholstered leather chairs. ⑤ *Average main: £20* ⊠ *25 Main St., Kenmare, Co. Kerry* ☎ *064/664–1589* ⊕ *www.tomcrean.ie* ⊗ *Closed Oct.–early Jan., Mon.–Thurs.; Jan. and Feb. call for hours. No lunch.*

$$ ✕ **The Wild Garlic.** Previously a pub, this street-level room has stylish
ECLECTIC contemporary place settings, with leather seats at small wooden tables, and a selection of homemade breads presented on a tray. Chef James Coffe's menu reflects his enthusiasm for fresh Irish produce, simply prepared. Dishes may include rabbit pie, slow cooked belly of pork with apple and raisin jus, or simple Angus rib eye steak with Béarnaise sauce. Some of the ingredients are foraged from the wild, including clams. The food is plated with such flamboyance that you will want to bring your camera. ⑤ *Average main: £22* ⊠ *36 Henry St., Kenmare, Co. Kerry* ☎ *064/664–2383* ⊕ *www.kenmarerestaurants.com* ⊗ *Closed Tues. and Wed. in Oct.–May, and last 2 wks Jan. No lunch.*

WHERE TO STAY

For expanded hotel reviews, visit Fodors.com.

$$ ⊞ **Brook Lane Hotel.** This small hotel may look like a traditional two-
HOTEL story stone building, with pointed gables and bay windows, but in fact it is an Irish-style boutique hotel—a product of the economic boom years. **Pros:** one-stop-shop with bar, restaurant, and parking on-site; genuine warm welcome; high standard of comfort. **Cons:** an uninspiring mile-long walk into village; live music in pub may shatter the rural idyll. **TripAdvisor:** "comfortable stay," "first-class food and

hospitality," "top class." $ *Rooms from: €160* ⊠ *Sneem Rd., Kenmare, Co. Kerry* ☎ *064/664–2077* ⊕ *www.brooklanehotel.com* ⇥ *20 rooms* ⊙| *Breakfast.*

$$$$ ⊞ **Park Hotel Kenmare.** One of Ireland's premier country-house hotels,
HOTEL   this 1897 stone château has spectacular views of the Caha Mountains.
Fodor'sChoice   **Pros:** amazingly friendly staff; great spa; impressive grounds. **Cons:**
★   a bit like living in a museum; basic room rates are quite steep. **Trip-Advisor:** "luxury and relaxation," "amazing experience," "simply perfect." $ *Rooms from: €470* ⊠ *Shelburne Rd., Kenmare, Co. Kerry* ☎ *064/664–1200* ⊕ *www.parkkenmare.com* ⇥ *35 rooms, 9 suites* ⊙ *Closed Nov. to Dec. 23 and Jan. 2–Easter* ⊙| *Breakfast.*

$ ⊞ **Sea Shore Farm.** Mary Patricia O'Sullivan offers a warm but pro-
B&B/INN   fessional welcome to her spacious farmhouse on Kenmare Bay. **Pros:** quiet rural spot with views of calm estuary; personal attention from owner-manager. **Cons:** on a working cattle farm; a mile out of town; no bar or restaurant. **TripAdvisor:** "charming hosts," "beautiful setting," "authentic farmhouse." $ *Rooms from: €100* ⊠ *Tubrid, Co. Kerry* ☎☎ *064/664–1270* ⊕ *www.seashorekenmare.com* ⇥ *6 rooms* ⊙ *Closed Nov.–mid-Mar.* ⊙| *Breakfast.*

$$$$ ⊞ **Sheen Falls Lodge Kerry Hotel.** The magnificence of this bright-yellow,
HOTEL   slate-roof stone manor is matched only by its setting: 300 secluded
Fodor'sChoice   acres of lawns, gardens, and forest between Kenmare Bay and the falls
★   of the River Sheen. **Pros:** fun and informal for the price range; good sports facilities. **Cons:** modern decor lacks traditional character; driving distance (2 km [1 mile]) from the village; room rates have been cut but are pricey for area. **TripAdvisor:** "idyllc setting," "excellent staff," "a wonderfully relaxing place." $ *Rooms from: €310* ⊠ *Sheen Falls, Co. Kerry* ☎ *064/664–1600* ⊕ *www.sheenfallslodge.ie* ⇥ *55 rooms, 11 suites* ⊙ *Closed Jan.* ⊙| *Breakfast.*

SHOPPING

Avoca Handweavers. At this scenic spot midway between Kenmare and Killarney, Avoca Handweavers sells wool clothing and mohair throws and rugs in remarkable palettes and a variety of weaves. ⊠ *N71, Moll's Gap on the road to Killarney, Kenmare, Co. Kerry* ☎ *064/663–4720.*

Kenmare Bookshop. A good selection of books of local interest and all the bestsellers can be found here. ⊠ *Shelburne St., Kenmare, Co. Kerry* ☎ *064/664–1578.*

Paul Kelly Jewellers. Paul Kelly makes striking, modern jewelry in gold and silver. ⊠ *18 Henry St., Kenmare, Co. Kerry* ☎ *064/664–2590* ⊕ *www.pfk.ie.*

Skyline Gallery. This gallery has stunning landscape images by international award-winning Irish photographer Eoghan Kavanagh. ⊠ *27 Henry St., Kenmare, Co. Kerry* ☎ *087/252–2807* ⊕ *www.skyline.ie.*

Sue Designer Knits. Here you'll find Irish-made knitwear in lambswool and cashmere. ⊠ *20 Henry St., Kenmare, Co. Kerry* ☎ *064/664–8986* ⊕ *suedesignerknits.com.*

The White Room. Irish lace and linen, both new and antique, are the specialty here. ⊠ *21 Henry St., Kenmare, Co. Kerry* ☎ *064/664–0600* ⊕ *www.thewhiteroomkenmare.com.*

SPORTS AND THE OUTDOORS

BICYCLING

Kenmare Cycle Centre. Pick up a free copy of the Ring of Kerry Cycle Route brochure from the tourist information office, and then explore the Ring using quiet country roads. The full trip is a blister-inducing 217 km (135 miles). Bikes are available for rent at this shop in town. ✉ *New Rd., Kenmare, Co. Kerry* ☎ *064/664–1083.*

BOAT TOURS

☾ **Seafari.** With complimentary tea and coffee for adults, plus lollipops for the kids, Seafari features fun two-hour ecotours and seal-watching cruises. Cruises cost €20 per adult, with special family rates. Reservations are essential. ✉ *Kenmare Pier, 3 Pier Rd., Kenmare, Co. Kerry* ☎ *064/664–2059* ⊕ *www.seafariireland.com.*

SNEEM

27 km (17 miles) southwest of Kenmare.

The pretty little village of Sneem (from the Irish for "knot") is settled around an English-style green on the Ardsheelaun River estuary, and its streets are filled with houses washed in different colors. The effect has been somewhat diminished by a cluster of new holiday home developments. The town has a cluster of souvenir shops that play Irish music over loudspeakers when the Ring of Kerry tour buses stop here.

GETTING HERE AND AROUND

It takes about 15 minutes to reach Sneem from Kenmare on N70. There's plenty of free street parking in the town's main square. ■ TIP➔ To see the best of Sneem, park near the Blue Bull pub, and walk down the narrow road beside it, signposted Pier. This quiet byway leads past a carefully tended community garden, terminating about 300 yards farther on at the village pier. Take a seat and look back toward the village to appreciate Sneem's unique location, nestled amid lush subtropical growth between the sea and the hills.

EXPLORING

Fodor'sChoice ★ **Derrynane House.** The Ring of Kerry has very few beautiful and historic country houses so many visitors here enjoy making a special excursion to Derrynane House, located 30 km (18 miles) west of Sneem. Famed as the home of Daniel O'Connell (1775–1847), "the Liberator," the mansion comes complete with a lovely garden and 320-acre seaside estate, now called the Derryname National Park. The house's south and east wings (which O'Connell himself remodeled) are decorated with much of the furniture and other items associated with the man who campaigned for Catholic Emancipation (the granting of full rights of citizenship to Catholics), which became a reality in 1829. ✉ *Near Caherdaniel, off N70, Sneem, Co. Kerry* ☎ *066/947–5113* ⊕ *www.heritageireland.com* ✂*€3* ☉ *Oct.–late Nov., Wed.–Sun. 10:30–5; early Apr.–Sept., daily 10:30–6; closed late Nov.–early Apr.*

Staigue Fort. The approximately 2,500-year-old, stone Staigue Fort, signposted 4 km (2 miles) inland at Castlecove, is almost circular and about 75 feet in diameter with a single south-side entrance. From the Iron Age

Continued on page 402

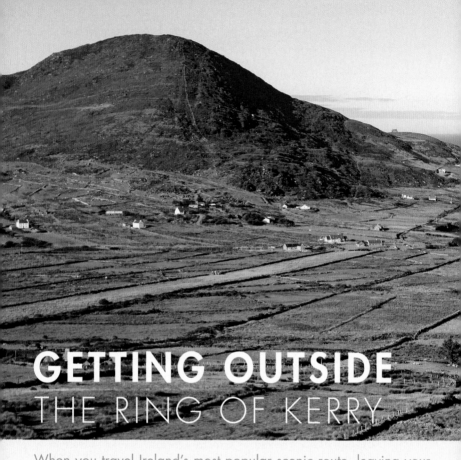

GETTING OUTSIDE
THE RING OF KERRY

When you travel Ireland's most popular scenic route, leaving your car behind makes all the difference. Here's how to get far from the madding crowd.

The Ring of Kerry is one of Europe's great drives. The common wisdom, though, is that it suffers from its own popularity: tour buses dominate the road from sunup to sundown. There's more than a grain of truth to this reputation, but that doesn't mean you should scratch the Ring from your itinerary. Instead, plan to turn off the main road and get out of your car. You'll make a blissful discovery: the Iveragh Peninsula—one of the most beautiful locations in all of Ireland—remains largely unspoiled. It's full of fabulous places to hike, bike, and boat—and best of all, there are views the tour bus passengers can only dream of.

Top, Elevated coastal view from the Ring of Kerry;
Below left, on horseback in Rossbeigh Strand, Kerry;
Below right, cycling around the Ring

AROUND THE RING BY FOOT AND BY BIKE

HIKING THE RING

Option number one for getting outdoors around the Ring of Kerry is to go by foot. There are appealing walking options for every degree of fitness and experience, from gentle, paved paths to an ascent up Ireland's tallest mountain.

THE KERRY WAY

The main hiking route across the peninsula is the Kerry Way, a spectacular 133-mile footpath that's easily broken down into day-trip-size segments. The path winds from **Killarney** through the foothills of the **MacGillicuddy's Reeks** and the **Black Valley** to Glencar and Glen-beigh, from where it parallels the Ring through **Cahirciveen, Waterville, Caherdaniel,** and **Sneem,** before ending in **Kenmare.** The route, indicated by way markers, follows grassy old paths situated at higher elevations than the Ring—meaning better, and more tranquil, views. Hiking the entire Kerry Way can take from 10 to 12 days. Numerous outfitters organize both guided and unguided tours. For a great day trip, hike the 10 km (6 mi) section from **Waterville** to **Caherdaniel,** which has great views of small islands and rocky coves. In the **Glencar** area near

HIKING RESOURCES

A copy of the **Kerry Way Map Guide,** available from Cork Kerry Tourism, is invaluable. For tours of the Way, try **Outdoors Ireland,** based in Beaufort, Killarney (☎ 086/860–4563 ⊕ www.-outdoorsireland.com). Climbers should check out the website of the **Mountaineering Council of Ireland** at ⊕ www.mountaineering.ie.

Blackstones Bridge, a series of shorter signposted walks, from 3 km (2 mi) upward, put you in the shadow of **Carrauntuohill,** Ireland's highest mountain.

TAKING IT EASY: THREE GENTLE STROLLS

MUCKROSS PARK in Killarney is a car-free zone with four signposted nature trails. Try the 4 km (2½ mi) Arthur Young's Walk through old yew and oak woods frequented by sika deer. You can also take an open boat from Ross Castle to the head of the **Upper Lake,** then walk back along the lakeside to Muckross House—about 10 km (6 mi).

The trails in **DERRYNANE NATIONAL PARK,** a 320-acre estate, run through mature woodland, bordering on rocky outcrops that lead to wide sandy beaches and dunes. At low tide, you can walk to **Abbey Island** offshore.

Even in high summer, **VALENTIA ISLAND** is a peaceful spot for walking, with little traffic. Walk the road from **Knightstown** through the subtropical vegetation of the Knight of Kerry's estate, to the historic **Slate Quarry** (3 km/2 mi), 900 ft above the sea, with views of the Skelligs offshore.

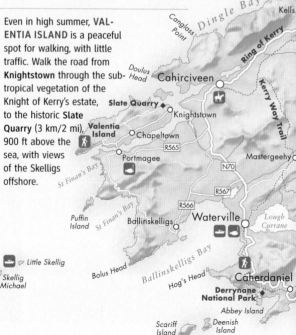

CYCLING THE RING

The Ring of Kerry Cycle Route follows the main road for about a third of its 134 miles, but the rest is on deserted roads, including a long, scenic loop through Ballinskelligs, Portmagee, and Valentia Island. There are significant climbs and strong winds along the way, so good fitness is a prerequisite.

EASY RIDES

From **Killarney**, the N71 road past **Muckross Park** and the **Upper Lake** takes you through ancient woodlands to **Ladies' View** (about 12 km/7.5 mi).

From here you have one of the area's best panoramas, with the sparkling blue lakes backed by purple mountains. The scene will be in front of you as you make the ride back.

From **Glenbeigh**, escape the traffic by riding inland to peaceful **Caragh Lake** through a bog and mountain landscape that's rich in wildlife. You might spot a herd of long-bearded wild goats, or a peregrine falcon hovering above its prey. The full circuit of the lake, returning to Glenbeigh, is about 35 km (22 mi).

BIKING RESOURCES

You can rent bikes and get route information at O'Sullivan's Cycles (☎ 064/663–1282) in Killarney. Along the Ring at Glenbeigh, bikes are for rent at **Glenross Caravan & Camping Park** (☎ 066/976-8451 ⊕ www.killarneycamping. com/glenross.html).

For an organized tour, contact **Irish Cycling Safaris** (⊕ www.cyclingsafaris.-com), which has trips along quiet back roads with local guides.

KEY

🚤 Boating
🚲 Cycling
🎣 Fishing
🥾 Hiking
🐴 Horseback Riding

TESTING THE WATERS

BOATING AROUND THE RING . . .

Kenmare Bay is the best spot for boating expeditions. **Kenmare Angling** (⊕ www.kenmareanglingandsightsee ing.com) offers customized tours, on which you can see castles, seals, dolphins, and salmon farms. Boats can take up to 10 people, and cost €300 for a full day, €200 for a half day. **Seafari** (⊕ www.seafariireland.com) at Kenmare Pier has a two-hour econature and seal watching cruise and also is an outfitter for kayaking, sailing, and windsurfing. The **Cappanalea Outdoor Education Centre** (⊕ www.cappanalea.ie), 7 mi west of Killorglin, near Caragh Lake, offers windsurfing, canoeing, rock climbing and guided hikes.

. . . AND FISHING

There's good fishing here, both inland and at sea. **Portmagee** and **Waterville** are the main deepsea angling centers; outings are generally from small open boats carrying up to 10 rods and run about €30 per person per day. Wreck and reef fishing promises pollock, ling, cod, conger, monkfish, and shark.

Inshore there are bass, turbot, dogfish, flounder, and tope.

The **Caragh Lake** and the rivers **Laune, Inny, Roughty,** and **Caragh** are all excellent for wild salmon—and all are beautiful wilderness locations. **Lough Currane** near Waterville is one of the great sea trout fisheries. The season runs from March to September, and fishing permits are available locally from hotels. You'll find tackle shops in Killarney and Waterville. For detailed information before you go, check out the Web site of the South Western Regional Fisheries Board (⊕ www.swrfb.com).

. . . AND SWIMMING

Swimming off the beaches around the coast is confined to July and August, when the water temperatures reach 55 to 60 degrees. There are dive centers at Caherdaniel, Kenmare, and Valentia Island; ⊕ www.scuba.ie is a good information resource.

Top left, fishing on the bay; Right, trout fishing; Bottom left, fishing boats in the Dingle harbor

THE TWIN PEAKS OF YOUR TRIP

Above and below left, ancient monastic site on Skellig Michael with Little Skellig in the background.

The distinctive conical **Skellig Rocks** hover offshore at the western end of the Iveragh Peninsula, surrounded by swirling blue sea. They're a haunting presence that seems to follow along as you travel the mainland from Valentia to Waterville and Caherdaniel.

A venture out to the twin peaks of **Skellig Michael** (shown above, also known as Great Skellig) is a truly awesome experience. Boats leave from Waterville, Ballinskelligs, and Portmagee for a white-knuckle ride lasting about 45 minutes. Along the way you pass Michael's companion, **Little Skellig,** where people aren't allowed but gannets flourish.

Skellig Michael rises steeply for 700 feet; you reach the summit by climbing 600 steps cut into the rockface. Once there, you find, amazingly, the remains of a monastery, occupied by hermit monks from the 7th to 12th century.

Looking back to the mainland and out at the wild expanse of open sea, you get an inkling of the monks' isolation from all things worldly. A visit to Skellig Michael may not be the most comfortable outing of you trip, but it will probably be the most memorable.

BIRDS OF THE SKELLIGS

The Ring of Kerry is one of the best places in Europe for observing seabirds, and the Skelligs are a particular treasure for birders. The gannet, with a wing span of 2 yards, is Ireland's largest seabird and up to 22,000 nesting pairs reside on Little Skellig, where they dive for food from heights of up to 120 feet.

If you are lucky enough to get out to Skellig Michael in May, you'll be warned to watch out for comical-looking **puffins** (below) nesting in burrows underfoot.

Below, two puffins standing on Skellig rocks

EQUITREKKING THE RING

Horses hold a special place in the hearts of the Irish. Horsemanship and breeding are sources of national pride—it's an oft-quoted fact that the Duke of Wellington rode an Irish horse at the Battle of Waterloo, while Napoleon's horse came from County Wexford. All over the country you'll find horses grazing in the fields, being ridden down country lanes, and galloping along beaches. If you share the Irish passion for all things equine, there's no better way to see the Ring than from the back of a horse.

You can gallop along the 3 mile stretch of **Rossbeigh Strand,** or take a trek around quiet country roads, on a horse from **Burke's Horse Trekking Center** in Glenbeigh (☎ 087/237–9110). They've been in the business for years and use mainly quiet-colored cobs (black and white all-rounders). Hats and boots are included in the price, which ranges from €20 to €30.

The six-day **Reeks Trail** riding led by **Killarney Riding Stables** (☎ 064/663–1686 ⊕ www.killarney-reeks-trail.com) takes you through the mountains and woodland of MacGillicuddy's Reeks. The stables also book half- and full-day rides.

Near **Cahirciveen,** the **Final Furlong Farmhouse B & B** has a riding stable and a gorgeous location overlooking the sea. Ride as little or as much as you like during your stay, in small groups supervised by members of the proprietors, the O'Sullivan family. Contact Kathleen O'Sullivan (☎ 066/947–3300 ⊕ www.thefinalfurlong.com.)

Top: Horse racing in Rossbeigh Strand;
Above left, Connemara Pony; Above right, Lakes of Killarney; Right, Bray Head, Valentia Island

WEATHER, FLORA, AND TOURING TIPS

Swimming at the Ring

THANKS TO
THE GULF STREAM . . .

The warm waters flowing from the Gulf of Mexico across the Atlantic, known as the Gulf Stream, give Ireland a mild climate, and the effects are particularly felt along the Ring of Kerry. The area is frost-free year round, with temperatures averaging 45 degrees Fahrenheit in winter and 60 in summer. But rain is a constant threat, brought in from the Atlantic by the prevailing southwesterly winds. Console yourself with this though: it may be wet, but it is never freezing.

Don't bother touring the Ring in heavy sea mist: you won't see a thing. But don't let other forms of rain deter you. Part of the attraction of the Ring is the interplay of light with sea, mountain, and distant horizons. Rain often enhances the view, and can give delightful effects. The sun is often shining before the rain has finished, so rainbows abound. Any weather, good or bad, seldom lasts more than half a day: if it's wet in the morning, it will probably be sunny in the afternoon, and vice versa.

SOCK IT TO ME

Bring a rain jacket and a warm fleece or sweater: sea winds can be chilly. Above all, wear sensible footwear. If you're venturing off-road, even in summer, you will be glad of strong, waterproof shoes. And bring plenty of socks. There's nothing more miserable than wet feet!

LAND OF EXOTIC PALMS

With no frost, Killarney and the Iveragh Peninsula are havens for subtropical vegetation. The New Zealand fern tree and the banana tree thrive. The "palm trees" you see here are usually yuccas that have been allowed to grow tall. Flax also grows to enormous size, and is often used as a shelter belt. The leaves of the gunnera can grow to the size of a compact car—look for them in Muckross Park. The lakes of Killarney are surrounded by luxuriant woods of oak, arbutus, birch, holly, and mountain ash, with undergrowth of ferns, saxifrages, and mosses. Rhododendron and azaleas thrive on pockets of acid soil, and are at their best from mid-April to May.

Valentia Island

THE ICE AGE COMETH, AND GOETH

Some 60 million years ago, the great rias, or drowned rivers, that became the bays of Bantry, Kenmare, and Dingle were formed. The sea penetrated far inland, forming the peninsulas of Beara, Iveragh, and Dingle. A million years ago, these lands were gripped by the Ice Age. When the ice receded, some 10,000 years ago, it left corries (or glacial hollows) gouged out of the mountains, great rocks scattered on the landscape (giving rise to legends of giants throwing stones), and outcrops of ice-smoothed sandstone.

(from 500 BC to the 5th century AD) and early Christian times (6th century AD), such "forts" were, in fact, the fortified homesteads for several families of one clan and their cattle. The walls at Staigue Fort are almost 13 feet wide at the base and 7 feet wide at the top; they still stand 18 feet high on the north and west sides. Within them, stairs lead to narrow platforms on which the lookouts stood. (Private land must be crossed to reach the fort, and a "compensation for trespass" of €1 is often requested by the landowner.)

WHERE TO STAY

For expanded hotel reviews, visit Fodors.com.

$$$
RESORT
Fodor's Choice
★
☾

🔲 **Parknasilla Resort.** For over a century Parknasilla, a towering, gray-stone mansion set on a stunningly beautiful inlet of the Kenmare estuary, has been synonymous with old-style resort luxury, attracting guests like George Bernard Shaw, Princess Grace, and Charles de Gaulle. **Pros:** excellent sports facilities and spa; sheltered coastal location; great family destination. **Cons:** grounds and hotel big enough to get lost in; hugely popular with Irish families in July and August. **TripAdvisor:** "amazing service and location," "lovely lodges," "haven of peace and tranquility." ⑤ *Rooms from: €180* ✉ *Sneem, Co. Kerry* ☎ *064/667–5600* ⊕ *www.parknasillahotel.ie* ⤳ *83 rooms* ☻ *Closed Jan.–mid-Mar.* ⑩ *Breakfast.*

$$
HOTEL

🔲 **Sneem Hotel.** Meet the locals and enjoy spacious accommodations at this waterfront hotel and apartment complex set on Goldens Cove, a rocky, sheltered spot with views of distant mountains. **Pros:** large, modern rooms; friendly service. **Cons:** some new development detracts from the views; large bar and restaurant can be a bit eerie when not busy. **TripAdvisor:** "lovely hotel," "friendly and relaxing," "peaceful." ⑤ *Rooms from: €160* ✉ *Goldens Cove, Sneem, Co. Kerry* ☎ *064/667–5100* ⊕ *www.sneemhotel.com* ⤳ *69 rooms, 25 apartments* ⑩ *No meals.*

WATERVILLE

35 km (22 miles) west of Sneem.

Waterville, a seaside village facing Ballinskelligs Bay, is famous for its sportfishing, its 18-hole championship golf course (adopted as a warm-up spot for the British Open by Tiger Woods), and for the fact that Charlie Chaplin and Charles de Gaulle spent summers here. The village, like many others on the Ring of Kerry, has a few restaurants and pubs, but little else. There's excellent salmon and trout fishing at nearby Lough Currane, and the area offers challenging hikes with stunning vistas.

GETTING HERE AND AROUND

Waterville, part of the Ring of Kerry driving loop, is a short half-hour drive from Sneem on the N70. You approach the town driving through the dramatically rocky Coomakesta Pass and Hog's Head. Stop at one of the viewing areas to take in the panoramic sea views, which look out at the distinctive Skellig Rocks. There is plenty of free parking in the village.

ESSENTIALS

Visitor Information Waterville Tourist Office ✉ *Town Center, Waterville, Co. Kerry* ☎ *066/947–4646* ⊙ *Open June–Sept. only.*

EXPLORING

Cill Rialaig. Outside Waterville and 1 km (½ mile) before Ballinskelligs, an Irish-speaking fishing village, is the Cill Rialaig Arts Centre. This is the best place in Kerry to see Irish and international art, along with fine crafts and gifts. Its attractive, thatched beehive-shaped roof is hard to miss. There's also a café run by an award-winning chef. ✉ *R566, Waterville, Co. Kerry* ☎ *066/947–9277* ⊕ *www.cillrialaig.org* ⊠ *Free* ⊙ *June–Sept., daily 11–6; other months call in advance.*

WHERE TO STAY

For expanded hotel reviews, visit Fodors.com.

$$
HOTEL
★

Butler Arms Hotel. Charlie Chaplin loved it here—so much so that the connection is now commemorated by a mini film festival held here in late August—and a whole host of families return year after year to this rambling old-world hotel, long a landmark on the Ring. **Pros:** charming old-world vibe; near beaches and village. **Cons:** village mainly a golfing and fishing center dominated by all-male groups; limited nightlife, shopping, dining. **TripAdvisor:** "beautiful seaside hotel," "spectacular views," "nice and quiet." ⑤ *Rooms from: €140* ✉ *Waterville, Co. Kerry* ☎ *35/3947–4144* ⊕ *www.butlerarms.com* ⊃ *24 rooms, 12 suites* ⊙ *Closed Nov.–Mar.* ⦿ *Breakfast.*

$
B&B/INN

Lakelands Farm Guesthouse. Amid rocky hills, this spacious, Dutch-gable modern house enjoys a stunning location about a mile off the Ring on the shore of Lough Currane (boats for hire), making it popular with game anglers, golfers, and scenery-lovers. **Pros:** good value; great scenery; huge bedrooms. **Cons:** nearly 2 miles outside village; won't win any style kudos. **TripAdvisor:** "nice hostess," "beautiful location," "good fishing." ⑤ *Rooms from: €70* ✉ *Lake Rd., look for signpost on the N70 on the south side of the village, Waterville, Co. Kerry* ☎ *066/947–4303* ⊕ *www.lakelandswaterville.com* ⊃ *12 rooms* ⊙ *Closed Oct., Feb., and early Mar.* ⦿ *Breakfast.*

NIGHTLIFE AND THE ARTS

Inny Tavern. Head to the Inny Tavern, a traditional country pub popular among locals, for live Irish music. ✉ *Inny Bridge, Waterville, Co. Kerry* ☎ *066/947–4512.*

SPORTS AND THE OUTDOORS

GOLF

Waterville Golf Links. Famously adopted by Tiger Woods and Mark O'Meara to practice their swings for the British Open, this 18-hole course remains one of the toughest and most scenic in Ireland or Britain. A championship links consisting of sand dunes, gorse, native grass, and sod-faced bunkers linked by firm fairways and carefully tended greens, Waterville is surrounded by the wild Atlantic on two of its three sides. This is one of Ireland's top five courses and is considered to be among the best in the world. Gary Player described the 11th hole, which runs for 500 yards through majestic dunes, as "the most beautiful

7

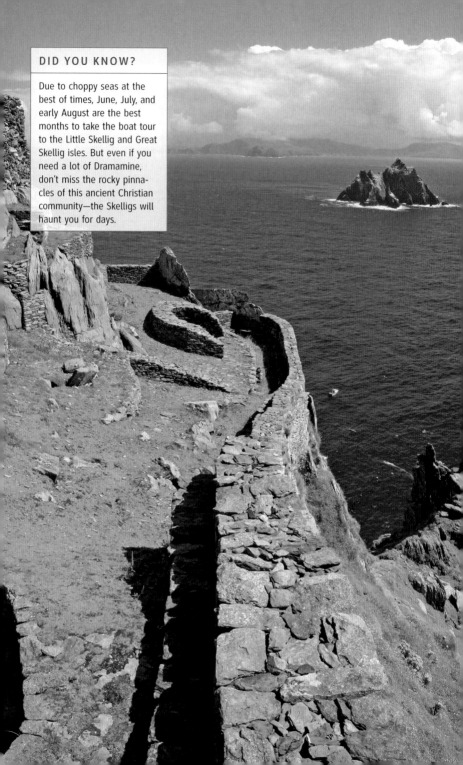

DID YOU KNOW?

Due to choppy seas at the best of times, June, July, and early August are the best months to take the boat tour to the Little Skellig and Great Skellig isles. But even if you need a lot of Dramamine, don't miss the rocky pinnacles of this ancient Christian community—the Skelligs will haunt you for days.

and satisfying par 5 of them all." Caddies must be booked in advance.
⊠ *Waterville, Co. Kerry* ☎ *066/947–4102* ⊕ *www.watervillegolfclub.ie*
🏌 *Greens fees: Apr.–Oct., weekdays €144, weekends €163. Nov.–Mar., €58* ⚑ *18 holes. Yardage: 7,355. Par 72. Practice area, caddies, caddy carts, buggies, catering.* ☺ *Visitors daily, year-round.*

THE SKELLIGS

Islands off the coastal town of Portmagee, 21 km (13 miles) northwest of Waterville.

GETTING HERE AND AROUND

To visit the Skelligs, you can take a half-day trip in an open boat—perfect for adventurers who pack plenty of Dramamine. The entire visit takes three to four hours, with 1½ hours on the Skellig Michael, where visitors are supervised by resident guides, and the remaining time in transit (the duration varies depending on the weather and tides). Note that the waters are choppy at the best of times, and trips are made when the weather permits. Even in fine weather, it can be a rough, white-knuckle ride (at least 45 minutes) as you cross the swell of the open sea, and it's not suitable for small children. One worthy outfitter to the Skelligs is Sea Quest, on Valentia Island. ■ TIP➔ From April to October the Valentia Island Car and Passenger Ferry operates a daily shuttle for cars and foot passengers between Knightstown on Valentia Island and Renard Point near Cahirciveen. The five-minute ferry ride saves a round trip of about 25 km (15 miles) by land.

ESSENTIALS

Transportation Contacts **Sea Quest** ⊠ *Valentia Island* ☎ *066/947–6214* ⊕ *www.skelligsrock.com* 🏷 *€45* ☺ *Apr.–Aug, daily 10 am, weather permitting (book in advance).* **Valentia Island Car and Passenger Ferry** ⊠ *Renard Point, Cahirciveen, Co. Kerry* ☎ *066/947–6141.*

Visitor Information **Skelligs Tourist Office** ⊠ *Skellig Experience, Valentia Island, Co. Kerry* ☎ *066/947–6306* ⊕ *www.discoverireland.ie* ☺ *June–Sept.*

EXPLORING

Fodor'sChoice **The Skellig Islands.** In the far northwestern corner of the Ring of Kerry,
★ across Portmagee Channel, lies **Valentia Island,** which is reachable by a bridge erected in 1971. Visible from Valentia, and on a clear day from other points along the coast, are the Skelligs, one of the most spectacular sights in Ireland. Sculpted as if by the hand of God, the islands of **Little Skellig, Great Skellig,** and the **Washerwoman's Rock** are distinctively cone-shaped, surrounded by blue swirling seas. The largest island, the Great Skellig, or Skellig Michael, distinguished by its twin peaks, rises 700 feet from the Atlantic. It has the remains of a settlement of early Christian monks, reached by climbing 600 increasingly precipitous steps. In spite of a thousand years of battering by Atlantic storms, the church, oratory, and beehive-shaped living cells are surprisingly well preserved.

During the journey to these islands you'll pass Little Skellig, the breeding ground of more than 22,000 pairs of gannets. Puffin Island, to the north, has a large population of shearwaters and storm petrel. Puffins nest in sand burrows on the Great Skellig in the month of May. But the masterpiece is the phenomenal Skellig Michael, home to that amazing 7th- to 12th-century village of monastic beehive dwellings, and offering vertigo-inducing views.

Skellig Experience. Located across the bridge to Valentia Island, the Skellig Experience offers an alternative for the less adventurous traveler. This center contains exhibits on local birdlife, the history of the lighthouse and keepers, and the life and work of the early Christian monks. There's also a 15-minute audiovisual show that allows you to "tour" the Skelligs without leaving dry land. The center also offers a 90-minute non-landing cruise around the islands. But if you're up for it, don't miss the boat ride from Portmagee that lets you land on the rocks; Skellig Michael is something you won't soon forget. ☒ *Valentia Island* ☎ *066/947–6306* ⊕ *www.skelligexperience.com* ☒ *€5, cruise €27.50* ☾ *Mar.–June and Sept., daily 10–6; July and Aug., daily 10–7; Oct. and Nov., daily 10–6.*

WHERE TO EAT AND STAY
For expanded hotel reviews, visit Fodors.com.

$$
IRISH
★

✕ **Bridge Bar.** Hungry mariners make a beeline for this simple bar on the windswept waterfront of the tiny fishing village of Portmagee. Overlooking the channel between the mainland and Valentia Island, its dramatic location has led the Bridge to being featured in ads as "the quintessential Irish pub." While not overly historic in decor, the low-beam interior—fitted out with red walls, rustic pine, and an open fire—is a sweet place to enjoy the renowned seafood chowder, or opt for daily specials like grilled haddock with lemon butter or steamed mussels with garlic. In July and August the pretty, adjoining Moorings restaurant serves a more ambitious, pricier menu most evenings. There are also 14 en-suite rooms overhead and an ace craft shop next door. Between Easter and October call to confirm. ⑤ *Average main: £18* ☒ *Portmagee, Co. Kerry* ☎ *066/947–7108* ⊕ *www.moorings.ie* ☾ *Closed (no food, but bar open) Mon., and totally closed Dec. 20–mid-Jan.*

$
B&B/INN
★

⛉ **Shealane Country House Bed & Breakfast.** A large, modern detached house set on Valentia Island, located beside the bridge to the mainland, Shealane is easily reached but also affords views of cows grazing in the adjoining field and a breakfast room with ocean views. **Pros:** friendly welcome from local family; quiet rural location. **Cons:** outside the village; rooms book far in advance for July and August. **TripAdvisor:** "beautiful stay," "lovely home," "top notch." ⑤ *Rooms from: €80* ☒ *Corha-Mor, Valentia Island, Co. Kerry* ☎ *066/947–6354* ⊕ *www. valentiaskelligs.com* ⟿ *5 rooms* ☾ *Closed Nov.–Feb.* ⵏⵓⵍ *Breakfast.*

CAHIRCIVEEN

18 km (11 miles) north of Waterville.

Cahirciveen (pronounced cah-her-sigh-*veen*), at the foot of Bentee Mountain, is the gateway to the western side of the Ring of Kerry and the main market town for southern Kerry. Following the tradition in this part of the world, the modest, terraced houses are each painted in different colors (sometimes two or three)—the brighter the better.

GETTING HERE AND AROUND

Cahurciveen is about a 15-minute drive from Waterville on N70, double that if you choose to detour to Portmagee for a visit to the Skellig Rock and Valentia Island. In summer you can return from Knightstown on Valentia Island to Cahirciveen by ferry. There is free parking on the side streets off the main road and outside the Tourist Office.

ESSENTIALS

Visitor Information **Cahirciveen Tourist Office** ⊠ *Church St., Cahirciveen, Co. Kerry* ☎ *066/947–1300* ⊕ *www.discoverireland.ie/southwest* ⊗ *June–Sept. only.*

EXPLORING

Cahersiveen Parish Daniel O'Connell Memorial Church. This large, elaborate, neo-Gothic structure dominates the main street. It was built in 1888 of Newry granite and black limestone to honor the local hero Daniel O'Connell—the only church in Ireland named after a layman. ⊠ *Cahirciveen, Co. Kerry* ☎ *066/947–2210* ⊕ *www.caherciveenparish.com.*

Old Barracks Heritage Centre. The converted former barracks of the Royal Irish Constabulary, an imposing, castlelike structure (built after the Fenian Rising of 1867 to suppress further revolts) now houses this museum. Well-designed displays depict scenes from times of famine, the life of Daniel O'Connell, and the restoration of this fine building from a blackened ruin. ⊠ *The Barracks, Cahirciveen, Co. Kerry* ☎ *066/947– 2777* ⊠ *€4* ⊗ *June–Sept., Mon.–Sat. 10–5:30, Sun. 1–5 pm; Mar.–May and Oct., Mon.–Fri.10–4:30, Sat. 11–4:30, Sun. 1–5 pm.*

GLENBEIGH

27 km (17 miles) northeast of Cahirciveen.

The road from Cahirciveen to Glenbeigh is one of the Ring's highlights. To the north is Dingle Bay and the jagged peaks of the Dingle Peninsula, which will, in all probability, be shrouded in mist. If they aren't, the gods have indeed blessed your journey. The road runs close to the water here, and beyond the small village of Kells it climbs high above the bay, hugging the steep side of Drung Hill before descending to Glenbeigh. Note how different the stark character of this stretch of the Ring is from the gentle, woody Kenmare Bay side.

On a boggy plateau by the sea, the block-long village of Glenbeigh is a popular holiday base—the hiking is excellent in the Glenbeigh Horseshoe, as the surrounding mountains are known, and the trout fishing exceptionally good in Lough Coomasaharn. The area south of Glenbeigh and west of Carrantouhill Mountain, around the shores of the Caragh River and the village of Glencar, is known as the Kerry Highlands. The scenery is wild and rough but strangely appealing. A series of circular walks have been signposted, and parts of the Kerry Way pass through here. The area attracts serious climbers who intend to scale Carrantouhill, Ireland's highest peak (3,408 feet).

GETTING HERE AND AROUND

The tiny roadside village of Glenbeigh is about 40 minutes from Cahirciveen on N70. There's free parking on the town's streets.

EXPLORING

Caragh Lake. A signpost to the right outside Glenbeigh points to Caragh Lake, a tempting excursion south to a beautiful expanse of water set among gorse- and heather-covered hills and majestic mountains. The road hugs the shoreline much of the way.

☼ **Kerry Bog Village Museum.** Worth a quick look, this museum is a cluster of reconstructed, fully furnished cottages that vividly portray the daily life of the region's working class in the early 1800s. The adjacent pub is famous for its Irish coffee. ⊠ *Beside Red Fox Bar, Glenbeigh, Co. Kerry* ☎ *066/976–9184* ⊕ *www.kerrybogvillage.ie* 🎫 *€6* ☼ *Daily 9–6.*

WHERE TO STAY

For expanded hotel reviews, visit Fodors.com.

$$$ ⊤ **Carrig Country House.** A rambling two-story Victorian house covered
HOTEL in flowering creepers and set on 4 acres of lush gardens along a secluded
Fodor's Choice lakeshore, this comes pretty close to most people's dream rural retreat.
★ **Pros:** lovely secluded location; real country-house atmosphere; affable owner-managers. **Cons:** tricky to find first time (see website for directions). **TripAdvisor:** "first class," "idyllic retreat," "perfection on all fronts." ⑤ *Rooms from: €180* ⊠ *Caragh Lake, Ring of Kerry, Killorglin, Co. Kerry* ☎ *066/976–9100* ⊕ *www.carrighouse.com* ⤴ *17 rooms* ☼ *Closed Dec.–Feb.* ¶⊙¶ *Breakfast.*

SPORTS AND THE OUTDOORS
BEACHES

☼ **Rossbeigh.** On the coast, 2 km (1 mile) west of Glenbeigh, Rossbeigh consists of a tombola (sand spit) of about 3 km (2 miles) backed by high dunes. It faces Inch Strand, a similar formation across the water on the Dingle Peninsula. Popular with families for its safe swimming, it also attracts walkers. **Amenities:** food and drink; lifeguards; parking (no fee). **Best for:** swimming; walking. ⊠ *Co. Kerry.*

KILLORGLIN

14 km (9 miles) east of Glenbeigh, 22 km (14 miles) west of Killarney.

Killorglin is on top of a hill beside the River Laune. At the "top of the town" is a Continental-style piazza, with outdoor tables in good weather and free entertainment in summer. (This is also the location of the tourist information office.) Venture down the hill to find an old-style traditional pub where you can savor a pint.

Killorglin is famed as the scene of the Puck Fair, three days of merry-making during the second weekend in August. A large billy goat with beribboned horns, installed on a high pedestal, presides over the fair. The origins of the tradition of King Puck are lost in time. Horse dealing takes place in an open field on the first morning of the fair. In the village the main attractions are fun fair rides, street traders, street performers, free outdoor concerts, and extended drinking hours. The crowds can be huge, so avoid Killorglin at fair time if you've come for peace and quiet. On the other hand, if you intend to join in the festivities, be sure to book accommodations well in advance.

GETTING HERE AND AROUND

The town is a 10-minute drive on the R70 from Glenbeigh. Street parking is available, and there is a free parking lot near the tourist information office.

ESSENTIALS

Visitor Information Killorglin Tourist Office ⊠ *Iveragh Rd., Killorglin, Co. Kerry* ☎ *066/976–1451* ⊙ *Open June–Sept.*

WHERE TO EAT

$$ ✕ **The Bianconi.** This hostelry opened in the 19th century, before the
IRISH days of railways, as the coaching inn for the national network of horse-drawn coaches known as Bianconis, after the Italian who set up the business. Today it's a busy pub, with guest rooms as well, at the riverside crossroads at the entrance to town. Its dark-wood Victorian interior has a rambling barroom with a tile floor, leatherette banquettes, and ancient stuffed animals above the booths. The menu includes such favorites as Dingle Bay prawns, local oak-smoked salmon, a steaming mussel pot in garlic sauce, and braised shank of Kerry lamb. Even though it's a pub, advance booking is advisable in summer and on weekends. $ *Average main: €20* ⊠ *Lower Bridge St., Killorglin, Co. Kerry* ☎ *066/976–1146* ⊕ *www.bianconi.ie* ⊙ *Closed Sun.*

CORCA DHUIBHNE: THE DINGLE PENINSULA   7

The gorgeously scenic Dingle Peninsula stretches for some 48 km (30 miles) between Tralee (pronounced tra-*lee*) in the east and Ceann Sleibne (Slea Head) in the west. Often referred to by its Irish name, Corca Dhuibhne (pronounced Cor-kah-guy-nay), the peninsula is made up of rugged mountains, seaside cliffs, and softly molded glacial valleys and lakes. Long sandy beaches and Atlantic-pounded cliffs unravel along the coast. Drystone walls enclose small, irregular fields, and exceptional prehistoric and early Christian remains dot the countryside. As you drive over its mountain passes, looking out past prehistoric remains to the wild Atlantic sea, Dingle can be a magical destination that makes you feel like you're living in an ancient legend. Unfortunately, Dingle is notorious for its heavy rainfall and impenetrable sea mists, which can strike at any time of year. If they do, sit them out in An Daingean (Dingle Town) and enjoy the friendly bars, cafés, and crafts shops. ■ TIP➔ West of Annascaul, the peninsula is Irish-speaking: English is considered a second language. A good Irish-English map can prove handy.

You can cover the peninsula in a long day trip of about 160 km (99 miles). If mist or continuous rain is forecast, postpone your trip until visibility improves. From Killarney, Killorglin, or Tralee, head for Castlemaine, and take the coast road (R561 and R559) to Dingle Town. Remember, it will be signposted in Irish: "An Daingean."

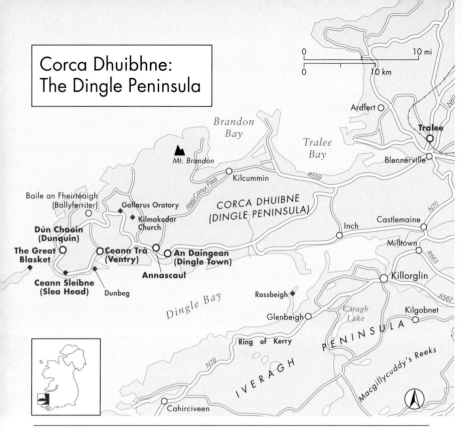

Corca Dhuibhne: The Dingle Peninsula

Brandon Bay

Mt. Brandon

Tralee Bay

Ardfert

Tralee

Blennerville

Kilcummin

R559

Conor Pass

R560

Baile an Fheirtéaigh (Ballyferriter)

Gallarus Oratory

CORCA DHUIBHNE (DINGLE PENINSULA)

Kilmakedar Church

Dún Chaoin (Dunquin)

Castlemaine

Inch

N70

The Great Blasket

Ceann Trá (Ventry)

An Daingean (Dingle Town)

Milltown

N70

R563

Annascaul

Ceann Sleibne (Slea Head)

Dunbeg

Killorglin

R562

Dingle Bay

Rossbeigh

Killorglin

Glenbeigh

Caragh Lake

Kilgobnet

N70

Ring of Kerry

PENINSULA

IVERAGH

Macgillycuddy's Reeks

Cahirciveen

0   10 mi
0   10 km

ANNASCAUL

47 km (30 miles) northwest of Killarney.

An important livestock center until the 1930s, this village near the junction of the Castlemaine and Tralee roads has a wide road, as cattle trading was once carried out in the streets. The town also has many pubs.

GETTING HERE AND AROUND

Annascaul is about one hour from Tralee on the N86, just over an hour from Killarney (take N70 then R561), and less than half an hour's drive from Dingle Town continuing on the main N86. There is abundant free parking in town.

EXPLORING

The South Pole Inn. This fascinating landmark was built by local hero Tom Crean (1877–1938). Crean enlisted in the English navy at the age of 15, and served on three expeditions to Antarctica—the *Discovery* (1901–04) and the *Terra Nova* (1910–13), both under the command of Captain Robert Falcon Scott, and the *Endurance* (1914–16), where he was second officer to Ernest Shackleton. Crean himself failed to reach the South Pole on any of these expeditions, and named his pub so that in his retirement he could go to work at the South Pole every day.

Dingle by Any Other Name

Residents of Dingle, especially those involved in the tourist business, are fighting a battle with the government for the right to continue to call their town and their peninsula by the name of Dingle. The problem arises because the western part of Dingle Peninsula—known in Irish as Corca Dhuibhne and its main town, Dingle (An Daingean, in Irish)—is officially an Irish-speaking area, part of the Kerry Gaeltacht. The Official Languages Act 2003 was introduced to strengthen the rights of Ireland's 90,000 Irish speakers to do business with the state in their native tongue—officially Ireland's first language. A side effect of this act was the necessity, under the new law, for all signposts for places where Irish is the official spoken language to be in Irish. So the name Dingle has disappeared from all signposts by official decree, to be replaced by An Daingean. The traders of Dingle claim that the name of their town is equivalent to an internationally recognized brand name, and are demanding that an exception be made in their case. The compromise suggested by the traders of Dingle, Dingle Daingean Uí Chúis, has yet to be approved by the government. Meanwhile, when heading for Dingle Town, follow signs to An Daingean. Only in Ireland.

Memorabilia at the pub fill in the details of Crean's Antarctic adventures. Crean was famed for his amazing strength and resilience. He walked 56 km (35 miles) through an Antarctic blizzard to bring help to his colleagues, with only two bars of chocolate and three biscuits for sustenance. For this he received the Albert Medal for Bravery. On another occasion he survived a 15-day journey across 1,280 km (800 miles) of ocean in an open boat.

The pub is the headquarters of the Tom Crean Society, which hosts occasional lectures and festivals and has been addressed by Sir Edmund Hillary and the grandsons of both Scott and Shackleton. ⊠ *Annascaul, Co. Kerry* ☎ *066/915–7388* ⊕ *No dedicated website; it has a Facebook page.*

AN DAINGEAN (DINGLE TOWN)

18 km (11 miles) west of Annascaul, 67 km (42 miles) west of Killarney, 45 km (28 miles) west of Killorglin.

Backed by mountains and facing a sheltered harbor, An Daingean, the chief town of its eponymous peninsula, has a year-round population of 1,400 that more than doubles in summer. Although many expect Dingle (to use its English name) to be a quaint and undeveloped Gaeltacht village, it has many crafts shops, seafood restaurants, and pubs.

Still, you can explore its main thoroughfares—the Mall, Main and Strand streets, and the Wood—in less than an hour. Celebrity hawks, take note: off-season Dingle is favored as a hideaway by the likes of Julia Roberts, Paul Simon, and Dolly Parton. These and others have their visits commemorated on Green Street's "path of stars."

The latest addition to the annual calendar is the **Dingle Food and Wine Festival** (⊕ *www.dinglefood.com*) on the first weekend in October. Sample local produce on the Taste Trail, enjoy special menus, try your hand at chocolate making, or learn about beekeeping and biodynamic vegetable growing. This is a major festival, and growing in popularity with every passing year.

GETTING HERE AND AROUND

Dingle Town is about an hour and 15 minute's drive from Tralee on the N86, and about two hours west of Killarney via Killorglin and Castlemaine. There are daily buses from Tralee, which is also the nearest railway station.

There is no public transportation west of Dingle Town, around Slea Head, where the best scenery is found. If you don't have a car, the 30-km (18-mile) circuit can be toured by minibus (€20 per person for two or more people). Coastline Tours is a good choice for these excursions, or ask at the tourist information office. Bear in mind that there are no gas stations and no ATMs west of Dingle Town, so load up on supplies before you leave.

Most boats to the Blasket Islands leave from Dunquin, 21 km (13 miles) west of town, but Dingle Bay Charters has boats from the marina in Dingle Town making ecotours of the Blasket Islands daily between May and September, weather permitting (€40).

ESSENTIALS

Transportation Contacts **Coastline Tours** ☎ *087/998–2230* ⊕ *www.coastlinetours.com.* **Dingle Bay Charters** ✉ *Dingle Marina, Dingle Town, Co. Kerry* ☎ *066/915–1344* ⊕ *www.dinglebaycharters.com.*

Visitor Information **An Daingean (Dingle Town) Tourist Office** ✉ *The Quay, Dingle Town, Co. Kerry* ☎ *066/915–1188* ⊕ *www.dingle-peninsula.ie.*

EXPLORING

☼ **Fungie.** Since 1985, An Daingean's central attraction, apart from its "trad" music scene, has been a winsome bottle-nosed dolphin that has taken up residence in the harbor. The Dingle dolphin, or Fungie, as he has been named, will play for hours with swimmers (a wet suit is essential) and scuba divers, and he follows local boats in and out of the harbor. It's impossible to predict whether he will stay, but boatmen have become so confident of a sighting that they offer trippers their money back if Fungie does not appear. Boat trips (€16) leave the pier hourly in July and August between 11 and 6, weather permitting.

WHERE TO EAT

$$$ ✗ **Chart House.** Host Jim McCarthy is often found in the early evening
IRISH leaning over the red half door of this low, cabinlike stone building.
★ The exterior gives little hint of the spacious, cleverly lighted dining room within, or of the beautiful pair of windows at the back that frame lovely views of Dingle Harbour's trawler fleet. Nautical artifacts complement the rusty red walls and matching tablecloths. The atmosphere is pleasantly informal, but both food and service are polished and professional. Top choices include the phyllo parcel of Annascaul black pudding with chutney, or the rack of Kerry mountain lamb with

An entry in Fodor's "Show Us Your Ireland" contest, this photo by Fodors.com member Michelle Nadal shows the coastal tip of the dramatic Dingle Peninsula.

redcurrant and rosemary jus. Finish the meal with a selection of Irish cheeses, served with a glass of port, or a homemade apple and clove tartlet with ginger-nut crumble. $ *Average main: €25* ⊠ *The Mall, Dingle Town, Co. Kerry* ☎ *066/915–2255* ⊕ *www.thecharthousedingle.com* ⊗ *Closed Jan.–mid-Feb., and Mon. and Tues. in Oct.–May (but call to confirm hrs Oct.–May). No lunch.*

$ EUROPEAN   ✕ **Chowder Cafe.** Look for the bright blue wooden shop front near the pier (about 3 minutes' walk from the tourist office) to find one of the best budget eateries in town. Enthusiastic young owner-chefs, Charlie and Joanna, welcome you to their restaurant, nicely brightened with artwork by local artists. The chowder is a star, but so is the steak sandwich with home fries, and some adore the goat cheese and red onion quiche. When the dinner menu kicks in during high season, more substantial seasonal mains are offered, perhaps slow-braised lamb shank, or cod with chorizo. Slow Fooders will like this place: fresh bread and cakes are home-baked daily. $ *Average main: €17* ⊠ *Strand St., Dingle Town, Co. Kerry* ☎ *066/915–1061* ⊗ *No dinner Oct.–May.*

$$$ SEAFOOD   ✕ **Out of the Blue.** Every fishing port should have a simple waterfront bistro like this one, serving the best seafood (owner Tim Mason won't open his tiny restaurant if there's no fresh-caught seafood available, which is almost never). Lobster, scallops, and crayfish are specialties, but also expect turbot, black sole, plaice, brill, monkfish, and even the humble pollack on the daily blackboard menu. The duo of French chefs put a modern twist on seafood classics, perhaps sole on the bone with almond cream, or John Dory with a pepper sauce and garlic eggplant. There's a short but well-chosen wine list, and a basic dessert selection. $ *Average main: €25* ⊠ *The Pier, Dingle Town, Co. Kerry*

☎ *066/915–0811* ⊲ *Reservations essential* ⊘ *Closed mid-Nov.–mid-March. No lunch Mon.–Sat.*

WHERE TO STAY

For expanded hotel reviews, visit Fodors.com.

$$$
HOTEL

⊡ **Dingle Skellig Hotel and Peninsula Spa.** This rambling and modern hotel's setting on Dingle Bay offers great views of the water. **Pros:** waterfront location; organized entertainment for children; separate floors for childless guests. **Cons:** still shows signs of its undistinguished 1970s architecture; edge-of-town location a bit bleak in bad weather. **TripAdvisor:** "great family hotel," "very friendly," "wonderful." ⑤ *Rooms from: €198* ⊠ *Dingle Harbour, Dingle Town, Co. Kerry* ☎ *066/915–0200* ⊕ *www.dingleskellig.com* ⤳ *99 rooms, 14 suites* ⦿| *Breakfast.*

$$$
B&B/INN

⊡ **Emlagh House.** Although many accommodations in An Daingean are cottagelike, the Kavanagh family chose the grander Georgian style, setting a tone of quiet, unostentatious luxury in this spacious, yellow, mansard-roof home on the water's edge. **Pros:** spacious, romantic rooms; waterside location. **Cons:** expensive for a B&B. **TripAdvisor:** "very beautiful house," "warm and inviting," "Irish hospitality at its finest." ⑤ *Rooms from: €180* ⊠ *Dingle Harbour, Dingle Town, Co. Kerry* ☎ *066/915–2345* ⊕ *www.emlaghhouse.com* ⤳ *10 rooms* ⊘ *Closed Nov.–mid-Mar.* ⦿| *Breakfast.*

$$
B&B/INN
Fodor'sChoice
★

⊡ **Greenmount House.** More like a boutique hotel than a B&B, the combination of comfort and elegance in the lobby sets the tone, as do the wonderful views of the town and harbor out the windows. **Pros:** plenty of private parking; wine license; nice common areas. **Cons:** new developments mar the foreground of an otherwise great view. **TripAdvisor:** "perfection in Dingle," "the most comfortable stay," "charming and sharp." ⑤ *Rooms from: €120* ⊠ *Upper John St., Dingle Town, Co. Kerry* ☎ *066/915–1414* ⊕ *www.greenmount-house.com* ⤳ *6 rooms, 6 suites* ⦿| *Breakfast.*

$
B&B/INN

⊡ **Heaton's Guesthouse.** To get to this traditional-style yellow house on the water's edge, drive through Dingle Town and out to its western fringe, following the signs for Slea Head. **Pros:** high standard of comfort and decor; ample parking; only a short walk from town. **Cons:** if it rains you'll be driving, not walking, to nearest bars and restaurants. **TripAdvisor:** "charming family staff," "best breakfast ever," "pure luxury." ⑤ *Rooms from: €80* ⊠ *The Wood, Dingle Town, Co. Kerry* ☎ *066/915–2288* ⊕ *www.heatonsdingle.com* ⤳ *16 rooms* ⊘ *Closed Dec.* ⦿| *Breakfast.*

NIGHTLIFE AND THE ARTS

Nearly every bar on the Corca Dhuibhne (Dingle Peninsula), particularly in the town of An Daingean, offers live music nightly in July and August.

An Droichead Beag (The Small Bridge). For a lively nighttime spot, try the Small Bridge, a large, busy pub in the town center known for live Irish music. ⊠ *Main St., Dingle Town, Co. Kerry* ☎ *066/915–1723.*

O' Flahertys. An Daingean's pubs are well known for their music, but among them O'Flaherty's, a simple, stone-floor bar, is something special and a hot spot for traditional musicians. Spontaneous sessions occur most nights in July and August, less frequently at other times. Even without music, this pub is a good place to compare notes with fellow travelers. ⊠ *Bridge St., at entrance to town, Dingle Town, Co. Kerry* ☎ *066/915–1983.*

SHOPPING

An Cafe Liteartha. Don't miss An Daingean's café-bookshop, which locals insist is one of the world's first (it has been here since the 1970s). Regardless, you can find friendly conversation as well as new and secondhand books. ⊠ *Bóthar An Dadhgaide, Dingle Town, Co. Kerry* ☎ *066/915–2204.*

Greenlane Gallery. Shows of contemporary Irish art with an emphasis on local landscapes are often held at Greenlane. ⊠ *Holy Ground, Dingle Town, Co. Kerry* ☎ *066/915–2018.*

Leác a Ré. For handmade Irish crafts, check out this noted emporium. ⊠ *Strand St., Dingle Town, Co. Kerry* ☎ *066/915–1138.*

Murphys Ice Cream. One of Ireland's more unusual culinary success stories is Murphys Ice Cream, which has won international awards. Find out why at this flagship parlor. ⊠ *Strand St., Dingle Town, Co. Kerry* ☎ *066/915–2644* ⊕ *www.murphysicecream.ie.*

Weaver's Shop. Lisbeth Mulcahy at the Weaver's Shop sells outstanding handwoven, vegetable-dyed woolen wraps, mufflers, and fabric for making skirts. ⊠ *Green St., Dingle Town, Co. Kerry* ☎ *066/915–1688.*

SPORTS AND THE OUTDOORS

BICYCLING

Foxy John's Hardware. You're likely to remember a bike ride around Slea Head for a long time. You can rent bicycles at Foxy John's Hardware, which also has a great old-style bar-cum-hardware store. ⊠ *Main St., Dingle Town, Co. Kerry* ☎ *066/915–1316.*

HORSEBACK RIDING

Dingle Horse Riding. Up in the hills behind Dingle Town, this stable offers some unforgettable treks. The two-hour rides (€65) follow mountain tracks then proceed through the town to visit the dolphin Fungie before galloping back along the beach. The half-day trek (€100) goes to Ventry Strand. ⊠ *Baile an Bualle, Dingle Town, Co. Kerry* ☎ *086/821–1225* ⊕ *www.dinglehorseriding.com.*

7

CEANN TRÁ (VENTRY)

8 km (5 miles) west of An Daingean (Dingle Town) on R561.

The next town after An Daingean along the coast, Ceann Trá has a small outcrop of pubs and small grocery stores (useful, since west of Dingle Town you'll find few shops of any kind), and a long sandy beach. Between Ventry and Dún Chaoin (Dunquin) are several interesting archaeological sites on the spectacular cliff-top road along Ceann Sleibne (Slea Head).

GETTING HERE AND AROUND

It takes about 10 minutes to reach Ventry by car on R561 from Dingle Town. Take extra care when driving these narrow scenic roads, which can be busy with cyclists, walkers, and sometimes sheep, as well as many other drivers unfamiliar with the locality.

EXPLORING

Dunbeg Fort. Perched on the very edge of a Dingle Bay cliff, and set in the small district of Fagan (which is part of the larger township of Ventry), the small, well-weathered Dunbeg Fort was an important Iron Age defensive promontory site, inhabited from about AD 800 until around AD 1200. Its drystone mound was defended against cattle raiders by four earthen rings—note the *souterraine* (underground) escape route, by the entrance. In addition, there are a number of archaeological artifacts here to interest the time traveler.

There is a 10-minute audiovisual show in the adjacent visitor center, but just as fascinating is the building itself, a modern replica of the drystone construction of the *clocháns* (pronounced cluk-*awns*), the famous prehistoric "beehive" cells first used by hermit monks in the Early Christian period. Beside it is a typical *naomhóg* (pronounced "na-*vogue*"), a tarred canvas canoe, resting upside down.

About half a mile farther on is another parking lot, and an interesting group of clocháns can be visited (€2 fee to resident farmer), built of drystone and set on the southern slopes of Mt. Eagle looking out directly across the sea to Skellig Michael. Far from being only prehistoric relics, as the signposts claim, clocháns were being built until a century ago; wood was scarce and stone abounded, so you'll find more than 400 of these clocháns exist between Ceann Sliebne and Dún Chaoin. ⊠ *Fahan, 8 km (5 miles) west of Ventry, Ventry, Co. Kerry* ☎ *066/915–9070* ⊕ *www.dunbegfort.com* ✉ *€3.50* ☉ *Easter–Apr., daily 9:30–7; May–Oct., 9:30–8; Nov.–Easter, phone in advance.*

SPORTS AND THE OUTDOORS

BEACHES

Ventry Beach. Ventry Beach (also known as Ventry Strand) is just southwest of the village of Ceann Trá (Ventry). This lovely stretch of golden sand, said by many to be one of Ireland's most beautiful beaches, runs for 8 km (5 miles) and is part of the Dingle Way walking route. There is a dune system with a small lake, wetlands, and a reed swamp, and abundant wildlife. In July and August it attracts families and swimmers. **Amenities:** food and drink; parking (no fee); lifeguards; toilets; water sports. **Best For:** surfing, swimming, walking, windsurfing. ⊠ *Ventry, Co. Kerry.*

CEANN SLEIBNE (SLEA HEAD)

16 km (10 miles) west of An Daingean (Dingle Town), 8 km (5 miles) west of Ceann Trá.

From the top of the towering cliffs of Ceann Sleibne at the southwest extremity of the Dingle Peninsula, the view of the Blasket Islands and the Atlantic Ocean is guaranteed to stop you in your tracks. Alas, Slea Head—to use its English name—has become so popular that tour buses, barely able to negotiate the narrow road, are causing traffic jams, particularly in July and August. Coumenole, the long sandy strand below, looks beautiful and sheltered, but swimming here is dangerous. This treacherous stretch of coast has claimed many lives in shipwrecks—most recently in 1982, when a large cargo boat, the *Ranga,* foundered on the rocks and sank. In 1588 four ships of the Spanish Armada were driven through the Blasket Sound; two made it to shelter, and two sank. One of these, the *Santa Maria de la Rosa,* is being excavated by divers.

GETTING HERE AND AROUND
Slea Head is a 10-minute drive from Ventry on R559.

SPORTS AND THE OUTDOORS
BEACHES
Clogher Strand. This dramatic, windswept stretch of rocks and sand visible below the coast road to the north of Slea Head is not a safe spot to swim, but it's a good place to watch the ocean dramatically pound the rocks when a storm is approaching or a gale is blowing. It may be familiar from David Lean's 1970 film *Ryan's Daughter.* **Amenities:** none. **Best For:** solitude; sunset; walking. ⊠ *Slea Head, Dunquin, Co. Kerry.*

DÚN CHAOIN (DUNQUIN)

13 km (8 miles) west of Ceann Trá, 5 km (3 miles) north of Ceann Sleibne (Slea Head).

Once the mainland harbor for the Blasket islanders (when there *were* islanders, as the Blaskets are deserted now), Dún Chaoin is at the center of the Gaeltacht, and attracts many students of Irish language and folklore.

EXPLORING

Fodor's Choice ★ ☺ **Blasket Centre.** The Blasket Islands (An Bhlaskaoid Mhóir) are among Ireland's most extraordinary islands. The largest visible from Ceann Sleibne is the Great Blasket, inhabited until 1953. The Blasket Islanders were great storytellers and were encouraged by Irish linguists to write their memoirs. The Blasket Centre explains the heritage of these islanders and celebrates their use of the Irish language with videos and exhibitions. ⊠ *Dún Chaoin (Dunquin), Co. Kerry* ☎ *066/915–6444* ⊕ *www.heritageireland.ie* ⊠ €4 ☉ *Apr.–Oct., daily 10–6.*

Dún Chaoin's Pier. Signposted from the main road, Dún Chaoin's pier is surrounded by cliffs of colored Silurian rock, more than 400 million years old and rich in fossils. Down at the pier you can see *naomhóga* (open fishing boats traditionally made of animal hide stretched over wooden laths and tarred) stored upside down. Three or four men walk the curraghs out to the sea, holding them over their heads. Similar boats are used in the Aran Islands, and when properly handled they're extraordinarily seaworthy.

Kruger's Pub. Long been frequented by artists and writers, including Brendan Behan, Kruger's Pub is known as Dunquin's social center. ⊠ *Dunquin, Co. Kerry* ☎ *066/915–6127.*

EN ROUTE

Louis Mulcahy Pottery. Overlooking the beach is the pottery studio of one of Ireland's leading ceramic artists. Louis Mulcahy produces large pots and urns that are both decorative and functional. You can watch the work in progress and buy items at workshop prices. There is also a coffee shop. ⊠ *Clogher Strand, Dunquin, Co. Kerry* ☎ *066/915–6229* ⊕ *www.louismulcahy.com* ⊙ *Daily 9:30–6.*

GREAT BLASKET ISLAND

The Great Blasket, which measures roughly 3 km by 1 km (2 miles by ½ mile), has no traffic, no pub, no hotel, and no electricity. Yet this island—centerpiece of the An Bhlaskaoid Mhóir (Blasket Islands)—is one of the most memorable places in Ireland to visit.

Until 1954 a small community of hardy fisherfolk and subsistence farmers eked out a living here.

Today, visitors are usually attracted by the literary heritage of the island—the Irish-language writings of Tomás Ó Criomhthain, Muiris Ó Suilleabhain, and Peig Sayers (also known in English as Tomás O Crohán and Maurice O'Sullivan)—but what makes people return is something else: a rare quality of light and an intense peace and quiet in beautiful, unspoiled surroundings.

The inadequacy of the existing piers limits visitors to the island to a maximum of about 400 per day, a figure that is reached only rarely, with the average under 200. Most visitors stay for three or four hours, walking, sketching, or taking photographs.

The silence strikes you at once. The seabirds, stonechats, and swallows sound louder than on the mainland; sheep graze silently on the steep hillside. The simple domestic ruins are very touching; you do not need to know the history to work out what happened to their owners (most departed for other places, with many settling in Springfield, Massachusetts).

■ TIP➔ Before you go, read Maurice O'Sullivan's Twenty Years a-Growing, a fascinating account of a simple way of life that has only recently disappeared on the Blaskets. For an overview of the island's more recent history, read Hungry for Home: Leaving the Blaskets: A Journey from the Edge of Ireland by Cole Moreton.

GETTING HERE AND AROUND

These days it takes only 15 minutes from Dún Chaoin (Dunquin) Pier to make the 3-km (2-mile) crossing of the Blasket Sound, but even on a calm day the swell can be considerable. In summer the island is usually accessible most days; in winter the island can be cut off for weeks.

Almost as memorable as the boat ride to the Skellig isles is the excursion out to the unspoiled Blasket Islands, a favorite escape for poets and writers.

ESSENTIALS

Transportation Contacts Blasket Islands Ferry. The ferry makes the 15-minute crossing from Dún Chaoin Pier to the island daily from April to September, weather permitting, costing €25 round-trip. The same company runs a 2½-hour ecotour around the island with the option of landing for €30. Sightings of seals are pretty well guaranteed. ☎ 086/335–3805 ⊕ www. blasketislands.ie ◁ €20. **Dingle Bay Charters.** A long-established charter boat company that sails from An Daingean (Dingle Town) to the Blaskets is Dingle Bay Charters. The trip usually takes about 40 minutes and costs €30 for a round-trip ticket. They also run a 3-hour guided ecotour (€40). ☎ 066/915–1344 ⊕ www.dinglebaycharters.com.

TRALEE

67 km (41 miles) west of Ballyferriter, 50 km (31 miles) northeast of An Daingean (Dingle Town) on R559.

County Kerry's capital and its largest town, Tralee (population 22,700), is a superb springboard to explore the adjoining Dingle Peninsula. It is also the transportation hub of the region. As such, people used to joke that the only good things to come out of Tralee were the buses shuttling travelers elsewhere. To a certain extent, that is still the case: apart from some Georgian town houses near the museum there is not much of architectural or antiquarian interest. Modern renovations, including concrete piazzas (which attract crowds of drinkers on weekends) have done little to ameliorate Tralee's medium-size-town-with-little-character feel. Accordingly, however, there are no tourists, so the local folk have been fashioning some worthwhile sights, including the town museum, and the Siamsa Tíre—the National Folk Theatre of Ireland—which stages impressive dances and plays based on Irish folklore.

The town has long been associated with the popular Irish song "The Rose of Tralee," the inspiration for the annual Rose of Tralee International Festival. The last week of August, Irish communities worldwide send young women to join native Irish competitors; one of them is chosen as the Rose of Tralee. Visitors, musicians, and entertainers pack the town then. A two-day horse-racing meet—with seven races a day—runs at the same time, which contributes to the crowds.

GETTING HERE AND AROUND

Tralee is at the junction of the N21 from Limerick (about an hour and a half away), the N21 and N22 from Killarney (about half an hour away), and the N86 from Dingle (an hour and 15 minutes away). It is also the terminus for the train from Dublin (the trip takes 3 hours and 45 minutes) and is well served by buses from Shannon Airport, Limerick, Killarney, and Dingle. There is a bus service that circles the town every hour, mainly to facilitate students: visit the tourist information office for details.

ESSENTIALS

Transportation Contacts **Tralee Bus Station** ⊠ *John Joe Sheey Rd., Tralee, Co. Kerry* ☎ *066/712–3566.* **Tralee Rail Station** ⊠ *Casement Station, John Joe Sheehy Rd., 4 Clounalour Mews, Tralee, Co. Kerry* ☎ *85/1105753* ⊕ *www.tralee.org/infra.html.*

Visitor Information **Tralee Tourist Office** ⊠ *Ashe Memorial Hall, Denny St., Tralee, Co. Kerry* ☎ *066/712–1288* ⊕ *www.discoverireland.ie/TraleeTIO.*

EXPLORING

⊕ **Kerry County Museum.** Tralee's major cultural attraction traces the history of Kerry's people since 5000 BC, using dioramas and an entertaining audiovisual show. You can also walk through a life-size reconstruction of a Tralee street in the Middle Ages. Admission for kids is free. ⊠ *Ashe Memorial Hall, Denny St., Tralee, Co. Kerry* ☎ *066/712–7777* ⊕ *www.kerrymuseum.ie* ⊠ *€8* ⊙ *Jan.–May, Sept.–Dec., Tues.–Sat. 9:30–5; June–Aug., daily 9:30–5:30.*

WHERE TO STAY

For expanded hotel reviews, visit Fodors.com.

$ ⊡ **Abbey Gate.** Built on the site of Tralee's old marketplace, in a
HOTEL   quiet spot behind the main shopping street, Abbey Gate is an attractive, modern hotel. **Pros:** good value; centrally located. **Cons:** Tralee town center largely rebuilt as concrete piazzas; bar can be noisy at night. **TripAdvisor:** "well worth a visit," "friendly staff," "beautiful food at a great price." ⑤ *Rooms from: €89* ⊠ *Main St., Tralee, Co. Kerry* ☎ *066/712–9888* ⊕ *www.abbeygate-hotel.com* ⊅ *100 rooms* ⑩ *Breakfast.*

$$ ⊡ **Ballygarry House Hotel.** A mile and a half outside town, this family-
HOTEL   run hotel with six acres of gardens and supremely stylish guest rooms
★   is a good choice if you're touring by car, and a better option than Tralee's busy town center. **Pros:** next to a woodland amenity area for

runners; in same family since 1958. **Cons:** no shops or cafés within walking distance. $ *Rooms from: €130* ✉ *Killarney Rd., Tralee, Co. Kerry* ☎ *066/712–3322* ⊕ *www.ballygarryhouse.com* ⤴ *53 rooms, 11 suites* ⦿❘ *Breakfast.*

$ 🏠 **Brook Manor Lodge.** Set against a dramatic backdrop of the Slieve
B&B/INN Mish Mountain, this large double-gable country house is a nice option. **Pros:** quiet and spacious; friendly personal welcome; delicious breakfast. **Cons:** no nearby village. **TripAdvisor:** "first class," "doesn't get better than this," "genuine comfort in luxury setting." $ *Rooms from: €100* ✉ *Fenit Rd., Tralee, Co. Kerry* ☎ *066/712–0406* ⊕ *www. brookmanorlodge.com* ⤴ *8 rooms* ⊗ *mid-Dec.–Jan.* ⦿❘ *Breakfast.*

NIGHTLIFE AND THE ARTS

National Folk Theater of Ireland (Siamsa Tire). Language is no barrier to the supremely colorful entertainment offered by this theater, which re-creates traditional rural life through music, mime, and dance. ✉ *Town Park, Tralee, Co. Kerry* ☎ *066/712–3055* ⊕ *www.siamsatire.com* ⊗ *Shows June, July, and Aug., Mon.–Sat. at 8:30 pm; May and Sept., Tues.–Sat. at 8:30 pm.*

The Abbey Inn. Slap-bang in the middle of the town center, the two-story Abbey Inn has late openings seven nights a week, live music and DJs, big screen sports, and poker classics. ✉ *Bridge St., Tralee, Co. Kerry* ☎ *066/712–3390* ⊕ *www.theabbeyinntralee.com.*

SPORTS AND THE OUTDOORS

BICYCLING

Tralee Bicycle Supplies. A top outfitter in town, this is a handy place to rent bicycles. ✉ *Strand St., Tralee, Co. Kerry* ☎ *066/712–2018.*

GOLF

Fodor's Choice **Ballybunion Golf Club.** President Bill Clinton will be eternally associated
★ in Irish golfers' minds with this revered course. In fact, there's even a brass statue of him teeing off in the nearby village, to commemorate his visit here in 1999. On the shore of the Atlantic next to the southern entrance of the Shannon, Ballybunion has the huge dunes of Lahinch without the blind shots. It's no pushover, but every hole is pleasurable. Watch out for "Mrs. Simpson," a double fairway bunker on the 1st hole, named after the wife of Tom Simpson, the architect who remodeled the course in 1937. (Tom Watson did the same in 1995.) The Cashen Course, which opened in 1985, was designed by Robert Trent Jones Sr. and currently is free to play if you've paid for a round on the Old Course. ✉ *Sandhill Rd., Ballybunion, Co. Kerry* ☎ *68/27611* ⊕ *www.ballybuniongolfclub.ie* ⛳ *Greens fees: May–Sept., €180 (Old), €65 (Cashen), €180 to play both on same day; Oct.–Apr. €95 (Old), €50 (Cashen)* ⛳ *36 holes. Yardage: 6,568 (Old), 6,306 (Cashen). Par 72 (Old), 70 (Cashen). Practice area, driving range, caddies, caddy carts, club rental, catering* ⊗ *Visitors: weekdays.*

Tralee Golf Club. Tralee is what all modern-golf-course architects *wish* they could do in the States: find unspoiled, seaside links and route a course on it that's designed for the modern game. This is an Arnold Palmer–Ed Seay design that opened in 1984, and the location is fantastic—cliffs, craters, dunes, and the gale-blowing ocean. Don't let the flat front 9 lull you to sleep—the back 9 can be a ferocious wake-up call. ⊠ *West Barrow, Ardfert, Co. Kerry* ☎ *066/713–6379* ⊕ *www. traleegolfclub.com* ⊠ *Greens fees: May–Oct. €170; Apr. and Oct. €80; Nov.–Mar. €50* ⚊. *18 holes. Yardage: 6,975. Par 72. Practice area, putting green, caddies, caddy carts, club rental, catering* ⊘ *Visitors: Mon., Tues., and Thurs.–Sat.*

NORTH KERRY AND SHANNONSIDE

Until several decades ago, Shannon meant little more to most people—if it meant anything at all—than the name of the longest river in Ireland and Great Britain, running from County Cavan to Limerick City in County Clare. But mention Shannon nowadays and people think immediately of the airport, which has become western Ireland's principal gateway. In turn, what also comes to mind are many of the glorious sights of North Kerry and Shannonside: Adare, sometimes called "Ireland's Prettiest Village" (and the neighboring Adare Manor, a grand country-house hotel); and Limerick City, which attracts visitors tracing the memories so movingly captured in Frank McCourt's international best seller *Angela's Ashes.*

If you want to leapfrog over the Shannon Estuary and head directly into the West of Ireland, head north on N69 18 km (11 miles) from Listowel to Tarbert, the terminus for the **Shannon Ferries** (☎ *065/905– 3124* ⊕ *www.shannonferries.com*) crossing to Killimer in West Clare, a convenient 20-minute shortcut to the West. The Shannon River is 273 km (170 miles) long, and its magnificent estuary stretches westward for another 96 km (60 miles) before reaching the sea.

ADARE

19 km (12 miles) southwest of Limerick City, 82 km (51 miles) northeast of Tralee.

Fodor's Choice
★
On the banks of the River Maigue, this once-upon-a-timefied village dotted with thatch cottages is famed as one of Ireland's prettiest spots. Perhaps it's more correct to say it's actually one of England's: the place was given a beauty makeover by a rich Anglo lord, the third earl of Dunraven, in the 1820s and 1830s, in an effort to create the "perfect rustic village." To a great extent, he succeeded.

Few local feathers were ruffled since Dunraven won goodwill by restoring many villagers' houses. Playing into the mid-19th-century vogue for romantic rusticity, the earl "picturesquely" restored many of the town's historic sights, including the remains of two 13th-century abbeys, a 15th-century friary, and the keep of the 13th-century **Desmond Castle** (now the centerpiece of a private golf course). Adjacent to the Adare Heritage Centre you'll find the **Trinitarian Priory,** founded in 1230 and now a convent. From the main bridge (where you can best view the castle), head to the **Augustinian Priory** and its gracious cloister. The most fetching time-burnished allure is provided by Adare's stone-built, thatch-roof cottages, often adorned with colorful, flower-filled window boxes and built for the earl's estate tenants.

Some now house boutiques selling Irish crafts and antiques, along with a fine restaurant called the Wild Geese. Adare Manor, an imposing Tudor–Gothic Revival mansion, which was once the grand house of the Dunraven peerage, is now a celebrated hotel; on its grounds you can view two 12th-century ruins, the **St. Nicholas Chapel** and the **Chantry Chapel.**

GETTING HERE AND AROUND

Adare is on the main road (N21) between Tralee and Limerick, just over an hour from Tralee and about 20 minutes from Limerick. The parking lot is in the center of town behind the Adare Heritage Centre; parking here is free. Buses on the Limerick–Tralee route stop at the Heritage Centre.

EXPLORING

Adare Heritage Centre. This center is home to an array of helpful facilities, including a restaurant and three retail outlets (one sells sweaters, another crafts, and the third heraldry items). There is also an exhibition on Adare's history since 1223, complete with a 15-minute audio-visual display, but some may feel it is not worth the extra fee. Guided tours of Desmond Castle (€6) depart from the center by coach from June to September. ⊠ *Main St., Adare, Co. Limerick* ☎ *061/396–666* ⊕ *www.adareheritagecentre.ie* 🕾 *Heritage center free, exhibition €5*

⊘ *Daily 9–6, historical exhibition Mar.–June, daily 9–5; July–Sept., daily 9–5:30; Oct.–Dec., weekdays 9–4, weekends 11–4.*

WHERE TO EAT AND STAY

For expanded hotel reviews, visit Fodors.com.

$$$
MODERN
EUROPEAN
★
✕ **The Wild Geese.** There's a charming, old-world atmosphere in the series of small dining rooms in this low-ceiling thatch cottage, one of the prettiest in a village famed for its fairy-tale looks. Co-owner and chef David Foley uses the best local produce to create imaginative and seriously good dishes. Try roast rack of lamb with a potato and garlic gratin, or pan-seared Castletownbere scallops with a potato pancake and cauliflower purée. Lobster—grilled with snow peas and shallots and topped with a chive mayonnaise—is a popular summer option. The house dessert platter for two lets you sample all desserts, including the fantastic homemade ice cream. For a real bargain, try their Sunday lunch (€25 for three courses). The restaurant is opposite the Dunraven Arms. ⑤ *Average main: €25* ⊠ *Rose Cottage, Adare, Co. Limerick* ☎ *061/396–451* ⊕ *www.thewild-geese.com* ⊘ *Dinner only Tues.-Sat; Suns lunch only.* ⊘ *Closed Mon. May–Sept; Sun.–Mon. Oct–Apr., and 3 wks Jan. No dinner Sun.*

$$$$
HOTEL
Fodor'sChoice
★
🏨 **Adare Manor Hotel.** Play king or queen for a day at this spectacular (and, interestingly, American-owned) Victorian Gothic mansion, once the abode of the earls of Dunraven and still a wonderland, thanks to 840 acres of French-style gardens outside and the 36-foot-high, 100-foot-long Minstrels' Gallery inside. **Pros:** an amazing and unforgettable Gothic experience. **Cons:** dominated by golfers; even the rich find it expensive. **TripAdvisor:** "absolutely lovely," "world class," "magnificent setting." ⑤ *Rooms from: €493* ⊠ *Adare, Co. Limerick* ☎ *061/396–566* ⊕ *www.adaremanor.ie* 🛏 *5 suites, 57 rooms* ⑩ *No meals.*

$$$
HOTEL
🏨 **Dunraven Arms Hotel.** Charles Lindbergh stayed here in Room 6 while he advised on the nearby Shannon Airport's design and he might still cotton to this tranquil, antique-adorned landmark coach-inn stop, established in 1792, even though it is now somewhat over-restored and generic. **Pros:** the staff make it a memorable Irish experience; pretty village; recent drop in room rates. **Cons:** decor verges on bland international; expensive for what it is. **TripAdvisor:** "excellent service," "fit for a queen," "a lovely, warm, friendly hotel." ⑤ *Rooms from: €190* ⊠ *Main St., Adare, Co. Limerick* ☎ *061/605–900* ⊕ *www.dunravenhotel.com* 🛏 *56 rooms, 30 suites* ⑩ *Breakfast.*

$$$
B&B/INN
Fodor'sChoice
★
🏨 **Mustard Seed at Echo Lodge.** This is the small country hotel of your dreams: a Victorian yellow-stucco jewel set atop a small hill overlooking Ballingarry, a village that time forgot, deep in rural Ireland, yet only 13 km (8 miles) southwest of Adare. **Pros:** quirky, memorable, and extremely comfortable; acclaimed restaurant. **Cons:** in the middle of nowhere; cock crows at dawn. **TripAdvisor:** "heavenly ambience," "a really lovely place," "excellent food and service." ⑤ *Rooms from: €190* ⊠ *Ballingarry, Co. Limerick* ☎ *069/68508* ⊕ *www.mustardseed.ie* 🛏 *14 rooms, 2 suites* ⊘ *Closed Jan.* ⑩ *Breakfast.*

As cute as a Fisher-Price toy village, Adare is a thatched-roof jewel laid out with characteristics that conjure up the English rather than the Irish countryside.

SPORTS AND THE OUTDOORS

GOLF

Adare Manor Golf Course. Connected with the celebrated Adare Manor luxury hotel, this parkland stretch is on the ancestral estate of the Earl of Dunraven. Its immediate success was virtually guaranteed by the international profile of its designer, Robert Trent Jones Sr. The front 9 are dominated by an artificial 14-acre lake with a $500,000 polyethylene base. It's in play at the 3rd, 5th, 6th, and 7th holes. The dominant hazards on the homeward journey are the River Mague and the majestic trees, which combine to make the par-5 18th one of the most challenging finishing holes imaginable. ⊠ *Adare, Co. Limerick* ☎ *061/395–044* ⊕ *www.adaremanor.com* ⊠ *Greens fees: May–Sept., €125; Oct. and Apr., €95; Nov., €90; Dec.–Mar., €80* ⅃ *18 holes. Yardage: 7,453. Par 72. Practice area, caddies, caddy carts, club rental, catering* ☉ *Visitors: daily.*

SHOPPING

Adare Cottage Shop. A gem of a gift and craft shop, this is found cozily ensconced in one of the village's thatched cottages. ⊠ *Main St., Adare, Co. Limerick* ☎ *061/396–422.*

George Stacpoole. Head here to find a nice selection of antiques large and small, plus books. ⊠ *Main St., Adare, Co. Limerick* ☎ *061/396–409.*

Lucy Erridge's. This cottage boutique has Irish-made jewelry and fine ladies' wear from Irish designer labels. ⊠ *Main St., Adare, Co. Limerick* ☎ *061/396–898.*

LIMERICK CITY

19 km (12 miles) northeast of Adare, 198 km (123 miles) southwest of Dublin.

Before you ask, there's *no* direct connection between Limerick City and the facetious five-line verse form known as a limerick, which was first popularized by the English writer Edward Lear in his 1846 *Book of Nonsense.* The city, at the head of the Shannon estuary and at the intersection of a number of major crossroads, is an industrial port and the republic's third-largest city (population 75,000). If you fly into or out of Shannon Airport, and have a few hours to spare, do take a look around. The attractions around the cathedral and the castle are linked by a riverside foot path, while the western part of the town center is dominated by mid-18th-century buildings with fine Georgian proportions. What's more, the city has undergone considerable revitalization since the days recounted in Frank McCourt's famed childhood memoir, *Angela's Ashes.*

GETTING HERE AND AROUND

Limerick is a major gateway to the Southwest and the West of Ireland, and is linked to Dublin by the M7 motorway (the drive is about two and a half hours). Cork is two hours south on the N20. A tunnel under the city links the Cork road with the road to Shannon Airport (N19) and the N18 to Galway (about an hour and a half). There are excellent express bus links to these cities and to Killarney. Limerick has a rail link to Dublin via Limerick Junction, and a smaller commuter line travels via Ennis to Galway (2 hours). Citylink buses, bookable online only, serve Dublin, Shannon, and Cork airports.

Within the city there is a regular bus service for shoppers connecting the historic center with the newer Crescent Shopping Centre at Dooradoyle.

In Limerick it's advisable to use a multistory parking garage, as on-street parking can be hard to find. If you do get lucky, you'll have to become familiar with "disk" parking regulations, which involve buying a ticket (or disk) for around €2 an hour from a machine or a shop and displaying it. Beware: car-clamper officers are active!

ESSENTIALS

Transportation Contacts Limerick Bus Station ⊠ *Colbert Station Forecourt, Parnell St., Limerick City, Co. Limerick* ☎ *061/313333.* **Limerick Rail Station** ⊠ *Colbert Station, Parnell St., Limerick City, Co. Limerick* ☎ *061/315555.*

Visitor Information Limerick City Tourist Office ⊠ *Arthur's Quay, Limerick City, Co. Limerick* ☎ *061/317–522* ⊕ *www.discoverlimerick.ie.*

EXPLORING

It doesn't help that the things for which Limerick is famous—rugby football, lace, and (Catholic) religious devotion—are all so uncool. This may explain why this big city still lacks a vibrant dining scene (many people prefer to head for the country to dine out, for instance in Adare). In addition, Limerick is still trying hard to counter a reputation for gang warfare, confined primarily to its less-privileged outer suburbs. Sadly, the city center feels like a ghost town once workers have gone home

Looming over Adare's Desmond Castle is the regal Adare Manor Hotel, once home to the town's lord of the manor, the earl of Dunraven.

at the end of the day (until the early hours, when young revelers are released from the nightclubs), in spite of the large sums of money spent recently on revitalizing Limerick's quays.

TOP ATTRACTIONS

Hunt Museum. In the Old Customs House on the banks of the Shannon in the city center, the Hunt Museum has the finest collection of Celtic and medieval treasures outside the National Museum in Dublin. Ancient Irish metalwork, European objets d'art, and a selection of 20th-century European and Irish paintings—including works by Jack B. Yeats—are on view. A café overlooks the river. ⊠ *Rutland St., Limerick City, Co. Limerick* ☎ *061/312–833* ⊕ *www.huntmuseum.com* ✑*€5* ☉ *Mon.–Sat. 10–5, Sun. 2–5.*

King John's Castle. First built by the Normans in the early 1200s, King John's Castle still bears traces on its north side of a 1691 bombardment. If you climb the drum towers (the oldest section), you'll have a good view of the town and the Shannon. Inside, a 22-minute audiovisual show illustrates the history of Limerick and Ireland; an archaeology center has three excavated, pre-Norman houses; and two exhibition centers display scale models of Limerick from its founding in AD 922. ⊠ *Castle St., Limerick City, Co. Limerick* ☎ *061/411–201* ⊕ *www. shannonheritage.com* ✑*€9* ☉ *Daily 10–5.*

St. Mary's Cathedral. Limerick is a predominantly Catholic city, but the Protestant St. Mary's Cathedral is the city's oldest religious building. Once a 12th-century palace—pilasters and a rounded Romanesque entrance were part of the original structure—it dates mostly from the 15th century (the black-oak carvings on misericords in the choir stalls are from this period). ✉ *Bridge St., Limerick City, Co. Limerick* ☎ *061/310–293* ⊕ *www.cathedral.limerick.anglican.org* ☉ *Mon.–Sat., 9:30–4:30; services only Sun.*

WORTH NOTING

Cruises Street. An inviting pedestrian thoroughfare, Cruises Street has chic shops and occasional street entertainers. It's on the opposite side of O'Connell Street from the Arthur's Quay Shopping Centre.

Georgian House and Garden. To see how people lived in Limerick's 18th-century heyday, head to this tall, narrow row house, which has been meticulously restored and filled with furnishings from the period. Out back, the garden has been planted in a manner true to the time. ✉ *Tontine Buildings, 2 Pery Sq., Limerick City, Co. Limerick* ☎ *061/314–130* ⊕ *www.limerickcivictrust.ie/georgian* 🎫 *€6* ☉ *Weekdays 10–4, weekends by appointment.*

O'Connell Street. On O'Connell Street you can find the main shopping area, which consists mostly of modest chain stores. However, the street lies one block inland from (east of) the Arthur's Quay Shopping Centre, through which it can be reached. Along with the futuristic tourist information center, this was part of a succesful campaign to develop the Shannonside quays.

WHERE TO EAT AND STAY

For expanded hotel reviews, visit Fodors.com.

$$ ✗ **Brasserie One.** The location—a second floor room on one of Limer-
IRISH ick's finest Georgian houses, recently converted into a luxury hotel—is
Fodor'sChoice naturally elegant but the aim here is to serve robust, brasserie-style
★ food in informal surroundings. Cream walls and gilt mirrors are lit by small crystal sconces and candelabra, while Victorian spoon-back chairs lend a raffish air as do the lunchtime paper napkins. Fresh local produce is simply and imaginatively presented: seared foie gras with polenta to start, or a tart of onion and Cashel Blue cheese, followed by grilled rib-eye steak with fries and béarnaise sauce. Don't miss the Earl Grey sabayon with aged prunes for dessert. The bar food served in a comfortable lounge on the ground floor is also excellent. $ *Average main: €23* ✉ *1 Pery Sq., Limerick City, Co. Limerick* ☎ *061/402–402* ⊕ *www.oneperysquare.com/brasserie-restaurants* ☉ *Closed for dinner Sun. and Mon.; lunch Sun. only.*

$ 🛏 **Jurys Inn.** Clean, airy, and in good shape (unlike some of Limer-
HOTEL ick's other inner-city lodgings), this big, well-run hotel is part of the Jurys budget chain. **Pros:** good value for couples and families; reliable hotel chain with consistently helpful staff. **Cons:** totally bland experience; "per room" pricing policy makes it expensive for singles; hugely popular with large groups of partying Irish people. **TripAdvisor:** "lovely view," "good location," "cozy and central." $ *Rooms from: €73* ✉ *Lower Mallow St., Mount Kennett Pl., Limerick City, Co. Limerick* ☎ *061/207–000* ⊕ *www.jurysinns.com* 🛏 *151 rooms* 🍴 *Breakfast.*

$ 🛏 **Patrick Punch's Hotel.** A striking, edgy glass-and-steel facade has been
HOTEL built onto a landmark Victorian pub to create a hotel where style and pizzazz are combined with a friendly Irish welcome. **Pros:** fun and

friendly; safe inner suburban location; easy access to bus and taxis. **Cons:** indoor parking is on a first-come, first-served basis; 20-minute walk or 5-minute bus or taxi ride to city center. **TripAdvisor:** "very comfortable," "pleasant stay," "extremely friendly." $ *Rooms from: €75* ✉ *Punch's Cross, New St. and O'Connell Ave., Limerick City, Co. Limerick* ☎ *35/3614–6080* ⊕ *www.patrickpunchshotel.com* ⇆ *71 rooms* ⦿ *Breakfast.*

NIGHTLIFE AND THE ARTS

ART GALLERIES

Belltable Arts Center. This noted exhibition space also has a small auditorium for touring productions. ✉ *69 O'Connell St., Limerick City, Co. Limerick* ☎ *061/319–866* ⊕ *www.belltable.ie.*

Limerick City Gallery of Art. Along with a small permanent collection of Irish art , this gallery also mounts exhibits of contemporary art. ✉ *Pery Sq., Limerick City, Co. Limerick* ☎ *061/310–633* ⊕ *gallery.limerick.ie.*

PUBS, CABARET, AND DISCOS

Curragower Pub. Across the river from King John's Castle, this is a favorite haunt of music students from Limerick University. You can hear good traditional music nightly from May through September, and Wednesday through Saturday in winter. ✉ *Clancy's Strand, Limerick City, Co. Limerick* ☎ *061/321–788* ⊕ *www.curragower.com.*

Dolan's Pub. A lively waterfront spot, Dolan's has traditional Irish music every night, and dancing classes from September to May. Dolan's Warehouse, under the same management and in the same location, is a live-music venue with top national and international acts. ✉ *3–4 Dock Rd., Limerick City, Co. Limerick* ☎ *061/314–483* ⊕ *www.dolanspub.com.*

The Locke Bar & Oyster House. Set on the riverside, this is one of Limerick's oldest bars, dating from 1724, and has live music every night except Sunday. It's also a great place for outdoor drinking in summer. ✉ *3 George's Quay, Limerick City, Co. Limerick* ☎ *061/413–733* ⊕ *www.lockebar.com.*

Nancy Blake's Pub. There's traditional music at this pub year-round Sunday–Wednesday from 9 pm. ✉ *19 Denmark St., Limerick City, Co. Limerick* ☎ *061/416–443.*

William G. South's Pub. An old-fashioned pub, this one is typical of the age of Frank McCourt's *Angela's Ashes.* There's no music, but do drop by for lunchtime bar food (weekdays 12:30–3) or a drink. ✉ *The Crescent, Limerick City, Co. Limerick* ☎ *061/318–850.*

SHOPPING

DEPARTMENT STORES

Brown Thomas. Limerick has a branch of Brown Thomas, Ireland's upscale department store. ✉ *O'Connell St., Limerick City, Co. Limerick* ☎ *061/417–222* ⊕ *www.brownthomas.com.*

Debenham's. A midrange department store, this is one of Limerick's largest. ✉ *O'Connell St., Limerick City, Co. Limerick* ☎ *1890/946–799.*

Dunnes Stores. This is, perhaps, Ireland's favorite department store chain. ✉ *Harvey's Quay, Limerick City, Co. Limerick* ☎ *061/431–200* ⊕ *www.dunnesstores.ie.*

Penneys. Also known as Primark, Penneys sells inexpensive clothing; it's a great place for low-price rain gear. ⊠ *137 O'Connell St., Limerick City, Co. Limerick* ☎ *061/416–033.*

SPECIALTY SHOPS

Arthur's Quay. A small indoor shopping mall near the tourist office, Arthur's Quay has a fine choice of Irish crafts and knitwear. ⊠ *Arthur's Quay, Limerick City, Co. Limerick* ☎ *061/419–888.*

O'Mahony's. Known for its good selection of Irish interest books, O'Mahony's has been selling books since 1902. ⊠ *120 O'Connell St., Limerick City, Co. Limerick* ☎ *061/418–155.*

Seoidin. An interesting selection of jewelry and gifts is available here. ⊠ *6 Sarsfield St., Limerick City, Co. Limerick* ☎ *061/318–011* ⊕ *www. seoidin.com.*

County Clare, Galway City, and the Aran Islands

WORD OF MOUTH

"Because the weather was once again dry and clear, we headed straight for the Cliffs of Moher. This was the one and only place where we saw a bunch of other tourists. There were lots of people and buses when we arrived but what a spectacular sight and wonderful photo op!"

—sessa

WELCOME TO COUNTY CLARE, GALWAY CITY, AND THE ARAN ISLANDS

TOP REASONS TO GO

★ **Ancient Aran:** Spend at least one night on one of the Oileáin Árainn (Aran Islands), three outposts of Gaelic civilization, which still have a strong whiff of the "old ways"—and not just the whiff of turf smoke.

★ **Foot-Tapping in Doolin and Ennis:** Tap your foot in time to "trad" Irish music—those heavenly strains of traditional Irish folk music—and sip your pint as you while away an afternoon and maybe an evening as well, in one of Doolin's or Ennis's noted music bars.

★ **High-Style Galway:** A university town and booming, buzzing hive of activity, with great theaters, bars, nightlife, shopping, and restaurants, Galway is the city that loves to celebrate and, as one of Europe's fastest-growing townships, has much to offer.

★ **The Mighty Cliffs of Moher:** Rising straight out of the sea to a height of 700 feet, these cliffs—standing in silence as they look out over the wild Atlantic—give you a new understanding of the word "awesome."

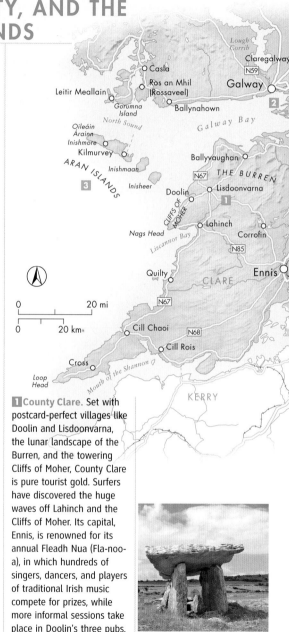

1 County Clare. Set with postcard-perfect villages like Doolin and Lisdoonvarna, the lunar landscape of the Burren, and the towering Cliffs of Moher, County Clare is pure tourist gold. Surfers have discovered the huge waves off Lahinch and the Cliffs of Moher. Its capital, Ennis, is renowned for its annual Fleadh Nua (Fla-noo-a), in which hundreds of singers, dancers, and players of traditional Irish music compete for prizes, while more informal sessions take place in Doolin's three pubs.

GETTING ORIENTED

Once you cross the Shannon in Limerick City you are officially in the West of Ireland. The rocky limestone plateau known as the Burren, dotted with megalithic remains, overlooks Galway Bay, lined with characterful villages like Ballyvaughan and Kinvara, and cradling the Aran Islands that lie across its entrance. Galway City is one of Ireland's liveliest, with a compact historic center bursting with artistic energy and a lively pub culture. This is the place to organize your trip to the Aran Islands, three windswept rocky islands where Irish is still spoken, with an almost total absence of traffic.

2 Galway City. This is easily the liveliest city in Ireland after Dublin. You've got to get your fill of its buzz when visiting, best done by checking out its eye-popping "g" hotel, stylish new boutiques and crafts shops, and dazzling weekend festivals.

3 Aran Islands. An hour or less away via ferry are the ageless Aran Islands. Once famed for their isolation, they are now disturbed a bit by 200,000-plus curious annual visitors, but even so they retain a distinctive identity, with traditional communities where Irish is still the daily language.

8

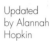
Updated
by Alannah
Hopkin

With some of the most westerly seaboard in Europe, Galway, in the province of Connaught, and Clare, in the province of Munster, together form the region where the Irish go to reconnect with their heritage, whether by practicing their jigs at the Fleadh Nua folk festival, enjoying "the craic" at the Lisdoonvarna Matchmaking Festival, visiting the ancient megalithic tombs of the Burren, or trading news with a Gaeltacht (Irish-speaking) resident. Wherever you go in the West, you'll not only see, but more important *hear,* how the best of traditional Ireland survives.

Even a Jackeen (Dubliner) will tell you that this area is distinctly different from the rest of Ireland and is bent on retaining its unspoiled, rugged way of life. With much of nature's magnificence on display—the majestic Cliffs of Moher, the rocky Burren, and the sublime Aran Islands—it's easy to see why. Visitors continue to relish the unique thrill of standing high above the pounding Atlantic, watching seabirds reel below, as the numerous Cliffs of Moher posts on YouTube demonstrate.

This area lies at the far western extremity of Europe, facing its nearest North American neighbors across thousands of miles of the Atlantic Ocean. Although other areas of Ireland were influenced by Norman, Scots, or English settlers, the West largely escaped systematic resettlement and, with the exception of the walled town of Galway, remained purely Irish in outlook. No wonder these western regions have the highest concentration of Irish-speaking communities and the best traditional musicians in the Republic.

West Clare, in fact, is the guardian of Ireland's musical traditions, where people still flock to learn new dance steps and fiddle riffs. The hub of the area remains Galway, the city that loves to celebrate. Saunter through its naturally festive, pedestrianized center and the city's many pubs, and you will find proof of Galway's reputation for good times. Not far away is the town of Ennis, and villages like Doolin and Kinvara, also noted as "trad"-music hot spots.

Visitors will find, particularly in western County Galway, the highest concentration of Gaeltacht (Irish-speaking) communities in Ireland, with roughly 40,000 native Irish speakers and the country's first Irish-language TV station based in tiny An Spidéal (Spiddle), a suburb of Galway City. You'll see plenty of signs printed in Irish only. This is especially the case out on the isolated Oileáin Árainn (Aran Islands), where many Irish schoolchildren have their first experience of a place where Irish is the main language during summer camps. These limestone islands are actually geological extensions of the mainland expanse known as the Burren, a craggy landscape rich in megalithic remains, unique geological formations, rare flora and fauna, and a bounty of myth and legend.

COUNTY CLARE, GALWAY CITY, AND THE ARAN ISLANDS PLANNER

WHEN TO GO
Be prepared for rain any time of year. Average rainfall in the rest of Ireland is between 31 inches and 47 inches, but here on the west coast, it can exceed 79 inches. Take comfort from the thought that while it may be damp, it is never really cold. In the coldest months, January and February, the mean daily temperature is around 6°C (43°F). That said, Ireland—like much of Northern Europe—has been experiencing colder winters in recent years with significant snow accumulations and prolonged below-normal temperatures. In the warmest months, July and August, average temperatures are around 15°C (60°F). ■ TIP→ If you're looking for authentic fun and festivity, skip St. Patrick's Day in March and plan to visit between May and September; yes, it's peak season, but you'll have your choice of local food and music festivals and you'll be able to catch a local hurling or Gaelic football match in the heated lead-up to All-Ireland finals in September.

FESTIVALS AND EVENTS
For visitors and locals alike, festivals provide both free entertainment and a chance to meet people from all backgrounds who share a common interest.

PLANNING YOUR TIME
There's much to see between Clare and Galway, so prioritizing your time means prioritizing your interests: if you want quintessential Irish castles, scenery, music, and history, spend all three days in Clare, allowing yourself time to stop and explore everything from Bunratty to the Burren and Craggaunowen to the Cliffs, as well as a night on the Aran Islands. If you want a little city buzz with your scenery, save the third day for Galway City—a vibrant city, rich in history and buzzing with artistic activity and festivals—and plan to spend the night so that you can sample the lively pub and music scene.

8

IF YOU HAVE 3 DAYS

Dedicate your first day to castles, *crannógs* (early Celtic dwellings), and *craic* (a good time). Begin with the magnificently restored Bunratty Castle, flanked by a lively folk village and a famous old riverside pub, Durty Nelly's. Allow a few hours to visit nearby Craggaunowen, where you'll find a medieval castle, a ring fort, Crannóg, and the Brendan Boat—a leather hulled boat built to reenact the voyage of St. Brendan, an early Christian monk said to have discovered America centuries before Columbus. Then, continue the castle theme with a quick visit to Knappogue Castle, a restored medieval manor, home to medieval banquets and beautiful walled gardens—perfect for a pre-dinner stroll. Finally, end the day in Ennis, with a hearty dinner, live music, and a well-earned pint.

Go coastal on Day 2 with an early start and a scenic drive that hugs the coastline of West Clare, taking in the seaside villages of Spanish Point, Lahinch, and Liscannor; the awe-inspiring Cliffs of Moher; the musical hot spot of Doolin; the beach of Fanore (noted for its edible seaweed); and the megalithic remains and limestone landscape of the Burren.■ TIP→ The drive along the coast from Doolin to Ballyvaughan (past Fanore and Black Head) is a favorite Sunday drive for Clare locals and especially lovely. If you're looking for a lively music scene, spend the night in a B&B in Doolin or Ballyvaughan. Otherwise, consider spending the night on the Aran Islands where you'll experience a taste of old Ireland—slow and peaceful. Take the ferry from Doolin; you can book a B&B with your ferry ticket.

Day three depends on your interests; if you want more of the raw quiet and countryside that inspired Irish writers like J. M. Synge, Liam O'Flaherty, and Máirtín Ó Díreíin, explore the forts and folklore of the Aran Islands. If you're ready for a little noise and excitement, head for Galway City, park the car, and take in the buzz on the streets. If you can, spend the night to sample Galway's lively and informal fine dining and music scene.

GETTING HERE AND AROUND

AIR TRAVEL

Flights to the Oileáin Árainn (Aran Islands) leave from Connemara Airport at Inverin, 30 km (18 miles) west of Galway on the R336, served by a minibus from Galway City (€3). There are hourly flights in July and August, and off-peak there are up to half a dozen flights a day. These flights call at all three Aran Islands. The journey takes eight minutes and costs about €40 round-trip. The airline will book a B&B for you when you book your flight. Ask about other special offers, including scenic routes, at the time of booking.

Carriers Aer Arann Islands ☏ *091/593–034* ⊕ *www.aerarannislands.ie.*

AIRPORTS   The West's most convenient international airport is Shannon, 25 km (16 miles) east of Ennis. Flying time from Dublin is about 30 minutes. Galway Airport (GWY) has no commercial flights at the time of writing, and is open only for charter business and private planes, but this may change as the recession eases. Connemara Airport at Inverin, which is 27 km (16 miles) west of Galway on R336, services the Aran Islands.

Ask about transport to the airport when buying your ticket: there is usually a courtesy bus from the center of Galway City.

Airport Information Connemara Airport ☎ *091/593–034* ⊕ *www.aerarannislands.ie.* **Shannon Airport** ☎ *061/471–444* ⊕ *www.shannonairport.com.*

AIRPORT TRANSFERS From Shannon Airport you can pick up a rental car to drive into the West, or you can take a bus to Galway or Ennis. Connemara Airport (for flights to the Aran Islands) is 27 km (16 miles) from Galway City, and is accessible by shuttle bus (€3).

BOAT AND FERRY TRAVEL

FROM KERRY TO CLARE The Tarbert–Killimer Ferry leaves every hour on the half hour and takes 20 minutes to cross the Shannon Estuary from North County Kerry to West County Clare; this saves you a 137-km (85-mile) drive through Limerick City. It is very handy if you are heading from the Ring of Kerry or Dingle area to the Cliffs of Moher. The ferry runs every day of the year except Christmas and costs €18 one-way, €28 round-trip. (Ferries return from Killimer every hour on the hour.)

Boat Companies Tarbert–Killimer Ferry ☎ *065/905–3124* ⊕ *www.shannonferries.com.*

TO THE ARAN ISLANDS The spell of the famed Oileáin Árainn (Aran Islands) is such that many travelers can't resist their siren call and make for the first ferry leaving from Doolin, which offers rates of €10 one-way. However, locals will tell you to hedge your bets and wait until you are in Galway City to make arrangements; that way, you can postpone your trip if the weather looks bad. You can do a day trip, leaving the city at 9:30 or noon and returning by 6:30, but staying overnight is more rewarding. Everyone wants to go to the islands, and it is made as easy as possible to organize by the various transport companies. They are all genuine and licensed: no one is going to rip you off. Book at the Galway Tourist Information Office in Forster Place, where the ferry companies and Aer Arann Islands have concessions.

The standard ferry deal on offer in Galway City is €25 round-trip and €7 for bus transfer to the ferry port at Ros an Mhil (Rossaveal). Look out for money-saving offers that may include bed-and-breakfast accommodations, free transfers to Ros an Mhill or Connemara Airport (both 40 minutes away), bicycle rental on the islands, or a ferry-out, flight-back plan. There are three different ferry operators, and tickets are not transferable, so check the return sailing times of your operator when you get on board. If you opt for the five-minute flight, for safety reasons, you (yes, you, not your bags!) will be weighed at check-in, and allocated an appropriate seat.

Boat Companies Doolin Ferries ⊠ *Doolin Pier* ☎ *065/707-4455* ⊕ *www.doolinferries.com* 🛥 *€10.* **Aran Island Ferries** ⊠ *Tourist Information Office, Forster St., Eyre Sq., 37–39 Forster St., Center, Galway City* ☎ *091/568–903* ⊕ *www.aranislandferries.com.* **O'Brien Line** ⊠ *Doolin Pier, Co. Clare* ☎ *065/707-5555* ⊕ *www.obrienline.com.* **Tarbert–Killimer Ferry** ☎ *065/905-3124* ⊕ *www.shannonferries.com.*

8

BUS TRAVEL

Bus Éireann runs several Expressway buses into Ennis and Galway City—the principal depots in the region—from Dublin, Cork City, and Limerick City. All buses mentioned are Bus Éireann (which includes Expressway) unless specified otherwise. Expect bus rides to last about one hour longer than the time it would take you to travel the distance by car. The Cliffs of Moher, Lisdoonvarna, Doolin, Liscannor, and Lahinch have two scheduled services a day (in each direction) from Galway, and only one from Ennis. Guided tours of the Cliffs of Moher and the Burren leave from the bus stations in Galway City and Ennis. Citylink operates frequent buses between Galway City and Shannon Airport as well as Dublin and Dublin Airport.

Bus Depots Ennis Bus Station ⊠ *Station Rd., Ennis* ☎ *065/682–4177*. **Galway Bus Station** (*Ceannt Railway Station*). ☎ *091/562–000*.

Bus Lines Bus Éireann ☎ *01/836–6111 in Dublin* ⊕ *www.buseireann.ie*. **Citylink** ☎ *091/564–163* ⊕ *www.citylink.ie*.

CAR TRAVEL

To do full justice to this region, you really need a car—and a good map: don't rely on GPS for the many small by-roads.

The 219-km (136-mile) Dublin–Galway trip takes about three hours. From Cork City take N20 through Mallow and N21 in the Limerick City direction, following signs for the tunnel (toll €1.80) before reaching the city, to join the N18/M18 Ennis–Galway road. The 209-km (130-mile) drive from Cork to Galway takes about three hours. From Killarney the shortest route to cover the 193 km (120 miles) to Galway (three hours) is to take N22 to Tralee, then N69 through Listowel to Tarbert and ferry across the Shannon Estuary to Killimer. From here, join N68 in Kilrush, and then pick up N18 in Ennis.

ROAD CONDITIONS The West has good, wide main roads (National Primary Routes) and better-than-average local roads (National Secondary Routes), both known as "N" routes. There is one stretch of motorway, the M18 north of Shannon, that bypasses Ennis and finishes north of Gort. If you stray off the beaten track on the smaller Regional ("R") routes, particularly in west Clare, you may encounter some challenging roads. Narrow and twisty, they are also used by hikers and cyclists from April to October, as well as local traffic (which can take the form of huge trucks serving the local agricultural co-ops, school buses, and tractors). The speed limits on these Regional routes is a whacking great 80 km per hour (50 mph), even for trucks and buses, but use your common sense and adjust your speed accordingly. ■TIP→ If traffic builds up behind you, it is customary to signal to the left and slow down/ pull over to let the locals fly by. Your kind gesture will usually be acknowledged with a nod or a wave.

TAXI TRAVEL

Taxis operate on the meter for journeys of up to 30 km (22 miles). For longer journeys, agree on the fare in advance. A Shannon Airport to Galway City journey will cost you about €120.

Taxi Companies **AAA Taxis** ✉ *Ennis* ☎ *065/689–2999.* **Big O Taxis**
✉ *21 Upper Dominick St., Galway City* ☎ *091/585–858* ⊕ *www.bigotaxis.com.*
Burren Taxi ✉ *Ennis* ☎ *065/682–3456.* **Galway Taxis** ✉ *Galway City*
☎ *091/561–111* ⊕ *www.galwaytaxis.com.*

TRAIN TRAVEL

The region's main rail stations are in Galway City and Ennis. Trains
for Galway and Ennis leave from Dublin's Heuston Station (on different lines). Trains run direct to Galway via Athlone, taking about three
hours, while for Ennis (which is reached via the Cork and Tralee line)
you must change twice. Journey time from Limerick to Ennis is 40 minutes (€11.80 round trip), while Limerick City to Galway takes about
two hours (€20 round trip).

Train Information **Irish Rail–Iarnod Éireann** ☎ *042/9334648*
⊕ *www.irishrail.ie.* **Ennis Station** ☎ *065/684–0444.*
Galway Station–Ceannt Railway Station ☎ *091/564–222.*

*For more information on getting here and around, see Travel Smart
Ireland.*

RESTAURANTS

Because the West provinces have a brief high season—from mid-June
to early September—and a quiet off-season, it doesn't have as broad
a choice of small, owner-operated restaurants as do other parts of
Ireland. Often the best place to eat is a local hotel—Gregan's Castle
Hotel near Ballyvaughan, for example. But some places landmark the
region, including Moran's Oyster Cottage in Kilcolgan near Galway
City, where the fare is simple, served in traditional pub surroundings,
but sea-leaping fresh. At the other extreme, are more dazzling experiments when you hit a grand blowout place like the superb formal restaurant at Dromoland Castle. For truly adventurous contemporary Irish
cooking, head to happening Galway and you'll find it at such showcases
as Kirwan's Lane, the Malt House, and Nimmo's: the town center is
so compact you can meander around and read the menus on display
outside before making your choice.

*Prices in the reviews are the average cost of a main course at dinner or,
if dinner is not served, at lunch.*

HOTELS

Some of Ireland's finest country-house and castle hotels are in this area.
Dromoland Castle, between Shannon Airport and Ennis, provides a
standard of luxury that you should experience at least once, if you
can stretch your budget. Star country-house destinations include the
creeper-clad Georgian house, known as Gregan's Castle Hotel, a tranquil retreat with views of the Burren and Galway Bay, and the more
modest but also charming Ballinalacken Castle, a shooting lodge set
in 100 acres of wildflower meadows next to the ruins of an O'Brien
castle. Other memorable destinations include the cliff-top Moy House
at Lahinch, and, in total contrast, the exuberantly glitzy "g" Hotel in
Galway. Among the newer, midrange hotels, Vaughan Lodge in Lahinch
and the Park House Hotel in Galway's city center offer exceptional
standards of comfort and design. Indoor pools and tennis courts are the

8

exception rather than the rule in this region, where business is largely seasonal and the emphasis is on outdoor pursuits. *Note: During peak events, such as the Galway Festival Race Week, hotel rates in Galway shoot up.*

Prices in the reviews are the lowest cost of a standard double room in high season.

TOURS

Galway City's TIO (tourist information office) has details of walking tours of Galway, including Neil Wilson's "Gore of Galway," an entertaining and interactive walking tour taking an hour and a quarter, which is based on Galway's hidden history—and promises "murder and mayhem," including the dramatic story of the Lynch family who gave the world the verb "to lynch"—departing from the TIO April to October 4 times a week (confirm schedule by phone).

Barratt Tours offers a day trip by coach visiting the Cliffs of Moher, the Burren, and Galway Bay (€27). Book at Ennis Tourist Information Office, which is also the departure point. The tour runs on Saturdays only from February to April, and daily from early May to mid-September.

Burren Wild runs a daily bus tour from Galway Bus Station that travels through Kinvara and along the coast of Galway Bay to a farm (with shop and café) in the village of Oughtmama in the Burren (€25). Here you stop for a one-hour guided walk of this unique landscape (included in tour price) before returning to the bus and continuing to the Cliffs of Moher. Burren Wild also has daily guided walks starting from their farm at 10:40 am (*see website for directions*) lasting 1½ hours (€10). Longer afternoon walks with qualified guide John A. Connolly, starting at 12:15 and lasting 2½ hours (€25), can be booked by appointment. Several companies including Lally Tours (€25) and O'Neachtain Day Tours (€20) run daily tours to the Cliffs of Moher and the Burren (each €25), returning to Galway around 4:30. Healy Tours offers historical sightseeing tours with professional guides, including the Cliffs of Moher and the Burren. Tickets, €20 each, can be purchased from the Galway Tourist Information Office or on the tour bus.

All tours run from mid-March to late September only. Book in advance or from 9 am on the day at Galway City's TIO. Buses leave from the bus station opposite. Heart of Burren Walks has guided walks leaving the Burren Display Center in Kilfenora with author Tony Kirby between April and August on Tuesday, Thursday, Saturday, and Sunday at 2:30 and lasting more than two hours (€20), visiting local antiquities and exploring the region's geology, including the Burren's biggest *turlough* (seasonal lake). Phone or check the website to confirm the schedule. Lally Tours also operates a vintage double-decker bus, departing from Eyre Square, which runs hourly tours of Galway City from 10:30 am until 4:30 pm from mid-March to October; tickets cost €12.

Tours **Barratt Tours** ☎ 087/237–5986 ⊕ www.4tours.biz. **Burren Wild Walks** ☎ 087/877–9565 ⊕ www.burrenwalks.com. **Ennis Tourist Information Office** ✉ Arthur's Row, Ennis, Co. Clare ☎ 065/682–8366 ⊕ www.discoverireland.ie/ shannon. **Galway City Tourist Information Office** ✉ Forster Pl., Center, Galway

City, Co. Galway ☎ *091/537–700* ⊕ *www.discoverireland.ie/west.*
Gore of Galway ☎ *086/727–4888* ✐ *neiladrianwilson@hotmail.com.*
Healy Tours ☎ *091/770–066* ⊕ *www.healytours.ie.* **Heart of Burren Walks**
☎ *065/682–7707* ⊕ *www.heartofburrenwalks.com* ☒ *€20.* **Lally Tours**
☎ *091/562–905* ⊕ *www.lallytours.com.* **O'Neachtain Day Tours**
☎ *091/553–188* ⊕ *www.ontours.biz.* **Salthill TIO** ☎ *091/520–500.*

VISITOR INFORMATION

Fáilte Ireland provides free information service, tourist literature, and an accommodations booking service at its TIOs (tourist information offices). The following offices are open all year, generally weekdays 9–6, daily during the high season: Aran Islands (Inis Mór), Ennis, and Galway City. Other TIOs that operate seasonally, generally weekdays 9–6 and Saturday 9–1, are open as follows: Cliffs of Moher (April–October; a concession within the main visitor center, which opens year round) and Salthill (May–September).

Information on Kinvara, Galway City and the Aran Islands can be found at Discover Ireland (⊕ *www.discoverireland.ie/Places-To-Go/ Galway*). Information on the main sights in County Clare—Ennis, the Burren, and the Cliff of Moher—can be found at Shannon Region Tourism (⊕ *www.shannonregiontourism.ie*).

COUNTY CLARE

County Clare claims two of Ireland's unique natural sights: the awesome Cliffs of Moher and the stark, mournful landscape of the Burren, which hugs the coast from Black Head in the north to Doolin and the Cliffs of Moher in the south. Yet western County Clare (West Clare for short) is widely beloved among native Irish for a natural phenomenon significantly less unique than these: its sandy beaches. Recently the surf that rolls in on these beaches, and on the rocky shores of the Aran Islands, has been attracting big-wave enthusiasts from all over the world. So whether you're looking for inimitable scenery, the perfect wave, or just a lovely beach to plunk down on to relax in the sun (or rain!) for a few hours, you can delightfully find it in West Clare.

This journey begins within minutes of Shannon Airport at Bunratty Castle and Folk Village, where you can kick-start your visit to the West of Ireland with castles and a famed pub.

BUNRATTY CASTLE

18 km (10 miles) west of Limerick City on N18 road to Shannon Airport.

GETTING HERE AND AROUND

Bunratty is about 15 minutes from Limerick's centre on the N18 Galway road. Most Bus Eiereann buses to Shannon Airport also stop at Bunratty: confirm when boarding.

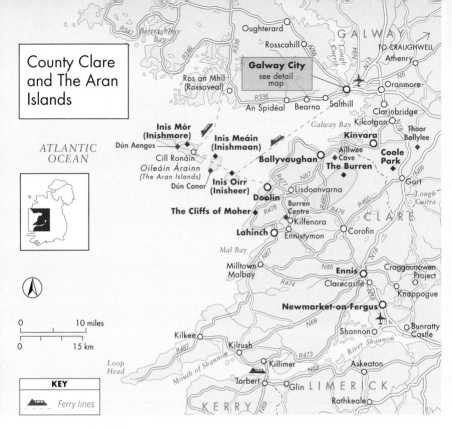

County Clare
and The Aran
Islands

ATLANTIC
OCEAN

0   10 miles
0   15 km

KEY

🚢 Ferry lines

EXPLORING

Bunratty Castle and Folk Park. Two of those rare attractions that appeal to all ages, Bunrattty Castle and Folk Park manage to be both educational and fun. Built in 1460, the castle—a stolid, massive affair with four square keep towers—has been fully restored and decorated with 15th- to 17th-century furniture and furnishings. It gives wonderful insight into the life of those times. As you pass under the walls of Bunratty, look for the three "murder holes" that allowed defenders to pour boiling oil on attackers below.

Bunratty medieval banquets are world famous and held nightly at 5:45 and 8:45; the cost is €59.95. You're welcomed by Irish colleens in 15th-century dress, who bear the traditional bread of friendship. Then you're led off to a reception, where you'll quaff mead made from fermented honey, apple juice, clover, and heather. Before sitting down at long tables in the candlelit great hall, you can don a bib. You'll need it, because you eat the four-course meal medieval-style: with your fingers. Serving "wenches" take time out to sing a few ballads or pluck harp strings. The banquets may not be authentic, but they're fun; they're also popular, so book as far in advance as possible. The Shannon website (⊕ *www.shannonheritage.com*) has good deals for advance booking, and includes a combination of castle visits and banquets.

On the castle grounds the quaint Bunratty Folk Park recreates a 19th-century village street and has examples of traditional rural housing. Exhibits include a working blacksmith's forge; demonstrations of flour milling, bread making, candle making, thatching, and other skills; and a variety of farm animals. An adjacent museum of agricultural machinery can't compete with the furry and feathered live exhibits. If you can't get a reservation for the medieval banquet at the castle, a *ceilí* folk-music session known as the Traditional Irish Night, held nightly May to September at 5:45 and 9 (€49.95) at the Folk Park is the next best thing. The program features traditional Irish dance and song and a meal of Irish stew, soda bread, and apple pie. Prices for banquets and entrance to Bunratty are generously discounted if you buy online. ✉ *Bunratty, Co. Clare* ☎ *061/360–788* ⊕ *www.shannonheritage.com* 🎟 *€15* ☽ *Sept.–May, daily 9–5:30, last entry at 4; June–Aug., daily 9–6, last entry at 5.*

WHERE TO EAT

$$
MODERN IRISH
✕ **J. P. Clarkes Country Pub.** Look left at the bend before Bunratty Castle and you will see a grouping of low thatched cottages, all gleaming with fresh whitewash. Inside the various cottages you will find an upmarket seafood restaurant, Gallagher's, and its affiliated gastropub, both of which enjoy a high reputation for food. The pub is an airy, high-ceilinged open-plan room, the rustic beams and sandstone floor smartly contrasting with snazzy leather-upholstered chairs. Its menu is an eclectic crowd-pleaser, with something for all tastes, from the pot of mussels in garlic and white wine cream to the char-grilled turkey steak with fiery pepper sauce, or char-grilled rib-eye steak with chunky chips. Such is its popularity that you can not only book a table online but you can also pre-order your food after doing so. *Éire nua*, or the "New Ireland," as the fellow says. ⑤ *Average main: €18* ✉ *Bunratty, Co. Clare* ☎ *061/363–363* ⊕ *www.gallaghersofbunratty.com.*

8

KNAPPOGUE

21 km (13 miles) north of Bunratty.

GETTING HERE AND AROUND

Knappogue Castle is about 20 minutes from Bunratty on minor roads; the route is well-marked.

EXPLORING

★
☾ **Knappogue Castle.** With a name that means "hill of the kiss," Knappogue is one of Ireland's most beautiful medieval tower-house castles. A 15th-century MacNamara stronghold, Knappogue Castle was renovated in the Victorian era and fitted with storybook details. Restored by a wealthy American family, the castle has now been retro-ed in 15th-century style.

By day you can enjoy a castle tour, including the walled garden, which looks like something out of a medieval book of hours. In the evenings it hosts fun and fabulous medieval banquets (€57). You're first greeted at the main door by the Ladies of the Castle who escort you to the Dalcassian Hall, where you enjoy a goblet of mead (honey wine), listen to harp and fiddle, then proceed to the banqueting hall for a four-course meal, great Irish choral music, and a theatrical set-piece in which the Butler and the Earl argue the virtues of Gallantry. As an added allure, the castle looks spectacular when floodlighted. Who can resist? ⊠ *R649, 5 km (3 miles) southeast of Quin, Bunratty, Co. Limerick* ☎ *061/360–788* ⊕ *www.shannonheritage.com* 🎫 *€8* ⊙ *May–Aug., daily 10–4:30.*

CRAGGAUNOWEN PROJECT

6 km (4 miles) northeast of Knappogue Castle.

GETTING HERE AND AROUND

Craggaunowen Castle is about 8 minutes from Knappogue Castle on minor roads.

EXPLORING

Craggaunowen Castle. It's a strange experience to walk across the little wooden bridge above reeds rippling in the lake into Ireland's Celtic past as a jumbo jet passes overhead on its way into Shannon Airport—1,500 years of history compressed into an instant. But if you love all things Celtic, you'll have to visit the Craggaunowen Project. The romantic centerpiece is Craggaunowen Castle, a 16th-century tower house restored with furnishings from the period. Huddling beneath its battlements are two replicas of early Celtic-style dwellings. On an island in the lake, reached by a narrow footbridge, is a clay-and-wattle *crannóg*, a fortified lake dwelling; it resembles what might have been built in the 6th or 7th century, when Celtic influence still predominated in Ireland. The reconstruction of a small ring fort shows how an ordinary soldier would have lived in the 5th or 6th century, at the time Christianity was being established here. Characters from the past explain their Iron Age (500 BC–AD 450) lifestyle, show you around their small holding stocked with animals, and demonstrate crafts skills from bygone ages. ⊠ *Signposted off road to Sixmilebridge, about 10 km (6 miles) east of Quin Town, Sixmilebridge, Co. Limerick* ☎ *061/360–788* ⊕ *www.shannonheritage.com* 🎫 *€9* ⊙ *Easter and mid-May–Aug., daily 10–4:15.*

NEWMARKET-ON-FERGUS

13 km (8 miles) north Shannon Airport on M18.

A small town in County Clare, Newmarket-on-Fergus is chiefly remarkable as the village nearest the famed hotel of Dromoland Castle, formerly the home of Lord Inchiquin, chief of the O'Brien clan.

GETTING HERE AND AROUND

Newmarket on Fergus is on the R472 between Shannon Airport and Ennis, 32 km (19 miles) west of Limerick. Head west on the M18, take exit 11, and follow the signs. There is a scheduled Bus Éireann service from Shannon Airport taking 25 minutes.

WHERE TO STAY

For expanded hotel reviews, visit Fodors.com.

$$
B&B/INN
★

Carrygerry Country House. Modest and gabled, this 1793 country house is only 8 km (5 miles) from Shannon Airport, but a world apart, with views across the plains where horses calmly graze, as they have done for centuries, to the distant Shannon estuary. **Pros:** proximity to airport; real Irish character; abundant wildlife, birdsong, peace and quiet; excellent restaurant. **Cons:** tricky to find the first time; no dinner Sundays and Mondays. **TripAdvisor:** "everything that draws people to Ireland," "great location and food," "lovely country setting." $ *Rooms from: €135* ✉ *Carrygerry, Newmarket-on-Fergus, Co. Clare* ☎ *061/360–500* ⊕ *www.carrygerryhouse.com* ⇲ *11 rooms.*

$$$$
HOTEL
Fodor's Choice
★
♺

Dromoland Castle Hotel and Country Estate. Dating from the 19th century and now one of Ireland's grandest hotels, Dromoland bristles with towers rising up over a picture-perfect lake like a storybook illustration from King Arthur. **Pros:** real old-fashioned luxury; friendly, helpful staff; genuine castle experience; beautiful grounds. **Cons:** golfers spoiling the romantic idyll; some standard rooms are a little ordinary; you'll want to stay much longer than you can afford. **TripAdvisor:** "a beautiful castle experience," "the spa is heavenly," "not to be missed." $ *Rooms from: €380* ✉ *5 km (3 miles) west of Newmarket-on-Fergus, signposted from N18, Newmarket-on-Fergus, Co. Clare* ☎ *061/368–144* ⊕ *www.dromoland.ie* ⇲ *12 suites, 87 rooms.*

SPORTS AND THE OUTDOORS

GOLF

Dromoland Golf Course. One of the most scenic courses in the country, Dromoland Golf Club is set in a 700-acre estate of rich woodland, rolling open pasture, and natural water features on the grounds of the famed Dromoland Castle hotel. The parkland course has streams and a natural lake that leaves little room for error on a number of holes. Views of the castle, expecially from the 7th hole, are little short of entrancing. Improvers take note: a state-of-the-art golf academy can help you to improve your swing. ✉ *Newmarket-on-Fergus, Co. Clare* ☎ *061/368–498* ⊕ *www.dromoland.ie* ✉ *Greens fees: Apr.–Sept. €63, Oct.–Mar. €72, twilight and early bird €58* ⚑ *18 holes. Yardage: 6,824. Par 72. Practice area, driving range, caddies, buggies, catering* ☉ *Visitors: daily (some restrictions).*

ENNIS

9½ km (6 miles) north of Newmarket-on-Fergus on M18.

A major crossroads and a convenient stop between the West and the Southwest, Ennis is the main town of County Clare. The pleasant market town has an attractively renovated, pedestrian-friendly center, bisected by the fast-flowing River Fergus.

GETTING HERE AND AROUND

Ennis is served by exits 12, 13, and 14 from the M18 Limerick–Galway motorway. It is 37 km (23 miles) northwest of Limerick. There are Expressway bus connections to Cork (3 hours), Limerick (1 hour

While the opulent interiors of Dromoland Castle will wow all guests, the hotel's parklands are even more enticing thanks to a vast array of sporting facilities.

15 minutes), Shannon Airport (1 hour), and Galway (1 hour 15 minutes). From Ennis there are two Bus Éireann buses a day to the Cliffs of Moher Visitor Centre (50 minutes); the same bus also calls at Lisdoonvarna and Doolin. Ennis Railway Station can be accessed from Limerick City and Galway on the Irish Rail commuter route linking Limerick and Galway; the trip to Limerick takes 40 minutes, and Galway is 1 hour 20 minutes.

TOURS

Local bus company Barratt Tours offers a guided tour of the Cliffs of Moher and the Burren leaving from the tourist information office in Ennis (€27; Saturdays only from March 21 to early May, then Saturday–Thursday from early May to mid-September). Or opt for taxis whose rates for long trips can be affordable if shared by four people.

ESSENTIALS

Visitor Information **Ennis Tourist Office** ⊠ *Arthur's Row, Town Center, Ennis, Co. Clare* ☎ *065/682–8366* ✆ *touristofficeennis@shannondev.ie.*

WHERE TO STAY

For expanded hotel reviews, visit Fodors.com.

$$ ⊤ **Old Ground Hotel.** Enter the original ivy-clad 18th-century manor
HOTEL house (which adjoins a new wing) and you'll see that old-fashioned charm meets contemporary élan at this winning entry to Ennis's hotel stakes—rest on the lobby's inviting brocade sofas as you study paintings on the wall from the hotel's striking collection of new Irish artists, including Donald Teskey, Cecil Maguire, and Mick O'Dea. **Pros:** genuine sense of history; handy town center location, lively bistro and

restaurant. **Cons:** extremely busy bar; hard to find initially due to town's one-way system (follow signs for Town Centre Hotels). **TripAdvisor:** "great food," "simply amazing," "perfect place to unwind." $ *Rooms from: €140* ✉ *O'Connell St., Ennis, Co. Clare* ☎ *065/682–8127* ⊕ *www.flynnhotels.com* ⥅ *1 suite, 82 rooms.*

$ ⊞ **Temple Gate Hotel.** Before its conversion, this lodging was a Gothic-
HOTEL style convent, and remnants of its previous existence (including the chapel, which is now a banquet hall) give character to this bright, modern hotel in the town center. **Pros:** more character than most modern hotels; good town center location. **Cons:** can get very busy with local functions at weekends; standard rooms a bit small; worth upgrading to executive if you need space. **TripAdvisor:** "perfect," "great location," "pleasant surprise." $ *Rooms from: €100* ✉ *The Square, Ennis, Co. Clare* ☎ *065/682–3300* ⊕ *www.templegatehotel.com* ⥅ *70 rooms* ⦿ *Breakfast.*

NIGHTLIFE AND THE ARTS

NIGHTLIFE

Although Ennis is not as fashionable as, say, Galway, it's one of the West's traditional-music hot spots. You're likely to hear sessions at many pubs, but keep in mind that sessions don't necessarily take place every night and that the scene is constantly changing. Phone ahead to check whether a session is happening.

Cruise's. A warm and lively bar in Queen's Hotel, a long-established town landmark near the old Friary, Cruise's has a romantic atmosphere with a roaring fire, candles on the tables, and live music most nights from about 9:30 pm. ✉ *Abbey St., Ennis, Co. Clare* ☎ *065/682–8963.*

Knox's Pub & Bistro. A Victorian-style high street bar with traditional plate glass shop front in the town centre, Knox's serves bar food until 9 pm, offers live traditional music from 9:30 pm Wednesday–Sunday, and a late bar until 2 am Thursday–Saturday. ✉ *18 Abbey St., Ennis, Co. Clare* ☎ *065/682–2871* ⊕ *www.knoxs.ie.*

Michael Kerin's Bar. Known as Mickey's Bar to locals, and far and wide for its Friday night traditional music sessions, Michael Kerin's is the oldest family-run bar in town and a classic Irish pub in every sense—welcoming, frequented by locals, and home to a decent pint. ✉ *Lifford Rd., Ennis, Co. Clare* ☎ *065/682–0582.*

Poet's Corner Bar. Located in Ennis's former town hall and now part of the Old Ground Hotel, the Poet's Corner is a spacious bar with a good reputation for hearty pub grub in the day, and regular traditional music sessions on weekends from 9:30. ✉ *Old Ground Hotel, Main St., Ennis, Co. Clare* ☎ *065/682–8155* ⊕ *www.flynnhotels.com/ Old_Ground_Hotel_Ennis/Dining/Poets_Corner.*

Preachers Pub. As you'd expect from the name, this bar has a church theme, and was formerly a chapel. That does not inhibit the devoted traditional musicians who congregate here from 9:30 pm on weekends to play traditional music. ✉ *Temple Gate Hotel, the Square, Ennis, Co. Clare* ☎ *065/682–3300* ⊕ *www.templegatehotel.com/preachers-pub.html.*

8

THE ARTS

Glór–Irish Music Centre. Ennis's venue for large concerts, the Glór–Irish Music Centre, hosts competitions of Irish music, song, and dance—including May's wildly popular Fleadh Nua (⊕ *www.fleadhnua.com*)—and big-name touring acts on the Irish music scene, including Mary Black, Paul Brady, and Aslan. There's also a crafts gallery, coffee shop, and free parking. ⊠ *Causeway Link, Ennis, Co. Clare* ☎ *065/684–3103* ⊕ *www.glor.ie.*

Fleadh Nua. Held in Ennis on a long bank-holiday weekend in late May, the Fleadh Nua festival is one of the country's biggest traditional music festivals, and offers a great program of workshops, concerts, trad sessions, parades, and street performances, as well as a great opportunity to mix with locals. ☎ *065/682-4276* ⊕ *www.fleadhnua.com.*

SHOPPING

Carraig Donn. A popular spot with locals for its own line of knitwear as well as its mix of Irish and international brands, Carraig Donn is also a sure thing for visitors looking for some contemporary Irish fashion, jewelry, crystal, and pottery. ⊠ *29 O'Connell Sq., Ennis, Co. Clare* ☎ *065/689–3433* ⊕ *www.carraigdonn.com.*

Ennis Bookshop. This long-established bookstore carries a big range of local history and Irish-interest titles. ⊠ *13 Abbey St., Ennis, Co. Clare* ☎ *065/682–9000* ⊕ *www.ennisbookshop.ie.*

Giftvenue. A wide array of top names is featured here, including Belleek china, Waterford crystal, Newbridge silverware, and Donegal Parian china, as well as Lladró, Hummel, and other collectible china. ⊠ *36 Abbey St., Ennis, Co. Clare* ☎ *065/686–7891* ⊕ *www.giftvenue.ie.*

Seodin. Stop here for a good selection of gold and silver jewelry as well as some lovely Irish-made gifts. ⊠ *52 O'Connell St., Ennis, Co. Clare* ☎ *065/682–3510* ⊕ *www.seoidin.com.*

Tony Honan Antiques. Established in 1966, and specializing in antique clocks as well as Irish and internationally sourced antiques, this old gem of a shop is handily located in the town center. ⊠ *14 Abbey St., Ennis, Co. Clare* ☎ *065/682–8137.*

SPORTS AND THE OUTDOORS

BICYCLING

Tierney Cycles & Fishing. Follow the scenic Burren Cycleway (69 km [43 miles]) to the famous Cliffs of Moher, or join the Clare 250 Mile Cycle charity event in May, on a bike rented from Tierney Cycles & Fishing. ⊠ *17 Abbey St., Ennis, Co. Clare* ☎ *065/682–9433.*

LAHINCH

6 km (4 miles) north of the Cliffs of Moher.

Noted for hotels packed with people touring the nearby Cliffs of Moher, Lahinch is a busy resort village beside a long, sandy beach backed by dunes. It is best known for its links golf courses and—believe it or not—its surfing. In 1972 the European Surfing Finals were held here, putting Lahinch on the world surfing map, and since then, it has achieved YouTube notoriety as the base from which surfers are towed by Jet Ski to surf the huge Atlantic wave known as the Aileens. Still, the center ring here is occupied by golf—with three world-class courses and a dazzling bay-view backdrop, Lahinch is often called the "St. Andrews of Ireland." Between golfers, surfers, and vacationers in general, the permanent winter population of 650 swells to 7,000 in the summer. Other Moher-bound people prefer to stay in Doolin.

GETTING HERE AND AROUND

Lahinch (also spelled Lehinch, on maps and in GPS systems) is a seaside resort 30 km (10 miles) west of Ennis on the N85. There is ample free parking on the seafront. It can be reached by bus from Ennis (1 hour).

WHERE TO EAT AND STAY

For expanded hotel reviews, visit Fodors.com.

$ ✕ **Morrissey's Seafood Bar and Grill.** Sporting distinctive colorful window boxes, this pretty family-run village pub has been transformed into an enormously popular seafood and steak restaurant. Burgundy leather banquettes line the walls, bentwood chairs sit at plain wooden tables beneath brass ceiling fans, while the cream walls are enlivened by a collection of paintings and photos of local scenes. There are no reservations, but you can take a drink at the bar while waiting your turn, or in summer, retreat to the wide deck overlooking the river. Happily, it's worth waiting for the fresh, simply prepared local food: Atlantic jumbo prawns with garlic and herb butter served with homemade breads, or smoked and barbecued salmon with capers, red onion, and crème fraîche. Angus sirloin steak is served with homemade onion rings, and kids love the Morrissey beef burger. There are also seven bedrooms overhead. ⑤ *Average main: €17* ⊠ *Doonbeg, Co. Clare* ☎ *065/905–5304* ⊕ *www.morrisseysdoonbeg.com* ⊘ *Closed Jan. and Feb., Mon. mid-May–Sept., and Mon. and Tues. in Oct., Nov., and Mar.–mid-May.*

SEAFOOD   ★

$$$$ **Moy House.** Built for Sir Augustine Fitzgerald, this enchanting, 18th-century Italianate-style lodge sits amid 15 private acres on an exhilarating, Wuthering Heights–like windswept cliff top that's a three-minute drive from Lahinch. **Pros:** romantic cliff-top location. **Cons:** Lahinch itself feels a bit downmarket in comparison. **TripAdvisor:** "simply the best," "pure luxury," "outstanding food." ⑤ *Rooms from: €220* ⊠ *Milltown Malbay Rd., Lahinch, Co. Clare* ☎ *065/708–2800* ⊕ *www. moyhouse.com* ⇆ *9 rooms* ⊘ *Closed Nov.–Apr.* ⑩ *Breakfast.*

B&B/INN
Fodor's Choice
★

$$$ **Vaughan Lodge.** Michael Vaughan is a fourth-generation Lahinch hotelier, and he and his wife, Maria, uphold the tradition splendidly in their Edwardian-style lodge—set at the quiet end of Lahinch, only a short walk from the busy village, it combines the facilities of a top hotel with the charm of a country house. **Pros:** quiet location; high standard of comfort; excellent restaurant on-site. **Cons:** location lacks scenic wham-bam; bedrooms may recall big-city hotels to those who travel for business. **TripAdvisor:** "exactly what an inn should be," "wonderful vegetarian food," "we'll be back again." ⑤ *Rooms from: €200* ⊠ *Road to Ennistymon, Co. Clare* ☎ *065/708–1111* ⊕ *www.vaughanlodge.ie* ⇆ *22 rooms* ⊘ *Closed Nov.–Mar.*

HOTEL

8

NIGHTLIFE AND THE ARTS

Galvin's. Established in 1840, and hosting traditional music sessions ever since, this popular spot has live music most nights in summer and on weekends in winter. ⊠ *Church St., Lahinch, Co. Clare* ☎ *065/708–1045.*

O'Looney's. Known as Lahinch's surfers' pub, O'Looney's offers music every night in summer and on Saturday night in winter. ⊠ *The Promenade, Lahinch, Co. Clare* ☎ *065/708–1414* ⊕ *www.olooneys.ie.*

SHOPPING

Lahinch Surf Shop. Tom and Rosemary Buckley's surf shop, the first in Ireland, dates from 1989, and is a landmark on Lahinch's Promenade. You'll find top quality boards, wet suits, and accessories, as well as lots of local tips and advice. Check their website for daily surf reports and a live webcam. ⊠ *The Promenade, Lahinch, Co. Clare* ☎ *065/708–1543* ⊕ *www.lahinchsurfshop.com.*

SPORTS AND THE OUTDOORS

BEACHES

Lahinch Beach. When the clouds part and the sun shows its prodigal face in Clare, locals drop everything and flock to Lahinch's Blue Flag beach, a wide sandy crescent about 2½ km (1 mile) long, facing southwest onto the Atlantic Ocean. The promenade ends with the village—where if you're in luck, you can find ice cream, seaweed, and periwinkle vendors—but continues as a footpath behind the beach, leading to a dune system and Lahinch's golf courses. The beach has long been a family favorite, offering safe bathing, and ideal conditions for beginner surfers. Arriving from Ennistymon on the N85, ignore the right hand turn at village entrance for the Cliffs of Moher (R478), and continue straight for about 50 meters to reach the promenade and car park. **Best For:** sunset, surfing, swimming, walking, shore fishing. **Amenities:** food and drink, lifeguards, parking, toilets, water sports. ⊠ *Village centre, Lahinch, Co. Clare.*

GOLF

Lahinch Golf Club. The grand old man of Irish links courses, Old Lahinch was originally designed by Old Tom Morris from St. Andrews in 1894, following the natural contours of the dunes, and is said to have a real Scottish flavor. In the 1920s design maestro Alister MacKenzie improved on the original, creating a memorably challenging 18 holes, with undulating greens, huge bunkers, and maddening blind shots. The Castle Course, built in 1963, is less of a challenge, but has some awkwardly placed bunkers and water hazards to negotiate. ⊠ *The Seafront, Lahinch, Co. Clare* ☎ *065/708–1003* ⊕ *www.lahinchgolfclub.com* ✉ *Greens fees: Standard: €160 (Old), €50 (Castle); Jan.–Mar. and Nov.–Dec. Mon.–Fri.: €50 (Old), €20 (Castle). See website for other seasonal offers* ⟲ *36 holes. Yardage 6,950 (Old), 5,700 (Castle). Practice area, caddies, club hire, buggies, catering* ⊙ *Visitors: daily (some restrictions).*

The Lodge Doonbeg Golf Club. Despite being held up for a time (due to government legislation to protect a rare local snail), Greg Norman-designed Doonbeg has arrived with a major splash on the Irish links scene. Physically stunning, this tough, unforgiving course stretches along nearly 2 miles of pristine Atlantic beach and dunes. The magnificent par-4 15th—with funnel-shaped green surrounded by huge dunes—is at the center of the whole course. Gamblers beware: anything long could easily run off the green and never be seen again. If you make it to the tricky 18th, you'll be rewarded with breathtaking views of the ocean. ⊠ *Doonbeg, Co. Clare* ☎ *065/905–5602* ⊕ *www.doonbeggolfclub.com* ⛳ *Greens fees: May–Sept., Mon.–Thurs. €130, Fri.–Sun. €150; Oct.–Apr., Mon.–Thurs. €90, Fri.–Sun. €100* 🏌 *18 holes. Yardage: 6,885. Par 72. Practice area, caddies, caddy carts, catering* ☉ *Visitors: daily.*

SURFING

Lahinch Surf School. Lahinch is a safe place to learn to surf if you stick to the beach. With enough practice—and Ireland's surfing champion, John MacCarthy, and his supercool crew teaching you—maybe it won't be too long before you can join the thrill-seeking surf dudes chasing huge waves (known as Aileens) a little farther up the coast at the Cliffs of Moher. ⊠ *Promenade, Lahinch, Co. Clare* ☎ *087/960–9667* ⊕ *www. lahinchsurfschool.com.*

THE CLIFFS OF MOHER

10 km (6 miles) northwest of Lahinch.

One of Ireland's most breathtaking natural sights, the majestic Cliffs of Moher rise vertically out of the sea in a wall that stretches over a long, 8-km (5-mile) swath and in places reaches a height of 710 feet. On a clear day you can see the Aran Islands and the mountains of Connemara to the north, as well as the lighthouse on Loop Head and the mountains of Kerry to the south. Get up close and you can study the stratified deposits of five different rock layers visible in the cliff face. But most visitors prefer to take in the grand distant vistas, especially as they open up every turn of the trail along the famous Burren Way that runs from Doolin to the Cliffs.

GETTING HERE AND AROUND

Head north and west from Lahinch through Liscannor on the R478 for 19 km (12 miles), (or west from Lisdoonvarna for about the same distance on the R478) and you will come to the visitor center, a lone feature dominating the otherwise empty landscape, and its huge car park (fee), which is the only parking option, and includes entrance to the visitor center and cliff walkways.

There is a bus service to the Cliffs of Moher Visitor Centre from both Ennis and Galway City. A bus from Ennis to the cliffs takes about 50 minutes. The bus trip from Galway City takes about 1 hour 50 minutes. ■ TIP➔ Avoid the parking fees and offloading buses at the Cliffs of Moher by parking in Doolin and walking over.

TOURS

You'd never know if you just headed to the main car park for the Cliffs of Moher but one of the most popular ways of viewing these natural wonders is by heading to Doolin (alternative port of departure: Liscannor) to pick up one of the famous Cliffs of Moher cruises. Two of the biggest outfitters heading out from Doolin Pier are Cliffs of Moher Cruises and the O'Brien Line. Cliffs of Moher Cruises has one-hour

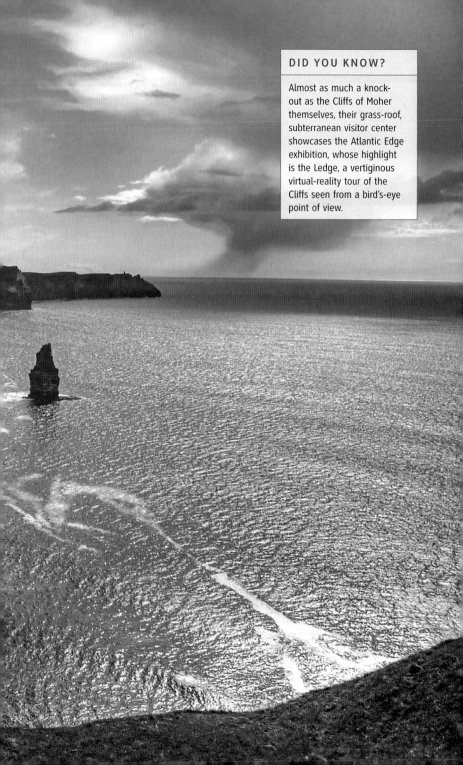

DID YOU KNOW?

Almost as much a knock-
out as the Cliffs of Moher
themselves, their grass-roof,
subterranean visitor center
showcases the Atlantic Edge
exhibition, whose highlight
is the Ledge, a vertiginous
virtual-reality tour of the
Cliffs seen from a bird's-eye
point of view.

cruises departing every day, weather permitting, from April to October at noon and 3 pm; tickets go for €20. O'Brien Lines operates mid-March to mid-November, with sailings usually at noon, 3, and 4 pm; tickets go for €10.

ESSENTIALS

Transportation Contacts Cliffs of Moher Cruises ☎ *065/707–5949* ⊕ *www.cliffs-of-moher-cruises.com.* **Ennis Bus Station** ✉ *Station Rd., Lahinch, Co. Clare* ☎ *065/682–4177.* **O'Brien Line** ☎ *065/707–5555* ⊕ *www.obrienline.com.*

Tour Contacts Cliffs of Moher Cruises. A coastal voyage under the command of Captain P. J. Garrihy will allow you to view the awesome Cliffs of Moher from the sea and the more than 20 species of seabirds that nest on its ledges. April through October there are two sailings per day, at noon and 3 pm; advance booking is highly recommended. ✉ *Doolin Pier, Lahinch, Co. Clare* ☎ *065/707–5949* ⊕ *www.cliffs-of-moher-cruises.com* 💷 *€10 for 1 hr.*

Visitor Information Cliffs of Moher Visitor Experience. ✉ *Near Liscannor, on road heading north to Lisdoonvarna, Lahinch, Co. Clare* ☎ *065/708–6141* ⊕ *www.discoverireland.ie/shannon* 💷 *€6.*

EXPLORING

Fodor'sChoice
★
☾

Cliffs of Moher. The Cliffs of Moher have a long and nearly hallowed history. They were sacred in the Celtic era and were a favorite hunting retreat of Brian Boru, the High King of Ireland. Numerous seabirds, including a large colony of puffins, make their homes in the shelves of rock on the cliffs. Built in 1835 by Cornelius O'Brien—of Bunratty Castle fame and a descendant of the kings of Thomond—**O'Brien's Tower** is a defiant, broody sentinel on the Cliffs' highest point, built to encourage tourism (yes, there were tourists even back then). Cornelius also erected here a wall of Liscannor flagstones (noted for their imprints of prehistoric eels).

Found on the road from Liscannor to Lisdoonvarna (R478), the grass-roof, subterranean **visitor center** (and adjacent car park) is built into the cliff face and is a good refuge from passing rain squalls. Note that there is no specific address for the Cliffs, which go on for miles, but you cannot miss the only road that gives access to the Cliffs, which is found on the main road from Liscannor to the north, a road which is heavily signposted. The visitor center interior imitates the limestone caves of County Clare and contains a gift shop, public toilets, and a tearoom. The Atlantic Edge exhibition is an optional extra, with information panels and interactive consoles for children—the highlight is the Ledge, a vertiginous virtual reality tour of the Cliffs from a bird's-eye point of view. Outside the center extensive hiking paths (some with elevated viewing platforms) gives access to the real thing, including O'Brien's Tower at the northern extremity. ✉ *Cliffs of Moher Visitor Centre (signposted on the R478 north from Liscannor), Lahinch, Co. Clare* ☎ *065/708–6141* ⊕ *www.cliffsofmoher.ie* 💷 *Parking €8 (includes access to visitor center, cliff-edge paths, and viewing platforms), Atlantic Edge €4.95* ☾ *Visitor center, daily 9–dusk; O'Brien's Tower daily 9–dusk (weather permitting).*

DOOLIN

6 km (4 miles) north of the Cliffs of Moher.

★ Once an enchanting, multihue-housed backwater, this tiny village—set at the point where the Cliffs of Moher flatten out and disappear into the sea as limestone plateaus—now seems to consist almost entirely of B&Bs, hostels, hotels, holiday homes, pubs, and restaurants, built on a flat plain about a mile from the pier and the sea. The reason for all this development (much of it newly built during Ireland's Celtic Tiger economic boom) is that Doolin is reputed to have three of the best pubs for traditional music in Ireland: McGann's, McDermott's, and O'Connor's. With the worldwide surge of interest in Irish music since the mid-1990s, the village has become more of a magnet for European and American musicians than it is for young, or even established, Irish artists. Amazingly, there is no tourist board office in Doolin but a sponsored website does offer plenty of listings for the town (⊕ *www. doolin-tourism.com*).

Popularity, of course, brings its own price: when every other person is witnessing the session through a camera screen, it can interrupt the connection and magic between the musicians and the audience. If you're disappointed with the music (or more likely, the crowd) in one pub, there are two more to try.

GETTING HERE AND AROUND
Doolin is on the R479 about 6 km (4 miles) north of the Cliffs of Moher Visitor Centre. There is one bus a day from Ennis and five from Galway. The town is a popular bus stop on the route that connects Ennis and Galway.

EXPLORING
Aran Doolin Ferries. Aran Doolin Ferries makes the 30-minute trip from Doolin Pier to Inis Oirr (Inisheer), the smallest of the Aran Islands, from spring until early fall (weather permitting, €15 round-trip). There are at least three round-trip sailings a day, and up to eight in July and August, but inquire on the day you plan to embark, as schedules vary according to weather and demand. There is also a day trip to the Aran Islands that includes a cruise under the Cliffs of Moher (€25). Usually more than one ferry company operates out of Doolin; your return ticket will be valid only with the company that took you out, so when boarding the outbound ferry, be sure to check the return schedule. ☎ *065/707–4455* ⊕ *www.doolinferries.com* 🖃 *€10.*

WHERE TO EAT AND STAY
For expanded hotel reviews, visit Fodors.com.

$$ ╳ **Cullinan's Restaurant & Guesthouse.** The small 25-seat restaurant, set in
SEAFOOD the back of an attractively renovated traditional farmhouse, is famed for its fresh, simply prepared seafood, but vegetarian and meat dishes are also served. Owner-chef James Cullinan uses fresh local ingredients—Inagh goat cheese, Burren smoked salmon, Doolin crabmeat, and Aran scallops—to form the basis of a light, imaginative menu. Try roast rack of Burren lamb with polenta galette and wild rosemary jus. Desserts are all homemade; or try a plate of farmhouse cheeses. A €30 early-bird set

menu is served from 6 to 6:45. The floor-to-ceiling windows on two sides of the restaurant overlook the Aille River. The eight (€90 double occupancy) cottage-style rooms have simple pine furniture, fresh cotton comforters, pleasant country views, Wi-Fi, and room TVs on request. ⑤ *Average main: €24* ✉ *Coast Rd., Doolin, Co. Clare* ☎ *065/707–4183* ⊕ *www.cullinansdoolin.com* ⊗ *Guesthouse closed Dec.–mid-Feb.; no dinner Wed. and Sun.; restaurant closed Oct.–Easter.*

$
B&B/INN

Aran View House Hotel. This extensively modernized 1736 house on 100 acres of farmland offers magnificent views in nearly every direction: the Aran Islands to the west, the Cliffs of Moher to the south, and the gray limestone rocks of the Burren to the north. **Pros:** well-located; amazing views; bar and restaurant on-site. **Cons:** a rather sprawling development, painted in an odd shade of pink; the exterior is less attractive than the interior. **TripAdvisor:** "true Ireland," "beautiful views," "loved everything about it." ⑤ *Rooms from: €110* ✉ *Coast Rd., Doolin, Co. Clare* ☎ *065/707–4061* ⊕ *www.aranview.com* ⇨ *19 rooms* ⊗ *Closed Nov.–Easter* ⧍ *Breakfast.*

$$
B&B/INN
★

Ballinalacken Castle Hotel. One hundred acres of wildflower meadows surround this restored, low-slung Victorian lodge—built alongside the 16th-century ruins of an O'Brien castle (hence its somewhat bogus name)—making this one of the most memorably sited of Ireland's coastal inns, with panoramic views of the Atlantic, the Aran Islands, and distant Connemara. **Pros:** fabulous location; warm old-fashioned welcome from the O'Callaghan family. **Cons:** not in fact a "castle." **TripAdvisor:** "lovely country house," "authentic Irish experience," "best owners ever." ⑤ *Rooms from: €160* ✉ *Coast Rd., about 1 km (½ mile) outside Doolin on the Lisdoonvarna Rd., Doolin, Co. Clare* ☎ *065/707–4025* ⊕ *www.ballinalackencastle.com* ⇨ *10 rooms, 2 suites* ⊗ *Closed Nov.–mid-Apr.* ⧍ *Breakfast.*

NIGHTLIFE AND THE ARTS

Famous for their traditional-music sessions, Doolin's three traditional pubs are designed to hold big crowds, which means you should expect minimal comfort: hard benches or bar stools if you're lucky, and spit-and-sawdust flooring. The theory is that the music will be so good, you won't notice anything else. However, interesting music-related memorabilia hang on the walls, and all three serve simple bar food from midday until 9 (Irish stew is a good bet). As you might imagine, the word is out about Doolin's "trad" scene—some nights the pubs overflow with crowds (and the video cams can get really annoying).

Gus O'Connor's. Set midway between the village center and the pier, popular Gus O'Connor's has tables outside near a stream and live music every night after 9.30 pm in summer. ✉ *Fisher St., Doolin, Co. Clare* ☎ *065/707–4168* ⊕ *www.gusoconnorsdoolin.com.*

McDermott's. Popular with locals, McDermott's is a great spot for soul-warming live music and belly-warming grub. Live music nightly early spring to late autumn, and weekends in winter. Note: it's sometimes closed during the day from autumn through spring. ✉ *Lisdoonvarna Rd., Doolin, Co. Clare* ☎ *065/707–4328* ⊕ *www. mcdermottspubdoolin.com.*

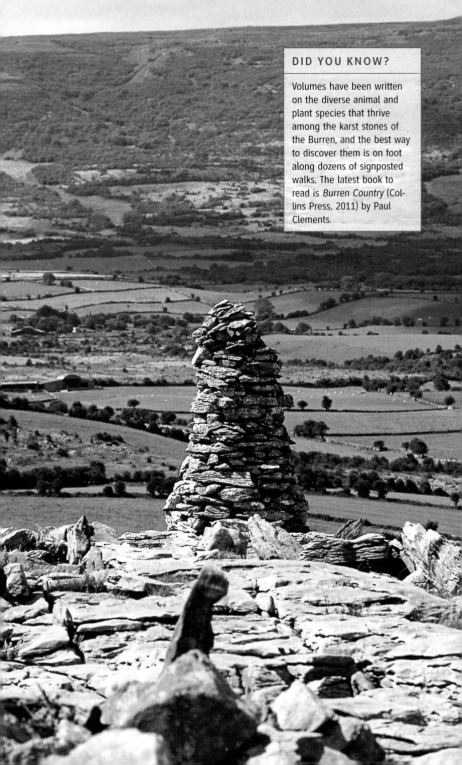

McGann's Pub & Restaurant. Across the road from McDermott's, McGann's is the smallest of Doolin's three famous pubs and has been run by the same family for 70 years. The music and food are so hearty you won't want to leave. Luckily, McGann's offers B&B, too (but you will need to book ahead). ✉ *Lisdoonvarna Rd., Doolin, Co. Clare* ☎ *065/707–4133* ⊕ *mcgannspubdoolin.com.*

THE BURREN

Extending throughout western County Clare from Cliffs of Moher in south to Black Head in north, and as far southeast as Corofin.

As you travel north toward Ballyvaughan, the landscape becomes rockier and stranger. Instead of the seemingly ubiquitous Irish green, gray becomes the prevailing color. You're now in the heart of the Burren, a 300-square-km (116-square-mile) expanse that is one of Ireland's strangest landscapes.

The Burren is aptly named: it's an Anglicization of the Irish word *bhoireann* (a rocky place). Stretching off in all directions, as far as the eye can see, are vast, irregular slabs of fissured limestone, known as *karst*, with deep cracks between them. From a distance, it looks like a lunar landscape, so dry that nothing could possibly grow on it. But in spring (especially from mid-May to mid-June), the Burren becomes a wild rock garden, as an astonishing variety of wildflowers blooms in the cracks between the rocks, among them at least 23 native species of orchid. The Burren also supports an incredible diversity of wildlife, including frogs, newts, lizards, badgers, stoats, sparrow hawks, kestrels, and dozens of other birds and animals. The wildflowers and other plants are given life from the spectacular caves, streams, and potholes that lie beneath the rough, scarred pavements. With the advent of spring, *turloughs* (seasonal lakes that disappear in dry weather) appear on the plateau's surface. Botanists are particularly intrigued by the cohabitation of Arctic and Mediterranean plants, many so tiny (and so rare, so please do not pick any) you can't see them from your car window; make a point of exploring some of this rocky terrain on foot. Numerous signposted walks run through both coastal and inland areas.

GETTING HERE AND AROUND

Take the R476 west from Lisdoonvarna for 9 km (5 miles) to Kilfenora where a visitor center will introduce you to the region. Continue for another 10 km (6 miles), turning left on to the R460 at the striking ruin of Leamaneh Castle (no access) to visit some of the major archaeological sites. Park only in designated car parks (free), which have been built adjacent to the major sites, and proceed by foot to avoid damaging the delicate ecology. The main bus stop for travelers to the Burren area is Lisdoonvarna.

EXPLORING

Burren Centre. Along with a café and a crafts shop with good maps and locally published guides, the tiny Burren Centre has a modest audiovisual display and other exhibits that explain the Burren's geology, flora, and archaeology. ✉ *8 km (5 miles) southeast of Lisdoonvarna on R476, Kilfenora, Co. Clare* ☎ *065/708–8030* ⊕ *www.theburrencentre.ie* 🎟 *€5* ⊙ *Mid-Mar.–May, Sept., and Oct., daily 10–5; June–Aug., daily 9:30–5:30.*

The Burren Way. You can explore the burren area by car, from a bike, or from the back of a bus, but the very best way to soak in the raw beauty of this craggy landscape is on foot. The Burren Way is a way-marked hiking trail from Lahinch to Ballyvaughan on the shores of Galway Bay, a distance of 35 km (22 miles). If you're short on time/breath, you may want to focus on the most spectacular and popular part of the trail that runs along the top of the Cliffs of Moher from Doolin to the coast near Lisdoonvarna, a distance of about 5 km (3 miles). The trail continues through the heart of the Burren's gray, rocky limestone landscape, with ever-changing views offshore of the Aran Islands and Galway Bay. Buy a map locally. ⊕ *www.shannonregiontrails.ie.*

Caherconnell Stone Fort. There are several stone forts in the Burren thought to have been in use between AD 400 and 1200, but Caherconnell—1 km (½ mile) south of Poulnabrone—is the best preserved, and the only one excavated and made accessible to visitors. The visitor center has an audio-visual display on the chief archaeological features of the area, including burial places marked by dolmens or cairns. Ongoing excavations continue to fill in the blanks of this impressive structure's history. Be sure to check out the sheepdog demonstrations and cafés. ⊠ *Carron, Co. Clare* ☏ *065/708–9999* ⊕ *www.burrenforts. ie* 🖃 *€5* 🕑 *Mar.–Oct., daily 10–5; July, Aug., daily 10–6.*

Cathedral of St. Fachtna. Beside the Burren Centre in Kilfenora, the ruins of a small 12th-century church, once the Cathedral of St. Fachtna, have been partially restored as a parish church. There are some interesting carvings in the roofless choir, including an unusual, life-size human skeleton. In a field about 165 feet west of the ruins is an elaborately sculpted high cross that is worth examining, though parts of it are badly weathered.

Poulnabrone Megalithic Tomb. The biggest and most famous of the Burren's megalithic tombs, Poulnabrone ("the hole of sorrows") is a portal grave/dolmen with a massive capstone and a majestic presence amid the craggy limestone fields shouldering the moody grey Burren skies. The monument was built around 4,500 years ago. Stand down the wind and you might hear ancient whispers. There is a designated car park nearby with an historical timeline, and a short gravel walkway to the dolmen (freely accessible). It's open and windy here, so grab an extra layer. ⊠ *(on R480, 8 km [5 miles] south of Ballyvaughan), Carron, Co. Clare.*

NIGHTLIFE AND THE ARTS

Vaughan's Pub. Known for its traditional-music sessions in a village famed for its Ceili Band, Vaughan's has been a local favorite for years. Free set dancing lessons are held in the barn during the summer. ⊠ *Main St., Kilfenora, Co. Clare* ☏ *065/708–8004* ⊕ *www.vaughanspub.ie.*

SPORTS AND THE OUTDOORS

BICYCLING

West Ireland Cycling. Either take an organized or self-guided Burren tour or hire a top-of-the-range bike from this Galway-based outfit. They can also deliver up to 80 bikes by trailer for groups, at €15 a day or €80s a week. ⊠ *Earl's Island, Galway, Co. Galway* ☏ *091/588–830* ⊕ *www. westirelandcycling.com.*

BALLYVAUGHAN

16 km (10 miles) north of Lisdoonvarna on N67.

A pretty little waterside village and a good base for exploring the Burren, Ballyvaughan attracts walkers and artists who enjoy the views of Galway Bay and access to the Burren.

GETTING HERE AND AROUND

Ballyvaughan is 16 km (10 miles) north of Lisdoonvarna on the N67. The coastal drive from Doolin is especially scenic.

EXPLORING

Aillwee Cave. A vast 2-million-year-old cave, Aillwee is the biggest and most impressive chamber in the region accessible to those who aren't spelunkers. Illuminated for about 3,300 feet, the cave contains an underground river and waterfall. Aboveground, there are a big crafts shop, cheese-making demonstrations, a cafe, and the **Burren Birds of Prey Centre,** which puts on flying displays from eagles, falcons, hawks, and owls daily at noon and 3 pm (weather permitting). ⊠ *5 km (3 miles) south of Ballyvaughan on R480, Ballyvaughan, Co. Clare* ☎ *065/707–7036* ⊕ *www.aillweecave.ie* 🎫 *Joint ticket for cave tour and birds of prey €17* ☉ *Jan.–mid-Nov, daily 10–dusk; mid-Nov.–Dec by appointment.*

WHERE TO STAY

For expanded hotel reviews, visit Fodors.com.

$
B&B/INN
Drumcreehy Country House. The pretty gabled facade with dormer windows is traditional in style, but, in fact, Bernadette Moloney and her German husband, Armin Grefkes, designed and built this house specifically as a B&B. **Pros:** big bedrooms for a B&B; nice waterfront location; peaceful nights. **Cons:** a long (1 mile-plus) walk down a narrow busy road to village. **TripAdvisor:** "pampered in a beautiful setting," "relaxing," "if only they were all this good." $ *Rooms from: €100* ⊠ *Ballyvaughan, Co. Clare* ☎ *065/707–7377* ⊕ *www.drumcreehyhouse.com* 🛏 *12 rooms* ☉ *Closed Dec.* ❑ *Breakfast.*

$$$$
HOTEL
Fodor's Choice
★
Gregan's Castle Hotel. One of Ireland's best-loved country-house hotels, this quiet, low-key retreat is a romantic, creeper-covered Georgian house, set amid pretty gardens with a splendid view of the rocky Burren hills and Galway Bay beyond. **Pros:** perfectly judged decor; birdsong morning and evening; excellent restaurant. **Cons:** 5 km (3 miles) from nearest village; almost a TV-free zone, limited channels; no elevator. **TripAdvisor:** "relaxed luxury in a stunning setting," "lovely views," "beautiful hotel." $ *Rooms from: €245* ⊠ *Base of Corkscrew Hill, Ballyvaughan, Co. Clare* ☎ *065/707–7005* ⊕ *www.gregans.ie* 🛏 *15 rooms, 6 suites* ☉ *Closed Dec.–mid-Feb., and Mon.–Thurs. from mid-Feb. until early Apr.* ❑ *Breakfast.*

$
HOTEL
Hyland's Burren Hotel. A turf fire greets you in the lobby of this unpretentious coaching inn, in the heart of the Burren, which dates from the early 18th century and has become a cheerful, welcoming spot with a reputation for friendliness and good entertainment. **Pros:** central location; bar and restaurant on-site; pleasant staff. **Cons:** won't win any style contests; bar and restaurant very busy July and August. **TripAdvisor:**

"beautiful," "nice staff," "a perfect undiscovered gem." $ *Rooms from: €118* ⊠ *Main St., Ballyvaughan, Co. Clare* ☎ *065/707–7037* ⊕ *www. hylandsburren.com* ⇩ *30 rooms* ☺ *Closed Jan.–Easter* ❖ *Breakfast.*

NIGHTLIFE AND THE ARTS

Fodor'sChoice ★ **Monk's Pub.** This friendly pub, near the waterfront, hosts sessions of traditional and folk music on Sunday from 4 pm and most evenings after 9:30 in July and August. The bar food is excellent (the seafood chowder has a cult following), but be warned—the prime location and well-regarded reputation mean it is often a busy spot. ⊠ *Main St., Ballyvaughan, Co. Clare* ☎ *065/707–7059* ⊕ *www.monks.ie.*

KINVARA

13½ km (8 miles) east of Ballyvaughan, 15 km (9 miles) northwest of Gort on N67, 25 km (15½ miles) south of Galway City.

★ The picture-perfect village of Kinvara is a growing holiday base, thanks to its gorgeous bay-side locale, great walking and sea angling, and numerous pubs. It's well worth a visit, whether you're coming from Ballyvaughan or Gort. Kinvara is best known for its longstanding early-August sailing event, **Cruinniú na mBád** (Festival of the Gathering of the Boats), in which traditional brown-sail Galway hookers laden with turf race across the bay. Hookers were used until the early part of this century to carry turf, provisions, and cattle across Galway Bay and out to the Aran Islands. A sculpture in Galway's Eyre Square honors their local significance.

GETTING HERE AND AROUND

The N67 coast road, a narrow but scenic route, follows the shore of Galway Bay from Ballyvaughan to Kinvara. From Kinvara, N67 joins the busy national route, the M18 at Clarenbridge and continues into Galway City (25km [15 miles]). There is free parking in Kinvara. Bus Éireann runs buses between Kinvara and Galway City; the journey takes about 30 minutes. The same bus continues to the Cliffs of Moher, Lisdoonvarna, and Doolin.

EXPLORING

Dunguaire Castle. On a rock north of Kinvara Bay, the 16th-century Dunguaire Castle spectacularly commands all the approaches to Galway Bay. It's said to stand on the site of a 7th-century castle built by the king of Connaught. Built in 1520 by the O'Hynes clan, the tiny storybook castle takes its name from the fabled king of Connaught, Guaire. In 1929 it was purchased by Oliver St. John Gogarty, the noted surgeon, man of letters, and model for Buck Mulligan, a character in James Joyce's *Ulysses*. To his outpost came many of the leading figures of the 19th-century Celtic revival in Irish literature. Today Dunguaire is used for a Middle Ages–style banquet that honors local writers and others with ties to the West, including Lady Gregory, W. B. Yeats, Sean O'Casey, and Pádraic O'Conaire (book online for banquet tickets to get substantial discounts).

8

WHERE TO EAT AND STAY

For expanded hotel reviews, visit Fodors.com.

$$$$
SEAFOOD
★

✕**Moran's Oyster Cottage.** Signposted off the main road on the south side of Clarinbridge, this waterside thatch cottage, the home of the Moran family since 1760, houses at its rear a simply furnished restaurant that serves only seafood: Gigas oysters, chowder, smoked salmon, seafood cocktail, lobster with boiled potatoes and garlic butter, and fresh crab salad. It's *the* place to sample the local oysters, grown on a nearby bed owned by the Moran family, who have had the pub for six generations. Hope for good weather, so that you can eat outside overlooking the weir and watch the swans float by. The front bar has been preserved in the "old style," which means it's small and cramped, but very interesting if you want to get an idea of what most pubs around here were like 50 years ago. ⑤ *Average main: €33* ✉ *The Weir, Kilcolgan, Co. Galway* ☎ *091/796–113* ⊕ *www.moransoystercottage.com.*

$$
IRISH
★

✕**The Pier Head.** Once the village pub, the Pier Head is still a bar, but it sells more food than pints these days. The location is idyllic, at the top (head) of the village's pier. Lunch ($) is served in the bustling, wooden-floored mahogany bar (restaurant lunch Sundays only), with outdoor seating and modest sea views. At dinner you can choose between the bar and the more formal upstairs restaurant with unforgettable views across Kinvara Bay to Dunguaire Castle. Both have roaring open fires, and friendly staff. Fresh local seafood and locally reared meat (beef, lamb, pork, and duck) feature on the simple, unfussy menu. Start with crab claws in garlic butter, or steamed mussels mariniere, then consider fillet of local lamb on a bed of creamed spinach, or honey-roast half duck with five spice and ginger sauce. Desserts are all made in-house: chocolate and ginger torte with vanilla ice cream perhaps, or a hazelnut pavlova with fresh strawberries and berry coulis. Top it all off with an Irish coffee. Don't forget that in summer there will be enough daylight until around 10 pm to enjoy the view. ⑤ *Average main: €23* ✉ *Kinvara, Co. Galway* ☎ *091/638–188* ⊕ *www.pierhead.ie.*

$
HOTEL

🛏**Merriman Inn.** Don't let its traditional looks deceive you: this whitewashed, thatch inn on the shores of Galway Bay is, in fact, a midsize hotel, decorated with locally made, well-designed furniture, and original crafts, paintings, and sculpture. **Pros:** center of village; secure car parking; decent restaurant; choice of other restaurants and bars nearby. **Cons:** bar gets very busy at weekends; bigger windows would be nice, to get more of the view. **TripAdvisor:** "amazing Ireland experience," "friendly staff," "comfortable." ⑤ *Rooms from: €118* ✉ *Main St., Kinvara, Co. Galway* ☎ *091/638–222* ⊕ *www.merrimanhotel.com* ⇱ *32 rooms* ⊙ *Closed Jan. and Feb.* ⦿| *Breakfast.*

NIGHTLIFE AND THE ARTS

Cuckoo Fleadh. The first weekend in May, Kinvara hosts the popular annual Cuckoo Fleadh, or Fleadh na gCuach, a traditional-music festival with a lovely view. ✉ *Main St., Kinvara, Co. Galway* ☎ *091/637–145* ⊕ *kinvara.com.*

Winkles Hotel bar. Traditional music is played most nights at the Winkles Hotel bar, where acclaimed Irish musician Sharon Shannon got her start in the music business. ☒ *The Square, Kinvara, Co. Galway* ☎ *091/637–137.*

COOLE PARK

24 km (15 miles) northeast of Corofin on M18.

EXPLORING

Coole Park & Gardens. Located north of the little town of Gort, Coole Park was once the home of Lady Augusta Gregory (1859–1932), patron of W.B. Yeats and cofounder with the poet of Dublin's Abbey Theatre. Yeats visited here often, as did almost all the other writers who contributed to the Irish literary revival in the first half of the 20th century, including George Bernard Shaw (1856–1950) and Sean O'Casey (1880–1964). Douglas Hyde (1860–1949), the first president of Ireland, was also a visitor. The house became derelict after Lady Gregory's death and was demolished in 1941; the grounds are now a national forest and wildlife park. Picnic tables make this a lovely alfresco lunch spot. The only reminder of its literary past is the Autograph Tree, a copper beech on which many of Lady Gregory's famous guests carved their initials. There's also a visitor center with displays on Lady Gregory and Yeats. ☒ *Galway Rd., Gort, Co. Galway* ☎ *092/8638–7888* ⊕ *www.coolepark. ie* ⬚ *Park free, visitor center €3* ☺ *Park: daily 8:30–7:30 (6 in winter); Visitor center: Apr. and Sept., Wed.–Sun. 10–5, May–Aug., daily 10–5.*

GALWAY CITY

Galway is often said to be a state of mind as much as it is a specific place. The largest city in the West today and the ancient capital of the province of Connaught, Galway, with a current population of 72,700, is also one of the fastest-growing cities in Europe. It's an astonishing fact, and you have to wonder where this city can possibly grow. For despite Galway's size, its commercially busy ring road, and its ever-spreading suburbs, its heart is *tiny*—a warren of streets so compact that if you spend more than a few hours here, you'll soon be strolling along with the sort of easy familiarity you'd feel in any small town.

For many Irish people, Galway is a favorite weekend getaway: known as the city of festivals, it's the liveliest place in the republic. It's also a university town: University College Galway (or UCG as it's locally known) is a center for Gaelic culture (Galway marks the eastern gateway to the West's large Gaeltacht). A fair share of UCG's 9,000 students pursue their studies in the Irish language. Galway is, in fact, permeated by youth culture. On festival weekends, you'll see as many pierced and tattooed teenagers and twentysomethings here as you'd find at a rock concert. But Galway's students aren't its only avant-garde, as Galway has long attracted writers, artists, and musicians. The latter whip up brand-new jigs while also keeping the traditional-music pubs lively year-round. And the city's two small but internationally acclaimed theater companies draw a steady stream of theater people.

Galway City

River Corrib

Waterside

Newcastle Rd.

University Rd.

Eglinton Canal

Nuns Island

Newcastle Rd.

Gaol Rd.

River Corrib

Nuns Island St.

Mill St.

New Rd.

St. Helens St.

Henry St.

Dominick St.

Wolfe Tone Bridge

Raleigh Row

Dominick St. Upper

Sea Rd.

Munster Ave.

Fr. Griffin Rd.

Fairhill

Claddagh Quay

St. Nicholas Rd.

Grattan Rd.

Nimmo's Pier

SOUTH PARK

CLADDAGH

Wood Quay

St. Vincents Ave.

Brendans Ave.

Headford Rd.

St. Bridget's Pl.

Prospect Hill

Forster St.

Eyre St.

Abbeygate St.

Post Office

Williamsgate St.

Eglinton St.

William St.

EYRE SQUARE

Kennedy Park

Eyre Square

Station Rd.

Bowling Green

Market St.

Lombard St.

Guard St.

High St.

Shop St.

Middle St.

Cross St.

St. Augustine St.

Eyre Square Shopping Centre

Lwr. Abbeygate St.

Queen St.

Victoria Pl.

CENTER

Train Station

Wm. O'Brien Bridge

Bridge St.

Quay St.

Flood St.

The Cornstore

Merchants Rd.

New Dock St.

Dock Rd.

Dock Rd.

SPANISH ARCH

Commercial Dock

The Long Walk

Old Dock

1/4 mi

0

1/4 km

Salthill

Legend

Cathedral of Our Lady Assumed into Heaven and St. Nicholas **11**	Lynch Memorial Window **4**	Spanish Arch **8**
	Lynch's Castle **3**	Tigh Neachtain **7**
Claddagh **13**	Nora Barnacle House **6**	Tourist Information Office (TIO) **2**
Collegiate Church of St. Nicholas **5**	Salmon Weir Bridge **10**	University College Galway (UCG) **12**
Eyre Square **1**		
Galway City Museum **9**	Salthill **14**	

City of the Tribes

Galway's founders were Anglo-Normans who arrived in the mid-13th century and fortified their settlement against "the native Irish," as local chieftains were called.

Galway became known as "the City of the Tribes" because of the dominant role in public and commercial life of the 14 families that founded it.

Their names are still common in Galway and elsewhere in Ireland: Athy,

Blake, Bodkin, Browne, D'Arcy, Dean, Font, French, Kirwan, Joyce, Lynch, Morris, Martin, and Skerret.

The city's medieval heritage, a fusion of Gaelic and Norman influences, is apparent in the intimate two- and three-story stone buildings, the winding streets, the narrow passageways, and the cobblestones underfoot.

■ TIP➜ If you're looking for the quiet, quaint side of Ireland depicted on travel posters, have a quick look at Galway City and push on to Clifden or Westport.

Although you're not conscious of it when you're in the center of town, Galway is spectacularly situated, on the north shore of Galway Bay, where the River Corrib flows from Lough Corrib to the sea. The seaside suburb of Salthill, on the south-facing shore of Galway Bay, has spectacular vistas across the vividly blue bay to Black Head and the Burren on the opposite shore.

Galway's growth and popularity mean that at its busiest moments, its narrow, one-way streets are jam-packed with pedestrians, while cars are gridlocked.

GETTING HERE AND AROUND

Galway is connected to Dublin by motorways M6–M4–M50 (four-lane highways with concrete dividers, some tolls), 20 km (129 miles) with a journey time of about 2 hours 20 minutes. There is a similarly good road to Limerick, the M18/N18 (100 km/62 miles), with a journey time of 1 hour.

Express bus services to Galway from Dublin are available from both Bus Éireann and Citylink. Both take about 3 hours 40 minutes from Dublin City Center. Bus services to Galway from Cork call at Limerick and Shannon Airport. Journey time from Cork is 4½ hours. There are also daily buses from Galway to Westport (1½ hours), Ballina (2½ hours), Sligo (2½ hours), and Belfast (6½ hours). For quick hops around the city, use a taxi, such as those of Big O.

Irish Rail–Iarnrod Éireann trains run from Dublin's Heuston Station to Galway City via Athlone. The journey takes 2 hours 10 minutes. There are trains from Limerick City via Ennis on the new commuter route, a two-hour journey.

At the time of writing there are no commercial flights to Galway Airport.

TOURS

Lally Tours. While Galway's historic center is compact and can be explored on foot, many visitors enjoy a quick orientation hop aboard Lally Tours' vintage double-decker bus for an hour-long Old Galway City Tour. Five buses a day leave from the tourist office in Forster Place on the corner of Eyre Square. ⊠ *Lally Tours, Galway City, Co. Galway* ☎ *091/562–905* ⊕ *www.lallytours.com* ⛟ *€10* ☉ *Daily 10:30 am–4:15 pm.*

ESSENTIALS

Transportation Contacts **Ceannt (Rail) Station** ⊠ *Eyre Sq., Galway City, Co. Galway* ☎ *091/564–222* ⊕ *www.irishrail.ie.* **Ceannt (Bus) Station** ⊠ *Eyre Sq., Galway City, Co. Galway* ☎ *091/562–000.* **Big O Taxis** ☎ *091/585–858* ⊕ *www.bigotaxis.com.*

Visitor Information **Galway Discover Ireland Centre.** This functions as Galway City's main tourist office. ⊠ *Forster St., Eyre Sq., Galway City, Co. Galway* ☎ *091/537–700* ⊕ *www.discoverireland.ie/places-to-go/visitgalway.*

EXPLORING

Most of the city's sights, aside from the cathedral and the university campus, can be found in a narrow sector of the medieval town center that runs in a southwesterly direction from Eyre Square to the River Corrib. Not only is the city center compact, but it's also largely pedestrian-friendly, so the best way to explore it is on foot. It takes only five minutes to walk straight down Galway's main shopping street, the continuation of the north side of Eyre Square, to the River Corrib, where it ends (note that the name of this street changes several times).

TOP ATTRACTIONS

Eyre Square. The largest open space in central Galway and the heart of the city, and a favorite chill-out spot on a sunny day for students, visitors, and lunching locals, Eyre Square on the east side of the River Corrib, incorporates a sculpture garden and children's play area on its east side, while its west side is bound by a heavily traveled road. In the center is **Kennedy Park,** a patch of lawn named in honor of John F. Kennedy, who spoke here when he visited the city in June 1963. At the north end of the park, a 20-foot-high steel sculpture standing in the pool of a fountain represents the brown sails seen on Galway hookers, the area's traditional sailing boats. Now the entrance to Kennedy Park, the **Browne Doorway** was taken in 1905 from the Browne family's town house on Upper Abbeygate Street; it has the 17th-century coats of arms of both the Browne and Lynch families (two of Galway's 14 founding families), called a "marriage stone" because when the families were joined in marriage their coats of arms were, too. Keep an eye out for similar if less elaborate Browne doorways as you walk around the old part of town.

Galway Discover Ireland Centre (*TIO*). Just off Eyre Square, east of the bus and train station and the Great Southern Hotel, this is the place to make reservations for events around town and find out about the latest happenings. You can also book tickets to the Aran Islands here. ⊠ *Forster Pl., Center, Galway City, Co. Galway* ☎ *091/537–700* ⊕ *www.discoverireland.ie/places-to-go/visitGalway* ☉ *Weekdays 9–6, Sat. 9–1.*

A Shopping Tour of Galway

There's no question about it: they have a different look in Galway. People have always dressed differently, because they dress for the Galway weather, which can be wet and windy at any time of year. But ever since Galway was transformed by Ireland's "Celtic Tiger" economic boom, they have also dressed—and decorated—with a real sense of style. Want proof? Just join the locals on the following walk.

Pick up a free map of Galway from the **tourist information office** on Forster Place. Turn left out the front door to reach the **Hotel Meyrick** (formerly the Great Southern), a monumental 19th-century grande dame in cut stone (its lobby is just the place for "scene-iors" to take their coffee or tea).

Turn left beyond the hotel and right into Merchants Road, location of the Blarney Woollen Mills, for Irish clothing, and (on the top floor) Meadows & Byrne for well-designed Irish goods for the home. Turn right out of the Woollen Mills, and take the next turn right along New Dock Street into **Flood Street**, the heart of medieval Galway, a tiny area where all the cutest shops are jam-packed together, including **Cobwebs**, abrim with off-beat antique jewelry, old binoculars, and bronze model airplanes. For a feel of the essential Galway, cross the road to the banks of the **River Corrib**, and walk to your left to the **Spanish Arch**. When natives feel homesick, this is the view they think of: white water breaking on the dark surface of the swift-flowing Corrib.

Staying on this side of the Corrib, cross over the bridge and take the riverside footpath past the contempo

Jurys Inn and some old warehouses. Turn left over O'Brien's Bridge for the historic **Bridge Mills**, now outfitted with a designer swap shop, a basement restaurant overlooking the river, and **Sam Beardon, Sculptor and Jeweller.** Cross the bridge again, taking the first right into Cross Street and right into Kirwan's Lane. Here, **Design Concourse Ireland/Judy Greene Pottery** has locally made turned-wood objects, basketware, and perfumery.

Medieval Kirwan's Lane leads you on to Quay Street and **Twice as Nice**, a vintage and antique clothing boutique with old Irish linen and gold and silver jewelry. Continue up High Street to **Faller's Sweaters and Tweeds**, just the place to buy an Aran sweater, and **The Kilkenny Shop**, Galway's largest emporium of Irish-designed products, with a dazzling selection of chic John Rocha crystal, Newbridge Silver, and Nicholas Mosse pottery.

Farther up on the right, **O'Maille** has some great mohair wraps and *the* essential Galway fashion item, a Jack Murphy raincoat. Top one off with a rainproof Stetson with a feather in it and you'll pass for a local.

High Street leads into William Street, where you'll find **The Treasure Chest**, a three-story shop selling upmarket Irish goods. Its exterior, painted in Wedgwood blue with white swags, just like the famous china, is a favorite with photographers. **Brown Thomas**, on William at the corner of Eglinton, has long been Galway's most upscale department store. The post office is on Eglinton Street. A few steps up Williamsgate Street brings us back to Eyre Square and your starting point at the TIO.

8

Nora Barnacle House. On June 16, 1904, James Joyce (1882–1941) had his first date with Nora Barnacle, who would later become his wife. He subsequently chose to set *Ulysses* on this day, now known universally as Bloomsday—"a recognition of the determining effect upon his life of his attachment to her," as Joyce's biographer Richard Ellman has said. Nora, the daughter of a poor baker, was born here. Today it has a modest collection of photographs, letters, and memorabilia, and a small gift shop. ⊠ *4 Bowling Green, Center, Galway City, Co. Galway* ☎ *087/901–7691* 🎫 *€2.50* ⊗ *June–mid-Sept., Tues.–Sat. 10–5; mid-Sept.–mid-May, by appointment.*

Salthill. A lively, hugely popular seaside resort, Salthill is beloved for its seaside promenade—the traditional place "to sit and watch the moon rise over Claddagh, and see the sun go down on Galway Bay," as Bing Crosby used to croon in the most famous song about the city. The main attraction of the village, set 3 km (2 miles) west of Galway, is the long sandy beach along the edge of Galway Bay and the promenade above it. The building of big new hotels along the seafront has nevertheless left plenty of room for the traditional amusement arcades (full of slot machines), seasonal cafés, and a fairground.

★ **Salmon Weir Bridge.** The bridge itself is nothing special, but in season—from mid-April to early July—shoals of salmon are visible from its deck as they lie in the clear river water before making their way upstream to the spawning grounds of Lough Corrib. ⊠ *West end of St. Vincent's Ave., Center, Galway City, Co. Galway.*

Spanish Arch. Built in 1584 to protect the quays where Spanish ships unloaded cargoes of wines and brandies, the hefty stone arch is now the central feature of the newly restored Spanish Parade, a riverside piazza located near Wolfe Tone Bridge. It's another reminder of Galway's—and Ireland's—past links with Spain, and is much loved locally. ⊠ *Spanish Parade, Spanish Arch, Galway City, Co. Galway.*

Fodor'sChoice
★
Tigh Neachtain (*Naughton's Pub*). Galway City's most famous pub, which stands at a busy little crossroads in the heart of the old town, is treasured for its unrenovated interior. Grab a spot at one of its old-fashioned partitioned snugs at lunchtime for an inexpensive selection of imaginative bar food. It's a good place to mingle with local actors, writers, artists, musicians, and students, although it can become sardine-can crowded. ⊠ *17 Cross St., Spanish Arch, Galway City, Co. Galway* ☎ *091/568–820* ⊕ *www.tighneachtain.com.*

WORTH NOTING

Cathedral of Our Lady Assumed into Heaven and St. Nicholas. On Nun's Island, which forms the west bank of the River Corrib beside the Salmon Weir Bridge, stands Galway's largest Catholic church, dedicated by Cardinal Cushing of Boston in 1965. The cathedral was built on the site of the old Galway jail; a white cross embedded in the pavement of the adjacent parking lot marks the site of the cemetery that stood beside the prison. A calm and peaceful spot, especially appealing to church-lovers. ⊠ *Nun's Island, Galway City, Co. Galway* ☎ *091/563–577* ⊕ *www. galwaycathedral.org* 🎫 *Free.*

Pedestrian alleys and high-style boutiques help make Galway into a stroller's paradise—keep your eye out for the many 19th-century footscrapers.

Claddagh. On the west bank of the Corrib estuary, this district was once an Irish-speaking fishing village outside the walls of the old town. The name is an Anglicization of the Irish *cladach*, which means "marshy ground." It retained a strong, separate identity until the 1930s, when its traditional thatch cottages were replaced by a conventional housing plan and its unique character and traditions were largely lost. One thing has survived: the Claddagh ring, composed of two hands clasped around a heart with a crown above it (symbolizing love, friendship, and loyalty), was designed some 400 years ago by a goldsmith in this village, and is still used by many Irish, and Irish diaspora, as a wedding ring. Reproductions in gold or silver are favorite Galway souvenirs.

Galway City Museum. The city's civic museum, housed in a modern building behind the Spanish Arch, contains materials relating to local history: old photographs, antiquities (the oldest is a stone ax head carbon-dated to 3500 BC), and other historical gewgaws. ⊠ *Spanish Parade, Spanish Arch, Galway City, Co. Galway* ☎ *091/532–640* ⊕ *www. galwaycitymuseum.ie* ⊡ *Free* ⊙ *June–Sept., daily 10–5; Oct.–May, Tues.–Sat. 10–5.*

Lynch Memorial Window. Embedded in a stone wall above a built-up Gothic doorway off Market Street, the window marks the spot where, according to legend, James Lynch FitzStephen, mayor of Galway in the early 16th century, condemned his son to death after the young man confessed to murdering a Spanish sailor who had romanced his girlfriend. When no one could be found to carry out the execution, Judge Lynch hanged his son himself, ensuring that justice prevailed, before retiring into seclusion. ⊠ *Market St., Center, Galway City, Co. Galway.*

Lynch's Castle. Now a branch of the Allied Irish Banks, this is the finest remaining example in Galway of a 16th-century fortified house—fortified because neighboring Irish tribes persistently raided the village, whose commercial life excluded them. The decorative details on its stone lintels are of a type usually found only in southern Spain. Historical material about the castle can be seen on the ground floor. ⊠ *Shop St., Center, Galway City, Co. Galway.*

NUI Galway (*UCG*). Opened in 1846 to promote the development of local industry and agriculture, the UCG today is a center for Irish-language and Celtic studies. The Tudor Gothic–style quadrangle, completed in 1848, is worth a visit, though much of the rest of the campus is architecturally undistinguished. The library here has an important archive of Celtic-language materials, and in July and August the university hosts courses in Irish studies for overseas students. The campus is across the River Corrib, in the northwestern corner of the city. ⊠ *Newcastle Rd., University, Galway City, Co. Galway* 🕾 *915/24411* ⊕ *www.galwaycity.ie.*

St. Nicholas' Collegiate Church Galway. Built by the Anglo-Normans in 1320 and enlarged in 1486 and again in the 16th century, the church contains many fine carvings and gargoyles dating from the late Middle Ages, and it's one of the best-preserved medieval churches in Ireland. Legend has it that Columbus prayed here on his last stop before setting off on his voyage to the New World. On Saturday mornings, a street market, held in the pedestrian way beside the church, attracts dozens of vendors and hundreds of shoppers. ⊠ *Lombard St., Junction of Mainguard St. and Lombard St., Center, Galway City, Co. Galway* 🕾 *091/564–648* ⊕ *www.stnicholas.ie* 🎫 *Free* ⊙ *Daily 8–dusk.*

WHERE TO EAT

$$
EUROPEAN
✕ **K.C. Blake's.** K.C. stands for Casey, as in owner-chef John Casey, a larger-than-life character, who turned a medieval stone town house once associated with the Blake family—one of the families that founded Galway—into an ultramodern eatery. The hard-edge, minimalist interior, with sleek black walls, provides a strong contrast with the old stone building. Dishes range from traditional-style stuffed roast quail with crispy potato croquettes, or sole meunière, to funky starter combinations like goat cheese salad with apple and vanilla purée. ⑤ *Average main: €23* ⊠ *10 Quay St., Spanish Arch, Galway City, Co. Galway* 🕾 *091/561–826* ⊕ *kcblakes.ie.*

$$$
EUROPEAN
✕ **Kirwan's Lane.** Look for Mike O'Grady's stylish modern restaurant in a revamped alley at the river end of Quay Street. Tables clad in white damask (covered with paper tablecloths at lunchtime), narrow floor-to-ceiling windows, and a quarry-tile floor set the stage for an informal, bistro-style menu. A seafood bar offers a tapas-style light menu, which includes sushi, local oysters, and fresh crab cocktail. On the main menu, a great starter of crisp julienne of ox tongue and pancetta is dressed with a fennel and orange cream. Main courses have similarly Mediterranean twists—fennel and courgette osso buco with saffron couscous, sautéed scallops with smoked garlic-infused spinach,

The Galway Saturday Market

Locals get up very early on Saturday in Galway in order to get the pick of the goods on offer at the Saturday food market. As many as 90 colorful stall-holders set out their wares in the area behind the Collegiate Church of St. Nicholas in the city center. Take your pick of the Mediterranean goods on offer at the Real Olive Company; sample a wide selection of Irish cheeses from Sheridan's Cheesemongers; treat yourself to an outdoor lunch at the Madras Curry Stall; get sushi from the Japanese-run Da Kappa-ya Sushi, and end on a sweet note with dessert from Yummy Crêpes. Organic-vegetable sellers, plant sellers, herbalists, cheese mongers, and bakers are joined by hat sellers, wood carvers, and knitwear stalls. A selection of Galway's famously wacky buskers entertain with music, juggling, and dance. Come early and hungry! ⊕ *www.galwaymarket.net.*

and a vegetarian favorite: wild mushroom and asparagus risotto with truffle oil and Parmesan shavings. $ *Average main: €25* ⊠ *Kirwan's La., Spanish Arch, Galway City, Co. Galway* ☎ *091/568–266* ⊗ *No lunch Sun., Nov.–Apr. closed Sun.*

$$ ╳ **Malt House.** Hidden away in a flower-filled courtyard off High Street
EUROPEAN in the center of old Galway is the lunch and dinner venue of choice for Galway's movers and shakers. A cool, contemporary space with leather tub chairs, small but with well-spaced wooden-top tables and a wooden floor, the specialty here is seasonal local seafood, with daily specials on the blackboard. Oysters come from Clarinbridge, fresh crab from Miltown Malbay, and smoked salmon from the Burren Smokehouse, Lisdoonvarna. Cooking is cool and contemporary, too: start with sushi rolls, or Galway Bay Oysters with bacon and cabbage and béarnaise sauce; sea bass fillets are pan-seared and served with parsley mash, braised fennel, and lemon caramel, while roast saddle of rabbit is stuffed with spinach, apricots, and pine nuts. Vegetarians can sample beetroot polenta with creamed leeks, Tipperary Brie, fig chutney, and roasted pumpkin seeds. Desserts include chocolate and chili tart, rhubarb trifle, or an Irish farmhouse cheese board. $ *Average main: €24* ⊠ *Old Malte Arcade, High St., Center, Galway City, Co. Galway* ☎ *091/567–866* ⊕ *themalthouse.ie* ⊗ *Closed Sun.*

$$ ╳ **Martine's Restaurant Galway.** With its red walls, its mahogany bar
ECLECTIC topped by a Victorian mirror, and Otis Redding crooning in the background, this cozy bistro-style wine bar is an excellent option for those evenings when you just want a simple meal nicely served in a pleasant ambience. Beyond the tiny wine bar are two more dining areas; go for a window table if you can in order to watch the passersby on busy Quay Street. Typical main courses could be Thai mussels in chili-lemongrass broth with chips, or the tandoori chicken with mint raita, or the splendid beef lasagna. Steaks from the charcoal oven and rack of lamb are also menu staples. Service is warm and attentive, even at the busiest times. For dessert, regulars recommend the bread-and-butter pudding, or opt for the fabulous *affogatto*—a scoop of vanilla ice topped with hot

espresso. ⑤ *Average main: €20* ✉ *21 Quay St., Spanish Arch, Galway City, Co. Galway* ☎ *091/565–662* ⊕ *www.winebar.ie.*

$$$ ✕ **McDonagh's Seafood House.** This longtime Galway landmark is partly
SEAFOOD a self-service fish-and-chips bar and partly a "real" fish restaurant. If
★ you haven't yet tried fish-and-chips, this is the place to start: cod, whiting, mackerel, haddock, or hake is deep-fried in a light batter while you watch. The gently priced fish is served with a heap of fabulous freshly cooked chips (which have won a nationwide competition for the best french fries in Ireland), and eaten at communal tables—a great way to meet the locals. Or go for the more sophisticated (and expensive) Seafood Restaurant menu: Galway oysters au naturel, perhaps, or scallops sautéed in creamed garlic butter, followed by flame-grilled turbot. The McDonaghs are one of Galway's biggest entrepreneurial families, in charge of several hotels in addition to this spot. ⑤ *Average main: €27* ✉ *22 Quay St., Spanish Arch, Galway City, Co. Galway* ☎ *091/565–001* ⊕ *mcdonaghs.net* ☉ *Restaurant closed Sun.*

$$ ✕ **Ard Bia at Nimmo's.** Good food and the friendly, enthusiastic staff make
EUROPEAN this bustling bistro one of Galway's most popular restaurants. The central location in an old stone boathouse overlooking the Corrib River adds to the pleasure. Downstairs is a one of Galway's busiest wine bar and luncheon spots, Ard Bia, which serves casual meals ($), while upstairs is a more sophisticated restaurant. The long, spacious, second-floor room has brightly colored paintings on the off-white walls, wooden floors, and well-spaced tables, with an eclectic mix of quirky white-painted stick or spoon-back chairs. The menu is short but well balanced, and while presentation is flamboyant, the food also tastes good. Try the west coast scallops with citrus salsa to start, then belly of pork with potato and celeriac, or grilled fillet of sea bass with spring-onion mashed potatoes, dill aioli, and organic leaves. Lobster and black sole are available in season. ⑤ *Average main: €24* ✉ *The Long Walk, Spanish Arch, Galway City, Co. Galway* ☎ *091/561–114* ⊕ *ardbia.com* ☉ *Closed Mon.*

WHERE TO STAY

■TIP→ If there's a city in Ireland that never sleeps, this must be it. If you want to get some shut-eye, ask for a room in the back of your city-center hotel or simply stay out of town.

For expanded hotel reviews, visit Fodors.com.

$ 🏠 **Adare Guest House.** A five-minute walk from the city center, across
B&B/INN the River Coribb, this family-run guesthouse, managed by the son of the original owners, makes a handy base for exploring Galway. **Pros:** convenient, quiet location; free parking; walking distance of pub-restaurant area. **Cons:** exterior of building very plain; bedrooms vary in size; hugely popular: book early. **TripAdvisor:** "amazing breakfast," "a different experience," "congenial owners." ⑤ *Rooms from: €110* ✉ *9 Father Griffin Pl., Spanish Arch, Galway City, Co. Galway* ☎ *091/582–638* ⊕ *www.adareguesthouse.ie* ⮌ *11 rooms* ◖⦿*Breakfast.*

$$$ 🏠 **the g Hotel.** "G" is for glamour—or good grief (depending on your
HOTEL taste)—at this flamboyant player at the top end of Galway's hotel scene,
★ whose architects worked with superstar hat designer Philip Treacy (a

native of Galway) to create an interior that is every bit as fanciful as Treacy's hats. **Pros:** a must for design lovers; it may be OTT, but it's fun and a much-loved reminder of Celtic Tiger Ireland. **Cons:** will wreck your budget; 1 km (½ mile) from town center. **TripAdvisor:** "amazing," "sorry I had to leave," "different and nice." $ *Rooms from:* €200 ⊠ *Wellpark, Galway City, Co. Galway* ☎ *091/865–200* ⊕ *www. theghotel.ie* ⤴ *98 rooms* ⧧*Breakfast.*

$$

B&B/INN

🛏 **The Huntsman Inn.** Situated 1 km (½ mile) from Eyre Square, across the road from the exotic "g" hotel and a stone's throw from Lough Atalia, this pub with rooms makes an excellent base for visiting Galway City if you're traveling by car. **Pros:** free car parking; within walking distance of city center, on bus route; bar is a good place to mix with locals. **Cons:** apart from the window boxes, nothing scenic or romantic about the place; rooms are a bit plain, as you'd expect for the price. **TripAdvisor:** "great food," "lovely room," "quiet." $ *Rooms from:* €150 ⊠ *164 College Rd., Galway City, Co. Galway* ☎ *091/562–849* ⊕ *www.huntsmaninn.com* ⤴ *12 rooms.*

$

HOTEL

🛏 **Jurys Inn Galway.** Expect good-quality budget accommodations at this four-story hotel set beside the historic Spanish Arch and the river. **Pros:** reliable Irish budget hotel chain; great location for pubs, clubs, and river views. **Cons:** rates subject to demand, so book early; favorite hotel chain for large groups of partying Irish. **TripAdvisor:** "top location," "central," "very friendly staff." $ *Rooms from:* €110 ⊠ *Quay St., Spanish Arch, Galway City, Co. Galway* ☎ *091/566–444* ⊕ *www. jurysinn.com* ⤴ *130 rooms.*

$$

HOTEL

★

🛏 **Park House Hotel.** Even though this is a large, luxury hotel in central Galway, snazzily converted from a 200-year-old warehouse, it feels like a home-away-from-home, thanks to attentive owner-managers. **Pros:** friendly, professional staff; a haven of quiet. **Cons:** tricky to find vehicle entrance first time. **TripAdvisor:** "service and food the way it should be," "a gem of a hotel," "classic charm and great hospitality." $ *Rooms from:* €140 ⊠ *Forster St., Center, Galway City, Co. Galway* ☎ *091/564–924* ⊕ *www.parkhousehotel.ie* ⤴ *84 rooms* ⧧*Breakfast.*

$$

HOTEL

Fodor'sChoice

★

🛏 **Radisson Blu Hotel and Spa.** Against several newcomers, the Radisson Blu has successfully defended its reputation as Galway's hippest hotel—indeed, its striking contemporary design has revived the run-down Lough Atalia area, a stone's throw from Eyre Square and overlooking a landlocked inflow of Galway Bay. **Pros:** stylish venue right at the heart of the social scene; sea views in the city center. **Cons:** very busy during Galway's many festivals; arriving by car can be a slow business in peak periods. **TripAdvisor:** "nice place, great little city," "high quality," "great service." $ *Rooms from:* €160 ⊠ *Lough Atalia Rd., Center, Galway City, Co. Galway* ☎ *091/538–300* ⊕ *www. radissonhotelgalway.com* ⤴ *261 rooms* ⧧*Breakfast.*

NIGHTLIFE AND THE ARTS

Because of its small size and concentration of pubs and restaurants, Galway can seem even livelier at 11 pm than it does at 11 am. On weekends, when there are lots of students and other revelers in town, Eyre Square and environs can be rowdy after pub-closing time—which is 2 am on Friday and Saturday. On the plus side, if you've been staying out in the country and you're ready for a little nightlife, you're certain to find plenty of it here.

NIGHTLIFE

The best spot for traditional music is the area between Eyre Square and the Spanish Arch. Although many pubs are open until 2 am on weekends, there is a big post-pub nightclub scene here, centered in the Eyre Square area.

CLUBS

The Cellar. Considering the fact that this place offers live entertainment seven nights, including DJs, and acoustic two-pieces, electro, techno, and house, it's amazing there is no cover charge. ⊠ *Eglinton St., Center, Galway City, Co. Galway* ☎ *091/563–966* ⊕ *www.thecellar.ie/.*

Central Park Night Club. Open every night from 11 pm, this venue's seven bars attract a dressy and young crowd (in their 20s) who like to dance the night away. ⊠ *36 Upper Abbey St., Center, Galway City, Co. Galway* ☎ *091/565–976.*

Fibber Magees. Late night hot spot in town center, slogan "cheap drinks and loud music," attracting mainly under 25s. Late nights Friday to Sunday. ⊠ *3 Eyre Square, Center, Galway City, Co. Galway* ☎ *091/564–633.*

PUBS

Áras na Gael. Cross O'Brien Bridge and take the first left to find this Irish-speaking social club-cum-pub, which is a great place to hear traditional music, watch (or join) dancing and language classes, and hear the Irish language in use. Non-Irish speakers very welcome. ⊠ *45 Dominick St., Galway City, Co. Galway* ☎ *091/567–824.*

The Crane Bar. There's traditional music from 9:30 most nights in a room above this tiny bar, to the west of Claddagh, but come early to get a seat. ⊠ *2 Sea Rd., Galway City, Co. Galway* ☎ *091/587–419.*

The Dail Bar. While it looks traditional with its dark-wood decor, the Dail is actually a recent arrival on the pub scene, and very popular with a younger crowd. ⊠ *42–44 Middle St., Center, Galway City, Co. Galway* ☎ *091/563–777.*

The Front Door. A lively spot for the twentysomethings, the Front Door has five bars spread over three floors, and a late bar until 2 am Wednesday to Sunday. ⊠ *3 High St., Center, Galway City, Co. Galway* ☎ *091/563–757.*

King's Head. You can usually find a session after about 9 pm at this local favorite. ⊠ *15 High St., Center, Galway City, Co. Galway* ☎ *091/566–630* ⊕ *www.thekingshead.ie.*

McSwiggan's. A huge Galway City place, McSwiggan's has everything from church pews to ancient carriage lamps contributing to its eclectic character. ⊠ *3 Eyre St., Wood Quay, Center, Galway City, Co. Galway* ☎ *091/568–917.*

Monroe's. A large and sociable pub, Monroe's has traditional music nightly and set dancing on Tuesday. ⊠ *20 Dominick St., Center, Galway City, Co. Galway* ☎ *091/583–397.*

The Quays. For many people the quintessential Galway bar is the Quays, a tall, narrow pub on three stories with live music upstairs. ⊠ *Quay St., Center, Galway City, Co. Galway* ☎ *091/568–347.*

Sally Longs. For late-night sounds heard from the comfort of your own table, try Sally Longs, Galway's hard-rock pub, much loved by bikers. ⊠ *Upper Abbeygate St., Center, Galway City, Co. Galway* ☎ *091/565–756.*

Róisín Dubh. A legend in its own right and a serious venue for emerging rock and traditional bands, Roisin Dubh often showcases big, if still-struggling, talents. ⊠ *Dominick St., Spanish Arch, Galway City, Co. Galway* ☎ *091/586–540* ⊕ *roisindubh.net.*

Taaffe's. In the midst of the shopping district, Taaffe's is very busy on afternoons. ⊠ *19 Shop St., Center, Galway City, Co. Galway* ☎ *091/564–066.*

Tigh Neachtain. If you're looking for *the* place to check out the quintessential Galway vibe, head here. Find a cozy corner and you'll stay longer than you should. ⊠ *17 Cross St., Spanish Arch, Galway City, Co. Galway* ☎ *091/568–820* ⊕ *www.tighneachtain.com.*

THE ARTS
THEATER

An Taibhdhearc Theatre. Founded in 1928 by Hilton Edwards and Micháel Macliammóir as the national Irish-language theater, An Taibhdhearc (pronounced *on tie*-vark) continues to produce first-class shows. Productions are mainly of Irish works in both the English and the Irish languages and it also hosts touring productions. ⊠ *Middle St., Center, Galway City, Co. Galway* ☎ *091/562–024* ⊕ *www.antaibhdhearc.com.*

Druid Theatre Company. Esteemed for its adventurous and accomplished productions, the Druid Theatre Company mainly showcases 20th-century Irish and European plays. The players have performed at Lincoln Center in New York, and several London venues. When they're home, they usually appear at the Town Hall, and they usually have a production at Galway Arts Festival in late July. ⊠ *Chapel La., Center, Galway City, Co. Galway* ☎ *091/568–660* ⊕ *www.druidtheatre.com.*

Macnas. An internationally renowned, roving Galway-based troupe of performance artists, Macnas has raised street theater in Ireland to new levels. Their participation in the Galway Arts Festival's annual parade is always much anticipated. ⊠ *Center, Galway City, Co. Galway* ☎ *091/561–462* ⊕ *www.macnas.com.*

GALLERIES

Norman Villa Gallery. Reflecting a passion for modern Irish art, this gallery exhibits work in the gallery owner's home and garden. ⊠ *86 Lower Salthill, Salthill, Galway City, Co. Galway* ☎ *091/521–131* ⊕ *www.normanvillagallery.com.*

NUI Galway. The art gallery at University College has a number of intriguing exhibitions each year. ⊠ *Newcastle Rd., University, Galway City, Co. Galway* ☎ *915/24411* ⊕ *www.nuigalway.ie.*

Continued on page 484

Gael Force

THE BOOM IN IRISH MUSIC & DANCE

Traditional Irish music and dance have taken the world by storm—but you need to journey to the West of Ireland to really get in step.

When the eye-popping spectacular of Riverdance first "tapped" its way into the Irish psyche in 1995 by jazzing up traditional step dancing and moving it from the local parish hall to the stages of Dublin's Point Theatre, it immediately sent its audiences reeling. The first troupe to introduce the Irish jig to world theaters, it has since performed before 18 million people and taken in more than $1 billion at the box office. Along the way, it gave once-languishing, "old-fashioned" arts of Ireland's folkloric music and dance a modern chic: today, thousands of young Irish are learning to play hornpipes, sing the old chanties, and dance the old jigs.

A GAELIC REBIRTH

Irish dancing has always been popular in American-Irish communities, as the first Riverdance stars proved: Jean Butler was born on Long Island to a mother from Mayo, while Michael Flatley was born in Chicago to emigrant parents. In 1995 Flatley founded his own triumphant show, Lord of the Dance, which spawned international troupes and, in turn, was followed by the Feet of Flames show, with more than 100 dancers.

Thanks to all these dance companies, the world has fallen in step—literally—as the passion for Irish dancing has taken hold. The World Irish Dancing Championship of 2011 attracted 4,500 competitors and some 20,000 supporters from 32 countries to Dublin. The 2012 event will be held in Belfast, and in 2013 the championships make the transatlantic hop to Boston (see ⊕ www.worldirishdancing.com).

GOING "TRAD"

Competitors, indeed: Irish dancing is now also a competitive sport, with thousands of passionate devotees (see its social networking site, ⊕ www.diddlyi.com) attending feis (festivals). Thousands of dollars are invested in costumes, wigs (you thought all those ringlets were real?) and, last but not least, shoes. Irish dancers are now found in far-off lands like Japan and Estonia. Whatever acccounts for Irish "Trad"'s continuing enormous crossover success—does it appeal because it is a return to a simpler time, or remains a dazzling slice of national culture in a blandly homogeneous age?—it certainly keeps growing more popular.

HARPING ON

Ireland is the only country to have a musical instrument as its national emblem. The harp appears on *garda* (police) caps, Irish Euro coins, and government stationery. The original Irish harp was a small, triangular instrument designed to be held on the knee (not the large version of today's concert halls). The harp was first used as a logo for Guiness stout in 1850. The Guinness harp faces right, while the national emblem faces left.

COME AND MEET THOSE DANCING FEET

Ireland was swept off its feet, and its collective feet onto the boards, by the spectacular success of Riverdance. Thanks to that phenomenon, the thunderous dancing, stomping, clacking feet of today's Irish youth have once again taken up the trigger-quick step dances of old and the traditional music of the past.

Before Riverdance, Irish dancing was something schoolchildren performed chiefly for competitions, and sometimes on civic occasions, with their arms rigidly held by their sides (only the legs would move—a holdover from religious teachings that felt that dancing was sinful), and an expression of grave concentration on their faces. Today, it's a big thing for young people and also, due to those glitzy costumes and contests, a very expensive hobby.

Riverdance was a conscious attempt to project a more modern image of Ireland, and central to its roaring success were two American step dancers, Michael Flatley and Jean Butler. Their dazzling innovations reflected their origin in the more flexible American step dance competition world. Before Riverdance, the only options for prize-winning Irish step-dancers were to teach or to retire—now hundreds of dancers are employed worldwide in touring shows inspired by Riverdance, such as Flatley's Celtic Tiger and Butler's Dancing on Dangerous Ground.

SET DANCING

Set dancing is also the name given to social dancing in which four couples face one another in a square in dances based on the French cotillion and the quadrilles. Nearly every town in Ireland once again has dancing at least one evening a week.

STEPS & SETS

Ireland has a long tradition of solo dancing, first introduced by the jigs, reels, and hornpipes that traveling dancing masters taught in the 18th century. Some are performed in hard shoes, with the dancer beating out rhythms on the floor to complement the music, while others are danced with soft shoes to emphasize their graceful, airborne nature. In both cases, the main interest of the dance is in the foot and lower leg. Some solo dances have specific patterns of steps and are only danced to one tune and are known as "set dances"—in some places, set dances are known as table dances because the dancer often jumped up on the table to display his or her skills.

FANCY FOOTWORK

Because there were no accompanying drums, the sound of the feet on wooden floors has always been an important element in Irish dancing. When dancing really took off in the 18th century, many cabins only had earth floors, so the custom was to remove the top half of the half-door, and dance on that. Dancing masters used to display their prowess on fair days by dancing on soapy barrel lids, so they developed the ability to vary their steps in a confined space. From this came the tradition of dancing solos on one spot.

The main interest of
the dance is in the
foot and lower leg

JUST FOLLOW THE SOUND OF THE MUSIC . . .

If you're interested in "Trad" music, the beat of a bodhrán or the tap of a shoe will likely lead you to Galway and County Clare's great folk *fleadhs* (festivals) and pub *seisiuns* (sessions).

THE BIGGEST FLEADH

The biggest festival of all is a three-day event called the All-Ireland finals at Fleadh Cheoil na hÉireann (pronounced flah-kwoil—"festival of music"). The 2010 event was held in Cavan, County Cavan, August 16–22, and was attended by nearly 10,000 musicians and 200,000 visitors, many of them second-generation Irish from overseas. This noncommercial festival of traditional music takes over a whole town, whose pubs become centers for casual music making. The All-Ireland rotates to different towns every year, much to the delight of the pub owners in the chosen town (⊕ www.fleadh2010.ie).

THE ENNIS BLOW-OUT

During the last week in May, the pleasant county town of Ennis hosts the **Fleadh Nua** (⊕ http://fleadhnua.com/), a massive eight-day-long celebration of dancing and song, with concerts, workshops, competitions, and *céilís*. Many of the events are open-air and free, and there is a great festive buzz. Ennis is home to a growing cadre of musicians:

the Custys, Siobhán and Tommy Peoples, flute player Kevin Crawford, and accordion whiz kid Murty Ryan. Check out **Knox's Pub** (⊠ Abbey St. ☎ 065/682–9264) and **Cruise's Bar** (⊠ Abbey St. ☎ 065/684–1800) for lively evening sessions.

TOE-TAPPING IN MILTOWN

Held during the first week in July, the **Willie Clancy Summer School** (⊕ http://www.setdancingnews.net/wcss) is Ireland's biggest traditional music summer school. Classes, lectures, and recitals attract around 1,500 students from 42 countries to this tiny village on the west coast of Clare near Spanish Point. Set dancing is a big draw here, and a surefire way to make friends.

CEOL AGUS RINCE

Ceol (pronounced coil) is the Irish for music. And what always goes with the Irish for music? *Rince* (pronounced rincha), the Irish for dance: Music and Dance: you often see *Ceol agus Rince* on a poster advertising a traditional session or a céili.

A Trad seisiun, Sligo, Co. Sligo, Ireland

Taafe's, Galway

DARLIN' DOOLIN

Doolin, County Clare, is little more than a dot on the map on the west coast of Clare. To traditional musicians its three main pubs— **O'Connor's** (✉ Fisher St. ☎ 065/707–4168 ⊕ www.oconnorspubdoolin.com), **McDermott's** (✉ Lisdoonvarna Rd. ☎ 065/707–4700 ⊕ www.mcdermottspubdoolin.com), and **McGann's** (✉ Lidoonvarna Rd. ☎ 065/707–4133 ⊕ www.esatclear.ie/mcgannsdoolin) are an irresistible magnet, as is the village's legendary charm.

CUCKOOS AND WINKLES

Kinvara, County Galway, is a pretty waterside village with a strong traditional music tradition. During the first weekend in May Kinvara hosts the annual **Cuckoo Fleadh** (✉ Main St. ☎ 091/637–145), a traditional music festival. Resident musicians like De Danann alumni Jackie Daly and Charlie Piggott play regularly at the town's **Winkles Hotel** (✉ The Square ☎ 091/637–137). Back in 1989, a young accordion player got together with her friends for a casual recording session. The resulting album, *Sharon Shannon*, became the most successful Trad-music recording ever released.

GIGGING IN GALWAY

Galway has nurtured some of the most durable names in Irish music: Dé Danann, Arcady, singers Dolores and Seán Keane, and the mercurial accordion genius, Mairtìn O'Connor. Seán Ryan, master of the tin whistle, has been playing every Sunday at **The**

Crane Bar (✉ 2 Sea Rd. ☎ 091/587–419) since the 1980s. **Áras na Gael** (✉ 45 Sráid Dominic ☎ 091/567824) has traditional Irish music sessions every day at 5:30 and 10 PM. **Monroe's Tavern** (✉ Dominick St. ☎ 091/583–397) has traditional music every night from 9:30 PM, and invites you to join the locals in set dancing. There is also plenty of music to be found at old favorites in the city center like **Tigh Neachtain** (✉ 17 Cross St. ☎ 091/568–820), **Taaffe's** (✉ 19 Shop St. ☎ 091/564–066), and **An Pucan** (✉ 11 Forster St. ☎ 091/561–528). **The Bard's Den** (✉ Main St. ☎ 091/41042) in Letterfrack, Co. Galway, is noted for its Trad sessions. **Molloy's Bar** (✉ Bridge St. ☎ 098/26655) in Westport, Co. Mayo, is owned by Matt Molloy, flute player of the Chieftains, and is renowned for its great sessions.

■ TIP➔ For details, log on to www.comhaltas.com or get a copy of the "trad" bible, Walton's Guide to Irish Music (www.waltonmusic.com).

GOOD BEHAVIOR

If you happen on a pub session there are a few ground rules. Don't talk during the solo, and don't stare at the singer; most people look at the floor. Buy the musicians a drink if it's a small session, and if at all possible, have a party piece to contribute yourself. It's the gesture that counts.

FIDDLING AROUND

Irish Traditional music is very much the music of the people, played on relatively simple, portable instruments: fiddle, flute, tin whistle, accordion, handheld drum, and, recent additions, guitar or banjo.

UILLEANN PIPES

The uilleann (pronounced "illun") pipes, literally "elbow" pipes, are a quieter indoor version of bagpipes. The player sits while playing with a bag under one arm, the bellows under the other, and the "chanter," which plays the melody, on the thigh. A temperamental instrument, it can be heartrenderingly beautiful in the hands of a master like Liam O'Flynn or Paddy Keenan of the Bothy Band.

FIDDLE

The classical violin all but in name, this is the most popular instrument in Trad music for its singing, swooping versatility, its portability, and its relative affordability. Local fiddle styles still persist, especially in Donegal, Sligo, and the Sliabh Luachra region of Cork and Kerry and virtuosos such as Frankie Gavin of Dé Dannan, Martin Hayes, Tommy Peoples, and Liz Doherty are famed for their rhythm, color, and ornamentation.

SQUEEZE-BOXES & ACCORDIONS

Squeeze-box is a generic term for a variety of melodeons, accordions, and concertinas. The concertina is a small, hexagonal-shaped button-key instrument. The simplest accordion is the one-row button accordion, usually called a melodeon. Styles of playing can vary enormously. Sharon Shannon is rooted in the highly rhythmic East Clare style but can veer into swing and Cajun styles as she plays her wildly energetic dance music.

FLUTES & WHISTLE

The tin whistle is the ideal beginner's instrument, but be sure to buy one in the key of D. It is still called the penny whistle because it costs so little to buy. But the flute used in Irish music is usually a simple wooden flute—hear it at its best in the hands of Matt Molloy and Paddy Moloney of the Chieftains, Mary Bergin, and Olean Masterson.

BODHRÁN

The Bodhrán (pronounced "bow-rawn") is a simple goat's skin drum played with the back of the hand or a small wooden stick. When played well, by Mel Mercier, John Joe Kelly, or Tommy Hayes, it makes an exciting addition to the running rhythms of Trad music. They make it look easy, but in the hands of an untrained amateur, a badly played bodhrán can wreck a session.

HAPPY LISTENING!

Olcan Masterson, on the whistle

SEÁN Ó RIADA The father of "modern" Trad music, this composer and visionary Irish language enthusiast (1931–71)—noted for his film score *Míse Éire* and his Irish language *Mass Cúil Aodha*—established the prototype traditional Irish group, Ceoltóiríc Chualann, in 1963, who evolved into the Chieftains.

DÉ DANNAN This famed group grew from regular sessions in Hughe's bar in Spiddal, Co. Galway, in 1974. Brilliant fiddle and flute player Frankie Gavin, bouzouki whiz Alec Finn, banjo master Carlie Piggot, and Johnny "Ringo" McDonagh on bodhrán were joined by singers Dolores Keane, Mary Black, and Maura O'Connell (all now solo artists). *Dé Dannan* (1975) and *Mist-Covered Mountain* (1980) are their timeless evocations of the West of Ireland.

THE CHIEFTAINS If you've seen a poster of Irish musicians wearing unhip cardigans, baggy trousers, and bad haircuts, it was probably the Chieftains, who went professional in 1975. Outstanding musicians, they include uilleann-piper Paddy Moloney, flute player Matt Molloy, harper Derek Bell (recently deceased), and Seán Keane and Martin Fay (fiddlers). Any of their famous 35 albums are worth owning.

PLANXTY The word *planxty* means a lively tune (without words) written to honor a patron, but it is now forever associated with a "supergroup" formed in 1972 by singer Christy Moore, with Dónal Lunny, Andy Irvine, and Liam O'Flynn. Their haunting debut album, *Planxty* (1972), is a must. Reincarnated in the later '70s as The Bothy Band, their 1975 debut album remains a classic.

ALTAN Donegal-born husband-and-wife duo, Frankie Kennedy on flute and Máiréead Mhaonaight (fiddle and vocals), showcase the special Donegal way with fiddle and flute.

ANÚNA This vocal and instrumental ensemble, founded in the 1990s, represents the mys-tical, spiritual aspect of Celtic music, and is widely known through performances with the original Riverdance production. *Anúna* (1993), their first album, is still their best.

KILA Touted by the under-30s to be the future of Irish music, this group shows African percussion, Andean flute, and Eastern European folk music among the influences on their debut album, *Tóg É Go Bog É*—roughly translated as "The Living is Easy."

Altan

8

IN FOCUS GAEL FORCE

SPORTS AND THE OUTDOORS

BICYCLING

Bike Hire Ireland. Prebook your bike of choice from a good range if you have strong preferences, then just go. Or opt for a self-guided tour: the company has handy drop-off points in Connemara, the Burren, and Kerry. ⊠ *Unit 1, West Side Business Centre, Galway City, Co. Galway* ☎ *091/525–007* ⊕ *www.bikehireireland.com.*

FISHING

Galway City is the gateway to Connemara, and Connemara is the place to fish.

Duffy's Fishing. They sell a good range of clothing for anglers, and tackle, too. ⊠ *5 Mainguard St., Center, Galway City, Co. Galway* ☎ *53/9156–2367* ⊕ *www.shoot.ie.*

Freeny's Sports. You can get fishing licenses, tackle, and bait, and arrange to hire a traditional fly-fishing guide or book a sea-angling trip at Freeny's Sports. ⊠ *19–23 High St., Center, Galway City, Co. Galway* ☎ *091/568–794.*

GOLF

Galway Bay Golf Resort. An 18-hole parkland course near the village of Renville, 14 km (8½ miles) from the city, Galway Bay Golf Resort is on the shores of Galway Bay, opposite the city, and was designed by former Ryder Cup and World Cup golfer, Christy O'Connor Jr. The Atlantic Ocean forms a dramatic backdrop to a course featuring mature trees, concealed bunkers, and highly praised putting surfaces. ⊠ *Renville, Oranmore, Co. Galway* ☎ *091/790–500* ⊕ *www.galwaybaygolfresort.com* ⚑ *Greens fees: Mon.–Thurs. €35, Fri. €30 (€25 via website), Sat. and Sun. €45* ⚑ *18 holes. Yardage 7,308. Par 72. Practice area, caddies, club hire, caddy carts, buggies, catering* ⊙ *Visitors daily (some restrictions).*

Galway Golf Club. Galway Golf Club was established in 1895, and moved to its present location in suburban Salthill in 1925. At that point it was redesigned by course architect Alister McKenzie, who was also responsible for Augusta, home of the U.S. Masters. It has been the home base of two famous Irish pros, Christy O'Connor Sr., and his nephew, Christy O'Connor Jr. In spite of its proximity to the city, there are excellent views of Galway Bay, the Burren, and the Aran Islands. It has an abundance of trees, prickly gorse bushes in the rough, and some tricky fairways that run close to the ocean. ⊠ *Blackrock, Salthill, Galway City, Co. Galway* ☎ *091/522–033* ⊕ *www.galwaygolf.com* ⚑ *Greens fees: €30 year-round, advance booking essential.* ⚑ *18 holes. Yardage 2,995 (Championship). Par 70. Practice area, caddies, carts, buggies, catering* ⊙ *Visitors: Mon. and Tues.–Sat., some restrictions.*

RIVER CRUISING

Corrib Princess. A lovely way to spend a fine afternoon is to take a Corrib Cruise from Wood Quay, behind the Town Hall Theatre, at the Rowing Club; it lasts 1½ hours and travels 8 km (5 miles) up the River Corrib and about 6 km (4 miles) around Lough Corrib. There's a bar on board, tea and coffee, and a commentary. The trip costs €14, and boats depart daily at 2:30 and 4:30 from May through September, with an additional departure at 12:30 July through August. You can also rent the boat for an evening. ☎ *091/592–447* ⊕ *www.corribprincess.ie.*

SHOPPING

ANTIQUES

Tempo Antiques. With an interesting collection of small antiques, Tempo also stocks jewelry, porcelain, and other small collectibles. ⊠ *9 Cross St., Center, Galway City, Co. Galway* ☎ *091/562–282* ⊕ *www. tempoantiques.com.*

Treasure Chest. Browse to your heart's content here for china, crystal, gifts, and classic clothing. ⊠ *William St., 31–33 William St., Center, Galway City, Co. Galway* ☎ *091/563–862* ⊕ *www.treasurechest.ie/ isapi/isapi.dll.*

BOOKS

Charlie Byrne's Bookshop. Book lovers should allow at least one hour for browsing at Charlie Byrne's, which not only sells a large, varied selection of new and used books and remainders but also has a wonderful emphasis on Irish interest. ⊠ *Middle St., Center, Galway City, Co. Galway* ☎ *091/561–766.*

CLOTHING

Blarney Woollen Mills. A great place for Irish souvenirs and clothing, Blarney is especially known for their casual Faller & Brown designer line. ⊠ *Merchants St., Center, Galway City, Co. Galway* ☎ *091/539–510.*

Faller's Sweater Shop. The choicest selection of Irish-made sweaters can be found here, and all competitively priced. ⊠ *25 High St., Center, Galway City, Co. Galway* ☎ *091/564–833.*

Galway Hat Shop. Not surprisingly, the home town of milliner-to-the-stars, Philip Treacey, has an excellent hat shop, with stock ranging from ladies' high fashion to men's cloth caps. ⊠ *Corbett Court, Eyre Square Shopping Centre, Eyre Square, Center, Galway City, Co. Galway* ☎ *091/561–052.*

O'Máille's. In addition to classically tailored clothing, O'Máille's is popular for its selection of Aran sweaters and handwoven tweeds. ⊠ *16 High St., Center, Galway City, Co. Galway* ☎ *091/562–696.*

CRAFTS AND GIFTS

Cloon Keen Atelier. A lovely little boutique stocked beautifully with packaged perfumes and candles, all made locally by dedicated artisans. ⊠ *Kirwan's Land, Center, Galway City, Co. Galway* ☎ *091/565–736.*

Galway Irish Crystal. A factory outlet on the city's ring road, Galway Irish Crystal sells hand-cut Irish glass, Belleek Pottery, and other fine porcelain. ⊠ *Dublin Rd., Merlin Park, Co. Galway* ☎ *091/757–311* ⊕ *www.galwaycrystal.ie.*

★ **Judy Greene.** Ceramics by Judy Greene—a local potter specializing in handthrown ceramics depicting Irish flora and landscape—and others can be found in this two-story treasure trove. ⊠ *Kirwan's La., Center, Galway City, Co. Galway* ☎ *091/561–753.*

Kilkenny Shop. Synonymous with good modern design in Ireland, the Kilkenny Shop stocks the best ceramics, crystal, leatherware, clothing, and other craft items from around the country. ⊠ *6–7 High St., Center, Galway City, Co. Galway* ☎ *091/566–110* ⊕ *www.kilkennyshop.com.*

Meadows & Byrne. A favorite with locals, and a great resource for visitors, Meadows & Byrne carries the best in modern Irish and international household items. ⊠ *Merchants St., Center, Galway City, Co. Galway* ☎ *091/567–776.*

FOOD

Sheridan's Cheesemongers. Together, Seamus and Kevin Sheridan know all of Ireland's artisan cheese makers personally and stock the widest possible range of delectable cheeses, complemented by charcuterie (mainly Italian). The wineshop upstairs will complete your picnic. ⊠ *16 Churchyard St., Center, Galway City, Co. Galway* ☎ *091/564–829* ⊕ *www. sheridanscheesemongers.com.*

JEWELRY

Cobwebs. Phyllis MacNamara's cute two-story boutique is filled with an irresistible selection of antique jewelry (real and costume) and collectibles for men and women, all with a witty twist. ⊠ *7 Quay St., Spanish Arch, Galway City, Co. Galway* ☎ *091/564–388* ⊕ *www.cobwebs.ie.*

Thomas Dillon's. Dating from 1750, Thomas Dillon's claims to be the original maker of Galway's famous Claddagh ring. In the back of the shop there's a small but interesting display of antique Claddagh rings and old Galway memorabilia. ⊠ *1 Quay St., Spanish Arch, Galway City, Co. Galway* ☎ *091/566–365* ⊕ *www.claddaghring.ie.*

MALLS

Eyre Square Shopping Centre. On the southwest side of Eyre Square and imaginatively designed to incorporate parts of the old town walls, the Eyre Square Shopping Centre is a good spot to pick up moderately priced clothing and household goods. ☎ *915/68302* ⊕ *www. eyresquarecentre.com.*

Galway Shopping Centre. This spacious indoor mall features more than 60 outlets just 10 minutes' walk from Eyre Square with ample parking. ⊠ *Headford Rd., Galway City, Co. Galway* ☎ *35/3156–1803* ⊕ *www. galwaysc.com/.*

MUSIC

Back2Music. This shop specializes in traditional Irish musical instruments, including the handheld drum, the *bodhrán* (pronounced baurawn). ⊠ *30 Upper Abbeygate St., Center, Galway City, Co. Galway* ☎ *091/565–272.*

Kieran Moloney. A display case of the craft of Irish luthiers, this lovely shop stocks acoustic stringed instruments and some wind instruments, including Irish hand-made Uillean pipes, and, more tempting for the traveler, pocket-size tin whistles. ⊠ *Olde Malt Arcade, 17 High St., Center, Galway City, Co. Galway* ☎ *091/566–488.*

P. Powell and Sons. The knowledgeable staff here can advise shoppers on buying traditional Irish musical instruments and CDs. ⊠ *The Four Corners, William St., Center, Galway City, Co. Galway* ☎ *091/562–295.*

THE OILEÁIN ÁRAINN (ARAN ISLANDS)

No one knows for certain when the Aran Islands—Inis Mór (Inishmore), Inis Meáin (Inishmaan), and Inis Oirr (Inisheer)—were first inhabited, but judging from the number of Bronze Age and Iron Age forts found here (especially on Inis Mór), 3000 BC is a safe guess. Why wandering nomads in deerskin jerkins would be attracted to these barren islets remains a greater mystery, not least because fresh water and farmable land were (and still are) scarce commodities. Remote western outposts of the ancient province of Connaught (though they are not the country's westernmost points; that honor belongs to the Blasket Islands), these three islands were once as barren as the limestone pavements of the Burren, of which they are a continuation.

> ## ISLAND NIGHTS
>
> To appreciate the fierce loneliness of the Aran Islands you must spend the night on one. Because all the islands, especially Inishmore, crawl with day-trippers, it's difficult to let their rugged beauty sink into your soul until 10 pm, when the sky is dark and the pubs fill with the acrid smell of peat smoke and Guinness. Once the day-trippers clear out, the islands' stunningly fierce and brooding beauty is disturbed only by the "baa" of the sheep and the incessant rush of the wind.

Today, the land is parceled into small, human-made fields surrounded by stone walls: centuries of erosion, generations of backbreaking labor, sheep, horses, and their attendant tons of manure have finally transformed this rocky wasteland into reasonably productive cropland.

While traditional Irish culture fights a rear-guard battle on the mainland, the islanders continue to preserve as best as they can a culture going back generations. Still, the Irish-speaking inhabitants enjoy a daily air service to Galway (subsidized by the government), motorized curraghs, satellite TV, and all the usual modern home conveniences. Yet they have retained a distinctness from mainlanders, preferring simple home decor, very plain food, and tightly knit communities, like the hardy fishing and farming folk from whom they are descended. Crime is virtually unknown in these parts; at your B&B, you'll likely find no locks on the guest-room doors, and the front-door latch will be left open. Many islanders have sampled life in Dublin or cities abroad but have returned to raise families, keeping the population stable at around 1,200. Tourists now flock here to see the ancient sights and savor the spectacular views: the uninterrupted expanse of the Atlantic on the western horizon; the Connemara coast and its Twelve Bens to the northeast; and County Clare's Burren and the Cliffs of Moher to the southeast.

There's a small hotel on Inisheer and one on Inishmore, but there's no shortage of guesthouses and B&Bs, mostly in simple family homes. The best way to book is through the Galway City TIO. Each island has at least one wine-licensed restaurant serving plain home cooking. Most B&Bs will provide a packed lunch and an evening meal (called high tea) on request. For general information about visiting the Aran Islands and useful links, try the islands' official website (⊕ *www.aranislands.ie*).

Aran Rediscovered

During the 1800s, the islands, wracked by famine and mass emigration, were virtually forgotten by mainland Ireland. At the turn of the 20th century, however, the books of J. M. Synge (1871–1909)—who learned Irish on Inishmaan and wrote about its people in his famous play *Riders to the Sea*—prompted Gaelic revivalists to study and document this isolated bastion of Irish culture. To this day, Synge's travel book *The Aran Islands,* first published in 1907, and reissued by Penguin with a brilliant introduction by artist and mapmaker Tim Robinson in 1992, remains the best book ever written about the islands. Liam O'Flaherty became one of the most famous sons of Inishmore through his novels, such as *Famine.* And in 1934, American director Robert Flaherty filmed his classic documentary *Man of Aran* on Inishmore, recording the islanders' dramatic battles with sea and storm, and bringing the islands into the world spotlight. The film is still highly esteemed by the islanders, and there are frequent showings on Inishmore during the summer months. Flaherty, incidentally, continues to be a common surname on the islands; it is hard to visit the islands *without* meeting a Flaherty.

GETTING HERE AND AROUND

The best place to book your trip to the Aran Islands is at the Galway Tourist Information Office.

Decide between a short flight, a 20-minute boat ride on a high-speed catamaran, or an hour-long trip on comfortable ferries.

Aer Arran Islands offers 10-minute flights to the Aran Islands. The fare is €45 round-trip, leaving from Connemara Airport near Inverin, 30 km (19 miles) west of Galway.

The majority of boats for the Aran Islands leave from Ros an Mhil (Rossaveale), 37 km (23 miles) west of Galway City. (You can also reach the islands from Doolin in County Clare.) Park at Ros an Mhil, or book a shuttle bus from the city when buying your ticket. There are at least two sailings a day, and four or more in high season, timed to facilitate day trips. Ask when boarding about interisland ferries if you intend to visit more than one island. Inishmore, the biggest island, is the only one with organized transport. Book a tour or taxi in advance (through the TIO in Galway), or hire a bicycle or pony and trap on landing. Galway-based Lally Tours sells a bus-and-ferry package.

Transportation Contacts **Aer Arann Islands** ☎ *091/593–034* ⊕ *www.aerarannislands.ie.* **Aran Bike Hire** ✉ *Kilronan Pier, Inishmore* ☎ *099/61132.* **Galway Discover Ireland Centre.** Galway City's tourist office is one of the best places to go for ferry tickets to Aran Islands. ✉ *Forster St., Eyre Sq., Galway City, Co. Galway* ☎ *091/537–700* ⊕ *www.discoverireland.ie/places-to-vist/galway.* **Noel Mahon Luxury Tours** ✉ *Killeany, Kilronan, Inishmore* ☎ *087/788–2775* ⊕ *www.tourbusaranislands.com.*

As you arrive by plane over the Aran Islands, their famous stone-wall fences—built by medieval farmers to clear lands for farms—come into view.

INIS MÓR (INISHMORE)

31 km (18 miles) southwest of Salthill docks, 48 km (30 miles) west of Galway Docks.

★ With a population of 900, Inis Mór is the largest of the islands and the closest to the Connemara coast. It's also the most commercialized, its appeal slightly diminished by road traffic.

In summer, ferries arriving at Cill Rónáin (Kilronan), Inis Mór's main village and port, are met by minibuses and pony-and-cart drivers, all eager to show visitors "the sights." More than 8 km (5 miles) long and about 3 km (2 miles) wide at most points, with an area of 7,640 acres, the island is just a little too large to explore comfortably on foot in a day. The best way to see it is really by bicycle; bring your own or rent one from one of the vendors operating near the quay.

GETTING HERE AND AROUND

If you are lucky enough to stay overnight on Inishmore island, try to get away from the crowds of day-trippers in the daytime, who clog up the road between Kilronan and Dún Aengus from 11 am to about 6 pm. Head for the less frequented west of the island, visiting Dún Dúchathair, a dramatically sited promontory fort (freely accessible), only slightly less impressive than Dún Aengus, or walk the secluded east coast. ■TIP→ Day-trippers: leave your luggage at Inishmore's Tourist Office (€1 per bag), or with the outfit that you are renting your bike from while you explore the island.

ESSENTIALS

Visitor Information Oileáin Árainn (Aran Islands)–Inis Mór (Inishmore) Tourist Office ⊠ *Cill Ronáin [Kilronan], Co. Galway* ☎ *099/61263* ⊕ *www.aranislands.ie.*

EXPLORING

Dún Aengus. Even if you have only a few hours to explore Inis Mór, rent a bike (next to the pier) and head straight for Dún Aengus, one of the finest prehistoric monuments in Europe, dating from about 2000 BC. Spectacularly set on the edge

> **WORD OF MOUTH**
>
> "In my opinion, the visit to Dún Aengus made the trip to Ireland worthwhile. It is a stunningly beautiful fort situated on cliffs that drop off dramatically into the Atlantic Ocean. The views are exhilarating. I can't begin to imagine how beautiful it would be on a sunny day."
>
> —Desiderado

of a 300-foot-tall cliff overlooking a sheer drop, the fort has defenses consisting of three rows of concentric circles. Whom the builders were defending themselves against is a matter of conjecture. From the innermost rampart there's a great view of the island and the Connemara coast. In order to protect this fragile monument from erosion, you should approach it only through the visitor center, which gives access to a 1-km (½-mile) uphill walk over uneven terrain—wear sturdy footwear. ⊠ *7 km (4 miles) west of Cill Ronáin (Kilronan), Kilmurvey* ☎ *099/61008* ⊕ *www.heritageireland.ie/en/West/DunAonghasa/* ⊠ *€3* ⊙ *Mar.–Oct., daily 10–6; Nov.–Feb., daily 10–4.*

WHERE TO STAY

For expanded hotel reviews, visit Fodors.com.

$$
B&B/INN
⊞ **Ard Einne Guesthouse.** Almost every window at this B&B on Inishmore looks out to the sea, making it the perfect place to de-stress. **Pros:** great location for getting away from it all; walking distance to pubs (half a mile) and restaurants (a mile and a half). **Cons:** one of the island's biggest guesthouses, thoroughly modernized; no elevator. **TripAdvisor:** "a taste of Aran," "clean and friendly," "very restful." $ *Rooms from: €120* ⊠ *Cill Ronáin (Kilronan), Co. Galway* ☎ *099/61126* ⊕ *www.ardeinne.com* ↝ *8 rooms* ⊙ *Closed Nov.–Jan.* ⦿ *Breakfast.*

NIGHTLIFE AND THE ARTS

Joe Mac's. Located right off the pier, Joe Mac's is a good place for a pint while waiting for the ferry home. ⊠ *Cill Ronáin (Kilronan)* ☎ *099/61248.*

Joe Watty's. This long-time favorite is a good bet for traditional music virtually every night in summer. ⊠ *Main Rd., Cill Ronáin (Kilronan)* ☎ *099/20892.*

Ostán Oileáin Árainn. Fans-in-the-know say this is the place to head for the best in traditional music on the Aran Islands. ⊠ *Cill Ronáin (Kilronan)* ☎ *099/61104.*

INIS MEÁIN (INISHMAAN)

3 km (2 miles) east of Inis Mór (Inishmore).

The middle island in both size and location, Inis Meáin has a population of about 300 and can be comfortably explored on foot.

EXPLORING

In fact, you have no alternative if you want to reach the island's major antiquities: **Dún Conor (Conor Fort)**, a smaller version of Dún Aengus; the ruins of two **early Christian churches**; and a chamber tomb known as the **Bed of Diarmuid and Grainne**, dating from about 2000 BC. You can also take wonderful cliff walks above secluded coves.

It's on Inishmaan that the traditional Aran lifestyle is most evident. Most islanders still don hand-knitted Aran sweaters, though nowadays they wear them with jeans and sneakers.

SHOPPING

Inis Meáin Knitting. Providing much needed local employment, Inis Meáin Knitting is a young company producing quality knitwear in luxury fibers for the international market, including Liberty of London, Barneys New York, and Bergdorf Goodman. The factory showroom has an extensive selection of garments at discount prices. To get here from the pier, walk five minutes due west. ⊠ *Carrown Lisheen* ☏ *099/73009.*

INIS OIRR (INISHEER)

4 km (2½ miles) east of Inis Meáin (Inishmaan), 8 km (5 miles) northwest of Doolin docks.

The smallest and flattest of the islands, Inis Oirr can be explored on foot in an afternoon, though if the weather is fine you may be tempted to linger on the long, sandy beach between the quay and the airfield. Only one stretch of road, about 500 yards long, links the airfield and the sole village.

"The back of the island," as Inis Oirr's uninhabited side facing the Atlantic is called, has no beaches, but people swim off the rocks. It's worth making a circuit of the island to get a sense of its utter tranquility. A maze of footpaths runs between the high stone walls that divide the fields, which are so small that they can support only one cow each, or two to three sheep.

EXPLORING

Church of Kevin. Signposted to the southeast of the quay, the Church of Kevin is a small, early Christian church that gets buried in sand by storms every winter. Each year the islanders dig it out of the sand for the celebration of St. Kevin's Day on June 14.

O'Brien's Castle. A pleasant walk through the village takes you up to this ruined 15th-century tower on top of a rocky hill—the only hill on the island.

8

WHERE TO STAY

For expanded hotel reviews, visit Fodors.com.

$$ ▦ **Hotel Inisheer.** A pleasant, modern
HOTEL   low-rise in the middle of the island's only village, a few minutes' walk from the quay and the airstrip, this simple, whitewashed building with a slate roof and half-slate walls has bright, plainly furnished rooms, with pine-frame beds, pine floors, and white bed linen. **Pros:** island's only all-in-one destination, with pub and restaurant; good location between pier and airstrip; very clean. **Cons:** basic standard of comfort: certainly no frills; very busy July and August. **TripAdvisor:** "perfect spot," "friendly staff and a good breakfast," "nice relaxing stay." ⑤ *Rooms from: €130* ✉ *Lurgan Village, Co. Galway* ☎ *099/75020* ⌂ *14 rooms* ⊘ *Closed Oct.–Mar.* ⎟⊙⎟ *Breakfast.*

EXTRA CREDIT

In summer, Inis Oírr's population of 300 is augmented by high school students from all over Ireland attending the Gaeltacht, or Irish-language, school.

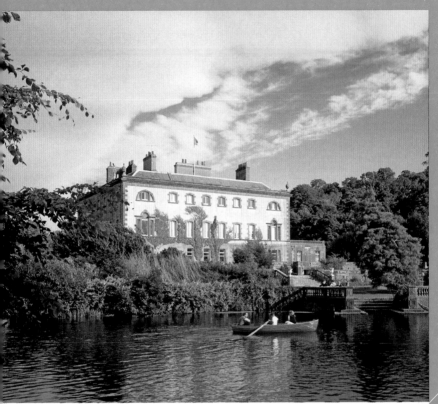

Connemara and County Mayo

INCLUDING COUNTIES GALWAY AND MAYO

WORD OF MOUTH

"We drove to Connemara National Park, Kylemore Abbey, and Ashford Castle our last full day in Ireland. Connemara was gorgeous. We only did the 45-minute hike, but when we go back we plan on doing the full shebang."

—Julies

WELCOME TO CONNEMARA AND COUNTY MAYO

TOP REASONS TO GO

★ **Captivating Connemara:** An almost uninhabited landscape of misty bogland, studded with deep blue lakes under huge Atlantic skies: painters have strived for generations to capture the ever-changing light.

★ **Cong à la Hollywood:** Fetching ivy-covered thatched cottages—including one commemorating the making of the archetypal "Irish" movie *The Quiet Man*—beside a ruined medieval monastery contrast with the baronial splendor of Ashford Castle, one of Ireland's most luxurious hotels.

★ **Clifden and the Sky Road:** Walk the Sky Road to take in its breathtaking scenery—sea views on one side, the Twelve Bens Mountains on the other—to the compact village of Clifden, the liveliest spot for miles around.

★ **Wordly Westport:** An engagingly old-fashioned country town, Westport has an octagonal market square that dates from the 18th century and a quayside (on Clew Bay) that offers spectacular Atlantic sunsets.

1 Connemara. The area west of Maam Cross and out to the rocky coast is the famed Connemara, and consists mainly of rugged, sparsely inhabited hills, enhanced by the ever-changing light of the Atlantic weather, with rainbows every time a shower crosses the sun. Get up close to a bog among the displays at the visitor center in Letterfrack, the heart of the 5,000-acre national park, to understand the fragile ecology of the peat lands. Then take a hike to explore the territory.

GETTING ORIENTED

With the most westerly seaboard in Europe, this region remains a place apart—the most Irish part of Ireland. While just to the west and north of hip Galway City, this area is famed for its wild and rural character. Connemara sits in the northwest corner of County Galway. County Mayo is Ireland's third-largest county, with coast on three of its four sides, and the River Moy and the huge expanse of Lough Conn and Lough Cullin on the fourth. Bright lights are to be found in Clifden and Westport, both lively small towns of great charm.

9

2 County Mayo. Outside the main towns—Castlebar and Westport—the rest of the county has long-empty roads leading to isolated shorelines, stunning vistas from remote peaks, and silent ghostly valleys that stretch along for miles. Apart from Achill Island and Westport, this is a relatively undeveloped destination, where the natives still provide a glimpse of the Ireland of old, and there is always time for a long chat.

HIKING THE WEST

More and more travelers are discovering that Ireland's western regions are hiking heaven. In fact, hikes or guided walks through Connemara or County Mayo are the best ways to explore these territories at first hand, or rather, foot.

(above) Eco-hiking in spectacular Connemara National Park; (right, top) Many "way-marked" hikes go past beautiful lakes like Lough Corrib; (right, bottom) Stop and smell the heather.

Why hike the West? It has some of the finest rugged scenery and dramatic indented coastline in all Ireland. In Connemara serried ranks of heather-clad mountains, interspersed with bright blue lakes, beckon to the walker as dramatic cloud formations scud across huge Atlantic skies. In County Mayo, the huge conical bulk of Croaghpatrick spectacularly looms above Clew Bar. Or what about earning some blisters along the black waters of Killary Fjord, set in the shadow of Mweelrea Mountain? The attraction lies in the terrific views nearly everywhere you look. Coastal views alternate with mountain vistas, often topped by a perfect rainbow. A daily highlight is the spectacular sunset over the Atlantic, at its biggest and best in late August.

WHAT TO BUY HERE

Walkers on way-marked trails are advised to buy an Ordnance Survey map of the area, which are sold locally. Most tourist offices also have free maps of less ambitious walks on roads and local footpaths. Because of the wind, most Irish walkers wear knitted or fleece hats, often decorated with a Guinness logo or a woolly sheep: shop around locally.

Hiking buffs will be glad to know that the last decade has seen the completion of various "way-marked" (signposted) walking routes, which can be sampled in easy one- or two-hour "loops," or, for more serious walkers, made the focus of a visit.

TOP HIKING DESTINATIONS

The Western Way's County Galway section extends from Oughterard on Lough Corrib through the mountains of Connemara to Leenane on Killary Harbour, a distance of 50 km (30 miles). Its 177-km (110-mile) County Mayo section, known as the Western Way (Mayo), continues past Killary Harbour to Westport on Clew Bay to the Ox Mountains east of Ballina. This trail should be the first choice of serious walkers, as it includes some of the finest mountain and coastal scenery in Ireland. The Great Western Greenway is a traffic-free 18-km (11-mile) cycling and walking trail that follows the line of Mayo's Newport–Mulranny Railway (closed since 1937) along the northern shore of Clew Bay, and offers scenic walking and cycling with very few inclines, suitable for moderately fit people. Another perfect hiking destination is Connemara National Park, which consists of some 5,000 acres of untamed mountain wilderness in and around the Twelve Bens peaks. Allow an hour or two to hike the Diamond Hill Loop, along 7 km (4 miles) of gravel

tracks and paved mountain paths, to a 1,493-foot peak, with a 360-degree vista taking in the distant sea, the turrets of Kylemore Abbey, and the higher peaks in the south. The nearby visitor center (March–October, free) has displays on the flora, fauna, and geology of Connemara.

WALKING IN COMPANY

Walking festivals are highly popular. Achill Island in County Mayo hosts the **Achill Walks Festival** (⊕ *www. achilltourism.com*) in March, to tempt people out again after the long dark winter, while Castlebar, in inland Mayo, has an **International Four Days Walks Festival** (⊕ *www.castlebar4dayswalks. com*) in early July.

BRING WITH YOU

You cannot hike Connemara and Mayo in sneakers, due to the combination of bog, rocky terrain, and frequent showers. Bring a pair of waterproof hiking boots, a lightweight waterproof rainsuit (preferably breathable), or at the very least waterproof boots, and a day pack to carry them in. A lightweight fleece over a T-shirt gives enough protection from the wind in summer.

9

Updated by Alannah Hopkin

This most distinct area of Ireland has always been one of contrasts—ancient history, sacred and savage; culture and literature, illuminating and unique; yesteryear and today, all in one memorable package. While the bustling town of Westport has assumed the identity of the ultrahip destination of a younger, newer, more confident Ireland, the surrounding countryside still provides endless fodder for the "rugged and rural" Irish stereotype.

This is a landscape where the thundering Atlantic forms the pounding backbeat to the most westerly seaboard in Europe, one richly endowed with magnificent vistas: Connemara's combination of rugged coastline, mountains, moorland, and lakes; the distinctive conelike shape of Croaghpatrick, towering over the 365 islands of Clew Bay, and the rippling waters of Lough Corrib, Lough Conn, and many smaller lakes. The Irish people are well aware of what a jewel they have in the largely unspoiled wilderness, grazed by sheep and herds of wild ponies, that is the 5,000-acre Connemara National Park, the result of a successful lobby for landscape preservation. Peat lands, or bogs as they are called around here, are at last being valued for their unique botanical character.

Time seems to have a different value out here, as if the 21st century had never begun. It is still not unusual to be stuck behind two cars parked on either side of the white line, drivers' windows open while local news is exchanged, and the drivers oblivious to your revving engine behind them. Unlike most of Ireland where the marks of Viking, Norman, and English invaders blotted out much of the rich heritage of the ancient Irish kingdoms, these western counties retained, by virtue of their remoteness, those essential Celtic characteristics of rebellion and individuality, and the accompanying graces of unstinting hospitality and courtly good manners. These traits survive, despite the purges of Cromwell's English armies and the all-pervasive trauma of the Great Famine (1845–49). That era started a tradition of emigration that continued to deprive the area of the majority of its youth well into the 1960s. Those who remained worked hard to eke a living from the produce of the rocky seashore and the harsh mountain territory. Where today's visitor, fleeing the stress and constant chatter of urban living, finds solace and romantic peacefulness in the emptiness of the area, its low population is also a reminder of how hard it is to make a living out in rocky territory.

These unspoiled regions possess a spirit that has always spoken to the hidden poet within all who travel here. Images of spectacular red sunsets lingering over the Atlantic, that shocking lapis-lazuli blue of your first Connemara *lough*, and the fleeting moments when the way ahead was framed by a completely semicircular rainbow will likely haunt your memory long after you leave. As will the ancient whispers, cries, and melodies carried on the Connemara breeze. Here is where the magic lies.

CONNEMARA AND COUNTY MAYO PLANNER

WHEN TO GO
There is a local saying in the Westport area: if you can't see the summit of Croaghpatrick, then it is raining; if you can see it, it is about to rain. Avoid visiting between November and February, when many places close for the winter and the days are short and overcast. In fact, you could have your umbrellas out constantly during all times but the warmest months, July and August, when the average temperatures are around 15°C (60°F).

PLANNING YOUR TIME
Visitors are often geared to a faster pace, but they should allow at least two days for exploring the region, four to six days if you intend to do some serious hiking or cycling, take a boat trip on Lough Corrib, visit Clare Island, and enjoy the village (and pub) life of Clifden and Westport. Although distances between sights are not great, you may want to take scenic—meaning slower—national secondary routes. Covering 80 to 112 km (50 to 70 miles) per day on these roads is a comfortable target.

If you love the outdoors, dramatic scenery, empty roads, and deserted coves, then you'll be in heaven in Connemara and Mayo. If you're a city lover, and tend to fade without daily doses of caffeine and retail therapy, then base yourself in Clifden for the first night, where there is coffee aplenty, and the shopping is surprisingly good for a very small town (Irish designer wear, locally made tweed, traditional hand-knits, and wackier hand-crafted knitwear).

IF YOU HAVE 3 DAYS
Allow a full day to meander slowly from Galway City to Clifden, perhaps stopping in Oughterard to take a boat trip to Cong for a little Quiet (Man) time, or climbing the slopes of the heather-clad mountains. Next morning, hire a Connemara pony, or take a stroll along the Sky Road before heading to the Connemara National Park in Letterfrack. A side trip to Renvyle to enjoy the view is worth it in clear weather.

Spend the night in the Letterfrack area, then take in Kylemore Abbey next day, and push on to Killary Harbour where you can take a boat trip on Ireland's only fjord. Drive the scenic Doolough Valley to Westport for your third night. Next day, climb Croagh Patrick, or take a walk on the big sandy beach at its base, or a day trip to Clare Island (long a haven for bird-watchers, archaeologists, and natural historians but also the venue for highly successful singles weekends—a novel way to meet your match). If the weather grounds you, head up to Turlough and the nostalgic Museum of Country Life (allow two hours).

GETTING HERE AND AROUND

A car is almost essential in Connemara and Mayo. Trains arrive from Dublin on separate lines to Westport and Ballina, but there is no service between these towns. The bus network is more flexible, but there are not many services each day, and the entire bus system goes into semihibernation during the winter months, so plan accordingly. If a rental car is out of the question, one option is to make Westport your base, and take a day trip to Connemara and Kylemore Abbey. There is no direct bus connection between Clifden and Westport, the two most attractive touring bases in the area. And the hardy can always consider making a biking trip through the region, even though it does get periods of strong rain.

AIR TRAVEL

Ryanair flies to Ireland West Airport Knock daily from London's Stansted Airport and Luton Airport; flying time is 80 minutes. BmiBaby has several flights to Knock from Manchester daily.

Carriers BmiBaby ☎ *44 8458/101–100 outside U.K.* ⊕ *www.bmibaby.com.*
Flybe ☎ *44 01392/268–529 outside U.K.* ⊕ *www.flybe.com.*
Ryanair ☎ *0818/303–030* ⊕ *www.ryanair.com.*

AIRPORTS The West's most convenient international airport is Shannon, 25 km (16 miles) east of Ennis.

Ireland West Airport Knock, at Charlestown—near Knock, in County Mayo—has direct daily service to London's Stansted, Luton, and Gatwick, and to Manchester and Birmingham, and several flights a week to Paris, Milan, and Frankfort.

No scheduled flights run from the United States to Knock; use Shannon Airport.

Airport Information Ireland West Airport Knock ☎ *94/936–8100*
⊕ *www.irelandwestairport.com.* **Shannon Airport** ☎ *061/471–444*
⊕ *www.shannonairport.com.*

BOAT AND FERRY TRAVEL

Corrib Cruises runs daily cruises on Lough Corrib from April to October, with great views of Ashford Castle and the Connemara mountains, and an optional visit to the monastic ruins on Inchagoill Island. The boat has indoor and outdoor seating and a licensed bar. Board either at Cong or at Oughterard, on the opposite side of the lake. You can use the cruise as a ferry service from one village to the other, or opt for a historic cruise with guide (both options €20). Their 6 pm traditional music cruise from Cong (June–September) is always popular.

Clare Island in Clew Bay and its smaller neighbor, Inisthturk Island, are increasingly popular day-trip destinations with hikers and natural historians. Clare Island Ferry Company sails to Clare Island and Inishturk between May and September, leaving the mainland at 10:45 am and returning at 4:45 pm (€15 round-trip). O'Malley Ferries is a year-round operator serving Clare Island. Both leave from Roonagh Pier at Louisburgh, a 35-minute drive from Westport. Tickets can be bought at the Westport Tourist Office.

From April through October, Killary Cruises runs 90-minute trips around Killary Harbour (€21), Ireland's only fjord, in an enclosed catamaran launch with seating for 150 passengers, plus a bar and restaurant. They offer a "no seasickness money-back guarantee."

Boat Companies **Tarbert–Killimer Ferry** ☎ *065/905–3124* ⊕ *www.shannonferries.com.*

BUS TRAVEL

Bus Éireann runs several expressway buses into the region from Dublin, Cork City, and Limerick City to Galway City (change for Connemara) and Westport, the principal depots in the region.

Citylink operates frequent buses, with up to 17 departures daily, between Clifden, Galway City, and Dublin and Dublin Airport. The trip costs €15 one-way.

Citylink also makes five daily trips in each direction between Shannon Airport and Galway City, costing €16 one-way.

Within Connemara and Mayo, bus routes are often slow and circuitous, and service can be erratic. A copy of the Bus Éireann Expressway timetable (€3 from any station) is useful for long trips. If possible use the website or phone the bus station (they are always very helpful) to plan local bus journeys.

Bus Éireann local buses travel from Galway City to Cong, Clifden, and Westport. There are no buses linking Cong, Clifden, and Westport: you must return to Galway City and take a different bus line out again to visit each place.

Bus Depots **Ballina Bus Station** ☎ *096/71800.* **Galway City Bus Station** (*Ceannt Station*). ☎ *091/562–000.* **Westport Bus Station** ☎ *098/25711.*

Bus Lines **Bus Éireann** ☎ *091/562–000 in Galway, 096/71800 in Ballina, 01/836–6111 in Dublin* ⊕ *www.buseireann.ie.* **Citylink** ✉ *Unit 1, Forster Ct., 17 Forster St., Galway City* ☎ *091/564–163* ⊕ *www.citylink.ie.*

CAR TRAVEL

The 207-km (129-mile) Dublin–Galway trip is on a motorway (four-lane expressway) and takes about two hours 20 minutes. The 196-km (122-mile) drive from Cork to Galway (opt for the toll tunnel under Limerick) takes about three hours, and another 45 minutes to Oughterard, where the Connemara scenery begins. From Killarney the shortest route to cover the 193 km (120 miles) to Galway (three hours) is to take N22 to Tralee, then N69 through Listowel to Tarbert and ferry across the Shannon Estuary to Killimer (*see "County Clare, Galway City, and the Aran Islands"*). From here, join N68 in Kilrush, and then pick up the M18.

ROAD
CONDITIONS
Connemara and Mayo have good, wide main roads (National Primary Routes) and better-than-average local roads (National Secondary Routes), both known as "N" routes. If you stray off the beaten track on the smaller Regional ("R") or Local ("L") routes you may encounter some hazardous mountain roads. Narrow, steep, and twisty, they are also frequented by untended sheep, cows, and ponies grazing "the long acre" (as the strip of grass beside the road is called) or simply straying in search of greener pastures. If you find a sheep in your path, just sound the horn, and it should scramble away. A good maxim for these roads is: "You never know what's around the next corner." Bear this in mind, and adjust your speed accordingly. Hikers and cyclists constitute an additional hazard on narrow roads. Within the Connemara Irish-speaking area, signs are in Irish only. The main signs to recognize are Gaillimh (Galway), Ros an Mhil (Rossaveal), An Teach Doite (Maam Cross), and Sraith Salach (Recess).

TAXI TRAVEL

Within Westport taxis operate on the meter. Outside the town, agree on the fare in advance.

Mickey's Cabs ☎ 087/222–6227 ⊕ www.westporttaxis.com.

TRAIN TRAVEL

The region's main rail stations are in Galway City, Westport, and Ballina. Trains for Galway and Westport, leave from Dublin's Heuston Station. The journey time to Galway is 3 hours; and to Westport, 3½ hours. Rail service within the region is limited. The major destinations of Galway City and Westport/Ballina are on different branch lines. Connections can be made only between Galway and the other two cities by traveling inland for about an hour to Athlone.

Train Information Irish Rail–Iarnod Éireann ☎ 098/25253 in Westport ⊕ www.irishrail.ie. **Ballina Station** ☎ 096/20229. **Dublin Heuston Station** ☎ 01/836–6222. **Galway Station** ☎ 091/564–222. **Westport Station** ☎ 098/25253.

For more information on getting here and around, see Travel Smart Ireland.

RESTAURANTS

Pubs and informal hotel restaurants are the main places to eat in this sparsely populated rural area. The only places with stand-alone restaurants are Clifden, the "capital" of Connemara (in fact a small village), and Westport, the chief resort in County Mayo. From Easter into the summer months many menus feature Connemara lamb: the sheep graze on wild herbs on the mountain slopes, which gives the meat a distinctive flavor. The other star is local seafood, including crab and lobster in summer, and superb Atlantic salmon all year-round, fresh or smoked. For seafood try the Tavern Bar and Restaurant near Westport, or Mitchell's in Clifden; for country house–style elegance go to Rosleague Manor in Letterfrack, or Renvyle House nearby. For memorable fine-dining experiences, there are two contenders: dinner beneath the crystal chandeliers at Ashford Castle's George V Restaurant, or the splendid river view from the Owenmore Restaurant in Ballynahinch Castle hotel in the heart of Connemara. Like all hotel restaurants in the area, they are open to nonresidents, but it is wise to reserve in advance.

Prices in the reviews are the average cost of a main course at dinner or, if dinner is not served, at lunch.

HOTELS

Accommodation in the area tends to the traditional; outside Westport there are few indoor pools and gyms: instead there are informal, friendly places where you will probably end up comparing notes with other travelers over a huge cooked breakfast. Add variety by alternating rural isolation with the lively towns. Both Clifden in Connemara and Westport in Mayo have lively pub scenes. Clifden attracts a younger, mainly single, crowd, especially in July and August, so be prepared: the music might be rock rather than Irish.

Lakeside Cong is a tiny village, but is a magnet for visitors. It is often pointed out that Ashford Castle, one of the most sumptuous of Ireland's castle hotels, is bigger than the village. All is perfectly manicured at this mock-Gothic baronial showpiece, built in 1870 as a country retreat for the Guinness family. Abbeyglen Castle Hotel in Clifden is a Victorian manor whose relaxed ambience and good value attract Irish holidaymakers on short breaks. Rosleague Manor, a pink-washed Georgian house on the waterside near Letterfrack, is among the prettiest Irish country-house hotels. The lake, sea, and mountain views from its 30 acres, its excellent restaurant, and elegant lounges mean you need not leave the estate at all.

Prices in the reviews are the lowest cost of a standard double room in high season. For expanded reviews, facilities, and current deals, visit Fodors.com.

TOUR OPTIONS

All TIOs in the West provide lists of suggested cycling tours. The only guided bus tours in the region, which take in the main sights of Connemara (€20), start from Galway and Westport and run only between June and September. Book at the bus station or tourist office. Lally Tours runs a day tour through Connemara and County Mayo. O'Neachtain Day Tours operates full-day tours of Connemara, also €20. The Galway Tour Company offers a Connemara tour that takes in Clifden, Kylemore Abbey, and Cong, the famed location of the classic movie *The Quiet Man*. Tickets can be purchased from the Galway tourist information office *(see "County Clare, Galway City, and the Aran Islands")* or on the tour bus. Michael Gibbons Walking Ireland in Clifden organizes everything from daylong mountain treks to weeklong holidays. Also based in Clifden, Connemara Safari Walking Holidays offers five- and seven-day residential walking holidays starting in either Clifden or Westport. They specialize in "island hopping" and remote-island hikes. Croagh Patrick Walking Holidays runs weeklong walking holidays between April and September, based in B&B accommodations near Westport; contact Gerry Greensmyth. Connemara Adventure Tours offers a range of self-guided or customized tours for walkers, cyclists, golfers, and horseback riders. Groups of 8 to 16 people participate in three-, four-, or seven-day programs, staying in a comfortable B&B

near Westport, or traveling to a new destination each night with luggage transfer. Walk Clare Island, climb Diamond Hill, or gallop along a sandy beach on Clew Bay. Clew Bay Bike Hire organizes cycling breaks and guided day-long cycle tours in the Westport area, as well as speedboat rides, sea kayaking, wake boarding, bungee jumps, and other adventure activities. Their most popular product however is day hire of electric bicycles that take the hard work out of cycling. They also offer a free drop-off and pick-up service via minibus and cycle trailer, invaluable if the weather takes a turn.

Tours Clew Bay Bike Hire and Outdoor Adventures ⊠ *Distillery Rd., Westport, Co. Mayo* ☎ *098/37675* ⊕ *www.clewbayoutdoors.ie.* **Connemara Adventure Tours** ⊠ *Leenane, Co. Galway* ☎ *095/42276* ⊕ *www.connemaraadventuretours.com.* **Croagh Patrick Walking Holidays** ⊠ *Belclare, Westport, Co. Mayo* ☎ *098/26090* ⊕ *www.walkingguideireland.com.* **Galway City TIO** ⊠ *Forster Pl., Center, Galway City, Co. Galway* ☎ *091/537–700* ⊕ *discoverireland.ie/places-to-go/Galway.* **Galway Tour Company** ☎ *091/566–566* ⊕ *www.galwaytourcompany.com.* **Lally Tours** ☎ *091/562–905* ⊕ *www.lallytours.com.* **Michael Gibbons Walking Ireland** ⊠ *Market St., Clifden, Co. Galway* ☎ *095/21379* ⊕ *www.walkingireland.com.* **O'Neachtain Day Tours** ☎ *091/553–188* ⊕ *www.ontours.biz.* **Connemara Safari Walking Holidays** ⊠ *Sky Rd., Clifden, Co. Galway* ☎ *095/21071* ⊕ *www.walkingconnemara.com.*

VISITOR INFORMATION

Discover Ireland provides free information service, tourist literature, and an accommodations booking service at its TIOs (tourist information offices). Oughterard and Westport TIOs are open all year, generally weekdays 9–6, daily during the high season. Other TIOs that operate seasonally, generally weekdays 9–6 and Saturday 9–1, are open as follows: Castlebar (May–mid-September), Clifden (March–October), and Cong (May–mid-September). Information on Connemara and Westport can be found at ⊕ *www.discoverireland.ie/places-to-go.* In addition to this main website, we sometimes also list a town website in individual town sections; this is occasionally an ad-supported site that is unofficial, but still helpful. Generally speaking, tourism has been carefully nurtured in this region. Ferry services to the islands and on Lough Corrib have been upgraded, while walking and cycling holidays are a big growth area.

CONNEMARA

Bordered by the long expanse of Lough Corrib on the east and the jagged coast of the Atlantic on the west is the rugged, desolate region of western County Galway known as Connemara. Like the American West, it's an area of spectacular, almost myth-making geography—of glacial lakes; gorgeous, silent mountains; lonely roads; and hushed, uninhabited boglands. To quote Tim Robinson in his exceptional book *Connemara: Listening to the Wind,* this is a place of "huge, luminous spaces." The glacially carved Twelve Bens mountain range, together with the Maamturk Mountains to their north, lord proudly over the area's sepia boglands. In the midst of this wilderness there are few people, since Connemara's population is sparse even by Irish standards. Especially in the off-season, you're far more likely to come across sheep strolling its roads than another car.

OUGHTERARD

27 km (17 miles) northwest of Galway City.

Bustling Oughterard (pronounced *ook*-ter-ard) is the main village on the western shores of Lough Corrib and one of Ireland's leading angling resorts. Boats can be hired for excursions to the many wooded islands studding the lakes. It is known as a fine center for exploring the beauty spots of the Twelve Bens, and other mountain ranges hereabouts, such as the Maamturk and Cloosh.

GETTING HERE AND AROUND

Oughterard is 27 km (17 miles) west of Galway City on the N59, a busy two-lane main road. The journey normally takes about half an hour by car. There is plenty of free parking. Bus Éireann and Citylink buses traveling from Galway to Clifden stop at Oughterard, a 40-minute journey.

Explore Lough Corrib with Corrib Cruises, which runs daily boat trips from Oughterard Pier from April to October. Take a day trip to Cong on the opposite side of the lake (€28), or opt for a historic cruise with guide (€20).

ESSENTIALS

Transportation Contacts CorribCruises ☎ *091/557–798* ⊕ *www.corribcruises.com.*

Visitor Information Oughterard Tourist Office ✉ *Main St., Oughterard, Co. Galway* ☎ *091/552-808* ⊕ *www.oughterardtourism.com.*

EXPLORING

The lough is signposted to the right in the village center, less than 1½ km (1 mile) up the road, near the gas station. From mid-June to early September, local boatmen offer trips on the lough, which has several islands. It's also possible to take a boat trip to the village of Cong, at the north shore of the lough. Midway between Oughterard and Cong, Inchagoill Island (the Island of the Stranger), a popular destination for a half-day trip, has several early Christian church remains. The prettiest part of the village is on the far (Clifden) side, beyond the busy commercial center, beside a wooded section of the River Corrib. Stop at the designated parking spot for a stroll beside the river.

WHERE TO STAY

For expanded hotel reviews, visit Fodors.com.

$$ ⌂ **Ross Lake House.** Built by James Edward Jackson, land agent for
B&B/INN Lord Iveagh at Ashford Castle, this well-off-the-beaten-path, white-
★ trim Georgian house, managed by the enthusiastic Henry and Elaine Reid, has a surprisingly stylish interior, with 19th-century antiques and welcoming open fires. **Pros:** country quiet—silence, in fact—with style; good restaurant on the premises. **Cons:** 3 miles out of town; no pubs nearby. **TripAdvisor:** "excellent hosts," "beautiful house," "a pleasant

stay." $ *Rooms from: €150* ⊠ *(5 km [3 miles] from Oughterard), Ross-cahill, Co. Galway* 🕿🕿 *091/550–109* ⊕ *www.rosslakehotel.com* 🛏 *11 rooms, 2 suites* ⊙ *Closed Nov.–mid-Mar.* ⏧*Breakfast.*

NIGHTLIFE

Flaherty's. For good traditional music, drop in to this popular spot. ⊠ *Main St., Oughterard, Co. Galway* 🕿 *091/552–194.*

RECESS

As you continue northwest from Oughterard on N59, you'll soon pass a string of small lakes on your left; their shining blue waters reflecting the blue sky are a typical Connemara sight on a sunny day. About 16 km (10 miles) northwest of Oughterard, the continuation of the coast road (R336) meets N59 at Maam Cross in the shadow of Leckavrea Mountain. Once an important meetingplace for the people of north and south Connemara, it's still the location of a large monthly cattle fair. Walkers will find wonderful views of Connemara by heading for any of the local peaks visible from the road.

Beyond Maam Cross, some of the best scenery in Connemara awaits on the road to Recess, 16 km (10 miles) west of Maam Cross on N59. At many points on this drive, a short walk away from either side of the main road will lead you to the shores of one of the area's many small loughs. Stop and linger if the sun is out—even intermittently—for the light filtering through the clouds gives splendor to the distant, dark-gray mountains and creates patterns on the brown-green moorland below. In June and July, it stays light until 11 pm or so, and it's worth taking a late-evening stroll to see the sun's reluctance to set.

WHERE TO STAY

For expanded hotel reviews, visit Fodors.com.

$$$$ HOTEL Fodor's Choice ★ 🍴 **Ballynahinch Castle Hotel.** More like a château than a castle in the Irish sense, this magnificent crenellated mansion sits amid 350 wooded acres and landscaped gardens, and against a rugged mountain back-drop. **Pros:** genuine Irish country-house experience; peaceful; stunning surroundings; friendly enthusiastic staff. **Cons:** doesn't come cheap. **TripAdvisor:** "beautiful," "a most relaxing stay," "old-world charm with therapeutic relaxation." $ *Rooms from: €240* ⊠ *Recess, Conne-mara, Co. Galway* 🕿🕿 *095/31006* ⊕ *www.ballynahinch-castle.com* 🛏 *3 suites, 37 rooms.*

SHOPPING

Joyce's. Joyce's crafts shop is owned by a family famed for its traditional Connemara tweeds. No surprise then that this emporium has a good selection of tweed, and also carries an enticing selection of contem-porary ceramics, handwoven shawls, books of Irish interest, original paintings, and small sculptures. 🕿 *095/34604.*

The village of Cong is world-famous as the setting for John Wayne's Oscar-winner *The Quiet Man*, and the Quiet Man Museum takes you behind the scenes.

CONG

23 km (14 miles) northeast of Maam Cross.

★ Set on a narrow isthmus between Lough Corrib and Lough Mask on the County Mayo border near Maam Cross, the pretty, old-fashioned village of Cong is still as camera-ready as it was when John Ford's *The Quiet Man* was filmed here. Dotted with ivy-covered thatch cottages and lorded over by one immensely posh hotel, Ashford Castle, this tiny village continues to have a worldwide fan base.

Just two blocks long, and bisected by the chocolate-brown River Cong, the village is surrounded on all sides by thickly forested hills. Almost larger than the village itself is the celebrated luxury hotel found here, Ashford Castle, much beloved by billionaires and off-duty celebrities. It was once the country estate of the powerful Guinness family. A public footpath runs from Cong Abbey through the grounds of Ashford Castle and out of its gates and is a pleasant walk of about two miles—or you could opt to drop by for lunch or dinner, or even afternoon tea, to get a peek at Ashford's aristocratic interior. A still more romantic way to see the castle is on a boat trip run by the local Corrib Cruises.

GETTING HERE AND AROUND

Cong is 23 km (14 miles) northeast of Maam Cross on the N59, a scenic drive skirting the shores of Lough Corrib. The main car parking area is on the edge of the village, a three-minute walk, and is clearly signposted. There is very limited parking in the village itself.

There is a limited Bus Éireann service from Galway Bus Station to Cong—be sure to get a bus that goes to Ryan's, the bus stop in the village center. The journey takes just over an hour. You can also take a delightful day-trip to Cong by Corrib Cruises boat from Oughterard between April and October.

ESSENTIALS

Visitor Information **Cong Tourist Office** ⊠ *Abbey St., Cong, Co. Galway* ☎ *094/954-6542* ⊕ *www.congtourism.com* ☉ *May–mid-Sept. only.*

EXPLORING

Augustine Abbey. Cong is surrounded by many stone circles and burial mounds, but its most notable ruins are those of the Augustine Abbey, overlooking a river. Dating from the early 12th century when it was founded by Turlough O'Connor, the High King of Ireland, this abbey still retains some finely carved details and a cloister. ⊠ *Abbey St., Cong, Co. Mayo.*

Quiet Man Museum and Gift Shop. Cong's 15 minutes of fame came in 1952, when John Ford filmed *The Quiet Man,* one of his most popular films, here; John Wayne plays a prizefighter who goes home to Ireland to court the fiery Maureen O'Hara. (Film critic Pauline Kael called the movie "fearfully Irish and green and hearty.") The Quiet Man Museum, in the village center, is an exact replica of the cottage used in the film, with reproductions of the furniture and costumes, a few original artifacts, and pictures of actors Barry Fitzgerald and Maureen O'Hara on location. O'Hara, a sprightly nonagenarian now living in Ireland, attended the film's 60th anniversary celebrations in 2012. Margaret and Gerry Collins host Quiet Man tours, leaving the cottage at 11 am daily, and exploring such Cong village sites as the river fight scene, the "hats in the air" scene, and Pat Cohan's Bar. ⊠ *Circular Rd., Cong Village Center, Cong, Co. Mayo* ☎ *094/954-6846* ⊕ *www.quietman-cong.com* ⊒ *€5* ☉ *Daily 10–4.*

WHERE TO STAY

For expanded hotel reviews, visit Fodors.com.

$$$$
HOTEL
★
☾

Ashford Castle. Massive, flamboyantly turreted, Ashord is the very picture of a romantic Irish castle and this famed mock-Gothic baronial showpiece, built in 1870 for the Guinness family, has been wowing visitors like President Reagan, John Travolta, Brad Pitt, and Pierce Brosnan—who got married here—ever since. **Pros:** baronial flamboyance; no-expense-spared facilities; regal grounds. **Cons:** so luxurious you are cut off from the normal hubbub of Irish life. **TripAdvisor:** "beautiful castle," "a destination for royalty," "feel like a king." ⓈRooms from: €375 ⊠ *Cong, Co. Mayo* ☎ *094/954-6003* ⊕ *www.ashford.ie* ⟳ *72 rooms, 11 suites.*

$
B&B/INN

Ryan's Hotel. With framed fishing ties and specimen fish given pride of place on the lobby wall, you know you are in a hostelry favored by anglers. **Pros:** you don't have to afford Ashford Castle to stay in Cong; central to village; good area for walkers and anglers. **Cons:** uninspiring views from most rooms. **TripAdvisor:** "friendly and helpful," "Ireland's secret gem," "best meal in Ireland." ⓈRooms from: €90 ⊠ *Main St., Cong, Co. Mayo* ☎ *094/954-6243* ⊕ *www.ryanshotelcong.ie* ⟳ *12 rooms.*

CLIFDEN

46 km (29 miles) southwest of Cong, 79 km (49 miles) northwest of Galway.

★ With roughly 1,100 residents, Clifden would be called a village by most, but in these parts it's looked on as something of a metropolis. It's far and away the prettiest town in Connemara, as well as its unrivaled "capital." Clifden's first attraction is its location—perched high above Clifden Bay on a forested plateau, its back to the spectacular Twelve Ben Mountains. The tapering spires of the town's two churches add to its alpine look.

Clifden is a popular base thanks to its selection of small restaurants, lively bars with music most summer nights, pleasant accommodations, and excellent walks. It's quiet out of season, but in July and August crowds flock here, especially for August's world-famous Connemara Pony Show. Year-round, unfortunately, Clifden's popularity necessitates a chaotic one-way traffic system and on summer Sunday afternoons loud techno music blasts out of certain bars. So if you're looking for a sleepy country town that time forgot, push on to Westport.

GETTING HERE AND AROUND

Clifden is 66 km (41 miles) southwest of Cong: travel via Maam Cross and take the N59 westwards. The town is 79 km (49 miles) northwest of Galway City on the N59, and takes about an hour and a half. It is a busy main road with only one lane in each direction, and delays can occur. Follow signs to find the car parks (and free parking).

Bus Éireann and Citylink have daily bus service from Galway Bus Station. Bus Éireann's route takes 2 hours (at least half of that through great scenery), while Citylink's service takes 1½ hours and continues from Galway to Dublin and Dublin Airport. Some of these services continue to Letterfrack (about 20 minutes) and Leenane (about an hour). Check with Galway Bus Station on day of travel.

ESSENTIALS

Visitor Information Clifden Tourist Office ✉ *Galway Rd., Clifden, Co. Galway* ☎ *095/21163* ⊕ *www.clifdenconnemara.com* ⊗ *Mid-Mar.–Oct. only.*

EXPLORING

Clifden Castle. Clifden Castle was built in 1815 by John D'Arcy, the town's founder, and High Sheriff of Galway, who wished to establish a center of law and order in what he saw as the lawless wilderness of Connemara. Before the founding of Clifden, the interior of Connemara was largely uninhabited, with most of its population clinging to the seashore. A 2-km (1-mile) walk along the beach road through the grounds of the now ruined Clifden Castle is the best way to explore the seashore.

Sky Road. Take the aptly named Sky Road to really appreciate Clifden's breathtaking scenery. Signposted at the west end of town, this high, narrow circuit of about 5 km (3 miles) heads west, giving phenomenal views of Clifden Bay's precipitous shores.

President Reagan, John Travolta, Brad Pitt, Pierce Brosnan … and now you? Lucky travelers call Ashford Castle their Cong home-away-from-home.

WHERE TO EAT AND STAY

For expanded hotel reviews, visit Fodors.com.

$$
SEAFOOD

✕**Mitchell's Seafood.** A town-center shop has been cleverly converted into a stylish, two-story eatery. On the first floor, beyond the plate-glass windows, there's a welcoming open fire, and you can eat at the bar or at one of the polished wood tables. Exposed stone walls and wooden floors are alluring accents on the quieter second level. Braised whole sea bass with fennel butter typifies the simple treatment given to seafood. The all-day menu also features lighter options like homemade spicy fish cakes and fresh crab salad. There are several meat options, including traditional Irish stew of Connemara lamb and fresh vegetables. $ *Average main: €18* ⊠ *Market St., Clifden, Co. Galway* ☎ *095/21867* ♺ *Closed Nov.–Feb.*

$$$$
HOTEL
Fodor's Choice
★

⛫**Abbeyglen Castle Hotel.** Creeper covered, as if under a Sleeping Beauty spell, the gorgeous Victorian castle-manor of Abbeyglen sits framed by towering trees at the foot of the glorious Twelve Bens Mountains—if time hasn't completely stopped here, it has certainly slowed down, but that's just the way the relaxed guests want it. **Pros:** laid-back, easygoing atmosphere; pleasantly homey for all its grandeur; friendly hosts and staff. **Cons:** uphill walk back from Clifden. **TripAdvisor:** "old-world hotel," "eat and relax," "very friendly." $ *Rooms from: €250* ⊠ *Sky Rd., Clifden, Co. Galway* ☎ *095/22832* ⊕ *www.abbeyglen.ie* ♺ *45 rooms* ♺ *Closed Jan.* ⦿ *Breakfast.*

$
B&B/INN

⛫**Dún Rí.** An old town house in the lower, quieter part of Clifden has been extended and converted into a comfortable guesthouse with private parking. **Pros:** hotel-grade rooms at B&B prices; quiet central location.

Cons: bland decor; parking lot is effectively on-street, not secured. **Trip-Advisor:** "wonderful small hotel," "clean and comfortable," "friendly atmosphere." ⑤ *Rooms from: €100* ⊠ *Hulk St., Clifden, Co. Galway* 🕾 *095/21625* ⊕ *www.dunri.ie* ⌇ *13 rooms* ⦿ *Breakfast.*

$$
B&B/INN
★

🛏 **Quay House.** Nineteenth-century time travelers would feel right at home walking into this three-story Georgian house, Clifden's oldest (1820), as ancestral portraits, mounted fish, Victorian engravings, and cosseting fabrics all lend a frozen-in-amber allure. **Pros:** fetching decor; harbor views. **Cons:** uphill walk into town. **TripAdvisor:** "just what I was looking for," "comfortable and friendly," "a quiet place." ⑤ *Rooms from: €160* ⊠ *The Quay, Connemara, Clifden, Co. Galway* 🕾 *095/21369* ⊕ *www.thequayhouse.com* ⌇ *14 rooms* ⊙ *Closed Nov.– mid-Mar.* ⦿ *Breakfast.*

THE ARTS

Clifden Arts Week. Held annually in mid-September for the past 35 years, the Clifden Arts Week has a great selection of music, arts, and poetry in a friendly informal atmosphere and scenic environment, making it an excellent time to tune in to local culture. ⊕ *www. clifdenartsweek.ie.*

SHOPPING

The Connemara Hamper. A small but well-stocked specialty food shop, this is an ideal place to pick up picnic fare, with its excellent Irish farmhouse cheeses, pâtés, smoked Connemara salmon, and handmade Irish chocolates. ⊠ *Market St., Clifden, Co. Galway* 🕾 *095/21054* ⊕ *www. connemarahamper.com.*

Millar's Connemara Tweeds. Millar's is a long-established emporium with a good selection of traditional tweeds and hand knits. ⊠ *Main St., Clifden, Co. Galway* 🕾 *095/21038.*

The Outdoor Shop/Faoin Tuath. You didn't pack hiking gear, but now that you're here you want to explore the raw landscape on foot. You'll find everything you need here as well as surfing gear and local knowledge for both activities. ⊠ *Market St., Clifden, Co. Galway* 🕾 *095/22838.*

Station House Courtyard. Set around a cobbled courtyard, the Station House has crafts studios, antiques dealers, and designer-wear outlets. ⊠ *Old Railway Station, Bridge St., Clifden, Co. Galway* 🕾 *095/21699* ⊕ *www.clifdenstationhouse.com.*

SPORTS AND THE OUTDOORS

BICYCLING

John Mannion & Son. Explore Connemara by renting a bike from this handy outfitter. ⊠ *Railway View, Clifden, Co. Galway* 🕾 *095/21160* ⊕ *www.clifdenbikes.com.*

GOLF

Connemara Golf Links. On a dramatic stretch of Atlantic coastline, the links course masterminded by Eddie Hackett, Ireland's finest course designer, is sited between the Twelve Bens mountains and the rugged coast, with unforgettable views of sea, hills, and the huge western sky. The opening hole has a challenging dogleg, while the back 9 offer a memorable golfing experience, considered equal to any in the world.

9

✉ *9 km (5½ miles) south of Clifden on R341, Ballyconneely, Co. Galway* ☎ *095/23502* ⊕ *www.connemaragolflinks.com* ✉ *Greens fees: Nov.–Mar. €35, Apr. and Oct. €45, May and Sept. €55, June €60, July €65, Aug. €70* ⚲ *18 holes. Yardage 7,055. Par 72. Practice area, caddies, club hire, catering* ☉ *Visitors: Mon.–Sun. (some restrictions).*

HORSEBACK RIDING

Errislannan Manor Connemara Pony Stud and Riding Centre. Ride a sure-footed Connemara pony in its native habitat at this long-established riding center, where these sturdy ponies are also bred. Treks are tailored to your ability, and the views of coast and hills from the mountain trails will be unforgettable. ✉ *6.5 km (4 miles) from Clifden on the Ballyconneely road (R341), Clifden, Co. Galway* ☎ *095/21134* ⊕ *www. errislannanmanor.com.*

LETTERFRACK

14 km (9 miles) north of Clifden.

This is one of the main gateway villages to the famous Connemara National Park. It also makes a handy base for those visiting spectacular Kylemore Abbey, one of Ireland's grandest ancestral estates.

GETTING HERE AND AROUND

Letterfrack is 14 km (9 miles) north of Clifden on the N59. The journey takes about 15 minutes. There is plenty of free parking in the village center. Bus Éireann has daily routes linking Letterfrack and Clifden, a 20-minute journey. The nonexpress service originates in Galway, and takes about 2 hours 30 minutes to reach Letterfrack. Citylink also operates between Letterfrack and Clifden (continuing to Galway).

EXPLORING

Connemara National Park. The 5,000-acre Connemara National Park lies southeast of the village of Letterfrack. Its visitor center covers the area's history and ecology, particularly the origins and growth of peat—and presents the depressing statistic that more than 80% of Ireland's peat, 5,000 years in the making, has been destroyed in the last 90 years. You can also get details on the many excellent walks and beaches in the area. The misleadingly named "park" is, in fact, just rocky or wooded wilderness territory, albeit with some helpful trails marked out to aid your exploration. It includes part of the famous **Twelve Bens** mountain range, which is for experienced hill walkers only. An easier hike is the Lower Diamond Hill Walk, at about 3 km (5 miles). Ask for advice on a hike suited to your abilities and interests at the Park and Visitor Centre, which is on the N59 as you arrive in Letterfrack from Clifden, on your right, clearly signposted, not too far southeast of the center of Letterfrack. ✉ *Park and Visitor Centre, on the N59 near Letterfrack, Letterfrack, Co. Galway* ☎ *95/41054* ⊕ *www.connemaranationalpark.ie* ✉ *Free* ☉ *Park daily, dawn–dusk; visitor center mid-Mar.–Oct., daily 9–5:30.*

WHERE TO EAT AND STAY

For expanded hotel reviews, visit Fodors.com.

$ ✕**The Bards Den.** Many visitors to Connemara share a memory of the

MODERN IRISH Den's huge stove, where weary travelers have dried their soaking clothes and warmed frozen hands while sipping restorative glasses of stout. While the low-ceilinged, warrenlike pub has long served food—and great traditional Irish music at night—it now has a restaurant with blackboard menu. The food is described as "fresh, local, and Irish," including smoked salmon, Connemara lamb stew, and prime Irish beef T-bone steaks. ⑤ *Average main: €18* ✉ *Main St., Letterfrack, Co. Galway* ☎ *095/41042* ⊕ *www.bardsden.com.*

$$ ⊞ **Renvyle House Hotel.** A lake at its front door, the Atlantic Ocean at its

HOTEL back door, and the mountains of Connemara as a backdrop form the

★ enthralling setting for this hotel 8 km (5 miles) north of Letterfrack, but

↻ don't count out the interior for it contains the Long Room, one of the most eminently civilized salons in Ireland—all polished wood, endless chairs, and pretty pictures. **Pros:** amazing views; secluded end-of-the-world location; recommended for artists and photographers; cheerful, unpretentious version of the country-house hotel experience. **Cons:** driving distance to anywhere else; bar and restaurant very busy at peak times. **TripAdvisor:** "lovely country-house hotel," "stress free Connemara gem," "exceptional hospitality." ⑤ *Rooms from: €170* ✉ *Renvyle, Co. Galway* ☎ *095/46100* ⊕ *www.renvyle.com* ⌁ *70 rooms* ⊘ *Closed Jan. 2–mid-Feb.* ⑩ *Breakfast.*

$$$ ⊞ **Rosleague Manor.** This pink, creeper-clad, two-story Georgian house

HOTEL occupies 30 lovely acres and has a jaw-dropping view: a gorgeous lawn

★ backdropped by Ballinakill Bay and the dreamy mountains of Connemara. **Pros:** quiet and elegant; mesmerizing views; excellent restaurant. **Cons:** can be very quiet off-season. **TripAdvisor:** "old-world charm," "great atmosphere and food," "one of a kind." ⑤ *Rooms from: €210* ✉ *Rosleague Bay, Letterfrack, Co. Galway* ☎ *095/41101* ⊕ *www. rosleague.com* ⌁ *20 rooms* ⊘ *Closed Nov.–mid-Mar.* ⑩ *Breakfast.*

NIGHTLIFE

The Bards Den. For traditional music, the best option in this region is the Bards Den. ✉ *Main St., Letterfrack, Co. Galway* ☎ *95/41042* ⊕ *www. bardsden.com.*

SHOPPING

Connemara Handcrafts. An extensive selection of crafts and women's fashions made by the stellar Avoca Handweavers is showcased here, along with a quaint coffee shop. ✉ *N59, west of village, Letterfrack, Co. Galway* ☎ *095/41058.*

KYLEMORE VALLEY

Runs for 6½ km (4 miles) between Letterfrack and intersection of N59 and R344.

One of the more conventionally beautiful stretches of road in Connemara passes through Kylemore Valley, which is between the Twelve Bens to the south and the naturally forested Dorruagh Mountains to the north. Kylemore (the name is derived from *Coill Mór,* Irish for "big

Few landscapes are as quintessentially Irish as the ravishing and rugged ones found in Connemara National Park.

wood") looks "as though some colossal giant had slashed it out with a couple of strokes from his mammoth sword," as artist and author John FitzMaurice Mills has written.

EXPLORING

Kylemore Abbey. One of the most magical "castles" in all of Europe, much-photographed Kylemore Abbey is visible across a reedy lake with a backdrop of wooded hillside. The storybook Gothic Revival, gray-stone mansion was built as a private home between 1861 and 1868 by Mitchell Henry, a member of Parliament for County Galway, and his wife, Margaret, who had fallen in love with the spot during a carriage ride while on their honeymoon. The Henrys spared no expense—the final bill for their house is said to have come to 1.5 million—and employed mostly local laborers, thereby abetting the famine relief effort (this area was among the worst hit in all of Ireland). Adjacent to the house is a spectacular neo-Gothic chapel, which, sadly, became the burial place for Margaret, who died after contracting "Nile fever" on a trip to Egypt. In 1920, nuns from the Irish Abbey of the Nuns of St. Benedict, who fled their abbey in Belgium during World War I, eventually sought refuge in Kylemore, which had gone through a number of owners and decades of decline after the Henrys died. Still in residence, the Benedictine nuns run a girls' boarding school here. Three reception rooms and the main hall are open to the public, as are a crafts center and cafeteria. There's also a 6-acre walled Victorian garden; a shuttle bus from the abbey to the garden departs every 15 minutes during opening hours. An exhibition and video explaining the history of the house can be viewed year-round at the abbey, and the grounds are freely accessible most of the year. Ask at the excellent crafts shop for directions to the **Gothic Chapel** (a five-minute walk from the abbey), a tiny replica of Norwich Cathedral built by the Henrys. ⊠ *About ¾ km (½ mile) back from Kylemore Valley Rd., Letterfrack, Co. Galway* ☎ *095/41146* ⊕ *www.kylemoreabbey.com* ☜ *€12, including shuttle bus to garden* ⊙ *Mid-Mar.–June and Sept.–Oct., daily 9:30–5:30; July–Aug., daily 9:30–7; Nov.–mid-Mar., daily 10–4:30.*

LEENANE

18 km (11 miles) east of Letterfrack.

Nestled idyllically at the foot of the Maamturk Mountains and overlooking the tranquil waters of Killary Harbour, Leenane is a tiny village noted for its role as the setting for the film *The Field*, which starred Richard Harris.

GETTING HERE AND AROUND

Leenane is 18 km (11 miles) east of Letterfrack on the N59. The journey takes just over 15 minutes. There is free parking in the village, on the streets and in designated car parks. Leenane has at least one Bus Éireann bus a day, traveling to Galway via Clifden, taking about 1 hour 15 minutes to Clifden. In summer there is also a bus to Westport, a 45-minute journey.

TOURS

Take a 90-minute trip around Killary Harbour in an enclosed Killary Cruises catamaran launch with seating for 150 passengers, bar, and restaurant.

ESSENTIALS

Transportation Contacts Killary Cruises ⊠ *Nancy's Point, Leenane, Co. Mayo* ☎ *091/566–736* ⊕ *www.killarycruises.com.*

EXPLORING

Fodor's Choice ★ **Killary Harbour.** Beyond Kylemore, N59 travels for some miles along Killary Harbour, a narrow fjord (the only one in Ireland) that runs for 16 km (10 miles) between County Mayo's Mweelrea Mountain to the north and County Galway's Maamturk Mountains to the south. The dark, deep water of the fjord reflects the magnificent steep-sided hills that border it, creating a haunting scene of natural grandeur. The harbor has an extremely safe anchorage, 13 fathoms (78 feet) deep for almost its entire length, and is sheltered from storms by mountain walls. The rafts floating in Killary Harbour belong to fish-farming consortia that raise salmon and trout in cages beneath the water. This is a matter of some controversy all over the West. Although some people welcome the employment opportunities, others bemoan the visual blight of the rafts. For cruises around the harbor, see Killary Cruises.

The Sheep and Wool Centre. The Sheep and Wool Centre, in the center of Leenane, focuses on the traditional industry of North Connemara and West Mayo. Several breeds of sheep graze around the house, and there are demonstrations of carding, spinning, weaving, and the dyeing of wool with natural plant dyes. ☎ *095/42323* ⊕ *www.sheepandwoolcentre. com* ☜ *Shop, cafe free; museum €5* ⊙ *Mid-Mar.–Oct., daily 10–6.*

WHERE TO STAY

For expanded hotel reviews, visit Fodors.com.

$$ **Delphi Lodge.** In the heart of what
B&B/INN   is arguably Mayo's most spectacu-
Fodor'sChoice   lar mountain and lake scenery,
★   5 km (3 miles) east of Leenane off N59, this attractive Georgian sporting lodge heavily stocked with fishing paraphernalia has a lovely lakeside setting. **Pros:** beautiful secluded location; abundant peace and quiet. **Cons:** you've got to like fishing or walking—and your fellow guests. **TripAdvisor:** "a dream come true," "great food," "unique location." $ *Rooms from: €160* ✉ *Leenane, Leenane, Co. Galway* ☎ *095/42222* ⊕ *www.delphilodge. ie* ⌂ *12 rooms, 5 cottages* ☉ *Closed mid-Oct.–mid-Mar.* ⦿ *Breakfast.*

$ **The Leenane Hotel.** Built in the 1790s at the entrance to Leenane village
★   as a coaching inn, and recently upgraded to modern standards (with the bigger rooms in the newest wing), only the main road separates this hotel from Killary Fjord. **Pros:** great value; comfortable and atmospheric one-stop base. **Cons:** some of the older bedrooms very small; lighting rather dim in bar and lounge. **TripAdvisor:** "a credit to Galway hospitality," "amazing surroundings," "a really lovely surprise." $ *Rooms from: €118* ✉ *Leenane, Co. Galway* ☎ *095/42249* ⊕ *www. leenanehotel.com* ⌂ *32* ☉ *Closed mid-Nov.–mid-Mar.*

> ### LEENANE AND THE ARTS
>
> Martin McDonagh's *Leenane Trilogy,* featuring a cast of tragicomic grotesques, presents an unflattering view of rural Irish life. An international hit, the plays brought a renown Leenane presumably could have done without. The plot thickened with Kevin Barry's "Fjord of Killary," a hilariously black short story set in Leenane and published in the *New Yorker* in February 2010.

COUNTY MAYO

County Mayo has long empty roads that stretch along for miles. The Museum of Country Life, the only branch of the National Museum outside Dublin, commemorates a disappearing way of life, and is fittingly located here in Turlough. Castlebar, the county town, has been overshadowed by its neighbor Westport, an elegantly laid-out 18th-century town with quays on the shore of island-studded Clew Bay, under the towering conical peak of St Patrick's holy mountain, Croagh Patrick. Not only does Westport have scenery, it also has some excellent hotels and bars, some a legacy of the boom years that brought metropolitan chic to the heart of the west.

WESTPORT

32 km (20 miles) north of Leenane.

★   By far the most attractive town in County Mayo, Westport is on an inlet of Clew Bay, a wide expanse of sea dotted with islands and framed by mountain ranges. It's one of the most attractive heritage towns in Ireland, its Georgian origins clearly defined by the broad streets skirting the gently flowing river and, particularly, by the lime-fringed central avenue called the Mall. Built as an O'Malley stronghold, the entire town received a face-lift when the Brownes, who had come from Sussex in the reign of Elizabeth I, constructed Westport House and much of the modern town, which was laid out by architect James Wyatt when he was employed to finish the grand estate of Westport House.

GETTING HERE AND AROUND

Westport is 32 km (20 miles) north of Leenane on the R335, and 78 km (48 miles) north of Clifden, a journey of about an hour. It is 106 km (66 miles) northwest of Galway on the N17, picking up the N60 at Claremorris and the N5 at Castlebar. The journey takes about 1 hour 45 minutes. There is ample parking in the town center, on the streets and in designated lots, with a nominal charge during business hours. There is more parking down on the quays.

There are Bus Éireann buses daily from Westport (the Octagon monument) to Galway, traveling on the nonscenic N17 via Claremorris. The express takes 1 hour 50 minutes, while the nonexpress bus takes more than two hours. There are also direct buses from Westport to Ballina, a journey of about an hour. There is no bus station in Westport. Irish Rail trains travel from Dublin's Heuston Station to Westport, a journey of 3½ hours.

ESSENTIALS

Visitor Information Croagh Patrick Information Centre. Located in the car park at the start of the Croagh Patrick ascent, the building houses a café, shop, and has shower and locker facilities. If you have any questions about climbing Croagh Patrick, this is the place to go. ⊠ *Murrisk, Westport, Co. Mayo* ☎ *098/64114* ⊕ *www.croagh-patrick.com.* **Westport Tourist Office** ⊠ *James St., Westport, Co. Mayo* ☎ *098/25711* ⊕ *www.westporttourism.com.*

EXPLORING

Clare Island. Clew Bay is said to have 365 islands, one for every day of the year. The biggest and most interesting to visit is Clare Island, at the mouth of the bay. In fine weather the rocky, hilly island, which is 8 km (5 miles) long and 5 km (3 miles) wide, affords beautiful views south toward Connemara, east across Clew Bay, and north to Achill Island. About 150 people live on the island today, but before the 1845–47 famine it had a population of about 1,700. A 15th-century tower overlooking the harbor was once the stronghold of Granuaile, the pirate queen, who ruled the area until her death in 1603. She is buried on the island, in its 12th-century Cistercian abbey. Today most visitors seek out the island for its unusual peace and quiet, golden beaches, and unspoiled landscape. A Singles Weekend (over 30s) held annually on the second weekend in June has proved a great success. Ferries depart from Roonagh Pier, near Louisburgh, a scenic 19-km (12-mile) drive from Westport on R335 past several long sandy beaches. The crossing takes about 15 minutes. Dolphins often accompany the boats on the trip, and there are large populations of seals under the island's cliffs. ☎ *098/25045 O'Malley's Ferries, 098/25212 Pirate Queen boat* ⊕ *www.clareisland.info* ⛴ *Ferry €15 round-trip* ☉ *May–mid-Sept., sailings usually twice daily, weather permitting.*

Croagh Patrick. Look out as you travel north for the great bulk of 2,500-foot-high Croagh Patrick; its size and conical shape make it one of the West's most distinctive landmarks. On clear days a small white

Connemara and County Mayo

building is visible at its summit (it stands on a ½-acre plateau), as is the wide path that ascends to it. The latter is the Pilgrim's Path. Each year about 25,000 people, many of them barefoot, follow the path to pray to St. Patrick in the oratory on its peak. St. Patrick spent the 40 days and nights of Lent here in 441, during the period in which he was converting Ireland to Christianity. The traditional date for the pilgrimage is the last Sunday in July; in the past, the walk was made at night, with pilgrims carrying burning torches, but that practice has been discontinued. The climb involves a gentle uphill slope, but you need to be fit and agile to complete the last half hour, over scree (small loose rocks with no trail). This is why most climbers carry a stick or staff (traditionally made of ash, and called an ash plant), which helps you to stop sliding backward. These can sometimes be bought in the parking area. The hike can be made in about three hours (round-trip) on any fine day and is well worth the effort for the magnificent views of the islands of Clew Bay, the Sheeffry Hills to the south (with the Bens visible behind them), and the peaks of Mayo to the north. The climb starts at Murrisk, a village about 8 km (5 miles) before Westport on the R335 Louisburgh road.

Octagon. Today Westport's streets radiate from its central Octagon, where an old-fashioned farmers' market is held on Thursday morning; look for work clothes, harnesses, tools, and children's toys for sale.

Traditional shops—ironmongers, drapers, and the like—line the streets that lead to the Octagon, while a riverside mall is shaded by tall lime trees. At Westport's Quay, about 2 km (1 mile) outside town, a large warehouse has been attractively restored as vacation apartments, and there are some good bars and decent restaurants.

Westport House. The showpiece of the town remains Westport House and Country Park, a stately home built on the site of an earlier castle (believed to have been the home of the 16th-century warrior queen, Grace O'Malley) and most famed for its setting right on the shores of a beautiful lake. The house was begun in 1730 to the designs of Richard Castle, added to in 1778, and completed in 1788 by architect James Wyatt for the Marquess of Sligo of the Browne family. The rectangular, three-story house is furnished with late-Georgian and Victorian pieces. Family portraits by Opie and Reynolds, a huge collection of old Irish silver and old Waterford glass, plus an opulent group of paintings—including *The Holy Family* by Rubens—are on display. A word of caution: Westport isn't your usual staid country house. The old dungeons now house video games and the grounds have given way to a small amusement park for children and a children's zoo. In fact, the lake is now littered with swan-shaped "pedaloes," boats that may be fun for families but help destroy the perfect Georgian grace of the setting. If these elements don't sound like a draw, arrive early when it's less likely to be busy. The Farmyard area has garden-plant sales, an indoor soft-play area, a gift shop, and a coffee shop. ⊠ *Off N59, south of Westport turnoff, clearly signposted from Octagon, Westport, Co. Mayo* ☎ *098/27766* ⊕ *www.westporthouse.ie* 🎫 *House €12, attractions €24, family day-ticket for house and attractions €59* ⊙ *House, gardens, and attractions: Mar. and Oct., weekends 10–4; Apr., May, June, and Sept., daily 10–6; July–Aug., daily 10–7.*

WHERE TO EAT AND STAY
For expanded hotel reviews, visit Fodors.com.

$ SEAFOOD
✕ **The Tavern Bar and Restaurant.** An outing to this traditional pub in the tiny village of Murrisk—at the foot of Croagh Patrick, just across the road from the seashore—is a popular excursion from Westport. Its distinctive, fuchsia-pink facade leads into a simple, family-run tavern where the emphasis is firmly on food. Carefully sourced local produce including Clew Bay seafood, Connemara lamb, and farmhouse cheese from the nearby village of Carrowholly are served in hearty portions. The bar also has a kids' menu. Connemara lamb sausages with spring-onion mash, or the house-special beef braised in Guinness with carrots, onions, and parsnips are two winners. Fishermen arrive regularly with freshly landed langoustine, which are then poached and served in garlic butter. Upstairs a more elaborate à la carte menu ($$$) is served in the restaurant, with a quieter, candlelit atmosphere. $ *Average main: €16* ⊠ *Murrisk, 5 km (3 miles) from Westport, Westport, Co. Mayo* ☎ *098/64060* ⊕ *www. tavernmurrisk.com/* ⊙ *Bar food daily. Restaurant upstairs closed Mon.– Thurs. in Nov. and Jan.–mid-Mar., but call to confirm.*

$ B&B/INN
Boffin Lodge. In a quiet part of town, just a short walk from the lively quayside area, the lodge is a traditional-style two-story gabled house with off-street parking. **Pros:** cozy and quiet; safe parking. **Cons:** a bit of a walk into town, and an uphill walk back from the quays.

TripAdvisor: "very friendly and welcoming," "surprisingly elegant," "relaxed atmosphere." ⑤ *Rooms from: €90* ⊠ *The Quay, Westport, Co. Mayo* ☎ *098/26092* ⊕ *www.boffinlodge.com* ➵ *10 rooms* ⓞ| *Breakfast.*

$

HOTEL

⌂ **Clew Bay Hotel.** In Westport's town center, this hotel welcomes guests with a warmly traditional wooden facade but once you are inside, however, a contemporary glass-roofed lobby comprises the centerpiece of a stylish modern interior decorated with original art works. **Pros:** central location; friendly owner-managers; good value. **Cons:** risk of late-night noise in front rooms; no private parking; bathrooms a bit old-fashioned. **TripAdvisor:** "very friendly," "lovely wee hotel," "five star service." ⑤ *Rooms from: €110* ⊠ *James St., Westport, Co. Mayo* ☎ *098/28088* ⊕ *www.clewbayhotel.com* ➵ *40 rooms.*

$$$

HOTEL

⌂ **Westport Plaza Hotel.** Walk in off the street of this small Irish town, past topiary balls in square wicker holders, to the vast marble lobby with its double-sided gas fire, some 16 giant sofas, and New Age mood music, and you could be in the heart of metropolitan anywhere. **Pros:** all the creature comforts; best of modern design; quiet and central. **Cons:** avoid the few bedrooms with street views; you might forget you're in Ireland. **TripAdvisor:** "heaven in the heart of Westport," "kid-friendly," "you have to love this place." ⑤ *Rooms from: €190* ⊠ *Castlebar St., Westport, Co. Mayo* ☎ *098/51166* ⊕ *www.westportplazahotel.ie* ➵ *85 rooms, 3 suites.*

NIGHTLIFE

Matt Molloy's. In Westport's town center try this favorite spot; Matt Malloy is not only the owner but also a member of the famed musical group, the Chieftains. Traditional music is, naturally, the main attraction. ⊠ *Bridge St., Westport, Co. Mayo* ☎ *098/26655* ⊕ *www.mattmolloy.com.*

SHOPPING

Carraig Donn. A good selection of crystal, jewelry, and ceramics are the main temptations here, along with Carraig Donn's own line of knitwear. ⊠ *Bridge St., Westport, Co. Mayo* ☎ *098/50300* ⊕ *www.carraigdonn.ie.*

Hewetson Bros. An old-fashioned fishing-tackle shop, Hewetson also stocks gear for surfing, climbing, and hiking. ⊠ *Bridge St., Westport, Co. Mayo* ☎ *098/26018.*

McCormack's. Downstairs is a traditional butcher shop but climb one flight up to find an attractive gallery and café with work by local artists for sale. ⊠ *Bridge St., Westport, Co. Mayo* ☎ *098/25619.*

O'Reilly/Turpin. Head here for the best in contemporary Irish design for knitwear, ceramics, and other decorative items. ⊠ *Bridge St., Westport, Co. Mayo* ☎ *098/28151.*

Thomas Moran's. For irresistibly unique gifts, Thomas Moran delivers with its locally made blackthorn sticks, bargain umbrellas, and some offbeat souvenirs. ⊠ *Bridge St., Westport, Co. Mayo* ☎ *098/25562.*

Treasure Trove. This spot has a good stock of antiques and curios, including linen and local memorabilia. ⊠ *Bridge St., Westport, Co. Mayo* ☎ *098/25118.*

SPORTS AND THE OUTDOORS

BICYCLING

Clew Bay Bike Hire. Explore the scenic bike trails of Clew Bay on a top-of-the-range bike, available by the hour, day, or multiday, and enjoy the minibus and bike trailer that offers a free drop-off and collection service. ✉ *Distillery Rd., Westport, Co. Mayo* ☎ *098/24818* ⊕ *www. clewbayoutdoors.ie.*

Electric Escapes. Take the hard work out of cycling and rent an electric bike to explore the Great Western Greenway between Newport and Mulranny, or join a guided cycle tour along the Bangor Trail, amid 1,000 square miles of wilderness. Even the young and fit find the electric bike greatly increases the miles you can cover in a day. ✉ *Distillery Rd., Westport, Co. Mayo* ☎ *098/56611* ⊕ *www.electricscapes.ie.*

J.P. Breheny & Sons. Enjoy the spectacular scenery of Clew Bay at a leisurely pace on a rented bike from this convenient shop. ✉ *Castlebar St., Westport, Co. Mayo* ☎ *098/25020.*

GOLF

Westport Golf Club. Twice this inland course hosted the Irish Amateur Championship. It lies in the shadows of religious history: rising 2,500 feet above Clew Bay, with its hundreds of islands, is Croagh Patrick, a mountain that legend connects with St. Patrick. The mountain is considered sacred, and it attracts multitudes of worshippers to its summit every year. All the prayers might pay off at the 15th, where your drive has to carry the ball over 200 yards of ocean. ✉ *Westport, Co. Mayo* ☎ *98/28262* ⊕ *www.westportgolfclub.com* ☑ *Greens fees: April–Sept. weekdays €27.50, weekends €37.50; Oct.–Mar. weekdays €20, weekends €30* ⚐ *18 holes. Yardage: 7,000. Par 73. Practice area, driving range, caddies, caddy carts, buggies, catering* ☾ *Visitors: daily.*

TURLOUGH

9

24 km (15 miles) east of Castlebar.

Before the opening of the Museum of Country Life, Turlough was chiefly visited for its round tower (freely accessible), which marks the site of an early monastery, traditionally associated with St. Patrick, and the nearby ruins of a 17th-century church.

Once a thriving hub, with a village school, two pubs, and a busy shop, Turlough now has a population of about 300, one pub with a small shop attached, and no school. Rather than working on the land, most of the locals commute to jobs in nearby Castlebar.

GETTING HERE AND AROUND

Turlough is 24 km (15 miles) east of Castlebar on the N5 Dublin road. The museum is clearly signposted from the main road. Bus Éireann buses from Westport to Ballina via Castlebar will stop at the Museum of Country Life on request (ask the driver as you board).

EXPLORING

Fodor's Choice
★
☾

Museum of Country Life. To understand the forces that have led to such dramatic changes in Turlough, pay a visit to the Museum of Country Life, which focuses on rural Ireland between 1860 and 1960—a way

CONNEMARA'S WILD PONIES

As you drive through Connemara, you will not only see sheep roaming the hillsides (lots of sheep: more sheep than people) but also herds of wild ponies, usually gray (the proper term for white horses) or dun (buckskin) in color.

Connemara ponies are strong, hardy, and companionable, highly intelligent, and also surprisingly elegant: averaging around 13 to 14 hands, they are much sought after for riding and show jumping. They are assumed to be a cross between a native Irish breed and Spanish-bred Arab horses imported in the Middle Ages.

The breed was only recognized in the early 20th century, and is celebrated on the third weekend in August at the Connemara Pony Show in Clifden. The whole town takes on a festive air and parties long into the night as breeders and competitors from all over Ireland enjoy their annual get-together. The show-jumping competitions are pretty nifty, too.

of life that remained unchanged for many years, then suddenly came to an end within living memory. At this highly acclaimed museum, the only branch of the National Museum of Ireland outside Dublin, you're invited to imagine yourself back in a vanished world, before the internal combustion engine, rural electrification, indoor plumbing, television, and increased education transformed people's lives and expectations. For many, this is a journey into a strange place, where water had to be carried from a well, turf had to be brought home from the bog, fires had to be lighted daily for heat and cooking, and clothes had to be made painstakingly by hand in the long winter evenings. Among the displayed items are authentic furniture and utensils; hunting, fishing, and agricultural implements; clothing; and objects relating to games, pastimes, religion, and education.

The museum experience starts in Turlough Park House, built in the High Victorian Gothic style in 1865 and set in pretty lakeside gardens. Just three rooms have been restored to illustrate the way the landowners lived. A sensational modern four-story, curved building houses the main exhibit. Cleverly placed windows afford panoramic views of the surrounding park and the distant round tower, allowing you to reflect on the reality beyond the museum's walls. Temporary exhibitions, such as one called "Romanticism and Reality," help illustrate the divide between the dreamy image of old rural life and its actual hardships. The shop sells museum-branded and handcrafted gift items as well as a good selection of books on related topics. A café with indoor and outdoor tables is in the stable yard, and you can take scenic lakeside walks in the park. Crafts demonstrations and workshops take place on Wednesday and Sunday afternoons. ⊠ *Turlough Park on the N4 (7 km [4 miles] east of Castlebar), Turlough, Co. Mayo* ☎ *094/903–1755* ⊕ *www.museum. ie* ⌨ *Free* ⊗ *Tues.–Sat. 10–5, Sun. 2–5.*

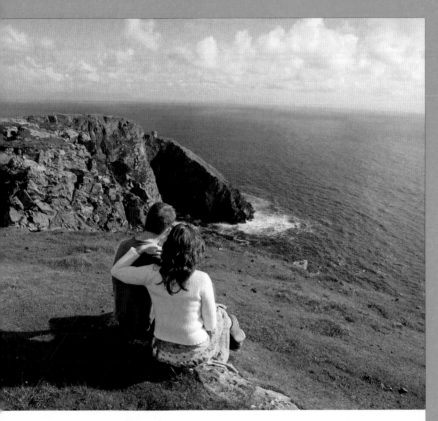

The Northwest

INCLUDING COUNTIES DONEGAL, LEITRIM, AND SLIGO

WORD OF MOUTH

"While finding Letterkenny, we came across Griannan Aileach, a stone fort on a high hill I had wanted to visit. It was a long, rather scary drive up the narrow road with high hedges and limited visibility, but it brought us most of the way to the top. We had the place to ourselves. The view was sublime, and it looked like you could see half of Ireland from the top."

—GreenDragon

WELCOME TO
THE NORTHWEST

TOP REASONS
TO GO

★ **Gaeltacht Country:** Venture to the seaside village of Ard an Ratha to listen to the seductive rhythms of locals conversing in full Irish (Gaelic) flight. Don't worry: everyone has English at the ready for lost visitors.

★ **The Yeats Trail:** From Sligo Town's museums head out to the majestic Ben Bulben peak to follow in the footsteps of the famous brother duo, W. B. Yeats, the great poet, and Jack B. Yeats, one of Ireland's finest 20th-century painters.

★ **Garbo's Castle:** The legendary screen actress was just one of the many notables who enjoyed a stay at Glenveagh Castle.

★ **Hiking the Slieve League Cliffs:** To truly humble yourself before ocean, cliff, and sky, hike these fabled headlands, the highest sea cliffs in Europe. The views will set your heart racing, and the Atlantic sea winds are sure to blow away the cobwebs. The cliffs are also the spectacular starting point for the newly designated Irish leg of the International Appalachian Trail.

1 Sligo and Environs.
What the poet William Butler Yeats would say about his native Sligo Town—a once idyllic spot now overrun with modern shopping malls—can only be imagined, but it makes a great jumping-off point for exploring Yeats Country: the Lake Isle at Innisfree, the cairn-crowned Knocknarea (a peak often painted by brother Jack), and Drumcliff, where W. B. lies buried under the shadow of Ben Bulben.

2 Donegal Bay. Donegal Town, with its fine medieval castle and abbey, is the gateway to County Donegal, regarded by many as the runner-up to Kerry as Ireland's most scenic region.

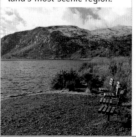

This is the ever-shrinking heart of the Donegal Gaeltacht (Irish-speaking region), where the moody hamlet of Gleann Cholm Cille and the majestic Slieve League Mountains beckon, as does the Belleek china of Ballyshannon. The nearby town of Bundoran has become synonymous with international surfing and hosts many championship events. Since 2010, a new 15-meter (50-foot) wave called Prowlers has brought surfers from all over the world to hit this monster Atlantic swell.

3 Northern Donegal.
This is the far Northwest, Ireland's back-of-the-beyond. The gateway town is Letterkenny, presided over by the 212-foot-high spire of St. Eunan's Cathedral. Westward lies Glenveagh National Park, where you'll find the storybook lair and gardens of Glenveagh Castle.

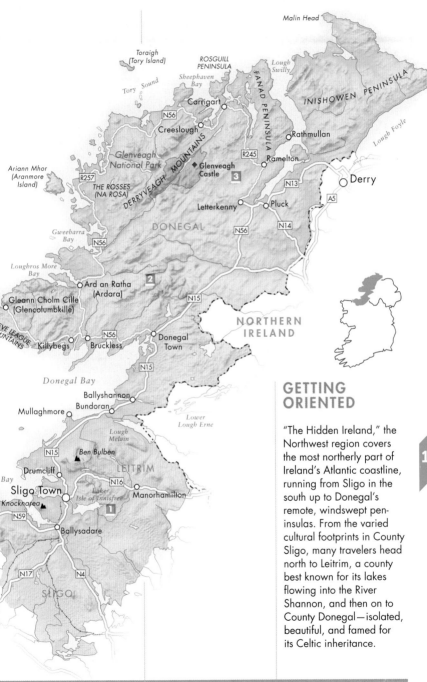

Malin Head

Toraigh
(Tory Island)

ROSGUILL
PENINSULA

Lough
Swilly

Sheephaven
Bay

INISHOWEN PENINSULA

Tory Sound

Carrigart

N56

Creeslough

Glenveagh
National Park

Rathmullan

Lough Foyle

R245

Ramelton

Ariann Mhor
(Aranmore
Island)

R257

THE ROSSES
(NA ROSA)

DERRYVEAGH MOUNTAINS

Glenveagh
Castle

3

N13

Derry

Letterkenny

Pluck

A5

Gweebarra
Bay

DONEGAL

N56

N14

Loughros More
Bay

N56

2

Ard an Ratha
(Ardara)

N15

NORTHERN
IRELAND

Gleann Cholm Cille
(Glencolumbkille)

SLIEVE LEAGUE MOUNTAINS

Killybegs

N56

Bruckless

Donegal
Town

N15

Donegal Bay

Ballyshannon

Bundoran

Mullaghmore

Lough
Melvin

Lower
Lough Erne

N15

Ben Bulben

LEITRIM

Drumcliff

N16

Sligo Town

Lake
Isle of Innisfree

Manorhamilton

Knocknarea

1

N59

Ballysadare

N17

N4

SLIGO

GETTING
ORIENTED

"The Hidden Ireland," the
Northwest region covers
the most northerly part of
Ireland's Atlantic coastline,
running from Sligo in the
south up to Donegal's
remote, windswept pen-
insulas. From the varied
cultural footprints in County
Sligo, many travelers head
north to Leitrim, a county
best known for its lakes
flowing into the River
Shannon, and then on to
County Donegal—isolated,
beautiful, and famed for
its Celtic inheritance.

Updated by
Paul Clements

Comprising counties Sligo, Leitrim, and Donegal, this most inaccessible and isolated corner of Ireland provides rich rewards for intrepid travelers willing to overcome vast distances and spotty transportation. While the rest of the Emerald Isle has been fully explored, the Northwest can still proclaim itself "the hidden Ireland"—and that's no blarney.

Glance at a map of Ireland that has scenic roads printed in green and chances are your eye will be drawn to the far-flung peninsulas of Northwest Ireland. At virtually every bend in the roads there will be something to justify all those green markings. On an island with no shortage of majestic scenery, the Northwest claims its full share. Cool, clean waters from the roaring Atlantic have carved the terrain into long peninsulas—creating a raw, sensual landscape that makes it seem as if the earth is still under construction.

But what you see *this moment* may not be what you will see an hour hence. Clouds and rain linger over mountains, glens, cliffs, beaches, and bogs, to be chased minutes later by sunshine and rainbows. The air, light, and colors of the countryside change as though viewed under a kaleidoscope. The writer William Butler Yeats and his brother Jack Butler Yeats, a painter, immortalized this splendidly lush and rugged countryside in their work.

Northwest Ireland is overwhelmingly rural and underpopulated. That's not to say there isn't a bit of action here. Sligo Town, for instance, has gone through a major renaissance. On a typical weekday, the little winding streets are as busy as those of Galway—an amazing feat for a town of only 18,000. Sligo Town pulses not only in the present but also with the charge of history, for it was the childhood home of W. B. and Jack B. Yeats, the place that, more than any other, gave rise to their particular geniuses—or, as Jack B. put it: "Sligo was my school and the sky above it."

THE NORTHWEST PLANNER

WHEN TO GO

When it rains, it really pours. Forget about the winter months, when inclement weather and a heavy fog swing in from the Atlantic and settle in until spring, masking much of the beautiful scenery. But in all seasons remember to pack a warm and waterproof coat (especially if you're headed to the coast) and bring a good pair of walking shoes. It's not all doom and gloom: the weather can be glorious in the summer months—just don't bet your house on it.

Try to plan your visit around one of the many festivals held in the Northeast. Each village tends to have its own *féile* (festival) during the summer months, and it's often worth the money and effort to attend. Music festivals are tops, from the traditional Irish Sligo Feis Ceoil in mid-April to the country-and-western Bundoran Music Festival in June, and the jazz and blues weekend féile in Gortahork, Donegal County, in April. But being an Irish-speaking stronghold, the emphasis is on Irish traditional music. Every summer weekend you are guaranteed a bit of *craic* (fun) with lively sessions in most pubs. Sligo Town, Ard an Ratha (Ardara), and Letterkenny are all hot spots. There are village festivals dedicated to hill walking, fishing, poetry, art, and food. As the saying goes "any excuse for a *féile*"

PLANNING YOUR TIME

The Northwest is one of Ireland's most compact regions, and beautifully designed so that you can see the best of it with a three- or five-day trip. The best starting place, of course, is the gateway town where all the trains deposit you: Sligo, an excellent base thanks to its first-class hotels and facilities.

IF YOU HAVE 3 DAYS

Start your tour with Sligo's walking trail, a signposted trail of the town with a free tourist-board booklet to help you identify the important buildings and architectural surprises. Whatever else you do, don't forget to call into Hargadon's time-burnished bar—unchanged in 160 years— for some fresh mussels and a glass of stout. You can drive or take an organized tour in the afternoon to the Lake Isle of Innisfree, south of Sligo town. Start early on day two for a short trip out to catch the sea breezes at Rosses Point or Mullaghmore on the coast followed by an onward drive north to Donegal. Stop en route at Drumcliff churchyard to pay your respects at Yeats's grave. Donegal town, with its Irish tweed shops, is good for a spot of shopping followed by a tour of the 15th-century Donegal Castle. After an hour's drive west over twisting roads and amid glorious mountain scenery via the fishing port of Killybegs, you will come to the "back of the beyonds," aka Glencolumbkille, where you can happily potter around the Folk Village Museum. You can overnight here or drive north to Letterkenny, a modest-sized town with decent hotels, cafés, and restaurants. After a morning pottering Letterkenny's streets you should devote the entire afternoon to Glenveagh: tour the castle and rhododendron-filled gardens, follow one of the short nature trails in search of the golden eagles that are found here, or join a ranger-guided hill walk and take a picnic with you.

10

CLOSE UP

Gaeltacht: Understanding the Language

County Donegal was part of the ancient kingdom of Ulster not conquered by the English until the 17th century. When the English withdrew in the 1920s, they had still not eradicated rural Donegal's Celtic inheritance. It thus shouldn't come as a surprise that it contains Ireland's largest Gaeltacht (Irish-speaking) area. Driving in this part of the country, you may either be frustrated or amused when you come to a crossroads whose signposts show only the Irish place-names, often so unlike the English versions as to be completely incomprehensible. To make things more confusing, some shop and hotel owners have opted to go with the English, not Irish, variant for their establishment's name. All is not lost, however, as maps generally give both the Irish and English names.

And locals are usually more than happy to help out with directions (in English)—often with a colorful yarn thrown in.

GETTING HERE AND AROUND
AIR TRAVEL

The principal international air-arrival point to Northwest Ireland is Ireland West Airport Knock, 55 km (34 miles) southwest of Sligo Town. City of Derry Airport, a few miles over the border, receives flights from Manchester and Glasgow. City of Derry (also called Eglinton) is a particularly convenient airport for reaching northern County Donegal. Donegal Airport, in Carrickfinn, typically receives flights from Dublin. BmiBaby flies from Knock to Manchester daily and to Birmingham six days a week. Ryanair has daily flights to Ireland West Airport Knock from London Stansted and London Gatwick, and also serves City of Derry Airport daily from London and Dublin. British Airways flies to City of Derry Airport from Glasgow and Dublin.

Airport Information City of Derry Airport ☎ 028/7181–0784 ⊕ www.cityofderryairport.com. **Donegal Airport** ☎ 074/954–8232 ⊕ www.donegalairport.ie. **Ireland West Airport Knock** ☎ 94/936–8100 ⊕ www.irelandwestairport.com. **Sligo Airport** ☎ 071/916–8280, 071/916–8318 ⊕ www.sligoairport.com.

Carriers Aer Arann. Aer Arann flights now handled by Aer Lingus. ☎ 0818/365–044, 0871/718–2020 in U.K. ⊕ www.aerlingus.com. **British Airways City Express** ☎ 0844/493–0787 ⊕ www.britishairways.com. **BmiBaby** ☎ 0844/848–4888 ⊕ www.bmibaby.com. **Ryanair** ☎ 0818/303-030 ⊕ www.ryanair.com.

AIRPORT TRANSFERS   If you aren't driving, Ireland West Airport Knock becomes less attractive; there are no easy public transportation links, except the once-a-day (in season) local bus to Charlestown, 11 km (7 miles) away. You can get taxis—both cars and minibuses—right outside Ireland West Airport Knock. The average rate is around €1.50 per kilometer. If you're not flying into Knock, you may have to phone a taxi company. Phone numbers of taxi companies are available from airport information desks and are also displayed beside pay phones.

BUS TRAVEL

Getting around by bus is easy enough if you plan to visit only the larger towns. Bus Éireann's routes are regular and reliable and there are also several privately run local bus companies, including McGeehan Coaches.

Bus Éireann helpfully offers a flexible Open Road bus pass ideally suited for travelers in the Northwest. A three-day pass costs €54 and each additional day's travel is €15. You can go anywhere in the republic on the nationwide network of services with this pass, but it is not valid across the border in Northern Ireland.

Bus Information **Bus Éireann** ☎ *01/836–6111 in Dublin, 071/916–0066 in Sligo, 074/912–1309 in Letterkenny* ⊕ *www.buseireann.ie.* **Bus Feda** ☎ *074/954–8114* ⊕ *www.feda.ie.* **Londonderry & Lough Swilly Railway Company** ☎ *028/7126–2017* ⊕ *www.loughswillybusco.com.* **McGeehan Coaches** ☎ *074/954–6150* ⊕ *www.mcgeehancoaches.com.* **North West Busways** ☎ *074/938–2619* ⊕ *www.foylecoaches.com.*

CAR TRAVEL

There is only one way to fully explore the rural Northwest of Ireland and that's by car. Once here, you can always rent a car at Ireland West Airport Knock or Sligo Town. But if coming from Dublin, many opt to rent from one of the bigger companies at the larger airports. If arriving from Northern Ireland, there are rental agencies aplenty in Derry or Belfast, but be sure to tell your agency if you are planning to cross the border.

The roads between the larger towns are fairly well maintained and signposted, but go slightly off the beaten track and conditions can vary from bad to dirt track. As long as you're not in a mad rush, this can add to the delight of your journey. This is rural Ireland and if the scenery doesn't make this blissfully clear, then the suspension on your rented car certainly will!

In the Irish-speaking areas, signposts are written only in the Irish (Gaelic) language, which can be confusing. Make sure that your map lists both English and Irish place-names.

TRAIN TRAVEL

Sligo Town is the northernmost direct rail link to Dublin. If you want to get to Sligo Town by rail from other provincial towns, you must make some inconvenient connections and take roundabout routes. The rest of the region has no railway service.

Train Information **Irish Rail** ☎ *01/836–6222, 071/916–9888 Sligo train station* ⊕ *www.irishrail.ie.*

For more information on getting here and around, see Travel Smart Ireland.

RESTAURANTS

Donegal mountain spring lamb, Glen Bay lobster and crab, Donegal Bay oysters and mussels, Lough Swilly wild salmon, freshly baked scones, crusty homemade brown bread, and Guinness cake are just some of the delicious reasons why you will not go hungry traveling through the Northwest. Sligo Town has established itself as a sort of last stop for food lovers, with a number of food-related shops worth visiting. Newcomers are serving up well-above-average food in memorable settings, though the majority of restaurants serve plain and simple fare, such as traditional Irish lamb stew or bacon and cabbage served with generous helpings of potatoes (often prepared in at least two ways on the same plate. You're likely to find the finest food at the higher-quality country houses, where chefs elegantly prepare local meat, fish, and produce in a hybrid Irish-French haute cuisine.

Prices in the reviews are the average cost of a main course at dinner or, if dinner is not served, at lunch.

HOTELS

True, it's the farthest-flung corner of Ireland, but thanks to the area's popularity, good bed-and-breakfasts and small hotels are abundant. In the two major towns—Sligo Town and Donegal Town—and the small coastal resorts in between, many traditional provincial hotels have been modernized (albeit not always elegantly). Yet most manage to retain some of the charm that comes with older buildings and personalized service. Away from these areas, your best overnight choice is usually a modest guesthouse that includes bed, breakfast, and an evening meal, though you can also find first-class country-house hotels with that gracious professionalism found elsewhere in Ireland. Consider staying in an Irish-speaking home to get to know members of the area's Gaeltacht population; the local tourist information office (TIO) can be helpful in making a booking with an Irish-speaking family.

Prices in the reviews are the lowest cost of a standard double room in high season.

TOURS

Bus Éireann has budget-price, guided, one-day bus tours of the Donegal Highlands and to Glenveagh National Park; they start from Bundoran, Sligo Town, Ballyshannon, and Donegal Town.

Bus Tours Bus Éireann ☎ *01/836–6111* ⊕ *www.buseireann.ie.*

VISITOR INFORMATION

The tourist information office (TIO) in Sligo Town provides a 24-page booklet detailing a sign-posted walking tour of Sligo, information about bus tours of Yeats Country as well as Yeats Trail leaflets, and details of boat tours of Lough Gill. It's also the main visitor information center for Northwest Ireland. Open hours are September to mid-March, weekdays 9–5; mid-March to August, weekdays 9–6, Saturday 10–4, and Sunday 11–3. If you're traveling in County Donegal in the north, try the TIO at Letterkenny, about 1½ km (1 mile) south of town. It's open September to May, weekdays 9–5; June to August, Monday–Saturday 9–6 and Sunday noon–3. The office at Bundoran is open only in summer (usually the first week in June to the second week in September).

SLIGO AND ENVIRONS

Just as James Joyce made Dublin his own through his novels and stories, Sligo and its environs, known locally as Yeats Country, are bound to the work of W. B. Yeats (1865–1939), Ireland's first of four Nobel laureates, and to the work of his brother Jack B. (1871–1957), one of Ireland's most important 20th-century painters, whose expressionistic landscapes and portraits are as emotionally fraught as his brother's poems are lyrical and plangent. The brothers intimately knew and eloquently celebrated in their art not only Sligo Town itself, but the surrounding countryside, with its lakes, farms, woodland, and dramatic mountains that rise up not far from the center of town. On the Sligo to Drumcliff route, you will often see glimpses of Ben Bulben Mountain, which looms over the western end of the Dartry range. The areas covered here are the most accessible parts of Northwest Ireland, easily reached from Galway.

SLIGO TOWN

60 km (37 miles) northeast of Ballina, 138 km (86 miles) northeast of Galway, 217 km (135 miles) northwest of Dublin.

Sligo, the only sizable town in the whole of Northwest Ireland, is the best place to begin a tour of Yeats Country. Squeezed onto a patch of land between Sligo Bay and Lough Gill, Sligo Town is clustered on the south shore between two bridges that span the River Garavogue, just east of where the river opens into the bay. Thanks to the pedestrian zone along the south shore of the river (between the two bridges), you can enjoy vistas of the river while right in the center of town.

Sligo was often a battleground in its earlier days. It was attacked by Viking invaders in 807; later, it was invaded by a succession of rival Irish and Anglo-Norman conquerors. In 1642 the British soldiers of Sir Frederick Hamilton fell upon Sligo, killing every visible inhabitant, burning the town, and destroying the interior of the beautiful medieval abbey. Between 1845 and 1849, more than a million inhabitants of Sligo County died in the potato famine or fled to escape it.

Since the early 2000s, the streets have been ringing with the bite of buzz saws as apartments, shopping malls, and cinema complexes have been erected behind tasteful, traditional facades, although with the demise of the Celtic Tiger building development has tapered off, and the area has been affected by the recession like most other parts of Ireland.

By day Sligo is as lively and crowded as its considerably larger neighbor to the southwest, Galway, with locals, students from the town's college, and tourists bustling past its historic buildings and along its narrow sidewalks and winding streets, and crowding its one-of-a-kind shops, restaurants, and traditional pubs. More than any other town in Northwest Ireland, the Sligo of today has an energy that would surprise anyone who hasn't been here in the past few years.

10

Sligo and Donegal Bay

Na Gleannta

Kilrean

N56 N250 R253

N56

Ard an Ratha (Ardara)

BLUE STACK MOUNTAINS

D O N E G A L

Glengesh Pass

Gleann Cholm Cille (Glencolumbkille)

Malin More

R262

TO LOUGH ESKE

SLIEVE LEAGUE MOUNTAINS

An Charraig (Carrick)

N56

N56

Donegal Town

N15

R263

Killybegs

Bruckless

Dunkineely

N15

Teileann

Cill Chaitaigh

Mac Swyne's Bay

Laghy

R234

TO LOUGH DERG

Inver Bay

St. John's Point

Rossnowlagh

Ballintra

Donegal Bay

R291

N15

Ballyshannon

TO LOUGH ERNE

Bundoran

Belleek

Lough Melvin

N
O
R
T
H
E
R
N

I
R
E
L
A
N
D

Mullaghmore

Kinlough

Cliffony

Creevykeel

Garrison

Grange

N15

R280

R282

Glenade

Carney

BEN BULBEN

Glencar Lough

Drumcliff Bay

Drumcliff

Rathcormack

N16

Sligo Bay

Rosses Point

R291

Cregg

N15

Sligo Town see detail map

Manorhamilton

Strandhill

R292

N286

R286

Parke's Castle

Knocknarea

Lough Gill

Creevelea Abbey

L E I T R I M

Templeboy

N59

Carrowmore

Lake Isle of Innisfree

Killarga

TO BALLINA

Beltra

N4

Dromahair

R280

R290

R287

Collooney

Ballygawley

Drumkeeran

R284

R280

Ropefield

N17

S L I G O

Drumfin

Riverstown

0   6 miles

0   9 km

N4

Lough Arrow

TO GALWAY

Ballymote

TO CARRICK-ON-SHANNON

Come Gather in 2013

During 2013, Sligo will be a key destination hub in what is billed as Ireland's biggest tourism event, The Gathering—an initiative to encourage Sligo diaspora to come "home" and rejoin their kin for some quintessential Sligo fun and festivity. Celebratory events include the Sligo Live Music Festival, the annual Choral Festival, and the Sligo Sea Shanty Festival at Rosses Point, 8 km (5 miles) from town. Alternatively, the returning peoples of Sligo may want to drop in to hear the magnificent Jazz Lads who've been together for 50 years and play at the Harp Tavern on Sunday mornings, or some might want to get straight to the bare bones of Sligo by joining in the "Dip in the Nip," an annual all-nude summer charity swim where more than 300 brave souls take to the Atlantic waters at a beach on the Sligo coast.

GETTING HERE AND AROUND

Sligo's two main pay car parks are in Wine Street and in the Quayside Shopping Centre. Prices are between €1 and €1.20 per hour. In other parts of the town, such as Temple Street (by the cathedral), you pay €3 for all-day parking. In the morning, school runs and store deliveries can cause congestion, but the town is mostly free of any serious traffic problems. Sligo is two hours north of Galway on the N17 and three hours driving time to Dublin on the N4.

Trains are in short supply in the Northwest region, but buses are plentiful. From Sligo Town, buses spider out frequently in all directions, serving rural towns and villages in counties Sligo, Leitrim, and much farther afield. The main service is operated by Bus Éireann, which has 47 departures daily from its McDiarmada Station at Lord Edward Street to many points of the Irish geographical compass. Seven daily express services link Sligo with Dublin Airport and Dublin city center's Busaras Station. There are daily services south to Ballina and Westport in County Mayo. Galway City is a 2½-hour journey. Main bus corridors north of Sligo run to Bundoran, Donegal Town, Letterkenny, and Derry. There are also four daily services between Sligo and Belfast, a trip that takes about three hours.

Iarnród Éireann, the Irish Rail company, operates efficient intercity train connections from Sligo to Dublin. However, other towns in County Donegal are not served by trains, nor are other nearby cities in Ireland: even if you're traveling to Galway or Belfast, you must transfer in Dublin first. Eight daily services run to and from Dublin's Connolly Station, taking three hours and five minutes to reach Sligo. ■TIP➜ Standard class round-trip fares are considerably cheaper if booked online. Sligo's McDiarmada Station is located on Lord Edward Street, a 10-minute walk to the city center (walk downhill and turn left).

TOURS

In the summer a good way to get your bearings is to join one of the guided walking tours of Sligo that leave from the tourist office on O'Connell Street. During June, July, and August (Tuesday–Friday 11

10

am–1 pm) these free two-hour tours are led by a knowledgeable guide and cover cultural history as well as stopping at many of the architectural highlights featured in the historic sites listed here.

ESSENTIALS

Transportation Information **Sligo Railway Station** ☎ *071/916–9888.*

Visitor Information **County Sligo Tourism** ✉ *O'Connell St., Sligo Town, Co. Sligo* ☎ *071/916–1201* ⊕ *www.sligotourism.ie.*

EXPLORING
TOP ATTRACTIONS

Fodor'sChoice ★ **The Model: Home of the Niland Collection.** Since its reopening in 2010, after a two-year €6 million renovation, this arts center housed in a beautifully renovated school built in 1862 has become one of Ireland's premier arts venues. The main attraction is one of Ireland's largest collections of works by 20th-century artists from Ireland and abroad. Periodically, the gallery displays works by famed Irish painter Jack B. Yeats, who once said, "I never did a painting without putting a thought of Sligo in it." At the heart of the collection is the work amassed by the woman whose name the gallery now bears, Nora Niland, who was the Sligo librarian from 1945 and who recognized the importance of Yeats' work. Paintings by John Yeats (father of Jack B. and W. B.), who had a considerable reputation as a portraitist, also hang here, as do portraits by Sean Keating and Paul Henry.

As part of the renovation, new performance and workshop spaces were built, a new gallery was opened to increase and complete the circuit on the first floor, and seven artists' studios were added. There is also a 214-seater cinema with a program run in conjunction with the Irish Film Institute. A revamped main entrance and the Slice Cafe complete the dynamic makeover. ✉ *The Mall, Sligo Town, Co. Sligo* ☎ *071/914–1405* ⊕ *www.themodel.ie* 🖾 *Free* ⊙ *Wed.–Sat. 11–5:30, Sun. noon–5.*

Sligo County Museum. The showpiece of this museum is its Yeats Hall, which houses a collection of W. B. Yeats's writings from 1889 to 1936, various editions of his plays and prose, the Nobel prize medal awarded to him in 1923, and the Irish tricolor (flag) that draped his coffin when he was buried at nearby Drumcliff. W. B. Yeats's letters to James Stephens and Oliver St. John Gogarty offer insight into Yeats's obsessive love for Sligo. The museum also has small sections on local society, history, and archaeology. ✉ *Stephen St., Sligo Town, Co. Sligo* ☎ *071/911–1850* ⊕ *www.sligolibrary.ie* 🖾 *Free* ⊙ *May–Sept., daily 9:30–12:30.*

★ **Yeats Memorial Building.** Set atop the stone Hyde Bridge, this structure makes for a suitably imposing address for the Yeats Society. On the first floor, a gallery hosts a rotating exhibition of contemporary art. In addition, the Yeats International Summer School is conducted here every August (in 2009 it celebrated its 50th School). A permanent photographic exhibition, "Yeats and his Circle," is on display and can be viewed along with a 15-minute film, "The Yeats Country." On the ground floor, drop in to the delightful Lily's café. Across the street

Sligo's most famous native son, poet W. B. Yeats, is honored by many memorials and statues found throughout the town.

is Rowan Gillespie's photo-worthy sculpture of the poet, draped in a flowing coat overlaid with excerpts from his work. It was unveiled in 1989 by Michael Yeats, W.B.'s son, in commemoration of the 50th anniversary of his father's death. ⊠ *Hyde Bridge, Sligo Town, Co. Sligo* ☎ *071/914–2693* ⊕ *www.yeats-sligo.com* ✉ *€2* ⊙ *Mon.–Fri. 10–5.*

The Yeats Trail. Yeatsian aficionados will want to follow the Yeats Trail, a tourist trail established jointly by Fáilte Ireland and the Yeats Society in January 2009 to mark the 70th anniversary of the poet's death. The trail takes in places strongly linked with W.B. Yeats, predominantly in Sligo, but also in County Galway and Dublin. It was launched by the Nobel Prize–winning poet Seamus Heaney, who proclaimed Yeats the greatest poet in the English language in the 20th century and one inextricably linked with Sligo. Amusingly, a local tourism official described Yeats as "the first public relations officer for the northwest of Ireland." A leaflet on the trail, with a detailed map, is available from the tourist office; once you have visited at least five of the locations—"the places of silence and solitude" to which W. B. Yeats retreated—you receive passport stamps and a personalized Yeats Trail certificate. ⊕ *www. discoverireland.com/gb/campaigns/yeats-trail/.*

WORTH NOTING

Sligo Abbey. A massive stone complex that is still redolent of "auld grandeur" and famed for its medieval tomb sculptures, Sligo Abbey is the town's only existing relic of the Middle Ages. Maurice FitzGerald erected the structure for the Dominicans in 1253. After a fire in 1414, it was extensively rebuilt, only to be destroyed again by Cromwell's Puritans under the command of Sir Frederick Hamilton, in 1642. Today the abbey consists of a ruined nave, aisle, transept, and tower. Some fine stonework remains, especially in the 15th-century cloisters. The visitor center is the base for guided tours, which are included with admission. ⊠ *Abbey St., Sligo Town, Co. Sligo* ☎ *071/914–6406* ⊕ *www. heritageireland.ie* ⊠ *€3* ⊙ *Apr.–Oct., daily 10–6.*

St. John's Cathedral. Designed in 1730 by Richard Castle—the architect who gave us the spectacular Powerscourt and Russborough stately houses in County Wicklow—this Church of Ireland cathedral has a handsome square tower and fortifications. In the north transept is a copper bronze memorial plaque to Susan Mary Yeats, mother of W. B. and Jack B. A beautiful stained-glass window commemorates William and Elizabeth Pollexfen, Yeats's maternal grandparents. Next door is the larger and newer Roman Catholic Cathedral of the Immaculate Conception (with an entrance on Temple Street), consecrated in 1874. Tours of St. John's can be arranged through the Yeats Society Memorial Building. ⊠ *John St., Sligo Town, Co. Sligo.*

WHERE TO EAT

$ ✕ **Bistro Bianconi.** In 2011, Bistro Bianconi moved its operation a
ITALIAN   short distance around the corner to Tobergal Lane and, happily, its 20-year-strong reputation in Sligo for top class pizzas baked in a wood-burning oven survived the move. The menu also includes classic and contemporary Italian dishes such as fresh pasta and lasagna while chicken *bocconcini*, the signature dish, is as popular as ever. A children's menu is available at lunchtime and until 7 pm. ⑤ *Average main: €15* ⊠ *Tobergal La., Sligo Town, Co. Sligo* ☎ *071/914–1744* ⊕ *www.bistrobianconi.ie.*

$$ ✕ **Eala Bhán.** Swans will be a leitmotif of your visit to Sligo: you will
MODERN IRISH   come across them in Yeats's poetry, see them in the Garavogue River, and find them depicted taking flight on the walls of Eala Bhán (meaning "White Swan") restaurant, a popular newcomer to the Sligo dining scene. The decor is modern but comfortable, and the food is Irish with a French twist. Steak and seafood—red snapper, monkfish, and lobster—are prominent on the evening dinner menu, as well as vegetarian dishes. The early-bird menu (5–6:30) is a good value with a choice of two or three courses, including, for main course, "posh" fish-and-chips (cooked in tempura and with pea purée), beef burgers, or pasta. Don't let the preening swans, visible from the dining-room window, distract you from the dessert menu. ⑤ *Average main: €19* ⊠ *Rockwood Parade, Sligo Town, Co. Sligo* ☎ *071/914–5823* ⊕ *www.ealabhan.ie* ⊙ *No lunch Mon.*

$ ✕ **Osta Café.** Osta Café's philosophy is a straightforward one: locally
IRISH   sourced food, preferably organic, simply prepared. There's also a simple pleasure in knowing that the seasonal vegetables are from the Crimlin Farm, free range and organic eggs are supplied by Bluebell Farm, the French Market in Sligo delivers fresh bread each day, honey is from Knocknaree, and the meat is supplied by Clarkes and Sheerins butchers. Sheep, cows, and goat cheese is made by Silke Cropp in Belturbet, while Carraig na Breac Smoke House in Drumshanbo provides smoked chicken and smoked cheddar cheese. Their 30-mile breakfast is named for the proud fact that all ingredients come from

within that distance—with the exception of the Fairtrade and organic Mexican and Peruvian Arabica coffee (but it's ethically sourced). The Osta Platter–homemade brown bread with roast ham, cheese, smoked chicken, and apple chutney packs a filling lunchtime punch. $ *Average main: €10* ⊠ *Garavogue Weir, Stephen St., Sligo Town, Co. Sligo* ☎ *071/914–4639.*

$$ ╳ **Source Sligo.** Since opening at the end of 2010, Sligonians have been
IRISH flocking to this new arrival, which occupies a three-story curving, glass-front building in the center of town. Everything on the menu is Irish, and food provenance is important to owners Ray and Eileen Monahan. Their company name, Source, inspired them to use local food from surrounding farms and fish suppliers. The result is that diners can choose from John Dory caught in the sea off Donegal, Sligo lamb, or Silverhill duckling from Monaghan. The platter dishes are the best value, with a choice of soups, mains, and desserts for €13.50 at lunch, while prices rise to an average of €18 for a main dinner course. Sit at a table of reclaimed timber and enjoy your food under the quirky fishing nets and waste bins used for lights. Then, if you're impressed with your lunch, head up to the top-floor cooking school; its wide repertoire of classes is sure to tempt the hungry stray visitor. $ *Average main: €19* ⊠ *1–2 John St., Sligo Town, Co. Sligo* ☎ *71/914–7605* ⊕ *www.sourcesligo.ie.*

10

WHERE TO STAY

For expanded hotel reviews, visit Fodors.com.

$$$$
HOTEL
Fodor's Choice
★

⚏ **Coopershill.** Seven generations of the O'Hara family have lived in this three-story Georgian farmhouse since it was built in 1774. **Pros:** enter a delightful haven of peace, sink into the roll-top bath or four-poster bed, and lose yourself in luxury; wander around the croquet lawn, admire the strutting peacocks, or feed the wild barn owls. **Cons:** rooms can be chilly on cold days; quite a trek to the nearest pub or shops. **Trip-Advisor:** "perfect in every way," "peace and relaxation," "romantic getaway." $ *Rooms from: €218* ⊠ *Off N4, 17 km (11 miles) southeast of Sligo, Riverstown, Co. Sligo* ☎ *071/916–5108* ⊕ *www.coopershill. com* ⤴ *8 rooms* ☾ *Closed Nov.–Mar.* ⏍*Breakfast.*

$$
HOTEL
Fodor's Choice
★

⚏ **The Glasshouse.** Cosmopolitan modernists will love this funky, shiny six-story riverside hotel—it elevates accommodations in Sligo to a brash new level: just take a look at the towering exterior, which has been designed to resemble a ship docked at the harbor. **Pros:** excellent location: Sligo's bustling heart is around the corner; underground car parking is included. **Cons:** bring your shades, as colors will dazzle until you adjust; lacks leisure facilities such as gym or pool. **TripAdvisor:** "super location," "great staff," "another fabulous Glasshouse experience." $ *Rooms from: €129* ⊠ *Swan Point, Sligo, Sligo Town, Co. Sligo* ☎ *071/919–4300* ⊕ *www.theglasshouse.ie* ⤴ *116 rooms, 4 suites* ⏍*Breakfast.*

$$
HOTEL
Fodor's Choice
★

⚏ **Markree Castle.** One of the most beautiful fortress fronts in Ireland greets you on arrival at Markree, Sligo's oldest inhabited castle and the home of the Cooper family for 350 years. **Pros:** nature lovers will be at home with walks across parkland and down to the Unsin River; luxurious but comfortable. **Cons:** bathroom water taps are slow; check out on time (11:30 am) or wind up with a €50 surcharge per hour. **TripAdvisor:** "in a beautiful bygone-age setting," "a right royal time," "real castle in stunning location." $ *Rooms from: €140* ⊠ *11 km (7 miles) south of Sligo Town, off N4, Collooney, Co. Sligo* ☎ *071/916–7800* ⊕ *www. markreecastle.ie* ⤴ *30 rooms* ⏍*Multiple meal plans.*

$
HOTEL

⚏ **Sligo Park Hotel & Leisure Club.** Expect a modern establishment designed for a contemporary traveler and those who want to tour Yeats Country: a first-rate fitness center, dancing and piano entertainment some evenings, and the Hazelwood restaurant as well as the popular Rathana bar. **Pros:** functional rooms; good facilities include a modern leisure center and ample car parking. **Cons:** as it's a suburban hotel, it's a 30-minute walk into town if you're feeling energetic; the dining focus is on pub grub rather than restaurant meals. **TripAdvisor:** "ticked all the boxes," "very helpful staff," "proper Irish hotel." $ *Rooms from: €110* ⊠ *Pearse Rd. off N4, Sligo Town, Co. Sligo* ☎ *071/919–0400* ⊕ *www. sligopark.com* ⤴ *138 rooms* ⏍*Multiple meal plans.*

NIGHTLIFE AND THE ARTS

NIGHTLIFE

Hargadons Bar. Part of the social fabric of Sligo since it opened over 150 years ago, Hargadons Bar preserves its unique historic character and local chef Joe Grogan has instilled new life into it since a tasteful makeover in 2008. Wood paneling, cozy snugs (small booths) for

Famed as a Sligo landmark since it opened its doors 150 years ago, Hargadons Bar has a time-burnished interior and also some of the freshest mussels around.

private powwows, marble-top counters, and little glass doors on hinges make this place especially conducive to that intangible Irish element, the craic. Check out the walls, covered with historical black-and-white photos as well as fading invoices from the bar's early days. Hearty food at great prices is served at lunchtime, and the evening dinner menu, featuring oysters, mussels, burgers, tiger prawns, or confit of duck, lists local suppliers. Walk through the bar and in separate premises at the back, you will find the well-stocked Hargadons Wine Shop in Johnston Court. ⊠ *4–5 O'Connell St., Sligo Town, Co. Sligo* ☎ *071/915–3709* ⊕ *www.hargadons.com.*

Thatch. A few miles south of town is a popular spot with the locals, the Thatch pub, which has traditional music sessions in the summer from Thursday to Sunday. ⊠ *Thatch, Ballysadare, Co. Sligo* ☎ *071/ 916–7288.*

Toffs. A sizable dance floor at Toffs teems with Sligo's younger set moving to a mix of contemporary dance music and older favorites. It stays open later than most places. ⊠ *Kennedy Parade, Sligo Town, Co. Sligo* ☎ *071/916–1250* ⊕ *www.toffs.eu.*

THE ARTS

THEATER **Hawk's Well Theatre.** With a jam-packed calendar year-round, Hawk's Well Theatre hosts amateur and professional companies from all over Ireland (and occasionally from Britain) in an eclectic mix of shows. Shows run €15–€30; the box office is open weekdays 10–5:30, Saturday 2–5:30, and on Sunday 30 minutes before the performance. ⊠ *Temple St., Sligo Town, Co. Sligo* ☎ *071/916–1526* ⊕ *www.hawkswell.com.*

Sligo Live Music and Arts Festival. If you're visiting in the fall, don't miss the Sligo Live Music and Arts Festival, held at various venues around town. Established in 2005, the festival runs over the bank-holiday weekend at the end of October. It is elbow room-only as hotels, pubs, and cafés are crammed with scores of live sessions while fiddlers, dancers, jugglers, and puppeteers fill the streets. For dates and details of gigs, visit the website, where you can buy tickets. ⊕ *www.sligolive.ie.*

SHOPPING

Sligo Town has Northwest Ireland's most thriving shopping scene, with lots of food-related, crafts, and hand-knits shops.

Carraig Donn. In addition to Irish knitwear, Carraig Donn carries pottery, glassware, linens, and Aran knits for children. ⊠ *41 O'Connell St., Sligo Town, Co. Sligo* ☎ *071/914–4158* ⊕ *www.carraigdonn.com.*

The Cat & the Moon. The Cat & the Moon specializes in eclectic and stylish Irish-made crafts, jewelry, pottery, ironwork, and scarves; it's named after the play by W. B. Yeats. Upstairs is the Hamilton gallery, featuring work by contemporary Irish artists. ⊠ *4 Castle St., Sligo Town, Co. Sligo* ☎ *071/914–3686* ⊕ *www.thecatandthemoon.com.*

Cosgrove and Son. The upscale deli Cosgrove and Son sells everything from Parma ham to carrageen moss boiled in milk (a local cure for upset stomachs). Stock up here for a picnic. ⊠ *32 Market St., Sligo Town, Co. Sligo* ☎ *071/914–2809.*

Cross Sections. Along with lovely tableware, this is the place to head for fine glassware and kitchenware. ⊠ *2 Grattan St., Sligo Town, Co. Sligo* ☎ *071/914–2265.*

Tír na nóg. Tír na nóg, Irish for "Land of the Ever-young," sells organic foods, including local cheeses and honeys, and other health-oriented items. A sister store across the street sells cards and posters. ⊠ *Grattan St., Sligo Town, Co. Sligo* ☎ *071/916–2752.*

LOUGH GILL

1½ km (1 miles) east of Sligo Town.

★ Lough Gill means simply "Lake Beauty." In fine weather the beautiful river-fed lough and its surroundings are serenity itself: sunlight on the meadows all around, lough-side cottages, the gentle sound of water, salmon leaping, a yacht sailing by.

GETTING HERE AND AROUND

To get to the lake from Sligo Town, take Stephen Street, which turns into N16 (signposted to Manorhamilton and Enniskillen). Turn right almost at once onto R286. Within minutes you can see gorgeous views of the lake so adored by the young W. B. Yeats.

EXPLORING

Creevelea Abbey. A few minutes' walk along a footpath south of Parke's Castle lie the handsome ruins of Creevelea Abbey. In fact not an abbey but a friary, Creevelea was founded for the Franciscans in 1508 by a later generation of O'Rourkes. It was the last Franciscan community to be founded before the suppression of the monasteries by England's

Continued on page 547

SHOPPING FOR
A PIECE OF
THE SHAMROCK

Prepping dishes for Spongeware patterns

With its Belleek porcelains and Waterford crystals, Ireland has always been a treasured island for shoppers. Today, its traditional crafts—centuries old yet very much alive—are enjoying a revival of the fittest.

A CRAFT REVIVAL

Remember all those traditional leprechaun figurines with "Made in China" stickers on their bottoms? Today, Irish traditional crafts are flourishing as never before. In a land where many villages are still redolent of a preindustrial age, "trad" culture has become commerce—big commerce. Claddagh friendship rings, spongeware pottery, heirloom Aran sweaters, Belleek china wedding plates, Carrickmacross lace, and Waterford crystal (so finely cut you'll need to don anti-brilliance eye goggles) are all objects endowed with vibrant personality. If Ireland has never been a country of great artists, it has always been one of great artistry.

Above: Claddagh ring.
Below: Louis Mulcahey at work on his pottery.
Dingle Peninsula, Southwest Ireland

WHERE TO BUY
While the entire country is blooming with craftsworkers, the Northwest region offers some seventh-level shopping, thanks to hand-knit Aran sweaters, fine Parian china, and handwoven tweeds. Those who want to make browsing—and buying—easy will find the famous multidealer town cooperatives (such as Midleton's Courtyard Crafts or Doolin's Celtic Waves) tempting. But, in general, the more interesting craftspeople are found outside the main cities, and intrepid consumers should head for smaller towns where overheads are lower (and the scenery is better). Don't buy the first blackthorn walking stick you see. Take a good look around and visit any number of crafts shops— you'll probably end up with a bogwood paperweight and basketweave china tureen as well!

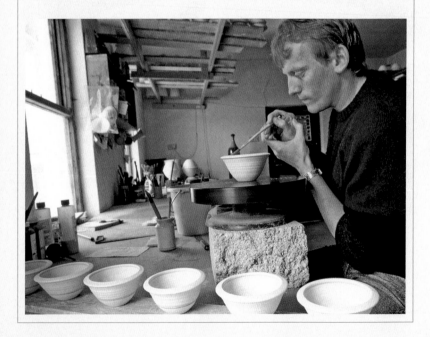

CHERISHED COLLECTIBLES

WATERFORD CRYSTAL

Founded in 1783, Waterford crystal is noted for its sparkle, clarity, and heft. Thicker glass means that each piece can be wedge-cut on a diamond wheel to dramatic effect (as you can see during the famous factory tour held at the Waterford factory in Southeast Ireland). Waterford artisans apprentice for *eight* years.

BELLEEK CHINA

China has been made in Belleek, a village just on the border with County Fermanagh, Northern Ireland, since 1857. This local product is a lustrous fine-bone china with a delicate green or yellow-on-white design and often incorporates weave-effect pottery. Americans love it. Old Belleek is an expensive collector's item, but modern Belleek is more reasonably priced and very likely to appreciate in value over the years (according to some experts).

TRADITIONAL LACEMAKING

Traditional Irish crochet and lace-making use a fine cotton and date back to the 1840s when they originated in the cottage homes and lace schools of Carrickmacross.

SPONGEWARE POTTERY

One of Ireland's most beautiful collectibles, Irish Spongeware first appeared in 18th-century potteries. With the use of a cut sponge, patterns and images—often "rural" in flavor, like plants and sheep—are applied to the lovely cream-colored surface.

CLADDAGH RINGS

Born in the Claddagh area of Galway during the 17th century, the Claddagh ring incorporates three symbols: a heart (for love), a pair of hands (for friendship), and a crown (for loyalty). Worn on the right hand, with crown and heart facing out, it symbolizes the wearer is still "free"; worn on the left, with symbols tucked under, indicates marriage.

ARAN: FROM FLEECE TO FASHION

Made of plain, undyed wool and knit with distinctive crisscross patterns, sometimes referred to as *bainin* sweaters or "ganseys," the Aran sweater is a combination of folklore and fashion.

Since harsh weather made warmth and protection vital out in the Atlantic Ocean, the women of Aran long ago discovered the solution to this problem in this strong, comfortable, hand-knit sweater. Indeed, these Arans can hold 30 percent of their weight in water before they even start to feel wet. The reason? Traditionally, the wool used was unwashed and retained its water-repellent natural sheep's lanolin.

LOOK FOR THE PATTERN

Not so long ago, these pullovers were worn by every County Donegal fisherman, usually made to a design belonging exclusively to his own family. It's said that a native can tell which family the knitter belongs to from the patterns used in a genuine Aran sweater. Often the patterns used religious symbols and folk motifs, such as the Tree of Life, the Honeycomb (standing for thrift and thought to be lucky), the SeaHorse, the Blackberry—all are patterns in the almost sculptured, deeply knitted work that characterizes the Aran method. Their famous basket stitch represents the fisherman's basket, a hope for a *curragh* (fisherboat) heavy with catch. A colorful belt called a *crios* (pronounced "criss")

is handcrafted in many traditional designs as a useful accessory.

MAKING YOUR PURCHASE

Most of the Aran sweaters you'll see throughout Ireland are made far north of the islands themselves, in County Donegal, an area most associated with high-quality, handwoven textiles. The best are painstakingly knitted by hand, a process that can take weeks. As a result, prices are not cheap, and if you think you've found a bargain, check the label before buying— it's more likely a factory copy. Still, the less expensive, lighter-weight, hand-loomed sweaters (knitted on a mechanical loom, not with needles) are less than half the price, and more practical for most lifestyles. But the real McCoy is still coveted: some of the finest examples woven by Inis Meáin are sold at luxury stores like Bergdorf Goodman and Wilkes Bashford. And young Irish designers like Liadain De Buitlear are giving the traditional Aran a newer-than-now spin, highly popular in Dublin boutiques.

Above left: A large selection of styles and sizes; Above right: Spun yarns ready to be knit into Aran sweaters

King Henry VIII. Like many other decrepit abbeys, the place still holds religious significance for the locals, who revere it. One curiosity here is the especially large south transept; notice, too, its cloisters, with well-executed carvings on the pillars of St. Francis of Assisi. ✉ *R288, Dromahair, Co. Sligo.*

Parke's Castle. This fortified house was built on the eastern shore of Lough Gill in the 17th century by an English Planter (a Protestant colonist settling on Irish lands confiscated from Catholic owners) who needed the strong fortifications to defend himself against a hostile populace. His relations with the people were made worse by the fact that he obtained his building materials mainly by dismantling a historic fortress on the site that had belonged to the clan leaders, the O'Rourkes of Breffni (once the name of the district). The entrance fee includes a short video show on the castle and local history; guided tours are available. In summer, boat tours of the lough leave from here. There's also a snack bar. ✉ *R288, Fivemile Bourne, Co. Sligo* ☎ *071/916–4149* ⊕ *www.heritageireland.ie/ en/north-west/parkescastle* 💷 *€3* ⏱ *Apr.–Sept., daily 10–6.*

WHERE TO STAY

For expanded hotel reviews, visit Fodors.com.

$ 🏠 **Stanford Village Inn.** With a 200-year-old pedigree and in the same
B&B/INN family for six generations this rustic stone-front inn is one of the few stops for sustenance near Lough Gill. **Pros:** blissful, pastoral location; lunch here will sustain you through the rest of the day. **Cons:** hard-to-find location; service can be hit or miss on busy days. 💲 *Rooms from: €55* ✉ *7 km (5 miles) from Parke's Castle, 19 km (12 miles) from Sligo Town, off R288, Dromahair, Co. Leitrim* ☎ *071/916–4140* ⊕ *www. stanfordinn.ie* 🛏 *9 rooms* ⏐⊖⏐ *Breakfast.*

LAKE ISLE OF INNISFREE

15 km (9 miles) south of Sligo Town via Dromahair.

In 1890 W. B. Yeats was walking through the West End of London when, seeing in a shop window a ball dancing on a jet of water, he was suddenly overcome with nostalgia for the lakes of his Sligo home. It was the moment, and the feeling, that shaped itself into his most famous poem, "The Lake Isle of Innisfree":

I will arise and go now, and go to Innisfree,

And a small cabin build there, of clay and wattles made:

Nine bean-rows will I have there, a hive for the honey-bee,

And live alone in the bee-loud glade.

And I shall have some peace there, for peace comes dropping slow.

Though there's nothing visually exceptional about Innisfree (pronounced *in-nish*-free), the "Lake Isle" is a must-see if you're a W. B. Yeats fan. To reach Innisfree from Dromahair, take R287, the minor road that heads back along the south side of Lough Gill, toward Sligo Town. Turn right at a small crossroads, after 4 or 5 km (2 or 3 miles), where signposts point to Innisfree. A little road leads another couple of miles down to the lakeside, where you can see the island just offshore.

10

ROSSES POINT

8 km (5 miles) northwest of Sligo Town.

It's obvious why W. B. and Jack B. Yeats often stayed at Rosses Point during their summer vacations: glorious pink-and-gold summer sunsets over a seemingly endless stretch of sandy beach. Coney Island lies just off Rosses Point. Local lore has it that the captain of the ship *Arathusa* christened Brooklyn's Coney Island after this one, but there's probably more legend than truth to this, as it's widely agreed that New York's Coney Island was named after the Dutch word *konijn* (wild rabbits, which abounded there during the 17th century).

GETTING HERE AND AROUND

Rosses Point is an 8-km (5-mile) drive west of Sligo town on the R291 around the northern arm of Sligo Harbor. There's a free car park with dramatic views overlooking Drumcliff Bay. Bus Éireann operates buses from Sligo bus station to Rosses Point and drops you off at the Roman Catholic church. The bus serves Rosses Point beach only in July and August.

SPORTS AND THE OUTDOORS

GOLF

County Sligo Golf Club. The popular County Sligo coastal links course at Rosses Point is one of Ireland's grand old venues; it's more than a century old and has hosted most of the country's major championships. Established in 1894 on land leased from Henry Middleton, an uncle of the famous Yeats brothers, the course offers magnificent views of the sea. From many of the holes—notably the 10th and 11th—there are stunning views of Ben Bulbin mountain. Sea winds are a constant factor and throw up a tremendous challenge, as do the wild dunes close to the shore. Another feature of the course is the array of wildlife; it teems with flora and fauna, a wonderful distraction for visitors. The club is the home of the West of Ireland Open amateur championship played every Easter since 1923. It has also hosted many other prestigious events including the Home Internationals, the Irish Close, and the Irish Professional Matchplay Championship. Some big-hitting names in the golfing world, including Sir Nick Faldo, Padraig Harrington, and Rory McIlroy, are honorary members. ☎ *071/917–7134* ⊕ *www. countysligogolfclub.ie* ✉ *Greens fees: 18-hole championship course, Apr.–Oct. €95; 9-hole Bomore course, Apr.–Oct. €25* ⚑ *18 holes. Yardage: 6,947. Par 71. Practice: putting, chipping, and bunker practice greens, short and long game practice areas, caddies, caddy carts, buggies, pull and electronic carts, catering* ⊗ *Visitors: daily, restricted hours at weekends from 12:06–1:26.*

SAILING

Sligo Yacht Club. With a fleet of some 90 boats, the Sligo Yacht Club has sailing and social programs, and regularly hosts races. ☎ *071/917–7168* ⊕ *www.sligoyachtclub.ie.*

DRUMCLIFF

15 km (9 miles) northeast of Rosses Point, 7 km (4½ miles) north of Sligo Town.

W. B. Yeats lies buried with his wife, Georgie, in an unpretentious grave in the cemetery of Drumcliff's simple Protestant church, where his grandfather was rector for many years. W. B. died on the French Riviera in 1939; it took almost a decade for his body to be brought back to the place that more than any other might be called his soul-land. In the poem "Under Ben Bulben," he spelled out not only where he was to be buried but also what should be written on the tomb-stone: "Cast a cold eye / On life, on death. / Horseman, pass by!" It is easy to see why the majestic Ben Bulben (1,730 feet), with its sawed-off peak (not unlike Yosemite's Half-Dome), made such an impression on the poet: the mountain gazes calmly down upon the small church, as it does on all of the surrounding landscape—and at the same time stands as a sentinel facing the mighty Atlantic.

HILLTOP DOINGS

The massive flat-dome plateau of Ben Bulben dominates the surrounding bogland. Dating to 574 when St. Columcille founded a monastery on its peak (these fellows were seriously into inaccessibility), it became a major religious destination until Oliver Cromwell extinguished it. The 1,729-foot climb has superb views, but, remember, it is always windy on top and frequently soggy underfoot.

Drumcliff is where St. Columba, a recluse and missionary who established Christian churches and religious communities in Northwest Ireland, is thought to have founded a monastic settlement around AD 575. The monastery that he founded before sailing off to the Scottish isle of Iona flourished for many centuries, but all that is left of it now is the base of a round tower and a carved high cross (both across N15 from the church) dating from around AD 1000, with scenes from the Old and New Testaments, including Adam and Eve with the serpent and Cain slaying Abel.

GETTING HERE AND AROUND

Follow the main N15 north of Sligo Town, taking the signposts for Donegal, and you will come to Drumcliff. There is ample parking at the church. It's a 15-minute drive from Sligo to Drumcliff. The Sligo–Donegal Town bus stops at Drumcliff and sets down passengers at the post office from where it's a five-minute walk to the grave of W. B. Yeats. Journey time is 15 minutes and a round-trip costs €6.20.

Drumcliff Tea House and Craft Shop. A good place to buy local crafts, books of W. B. Yeats's poetry, and books about the poet's life, the Drumcliff Tea House and Craft Shop also sells light lunches and snacks, including soup, sandwiches, and paninis. ⊠ *Next to Protestant church, Drumcliff, Co. Sligo* ☎ *071/914–4956* ⊙ *Mon.–Sun. 9–5.*

10

DONEGAL BAY

As you drive north to Donegal Town, the glens of the Dartry Mountains (to which Ben Bulben belongs) gloriously roll by to the east. Look across coastal fields for views of the waters of Donegal Bay to the west. In the distant horizon the Donegal hills beckon. This stretch, dotted with numerous prehistoric sites, has become Northwest Ireland's most popular vacation area. There are a few small and unremarkable seashore resorts, and in some places you may find examples of haphazard and fairly tasteless construction that detracts from the scenery. In between these minor resort developments, wide-open spaces are free of traffic. The most intriguing area lies on the north side of the bay—all that rocky indented coastline due west of Donegal Town. Here you enter the heart of away-from-it-all: County Donegal.

MULLAGHMORE

37 km (24 miles) north of Sligo Town.

In July and August, the sleepy fishing village of Mullaghmore becomes congested with tourists. Its main attractions: a 3-km-long (2-mile-long) sandy beach; and the turreted, fairy-tale Classie Bawn—the late Lord Louis Mountbatten's home (he, his grandson, and a local boy were killed when the IRA blew up his boat in the bay in 1979; the castle is still privately owned and not open to the public). A short drive along the headland is punctuated by unobstructed views beyond the rocky coastline out over Donegal Bay. When the weather is fair, you can see all the way across to St. John's Point and Drumanoo Head in Donegal.

GETTING HERE AND AROUND

Mullaghmore is a 30-minute drive from Sligo along the N15 main road to Donegal. Look for the turnoff signpost at the village of Cliffony; from there it's a 5-minute drive along a narrow country road to reach Mullaghmore. There is a large free car park.

EXPLORING

★ **Creevykeel.** One of Ireland's best megalithic court-tombs, Creevykeel contains a burial area and an enclosed open-air court where rituals were performed around 3000 BC. Bronze artifacts found here are now in the National Museum in Dublin. The site (signposted from N15) lies off the road, just beyond the edge of the village of Cliffony. ⊠ *3 km (2 miles) southeast of Mullaghmore off N15, Mullaghmore, Co. Sligo.*

BALLYSHANNON

23 km (15 miles) north of Mullaghmore, 42 km (26 miles) northeast of Sligo Town.

The former garrison town of Ballyshannon rises gently from the banks of the River Erne and has good views of Donegal Bay and the surrounding mountains. Come early August, this quiet village springs to life with a grand fest of traditional music, the **Ballyshannon Folk Festival** (☎ *086/252–7400* ⊕ *www.ballyshannonfolkfestival.com*), Ireland's longest-running music gathering. The town is a hodgepodge of shops, arcades, and hotels. Its triangular central area has several bars and places to grab a snack. The town was also the birthplace of the prolific poet William Allingham.

A few kilometers down the road are several factories where, for generations, master craftsmen have made eggshell-thin Irish porcelain. It's said that if a newlywed couple receives a piece of this china, their marriage will be blessed with everlasting happiness.

GETTING HERE AND AROUND

Ballyshannon is on the main N15 Sligo–Donegal route, about 20 minutes south of Donegal Town. There are several free car parks around the town, but parking on the main street is metered.

EXPLORING

Belleek Pottery Ltd. The name Belleek has become synonymous with much of Ireland's delicate ivory porcelain figurines and woven china baskets (sometimes painted with shamrocks). Belleek Pottery Ltd. is the best known of the producers, in operation since 1857. The main factories are just down the road from Ballyshannon in Northern Ireland (which is why their prices are quoted in pounds sterling, not euros). Watch the introductory film, take the 30-minute tour, stop by for refreshment in the tearoom, or just head to the on-site shop. The factory-museum-store is near the border with Northern Ireland. Company products can also be found in the shops of Donegal and Sligo. ⊠ *6 km (4 miles) east of Ballyshannon, 3 Main St., Belleek* ☎ *028/6865–9300 in Northern Ireland* ⊕ *www.belleek.ie* ☜*€5* ⊗ *Jan.–Dec., weekdays 9–5:30; Mar.,–Dec., Sat. 10–5.30, Sun 2–5.*

Celtic Weave China. The fourth generation (since 1866) of the Daly family hand crafts and paints the elaborate floral and basket-weave designs at Celtic Weave China. Because it's a small, personal operation, they can make a single piece of china to your specifications. They also carry out design work for Tiffany Jewelers of New York and have worked with the Los Angeles-based architect Frank Gehry. Prices start at €10, and most pieces cost less than €125, although you can spend up to €3,000 on a double photo frame. ⊠ *R230, 5 km (3 miles) east of Ballyshannon, Cloghore, Co. Donegal* ☎ *071/985–1844* ⊕ *www.celticweavechina.ie* ☜*Free* ⊗ *Weekdays 8–6, Sat. 9–5.*

Lough Derg. From Whitsunday to the Feast of the Assumption (June to mid-August), tens of thousands beat a path to the shores of Lough Derg, ringed by heather-clad slopes. In the center of the lake, Station Island—known as St. Patrick's Purgatory (the saint is said to have fasted here for 40 days and nights)—is one of Ireland's most popular pilgrimage sites. It's also the most rigorous and austere of such sites in the country. Pilgrims stay on the island for three days without sleeping, and ingest only black tea and dry toast. They pay €70 to walk barefoot around the island, on its flinty stones and pray at a succession of shrines. Non-pilgrims may not visit the island from June to mid-August. You can also visit the island for a "Quiet Day" trip (10–4) that costs €35 including the boat journey and lunch. In 2010 all-day mother-and-daughter or parent-and-child retreats were introduced

OFF THE
BEATEN
PATH

10

(costing €45 per person). To find out how to become a pilgrim, write to the Reverend Prior. To reach the shores of Lough Derg, turn off the main N15 Sligo–Donegal road in the village of Laghy on to the minor R232 Pettigo road, which hauls itself over the Black Gap and descends sharply into the border village of Pettigo, about 21 km (13 miles) from N15. From here, take the Lough Derg access road for 8 km (5 miles). During pilgrim season, buses connect Pettigo with Ballyshannon and Enniskillen from Thursday to Monday. There are no services on Tuesday or Wednesday. It's a 30-minute journey from both towns and the return taxi fare is €30. There is also a direct Bus Éireann service in the Pilgrim Season from Dublin to Lough Derg from Thursday to Monday. Journey time is just over four hours. ⊠ *Pettigo, Co. Donegal* ☎ *071/986–1518* ⊕ *www.loughderg.org.*

NIGHTLIFE

Seán Óg's. The biggest and most popular pub, Seán Óg's, has live music on Friday, Saturday, and Sunday evenings. ⊠ *Market St., Ballyshannon, Co. Donegal* ☎ *071/985–8964.*

DONEGAL TOWN

21 km (13 miles) north of Ballyshannon, 66 km (41 miles) northeast of Sligo Town.

With a population of about 3,000, Donegal is Northwest Ireland's largest small village—marking the entry into the back-of-the-beyond of the wilds of County Donegal. The town is centered on the triangular Diamond, where three roads converge (N56 to the west, N15 to the south and the northeast) and the mouth of the River Eske pours gently into Donegal Bay. You should have your bearings in five minutes, and seeing the historical sights takes less than an hour; if you stick around any longer, it'll probably be to do some shopping—arguably Donegal's top attraction.

The town of Donegal was previously known in Irish as *Dun na nGall,* "Fort of the Foreigners." The foreigners were Vikings, who set up camp here in the 9th century to facilitate their pillaging and looting. They were driven out by the powerful O'Donnell clan (originally Cinel Conail), who made it the capital of Tyrconail, their extensive Ulster territories. Donegal was rebuilt in the early 17th century, during the plantation period, when Protestant colonists were planted on Irish property confiscated from its Catholic owners.

The **Diamond,** like that of many other Irish villages, dates from this period. Once a marketplace, it has a 20-foot-tall obelisk monument (1937), which honors the town monks who, before being driven out by the English in the 17th century, took the time to copy down a series of old Irish legends in what they called *The Annals of the Four Masters.*

GETTING HERE AND AROUND

Donegal is a 60-minute drive from Sligo north along the N15. The main pay car park is at the Quay beside the tourist information office on the approach road from the south. Catch the wrong day in the height of summer and Donegal town is a bottleneck. Fortunately it doesn't occur very often—the reason may be a local wedding, a festival, a funeral, or a Gaelic football match. The main delays focus on the one-way system operating around the Diamond. Try to avoid this area around 5 pm.

Public transport throughout Donegal is limited to buses. Bus Éireann operates direct daily services from Donegal Town to Dublin Airport and the city center, which also stop in the nearby towns of Ballyshannon and Belleek. They run regular services between the bigger towns linking Donegal Town with Bundoran, Letterkenny, and west to Killybegs, Glencolumbkille, Glenties, and Dungloe. There is no bus station but buses stop outside the Abbey Hotel in the Diamond. A raft of smaller independently run buses crisscrosses Donegal's roads—including McGeehan Coaches, Patrick Gallagher Coaches, Feda O'Donnell Coaches, John McGinley Coach Travel, and Donegal Coaches—and these companies pick up and drop off in Quay Street.

ESSENTIALS

Visitor Information **Discover Ireland Centre, Donegal Town** ✉ *The Quay, Donegal Town, Co. Donegal* ☎ *074/972–1148* ⊕ *www.discoverireland.ie.*

EXPLORING

Donegal Castle. Donegal Castle was built by clan leader Hugh O'Donnell in the 1470s. More than a century later, this structure was the home of his descendant Hugh Roe O'Donnell, who faced the might of the invading English and was the last clan chief of Tyrconail. In 1602 he died on a trip to Spain while trying to rally reinforcements from his allies. In 1610 its new English owner, Sir Basil Brooke, modified the little castle, fitting Jacobean towers and turrets to the main fort and adding a Jacobean mansion (which is now a ruin). Inside, you can peer into the *garderobe* (the restroom) and the storeroom, and survey a great banqueting hall with an exceptional vaulted wood-beam roof. Also of note is the gargantuan sandstone fireplace nicely wrought with minute details. Mind your head on the low doorways and be careful on the narrow trip stairwell. The small, enclosed grounds are pleasant. ✉ *Tirchonaill St., near north corner of Diamond, Donegal Town, Co. Donegal* ☎ *074/972–2405* ⌑ *€4* ⊙ *Apr.–Sept., daily 10–6; Oct.–Mar., Thurs.–Mon. 9:30–3:45.*

Franciscan Abbey. The ruins of the Franciscan Abbey, founded in 1474 by Hugh O'Donnell, are a five-minute walk south of town at a spectacular site perched above the Eske River, where it begins to open up into Donegal Bay. The complex was burned to the ground in 1593, razed by the English in 1601, and ransacked again in 1607; the ruins include the choir, south transept, and two sides of the cloisters, between which lie hundreds of graves dating to the 18th century. The abbey was probably where *The Annals of the Four Masters,* which chronicles the whole of Celtic history and mythology of Ireland from earliest times up to the year 1618, was written from 1632 to 1636. "The Four Masters" were monks who believed (correctly, as it turned out) that Celtic culture was doomed by the English conquest, and they wanted to preserve as much of it as they could. At the National Library in Dublin, you can see copies of the monks' work; the original is kept under lock and key. ✉ *Off N15 behind Central Hotel, Donegal Town, Co. Donegal* ⌑ *Free* ⊙ *Freely accessible.*

10

WHERE TO EAT AND STAY

For expanded hotel reviews, visit Fodors.com.

$ ✕ **Blueberry Tea Room and Restaurant.** Proprietors Brian and Ruperta Gal-
CAFÉ   lagher serve breakfast, lunch, afternoon tea, and a light early evening
★   meal—always using homegrown herbs. Daily specials—Irish lamb stew,
pasta dishes, and quiche—are served from 9 am to 7 pm. Soups, sandwiches, salads, and fruit are on the regular menu, along with homemade desserts, breads, scones, and jams. Upstairs is an Internet café but
check in downstairs first. It's across the street from Donegal Castle. Get
there early for lunch, as the lines stretch out onto the street on busy
days. ⑤ *Average main: €10* ⊠ *Castle St., Donegal Town, Co. Donegal*
🕾 *074/972–2933* ◷ *Closed Sun.*

$ 🖃 **The Central Hotel, Donegal.** With its bright white shutters and boldly
HOTEL red facade, this pretty-as-an-Irish-picture inn sits smack on Done-
Fodor's Choice gal's central square, more correctly called the "Diamond." **Pros:** top
★   marks for convenience for exploring the town and its history; friendly
and knowledgeable staff. **Cons:** no frills; relentless surge of taxis and
motorbikes circling the Diamond. **TripAdvisor:** "good location,"
"revive the nostalgia," "best hotel experience." ⑤ *Rooms from: €110*
⊠ *The Diamond, Donegal Town, Co. Donegal* 🕾 *74/9721027* ⊕ *www.
centralhoteldonegal.com* ⤴ *112 rooms* ⦿ *Multiple meal plans.*

$$ 🖃 **Harvey's Point Country Hotel.** Set in a remote and breathtaking loca-
HOTEL tion in landscaped gardens on the shores of Lough Eske at the foot
Fodor's Choice of the Blue Stack Mountains, Harvey's Point has, since 1989, been a
★   spirit-lifting escape. **Pros:** luxury and style in timeless grandeur; peaceful
surroundings; great concierge Brendan Brien. **Cons:** older rooms lack
the opulence of new ones; long walk to ATM. **TripAdvisor:** "a piece of
paradise," "pure bliss," "old-school fun." ⑤ *Rooms from: €158* ⊠ *6
km (4 miles) northwest of Donegal Town, off N15, Lough Eske, Co.
Donegal* 🕾 *074/972–2208* ⊕ *www.harveyspoint.com* ⤴ *70 rooms, 4
suites* ⦿ *Some meals.*

$$$$ 🖃 **Solis Lough Eske Castle.** Most guests gasp as they come down the
HOTEL sweeping drive through ancient woodland and arrive at this magnifi-
Fodor's Choice cent Tudor-style baronial castle—complete with Sleeping Beauty tower
★   and crenellations and a suitably regal backdrop of Lough Eske and
the Blue Stack Mountains. **Pros:** calming sheltered oasis in stunning
location; attentive, slick, and impressive service. **Cons:** queues form
at busy breakfast times; limited choice on the dinner menu. **TripAd-
visor:** "excellent staff," "haven of gentle luxury," "beautiful place."
⑤ *Rooms from: €235* ⊠ *3 km (2 miles) north of Donegal town, Lough
Eske, Co. Donegal* 🕾 *074/972–5100* ⊕ *www.solishotels.com/lougheske*
⤴ *96 rooms, 16 suites.*

NIGHTLIFE

The Abbey Hotel, Donegal Town. Visit for music every night in July and
August and a disco every Saturday and Sunday night throughout the
year. ⊠ *The Diamond, Donegal Town, Co. Donegal* 🕾 *074/972–1014*
⊕ *www.abbeyhoteldonegal.com.*

O'Donnell's Bar. In summer, people pack O'Donnell's Bar to hear contemporary music on weekends. ⊠ *The Diamond, Donegal Town, Co. Donegal* ☎ *074/972–1049.*

SPORTS AND THE OUTDOORS

BEACHES

Silver Strand Beach. The Silver Strand Beach, or in Irish *An Trá Bhán*, at Gleann Cholm Cille lives up to its name. It's a beautifully enclosed small, silvery white, sandy beach, quiet and hidden from view/visitor traffic. Peaceful solitude is the name of the game here but if your hair is standing on your arms it's because you're being watched; there are a few peeping sheep on the surrounding hillsides. When you've had your fill of sand and serenity, explore the ruined promontory fort, Dun Alt, directly above the beach. It was built around 300 BC, and archaeologists believe it was used as a defensive fortification when the community was in danger of attack. **Amenities:** small car park (no fee), short walk to nearby shop. **Best for:** paddling, swimming, walking, sunbathing, or simply hiding from the crowds. ⊠ *Gleann Cholm Cille, Gleann Cholm Cille, Co. Donegal.*

GOLF

Donegal Golf Club. Famously named by *Golf World* as one of Ireland's top 10 clubs, this is a course that has always rated high in the estimation of local golfers. On the shores of Donegal Bay and approached through a forest, the windswept links are shadowed by the Blue Stack Mountains, with the Atlantic as a backdrop. The greens are large, but the rough is deep and penal, and there's a constant battle against erosion by the sea. The par-3 5th, fittingly called the "Valley of Tears," begins a run of four of the course's biggest challenges, which could have you discreetly hiding your scorecard by the time you reach the 18th. ⊠ *Murvagh, Laghey, Co. Donegal* ☎ *074/973–4054* ⊕ *www.donegalgolfclub.ie* 🏌 *Greens fees: Mar.–Oct., weekdays €60, weekends €70; Nov.–Feb., weekdays €35, weekends €40 ℸ 18 holes. Yardage: 6,753. Par 73. Practice area, caddy carts, buggies, club rental, catering* ☉ *Visitors: daily.*

SHOPPING

Long the principal marketplace for the region's wool products, Donegal Town has several smaller shops with local hand weaving, knits, and crafts.

Donegal Craft Village. Explore this complex of workshops where you can buy pottery, handwoven goods, jewelry, and ceramics from young, local craftspeople. You can even watch the items being made Monday to Saturday 9–5:30. The Aroma Café in the Craft Village is a top-class spot for homemade cakes and breads, and also serves dishes with a Mexican twist. ⊠ *N15, 1½ km (1 mile) south of town, Donegal Town, Co. Donegal* ☎ *074/972–3222* ⊕ *www.donegalcraftvillage.com.*

Four Masters Bookshop. For the best selection of local history books on Donegal and Ireland in general, Ordnance Survey maps, and travel guides, as well as CDs, DVDs, and Celtic jewelry, the Four Masters Bookshop is a great place to browse. ⊠ *The Diamond, Donegal Town, Co. Donegal* ☎ *074/972–1526.*

10

Magee's. The main hand-weaving store in town, Magee's carries renowned private-label tweeds for both men and women (jackets, hats, scarves, suits, and more), as well as pottery, linen, and crystal. ⊠ *The Diamond, Donegal Town, Co. Donegal* ☎ *28/2566–1064* ⊕ *www. mageeireland.com.*

EN ROUTE

As you travel west on N56, which runs slightly inland from a magnificent shoreline of rocky inlets with great sea views, it's worthwhile to turn off the road from time to time to catch a better view of the coast. About 6 km (4 miles) out of Donegal Town, N56 skirts Mountcharles, a bleak hillside village that looks back across the bay.

KILLYBEGS

28 km (17 miles) west of Donegal Town.

Trawlers from Spain and France are moored in the harbor at Killybegs, one of Ireland's busiest fishing ports. Though it's one of the most industrialized places along this coast, it's not without some charm thanks to its waterfront location. Killybegs once served as a center for the manufacture of Donegal hand-tufted carpets, examples of which are in the White House and the Vatican.

GETTING HERE AND AROUND

Killybegs is a 45-minute drive west of Donegal Town along the N56. It's a busy fishing and tourist port in the summer months but there are plenty of parking spaces at the harbor front or along the side roads off the main street, which is a one-way system. Regular daily bus connections link Killybegs with Donegal Town or north to Ardara. Services west to Glencolumbkille along the narrow and twisty R263 are much less frequent.

EXPLORING

Maritime and Heritage Centre. This factory produces high-quality hand-knotted and hand-tufted carpets to order: a square meter costs around €2,000. Visitors are welcome to commission a piece, but examples of the carpets are not sold off the peg. For €1 you can play with the Ship Simulator and steer your own boat through the tricky waters of the harbor. ⊠ *Kilcar Rd., Killybegs, Co. Donegal* ☎ *074/974–1944* ⊕ *www. visitkillybegs.com* 🖾 *€5* ⊗ *Sept.–June, weekdays 10–6; July and Aug., weekdays 10–6, weekends 1–5.*

Sliabh League Cultural Centre. Stop off at Tí Linn, the Slieve League Cultural Centre, where they serve Italian Illy coffee; sample their delectable traditional home-baked cakes that include carrot, banana and date, coconut, as well as the apple sultana pancakes with maple-syrup butter. The tomato, orange, and lentil soup is also a lunchtime winner. At the same time you can stock up on information about the cultural history of the region. Paddy Clarke runs the center and is a rich source of information about the area, especially the archaeological heritage. ⊠ *Cliffs Rd., Teileann, Carrick, Killybegs, Co. Donegal* ☎ *074/973–9077* ⊕ *www. slieveleaguecliffs.com* ⊗ *Daily 10:30–5.*

To make the Slieve League mountains—Ireland's highest—more accessible, a viewing station now allows access to one of Europe's grandest sea vistas.

Slieve League Mountains. You'll be a long time walking but, as of 2011, Donegal is now part of the famed Appalachian Trail. The dramatic Slieve League cliffs and mountains have become the starting point for the newly designated Irish leg of the International Applachian Trail, an extension to the original route stretching from Georgia to Maine and then on to Newfoundland. And what more spectacular setting could you have for such a renowned trail linking two pieces of land separated by thousands of kilometers of ocean?

Make no mistake: the landscape hereabouts is awe-inspiring. The narrows and twists of R263 afford terrific views of Donegal Bay before descending into pretty Cill Chartaigh (Kilcar), a traditional center of tweed making. Signposted by its Irish name, the next village, An Charraig (Carrick), clings to the foot of the Slieve League Mountains, whose color-streaked ocean cliffs are, at 2,000 feet, the highest in Ireland. Slieve League (Sliah Liec, or Mountain of the Pillars) is a ragged, razorback rise bordered by the River Glen. To see the cliffs, follow the little road to the Irish-speaking village of Teileann, 1½ km (1 mile) south from Carrick. Then take the narrow lane (signposted to the Bunglass Cliffs) that climbs steeply to the top of the cliffs. The mountain looks deceptively easy from the back (the inaccessible point borders the Atlantic), but once the fog rolls in, the footing can be perilous. If you want to take in this thrilling perspective—presuming you're hardy and careful—walk along the difficult coastal path from Teilann: not for the dizzily squeamish. The cliffs have been made more accessible by widening the road to the top and enhancing it with parking lots, turnouts, fencing, and an information panel as part of the Donegal Interpretative

10

Project, the first of its kind anywhere in Ireland. A newly erected viewing point over the sea cliffs ensures visitors can appreciate one of the finest panoramas in Europe in safety.

WHERE TO STAY

For expanded hotel reviews, visit Fodors.com.

$ ⊞ **Tara Hotel.** Since opening in 2004, this modern, bright, and airy
HOTEL   harborside hotel has gained a sterling reputation for professional and friendly service. **Pros:** attractive guest rooms; leisure club is one of the finest in County Donegal. **Cons:** no pool; noisy when big sporting events bring out supporters. **TripAdvisor:** "great food," "still excellent," "lovely view." ⑤ *Rooms from: €110* ⊠ *Harbor front, Killybegs, Co. Donegal* ☎ *074/974–1700* ⊕ *www.tarahotel.ie* ➪ *31 rooms* �|◎| *Multiple meal plans.*

SHOPPING

Harbour Store. Right on the wharf, the Harbour Store has plenty to make both fisherfolk and landlubbers happy, including boots and rain gear, competitively priced sweaters, and unusual bright yellow or orange fiberglass-covered gloves (made in Taiwan). ⊠ *Main St., Killybegs, Co. Donegal* ☎ *074/973–2122.*

GLEANN CHOLM CILLE (GLENCOLUMBKILLE)

27 km (17 miles) west of Killybegs on R263, 54 km (27 miles) west of Donegal Town.

Fodor's Choice
★

"The back of beyond" at the far end of a stretch of barren moorland, the tiny hamlet of Gleann Cholm Cille clings dramatically to the rockbound harbor of Glen Bay. Known alternatively as Glencolumbkille (pronounced glen-colm-*kill*), it remains the heart of County Donegal's shrinking Gaeltacht region and retains a strong rural Irish flavor, as do its pubs and brightly painted row houses. The name means St. Columba's Glen; the legend goes that St. Columba, the Christian missionary, lived here during the 6th century with a group of followers before many of them moved on to find greater glory by settling Scotland's Isle of Iona. Some 40 prehistoric cairns, scattered around the village, have become connected locally with the St. Columba myths. The village has a website (⊕ *www.gleanncholmcille.ie*) where hopeful overnighters can track down one of the village B&Bs. There are no hotels in town, but walking lodges, friendly inns that cater to hikers, are worth checking out.

Cliffs surrounding Gleann Cholm Cille rise up to more than 700 feet, including Glen Head; many cliffs are studded with ancient hermit cells. Also of note is a squat martello tower, built by the British in 1804 to protect against an anticipated French invasion that never happened. Another good walk is the 8-km (5-mile) trek to Malinbeg, reached by the coast road running past Doon Point. Look for the ruins of no less than five burial cairns, a ring fort, a second martello tower, and one of the best beaches in Ireland, renowned for its calm waters, dramatic scenery, and lovely golden sand.

To step back in time, just head to Gleann Cholm Cille—if you're lucky you'll catch the locals rethatching their roofs.

GETTING HERE AND AROUND

It's a rollercoaster mountain road to Glencolumbkille, and you need your wits about you on the R263 from Killybegs. The journey time is 30 minutes (at a top speed of 40 mph). Once you get to Glencolumbkille, car parking is not a problem. Ardara, to the northeast along the R230 is a 45-minute drive (but it'll take much longer if you stop to drink in the stunning scenery).

The main Donegal Town–Dungloe Bus Éireann service does not go to Glencolumbkille, but there is a morning Bus Éireann bus service (Tuesday, Thursday, and Saturday only) that leaves Donegal Town for Glencolumbkille year-round. There is also a Monday–Saturday bus from Glencolumbkille to Donegal Town at 7:30 am. From July 7 to August 22, a Hills of Donegal Bus Éireann scheduled service runs Tuesday–Saturday from Donegal Town to top attractions like Glencolumbkille, Teelin Village (for the Slieve League cliffs), and Glenveagh National Park.

ESSENTIALS

Transportation Contacts Stranorlar Bus Station ☎ *074/913–1008.*

EXPLORING

★ **Glencolmcille Folk Village Museum.** Walk through the beachfront Folk Village Museum to explore rural life. This *clachan*, or tiny village, comprises eight cottages, all of which are whitewashed, thatch-roofed, and extremely modest in appearance. Three showcase particular years in Irish culture: 1720, 1820, and 1920; pride of place goes to the 1881 schoolhouse and the re-created *shebeen* (pub). Two new exhibition houses, a fisherman's cottage and a traditional pub/grocery and shoemaker's shop, opened in 2011. The complex was built after local priest Father McDyer started a cooperative to help combat rural depopulation. You'll also find an interpretive center, teashop, and crafts shop selling local handmade products. In summer the museum hosts traditional music evenings. Three small cottages, with bare-earth floors, represent the very basic living conditions of the 1720s, 1820s, and 1920s. ⊠ *Near beach, Glencolumbkille, Co. Donegal* ☎ *074/973–0017* ⊕ *www.glenfolkvillage.com* 🎫 *€3.50* ☉ *Easter–Sept., Mon.–Sat. 10–6, Sun. noon–6.*

House of St. Columba. The House of St. Columba, on the cliff top rising north of the village, is a small oratory said to have been used by the saint himself. Inside, stone constructions are thought to have been his bed and chair. Every year on June 9, starting at midnight, local people make a 3-km (2-mile) barefoot procession called An Turas (the journey) around 15 medieval crosses and ancient cairns, collectively called the Stations of the Cross.

WHERE TO STAY

For expanded hotel reviews, visit Fodors.com.

$ **▦ Ionad Siúl Walking Lodge.** Lovely Gleann Cholm Cille has enough
B&B/INN charms to entice loads of travelers but, until recently, it was short a few beds for those same travelers. **Pros:** set in spectacular countryside; friendly service; good value. **Cons:** rooms are basic; local facilities are limited. **TripAdvisor:** "great accommodation," "beautiful place at the end of the world," "beautiful scenery." ⑤ *Rooms from: €50* ⊠ *Gleann Cholm Cille, Co. Donegal* ☎ *074/973–0302* ⊕ *www.ionadsiul.ie* ⊅ *11 rooms.*

ARD AN RATHA (ARDARA)

28 km (17 miles) northeast of Gleann Cholm Cille, 40 km (25 miles) northwest of Donegal Town.

★ At the head of a lovely ocean inlet, the unpretentious, old-fashioned hamlet of Ard an Ratha (Ardara) is built around the L-shaped intersection of its two main streets. (If you come from Gleann Cholm Cille, expect a scenic drive full of hairpin curves and steep hills as you cross over Glengesh Pass.) For centuries, great cloth fairs were held on the first of every month; cottage workers in the surrounding countryside still provide Ard an Ratha (and County Donegal) with high-quality, handwoven cloths and hand knits. The village was thrust into the spotlight on St. Patrick's Day 2012 when it set a record for the most St. Patricks gathered in one place. A total of 229 such saints turned up with their crosiers, including visiting saint clones from Europe. It has yet to be declared a record in the *Guinness World Records*.

GETTING HERE AND AROUND

Three main roads from the north, east, and south converge on Ardara, which really only gets busy in the summer months. There is ample free on-street car parking in the town. It's 30 minutes from Killybegs and 75 minutes from Donegal Town to the south and east. Letterkenny is a 75-minute drive north along the N56 to Glenties, then switch to the narrower R250.

Set at the "back of beyond," the seaside hamlet of Gleann Cholm Cille welcomes travelers at its beachfront Folk Village Museum.

WHERE TO EAT AND STAY

For expanded hotel reviews, visit Fodors.com.

$$$ ✕**Nesbitt Arms Hotel.** Offering casual pub grub and more substantial
IRISH fare, this old-fashioned inn gets understandably busy in summer. Decor
harks back to the days when Ard an Ratha was Donegal's foremost
weaving and wool center, which explains the wooden loom in the cor-
ner of the dining room. And what about the weaver depicted on the
menu? He's the grandfather of the owner, Marie Gallagher, who runs
the business, which has a long pedigree stretching back to 1838. If you
want a quick bite, check out the daily specials in the Weavers Bistro.
Upstairs in the dining room, a standout is the Hangman's Steak Kebab
with onions and peppers served on a breadboard (replete with hang-
ing spike). There's music in the bar every Saturday night. The hotel
also rents simple rooms. ⑤ *Average main: €25* ⊠ *Main St., Ardara, Co.
Donegal* ☎ *074/954–1103* ⊕ *www.nesbittarms.com.*

$ 🏠 **Green Gate.** For an alternative to country estates and village hotels,
B&B/INN make a beeline for Frenchman Paul Chatenoud's remote cottage B&B
Fodor'sChoice overlooking Ard an Ratha, the Atlantic, and some spectacular Done-
★ gal scenery—it's one of Ireland's most beautiful little guesthouses.
Pros: tons of local information; great camaraderie with fellow travel-
ers. **Cons:** cottages have few extras; hard to find on a dark drunken
night. **TripAdvisor:** "green gloriousness," "peace and quiet," "unique
romantic place." ⑤ *Rooms from: €45* ⊠ *Ardvally, Co. Donegal*
☎ *074/954–1546* ⊕ *www.thegreengate.eu* 🛏 *4 rooms* ⊟ *No credit
cards* ⦿ *Breakfast.*

Aran Sweaters

Most of the Aran sweaters you'll see throughout Ireland are made in County Donegal, the area most associated with high-quality, handwoven tweeds and hand-knit items. Made of plain, undyed wool and knit with distinctive crisscross patterns, Aran sweaters are durable, soft, often weatherproof, and can be astonishingly warm. They once provided essential protection against the wild, stormy Atlantic Ocean. Indeed, these Arans can hold 30% of their weight in water before they even start to feel wet.

Not so long ago, these pullovers were worn by every County Donegal fisherman, usually made to a design belonging exclusively to his own family. It's said that a native can tell which family the knitter belongs to from the patterns used in a genuine Aran sweater. Produced for centuries in the fishing communities of Northern and West Ireland, they are painstakingly knitted by hand, a process that can take weeks. As a result, prices are not cheap, and if you think you've found a bargain, check the label before buying—it's more likely a factory copy.

When it comes to Donegal tweed, weavers—inspired by the soft greens, red rusts, and dove grays of the famed Donegal landscape—have been producing it for centuries. In long-gone days, crofters' wives concocted the dyes to give Donegal tweed its distinctive flecks, and their husbands wove the cloth into tweed. Traditional Donegal tweed was a salt-and-pepper mix, but gradually weavers began adding dyes distilled from yellow gorse, purple blackberries, orange lichen, and green moss. Today most tweed comes from factories. However, there are still about 25 local craftsmen working from their cottages. Chic fashion designers such as Armani, Ralph Lauren, and Burberry all use handwoven Donegal tweed—obviously, more fashionable than ever.

The sweaters are enjoying a revival thanks partly to the traditional music group the High Kings, who toured the United States in 2008, impressing critics and audiences not only with their tunes and *bodhráns,* but also their Aran jumpers. There is a huge amount of romance and folklore attached to the sweaters, and many regard them as a badge of iconic chic—a 21st-century symbol of Irish folk art.

$

B&B/INN

Fodor's Choice

★

Woodhill House. The cream-color exterior of John Yates's spacious manor house is Victorian, but parts of the interior and the coach house date from the 17th century. **Pros:** quiet location; beautifully maintained house where visitors fall in love with the gardens. **Cons:** some don't like the library-like breakfast-time silences; complaints about poor TV reception. **TripAdvisor:** "charm and comfort," "magical place," "relaxing home from home." $ *Rooms from: €110* ⊠ *Wood Rd., Ardara, Co. Donegal* ☎ *074/954–1112* ⊕ *www.woodhillhouse.com* ⋙ *13 rooms* ⊗ *Closed Christmas wk* ⊠ *Breakfast.*

NIGHTLIFE

For a small, old-fashioned village, Ard an Ratha has a surprising number of pubs, many of which have traditional music in the evening.

The Corner Bar. You'll find this place usually packed, as it features music almost every night in July and August and on weekends the rest of the year. ⊠ *Main St., Ardara, Co. Donegal* ☎ *074/954–1736.*

Nancy's Pub. One of the smallest bars in the Republic, Nancy's makes you wonder if you've wandered into the owner's sitting room, but it occasionally finds space for a folk group. Seafood, in the form of oysters, smoked salmon, prawns, and mussels, dominates the menu served noon to 9. ⊠ *Front St., Ardara, Co. Donegal* ☎ *074/954–1187.*

SHOPPING

Many handwoven and locally made knitwear items are on sale in Ard an Ratha. Some stores commission goods directly from knitters, and prices are about as low as anywhere. Handsome, chunky Aran hand-knit sweaters (€80–€130), cardigans (similar prices), and scarves (€25) are all widely available.

Campbells Tweed Shop. Stores such as Campbells are treasure troves of ready-to-wear tweeds—sports jackets can run up to €120. ⊠ *Front St., Ardara, Co. Donegal.*

C. Bonner and Son. Factory knitwear from €30 to €120 is for sale here, as well as pottery, tweeds, jewelry, and gifts. There's also a good selection of hand-knit Aran sweaters and cardigans available. ⊠ *Front St., Ardara, Co. Donegal.*

E. Doherty (Ardara) Ltd. This store showcases handwoven tweeds, from scarves for €25 to capes for €195, from Ard an Ratha and other parts of the country. ⊠ *Front St., Ardara, Co. Donegal* ☎ *074/954–1304* ⊕ *www.handwoventweed.ie.*

John Molloy. This factory shop, on the Killybegs Road, on the outskirts of town, offers high-quality, handwoven Donegal tweed, and hand-knit Aran sweaters. ⊠ *Killybegs Rd, Ardara, Co. Donegal* ☎ *074/954–1133* ⊕ *www.johnmolloy.com.*

10

NORTHERN DONEGAL

Traveling on northern County Donegal's country roads, you've escaped at last from the world's hurry and hassle. There's almost nothing up here but scenery, and plenty of it: broad, island-studded loughs of deep, dark tranquility; unkempt, windswept, sheep-grazed grasses on mountain slopes; ribbons of luminous greenery following sparkling streams; and the mellow hues of wide boglands, all under shifting and changing cloudscapes. This trip begins in Letterkenny, the largest town in the county (population 6,500), and makes a beeline to the Irish Xanadu of Henry P. McIlhenny's Glenveagh Castle. Just one word of warning—don't be surprised if you find a sheep standing in the middle of a mountain road looking as though you, rather than it, are in the wrong place.

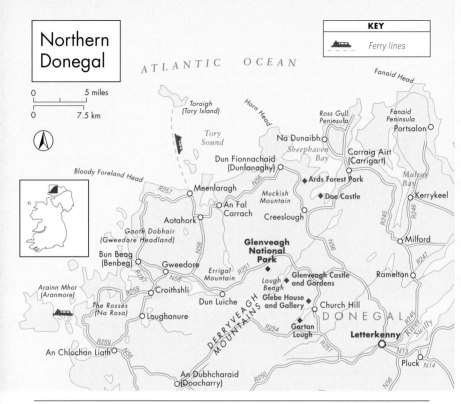

LETTERKENNY

55 km (34 miles) northeast of Ard an Ratha, 51 km (32 miles) northeast of Donegal Town, 35 km (21 miles) west of Derry.

Letterkenny, like Donegal to the south, is at the gateway to the far Northwest; you're likely to come through here if you're driving west out of Northern Ireland. Letterkenny's claim to fame has been that it has the longest main street in the whole country. None of Letterkenny's shops or pubs are particularly special, but lots of locals bustling around make it an interesting place to get a feel for what it's like to live in a modest-size Irish town.

GETTING HERE AND AROUND

Standing at the intersection of the main roads linking Derry and Donegal town, Letterkenny is at the southern end of Lough Swilly and serves as a handy refueling stop for many drivers. Parking along the main street is free for the first 30 minutes only; use the pay-and-display ticketing system at €1 per hour when your free time is up. There are three main car parks that also have a metered charge but you can park free in the grounds of the cathedral.

Derry is just 30 minutes away along the N13 on a wide fast road, while Donegal is 60 minutes south. The area's major tourist attraction, Glenveagh National Park is a 30-minute drive northwest along the N56 and then R256.

Bus Éireann runs nine daily services to and from Dublin city center (via Dublin Airport) and Letterkenny with a journey time of four hours. This part of Donegal is served well by independent operators, with many routes connecting with Derry and the Inishowen Peninsula. Most buses leave Derry city's bus station in Foyle Street.

ESSENTIALS

Visitor Information Failte Ireland Northwest Tourism Office
✉ *Neil T. Blaney Rd., Letterkenny, Co. Donegal* ☎ *074/912–1160*
⊕ *www.discoverireland.ie/northwest.*

EXPLORING

St. Eunan's Cathedral. The 212-foot-high spire of St. Eunan's Cathedral dominates the town, especially when illuminated at night. This striking, ornate neo-Gothic structure was finally finished in 1901, and is the only cathedral in the county. Designed by William Hague of Dublin and built of white Donegal sandstone, the exterior of the building is said to be in perfect classical-rule proportion. Inside, the intricate decorative ceilings and ceramic floor mosaics are the work of an Italian artist, Signor Amici of Rome. The main and side altars are carved from the finest Italian marble, while the great nave arch depicts the lives of St. Eunan and St. Columba in meticulous detail. ✉ *Convent Rd., Letterkenny, Co. Donegal.*

WHERE TO STAY

For expanded hotel reviews, visit Fodors.com.

$ **Ardeen House.** Overlooking Lough Swilly and the River Lennon and
B&B/INN set at the edge of Ramelton, 13 km (8 miles) north of Letterkenny, Ardeen House makes an ideal base for exploring the region, especially Glenveagh National Park. **Pros:** handsome house in a town brimming with the juxtaposition of new and old Ireland; well-run with finely appointed rooms. **Cons:** one bathroom is private but not en suite; no bar, but try Conway's, rethatched and expanded in 2010, where you're likely to stumble across a music session. **TripAdvisor:** "nice Victorian house," "don't miss this gem," "very friendly." ⑤ *Rooms from: €70* ✉ *Ramelton, Co. Donegal* ☎ *074/915–1243* ⊕ *www.ardeenhouse.com* ⌁ *8 rooms, 3 self-catering* ☼ *Closed Oct.–Mar.* ⑩ *Breakfast.*

$ **Clanree Hotel.** Formerly a Holiday Inn, this hotel has reinvented itself
HOTEL with flair, and the spacious entrance hall strikes the right welcoming note. **Pros:** fully equipped health and fitness center; staff friendly and helpful. **Cons:** room service lackadaisical; be prepared to queue for the breakfast buffet. **TripAdvisor:** "must go," "nice during cold winter days," "interesting." ⑤ *Rooms from: €99* ✉ *Derry Rd., Letterkenny, Co. Donegal* ☎ *074/912–4369* ⊕ *www.clanreehotel.com* ⌁ *120 rooms* ⑩ *Multiple meal plans.*

10

GLENVEAGH NATIONAL PARK

21 km (13 miles) northwest of Letterkenny.

GETTING HERE AND AROUND

Glenveagh National Park is 30 minutes northwest of Letterkenny along the N56 through Kilmacrenan and then left on to the R255, a road that leads on to Gweedore on the west Donegal coastline. There is a free car park at the visitor center.

EXPLORING

Fodor's Choice
★

Glenveagh National Park. Bordered by the Derryveagh Mountains (Derryveagh means "forest of oak and birch"), Glenveagh National Park encompasses 24,000 acres of wilderness—mountain, moorland, lakes, and woods—that has been called the largest and most dramatic tract in the wildest part of Donegal. Within its borders, a thick carpet of russet-color heath and dense woodland rolls down the Derryveagh slopes into the broad open valley of the River Veagh (or Owenbeagh), which opens out into Glenveagh's spine: long and narrow, dark and clear Lough Beagh.

The lands of Glenveagh (pronounced glen-*vay*) have long been recognized as a remote and beautiful region. Between 1857 and 1859, John George Adair, a ruthless gentleman farmer, assembled the estate that now makes up the park. In 1861 he evicted the estate's hundreds of poor tenants without compensation and destroyed their cottages. Nine years later Adair began to build **Glenveagh Castle** on the eastern shore of Lough Veagh, but he soon departed for Texas. He died in 1885 without returning to Ireland, but his widow, Cornelia, moved back to make Glenveagh her home. She created four gardens, covering 27 acres; planted luxuriant rhododendrons; and began the job of making this turret-and-battlement-laden 19th-century folly livable. At the end of a dramatic 3-km-long (2-mile-long) entryway, perched over the lake waters, this is a true fairy-tale castle. Like a dollhouse Balmoral, its castellated, rectangular keep, battlemented ramparts, and a round tower enchantingly conjure up all the Victorian fantasies of a medieval redoubt.

The gardens and castle as they appear today are almost entirely an American invention, the product of the loving attentions of Glenveagh's last owners, including Mr. Kingsley Porter, a venerated professor of medieval art history at Harvard. He then passed the property over to U.S. millionaire Henry P. McIlhenny, who bought the estate in 1937 and, beginning in 1947, lived here for part of every year for almost 40 years. An avid art collector and philanthropist (his collection of Degas, Toulouse-Lautrec, and Ingres masterworks now resides at the Philadelphia Museum of Art), McIlhenny decorated every inch of the house himself in faux-baronial fashion and entertained the beau monde (Greta Garbo once slept in the Pink Room) lavishly. The house has been maintained just as it was on his last occupancy in 1983; later that year, he made a gift of the house to the nation. He had sold the government the surrounding land in 1975, which it opened to the public in 1984 as Ireland's third national park.

Beyond the castle, footpaths lead into more remote sections of the park, including the **Derrylahan Nature Trail,** a 1½-km (1-mile) signposted trail where you may suddenly catch sight of a soaring golden eagle or chance upon a shy red deer. The park is the home of one of Ireland's two largest herds; the other is at Killarney. The eagles, which became extinct in Ireland in 1912, have flourished here since their reintroduction in 2001. Guided ranger-led walks are held from March through November and 2010 saw the initiation of guided tours of the extensive gardens (45 minutes, from mid-April to mid-September). In 2012 new history tours started and take visitors to the Derryveagh eviction sites focusing on the built heritage. The visitor center at the park's entrance has a permanent exhibition on the local way of life and on the influence of climate on the park's flora and fauna. Have a bite to eat in the castle tea rooms, or enjoy your own picnic on the extensive estate grounds, which are free for walkers. A shuttle bus runs from the visitor center to the castle and at weekends there's a free bus service to the 90-minute Bridal Path—so-named because local men used to walk it looking for brides. ⊠ *R251, Church Hill, Co. Donegal* ☎ *074/913–7090* ⊕ *www.glenveaghnationalpark.ie* ✉ *Castle tour €5, garden tour €5, shuttle bus €3 round-trip* ☉ *Mar.–Oct., daily 9–6, Nov.–Feb., daily 9–5.*

10

Northern Ireland

INCLUDING COUNTIES OF ANTRIM, ARMAGH, DERRY, DOWN, FERMANAGH, AND TYRONE

WORD OF MOUTH

"We drove along the Causeway Coastal Route, which is similar in beauty to California's Highway 1, and saw Carrickfergus Castle, Dunluce Castle, the famous Carrick-a-Rede rope bridge, the Giant's Causeway, and Bushmills. It was an amazing trip and the drive was one of the most scenic I've seen on my travels."

—aladyinlondon

WELCOME TO NORTHERN IRELAND

TOP REASONS TO GO

★ **Belfast, Gateway City:** As the locals put it, "Despite what you've probably heard, Belfast is not what you expect"—so get ready to love this bustling city that bristles with Victorian shop fronts and hip restaurants.

★ **The Giant's Causeway:** This spectacular remnant of Ireland's volcanic period will steal you away from your 21st-century existence and transport you to a time when the giant Finn McCool roamed the land.

★ **Nine Glens of Antrim:** Fabled haunt of "the wee folk," the glacier-carved valleys have a beauty that has become synonymous with Irishness. Don't miss Glenariff, dubbed "Little Switzerland" by Thackeray.

★ **Ulster-American Folk Park:** A tale of two countries joined by a common people is told at this impressive open-air museum, which re-creates a 19th-century Tyrone village and boasts the Centre for Migration Studies.

1 Belfast. Belfast's location is striking, nestled on the coast, buffered by green water on one side and by heath-covered hills on the other. Once you tour the Victorian city, head to its outskirts to visit three marvels: Belfast Castle, the Mount Stewart estate, and the Ulster Folk and Transport Museum.

2 The Giant's Causeway Coast. North of the famously beautiful Glens of Antrim—still considered "gentle" (supernatural) in spirit—the coast continues up to Northern Ireland's premier attraction, the Giant's Causeway. Farther along the North Antrim coast are Bushmills, the oldest distillery in the world; Dunluce Castle, spectacularly perched over its "Mermaid's Cave"; and the heart-stopping Carrick-a-Rede rope bridge.

4 The Border Counties.
To the west, the Fermanagh Lakeland is an intricate patchwork quilt of undulating hillsides and some of the most uncongested lakes in Europe. A paradise of open horizons and opportunities for those who love the outdoor life,

GETTING ORIENTED

With peace—precious peace—nearly always now abiding, Northern Ireland can finally go about the business of charming visitors full-time. North of the vibrant Victorian city of Belfast, you'll find the ageless wonders of the Causeway Coast while south of the inspiring skyline of Derry lie the Border Counties, where tiny "Ulster" towns dot the scenic landscapes around the Lakes of Fermanagh and Mountains of Mourne. Occasional outbreaks of violence do erupt still in Northern Ireland, so it's best not to stray into trouble areas featured on the news; if in doubt ask at the tourist offices for guidance.

3 Derry. A walk through Ireland's only walled city provides a unique way to view the layout of the 17th-century inner town, particularly noticeable in the streets and alleys that fan outward from the Diamond, where fine examples of Georgian and Victorian architecture rub shoulders with old-style pubs and museums.

it is also home to stately mansions such as Florence Court and Castle Coole, the Ulster-American Folk Park in next-door County Tyrone, and Belleek, a town famous for its porcelain. South of Belfast past the Ards Peninsula is St. Patrick Country: Downpatrick, reputed to be the burial place of the saint; Armagh's two St. Patrick cathedrals; and the seaside Mountains of Mourne.

ALL ABOUT IRISH WHISKEYS

Located on the Antrim coast, the small town of Bushmills lays claim to the world's oldest distillery. Today, its name is synonymous with the best in whiskey. Taste one drop and you may never drink Tennessee whiskey or Jack Daniels again.

(above) Liquid history on view at Bushmills Distillery; (right, top) Learn how malted barley and yeasts are alchemized into whiskey; (right, bottom) Drink Bushmills neat.

Some 125 years ago, Ireland had 28 whiskey distilleries in what was a great industry. Today, only four working ones remain: Bushmills in Antrim, Midleton in Cork, Kilbeggan in Westmeath, and Cooley in Louth. For some, Bushmills is the best, literally: at the 2009 San Francisco Wine and Spirit Awards, it won the Best Irish Whiskey title. And to celebrate its 400th anniversary in 2008, it was selected as the icon of Northern Ireland, and was featured on Bank of Ireland notes. Where does the whiskey drinker start? Some prefer the classic melt-in-the-mouth Black Bush (drunk neat) to the more expensive malt. Other delights include the limited-edition 1608, the Original, and four single malts: aged 10 years, 12 years, 16 years, and 21 years.

OLD BUSHMILLS

✉ *2 Distillery Rd., Bushmills, Co. Antrim* ☎ *028/2073-3218* ⊕ *www.bushmills.com* 🎫 *£6* ⊙ *Tours Apr.–Oct., Mon.–Sat. 9:15–5, Sun. noon–5; Nov.–Mar., weekdays 9:30–3:30, weekends 12:30–3:30. For more information on the Distillery tours, see our listing under Bushmills, below.*

THE "WATER OF LIFE"

Whiskey is a word that comes from the Irish *uisce beatha,* meaning "water of life." Water is a major factor influencing the flavor of any whiskey. For Bushmills, it flows from the crystal-clear St. Columb's Rill, taking its character from the basalt and turf bed of the River Bush. Another key ingredient is malted barley, which is here ground into grist in the mash house and added to boiling water in vats to become wort. Yeast is then added to the mix, and the fermentation turns the sugars to alcohol. The wash goes into a copper pot and is distilled three times, each distillation making the alcohol purer. By comparison, American whiskey is distilled only once. The spirit is diluted, then matured in oak casks, and seasoned by sherry, bourbon, or port. A small portion, about 2% of the distillate, evaporates and is affectionately known as the Angels' Share. Remember to first try Bushmills neat and then add water in teaspoonful increments, as a soupçon of water unlocks the flavor while knocking a little fire out of the whiskey—there's a crucial tipping point so don't dilute too much!

WHAT'S IRISH ABOUT WHISKEY?

First off, it is spelled with an "e," to distinguish it from Scotch whisky. "Irish" has a characteristic flavor that distinguishes it from Scotch, bourbon, or rye; try it straight or with water, as it is best without a mixer. And don't go chasing after poteen (pronounced "potcheen"), the famed Irish moonshine. Any attempts by a "stranger" to procure it will result either in meeting a brick wall or a wild goose chase. Just as well: it produces one of the worst hangovers known to man or woman.

TOURING THE DISTILLERY

Set in an area of natural beauty a short distance from the Giant's Causeway, Bushmills was granted its first license in 1608, although records refer as far back as 1276. Visitors to the distillery are shown around a higgledy-piggledy collection of redbrick and whitewashed buildings that include 11 warehouses brimming with 187,000 barrels of whiskey. Look out for the long rows of Oloroso sherry casks, where the drink is aged in some instances, for more than 25 years (they favor a generous gestation here). Tours run every half hour and cost £7. If you're in the mood to splurge, take the two-hour deluxe Bush Experience tour, which offers eight varieties of whiskey and costs £60 (reservations required, with a minimum of six). Tasting sessions all take place in the 1608 pub where American troops were once billeted during World War II.

Updated by
Paul Clements

Legend has it that a millennium ago a seafaring chieftain caught sight of the green shores of Northern Ireland, and offered the land to whichever of his two sons would be first to lay a hand upon it. As the two rivals rowed toward shore in separate boats, one began to draw ahead, whereupon the other drew his sword, cut off his own hand, and hurled it onto the beach—and so, by blood and sacrifice, gained the province. To this day the coat of arms of Northern Ireland bears the severed limb: the celebrated "Red Hand of Ulster."

From this ancient bardic tale to the recent Troubles—civil strife that lasted from 1969 to 1994—Northern Ireland has had a long and often ferocious history. But all such thoughts vanish in the face of the country's natural beauty, magnificent stately houses, and the warm hospitality of its people. The Six Counties, or Ulster (as Northern Ireland is often called), cover less than 14,245 square km (5,500 square miles)—the country is about half the size of Delaware and less than one-fifth the size of the Republic of Ireland, its neighbor to the south. But within Northern Ireland's boundaries are some of the most unspoiled scenery you could ever hope to find on this earth: the granite Mountains of Mourne; the Giant's Causeway, made of extraordinary volcanic rock; more than 320 km (200 miles) of coastline beaches and hidden coves; and rivers and leaf-sheltered lakes, including Europe's largest freshwater lake, Lough Neagh, that provide fabled fishing grounds. Ancient castles and Palladian-perfect 18th-century houses are as numerous here as almost anywhere else in Europe, and each has its own tale of heroic feats, dastardly deeds, and lovelorn ghosts.

Northern Ireland not only houses this heritage within its native stone, but has also given the world perhaps an even greater legacy: its roster of celebrated descendants. Nearly one in six of the millions of Irish who journeyed across the Atlantic in search of fortune in the New World came from Ulster, and of this group (and from their family stock), more than a few left their mark in America: Davy Crockett, President Andrew Jackson, General Ulysses S. Grant, President Woodrow Wilson, General Stonewall Jackson, financier Thomas Mellon, merchant J. Paul Getty, writers Edgar Allan Poe and Mark Twain, and astronaut Neil Armstrong.

Present-day Northern Ireland, a province under the rule of the United Kingdom, includes six of the old Ulster's nine counties and retains its sense of separation, both in the vernacular of the landscape and, some would say, in the character of the people. The hardheaded and industrious Scots-Presbyterians, imported to make Ulster a bulwark against Ireland's Catholicism, have had a profound and ineradicable effect on the place. For all that, the border between north and south is of little consequence if you're just here to see the country.

On the political front, peace reigns in Northern Ireland today. There are no checkpoints anymore—not security-related ones anyway. As far as border issues go (with the Republic of Ireland to the south), the border is there in name only. No one is stopped or questioned, no passports are checked, and there isn't even a sign announcing you are passing into the Republic. Visitors—even ones with English accents—are not hassled in any way, and Americans are more than warmly welcomed. The "peace dividend" has led to massive investment in places such as Belfast and Derry. Every year, Derry gets dolled up for its annual Halloween fancy-dress party and Northern Ireland's vivacious spirit truly takes center stage. More significantly, the city has been awarded the very first U.K. City of Culture prize; during 2013 a calendar filled with special events and celebrations will take over the city, which will hopefully reap social and economic benefits. The Turner Prize, regarded as one of the most important events in the contemporary European art calendar and the Fleadh Cheol, Ireland's most prestigious music festival, are also coming to Derry in 2013.

NORTHERN IRELAND PLANNER

WHEN TO GO

If the weather is good—and most of the year it isn't—touring Northern Ireland can be a real pleasure. But the place is so green for a reason: lots of rain, which means you should certainly pack your Burberry. Because you're on the coast, even on bright summer days you can feel the chill from the sea, so it's best to wear layers. Needless to say, the weather from May to September is a little friendlier to tourists.

When planning your visit, remember that Northern Ireland is a great place for festivals: almost every town has its own theme festival of some sort. The **Belfast Festival** (⊕ *www.belfastfestival.com*), held in October at Queen's University, is one of the biggest, with a packed program of arts, music, and literature. Belfast's **Cathedral Arts Quarter Festival** (⊕ *www.cqaf.com*), held late April–early May, uses established, new, and unusual venues throughout the oldest part of the city center for two weeks of music, theater, and visual arts. In early April the Titanic Festival commemorates the anniversary of the sinking in 1912 of RMS *Titanic*, built in Belfast and the focus of renewed interest following the opening of the new Belfast Titanic Visitor Centre in 2012. **Féile an Phobail,** the West Belfast Festival (⊕ *www.feilebelfast.com*), held in early August, is a 10-day schedule of events with a political and international theme. **Hillsborough International Oyster Festival** (⊕ *www.hillsboroughoysterfestival.com*), held in September, is three days of good food and entertainment. For a rundown on many other festivals, contact the Northern Ireland Tourist Board.

PLANNING YOUR TIME

Though Northern Ireland may not look that big on paper, tackling a fair share of its many attractions in less than a week isn't possible without exhausting yourself in the process. If your time is limited, choose the eastern half (Belfast, the Antrim Coast, and the Mountains of Mourne) or the western half (Derry and the Border Counties). The cities are small enough to tour in a day or two. But remember that the rural wonders—the Antrim Coast, the Fermanagh lakes, the Mountains of Mourne—cast their spell easily. You may head out to enjoy them for a day trip and find yourself wishing that you'd factored in more time to explore the endless string of postcard-worthy villages, misty glens, and rugged mountains. And although distances are not great, neither are the roads—you'll spend most of your time traveling smaller roads, not major express highways. If you have three days, then spend an extra night and day in Derry. The city has many shiny new attractions such as Ebrington Square and the Peace Bridge, and its old shirt factories and warehouses have been reinvented as bistros, wine bars, and arts centers. A half-day side trip should also be made to the top-class Ulster-American Folk Park at Omagh, where the contribution of Northern Irish people to American history is traced.

GETTING HERE AND AROUND

Because Northern Ireland is so small, one option is to simply base yourself in the two main cities, Belfast and Derry, and make day trips out. However, one of the real glories of Ulster is its endless supply of spectacular rural scenery. The good news is that bus travel is both quick and fairly priced, with express buses operating on all the high-traffic routes. The bad news is that rail options are somewhat limited: there are just three main routes out of Belfast. That said, you can easily access much of the country by bus or train, though in some areas, including the wildly popular Causeway Coast, you'll may end up on smaller bus routes such as the Causeway Coast Express if you don't drive a car.

AIR TRAVEL

Scheduled services from the United States and Canada are mostly routed through Dublin, Glasgow, London, or Manchester. Frequent services to Belfast's two airports are scheduled throughout the day from London Heathrow, London Gatwick, and Luton (all of which have fast coordinated subway or rail connections to central London) and from 17 other U.K. airports.

AIRPORTS Belfast International Airport at Aldergove is the North's principal airport, 30½ km (19 miles) north of town. George Best Belfast City Airport is the secondary airport, 6½ km (4 miles) east of the city. It receives flights from U.K. provincial airports, from London's Gatwick and Heathrow, and from Stansted and Luton (both near London). City of Derry Airport is 8 km (5 miles) from Derry and receives flights from Dublin, Glasgow, London, and Manchester. United Airlines and several Europe-based airlines are the major carriers serving Northern Ireland's airports.

Airport Information Belfast International Airport at Aldergove
☎ *028/9448–4848* ⊕ *www.belfastairport.com.* **City of Derry Airport**
☎ *028/7181–0784* ⊕ *www.cityofderryairport.com.* **George Best Belfast City Airport** ☎ *028/9093–9093* ⊕ *www.belfastcityairport.com.*

Airline Information Aer Arann ☎ *081/8365–0044 00353*
⊕ *www.aerlingus.com.* **Aer Lingus** ☎ *0871/718–5000* ⊕ *www.aerlingus.com.*
British Airways ☎ *0844/493–0787* ⊕ *www.britishairways.com.*
British Midland Airways ☎ *0844/848–4888* ⊕ *www.bmibaby.com.*
United ☎ *0845/607–6760* ⊕ *www.united.com.* **EasyJet** ☎ *084/3104–5000*
⊕ *www.easyjet.com.* **Flybe** ☎ *0871/700–2000* ⊕ *www.flybe.com.*
Jet2 ☎ *0871/226–1737* ⊕ *www.jet2.com.* **Ryanair** ☎ *0871/246–0000*
⊕ *www.ryanair.com.*

AIRPORT
TRANSFERS
Ulsterbus, a branch of Translink, operates Airport Express 300 buses (one-way £7, round-trip £10) several times an hour between Belfast International Airport and Belfast city center (6:50 am–6:15 pm), and Airport Express 600 buses between George Best Belfast City Airport and the city center (one-way £2, round-trip £3; weekdays every 20 minutes, 6 am–10:05 pm). From the City Airport, you can also travel into Belfast by train from Sydenham Halt to Central Station or catch a taxi from the airport to your hotel. Value Cabs serves both Belfast airports. The fare from Belfast International to Belfast city center is around £25; from Belfast City Airport to the city center is around £6.

If you arrive at the City of Derry Airport, you may need to call a taxi to get to your destination. The fare for Delta or Foyle cabs is about £12 to the city center. A direct bus service, the Airporter, links Derry with both Belfast International and George Best Belfast City airports (one way £17.50, round-trip £27.50).

Airport Transfer Contacts Airporter ☎ *028/7126–9996*
⊕ *www.airporter.co.uk.* **City Cabs** ✉ *Derry, Co. Antrim, Northern Ireland*
☎ *028/7126–4466* ⊕ *www.citycabsderry.com.* **Delta Cabs** ☎ *028/7127–9999*
⊕ *www.foyledeltacabs.com.* **Foyle Taxis** ☎ *028/7126–3905*
⊕ *www.foyledeltacabs.com.* **Translink Airport Services** ☎ *028/9066–6630*
⊕ *www.translink.co.uk/services/other-translink-services.* **Value Cabs** ✉ *Belfast, Co. Antrim, Northern Ireland* ☎ *028/9080–9080* ⊕ *www.valuecabs.co.uk.*

BOAT AND FERRY TRAVEL

P&O European Ferries has a one-hour sailing from Cairnryan, Scotland, to Larne, and a two-hour ferry, both with train (more convenient) or bus connections to Belfast, 35½ km (22 miles) to the south. Stena Line has eight-hour daytime or overnight car ferries that connect Belfast with the English west-coast port of Liverpool every day. Stena Line also operates a fast catamaran (1½ hours) between Belfast and Stranraer, Scotland.

Boat and Ferry Information P&O European Ferries ☎ *0871/664–4777*
⊕ *www.poferries.com.* **Stena Line** ✉ *Victoria Terminal 2, W. Bank Rd., Belfast, Northern Ireland* ☎ *028/9077–9090* ⊕ *www.stenaline.co.uk.*

BUS TRAVEL

Northern Ireland's main bus company, Ulsterbus, operates direct Gold-line service—superior express buses with modern, comfortable seats—between Dublin and Belfast. Bus Éireann runs direct service to Belfast from Dublin, calling at Dublin Airport. The ride takes three hours; both company's buses arrive at Belfast's Europa Buscentre, just behind the Europa Hotel.

You can take advantage of frequent and inexpensive Ulsterbus links between all Northern Ireland towns. If you want to tour the North by bus and train, contact Translink: an iLink ticket allows unlimited travel on bus or train (£15 per day, or £55 per week; it costs £1.50 to buy the card). Best buy: the Sunday Rambler Ticket for £8 for unlimited travel on all scheduled Ulsterbus services.

Bus Depot Europa Buscentre ✉ *Great Victoria St., Golden Mile, Belfast, Co. Antrim, Northern Ireland* ☎ *028/9066–6630.*

Bus Lines Bus Éireann ☎ *01/836–6111 in Dublin* ⊕ *www.buseireann.ie.* **Translink Ulsterbus** ☎ *028/9066–6630* ⊕ *www.translink.co.uk/ulsterbus.*

CAR TRAVEL

The fast N1/A1 road connects Belfast to Dublin in 160 km (100 miles) with an average driving time of just over two hours. Only a few customs formalities are observed at the border. When in Belfast, it's best to avail yourself of the many parking garages. If you opt for street meter-ticket parking, check the posted regulations because many spots become no-parking during rush hours. Throughout Northern Ireland, there are plenty of parking lots in the towns, and you should use them.

TAXI TRAVEL

Most taxis operate on the meter; ask for a price for longer journeys. You can order in advance. The minimum fare is usually £2.70 and £1.05 per mile thereafter.

Taxi Companies FonACAB ✉ *Belfast, Northern Ireland* ☎ *028/9033–3333* ⊕ *www.fonacab.com.* **Foyle Delta Cabs** ✉ *10a Market St., Derry, Northern Ireland* ☎ *028/7126–3905* ⊕ *www.foyledeltacabs.com.* **Value Cabs** ✉ *Belfast, Co. Antrim, Northern Ireland* ☎ *028/9080–9080* ⊕ *www.valuecabs.co.uk.*

TRAIN TRAVEL

The Dublin to Belfast Enterprise Service, run jointly by Northern Ireland Railways (a company operated by Translink) and Irish Rail–Iarnród Éireann (which only services the Republic of Ireland), operates trains, the fastest of which take about two hours, between Dublin and Belfast's Central Station. A single journey costs £28; a day return is £30. You can change trains at Central Station—which, in fact, is not that central—for the city-center Great Victoria Street Station, which is adjacent to the Europa Buscentre.

Northern Ireland Railways (NIR) runs four rail routes from Belfast's Central Station: northwest to Derry via Coleraine; east to Bangor along the shore of Belfast Lough; northeast to Larne (for the P&O European ferry to Scotland); and south to Dublin. Nine daily weekday trains operate between Belfast and Derry, with seven trains on Saturday and five on Sunday. The journey time is about two hours, and a round-trip ticket costs £16. If you travel after 9:30 am, you'll get a third off the standard fare. Best buy: the £6 Sunday Day Tracker gives you unlimited travel on all scheduled train services within Northern Ireland.

There are frequent connections to Central Station from the city-center Great Victoria Street Station and from Botanic Station in the university area. If you want to tour the North by train, contact Translink: an iLink ticket allows unlimited travel on bus or train (£15 per day, or £55 per week; it costs £1.50 to buy the card).

Train Info **Enterprise Service** ☎ 028/9066–6630 ⊕ www.translink.co.uk/ Enterprise. **Iarnród Éireann** ☎ 1850/366–222 timetables ⊕ www.irishrail.ie. **Northern Ireland Railways** ✉ Central Station, E. Bridge St., Belfast, Northern Ireland ☎ 028/9066–6630 ⊕ www.translink.co.uk/ni-railways.

Train Stations **Botanic Station** ✉ Botanic Ave., Belfast, Northern Ireland ☎ 028/9089–9400. **Central Station** ✉ E. Bridge St., Belfast, Northern Ireland ☎ 028/9089–9400 ⊕ www.translink.co.uk.

RESTAURANTS

Belfast has experienced an influx of au courant and internationally influenced restaurants, bistros, wine bars, and—as in Dublin—European-style café-bars where you can get good food most of the day and linger over a drink. New York City itself might not have a restaurant as hip as Belfast's eye-popping "restolounge," Made in Belfast. By and large, though, hearty, unpretentious cooking predominates, with good-quality, fresh local fish and meat simply prepared. Among the traditional dishes on menus here are Guinness and beef pie; steak, chicken and pork; champ (creamy, buttery mashed potatoes with scallions); oysters from Strangford Lough; Ardglass herring; mussels from Dundrum; and smoked salmon from Glenarm. A widespread favorite is the Ulster fry, an inexpensive pub plate of bacon, black pudding, mushrooms, sausages, tomatoes, and eggs, served with potato or soda bread—one of the reasons Northern Ireland has a high rate of heart disease. The delights of ethnic restaurants, including Chinese, Japanese, Indian, Persian, and Thai, are available in Belfast, Derry, and in some smaller cities and towns. By the standards of the Republic or the United States, or even the rest of the United Kingdom, restaurant prices can be surprisingly moderate. A service charge of 10% may be indicated on the bill; it's customary to pay this, unless the service was bad.

Prices in the reviews are the average cost of a main course at dinner or, if dinner is not served, at lunch.

HOTELS

Major hotel chains based in both the Republic and abroad have invested in Northern Ireland's cities. In Belfast's environs, you can also choose from the humblest terraced town houses or farm cottages to the grandest country houses. Dining rooms of country-house lodgings frequently match the standard of top-quality restaurants. All accommodations in the province are inspected and categorized by the Northern Ireland Tourist Board Information Centre, which publishes hostelry names, addresses, and ratings in the free guidebooks *Hotel and Guest House Guide* and *Bed & Breakfast Guide*, also available online. Hundreds of excellent-value specials—single nights to weekend deals, the most intimate bed-and-breakfasts to Belfast's finest hotels—become available in the low season, from October to March. Assume that all hotel rooms reviewed have in-room phones and TVs, along with private bathrooms, unless otherwise indicated.

Prices in the reviews are the lowest cost of a standard double room in high season. For expanded reviews, facilities, and current deals, visit Fodors.com.

MONEY

Northern Ireland uses British currency. Euros are accepted in some shops along the border areas and in some shopping centers in Belfast. You may sometimes be given bank notes, drawn on Ulster banks. Be sure not to get stuck with a lot of these when you leave, because they're accepted with reluctance, if at all, in the rest of the United Kingdom and will be difficult to change at banks back home.

TOURS

Allen's Tours (from £15) and McComb's/MiniCoach operate day tours of Belfast (£8–£16) and to the Giant's Causeway, Bushmills Distillery, and Carrickfergus (£17.50). Ulsterbus Tours conducts its Day Tours, half- or full-day trips (prices vary) during the summer from Belfast to the Glens of Antrim, the Giant's Causeway, the Fermanagh lakes, Lough Neagh, the Mountains of Mourne, and the Ards Peninsula. Ulsterbus has also teamed up with the Old Bushmills Distillery on an open-top tour bus running in summer from Coleraine (via Bushmills to observe whiskey making) to the Giant's Causeway and the coastal resorts. *See Tours at the beginning of Belfast coverage for more tours of the capital city.*

Cyclists have several touring options. Iron Donkey Bicycle Touring organizes multiday tours of the Mournes, Glens of Antrim, Causeway Coast, Sperrin Mountains, and other destinations. Mourne Cycle Tours runs bike tours complete with hotel accommodations (bikes are delivered to the hotel).

Bus Tours Allens Tours ☎ *028/9091–5613* ⊕ *www.allenstours.co.uk.* **Ulsterbus Tours** ☎ *028/9033–7004* ⊕ *www.ulsterbustours.com.*

Cycle Tours Iron Donkey Bicycle Touring ☎ *028/9081–3200* ⊕ *www.irondonkey.com.* **Mourne Cycle Tours** ☎ *028/4372–4348.*

VISITOR INFORMATION

The Northern Ireland Tourist Board provides information about attractions, accommodations, and activities online and at its central and regional tourist information offices (TIOs). The offices in Belfast and Derry are open year-round; other useful TIOs are in Enniskillen, Armagh, Newcastle, Carrickfergus, and at the Giant's Causeway on the North Antrim coast.

Contact Northern Ireland Tourist Board ⊠ *59 North St., Belfast, Co. Antrim, Northern Ireland* ☎ *028/9023–1221* ⊕ *www.discovernorthernireland.com.*

BELFAST

The city of Belfast was a great Victorian success story, an industrial boomtown whose prosperity was built on trade—especially linen and shipbuilding. Famously (or infamously), the *Titanic* was built here, giving Belfast, for a time, the nickname "Titanic Town."

In 2012 the city commemorated the 100th anniversary of the liner's sinking on April 15, 1912, by opening a dazzling Titanic Belfast exhibition center. With nine galleries spread over six floors, the enormous multi-prow-shaped building—about the same height as *Titanic* and twice the size of City Hall—the center certainly has the wow factor. It has generated international interest, bringing in much-needed revenue and creating jobs at a difficult economic time.

This is all a welcome change from the period when news about Belfast meant reports about "the Troubles." Since the 1994 ceasefire, Northern Ireland's capital city has benefited from major hotel investment, gentrified quaysides (or strands), a sophisticated new performing arts center, and major initiatives to boost tourism. Although the 1996 bombing of offices at the Canary Wharf in London disrupted the 1994 peace agreement, the cease-fire was officially reestablished on July 20, 1997, and this embattled city began its quest for a newfound identity.

Belfast's city center is made up of three roughly contiguous areas that are easy to navigate on foot. From the south end to the north it's about an hour's leisurely walk.

GETTING HERE AND AROUND

CAR TRAVEL Belfast is 167 km (104 miles) north of Dublin. Motorways, or dual carriageways, lead into Belfast's city center from the main airports and seaports, and the fast N1/A1 motorway links the city with Dublin. The trip takes about two hours. The drive from Derry takes 90 minutes. The main arterial routes into central Belfast are busy only at peak commuter times, between 8 and 9 am and 5 and 6 pm.

Street parking costs £1.30 per hour for a pay-and-display ticket from a meter. The maximum parking time is two hours for such street spaces. Be careful not to overstay, as zealous clamping wardens operate. Multistory car park garages are at the Victoria Square and Castle Court shopping centers. Some, but not all, hotels have car parking. If you'll need parking, ask a hotel or inn prior to booking.

BUS TRAVEL Pink-and-white Metro buses are the best way to get around. Fares range from £1.40 to £2, depending on the zone. If you're staying a few days, buy a Smartlink Travel Card for more than five journeys, which is a 30% saving; a weekly card is £14.50, plus £1.50 for the card. A Metro day ticket costs £3.50 (£2.90 after 9:30 am) and takes you anywhere on the network. Most bus routes start from Donegall Square or adjoining streets, where the Metro Kiosk, on Donegall Square West, has details and timetables.

TRAIN TRAVEL As the capital city of Northern Ireland, Belfast is well served by an efficient train network. Most trains arrive and leave from Central Station, a 15-minute walk from the city center.

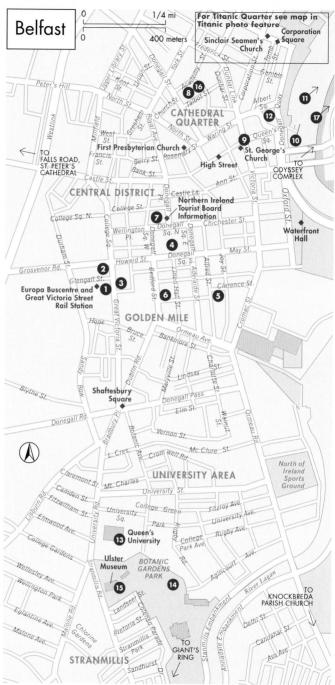

Belfast

0   1/4 mi

0   400 meters

For Titanic Quarter see map in Titanic photo feature

Transportation Contacts Belfast Metro Service ⊠ *Donegall Square West, Belfast, Northern Ireland* ☎ *028/9066–6630* ⊕ *www.translink.co.uk/metro.* **Central Rail Station** ⊠ *E. Bridge St., Belfast, Co. Antrim, Northern Ireland* ☎ *028/9089–9400.*

TOURS

Belfast City Sightseeing runs the most comprehensive open-top tour through Belfast. The Belfast City Tour covers the City Hall, University Quarter, Shipyard, Titanic Quarter, Stormont, Shankill Road, peace line, and Falls Road, and goes past the Grand Opera House on Great Victoria Street. You can hop off and hop on as you please. The entire route, without stops, takes about an hour and a half. The company's Titanic Explorer (⊕ *www.titanicexplorer.com*) bus, scheduled to run through 2013, embarks on a two-hour hop-off, hop-on excursion that takes in Titanic's Dock and Pump House, stops at the Titanic Belfast Visitor Centre, and includes a 45-minute walking tour of the Titanic shipyard. The bus will pick you up from your hotel.

Belfast Ghost Walk tours leave from City Hall's front gates to reveal some of Belfast darkest secrets and most haunted sites.

Belfast Pub Tours, walks that sample a dozen or so of the city's historic pubs, leave from the Crown Dining Room (above the Crown Liquor Saloon).

Belfast Splash Tours, the favorite of many kids, are sightseeing "Duck" boat excursions that take in Titanic Quarter and other notable city landmarks before splashing into the River Lagan. Tours leave five times daily from Victoria Square shopping mall on Chichester Street.

Belfast Welcome Centre *(see Essentials, below; note that the center is moving in 2013)* is the starting point for two worthy 90-minute walking tours. On the Blackstaff Way tour (£6; Saturday at 11 am), you'll learn how Belfast developed between three rivers—the Blackstaff, the Farset, and the Lagan. You'll also take in the Boyne Bridge, Belfast's oldest bridge, and discover the significance of the Mystery Stone from Belfast Castle. The Historic Belfast tour (£6; Wednesday, Friday, Saturday, and Sunday at 2 pm) focuses on the city's origins and its Victorian architecture.

Black taxi tours are another way to experience Belfast's history. Belfast City Black Taxi Tours conducts 75-minute tours in a London-style black taxi, visiting both Loyalist and Nationalist sights. Official Black Taxi Tours and the popular TaxiTrax Tours provide similar itineraries. For all companies, the Loyalist tours leave from North Street or Bridge Street and prices can vary depending on pick-up point; the Nationalist tours pick you up at your hotel.

Bus Tours Allen's Tours ☎ *028/9091–5613* ⊕ *www.allenstours.co.uk.* **Belfast City Sightseeing** ⊠ *City Tour departs from Castle Place (opposite McDonald's); Titanic Explorer pickups at Odyssey Complex and the Premier Inn Hotel and other city-center hotels* ☎ *028/9032–1321* ⊕ *www.belfastcitysightseeing.com* 🚌 *City Tour £12.50, valid 48 hrs on a hop-on, hop-off basis; Titanic Explorer £10 (£28.00 for 2 adults and 2 children)* ☉ *City Tour daily 10–4 every 15 mins. Mar.–Sept., every 30 minutes Oct.–Feb.; Titanic*

Explorer departs 9:45–3:45 each hr at a quarter to the hr.
Belfast Ghost Walk ✉ *Departs from City Hall front gates, Donegall Sq., Central District, Belfast, Northern Ireland* ☎ *079/0725–1414*
⊕ *www.ghostwalkbelfast.com* ✑ *£8* ⏲ *Mar.–Oct., Wed., Fri., and Sun. at 7.30 pm.* **Belfast Splash Tours** ☎ *028/9077–0990* ⊕ *www.belfastsplashtours.com*
✑ *£15.* **Belfast Pub Tours** ✉ *Depart from the Crown Rooms, 46 Great Victoria St., Golden Mile, Belfast, Northern Ireland* ☎ *028/9268–3665*
⊕ *www.belfastpubtours.com* ✑ *£6* ⏲ *Tours May–Oct., Thurs. 7 pm, Sat. 4 pm; check in advance.* **McComb's Coach Travel** ✉ *22 Donegall Rd., Central District, Belfast, Northern Ireland* ☎ *028/9077–7440* ⊕ *www.minicoachni.co.uk/tours.cfm.*

Taxi Tours **Belfast City Black Taxi Tours** ☎ *077/1267–3178*
⊕ *www.belfastcityblacktaxitours.com* ✑ *£25 for 1–2 passengers, £30 for 3 and £33 for 4.* **The Official Black Taxi Tours** ☎ *028/9064–2264*
⊕ *www.belfasttours.com* ✑ *£30 1–2 passengers, £10 per add'l person.*
TaxiTrax Tours ☎ *028/9031–5777* ⊕ *www.taxitrax.com* ✑ *£30 1–3 passengers, £10 per add'l person.*

ESSENTIALS

After April 2013, you'll find the Belfast Welcome Centre, the city's main tourist office, at 8–10 Donegall Square North, directly opposite the front of City Hall. (Until the move, the center can be found around the corner at 47 Donegall Place.) Some walking tours *(see above)* leave from the center, which also sells the Belfast Visitor pass—good for unlimited travel within a specified zone, as well as for discounts on tours and entrance to major attractions such as the Ulster Folk & Transport Museum and W5 at the Odyssey. The pass costs £6.50 for one day, £10.50 for two, and £14 for three, plus an initial £1.50 charge.

Visitor Information **Belfast Welcome Centre** ✉ *After April 2013, directly opposite the front of City Hall, 8–10 Donegall Square N, Central District, Belfast, Co. Antrim, Northern Ireland* ☎ *028/9024–6609* ⊕ *www.gotobelfast.com*
⏲ *Oct.–May, Mon.–Sat. 9–5:30; June–Sept., Mon.–Sat. 9–7, Sun. 11–4.*

EXPLORING

Magnificent Victorian structures still line the streets of the city center, but instead of housing linen mills or cigarette factories, they are home to chic new hotels and fashionable bars. Smart restaurants abound, and the people of Belfast, who for years would not venture out of their districts, appear to be making up for lost time. Each area of the city has changed considerably in the new peaceful era, but perhaps none more than the docklands around the Harland and Wolff shipyards, whose historic and enormous cranes, known to the locals as Samson and Goliath, still dominate the city's skyline. New developments—such as the Titanic Quarter—are springing up all around deserted shipyards, ranging from luxury hotels to modern office blocks. And in the center of the city, Victoria Square is a gigantic shopping and residential complex, replete with a geodesic dome, floors of glossy shops, and renovated Victorian row houses. In the west of the city, the physical scars of the Troubles are still evident, from the peace line that divides Catholic and Protestant

THE TROUBLES

11

Northern Ireland's historic conflict between Catholic and Protestant, Irish and English, had its roots in the first Norman incursions in the 12th century, when the English endeavored to subdue the potential enemy they saw as Ireland. The northern province of Ulster proved the hardest to conquer, but in 1607, its Irish nobility fled, their lands then given by the English to "the Planters"—staunch Protestants from England and Scotland.

Fast-forward through three centuries of smoldering tensions and religious strife to the overwhelming 1918 Nationalist vote across Ireland for Sinn Féin ("Ourselves Alone"), the party that believed in independence for all of Ireland. In Ulster, however, 22 (out of 29) seats went to the Unionists, who believed in maintaining British rule. After 50 years of living with a Unionist majority, students in Belfast's Queen's University launched a civil rights protest in 1968, claiming equal rights in jobs, housing, and opportunity. They were met by brutal British suppression, which, in turn, awoke the Irish Republican Army (IRA), dormant for decades. Britain then imposed Direct Rule. This struggle tragically came to a head on Bloody Sunday, January 30, 1972, when British paratroopers opened fire on people participating in a nonviolent protest in Derry against the British policy of internment without trial. When the smoke cleared, 13 people, all Catholic and unarmed, had been killed.

Decades of guerrilla conflict ensued between the IRA, the UDA/UVF (Protestant/Loyalist paramilitaries), and the British government and continued until 1998's Good Friday Agreement, which finally gave the province its own parliament. But a mere two months later, the province's fragile peace was shattered when a massive car bomb exploded in the quiet market town of Omagh on August 15. A minority of dissident Republicans had succeeded in killing 31 people. Despite this appalling act, the peace process continued and Unionists eventually entered government proceedings with Sinn Féin at the end of 1999.

Today, despite ongoing assembly battles between pro- and anti-agreement camps, Northern Ireland is enjoying the longest period of peace in its history. In September 2005, the IRA decommissioned all its weapons. In 2009, the Loyalist paramilitaries, the Ulster Volunteer Force and its splinter group, the Red Hand Commando, destroyed their weapons. By early 2010, the biggest Loyalist paramilitary group, the Ulster Defence Association, decommissioned all weapons. Two Irish Republican terror groups—the extreme Irish National Liberation Army and the Official IRA—also announced they had put weapons beyond use. In February 2010, the endorsement of a final political deal culminated in the Hillsborough Castle Agreement, securing the stability of the Northern Ireland Assembly.

For many nationalists, the icing on the political cake came with the announcement in June 2010 by the British government apologizing for Bloody Sunday and saying it "had been unjustified and unjustifiable." For the people of Derry this has been liberating and has brought about a wind of change that has had a positive impact on the city.

West Belfast to the murals on every gable wall. Visitors are discovering that it's safe to venture beyond the city center; indeed, backpackers are a regular sight on the Falls Road, and taxi tours of these once troubled areas are very popular.

GOLDEN MILE

The arrowhead-shaped district extending from Howard Street in the north to Shaftesbury Square at the southern tip, and bordered on the west by Great Victoria Street and on the east by Bedford Street and Dublin Road, is a great area from which to begin an exploration of Belfast. Although it doesn't glow quite the way the name suggests, the bustling Golden Mile and its immediate environs harbor noteworthy historic buildings. In addition, the area is filled with hotels and major civic and office buildings, as well as some restaurants, cafés, and shops. Even if you don't end up staying here, you're likely to pass through it often.

TOP ATTRACTIONS

Fodor's Choice
★

City Hall. After an £11 million, two-year restoration that saw the marbles freshly cleaned, the massive dome repainted, and the chandeliers polished, the exuberant Renaissance Revival–style City Hall has attracted sightseers in large numbers since reopening its doors in 2009. Built of Portland stone between 1898 and 1906 and modeled on St. Paul's Cathedral in London, the edifice was designed by Brumwell Thomas (who was knighted but had to sue to get his fee). Before you enter, take a stroll around Donegall Square, to see statues of Queen Victoria and a column honoring the U.S. Expeditionary Force, which landed in the city on January 26, 1942—the first contingent of the U.S. Army to land in Europe during World War II. A monument commemorating the *Titanic* stands in the grounds, and in 2012 a granite memorial was unveiled in a newly opened *Titanic* memorial garden in commemoration of the 100th anniversary of the sinking. The new memorial, on the east side of the grounds, lists the names of everyone who died in the tragedy. Enter the building under the porte cochere at the front. From the entrance hall (the base of which is a whispering gallery), the view up to the heights of the 173-foot-high Great Dome is a feast for the eyes. With its complicated series of arches and openings, stained-glass windows, Italian-marble inlays, decorative plasterwork, and paintings, this is Belfast's most ornate public space—a veritable homage to the might of the British Empire. Now the modernized building has been brought into the 21st century. It comes replete with the Bobbin coffee shop and the "Waking a Giant" exhibition, in which historic photographs tell the story of Belfast's industrial development. Another exhibition, "No Mean City," an interactive and photographic display, celebrates 68 inspirational people of the last 100 years, including Thomas Andrews (the designer of the *Titanic*), singer Van Morrison, and footballer George Best. In the courtyard a 60-jet fountain has been dedicated to Belfast City Council members killed during the Troubles. Free, guided one-hour tours are given. ⊠ *Donegall Sq., Golden Mile, Belfast, Co. Antrim, Northern Ireland* ☎ *028/9027–0456* ⊕ *www.belfastcity.gov.uk* ☜ *Tours free* ☾ *Tours weekdays at 11, 2, and 3; Sat. at 2 and 3.*

A monument of the High Victorian style, Belfast's City Hall towers over Donegall Place in the heart of the city center.

Fodor's Choice
★

Crown Liquor Saloon. Opposite the Europa Hotel on Great Victoria Street and owned by the National Trust (the United Kingdom's official conservation organization), the Crown is one of Belfast's glories. It began life in 1826 as the Railway Tavern; in 1885 the owner asked Italian craftsmen working on churches in Ireland to moonlight on rebuilding it, and its place in Irish architectural pub history was assured. The bar has richly carved woodwork around cozy snugs (cubicles—known to regulars as "confessional boxes"), leather seats, color tile work, and an abundance of mirrors. The Crown entered a new phase in its history in 2007 when the Trust spent £500,000 on a major restoration project. An ostentatious box of delights, it has been immaculately preserved—it is still lighted by gas. The pièce de résistance is the embossed ceiling with its swirling arabesques and rosettes of burnished primrose, amber, and gold, as dazzling again now as the day it was installed. The Crown claims to serve the perfect pint of Guinness—so no need to ask what anyone's drinking—and you can order a great plateful of warming Irish stew. When you settle down in your snug, note the little gunmetal plates used by the Victorians for lighting their matches as well as the newly restored antique push-button bells for ordering another round. Ageless, timeless, and classless—some would say the Crown is even priceless. ⊠ *46 Great Victoria St., Golden Mile, Belfast, Northern Ireland* ☎ *028/9024–3187* ⊕ *www.crownbar.com* ☼ *Mon.–Wed. 11:30 am–11 pm, Thurs.–Sat until midnight, Sun. 12:30–10.*

★ **Grand Opera House.** Belfast's opera house exemplifies the Victorians' fascination with ornamentation, opulent gilt moldings, and intricate plasterwork. The renowned theater architect Frank Matcham beautifully designed the building in 1894. Since 2005, the theater has undergone a massive extension program that has almost doubled its size, thanks to a new foyer bar, café, and party room. Contemporary Irish artist Cherith McKinstry's exquisite angel-and-cherub-laden fresco floats over the auditorium ceiling. You can take a one-hour behind-the-scenes tour, but by far the best way to see and enjoy the place is to attend a show. The theater regularly hosts musicals, operas, plays, and concerts. ✉ *2 Great Victoria St., Golden Mile, Belfast, Co. Antrim, Northern Ireland* ☎ *028/9024–1919* ⊕ *www.goh.co.uk* ✒ *bp]4* ☉ *Tours Thurs. and Sat. 11 am.*

St. Malachy's Church. In 2009 the wrappers came off the renovated St. Malachy's Church and, after a 15-month restoration program, one of the most impressive redbrick Tudor Revival churches in Ireland was reintroduced to the public. The extensive makeover included replacing brickwork and rebuilding the stone-dressed castellated towers and the slender octagonal corner turrets. Opened in 1844, St. Malachy's was designed by Thomas Jackson of Waterford. One of the interior highlights is the densely patterned fan-vaulted ceiling, a delightfully swirling masterpiece of plasterwork—whose inspiration was taken from the chapel of Henry VII at Westminster Abbey in London—tastefully repainted in cream. The high altarpiece featuring Pugin's *Journey to Calvary* was originally carried out by the portraitist Felix Piccioni whose family were refugees to Belfast from Austrian Italy. In 1868 the largest bell in Belfast was added to the church but after complaints that its deafening noise was interfering with the maturing of whiskey in the nearby Dunville distillery, it was wrapped in felt to soften its peal and vibration. Today, along the southeast wall of the church gazing out in contemplative mood with his brown eyes and torn chocolate brown coat, the delicate Statue of the Ragged Saint has also been cleaned. St. Benedict Joseph Labre, the patron saint of the unemployed, once again welcomes visitors into the ethereal elegance of one of Belfast's most architecturally romantic buildings. ✉ *Alfred St., Golden Mile, Belfast, Northern Ireland* ☎ *028/9032–1713* ⊕ *www.saintmalachys.ie* ✒ *Free.*

Ulster Hall. It has hosted Charles Dickens, the Rolling Stones, and Rachmaninov as well as a diverse range of Irish politicians from Charles Stewart Parnell to Ian Paisley. Built in 1862 as a ballroom, the Ulster Hall, affectionately known as the Grand Dame of Bedford Street, reopened in 2009 after an £8.5 million renovation and celebrated its 150th anniversary in 2012 with a special program of talks and musical events. Much of W. J. Barrie's original decor has now been restored and 13 historic oil paintings reflecting the history and mythology of Belfast by local artist Joseph Carey are on display in their original magnificence in the Carey Gallery. Another highlight of the restoration is an interpretative display featuring poetry, pictures, and sound telling the history of the hall through personal reminiscences. During World War II the building was used as a dance hall by U.S. troops based in Northern Ireland. The hall is also the permanent home of the Ulster Orchestra. Stop by the Café Grand Dame, drink in some of Belfast's colorful history, and reflect on the fact that it was here in

March 1971 that Led Zeppelin performed the stage debut of "Stairway to Heaven." At the box office you can buy tickets for all upcoming events at both Ulster Hall and Waterfront Hall. ⊠ *Bedford St., Golden Mile, Belfast, Northern Ireland* ☎ *028/9033–4400* ⊕ *www.belfastcity.gov.uk* ☉ *Guided tours by appointment.*

WORTH NOTING

Europa Hotel. A landmark in Belfast, the Europa is a monument to the resilience of the city in the face of the Troubles. The most bombed hotel in Western Europe, it was targeted 11 times by the IRA starting in the early 1970s and was refurbished every time; today it shows no signs of its explosive history. Indeed, even with this track

> ### VICTORIAN GRISLY
>
> Most of Belfast's landmarks were built during the reign of Queen Victoria. Once considered unappealing—"Victorian Grisly" was the epithet used by more than one critic—today they are marvelous remnants of an age that considered show, pomp, and circumstance paramount. Most of these buildings are found within 20 blocks of each other and a time-travel walk can hit many of them, including City Hall, Linen Hall Library, the Grand Opera House, Crown Liquor Saloon, Ulster Hall, St. Malachy's Church, and St. Anne's Cathedral.

record, President Bill Clinton and his wife, Hillary, chose the hotel for an overnight visit during their 1995 visit—for 24 hours the phones were answered with "White House Belfast, can I help you?" The president's room is now called the Clinton Suite and contains memorabilia from the presidential stay. In 2008 the Europa was outfitted with an Italian marble lobby and expanded to 272 rooms, including six suites. A photographic timeline was added in 2011 to commemorate the hotel's 40th anniversary. The property is owned by the affable Ulster millionaire and hotel magnate Billy Hastings. ⊠ *38 Great Victoria St., at Glengall St., Golden Mile, Belfast, Northern Ireland* ☎ *028/9027–1066* ⊕ *www.hastingshotels.com.*

CENTRAL DISTRICT

Belfast's Central District, immediately north of the Golden Mile, extends from Donegall Square north to St. Anne's Cathedral. It's not geographically the center of the city, but it's the old heart of Belfast. It's a frenetic place—the equivalent of Dublin's Grafton and Henry streets in one—where both locals and visitors shop. Cafés, pubs, offices, and shops of all kinds, from department stores to the Gap and Waterstones (there's even a Disney store), occupy the redbrick, white Portland-stone, and modern buildings that line its narrow streets. Many streets are pedestrian-only, so it's a good place to take a leisurely stroll, browse, and see some sights to boot. It's easy to get waylaid shopping and investigating sights along the river when taking this walk, so give yourself at least two hours to cover the area comfortably.

The Central District contains what locals call the **Cathedral Quarter**: radiating out from the new mock neo-Palladian development St. Anne's Square. Along its narrow, cobbled redbrick streets a former banana warehouse is now a circus school; an architectural firm has moved into a converted jute sack warehouse; and a busy brasserie given new life to a derelict building. Small privately owned art galleries, alongside the Black Box—a major performance venue—line the side streets and are crammed in alongside bars, cafés, and lively restaurants. Crowning it all is the dramatic Metropolitan Arts Centre. Northern Ireland's new flagship for the arts, the center opened in 2012. With its bright airy galleries, the MAC unashamedly contrasts with the neighboring Victorian warehouses and mills. It looms over its quarter the way the

> ### POOR PHIOMENA
>
> One of the largest private collections of *Titanic* memorabilia in Ireland is on display in Robinson's Bar in Great Victoria Street (opposite Europa Hotel, at Great Victoria and Glengall streets). It includes letters and postcards written on board the ship and poignant items such as "Philomena," the doll recovered floating at the wreck site.

Titanic Belfast looms over the Titanic Quarter. Both are important new landmarks for a reinvigorated city.

TOP ATTRACTIONS

★ **High Street.** Off High Street, especially down to Ann Street (parallel to the south), run narrow lanes and alleyways called entries. Though mostly cleaned up and turned into chic shopping lanes, they still hang on to something of their raffish character, and have distinctive pubs with little-altered Victorian interiors. Among the most notable are the Morning Star (Pottinger's Entry off High Street), with its large windows and fine curving bar; White's Tavern (entry off High Street), Belfast's oldest pub, founded in 1630, which, although considerably updated, is still warm and comfortable, with plush seats and a big, open fire; Ronnie Drew's (on May Street), in splendid counterpoint to the Waterfront's space-age style; and McHugh's (in Queen's Square), in what is reckoned to be the city's oldest extant building, dating from 1711.

Lagan Boat Company N.I. Ltd. A 75-minute *Titanic* tour takes in the shipyard where the famous liner was built. The Lagan Company also runs a separate two-hour boat trip, the Belfast Lough Tour at 3:30 on Sundays. The departure point for both tours is from Donegall Quay near the *Bigfish* sculpture (a gigantic salmon covered in tiles and printed with text and imagery about Belfast). Tickets can be bought in the Maritime Emporium shop beside the Obel tower at Donegall Quay. ⊠ *66 Donegall Quay, Central District, Belfast, Northern Ireland* ☎ *028/9033–0844* ⊕ *www.titanicboattours.com* ⊠ *Tours £10* ⊗ *Titanic tour Apr.–Oct., daily 12:30, 2, and 3.30; Nov.–Mar., weekends 12:30 and 2.*

Metropolitan Arts Centre. Starkly, eye-catchingly beautiful, the Metropolitan Arts Centre (MAC) is Northern Ireland's new flagship home for the arts. Six stories tall and with two theaters, three art galleries, and artists' studios—along with a café, a bar, and a restaurant—the MAC opened in April 2012. The centerpiece of the neo-Palladian St. Anne's Square development, with its semicolonnaded piazza, the MAC makes an astonishing statement all by itself with red brick and dark basalt, oak furnishings, Danish fabric panels, steel balustrades, bronze window frames, and dark-gray terrazzo flooring. The galleries present everything from the debut efforts of students from the nearby College of Art to attention-grabbing temporary exhibitions incorporating the works of world-renowned artists. ✉ *St. Anne's Square, Cathedral Quarter, Belfast, Northern Ireland* ☎ *028/9023–5053* ⊕ *www.themaclive.com* ◪ *Galleries free* ⊙ *Daily 10–7, later on performance nights.*

Fodor'sChoice **Titanic Belfast Visitor Centre.** This world-class attraction headlines a
★ Titanic Experience exhibition along with showcasing nine linked
♺ interpretative galleries that outline the *Titanic*'s dramatic story as well as the wider theme of Belfast's seafaring and industrial heritage. The stunning bow-shaped facade of the six-story building reflects the lines of the great ship, the shardlike appearance created from 3,000 different-shaped panels each folded from silver anodized aluminum sheets into asymmetrical geometries. The ultimate, startling effect is of light caught by a cut diamond. As you wander through Titanic Belfast you will learn about the thriving boomtown at the turn of the century; the ride through the reconstruction of the shipyards echoes with the sounds and sensations of 100 years ago. In one of the galleries, the ship's saga is brought up to the present with the discovery of the wreck and into the future with live links to contemporary undersea exploration. Also on-site is a movie theater designed by the *Titanic* explorer Robert Ballard (he discovered the wreck in 1985), which shows films about the ship. Tours are self-guided, and audio tours are available in seven languages. ■TIP➔ Tickets can be bought online (5% cheaper); the least crowded time to go is on Sunday morning. ✉ *Titanic House, 6 Queen's Rd., Titanic Quarter, East Belfast, Belfast, Northern Ireland* ☎ *028/9076–6386* ⊕ *titanicbelfast.com* ◪ *£13.50* ⊙ *Apr.–Sept., Mon.–Sun. 9–7; Oct.–Mar., Tues.–Sun. 10–5.*

Fodor'sChoice **Titanic's Dock and Pump-House Tour.** The atmospheric 900-foot-long dock
★ where *Titanic* was built—in its time the biggest in the world—is open to the public and ranks as one of *the* great attractions in Northern Ireland. Since spring 2012, and the events held for the 100th anniversary, *Titanic*'s Dock—officially known as the Thompson Dry Dock—has been accessible to visitors. Steps lead deep down 44 feet (13½ meters) to the floor of the dock, and for the first time in history you can bask in the evocative spirit of this remarkable place well below sea level. In its heyday in the early 20th century, the dock could hold 21 million gallons of water. Today it is Belfast's outstanding relic of *Titanic*'s legacy and strikingly represents the ship's physical footprint. Built by 500 men over a period of seven years, it was the beating heart of the shipyard's operation during the construction of the great White Star Liners—*Britannic*, *Olympic*, and RMS *Titanic*. But it was a tight squeeze because the *Titanic* barely fitted in. The original steel-casing gate (now showing some signs of rust) that enclosed the dock and kept ships watertight weighs a staggering 1,000 tons. To access the dock and pump house, you must join one of Colin Cobb's fascinating, fact-filled walks that help visitors—through visual aids of the *Titanic*—imagine, relive, and reflect on both a singular marvel of engineering and the importance of shipbuilding in Belfast's heritage. Hot snacks and sandwiches are available in the pump-house café and visitor center (open March–October, daily 10–6), where you can buy *Titanic* postcards and other souvenirs, including a deck-plan poster. Taking Metro Bus No. 26, 26b, or 26c

from City Hall is the easiest way to get to the Dock and Pump-House Tour; you can take a train to the new Titanic Quarter halt or opt for a 20-minute walk from Belfast city center to Queen's Road (home to the Odyssey Arena and W5 science center). ⊠ *Queen's Rd., Titanic Quarter, Belfast, Northern Ireland* ☎ *028/9073–7813* ⊕ *www.titanicsdock.com* ⊠ *£7* ☽ *Tours Mar.–Oct., daily on the hour 11–3.*

NEED A BREAK?

Kelly's Cellars. At the start of Royal Avenue, turn left onto Bank Street to find Kelly's Cellars, a circa-1720 pub with loads of character. Try the specialty: Irish stew. Two centuries ago, Kelly's Cellars was the regular meeting place of a militant Nationalist group, the Society of United Irishmen, whose leader, Wolfe Tone (who was a Protestant), is remembered as the founder of Irish Republicanism. Traditional music and plenty of local banter make the pub particularly lively on weekends. ⊠ *30–32 Bank St., Central District, Belfast, Northern Ireland* ☎ *028/9024–6058.*

☽ **W5: WhoWhatWhereWhyWhen.** Part of the Odyssey complex in Belfast's docks, the W5 science discovery center takes a high-tech, hands-on approach to interpreting science and creativity for adults and children. Video displays and flashing lights enhance the futuristic feel, and with more than 180 interactive exhibits you can do everything from explore the weather to build bridges and robots. ⊠ *2 Queen's Quay, Central District, Belfast, Northern Ireland* ☎ *028/9046–7700* ⊕ *www.w5online.co.uk* ⊠ *£7.90* ☽ *Mon.–Fri. 10–5, Sat. 10–6, Sun. noon–6; last entry 1 hr before closing.*

WORTH NOTING

Custom House. The 19th-century architect Charles Lanyon designed the Custom House. This building, along with many others in Belfast, including Queen's University and the unusual Sinclair Seaman's Church, bear the hallmarks of his skill. It's not open to the public, but it's worth circling the house to view the lofty pediment of Britannia, Mercury, and Neptune on the front, carved by acclaimed stonemason Thomas Fitzpatrick. A blue plaque records the fact that the 19th-century novelist Anthony Trollope worked in the building as a post-office surveyor. During the historic Dockers' Strike of 1907, the labor organizer Jim Larkin addressed crowds of up to 20,000 people from the steps of the Custom House. The steps became known as "Speaker's Corner." A life-size bronze statue with arms raised commemorates the orator and his cause. ⊠ *Donegall Quay, Central District, Belfast, Northern Ireland.*

☽ **Linen Hall Library.** This gray building on Donegall Square's northwest corner is in fact a comfortable private library, founded in 1788 and designed by Charles Lanyon. The library has an unparalleled collection of 80,000 documents and books relating to the Troubles, regarded as the definitive archive. One early librarian, Thomas Russell, was hanged in 1803 for supporting an Irish uprising. On the walls are paintings and prints depicting Belfast views and landmarks. Much of this artwork is for sale. It's an ideal hideaway for relaxing with a newspaper and enjoying the library's café. ⊠ *17 Donegall Sq. N, Central District, Belfast, Northern Ireland* ☎ *028/9032–1707* ⊕ *www.linenhall.com* ⊠ *Free* ☽ *Weekdays 9:30–5:30, Sat. 9:30–4.*

Continued on page 598

THE *TITANIC*: BORN IN BELFAST

"The *Titanic* has at last sailed home." That, in the words of one newspaper headline, fittingly described the 2012 Centennial commemorations held in Belfast to honor the 1912 sinking of the *Titanic*. Not far from the famous shipyards that built her, the city has opened a gloriously dramatic Titanic Belfast Visitor Centre (cost: an eye-watering £77 million), a towering building stuffed with spectacular exhibits, virtual tours, GCI effects, and even a ride through 1912 Belfast. Commentators predict this center could do for Belfast what the Guggenheim did for Bilbao. Only time will tell.

NOW OPEN: BELFAST TITANIC VISITOR CENTRE

Tragically touted as "unsinkable," the RMS *Titanic* set sail from Belfast's famed Harland & Wolff shipyards on April 2, 1912. Five miles of decks, twenty-nine boilers, a sixteen-ton forward anchor . . . and just 62 seconds to launch. But four days into her maiden voyage to New York—at precisely 11:40 pm on the night of April 14th—lookouts alarmingly sounded the ship's bell: "Iceberg, Straight Ahead!"

Too late: even though the Marconi wireless service on-board had received iceberg warnings from other ships—disregarded in favor of messages for first-class passengers—the ship hit the huge iceberg, which sliced open five watertight compartments (only four and the ship would have stayed afloat). With a 300-foot gash in her hull, the doomed liner sank two hours and forty minutes later—at 2:20 am—the next morning. Of the 2,201 passengers and

Top, left: view of Gallery 7's *Titanic* lifeboat; Top, right above: *Titanica* sculpture on main Plaza; Top, right below: the Fit-Out gallery—how the most elegant ship afloat was furnished; Right page, top: view of the museum exterior.

crew, only 711 survived . . . because there were not enough lifeboats.

THE WORLD'S LARGEST TITANIC ATTRACTION

Opened on March 31, 2012, and designed by Eric Kuhne Associates, the eye-catching, multi-prow shaped Titanic Belfast Visitor Centre rises right on the spot where the ship was built. Many Titanoraks (the term for Titanic groupies) feel it is a great success, if only because it has reclaimed Belfast's Titanic legacy. In the past, the tragedy had cast a shadow across the city's great shipyards (thanks to whispers about low-quality steel and a rushed production schedule) but the recent centenary uncovered the true story.

THE REAL REASONS SHE SANK

Surviving relatives of key players only revealed in 2012 the real missteps: due to a mix-up between steam-ship and sailing-ship steering systems, Second Officer Charles Lightoller's direction to steer "hard a-starboard" meant that Quartermaster Robert Hitchins panicked and steered right into the ice. But for the fact that Bruce Ismay, owner

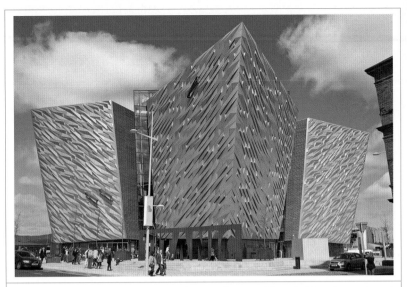

of the White Star Line, then gave the order to dislodge the berg, the *Titanic* would never have sunk.

TOURING THE GALLERIES

Gallery 1: Walk through the Harland & Wolff shipyard gates to discover Boomtown Belfast, as newspaper billboards and other memorabilia transport you back to 1912.

Gallery 2: Rise to the top of the Arrol Gantry as a six-seater fiberglass cart whisks you on a 5-minute ride through the busy shipyard.

Gallery 3: Through innovative special effects, experience the exciting launch on May 31, 1911, when 100,000 people saw *Titanic* hit the water for the first time.

Gallery 4: The Fit-Out is a custom-designed CGI show that takes you on a virtual tour of the liner from the engine room to the opulent restaurant (where a string orchestra serenades you).

Gallery 5: On the Maiden Voyage, get to know the passengers (of 38 nationalities) as the liner sails from Belfast via Southampton, Cherbourg, and Queenstown.

Gallery 6: The Sinking is portrayed through a dramatically chilly room that re-creates the harrowing last moments as *Titanic* plunges to disaster.

Gallery 7: In the Aftermath gallery a poignant wall of 400 life-vests leads to visual and audio displays centered on a 25-foot replica of a *Titanic* lifeboat. Use the touch-screen passenger and crew database.

Gallery 8: Sort fact from fiction amid the plethora of films, plays, song, poetry, novels and non-fiction works.

Gallery 9: Titanic Beneath dives to the wreck, two-and-a-half miles below the surface of the North Atlantic, by letting visitors stand on a transparent floor; nearby a film explores Robert Ballard's 1985 discovery of the wreck.

YOUR KATE WINSLET MOMENT

Pose on the painstaking replica of the magnificent staircase that leads up to the Astor Banqueting Suite, but note that this area is usually limited to functions and only open to the public on selected dates (check the website in advance).

THE TITANIC TRAIL: TOURING THE LANDMARKS

Titanic's Dock and Pump-House

Running along Queen's Road, the new Titanic Trail passes the main landmarks of the giant Harland & Wolff shipyards, the actual birthplace of the *Titanic*. Note that several attractions can only be seen as part of an organized tour. (*See the sightseeing outfits listed in the Belfast Tour Options Close-Up box.*) For others, you can only view the exteriors. Several of these Titanic tours pass the largest waterfront development in Europe, the eponymously named Titanic Quarter. It is budgeted at £1 billion and is remaking the former shipyard region in the Queen's Island sector (accessed by the Queen Elizabeth or Queen's bridges), northeast of the city center, into a mini-city (15 years in the building) of repurposed Victorian harbor buildings, plus hotels and marinas.

Heart of Titanic Quarter

❶ Titanic Belfast Visitor Centre. Completed in March 2012, this world-class attraction showcases nine linked interpretive galleries that outline the dramatic saga as well as the wider theme of Belfast's seafaring heritage. Framed by "Titanica"—a life-size female sculpted by Rowan Gillespie—and a gigantic 15-ton Titanic sign, the entrance plaza is embedded with the world's largest map, dotted with LED lights that track the *Titanic*'s route. To do justice to the center, allow up to three hours. Audio guides in seven languages are available for rent. ✉ Titanic House, 6 Queen's Rd., Queen's Island, Titanic Quarter ☎ 028/9076-6386 (ticket inquiries: 028/9076-6399) ⊕ www.titanicbelfast.com ✒ £13.50 ⊗ Apr.–Sept., Mon.–Sat., 9–7, Sun., 10–5; Oct.–Mar., daily 10–5.

❷ Titanic's Dock and Pump-House. Located at the Thompson Graving Dock, these fascinating attractions represent the liner's physical footprint and the last place she rested on dry ground. The giant ship fit into this dock with just a few feet to spare, giving you a sense of her amazing size. *See our full write-up on this attraction in the Belfast Exploring section.*

❸ Titanic and Olympic Slipways. Set in the Titanic Quarter, these massive twin slipways at Queen's Yard, where RMS *Titanic* and *Olympic* were built, are a part of the walking trail, but they can best be studied on one of the harbor boat tours.

Samson and Goliath

SS *Nomadic*

A 1911 view of the Queen's Yard Slipways

The 30-foot-tall Reconstructed Bow, built to scale

④ Harland & Wolff Drawing Offices. This long and elegant three-story former drawing office block in sandstone and brick is where the concept design and detailed construction drawings for *Titanic* were laid out. Nearby is the Paint Hall, built in 1974, and now used to film international movies such as *City of Ember, MickyBo & Me* and *Breakfast on Pluto*.

⑤ SS *Nomadic*, Hamilton Dock. Right next door to Titanic Belfast lies the tender ship to *Titanic* and last White Star Line ship in existence, SS *Nomadic*. It operated as a shuttle ship delivering 142 first-class passengers—including John Jacob Astor and Benjamin Guggenheim—to *Titanic* in Cherbourg (whose harbor was too small for the big liners to berth) before its departure for New York. Inside, interpretive galleries bring to life a time capsule of what it was like for workers and passengers. The ship is berthed at the Hamilton Graving Dock, a unique part of the shipyard's heritage which has also been sensitively

restored. ✉ 47 Donegall Pl., Central District ☎ 028/9024–6609 ⊕ www.nomadicbelfast. com ⊗ Oct.–May, Mon.–Sat. 9–5:30; June–Sept., Mon.–Sat. 9–7, Sun. 11–4.

⑥ Reconstructed Bow. *Titanic* enthusiasts will love a replica 30-ft. section of the bow of the liner, a new permanent "sculpture" unveiled in 2010. A team of engineers rebuilt the bow section using both modern and Edwardian techniques. It's on display on Queen's Island right beside the dock where the ship was built.

⑦ Samson and Goliath. Towering over everything, the giant yet noble yellow gantry cranes provide a top photo-op for tourists; sadly you can't climb them as there is no public access. The Big Crane tour, run by Lagan Boat Company, gives visitors an insight into their history—a relatively recent addition to the yard as these replacements to the originals were built in 1969.

St. Anne's Cathedral. A somber heaviness—a hallmark of the Irish neo-Romanesque style—marks this large, turn-of-the-20th-century edifice. Lord Carson (1854–1935), who was largely responsible for keeping the six counties inside the United Kingdom, is buried here. His is the only tomb; he was buried here by virtue of a special Act of Parliament. The guides on duty show you around for no charge. In April 2007, the 175-foot stainless steel Spire of Hope was erected atop the cathedral's roof, adding a new feature to the city's skyline and shining brightly as a beacon of the newfound optimism for the future. In 2012, as part of the *Titanic* centennial, an elegant Titanic Funeral Pall was unveiled. The German Luftwaffe bombed this section of Belfast during World War II. On the cathedral's Talbot Street side, at No. 21, the Northern Ireland War Memorial has an interactive exhibit about the war. ⊠ *Donegall St., Cathedral Quarter, Belfast, Northern Ireland* ☎ *028/9032–8332* ⊕ *www.belfastcathedral. org* 🖃 *Free* ☉ *Mon.–Sat. 10–4, Sun.services at 10, 11, 3:30.*

UNIVERSITY AREA

At Belfast's southern end, the part of the city around Queen's University is dotted with parks, botanical gardens, and leafy streets with fine, intact, two- and three-story 19th-century buildings. The area evokes an older, more leisurely pace of life. The many pubs and excellent restaurants make this area the hub of the city's nightlife. However, remember that Belfast is a student town and this is the main university area—the pace of life here can be fast (and sometimes a little furious) during school-term weekends.

★ **Botanic Gardens.** In the Victorian heyday, it was not unusual to find 10,000 of Belfast's citizens strolling about here on a Saturday afternoon. These gardens are a glorious haven of grass, trees, flowers, curving walks, and wrought-iron benches, all laid out in 1827 on land that slopes down to the River Lagan. The curved-iron and glass Palm House is a conservatory marvel designed in 1839 by Charles Lanyon. The Tropical Ravine House, though not architecturally distinguished, has an outstanding collection of tropical flora, in addition to some indigenous plants (it was famously said that it once held more Killarney ferns than could be found in Killarney itself). Once known as "the Glen," the Ravine House is unusually and exotically built over a faux ravine that you walk around. ⊠ *Stranmillis Rd., University Area, Belfast, Co. Antrim, Northern Ireland* ☎ *028/9031–4762* 🖃 *Free* ☉ *Gardens daily dawn–dusk; Palm House and Tropical Ravine House Apr.–Sept., weekdays 10–5, weekends 1–5; Oct.–Mar., weekdays 10–4, weekends 1–4.*

Queen's University Belfast. Dominating University Road is Queen's University. The main buildings, modeled on Oxford's Magdalen College and designed by the ubiquitous Charles Lanyon, were built in 1849 in the Tudor Revival style. The long, handsome redbrick-and-sandstone facade of the main building features large lead-glass windows, and is topped with three square towers and crenellations galore. University Square, really a terrace, is from the same era. The Seamus Heaney Library is named after the Ulster-born 1997 Nobel Prize–winning poet. In 2009 the McClay Library in College Park opened at a cost of £50 million. Designed by Boston-based architects Shepley, Bulfinch, Richardson & Abbot (SBRA)—who also worked on libraries at Yale, Cornell, and Harvard—the library features a multistory open atrium, 1.5 million volumes, and the Brian Friel Theatre, named in honor of one of Ireland's most illustrious playwrights. The C. S. Lewis reading room on the first floor has a replica of the wardrobe door used in the film *The Lion, the Witch, and the Wardrobe.* The Queen's Welcome Centre hosts a regular program of exhibitions and serves as a visitor information point. Guided tours are available but must be booked in advance. ⊠ *University Rd., University Area, Belfast, Northern Ireland* ☎ *28/9024–5133* ⊕ *www.qub.ac.uk* ⊠ *Free* ☉ *Welcome Centre Mon.–Fri. 8–6, weekends 11–4.*

> ## DORMANT ED ISN'T DEAD
>
> The Ulster Museum's showstopper, *Edmontosaurus,* is the most complete dinosaur fossil on display in Ireland. "Ed," as he's affectionately known, roamed America about 70 million years ago and would have looked a bit like a plucked turkey. At 20 feet long, Ed has settled into his 21st-century home and is now a big attraction.

Fodor's Choice ★ Ⓒ **Ulster Museum.** Set in an impressive edifice at the southwest corner of the Botanic Gardens, the Ulster Museum reopened in 2009 following a £17 million redevelopment project and has proved a hit with visitors. The rejuvenated museum with its spacious light-filled atrium and polished steel is a world away from the tenebrous galleries of old. The museum's forte is the history and prehistory of Ireland using exhibitions to colorfully trace the rise of Belfast's crafts, trade, and industry, and offering a reflective photographic archive of the Troubles. In addition, the museum has a large natural history section, with famed skeleton of the extinct Irish giant deer, and a trove of jewelry and gold ornaments recovered from the Spanish Armada vessel *Girona,* which sank off the Antrim coast in 1588. Take time to seek out the *Girona*'s stunning gold salamander studded with rubies and still dazzling after 400 years in the Atlantic. The museum includes a first-rate collection of 19th- and 20th-century art from Europe, Britain, and America. The new art, history, and nature discovery zones are jam-packed with hands-on activities for children. Kids also enjoy Peter the polar bear exhibit, and the famed Egyptian mummy, Takabuti. There's also an innovative 360-degree light-and-sound immersive experience, museum shop, café, and restaurant. ⊠ *Stranmillis Rd., University Area, Belfast, Northern Ireland* ☎ *028/9044–0000* ⊕ *www.nmni.com/um* ⊠ *Free* ☉ *Tues.–Sun. 10–5.*

BELFAST ENVIRONS

The sights along the Ards Peninsula and the north coast are a short drive from Belfast—an hour or less, perfect for day trips.

Fodor's Choice ★ **Belfast Castle.** In 1934 this spectacularly baronial castle, built for the Marquis of Donegall in 1865, was passed to the Belfast Corporation. Although the castle functions primarily as a restaurant, it also houses, on the second floor, the Cave Hill Visitor Centre, which provides information about the castle's history and its natural surroundings in Cave Hill Country Park. Views across Belfast are spectacular, taking in a vast swath of the city and stretching, for miles, in all directions. Guided tours (by reservation) of the reception rooms built by the Earls of Shaftesbury are sometimes offered on weekends. For a fine introduction to the castle

Anchoring Freedom Corner are loyalist murals found on Lower Newtownards Road, near the center of Protestant East Belfast.

and its park, check out the excellent eight-minute video "Watching over Belfast." In fact, the best reason to visit the castle is to take a stroll in its ornamental gardens and then make the ascent to McArt's Fort. This promontory, at the top of sheer cliffs 1,200 feet above the city, also affords an excellent view across Belfast. Take the path uphill from the parking lot, turn right at the next intersection of pathways, and then keep left as you journey up the, at some points, steep hill to the fort. ■ TIP→ After your walk, the Castle Tavern is a great place for drinks, snacks and bar meals. ⊠ *Antrim Rd., 4 km (2½ miles) north of Belfast, Belfast, Northern Ireland* ☎ *028/9077–6925* ⊕ *www.belfastcastle.co.uk* ⊠ *Free* ☉ *Visitor center, Tues.–Sat. 9 am–10 pm, Sun.–Mon. 9–6.*

★ **Mount Stewart.** The grandest stately house near Belfast, this was the country estate of the Marquesses of Londonderry, whose fame, or infamy, became known around the world thanks to the historical role played by the second Marquess. Known as Castlereagh, this Secretary of Ireland put down the Rising of 1798, helped forge the Act of Union, and killed himself by cutting his own throat. Mount Stewart was constructed in two stages where an earlier house had stood: George Dance designed the west facade (1804–05), and William Vitruvius Morrison designed the neoclassical main part of the building (1845–49), complete with an awe-inspiring Grecian portico facade. The seventh Marchioness, Edith, managed to wave her wand over the interior—after a fashion: Chinese vases, Louis-Philippe tables, and Spanish oak chairs do their worst to clutter up the rooms here. Still, the house does have some noted 18th-century interiors, including the Central Hall and the grand staircase hung with one of George Stubbs's most famous portraits, that of the celebrated

Belfast's Wall Murals

In Northern Ireland they say the Protestants make the money and the Catholics make the art, and as with all clichés, there is some truth in it. It's a truth that will become clear as you look up at the gable walls of blue-collar areas of Belfast on which the two communities—Catholic and Protestant—have expressed themselves in colorful murals that have given rise to one of the more quirky tours of the city.

Although the wildly romantic Catholic murals often aspire to the heights of Sistine Chapel–lite, those in Protestant areas (like the tough, no-nonsense Shankill and the Newtownards Road) are more workmanlike efforts that sometimes resemble war comics without the humor. It was not always this way.

In Protestant areas, murals were once painted by skilled coachbuilders to mark the July 12 celebrations of the defeat of the Catholic King James by King William at the Battle of the Boyne. As such, they typically depicted William resplendent in freshly laundered scarlet tunic and plumed cap, sitting on a white stallion that has mastered the art of walking on water. On the banks of the Boyne sits a mildly disheveled James, the expression on his face making him look as if he has just eaten an overdose of anchovies. Other popular themes in Protestant areas are the Red Hand of Ulster, symbolizing the founding of the province, and, on Carnmore Street, the 13 Protestant apprentice boys shutting the gates of Derry against King James in 1688, leading to the famous siege.

More recently, though, Protestant murals have taken on a grimmer air, and typical subjects include walleyed paramilitaries perpetually standing firm against increasing liberalism, nationalism, and all the other isms that Protestants see eroding their stern, Bible-driven way of life. Nationalist murals, on the other hand, first sprang up in areas like the Falls Road in 1981, when IRA inmates of the Maze prison began a hunger strike in an unsuccessful bid to be recognized by the British government as political prisoners rather than common criminals. Ten died, and the face of the most famous, Bobby Sands, looks down now from a gable wall on the Falls Road alongside the words "Our revenge will be the laughter of our children."

Since then, themes of freedom from oppression and a rising nationalist confidence have expressed themselves in murals that romantically and surreally mix and match images from the *Book of Kells,* the Celtic Mist mock-heroic posters of Irish artist Jim Fitzpatrick, assorted phoenixes rising from ashes, and revolutionaries clad in splendidly idiosyncratic sombreros and bandannas from ideological battlegrounds in Mexico and South America. Irish words and phrases that you will see springing up regularly include the much-used slogan *Tiocfaidh ár lá* (pronounced *chuck-y ohr law* and meaning "Our day will come") and the simple cry *Saoirse* (pronounced *seer-she*), meaning "Freedom."

The murals in both Protestant and Catholic areas are safe to view in daylight and outside the sensitive week of the July 12 marches by Protestant Orangemen. However, the most sensible way to view them would be to take a guided tour with Belfast City Sightseeing or one of the other bus or taxi tour companies.

racehorse Hambletonian, after he won one of the most prominent contests of the 18th century—this is perhaps the greatest in situ setting for a painting in Ireland. During 2013 the National Trust, which manages the property, is carrying out a major conservation and renovation project at Mount Stewart. Some rooms normally open to the public, will not be accessible, although the work will open new doors to areas which have never been seen by the public before. Visitors will be able to watch some of the restoration program—scheduled for completion in 2014—taking place during guided tours. On the grounds, don't miss the octagonal Temple of the Winds, a copy of a similar structure in Athens, and

> **THE GREENING OF BELFAST**
>
> It was due to Edith, the 7th Marchioness of Londonderry, that Mount Stewart was transformed into a garden showplace in the 1920s. Taking advantage of the salubrious microclimate of the Ards Peninsula, she created, in short order, a Shamrock Garden, Dodo Garden (note the stone figures that honor her close circle of friends—the "Warlock" is Winston Churchill), and Lady Mairi's Garden, complete with a "Mary, Mary, Quite Contrary" statue surrounded with silver bells and cockleshells.

the remarkable bathhouse and pool at the end of the wooded peninsula just before the entrance to the grounds. Ask for a free copy of the *Mount Stewart Garden Guide*, with a folding map showing the scale and diversity of the 18 named garden walks—you'll need more than one day to explore them all. Opening times often change here—it's prudent to phone ahead or log on to the website for the complete schedule. ✉ *Portaferry Rd., Newtownards, Northern Ireland* 🕾 *028/4278–8387* ⊕ *www.nationaltrust.org.uk* 🎫 *£7.30* ⊙ *Gardens: All year daily 11–6. House: by guided tour, Mar.–Oct., daily 12–6; July; closed Nov.–Feb.*

NEED A BREAK?

Grace Neill's Bar. Reputed to be the oldest pub in Ireland, Grace Neill's served its first pint in 1611 and has hosted such luminaries as Peter the Great, Franz Liszt, and John Keats. Behind the original pub, a cubby under the stairs with bar stools, is a larger bar where you can try a simple peppered beef sandwich with a pint of Guinness. There's live music on Friday and Saturday nights. ✉ *33 High St., 22 km (13 miles) from Mount Stewart, Donaghadee, Northern Ireland* 🕾 *028/9188–4595* ⊕ *www.graceneills.com.*

Fodor'sChoice
★

Ulster Folk and Transport Museum. Devoted to the province's social history, the excellent Ulster Folk and Transport Museum vividly brings Northern Ireland's past to life. With the installation in 2012 of a *Titanic* exhibition—set to run for at least the next few years—even more visitors have been heading here. The Folk Museum first invites you to visit Ballycultra—a typical Ulster town of the early 1900s—which comes alive thanks to costumed guides who practice such regional skills as lace making, sampler making, spinning, weaving, wood turning, forgework, printing, open-hearth cooking, carpentry, basket making, and needlework. The setting is evocative: a score of reconstructed buildings moved here from around the region, including a traditional weaver's dwelling, terraces of Victorian town houses, an 18th-century country church, a

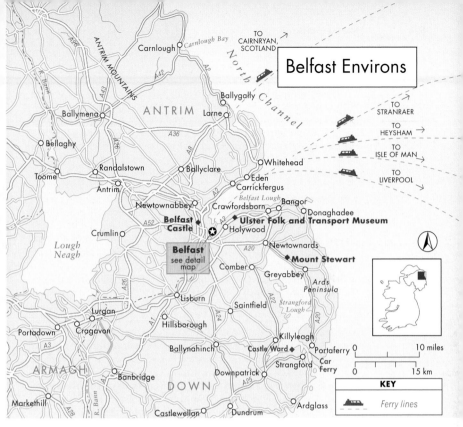

village flax mill, a farmhouse, and a rural school. Across the main road (by footbridge) is the beautifully designed Transport Museum, where exhibits include locally built airplanes and motorcycles, as well as the iconoclastic car produced by former General Motors whiz kid John DeLorean in his Belfast factory in 1982. The museum is on the 70 acres of Cultra Manor, encircled by a larger park and recreation area.

As for "TITANICa: The People's Story," this £1-million photographic and artifact exhibition explores the liner's history and reflects on the significance of the 100th centenary of the sinking in 2012. More than 500 original artifacts are on display as well as letters, brochures, and postcards, and there's even a first-class chamber pot from the great liner itself. A trail links the permanent transportation galleries to the special People's Story show in the outdoor Folk Museum. Visitors explore the living history experience of the *Titanic* and its times through people's daily routines with the main spotlight thrown on hearing stories in the period before, during, and after the maiden voyage of the doomed ocean liner. ⊠ *163 Bangor Rd., 16 km (10 miles) northeast of Belfast on A2, Cultra, Northern Ireland* ☎ *028/9042–8428* ⊕ *www.nmni.com* ⊡ *£7.50* ⊘ *Mar.–June, Tues.–Fri. 10–4, Sat. 10–6, Sun. 11–6; July–Sept., Tues.–Sat. 10–6, Sun. 11–6; Oct.–Feb., Tues.–Sat. 10–4, Sun. 11–4; last entry 1½ hrs before closing.*

WHERE TO EAT

GOLDEN MILE

$$ × **Cayenne.** One of Belfast's most exciting restaurants, Cayenne explodes
EUROPEAN with culinary fireworks. To wit, the salt-and-chili squid, crispy-duck
Fodor'sChoice salad, and millefeuille of Strangford crab are just a few of the worthy
★ starters, all fine introductions to the cutting-edge fusion cuisine of celeb-
rity chef Paul Rankin. Always with an Asian twist, the restaurant comes
up with such winning mains as seared diver scallops, soy-glazed halibut,
and braised spring lamb shoulder. As for desserts, few can resist the
rhubarb and raspberry crumble or the saltine panna cotta. A favorite
with theatergoers, Cayenne also offers a two-course pre-theater menu
for £16.95 or £19.95 for three courses. Cayenne accepts orders until
11 on Friday and Saturday evenings. $ *Average main: £18* ⊠ *7 Ascot
House, Shaftesbury Sq. at Great Victoria St., Golden Mile, Belfast,
Northern Ireland* ☎ *028/9033–1532* ⊕ *www.cayenne-restaurant.co.uk*
⊘ *Closed Mon., Tues. No lunch Sat.*

$$ × **The Ginger Bistro.** Chef-owner Simon McCance's modern Irish classics
EUROPEAN with an international twist attract foodies to this gem just off Great
Fodor'sChoice Victoria Street. A short but perfectly balanced menu emphasizes locally
★ sourced seafood and lean meats. Fishy dinner highlights include fillet
of hake, or sea bass; pan-roasted breast of duck or roasted loin of rare-
breed pork are also highly recommended, but the flavorsome fried squid
far outsells anything else on the menu. For lunchgoers in a hurry there
is an excellent-value menu offering haddock and chips, fish pie, and rib-
eye steak. The wines are outstanding, or try malt-flavored handcrafted
Belfast ales or lagers from the Mourne Mountains. Chalked-up black-
boards warn: "Can't have any pudding if you don't eat your greens."
For those who do, the desserts include the delectable crème brûlée with
raspberry compote, the soft-centered chocolate cake with berries, and
the unforgettable sticky-toffee pudding. $ *Average main: £18* ⊠ *7–8
Hope St., Golden Mile, Belfast, Northern Ireland* ☎ *028/9024–4421*
⊕ *www.gingerbistro.com* ⊘ *Closed Sun. No lunch Mon.*

CENTRAL DISTRICT

$ × **Deanes Deli Bistro.** Half take-out deli, half comfort-food eatery, this
EUROPEAN Michael Deane outpost is a few blocks away from his flagship Deanes
★ Restaurant. You'll rarely find an empty seat at this all-day affair. Try the
old-fashioned beer-battered fish-and-chips or one of the ever-changing
daily specials. Next door at the gourmet deli, the shelves groan with
homemade cheeses, breads, chocolates, and chutneys, many of them
from the local farmers' market. The deli is a smart stop for take-away
sandwiches. $ *Average main: £8* ⊠ *44 Bedford St., Central District,
Belfast, Northern Ireland* ☎ *028/9024–8800* ⊕ *www.michaeldeane.
co.uk/deanes-deli-bistro* ⊘ *Closed Sun.*

$$$ × **Deanes Restaurant.** Michael Deane is credited with revolutionizing the
EUROPEAN 21st-century culinary scene in Belfast. His flagship, Deanes Restaurant,
Fodor'sChoice is packed with Belfast's dining elite feasting on such delights as slow-
★ braised veal shin with creamed polenta and gremolata and roast monk-
fish with *pommes mousseline* (fancy mashed potatoes), pancetta, and a
bourguignon garnish. Steak, lamb, chicken, and venison dishes are all

In the early 20th century, the marchioness of Londonderry remade her Mount Stewart estate into the horticultural showplace of Northern Ireland.

menu staples. For fabulously fresh fish, head to the informal 20-seater all-white Seafood Bar, where the feel is strictly Cape Cod: coral curtains, shells, and nautical memorabilia create a seaside effect complemented by two large and boldly stylized Graham Knuttel paintings and his colorful wooden sculpture of a mackerel. The food is equally distinctive: the highlights include salt-and-chili squid, fishcakes, and the delicately glazed salmon burger. If you want a light and inexpensive lunch, the Seafood Bar serves a filling bowl of chowder or mussels with bread. The Deanes empire also includes ⇨ *Deanes Deli Bistro and, in the leafy University Area, Deanes at Queens (also open on Sunday; see website for details).* ⑤ *Average main: £19* ✉ *36–40 Howard St., Central District, Belfast, Northern Ireland* ☎ *028/9033–1134* ⊕ *www.michaeldeane. co.uk* ☉ *Closed Sun.*

$$$$
EUROPEAN
Fodor's Choice
★

✕ **The Great Room.** Inside the swank and lavish Merchant Hotel, beneath the grand dome of this former bank's great hall and Ireland's biggest chandelier, you'll find the perfect setting for a memorable dinner of adventurous European fare. Exceptional offerings from the kitchen include Dover sole *niçoise*, rib of Kettyle beef, or, for vegetarians, pappardelle pasta with black truffles and olive oil. The wonderful extravaganza of profiterole swans swimming delicately in a small lake of chocolate sauce is just one delight found on the dessert trolley. First-class service in truly opulent surroundings makes this restaurant worth a detour. The set £22.50 per person dinner menu from Monday through Thursday is great value; on the weekend it increases to between £80 and £100 for two, with a bottle of wine included. ⑤ *Average main: £23* ✉ *35 Waring St., Cathedral Quartert, Belfast, Northern Ireland* ☎ *028/9023–4888* ⊕ *www.themerchanthotel.com.*

$ ✕**Long's.** For nigh on a hundred years—the place opened in 1914—
IRISH Long's has been serving fish-and-chips in its tiny, completely basic
★ Athol Street premises. Garbage collectors, millionaires, and patrons
from every sector in between flock here for the secret-batter-recipe fish,
served with chips, bread and butter, and a mug of tea. Long's closes
at 6:30 pm. ⑤ *Average main: £7* ✉ *39 Athol St., Golden Mile, Belfast,
Northern Ireland* ☎ *028/9032–1848* ▭ *No credit cards* ⊘ *Closed Sun.
No dinner.*

$ ✕**Made in Belfast: Cathedral Quarter.** Could this self-styled "restolounge"
MODERN IRISH start a new worldwide trend? Touted as "violently chic" yet with a
Fodor'sChoice bohemian, casual vibe, flaunting one of Belfast's most eye-popping
★ decors yet given a menu packed with classic old favorites, this 2010
addition to the happening Cathedral Quarter is one of Belfast's buzzi-
est bistros. Following the big success of its sister restaurant located
just a block from City Hall (at Units 1 and 2 Wellington Buildings on
Wellington St.) and on a street lined with stylish stores, this Cathedral
Quarter outlet changed its name from the Beautiful Hooligan to cash in
on the fame of the original. Redecorated in a giant mish-mash of retro
lamps, vintage fabrics, and '50s collectibles, this newer outlet follows
the Cuisinart school of design, mix n' matching all sorts of
antiques and objects, including a ceiling adorned with glossy magazine photographs. The typewritten menu, set on clipboards, showcases
"seasonal" and retro dishes, best downed with one of the fab cocktails such as Apple Poshmopolitan. Start with the trio of potted fish
with dill, gherkin, and mayo or the delicious melted baked Camembert
with applesauce and warm toast. Mains average £11, with the choice
ranging from spinach falafels with fattoush salad and cumin yogurt
to Finnebrogue Irish venison burger with chili and coffee chutney and
apricot coleslaw. And you thought New York City was hip! ⑤ *Average main: £11* ✉ *23 Talbot St., Cathedral Quarter, Belfast, Northern
Ireland* ☎ *028/9024–4107* ⊕ *www.madeinbelfastni.com.*

$ ✕**The Morning Star.** Halfway down a narrow lane is the 19th-century
IRISH Morning Star, one of the city's most historic pubs, first built as a coach-
Fodor'sChoice ing stop for the Belfast to Dublin post. There's a traditional bar down-
★ stairs and a cozy velvet and wood-panel restaurant upstairs. On the
menu you might find venison and game in winter, lamb in spring, and
grilled haddock with dark rum or roast Antrim pork in summer. Also
notable is the steak menu; you'd be hard-pressed to find a larger assort-
ment of aged-beef cuts. And they are enormous: sizzling steaks, some
up to 48 ounces, arrive at the table in red-hot cast-iron skillets and
are served with a flourish by the friendly staff. There's also a great
value buffet at which you select from chicken, seafood, and pork. This
place tends to the pangs of visitors, on Sundays enticing Australians
with a Jolly pie and a pint for £3, and providing BBQ sauce daily to
keep the Americans happy. ⑤ *Average main: £9* ✉ *17–19 Pottinger's
Entry, Central District, Belfast, Northern Ireland* ☎ *028/9023–5986*
⊕ *themorningstarbar.com.*

$$$ ✕**Mourne Seafood Bar.** This seafood bar hidden down a side street
SEAFOOD has established itself as a firm favorite on the Belfast dining scene.
Cofounder Bob McCoubrey was originally a marine biologist and has

teamed up with experienced head chef Andy Rae to create a restaurant that has helped to reinvigorate the city's gastronomic scene. Daily specials might include seafood dumplings with nam jim dressing and Napa slaw or seared king scallops with butternut-squash risotto and crispy sage. The salmon, cod, hake, and sea bream are all done to perfection, but the standout dish for many is the gurnard, a whole fish served with bacon and clam velouté. The upstairs Oyster Bar, a cheaper alternative to the main dining room, offers small and big plates. Small plates (they're brimful) costing £4 include the Mourne Oyster Bar mini casserole, the Indian-spiced mackerel with focaccia crisps, and the Thai seafood dumplings with chili jam. The big plates average £9, for which you get a filling portion of mussels, fish fingers, prawn linguine, or the cold seafood platter with wheaten bread—a big hit with a glass of the Oyster stout (don't ask for Guinness here) made by the Whitewater brewery in Kilkeel. $ *Average main: £19* ⊠ *Central District, Belfast, Northern Ireland* ☎ *028/9024–8544* ⊕ *www.mourneseafood.com* ⊗ *No dinner Sun. No reservations for lunch.*

$$ ⤬ **Nick's Warehouse.** Ever since 1989, the energetic Nick Price has presided over a cozy wine bar and buzz-filled restaurant on a narrow cobbled street in the now fashionable Cathedral Quarter. The informal ground-floor Anix restaurant is frequented by legal, financial, and media types for lunch. Using local ingredients and produce, the menu draws on a wide range of influences in dishes ranging from fillet of sea bass with fennel to rump of lamb with Boulangère potatoes. The upstairs restaurant, which serves dinner on Saturday night, was refurbished in 2012. It has a different persona and a more expensive menu to go with it. Even the bread is made on the premises: a pastry chef bakes wonderful soda, wheaten, and whole-grain breads. $ *Average main: £17* ⊠ *35–39 Hill St., Cathedral Quarter, Belfast, Northern Ireland* ☎ *028/9043–9690* ⊕ *www.nickswarehouse.co.uk* ⤳ *Reservations essential* ⊗ *Closed Sun. and Mon.*

EUROPEAN
Fodor'sChoice
★

$ ⤬ **The Northern Whig.** Housed in an elegant former newspaper building, the Northern Whig is spacious and stylish. Three 30-foot-high statues of Soviet heroes that once topped Communist Party headquarters in Prague dominate the wood-and-leather interior. In the evenings, one wall slides away so you can watch classic movies, a jazz band, or a DJ playing laid-back blues, soul, or retro music. The food is brasserie style—not astonishing, but good. The environment, the wine selection, and the bar are the main draws, though. $ *Average main: £12* ⊠ *2–10 Bridge St., Central District, Belfast, Northern Ireland* ☎ *028/9050–9888* ⊕ *www.thenorthernwhig.com.*

EUROPEAN

$$ ⤬ **Red Panda.** It comes as a surprise to visitors to learn that Belfast has a large Chinese community, a sizable portion of which seems to favor this bustling spot—making reservations always a good idea here. This venue (there's another in Odyssey Arena complex) is large, spacious, and modern. A five-course set dinner might include crispy aromatic duck pancakes or stirfried king prawns with scallops with broccoli. $ *Average main: £16* ⊠ *60 Great Victoria St., Central District, Belfast, Northern Ireland* ☎ *028/9080–8700* ⊕ *www.theredpanda.co.uk* ⊗ *No lunch Sat.*

CHINESE

$$ **✕Zen.** Entrepreneur Eddie Fung

JAPANESE has miraculously transformed a red-brick 19th-century Belfast mill into an Asian oasis housing the city's finest Japanese restaurant. Upstairs you traverse a 30-foot-long mirrored catwalk with a glass walkway to get to the seating area. Choose between wooden booths, or, if you're prepared to hunker down on the floor, Japanese-style, opt for the traditional dining area. Downstairs, handpick your meal at the sushi bar, or choose a discreet table for two under the serene gaze of (reputedly) Ireland's largest Buddha. Zen has a reputation for authentic fresh sushi and sashimi. Purists may raise an eyebrow over the crispy prawns, but everyone declares them delicious. Finish your meal with a Japanese malt whiskey: Nikka Black is smoky and mellow and will round off the perfect dinner. $ *Average main: £15* ✉ *55–59 Adelaide St., behind City Hall, Central District, Belfast, Northern Ireland* ☎ *028/9023–2244* ⊕ *www.zenbelfast.co.uk* ⊗ *No lunch Sat.*

> **CARBING UP**
>
> When it comes to food, Northern Ireland is most famed (or notorious) for its Ulster Fry, a fried-up, carbohydrate blowout of a breakfast that is a cardiologist's nightmare. Sausage, bacon, eggs, black pudding, fried soda bread, and potato bread (perhaps a grilled tomato or fried mushrooms) all make a meal that sounds as dangerous to your health as bungee jumping without a rope. After a night on the Guinness, however, you'll understand why this breakfast is so popular: it makes a great cure for a hangover.

UNIVERSITY AREA

$$ **✕Drennans Restaurant.** A magnificently restored stained-glass window

IRISH featuring St. Cecilia (the patron saint of musicians) playing her pipes and looking down on diners sets the mood in this classy restaurant run by Lawrence Delaney, who has years of experience pleasing hungry customers. Delaney is interested in Irish history and named his restaurant after Dr. William Drennan, who coined the sobriquet the "Emerald Isle." Reminiscent of a Parisian-style bistro, it offers an early-bird menu (£12.95 for two courses) laden with sirloin steak, buttered chicken, pork belly, lamb, and fish. Options from the regular dinner menu include sea bass over tagliatelle with asparagus and Parmesan shavings. For dessert, the warm sticky toffee pudding in butterscotch sauce will linger long on the taste buds. The restaurant is BYOB. As befits a restaurant with a musical saint, each night a pianist switches effortlessly between blues, pop, and jazz. $ *Average main: £17* ✉ *43 University Rd., University Area, Belfast, Northern Ireland* ☎ *028/9020–4556* ⊕ *www.drennans. co.uk* ⚐ *Reservations essential.*

WHERE TO STAY

For expanded hotel reviews, visit Fodors.com.

CENTRAL DISTRICT

$ **Benedict's of Belfast.** Friendly, lively, and convenient, Benedict's looms

HOTEL large on Shaftesbury Square—guest rooms on the second floor are bright and colorful, and have wooden floors; the carpeted rooms on the third floor are darker, with an Asian influence, simple but comfortable. **Pros:** rooms are plain but functional and clean; great value dining. **Cons:** guests have experienced late check-in due to rooms not being ready; some parts of hotel show wear and tear. **TripAdvisor:** "friendly staff," "a really lovely place to stay," "highly recommended." $ *Rooms from: £75* ✉ *7–21 Bradbury Pl., Golden Mile, Belfast, Co. Down, Northern Ireland* ☎ *028/9059–1999* ⊕ *www.benedictshotel. co.uk* ⤴ *32 rooms* ⦿| *Breakfast.*

$$$
B&B/INN

🛏 **Holiday Inn Belfast.** Still fresh from a £1.6 million renovation in 2011, the Holiday Inn is only a 10-minute walk from the city center and offers outstanding facilities at a reasonable price. **Pros:** value deals; health club and facilities are top-notch; TV celebrities often spotted in front of nearby BBC studios. **Cons:** queues at busy times at check-in and checkout; no car parking spaces available. **TripAdvisor:** "friendly staff," "brilliant stay," "wonderful surprise." $ *Rooms from: £140* ✉ *22 Ormeau Ave., Golden Mile, Belfast, Co. Down, Northern Ireland* ☎ *087/1942–9005* ⊕ *www.holidayinn.com* ⤴ *170 rooms* ⦿| *Multiple meal plans.*

$
HOTEL

🛏 **Jurys Inn Belfast.** Within walking distance of the main city-center attractions—pubs, cinemas, shops, restaurants, and the Grand Opera House are all nearby—this inn has newish furnishings, and the spacious lobby has a welcoming feel. **Pros:** central location; staff helpful and friendly; spacious rooms recently refurbished. **Cons:** complaints of bedrooms not being properly cleaned; lack of car parking. **TripAdvisor:** "professional and clean," "very good quality accommodation," "friendly staff." $ *Rooms from: £69* ✉ *Fisherwick Pl., at Great Victoria St., Golden Mile, Belfast, Co. Down, Northern Ireland* ☎ *028/9053–3500* ⊕ *www.jurysinns.com* ⤴ *190 rooms* ⦿| *Breakfast.*

$$$$
HOTEL
Fodor's Choice
★

🛏 **Malmaison.** "A hotel that dares to be different," trumpets the promotional blurb for Malmaison, and the place certainly lives up to the claim. **Pros:** imaginative and glamorous; five-minute walk to major Belfast shopping. **Cons:** lack of car parking; if you don't like the bar's subtle darkness, bring a flashlight. **TripAdvisor:** "friendly but luxurious," "stunning," "perfect location." $ *Rooms from: £180* ✉ *34–38 Victoria St., Central District, Belfast, Co. Down, Northern Ireland* ☎ *028/9022–0200* ⊕ *www.malmaison.com* ⤴ *62 rooms, 2 suites.*

$$$$
HOTEL
Fodor's Choice
★

🛏 **The Merchant Hotel.** Upon opening in 2006, this was quickly heralded as Northern Ireland's—perhaps all of Ireland's—most spectacular and sumptuous hotel, built as the headquarters of Ulster Bank in the mid-19th century. **Pros:** opulent place with attentive reception and friendly bar staff; deep King Koil mattresses leave a mellow afterglow; history and architecture buffs will love it. **Cons:** revelers from pubs and clubs in the surrounding streets detract from the internal serenity; at £15, breakfast room service is for high rollers only. **TripAdvisor:** "excellent staff," "gorgeous," "superb boutique hotel." $ *Rooms from: £220* ✉ *16 Skipper St., Cathedral Quarter, Belfast, Co. Down, Northern Ireland* ☎ *028/9023–4888* ⊕ *www.themerchanthotel.com* ⤴ *63 rooms, 5 suites.*

$$$
HOTEL
★

🛏 **Ten Square.** You don't get much more downtown or contemporary than this fashionable boutique hotel right behind City Hall. **Pros:** luxurious surroundings; attention to detail in the attractive rooms;

super-king beds; convivial feel to the Grill Room. **Cons:** the noisy bar can be sweaty; sit outside, but only if you don't mind the fumes from taxis, cars, and buses. **TripAdvisor:** "very comfortable," "a hidden gem," "so friendly." ⑤ *Rooms from: £129 ✉ 10 Donegall Sq. S, Golden Mile, Belfast, Co. Down, Northern Ireland ☎ 028/9024–1001 ⊕ www. tensquare.co.uk ↻ 22 rooms ⧉ Multiple meal plans.*

UNIVERSITY AREA

$
B&B/INN

All Seasons. Enjoying a superb location on the fashionable Lisburn Road in the south of the city, this spot is steps from some of the city's most stylish boutiques and trendiest bars. **Pros:** top-notch location for exploring the cafés and bars on Lisburn Road; warm, welcoming, and inviting owner. **Cons:** family rooms can be a tight squeeze; few toiletries and no hair dryers. **TripAdvisor:** "very enjoyable stay," "very warm and welcoming," "budget accommodation with a smile." ⑤ *Rooms from: £50 ✉ 356 Lisburn Rd., Belfast, Co. Down, Northern Ireland ☎ 028/9068–2814 ⊕ www.allseasonsbelfast.com ↻ 7 rooms ⧉ Breakfast.*

$
HOTEL
★

Dukes at Queens. The handsomely transformed hotel reopened in 2009, bringing a whiff of trendiness to an area that's about as bohemian as Belfast gets—although it has retained its distinguished redbrick Victorian facade, the inside has been revamped in a cool contemporary style. **Pros:** stylish hotel offering excellent service; good value for the money; convenient location. **Cons:** area is thronged at lunchtime with office workers and even busier at night—noise is an ever-present reality. **TripAdvisor:** "chic," "very comfortable and welcoming," "wonderful surprise." ⑤ *Rooms from: £75 ✉ 65–67 University St., University Area, Belfast, Co. Down, Northern Ireland ☎ 028/9023–6666 ⊕ www. dukesatqueens.com ↻ 32 rooms ⧉ Breakfast.*

$
HOTEL

Madison's Hotel. A 2011 upgrade has revitalized this gracious hotel surrounded by the shops and cafés of tree-lined and mildly bohemian Botanic Avenue—the facade and public areas are decorated in a modish Barcelona-inspired take on art nouveau, and all the rooms have new furnishings and carpets. **Pros:** appealing hotel with friendly service; Madison's Irish whiskey and white chocolate cheesecake demands second helping. **Cons:** late-night student rowdiness on Botanic Avenue; some standard rooms on the smallish side. **TripAdvisor:** "ideal place to stay," "wonderful staff," "excellent food." ⑤ *Rooms from: £74 ✉ 59–63 Botanic Ave., University Area, Belfast, Northern Ireland ☎ 028/9050–9800 ⊕ www.madisonshotel.com ↻ 35 rooms ⧉ Breakfast.*

BELFAST ENVIRONS

$$$$
HOTEL
★

Culloden Estate & Spa. Built in 1876, this imposingly grand vision in Belfast stone presides over the forested slopes of the Holywood hills and the busy waters of Belfast Lough—antiques and silk-and-velvet fabrics grace guest rooms both in the original section and in a newer wing; all rooms have fine views. **Pros:** building oozes character and personality; top-class service. **Cons:** suites are just big rooms and don't measure up; the restaurant can be stuffy; massages, manicures, and vintage champagne don't come cheap. **TripAdvisor:** "beautiful location and facilities," "luxurious pampering," "beautiful." ⑤ *Rooms* *from: £240 ✉ 142 Bangor Rd., 8 km (5 miles) east of Belfast on A2, Holywood, Co. Down, Northern Ireland* ☎ 028/9042–1066 ⊕ *www. hastingshotels.com/culloden-estate-and-spa* ↘ *105 rooms, 22 suites* ⦿ *Multiple meal plans.*

$ | B&B/INN | Fodor's Choice ★

⌂ The Old Inn. Set in the village of Crawfordsburn, this 1614 coach inn, reputedly Ireland's oldest, certainly looks the part: it's pure 17th-century with a sculpted thatch roof, half doors, and leaded-glass windows. **Pros:** a proverbial step back in time; lots of character; comfortable rooms. **Cons:** slow service; breakfasts not always up to snuff. **TripAdvisor:** "good old-fashioned excellence," "sumptuous surroundings," "old-world charm." $ *Rooms from: £80 ✉ 15 Main St., 16 km (10 miles) east of Belfast on A2, Crawfordsburn, Co. Down, Northern Ireland* ☎ 028/9185–3255 ⊕ *www. theoldinn.com* ↘ *31 rooms, 8 suites* ⦿ *Breakfast.*

$ | B&B/INN ★

⌂ Rayanne House. Famous both for its food and for its hospitality, this country house run by the devoted Bernadette McClelland offers guest rooms that are airy, each in a contemporary style with garden views, along with lunch and dinner available by request 24 hours in advance. **Pros:** well-appointed bright and comfortable rooms; handsome furnishings, tastefully presented; the *Titanic* dinner is a true conversation piece. **Cons:** Holywood nightlife is limited to a few bars. **TripAdvisor:** "great service," "a true gem," "food for the soul." $ *Rooms from: £80 ✉ 60 Demesne Rd., 8 km (5 miles) east of Belfast on A2, Holywood, Co. Down, Northern Ireland* ☎☎ 028/9042–5859 ⊕ *www.rayannehouse. com* ↘ *11 rooms* ⦿ *Multiple meal plans.*

$ | B&B/INN

⌂ Roseleigh House. This Victorian guesthouse on a tree-filled avenue in residential south Belfast is a friendly option. **Pros:** the breakfasts are healthy and robust; terrific suburban location well away from city-center noise and just a 15-minute bus ride into town. **Cons:** no bar, but around the corner on the fashionable Ormeau Road you'll find clubs aplenty. **TripAdvisor:** "excellence in simplicity," "beautiful and cozy home," "simply perfection." $ *Rooms from: £70 ✉ 19 Rosetta Park, Belfast, Co. Down, Northern Ireland* ☎ 028/9064–4414 ⊕ *www. roseleighhouse.co.uk* ↘ *6 rooms* ⦿ *Breakfast.*

$$ | HOTEL

⌂ Dunadry Hotel. This spacious, whitewashed former mill on 10 acres of land is a hotel of considerable charm. **Pros:** charming location; large bedrooms; 10-minute drive from Belfast Airport. **Cons:** those wedding parties can get boisterous. **TripAdvisor:** "best in Belfast," "excellent service," "lovely cozy hotel." $ *Rooms from: £90 ✉ 2 Islandreagh Dr., off M2, Dunadry, Co. Antrim, Northern Ireland* ☎ 028/9443–4343 🖷 028/9443–3389 ⊕ *www.dunadry.com* ↘ *83 rooms* ⦿ *No meals.*

$$$ | HOTEL

⌂ Hilton Templepatrick Hotel & Country Club. During 2011 the Hilton refurbished all its rooms, refreshing the decor and changing furnishings; rooms all come with satellite TV. **Pros:** relaxing surroundings; great

---

HIDEOUT HISTORY

If you're lucky enough to stay in the oldest parts of the Old Inn, you still may be able to uncover a secret hiding place for contraband, as smugglers, like the famous highwayman Dick Turpin, made this one of their favored homes away from home.

location near the airport and short distance from Belfast; championship golf course. **Cons:** bland chain lacks individual character; large parties equal noisy nights. **TripAdvisor:** "a relaxing break," "great staff," "nice surroundings." ⑤ *Rooms from: £120 ⊠ 6 km (4 miles) from Belfast Airport on A57, Castle Upton Estate, Templepatrick, Co. Antrim, Northern Ireland* ☎ *028/9443–5500* 🖹 *028/9443–5511* ⊕ *www.hilton. com* ↬ *129 rooms, 2 suites.*

NIGHTLIFE AND THE ARTS

NIGHTLIFE

Belfast has dozens of pubs packed with relics of the Victorian and Edwardian periods. Although pubs typically close around 11:30 pm, many city-center–Golden Mile nightclubs stay open until 1 am.

GOLDEN MILE

The glorious Crown Liquor Saloon is far from being the only old pub in the Golden Mile area—some, but by no means all, of Belfast's evening life, takes place in bars and restaurants here. At several replicated Victorian bars, more locals and fewer visitors gather.

★ **Benedict's Bar.** The faux-Gothic exterior of Benedict's hotel belies its modern origins. Within you'll find a bar, music venue, disco, 150-seat restaurant, and high-style hotel. ⊠ *7–21 Bradbury Pl., Golden Mile, Belfast, Northern Ireland* ☎ *028/9059–1999* ⊕ *www.benedictshotel.co.uk.*

Limelight. Straying from the model of the Victorian-style public house, the Limelight is a disco-nightclub with cabaret on Tuesdays, Fridays, and Saturdays, and recorded music on other nights. Extremely popular with students, it books musicians as well as DJs. ⊠ *17 Ormeau Ave., Golden Mile, Belfast, Northern Ireland* ☎ *028/9032–7007* ⊕ *www. limelightbelfast.com.*

Morrisons. Across the road from the BBC, Morrisons is a haunt of media types and beloved by PR and advertising execs. ⊠ *21 Bedford St., Golden Mile, Belfast, Northern Ireland* ☎ *028/9032–0030* ⊕ *www. morrisonsbar.com.*

Robinsons. A popular pub two doors from the Crown Liquor Saloon, Robinsons draws a young crowd with folk music in its Fibber Magees bar on Sunday and funk in the trendy BT1 karoke bar on weekends. ⊠ *38–42 Great Victoria St., Golden Mile, Belfast, Northern Ireland* ☎ *028/9024–7447* ⊕ *www.robinsonsbar.co.uk.*

CENTRAL DISTRICT

★ **Apartment.** One of the city center's trendiest bars, the Apartment, set beside City Hall, serves drinks and brasserie-style pub grub to Belfast's cool young things. Extensive but inexpensive wine and cocktail lists attract a good crowd. ⊠ *2 Donegall Sq. W, Central District, Belfast, Northern Ireland* ☎ *028/9050–9777* ⊕ *www.apartmentbelfast.com.*

Bittles Bar. Gilded shamrocks bedeck this interesting triangular Victorian pub on the fringes of the Cathedral Quarter. Paintings of literary characters and local landmarks adorn the walls, while a high, wood-panel ceiling gives an illusion of spaciousness. Bittles serves pub grub.

✉ *On Victoria Square, 70 Upper Church La., Central District, Belfast, Northern Ireland.*

Fodor's Choice **Café Vaudeville.** Enjoying a glamorous and ornate setting, Café Vaudeville
★ is an orgy of leopard-spot chairs, ravishing textiles, and grandly cano-
pied daybeds, while its inner sanctum, located upstairs, is the ab-fab Bolli
Bar, which just happens to be one of the top hot spots for local celebrities and the beautiful people. ✉ *25 Arthur St., Central District, Belfast,
Northern Ireland* ☎ *028/9043–9160* ⊕ *www.cafevaudeville.com.*

★ **The John Hewitt Bar.** A must for every traveler's hit list, this bar named
after one of Ulster's most famous poets, is traditional in style with a
marble counter, waist-high wooden paneling, high ceilings, and open
fire. It channels Hewitt's socialist sensibility, as it's owned by the Belfast
Unemployed Centre (which it helps fund with its profits)—top pub grub
is served at lunch and live music is featured most nights, including the
excellent Panama Jazz Band on Friday (except the first Friday of each
month). ✉ *51 Donegall St., Central District, Belfast, Northern Ireland*
☎ *028/9023–3768* ⊕ *www.thejohnhewitt.com.*

Kelly's Cellars. Open since 1720 (more or less), Kelly's Cellars hosts blues
bands on Saturday night. Lunchtime tip: the large bowls of nourish-
ing Irish stew available here are a delight. ✉ *30–32 Bank St., Central
District, Belfast, Northern Ireland* ☎ *028/9024–6058.*

Kremlin. A massive statue of Lenin above the front door greets patrons
of the city's oldest and most outrageous gay-oriented club, and the
over-the-top Soviet theme continues inside. Superstar DJs regularly fly
in to perform. ✉ *96 Donegall St., Cathedral Quarter, Belfast, Northern
Ireland* ☎ *028/9031–6060* ⊕ *www.kremlin-belfast.com.*

Madden's Bar. A popular locals' favorite near the Castle Court mall,
Madden's has live music nightly and traditional tune fests on occasion.
✉ *Berry St. behind Castle Court, Central District, Belfast, Northern
Ireland* ☎ *028/9024–4114.*

The Morning Star. Regulars perch themselves at the horseshoe-shaped bar
of this Victorian showpiece from noon on. Strike up a conversation with
a local, and you're guaranteed a bit of craic. ✉ *17–19 Pottinger's Entry,
Central District, Belfast, Northern Ireland* ☎ *028/9023–5986* ⊕ *www.
themorningstarbar.com.*

McHugh's. In Belfast's oldest building (1711), McHugh's has three floors
of bars and restaurants, and live music on weekends. Food is served
from lunchtime on. McHugh's retains the character of an early-18th-
century dockside inn and exudes a homely feel with open fires. To
mark the bar's 300th anniversary, Whitewater Brewery created the
McHugh's 300 Beer in 2011. ✉ *29–31 Queen's Sq., Central District,
Belfast, Northern Ireland* ☎ *028/9050–9999* ⊕ *www.mchughsbar.com.*

Union Street Pub. A gay-friendly bar near the Cathedral Quarter, Union
Street is housed in a converted 19th-century shoe factory. The three-
story redbrick Victorian is one of the city's few gastropubs, with a more
formal upstairs restaurant that's popular with local foodies. ✉ *8–14
Union St., Central District, Belfast, Northern Ireland* ☎ *028/9031–
6060* ⊕ *www.unionstreetpub.com.*

Get your perfect pint of Guinness at the Crown Liquor Saloon, a Victorian extravaganza of embossed ceilings, gilded arabesques, and carved woodwork.

White's Tavern. Enjoy traditional Irish sessions on Friday and Saturday nights at White's Tavern, which claims to be the oldest public house in Belfast. In winter a roaring fire greets you as soon as you enter the bar. Friendly staff serve good pub grub, including the famous creamy, buttery, cholesterol-laden potato champ. ⊠ *2–12 Winecellar Entry, Central District, Belfast, Northern Ireland* ☎ *028/9024–3080* ⊕ *www. whitestavern.co.uk.*

UNIVERSITY AREA

Bar Twelve. The stylish and modern Bar Twelve is an excellent venue for fashionable wine sipping. On weekends, DJs spin 1960s and '70s soul and funk tunes. ⊠ *Crescent Town House, 13 Lower Crescent, University Area, Belfast, Northern Ireland* ☎ *028/9032–3349* ⊕ *www. crescenttownhouse.com/bar-twelve.*

Fodor's Choice
★

Belfast Empire Music Hall. Inside a deconsecrated church, the Music Hall is the city's leading music venue. Most nights are devoted to concerts from groups such as local heroes Snow Patrol. Stand-up comedy nights are usually on Tuesdays—Patrick Kielty was a regular until he hit the big time in London. The Rab McCullough blues nights on Thursdays are popular, as are Friday Glamaramas, devoted to Queen, Bowie, and the like. ⊠ *42 Botanic Ave., University Area, Belfast, Northern Ireland* ☎ *028/9024–9276* ⊕ *www.thebelfastempire.com.*

Botanic Inn. Known as "the Bot" to its student clientele, the Botanic is a big, popular disco-pub. ⊠ *23–27 Malone Rd., University Area, Belfast, Northern Ireland* ☎ *028/9050–9740* ⊕ *www.thebotanicinn.com.*

Chelsea Wine Bar. Packed with affluent professionals determined to prove that life begins at 30, the Chelsea serves contemporary cuisine that is reasonably priced and has 100-plus wines on its list. ✉ *346 Lisburn Rd., University Area, Belfast, Co. Antrim, Northern Ireland* ☎ *028/9068–7177* ⊕ *www.chelseawinebar.com.*

Cutters Wharf. Down by the river south of the university, this bar and restaurant is at its best on summer evenings and during music performances on Sundays after 6. Spacious and light inside, it rarely gets too packed; if seating is limited, try the picnic tables and chairs on the wooden deck outside. ✉ *4 Lockview Rd., University Area, Belfast, Co. Antrim, Northern Ireland* ☎ *028/9066–3388* ⊕ *www. cutterswharf.co.uk.*

Lavery's Bar. This hot-blooded spot mixes old-fashioned beer-drinking downstairs with dancing upstairs. ✉ *12–18 Bradbury Pl., University Area, Belfast, Co. Antrim, Northern Ireland* ☎ *028/9087–1106* ⊕ *www. laverysbelfast.com.*

Fodor'sChoice ★ **Lily's Pub & Eatery.** Spacious and chic Lily's attracts a cool, youngish crowd. The restaurant serves lunch and dinner and hosts live music most nights. ✉ *701 Lisburn Rd., University Area, Belfast, Co. Antrim, Northern Ireland* ☎ *028/9066–4442* ⊕ *www.lilysbelfast.com.*

M-Club. Belfast's place for dedicated clubbers, M-Club even flies in soap-opera celebrities to mix with the local nighthawks. ✉ *23–31 Bradbury Pl., University Area, Belfast, Co. Antrim, Northern Ireland* ☎ *028/9023–3131* ⊕ *www.mclub.co.uk.*

THE ARTS

★ **Culture Northern Ireland.** A useful resource for visitors, this organization's website provides information about music, film, multimedia, literature, heritage, sports, and the visual and performing arts, and it has searchable "What's On" listings. ☎ *289/044–9863* ⊕ *www. culturenorthernireland.org.*

ARTS CENTERS

The Crescent Arts Centre. After a £7.2 million renovation, the Crescent returned to its rambling stone building—a former girls' high. The center presents experimental dance and theater, concerts, and workshops and hosts the Belfast Book Festival, during which writers from around the world participate in talks, lectures, and readings. Nature note: between May and July, common swifts fly in from southern Africa to nest above the center's stone walls. During the renovation, special "swift bricks" were installed to provide nesting sites. ✉ *2 University Rd., University Area, Belfast, Co. Antrim, Northern Ireland* ☎ *028/9024–2338* ⊕ *www. crescentarts.org.*

★ **Cultúrlann McAdam Ó Fiaich.** A £2 million renovation and extension in 2011 to mark its 20th anniversary has breathed new life into this venue. Celebrating Gaeilge (Irish language) and culture, this cosmopolitan arts center hosts exhibitions, book launches, concerts, theater, and poetry readings. For travelers interested in the Gaeltacht experience, this is a great place to start. On the ground floor, the Dillon Gallery, named after the Falls Road artist Gerard Dillon, who spent much time painting in Connemara in the West of Ireland, mounts shows by top local and international artists. A shop sells Irish-language and English books as well as gifts and crafts. Also here are a tourist information point, Wi-Fi access, and a café. The center's staff can arrange regional tours and book accommodations. ⊠ *216 Falls Rd., West Belfast, Belfast, Northern Ireland* ☎ *028/9096–4180* ⊕ *www. culturlann.ie* ⊙ *Daily 9–9.*

ARTS FESTIVALS

Arts Council of Northern Ireland. The country's main arts agency supports a range of cultural events, including many Belfast festivals, and has information about them. ☎ *028/9038–5200* ⊕ *www.artscouncil-ni.org.*

GALLERIES

Central Belfast, especially in Cathedral Quarter, is awash with small, quirky galleries that exhibit painting, sculpture, photography, and prints, as well as installations of digital and video work. Check ⊕ *www. belfastgalleries.com* for detailed listings.

Craft Northern Ireland Gallery. Opposite the Merchant Hotel, this gallery is a hotbed of crafts where street performers at Cotton Court regularly entertain crowds on summer Sundays. ⊠ *42 Waring St., Central District, Belfast, Northern Ireland* ☎ *028/9032–3059* ⊕ *www.craftni.org.*

Golden Thread Gallery. One of Belfast's best arts venues, the Golden Thread has links to the Venice Biennale and the International Symposium for Electronic Art. The gallery presents visual art, from paintings on canvas to the latest digital arts. ⊠ *84–94 Great Patrick St., Cathedral Quarter, Belfast, Northern Ireland* ☎ *028/9033–0920* ⊕ *www. goldenthreadgallery.co.uk.*

The Red Barn. Popular with visitors, the Red Barn often exhibits photographs reflecting the history of the Troubles. The gallery also presents installations by students from Belfast Metropolitan College and watercolors by local artists. ⊠ *43b Rosemary St., Cathedral Quarter, Belfast, Northern Ireland* ☎ *028/9023–1901* ⊕ *www.rbgbelfast.com.*

THEATER

★ **Belfast Waterfront.** Everyone in Belfast sings the praises of this striking civic structure. From the looks of it, the hall is an odd marriage of *Close Encounters* modern and Castel Sant'Angelo antique. It houses a 2,235-seat concert hall (for ballet and classical, rock, and Irish music) and a 500-seat studio space (for modern dance, jazz, and experimental theater). The Arc Brasserie and two bars make the Waterfront a convenient place to eat, have a pint, and enjoy the river views before or after your culture fix. ⊠ *2 Lanyon Pl., Central District, Belfast, Northern Ireland* ☎ *28/9033–4400* ⊕ *www.waterfront.co.uk.*

Fodor'sChoice **Grand Opera House.** Shows from all over the British Isles—and some-
★ times farther afield—play at this beautifully restored Victorian theater. Though it has no resident company of its own, major West End musicals and plays pass through, plus the occasional opera or ballet. It's worth attending a show just to enjoy the gigantic and splendid opera house itself. The Baby Grand—a theater within a theater—hosts comedy, live music, and educational workshops as well as film and special events. Hour-long guided tours take place on Thursdays and Saturdays, and you can peruse a theater-history exhibition on the second floor. Luciano's Café Bar (named after the opera giant Pavarotti) serves snacks and light lunches. For a more extensive choice the

Hippodrome Restaurant on the first floor opens two hours before the show and allows you to split your meal: have a main course before the performance and come back for puddings at the interval. ⊠ *2 Great Victoria St., Golden Mile, Belfast, Northern Ireland* ☎ *028/9024–1919* ⊕ *www.goh.co.uk.*

Fodor's Choice
★

Lyric Theatre. One of Northern Ireland's most prized cultural organizations, the Lyric, presents a diverse repertory of classical, popular, and contemporary drama. With its angular brick bulk topped by three distinctive sloping roofs, the theater, completed in 2011, is an impressive modernist achievement. To fund it a total of £18 million was raised with money from local companies as well as the Lyric's famed patron Liam Neeson, who made his 1976 stage debut in Brian Friel's *Philadelphia, Here I Come!*

Strong emphasis is placed on the use of natural light, with a glass-walled Long Hall running the length of the first floor and looking out over the River Lagan. The main auditorium is lined with iroko wood and has 33 different styles of brick, all specially fired so each one is complete and uncut. The work was undertaken by the Dublin architectural firm O'Donnell & Tuomey. In addition to the main 390-seat venue, presided over by the Northern Bank Stage, there is the Naughton Studios, a theater space that can hold up to 125 people. ⊠ *55 Ridgeway St., University Area, Belfast, Co. Antrim, Northern Ireland* ☎ *28/9038–5685* ⊕ *www.lyrictheatre.co.uk.*

Odyssey Arena. The Belfast Giants hockey team is the main tenant of the 10,000-seat Odyssey Arena, but Northern Ireland's biggest indoor venue also hosts rock, pop, and classical concerts. The adjacent Odyssey Pavilion complex has bars, restaurants, shops, and nightclubs. ⊠ *2 Queen's Quay, Central District, Belfast, Northern Ireland* ☎ *028/9076–6000* ⊕ *www.theodyssey.co.uk.*

Ulster Hall. The historic Ulster Hall became the permanent home of the Ulster Orchestra shortly after the building reopened in 2009 following its multimillion-pound refit. At the gala civic ceremony on the reopening night the orchestra played "Rhapsody on a Theme of Paganini" by Sergei Rachmaninov, who himself once played in the hall. The classical music season runs here from September through April. Concerts are mostly held on Fridays, but you can call or check online (⊕ *www.ulsterorchestra.com*) to learn about other dates and free open rehearsals and 50-minute lunchtime concerts. Apart from classical, the hall presents rock, folk, traditional Irish, blues, jazz, and other forms, along with comedy and cabaret acts. With its superb acoustics, Ulster Hall provides the perfect listening and foot-tapping experience. ⊠ *Bedford St., Central District, Belfast, Northern Ireland* ☎ *028/9033–4455* ⊕ *www.waterfront.co.uk.*

SHOPPING

Belfast's main shopping streets include High Street, Donegall Place, Royal Avenue, and several of the smaller streets connecting them. Except for buses and delivery vehicles, the area is mostly traffic-free. The long thoroughfare of Donegall Pass, running from Shaftesbury

Square at the point of the Golden Mile east to Ormeau Road, contains a mix of biker shops, ethnic restaurants, and antiques arcades. Another retail haven is Lisburn Road, jam-packed with nearly a hundred trendy designer shops, lifestyle emporia, galleries, and antiques stores. The Lisburn Road Business Association (LRBA) has special offers on its website (⊕ *www.thevisitlisburnroad.com*). For a break from shopping, let the Victorian-style Maryville House Tea Rooms (⊕ *www.maryvillehouse. co.uk),* just off Lisburn Road, transport you back to another era, starting with the foyer's 1792 map of Ireland dedicated to His Majesty King George III. The 20 different house teas range from a zesty Rooibos citrus to lemongrass with ginger twist.

GOLDEN MILE

CLOTHING

Smyth and Gibson. This noted shop makes and sells beautiful, luxurious linen and cotton shirts and accessories. Upstairs you'll find a small and lovely café. ⊠ *Bedford House, Bedford St., Central District, Belfast, Northern Ireland* ☎ *028/9023–0388* ⊕ *www.smythandgibson.com.*

JEWELRY

The Steensons. Locally designed, the superb jewelry sold here has a worldwide fan base. ⊠ *Bedford House, Bedford St., Golden Mile, Belfast, Northern Ireland* ☎ *028/9024–8269* ⊕ *www.thesteensons.com.*

CENTRAL DISTRICT

MARKETS AND MALLS

Castle Court. The city's second-largest shopping mall is euro-friendly, with most shops accepting both sterling and euros. Trendy stores such as Gap can be found under Castle Court's glass roof, alongside British clothing chains such as Miss Selfridge, Warehouse, and Blue Inc. For one-stop shopping, head for Debenham's department store, which has everything from cosmetics to kitchenware. When you tire of the shops, try a pedicure at Appyfeet, a "fish foot spa" that will relax you and in the process help the welfare of the Turkish Garra Rufa Fish. Plenty of parking makes shopping easy. ⊠ *10 Royal Ave., Central District, Belfast, Northern Ireland* ☎ *028/9023–4591* ⊕ *www.castlecourt-uk.com.*

★ **St. George's Market.** If you've an interest in bric-a-brac, visit the enormous St. George's Market, an indoor market that takes place on Friday, Saturday, and Sunday mornings. When it opened in the 1890s, this historic market sold butter, eggs, poultry, and fruit. In those days Belfast was known as the "City of Seven Smells": these came from such fixtures as gasworks, slaughterhouses, and soap factories. Today the market is a vibrant place with a hundred or so traders selling everything from apples to zippers and antiques to shark meat. Arrive early on Saturday for the farmers' market—lots of organically grown produce—as well as treats such as homemade cakes and bread. At Piece of Cake Bakery, you can choose from 20 terrific breads, including rye, spelt, olive, walnut, and banana, or sample the delicious baklava. Next door is S. D. Bell's coffee stand; the company is older than the market, as it was set up in 1887 and has been brewing nonstop ever since. ⊠ *May St., Central District, Belfast, Northern Ireland* ☎ *028/9043–5704* ⊕ *www. belfastcity.gov.uk/stgeorgesmarket.*

Fodor's Choice ★ **Victoria Square.** Occupying an eight-block site in central Belfast, Victoria Square has changed the Belfast skyline with a Disneyland-like complex of shopping malls and residences adding a fresh dimension to the retail world. The flagship 800,000-square-foot Victoria Square shopping complex, all glittering steel, is presided over by a vast geodesic glass dome eight stories high and complete with viewing platforms—you need a ticket to enter the viewing gallery, but admission is free. The center has attracted leading London brand names to Northern Ireland. The House of Fraser department store is the main anchor tenant and designer shops such as Cruise, Hugo Boss, Reiss, and All Saints also provide shoppers their fix of happiness. Coffee shops, fast-food restaurants, and an eight-screen cinema are also on-site. Offering a delightful architectural contrast, the complex incorporates noted Victorian landmarks such as the McErvel's Seed Warehouse and the Royal Belfast Ginger Ale Manufactury. With the opening of the complex, many commentators feel that consumerism has at last trumped terrorism in Northern Ireland. The **Q-Park** (⊕ *www.q-park.co.uk*) provides 1,000 parking spaces and is open 24/7. ⊠ *Chichester, Montgomery, and Ann Sts., and Victoria Square, 1 Victoria Sq., Central District, Belfast, Northern Ireland* ☎ *028/9032–2277* ⊕ *www.victoriasquare.com.*

BOOKS
The Good Bookshop. Run by the Church of Ireland, this shop stocks new Christian and secular books. Spirituality and pilgrimages are also a popular theme. ⊠ *61–67 Donegall St., Cathedral Quarter, Belfast, Northern Ireland* ☎ *028/9082–8890* ⊕ *www.goodbookshop.com.*

GIFTS
Smyth's Irish Linens. Looking for linen souvenirs? Smyth's Irish Linens carries a large selection of handkerchiefs, tablecloths, napkins, knitwear, Belleek china, Galway crystal, and other traditional goods. It's opposite the Castle Court mall. ⊠ *65 Royal Ave., Central District, Belfast, Northern Ireland* ☎ *028/9031–4272.*

Utopia. Stocked with everything from toys to costume jewelery, Utopia sells intricate silver pendants and earrings made by local designer Alpha Zed. Also worth a look are the wooden, alabaster, and metal chess sets. ⊠ *Fountain Centre, College St., Central District, Belfast, Northern Ireland* ☎ *028/9024–1342.*

UNIVERSITY AREA
BOOKS
No Alibis. Just the way a bookstore should be, No Alibis specializes in British and American crime thrillers, as well as general fiction and nonfiction, plus a smattering of local books. All in all, it's a bibliophile's delight. The shop hosts jazz, blues, and other music events on Friday nights. ⊠ *83 Botanic Ave., University Area, Belfast, Co. Antrim, Northern Ireland* ☎ *028/9031–9601* ⊕ *www.noalibis.com.*

CLOTHING
Clarke and Dawe. This shop, located on the retail-haven of Lisburn Road, is noted for its men's and women's suits and shirts. ⊠ *485 Lisburn Rd., University Area, Belfast, Co. Antrim, Northern Ireland* ☎ *028/9066–8228* ⊕ *www.clarkeanddawe.com.*

THE GIANT'S CAUSEWAY COAST

Starting in Belfast, stretching for 80 km (50 miles) along Northern Ireland's Atlantic shore, the Causeway Coast holds many of the province's don't-miss attractions. The man-made brilliance of the castle at Dunluce, the endless string of whitewashed fishing villages along the sea, and the world-famous natural wonder that is the Giant's Causeway are just some of the delights to be discovered here. The sparkling visitor center opened in 2012. Once your car or mountain bike (ideal for the Causeway's flat terrain) makes its way past some fair-size towns, you'll enter the splendid Glens area—one of the more "gentle" (an Irish turn of phrase for supernatural) places in all Ireland. Here, ageless villages, still inhabited by descendants of the ancient Irish and the Hebridean Scots who hailed from across the narrow Sea of Moyle, are set in peaceful, old-growth forests that have become synonymous with Irishness. But once past the Giant's Causeway you'll find more cosmopolitan pleasures, including Bushmills—the oldest licensed distillery in the world—and the old walled city of Derry.

CARRICKFERGUS

16 km (10 miles) northeast of Belfast.

Carrickfergus, on the shore of Belfast Lough, grew up around its ancient castle. When the town was enclosed by ramparts at the start of the 17th century, it was the only English-speaking town in Ulster. Not surprisingly, this was the loyal port where William of Orange chose to land on his way to fight the Catholic forces at the Battle of the Boyne in 1690. However, the English did have one or two small setbacks, including the improbable victory in 1778 of John Paul Jones, the American naval hero, over the British warship HMS *Drake*. Although a long way from home, this stands as the first naval victory of America's fledgling naval fleet. After this battle, which was waged in Belfast Lough, the inhabitants of Carrickfergus stood on the waterfront and cheered Jones when his ship passed the town castle, demonstrating their support for the American Revolution. Carrickfergus's past can still be seen in some of its old buildings. St. Nicholas's Church, built by John de Courcy in 1205 (remodeled in 1614), and the North Gate in the town's medieval walls are worth checking. Dobbins Inn on High Street has been a hotel for more than three centuries and is a popular local watering hole.

GETTING HERE AND AROUND

CAR TRAVEL   A 15-minute drive northeast of Belfast on A2, Carrickfergus, is an easy town to negotiate. There's a huge free car park beside the castle, and parking on the main streets is free, though limited to one hour. Pay and display car parks, costing 40 pence per hour, operate at Joymount, Bride, and Lancastrian streets.

TRAIN TRAVEL   Trains run by Northern Ireland Railways from Belfast on this section of the Antrim coast go only as far as the 40 km (25 miles) to Larne. Daily service stops at a number of towns, including Carrickfergus, Whitehead, and Glynn. A round-trip ticket from Belfast's Yorkgate or Central Station to Carrickfergus costs £5.50; from Belfast to Larne, it's £9.30.

Giant's
Causeway
Coast

ESSENTIALS

Visitor Information Carrickfergus Borough ✉ *11 Antrim St., Carrickfergus,
Co. Antrim, Northern Ireland* ☎ *028/9335–8049* ⊕ *www.carrickfergus.org.*

EXPLORING

Andrew Jackson Cottage and U.S. Rangers Centre. The center tells the tale
of the U.S. president, whose parents emigrated from here in 1765.
This thatch cottage just outside of town is a reconstruction of an
18th-century structure thought to resemble their home. The cottage
is open year-round, but access is by arrangement through Carrickfergus tourist office. ✉ *1½ km (1 mile) northeast of Carrickfergus,
Larne Rd., Boneybefore, Northern Ireland* ☎ *028/9335–8049* ⊕ *www.
carrickfergus.org* ✉ *Free.*

★ **Carrickfergus Castle.** Carrickfergus Castle, one of the first and one of
the largest of Irish castles, is still in good shape. It was built atop a
rock ledge in 1180 by John de Courcy, provincial Ulster's first Anglo-
Norman invader. Apart from being captured briefly by the French in
1760, the castle stood as a bastion of British rule until 1928, at which
time it still functioned as an English garrison. Walk through the castle's
13th-century gatehouse into the Outer Ward. Continue into the Inner
Ward, the heart of the fortress, where the five-story keep stands, a
massive, sturdy building with walls almost 8 feet thick. If you're here

at the end of July, you can enjoy the annual Lughnasa festival, a lively medieval-costume entertainment. ⊠ *Off A2, Carrickfergus, Northern Ireland* ☎ *028/9335–1273* ⊕ *www.doeni.gov.uk/niea/carrick.htm* ⊠ *£5* ⊙ *Apr–Sept., daily 10–6; Oct.–Mar., daily 10–4.*

GLENS OF ANTRIM

Beginning 24 km (15 miles) north of Carrickfergus at Larne.

★ North of Carrickfergus after Larne, the coast of County Antrim becomes spectacular—wave upon wave of high green hills that curve down to the hazy sea are dotted with lush glens, or valleys, first carved out by glaciers at the end of the last ice age. Nine wooded river valleys occupy the 86 km (54 miles) between Larne and Ballycastle, the two largest towns in the Glens of Antrim. Until the building of the narrow coastal road in 1834, the Glens were home to isolated farming communities whose residents adhered to the romantic, mystical Celtic legends and the everyday use of the Irish language. Steeped in Irish mythology, the Glens were first inhabited by small bands of Irish monks as early as AD 700. Some residents proudly note that Ossian, the greatest of the Celtic poets, is supposedly buried near Glenaan. The Glens are famed beauty spots and popular destinations: for tourist offices, head to the larger towns such as Larne, Ballymena, and Ballycastle. Cushendall, Cushendun, and Carnlough are extremely small and can't support tourist offices even in high season, though McKillop's (⊠ *14–16 Main St.* ☎ *028/2888–5236*), a shop in Carnlough, has leaflets describing local attractions, and the folks there are happy to offer tips about the Glens. Also helpful is the Causeway Coast and Glens website.

GETTING HERE AND AROUND

CAR TRAVEL   Oft-lauded as one of Ireland's most scenic drives—on a clear day you can see Scotland—the A2 Antrim coastal route is a delightful narrow, winding, two-lane road that hugs the slim strip of land between the hills and sea, bringing you to the magnificent Glens of Antrim. In most towns, cars park free of charge on the main street or in parking lots overlooking the harbor. The road is busy in summer, so allow extra travel time.

BUS TRAVEL   The scenic Antrim Coaster Goldline trains from Belfast traverse the entire County Antrim coastline all the way to Coleraine—a 160-km (100-mile), four-hour journey (£15, and worth every penny) with many stops en route. The service operates daily except Sundays year-round and on Sundays too from early July to mid-September. Because reservations are not accepted, arrive early in summer to be assured a window seat. Departures are from the Europa Buscentre in Belfast.

Visitor Information Ballymena Tourist Information Office ⊠ *The Braid, Ballymena Town hall Museum and Arts Centre, 1–29 Bridge St., Ballymena, Co. Antrim, Northern Ireland* ☎ *028/2563–5900* ⊕ *www.gatewaytotheglens.com.* **Causeway Coast and Glens** ⊠ *Northern Ireland* ⊕ *www.causewaycoastandglens.com.* **Larne Tourist Information Office** ⊠ *Narrow Gauge Rd., Larne, Co. Antrim, Northern Ireland* ☎ *028/2826–0088* ⊕ *www.larne.gov.uk.*

EXPLORING

The Glens merit several days of serious exploration. Supernarrow B-roads curl west off A2, up each of the beautiful glens, where trails await hikers. You'll need a full week and a rainproof tent to complete the nine-glen circuit (working from south to north, Glenarm, Glencloy, Glenariff, Glenballyeamon, Glenaan, Glencorp, Glendun, Glenshesk, and Glentasie); or you could just head for Glenariff Park, the most accessible glen.

> **WATCH YOUR BACK**
>
> In the beautiful Glens of Antrim, locals often talk of "the wee folk," said to reside in and around the "gentle" (i.e., supernatural) places of Lurigethan Mountain and Tiveragh Hill. The fairies inhabiting these places are mischievous creatures who mostly mind their own business, but woe betide anyone rash enough to cut off a fairy thorn (a type of bush).

Carnlough. A little resort made of white limestone, Carnlough overlooks a charming harbor that is surrounded by stone walls. The harbor can be reached by crossing over the limestone bridge from Main Street, built especially for the Marquis of Londonderry. The small harbor, once a port of call for fishermen, now shelters pleasure yachts. Carnlough is surrounded on three sides by hills that rise 1,000 feet from the sea. ⊠ *24 km (15 miles) north of Larne on A2, Co. Antrim, Northern Ireland* ☎ *028/2888–5236.*

Cushendall. Turnley's Tower—a curious, fortified square tower of red stone, built in 1820 as a curfew tower and jail for "idlers and rioters"—stands in Cushendall, at a crossroads in the middle of the village. Cushendall is called the capital of the Glens because it has a few more streets than the other villages hereabouts. The road from Waterfoot to Cushendall is barely a mile long and worth the stroll or cycle out to see the coastal caves (one of which had a resident called Nun Marry) that line the route. ⊠ *3 km (2 miles) north of Glenariff on A2, Co. Antrim, Northern Ireland* ⊕ *www.moyle-council.org/tourism.*

Fodor's Choice ★ **Cushendun.** Off the main A2 route, the road between Cushendall and Cushendun turns into one of a Tour-de-France hilliness, so cyclists beware. Your reward, however, will be the tiny jewel of a village, Cushendun, which was designed in 1912 by Clough Williams-Ellis (who also designed the famous Italianate village of Portmeirion in Wales) at the request of Ronald John McNeill, Baron Cushendun. Up sprang a series of cottages and a village square of seven houses, all done up in the Cornish taste courtesy of the Penzance-born wife of the baron. To top it all off, the baron had Glenmona House built in the regal neo-Georgian style. From this part of the coast you can see the Mull of Kintyre on the Scottish mainland. Hikes along the beachy strand have inspired poets and artists, including John Masefield. ⊠ *2 km (1½ miles) north of Cushendall on Coast Rd., Co. Antrim, Northern Ireland.*

EN ROUTE The precipitous Antrim Coast Road cuts off from A2 and heads north from Cushendun past dramatically beautiful Murlough Bay to Fair Head and on to Ballycastle. In this area are Drumnakill, a renowned pagan site; Torr Head, a jutting peninsula; and three state parks that allow for some fabulous hikes, fine hill-walking, and great views of

Scotland from Fair Head. Or you can rejoin A2 at Cushendun via B92 (a left turn). After a few miles the road descends, passing ruins of the Franciscans' 16th-century Bonamargy Friary, into Ballycastle.

Fodor'sChoice ★ **Glenariff Forest Park.** Head to this natural preserve to explore the most beautiful and unsettled of Antrim's glens. Glenariff was christened "Little Switzerland" by Thackeray for its spectacular combination of rugged hills and lush vales. The main valley opens onto Red Bay at the village of Glenariff (also known as Waterfoot). Inside the park are picnic facilities and dozens of good hikes. Bisecting the park are two lovely rivers, the Inver and the Glenariff, which help sculpt the rocky gorges here and culminate in the famous 5½-km (3½-mile) **Waterfall Trail,** marked with blue arrows, which passes outstanding views of Glenariff River, its three waterfalls, and small but swimmable loughs. Escape from the summer crowds by taking one of the longest trails, such as the **Scenic Hike.** Pick up a detailed trail map at the park visitor center, which also has a small cafeteria. ⊠ *98 Glenariff Rd., 7 km (5 miles) north of Carnlough, off A2, Glenariff, Co. Antrim, Northern Ireland* ☎ *028/2955–6000* ⊕ *www. causewaycoastandglens.com* ⊠ *Vehicles £4.50, pedestrians £2* ☉ *Apr.–Sept., daily 8:30–8; Oct.–Mar., daily 10–dusk.*

> ### CAVE DWELLING
>
> The coastal caves of Cushendall have been used for various purposes, including housing. One of the more colorful residents was a lady called Nun Marry who lived in one cave for 50 years, supplementing her income as one of the region's best potion brewers. The damp and windy conditions obviously agreed with her—as did perhaps a taste of her own brew?—for she lived to the ripe old age of 100.

WHERE TO STAY

For expanded hotel reviews, visit Fodors.com.

$$$$
HOTEL
☖ **Ballygally Castle.** Set between the Glens of Antrim and the Giant's Causeway, this baronial castle, built by a Scottish lord in 1625 to rise dramatically beside Ballygally Bay, can be booked solid much of the time so you will want to reserve well in advance. **Pros:** guests are well looked after; handy stopover en route to the Giant's Causeway. **Cons:** can fill up quickly, leading to delays particularly at peak holiday times; the room heating system seems to have a mind of its own. **TripAdvisor:** "nice lunch," "nice place," "what a great time." ⑤ *Rooms from: £165* ⊠ *274 Coast Rd., Ballygally, Co. Antrim, Northern Ireland* ☎ *028/2858–1066* ⊕ *www.hastingshotels.com* ⬎ *44 rooms* ⑩ *Breakfast.*

$$
RESORT
Fodor'sChoice ★
☖ **Galgorm Resort & Spa.** The manor house itself is photogenic, and the 160 acres of estate grounds—where you may go riding, practice archery, and shoot clay pigeons—cinematic. **Pros:** an elegant mix of the cozy and luxurious; perfect place for pampering. **Cons:** if you're not a golfer, swimmer, or spa fan, there's not a lot to do apart from relaxing; hovers on the edge of remoteness and a long walk to shops. **TripAdvisor:** "out of this world," "a piece of Irish natural beauty," "fabulous luxury in idyllic surroundings." ⑤ *Rooms from: £115* ⊠ *136 Fenaghy Rd., 40 km (25 miles) east of Larne on A36, Ballymena, Co. Antrim,*

Northern Ireland ☎ *028/2588–1001* ⊕ *www.galgorm.com* ⤳ *75 rooms* ⑂*Multiple meal plans.*

$ ⌂ **The Londonderry Arms Hotel.** What awaits at this lovely traditional
HOTEL inn are ivy-clad walls, gorgeous antiques, astonishing wallpaper,
★ regional paintings, prints and maps, and lots of fresh flowers—all
time-burnished accents well befitting an estate once inherited by Sir
Winston Churchill. **Pros:** fine historic vibe; cheerful staff; free newspapers. **Cons:** chattering birds in the ivy sometimes provide unsched-
uled early wake-up call; old-fashioned hotels (and creaky floorboards)
aren't everyone's taste. **TripAdvisor:** "top class," "friendly," "stay in a
bit of history." ⑂ *Rooms from: £70* ⊠ *20 Harbor Rd., Carnlough, Co.
Antrim, Northern Ireland* ☎ *028/2888–5255* ⊕ *www.glensofantrim.
com* ⤳ *35 rooms* ⑂*Multiple meal plans.*

BALLYCASTLE

86 km (54 miles) northeast of Larne.

Ballycastle is the main resort at the northern end of the Glens of Antrim.
People flock here in summer, but apart from peak season, this is a quiet
town. Ballycastle is shaped like an hourglass, with its strand and dock
on one end, its pubs and chippers on the other, and the 1-km (½-mile)
Quay Road in between. Beautifully aged shops and pubs line its Castle,
Diamond, and Main streets.

GETTING HERE AND AROUND

CAR TRAVEL Ballycastle is an hour's drive north of Belfast on the M2, which leads
on to A26 before branching off to the narrower A44. You can park
free along the seafront and at the marina. Other car parks are on Quay
Road and Ann Street.

BUS TRAVEL Regular bus services link Ballycastle with the main towns of Bushmills, Coleraine, Ballymoney, and Ballymena. Translink buses run daily
between the towns. The Antrim Coaster 252 also stops in Ballycastle.

ESSENTIALS

Visitor Information Ballycastle Tourist Office ⊠ *7 Mary St., Ballycastle, Co.
Antrim, Northern Ireland* ☎ *028/2076–2024* ⊕ *www.moyle-council.org/tourism.*

EXPLORING

Rathlin Island. From Ballycastle town you have a view of L-shaped Rathlin Island, where in 1306 the Scottish king Robert the Bruce took shelter in a cave (under the east lighthouse) and, according to the popular
legend, was inspired to continue his armed struggle against the English
by watching a spider patiently spinning its web. It was on Rathlin in
1898 that Guglielmo Marconi set up the world's first cross-water radio
link, from the island's lighthouse to Ballycastle. Hiking and bird-watching—watch for the Atlantic nomads: puffins, guillemots, and razorbills
nesting on the cliffs and sea stacks in the summer—are the island's main
activities. The **Boathouse Visitor Centre** (☎ *028/2076–2024*) houses
a collection of photographs, tools, and implements from the island's
past. The center is open from May through mid-September, and admission is free. A high-speed double-decker catamaran, the M. V. *Rathlin Express,* cuts the 10-km (6-mile) journey time crossing over the

Sea of Moyle to 25 minutes; from July to September it runs six round-trips daily (£11.60; reservations 24 hours ahead essential). Unless the sea is extremely rough, the M. V. *Canna* ferryboat also makes four daily round-trips (£11.60, reservations also essential). This more leisurely trip can take up to 45 minutes; be mindful of the weather to ensure that you can return on the

same day. The last return to Ballycastle is at 4:15 pm for the *Rathlin* and 5:30 pm for the *Canna*. ⊠ *18 Bayview Rd., 9½ km (6 miles) from Ballycastle, Ballycastle, Northern Ireland* ☎ *028/2076–9299* ⊕ *www. rathlinballycastleferry.com.*

★ **Carrick-a-Rede.** In the summer of 2012, the Carrick-a-Rede rope bridge played its part in the buildup to the London Olympic Games. Torchbearers carried the Olympic flame across the bridge as part of an 8,000-mile relay around the United Kingdom and Ireland. Adrenalin junkies love the rope bridge—off the coast at Ballintoy in Larrybane—which spans a 60-foot gap between the mainland and tiny Carrick-a-Rede Island. The island's name means "rock in the road" and refers to how it stands in the path of the salmon that follow the coast as they migrate to their home rivers to spawn. The bridge is open to the public daily, weather-permitting. More than 227,000 visitors cross it (or at least take a look at it) each year. It has some heart-stopping views of the crashing waves 100 feet below. For an exhilarating cliff-top experience, the rope bridge walk is hard to beat. ⊠ *119a White Park Rd.(8 km [5 miles] west of Ballycastle on B15), Ballintoy, Northern Ireland* ☎ *028/2076–9839* ⊕ *www.nationaltrust.org.uk* ☎ *£5.60* ⊙ *Nov.–Jan., daily 10:30–3:30; Feb.–May and Sept.–Oct., daily 10–6; June–Aug., daily 10–7; last entry 45 mins before closing.*

The Ould Lammas Fair. Every year since 1606, on the last Monday and Tuesday in August, Ballycastle has hosted the Oul' Lammas Fair, a modern version of the ancient Celtic harvest festival of Lughnasa (Irish for "August"). Ireland's oldest fair, this is a very popular two-day event with entertainers, several hundred shopping stalls, and even a pony show. Treat yourself to the fair's traditional snacks, dulse (sun-dried seaweed), and yellowman (rock-hard yellow toffee). ⊕ *www. irishcultureandcustoms.com/ACalend/LammasFair.html.*

GIANT'S CAUSEWAY

19½ km (12 miles) west of Ballycastle.

GETTING HERE AND AROUND

CAR TRAVEL   The Causeway is just off the A2 coast road. The nearest towns are Coleraine (a 20-minute drive), Ballycastle (10 minutes) and Ballymoney (35 minutes) In summer, the roads are congested, particularly on bank holidays and festival weekends. You can park your car at the center itself, which has 400 spaces (the parking fee is included in the

Grand Prize winner of Fodor's "Show Us Your Ireland" contest, this entry by Fodors.com member Traveling shows the famed Carrick-a-Rede rope bridge.

admission price), or leave it in nearby Bushmills, where a park-and-ride service operates. The National Trust, which runs this site, has introduced a Green Travel Admission Ticket for visitors arriving by park and ride or public transportation; you'll save £1.50 off the standard adult admission price.

BUS TRAVEL The Antrim Coaster 252 bus (£15 round-trip) is a great way to take in the dramatic coastline. The bus departs at 9:05 am for the Giant's Causeway from Belfast's Europa Buscentre. The Coaster stops on the Nook Main Road, where you can catch a shuttle bus (£2 round-trip) down to the Causeway itself. If coming from Coleraine, a fun way to access the Causeway is aboard the Translink North Coast Open Topper Service, a double-decker bus (£5.20) that runs in July and August, weather permitting. Kids love it. This bus also links with the Translink Causeway Rambler high-frequency service (from June to mid-September), which hits all the main visitor attractions, including Bushmills Distillery, the Giant's Causeway, and the Carrick-a-Rede rope bridge. An all-day Rambler ticket allows you to hop on and off as many times as you like. It costs £4.50 and is valid only the day of purchase—at the Europa Buscentre in Belfast or at any Translink station. For a more direct bus between Belfast and Coleraine, catch the Translink Goldline Express service for £15.

TOURS Two bus tours from Belfast (among many) are the Giant's Causeway Tour by Allen's Tours and a same-named offering from McComb's.

TRAIN TRAVEL No regular public trains serve the Giant's Causeway, but a fun passenger link is provided on a narrow-gauge train running from Bushmills. The Giant's Causeway and Bushmills Railway leaves Runkerry Road,

Bushmills, for the 3-km (2-mile) journey along the track bed of the former causeway tram. The train operates every weekend from Easter until the end of June, and daily in July and August. The nearest Translink train stations are 21 km (14 miles) away in Portrush or 18 km (11 miles) west in Coleraine, where the main Belfast–Derry train stops (£15 round-trip). If you buy a one-day iLink ticket, you can ride buses and trains to get to and from the Giant's Causeway.

ESSENTIALS

Transportation Contacts Allen's Giant's Causeway Tour ☎ *028/9091–5613* ⊕ *www.allensbelfastbustours.com.* **Giant's Causeway and Bushmills Railway** ☎ *028/2073–2844* ⊕ *www.freewebs.com/giantscausewayrailway.* **McComb's Giant's Causeway Tour** ☎ *028/9031–5333* ⊕ *www.minicoachni.co.uk.*

Visitor Information Giant's Causeway Tourist Office ✉ *Visitor Centre, Giant's Causeway Centre, 44a Causeway Rd., Bushmills, Co. Antrim, Northern Ireland* ☎ *028/2073–1855* ⊕ *nationaltrust.org.uk/giants-causeway.* **Causeway Coast and Glens Tourism Partnership** ✉ *11 Lodge Rd., Coleraine, Bushmills, Northern Ireland* ☎ *028/7032–7720* ⊕ *www.causewaycoastandglens.com.*

EXPLORING

Fodor's Choice
★
☺
Giant's Causeway. "When the world was moulded and fashioned out of formless chaos, this must have been a bit over—a remnant of chaos," said the great Thackeray about Northern Ireland's premier tourist draw, the Giant's Causeway. Imagine a mass of 37,000 mostly hexagonal pillars of volcanic basalt, clustered like a giant honeycomb and extending hundreds of yards into the sea. Legend has it this "causeway" was created 60 million years ago, when boiling lava, erupting from an underground fissure that stretched from the North of Ireland to the Scottish coast, crystallized as it burst into the sea, and formed according to the same natural principle that structures a honeycomb. As all Ulster folk know, though, the truth is that the giant Finn McCool, in a bid to reach a giantess he'd fallen in love with on the Scottish island of Staffa (where the causeway resurfaces), created the columns as stepping-stones. Unfortunately, the giantess's boyfriend found out, and in the ensuing battle, Finn pulled out a huge chunk of earth and flung it toward Scotland. The resulting hole became Lough Neagh, and the sod landed to create the Isle of Man.

■TIP➜ The Causeway is Northern Ireland's only UNESCO World Heritage Site. In the peak summer months it can be very busy—get there early before the crowds or leave your visit until late afternoon, when it's generally quieter.

To reach the causeway, you can either walk 1½ km (1 mile) down a long, scenic hill or take the Causeway Coaster minibus. A popular option with many visitors is to take the 20-minute walk downhill to the main causeway rock formation and catch the shuttle bus back uphill. ■TIP➜ When out on the causeway, small children will need to be properly supervised.

A good place to start, though, is at the sparkling new glass-fronted **Giant's Causeway Visitor Experience**, which opened in summer 2012. Designed by the Irish architectural firm Heneghan Peng and built at

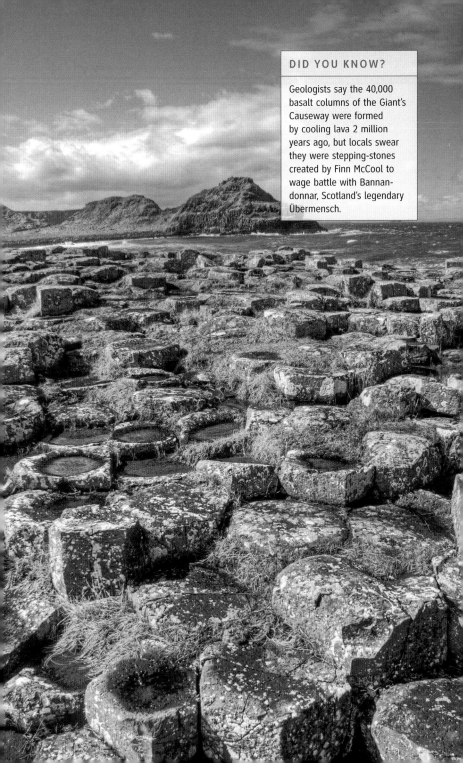

a cost of £18.5 million, the center is made of locally quarried basalt. The glass front ensures that all visitors can enjoy the spectacular coastal views, and the building is sunken into the ground, blending so effectively into the landscape that the indigenous grasses on the roof restore the natural ridgeline and provide a habitat for wildlife. Special environmental features include water-permeable paving, natural lighting, and rainwater harvesting.

> **WORD OF MOUTH**
>
> "I really didn't feel like walking all the way down to the Giant's Causeway. And the thought of walking back up was even less fun. So it's a good thing that they have the Causeway Coaster bus that goes every tenth minute. Cost 1 pound for a single ticket, 2 pounds for a return ticket."
>
> —anyegr

Inside the building, a stunning exhibition, complete with the 21st-century commercialization of Finn McCool, is made up of five parts: coastal map, geological history, people and their stories, natural life, and the power of the landscape. Through some fun animation, visitors meet the McCool family, which is promoted as ambassadors across the world. Guided one-hour tours of the exhibitions are included in admission price, and visitors are issued a hand-held device on which snippets of oral history—people relating stories and experiences of the causeway—can be heard. ■TIP→ Kids love the new center, so make sure you allow enough time on your visit to let them take in everything.

Outside, be aware that not all stones are created equal. Be sure to take a seat in the "Wishing Chair" and also look out for the "Giant's Boot," "Camel," "Harp," and the "Giant's Organ" pipes. Heading west of the causeway, keep an eye out for Port-na-Spania, the spot where the 16th-century Spanish Armada galleon *Girona* went down on the rocks. The ship was carrying an astonishing cargo of gold and jewelry, some of which was recovered in 1967. Beyond this, Chimney Point is the name given to one of the causeway structures on which the Spanish fired, thinking that it was Dunluce Castle, which is 8 km (5 miles) west.

You can park at the center—the fee is included in the admission price—or use the park and ride service between Bushmills and the causeway. Visitors who opt for the park and ride, or who arrive by public transportation, save £1.50 on the standard adult admission price (£3 per family) as part of a new Green Travel Admission Ticket.

■TIP→ Booking online far enough in advance to receive email confirmation of your date and time slot is recommended. ⊠ *44 Causeway Rd., Bushmills, Northern Ireland* ☎ *028/2073–1582* ⊕ *www.nationaltrust. org.uk/giantscauseway* 🖃 *£8.50* 🕙 *Visitor center Mar.–June, Sept., and Oct., daily 10–5; July and Aug., daily 10–6; Nov.–Feb., daily 10–4:30.*

BUSHMILLS

3 km (2 miles) west of Giant's Causeway.

GETTING HERE AND AROUND

CAR TRAVEL Bushmills is on the A2 coastal route and an ideal stopping place for refueling. It has the best parking facilities if you'll be exploring the Giant's Causeway. A park-and-ride service operates from the town to the visitor center and saves you the trouble of finding a space. If you're visiting Bushmills Distillery, there's a large free car park out front. Parking is free in the town along main streets.

EXPLORING

Bushmills. Reputedly the oldest licensed distillery in the world, Bushmills was first granted a charter by King James I in 1608, though historical records refer to a distillery here as early as 1276. Bushmills produces the most famous of Irish whiskeys—its namesake—and what is widely regarded as the best, the rarer black-label version known to aficionados as Black Bush. On the guided tour you will discover the secrets of the special water from St. Columb's Rill, the story behind malted Irish barley, and learn about triple distillation in copper stills and aging (which happens for long years in oak casks). You begin in the mashing and fermentation room, proceed to the maturing and bottling warehouse, and conclude, yes, with the much anticipated, complimentary shot of *uisce beatha,* the "water of life." You can also have a light lunch in the Distillery Kitchen or buy souvenirs in the distillery gift shop. To mark its 400th anniversary, the company produced Bushmills 1608, a limited edition whiskey distilled with crystal malt, a special type of malted barley with an alluring aroma and sweet toffeelike smoothness. It's a buy at £45 (£5 off if you take the tour). Bushmills Master Distiller, Colum Egan, describes it with the following colorful personification: "It is a very approachable whiskey with great depth of character, and in true Irish style, it has plenty of personality and a gentle touch." *For more on Bushmills, see our Spotlight feature, "All About Irish Whiskeys."* ✉ *2 Distillery Rd., off A2, Bushmills, Co. Antrim, Northern Ireland* ☎ *028/2073–3218* ⊕ *www.bushmills.com/visit* ✉ *£7; children under 8 not permitted on tour* ⊗ *Tours Apr.–Oct., Mon.–Sat. 9:15–5, Sun. noon–5; Nov.–Mar., weekdays 9:30–4:30, weekends 12:30–3:30.*

WHERE TO STAY

For expanded hotel reviews, visit Fodors.com.

$$$$ ▦ **The Bushmills Inn.** Owner Alan Dunlop oversees this cozy old coach
B&B/INN   inn where you'll be welcomed by stripped pine, peat fires, and gaslights
★   warming the public rooms; a 2009 revamp added nine bedrooms with four-poster beds. **Pros:** the proximity to the distillery—never mind the Giant's Causeway—helps ensure it's a choice location with comfortable rooms; tourists and chatty locals cross paths in the bar. **Cons:** if you're tall, look out for the low timber beams; it's hard to leave—even with the distractions of the surrounding area. **TripAdvisor:** "rural Ireland with a modern twist," "bowled us over with their hospitality," "perfect room in a perfect setting." ⑤ *Rooms from: £178* ✉ *9 Dunluce Rd., Bushmills, Co. Antrim, Northern Ireland* ☎ *028/2073–3000, 028/2073–2339* ⊕ *www.bushmillsinn.com* ⤴ *41 rooms, 9 suites* ⑩ *Breakfast.*

$ ⚓ **Causeway Hotel.** Owned by England's National Trust and flaunting a stunning location overlooking the Atlantic Ocean, this hotel that can trace its origins to the 1840s is only a half-mile from the celebrated Giant's Causeway. **Pros:** bracing coastal walks (often chilly even in summer) but you'll feel the warmth when you enter; worth it for the views. **Cons:** too many family parties; service can be a tad churlish. **TripAdvisor:** "great food and service," "splendid location," "perfect retreat." $ *Rooms from: £50* ✉ *40 Causeway Rd., Bushmills, Co. Antrim, Northern Ireland* ☎ *028/2073–1210* ⊕ *www. giants-causeway-hotel.com* ⇨ *28 rooms* ⦵*Some meals.*

HOTEL

DUNLUCE CASTLE

3 km (2 miles) west of Bushmills.

GETTING HERE AND AROUND

CAR AND BUS TRAVEL

Dunluce is midway between Bushmills and Portrush. There is a small, free car park at the castle. It isn't big enough to accommodate large numbers at busy times, though a planned expansion may be in place by 2013. A tip: park free in Bushmills or Portrush, both a 10-minute drive away, and hop on the Causeway Rambler bus, which operates in summer along the A2 coastal route and will drop you at the castle. Coleraine is the nearest big town. Derry is an hour's drive west.

EXPLORING

★ **Dunluce Castle.** Halfway between Portrush and the Giant's Causeway, ☾ dramatically perched on a 100-foot-high basalt-rock cliff, Dunluce Castle is one of the north's most evocative ruins. Even roofless, this shattered bulk conjures up a strength and aura that is quintessentially Antrim. Originally a 13th-century Norman fortress, Dunluce was captured in the 16th century by the local MacDonnell clan chiefs—the so-called Lords of the Isles. They enlarged it, in part using profits from salvaging the Spanish galleon *Girona,* and made it an important base for ruling northeastern Ulster. Perhaps the MacDonnells expanded the castle a bit too much, for in 1639 faulty construction caused the kitchens (with all the cooks) to plummet into the sea during a storm.

Between 2009 and 2012, archaeologists held digs at the site and uncovered belt buckles, thimbles, dress fastenings, jewelry, clay pipes, animal bones, and shards of pottery that are now on display in the Discovery Room. A new 8-minute introductory film explores the castle's history, and a 10-minute film details the excavations. ■**TIP**➔ Children love the sand pit where they handle tools and dress up. ✉ *87 Dunluce Rd., Bushmills, Northern Ireland* ☎ *028/2073–1938* ⊕ *www.ni-environment.gov.*

uk ✉ *£5* ⏱ *Apr.–Sept., Mon.–Sun. 10–6; Oct.–Mar., Mon.–Sun. 10–4; last entry 30 mins before closing.*

Dunluce Centre. An entertainment complex, the Dunluce Centre has three floors of interactive play zones—among them a 4-D motion simulator, a Finn McCool–themed playground, and a laser drome—plus a viewing tower, shops, a café, and a tourist center. ✉ *10 Sandhill Dr., Portrush, Northern Ireland* ☎ *028/7082–4444* ⊕ *www.dunlucecentre. co.uk* ✉ *£4.60–£4.75 for 1 attraction, £7.80 for 2, £9.30 for 3* ⏱ *Easter week, July, and Aug., daily 10.30–5.30; end of Apr.–June, Sept., and Oct., weekends noon–5.*

WHERE TO EAT

$
ECLECTIC
★
☕

✕ **Ramore Wine Bar.** Options abound at this spot with panoramic views of Portrush's attractive harbor. The wine bar serves nibbles and contemporary cuisine along with fine wines. The Oriental Restaurant offers two- and three-course menus with such dishes as chili monkfish, salmon teriyaki, and Peking duck. The more informal Harbour Bistro serves the basics, including burgers and chicken and ham pie, and the Coast Restaurant specializes in pizzas and pasta. Also on-site are a bar and a lounge with live or DJ music. $ *Average main: £13* ✉ *The Harbor, Portrush, Northern Ireland* ☎ *028/7082–4313* ⊕ *www. ramorerestaurant.com.*

SPORTS AND THE OUTDOORS

BEACHES

Portstewart Strand. Portstewart Strand is signposted as "The Strand" at all major junctions in town. The magnificent 2 miles of golden sand is one of the north coast's finest beaches suitable for all ages. Owned by the National Trust and well maintained and clean, it's the ideal spot for picnics, swimming, or long walks into sand dunes that are a haven for wildflowers and butterflies. Lifeguards are on duty from June to August. The beach has an undertow at certain points and small sections have seaweed, but it's not a big nuisance. On hot summer days the beach fills with cars, but its size ensures that it is never completely crowded. **Amenities:** car park, changing rooms, toilets, outdoor shower, lifeguards, shop, café. **Best for:** swimming, sunbathing, snorkeling, windsurfing, kite-surfing, walks, sand dunes. ✉ *118 Strand Rd., Portstewart, Northern Ireland* ☎ *028/7083–6396* ✉ *£4.50 per car* ⏱ *Facilities Mar., Oct., daily 10–4; Apr. and Sept., daily 10–5; May, daily 10–6; June–Aug., daily 10–7.*

GOLF

Fodor's Choice
★

Royal Portrush Golf Club. In addition to Royal County Down, Portrush also makes *Golf Digest's* top 10 non-U.S. courses. A legend in Irish golfing circles, Portrush is the only Irish club to have hosted a British Open. The championship Dunluce course is named for the ruins of the nearby castle and is a sea of sand hills and curving fairways. Despite its understated appearance it poses many and varied challenges. "White Rocks," the par-5 5th hole, is quite literally a cliff-hanger. It's a wicked dogleg with the green perched on the edge of a cliff. The Valley course is a less exposed, tamer track. Both are conspicuous for their lack of bunkers. In a poll of Irish golf legends, Dunluce was voted the best

While cliff erosion has played havoc with what's left of its battlements, Dunluce Castle still remains one of Northern Ireland's most intensely beautiful sights.

in Ireland. ⊠ *Dunluce Rd., Portrush, Co. Antrim, Northern Ireland* ☎ *048/7082–2311* ⊕ *www.royalportrushgolfclub.com* ✍ *Greens fees: Apr.–Oct. weekdays £140 (Dunluce), £37.50 (Valley); weekends £160 (Dunluce), £45 (Valley). Nov.–Mar. £70 (Dunluce), £25 (Valley)* ⅃ *36 holes. Yardage: 7,143 (Dunluce), 6,304 (Valley). Par 72 (Dunluce), 75 (Valley). Practice area, caddies, caddy carts, buggies, catering* ☺ *Visitors: daily (some restrictions).*

Portstewart Golf Club. More than a century old, Portstewart may scare you with its opening hole, generally regarded as the toughest starter in Ireland. Picture a 425-yard par-4 that descends from an elevated tee to a small green tucked between the dunes. The greens are known for uniformity and speed, and seven of the holes have been redesigned to toughen the course. If you want a break from the grand scale of the Strand championship links, there's the Old Course and the Riverside, 36 holes of downsize, executive-style golf. A modern clubhouse opened in 2009 with a bar and restaurant. ⊠ *117 Strand Rd., Portstewart, Northern Ireland* ☎ *048/7083–2015* ⊕ *www.portstewartgc. co.uk* ✍ *Greens fees: weekdays £80 (The Strand), £10 (Old Course), £20 (Riverside); weekends £95 (The Strand), £15 (Old Course), £25 (Riverside)* ⅃ *54 holes. Yardage: 6,895 (The Strand), 4,730 (Old Course), 5,725 (Riverside). Par 72 (The Strand), 64 (Old Course), 68 (Riverside). Practice area, caddies, caddy carts, buggies, catering* ☺ *Visitors: daily.*

LIMAVADY

27 km (17 miles) east of Derry.

In 1851, at No. 51 on Limavady's Georgian main street, Jane Ross wrote down the tune played by a traveling fiddler and called it "Londonderry Air," better known now as "Danny Boy." While staying at an inn on Ballyclose Street, William Thackeray (1811–1863) wrote his rather lustful poem "Peg of Limavaddy" about a barmaid. Among the many Americans descended from Ulster emigrants was President James Monroe, whose relatives came from the Limavady area.

GETTING HERE AND AROUND

CAR TRAVEL On the main route between Derry and Coleraine, Limavady is well served with car parking. Motorists park free on the main street with a one-hour time limit. Pay and display parking, costing 40 pence per hour, is available at Newtown Square (off Linenhall Street) and on Connell Street.

BUS TRAVEL Translink buses leave Limavady every hour during the day for Derry; journey time is 35 minutes. There is no train station, but you can connect with the train to Belfast by taking a bus to Coleraine or Ballymena.

ESSENTIALS

Visitor Information Limavady Tourist Office ✉ *Roe Valley Arts Centre, 24 Main St., Limavady, Northern Ireland* ☎ *028/7776–0650* ⊕ *www.limavady.gov.uk/visiting.*

WHERE TO STAY

For expanded hotel reviews, visit Fodors.com.

$$$ **Roe Park Resort.** A country estate serves as the model for this deluxe
RESORT modern resort on 155 acres straddling the banks of the River Roe—the place is relatively large and impersonal, although the lobby is a feast of welcoming ruby-hue carpets and gilt lanterns. **Pros:** ideal location for pampering and relaxation; lively bars good for post-golf analysis. **Cons:** can be noisy with evening wedding parties; older rooms have a somewhat tired appearance. **TripAdvisor:** "lovely relaxing break," "superb staff," "first class and service." ⑤ *Rooms from: £155* ✉ *Roe Park, Limavady, Northern Ireland* ☎ *028/7772–2222* ⊕ *www.roeparkresort. com* ⤴ *118 rooms, 3 suites* ⦿ *Multiple meal plans.*

DERRY

In 2013, Northern Ireland's second-largest city, Derry/Londonderry (as it's now known) hosts the U.K. City of Culture. By a happy coincidence, 2013 is also the 400th anniversary of the building of the historic 20-foot-tall walls enclosing the old city. Derry's stint as City of Culture will bring writers, painters, poets, musicians, sculptors, and other artists to town to showcase their work, and many cultural events will take place. Derry will also host the 2013 All-Ireland Fleadh Cheoil (⊕ *2013fleadh.ie*), the most prestigious event on the Irish traditional music and culture calendar. From August 11th through the 17th, thousands will flock to watch dancers and listen to singers, tin whistlers, fiddlers, and bodhrán players. This is the first time that Northern

Ireland has hosted this event. As if that's not enough, the Turner Prize—regarded as the most important event on the contemporary art calendar in the United Kingdom—is coming to Derry in 2013.

Recent changes in Derry also include the 2011 opening of the spectacular Peace Bridge across the River Foyle. The bridge links the city center with Ebrington Square, a redeveloped military base that figured in World War II's Battle of the Atlantic. The base's developers are building a gallery, a modern art center, studios, bars, hotels, shops, and eventually a maritime museum. Collectively, the changes of recent years are being seen as a huge opportunity to build on progress born of the peace process and to send out a message to the world that this city's communities, so long divided, now desire to work together.

GETTING HERE AND AROUND

CAR TRAVEL   The city's two main shopping centers, Foyleside and Quayside, have multistory car parking garages. Collect a ticket on entry and pay at a machine on departure. Other main car parks, which are mostly pay-by-the-hour via metered ticket machines, are located at Foyle Street, Carlisle Road, William Street, Society Street, Queens Quay, Alfred Street, and Victoria Market. Derry is a 75-minute drive from Belfast; A6 takes you over the mountainous Glenshane Pass. Roads lead south to Strabane and Omagh on A5 and on to Dublin (about four hours away, depending on road conditions and traffic). Derry is also the jumping off point for exploring the Inishowen peninsula by car and the beautifully remote Northern Donegal region.

BUS TRAVEL   Fast Translink Goldline Express buses (£16 round-trip) link Derry and Belfast on a trip over the Glenshane Pass. Journey time is one hour and 40 minutes. Weekend service, especially on Sundays, is less frequent. An alternative, slightly longer route, operated by Translink Goldline between Belfast and Derry, travels along the M1 motorway and through County Tyrone—it takes about two hours. Translink buses run from Derry to neighboring towns, with fares averaging about £12.50 round-trip. You can also catch a bus from City of Derry Airport into the Foyle Street bus station in the city center (£6 round-trip). The Airporter Coach operates between Derry and Belfast International Airport and George Best Belfast City Airport. Tickets to both airports cost £27.50 round-trip. If you're traveling across the border from Derry into Donegal, then you have a choice of using Bus Éireann or the Lough Swilly Bus Company.

TRAIN TRAVEL   One of the most relaxing ways to arrive in Derry is by train. Frequent daily services on Northern Ireland Railways link it with Coleraine, Ballymena, Antrim, and Belfast. For the final 20-minute section of the journey—along the County Derry coastline—the track runs parallel to the sea and is one of Ireland's most stunning routes. The journey time from Belfast to Derry is about two hours (£15 round-trip). The main station is in the Waterside area of the city—catch a free 10-minute shuttle bus across Craigavon Bridge to get to the West Bank, where most attractions are concentrated.

Transportation Contacts Airporter Coach ☎ 028/7126–9996 ⊕ *www.airporter.co.uk*. **Lough Swilly** ☎ 74/912–2873 00353.

TOURS

BICYCLE TOURS City Bike Tours (£15, includes bike rental and gear) are led by Martin McCrossan, also known for his popular City Tours walks *(see Walking Tours)*. The 75-minute ride, on a mostly flat route, takes in city sights and some out-of-the-way delights and ends with a gentle pedal along the Derry City Walls. Tours depart on weekends at 10 and 2 from the Derry Visitor and Convention Bureau *(see Visitor Information)*.

BUS TOURS Top Tours Ireland operates double-decker bus tours (£8) daily from 10 to 5. Departing from the visitor bureau and Guildhall, the tours last an hour, hit all the sightseeing spots, and have guides offering commentary.

WALKING TOURS City Tours (£4), walks led by Martin McCrossan, leave daily at 10, noon, and 2 (also 4 pm from April to October). For two decades, Martin has shared his great passion for Derry with visitors. His tour, which departs from 11 Carlisle Road (just show up; reservations not necessary), lasts one hour and incorporates not only history and centuries-old stories but also architecture and engaging bits of local lore and humor.

Two other good walking tours leave from the visitor bureau. Tours 'n Trails (£6) leaves at 11 and 3 except Sunday and includes a visit inside St. Columb's Cathedral. Historic Derry (£4), a tour led by Stephen McPhilemy, leaves daily at 4 pm. Ask about these and other city tours at the visitor bureau.

City Tours ⊠ *11 Carlisle Rd., West Bank, Derry, Northern Ireland* ☎ *028/7127–1996* ⊕ *derrycitytours.com.*

Top Tours Ireland ☎ *028/7137–0067* ⊕ *toptoursireland.com.*

Visitor Information Derry Visitor and Convention Bureau ⊠ *44 Foyle St., West Bank, Derry, Northern Ireland* ☎ *028/7126-7284* ⊕ *www.derryvisitor.com.*

EXPLORING

Derry's name shadows its history. Those in favor of British rule call the city Londonderry, its old plantation-period name: the "London" part was tacked on in 1613 after the Flight of the Earls, when the city and county were handed over to the Corporation of London, which represented London's merchants. The corporation brought in a large population of English and Scottish Protestant settlers, built towns for them, and reconstructed Derry within the city walls, which survive almost unchanged to this day. Both before this and after, Derry's sturdy ramparts withstood many fierce attacks—they have never been breached, which explains the city's coy sobriquet, "The Maiden City." The most famous attack was the siege of 1688–89, begun after 13 apprentice boys slammed the city gates in the face of the Catholic king, James II. Inhabitants, who held out for 105 days and were reduced to eating dogs, cats, and laundry starch, nevertheless helped to secure the British throne for the Protestant king, William III. Whatever you choose to call it, Derry is one of Northern Ireland's most underrated towns.

TOP ATTRACTIONS

Derry City Walls. In 2013, Derry's famed walls celebrate their 400th anniversary. Established under a charter by James I in 1613, the walls took from 1614 to 1618 to build. Today, most of the life of the city takes place outside these walls—they're among Europe's few remaining sets of intact city walls—but you can get a feel for Derry's deep history by strolling along the parapet walkway atop the ramparts. Pierced by eight gates (originally four) and as much as 30 feet thick, the gray-stone ramparts are only 1½ km (1 mile) all around. On your walk, take a break at a strategically placed café or simply drink in the historic atmosphere of this most photogenic of cities. In summer when the walls are awash with tourists, "Ambassadors" are on hand to help show you around. ⊕ *www.derryswalls.com.*

Derry Wall Murals. Dramatic wall murals throughout Derry testify to the power of art as historical document, while also serving as a reminder of painful pasts. Symbolic of the different communities, the murals attract considerable curiosity from tourists. The Bogside Gallery of Murals, painted by William Kelly, Kevin Hasson, and Tom Kelly, are made up of 12 wall paintings known collectively as "The Peoples Gallery." They include the *Bloody Sunday Commemoration, The Death of Innocence, Civil Rights, The Hunger Strikes*, and a poignant one featuring the Nobel Peace Prize–winning Derry politician John Hume along with Martin Luther King Jr., Nelson Mandela, and Mother Teresa—all beside Brooklyn Bridge. The paintings span the length of Rossville Street in the heart of the Bogside. Some of the guided walking tours that leave from the tourist information center include the story of the murals. On the other side of the political divide, close to the city walls, the Protestant Fountain estate is home to one of the oldest King Billy murals along with other colorful ones linked to the siege of Derry. ⊠ *Rossville St., Bogside, Derry, Northern Ireland* ☎ *028/7126–7284.*

★ **Ebrington Square.** In 2012, this 26-acre development on the River Foyle's East Bank made its debut as a dynamic cultural hub, with the Ebrington Centre arts venue, as well as studios, a café, a bar, and shops. A former military barracks, Ebrington Square is expected to play a key role in the U.K. City of Culture festivities in 2013. The square is named for Lord Ebrington, the Lord Lieutenant of Ireland during the years (1839–41) when many of the military buildings here were erected, including the Star Fort, one of the architectural highlights. During World War II, the barracks became part of a naval base that later functioned as an anti-submarine school. The base closed in 2004 and will be developed over the next decade. The former officers' mess, for instance, is being transformed into a boutique hotel.

Storyboards along a tourism trail relate the history of this site that was a Jacobite camp during the Derry's 17th-century siege, but the new development's cutting-edge infrastructure is an equally compelling tale. With its built-in geothermal heating deep underground, Erbington Square, linked to the old city by the Peace Bridge, has a reduced carbon footprint. Water is partially heated by the surrounding earth before being pumped to the square's buildings. Ebrington Square's transformation won't be complete for several years, but already this development has breathed new life into the East Bank, or waterside as it's commonly known. ✉ *Ebrington Sq., East Bank, Derry, Northern Ireland* ☎ *028/7126–4226* ⊕ *www.ilex-urc.com* 🖃 *Free.*

Fodor's Choice ★ **Guildhall.** In 2013, the Guildhall, one of Derry's most ornate Victorians—it dates from 1890—emerges from a three-year makeover that included replacement of the Dumfries-sandstone facade, repair of the beautiful stained-glass windows, and renovation of the main hall. An outstanding example of the city's architecture, the Guildhall should be on every tourist's itinerary, and now that it's been refashioned as a tourist information point, there's all the more reason to come. Permanent touch-screen displays explain the building's special features; the many delights for the eye here include the neo-Gothic strutwork, elaborate ceilings, baronial wood paneling, and magnificent organ. Another interactive exhibit explores the Plantation of Ulster and how it shaped the city. The building is expected to play a vital role in the U.K. City of Culture 2013 celebrations as a premier location for musical recitals and other events. With the gleaming restoration, one of the most famous of all Derry's local sayings, "You've more faces than the Guildhall clock" (not to be taken as a compliment), has renewed resonance. ✉ *Guildhall Sq., West Bank, Derry, Northern Ireland* ☎ *028/7137–7335* ⊕ *www. derryvisitor.com/P3062-The-Guildhall-Londonderry-Derry.aspx* 🖃 *Free* ⊙ *Weekdays 9–5.*

★ **Museum of Free Derry.** At Free Derry Corner stands the white gable wall where Catholics defiantly painted the slogan "You are now entering Free Derry" as a declaration of a zone from which police and the British Army were banned until 1972, when the army broke down the barricades. That year, on January 30, 13 civil-rights marchers were shot and killed by British soldiers. Thirty-eight years later, the British government released its official report on the shootings from Lord Saville, which resulted in an official apology from Prime Minister David Cameron saying that he was "deeply sorry" for what happened on Bloody Sunday and that it "had been unjustified and unjustifiable." Historical homage to this tragic moment in time is rendered by the Museum of Free Derry, which has become one of the major tourist attractions in Derry. It opened in 2007 in a derelict block of flats right on the spot where Bloody Sunday happened; the building still retains bullet scars and was conserved to preserve the "line of sight" that fateful day. Inside, visitors will find a real-time recording of the event as well as a gallery with newspaper reports, photographs, and posters about the "Battle of the Bogside." ✉ *55 Glenfada Park, off Rossville St., West Bank, Derry, Northern Ireland* ☎ *028/7136–0880* ⊕ *www. museumoffreederry.org* 🖃 *£3* ⊙ *Weekdays 9:30–4:30; also Apr.–Sept., Sat. 1–4; and July–Sept., Sun. 1–4.*

★ **St. Columb's Cathedral.** The first Protestant cathedral built in the United Kingdom after the Reformation, this houses the oldest and largest bells in Ireland (dating from the 1620s). It's a treasure house of Derry Protestant emblems, memorials, and relics from the siege of 1688–89; most visitors come to see the keys that locked the four main gates of the city during the siege. The church was built in 1633 in simple Planter's Gothic style, with an intricate corbeled roof and austere

Derry

St. Columb's Park

EBRINGTON

River Foyle

Browning Dr.

Peace Bridge

spire. In the vestibule is the 270-pound mortar ball that was fired over the wall during the Siege of Derry, with an invitation to surrender sent by King James. Legend has it that when it was read, every man, woman, and child in the city rushed to the walls and shouted, "No surrender!"—a Protestant battle cry to this day. The attached Chapter House Museum has the oldest surviving copy of a map of Derry (from 1600) and the Bible owned by Governor George Walker during the siege. View the interesting display cases and information panels. In recent years the tower and spire have been restored and the stonework and stained-glass windows repaired. A new LED lighting system reveals the beauty of the elegant Canadian pine ceiling. Knowledgeable tour guides are on hand, or you can hire an audio tour for £3. ⊠ *London St., off Bishop St., West Bank, Derry, Northern Ireland* ☎ *028/7126–7313* ⊕ *www.stcolumbscathedral.org* ✉ *£2 suggested donation* ⊗ *Mon.–Sat. 9–5.*

★ **Tower Museum.** Tall, brooding, medieval, and magical, the reconstructed granite-stone O'Dohertys Tower contains the Tower Museum, which chronicles the history of Derry. The original building was constructed in 1615 by the O'Dohertys for their overlords, the O'Donnells, in lieu of tax payments. Highlights of the museum include a small section on the eccentric Bishop Frederick Augustus Hervey (1763–1803), who conducted a lifelong affair with the mistress of Frederick William II of Prussia, built the now derelict Downhill Castle above the cliffs outside the city, and allegedly had his curates stage naked sprints along the beach while he horsewhipped them. The winners were awarded the most lucrative parishes in the district. There's excellent information celebrating the life and legacy of St. Columba. The vivid "Story of Derry" exhibition covers the city's history, from its origins as a monastic settlement in an oak grove up to the Troubles, beginning in 1969 after years of institutionalized discrimination in jobs and public housing. (A well-known Derry joke is that the skeleton in the city's coat of arms was actually a Catholic waiting for a house.) There's also an exhibition, spread over four floors, on the Spanish Armada, thanks to the fact that its fourth-largest ship, *La Trinidad Valencera*, foundered in Kinnagoe Bay, in County Donegal, in 1588. ⊠ *Union Hall Pl., West Bank, Derry, Northern Ireland* ☎ *028/7137–2411* ⊕ *www.derrycity.gov.uk/ museums* ✉ *£4.20* ⊗ *Sept.–June, Tues.–Sat. 10–5; July and Aug., Mon.– Sat. 10–5, Sun. 11–4; last entry 30 mins before closing.*

WORTH NOTING

Apprentice Boys' Memorial Hall. Imposing in its Scottish Baronial fortified grandeur, this is a meeting place for the exclusively Protestant organization set up in 1715 to honor 13 apprentice boys who slammed the city gate in the face of the Catholic King James in 1688 and sparked the Siege of Derry, and it has remained a symbol of Protestant stubbornness ever since. Inside there's an initiation room in which 20,000 have pledged to uphold Protestant values, and a magnificently chaotic museum filled to the brim with furniture, firearms, books, bombs, swords, and sculpture. It's a fascinating glimpse into a mostly closed world. An upstairs bar and dance hall—now used for meetings, initiations, and social events organized by the Apprentice Boys—has walls lined with 12 banners representing the lost tribes of Israel. (Some Protestants believe the lost tribes of Israel ended up in Northern Ireland and are their forebears.) More recent exhibitions showcase the story of the siege and show a scale model of how the city walls looked at the time of the city siege. In 2010 four murals on boards depicting scenes from the siege were transferred from the walls of the Protestant Fountain estate into one of the hall's exhibition rooms. ⊠ *Society St., West Bank, Derry, Northern Ireland* ☎ *028/7126–3571* ✉ *£3* ⊙ *June–Oct., weekdays 10–4:30; tours by appointment.*

THE HIGH AND THE FLIGHTY
Aviation fans, take note: Derry was where Amelia Earhart touched down on May 21, 1932, after her historic solo flight across the Atlantic. Local lore has it that the first man to reach her airplane greeted her in typically unfazed Derry fashion: "Aye, and what do you want, then?"

Walker Memorial. The memorial, a statue of George Walker, the governor of Derry during the siege, is a symbol of the city's divided nature. It was blown up by the IRA in 1973, and the story goes that the statue's head rolled down the hill into the Catholic Bogside, where it was captured by a local youth. He ransomed it back to the Protestants for a small fortune, and today it sits on the shoulders of a replica of the original statue beside the Apprentice Boys' Memorial Hall. ⊠ *Apprentice Boys' Memorial Hall, Society St., West Bank, Derry, Northern Ireland.*

WHERE TO EAT

$
EUROPEAN
Fodor's Choice
★

✕ **Custom House Restaurant.** The food is top class and the river views are stunning, but at this new restaurant on Derry's quays it's the chandelier that truly wows diners. Made in Italy from thousands of octagonal glass crystals and weighing 150 kg, it is illuminated by 30 color-changing LEDs. Signature dishes for dinner, served upstairs in the main dining area, include crispy pork belly, black pudding and crispy hen's egg, and delicious salt-and-chili squid. Snacks and bar food are available in the more informal downstairs lounge. The restaurant occupies an 1876 building where taxes were collected from ships arriving at the port. $ *Average main: £12* ⊠ *Custom House St., Queen's Quay, Central District, Derry, Northern Ireland* ☎ *028/7137–3366* ⊕ *www.customhouserestaurant.com* ⊙ *No lunch Sun.*

$$
IRISH

✕ **The Exchange Restaurant and Wine Bar.** Overdressed twentysomethings lounge by the circular and ultramodern bar in this chic restaurant-cum-wine bar. It's become *the* place to be seen in Derry, so weekend evenings can be extremely busy. Unfortunately, reservations are not taken, so be prepared to wait at the bar—with a chilled glass of sauvignon blanc from the excellent wine list, it's no hardship. The locally caught seafood served here is delicious; the standout dish is the medallions of monkfish with tiger prawns. Service is superefficient but can be a touch brisk. At £10.95, the early-bird menu is a great value. $ *Average main: £15* ⊠ *Exchange House, Queen's Quay, Central District, Derry, Northern Ireland* ☎ *028/7127–3990* ⊕ *www.exchangerestaurant.com* ⊙ *No lunch Sun.*

$

EUROPEAN

☺

✕ Fitzroy's. This popular city-center brasserie gives "quare packin" (Derry-speak for good value for money), with belt-busting portions of old favorites like burgers, steaks, and caesar salads in the evening. Lunchtimes are busy, with weary shoppers and office staff stopping by for seafood chowder or the popular chicken melter, made up of cheese, tobacco onions, and bacon with Mexican spices. Fitzroy's frequently offers discount deals—check the website for the latest specials. $ *Average main: £11* ⊠ *2–4 Bridge St., Central District, Derry, Northern Ireland* ☎ *028/7126–6211* ⊕ *www.fitzroysrestaurant.com.*

$

IRISH

Fodor's Choice

★

✕ Thompson's Restaurant. The main restaurant of the City Hotel takes its name from the old Thompsons Mill that once occupied this site on the banks of the River Foyle. The decor is airy and cool, while the cuisine is stylish and hot: best bets include honey loin of pork and salmon or sea bass dishes. Thanks to its popularity, reservations are recommended (and practically essential on weekends). The Two's Company menu, based on two people sharing two courses, is a good value at £29.95 for two people. Throw in an impressive but not expensive wine list, and this adds up to a fine place to chill while taking in some great river views. Breakfast is served daily, but lunch only on Sundays. $ *Average main: £13* ⊠ *City Hotel on Queen's Quay, Central District, Derry, Northern Ireland* ☎ *028/7136–5800* ⊕ *www.cityhotelderry.com* ☽ *No lunch except Sun.*

WHERE TO STAY

For expanded hotel reviews, visit Fodors.com.

$

B&B/INN

Fodor's Choice

★

The Merchant's House. No. 16 Queen Street was originally a Victorian merchant's family town home built to Georgian proportions, then a rectory and bank, before Joan Pyne turned it into the city's grandest B&B—garnet-color walls, elaborate plasterwork, and a fireplace make the parlor warm and welcoming. **Pros:** graceful and elegant; great value; for the discriminating traveler; resident pooch, Bertie the bulldog. **Cons:** rooms next to kitchen noisy in morning; small bathrooms. **TripAdvisor:** "friendly people," "great location," "super comfy." $ *Rooms from: £60* ⊠ *16 Queen St., West Bank, Derry, Northern Ireland* ☎ *028/7126–9691* ⊕ *www.saddlershouse.com* ⤵ *9 rooms in Merchant's House; 7 rooms with shared bath in Saddler's House* ⦿ *Breakfast.*

$$

HOTEL

Tower Hotel. The only hotel within Derry city's historic walls, this modern building has more to offer than its unequaled location. **Pros:** top-notch location for exploring Derry's walls, sights, shops, and idiosyncrasies; practical, clean, and tastefully decorated rooms with modern facilities. **Cons:** limited parking available; wedding guests and conference delegates spill over into the sometimes-noisy, crowded lobby. **TripAdvisor:** "nice stop after a busy day," "the heart of the citty," "fabulous location." $ *Rooms from: £99* ⊠ *Tower Hotel, Butcher Street, Central District, Derry, Northern Ireland* ☎ *028/7137–1000* ⊕ *www.towerhotelderry.com* ⤵ *90 rooms, 3 suites* ⦿ *Multiple meal plans.*

NIGHTLIFE AND THE ARTS

NIGHTLIFE

Gweedore Bar. A favorite for hip-hop, Gweedore also pleases fans of house music. ✉ *59–63 Waterloo St., West Bank, Derry, Northern Ireland* ☎ *028/7137–2318* ⊕ *www.peadars-gweedorebar.com.*

Peadar O'Donnell's. This is one of the top places to listen to traditional Irish music in Derry. ✉ *63 Waterloo St., West Bank, Derry, Northern Ireland* ☎ *028/7137–2318* ⊕ *www.peadars-gweedorebar.com.*

Sugar Nightclub. Many night owls consider this *the* place for dance music in Derry. ✉ *33 Shipquay St., West Bank, Derry, Northern Ireland* ☎ *028/7126–6017.*

THE ARTS

Its organizers are calling 2013's U.K. City of Culture extravaganza "a joyous celebration." During 2013, the annual festivals for which the city is renowned will receive substantially increased support. These include the St Patrick's Spring Carnival, the wildly popular City of Derry Jazz Band Festival, in May; the Colmcille Pageant, in June, to celebrate Derry's patron saint; and the Halloween Carnival. Also on tap are a "Sons and Daughters" concert in January by local musical celebs, street performances, a choral festival, and, in August, a musical pageant to commemorate Derry's 17th-century siege. The pageant will take place in the new Ebrington Square, where many of 2013's other cultural activities will occur.

Apart from festivals, new theatrical commissions from the local Field Day group will be staged alongside international premieres of plays (including one by Sam Shepard), and there will be lectures, readings, and symposiums. Other highlights include a Battle of the Atlantic commemoration in May; an Amelia Earhart Festival, also in May; and Banquet on the Bridge, a food banquet to be held in September on the Peace Bridge. Even during a short stay in the city, visitors should find something to tap into. For the full line-up of events, contact City of Culture 2013 (☎ *028/7131–0560* ⊕ *www.cityofculture2013.com*).

ART GALLERIES **CCA Derry/Londonderry.** This cutting-edge gallery that exhibits works by emerging Irish and international artists, reinvented itself in 2012 with a new identity as a Centre for Contemporary Art. As part of the U.K. City of Culture celebrations for 2013, CCA is affiliating with international exhibitions in Scotland, London, and Holland. The gallery will also be associated with the Turner Prize in 2013. ✉ *10–12 Artillery St., West Bank, Derry, Northern Ireland* ☎ *028/7137–3538* ⊕ *www. cca-derry-londonderry.org.*

Cowley Cooper Fine Art. Clare Cooper runs this busy art gallery in the city center. She mounts several exhibitions each year, featuring works of, among others, the abstract artists Gerard Moran and George Callaghan, as well as Eva O'Connor, who produces figurative and landscape paintings, and Marina Hamilton, known for animal paintings. Wine is often served on Friday evenings until 9 pm during the run of exhibitions. ✉ *15–17 Shipquay St., West Bank, Derry, Northern Ireland* ☎ *028/7136–6011* ⊕ *www.cowleycooperfineart.com.*

Millennium Forum. This catch-all venue hosts everything from boy bands and comedians to plays, musicals, tattoo conventions, and even weddings (invitations required). ✉ *Newmarket St., West Bank, Derry, Northern Ireland* ☎ *028/7126–4455* ⊕ *www.millenniumforum.co.uk.*

★ **Playhouse.** With its impressive auditorium and workshop spaces, the Playhouse stages traditional and contemporary plays and also holds contemporary music concerts. ✉ *5–7 Artillery St., West Bank, Derry, Northern Ireland* ☎ *028/7126–8027* ⊕ *www.derryplayhouse.co.uk.*

★ **Verbal Arts Centre.** A hotbed of literary activity promoting the spoken and written word, the Verbal Arts presents events such as storytelling re-created in the old Irish tradition of fireside tales. The center also promotes the work of emerging artists and hosts the annual 2D Northern Ireland Comics Festival. Book hounds love to chill at Blooms Café, a delightful spot looking out over Derry's walls. ✉ *Stable La. and Mall Wall, Bishop St., West Bank, Derry, Northern Ireland* ☎ *028/7126–6946* ⊕ *www.verbalartscentre.co.uk.*

SHOPPING

Shopping in town is generally low-key and unpretentious, but there are some upscale gems of Irish craftsmanship. Stroll up Shipquay Street to find small arts-and-crafts stores and an indoor shopping center.

★ **Foyle Books.** Derry's largest selection of secondhand and antiquarian titles can be found here. The specialties include English lit, Irish-language books, criticism, poetry, biography, travel, music, and sports. ✉ *12 Magazine St., West Bank, Derry, Northern Ireland* ☎ *028/7137–2530* ⊕ *www.derrycraftvillage.com/foylebooks.html.*

Occasions. This remains one of Derry's best showcases for Irish crafts and gifts. ✉ *48 Spencer Rd., East Bank, Derry, Northern Ireland* ☎ *028/7132–9595.*

Pauline's Patch. Stop at this gift shop for the perfect knickknack. ✉ *32 Shipquay St., West Bank, Derry, Northern Ireland* ☎ *028/7127–9794* ⊕ *www.paulinespatch.com.*

Thomas the Goldsmith. Head here for exquisite work by international jewelry designers. ✉ *7 Pump St., West Bank, Derry, Northern Ireland* ☎ *028/7137–4549* ⊕ *www.thomasgoldsmiths.com.*

Trip. Off Shipquay Street, the Trip is a teenage-clothing shop that specializes in knitwear. ✉ *29 Ferryquay St., West Bank, Derry, Northern Ireland* ☎ *028/7137–2382.*

THE BORDER COUNTIES

While blissfully off the beaten track, this region contains some dazzling sights: the Ulster-American Folk Park; the great stately houses of Castle Coole and Florence Court; the pottery town of Belleek; the breathtaking Mountains of Mourne; and the blessed St. Patrick sites in Armagh and Downpatrick. During the worst of the Troubles, the counties of Tyrone, Fermanagh, Armagh, and Down, which border the republic, were known as "bandit country," but now you can enjoy a worry-free trip through the calm countryside and stop in at some very "Ulster" towns, delightfully distinct from the rest of Ireland.

OMAGH

55 km (34 miles) south of Derry.

Omagh, the county town of Tyrone, lies close to the Sperrin Mountains, with the River Strule to the north. The playwright Brian Friel was born here. Sadly, it's better known as the scene of the worst atrocity of the Troubles, when an IRA bomb killed 31 people in 1998. On the 10th anniversary of the bombing, the Garden of Light, a touching memorial by artist Sean Hillen and landscape architect Desmond Fitzgerald, was opened. A heliostatic mirror in the memorial park tracks the sun and directs a beam of light onto 31 small mirrors, each etched with the name of a victim. They in turn bounce the light via another hidden mirror onto a heart-shaped crystal in an obelisk at the bomb site.

GETTING HERE

CAR TRAVEL   Omagh, 55 km (34 miles) south of Derry on A5, is a busy hub. Free car parking on the town's two main central streets, High and Market, is available for one hour. Pay-and-display ticket machines, costing 40 pence per hour, operate in car parks at Mountjoy Road (beside the bus station) and Kevlin Avenue. You can also park free for two hours in the retail park at the Showgrounds, on Sedan Avenue.

BUS TRAVEL   The Translink Goldline service operates buses aplenty between Derry and Belfast and traverses a delightful incantation of mellifluous-sounding Tyrone towns, from Strabane to Ballygawley, and thence along the M1 into Belfast. Journey time is just under two hours (£15 round-trip). Services in both directions stop on request at the popular Ulster-American Folk Park.

EXPLORING

Fodor's Choice   **Ulster American Folk Park.** Several miles north of Omagh is the big attrac-
★   tion of the region: the excellent Ulster American Folk Park re-creates a Tyrone village of two centuries ago, a log-built American settlement of the same period, and the docks and ships that the emigrants to America would have used. The centerpiece of the park is an old whitewashed cottage, now a museum, which is the ancestral home of Thomas Mellon (1813–1908), the U.S. banker and philanthropist. Another thatch cottage is a reconstruction of the boyhood home of Archbishop John Hughes, founder of New York's St. Patrick's Cathedral. There are also full-scale replicas of Irish peasant cottages, Pennsylvania farmhouses, a New York tenement room, immigrant transport ship holders, plus a

Beautiful Belleek

11

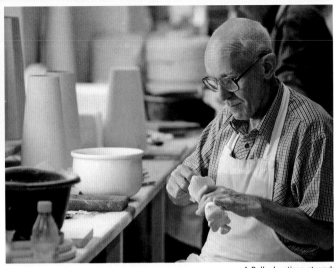

A Belleek artisan at work

The origins of Belleek china are every bit as romantic as the Belleek blessing plates traditionally given to brides and grooms on their wedding day—that is, if you believe the legends. The story goes that in the mid-1800s, John Caldwell Bloomfield, the man behind the world-famous porcelain, accidentally discovered the raw ingredients necessary to produce china. After inheriting his father's estate in the Fermanagh Lakelands on the shore of the Erne River, he whitewashed his cottage using a flaky white powder dug up in his backyard. A passerby, struck by the luminescent sheen of the freshly painted cottage, commented on the unusual brightness of the walls to Bloomfield, who promptly ordered a survey of the land, which duly uncovered all the minerals needed to make porcelain. The venture was complete when Bloomfield met his business partners—London architect

Robert Armstrong and the wealthy Dublin merchant David McBirney. They decided to first produce earthenware, and then porcelain. And the rest, as they say, is history. The delicate, flawless porcelain (Bloomfield declared that any piece with even the slightest blemish should be destroyed) soon attracted the attention of Queen Victoria and many other aristos. Other companies tried to mimic the china's delicate beauty, but genuine Belleek porcelain is recognizable by its seashell designs, basket weaves, and marine themes. The company is now owned by an Irish-born American businessman, Dr. George Moore, and continues to flourish. It has become a favored tradition in Ireland to give a piece of Belleek china at weddings, giving rise to a saying: "If a newly married couple receives a piece of Belleek, their marriage will be blessed with lasting happiness."

19th-century Ulster village, complete with staff dressed in 19th-century costumes. In 2012, the Centre for Migration Studies was rebranded the Mellon Centre for Migration Studies and was opened by James R. Mellon II, great-great-grandson of Thomas Mellon. It contains 12,000 books and periodicals, an Irish emigration database including passenger lists from 1800 to 1860, and emigrant letters. During 2013, an exhibition exploring the stories of Irish steerage passengers on the *Titanic* continues. Highlights include artifacts such as clothing like that worn by third-class passengers, as well as jewelry and personal items from the era. ⊠ *Mellon Rd., Castletown, 10 km (6 miles) north of town on A5, Omagh, Northern Ireland* ☏ *028/8224–3292* ⊕ *www.nmni.com/ uafp* ⧉ *£6.50* ⊙ *Mar.–Sept., Tues.–Sun. 10–5; Oct.–Mar., Tues.–Sun. 10–4; weekends 11–4.*

BELLEEK

42 km (25 miles) southwest of Omagh.

World-famous Belleek Pottery is made in the old town of Belleek on the northwestern edge of Lower Lough Erne, at the border with Northwest Ireland. Other porcelain-ware makers are a few kilometers across the border.

GETTING HERE AND AROUND
Belleek is on A46, a scenic route running along the southern shore of Lower Lough Erne between Enniskillen (a 30-minute drive), in County Fermanagh, and Ballyshannon (15 minutes), in County Donegal. There is ample car parking at the pottery factory—the reason most people come here—with no time restrictions. You can also park free along main or side streets.

EXPLORING
★ **Belleek Pottery.** On the riverbank stands the visitor center of Belleek Pottery Ltd., producers of Parian china, a fine, eggshell-thin, ivory porcelain shaped into dishes, figurines, vases, and baskets. There's a factory, showroom, exhibition, museum, and café. On tours of the factory you can get up close and talk to craftspeople—there's hardly any noise coming from machinery in the workshops. Everything here is made by hand just as workers did back in 1857. The showroom is filled with beautiful but pricey gifts: a shamrock cup-and-saucer set costs about £42, and a bowl in a basket-weave style (typical of Belleek) runs £95 and up. The company has a jewelry portfolio called Belleek Living. The designs are inspired by the Irish landscape. To commemorate the 100th anniversary of the sinking of the *Titanic* the company produced a hand-painted Belleek Titanic Plate. ⊠ *3 Main St., Belleek, Co. Fermanagh, Ireland* ☏ *028/6865–8501* ⊕ *www.belleek.ie* ⧉ *£5* ⊙ *Mar.–Oct., weekdays 9–5:30, Sat. 10–5:30, Sun. noon–5:30; Nov. and Dec., weekdays 9–5:30, Sat. 10–5:30; Jan. and Feb., weekdays 9–5:30.*

WHERE TO EAT
$ ✕ **The Thatch.** Housed in a lovely building dating to the 18th century,
CAFÉ this simple café is worth a visit—not just for the excellent soups, sandwiches, baked potatoes, and similarly light fare—but also because

An annual bluegrass music festival at the Ulster-American Folk Park reaffirms the strong links between Northern Ireland and the United States.

it's the only thatch-roof establishment in the entire county. Full of locals and rife with the sounds of easy banter, it's the perfect place to glean local knowledge and gossip about the surrounding area. $ *Average main: £12* ✉ *20 Main St., Belleek, Ireland* ☎ *028/6865–8181* ☉ *Closed Sun.*

ENNISKILLEN

5 km (3 miles) south of Devenish Island, Lower Lough Erne.

Enniskillen is the pleasant, smart-looking capital of County Fermanagh and the only place of any size in it. The town center is, strikingly, on an island in the River Erne between Lower and Upper Lough Erne. The principal thoroughfares, Townhall and High streets, are crowded with old-style pubs and rows of redbrick Georgian flats. The tall, dark spires of the 19th-century St. Michael's and St. Macartin's cathedrals, both on Church Street, tower over the leafy town center.

GETTING HERE

CAR TRAVEL Enniskillen is 85 km (52 miles) south of Derry on A32 and A5. The town has many car parks, including ones at East Bridge, Eden, Market, and Townhall streets. Be warned: parking attendants clamp down on all drivers lacking a ticket for the required duration of their stay. On the street there are few free street spaces, so be careful where you park.

BUS TRAVEL Translink's Goldline Express buses connect Enniskillen with Belfast, 145 km (90 miles) east. Buses run from early morning to late evening, with a two-hour journey time (£15 round-trip). Local service operates

The Western Border Counties

from the bus depot on Wellington Road, beside the tourist information office; an all-day ticket is £2.30. The bus to visit some of Fermanagh's attractions, such as Castle Coole historic house, costs £1.30. The driver will drop you off on request at the entrance gates. Enniskillen also has a slew of cross-border services in many directions. Bus Éireann operates Expressway routes west to Sligo.

TOURS

Erne Tours. On Lower Lough Erne, this company operates tours, about 90 minutes long, aboard the *Kestrel,* a 56-seat water bus. Tours leave from Round O Pier at Enniskillen. On weekdays the boat stops for 45 minutes at Devenish Island. From early May to the end of September the company also has a Saturday-evening dinner cruise departing at 6:30. The three-course meal costs £27, and the cruise, which leaves from the Killyhevlin Hotel near Enniskillen, lasts two hours. ⊠ *Round O Pier, Enniskillen, Co. Fermanagh, Ireland* ☎ *028/6632–2882* ⊕ *www. ernetoursltd.com* ✉ *90-min tours £10* ⊙ *90-min tours May and Sept., Tues., Sat., and Sun. at 2:15 and 4:15; June, daily at 2:15 and 4:15; July and Aug., daily at 10:30, 12:15, 2:15, and 4:15.*

ESSENTIALS

Visitor Information **Enniskillen Tourist Office** ⊠ *Lakeland Visitor Centre, Wellington Rd., Enniskillen, Co. Fermanagh, Ireland* ☎ *028/6632–3110* ⊕ *www. fermanagh.gov.uk.*

EXPLORING

★ **Blake's of the Hollow.** Among the several relaxed and welcoming old pubs in Enniskillen's town center, the one with the most appeal is Blake's, a place hardly altered since it opened in 1887. Its name derives from the fact that the heart of the town lies in a slight hollow and the pub's landlord is named William Blake. (Don't ask: he's not related to the English poet, painter, and engraver.) ⊠ *6 Church St., Enniskillen, Co. Fermanagh, Ireland* ☎ *028/6632–2143.*

Buttermarket. Sixteen wonderful arts and crafts shops selling pottery, jewelry, and paintings are gathered at the Buttermarket. This restored dairy market built in 1835 also has a café. ⊠ *Down St., Enniskillen, Co. Fermanagh, Ireland* ☎ *028/6632–3117.*

Enniskillen Castle. Enniskillen's main sight is the waterfront Enniskillen Castle, one of the best-preserved monuments in the North. This stronghold on land once ruled by the Maguire clan houses the local history collection of the Fermanagh County Museum and the polished paraphernalia of the Royal Inniskilling Fusiliers Regimental Museum. A Heritage Centre—Fermanagh County Museum, with displays of pottery and lace—also stands within the curtilage of the castle. In 2009 the castle keep was redeveloped with new exhibitions and interactive displays, and the following year a Roll of Honor containing the names of the 9,100 people from all over Ireland who died in World War II was presented to the Regimental Museum. ⊠ *Castlebarracks, Enniskillen, Co. Fermanagh, Ireland* ☎ *028/6632–5000* ⊕ *www.enniskillencastle. co.uk* ⊡ *£4* ⊘ *Apr., May, June, and Sept, Oct., Mon. and Sat. 2–5, Tues.–Fri. 10–5; July and Aug., Mon. and weekends 2–5, Tues.–Fri. 10–5; Nov.–Mar., Mon. 2–5, Tues.–Fri. 10–5.*

Portora Royal School. Beyond the West Bridge is Portora Royal School, established in 1608 by King James I. On the grounds are some ruins of Portora Castle. Among writers educated here are Samuel Beckett and Oscar Wilde, the pride of the school (until his trial for homosexuality).

Water Gate. At the Erne riverside, the 16th-century Water Gate, between two handsome turrets, protected the town from invading armies.

WHERE TO STAY

For expanded hotel reviews, visit Fodors.com.

$$$$
RESORT
★

Lough Erne Resort. Flickering beech-log fires greet you on arrival in the lobby of this sumptuous five-star hotel, a resort set between two of Fermanagh's lakes on the small island of Ely—the headliner is the 18-hole Faldo Course, designed by the touring pro Nick Faldo, but a Thai spa is among the other delights. **Pros:** binoculars in rooms for bird-watching; velour slippers and bathrobe; luxury Irish bed linen; Egyptian cotton towels. **Cons:** luxury comes at a steep price; queues at busy breakfast times. **TripAdvisor:** "beautiful and peaceful location," "lovely rooms," "an unforgettable experience." ⑤ *Rooms from: £204*

Fabled haunt of "the little people," the stately abode of Florence Court sits in a vale reputedly populated by leprechauns and fairies.

✉ *Belleek Rd., 5 km (3 miles) north of Enniskillen, Enniskillen, Co. Fermanagh, Ireland* ☎ *028/6632–3230* ⊕ *www.lougherneresort.com* ⇗ *120 rooms, 6 suites, 25 lodges* ❏ *Breakfast.*

Marble Arch Caves Global Geopark. If it's raining in Fermanagh, an ideal half-day activity is to go underground to visit this geopark, one of Europe's finest show caves. Stalactites glisten above streams as you admire fragile mineral veils and cascades of calcite-coated walls and waterfalls. Guided tours last 75 minutes; bring walking shoes and a warm sweater. Tours begin at Marlbank Scenic Loop Centre, Florence-court. ☎ *028/6634–8855* ⊕ *www.marblearchcavesgeopark.com* ✉ *£8* ☉ *Mar.–Sept., daily 10–4:30.*

OFF THE BEATEN PATH

FLORENCE COURT

11 km (7 miles) south of Enniskillen.

GETTING HERE AND AROUND

CAR TRAVEL Take A4 south from Enniskillen and continue south on A32 (also signed as Swanlinbar Road) to reach Florence Court. The drive takes 10 minutes. There is ample car parking at Florence Court, and in summer an overflow car park operates. The admission price to the house and grounds includes parking.

BUS TRAVEL There is no direct bus service, but the main Enniskillen–Swanlinbar Translink bus will pull over on request to allow you to hop off at the Creamery Corner stop. From there, it's a 2-mile walk to the estate's entrance, and a further long walk along the avenue to reach the main house.

EXPLORING

Fodor's Choice ★ **Florence Court.** When it comes to Early Irish Georgian houses, there are few as magical as Florence Court. Less known than some showier estates, this three-story Anglo-Irish mansion was built around 1730 for John Cole, father of the first earl of Enniskillen. Topped off about 1760 with its distinctive two flanking colonnaded wings, the central house is adorably adorned with a positive surfeit of Palladian windows, keystones, and balustrades thanks to, as one architectural historian put it, "the vaingloriousness of a provincial hand." Even more impressive is its bucolically baroque setting, as the Cuilcagh Mountains form a wonderful contrast to the shimmering white-stone facade. Up until a few years ago, the house was barely furnished but a magnificent National Trust restoration has returned many family heirlooms to these interiors. Showstoppers in terms of decor are the rococo plasterwork ceilings in the dining room; the Venetian Room; and the famous staircase, all ascribed to Robert West, one of Dublin's most famous *stuccadores* (plasterworkers). For a peek at the "downstairs" world, check out the restored kitchen and other service quarters. In 2009 a shop, reception area, and secondhand bookstore were added, and the Men's Way and South Yard were converted into a holiday apartment. Children's tours, lasting 20 minutes, were introduced in 2011 and cost £2. ⊠ *11 km (7 miles) south of Enniskillen on A4 and A32, Enniskillen, Co. Fermanagh, Ireland* ☎ *028/6634–8249* ⊕ *www.nationaltrust.org.uk/florence-court* ⊠ *£5 house, £4 grounds* ☉ *Grounds: Nov.–Feb., daily 10–4; Mar.–Oct., daily 10–7. House: Mar. and Oct., weekends 11–5; Apr., daily 11–5; May–June and Sept., Wed.–Mon. 11–5 (closed Fri. in Sept.); July and Aug., daily 11–5.*

> **LISTEN CLOSELY AND YOU SHALL HEAR…**
>
> Florence Court's ancestral park is one of Northern Ireland's glories—dotted with noted heirloom trees (including the Florence Court weeping beech), it also has nooks and dells where, legend has it, you can hear the "song of the little people."

CASTLE COOLE

3 km (2 miles) east of Enniskillen.

GETTING HERE AND AROUND

CAR TRAVEL A five-minute drive from Enniskillen on A4, Castle Coole has a car park (£2.50 per car) that overflows in the summer.

BUS TRAVEL There is no bus service to Castle Coole. You can request the driver to stop on the Translink Enniskillen–Clones route only. The main express bus services heading for Belfast will not stop here.

EXPLORING

★ **Castle Coole.** In the 18th century and through most of the 19th, the Loughs of Erne and their environs were remote places far from Ireland's bustling cities. But it was just this isolated green and watery countryside that attracted the Anglo-Irish gentry, who built grand houses. This "uncommonly perfect" mansion (to quote the eminent architectural historian Desmond Guinness) is on its own landscaped oak woods and gardens at the end of a long tree-lined driveway. Although the Irish architect Richard Johnston made the original drawings in the 1790s, and was responsible for the foundation, the castle was, for all intents and purposes, the work of James Wyatt, commissioned by the first earl of Belmore. One of the best-known architects of his time, Wyatt was based in London but visited Ireland only once, so Alexander Stewart was drafted as the resident builder-architect. The designer wasn't the only imported element; in fact, much of Castle Coole came from England, including the main facade, which is clad in Portland stone and hauled here by bullock carts. And what a facade it is—in perfect symmetry, white colonnaded wings extend from either side of the mansion's three-story, nine-bay center block, with a Palladian central portico and pediment. It is perhaps the apotheosis of the 18th century's reverence for the Greeks.

Inside, the house is remarkably preserved; most of the lavish plasterwork and original furnishings are in place. On its completion in September 1798, the construction had cost £70,000 and the furnishings another £22,000, compared with the £6 million cost of a restoration in 1995–96. The saloon is one of the finest rooms in the house, with a vast expanse of oak flooring, gilded Regency furniture, and gray scagliola pilasters with Corinthian capitals. The Life Below Stairs exhibition features tours of the servants' rooms and service quarters; above stairs, so to speak, is the present earl of Belmore, who still lives on the estate. In 2012, an extended tearoom was opened. ⊠ *Dublin Rd., A4, Enniskillen, Co. Fermanagh, Ireland* ☎ *028/6632–2690* ⊕ *www. nationaltrust.org.uk/castle-coole* ☜ *House £5; grounds £2; car (per adult): £3* ☉ *House Mar.–May and Sept., weekends 11–5 (open daily Easter wk); June–Aug., daily 11–5. Grounds Nov.–Feb., daily 10–4; Mar.–Oct., daily 10–7.*

ARMAGH

75 km (42 miles) east of Enniskillen.

The spiritual capital of Ireland for 5,000 years, and the seat of both Protestant and Catholic archbishops, Armagh is the most venerated of Irish cities. St. Patrick called it "my sweet hill" and built his stone church on the hill where the Anglican cathedral now stands. On the opposite hill, the twin-spire Catholic cathedral is flanked by two large marble statues of archbishops who look across the land. Despite the pleasing Georgian terraces around the elegant Mall east of the town center, Armagh can seem drab. Having suffered as a trouble spot in the sectarian conflict, though, it's now the scene of some spirited and sympathetic renovation.

GETTING HERE AND AROUND

CAR TRAVEL   Armagh is a one-hour drive from Belfast along A3 before joining the M1 at Port Down. Dublin is just over two hours south via Newry on A28 and A1, before crossing the Irish border to join the motorway for the rest of your journey. There are several pay-and-display car parks in Armagh city center. The main one is next to the tourist office, on

Thackeray admired the Church of Ireland's St. Patrick's Cathedral which, with St. Patrick's Roman Catholic Cathedral, jointly presides over Armagh.

English Street. You can also park at the Mall, and there is free parking on side streets.

BUS TRAVEL Buses link Armagh with neighboring towns as well as Belfast, an 80-minute journey. You can catch a Translink Goldline Express from the Buscentre on the Lonsdale Road in Armagh (£14.50 round-trip). Cross-border buses also operate out of Armagh—you can hop aboard the Belfast–Galway Bus Éireann bus that runs via Cavan town and Athlone. Round-trip to Galway is £33.15. Bus Éireann Expressway connections run from Dublin to Portrush on the north coast and stop in Armagh. The Armagh–Dublin bus journey takes 2¾ hours and costs £22.15 round-trip.

ESSENTIALS

Visitor Information Armagh Tourist Information Centre ✉ *40 English St., Armagh, Northern Ireland* ☎ *028/3752–1800* ⊕ *www.armagh.co.uk.*

EXPLORING

☾ **Armagh Planetarium.** Displayed here in all its nickel-iron glory is Ireland's largest meteorite, an astonishing 4.5 billion years old and weighing 24 stone (336 pounds). Elsewhere, you'll find a spaceship, satellite models, and the Digital Theater—sit back and navigate the night sky in the company of experts. Children's activities include building and launching rockets. Outside, stroll through the solar system and into the Milky Way at the huge scale model of the universe. ✉ *College Hill, Armagh, Northern Ireland* ☎ *028/3752–3689* ⊕ *www.armaghplanet.com* ✇ *£6* ⊙ *Mon.–Sat. 10–5; July and Aug., also Sun. 10–5.*

★ **Navan Centre and Fort.** Just outside Armagh is Ulster's Camelot—the ☼ region's ancient capital. Excavations date evidence of activity to 700 BC. The fort has strong associations with figures of Irish history. Legend has it that thousands of years ago this was the site of the palace of Queen Macha; subsequent tales call it the barracks of the legendary Ulster warrior Cuchulainn and his Red Branch Knights. Remains dating from 94 BC are particularly intriguing: a great conical structure, 120 feet in diameter, was formed from five concentric circles made of 275 wooden posts, with a 276th, about 12 yards high, situated in the center. In a ritual whose meaning is not known, it was filled with brushwood and set on fire. Young children can dig into the past in the Archeo Pit, dress up as a Celt, and touch history with "feely boxes." ⊠ *81 Killyleagh Rd., 3 km (2 miles) west of Armagh on A28, Armagh, Northern Ireland* ☎ *028/3752–9644* ⊕ *www.navan.com* £6 ☉ *Apr.– Sept., daily 10–7; Oct.–Mar., daily 10–4.*

St. Patrick's Anglican Cathedral. Near the city center, a squat battlement tower identifies the cathedral, in simple, early-19th-century, low-Gothic style. On the site of much older churches, it contains relics of Armagh's long history. Brian Boru, the High King (King of All Ireland) is buried here. In 1014, he drove the Vikings out of Ireland but was killed after the battle was won. Some memorials and tombs here are by important 18th-century sculptors such as Roubilliac and Rysbrack, and in 2012, the cathedral opened its atmospheric crypt to visitors. Dating from the Middle Ages, this sanctuary where law-abiding citizens safely stored their valuable goods—a few archbishops are buried here, too—is worth a look. ⊠ *43 Abbey St., Cathedral Close, Armagh, Northern Ireland* ☎ *028/3752–3142* ⊕ *www.stpatricks-cathedral.org* £3 ☉ *Nov.–Mar., weekdays 10–4; Apr.–Oct., weekdays 10–5.*

St. Patrick's Roman Catholic Cathedral. The pale limestone, St. Patrick's, the seat of a Roman Catholic archdiocese, rises above a hill to dominate the north end of Armagh. The cathedral's rather gloomy interior is enlivened by a magnificent organ, the potential of which is fully realized at services. Construction of the twin-spire structure started in 1840 in the neo-Gothic style, but the Great Famine brought work to a halt until 1854, and it wasn't completed until 1873. An arcade of statues over the main doorway on the exterior is one of the cathedral's most interesting features. The altar is solid Irish granite and the woodwork is Austrian oak. ⊠ *Cathedral Rd., Armagh, Northern Ireland* ☎ *028/3752–2802* ⊕ *www.archdioceseofarmagh.org.*

☼ **St. Patrick's Trian.** A former church behind the tourist office has been reinvented as a visitor complex called St. Patrick's Trian. It contains two main exhibitions: the Armagh Story, exploring the city's rich history and pagan monuments; and the Land of Lilliput, the story of Jonathan Swift's most famous book *Gulliver's Travels,* as told by one of the book's "giants"—a big hit with children who dress up in costumes provided. ⊠ *40 English St., Armagh, Northern Ireland* ☎ *028/3752–1801* ⊕ *www.saintpatrickstrian.com* £6 ☉ *Mon.–Sat. 10–5, Sun. 2–5.*

The Eastern
Border Counties

THE MOUNTAINS OF MOURNE

52½ km (32½ miles) southeast of Armagh on A28, 51 km (32 miles) south of Belfast.

Subjects of a song that is sung on every Irish occasion from baptisms to funerals, the Mountains of Mourne must surely qualify as one of Ireland's best-known ranges. According to those lyrics by Percy French, the Mountains of Mourne "sweep down to the sea," from 2,000-foot summits. East of the unprepossessing border city of Newry, this area was long considered ungovernable, its hardy inhabitants living from smuggling contraband into the numerous rocky coves on the seashore. Much of the Mourne range is still inaccessible except on foot. The countryside is gorgeous: high, windswept pasture and moorland threaded with bright streams, bound by a tracery of drystone walls and dotted with sheep and whitewashed farmhouses snuggled in stands of sycamore. It's the perfect landscape for away-from-it-all walkers, cyclists, and serious climbers.

GETTING HERE AND AROUND

CAR TRAVEL Newcastle is a 45-minute drive south of Belfast on A24 through Ballynahinch. A one-way system operates through the town and is especially crowded during summer. Car parks are at the seafront near the Slieve Donard Hotel, beside the bus station, and at Donard Park. The nearest city is Newry, a 35-minute drive west on A25.

BUS TRAVEL   Newcastle bus station on Railway Street is the arrival and departure point for all routes to one of the most scenic parts of Northern Ireland. Ulsterbus service leaves Belfast regularly for the 48-km (30-mile) trip to Newcastle (70 minutes, £12.50 round-trip). If you wish to appreciate the panoramic glory of the Mountains of Mourne, take a bus from Newcastle along the coast to the foothill towns of Annalong and Kilkeel (£6.80 round-trip). To truly get an up-close feel for the mountains, board the Mourne Rambler (info found on Rambler Services on the Translink website), a 23-seat rural bus that transports you to the heart of Mourne country. A complete circuit on the Rambler, which runs only in July and August, takes 90 minutes (£5.80). You can also catch a bus from Newcastle to Dublin. This service starts from Downpatrick and runs from Newcastle to Castlewellan, Newry, and across the border to Dublin (£19.15 round-trip).

> ### WORD OF MOUTH
>
> "If you like hiking, consider the Mountains of Mourne—wonderful scenery and very few other people other than walkers and locals know about their beauty. It is also the area where the Brontë family originated. The Silent Valley drive is wonderful."
>
> —Cambe

EXPLORING

Castlewellan Forest Park. A huge maze, grown to symbolize the convoluted path to peace, is the latest addition to Castlewellan Forest Park, which comprises 1,150 acres of forested hills running between the Mourne Mountains and Slieve Croob. With the maze, lake, secluded arbors, and arboretum, the park makes an excellent introduction to the area. ✉ *Castlewellan, Northern Ireland* ☎ *028/4377–8664* ⊕ *www.forestserviceni.gov.uk* ✉ *Free; vehicles £4.40* ⊙ *Daily 10 am–dusk.*

Newcastle. A bracing Victorian cold-water bathing station, Newcastle is the main center for visitors to the hills. ⊕ *www.downdc.gov.uk.*

Silent Valley. The road to the Silent Valley reservoir park leads to mountain views and excellent photo ops. Also here is a visitor center with an informative exhibition explaining the history of Silent Valley. ✉ *6 km (4 miles) north of Kilkeel off B27, right turn, Northern Ireland* ☎ *028/9074–6581* ⊕ *www.visitnewryandmourne.com* ✉ *£1.60; vehicles £4.50* ⊙ *June–Aug., daily 10–6:30; Oct.–Apr, daily 10–4.*

★   **Slieve Donard.** Looming above Newcastle is Slieve Donard, its panoramic, 2,796-foot-high summit grandly claiming views into England, Wales, and Scotland "when it's clear enough"—in other words, "rarely," say the pessimists. It's not possible to drive up the mountain, so leave your car in the Donard parking lot. It should take roughly three hours to climb to the summit and no longer than two hours to descend. Experienced hikers should not find it difficult, but if you prefer an easier trek, follow the trails signposted in Tollymore Forest Park. Hiking boots are essential and, as the weather can be unpredictable, it's advisable to take an extra layer of clothing, even in summer.

★   **Tollymore Forest Park.** Covering 1,200 acres and entered through Gothic gateways, Tollymore Forest Park extends up the valley of the River

A four-hour ascent of the Slieve Donard peak—queen of the magnificent Mountains of Mourne—offers vistas that reach as far as Scotland and the Isle of Man.

Shimna. Many pretty stone bridges cross over the sparkling waters here. The arboretum at Tollymore has the widest range of tree species of any park in Ireland. Apart from the better-known oak, birch, beech, and Sitka spruce, the eucalyptus from Australia and Tasmania stand out and bring a cheerful note. ✉ *Tullybrannigan Rd., Newcastle, Northern Ireland* ☎ *028/4372–2428* ⊕ *www.forestserviceni.gov.uk* 🛋 *Free; vehicles £4.50* 🕑 *Daily 10–dusk.*

WHERE TO STAY

For expanded hotel reviews, visit Fodors.com.

$$$
B&B/INN
Fodor's Choice
★

🍴 **Glassdrumman Lodge.** For those who wish to be pampered as well as immersed in the ancient Kingdom of Mourne, brothers Johnny and Ben Hall's eclectically simple and stylish lodge is the place. **Pros:** stunning location in the heart of the mountains with the sea on your doorstep; rooms well appointed with pleasant en suite bathrooms. **Cons:** some say the restaurant is overrated; pity they've stopped churning their own butter. **TripAdvisor:** "relaxing stay," "first-class service," "perfect for a group of golfers." ⑤ *Rooms from: £120* ✉ *85 Mill Rd., Annalong, Co. Down, Northern Ireland* ☎ *028/4376–8451* ⊕ *www.glassdrummanlodge.com* ⤳ *10 rooms, 2 suites* 🍽 *Breakfast.*

$$$$
RESORT
Fodor's Choice
★

🍴 **Slieve Donard Resort & Spa.** A lavish redbrick monument to Victoriana, this turreted hotel, built in 1898, stands like a palace on green lawns at one end of Newcastle's 6½-km (4-mile) sandy beach—the traditional furnishings may make you feel as if you're stepping back in time to the town's turn-of-the-20th-century heyday as an elegant seaside resort, though the guest rooms have modern comforts and are bright and airy. **Pros:** appealing mix of luxury, history, and style; renovations brought hotel into the 21st century; fireplaces in lobby welcome on chilly days. **Cons:** housekeeping slow with requests; occasional cacophony from wedding receptions. **TripAdvisor:** "amazing hotel," "fantastic setting," "stunning mountain and sea views." ⑤ *Rooms from: £200* ☒ *Downs Rd., Newcastle, Co. Down, Northern Ireland* ☎ *028/4372–1066* ⊕ *www.hastingshotels.com/slieve-donard-resort-and-spa* ⟳ *178 rooms, 6 suites* ⎢⊙⎥ *Multiple meal plans.*

SPORTS AND THE OUTDOORS

★ **Tollymore National Outdoor Centre.** If you need advice on mountain climbing, canoeing, and hiking trails, this impressive center is the place to head. ☒ *Bryansford, Newcastle, Northern Ireland* ☎ *028/4372–2158* ⊕ *www.tollymore.com.*

GOLF

Fodor'sChoice ★ **Royal County Down.** Recently ousting the Old Course at St. Andrews as the best course outside the United States in *Golf Digest*'s annual survey, Royal County Down is a links course with a sea of craterlike bunkers and small dunes; catch it on the right day at the right time and you may think you're on the moon. And for better players, every day is the right one. Back in his day, Harry Vardon labeled it the toughest course on the Emerald Isle, and if you can't hit your drive long and straight, you might find it the toughest course in the world. ☒ *Golf Links Rd., 36 Golf Links Rd., Newcastle, Co. Down, Northern Ireland* ☎ *28/4372–3314* ⊕ *www.royalcountydown.org* ⌦ *Greens fees: weekdays £100–£165 (Championship), £25 (Annesley); weekends £180 (Championship), £25 (Annesley)* ⅄ *36 holes. Yardage: 7,204 (Championship), 4,617 (Annesley). Par 71 (Championship), 66 (Annesley). Practice area, caddies, caddy carts, catering* ⊘ *Visitors: Sun.–Tues., Thurs., and Fri. (Championship); daily (Annesley).*

DOWNPATRICK

21 km (14 miles) east of Newcastle.

Downpatrick once was called plain and simple "Down" but had its name changed by John de Courcy, a Norman knight who moved here in 1176. De Courcy set about promoting St. Patrick, the 5th-century Briton who was captured by the Irish and served as a slave in the Down area before he escaped to France, where he learned about Christianity and bravely returned to try to convert the local chiefs. Although it's not true that Patrick brought a new faith to Ireland—there was already a bishop of Ireland before Patrick got here—he must have been a better missionary than most because he did indeed win influential converts. The clan chief of the Down area gave him land at the village of Saul, near Downpatrick, to build a monastery.

GETTING HERE AND AROUND

CAR TRAVEL   Downpatrick is 21 km (14 miles) east of Newcastle on A2 and A25 and 30km (22 miles) south of Belfast on A24. On-street parking is free but restricted to either 30 or 60 minutes. The car park at the Grove shopping center is pay-and-display and costs 40 pence per hour. There is free parking on English and Market streets and beside the bus station.

BUS TRAVEL Buses arrive at the main station in Downpatrick from many points of County Down and beyond. Frequent Translink Goldline Express services run to and from Belfast. The journey time is one hour (£9.10 round-trip). Some services link up with the Belfast Metro network of suburban routes. To visit Strangford, there are daily services from Downpatrick (£5.40 round-trip); to visit Castle Ward, ask the driver to stop by the roadside. Buses also leave Downpatrick for Dublin; the journey takes just over three hours (£19.15 round-trip).

> **A DAY LIKE ANY OTHER**
>
> St. Patrick's Day—March 17—is a great time to visit Downpatrick, as the whole town turns out in carnival dress for the holiday parade. But why is St. Paddy fêted on March 17? Legend has it he died on that date, perhaps in AD 461. Others point to the fact that this date marked one of the great pagan festivals celebrating the onset of spring and the sowing of crops.

ESSENTIALS

Visitor Information Downpatrick Tourist Office ✉ *53A Market St., Downpatrick, Co. Down, Northern Ireland* ☎ *028/4461–2233* ⊕ *www.downdc.gov.uk.*

EXPLORING

Down Cathedral. Down Cathedral is one of the disputed burial places of St. Patrick. In the churchyard, a somber slab inscribed "Patric" is supposedly the saint's tomb, but no one knows where he's actually buried. It might be here, at Saul, or, some scholars argue, more likely at Armagh. The church, which lay ruined from 1538 to 1790 (it reopened in 1818), preserves parts of some of the earlier churches and monasteries that have stood on this site, the oldest of which dates to the 6th century. Even by then, the cathedral site had long been an important fortified settlement: Down takes its name from the Celtic word *dun*, or fort. ✉ *35 English St., Downpatrick, Northern Ireland* ☎ *028/4461–4922* ⊕ *www.downcathedral.org* 🎟 *£1* ⊙ *Mon.–Sat. 9:30–4:30, Sun. 2–5.*

Down County Museum. Housed in an elegantly restored 18th-century jail between the cathedral and the courthouse, this museum is brimful of living history. Behind, a short signposted trail leads to the Mound of Down, an example of a Norman motte and bailey. ✉ *The Mall, English St., Downpatrick, Northern Ireland* ☎ *028/4461–5218* ⊕ *www.downcountymuseum.com* 🎟 *Free* ⊙ *Weekdays 10–5, weekends 1–5.*

★ **St. Patrick Centre.** For some hard facts concerning the patron saint of Ireland, visit the interactive exhibits of St. Patrick Centre, where the ancient myths and stories of early Christian Ireland are brought to life. You can explore how St. Patrick's legacy developed in early Christian times and examine the art and metalwork that was produced during this golden age. The Grove gift store exhibits jewelry, textiles, photographs, sculpture, and paintings by local artists and craftsmen. After lunch at Daisy's Café, browse through the gift shop and buy your own crock of shamrock. The center also includes an art gallery, terraced gardens, and a tourist information kiosk. ✉ *53A Lower Market St., Downpatrick, Northern Ireland* ☎ *028/4461–9000* ⊕ *www.saintpatrickcentre.com* 🎟 *£4.95* ⊙ *Mon.–Sat. 9–5; July and Aug., Sun. 1–5. Off-season hrs can vary, so check ahead.*

St. Patrick's Trail. After returning to Ireland in the year AD 432, Ireland's patron saint popped up everywhere on his peregrinations. You can explore some places associated with him along the St. Patrick's Trail, an automobile route linking 15 historic and ecclesiastical sites across the beautiful drumlin hills of counties Down and Armagh. ⊕ *www. discovernorthernireland.com/stpatrick.*

WHERE TO EAT AND STAY

For expanded hotel reviews, visit Fodors.com.

$

IRISH

✕**Denvir's.** In this wonderfully atmospheric pub and hotel—an old coaching inn dating to 1642—oak beams, stone floors, meat hooks hanging from the ceiling, and a large open fireplace testify to the antiquity. The bar top was crafted from the timbers of ships wrecked in Lough Foyle. Back in the mists of time, it was a member of the same Denvir family who gave the family name to a small settlement in Colorado, its name later modified to Denver. Six guest rooms have been sympathetically refurbished to retain the character of the old inn and come with original wooden floors and period wooden beds. Solid traditional dishes dominate the menu—steak, roast chicken, spring lamb, and the daily fresh fish. Live music in the bar features traditional Irish as well as old classics on Fridays and weekend nights. $ *Average main: £10 ⊠ 14–16 English St., Downpatrick, Northern Ireland ☎ 028/4461–2012 ⊕ www.denvirshotel.com.*

$

B&B/INN

Fodor'sChoice

★

⌂ **Dufferin Coaching Inn.** Leontine Haines presides over this 1803 inn next to picture-perfect, grandly gracious Killyleagh Castle—reputedly the longest-inhabited castle in Ireland and arguably the country's prettiest. **Pros:** ideal for exploring Strangford Lough attractions; good value for the money. **Cons:** pub noise can be a problem; far from the bright city lights; no elevator. **TripAdvisor:** "friendly and helpful owners," "cozy," "old Irish charm." $ *Rooms from: £65 ⊠ 33 High St., 10 km (6 miles) north of Downpatrick, Killyleagh, Co. Down, Northern Ireland ☎ 028/4482–1134 ⊕ www.dufferincoachinginn.com ⇗ 7 rooms* ⦁⊚⦁ *Breakfast.*

Travel Smart Ireland

WORD OF MOUTH

"I really do think renting a car is the best way to see the country, it was so nice to be able to go at our own pace and stop when we wanted to. My suggestion: definitely rent a car, get all the insurance so you don't have to worry, study the maps and ask the locals for help and you will be fine. Go at the speed you are comfortable with and pull over to let others pass you if they need to."

—Nspotz

GETTING HERE AND AROUND

▮ AIR TRAVEL

Flying time to Ireland is 6½ hours from New York, 7½ hours from Chicago, 10 hours from Los Angeles, and 1 hour from London.

Flying into Ireland involves few hassles, although an increase in traffic in the last decade has caused a slight increase in flight delays and time spent waiting for baggage to clear customs. Flights within Ireland tend to be filled with business travelers. Increased competition on internal routes has led internal flights to be competitive with rail travel if you can travel outside peak business hours. However, given problems with passenger numbers and long lines for security clearance at Dublin Airport, rail is often preferable.

Checking in and boarding an outbound plane tends to be civilized. Security is professional but not overbearing, and airport staffers are usually helpful and patient. In the busy summer season lines can get long, and you should play it safe and arrive a couple of hours before your flight.

Airlines and Airports Airline and Airport Links.com. This website has links to many of the world's airlines and airports. ⊕ www.airlineandairportlinks.com.

Airline Security Issues Transportation Security Administration. Everything you need to know about security before you go to an airport. ⊕ www.tsa.gov.

AIRPORTS

The major gateways to Ireland are Dublin Airport (DUB) on the east coast, 10 km (6 miles) north of the city center, and Shannon Airport (SNN) on the west coast, 25 km (16 miles) west of Limerick. Two airports serve Belfast: Belfast International Airport (BFS) at Aldergrove, 24 km (15 miles) from the city, handles local and U.K. flights, as well as all other international traffic; Belfast City Airport (BHD), 6½ km (4 miles) from the city, handles local and U.K. flights only. In addition, the City of Derry Airport (LDY) receives flights from Liverpool, London Stansted, and Glasgow in the United Kingdom. If you plan to visit mainly the Southwest of Ireland, use Cork Airport (ORK), which handles flights from Dublin and the U.K., and has direct flights from Paris, Malaga, and Rome.

Airport Information City of Derry Airport ☎ 028/7181-0784 ⊕ www.cityofderryairport. com. **Cork Airport** ☎ 021/431-3131 ⊕ www.corkairport.com. **Dublin Airport** ☎ 01/814-1111 ⊕ www.dublinairport. com. **George Best Belfast City Airport** ☎ 028/9093-9093 ⊕ www.belfastcityairport. com. **Belfast International Airport at Aldergrove** ☎ 028/9448-4848 ⊕ www. belfastairport.com. **Shannon Airport** ☎ 061/712-000 ⊕ www.shannonairport.com.

FLIGHTS

From North America and the United Kingdom, Aer Lingus, the national flag carrier, has the greatest number of direct flights to Ireland.

Aer Lingus operates regularly scheduled flights to Shannon and/or Dublin from New York's JFK (John F. Kennedy Airport), Chicago's O'Hare, Boston, and Orlando. Delta has a daily departure from New York's JFK that flies first to Shannon and then to Dublin. Continental flies daily direct to Dublin, Shannon, and Belfast, departing from Newark Liberty International Airport in New Jersey. With the exception of special offers, the prices of the three airlines tend to be similar. London to Dublin is one of the world's busiest international air routes. Aer Lingus, British Airways, BMI, and CityJet all have several daily flights. Ryanair—famous for its cheap, no-frills service—offers several daily flights from London Gatwick, Luton, and Stansted airports. With such healthy competition, bargains abound. British Airways, BMI, and EasyJet offer regularly scheduled flights to Belfast from London Gatwick, Luton, and Stansted airports.

Within Ireland, Aer Lingus provides service to Dublin, Galway, Kerry, and Shannon. Aer Arann Express flies from Dublin to Derry, Donegal, Galway, Knock, and Sligo. British Airways has daily service between Dublin and Derry.

Airline Contacts Aer Arann ☎ *0800/587–2324, 353/1844–7700 in Republic of Ireland* ⊕ *www.aerarann.com.* **Aer Lingus** ☎ *800/474–7424, 353/818-365000* ⊕ *www.aerlingus.com.* **American Airlines** ☎ *800/433–7300, 353/818–286597* ⊕ *www.aa.com.* **BMI** ☎ *800/788–0555, 353/1283–0700* ⊕ *www.flybmi.com.* **British Airways** ☎ *800/247–9297, 353/1890–626747* ⊕ *www.ba.com.* **CityJet** ☎ *818/776–057* ⊕ *www.cityjet.com.* **Delta Airlines** ☎ *800/221–1212* ⊕ *www.delta.com.* **EasyJet** ⊕ *www.easyjet.com.* **Ryanair** ☎ *15/5092–7030* ⊕ *www.ryanair.com.* **United Airlines** ☎ *800/231–0856* ⊕ *www.united.com.*

∎ BOAT TRAVEL

TO AND FROM IRELAND

The ferry is a convenient way to travel between Ireland and elsewhere in Europe, particularly the United Kingdom. There are five main ferry ports to Ireland; four in the republic at Dublin Port, Dun Laoghaire, Rosslare, and Cork, and two in Northern Ireland at Belfast and Larne. The cost of your trip can vary substantially, so spend time with a travel agent and compare prices carefully. Bear in mind, too, that flying can be cheaper, so look into all types of transportation before booking.

Irish Ferries operates the *Ulysses,* the world's largest car ferry, on its Dublin to Holyhead, Wales, route (3 hrs, 15 mins); there's also a swift service (1 hr, 50 mins) between these two ports. There are several trips daily. The company also runs between Rosslare and Pembroke, Wales (3 hrs, 45 mins), and has service to France. Stena Line sails several times a day between Dublin and Holyhead (3 hrs,

15 mins) and has swift service to Dun Laoghaire (2 hrs). The company also runs a fast craft (2 hrs) and a superferry (3 hrs) between Belfast and Stranraer, Scotland, as well as a fast craft (2 hrs) between Rosslare and Fishguard, Wales. There are several trips daily on both routes.

Norfolk Line offers a Dublin and Belfast to Liverpool service (8 hrs). P&O Irish Sea vessels run between Larne and Troon, Scotland (2 hrs), a couple of times a day. The company also sails from Dublin to Liverpool twice daily (8 hrs) with a choice of daytime or overnight sailings.

WITHIN IRELAND

There are regular services to the Aran Islands from Ros an Mhil (Rossaveal) in County Galway, and Doolin in County Clare. Ferries also sail to Inishbofin off the Galway coast and Arranmore off the Donegal coast, and to Bere, Whiddy, Sherkin, and Cape Clear Islands off the coast of County Cork. Bere and Whiddy have a car ferry, but the other islands are all small enough to explore on foot, so the ferries are for foot passengers and bicycles only. Other islands—the Blaskets and the Skelligs in Kerry, Rathlin in Antrim, and Tory, off the Donegal coast—have seasonal ferry services running daily between May and September, less frequently outside these months. Failte Ireland publishes a free guide and map with ferry details, *Ireland's Islands,* or see ⊕ *www.irelandsislands. com.* Alternatively, check with the nearest Tourist Information Office near the time of your visit, or see ⊕ *www.discoverireland. ie.* Boating the Shannon River system is an appealing alternative to traveling overland. In some places bicycles can be rented so you can drop anchor and explore. *See the Getting Here and Around sections in the various regional towns and cities for other ferry routes.*

FARES AND SCHEDULES

You can get schedules and purchase tickets, with a credit card if you like, directly from the ferry lines. You can also pick up tickets at Dublin tourism offices and at any major travel agent in Ireland or the United Kingdom. Payment must be made in the currency of the country of the port of departure. Bad weather can delay or cancel ferry sailings so it's always a good idea to call before departing for the port.

Information Irish Ferries ☎ *0818/300–400 in Ireland, 08717/300–400 in U.K.* ⊕ *www.irishferries.com.* **Norfolk Line.** ☎ *01/819–2999 in Ireland, 0844/499–0007 in U.K.* ⊕ *www.norfolkline.com.* **P&O Irish Sea** ☎ *01/407–3434 in Ireland, 0871/664–4999 in U.K.* ⊕ *www.poferries.com.* **Stena Line** ☎ *01/204–7777 in Ireland, 028/9074–7747 in Northern Ireland, 084/4770–7070 in U.K.* ⊕ *www.stenaline.co.uk.*

Boat Travel on the Shannon
Carrickcraft ✉ *Lurgan* ☎ *028/3834–4993* ⊕ *www.carrickcraft.com.* **Emerald Star** ✉ *Connaught Harbor, Portumna* ☎ *071/962–7633* ⊕ *www.emeraldstar.ie.* **Riversdale Barge Holidays** ✉ *Ballinamore* ☎ *071/964–4122* ⊕ *www.riversdalebargeholidays.com.* **Shannon Cruisers** ✉ *Williamstown Harbor, Whitegate* ☎ *061/927–042* ⊕ *www.shannoncruisers.com.* **Silver Line Cruisers** ✉ *The Marina, Banagher* ☎ *057/915–1112* ⊕ *www.silverlinecruisers. com.* **Waveline Cruisers** ✉ *Quigley's Marina, Killinure Point, Glassan* ☎ *0906/485–711* ⊕ *www.waveline.ie.*

▌ BUS TRAVEL

In the Republic of Ireland, long-distance bus services are operated by Bus Éireann, which also provides local service in Cork, Galway, Limerick, and Waterford. There's only one class, and prices are similar for all seats. Note, though, that outside of the peak season, services are limited; some routes (e.g., Ring of Kerry) disappear altogether.

A new chapter in Bus Éireann service opened several years ago with the addition of their Expressway service. Expressway buses go directly, in the straightest available line, from one biggish town to another, and stop at a limited number of designated places only. There's sometimes only one trip a day on express routes. Their other divisions comprise commuter buses, as in the rest of the world, and then a kind of community service bus that rambles around the countryside passing through as many villages as possible, and stopping wherever anyone wants to get on or off, allowing as many people as possible to get to the nearest big town at least once a week. This used to be the *only* kind of bus service 30 years ago, which is why Bus Éireann so proudly trumpets their Expressway network.

Rural bus services shut down at around 7 or 8 pm. To ensure that a bus journey is feasible, buy a copy of Bus Éireann's timetable—€3 from any bus terminal— or check online. Many of the destination indicators are in Irish (Gaelic), so make sure you get on the right bus.

IN NORTHERN IRELAND

In Northern Ireland, all buses are operated by the state-owned Ulsterbus. Service is generally good, with particularly useful links to those towns not served by train. Ulsterbus also offers tours. Buses to Belfast run from London and from Birmingham, making the Stranraer–Port of Belfast crossing. Contact National Express for that specific route.

▌TIP→ Prepaid tickets don't apply to a particular bus time, just a route, so show up at least 30 minutes early to get a seat. If one vehicle is full, you will have to wait for the next bus.

FARES AND PASSES

You can buy tickets online, or at the main tourist offices, at the bus station, or on the bus (though it's cash only for the latter option). A round-trip from Dublin to Cork costs €22 and Dublin to Galway return is €19.

You can save money by buying a multi-day pass, some of which can be combined with rail service. There are also cost-cutting passes that will give access to travel in both Northern Ireland and the Republic of Ireland. An iLink Card costs £55 for seven days' unlimited bus and rail travel in all parts of Northern Ireland—a really good deal when you consider that a one-day ticket costs £15. In the republic, passes include the Irish Explorer Rail and Bus Pass, which gives you eight days' bus travel out of 15 consecutive days for €245. The bus-only Irish Rover Card costs €190 for eight days' travel out of 15 consecutive days across both Northern Ireland and the republic. Contact Bus Éireann or Ulsterbus for details.

An Irish Rover bus ticket from Ulsterbus covers Ireland, north and south, and costs £56 for 3 days, £127 for 8, and £188 for 15. It also includes city center bus travel in Cork, Waterford, Limerick, Galway, and on the Metro services in Belfast—but not Dublin.

Bus Information Bus Éireann ☎ 01/836–6111 in Republic of Ireland ⊕ www.buseireann.ie. Eurolines ☎ 08717/818–178 in U.K. ⊕ www.eurolines. co.uk. Ulsterbus ☎ 028/9066–6630 in Northern Ireland ⊕ www.ulsterbus.co.uk.

▌ CAR TRAVEL

U.S. driver's licenses are recognized in Ireland.

Roads in the Irish Republic are generally good, though four-lane highways, or motorways, are the exception rather than the rule. In addition, many roads twist and wind their way up and down hills and through towns, which can slow you down. On small, rural roads, watch out for cattle and sheep; they may be just around the next bend. Reckless drivers (surveys says that Irish drivers are among the worst) are also a problem in the countryside, so remain cautious and alert.

ROAD SIGNS

Road signs in the republic are generally in both Irish (Gaelic) and English; destinations in which Irish is the spoken language are signposted only in Irish. The most important one to know is An Daingean, which is now the official name of Dingle Town. ▌TIP→ Get a good bilingual road map and know the name of the next town on your itinerary; neither the small local signposts nor the local people refer to roads by official numbers. Traffic signs are the same as in the rest of Europe, and roadway markings are standard. On the new green signposts in the republic distances are in kilometers; on some of the old white signposts they're still miles, but the majority of signposts are in kilometers. Most important, remember that speed limits are signposted in the republic (but not in Northern Ireland) in kilometers.

There are no border checkpoints between the republic and Northern Ireland, where the road network is excellent and, outside Belfast, uncrowded. Road signs and traffic regulations conform to the British system.

CAR FERRIES

All ferries on both principal routes to the Irish Republic take cars. Fishguard and Pembroke are relatively easy to reach by road. The car trip to Holyhead, on the other hand, is sometimes difficult: delays on the A55 North Wales coastal road aren't unusual. *See Boat Travel.*

GASOLINE

You can find gas stations along most roads. Self-service is the norm. Major credit cards and traveler's checks are usually accepted. Prices are near the lower end for Europe, with unleaded gas priced around €1.25 in Ireland and £1.12 a liter in Northern Ireland—gasoline prices in the United States are a bit more than half the price in Ireland. Prices vary significantly from station to station, so it's worth driving around the block (if you have enough gas!).

ROAD CONDITIONS

Most roads are paved and make for easy travel. Roads are classified as M, N, or R: those designated with an M for "motorway" are double-lane divided highways with paved shoulders; N, or national, routes are generally undivided highways with shoulders; and R, or regional, roads tend to be narrow and twisty.

Rush-hour traffic in Dublin, Cork, Limerick, Belfast, and Galway can be intense. Rush hours in Dublin run 7 am to 9:30 am and 5 pm to 7 pm; special events such as football (soccer) games will also tie up traffic in and around the city, as will heavy rain.

ROADSIDE EMERGENCIES

Membership in an emergency car service is a good idea if you're using your own vehicle in Ireland. The Automobile Association of Ireland is a sister organization of its English counterpart and is highly recommended. Note that the AA can help you or your vehicle only if you are a member of the association. If not, contact your car-rental company for assistance. If involved in an accident you should note the details of the vehicle and the driver and witnesses and report the incident to a member of the Garda Síochána (the Irish Police) or the Police Service of Northern Ireland (PSNI) as soon as possible. Since traffic congestion is chronic in Dublin, emergency services are more likely to be dispatched quickly to help you and to clear the road. If your car does break down, if at all possible try to stop it in a well-lighted area near a public phone. If you're on a secondary or minor road, remain in your car with the doors locked after you call for assistance. If you break down on the motorway, you should pull onto the hard shoulder and stay out of your car with the passenger side door open and the other doors locked. This will allow you to jump into the car quickly if you sense any trouble. Make sure you check credentials of anyone who offers assistance—note the license-plate number and color of the assisting vehicle before you step out of the car.

Emergency Services An Garda Síochána (Police) ☎ 112, 999 ⊕ www.garda.ie.
Automobile Association of Ireland ☎ 01/617–9999 in Ireland, 0800/887–766 in Northern Ireland, 08457/887–766 from cell phone in Northern Ireland ⊕ www.aaireland.ie.
Police Service of Northern Ireland ☎ 999 ⊕ www.psni.police.uk.

RULES OF THE ROAD

The Irish, like the British, drive on the left-hand side of the road in whatever direction they are headed (not, as in America, on the right-hand side). Safety belts must be worn by the driver and all passengers, and children under 12 must travel in the back unless riding in a car seat. It's compulsory for motorcyclists and their passengers to wear helmets. Speed limits in Ireland are posted in kilometers per hour and in Northern Ireland in miles per hour, so if crossing the border, be sure to make the adjustment. In towns and cities the speed limit is 50 kph (31 mph). On Regional (R) and Local (L) roads, the speed limit is 80 kph (50 mph), indicated by white signs. On National (N) roads, the speed limit is 100 kph (62 mph), indicated by green signs. On Motorways (M), the speed limit is 120 kph (74 mph), indicated by blue signs.

Drunk-driving laws are strict. The legal limit is 50 mg of alcohol per 100 ml of blood. Ireland has a Breathalyzer test, which the police can administer anytime. If you refuse to take it, the odds are you'll be prosecuted anyway. As always, the best advice is don't drink if you plan to drive.

Speed cameras and radar are used throughout Ireland. Speeding carries an on-the-spot fine of €80, and if the Gardaí (police) charge you with excessive speeding you could be summoned to court. This carries a much higher fine, and you will be summoned within six months (meaning you could be required to return to Ireland).

Note that a continuous white line down the center of the road prohibits passing. Barred markings on the road and flashing yellow beacons indicate a crossing, where pedestrians have right of way. At a junction of two roads of equal importance, the driver to the right has right of way. On a roundabout, vehicles approaching from the right have right of way. Also, remember there are no left turns permitted on a red light. ■ TIP→ If another motorist flashes their headlights at you, they are giving you right of way (or warning of a Gardaí/police checkpoint up ahead).

Despite the relatively light traffic, parking in towns can be a problem. Signs with the letter *P* indicate that parking is permitted; a stroke through the *P* warns you to stay away or you'll be liable for a fine of €20–€65; however, if your car gets towed away or clamped, the fine is around €180. In Dublin and Cork, parking lots are your best bet, but check the rate first in Dublin; they vary wildly.

In Northern Ireland there are plenty of parking lots in the towns (usually free except in Belfast), and you should use them. In Belfast, you can't park your car in some parts of the city center, more because of congestion than security problems.

RENTAL CARS

When you reserve a car, ask about cancellation penalties, taxes, drop-off charges (if you're planning to pick up the car in one city and leave it in another), and surcharges (for being under or over a certain age, for additional drivers, or for driving across state or country borders or beyond a specific distance from your point of rental). All these things can add substantially to your costs. Request car seats and extras such as GPS when you book.

Rates are sometimes—but not always—better if you book in advance or reserve through a rental agency's website. There are other reasons to book ahead, though: for popular destinations, during busy times of the year, or to ensure that you get certain types of cars (vans, SUVs, exotic sports cars).

■ TIP→ Make sure that a confirmed reservation guarantees you a car. Agencies sometimes overbook, particularly for busy weekends and holiday periods.

If you're renting a car in the Irish Republic and intend to visit Northern Ireland (or vice versa), make this clear when you get your car, and check that the rental insurance applies when you cross the border.

Renting a car in Ireland is far more expensive than organizing a rental before you leave home. Rates in Dublin for an economy car with a manual transmission and unlimited mileage are from about €35 a day and €160 a week to €50 a day and €190 a week, depending on the season. This includes the republic's 12.5% tax on car rentals. Rates in Belfast begin at £25 a day and £130 a week, including the 17.5% tax on car rentals in the North.

Both manual and automatic transmissions are readily available, though automatics cost extra. Typical economy car models include Volkswagen Lupo, Ford Focus, Fiat Panda, and Nissan Micra. Minivans, luxury cars (Mercedes or Alfa Romeos), and four-wheel-drive vehicles (say, a Jeep Cherokee) are also options, but the daily rates are high. Argus Rent A Car and Dan Dooley have convenient locations at Dublin, Shannon, Belfast, and Belfast City airports as well as at ferry ports.

Most rental companies require you to be over 24 to rent a car in Ireland (a few will rent to those over 21) and to have had a license for more than a year. Some companies refuse to rent to visitors over 70, or in some cases 74. Children under 12 years of age aren't allowed to ride in the front seat unless they're in a properly fitted child seat.

Drivers between the ages of 21 and 26, and 70 and 76 will probably be subject to an insurance surcharge—if they're allowed to drive a rental car at all. An additional driver will add about €5 a day to your car rental, and a child seat costs about €20 for the rental and will require 24-hour advance notice.

Your driver's license may not be recognized outside your home country. You may not be able to rent a car without an International Driving Permit (IDP), which can be used only in conjunction with a valid driver's license and which translates your license into 10 languages. Check the AAA website for more info as well as for IDPs ($10) themselves. Happily, U.S. driver's licenses are recognized in Ireland.

CAR RENTAL RESOURCES

Local Agencies Local and international car hire companies in both the Republic and Northern Ireland are listed on ⊕ *www.carhireireland.com*. **Argus Rent A Car** ☎ *023/888–3002 in Ireland and Northern Ireland* ⊕ *www.argus-rentacar.com*. **Dooley Car Rentals** ☎ *800/331–9301 in U.S., 062/53103 in Ireland* ⊕ *www.dan-dooley.ie*.

Major Agencies Avis ☎ *800/331–1212 in U.S., 021/428–1111 in Ireland* ⊕ *www.avis.com*. **Budget** ☎ *800/472–3325 from U.S., 09/066–27711 in Ireland* ⊕ *www.budget.com*. **Dollar** ☎ *800/800–6000 in U.S., 01/670–7890 in Dublin* ⊕ *www.dollar.com*. **Hertz** ☎ *800/654–3001, 01/676–7476 in Ireland* ⊕ *www.hertz.com*. **National Car Rental** ☎ *877/222–9058, 01/812–2800 in Dublin (serviced by Europcar)* ⊕ *www.nationalcar.com*.

Wholesalers Auto Europe ☎ *888/223–5555 in U.S., 800/943–075 in Ireland* ⊕ *www.autoeurope.com*. **Europe by Car** ☎ *800/223–1516, 212/581–3040 in U.S.* ⊕ *www.europebycar.com*. **Eurovacations** ☎ *877/471–3876* ⊕ *www.eurovacations.com*. **Kemwel** ☎ *800/678–0678* ⊕ *www.kemwel.com*.

▮ TRAIN TRAVEL

The republic's Irish Rail trains are generally reliable, reasonably priced, and comfortable. You can easily reach all the principal towns from Dublin, though services between provincial cities are roundabout. To get to Cork City from Wexford, for example, you have to go via Limerick Junction. It's often quicker, though perhaps less comfortable, to take a bus. Most mainline trains have one standard class. Round-trip tickets are usually cheapest. Northern Ireland Railways has three main rail routes, all operating out of Belfast's Central Station. These are north to Derry, via Ballymena and Coleraine; east to Bangor along the shores of Belfast Lough; and south to Dublin and the Irish Republic. Note that Eurail Passes aren't valid in Northern Ireland.

▮TIP→ Get to the train station at least 30 minutes before your train departs to ensure you'll get a seat. It's not uncommon on busier routes to find that you have to stand since all seats have been sold and taken.

FARES AND PASSES

Tickets can be purchased online or at the train station. Cash, traveler's checks, and credit-card payments are accepted. You must pay in the local currency. Dublin, Connolly, and Heuston stations have automated ticket machines that take either cash or credit-card payments, offering a convenient way to avoid long lines at ticket windows.

Sample fares? A return ticket from Dublin to Cork will cost around €60; Dublin to Belfast is approximately €55. Considerable savings can be made by booking online where off-peak tickets cost as little as €10 each way on most long journeys.

Ireland (excluding Northern Ireland) is one of 22 countries in which you can use an **InterRail Pass**, which provides unlimited rail travel in all of the participating countries for the duration of the pass. If you plan to rack up the miles, get a standard pass. These are available from Rail Europe (the company that services many of the passes listed here), for 15 days (€769), 21 days (€989), and one month (€1,219). In addition to standard Eurail Passes, ask about special rail-pass plans. Among these are the **Eurail Youth Pass** (for those under age 26), the **Eurail Saver Pass** (which gives a discount for two or more people traveling together), the **EurailDrive Pass**, and the **Eurail Select Pass 'n Drive** (which combines travel by train and rental car). Whichever pass you choose, you must purchase your pass before you leave for Europe. For these passes, buy online from ⊕ *www.Eurail. com* or through your travel agent.

The **Irish Explorer Rail & Bus Pass** covers all the state-run and national railways and bus lines throughout the republic. It does not apply to the North or to transportation within cities. An eight-day ticket for use on buses *and* trains during a 15-day period is €245. Irish Rail provides details on both (bus and rail) passes.

In Northern Ireland, the iLink Card entitling you to up to seven days' unlimited travel on scheduled bus and rail services throughout Northern Ireland is available from main Northern Ireland Railways stations. It costs about £55 for adults (half price for children under 12 and senior citizens). InterRail tickets are also valid in Northern Ireland.

There's only one class of train travel in Ireland (with the exception of the Enterprise, the express train that travels from Dublin to Belfast, for which you can purchase a First Class or Standard Class ticket, and the Dublin to Cork train). All tickets bought online on the Cork–Dublin train include a seat reservation. Otherwise, specific seat reservations can be made only for trains deemed to be busy (ask when buying your ticket if they're taking reservations for your route).

Information and Passes

Eurail ⊕ *www.eurail.com.* **Fáilte Ireland** ⊕ *www.discoverireland.com.*

Train Information Irish Rail (*Iarnrod Éireann*). ☏ *01/836–6222* ⊕ *www.irishrail.ie.* **Northern Ireland Railways** ☏ *028/9066–6630* ⊕ *www.translink.co.uk/NI-Railways.*

Train Station Information Belfast Central Station ✉ *East Bridge St., Belfast, Northern Ireland* ☏ *028/9089–9400* ⊕ *www.translink. co.uk.* **Connolly Station** ✉ *Amiens St., Dublin* ☏ *01/703–2358* ⊕ *www.irishrail.ie.* **Galway Station** ✉ *Station Rd., Galway* ☏ *091/564–222* ⊕ *www.irishrail.ie.* **Heuston Station** ✉ *Dublin* ☏ *01/703–2132* ⊕ *www.irishrail.ie.* **Kent Station** ✉ *Lower Glanmire Rd., Cork* ☏ *021/450–6766* ⊕ *www.irishrail.ie.*

ESSENTIALS

▌ACCOMMODATIONS

From cottages to castles, Ireland has a vast range of accommodations. And while some of them rank among Europe's prettiest and priciest, the recent economic downturn has meant one thing: bargains galore. One minute of research will uncover deals like two nights and a B&B with two dinners, all for about half of the full price, sometimes with a third night free. Many hotels have halved their prices since 2008, the height of the Celtic Tiger boom years. So remember to ask for a discount and see what they offer.

In Dublin and other cities, boutique hotels combine luxury with contemporary (and often truly Irish) design. Manors and castles offer a unique combination of luxury and history. Less impressive, but equally charming, are the provincial inns and country hotels with simple but adequate facilities.

You can meet a wide cross section of Irish people by hopping from one bed-and-breakfast to the next, or you can keep to yourself for a week or two in a thatched cottage. B&Bs approved by Tourism Ireland display a green shamrock outside and are usually considered more reputable than unregistered ones. Hotels and other accommodations in Northern Ireland are similar to those in the Republic of Ireland.

Fáilte Ireland has a grading system and maintains a list of registered hotels, guesthouses, B&Bs, farmhouses, hostels, and campgrounds. For each accommodation, the list gives a maximum charge that can't be exceeded without special authorization. Prices must be displayed in every room; if the hotel oversteps its limit, don't hesitate to complain to the hotel manager and/or Fáilte Ireland.

Prices in the reviews are the lowest cost of a standard double room in high season.

APARTMENT AND HOUSE RENTALS

Local Agents Fáilte Ireland ☎ 1890/324–583 ⊕ www.discoverireland.ie. **Premier Suites Dublin** ☎ 01/638–1111 ⊕ www.premiersuitesdublin.com.

ONLINE BOOKING RESOURCES

Contacts At Home Abroad ☎ 212/421–9165 ⊕ www.athomeabroadinc.com. **Barclay International Group** ☎ 516/364–0064, 800/845–6636 ⊕ www.barclayweb.com. **Drawbridge to Europe** ☎ 541/482–7778, 888/268–1148 ⊕ www.drawbridgetoeurope. com. **Interhome** ☎ 800/882–6864 ⊕ www.interhomeusa.com. **Suzanne B. Cohen & Associates** ☎ 207/622–0743 ⊕ www.villaeurope.com. **Villas & Apartments Abroad** ☎ 212/213–6435, 800/433–3020 ⊕ www.vaanyc.com. **Villas International** ☎ 415/499–9490, 800/221–2260 ⊕ www.villasintl.com.

BED AND BREAKFASTS

B&Bs are classified either as town homes, country homes, or farmhouses. Most B&Bs now have private bathrooms for most bedrooms, but don't expect this as a matter of course. Some B&Bs are on farms, but the "farmhouses" are more likely to be modern bungalows than undistinguished two-story houses than creeper-clad Georgian mansions. However, there are some mansions offering B&B, and rooms are priced accordingly. At the lower end of the price scale, expect to pay an average of €35–€40 per person per night. Ask for a reduction if you are staying more than one night. Many travelers don't bother booking a B&B in advance. They are so plentiful in rural areas that it's often more fun to leave the decision open, allowing yourself a choice of final destinations for the night. Long weekends are the exception to this rule, with B&Bs often getting booked up far in advance, so keep an eye on the calendar of local holidays. If you want to be sure of staying in a family home, check out the places listed by Family Homes of Ireland.

To qualify as a guesthouse, establishments must have at least five bedrooms. Some guesthouses are above a bar or restaurant; others are part of a home. As a rule, they're cheaper (some include an optional evening meal) and offer fewer amenities than hotels. But often that's where the differences end. Most have high standards of cleanliness and hospitality, and most have a bathroom, a TV, and a direct-dial phone in each room. Premier Guesthouses are generally small inns, run by the owner, and hard to distinguish from hotels.

Local Services Family Homes of Ireland ☎ *091/552–000* ⊕ *www.familyhomes. ie.* **B&B Ireland** ☎ *071/982–2222* ⊕ *www.bandbireland.com.* **Premier Guesthouses of Ireland** ☎ *01/205–2826* ⊕ *www.premierguesthouses.com.*

CASTLES AND MANORS

Among the most magical experiences on an Irish vacation are stays at some of the country's spectacular castle-hotels, such as Dromoland (Co. Clare), Ashford (Co. Galway), and Waterford Castle (near Waterford City). For directories to help you get to know the wide array of manor house and castle accommodations, including a goodly number of private country estates and castles, contact Ireland's Blue Book of Country Houses & Restaurants, or Hidden Ireland.

Reservations Services Hidden Ireland ☎ *098/66650* ⊕ *www.hiddenireland.com.* **Ireland's Blue Book** ☎ *01/676–9914* ⊕ *www.irelands-blue-book.ie.*

COTTAGES

Vacation cottages, which are usually in clusters, are rented by the week. Although often built in the traditional style, most have central heating and all the other modern conveniences. It's essential to reserve in advance.

Reservations Services Discover Northern Ireland ⊠ *59 North St., Belfast, Northern Ireland* ☎ *44 28/9024–6609* ⊕ *www.discovernorthernireland.com.* **Irish Cottage Holiday Homes** ⊠ *Bracken Court, Bracken Rd., Sandyford, Dublin* ☎ *01/205–2777* ⊕ *www.irishcottageholidays.com.*

HOTELS

Standard features in most hotels include private bath, two twin beds (you can usually ask for a king-size instead), TV (often with DVD), free parking, and no-smoking rooms. There's usually no extra charge for these services. All hotels listed have private bath unless otherwise noted.

Information Irish Hotels Federation ☎ *01/808–4419* ⊕ *www.irelandhotels. com.* **Northern Ireland Hotels Federation** ☎ *048/9077–6635* ⊕ *www.nihf.co.uk.* **Discover Ireland** ☎ *800/7426–7025* ⊕ *www.discoverireland.com.*

❚ COMMUNICATIONS

INTERNET

If you're traveling with a laptop, carry a spare battery and adapter. Most laptops will work at both 120V and 220V, but you will need an adapter so the plug will fit in the socket. In the countryside, a surge protector is a good idea.

Going online is becoming routine in Dublin, thanks, in part, to the Wi-Fi hotspots—which allow you to make a wireless connection from your laptop onto a network—popping up across the city. Net House, an Internet café chain, has the most locations in the country, with nine in Dublin and one in Cork.

There are also many independent Internet cafés across the country. Prices vary from the low end in Dublin of €2.60 per hour to €5 per hour in smaller cities. There are also many Wi-Fi hotspots (not just focused on Internet users) throughout the country, such as the Insomnia Coffee/Sandwich Bar chain in Galway. Dublin Airport and Dun Laoghaire Harbor have facilities to access wireless connection to the Internet. Most hotels in cities and large towns now offer a Wi-Fi hotspot in the lobby or lounge. A Wi-Fi connection can cost about €9 for an hour or €22 for unlimited access within a 24-hour period. In most cases, however, Wi-Fi access is free if you are using the facilities of the hotel or café.

Contacts Cybercafes. Cybercafes lists over 4,000 Internet cafés worldwide. ⊕ www.cybercafes.com.

PHONES

Ireland's telephone system is up to the standards of the United Kingdom and the United States. Direct-dialing is common; local phone numbers have five to eight digits. You can make international calls from most phones, and some cell phones also work here, depending on the carrier.

Do not make calls from your hotel room unless it's absolutely necessary. Practically all hotels add 200% to 300% to the cost. As expensive as mobile phone calls can be, they are still usually a much cheaper option than calling from your hotel.

The country code for Ireland is 353; for Northern Ireland, which is part of the United Kingdom telephone system, it's 44. The local area code for Northern Ireland is 028. However, when dialing Northern Ireland from the republic you can simply dial 048 without using the U.K. country code. When dialing an Irish number from abroad, drop the initial 0 from the local area code. The country code is 1 for the United States and Canada, 61 for Australia, 64 for New Zealand, and 44 for the United Kingdom.

Public pay phones can be found in street booths and in restaurants, hotels, bars, and shops, some of which display a sign saying "you can phone from here." There are at least three models of pay phones; read the instructions or ask for assistance.

CALLING WITHIN IRELAND

If the operator has to connect your call, it will cost at least one-third more than direct dial.

Directory Information Republic of Ireland ☎ *11811 for directory inquiries and operator assistance in the republic and Northern Ireland, 11818 for U.K. and international numbers.* **Northern Ireland.** ☎ *118118 for directory inquiries in Northern Ireland, 118505 for international directory inquiries, which includes the republic, 155 for the international operator, 100 for operator assistance for calls in Northern Ireland.*

Public phones take either coins or cards, but not both. Card phones are rapidly replacing coin-operated phones, and are also cheaper. Phone cards can be bought at newsagents, convenience stores, and post offices in units of €5 upwards. It's worth carrying one, especially in rural areas where coin-operated phones are a rarity. In the republic, €0.40 will buy you a three-minute local call; around €1.50 is needed for a three-minute long-distance call within the republic. In Northern Ireland, a local call costs 20p.

To make a local call, just dial the number direct. To make a long-distance call, dial the area code, then the number. The local code for Northern Ireland is 028, unless you're dialing from the republic, in which case you dial 048 or 004428, followed by the eight-digit number.

CALLING OUTSIDE IRELAND

The country code for the United States is 1.

The international prefix from Ireland is 00. For calls to Great Britain (except Northern Ireland), dial 0044 before the exchange code, and drop the initial zero of the local code. For the United States and Canada dial 001, for Australia 0061, and for New Zealand 0064.

Access Codes AT&T Direct ☎ *1800/550–000 from Republic of Ireland, 0500/890–011 from Northern Ireland.* **MCI WorldPhone** ☎ *1800/551–001 from Republic of Ireland, 0800/890–222 from Northern Ireland using British Telecom [BT], 0500/890–222 using Cable & Wireless [C&W].* **Sprint International Access** ☎ *1800/552–001 from Republic of Ireland, 0800/890–877 from Northern Ireland using BT, 0500/890–877 using C&W.*

CALLING CARDS

"Callcards" are sold in post offices and newsagents. These range in price from €5 to €30.

MOBILE PHONES

If you have a multiband phone (some countries use different frequencies from those used in the United States) and your service provider uses the world-standard GSM network (as do T-Mobile and Verizon), you can probably use your phone abroad. Roaming fees can be steep, however: 99¢ a minute is considered reasonable. And overseas you normally pay the toll charges for incoming calls. It's almost always cheaper to send a text message than to make a call, since text messages have a very low set fee (often less than 5¢).

If you just want to make local calls, consider buying a new SIM card (note that your provider may have to unlock your phone for you to use a different SIM card) and a prepaid service plan in the destination. You'll then have a local number and can make local calls at local rates. If your trip is extensive, you could also simply buy a new cell phone in your destination, as the initial cost will be offset over time.

■TIP➔ If you travel internationally frequently, save one of your old mobile phones or buy a cheap one on the Internet; ask your cell phone company to unlock it for you, and take it with you as a travel phone, buying a new SIM card with pay-as-you-go service in each destination.

Contacts **Cellular Abroad**. Cellular Abroad rents and sells GMS phones and sells SIM cards that work in many countries. ☎ *800/287–5072* ⊕ *www.cellularabroad.com*. **Mobal**. Mobal rents mobiles and sells GSM phones (starting at $49) that will operate in 140 countries. Per-call rates vary throughout the world. ☎ *888/888–9162* ⊕ *www.mobal.com*. **Planet Fone**. Planet Fone rents cell phones, but the per-minute rates are expensive. ☎ *888/988–4777* ⊕ *www.planetfone.com*.

▌CUSTOMS AND DUTIES

You're always allowed to bring goods of a certain value back home without having to pay any duty or import tax. But there's a limit on the amount of tobacco and liquor you can bring back duty-free, and—if you are traveling to additional destinations after your visit to Ireland—some countries have separate limits for perfumes; for exact figures, check with your customs department. The values of so-called "duty-free" goods are included in these amounts. When you shop abroad, save all your receipts, as customs inspectors may ask to see them as well as the items you purchased. If the total value of your goods is more than the duty-free limit, you'll have to pay a tax (most often a flat percentage) on the value of everything beyond that limit.

Duty-free allowances have been abolished for those traveling between countries in the EU. For goods purchased outside the EU, you may import duty-free: (1) 200 cigarettes or 100 cigarillos or 50 cigars or 250 grams of smoking tobacco; (2) 2 liters of wine, and either 1 liter of alcoholic drink over 22% volume or 2 liters of alcoholic drink under 22% volume (sparkling or fortified wine included); (3) 50 grams (60 ml) of perfume and ¼ liter of eau de toilette; and (4) other goods (including beer) to a value of €175 per person (€90 per person for travelers under 15 years of age).

Goods that cannot be freely imported to the Irish Republic include firearms, ammunition, explosives, indecent or obscene books and pictures, oral smokeless tobacco products, meat and meat products, poultry and poultry products. Plants and plant products (including shrubs, vegetables, fruit, bulbs, and seeds) can be imported from other countries within the EU only, provided they are eligible under the EU's plant passport scheme. Domestic cats and dogs from outside the United Kingdom and live animals from outside Northern Ireland

LANGUAGE DO'S AND TABOOS

In the old days, Ireland's native language was called Gaelic and some people chuckled that it was the world's most perfect medium for prayers, curses, and lovemaking.

These days, Gaelic is called Irish and no one is joking any longer.

In March 2005, legislation was passed to restore the sovereignty of Irish, originally a Celtic language related to Scots Gaelic, Breton, and Welsh, as Ireland's official national language.

English is technically the second language of the country but it is, in fact, the everyday tongue of 95% of the population.

However, the western coastlands of Ireland are still home to the Gaeltacht (pronounced *gale*-taukt).

These Irish-speaking communities are found mainly in sparsely populated rural areas along the western seaboard, on some islands, and in pockets in West Cork and County Waterford.

Travelers to these western seaboard regions in counties Donegal and Galway should note that new laws have mandated Irish as the sole language for signage.

In these Gaeltacht areas, English is now outlawed on road signs and official maps.

As the Associated Press reported, "Locals concede the switch will confuse foreigners in an area that depends heavily on tourism, but they say it's the price of patriotism."

The Gaeltacht includes some big tourist destinations.

For instance, if travelers are in Killarney and now wish to go to Dingle, they will have to follow signposts that say "An Daingean," which is Dingle in Irish.

Other instances include: Oileáin Árainn (Aran Islands); Corca Dhuibne (Dingle Peninsula); and Arainn Mhor (Aranmore Island).

As this changeover affects more than 2,000 other place-names, have an updated or Irish-friendly map if touring these Gaeltacht regions.

Don't rely on official Ordnance Survey maps, which can now print only Irish place-names in these areas.

This is even in cases where the English versions remain popular in local parlance (many hotels will retain their English names, such as the Dingle Bay Hotel).

Main place-names are given in both Irish and English in this guidebook for the affected regions.

Outside these Gaeltacht areas, Ireland remains officially bilingual in its road signs.

With just 55,000 native Irish speakers in a population of 4 million, a major national debate has sprung up, with local councils and tourist authorities beginning to protest the new laws.

Follow the debate by searching online for "Official Languages Act 2003."

Of course, some basic Irish vocabulary certainly wouldn't hurt: *fir* (men) and *mná* (women) should prove useful when using public restrooms.

must be quarantined for six months, unless they are traveling under the EU's Pet Travel Scheme.

Information in Ireland Customs and Excise ⊠ *Government Buildings, St Conlon's Rd., Nenagh, Co. Tipperary* ☎ *067/63400* ⊕ *www.revenue.ie.* **HM Customs and Excise** ⊠ *Crownhill Ct., Tailyour Rd., Plymouth, England* ☎ *0845/010–9000* ⊕ *www.hmrc.gov. uk.* **Pet Travel Scheme.** For details of the Pet Travel Scheme see: ⊕ *www.agriculture.gov.ie.*

U.S. Information U.S. Customs and Border Protection ⊕ *www.cbp.gov.*

▊ EATING OUT

MEALS AND MEALTIMES
Unless otherwise noted, the restaurants listed here are open daily for lunch and dinner.

No longer will you "enjoy" your favorite tipple in the blue haze of a smoke-filled pub. The Republic of Ireland became the first European country to ban smoking in all pubs and restaurants in March 2004. A smoking ban was introduced in Northern Ireland in 2007.

Breakfast is served from 7 to 10, lunch runs from 12:30 to 2:30, and dinners are usually midevening occasions.

Pubs are generally open Monday and Tuesday 10:30 am–11:30 pm and Wednesday–Saturday 10:30 am–12:30 am. On Sunday, pubs are open 12:30 pm–11 pm or later on certain Sundays. All pubs close on Christmas Day and Good Friday, but hotel bars are open for guests.

Pubs in Northern Ireland are open 11:30 am–11 pm Monday–Saturday and 12:30 pm–2:30 pm and 7 pm–10 pm on Sunday (note that Sunday openings are at the owner's or manager's discretion).

PAYING
Traveler's checks and credit cards are widely accepted, although it's cash-only at smaller pubs and takeout restaurants.

WORD OF MOUTH

Was the service stellar or not up to snuff? Did the food give you shivers of delight or leave you cold? Did the prices and portions make you happy or sad? Rate restaurants and write your own reviews in Travel Ratings or start a discussion about your favorite places in Travel Talk on ⊕ *www.fodors.com.* Your comments might even appear in our books. Yes, you, too, can be a correspondent!

Prices in the reviews are the average cost of a main course at dinner or, if dinner is not served, at lunch.

For guidelines on tipping see Tipping, below.

RESERVATIONS AND DRESS
Regardless of where you are, it's a good idea to make a reservation if you can. In some places, it's expected. We mention them specifically only when reservations are essential (there's no other way you'll ever get a table) or when they are not accepted. For popular restaurants, book as far ahead as you can (often 30 days), and reconfirm as soon as you arrive. (Large parties should always call ahead to check the reservations policy.) We mention dress only when men are required to wear a jacket or a jacket and tie.

WINES, BEER, AND SPIRITS
All types of alcoholic beverages are available in Ireland. Beer and wine are sold in shops and supermarkets, and you can get drinks "to go" at some bars, although at inflated prices. Stout (Guinness, Murphy's, Beamish) is the Irish beer; whiskey comes in many brands, the most notable being Bushmills and Jameson, and is smoother than Scotch.

■ ELECTRICITY

The current in Ireland is 220 volts, 50 cycles alternating current (AC); wall outlets take plugs with three prongs.

Consider making a small investment in a universal adapter, which has several types of plugs in one lightweight, compact unit. Most laptops and mobile phone chargers are dual voltage (i.e., they operate equally well on 110 and 220 volts), and so require only an adapter. These days the same is true of small appliances such as hair dryers. Always check labels and manufacturer instructions to be sure. Don't use 110-volt outlets marked "for shavers only" for high-wattage appliances such as hair dryers.

Contacts Steve Kropla's Help for World Travelers. This website has information on electrical and telephone plugs around the world. ⊕ *www.kropla.com.*

■ EMERGENCIES

The police force in the Republic of Ireland is called the Garda Síochána ("Guardians of the Peace," in English), usually referred to as the Gardaí (pronounced gar-*dee*). The force is unarmed and is headed by a government-appointed commissioner, who is answerable to the Minister for Justice, who in turn is accountable to the Dáil (the Irish legislature). Easily identified by their fluorescent yellow blazers in winter, or, if weather permits in summer, by a dark blue shirt and peaked cap, the Gardaí are generally very helpful. They, and all other emergency forces, can be contacted by dialing 999 (in the Republic of Ireland, 112, the European standard, is also in use). These numbers will connect you with local police, ambulance, and fire services. You can expect a prompt response to your call. The Garda Síochána website provides contact information for local stations. In Northern Ireland the police force is the Police Service of Northern Ireland (PSNI). They are distinguished by their dark blue coats and white shirts. They can be contacted by dialing 999 in Northern Ireland.

United States Embassy ✉ *42 Elgin Rd., Ballsbridge, Dublin* ☎ *01/668–8777* ⊕ *dublin.usembassy.gov.*

Consulate General of the United States ✉ *Danesfort House, 223 Stranmills Rd., Belfast, Northern Ireland* ☎ *028/9038–6100* ⊕ *belfast.usconsulate.gov.*

General Emergency Contacts Ambulance, fire, police. In Northern Ireland, 999 only. ☎ *999, 112.* **An Garda Síochána** ⊕ *www.garda.ie.* **Police Service of Northern Ireland** ⊕ *www.psni.police.uk.*

■ GUIDED TOURS

Guided tours are a good option when you don't want to do it all yourself. The companies here all offer tours to Ireland on a "land-only" basis. A "land-only" tour includes all your travel (by bus, in most cases) once you arrive in the destination country, but not necessarily your flights to your destination. And remember that you'll be expected to tip your guide (in cash) at the end of the tour.

GENERAL TOURS

CIE Tours International is one of the biggest and longest-established (75 years) tour operators in the Irish market. They offer a selection of fully inclusive, escorted bus tours, or independent fly-drive vacations. An eight-day itinerary with car rental and confirmed hotel bookings starts at $796 per person, with two people traveling. The Heritage Tour is an eight-day bus tour, starting with two nights in Dublin, and taking in Bunratty Castle and Folk Park, Blarney Castle, the Cliffs of Moher, the Skellig Experience, and the Lakes of Killarney, among other attractions, with accommodation in top hotels.

Myguideireland, a young company set up by three friends on their return to Ireland from living and working in Philadelphia, aims to create the best holiday experience by using enthusiastic local guides. A customized seven-day self-drive tour across Ireland starts from $513 per person, with two people traveling. The price includes six nights at a B&B, car rental, and toll-free calls to your vacation specialist. Escorted bus tours include the Irish Jaunt, which includes one day in Dublin, a drive to Blarney Castle via the Rock of Cashel, Killarney, the Ring of Kerry, and the Cliffs of Moher, and offers five days, four nights, five meals, and accommodation in superior hotels, and costs from $708 per person.

Contacts **CIE Tours International** ☎ *800/243–8607* ⊕ *www.cietours.com.* **myguideireland** ☎ *800/965–9612* ⊕ *www.myguideireland.com.*

SPECIAL-INTEREST TOURS
BIKING

Irish Cycling Safaris. Irish Cycling Safaris pioneered cycling holidays in Ireland, and offer easygoing to moderate cycling trips along rural back roads with luggage transfer and accommodation in small family-run hotels and guesthouses. A weeklong tour of west Cork and Kerry, including Killarney, costs €705 per person sharing. Tour groups are accompanied by a local guide who drives the support van. Alternatively, you can opt for a self-led tour that includes bike rental, itinerary, and prebooked accommodation, also €705 per person sharing.

Iron Donkey. Iron Donkey gets raves from Fodor's readers. Offering something for everyone from novices to hammerheads, their mainstay are guided group tours: for instance, the Clare and Burren itinerary sets out from Ennis and includes Kilkee, Loop Head, Spanish Point, the Cliffs of Moher, the Burren coastline, and Bunratty Castle (cost is about €1,475 per person sharing). But others swear by the super-thorough and well-run custom tours, where they meet you at the first lodging (all great options, incidentally) with your bikes and size them to you, go over your route, and beautifully prep you for the ride.

■ TIP→ Most airlines accommodate bikes as luggage, provided they're dismantled and boxed.

Contacts **Irish Cycling Safaris** ☎ *01/260–0749* ⊕ *www.cyclingsafaris.com.* **Iron Donkey** ☎ *028/90–813200* ⊕ *www.irondonkey.com.*

CULTURE

Adams & Butler. Adams & Butler is Ireland's leading purveyor of customized vacations, with an unbeatable range of contacts in the upper end of the market. Most of their tours are customized for small groups in chauffeur-driven cars or on small luxury buses. They can offer you a week in Ireland with a self-drive car, with and itinerary and B&B in 4-star luxury hotels from $650; up that price to $4,000 per person for a luxury hotel with driver guide and 5-star accommodation. Should you prefer to travel by helicopter and stay in the presidential suites of Ireland's top hotels your week could run to $48,000. Charter a whole country house hotel for the family, or stay in a smaller historic or haunted house: whatever your whim, Adams & Butler will be able to indulge it—or so they say.

Contacts **Adams & Butler** ☎ *800/894–5712, 01/288–9355* ⊕ *www.adamsandbutler.com.*

GOLF

Executive Golf & Leisure. These Scotland-based golf specialists offer customized golf breaks or packages, such as an eight-day golf tour of the west of Ireland for about $7,222 with luxury accommodation, transfers, and rounds on some of the finest courses: the K Club, Old Portmarnock, Waterville, Ballybunion, Killarney, and the Old Head of Kinsale. ⊕ *www.execgolf-leisure.com.*

Golfbreaks.com. This company will customize a golf tour for you and also has tours of different regions of Ireland. Their Northern Ireland and the Northwest package includes rounds at the legendary Royal County Down and Royal Portrush courses.

Contacts **Executive Golf & Leisure** ☎ *877/295–2247, 1786/832–244* ⊕ *www.execgolf-leisure.com.* **Golfbreaks.com** ☎ *800/279–7988* ⊕ *www.golfbreaks.com.*

HIKING

Isle Inn. A long-established concern, Isle Inn offers self-drive holidays and escorted tours, and has an interesting range of activity holidays and escorted hiking holidays averaging 10 to 12 miles a day, staying in family-run guesthouses and characterful small hotels, while walking through scenic areas, including Donegal coast, the Glens of Antrim, and Achill Island and Mayo. Escorted hiking holidays start from $1,385 and cycling from $1035. A chauffeur-driven itinerary (from $1,170) combines culture and cuisine, offering six nights at top hotels with gourmet dinners and a driver to escort you.

Contacts Isle Inn Tours ☎ 800/237-9376 ⊕ www.isleinntours.com.

RAIL

Railtours Ireland. This top outfitter uses the Irish railway network for major transfers, and coaches for sightseeing at the destination, avoiding long, leg-numbing stretches of coach travel. The five-day tour starts with a train ride from Dublin to Cork (2 hours, 45 minutes) including breakfast, and continues with a bus tour to Blarney, train to Killarney, bus tour of the Ring of Kerry, and also visits Galway, the Cliffs of Moher, and Connemara, starting at €599 per person, with accommodation in B&Bs and modest hotels. ☎ 01/856-0045 ⊕ *www.railtoursireland.com.*

Contacts Railtours Ireland ☎ 01/856-0045 ⊕ www.railtoursireland.com.

▌HOURS OF OPERATION

Business hours are 9–5, sometimes later in the larger towns. In smaller towns, stores often close from 1 to 2 for lunch. If a holiday falls on a weekend, most businesses are closed on Monday.

Banks are open 10–4 weekdays. In small towns banks may close from 12:30 to 1:30. They remain open until 5 one afternoon per week; the day varies but it's usually Thursday. Post offices are open weekdays 9–5 and Saturday 9–1; some of the smaller branches close for lunch.

In Northern Ireland bank hours are weekdays 9:30–4:30. Post offices are open weekdays 9–5:30, Saturday 9–1. Some close for an hour at lunch (1–2).

There are some 24-hour gas stations along the highways; otherwise, hours vary from morning rush hour to late evenings.

Museums and sights are generally open Tuesday–Saturday 10–5 and Sunday 2–5.

Most pharmacies are open Monday–Saturday 9–5:30 or 6. Larger towns and cities often have 24-hour establishments.

Most shops are open Monday–Saturday 9–5:30 or 6. Once a week—normally Wednesday, Thursday, or Saturday—shops close at 1 pm. These times do *not* apply to Dublin, where stores generally stay open later, and they can vary from region to region, so it's best to check locally. Larger malls usually stay open late once a week—generally until 9 on Thursday or Friday. Convenience stores, supermarkets, and gas stations in both Dublin and rural Ireland are generally open until 8 or 9 pm.

Shops in Belfast are open weekdays 9–5:30, with a late closing on Thursday, usually at 9. Elsewhere in Northern Ireland, shops close for the afternoon once a week, usually Wednesday or Thursday. In addition, most smaller shops close for an hour or so at lunch.

HOLIDAYS

Irish national holidays in 2013 are as follows: January 1 (New Year's Day); March 17 (St. Patrick's Day); March 29 (Good Friday); April 1 (Easter Monday); May 6 (May Day); June 3 and August 5 (summer bank holidays); October 28 (autumn bank holiday); and December 25 and 26 (Christmas and St. Stephen's Day). If you plan to visit at Easter, remember that theaters and cinemas are closed for the last three days of the preceding week.

In Northern Ireland the following are holidays: January 1 (New Year's Day);

March 17 (St. Patrick's Day); April 6 (Good Friday); April 9 (Easter Monday); May 6 (early May bank holiday); May 27 and 26 (spring bank holiday); July 12 (Battle of the Boyne); August 26 (summer bank holiday); and December 25 and 26 (Christmas and Boxing Day).

MAIL

Outside of Dublin and Northern Ireland, postal codes aren't used; what's more important here is the county, so be sure to include it when addressing an envelope.

Letters by standard post take a week to 10 days to reach the United States and Canada, three to five days to reach the United Kingdom.

Airmail rates to the United States and Canada from the Irish Republic are €0.82 for letters and postcards. Rates are also €0.82 for letters and postcards to Europe. Mail to overseas can be sent economy or airmail. Letters and postcards within the Irish Republic cost €0.55.

Rates from Northern Ireland are 68p for letters and postcards (not over 10 grams) to continental Europe, and 76p to the United States and Canada, Australia, and New Zealand. To the rest of the United Kingdom and the Irish Republic, rates are 46p for first-class letters and 36p for second-class.

Mail can be held for collection at any post office for free for up to three months. It should be addressed to the recipient "c/o Poste Restante." In Dublin, use the General Post Office. The postal service in the Republic of Ireland, known as An Post, has a website with a branch locator and loads of other postal information. In Northern Ireland mail service is run by the Royal Mail.

Contact **An Post** ☎ 01/705-7600
⊕ *www.anpost.ie.* **General Post Office**
✉ *O'Connell St., Dublin* ☎ 01/705-8833.

MONEY

A modest hotel in Dublin costs about €140 a night for two; this figure can be reduced to under €90 by staying in a registered guesthouse or inn, and reduced to about €70 by staying in a suburban B&B. Lunch, consisting of a good one-dish plate of bar food at a pub, costs around €10–€14; a sandwich at the same pub costs about €5. In Dublin's better restaurants, dinner will run €45–€60 (dinner being a three-course meal) per person, excluding drinks and tip.

Theater and entertainment in most places are inexpensive—about €18 for a good seat, and double or triple that for a big-name, pop-music concert. For the price of a few drinks and (in Dublin and Killarney) a small entrance fee of about €2, you can spend a memorable evening at a *seisun* (pronounced say-*shoon* when referring to this folk music session), in a music pub. Entrance to most public galleries is free, but stately homes and similar attractions charge anywhere from €4 to a whopping €16 per person.

Just about everything is more expensive in Dublin, so add at least 10% to these sample prices: cup of coffee, €2.20; pint of beer, €5; soda, €2.40; and 2-km (1-mile) taxi ride, €8. Due to the exchange rate, Canadians, Australians, New Zealanders, Americans, and U.K. residents will find Ireland a little pricey when they convert costs to their home currency.

Hotels and meals in Northern Ireland are less expensive than in the United Kingdom and the Republic of Ireland. Also, the lower level of taxation makes taxable goods such as gasoline, alcoholic drinks, and tobacco cheaper.

Prices throughout this guide are given for adults. Substantially reduced fees are almost always available for children, students, and senior citizens.

■TIP➜ Banks never have every foreign currency on hand, and it may take as long as a week to order. If you're planning to exchange funds before leaving home, don't wait until the last minute.

ATMS AND BANKS

Your own bank will probably charge a fee for using ATMs abroad; the foreign bank you use may also charge a fee. Nevertheless, you'll usually get a better rate of exchange at an ATM than you will at a currency-exchange office or even when changing money in a bank. And extracting funds as you need them is a safer option than carrying around a large amount of cash.

■TIP➜ PINs with more than four digits are not recognized at ATMs in many countries. If yours has five or more, remember to change it before you leave.

ATMs are found in all major towns and are, by far, the easiest way to keep yourself stocked with euros and pounds. Most major banks are connected to Cirrus or PLUS systems; there's a four-digit maximum for your PIN.

CREDIT CARDS

It's a good idea to inform your credit-card company before you travel, especially if you're going abroad and don't travel internationally very often. Otherwise, the credit-card company might put a hold on your card owing to unusual activity—not a good thing halfway through your trip. Record all your credit-card numbers— as well as the phone numbers to call if your cards are lost or stolen—in a safe place, so you're prepared should something go wrong. Both MasterCard and Visa have general numbers you can call (collect if you're abroad) if your card is lost, but you're better off calling the number of your issuing bank, since Master-Card and Visa usually just transfer you to your bank; your bank's number is usually printed on your card.

If you plan to use your credit card for cash advances, you'll need to apply for a PIN at least two weeks before your trip.

Although it's usually cheaper (and safer) to use a credit card abroad for large purchases (so you can cancel payments or be reimbursed if there's a problem), note that some credit-card companies *and* the banks that issue them add substantial percentages to all foreign transactions, whether they're in a foreign currency or not. Check on these fees before leaving home, so there won't be any surprises when you get the bill.

When using your credit card, check that the merchant is putting the transaction through in euros or pounds sterling. If he or she puts it through in the currency of your home country—a transaction called a dynamic currency conversion— the exchange rate might be less favorable and the service charges higher than if you allow the credit-card company to do the conversion for you. Be sure to ask at the time, and insist on being billed in euros to get the most advantageous rate and avoid the service charge.

Reporting Lost Cards **American Express** ☎ *800/992–3404 in U.S., 336/393–1111 collect from abroad* ⊕ *www.americanexpress. com.* **Diners Club** ☎ *800/234–6377 in U.S., 303/799–1504 collect from abroad* ⊕ *www.dinersclub.com.* **MasterCard** ☎ *800/622–7747 in U.S., 636/722–7111 collect from abroad* ⊕ *www.mastercard.com/ie.* **Visa** ☎ *800/847–2911 in U.S., 410/581–9994 collect from abroad* ⊕ *www.visa.com.*

CURRENCY AND EXCHANGE

The Irish Republic is a member of the European Monetary Union (EMU). Euro notes come in denominations of €500, €200, €100, €50, €20, €10, and €5. The euro is divided into 100 cents, and coins are available as €2 and €1 and 50, 20, 10, 5, 2, and 1 cent.

The unit of currency in Northern Ireland is the pound sterling (£), divided into 100 pence (p). The bills (called notes) are £50, £20, £10, and £5. Coins are £2, £1, 50p, 20p, 10p, 5p, 2p, and 1p. The bank of Northern Ireland prints its own notes, which look different from the English or Scottish sterling.

Check out today's rates at ⊕ *www.oanda. com.*

At this writing, €1 is equal to U.S. $1.46. One pound sterling is equal to U.S. $1.65. Rates fluctuate regularly, though, particularly for the euro, so monitor them closely.

■TIP→ Even if a currency-exchange booth has a sign promising no commission, rest assured that there's some kind of huge, hidden fee. (Oh . . . that's right. The sign didn't say no fee.) And as for rates, you're almost always better off getting foreign currency at an ATM or exchanging money at a bank.

TRAVELER'S CHECKS AND CARDS

Some consider this the currency of the cave man, and it's true that fewer establishments accept traveler's checks these days. Nevertheless, they're a cheap and secure way to carry extra money, particularly on trips to urban areas. Both Citibank (under the Visa brand) and American Express issue traveler's checks in the United States, but Amex is better known and more widely accepted. Whatever you do, keep track of all the serial numbers in case the checks are lost or stolen.

Contacts **American Express** ☎ *888/412-6945 in U.S., 801/945–9450 collect outside of U.S. to add value or speak to customer service* ⊕ *www.americanexpress.com.*

▍PACKING

In Ireland you can experience all four seasons in a day. There can be damp chilly stretches even in July and August, the warmest months of the year. Layers are the best way to go. Pack several long- and short-sleeve T-shirts (in winter, some should be thermal or silk), a sweatshirt, a lightweight sweater, a heavyweight sweater, and a hooded, waterproof windbreaker that's large enough to go over several layers if necessary. A portable umbrella is absolutely essential, and the smaller and lighter it is, the better, as

you'll want it with you every second. You should bring at least two pairs of walking shoes; footwear can get soaked in minutes and then take hours to dry.

The Irish are generally informal about clothes. In the more expensive hotels and restaurants, people dress formally for dinner, and a jacket and tie may be required in bars after 7 pm, but very few places operate a strict dress policy. Old or tattered blue jeans and running shoes are forbidden in certain bars and dance clubs.

If you're used to packing things or stowing dirty clothes in plastic shopping or drawstring bags, bring your own. About the only place you can find the latter here is in the closets of better hotel rooms (for on-site dry cleaning and laundry). Plastic bags carry a 22¢ government levy and can be sold by supermarkets, but it's illegal to give them away. Most stores use paper bags or recycle boxes.

▍PASSPORTS

All U.S. citizens, even infants, need a valid passport to enter Ireland for stays of up to 90 days. Citizens of the United Kingdom, when traveling on flights departing from Great Britain, do not need a passport to enter Ireland but it's advisable to carry some form of photo ID. Passport requirements for Northern Ireland are the same as for the republic.

We're always surprised at how few Americans have passports—only 25% at this writing. This number is expected to grow in coming years, now that it is impossible to reenter the United States from trips to neighboring Canada or Mexico without one.

U.S. passports are valid for 10 years. You must apply in person if you're getting a passport for the first time; if your previous passport was lost, stolen, or damaged; or if your previous passport has expired and was issued more than 15 years ago or when you were under 16. All children under 18 must appear in person to apply for or renew a passport. Both parents must accompany any child under 14 (or send a notarized statement with their permission) and provide proof of their relationship to the child.

■ TIP→ Before your trip, make two copies of your passport's data page (one for someone at home and another for you to carry separately). Or scan the page and e-mail it to someone at home and/or yourself.

There are 13 regional passport offices, as well as 7,000 passport acceptance facilities in post offices, public libraries, and other governmental offices. If you're renewing a passport, you can do so by mail. Forms are available at passport acceptance facilities and online.

The cost to apply for a new passport is $100 for adults, $85 for children under 16; renewals are $75. Allow six weeks for processing, both for first-time passports and renewals. For an expediting fee of $60 you can reduce this time to about two weeks. If your trip is less than two weeks away, you can get a passport even more rapidly by going to a passport office with the necessary documentation. Private expediters can get things done in as little as 48 hours, but charge hefty fees for their services.

U.S. Passport Information **U.S. Department of State** ☎ 877/487–2778 ⊕ travel.state.gov/passport.

U.S. Passport and Visa Expediters **A. Briggs Passport & Visa Expeditors** ☎ 800/806–0581, 202/338–0111 ⊕ www.abriggs.com. **American Passport Express** ☎ 800/455–5166, 603/559–9888 ⊕ www.americanpassport.com. **Passport Express** ☎ 800/362–8196 ⊕ www.passportexpress.com. **Travel Document Systems** ☎ 800/874–5100, 202/638–3800 ⊕ www.traveldocs.com. **Travel the World Visas** ☎ 202/223–8822, 866/886–8472 ⊕ www.world-visa.com.

▌RESTROOMS

Public restrooms are in short supply in Ireland. They'll be easy enough to find in public places such as airports, train stations, and shopping malls, but if you don't find yourself in one of these locations your best bet is to look for the nearest pub (never more than a few minutes away in Ireland!). Restrooms are often labeled in Irish—*fir* (men) and *mná* (women). Pubs are increasingly putting up signs saying that restrooms are for customers only—but this is difficult to enforce. If it's outside of shopping or pub hours, your last option may be the nearest hotel. Most gas stations will have toilets available. Only toilets in hotels or shopping centers will be up to a polished North American standard. Although many toilets look well worn, they are generally clean. Unfortunately, few toilets are heated and an open window is typically used for ventilation, making for uncomfortably cold restrooms in the colder months.

▌TAXES

When leaving the Irish Republic, U.S. and Canadian visitors get a refund of the value-added tax (V.A.T.), which currently accounts for a hefty 23% of the purchase price of many goods and 13.5% of those that fall outside the luxury category. Apart from clothing, most items of interest to visitors, right down to ordinary toilet soap, are rated at 23%. V.A.T. is not refundable on accommodations, car rental, meals, or any other form of personal services received on vacation.

Many crafts outlets and department stores operate a system that enables U.S. and Canadian visitors to collect V.A.T. rebates in the currency of their choice at Dublin or Shannon Airport on departure. Some stores give you the rebate at the register; with others you claim your refund after you've returned home. Refund forms, known as tax-free shopping cheques, must be picked up at the time of purchase, and they must be stamped by customs, and mailed back to the store before you leave for home. It may take months for your refund to be processed. Many merchants work with a service such as Global Blue, which has offices at major ports and airports, and will refund your money immediately in return for a 4% fee. If a store gives you a refund at the register, you'll also be given papers to have stamped by customs; you'll then put the papers in an envelope (also provided by the store) and mail it before you leave. Most major stores deduct V.A.T. at the time of sale if goods are to be shipped overseas; however, there's a shipping charge.

When leaving Northern Ireland, U.S. and Canadian visitors can also get a refund of the 17.5% V.A.T. by the over-the-counter and the direct-export methods. Most larger stores provide these services on request and will handle the paperwork. For the over-the-counter method, you must spend more than £75 in one store. Ask the store for Form V.A.T. 407 (you must have identification—passports are best), to be given to customs when you leave the country. The refund will be forwarded to you in about eight weeks (minus a small service charge) either in the form of a sterling check or as a credit to your charge card. The direct-export method, where the goods are shipped directly to your home, is more cumbersome. V.A.T. Form 407/1/93 must be certified by customs, police, or a notary public when you get home and then sent back to the store, which will refund your money.

When making a purchase, ask for a V.A.T. refund form and find out whether the merchant gives refunds—not all stores do, nor are they required to. Have the form stamped like any customs form by customs officials when you leave the country or, if you're visiting several EU countries, when you leave the European Union. After you're through passport control, take the form to a refund-service counter for an on-the-spot refund (which is usually the quickest and easiest option), or mail it to the address on the form (or the envelope with it) after you arrive home. You receive the total refund stated on the form, but the processing time can be long, especially if you request a credit-card adjustment.

Global Blue is a Europe-wide service with 225,000 affiliated stores and more than 700 refund counters at major airports and border crossings. Its refund form is the most common across the European continent. The service issues refunds in the form of cash, check, or credit-card adjustment.

Global Blue ☎ *866/706–6090 in U.S.* ✉ *taxfree@global-blue.com* ⊕ *www. global-blue.com.*

▌ TIME

Dublin is five hours ahead of New York and eight hours ahead of Los Angeles.

▌ TIPPING

In some hotels and restaurants a service charge of around 10%—rising to 15% in plush spots—is added to the bill. If in doubt, ask whether service is included. In places where it's included, tipping isn't necessary unless you have received particularly good service. If there's no service charge, add a minimum of 10% to the total. Taxi drivers or hackney cab drivers, who make the trip for a prearranged sum, don't expect tips. There are few porters and plenty of baggage trolleys at airports, so tipping is usually not an issue; if you use a porter, €1 is the minimum. Tip hotel porters at least €1 per suitcase. Hairdressers normally expect about 10% of the total spent. You don't tip in pubs, but for waiter service in a bar, a hotel lounge, or a Dublin lounge bar, leave about €1. It's not customary to tip for regular concierge service.

TIPPING GUIDELINES FOR IRELAND	
Bellhop	€1 to €2, depending on the level of the hotel
Hotel Concierge	€5 or more if he or she performs a special service for you
Hotel Doorman	€1–€2 if he helps you get a cab
Hotel Maid	€1–€3 a day (either daily or at the end of your stay, in cash)
Hotel Room-Service Waiter	€1 to €2 per delivery, even if a service charge has been added
Taxi Driver	10%, or just round up the fare to the next euro amount
Tour Guide	10% of the cost of the tour
Valet Parking Attendant	€1–€2, but only when you get your car
Waiter	Just small change (up to a euro or two) to round out your bill if service is included
Restroom Attendant	Restroom attendants in more expensive restaurants expect some small change or €1.

▌ VISITOR INFORMATION

For information on travel in the Irish Republic, contact Tourism Ireland, the international marketing authority for Fáilte Ireland (pronounced *fal*-cha), as the tourist information network is called within the Republic of Ireland. They have two websites, one for people logging on internationally (⊕ *www.discoverireland. com*) and one for people logging on domestically (⊕ *www.discoverireland. ie*). Information on travel in the north is available from the Northern Ireland Tourist Board.

Information Fáilte Ireland ✉ *88–95 Amiens St., Dublin* ☎ *01/884-7700, 1890/324-583 toll-free within Ireland* ⊕ *www.failteireland.ie.* **Northern Ireland Tourist Board** (*NITB*). ✉ *59 North St., Belfast, Northern Ireland* ☎ *028/9023-1221* ⊕ *www.discovernorthernireland.com.* **Discover Ireland** ⊕ *www.discoverireland.com.* **Tourism Ireland, Canada office** ✉ *2 Bloor St.*

W, Suite 3403, Toronto, Ontario ☎ *416/925-6368, 1800/223-6470.* **Tourism Ireland, U.K. office** ✉ *Nation House, 103 Wigmore St., London, England* ☎ *44 207/518-0800, 800/039-7000* ⊕ *www.discoverireland.com.* **Tourism Ireland** ✉ *345 Park Ave., 17th fl., New York, New York, USA* ☎ *212/418-0800, 800/223-6470* ⊕ *www.tourismireland.com.*

ONLINE TRAVEL TOOLS

The main website for the Irish tourist board, Tourism Ireland is ⊕ *www. discoverireland.com*; this is meant for people logging on internationally. Fáilte Ireland (the National Tourism Development Authority) sponsors Discover Ireland, at ⊕ *www.discoverireland.ie*, which is geared for people logging on domestically. For lots of entertaining bits—Irish and otherwise—visit ⊕ *www.irishabroad. com*. The website ⊕ *www.ireland-information.com* is dedicated to providing as many free resources and as much free information about Ireland as possible on an array of topics from genealogy to shopping. For a central directory of links to all things Irish, log on to ⊕ *www. finditireland.com*. Comhaltas Ceoltóirí Éireann is an association that promotes the music, culture, and art of Ireland, and its website ⊕ *www.comhaltas.ie* has helpful news about the Irish traditional music scene. For listings of all music, film, and theater events and festivals, see ⊕ *www. entertainment.ie*. For general information on Irish current affairs, sports, entertainment, and more, log on to ⊕ *www. ireland.com*. Keep in mind that many of the leading newspapers of Ireland have websites, which can be gold mines of timely information. See, for example, the *Irish Times*' website, ⊕ *www.irishtimes. com*. To keep Irish people abroad up to date on events at home, visit ⊕ *www. irishcentral.com*.

Officially designated Heritage Towns are featured on ⊕ *www.heritagetowns.com*. A range of heritage attractions are flagged on ⊕ *www.heritageisland.com*, while ⊕ *www.heritageireland.ie* is the website for the prime heritage attractions in the care of the Irish State, from the Rock of Cashel to Killarney National Park. For more information on counties in the west of Ireland, try ⊕ *www.discoverireland.com/west*. A handy regional site for the area near Shannon Airport is ⊕ *www.shannonregiontourism.com*, while ⊕ *www.visitdublin.com* has all you need to know about the capital. Portions of the Tourism Ireland's eloquent magazine, *Ireland of the Welcomes*, are available online at ⊕ *www.irelandofthewelcomes.com*. Castle lovers will enjoy ⊕ *www.celticcastles.com*, while foodies should check out ⊕ *www.bordbia.ie* and ⊕ *www. goodfoodireland.ie*.

BASICS

Currency Conversion Google. Google does currency conversion. Just type in the amount you want to convert and an explanation of how you want it converted (e.g., "14 Swiss francs in dollars"), and then voilà. ⊕ *www.google.com*. **Oanda.com.** Oanda.com also allows you to print out a handy table with the current day's conversion rates. ⊕ *www.oanda.com*. **XE.com.** XE.com is a good currency conversion website. ⊕ *www.xe.com*.

Safety Transportation Security Administration (*TSA*). ⊕ *www.tsa.gov*.

Time Zones Timeanddate.com. This site can help you figure out the correct time anywhere. ⊕ *www.timeanddate.com/worldclock*.

Weather Accuweather.com. This is one of the better independent weather-forecasting services. ⊕ *www.accuweather.com*. **Weather.com.** This is the website for the Weather Channel. ⊕ *www.weather.com*.

Other Resources CIA World Factbook. This noted resource has profiles of every country in the world. It's a good source if you need some quick facts and figures. ⊕ *www.cia.gov/library/publications/the-world-factbook*.

INDEX

PHOTO CREDITS